CREDE BYRON
THE
ILLUSTRATED
BYRON
WITH UPWARDS OF
TWO HUNDRED ENGRAVINGS
From Original Drawings
BY
KENNY MEADOWS
BIRKET FOSTER
HABLET K. BROWNE
GUSTAVE JANET
AND
EDWARD MORIN.
D. APPLETON & CO.,
NEW YORK:
90, 92 & 94 GRAND ST.

CONTENTS.

THE

ILLUSTRATED BYRON.

THE CORSAIR.

TO THOMAS MOORE, ESQ.

My dear Moore,

I dedicate to you the last production with which I shall trespass on public patience, and your indulgence, for some years; and I own that I feel anxious to avail myself of this latest and only opportunity of adorning my pages with a name, consecrated by unshaken public principle, and the most undoubted and various talents. While Ireland ranks you among the firmest of her patriots; while you stand alone the first of her bards in her estimation, and Britain repeats and ratifies the decree, permit one, whose only regret, since our first acquaintance, has been the years he had lost before it commenced, to add the humble but sincere suffrage of friendship, to the voice of more than one nation. It will at least prove to you, that I have neither forgotten the gratification derived from your society, nor abandoned the prospect of its renewal, whenever your leisure or inclination allows you to atone to your friends for too long an absence. It is said among those friends, I trust truly, that you are engaged in the composition of a poem whose scene will be laid in the East; none can do those scenes so much justice. The wrongs of your own country, the magnificent and fiery spirit of her sons, the beauty and feeling of her daughters, may there be found; and Collins, when he denominated his Oriental his Irish Eclogues, was not aware how true, at least, was a part of his parallel. Your imagination will create a warmer sun, and less clouded sky; but wildness, tenderness, and originality, are part of your national claim of oriental des-

cent, to which you have already thus far proved your title more clearly than the most zealous of your country's antiquarians.

May I add a few words on a subject on which all men are supposed to be fluent, and none agreeable?—Self. I have written much, and published more than enough to demand a longer silence than I now meditate; but, for some years to come, it is my intention to tempt no further the award of "Gods, men, nor columns." In the present composition I have attempted not the most difficult, but, perhaps, the best adapted measure to our language, the good old and now neglected heroic couplet. The stanza of Spenser is perhaps too slow and dignified for narrative; though, I confess, it is the measure most after my own heart: Scott alone, of the present generation, has hitherto completely triumphed over the fatal facility of the octosyllabic verse; and this is not the least victory of his fertile and mighty genius: in blank verse, Milton, Thomson, and our dramatists, are the beacons that shine along the deep, but warn us from the rough and barren rock on which they are kindled. The heroic couplet is not the most popular measure, certainly; but as I did not deviate into the other from a wish to flatter what is called public opinion, I shall quit it without further apology, and take my chance once more with that versification, in which I have hitherto published nothing but compositions whose former circulation is part of my present, and will be of my future, regret.

With regard to my story, and stories in general, I should have been glad to have rendered my personages more perfect and amiable, if possible, inasmuch as I have been sometimes criticised, and considered no less responsible for their deeds and qualities than if all had been personal. Be it so—if I have deviated into the gloomy vanity of "drawing from self," the pictures are probably like, since they are unfavourable; and if not, those who know me are undeceived, and those who do not, I have little interest in undeceiving. I have no particular desire that any but my acquaintance, should think the author better than the beings of his imagining; but I cannot help a little surprise, and perhaps amusement, at some odd critical exceptions in the present instance, when I see several bards (far more deserving, I allow) in very reputable plight, and quite exempted from all participation in the faults of those heroes, who, nevertheless, might be found with little more morality than "The Giaour," and perhaps—but no—I must admit Childe Harold to be a very repulsive personage; and as to his identity, those who like it must give him whatever "alias" they please.

If, however, it were worth while to remove the impression, it might be of some service to me, that the man who is alike the delight of his readers and his friends, the poet of all circles, and the idol of his own, permits me here and elsewhere to subscribe myself,

Most truly,

And affectionately,

His obedient servant,

BYRON,

January 2, 1814.

THE LIFE

OF

GEORGE GORDON, LORD BYRON.*

(1788-1824.)

"O'er the harp, from earliest years beloved,
He threw his fingers hurriedly, and tones
Of melancholy beauty died away
Upon its strings of sweetness."

It was reserved for the present age to produce one distinguished example of the Muse having descended upon a bard of a wounded spirit, and lent her lyre to tell afflictions of no ordinary description—afflictions originating probably in that singular combination of feeling with imagination which has been called the poetical temperament, and which has so often saddened the days of those on whom it has been conferred. If ever a man was entitled to lay claim to that character in all its strength and all its weakness, with its unbounded range of enjoyment, and its exquisite sensibility of pleasure and of pain, that man was Lord Byron. Nor does it require much time, or a deep acquaintance with human nature, to discover why these extraordinary powers should in so many cases have contributed more to the wretchedness than to the happiness of their possessor.

We think that many points of resemblance may be traced between Byron and Rousseau. Both are distinguished by the most ardent and vivid delineation of intense conception, and by a deep sensibility of passion rather than of affection. Both too, by this double power, have held a dominion over the sympathy of their readers far beyond the range of those ordinary feelings which are excited by the mere efforts of genius. The impression of this interest still accompanies the perusal of their writings; but there is another interest, of more lasting and far stronger power, which each of them possessed,—the continual embodying of the individual character, it might almost be said of the very person, of the writer. When we speak or think of Rousseau or Byron, we are not conscious of speaking or thinking of an author; we have a vague but impassioned remembrance of men of surpassing genius, eloquence, and power,—of prodigious capacity both of misery and happiness: we feel as if we had transiently met such beings in real life, or had known them in the obscure communion of a dream. Each of their works presents, in succession, a fresh idea of themselves; and while the productions of other great men stand out from them, like something they have created, theirs, on the contrary, are images, pictures, busts of their living selves,—clothed, no doubt, at different times in different drapery, and prominent from a different background, but still impressed with the same form and mien and lineaments, and not to be mistaken for the representations of any other of the children of men.

But this view of the subject, though universally felt to be a true one, requires perhaps

* Written in 1831 by Sir Henry L. Bulwer, and now reprinted by his permission.

a little explanation. The personal character to which we allude is not altogether that on which the seal of life has been set, and to which, therefore, moral approval or condemnation is necessarily annexed, as to the language or conduct of actual existence; it is the character, so to speak, which is prior to conduct, and yet open to good and to ill—the constitution of the being in body and in soul. Each of these illustrious writers has, in this light, filled his works with expressions of his own character—has unveiled to the world the secrets of his own being. They have gone down into those depths which every man may sound for himself, though not for another; and they have made disclosures to the world of what they beheld and knew there—disclosures that have excited a profound and universal sympathy, by proving that all mankind, the troubled and the untroubled, the lofty and the low, the strongest and the weakest, are linked together by the bonds of a common but inscrutable nature.

Thus, each of these wayward and richly-gifted spirits made himself the object of profound interest to the world, and that, too, during periods of society when ample food was everywhere spread abroad for the meditation and passions of men.

Although of widely dissimilar fortunes and birth, a close resemblance in their passions and their genius may be traced, too, between Byron and Robert Burns. Their careers were short and glorious, and they both perished in the "rich summer of their life and song," and in all the splendour of a reputation more likely to increase than diminish. One was a peasant, and the other a peer; but nature is a great leveller, and makes amends for the injuries of fortune by the richness of her benefaction: the genius of Burns raised him to a level with the nobles of the land; by nature, if not by birth, he was the peer of Byron. They both distinguished themselves by the force of their genius, and fell by the strength of their passions: one wrote from a love, and the other from a scorn of mankind; and both sung of the emotions of their own hearts with a vehemence and an originality which few have equalled, and none have surpassed.

Lord Byron was descended from an illustrious line of ancestry. From the period of the Conquest, his family, who possessed extensive manors in Lancashire and other parts of the kingdom, were highly distinguished for their prowess in arms. John de Byron attended Edward I. in several warlike expeditions. Two of the Byrons fell at the battle of Cressy. Another member of the family, Sir John de Byron, rendered good service in Bosworth field to the Earl of Richmond, and contributed by his valour to transfer the crown from the head of Richard III. to that of Henry VII. Sir John was a man of honour as well as a brave warrior. He was very intimate with his neighbour Sir Gervase Clifton; and although Byron fought under Henry and Clifton under Richard, it did not diminish their friendship, though it put it to a severe test. Previous to that battle, they had mutually promised, that whichever should be vanquished, the other should endeavour to prevent the forfeiture of his friend's estate. While Clifton was bravely fighting at the head of his troop, he was struck off his horse: Byron perceiving the accident, quitted the ranks and ran to the relief of his friend, who died in his arms. Sir John de Byron kept his word; he interceded with the king; and the estate, preserved to the Clifton family, is now in the possession of a descendant of Sir Gervase.

In the wars between Charles I. and the parliament, the Byrons adhered to the royal cause. Sir Nicholas Byron, the eldest brother and representative of the family, was an eminent royalist, who having distinguished himself in the wars of the Low Countries,

was appointed governor of Chelsea in 1642. He had two sons, who both died without issue; and his younger brother, Sir John, became heir. This person was made a knight of the Bath at the coronation of James I. He had eleven sons, most of whom distinguished themselves by their loyalty and gallantry on the side of Charles I. Seven of these brothers were engaged at the battle of Marston Moor, and four fell in the defence of the royal cause. Sir John Byron, one of the survivors, was appointed to several important commands; and on the 26th of October, 1643, was created Lord Byron, with a collateral remainder to his brothers. On the decline of the king's affairs, he was appointed governor to the Duke of York, and while holding this office died without issue, in France, in 1652; upon which his brother Richard, a celebrated cavalier, became the second Lord Byron. He was governor of Appleby Castle, and distinguished himself at Newark. He died in 1697, aged seventy-four, and was succeeded by his eldest son William, who married Elizabeth, the daughter of John Viscount Chaworth, of the kingdom of Ireland, by whom he had five sons, all of whom died young, except William, whose eldest son, William, was born in 1722, and came to the title in 1736.

William Lord Byron passed the early part of his life in the navy. In 1763 he was made master of the stag-hounds; and in 1765 was sent to the Tower, and tried before the House of Peers, for killing his relation and neighbour, Mr. Chaworth, in a duel. The following details of this fatal event are peculiarly interesting from subsequent circumstances connected with the subject of our memoir.

William Lord Byron belonged to a club of which Mr. Chaworth was also a member. It met at the Star and Garter tavern, Pall Mall, and was called the Nottinghamshire Club. On the 29th January, 1765, they assembled at four o'clock to dinner as usual; and everything went on agreeably until about seven o'clock, when an angry dispute arising betwixt Lord Byron and Mr. Chaworth concerning the quantity of game on their estates, the latter gentleman paid his share of the bill and retired. Lord Byron followed him out of the room, and, stopping him on the landing of the stairs, called to the waiter to show them into an empty room. They were shown into one, and a single candle placed on the table: in a few minutes the bell was rung, and Mr. Chaworth found mortally wounded. He said that Lord Byron and he entered the room together; that his lordship, in walking forward, said something relative to the former dispute, on which he proposed fastening the door; that on turning himself round from this act, he perceived his lordship with his sword half drawn, or nearly so; on which, knowing his man, he instantly drew his own, and made a thrust at him, which he thought had wounded or killed him; that then, perceiving his lordship shorten his sword to return the thrust, he thought to have parried it with his left hand; that he felt the sword enter his body, and go deep through his back; that he struggled, and being the stronger man, disarmed his lordship, and expressed some concern, as under the apprehension of having mortally wounded him; that Lord Byron replied by saying something to the like effect, adding, at the same time, that he hoped "he would now allow him to be as brave a man as any in the kingdom."

For this offence he was unanimously convicted of manslaughter; but, on being brought up for judgment, pleaded his privilege as a peer, and was, in consequence, discharged. After this affair he was abandoned by his relations, and retired to Newstead Abbey; where, while he lived in a state of exile from persons of his own rank, his unhappy

temper found abundant exercise in continual war with his neighbours and tenants, and sufficient punishment in their hatred. One of his amusements was feeding crickets, which he rendered so tame as to crawl over him, and used to whip them with a wisp of straw when too familiar. In this forlorn condition he lingered out a long life, doing all in his power to ruin the paternal mansion for that other branch of the family to which he was aware it must pass at his death, all his own children having descended before him to the grave.

John, the next brother to William, and born in the year after him, that is in 1723, was of a very different disposition; but his career in life was almost an unbroken series of misfortunes. The hardships he endured while accompanying Commodore Anson in his expedition to the South Seas are well known, from his own highly popular and affecting narrative. His only son, born in 1751, who received an excellent education, and held a commission in the Guards, was so dissipated, that he was known by the name of "mad Jack Byron." He was one of the handsomest men of his time; but his character was so notorious that his father was obliged to desert him, and his company was shunned by the better part of society. In his twenty-seventh year he seduced the Marchioness of Carmarthen, who had been but a few years married to a husband with whom she lived in the greatest happiness until the commencement of this unfortunate connection. After a fruitless attempt at reclaiming his lady, the marquis obtained a divorce; and a marriage was brought about between her and her seducer, which, after the most brutal conduct on his part, and the greatest misery and keenest remorse on hers, was dissolved in two years by her sinking to the grave, the victim of a broken heart. About three years subsequently, Captain Byron sought to recruit his fortune by matrimony; and having made a conquest of Miss Catherine Gordon, an Aberdeenshire heiress (lineally descended from the Earl of Huntly and the princess Jane, daughter of James II. of Scotland), he united himself to her, ran through her property in a few years, and leaving her and her only child, the subject of this memoir, fled to France to avoid his creditors, and died at Valenciennes in 1791.

George Byron Gordon (for so he was called, on account of the neglect his father's family had shown to his mother) was born at Dover, on the 22nd of January, 1788. On the flight of his father, the entire care of his infant years devolved upon his mother, who retired to Aberdeen, where she lived in almost perfect seclusion, on the remains of her fortune. Her excessive maternal indulgence, and the absence of that salutary discipline and control so necessary to childhood, doubtless contributed to the formation of the less pleasing features of Lord Byron's character. It must, however, be remembered, in Mrs. Byron's extenuation, not only that the circumstances in which she had been left with her son were of a very peculiar nature, but also that a slight malformation of one of his feet, and great weakness of constitution, naturally obtained for him in the heart of a mother a more than ordinary portion of tenderness.

When George was seven years of age, his mother sent him to the grammar-school at Aberdeen, where he remained till his removal to Harrow, with the exception of some intervals of absence, which were deemed requisite for the preservation of his health. His progress beyond that of the general run of his class-fellows was never so remarkable as after those occasional intervals of recreation, when, in a few days, he would master exercises which, in the ordinary school routine, it had required weeks to accomplish.

But when he had overtaken the rest of the class, he always relaxed his exertions, and, contenting himself with being considered a tolerable scholar, never made any extraordinary effort to place himself at the head of the highest form. It was only out of school that he aspired to be the leader of everything: in all boyish games and amusements he would be first if possible. For this he was eminently calculated; quick, enterprising, and daring, the energy of his mind enabled him to overcome the impediments which nature had thrown in his way. Even at that early period (from eight to ten years of age) all his sports were of a manly character: fishing, shooting, swimming, managing a horse, or steering and trimming the sails of a boat, constituted his chief delight, and to the superficial observer seemed his sole occupation.

He was exceedingly brave; and in the juvenile wars of the school he generally gained the victory. Upon one occasion, a boy pursued by another took refuge in Mrs. Byron's house: the latter youth, who had been much abused by the former, proceeded to take vengeance on him on the landing-place of the drawing-room stairs, when George interposed in his defence, declaring that nobody should be ill-used while under his roof and protection. Upon this the aggressor dared him to fight; and although the former was by much the stronger of the two, the spirit of young Byron was so determined, that after the combat had lasted nearly two hours, it was suspended only in consequence of their complete exhaustion.

It is the custom of the grammar-school at Aberdeen, that the boys of all the five classes of which it is composed should be assembled for prayers in the public school at eight o'clock in the morning; after prayers, a censor calls over the names, and those who are absent are punished. The first time that Lord Byron had come to school after his accession to his title, the rector had caused his name to be inserted in the censor's book, "Georgius Dominus de Byron," instead of "Georgius Byron Gordon," as formerly. The boys, unaccustomed to this aristocratic sound, set up a loud and involuntary shout, which had such an effect on his sensitive mind that he burst into tears, and would have fled from the school had he not been restrained by the master.

The answer which Lord Byron made to a fellow-scholar, who questioned him as to the cause of the honorary addition of "Dominus de Byron" to his name, served at that time, when he was only ten years of age, to point out that he would be a man who would speak and act for himself; who, whatever might be his vices or his virtues, would not condescend to receive them at second-hand. It took place the very day after he had been menaced with a flogging round the school for a fault which he had not committed. When the question was put to him, he replied, "It is not my doing: Fortune was to whip me yesterday for what another did, and she has this day made me a lord for what another has ceased to do. I need not thank her in either case, for I have asked nothing at her hands."

On the 17th of May, 1798, William, the fifth Lord Byron, departed this life at Newstead. The son of this eccentric nobleman died when George was five years old; and as the descent both of the titles and estates was to heirs male, the latter of course succeeded his great uncle. Upon this change of fortune, Lord Byron, now ten years of age, was removed from the immediate care of his mother, and placed as a ward under the guardianship of the Earl of Carlisle, whose father had married Isabella, the sister of the preceding Lord Byron. In one or two points of character this great aunt resembled the

bard: she also wrote beautiful poetry; and after adorning the gay and fashionable world for many years, she left it without any apparent cause and with perfect indifference, and in a great measure secluded herself from society.

The young nobleman's guardian decided that he should receive the usual education given to England's titled sons, and that he should in the first instance be sent to the public school at Harrow. He was accordingly placed there under the tuition of the Rev. Dr. Drury, to whom he has testified his gratitude in a note to the fourth canto of *Childe Harold*, in a manner which does equal honour to the tutor and the pupil. A change of scene and circumstances so rapid would have been hazardous to any boy, but it was doubly so to one of Byron's ardent mind and previous habits. Taken at once from the society of boys in ordinary life, and placed among youths of his own newly-acquired rank, with means of gratification which to him must have appeared considerable, it is by no means surprising that he should have been betrayed into every sort of extravagance: none of them appear, however, to have been of a very culpable nature.

"Though he was lame," says one of his schoolfellows, "he was a great lover of sports, and preferred hockey to Horace, relinquished even Helicon for 'duck-puddle,' and gave up the best poet that ever wrote hard Latin for a game of cricket on the common. He was not remarkable (nor was he ever) for his learning; but he was always a clever, plain-spoken, and undaunted boy. I have seen him fight by the hour like a Trojan, and stand up against the disadvantage of his lameness with all the spirit of an ancient combatant. 'Don't you remember your battle with Pitt?' (a brewer's son), said I to him in a letter (for I witnessed it); but it seems that he had forgotten it. 'You are mistaken, I think,' said he in reply; 'it must have been with Rice-Pudding Morgan, or Lord Jocelyn, or one of the Douglasses, or George Raynsford, or Pryce (with whom I had two conflicts), or with Moses Moore (the 'clod'), or with somebody else, and not with Pitt; for with all the above-named and other worthies of the fist had I an interchange of black eyes and bloody noses, at various and sundry periods: however, it may have happened for all that.'"

Byron long retained a friendship for several of his Harrow school-comrades. Lord Clare was one of his constant correspondents; and Scroope Davies was also one of his chief companions before his lordship went to the Continent. The latter gentleman and Byron once lost all their money at "chicken-hazard," in one of the hells of St. James's, and the next morning Davies sent for Byron's pistols to shoot himself with. Byron sent a note refusing to give them, on the ground that they would be forfeited as a deodand and this comic excuse had the desired effect.

Byron, whilst living at Newstead during the Harrow vacation, saw and became enamoured of Miss Chaworth, the Mary of his poetry, and the maiden of his beautiful "Dream." Miss Chaworth was older than his lordship by a few years, was light and volatile; and though no doubt highly flattered by his attachment, treated our poet less as an ardent lover than as a younger brother. She was punctual to their assignations, which took place at a gate dividing the grounds of the Byrons from the Chaworths, and received all his letters; but her answers, it is said, were written with more of the caution of coquetry than the romance of "love's young dream." She, however, gave him her picture, but her hand was reserved for another.

It was somewhat remarkable that Lord Byron and Miss Chaworth should both have

been under the guardianship of Mr. White, who was associated with Lord Carlisle in that office over Byron. Mr. White particularly wished that his wards should be united in marriage; but Miss C., as young ladies generally do in such circumstances, differed from him, and was resolved to please herself in the choice of a husband. The celebrated Mr. M., commonly known by the name of Jack M., was at this time quite the rage, and Miss C. was not subtle enough to conceal the *penchant* she had for him. It was in vain that Mr. W. took her from one watering-place to another; still the lover, like an evil spirit, followed; and at last, being somehow more persuasive than the "child of song," he carried off the lady, to the great grief of Lord Byron. The marriage, however, was not a happy one; the parties soon separated; and Mrs. M. afterwards proposed an interview with her former lover, which, by the advice of his sister, he declined.

Then it was that Lord Byron published his first poems, under the title of *Hours of Idleness*, which gave little promise of that eminent genius which afterwards distinguished their author. The history of the attack upon this first essay of the noble young poet, by a critic in the *Edinburgh Review*, and his lordship's caustic poem, *English Bards and Scotch Reviewers*, in retaliation, are well known. The latter, besides giving a present triumph to the poet, exhibited the first germs of those matchless powers which in a few years afterwards were felt and acknowledged throughout Europe and the world.

From Harrow Lord Byron was removed to Trinity College, Cambridge: there, however, he did not mend his manners, nor hold the sages of antiquity in higher esteem than when under the command of his reverend tutor at Harrow. He was above studying the poets, and held the rules of the Stagyrite in as little esteem as in after-life he did the "invariable principles" of the Rev. Mr. Bowles. Reading after the fashion of the studious men of Cam was to him a bore, and he held a senior wrangler in the greatest contempt. Persons of real genius are seldom candidates for college prizes; and Byron left them to those plodding characters who perhaps deserve them, as the guerdon of the unceasing labour necessary to overcome the all-but invincible dulness of their intellects. Instead of reading what tutors pleased, Byron read what pleased himself, and wrote what could not fail to displease those connected with the university. He did not admire their system of education; and they, as is the case with most scholars, could admire no other. He took to quizzing them; and as no one likes to be laughed at, doctors frowned, fellows fumed, and Byron at the age of nineteen left college without a degree.

Among other means which he adopted to show his contempt for academical honours, he kept a young bear in his room for some time, which he told all his friends was in training for a fellowship.

When Lord Byron bade adieu to the university, he took up his residence at Newstead Abbey, where his pursuits were principally those of amusement. Among others he was extremely fond of the water. In his aquatic exercises he had seldom any other companion than a large Newfoundland dog, to try whose sagacity and fidelity he used to let himself fall out of the boat, as if by accident, when the dog would seize him and drag him ashore. On losing this dog, in the autumn of 1808, he caused a monument to be erected, upon which are inscribed some verses commemorative of its attachment.

The following descriptions of Newstead will be found interesting:—

"This abbey was founded in the year 1170, by Henry II., as a priory of Black Canons,

and dedicated to the Virgin Mary. It continued in the family of the Byrons until the time of our poet, who sold it first to Mr. Claughton for the sum of 140,000*l.*; and on that gentleman's not being able to fulfil the agreement, and paying 20,000*l.* of a forfeit, it was afterwards sold to another person, and most of the money vested in trustees for the jointure of the Hon. Mrs. Byron. The greater part of the edifice still remains. The present possessor, Major Wildman, is, with genuine taste, repairing this beautiful specimen of Gothic architecture. The late Lord Byron repaired a considerable part of it; but, forgetting the roof, he turned his attention to the inside; and the consequence was, that in a few years the rain, penetrating to the apartments, soon destroyed all those elegant devices which his lordship contrived. Lord Byron's own study was a neat little apartment, decorated with some good classic busts, a select collection of books, an antique cross, a sword in a gilt case, and, at the end of the room, two finely-polished skulls on a pair of light fancy stands. In the garden, likewise, there was a great number of these skulls, taken from the burial-ground of the abbey, and piled up together: but they were afterwards re-committed to the earth." A writer, who visited it soon after Lord Byron had sold it, says: "In one corner of the servants' hall lay a stone coffin, in which were fencing-gloves and foils; and on the walls of the ample but cheerless kitchen was painted in large letters, 'Waste not, want not.' During the minority of Lord Byron, the abbey was in the possession of Lord G——, his hounds, and divers colonies of jackdaws, swallows, and starlings. The internal traces of this Goth were swept away; but without, all appeared as rude and unreclaimed as he could have left it. With the exception of the dog's tomb, a conspicuous and elegant object, I do not recollect the slightest trace of culture or improvement. The late lord, a stern and desperate character, who is never mentioned by the neighbouring peasants without a significant shake of the head, might have returned and recognised everything about him, except, perhaps, an additional crop of weeds. There still slept that old pond, into which he is said to have hurled his lady in one of his fits of fury, whence she was rescued by the gardener, a courageous blade, who was his lord's master, and chastised him for his barbarity. There still, at the end of the garden, in a grove of oak, two towering satyrs, he with his goat and club, and Mrs. Satyr with her chubby cloven-footed brat, placed on pedestals at the intersections of the narrow and gloomy pathways, struck for a moment, with their grim visages and silent shaggy forms, the fear into your bosom which is felt by the neighbouring peasantry at 'th'oud laird's devils.' I have frequently asked the country people near Newstead, what sort of a man his lordship (our Lord Byron) was. The impression of his eccentric but energetic character was evident in the reply, 'He's the devil of a fellow for comical fancies. He flogs th'oud laird to nothing; but he's a hearty good fellow for all that.'"

Walpole, who had visited Newstead, gives, in his usual bitter, sarcastic manner, the following account of it:

"As I returned I saw Newstead and Althorp; I like both. The former is the very abbey. The great east window of the church remains, and connects with the house; the hall entire, the refectory entire, the cloister untouched, with the ancient cistern of the convent, and their arms on it: it has a private chapel quite perfect. The park, which is still charming, has not been so much unprofaned. The present lord has lost large sums, and paid part in old oaks, five thousand pounds' worth of which have been cut near the

house. *En revanche*, he has built two baby forts, to pay his country in castles for damage done to the navy; and planted a handful of Scotch firs, that look like ploughboys dressed in old family liveries for a public day. In the hall is a very good collection of pictures, all animals. The refectory, now the great drawing-room, is full of Byrons; the vaulted roof remaining, but the windows have new dresses making for them by a Venetian tailor."

It was at Newstead, just before his coming of age, that he planned his future travels; and his original intention included a much larger portion of the world than that which he afterwards visited. He first thought of Persia, to which idea, indeed, he for a long time adhered. He afterwards meant to sail for India; and had so far contemplated this project as to write for information to the Arabic professor at Cambridge, and to ask his mother to inquire of a friend who had lived in India, what things would be necessary for his voyage. He formed his plan of travelling upon very different grounds from those which he afterwards advanced. All men should travel at one time or another, he thought, and he had then no connexions to prevent him; when he returned he might enter into political life, for which travelling would not incapacitate him; and he wished to judge of men by experience.

At length, in July 1809, in company with John Cam Hobhouse, Esq. (with whom his acquaintance commenced at Cambridge), Lord Byron embarked at Falmouth for Lisbon, and thence proceeded, by the southern provinces of Spain, to the Mediterranean The objects that he met with as far as Gibraltar seem to have occupied his mind, to the temporary exclusion of his gloomy and misanthropic thoughts; for a letter which he wrote to his mother from thence contains much playful description of the scenes through which he had passed. At Seville Lord Byron lodged in the house of two ladies, one of whom was about to be married, and who, though he remained there only three days, paid him the most particular attention. At parting, she embraced him with great tenderness, cutting off a lock of his hair, and presenting him with one of her own. With this specimen of Spanish female manners, he proceeded to Cadiz, where various incidents occurred to confirm the opinion he had formed at Seville of the Andalusian belles, and which made him leave it with regret, but with a determination to return to it. He wrote to his mother from Malta, announcing his safety, and again from Previsa in November. Upon arriving at Yanina, he found that Ali Pacha was with his troops in Illyrium, besieging Ibrahim Pacha in Berat; but the vizier, having heard that an English nobleman was in his country, had given orders at Yanina to supply him with every kind of accommodation free of expense. From Yanina Lord Byron went to Tepaleen. Here he was lodged in the palace, and the next day introduced to Ali Pacha, who declared that he knew him to be a man of rank from the smallness of his ears, his curling hair, and his white hands.

In going in a Turkish ship of war, provided by Ali Pacha, from Previsa, intending to sail for Patras, Lord Byron was very nearly lost in a moderate gale of wind, from the ignorance of the Turkish officers and sailors, and was driven on the coast of Suli, where an instance of disinterested hospitality in the chief of a Suliote village occurred. The honest Albanian, after assisting him in his distress, supplying his wants, and lodging him and his suite, refused to receive any remuneration. When Lord Byron pressed him to accept some money, he said, "I wish you to love me, not to pay me!" At Yanina, on

his return, he was introduced to Hussein Bey and Mahmout Pacha, two young children of Ali Pacha. He afterwards visited Smyrna, whence he went in the Salsette frigate to Constantinople.

On the 3rd of May, 1810, while the Salsette was lying at anchor in the Dardanelles, Lord Byron, accompanied by Lieutenant Ekenhead, swam across the Hellespont from the European shore to the Asiatic—about two miles wide. The tide of the Dardanelles runs so strong, that it is impossible either to swim or to sail to any given point. Lord Byron went from the castle to Abydos, landing full three miles below his meditated place of approach. He had a boat in attendance all the way; so that no danger could be apprehended, even if his strength had failed. His lordship records, in one of his minor poems, that he got the ague by the voyage; but it was well known, that after landing he was so much exhausted, that he gladly accepted the offer of a Turkish fisherman, and reposed in his hut for several hours. He was then very ill; and as Lieutenant Ekenhead was compelled to go on board his frigate, he was left alone. The Turk had no idea of the rank or consequence of his inmate, but paid him most marked attention. His wife was his nurse; and at the end of five days he left this asylum, completely recovered. When about to embark, the Turk gave him a large loaf, a cheese, a skin filled with wine, and a few paras (about a penny each), prayed Allah to bless him, and wished him safe home. When his lordship arrived at Abydos, he sent over his man Stefano to the Turk, with an assortment of fishing nets, a fowling-piece, a brace of pistols, and twelve yards of silk to make gowns for his wife. The poor Turk was astonished. "What a noble return," said he, "for an act of humanity!" He then formed the resolution of crossing the Hellespont, in order to thank his lordship in person. H[illegible] wife approved of the plan; and he had sailed about half way across, when a sudden squall upset his boat, and the poor Turkish fisherman found a watery grave. Lord Byron was much distressed on hearing of the catastrophe, and, with all that kindness of heart which was natural to him, he sent the widow fifty dollars, and told her he would ever be her friend. This anecdote, so highly honourable to his lordship's memory, is very little known. Lieutenant Hare, who was on the spot at the time, furnished the particulars; and added that, in the year 1817, Lord Byron, then proceeding to Constantinople, landed at the same spot, and made a handsome present to the widow and her son.

It was not till after Lord Byron arrived at Constantinople that he decided on not going to Persia, but to pass the following summer in the Morea. At Constantinople, Mr. Hobhouse left him to return to England. On losing his companion, Lord Byron went alone to many of the places which he had already visited, and studied scenery and manners, especially those of Greece, with the searching eye of a poet. His mind appeared occasionally to have some tendency towards a recovery from the morbid state of apathy which it had previously evinced; and the gratification he manifested on observing the superiority of England over other countries, proved that patriotism was far from being extinct in his bosom. The embarrassed state of his affairs at length induced him to return home; and he arrived in the *Volage* frigate on the 2nd of July, 1811, having been absent two years. His health had not suffered by his travels, although it had been interrupted by two sharp fevers, in consequence of which he put himself on a vegetable diet, and drank no wine.

Soon after his arrival, the serious illness of his mother summoned him to Newstead; but on reaching the Abbey he found that she had breathed her last. He suffered much

from this loss, and from the disappointment of not seeing her before her death; and while his feelings on the subject were still acute, he received the intelligence that a friend, whom he highly esteemed, had been drowned in the Cam. Not long before, he had heard of the death at Coimbra of a schoolfellow to whom he was much attached. These three melancholy events, occurring within the space of a month, had a powerful effect on Lord Byron's feelings.

Towards the termination of his *English Bards and Scotch Reviewers*, the noble author had declared that it was his intention to break off, from that period, his connexion with the Muses. Such resolutions are seldom maintained. In February 1812 the first two cantos of *Childe Harold's Pilgrimage* (with the manuscript of which he had presented Mr. Dallas) made their appearance, and produced an effect on the public equal to that of any work which has been published within this or the last century.

The indications of a powerful and original mind which glance through every line of *Childe Harold* electrified the mass of readers, and placed at once upon Lord Byron's head the garland for which other men of genius have toiled long and obtained late. He became pre-eminent among the literary men of his country by general acclamation. Those who had so mercilessly censured his juvenile essays were the first to pay homage to his more matured efforts; while others, who saw in the sentiments of Childe Harold much to regret and censure, did not withhold their tribute of applause to the depth of thought and force of expression which animated the *Pilgrimage*. Thus, as all admired the poem, all were prepared to greet the author with that fame which is the poet's best reward. It was amidst such feelings of admiration that Lord Byron fully entered on that public stage, where, to the close of his life, he made so distinguished a figure.

At one of the fashionable parties to which the noble bard was invited, his Majesty, then Prince Regent, happened to be present. Lord Byron was at some distance when he entered the room, but, on learning who he was, his Royal Highness sent a gentleman to desire that he would be presented. Of course the presentation took place: the Regent expressed his admiration of *Childe Harold's Pilgrimage*, and entered into a conversation which so fascinated the poet, that had it not been for an accident which deferred a levee intended to have been held the next day, he would have gone to court. Soon after, however, an unfortunate influence counteracted the effect of royal praise, and Byron permitted himself to write and speak disrespectfully of the Prince.

The whole of Byron's political career may be summed up in the following anecdotes:

The Earl of Carlisle having declined to introduce him to the House of Peers, he resolved to introduce himself, and accordingly went there a little before the usual hour, when he knew few of the lords would be present. On entering he appeared rather abashed, and looked very pale, but, passing the woolsack where the Chancellor (Lord Eldon) was engaged in some of the ordinary routine of the house, he went directly to the table, where the oaths were administered to him. The Lord Chancellor then approached, and offered his hand in the most open, friendly manner, congratulating him on his taking possession of his seat. Lord Byron only placed the tips of his fingers in the Chancellor's hand: the latter returned to his seat: and Byron, after lounging a few minutes on one of the opposition benches, retired. To Mr. Dallas, who followed him out, he gave as a reason for not entering into the spirit of the Chancellor, "that it might have been supposed he would join the court party, whereas he intended to have nothing at all to do with politics."

He only addressed the house three times: the first of his speeches was on the Frame-work Bill; the second in favour of the Catholic claims, which gave good hopes of his becoming an orator; and the other related to a petition from Major Cartwright. Byron himself says, the lords told him "his manner was not dignified enough for them, and would better suit the lower house;" others say, they gathered round him while speaking, listening with the greatest attention—a sign, at any rate, that he was interesting. He always voted with the Opposition, but evinced no likelihood of becoming the partisan of either side.

The enmity that Byron entertained towards the Earl of Carlisle was owing to two causes: the earl had spoken rather irreverently of the *Hours of Idleness;* and had also refused to introduce his kinsman to the House of Lords, even, it is said, doubting his right to a seat in that honourable house. The Earl was a great admirer of the classic drama, and once published a pamphlet, in which he strenuously argued in behalf of the propriety and necessity of small theatres: the same day that this weighty publication appeared, he subscribed a thousand pounds for some public purpose. On this occasion Byron composed the following epigram:

"Carlisle subscribes a thousand pound
Out of his rich domains;
And for a sixpence circles round
The produce of his brains:
'Tis thus the difference you may hit
Between his fortune and his wit."

Byron retained to the last his antipathy to this relative. On reading some lines addressed to Lady Holland by the Earl of Carlisle, persuading her to reject the snuff-box bequeathed to her by Napoleon, beginning

"Lady, reject the gift," &c

he immediately wrote the following parody:

"Lady, accept the gift a hero wore,
In spite of all this elegiac stuff:
Let not seven stanzas written by a bore
Prevent your ladyship from taking snuff."

On the 2d of January, 1815, Lord Byron married, at Seaham, in the county of Durham, Anne Isabella, only daughter of Sir Ralph Millbank (since Noel), Bart. To this lady he had made a proposal twelve months before, but was rejected: well would it have been for their mutual happiness had that rejection been repeated. After their marriage, Lord and Lady Byron took a house in London, gave splendid dinner-parties, and launched into every sort of fashionable extravagance. This could not last long; the portion which his lordship received with Miss Millbank (ten thousand pounds) soon melted away; and at length an execution was actually levied on the furniture of his residence. It was then agreed that Lady Byron, who on the 10th of December, 1815, had presented her lord with a daughter, should pay a visit to her father till the storm was blown over, and some arrangements had been made with their creditors. From that visit she never returned, and a separation ensued, for which various reasons have been assigned: the real cause or causes, however, are up to this moment involved in mystery; though, as might be expected, a wonderful

sensation was excited at the time, and every description of contradictory rumour was in active circulation.

Byron was first introduced to Miss Millbank at Lady ——'s. In going up stairs he stumbled, and remarked to Moore, who accompanied him, that it was a bad omen. On entering the room, he perceived a lady, more simply dressed than the rest, sitting on a sofa. He asked Moore if she was a humble companion to any of the ladies. The latter replied, "She is a great heiress; you'd better marry her, and repair the old place at Newstead."

The following anecdotes on the subject of his marriage are given from Lord Byron's Conversations, in his own words:

"There was something piquant, and what we term pretty, in Miss Millbank; her features were small and feminine, though not regular; she had the fairest skin imaginable; her figure was perfect for her height; and there was a simplicity, a retired modesty about her, which was very characteristic, and formed a happy contrast to the cold artificial formality and studied stiffness which is called fashion: she interested me exceedingly. It is unnecessary to detail the progress of our acquaintance: I became daily more attached to her, and it ended in my making her a proposal that was rejected; her refusal was couched in terms that could not offend me. I was besides persuaded that in declining my offer she was governed by the influence of her mother, and was the more confirmed in this opinion by her reviving our correspondence herself twelve months after. The tenor of her letter was that although she could not love me, she desired my friendship. Friendship is a dangerous word for young ladies; it is love full-fledged, and waiting for a fine day to fly.

"I was not so young when my father died, but that I perfectly remember him, and had very early a horror of matrimony, from the sight of domestic broils; this feeling came over me very strongly at my wedding. Something whispered me that I was sealing my own death-warrant. I am a great believer in presentiments: Socrates' demon was not a fiction; Monk Lewis had his monitor; and Napoleon many warnings. At the last moment I would have retreated if I could have done so. I called to mind a friend of mine, who had married a young, beautiful, and rich girl, and yet was miserable; he had strongly urged me against putting my neck in the same yoke: and, to show you how firmly I was resolved to attend to his advice, I betted Hay fifty guineas to one that I should always remain single. Six years afterwards, I sent him the money. The day before I proposed to Lady Byron, I had no idea of doing so.

"It had been predicted by Mrs. Williams, that twenty-seven was to be a dangerous age for me: the fortune-telling witch was right; it was destined to prove so. I shall never forget the 2nd of January! Lady Byron (Byrn, he pronounced it) was the only unconcerned person present; Lady Noel, her mother, cried; I trembled like a leaf, made the wrong responses, and after the ceremony, called her Miss Millbank.

"There is a singular history attached to the ring: the very day the match was concluded, a ring of my mother's that had been lost was dug up by the gardener at Newstead. I thought it was sent on purpose for the wedding; but my mother's marriage had not been a fortunate one, and this ring was doomed to be the seal of an unhappier union still.

"After the ordeal was over, we set off for a country seat of Sir Ralph's; and I was surprised at the arrangements for the journey, and somewhat out of humour to find a lady's maid stuck between me and my bride. It was rather too early to assume the husband, so I was forced to submit, but it was not with a very good grace.

"I have been accused of saying, on getting into the carriage, that I had married Lady Byron out of spite, and because she had refused me twice. Though I was for a moment vexed at her prudery, or whatever it may be called, if I had made so uncavalier, not to say brutal, a speech, I am convinced Lady Byron would instantly have left the carriage to me and the maid (I mean the lady's); she had spirit enough to have done so, and would properly have resented the affront.

"Our honeymoon was not all sunshine, it had its clouds; and Hobhouse has some letters which would serve to explain the rise and fall in the barometer; but it was never down at zero.

"A curious thing happened to me shortly after the honeymoon, which was very awkward at the time, but has since amused me much. It so happened that three married women were on a wedding visit to my wife (and in the same room at the same time), whom I had known to be all birds of the same nest. Fancy the scene of confusion that ensued!

"The world says I married Miss Millbank for her fortune, because she was a great heiress. All I have ever received, or am likely to receive (and that has been twice paid back too), was 10,000*l.* My own income at this period was small and somewhat bespoke. Newstead was a very unprofitable estate, and brought me in a bare 1500*l.* a year; the Lancashire property was hampered with a lawsuit, which has cost me 14,000*l.*, and is not yet finished.

"I heard afterwards that Mrs. Charlment had been the means of poisoning Lady Noel's mind against me; that she had employed herself and others in watching me in London, and had reported having traced me into a house in Portland Place. There was one act unworthy of any one but such a confidante; I allude to the breaking open my writing-desk: a book was found in it that did not do much credit to my taste in literature, and some letters from a married woman with whom I had been intimate before my marriage. The use that was made of the latter was most unjustifiable, whatever may be thought of the breach of confidence that led to their discovery. Lady Byron sent them to the husband of the lady, who had the good sense to take no notice of their contents. The gravest accusation that has been made against me is that of having intrigued with Mrs. Mardyn in my own house, introduced her to my own table, &c.: there never was a more unfounded calumny. Being on the Committee of Drury Lane Theatre, I have no doubt that several actresses called on me; but as to Mrs. Mardyn, who was a beautiful woman, and might have been a dangerous visitress, I was scarcely acquainted (to speak) with her. I might even make a more serious charge against —— than employing spies to watch suspected amours. I had been shut up in a dark street in London, writing *The Siege of Corinth*, and had refused myself to every one till it was finished. I was surprised one day by a doctor and a lawyer almost forcing themselves at the same time into my room; I did not know till afterwards the real object of their visit. I thought their questions singular, frivolous, and somewhat importunate, if not impertinent; but what should I have thought if I had known that they were sent to provide proofs of my insanity! I have no doubt that my answers to these emissaries' interrogations were not very rational or consistent, for my imagination was heated by other things; but Dr. Baillie could not conscientiously make me out a certificate for Bedlam, and perhaps the lawyer gave a more favourable report to his employers. The doctor said afterwards he had been told that I always looked down when Lady Byron bent her eyes on me, and exhibited other symptoms equally infallible, particularly those that

marked the late king's case so strongly. I do not, however, tax Lady Byron with this transaction: probably she was not privy to it; she was the tool of others. Her mother always detested me: she had not even the decency to conceal it in her own house. Dining one day at Sir Ralph's (who was a good sort of man, and of whom you may form some idea, when I tell you that a leg of mutton was always served at his table, that he might cut the same joke upon it), I broke a tooth, and was in great pain, which I could not avoid showing. 'It will do you good,' said Lady Noel; 'I am glad of it!' I gave her a look!

"Lady Byron had good ideas, but could never express them; wrote poetry too, but it was only good by accident; her letters were always enigmatical, often unintelligible. She was easily made the dupe of the designing, for she thought her knowledge of mankind infallible. She had got some foolish idea of Madame de Staël's into her head, that a person may be better known in the first hour than in ten years. She had the habit of drawing people's characters after she had seen them once or twice. She wrote pages on pages about my character, but it was as unlike as possible. She was governed by what she called fixed rules and principles, squared mathematically. She would have made an excellent wrangler at Cambridge. It must be confessed, however, that she gave no proof of her boasted consistency. First she refused me, then she accepted me, then she separated herself from me—so much for consistency. I need not tell you of the obloquy and opprobrium that were cast upon my name when our separation was made public. I once made a list from the journals of the day of the different worthies, ancient and modern, to whom I was compared: I remember a few,—Nero, Apicius, Epicurus, Caligula, Heliogabalus, Henry the Eighth, and lastly, the ——. All my former friends, even my Cousin George Byron, who had been brought up with me, and whom I loved as a brother, took my wife's part: he followed the stream when it was strongest against me, and can never expect anything from me; he shall never touch a sixpence of mine. I was looked upon as the worst of husbands, the most abandoned and wicked of men; and my wife as a suffering angel, an incarnation of all the virtues and perfections of the sex. I was abused in the public prints, made the common talk of private companies, hissed as I went to the House of Lords, insulted in the streets, afraid to go to the theatre, whence the unfortunate Mrs. Mardyn had been driven with insult. The *Examiner* was the only paper that dared say a word in my defence, and Lady Jersey the only person in the fashionable world that did not look upon me as a monster.

"In addition to all these mortifications, my affairs were irretrievably involved, and almost so as to make me what they wished. I was compelled to part with Newstead, which I never could have ventured to sell in my mother's lifetime. As it is, I shall never forgive myself for having done so, though I am told that the estate would not now bring half so much as I got for it: this does not at all reconcile me to having parted with the old Abbey. I did not make up my mind to this step but from the last necessity; I had my wife's portion to repay, and was determined to add 10,000*l.* more of my own to it, which I did: I always hated being in debt, and do not owe a guinea. The moment I had put my affairs in train, and in little more than eighteen months after my marriage, I left England, a voluntary exile, intending it should be for ever."

We shall here avail ourselves of some observations by a powerful and elegant critic,* whose opinions on the personal character of Lord Byron, as well as on the merits of his poems, are, from their originality, candour, and discrimination, of considerable weight.

* Sir Egerton Brydges, Bart.

"The charge against Lord Byron," says this writer, "is not that he fell a victim to excessive temptations, and a combination of circumstances, which it required a rare and extraordinary degree of virtue, wisdom, prudence, and steadiness to surmount; but that he abandoned a situation of uncommon advantages, and fell weakly, pusillanimously, and selfishly, when victory would have been easy, and when defeat was ignominious. In reply to this charge I do not deny that Lord Byron inherited some very desirable, and even enviable privileges, in the lot of life which fell to his share. I should falsify my own sentiments if I treated lightly the gift of an ancient English peerage, and a name of honour and venerable antiquity; but without a fortune competent to that rank, it is not a bed of roses, nay, it is attended with many and extreme difficulties; and the difficulties are exactly such as a genius and temper like Lord Byron's were least calculated to meet—at any rate, least calculated to meet under the peculiar collateral circumstances in which he was placed. His income was very narrow; his Newstead property left him a very small disposable surplus; his Lancashire property was, in its condition, &c. unproductive. A profession, such as the army, might have lessened, or almost annihilated the difficulties of his peculiar position; but probably his lameness rendered this impossible. He seems to have had a love of independence, which was noble, and probably even an intractability; but this temper added to his indisposition to bend and adapt himself to his lot. A dull, or supple, or intriguing man, without a single good quality of head or heart, might have managed it much better; he might have made himself subservient to government, and wormed himself into some lucrative place; or might have lived meanly, conformed himself stupidly or cringingly to all humours, and been borne onward on the wings of society with little personal expense.

"Lord Byron was of another quality and temperament. If the world would not conform to him, still less would he conform to the world. He had all the manly baronial pride of his ancestors, though he had not all their wealth, and their means of generosity, hospitality, and patronage. He had the will, alas! without the power.

"With this temper, these feelings, this genius, exposed to a combination of such untoward and trying circumstances, it would indeed have been inimitably praiseworthy if Lord Byron could have been always wise, prudent, calm, correct, pure, virtuous, and unassailable:—if he could have shown all the force and splendour of his mighty poetical energies, without any mixture of their clouds, their baneful lightnings, or their storms: if he could have preserved all his sensibility to every kind and noble passion, yet have remained placid, and unaffected by the attack of any blameable emotion;—that is, it would have been admirable if he had been an angel, and not a man!

"Unhappily, the outrages he received, the gross calumnies which were heaped upon him, even in the time of his highest favour with the public, turned the delights of his very days of triumph to poison, and gave him a sort of moody, fierce, and violent despair, which led to humours, acts, and words, that mutually aggravated the ill-will and the offences between him and his assailants. There was a daring spirit in his temper and his talents, which was always inflamed rather than corrected by opposition.

"In this most unpropitious state of things, everything that went wrong was attributed to Lord Byron, and, when once attributed, was assumed and argued upon as an undeniable fact. Yet, to my mind, it is quite clear,—quite unattended by a particle of doubt,—that in many things in which he has been the most blamed, he was the absolute victim of

misfortune; that unpropitious trains of events (for I do not wish to shift the blame on others) led to explosions and consequent derangements, which no cold, prudent pretender to extreme propriety and correctness could have averted or met in a manner less blameable than that in which Lord Byron met it."

By his ill-assorted marriage, Lord Byron had one child, a daughter, for whom he felt to the hour of his death the strongest and most anxious affection. She was named Ada: the beautifully pathetic stanza at the opening of the third canto of *Childe Harold* touchingly expresses his paternal feelings towards this "sole daughter of his house and heart."

In the spring of 1816, Lord Byron quitted England, to return to it no more. He crossed over to France, through which he passed rapidly to Brussels, taking in his way a survey of the field of Waterloo. He then proceeded to Coblentz, and up the Rhine to Basle. He passed the summer on the banks of the lake of Geneva. With what enthusiasm he enjoyed its scenery, his own poetry soon exhibited to the world. The third canto of *Childe Harold*, *Manfred*, and the *Prisoner of Chillon* were composed at the Campagno Diodati, at Coligny, a mile from Geneva.

Lord Byron avoided as much as possible any intercourse with his countrymen at Venice; and this seems to have been in a great measure necessary, in order to prevent the intrusion of impertinent curiosity. In the appendix to one of his poems, written with reference to a book of travels, the author of which disclaimed any wish to be introduced to the noble lord, he loftily and sarcastically chastises the incivility of such a gratuitous declaration, expresses his "utter abhorrence of any contact with the travelling English;" and thus concludes: "Except Lords Lansdowne, Jersey, and Lauderdale, Messrs. Scott, Hammond, Sir Humphry Davy, the late Mr. Lewis, Bankes, W. Hoppner, Thomas Moore, Lord Kinnaird, his brother, Mr. Joy, and Mr. Hobhouse, I do not recollect to have exchanged a word with another Englishman, since I left their country; and almost all these I had known before. The others, and God knows there were some hundreds, who bored me with letters or visits, I refused to have any communication with, and shall be proud and happy when that wish becomes mutual."

After a residence of three years at Venice, Lord Byron removed to Ravenna, towards the close of the year 1819. Here he wrote the *Prophecy of Dante*, which exhibited a new specimen of the astonishing variety of strength and expansion of faculties he possessed and exercised. About the same time he wrote *Sardanapalus*, a tragedy; *Cain*, a mystery; and *Heaven and Earth*, a mystery. Though there are some obvious reasons which render *Sardanapalus* unfit for the English stage, it is, on the whole, the most splendid specimen which our language affords of that species of tragedy which was the exclusive object of Lord Byron's admiration. *Cain* is one of the productions which has subjected its noble author to the severest denunciations, on account of the crime of impiety alleged against it, as it seems to have a tendency to call in question the benevolence of Providence. In answer to the loud and general outcry which this production occasioned, Lord Byron observed, in a letter to his publisher, "If *Cain* be blasphemous, *Paradise Lost* is blasphemous, and the words of the Oxford gentleman, 'Evil, be thou my good,' are from that very poem from the mouth of Satan; and is there anything more in that of Lucifer in the mystery? *Cain* is nothing more than a drama, not a piece of argument: if Lucifer and Cain speak as the first rebel and first murderer may be supposed to speak, nearly all the

rest of the personages talk also according to their characters; and the stronger passions have ever been permitted to the drama. I have avoided introducing the Deity as in Scripture, though Milton does, and not very wisely either: but have adopted his angel, as sent to Cain, instead, on purpose to avoid shocking any feelings on the subject, by falling short of what all uninspired men must fall short in, viz. giving an adequate notion of the effect of the presence of Jehovah. The old mysteries introduced him liberally enough, and all this I avoided in the new one."

An event occurred at Ravenna, during his lordship's stay there, which made a deep impression on him, and to which he alludes in the fifth canto of *Don Juan*. The military commandant of the place, suspected of being secretly a Carbonaro, but too powerful a man to be arrested, was assassinated opposite Lord Byron's palace. His lordship had his foot in the stirrup at the usual hour of exercise, when his horse started at the report of a gun: on looking up, Lord Byron perceived a man throw down a carbine and run away at full speed, and another man stretched upon the pavement a few yards distant; it was the unhappy commandant. A crowd was soon collected, but no one ventured to offer the least assistance. Lord Byron directed his servant to lift up the bleeding body, and carry it into his palace; though it was represented to him that by doing so he would confirm the suspicion, which was already entertained, of his belonging to the same party. Such an apprehension could have had no effect on Byron's mind when an act of humanity was to be performed: he assisted in bearing the victim of assassination into the house, and putting him on a bed; but he was already dead from several wounds. "He appeared to have breathed his last without a struggle," said his lordship, when afterwards recounting the affair. "I never saw a countenance so calm. His adjutant followed the corpse into the house; I remember the lamentation over him:—'Povero diavalo! non aveva fatto male, anchè ad un cane.'" The following were the noble writer's poetical reflections (in *Don Juan*) on viewing the dead body:—

"—— I gazed (as oft I have gazed the same
To try if I could wrench aught out of death
Which should confirm, or shake, or make a faith.
But it was all a mystery:—here we are,
 And there we go:—but where? Five bits of lead,
Or three, or two, or one, send very far!
 And is this blood, then, form'd but to be shed?
Can every element our elements mar?
 And air, earth, water, fire, live,—and we dead?
 We whose minds comprehend all things?"

That a being of such capabilities should abstractedly, and without an attempt to throw the responsibility on a fictitious personage, have avowed such startling doubts, was a daring which, whatever might have been his private opinion, he ought not to have hazarded.

"It is difficult," observes Captain Medwin, "to judge, from the contradictory nature of his writings, what the religious opinions of Lord Byron really were. From the conversations I held with him, on the whole, I am inclined to think that, if he were occasionally sceptical, and thought it, as he says in *Don Juan*,

'—— a pleasant voyage, perhaps, to float
Like Pyrrho, in a sea of speculation,'

yet his wavering never amounted to a disbelief in Christianity.'"

In the autumn of 1821, the noble bard removed to Pisa, in Tuscany. He took up his residence in the Lanfranchi Palace, and engaged in an intrigue with the beautiful Guiccioli, wife of the count of that name, which connexion, with more than his usual constancy, he maintained for nearly three years; during which period the countess was separated from her husband, on an application from the latter to the Pope.

The following is a sketch of this "fair enchantress," as taken at the time the *liaison* was formed between her and Byron. "The countess is twenty-three years of age, though she appears no more than seventeen or eighteen. Unlike most of the Italian women, her complexion is delicately fair. Her eyes, large, dark, and languishing, are shaded by the longest eye-lashes in the world; and her hair, which is ungathered on her head, plays over her falling shoulders in a profusion of natural ringlets of the darkest auburn. Her figure is, perhaps, too much embonpoint for her height; but her bust is perfect. Her features want little of possessing a Grecian regularity of outline; and she has the most beautiful mouth and teeth imaginable. It is impossible to see without admiring—to hear the Guiccioli speak without being fascinated. Her amiability and gentleness show themselves in every intonation of her voice, which, and the music of her perfect Italian, give a peculiar charm to everything she utters. Grace and elegance seem component parts of her nature. Notwithstanding that she adores Lord Byron, it is evident that the exile and poverty of her aged father sometimes affect her spirits, and throw a shade of melancholy on her countenance, which adds to the deep interest this lovely woman creates. Her conversation is lively, without being learned; she has read all the best authors of her own and the French language. She often conceals what she knows, from the fear of being thought to know too much, possibly from being aware that Lord Byron was not fond of *blues*. He is certainly very much attached to her, without being actually in love. His description of the Giorgioni in the Manfrini Palace at Venice is meant for the countess. The beautiful sonnet prefixed to the *Prophecy of Dante* was addressed to her."

It is impossible to conceive a more unvaried life than Lord Byron led at this period, in the society of a few select friends. Billiards, conversation, or reading, filled up the intervals till it was time to take the evening drive, ride, and pistol-practice. He dined at half an hour after sunset, then drove to Count Gamba's, the Countess Guiccioli's father, passed several hours in her society, returned to his palace, and either read or wrote till two or three in the morning; occasionally drinking spirits diluted with water as a medicine, from a dread of a nephritic complaint to which he was, or fancied himself, subject.

While Lord Byron resided at Pisa, a serious affray occurred, in which he was personally concerned. Taking his usual ride with some friends, one of them was violently jostled by a serjeant-major of hussars, who dashed at full speed through the midst of the party. They pursued and overtook him near the Piaggia gate; but their remonstrances were answered only by abuse and menace, and an attempt on the part of the guard at the gate to arrest them. This occasioned a severe scuffle, in which several of Lord Byron's party were wounded, as was also the hussar. The consequence was, that all Lord Byron's servants (who were warmly attached to him, and had shown great ardour in his defence), were banished from Pisa; and with them the Counts Gamba, father and son. Lord Byron was himself advised to leave it; and as the countess accompanied her father, he soon after joined them at Leghorn, and passed six weeks at Monte Nero. His return to Pisa was occasioned by a new persecution of the Counts Gamba. An order was issued for

them to leave the Tuscan states in four days; and after their embarkation for Genoa, the countess and Lord Byron openly lived together at the Lanfranchi Palace.

It was at Pisa that Byron wrote *Werner*, a tragedy; the *Deformed Transformed;* and continued his *Don Juan* to the end of the sixteenth canto.

Lord Byron's friendship for Leigh Hunt, the late editor of the *Examiner*, was increased by his grateful feeling for the manner in which Mr. Hunt stood forward in his justification at a time when the current of public opinion ran strongly against him. This feeling induced him to invite Mr. Hunt to the Lanfranchi Palace, where a suite of apartments was fitted up for him. On his arrival in the spring of 1822,—a periodical publication was projected under the title of the *Liberal*, of which Hunt was to be the editor, and to which Lord Byron and the celebrated—though yet less celebrated than he merits—poet Shelley (who was on terms of great intimacy with his lordship) were to contribute. Three numbers of the *Liberal* were published in London, when, in consequence of the unhappy fate of Mr. Shelley (who perished in the Mediterranean by the upsetting of a boat), and of other discouraging circumstances, it was discontinued.

The enmity between Byron and Southey, the poet-laureate, is as well known as that between Pope and Colley Cibber. Their politics were diametrically opposite, and the noble bard regarded the bard of royalty as a renegade from his early principles. It was not, however, so much on account of political principles that the enmity between Byron and Southey was kept up. The peer, in his satire, had handled the epics of the laureate "too roughly," and this the latter deeply resented. Whilst travelling on the continent, Southey observed Shelley's name in the album at Mont Anvert, with Αθεος written after it, and an indignant comment in the same language written under it; also the names of some of Byron's other friends. The laureate, it is said, copied the names and the comment, and, on his return to England, reported the whole circumstances, and hesitated not to conclude that Byron was of the same principles as his friends. In a poem he subsequently wrote, called the *Vision of Judgment*, he stigmatised Lord Byron as the father of the "Satanic school of poetry." His lordship, in a note appended to the *Two Foscari*, retorted in a severe manner, and even permitted himself to ridicule Southey's wife, the sister of Mrs. Coleridge, they having been at one time "milliners of Bath." The laureate wrote an answer to this note in the *Courier* newspaper, which, when Byron saw it, enraged him so much, that he consulted with his friends whether or not he ought to go to England to answer it personally. In cooler moments, however, he resolved to write the *Vision of Judgment*, a parody on Southey's; and it appeared in one of the numbers of the *Liberal*, on account of which Hunt, the publisher, was prosecuted by the "Constitutional Association," and found guilty.

As our readers may be curious to know the rate at which Lord Byron was paid for his productions, we annex the following statement, by Mr. Murray the bookseller, of the sums given by him for the copyrights of most of his lordship's works:

Childe Harold, I. II.	£ 600
————, III.	1575
————, IV.	2100
Giaour	525
Bride of Abydos	525
Corsair	525
Lara	700

Siege of Corinth	£ 525
Parisina	525
Lament of Tasso	315
Manfred	315
Beppo	525
Don Juan, I. II.	1525
———, III. IV. V.	1525
Doge of Venice	1050
Sardanapalus, Cain, and Foscari	1100
Mazeppa	525
Prisoner of Chillon	525
Sundries	450
Total	£15,455

Several years ago, Lord Byron presented his friend, Mr. Thomas Moore, with his *Memoirs*, written by himself, with an understanding that they were not to be published until after his death. Mr. Moore, with the consent and at the desire of Lord Byron, sold the manuscript to Mr. Murray, the bookseller, for the sum of 2000 guineas. The following statement by Mr. Moore will, however, show its fate: "Without entering into the respective claims of Mr. Murray and myself to the property in these memoirs (a question which, now that they are destroyed, can be but of little moment to any one), it is sufficient to say that, believing the manuscript still to be mine, I placed it at the disposal of Lord Byron's sister, Mrs. Leigh, with the sole reservation of a protest against its total destruction; at least, without previous perusal and consultation among the parties. The majority of the persons present disagreed with this opinion, and it was the *only point* upon which there did exist any difference between us. The manuscript was accordingly torn and burnt before our eyes, and I immediately paid to Mr. Murray, in the presence of the gentlemen assembled, 2000 guineas, with interest, &c., being the amount of what I owed him upon the security of my bond, and for which I now stand indebted to my publishers, Messrs. Longman and Co. Since then, the family of Lord Byron have, in a manner highly honourable to themselves, proposed an arrangement, by which the sum thus paid to Mr. Murray might be reimbursed me; but from feelings and considerations which it is unnecessary here to explain, I have respectfully, but peremptorily, declined their offer."

As is the case with many men in affluent circumstances, Byron was at times more than generous, and at other times what might be called mean. He once borrowed 500*l.* in order to give it to the widow of one who had been his friend; he frequently dined on five pauls, and once gave his bills to a lady to be examined, because he thought he was cheated. He paid 1000*l.* for a yacht, which he sold again for 300*l.*, and refused to give the sailors their jackets. It ought, however, to be observed, that generosity was natural to him, and that his avarice, if it can be so termed, was a mere whim or caprice of the moment—a character he could not long sustain. He once borrowed 100*l.* to give to Coleridge, the poet, the brother-in-law of Southey, when in distress. In his quarrel with the laureate he was provoked to allude to this circumstance, which certainly he ought not to have done.

Byron was a great admirer of the Waverley novels, and never travelled without them. "They are," said he to Captain Medwin, one day, "a library in themselves, a perfect literary treasure. I could read them once a-year with new pleasure." During that

morning he had been reading one of Sir Walter's novels, and delivered, according to Medwin, the following criticism: "How difficult it is to say anything new! Who was that voluptuary of antiquity who offered a reward for a new pleasure? Perhaps all nature and art could not supply a new idea."

The motives which ultimately induced Lord Byron to leave Italy and join the Greeks, struggling for emancipation, are sufficiently obvious. It was in Greece that his high poetical faculties had been first fully developed. It was necessarily the chosen and favourite spot of a man of powerful and original intellect, of quick and sensible feelings, of varied information, and who, above all, was satiated with common enjoyments, and disgusted with what appeared to him to be the formality and sameness of daily life. Dwelling upon that country, as it is clear from all Lord Byron's writings he did, with the fondest solicitude, and being an ardent, though perhaps not a very systematic lover of freedom, he could be no unconcerned spectator of its revolution. As soon as it seemed to him that his presence might be useful, he prepared to visit once more the shores of Greece.

Lord Byron embarked at Leghorn, and arrived in Cephalonia in the early part of August, 1823, attended by a suite of six or seven friends, in an English vessel (the *Hercules*, Captain Scott), which he had chartered for the express purpose of taking him to Greece. His lordship had never seen any of the volcanic mountains, and for this purpose the vessel deviated from its regular course, in order to pass the island of Stromboli, and lay off that place a whole night, in the hopes of witnessing the usual phenomena; but, for the first time within the memory of man, the volcano emitted no fire. The disappointed poet was obliged to proceed, in no good humour with the fabled forge of Vulcan.

Greece, though with a fair prospect of ultimate triumph, was at that time in an unsettled state. The third campaign had commenced, with several instances of distinguished success: her arms were everywhere victorious, but her counsels were distracted. Western Greece was in a critical situation; and although the heroic Marco Botzaris had not fallen in vain, yet the glorious enterprise in which he perished only checked, but did not prevent, the advance of the Turks towards Anatolica and Missolonghi. This gallant chief, worthy of the best days of Greece, hailed with transport Lord Byron's arrival in that country; and his last act, before proceeding to the attack in which he fell, was to write a warm invitation to his lordship to come to Missolonghi. In his letter, which he addressed to a friend at Missolonghi, Botzaris alludes to almost the first proceeding of Lord Byron in Greece, which was the arming and provisioning of forty Suliotes, whom he sent to join in the defence of Missolonghi. After the battle Lord Byron transmitted bandages and medicines, of which he had brought a large store from Italy, and pecuniary succour to those who had been wounded. He had already made a generous offer to the government. He says, in a letter, "I offered to advance a thousand dollars a month for the succour of Missolonghi, and the Suliotes under Botzaris (since killed); but the government have answered me through ——, of this island, that they wish to confer with me previously, which is in fact saying they wish me to spend my money in some other direction. I will take care that it is for the public cause, otherwise I will not advance a para. The opposition say they want to cajole me, and the party in power say the others wish to seduce me; so between the two I have a difficult part to play. However, I will have nothing to do with the factions, unless to reconcile them, if possible."

Lord Byron established himself for some time at the small village of Metaxata, in Cephalonia, and despatched two friends, Mr. Trelawney and Mr. Hamilton Browne, with a letter to the Greek government, in order to collect intelligence as to the real state of things. His lordship's generosity was almost daily exercised in his new neighbourhood. He provided for many Italian families in distress, and even indulged the people of the country in paying for the religious ceremonies which they deemed essential to their success.

While at Metaxata, an embankment, near which several persons had been engaged digging, fell in, and buried some of them alive. He was at dinner when he heard of the accident; starting up from table, he ran to the spot, accompanied by his physician. The labourers employed in extricating their companions soon became alarmed for themselves, and refused to go on, saying they believed they had dug out all the bodies which had been covered by the rubbish. Byron endeavoured to force them to continue their exertions; but finding menaces in vain, he seized a spade and began to dig most zealously, when the peasantry joined him, and they succeeded in saving two more persons from certain death.

In the mean while, Lord Byron's friends proceeded to Tripolitza, and found Colocotroni (the enemy of Mavrocordato, who had been compelled to flee from the presidency) in great power: his palace was filled with armed men, like the castle of some ancient feudal chief; and a good idea of his character may be formed from the language he held. He declared that he had told Mavrocordato that, unless he desisted from his intrigues, he would put him on an ass, and whip him out of the Morea; and that he had only been withheld from doing so by the representation of his friends, who had said that it would injure the cause.

They next proceeded to Salamis, where the congress was sitting; and Mr. Trelawney agreed to accompany Odysseus, a brave mountain chief, into Negropont. At this time the Greeks were preparing for many active enterprises. Marco Botzaris' brother, with his Suliotes, and Mavrocordato, were to take charge of Missolonghi, which at that time (October, 1823) was in a very critical state, being blockaded both by land and sea. "There have been," says Mr. Trelawney, "thirty battles fought and won by the late Marco Botzaris and his gallant tribe of Suliotes, who are shut up in Missolonghi. If it fall, Athens will be in danger, and thousands of throats cut. A few thousand dollars would provide ships to relieve it: a portion of this sum is raised; and I would coin my heart to save this key of Greece!" A report like this was sufficient to show the point where succour was most needed; and Lord Byron's determination to relieve Missolonghi was still more decidedly confirmed by a letter which he received from Mavrocordato.

Mavrocordato was at this time endeavouring to collect a fleet for the relief of Missolonghi, and Lord Byron generously offered to advance 400,000 piastres (about 12,000*l.*) to pay for fitting it out. In a letter in which he announced this noble intention, he alluded to the dissensions in Greece, and stated that if these continued, all hope of a loan in England, or of assistance from abroad, would be at an end.

"I must frankly confess," he says in his letter, "that unless union and order are confirmed, all hopes of a loan will be in vain; and all the assistance which the Greeks could expect from abroad, an assistance which might be neither trifling nor worthless, will be suspended or destroyed; and, what is worse, the great powers of Europe, of whom no one

was an enemy to Greece, but seemed inclined to favour her in consenting to the establishment of an independent power, will be persuaded that the Greeks are unable to govern themselves, and will, perhaps, themselves undertake to arrange your disorders in such a way as to blast the brightest hopes you indulge, and that are indulged by your friends. And allow me to add once for all, I desire the well-being of Greece, and nothing else; I will do all I can to secure it; but I cannot consent, I never will consent, to the English public or English individuals being deceived as to the real state of Greek affairs. The rest, gentlemen, depends on you. You have fought gloriously: act honourably towards your fellow-citizens and towards the world, and then it will no more be said, as has been repeated for 2000 years with the Roman historian, that Philopœmen was the last of the Grecians. Let not calumny itself (and it is difficult to guard against it in so difficult a struggle) compare the Turkish pacha with the patriot Greek in peace, after you have exterminated him in war."

The dissensions among the Greek chiefs evidently gave great pain to Lord Byron, whose sensibility was keenly affected by the slightest circumstance which he considered likely to retard the deliverance of Greece. "For my part," he observes, in another of his letters, "I will stick by the cause while a plank remains which can be honourably clung to: if I quit it, it will be by the Greeks' conduct, and not the Holy Allies, or the holier Mussulmans." In a letter to his banker at Cephalonia he says: "I hope things here will go well, some time or other; I will stick by the cause as long as a cause exists."

His playful humour sometimes broke out amidst the deep anxiety he felt for the success of the Greeks. He ridiculed with great pleasantry some of the supplies which had been sent out from England by the Greek committee. In one of his letters, after alluding to his having advanced 4000*l.*, and expecting to be called on for 4000*l.* more, he says: "How can I refuse, if they (the Greeks) will fight, and especially if I should happen to be in their company? I therefore request and require that you should apprise my trusty and trustworthy trustee and banker, and crown and sheet-anchor, Douglas Kinnaird the honourable, that he prepare all monies of mine, including the purchase-money of Rochdale manor, and mine income for the year A.D. 1824, to answer and anticipate any orders or drafts of mine, for the good cause, in good and lawful money of Great Britain, &c. &c. &c. May you live 1000 years! which is 999 longer than the Spanish Cortes constitution."

When everything was arranged, two Ionian vessels were ordered; and, embarking his horses and effects, Lord Byron sailed from Argostoli on the 29th of December. At Zante his lordship took a considerable quantity of specie on board, and proceeded towards Missolonghi. Two accidents occurred in this short passage. Count Gamba, who accompanied his lordship from Leghorn, had been charged with the vessel in which the horses and part of the money were embarked. When off Chiarenza, a point which lies between Zante and the place of their destination, they were surprised at daylight on finding themselves under the bows of a Turkish frigate. Owing, however, to the activity displayed on board Lord Byron's vessel, and her superior sailing, she escaped, while the other was fired at, brought to, and carried into Patras. Count Gamba and his companions being taken before Yusuff Pacha, fully expected to share the fate of some unfortunate men whom that sanguinary chief had sacrificed the preceding year at Previsa; and their fears would most probably have been realised, had it not been for the presence of mind displayed by

the count, who, assuming an air of hauteur and indifference, accused the captain of the frigate of a scandalous breach of neutrality, in firing at and detaining a vessel under English colours; and concluded by informing Yusuff, that he might expect the vengeance of the British government in thus interrupting a nobleman who was merely on his travels, and bound to Calamos. The Turkish chief, on recognising in the master of the vessel a person who had saved his life in the Black Sea fifteen years before, not only consented to the vessel's release, but treated the whole of the passengers with the utmost attention, and even urged them to take a day's shooting in the neighbourhood.

Owing to contrary winds, Lord Byron's vessel was obliged to take shelter at the Scropes, a cluster of rocks within a few miles of Missolonghi; and while detained here he was in considerable danger of being captured by the Turks.

Lord Byron was received at Missolonghi with enthusiastic demonstrations of joy. No mark of honour or welcome which the Greeks could devise was omitted. The ships anchored off the fortress fired a salute as he passed. Prince Mavrocordato and all the authorities, with the troops and the population, met him on his landing, and accompanied him to the house which had been prepared for him, amidst the shouts of the multitude and the discharge of cannon.

One of the first objects to which he turned his attention was to mitigate the ferocity with which the war had been carried on. The very day of his lordship's arrival was signalised by his rescuing a Turk who had fallen into the hands of some Greek sailors. The individual thus saved, having been clothed by his orders, was kept in the house until an opportunity occurred of sending him to Patras. Nor had his lordship been long at Missolonghi before an opportunity presented itself for showing his sense of Yusuff Pacha's moderation in releasing Count Gamba. Hearing that there were four Turkish prisoners in the town, he requested that they might be placed in his hands. This being immediately granted, he sent them to Patras, with a letter addressed to the Turkish chief, expressing his hope that the prisoners thenceforward taken on both sides would be treated with humanity. This act was followed by another equally praiseworthy, which proved how anxious Lord Byron felt to give a new turn to the system of warfare hitherto pursued. A Greek cruiser having captured a Turkish boat, in which there was a number of passengers, chiefly women and children, they were also placed in the hands of Lord Byron, at his particular request; upon which a vessel was immediately hired, and the whole of them, to the number of twenty-four, were sent to Previsa, provided with every requisite for their comfort during the passage. The Turkish governor of Previsa thanked his lordship, and assured him that he would take care equal attention should be in future shown to the Greeks who might become prisoners.

Another grand object with Lord Byron, and one which he never ceased to forward with the most anxious solicitude, was to reconcile the quarrels of the native chiefs, to make them friendly and confiding towards one another, and submissive to the orders of the government. He had neither time nor opportunity to carry this point to any great extent; some good was, however, done.

Lord Byron landed at Missolonghi animated with military ardour. After paying the fleet,—which, indeed, had only come out under the expectation of receiving its arrears from the loan which he promised to make to the provisional government,—he set about forming a brigade of Suliotes. Five hundred of these, the bravest and most resolute of

the soldiers of Greece, were taken into his pay on the 1st of January, 1824. An expedition against Lepanto was proposed, of which the command was given to Lord Byron. This expedition, however, had to experience delay and disappointment. The Suliotes, conceiving that they had found a patron whose wealth was inexhaustible, and whose generosity was boundless, determined to make the most of the occasion, and proceeded to the most extravagant demands on their leader for arrears, and under other pretences. These mountaineers, untameable in the field, and unmanageable in a town, were, at this moment, peculiarly disposed to be obstinate, riotous, and mercenary. They had been chiefly instrumental in preserving Missolonghi when besieged the previous autumn by the Turks; had been driven from their abodes; and the whole of their families were at this time in the town, destitute of either home or sufficient supplies. Of turbulent and reckless character, they kept the place in awe; and Mavrocordato having, unlike the other captains, no soldiers of his own, was glad to find a body of valiant mercenaries, especially if paid for out of the funds of another, and consequently was not disposed to treat them with harshness. Within a fortnight after Lord Byron's arrival, a burgher refusing to quarter some Suliotes who rudely demanded entrance into his house, was killed, and a riot ensued, in which some lives were lost. Lord Byron's impatient spirit could ill brook the delay of a favourite scheme: but he saw, with the utmost chagrin, that the state of his troops was such as to render any attempt to lead them out at that time impracticable.

The project of proceeding against Lepanto being thus suspended, at a moment when Lord Byron's enthusiasm was at its height, and when he had fully calculated on striking a blow which could not fail to be of the utmost service to the Greek cause, the unlooked-for disappointment preyed on his spirits, and produced a degree of irritability which, if it was not the sole cause, contributed greatly to a severe fit of epilepsy with which he was attacked on the 15th of February. His lordship was sitting in the apartment of Colonel Stanhope, talking in a jocular manner with Mr. Parry, the engineer, when it was observed, from occasional and rapid changes in his countenance, that he was suffering under some strong emotion. On a sudden he complained of a weakness in one of his legs, and rose; but finding himself unable to walk, he cried out for assistance. He then fell into a state of nervous and convulsive agitation, and was placed on a bed. For some minutes his countenance was much distorted. He, however, quickly recovered his senses, his speech returned, and he soon appeared perfectly well, although enfeebled and exhausted by the violence of the struggle. During the fit, he behaved with his usual extraordinary firmness; and his efforts in contending with, and attempting to master, the disease, are described as gigantic. In the course of the month, the attack was repeated four times; the violence of the disorder at length yielded to the remedies which his physicians advised, such as bleeding, cold bathing, perfect relaxation of mind, &c., and he gradually recovered. An accident, however, happened a few days after his first illness, which was ill calculated to aid the efforts of his medical advisers. A Suliote, accompanied by another man, and the late Marco Botzaris' little boy, walked into the Seraglio; a place which, before Lord Byron's arrival, had been used as a sort of fortress and barrack for the Suliotes, and out of which they were ejected, with great difficulty, for the reception of the committee-stores, and for the occupation of the engineers, who required it for a laboratory. The sentinel on guard ordered the Suliote to retire, which being a species of motion to which Suliotes are not accustomed, the man carelessly advanced; upon which the serjeant of the guard (a

German) demanded his business, and receiving no satisfactory answer, pushed him back. These wild warriors, who will dream for years of a blow if revenge is out of their power, are not slow to resent even a push. The Suliote struck again, the serjeant and he closed and struggled, when the Suliote drew a pistol from his belt; the serjeant wrenched it out of his hand, and blew the powder out of the pan. At this moment, Captain Sass, a Swede, seeing the fray, came up, and ordered the man to be taken to the guard-room. The Suliote was then disposed to depart, and would have done so if the serjeant would have permitted him. Unfortunately, Captain Sass did not confine himself to merely giving the order for his arrest; for when the Suliote struggled to get away, Captain Sass drew his sword and struck him with the flat part of it; whereupon the enraged Greek flew upon him, with a pistol in one hand and a sabre in the other, and at the same moment nearly cut off the captain's right arm, and shot him through the head. Captain Sass, who was remarkable for his mild and courageous character, expired in a few minutes. The Suliote also was a man of distinguished bravery. This was a serious affair, and great apprehensions were entertained that it would not end here. The Suliotes refused to surrender the man to justice, alleging that he had been struck, which, in Suliote law, justifies all the consequences which may follow.

In a letter written a few days after Lord Byron's first attack, to a friend in Zante, he speaks of himself as rapidly recovering. "I am a good deal better," he observes, "though of course weakly. The leeches took too much blood from my temples the day after, and there was some difficulty in stopping it; but I have been up daily, though not in boats or on horseback. To-day I have taken a warm bath, and live as temperately as well can be, without any liquid but water, and without any animal food." After adverting to some other subjects, the letter thus concludes: "Matters are here a little embroiled with the Suliotes, foreigners, &c.; but I still hope better things, and will stand by the cause as long as my health and circumstances will permit me to be supposed useful."

Notwithstanding Lord Byron's improvement in health, his friends felt from the first that he ought to try a change of air. Missolonghi is a flat, marshy, and pestilential place, and, except for purposes of utility, never would have been selected for his residence. A gentleman of Zante wrote to him early in March, to induce him to return to that island for a time. To his letter the following answer was received:

"I am extremely obliged by your offer of your country-house, as for all other kindness, in case my health should require my removal; but I cannot quit Greece while there is a chance of my being of (even supposed) utility. There is a stake worth millions such as I am; and while I can stand at all, I must stand by the cause. While I say this, I am aware of the difficulties, and dissensions, and defects of the Greeks themselves; but allowance must be made for them by all reasonable people."

It may be well imagined, after so severe a fit of illness, and that in a great measure brought on by the conduct of the troops he had taken into his pay and treated with the utmost generosity, that Lord Byron was in no humour to pursue his scheme against Lepanto, even supposing that his state of health had been such as to bear the fatigue of a campaign in Greece. The Suliotes, however, showed some signs of repentance, and offered to place themselves at his lordship's disposal. But still they had an objection to the nature of the service: "they would not fight against stone walls!" It is not surprising that the expedition to Lepanto was no longer thought of.

The *luxury* of Lord Byron's living at this time may be seen from the following order which he gave his superintendent of the household, for the daily expenses of his own table. It amounts to no more than one piastre:

Bread, a pound and a half	15 paras
Wine	7
Fish	15
Olives	3
	40

This was his dinner; his breakfast consisted of a single dish of tea, without milk or sugar.

The circumstances that attended the death of this illustrious and noble-minded man are described in the following plain and simple statement by his faithful valet and constant follower, Mr. Fletcher:

"My master," says Mr. Fletcher, "continued his usual custom of riding daily, when the weather would permit, until the 9th of April. But on that ill-fated day he got very wet, and on his return home his lordship changed the whole of his dress; but he had been too long in his wet clothes; and the cold, of which he had complained more or less ever since we left Cephalonia, made this attack be more severely felt. Though rather feverish during the night, his lordship slept pretty well, but complained in the morning of a pain in his bones and a headache; this did not, however, prevent him from taking a ride in the afternoon, which, I grieve to say, was his last. On his return, my master said that the saddle was not perfectly dry, from being so wet the day before; and observed that he thought it had made him worse. His lordship was again visited by the same slow fever; and I was sorry to perceive, on the next morning, that his illness appeared to be increasing. He was very low, and complained of not having had any sleep during the night. His lordship's appetite was also quite gone. I prepared a little arrowroot, of which he took three or four spoonfuls, saying it was very good, but he could take no more. It was not till the third day, the 12th, that I began to be alarmed for my master. In all his former colds he always slept well, and was never affected by this slow fever. I therefore went to Dr. Bruno and Mr. Millingen, the two medical attendants, and inquired minutely into every circumstance connected with my master's present illness; both replied that there was no danger, and I might make myself perfectly easy on the subject, for all would be well in a few days. This was on the 13th. On the following day I found my master in such a state that I could not feel happy without supplicating that he would send to Zante for Dr. Thomas. After expressing my fears lest his lordship should get worse, he desired me to consult the doctors, which I did; and was told there was no occasion for calling in any person, as they hoped all would be well in a few days. Here I should remark that his lordship repeatedly said, in the course of the day, he was sure the doctors did not understand his disease; to which I answered, 'Then, my lord, have other advice by all means.' 'They tell me,' said his lordship, 'that it is only a common cold, which, you know, I have had a thousand times.' 'I am sure, my lord,' said I, 'that you never had one of so serious a nature.' 'I think I never had,' was his lordship's answer. I repeated my supplications that Dr. Thomas should be sent for on the 15th, and was again assured that my master would be better in two or three days. After these con-

fident assurances, I did not renew my entreaties until it was too late. With respect to the medicines that were given to my master, I could not persuade myself that those of a strong purgative nature were the best adapted for his complaint; concluding that, as he had nothing in his stomach, the only effect would be to create pain. Indeed, this must have been the case with a person in perfect health. The whole nourishment taken by my master for the last eight days consisted of a small quantity of broth at two or three different times, and two spoonfuls of arrowroot on the 18th, the day before his death. The first time I heard of there being any intention of bleeding his lordship was on the 15th, when it was proposed by Dr. Bruno, but objected to at first by my master, who asked Mr. Millingen if there was any great reason for taking blood. The latter replied that it might be of service, but added it might be deferred till the next day; and accordingly my master was bled in the right arm on the evening of the 16th, and a pound of blood was taken. I observed at the time that it had a most inflamed appearance. Dr. Bruno now began to say, that he had frequently urged my master to be bled, but that he always refused. A long dispute now arose about the time that had been lost, and the necessity of sending for medical aid to Zante; upon which I was informed, for the first time, that it would be of no use, as my master would be better or no more before the arrival of Dr. Thomas. His lordship continued to get worse, but Dr. Bruno said he thought letting blood again would save his life; and I lost no time in telling my master how necessary it was to comply with the doctor's wishes. To this he replied by saying, he feared they knew nothing about his disorder; and then, stretching out his arm, said, 'Here, take my arm, and do whatever you like.' His lordship continued to get weaker, and on the 17th he was bled twice, in the morning and at two o'clock in the afternoon; the bleeding at both times was followed by fainting fits, and he would have fallen down more than once had I not caught him in my arms. In order to prevent such an accident, I took care not to permit his lordship to stir without supporting him. On this day my master said to me twice, 'I cannot sleep, and you well know I have not been able to sleep for more than a week. I know,' added his lordship, 'that a man can only be a certain time without sleep, and then he must go mad, without any one being able to save him; and I would ten times sooner shoot myself than be mad, for I am not afraid of dying—I am more fit to die than people think.'

"I do not, however, believe that his lordship had any apprehension of his fate till the day after the 18th, when he said, 'I fear you and Tita will be ill by sitting continually night and day.' I answered, 'We shall never leave your lordship till you are better.' As my master had a slight fit of delirium on the 16th, I took care to remove the pistol and stiletto which had hitherto been kept at his bedside in the night. On the 18th his lordship addressed me frequently, and seemed to be very much dissatisfied with his medical treatment. I then said, 'Do allow me to send for Dr. Thomas!' to which he answered, 'Do so, but be quick; I am sorry I did not let you do so before, as I am sure they have mistaken my disease. Write yourself, for I know they would not like to see other doctors here.' I did not lose a moment in obeying my master's orders; and, on informing Dr. Bruno and Mr. Millingen of it, they said it was very right, as they now began to be afraid themselves. On returning to my master's room, his first words were, 'Have you sent?' 'I have, my lord,' was my answer. Upon which he said, 'You have done right; for I should like to know what is the matter with me.' Although his lord-

ship did not appear to think his dissolution was so near, I could perceive he was getting weaker every hour; and he even began to have occasional fits of delirium. He afterwards said, 'I now begin to think I am seriously ill; and in case I should be taken off suddenly, I wish to give you several directions, which I hope you will be particular in seeing executed.' I answered I would, in case such an event came to pass; but expressed a hope that he would live many years to execute them much better himself than I could. To this my master replied, 'No, it is now nearly over;' and then added, 'I must tell you all without losing a moment.' I then said, 'Shall I go, my lord, and fetch pen, ink, and paper?' 'Oh, my God! no; you will lose too much time, and I have it not to spare, for my time is now short,' said his lordship; and immediately after, 'Now pay attention!' His lordship commenced by saying, 'You will be provided for.' I begged him, however, to proceed with things of more consequence. He then continued, 'Oh, my poor dear child! my dear Ada! My God! could I but have seen her! Give her my blessing; and my dear sister Augusta and her children. And you will go to Lady Byron, and say—tell her everything—you are friends with her.' His lordship seemed to be greatly affected at this moment. Here my master's voice failed him, so that I could only catch a word at intervals: but he kept muttering something very seriously for some time, and would often raise his voice: and said, 'Fletcher, now if you do not execute every order which I have given you, I will torment you hereafter if possible.' Here I told his lordship, in a state of the greatest perplexity, that I had not understood a word of what he said; to which he replied, 'Oh, my God; then all is lost, for it is now too late! Can it be possible you have not understood me?' 'No, my lord,' said I; 'but I pray you to try and inform me once more.' 'How can I?' rejoined my master; 'it is now too late, and all is over;' I said, 'Not our will, but God's be done;' and he answered, 'Yes, not mine be done; but I will try.' His lordship did, indeed, make several efforts to speak, but could only speak two or three words at a time, such as, 'My wife! my child! my sister!—you know all—you must say all—you know my wishes.' The rest was quite unintelligible. A consultation was now held (about noon), when it was determined to administer some Peruvian bark and wine. My master had now been nine days without any sustenance whatever, except what I have already mentioned. With the exception of a few words, which can only interest those to whom they were addressed,—and which, if required, I shall communicate to themselves,—it was impossible to understand anything his lordship said after taking the bark. He expressed a wish to sleep. I at one time asked whether I should call Mr. Parry; to which he replied, 'Yes, you may call him.' Mr. Parry desired him to compose himself. He shed tears, and apparently sank into a slumber. Mr. Parry went away, expecting to find him refreshed on his return; but it was the commencement of the lethargy preceding his death. The last words I heard my master utter were at six o'clock on the evening of the 18th, when he said, 'I must sleep now;' upon which he lay down, never to rise again; for he did not move hand or foot during the following twenty-four hours. His lordship appeared, however, to be in a state of suffocation at intervals, and had a frequent rattling in the throat; on these occasions I called Tita to assist me in raising his head; and I thought he seemed to get quite stiff. The rattling and choking in the throat took place every half-hour; and we continued to raise his head whenever the fit came on, till six o'clock on the evening of the 19th, when I saw my master open his eyes and then shut them, but without showing any symptom of pain, or moving hand or foot.

'Oh, my God!' I exclaimed; 'I fear his lordship is gone!' The doctors then felt his pulse, and said, 'You are right; he is gone!'"

On the day of this melancholy event, Prince Movrocordato issued a proclamation expressive of the deep and unfeigned grief felt by all classes, and ordering every public demonstration of respect and sorrow to be paid to the memory of the illustrious deceased, by firing minute-guns, closing all the public offices and shops, suspending the usual Easter festivities, and by a general mourning and funeral prayers in all the churches. It was resolved that the body should be embalmed, and after suitable funeral honours had been performed, should be embarked for Zante, thence to be conveyed to England. Accordingly the medical men opened the body and embalmed it; and having enclosed the heart, and brain, and intestines in separate vessels, they placed it in a chest lined with tin, as there were no means of procuring a leaden coffin capable of holding the spirits necessary for its preservation on the voyage. Dr. Bruno drew up an account of the examination of the body, by which it appeared his lordship's death had been caused by an inflammatory fever. Dr. Meyer, a Swiss physician who was present, and had accidentally seen Madame de Staël after her death, stated that the formation of the brain in both these illustrious persons was extremely similar, but that Lord Byron had a much greater quantity.

On the 22d of April, 1824, in the midst of his own brigade, the troops of the government, and the whole population, the most precious portion of his honoured remains was carried to the church, where lie the bodies of Marco Botzaris and of General Normann. The coffin was a rude, ill-constructed chest of wood; a black mantle served for a pall; and over it were placed a helmet, a sword, and a crown of laurel. But no funeral pomp could have left the impression or spoken the feelings of this simple ceremony. The wretchedness and desolation of the place itself, the wild and half-civilised warriors present, their deep-felt, unaffected grief, the fond recollections, the disappointed hopes, the anxieties and sad presentiments which might be read on every countenance,—all contributed to form a scene more truly affecting than perhaps was ever before witnessed round the grave of a great man. When the funeral service was over, the bier was left in the middle of the church, where it remained until the evening of the next day, guarded by a detachment of his own brigade, when it was privately carried back by his officers to his own house. The coffin was not closed till the 29th of the month.

On the 2nd of May the remains of Lord Byron were embarked, under a salute from the guns of the fortress. "How different," exclaims Count Gamba, "from that which had welcomed the arrival of Byron only four months ago!" After a passage of three days, the vessel reached Zante, and the precious deposit was placed in the quarantine-house. Here some additional precautions were taken to ensure its safe arrival in England, by providing another case for the body. On the 10th May, Colonel Stanhope arrived at Zante from the Morea; and as he was on his way back to England, he took charge of Lord Byron's remains, and embarked with them on board the *Florida*. On the 25th of May she sailed from Zante, on the 29th of June entered the Downs; and from thence proceeded to Stangate Creek to perform quarantine, where she arrived on Thursday, July 1.

John Cam Hobhouse, Esq., and John Hanson, Esq., Lord Byron's executors, after having proved his will, claimed the body from the *Florida;* and under their directions it was removed to the house of Sir Edward Knatchbull, Westminster, where it lay in state several days.

A few select friends and admirers of the noble bard followed his remains to the grave. As the funeral procession passed through the streets of London, a fine-looking honest tar was observed to walk near the hearse uncovered; and on being asked whether he formed part of the *cortège*, he replied he came there to pay his respects to the deceased, with whom he had served in the Levant, when he made the tour of the Grecian islands. The poor fellow was offered a place by some of the servants; but he said he was strong, and had rather walk near the hearse.

The interment took place on Friday, July 16th. Lord Byron was buried in the family vault, at the village of Hucknall, eight miles beyond Nottingham, and within two miles of the venerable abbey of Newstead. He was accompanied to the grave by crowds of persons eager to show this last testimony of respect to his memory. As in one of his earlier poems he had expressed a wish that his dust might mingle with his mother's, his coffin was placed in the vault next to hers.

It bore the following inscription:

George Gordon Noel Byron,
Lord Byron,
of Rochdale,
born in London,*
Jan. 22, 1788,
died at Missolonghi,
in Western Greece,
April 19th, 1824.

An urn accompanied the coffin; and on it was inscribed:

Within this urn are deposited the heart,
brain, &c.,
of the deceased Lord Byron.

* Mr. Dallas says Dover.

THE CORSAIR:

CANTO THE FIRST.

"——— nessun maggior dolore,
Che ricordarsi del tempo felice
Nella miseria, ———."—DANTE.

I.

'O'ER the glad waters of the dark blue sea,[1]
Our thoughts as boundless, and our souls as free,
Far as the breeze can bear, the billows foam,
Survey our empire, and behold our home!
These are our realms, no limits to their sway—
Our flag the sceptre all who meet obey.
Ours the wild life in tumult still to range
From toil to rest, and joy in every change.

Oh, who can tell? not thou, luxurious slave!
Whose soul would sicken o'er the heaving wave;
Not thou, vain lord of wantonness and ease!
Whom slumber soothes not—pleasure cannot please—
Oh, who can tell, save he whose heart hath tried,
And danced in triumph o'er the waters wide,
The exulting sense—the pulse's maddening play,
That thrills the wanderer of that trackless way?
That for itself can woo the approaching fight,
And turn what some deem danger to delight;
That seeks what cravens shun with more than zeal,
And where the feebler faint—can only feel—
Feel—to the rising bosom's inmost core,
Its hope awaken and its spirit soar?
No dread of death—if with us die our foes—
Save that it seems even duller than repose:
Come when it will—we snatch the life of life—
When lost—what recks it—by disease or strife?
Let him who crawls enamour'd of decay,
Cling to his couch, and sicken years away;
Heave his thick breath, and shake his palsied head;
Ours—the fresh turf, and not the feverish bed.
While gasp by gasp he falters forth his soul,
Ours with one pang—one bound—escapes control.
His corse may boast its urn and narrow cave,
And they who loath'd his life may gild his grave:
Ours are the tears, though few, sincerely shed,
When Ocean shrouds and sepulchres our dead.
For us, even banquets fond regret supply
In the red cup that crowns our memory;
And the brief epitaph in danger's day,
When those who win at length divide the prey,
And cry, Remembrance saddening o'er each brow,
How had the brave who fell exulted *now!*"

II.

Such were the notes that from the Pirate's isle,
Around the kindling watch-fire rang the while;
Such were the sounds that thrill'd the rocks along,
And unto ears as rugged seemed a song!
In scatter'd groups upon the golden sand,
They game—carouse—converse—or whet the brand;
Select the arms—to each his blade assign,
And careless eye the blood that dims its shine;
Repair the boat, replace the helm or oar,
While others straggling muse along the shore;
For the wild bird the busy springes set,
Or spread beneath the sun the dripping net;
Gaze where some distant sail a speck supplies,
With all the thirsting eye of Enterprise;
Tell o'er the tales of many a night of toil,
And marvel where they next shall seize a spoil:
No matter where—their chief's allotment this;
Theirs, to believe no prey nor plan amiss.
But who that CHIEF? his name on every shore
Is famed and fear'd—they ask and know no more.
With these he mingles not but to command;
Few are his words, but keen his eye and hand.
Ne'er seasons he with mirth their jovial mess,
But they forgive his silence for success.
Ne'er for his lip the purpling cup they fill,
That goblet passes him untasted still—
And for his fare—the rudest of his crew
Would that, in turn, have pass'd untasted too;
Earth's coarsest bread, the garden's homeliest roots,
And scarce the summer luxury of fruits,
His short repast in humbleness supply
With all a hermit's board would scarce deny.
But while he shuns the grosser joys of sense,
His mind seems nourished by that abstinence.
"Steer to that shore!"—they sail. "Do this!"—'tis done:
"Now form and follow me!"—the spoil is won.
Thus prompt his accents and his actions still,
And all obey and few inquire his will;
To such, brief answer and contemptuous eye
Convey reproof, nor further deign reply.

III.

"A sail!—a sail!"—a promised prize to Hope!
Her nation—flag—how speaks the telescope?
No prize, alas!—but yet a welcome sail:
The blood-red signal glitters in the gale.
Yes—she is ours—a home-returning bark—
Blow fair, thou breeze!—she anchors ere the dark.
Already doubled is the cape—our bay
Receives that prow which proudly spurns the spray.
How gloriously her gallant course she goes!
Her white wings flying—never from her foes—
She walks the waters like a thing of life,
And seems to dare the elements to strife.
Who would not brave the battle-fire—the wreck—
To move the monarch of her peopled deck?

IV.

Hoarse o'er her side the rustling cable rings;
The sails are furled; and anchoring round she swings;
And gathering loiterers on the land discern
Her boat descending from the latticed stern.
'Tis mann'd—the oars keep concert to the strand
Till grates her keel upon the shallow sand.
Hail to the welcome shout!—the friendly speech!
When hand grasps hand uniting on the beach;
The smile, the question, and the quick reply,
And the heart's promise of festivity!

V.

The tidings spread, and gathering grows the crowd:
The hum of voices, and the laughter loud,
And woman's gentler anxious tone is heard—
Friends'—husbands'—lovers' names in each dear word:
"Oh! are they safe? we ask not of success—
But shall we see them? will their accents bless?
From where the battle roars—the billows chafe—
They doubtless boldly did—but who are safe?

Here let them haste to gladden and surprise,
And kiss the doubt from these delighted eyes!"

VI.

"Where is our chief? for him we bear report—
And doubt that joy—which hails our coming—short;
Yet thus sincere—'tis cheering, though so brief;
But, Juan! instant guide us to our chief:
Our greeting paid, we'll feast on our return,
And all shall hear what each may wish to learn."
Ascending slowly by the rock-hewn way,
To where his watch-tower beetles o'er the bay,
By bushy brake, and wild flowers blossoming,
And freshness breathing from each silver spring,
Whose scatter'd streams from granite basins burst,
Leap into life, and sparkling woo your thirst;

From crag to cliff they mount—Near yonder cave,
What lonely straggler looks along the wave?
In pensive posture leaning on the brand,
Not oft a resting-staff to that red hand?
"'Tis he—'tis Conrad—here—as wont—alone;
On—Juan!—on—and make our purpose known.
The bark he views—and tell him we would greet
His ear with tidings he must quickly meet:
We dare not yet approach—thou know'st his mood,
When strange or uninvited steps intrude."

VII.

Him Juan sought, and told of their intent;—
He spake not—but a sign express'd assent.
These Juan calls—they come—to their salute
He bends him slightly, but his lips are mute.

"These letters, Chief, are from the Greek—the spy,
Who still proclaims our spoil or peril nigh:
Whate'er his tidings, we can well report
Much that"—"Peace, peace!"—he cuts their prating short.
Wondering they turn, abash'd, while each to each
Conjecture whispers in his muttering speech:
They watch his glance with many a stealing look,
To gather how that eye the tidings took;
But, this as if he guess'd, with head aside,
Perchance from some emotion, doubt, or pride,
He read the scroll—"My tablets, Juan, hark—
Where is Gonsalvo?"
"In the anchor'd bark."
"There let him stay—to him this order bear.
Back to your duty—for my course prepare:
Myself this enterprise to-night will share."
"To-night, Lord Conrad?"
"Ay! at set of sun:
The breeze will freshen when the day is done.
My corslet—cloak—one hour—and we are gone.
Sling on thy bugle—see that free from rust
My carbine-lock springs worthy of my trust;
Be the edge sharpen'd of my boarding-brand,
And give its guard more room to fit my hand.
This let the Armourer with speed dispose;
Last time, it more fatigued my arm than foes:
Mark that the signal-gun be duly fired,
To tell us when the hour of stay 's expired."

VIII.

They make obeisance, and retire in haste,
Too soon to seek again the watery waste:
Yet they repine not—so that Conrad guides,
And who dare question aught that he decides?
That man of loneliness and mystery,
Scarce seen to smile, and seldom heard to sigh;
Whose name appals the fiercest of his crew,
And tints each swarthy cheek with sallower hue;
Still sways their souls with that commanding art
That dazzles, leads, yet chills the vulgar heart.
What is that spell, that thus his lawless train
Confess and envy, yet oppose in vain?
What should it be, that thus their faith can bind?
The power of Thought—the magic of the Mind!
Link'd with success, assumed and kept with skill,
That moulds another's weakness to its will;
Wields with their hands, but, still to these unknown,
Makes even their mightiest deeds appear his own.
Such hath it been—shall be—beneath the sun
The many still must labour for the one!
'T is Nature's doom—but let the wretch who toils,
Accuse not, hate not *him* who wears the spoils.
Oh! if he knew the weight of splendid chains,
How light the balance of his humbler pains!

IX.

Unlike the heroes of each ancient race,
Demons in act, but Gods at least in face,
In Conrad's form seems little to admire,
Though his dark eyebrow shades a glance of fire:
Robust but not Herculean—to the sight
No giant frame sets forth his common height;
Yet, in the whole, who paused to look again,
Saw more than marks the crowd of vulgar men;
They gaze and marvel how—and still confess
That thus it is, but why they cannot guess.
Sun-burnt his cheek, his forehead high and pale
The sable curls in wild profusion veil;
And oft perforce his rising lip reveals
The haughtier thought it curbs, but scarce conceals.
Though smooth his voice, and calm his general mien,
Still seems there something he would not have seen:
His features' deepening lines and varying hue
At times attracted, yet perplex'd the view,
As if within that murkiness of mind
Work'd feelings fearful, and yet undefin'd;
Such might it be—that none could truly tell—
Too close inquiry his stern glance would quell.
There breathe but few whose aspect might defy
The full encounter of his searching eye:
He had the skill, when Cunning's gaze would seek
To probe his heart and watch his changing cheek,
At once the observer's purpose to espy,
And on himself roll back his scrutiny,
Lest he to Conrad rather should betray
Some secret thought, than drag that chief's to day.
There was a laughing Devil in his sneer,
That raised emotions both of rage and fear;
And where his frown of hatred darkly fell,
Hope withering fled—and Mercy sigh'd farewell!

X.

Slight are the outward signs of evil thought,
Within—within—'t was there the spirit wrought!
Love shows all changes—Hate, Ambition, Guile,
Betray no further than the bitter smile;
The lip's least curl, the lightest paleness thrown
Along the govern'd aspect, speak alone
Of deeper passions; and to judge their mien,
He, who would see, must be himself unseen.
Then—with the hurried tread, the upward eye,
The clenched hand, the pause of agony,
That listens, starting, lest the step too near
Approach intrusive on that mood of fear:
Then—with each feature working from the heart,
With feelings loosed to strengthen—not depart:
That rise—convulse—contend—that freeze, glow,
Flush in the cheek, or damp upon the brow;

Then — Stranger! if thou canst, and tremblest not,
Behold his soul—the rest that soothes his lot!
Mark—how that lone and blighted bosom sears
The scathing thought of execrated years!
Behold—but who hath seen, or e'er shall see,
Man as himself—the secret spirit free?

XI.

Yet was not Conrad thus by Nature sent
To lead the guilty—guilt's worst instrument—
His soul was changed, before his deeds had driven
Him forth to war with man and forfeit heaven.
Warp'd by the world in Disappointment's school,
In words too wise, in conduct *there* a fool;

Too firm to yield, and far too proud to stoop,
Doom'd by his very virtues for a dupe,
He cursed those virtues as the cause of ill,
And not the traitors who betray'd him still;
Nor deem'd that gifts bestow'd on better men
Had left him joy, and means to give again.
Fear'd—shunn'd—belied—ere youth had lost her force,
He hated man too much to feel remorse,
And thought the voice of wrath a sacred call,
To pay the injuries of some on all.
He knew himself a villain—but he deem'd
The rest no better than the thing he seem'd;
And scorn'd the best as hypocrites who hid
Those deeds the bolder spirit plainly did.
He knew himself detested, but he knew

The hearts that loath'd him, crouch'd and dreaded too.
Lone, wild, and strange, he stood alike exempt
From all affection and from all contempt:
His name could sadden, and his acts surprise;
But they that fear'd him dared not to despise.
Man spurns the worm, but pauses ere he wake
The slumbering venom of the folded snake:
The first may turn—but not avenge the blow;
The last expires—but leaves no living foe;
Fast to the doom'd offender's form it clings,
And he may crush—not conquer—still it stings!

XII.

None are all evil—quickening round his heart,
One softer feeling would not yet depart;
Oft could he sneer at others as beguiled
By passions worthy of a fool or child;
Yet 'gainst that passion vainly still he strove,
And even in him it asks the name of Love!
Yes, it was love—unchangeable—unchanged,
Felt but for one from whom he never ranged;
Though fairest captives daily met his eye,
He shunn'd, nor sought, but coldly pass'd them by;
Though many a beauty droop'd in prison'd bower,
None ever soothed his most unguarded hour.
Yes—it was Love—if thoughts of tenderness,
Tried in temptation, strengthen'd by distress,
Unmoved by absence, firm in every clime,
And yet—Oh more than all!—untired by time;
Which nor defeated hope, nor baffled wile,
Could render sullen were she near to smile,
Nor rage could fire, nor sickness fret to vent
On her one murmur of his discontent;
Which still would meet with joy, with calmness part,
Lest that his look of grief should reach her heart;
Which naught removed, nor menaced to remove—
If there be love in mortals—this was love!
He was a villain—ay—reproaches shower
On him—but not the passion, nor its power,
Which only proved, all other virtues gone,
Not guilt itself could quench this loveliest one!

* * * * * *

XIII.

He paused a moment—till his hastening men
Pass'd the first winding downward to the glen.
"Strange tidings!—many a peril have I past,
Nor know I why this next appears the last!
Yet so my heart forebodes, but must not fear,
Nor shall my followers find me falter here.
'T is rash to meet, but surer death to wait
Till here they hunt us to undoubted fate;
And, if my plan but hold, and Fortune smile,
We'll furnish mourners for our funeral-pile.
Ay—let them slumber—peaceful be their dreams!
Morn ne'er awoke them with such brilliant beams
As kindle high to-night (but blow, thou breeze!)
To warm these slow avengers of the seas.
Now to Medora—Oh! my sinking heart,
Long may her own be lighter than thou art!
Yet was I brave—mean boast where all are brave!
Ev'n insects sting for aught they seek to save.
This common courage which with brutes we share,
That owes its deadliest efforts to despair,
Small merit claims—but 't was my nobler hope
To teach my few with numbers still to cope;
Long have I led them—not to vainly bleed:
No medium now—we perish or succeed!
So let it be—it irks not me to die;
But thus to urge them whence they cannot fly.
My lot hath long had little of my care,
But chafes my pride thus baffled in the snare:
Is this my skill? my craft? to set at last
Hope, power, and life upon a single cast?
Oh, Fate!—accuse thy folly, not thy fate—
She may redeem thee still—nor yet too late."

XIV.

Thus with himself communion held he, till
He reach'd the summit of his tower-crown'd hill:
There at the portal paused—for wild and soft
He heard those accents never heard too oft;
Through the high lattice far yet sweet they rung,
And these the notes his bird of beauty sung:

1.

"Deep in my soul that tender secret dwells,
Lonely and lost to light for evermore,
Save when to thine my heart responsive swells,
Then trembles into silence as before.

2.

"There, in its centre, a sepulchral lamp
Burns the slow flame, eternal—but unseen;
Which not the darkness of despair can damp,
Though vain its ray as it had never been.

3.

"Remember me—Oh! pass not thou my grave
Without one thought whose relics there recline:
The only pang my bosom dare not brave
Must be to find forgetfulness in thine.

4.

"My fondest—faintest—latest accents hear:
Grief for the dead not Virtue can reprove;
Then give me all I ever ask'd—a tear,
The first—last—sole reward of so much love!"

He pass'd the portal—cross'd the corridore,
And reach'd the chamber as the strain gave o'er:
"My own Medora! sure thy song is sad—"

"In Conrad's absence wouldst thou have it glad?

Without thine ear to listen to my lay,
Still must my song my thoughts, my soul betray:
Still must each accent to my bosom suit,
My heart unhush'd — although my lips were mute!
Oh! many a night on this lone couch reclined,
My dreaming fear with storms hath wing'd the wind,
And deem'd the breath that faintly fann'd thy sail
The murmuring prelude of the ruder gale;
Though soft, it seem'd the low prophetic dirge,
That mourn'd thee floating on the savage surge:
Still would I rise to rouse the beacon fire,
Lest spies less true should let the blaze expire:
And many a restless hour outwatch'd each star,
And morning came—and still thou wert afar.
Oh! how the chill blast on my bosom blew,
And day broke dreary on my troubled view,
And still I gazed and gazed—and not a prow
Was granted to my tears—my truth—my vow!
At length—'t was noon—I hail'd and blest the mast
That met my sight—it near'd—Alas! it pass'd!
Another came—Oh God! 't was thine at last?
Would that those days were over! wilt thou ne'er,
My Conrad! learn the joys of peace to share?
Sure thou hast more than wealth, and many a home
As bright as this invites us not to roam:
Thou know'st it is not peril that I fear,
I only tremble when thou art not here;
Then not for mine, but that far dearer life,
Which flies from love and languishes for strife—
How strange that heart, to me so tender still,
Should war with nature and its better will!"

"Yea, strange indeed—that heart hath long been changed;
Worm-like 't was trampled—adder-like avenged,
Without one hope on earth beyond thy love,
And scarce a glimpse of mercy from above.
Yet the same feeling which thou dost condemn,
My very love to thee is hate to them,
So closely mingling here, that disentwined,
I cease to love thee when I love mankind:
Yet dread not this—the proof of all the past
Assures the future that my love will last;
But—Oh, Medora! nerve thy gentler heart,
This hour again—but not for long—we part."

"This hour we part!—my heart foreboded this:
Thus ever fade my fairy dreams of bliss.
This hour—it cannot be—this hour away!
Yon bark hath hardly anchor'd in the bay:
Her consort still is absent, and her crew
Have need of rest before they toil anew:
My love! thou mock'st my weakness; and wouldst steel
My breast before the time when it must feel;
But trifle now no more with my distress,
Such mirth hath less of play than bitterness.
Be silent, Conrad!—dearest! come and share
The feast these hands delighted to prepare;
Light toil! to cull and dress thy frugal fare!
See, I have pluck'd the fruit that promised best,
And where not sure, perplex'd, but pleased, I guess'd
At such as seem'd the fairest: thrice the hill
My steps have wound to try the coolest rill;
Yes! thy sherbet to-night will sweetly flow,
See how it sparkles in its vase of snow!
The grapes' gay juice thy bosom never cheers;
Thou more than Moslem when the cup appears:
Think not I mean to chide—for I rejoice
What others deem a penance is thy choice.
But come, the board is spread; our silver lamp
Is trimm'd, and heeds not the Sirocco's damp:
Then shall my handmaids while the time along,
And join with me the dance, or wake the song;
Or my guitar, which still thou lov'st to hear,
Shall soothe or lull—or, should it vex thine ear,
We'll turn the tale, by Ariosto told,
Of fair Olympia loved and left of old.[2]
Why—thou wert worse than he who broke his vow
To that lost damsel, shouldst thou leave me now;
Or even that traitor chief—I've seen thee smile,
When the clear sky show'd Ariadne's Isle,
Which I have pointed from these cliffs the while:
And thus, half sportive, half in fear, I said,
Lest Time should raise that doubt to more than dread,
Thus Conrad, too, will quit me for the main:
And he deceived me—for—he came again!"

"Again—again—and oft again—my love!
If there be life below, and hope above,
He will return—but now, the moments bring
The time of parting with redoubled wing:
The why—the where—what boots it now to tell?
Since all must end in that wild word—farewell!
Yet would I fain—did time allow—disclose—
Fear not—these are no formidable foes;
And here shall watch a more than wonted guard,
For sudden siege and long defence prepared:
Nor be thou lonely—though thy lord's away,
Our matrons and thy handmaids with thee stay;
And this thy comfort—that, when next we meet,
Security shall make repose more sweet.
List!—'t is the bugle"—Juan shrilly blew—
"One kiss—one more—another—Oh! Adieu!"

She rose—she sprung—she clung to his embrace,
Till his heart heaved beneath her hidden face.

He dared not raise to his that deep-blue eye,
Which downcast droop'd in tearless agony.
Her long fair hair lay floating o'er his arms,
In all the wildness of dishevel'd charms;
Scarce beat that bosom where his image dwelt
So full—*that* feeling seem'd almost unfelt!
Hark—peals the thunder of the signal-gun!
It told 't was sunset—and he cursed that sun.
Again—again—that form he madly press'd,
Which mutely clasp'd, imploringly caress'd!
And tottering to the couch his bride he bore,
One moment gazed—as if to gaze no more;
Felt—that for him earth held but her alone,
Kiss'd her cold forehead — turn'd — is Conrad gone?

XV.

"And is he gone?"—on sudden solitude
How oft that fearful question will intrude!
"'T was but an instant past—and here he stood!
And now"—without the portal's porch she rush'd,
And then at length her tears in freedom gush'd;
Big—bright—and fast, unknown to her they fell;
But still her lips refused to send—"Farewell!"
For in that word—that fatal word—howe'er
We promise—hope—believe—there breathes despair.
O'er every feature of that still, pale face,
Had sorrow fix'd what time can ne'er erase:
The tender blue of that large loving eye
Grew frozen with its gaze on vacancy,

Till—Oh, how far!—it caught a glimpse of him,
And then it flow'd—and phrensied seem'd to swim,
Through those long, dark, and glistening lashes dew'd
With drops of sadness oft to be renew'd.
"He's gone!"—against her heart that hand is driven,
Convulsed and quick—then gently raised to heaven;
She look'd and saw the heaving of the main;
The white sail set—she dared not look again;
But turn'd with sickening soul within the gate—
"It is no dream—and I am desolate!"

XVI.

From crag to crag descending—swiftly sped
Stern Conrad down, nor once he turn'd his head;
But shrunk whene'er the windings of his way
Forced on his eye what he would not survey,
His lone, but lovely dwelling on the steep,
That hailed him first when homeward from the deep:

And she—the dim and melancholy star,
Whose ray of beauty reach'd him from afar,
On her he must not gaze, he must not think,
There he might rest—but on Destruction's brink;
Yet once almost he stopp'd—and nearly gave
His fate to chance, his projects to the wave;
But no—it must not be—a worthy chief
May melt, but not betray to woman's grief.
He sees his bark, he notes how fair the wind,
And sternly gathers all his might of mind:
Again he hurries on—and as he hears
The clang of tumult vibrate on his ears,
The busy sounds, the bustle of the shore,
The shout, the signal, and the dashing oar;
As marks his eye the seaboy on the mast,
The anchors rise, the sails unfurling fast,
The waving kerchiefs of the crowd that urge
That mute adieu to those who stem the surge;
And more than all, his blood-red flag aloft,
He marvell'd how his heart could seem so soft.
Fire in his glance, and wildness in his breast,
He feels of all his former self possest;
He bounds—he flies—until his footsteps reach
The verge where ends the cliff, begins the beach,
There checks his speed; but pauses less to breathe
The breezy freshness of the deep beneath,
Than there his wonted statelier step renew;
Nor rush, disturb'd by haste, to vulgar view:
For well had Conrad learn'd to curb the crowd,
By arts that veil, and oft preserve the proud;
His was the lofty port, the distant mien,
That seems to shun the sight—and awes if seen:
The solemn aspect, and the high-born eye,
That checks low mirth, but lacks not courtesy;
All these he wielded to command assent:
But where he wished to win, so well unbent,
That kindness cancell'd fear in those who heard,
And others' gifts show'd mean beside his word,
When echo'd to the heart as from his own
His deep yet tender melody of tone:
But such was foreign to his wonted mood,
He cared not what he soften'd, but subdued;
The evil passions of his youth had made
Him value less who loved—than what obey'd.

XVII.

Around him mustering ranged his ready guard.
Before him Juan stands—"Are all prepared?"

"They are—nay more—embark'd: the latest boat
Waits but my chief——"
"My sword, and my capote."
Soon firmly girded on, and lightly slung,
His belt and cloak were o'er his shoulders flung:
"Call Pedro here!"—He comes—and Conrad bends,
With all the courtesy he deign'd his friends;
"Receive these tablets, and peruse with care,
Words of high trust and truth are graven there;
Double the guard, and when Anselmo's bark
Arrives, let him alike these orders mark:
In three days (serve the breeze) the sun shall shine
On our return—till then all peace be thine!"
This said, his brother Pirate's hand he wrung,
Then to his boat with haughty gesture sprung.
Flash'd the dipt oars, and sparkling with the stroke,
Around the waves' phosphoric[3] brightness broke;
They gain the vessel—on the deck he stands,
Shrieks the shrill whistle—ply the busy hands—
He marks how well the ship her helm obeys,
How gallant all her crew—and deigns to praise.
His eyes of pride to young Gonsalvo turn—
Why doth he start, and inly seem to mourn?
Alas! those eyes beheld his rocky tower,
And live a moment o'er the parting hour;
She—his Medora—did she mark the prow?
Ah! never loved he half so much as now!
But much must yet be done ere dawn of day—
Again he mans himself and turns away;
Down to the cabin with Gonsalvo bends,
And there unfolds his plan—his means—and ends;
Before them burns the lamp, and spreads the chart,
And all that speaks and aids the naval art;
They to the midnight watch protract debate;
To anxious eyes what hour is ever late?
Meantime, the steady breeze serenely blew,
And fast and falcon-like the vessel flew;
Pass'd the high headlands of each clustering isle,
To gain their port—long—long ere morning smile:
And soon the night-glass through the narrow bay
Discovers where the Pacha's galleys lay.
Count they each sail—and mark how there supine
The lights in vain o'er heedless Moslem shine.
Secure, unnoted, Conrad's prow pass'd by,
And anchor'd where his ambush meant to lie;
Screen'd from espial by the jutting cape,
That rears on high its rude fantastic shape.
Then rose his band to duty—not from sleep—
Equipp'd for deeds alike on land or deep;
While lean'd their leader o'er the fretting flood,
And calmly talk'd—and yet he talk'd of blood!

CANTO THE SECOND.

Conosceste i dubiosi desiri?—Dante.

I.

In Coron's bay floats many a galley light,
Through Coron's lattices the lamps are bright,
For Seyd, the Pacha, makes a feast to-night:
A feast for promised triumph yet to come,
When he shall drag the fetter'd Rovers home;
This hath he sworn by Alla and his sword,
And faithful to his firman and his word,
His summon'd prows collect along the coast,
And great the gathering crews, and loud the boast;
Already shared the captives and the prize,
Though far the distant foe they thus despise;
'T is but to sail—no doubt to-morrow's Sun
Will see the Pirates bound—their haven won!
Meantime the watch may slumber, if they will,
Nor only wake to war, but dreaming kill.

Though all, who can, disperse on shore and seek
To flesh their glowing valour on the Greek;
How well such deed becomes the turban'd brave—
To bare the sabre's edge before a slave!
Infest his dwelling—but forbear to slay,
Their arms are strong, yet merciful to-day,
And do not deign to smite because they may!
Unless some gay caprice suggests the blow,
To keep in practice for the coming foe.
Revel and rout the evening hours beguile,
And they who wish to wear a head must smile;
For Moslem mouths produce their choicest cheer,
And hoard their curses, till the coast is clear.

II.

High in his hall reclines the turban'd Seyd;
Around—the bearded chiefs he came to lead.
Removed the banquet, and the last pilaff—
Forbidden draughts, 't is said, he dared to quaff,
Though to the rest the sober berry's juice,[4]
The slaves bear round for rigid Moslems' use;
The long Chibouque's[5] dissolving cloud supply,
While dance the Almas[6] to wild minstrelsy.
The rising morn will view the chiefs embark;
But waves are somewhat treacherous in the dark:
And revellers may more securely sleep
On silken couch than o'er the rugged deep,
Feast there who can—nor combat till they must,
And less to conquest than to Korans trust;
And yet the numbers crowded in his host
Might warrant more than even the Pacha's boast.

III.

With cautious reverence from the outer gate,
Slow stalks the slave, whose office there to wait,
Bows his bent head—his hand salutes the floor,
Ere yet his tongue the trusted tidings bore:
" A captive Dervise, from the pirate's nest
Escaped, is here—himself would tell the rest."[7]
He took the sign from Seyd's assenting eye,
And led the holy man in silence nigh.
His arms were folded on his dark-green vest,
His step was feeble, and his look deprest;
Yet worn he seem'd of hardship more than years,
And pale his cheek with penance, not from fears.
Vow'd to his God—his sable locks he wore,
And these his lofty cap rose proudly o'er:
Around his form his loose long robe was thrown,
And wrapt a breast bestow'd on Heaven alone;
Submissive, yet with self-possession mann'd,
He calmly met the curious eyes that scann'd;
And question of his coming fain would seek,
Before the Pacha's will allow'd to speak.

IV.

" Whence com'st thou, Dervise?"
" From the outlaw's den,
A fugitive—"
" Thy capture where and when?"
" From Scalanovo's port to Scio's isle,
The Saick was bound; but Alla did not smile
Upon our course—the Moslem merchant's gains
The Rovers won: our limbs have worn their chains.
I had no death to fear, nor wealth to boast,
Beyond the wandering freedom which I lost;
At length a fisher's humble boat by night
Afforded hope, and offer'd chance of flight:
I seized the hour, and find my safety here—
With thee—most mighty Pacha! who can fear?"

" How speed the outlaws? stand they well prepared
Their plunder'd wealth, and robber's rock, to guard?
Dream they of this our preparation, doom'd
To view with fire their scorpion nest consumed?"

" Pacha! the fetter'd captive's mourning eye,
That weeps for flight, but ill can play the spy;
I only heard the reckless waters roar,
Those waves that would not bear me from the shore;
I only mark'd the glorious sun and sky,
Too bright—too blue—for my captivity;
And felt—that all which Freedom's bosom cheers,
Must break my chain before it dried my tears.
This may'st thou judge, at least, from my escape,
They little deem of aught in peril's shape;
Else vainly had I pray'd or sought the chance
That leads me here—if eyed with vigilance:
The careless guard that did not see me fly,
May watch as idly when thy power is nigh.
Pacha!—my limbs are faint—and nature craves
Food for my hunger, rest from tossing waves:
Permit my absence—peace be with thee! Peace
With all around!—now grant repose—release."

" Stay, Dervise! I have more to question—stay,
I do command thee—sit—dost hear?—obey!
More I must ask, and food the slaves shall bring;
Thou shalt not pine where all are banqueting:
The supper done—prepare thee to reply,
Clearly and full—I love not mystery."

'T were vain to guess what shook the pious man,
Who look'd not lovingly on that Divan;
Nor show'd high relish for the banquet prest,
And less respect for every fellow guest.
'T was but a moment's peevish hectic past
Along his cheek, and tranquillized as fast:
He sate him down in silence, and his look
Resumed the calmness which before forsook:
The feast was usher'd in—but sumptuous fare
He shunn'd as if some poison mingled there.
For one so long condemn'd to toil and fast,
Methinks he strangely spares the rich repast.

" What ails thee, Dervise? eat—dost thou suppose
This feast a Christian's? or my friends thy foes?

Why dost thou shun the salt? that sacred pledge,
Which, once partaken, blunts the sabre's edge,
Makes even contending tribes in peace unite,
And hated hosts seem brethren to the sight!"

"Salt seasons dainties—and my food is still
The humblest root, my drink the simplest rill;
And my stern vow and order's[8] laws oppose
To break or mingle bread with friends or foes;
It may seem strange--if there be aught to dread,
That peril rests upon my single head;
But for thy sway—nay more—thy Sultan's throne,
I taste nor bread nor banquet—save alone;
Infringed our order's rule, the Prophet's rage
To Mecca's dome might bar my pilgrimage."

"Well—as thou wilt—ascetic as thou art—
One question answer; then in peace depart.
How many?—Ha! it cannot sure be day?
What star—what sun is bursting on the bay?
It shines a lake of fire!—away—away!
Ho! treachery! my guards! my scimitar!
The galleys feed the flames—and I afar!
Accursèd Dervise!—these thy tidings—thou
Some villain spy—seize—cleave him—slay him now!

Up rose the Dervise with that burst of light,
Nor less his change of form appall'd the sight:
Up rose that Dervise—not in saintly garb,
But like a warrior bounding on his barb,
Dash'd his high cap, and tore his robe away—
Shone his mail'd breast, and flash'd his sabre's ray!
His close but glittering casque, and sable plume,
More glittering eye, and black brow's sabler gloom
Glared on the Moslems' eyes some Afrit sprite,
Whose demon death-blow left no hope for fight.
The wild confusion, and the swarthy glow
Of flames on high, and torches from below;
The shriek of terror, and the mingling yell—
For swords began to clash, and shouts to swell—
Flung o'er that spot of earth the air of hell!
Distracted, to and fro, the flying slaves
Behold but bloody shore and fiery waves;
Nought heeded they the Pacha's angry cry,
They seize that Dervise!—seize on Zatanai![9]
He saw their terror—checked the first despair
That urged him but to stand and perish there,
Since far too early and too well obey'd,
The flame was kindled ere the signal made;
He saw their terror—from his baldric drew
His bugle—brief the blast—but shrilly blew:
'T is answer'd—"Well ye speed, my gallant crew!
Why did I doubt their quickness of career?
And deem design had left me single here?"
Sweeps his long arm—that sabre's whirling sway
Sheds fast atonement for its first delay;
Completes his fury what their fear begun,
And makes the many basely quail to one.
The cloven turbans o'er the chamber spread,
And scarce an arm dare rise to guard its head:
Even Seyd, convulsed, o'erwhelmed with rage, surprise,
Retreats before him, though he still defies.
No craven he—and yet he dreads the blow,
So much confusion magnifies his foe!
His blazing galleys still distract his sight,
He tore his beard, and foaming fled the fight;[10]
For now the pirates passed the Haram gate,
And burst within—and it were death to wait;
Where wild Amazement shrieking—kneeling throws
The sword aside—in vain—the blood o'erflows!
The Corsairs pouring, haste to where within,
Invited Conrad's bugle, and the din
Of groaning victims, and wild cries for life,
Proclaim'd how well he did the work of strife.
They shout to find him grim and lonely there,
A glutted tiger mangling in his lair!
But short their greeting—shorter his reply—
"'T is well—but Seyd escapes—and he must die—
Much hath been done—but more remains to do—
Their galleys blaze—why not their city too?"

V.

Quick at the word—they seized him each a torch,
And fire the dome from minaret to porch.
A stern delight was fixed in Conrad's eye,
But sudden sunk—for on his ear the cry
Of women struck, and like a deadly knell
Knock'd at that heart unmoved by battle's yell.
"Oh! burst the Haram—wrong not on your lives
One female form—remember—*we* have wives.
On them such outrage Vengeance will repay;
Man is our foe, and such 't is ours to slay;
But still we spared—must spare the weaker prey.
Oh! I forgot—but Heaven will not forgive
If at my word the helpless cease to live:
Follow who will—I go—we yet have time
Our souls to lighten of at least a crime."
He climbs the crackling stair—he bursts the door,
Nor feels his feet glow scorching with the floor;
His breath choked gasping with the volumed smoke,
But still from room to room his way he broke.
They search—they find—they save: with lusty arms
Each bears a prize of unregarded charms;
Calm their loud fears; sustain their sinking frames
With all the care defenceless beauty claims:
So well could Conrad tame their fiercest mood,
And check the very hands with gore imbrued.
But who is she? whom Conrad's arms convey
From reeking pile and combat's wreck—away—
Who but the love of him he dooms to bleed?
The Haram queen—but still the slave of Seyd!

VI.

Brief time had Conrad now to greet Gulnare,
Few words to re-assure the trembling fair;
For in that pause compassion snatch'd from war,
The foe before retiring, fast and far,
With wonder saw their footsteps unpursued,
First slowlier fled—then rallied—then withstood.
This Seyd perceives, then first perceives how few,
Compared with his, the Corsair's roving crew,
And blushes o'er his error, as he eyes
The ruin wrought by panic and surprise.
Alla il Alla! Vengeance swells the cry—
Shame mounts to rage that must atone or die!
And flame for flame and blood for blood must tell,
The tide of triumph ebbs that flow'd too well—
When wrath returns to renovated strife,
And those who fought for conquest strike for life.
Conrad beheld the danger—he beheld
His followers faint by freshening foes repelled:
"One effort—one—to break the circling host!"
They form—unite—charge—waver—all is lost!
Within a narrower ring compress'd, beset,
Hopeless, not heartless, strive and struggle yet—
Ah! now they fight in firmest file no more,
Hemm'd in—cut off—cleft down—and trampled o'er;
But each strikes singly, silently, and home,
And sinks outwearied rather than o'ercome,
His last faint quittance rendering with his breath,
Till the blade glimmers in the grasp of death!

VII.

But first, ere came the rallying host to blows,
And rank to rank, and hand to hand oppose,
Gulnare and all her Haram handmaids freed,
Safe in the dome of one who held their creed,
By Conrad's mandate safely were bestow'd,
And dried those tears for life and fame that flow'd:
And when that dark-eyed lady, young Gulnare,
Recall'd those thoughts late wandering in despair,
Much did she marvel o'er the courtesy
That smooth'd his accents; soften'd in his eye:
'T was strange—*that* robber thus with gore bedew'd
Seem'd gentler then than Seyd in fondest mood.
The Pacha woo'd as if he deem'd the slave
Must seem delighted with the heart he gave;
The Corsair vow'd protection, soothed affright,
As if his homage were a woman's right.

"The wish is wrong—nay, worse for female—vain:
Yet much I long to view that chief again;
If but to thank for, what my fear forgot,
The life—my loving lord remember'd not!"

VIII.

And him she saw, where thickest carnage spread,
But gather'd breathing from the happier dead;
Far from his band, and battling with a host
That deem right dearly won the field he lost,
Fell'd—bleeding—baffled of the death he sought,
And snatch'd to expiate all the ills he wrought;
Preserved to linger and to live in vain,
While Vengeance ponder'd o'er new plans of pain,
And stanch'd the blood she saves to shed again—
But drop by drop, for Seyd's unglutted eye
Would doom him ever dying—ne'er to die!
Can this be he? triumphant late she saw,
When his red hand's wild gesture waved, a law!
'T is he indeed—disarm'd but undeprest,
His sole regret the life he still possest;
His wounds too slight, though taken with that will,
Which would have kiss'd the hand that then could kill.
Oh were there none, of all the many given,
To send his soul—he scarcely ask'd to heaven?
Must he alone of all retain his breath,
Who more than all had striven and struck for death?
He deeply felt—what mortal hearts must feel,
When thus reversed on faithless fortune's wheel,
For crimes committed, and the victor's threat
Of lingering tortures to repay the debt—
He deeply, darkly felt; but evil pride
That led to perpetrate—now nerves to hide.
Still in his stern and self-collected mien
A conqueror's more than captive's air is seen,
Though faint with wasting toil and stiffening wound,
But few that saw—so calmly gazed around:
Though the far-shouting of the distant crowd,
Their tremors o'er, rose insolently loud,
The better warriors who beheld him near,
Insulted not the foe who taught them fear;
And the grim guards that to his durance led,
In silence eyed him with a secret dread.

IX.

The Leech was sent—but not in mercy—there,
To note how much the life yet left could bear;
He found enough to load with heaviest chain,
And promise feeling for the wrench of pain:
To-morrow—yea—to-morrow's evening sun
Will sinking see impalement's pangs begun,
And rising with the wonted blush of morn
Behold how well or ill those pangs are borne.
Of torments this the longest and the worst,
Which adds all other agony to thirst,
That day by day death still forbears to slake,
While famish'd vultures flit around the stake.
"Oh! water—water!"—smiling Hate denies
The victim's prayer—for if he drinks—he dies.
This was his doom:—the Leech, the guard, were gone,
And left proud Conrad fetter'd and alone.

X.

'T were vain to paint to what his feelings grew—
It even were doubtful if their victim knew.
There is a war, a chaos of the mind,
When all its element convulsed—combined—
Lie dark and jarring with perturbêd force,
And gnashing with impenitent Remorse;
That juggling fiend—who never spake before—
But cries "I warn'd thee!" when the deed is o'er.
Vain voice! the spirit burning but unbent,
May writhe—rebel—the weak alone repent!
Even in that lonely hour when most it feels,
And, to itself, all—all that self reveals,
No single passion, and no ruling thought
That leaves the rest as once unseen, unsought;
But the wild prospect when the soul reviews—
All rushing through their thousand avenues,
Ambition's dreams expiring, love's regret,
Endanger'd glory, life itself beset;
The joy untasted, the contempt or hate
'Gainst those who fain would triumph in our fate;
The hopeless past, the hasting future driven
Too quickly on to guess if hell or heaven;
Deeds, thoughts, and words, perhaps remember'd not
So keenly till that hour, but ne'er forgot;
Things light or lovely in their acted time,
But now to stern reflection each a crime;
The withering sense of evil unreveal'd,
Not cankering less because the more conceal'd—
All, in a word, from which all eyes must start,
That opening sepulchre—the naked heart
Bares with its buried woes, till Pride awake,
To snatch the mirror from the soul—and break.
Ay—Pride can veil, and Courage brave it all,
All—all—before—beyond—the deadliest fall.
Each hath some fear, and he who least betrays,
The only hypocrite deserving praise:
Not the loud recreant wretch who boasts and flies;
But he who looks on death—and silent dies.
So steel'd by pondering o'er his far career,
He half-way meets him should he menace near!

XI.

In the high chamber of his highest tower.
Sate Conrad, fetter'd in the Pacha's power.
His palace perish'd in the flame—this fort
Contain'd at once his captive and his court.
Not much could Conrad of his sentence blame,
His foe, if vanquish'd, had but shared the same:—
Alone he sate—in solitude and scann'd
His guilty bosom, but that breast he mann'd:
One thought alone he could not—dared not meet—
"Oh, how these tidings will Medora greet?"

Then—only then—his clanking hands he raised,
And strain'd with rage the chain on which he gazed;
But soon he found—or feign'd—or dream'd relief,
And smiled in self-derison of his grief,
"And now come torture when it will—or may,
More need of rest to nerve me for the day!"

This said, with languor to his mat he crept,
And, whatso'er his visions, quickly slept.
'T was hardly midnight when that fray begun,
For Conrad's plans matured, at once were done:
And Havoc loathes so much the waste of time,
She scarce had left an uncommitted crime.

One hour beheld him since the tide he stemm'd—
Disguised — discover'd — conquering — ta'en — condemn'd—
A chief on land—an outlaw on the deep—
Destroying—saving—prison'd—and asleep!

XII.

He slept in calmest seeming—for his breath
Was hush'd so deep—Ah! happy if in death!
He slept—Who o'er his placid slumber bends?
His foes are gone—and here he hath no friends;

Is it some seraph sent to grant him grace?
No, 'tis an earthly form with heavenly face!
Its white arm raised a lamp—yet gently hid,
Lest the ray flash abruptly on the lid
Of that closed eye, which opens but to pain,
And once unclosed—but once may close again.
That form, with eye so dark, and cheek so fair,
And auburn waves of gemm'd and braided hair;
With shape of fairy lightness—naked foot,
That shines like snow, and falls on earth as mute—
Through guards and dunnest night how came it there?
Ah! rather ask what will not woman dare?
Whom youth and pity lead like thee, Gulnare!
She could not sleep—and while the Pacha's rest
In muttering dreams yet saw his pirate-guest,
She left his side—his signet-ring she bore,
Which oft in sport adorn'd her hand before—
And with it, scarcely question'd, won her way
Through drowsy guards that must that sign obey.
Worn out with toil, and tired with changing blows,
Their eyes had envied Conrad his repose;
And chill and nodding at the turret door,
They stretch their listless limbs, and watch no more:
Just raised their heads to hail the signet-ring,
Nor ask or what or who the sign may bring.

XIII.

She gazed in wonder, "Can he calmly sleep,
While other eyes his fall or ravage weep?
And mine in restlessness are wandering here—
What sudden spell hath made this man so dear?
True—'tis to him my life, and more, I owe,
And me and mine he spared from worse than woe:
'T is late to think—but soft—his slumber breaks—
How heavily he sighs!—he starts—awakes!"

He raised his head—and dazzled with the light,
His eye seem'd dubious if it saw aright:
He moved his hand—the grating of his chain
Too harshly told him that he lived again.
"What is that form? if not a shape of air,
Methinks, my jailor's face shows wondrous fair!"

"Pirate! thou know'st me not—but I am one,
Grateful for deeds thou hast too rarely done;
Look on me—and remember her, thy hand
Snatch'd from the flames, and thy more fearful band.
I come through darkness—and I scarce know why—
Yet not to hurt—I would not see thee die."

"If so, kind lady! thine the only eye

That would not here in that gay hope delight:
Theirs is the chance—and let them use their right.
But still I thank their courtesy or thine,
That would confess me at so fair a shrine!"

Strange though it seem—yet with extremest grief
Is link'd a mirth—it doth not bring relief—
That playfulness of Sorrow ne'er beguiles,
And smiles in bitterness—but still it smiles;
And sometimes with the wisest and the best,
Till even the scaffold[12] echoes with their jest!
Yet not the joy to which it seems akin—
It may deceive all hearts, save that within.
Whate'er it was that flash'd on Conrad, now
A laughing wildness half unbent his brow:
And these his accents had a sound of mirth,
As if the last he could enjoy on earth;
Yet 'gainst his nature—for through that short life,
Few thoughts had he to spare from gloom and strife.

XIV.

"Corsair! thy doom is named—but I have power
To soothe the Pacha in his weaker hour.
Thee would I spare—nay more—would save thee now,
But this—time—hope—nor even thy strength allow;
But all I can, I will: at least, delay
The sentence that remits thee scarce a day.
More now were ruin—even thyself were loth
The vain attempt should bring but doom to both."

"Yes!—loth indeed:—my soul is nerved to all,
Or fall'n too low to fear a further fall:
Tempt not thyself with peril; me with hope
Of flight from foes with whom I could not cope:
Unfit to vanquish—shall I meanly fly,
The one of all my band that would not die?
Yet there is one—to whom my memory clings,
Till to these eyes her own wild softness springs.
My sole resources in the path I trod
Were these—my bark—my sword—my love—my God!
The last I left in youth—He leaves me now—
And Man but works His will to lay me low.
I have no thought to mock His throne with prayer
Wrung from the coward crouching of despair;
It is enough—I breathe—and I can bear.
My sword is shaken from the worthless hand
That might have better kept so true a brand;
My bark is sunk or captive—but my love—
For her in sooth my voice would mount above:
Oh! she is all that still to earth can bind—
And this will break a heart so more than kind,
And blight a form—till thine appear'd, Gulnare!
Mine eye ne'er ask'd if others were as fair."

"Thou lov'st another then?—but what to me
Is this—'t is nothing—nothing e'er can be:
But yet—thou lov'st—and—Oh! I envy those
Whose hearts on hearts as faithful can repose,
Who never feel the void—the wandering thought
That sighs o'er visions—such as mine hath wrought."

"Lady—methought thy love was his, for whom
This arm redeem'd thee from a fiery tomb."

"My love stern Seyd's! Oh—No—No—not my love—
Yet much this heart, that strives no more, once strove
To meet his passion—but it would not be.
I felt—I feel—love dwells with—with the free.
I am a slave, a favour'd slave at best,
To share his splendour, and seem very blest!
Oft must my soul the question undergo,
Of—'Dost thou love?' and burn to answer, 'No!'
Oh! hard it is that fondness to sustain,
And struggle not to feel averse in vain;
But harder still the heart's recoil to bear,
And hide from one—perhaps another there.
He takes the hand I give not—nor withhold—
Its pulse nor check'd—nor quicken'd—calmly cold:
And when resign'd, it drops a lifeless weight
From one I never loved enough to hate.
No warmth these lips return by his imprest,
And chill'd remembrance shudders o'er the rest.
Yes—had I ever proved that passion's zeal,
The change to hatred were at least to feel:
But still—he goes unmourn'd—returns unsought—
And oft when present—absent from my thought.
Or when reflection comes, and come it must—
I fear that henceforth 't will but bring disgust;
I am his slave—but, in despite of pride,
'T were worse than bondage to become his bride.
Oh! that this dotage of his breast would cease!
Or seek another and give mine release,
But yesterday—I could have said, to peace!
Yes—if unwonted fondness now I feign,
Remember—captive! 't is to break thy chain;
Repay the life that to thy hand I owe;
To give thee back to all endear'd below,
Who share such love as I can never know.
Farewell—morn breaks—and I must now away:
'T will cost me dear—but dread no death to-day!"

XV.

She press'd his fetter'd fingers to her heart,
And bow'd her head, and turn'd her to depart,
And noiseless as a lovely dream is gone.
And was she here? and is he now alone?
What gem hath dropp'd and sparkles o'er his chain?
The tear most sacred, shed for others' pain,
That starts at once—bright—pure—from Pity's mine,
Already polish'd by the hand divine!

Oh! too convincing—dangerously dear—
In woman's eye the unanswerable tear!
That weapon of her weakness she can wield,

To save, subdue—at once her spear and shield:
Avoid it—Virtue ebbs and Wisdom errs,
Too fondly gazing on that grief of hers!
What lost a world, and bade a hero fly?
The timid tear in Cleopatra's eye.
Yet be the soft triumvir's fault forgiven;
By this—how many lose not earth—but heaven!
Consign their souls to man's eternal foe,
And seal their own to spare some wanton's woe.

XVI.

'T is morn—and o'er his alter'd features play
The beams—without the hope of yesterday.
What shall he be ere night? perchance a thing
O'er which the raven flaps her funeral wing:
By his closed eye unheeded and unfelt,
While sets that sun, and dews of evening melt,
Chill—wet—and misty round each stiffen'd limb,
Refreshing earth—reviving all but him!—

CANTO THE THIRD.

"Come vedi—ancor non m'abbandona."—Dante.

I.

Slow sinks, more lovely ere his race be run,
Along Morea's hills the setting sun;
Not, as in northern climes, obscurely bright,
But one unclouded blaze of living light!
O'er the hush'd deep the yellow beam he throws,
Gilds the green wave, that trembles as it glows.
On old Ægina's rock, and Idra's isle,
The god of gladness sheds his parting smile:

O'er his own regions lingering, loves to shine,
Though there his altars are no more divine.
Descending fast the mountain shadows kiss
Thy glorious gulf, unconquer'd Salamis!
Their azure arches through the long expanse
More deeply purpled meet his mellowing glance,
And tenderest tints, along their summits driven,
Mark his gay course, and own the hues of heaven;
Till, darkly shaded from the land and deep,
Behind his Delphian cliff he sinks to sleep.

On such an eve, his palest beam he cast,
When—Athens! here thy Wisest look'd his last.
How watch'd thy better sons his farewell ray,
That closed their murder'd sage's[13] latest day!
Not yet—not yet—Sol pauses on the hill—
The precious hour of parting lingers still;
But sad his light to agonising eyes,
And dark the mountain's once delightful dyes:
Gloom o'er the lovely land he seem'd to pour,
The land, where Phœbus never frown'd before;
But ere he sank below Cithæron's head,
The cup of woe was quaff'd—the spirit fled;
The soul of him who scorn'd to fear or fly—
Who lived and died, as none can live or die!

But lo! from high Hymettus to the plain,
The queen of night asserts her silent reign.[14]
No murky vapour, herald of the storm,
Hides her fair face, nor girds her glowing form;
With cornice glimmering as the moon-beams play,
There the white column greets her grateful ray,
And, bright around with quivering beams beset,
Her emblem sparkles o'er the minaret:
The groves of olive scatter'd dark and wide
Where meek Cephisus pours his scanty tide,
The cypress saddening by the sacred mosque,
The gleaming turret of the gay kiosk,[15]
And, dun and sombre 'mid the holy calm,
Near Theseus' fane yon solitary palm,
All tinged with varied hues arrest the eye—
And dull were his that pass'd them heedless by.

Again the Ægean, heard no more afar,
Lulls his chafed breast from elemental war;
Again his waves in milder tints unfold
Their long array of sapphire and of gold,
Mix'd with the shades of many a distant isle,
That frown—where gentler ocean seems to smile.[16]

II.

Not now my theme—why turn my thoughts to thee?
Oh! who can look along thy native sea,
Nor dwell upon thy name, whate'er the tale,
So much its magic must o'er all prevail?
Who that beheld that Sun upon thee set,
Fair Athens! could thine evening face forget?
Not he—whose heart nor time nor distance frees,
Spell-bound within the clustering Cyclades!
Nor seems this homage foreign to his strain,
His Corsair's isle was once thine own domain—
Would that with freedom it were thine again!

III.

The Sun hath sunk—and, darker than the night,
Sinks with its beam upon the beacon height—
Medora's heart—the third day's come and gone—
With it he comes not—sends not—faithless one!
The wind was fair though light; and storms were none.
Last eve Anselmo's bark return'd, and yet
His only tidings that they had not met!
Though wild, as now, far different were the tale
Had Conrad waited for that single sail.

The night-breeze freshens—she that day had pass'd
In watching all that Hope proclaim'd a mast;
Sadly she sate—on high—Impatience bore
At last her footsteps to the midnight shore,
And there she wander'd, heedless of the spray
That dash'd her garments oft, and warn'd away:
She saw not—felt not this—nor dared depart,
Nor deem'd it cold—her chill was at her heart;
Till grew such certainty from that suspense—
His very Sight had shock'd from life or sense!

It came at last—a sad and shatter'd boat,
Whose inmates first beheld whom first they sought;
Some bleeding—all most wretched—these the few—
Scarce knew they how escaped—*this* all they knew.
In silence, darkling, each appear'd to wait
His fellow's mournful guess at Conrad's fate:
Something they would have said; but seem'd to fear
To trust their accents to Medora's ear.
She saw at once, yet sank not—trembled not—
Beneath that grief, that loneliness of lot,
Within that meek fair form, were feelings high,
That deem'd not till they found their energy.
While yet was Hope—they soften'd—flutter'd—wept—
All lost—that softness died not—but it slept;
And o'er its slumber rose that Strength which said,
"With nothing left to love—there's nought to dread."
'T is more than nature's; like the burning might
Delirium gathers from the fever's height.

"Silent you stand—nor would I hear you tell
What—speak not—breathe not—for I know it well—
Yet would I ask—almost my lip denies
The—quick your answer—tell me where he lies."

"Lady! we know not—scarce with life we fled;
But here is one denies that he is dead:
He saw him bound; and bleeding—but alive."

She heard no further—'t was in vain to strive—

So throbb'd each vein—each thought—till then withstood;
Her own dark soul—these words at once subdued:
She totters—falls—and senseless had the wave
Perchance but snatch'd her from another grave;
But that with hands though rude, yet weeping eyes,
They yield such aid as Pity's haste supplies:
Dash o'er her death-like cheek the ocean dew,
Raise—fan—sustain—till life returns anew;
Awake her handmaids, with the matrons leave
That fainting form o'er which they gaze and grieve;
Then seek Anselmo's cavern, to report
The tale too tedious—when the triumph short.

IV.

In that wild council words wax'd warm and strange
With thoughts of ransom, rescue, and revenge;
All, save repose or flight: still lingering there
Breathed Conrad's spirit, and forbade despair;
Whate'er his fate—the breasts he form'd and led,
Will save him living, or appease him dead.
Woe to his foes! there yet survive a few,
Whose deeds are daring, as their hearts are true.

V.

Within the Haram's secret chamber sate
Stern Seyd, still pondering o'er his Captive's fate;
His thoughts on love and hate alternate dwell,
Now with Gulnare, and now in Conrad's cell;

Here at his feet the lovely slave reclined
Surveys his brow—would soothe his gloom of mind:
While many an anxious glance her large dark eye
Sends in its idle search for sympathy,
His only bends in seeming o'er his beads,[17]
But inly views his victim as he bleeds.

"Pacha! the day is thine; and on thy crest
Sits Triumph—Conrad taken—fall'n the rest!
His doom is fix'd—he dies: and well his fate
Was earn'd—yet much too worthless for thy hate:
Methinks, a short release, for ransom told
With all his treasure, not unwisely sold;
Report speaks largely of his pirate-hoard—
Would that of this my Pacha were the lord!
While baffled, weaken'd by this fatal fray—
Watch'd—follow'd—he were then an easier prey;
But once cut off—the remnant of his band
Embark their wealth, and seek a safer strand."

"Gulnare!—if for each drop of blood a gem
Were offer'd rich as Stamboul's diadem;
If for each hair of his a massy mine
Of virgin ore should supplicating shine;
If all our Arab tales divulge or dream
Of wealth were here—that gold should not redeem!
It had not now redeem'd a single hour,
But that I know him fetter'd, in my power;
And, thirsting for revenge, I ponder still
On pangs that longest rack, and latest kill."

"Nay, Seyd!—I seek not to restrain thy rage,
Too justly moved for mercy to assuage;
My thoughts were only to secure for thee
His riches—thus released, he were not free:
Disabled, shorn of half his might and band,
His capture could but wait thy first command."

"His capture *could!*—and shall I then resign
One day to him—the wretch already mine?
Release my foe!—at whose remonstrance?—thine!
Fair suitor!—to thy virtuous gratitude,
That thus repays this Giaour's relenting mood,
Which thee and thine alone of all could spare,
No doubt—regardless if the prize were fair,
My thanks and praise alike are due—now hear!
I have a counsel for thy gentler ear:
I do mistrust thee, woman! and each word
Of thine stamps truth on all Suspicion heard.
Borne in his arms through fire from yon Serai—
Say, wert thou lingering there with him to fly?
Thou need'st not answer—thy confession speaks,
Already reddening on thy guilty cheeks;
Then, lovely dame, bethink thee! and beware:
'T is not *his* life alone may claim such care!
Another word and—nay—I need no more.
Accursed was the moment when he bore
Thee from the flames, which better far—but—no—
I then had mourn'd thee with a lover's woe—
Now, 't is thy lord that warns—deceitful thing!
Know'st thou that I can clip thy wanton wing?
In words alone I am not wont to chafe:
Look to thyself—nor deem thy falsehood safe!"

He rose—and slowly, sternly thence withdrew,
Rage in his eye and threats in his adieu:
Ah! little reck'd that chief of womanhood—
Which frowns ne'er quell'd, nor menaces subdued;
And little deem'd he what thy heart, Gulnare!
When soft could feel, and when incensed could dare.
His doubts appear'd to wrong—nor yet she knew
How deep the root from whence compassion grew—
She was a slave—from such may captives claim
A fellow-feeling, differing but in name;
Still half unconscious—heedless of his wrath,
Again she ventured on the dangerous path,
Again his rage repell'd—until arose
That strife of thought—the source of woman's woes!

VI.

Meanwhile—long anxious—weary—still—the same
Roll'd day and night—his soul could never tame—
This fearful interval of doubt and dread,
When every hour might doom him worse than dead,
When every step that echo'd by the gate
Might entering lead where axe and stake await;
When every voice that grated on his ear
Might be the last that he could ever hear;
Could terror tame—that spirit stern and high
Had proved unwilling as unfit to die;
'T was worn—perhaps decay'd—yet silent bore
That conflict deadlier far than all before:
The heat of fight, the hurry of the gale,
Leave scarce one thought inert enough to quail;
But bound and fix'd in fetter'd solitude,
To pine, the prey of every changing mood;
To gaze on thine own heart; and meditate
Irrevocable faults, and coming fate—
Too late the last to shun—the first to mend—
To count the hours that struggle to thine end,
With not a friend to animate, and tell
To other ears that death became thee well;
Around thee foes to forge the ready lie,
And blot life's latest scene with calumny;
Before thee tortures, which the soul can dare,
Yet doubts how well the shrinking flesh may bear;
But deeply feels a single cry would shame,
To valour's praise thy last and dearest claim;
The life thou leav'st below, denied above
By kind monopolists of heavenly love;
And more than doubtful paradise—thy heaven
Of earthly hope—thy loved one from thee riven.

Such were the thoughts that outlaw must sustain,
And govern pangs surpassing mortal pain:
And those sustain'd he—boots it well or ill?
Since not to sink beneath, is something still!

VII.

The first day pass'd—he saw not her—Gulnare—
The second—third—and still she came not there;
But what her words avouch'd, her charms had done,
Or else he had not seen another sun.
The fourth day roll'd along, and with the night
Came storm and darkness in their mingling might:
Oh! how he listen'd to the rushing deep,
That ne'er till now so broke upon his sleep;
And his wild spirit wilder wishes sent,
Roused by the roar of his own element!
Oft had he ridden on that wingèd wave,
And loved its roughness for the speed it gave;
And now its dashing echo'd on his ear,
A long known voice—alas! too vainly near!
Loud sung the wind above; and, doubly loud,
Shook o'er his turret cell the thunder-cloud;
And flash'd the lightning by the latticed bar,
To him more genial than the midnight star:
Close to the glimmering grate he dragg'd his chain,
And hoped *that* peril might not prove in vain.
He raised his iron hand to Heaven, and pray'd
One pitying flash to mar the form it made:
His steel and impious prayer attract alike—
The storm roll'd onward, and disdain'd to strike;
Its peal wax'd fainter—ceased—he felt alone,
As if some faithless friend had spurn'd his groan!

VIII.

The midnight pass'd—and to the massy door
A light step came—it paused—it moved once more;
Slow turns the grating bolt and sullen key:
'T is as his heart foreboded—that fair she!
Whate'er her sins, to him a guardian saint,
And beauteous still as hermit's hope can paint;
Yet changed since last within that cell she came,
More pale her cheek, more tremulous her frame:
On him she cast her dark and hurried eye,
Which spoke before her accents—"Thou must die!
Yes, thou must die—there is but one resource,
The last—the worst—if torture were not worse."

"Lady! I look to none—my lips proclaim
What last proclaimed they—Conrad still the same:
Why shouldst thou seek an outlaw's life to spare,
And change the sentence I deserve to bear?
Well have I earn'd—nor here alone—the meed
Of Seyd's revenge, by many a lawless deed."

"Why should I seek? because—Oh! didst thou not
Redeem my life from worse than slavery's lot?
Why should I seek?—hath misery made thee blind
To the fond workings of a woman's mind!
And must I say? albeit my heart rebel
With all that woman feels, but should not tell—
Because—despite thy crimes—that heart is moved:
It fear'd thee—thank'd thee—pitied—madden'd—loved.
Reply not, tell not now thy tale again,
Thou lov'st another—and I love in vain;
Though fond as mine her bosom, form more fair,
I rush through peril which she would not dare.
If that thy heart to hers were truly dear,
Were I thine own—thou wert not lonely here:
An outlaw's spouse—and leave her lord to roam!
What hath such gentle dame to do with home?
But speak not now—o'er thine and o'er my head
Hangs the keen sabre by a single thread;
If thou hast courage still, and wouldst be free,
Receive this poinard—rise—and follow me!"

"Ay—in my chains! my steps will gently tread,
With these adornments, o'er each slumbering head!
Thou hast forgot—is this a garb for flight?
Or is that instrument more fit for fight?"

"Misdoubting Corsair! I have gain'd the guard,
Ripe for revolt, and greedy for reward.
A single word of mine removes that chain:
Without some aid how here could I remain?
Well, since we met, hath sped my busy time,
If in aught evil, for thy sake the crime:
The crime—'t is none to punish those of Seyd.
That hated tyrant, Conrad—he must bleed!
I see thee shudder—but my soul is changed—
Wrong'd, spurn'd, reviled—and it shall be avenged—
Accused of what till now my heart disdain'd—
Too faithful, though to bitter bondage chain'd.
Yes, smile!—but he had little cause to sneer,
I was not treacherous then—nor thou too dear:
But he has said it—and the jealous well,
Those tyrants, teasing, tempting to rebel,
Deserve the fate their fretting lips foretell.
I never loved—he bought me—somewhat high—
Since with me came a heart he could not buy.
I was a slave unmurmuring: he hath said,
But for his rescue I with thee had fled.
'T was false thou know'st—but let such augurs rue,
Their words are omens Insult renders true.
Nor was thy respite granted to my prayer;
This fleeting grace was only to prepare
New torments for thy life, and my despair.
Mine too he threatens; but his dotage still
Would fain reserve me for his lordly will;
When wearier of these fleeting charms and me,
There yawns the sack—and yonder rolls the sea.
What, am I then a toy for dotard's play,
To wear but till the gilding frets away?

I saw thee—loved thee—owe thee all—would save,
If but to show how grateful is a slave.
But had he not thus menaced fame and life,
(And well he keeps his oaths pronounced in strife,)
I still had saved thee—but the Pacha spared.
Now I am all thine own—for all prepared:
Thou lov'st me not—nor know'st—or but the worst.
Alas! this love—that hatred are the first—
Oh! couldst thou prove my truth, thou would'st not start,
Nor fear the fire that lights an Eastern heart,
'T is now the beacon of thy safety—now
It points within the port a Mainote prow:
But in one chamber, where our path must lead,
There sleeps—he must not wake—the oppressor Seyd!"

"Gulnare—Gulnare—I never felt till now
My abject fortune, wither'd fame so low:
Seyd is mine enemy: had swept my band
From earth with ruthless but with open hand,
And therefore came I, in my bark of war,
To smite the smiter with the scimitar;
Such is my weapon—not the secret knife—
Who spares a woman's seeks not slumber's life.
Thine saved I gladly, Lady, not for this—
Let me not deem that mercy shown amiss.
Now fare thee well—more peace be with thy breast!
Night wears apace—my last of earthly rest!"

"Rest! rest! by sunrise must thy sinews shake,
And thy limbs writhe around the ready stake.
I heard the order—saw—I will not see—
If thou wilt perish, I will fall with thee.
My life—my love—my hatred—all below
Are on this cast—Corsair! 't is but a blow!
Without it flight were idle—how evade
His sure pursuit? my wrongs too unrepaid,
My youth disgraced—the long, long wasted years,
One blow shall cancel with our future fears;
But since the dagger suits thee less than brand,
I'll try the firmness of a female hand.
The guards are gain'd—one moment all were o'er—
Corsair! we meet in safety or no more;
If errs my feeble hand, the morning cloud
Will hover o'er thy scaffold, and my shroud."

IX.

She turn'd, and vanish'd ere he could reply,
But his glance followed far with eager eye;
And gathering, as he could, the links that bound
His form, to curl their length, and curb their sound,
Since bar and bolt no more his steps preclude,
He, fast as fetter'd limbs allow, pursued.
'T was dark and winding, and he knew not where
That passage led; nor lamp nor guard were there:
He sees a dusky glimmering—shall he seek
Or shun that ray so indistinct and weak?
Chance guides his steps—a freshness seems to bear
Full on his brow, as if from morning air—
He reached an open gallery—on his eye
Gleam'd the last star of night, the clearing sky:
Yet scarcely heeded these—another light
From a lone chamber struck upon his sight.
Towards it he moved; a scarcely closing door
Reveal'd the ray within, but nothing more.
With hasty step a figure outward past,
Then paused—and turn'd—and paused—'t is She at last!
No poniard in that hand—nor sign of ill—
"Thanks to that softening heart—she could not kill!"
Again he look'd, the wildness of her eye
Starts from the day abrupt and fearfully.
She stopp'd—threw back her dark far-floating hair,
That nearly veil'd her face and bosom fair:
As if she late had bent her leaning head
Above some object of her doubt or dread.
They meet—upon her brow—unknown—forgot—
Her hurrying hand had left—'t was but a spot—
Its hue was all he saw, and scarce withstood—
Oh! slight but certain pledge of crime—'t is blood!

X.

He had seen battle—he had brooded lone
O'er promised pangs to sentenced guilt foreshown;
He had been tempted—chastened—and the chain
Yet on his arms might ever there remain:
But ne'er from strife—captivity—remorse—
From all his feelings in their inmost force—
So thrill'd—so shudder'd every creeping vein,
As now they froze before that purple stain.
That spot of blood, that light but guilty streak,
Had banish'd all the beauty from her cheek!
Blood he had view'd—could view unmoved—but then
It flow'd in combat, or was shed by men!

XI.

"'T is done—he nearly waked—but it is done.
Corsair! he perish'd—thou art dearly won.
All words would now be vain—away—away!
Our bark is tossing—'t is already day.
The few gain'd over, now are wholly mine,
And these thy yet surviving band shall join:
Anon my voice shall vindicate my hand,
When once our sail forsakes this hated strand."

XII.

She clapp'd her hands—and through the gallery pour,
Equipp'd for flight, her vassals—Greek and Moor;
Silent but quick they stoop, his chains unbind;
Once more his limbs are free as mountain wind!

But on his heavy heart such sadness sate,
As if they there transferr'd that iron weight.
No words are utter'd—at her sign, a door
Reveals the secret passage to the shore;
The city lies behind—they speed, they reach
The glad waves dancing on the yellow beach;
And Conrad following, at her beck, obey'd,
Nor cared he now if rescued or betray'd;
Resistance was as useless as if Seyd
Yet lived to view the doom his ire decreed.

XIII.

Embark'd, the sail unfurl'd, the light breeze blew—
How much had Conrad's memory to review!
Sunk he in Contemplation, till the cape
Where last he anchor'd rear'd its giant shape.
Ah!—since that fatal night, though brief the time,
Had swept an age of terror, grief, and crime.
As its far shadow frown'd above the mast,
He veil'd his face, and sorrow'd as he pass'd;
He thought of all—Gonsalvo and his band,
His fleeting triumph and his failing hand;
He thought on her afar, his lonely bride:
He turn'd and saw—Gulnare, the homicide!

XIV.

She watch'd his features till she could not bear
Their freezing aspect and averted air,

And that strange fierceness foreign to her eye,
Fell quench'd in tears, too late to shed or dry.
She knelt beside him and his hand she press'd,
"Thou may'st forgive though Alla's self detest;
But for that deed of darkness what wert thou?
Reproach me—but not yet—O! spare me *now!*
I am not what I seem—this fearful night
My brain bewilder'd—do not madden quite!
If I had never loved—though less my guilt,
Thou hadst not lived to—hate me—if thou wilt."

XV.

She wrongs his thoughts, they more himself upbraid
Than her, though undesign'd, the wretch he made;
But speechless all, deep, dark, and unexprest,
They bleed within that silent cell—his breast.
Still onward, fair the breeze, nor rough the surge,
The blue waves sport around the stern they urge;
Far on the horizon's verge appears a speck,
A spot—a mast—a sail—an armed deck!
Their little bark her men of watch descry,
And ampler canvas woos the wind from high;
She bears her down majestically near,
Speed on her prow, and terror in her tier;
A flash is seen—the ball beyond their bow
Booms harmless, hissing to the deep below.
Up rose keen Conrad from his silent trance,
A long, long absent gladness in his glance;
"'T is mine—my blood-red flag! again—again—
I am not all deserted on the main!"
They own the signal, answer to the hail,
Hoist out the boat at once, and slacken sail.
"'T is Conrad! Conrad!" shouting from the deck,
Command nor duty could their transport check!
With light alacrity and gaze of pride,
They view him mount once more his vessel's side;
A smile relaxing in each rugged face,
Their arms can scarce forbear a rough embrace.
He, half forgetting danger and defeat,
Returns their greeting as a chief may greet,
Wrings with a cordial grasp Anselmo's hand,
And feels he yet can conquer and command!

XVI.

These greetings o'er, the feelings that o'erflow,
Yet grieve to win him back without a blow;
They sail'd prepar'd for vengeance—had they known
A woman's hand secured that deed her own,
She were their queen—less scrupulous are they
Than haughty Conrad how they win their way.
With many an asking smile, and wondering stare,
They whisper round, and gaze upon Gulnare;
And her, at once above—beneath her sex,
Whom blood appall'd not, their regards perplex.
To Conrad turns her faint imploring eye,
She drops her veil, and stands in silence by;
Her arms are meekly folded on that breast,
Which—Conrad safe—to fate resign'd the rest.
Though worse than frenzy could that bosom fill,
Extreme in love or hate, in good or ill,
The worst of crimes had left her woman still!

XVII.

This Conrad mark'd, and felt—ah! could he less?—
Hate of that deed—but grief for her distress;
What she has done no tears can wash away,
And Heaven must punish on its angry day:
But—it was done: he knew, whate'er her guilt,
For him that poniard smote, that blood was spilt;
And he was free!—and she for him had given
Her all on earth, and more than all in heaven!
And now he turn'd him to that dark-eyed slave,
Whose brow was bow'd beneath the glance he gave,
Who now seem'd changed and humbled:—faint and meek,
But varying oft the colour of her cheek
To deeper shades of paleness—all its red
That fearful spot which stain'd it from the dead!
He took that hand—it trembled—now too late—
So soft in love—so wildly nerved in hate;
He clasp'd that hand—it trembled—and his own
Had lost its firmness, and his voice its tone.
"Gulnare!"—but she replied not—"dear Gulnare!"
She raised her eye—her only answer there—
At once she sought and sunk in his embrace:
If he had driven her from that resting-place,
His had been more or less than mortal heart,
But—good or ill—it bade her not depart.
Perchance, but for the bodings of his breast,
His latest virtue then had join'd the rest.
Yet even Medora might forgive the kiss
That ask'd from form so fair no more than this,
The first, the last that Frailty stole from Faith—
To lips where Love had lavish'd all his breath,
To lips—whose broken sighs such fragrance fling
As he had fann'd them freshly with his wing!

XVIII.

They gain by twilight's hour their lonely isle.
To them the very rocks appear to smile;
The haven hums with many a cheering sound,
The beacons blaze their wonted stations round,
The boats are darting o'er the curly bay,
And sportive dolphins bend them through the spray;
Even the hoarse sea-bird's shrill, discordant shriek,
Greets like the welcome of his tuneless beak!
Beneath each lamp that through its lattice gleams,
Their fancy paints the friends that trim the beams.
Oh! what can sanctify the joys of home,
Like Hope's gay glance from Ocean's troubled foam!

XIX.

The lights are high on beacon and from bower,
And 'midst them Conrad seeks Medora's tower:

He looks in vain—'t is strange—and all remark,
Amid so many, hers alone is dark.
'T is strange—of yore its welcome never fail'd,
Nor now, perchance, extinguish'd, only veil'd.
With the first boat descends he to the shore,
And looks impatient on the lingering oar.
O! for a wing beyond the falcon's flight,
To bear him like an arrow to that height!
With the first pause the resting rowers gave,
He waits not—looks not—leaps into the wave,
Strives through the surge, bestrides the beach, and high
Ascends the path familiar to his eye.

He reach'd his turret door—he paused—no sound
Broke from within; and all was night around.
He knock'd, and loudly—footstep nor reply
Announced that any heard or deem'd him nigh;
He knock'd—but faintly—for his trembling hand
Refused to aid his heavy heart's demand.
The portal opens—'t is a well-known face—
But not the form he panted to embrace.
Its lips are silent—twice his own essay'd,
And fail'd to frame the question they delay'd;
He snatch'd the lamp—its light will answer all—
It quits his grasp, expiring in the fall.
He would not wait for that reviving ray—
As soon could he have linger'd there for day;
But, glimmering through the dusky corridore,
Another chequers o'er the shadow'd floor;
His steps the chamber gain—his eyes behold
All that his heart believed not—yet foretold!

XX.

He turn'd not—spoke not—sunk not—fix'd his look,
And set the anxious frame that lately shook:
He gazed—how long we gaze despite of pain,
And know, but dare not own, we gaze in vain!
In life itself she was so still and fair,
That death with gentler aspect wither'd there;
And the cold flowers her colder hand contain'd,[18]
In that last grasp as tenderly were strain'd
As if she scarcely felt, but feign'd a sleep,
And made it almost mockery yet to weep:
The long dark lashes fringed her lids of snow,
And veil'd—thought shrinks from all that lurk'd below—
Oh! o'er the eye death most exerts his might,
And hurls the spirit from her throne of light:
Sinks those blue orbs in that long last eclipse,
But spares, as yet, the charm around her lips—

Yet, yet they seem as they forbore to smile,
And wish'd repose—but only for a while;
But the white shroud, and each extended tress,
Long—fair—but spread in utter lifelessness,
Which, late the sport of every summer wind,
Escaped the baffled wreath that strove to bind;
These—and the pale pure cheek, became the bier,
But she is nothing—wherefore is he here?

XXI.

He ask'd no question—all were answer'd now
By the first glance on that still—marble brow.
It was enough—she died—what reck'd it how?
The love of youth, the hope of better years,
The source of softest wishes, tenderest fears,
The only living thing he could not hate,
Was reft at once—and he deserved his fate,
But did not feel it less;—the good explore,
For peace, those realms where guilt can never soar:
The proud—the wayward—who have fix'd below
Their joy, and find this earth enough for woe,
Lose in that one their all—perchance a mite—
But who in patience parts with all delight?
Full many a stoic eye and aspect stern
Mask hearts where grief hath little left to learn;
And many a withering thought lies hid, not lost,
In smiles that least befit who wear them most.

XXII.

By those, that deepest feel, is ill exprest
The indistinctness of the suffering breast;
Where thousand thoughts begin to end in one,
Which seeks from all the refuge found in none;
No words suffice the secret soul to show,
For Truth denies all eloquence to Woe.
On Conrad's stricken soul exhaustion prest,
And stupor almost lull'd it into rest;
So feeble now—his mother's softness crept
To those wild eyes, which like an infant's wept:
It was the very weakness of his brain,
Which thus confess'd without relieving pain.
None saw his trickling tears—perchance, if seen,
That useless flood of grief had never been:
Nor long they flow'd—he dried them to depart,
In helpless—hopeless—brokenness of heart:
The sun goes forth—but Conrad's day is dim;
And the night cometh—ne'er to pass from him.

There is no darkness like the cloud of mind,
On Grief's vain eye—the blindest of the blind!
Which may not—dare not see—but turns aside
To blackest shade—nor will endure a guide!

XXIII.

His heart was form'd for softness — warp'd to wrong;
Betray'd too early, and beguiled too long;
Each feeling pure—as falls the dropping dew
Within the grot; like that had harden'd too;
Less clear, perchance, its earthly trials pass'd,
But sunk, and chill'd, and petrified at last.
Yet tempests wear, and lightning cleaves the rock;
If such his heart, so shatter'd it the shock.
There grew one flower beneath its rugged brow,
Though dark the shade — it shelter'd — saved till now.
The thunder came—that bolt hath blasted both,
The Granite's firmness, and the Lily's growth:
The gentle plant hath left no leaf to tell
Its tale, but shrunk and wither'd where it fell;
And of its cold protector, blacken round
But shiver'd fragments on the barren ground!

XXIV.

'T is morn—to venture on his lonely hour
Few dare; though now Anselmo sought his tower.
He was not there—nor seen along the shore;
Ere night, alarm'd, their isle is travers'd o'er:
Another morn—another bids them seek,
And shout his name till echo waxeth weak;
Mount—grotto—cavern—valley search'd in vain,
They find on shore a sea-boat's broken chain:
Their hope revives—they follow o'er the main.
'T is idle all—moons roll on moons away,
And Conrad comes not — came not since that day:
Nor trace, nor tidings of his doom declare
Where lives his grief, or perish'd his despair!
Long mourn'd his band whom none could mourn beside;
And fair the monument they gave his bride:
For him they raise not the recording stone—
His death yet dubious, deeds too widely known;
He left a Corsair's name to other times,
Link'd with one virtue, and a thousand crimes.[19]

NOTES TO THE CORSAIR.

NOTE 1, page 1.

O'er the glad waters of the dark blue sea.

The time in this poem may seem too short for the occurrences, but the whole of the Ægean isles are within a few hours' sail of the continent, and the reader must be kind enough to take the *wind* as I have often found it.

NOTE 2, page 7.

Of fair Olympia loved and left of old.

Orlando Furioso, Canto 10.

NOTE 3, page 10.

Around the waves' phosphoric brightness broke.

By night, particularly in a warm latitude, every stroke of the oar, every motion of the boat or ship, is followed by a slight flash like sheet-lightning from the water.

NOTE 4, page 12.

Though to the rest the sober berry's juice.

Coffee.

NOTE 5, page 12.

The long Chibouque's dissolving cloud supply.

Pipe.

NOTE 6, page 12.

While dance the Almas to wild minstrelsy.

Dancing girls.

NOTE 7, page 12.

A captive Dervise, from the pirate's nest
Escaped, is here—himself would tell the rest.

It has been objected that Conrad's entering disguised as a spy is out of nature;—perhaps so. I find something not unlike it in history.

"Anxious to explore with his own eyes the state of the Vandals, Majorian ventured, after disguising the colour of his hair, to visit Carthage in the character of his own Ambassador; and Genseric was afterwards mortified by the discovery, that he had entertained and dismissed the Emperor of the Romans. Such an anecdote may be rejected as an improbable fiction; but it is a fiction which would not have been imagined unless in the life of a hero." —*Gibbon, Decline and Fall*, vol. vi. p. 180.

That Conrad is a character not altogether out of nature, I shall attempt to prove by some historical coincidences which I have met with since writing "The Corsair."

"Eccelin prisonnier," dit Rolandini, "s'enfermoit dans un silence menaçant, il fixoit sur la terre son visage féroce, et ne donnoit point d'essor à sa profonde indignation.—De toutes parts cependant les soldats et les peuples accouroient; ils vouloient voir cet homme, jadis si puissant, et la joie universelle éclatoit de toutes parts.

.

"Eccelin étoit d'une petite taille; mais tout l'aspect de sa personne, tous ses mouvemens, indiquoient un soldat.—Son langage étoit amer, son déportement superbe—et par son seul égard, il faisoit trembler les plus hardis."—*Sismondi*, tome iii., pp. 219, 220.

"Gizericus (Genseric, king of the Vandals, the conqueror of both Carthage and Rome), staturâ mediocris, et equi casu claudicans, animo profundus, sermone rarus, luxuriæ contemptor, irâ turbidus, habendi cupidus, ad solicitandas gentes providentissimus," etc., etc.—*Jornandes de Rebus Geticis*, c. 33.

I beg leave to quote these gloomy realities to keep in countenance my Giaour and Corsair

NOTE 8, page 13.

And my stern vow and order's laws oppose.

The Dervises are in colleges, and of different orders, as the monks.

NOTE 9, page 13.

They seize that Dervise!—seize on Zatanai

Satan.

NOTE 10, page 13.

He tore his beard, and foaming fled the fight.

A common and not very novel effect of Mussulman anger. See Prince Eugene's Memoirs, page 24. "The Seraskier received a wound in the thigh; he plucked up his beard by the roots, because he was obliged to quit the field."

NOTE 11, page 14.

Brief time had Conrad now to greet Gulnare.

Gulnare, a female name; it means, literally, the flower of the pomegranate.

NOTE 12, page 18.

Till even the scaffold echoes with their jest!

In Sir Thomas More, for instance, on the scaffold, and Anne Boleyn, in the Tower, when, grasping her neck, she remarked, that it "was too slender to trouble the headsman much." During one part of the French Revolution, it became a fashion to leave some "mot" as a legacy; and the quantity of facetious last words spoken during that period would form a melancholy jest-book of a considerable size.

NOTE 13, page 20.

That closed their murder'd sage's latest day!

Socrates drank the hemlock a short time before sunset (the hour of execution), notwithstanding the entreaties of his disciples to wait till the sun went down.

NOTE 14, page 20.

The queen of night asserts her silent reign.

The twilight in Greece is much shorter than in our own country; the days in winter are longer, but in summer of shorter duration.

NOTE 15, page 20.

The gleaming turret of the gay kiosk.

The Kiosk is a Turkish summer-house: the palm is without the present walls of Athens, not far from the temple of Theseus, between which and the tree the wall intervenes.—Cephisus' stream is indeed scanty, and Ilissus has no stream at all.

NOTE 16, page 20.

That frown—where gentler ocean seems to smile.

The opening lines, as far as section ii., have, perhaps, little business here, and were annexed to an unpublished (though printed) poem; but they were written on the spot in the Spring of 1811, and—I scarce know why—the reader must excuse their appearance here if he can.

Note 17, page 22.

His only bends in seeming o'er his beads.

The Comboloio, or Mahometan rosary; the beads are in number ninety-nine.

Note 18, page 27.

And the cold flowers her colder hand contain'd.

In the Levant it is the custom to strew flowers on the bodies of the dead, and in the hands of young persons to place a nosegay.

Note 19, page 28.

Link'd with one virtue, and a thousand crimes.

That the point of honour which is represented in one instance of Conrad's character has not been carried beyond the bounds of probability, may perhaps be in some degree confirmed by the following anecdote of a brother buccaneer in the year 1814:—

"Our readers have all seen the account of the enterprise against the pirates of Barrataria; but few, we believe, were informed of the situation, history, or nature of that establishment. For the information of such as were unacquainted with it, we have procured from a friend the following interesting narrative of the main facts, of which he has personal knowledge, and which cannot fail to interest some of our readers.

"Barrataria is a bay, or a narrow arm of the gulf of Mexico: it runs through a rich but very flat country, until it reaches within a mile of the Mississippi river, fifteen miles below the city of New Orleans. The bay has branches almost innumerable, in which persons can lie concealed from the severest scrutiny. It communicates with three lakes which lie on the south-west side, and these, with the lake of the same name, and which lies contiguous to the sea, where there is an island formed by the two arms of this lake and the sea. The east and west points of this island were fortified in the year 1811, by a band of pirates, under the command of one Monsieur La Fitte. A large majority of these outlaws are of that class of the population of the state of Louisiana who fled from the island of St. Domingo during the troubles there, and took refuge in the island of Cuba; and when the last war between France and Spain commenced, they were compelled to leave that island with the short notice of a few days. Without ceremony, they entered the United States, the most of them the state of Louisiana, with all the negroes they had possessed in Cuba. They were notified by the Governor of that state of the clause in the constitution which forbad the importation of slaves; but, at the same time, received the assurance of the Governor that he would obtain, if possible, the approbation of the General Government for their retaining this property.

"The island of Barrataria is situated about lat. 29 deg. 15 min., lon. 92 deg. 30 min., and is as remarkable for its health as for the superior scale and shell fish with which its waters abound. The chief of this horde, like Charles de Moor, had mixed with his many vices some virtues. In the year 1813, this party had, from its turpitude and boldness, claimed the attention of the Governor of Louisiana; and to break up the establishment, he thought proper to strike at the head. He therefore offered a reward of 500 dollars for the head of Monsieur La Fitte, who was well known to the inhabitants of the city of New Orleans, from his immediate connection, and his once having been a fencing-master in that city of great reputation, which art he learnt in Buonaparte's army, where he was a captain. The reward which was offered by the Governor for the head of La Fitte was answered by the offer of a reward from the latter of 15,000 dollars for the head of the Governor. The Governor ordered out a company to march from the city to La Fitte's island, and to burn and destroy all the property, and to bring to the city of New Orleans all his banditti. This company, under the command of a man who had been the intimate associate of this bold captain, approached very near to the fortified island, before he saw a man, or heard a sound, until he heard a whistle, not unlike a boatswain's call. Then it was he found himself surrounded by armed men, who had emerged from the secret avenues which led into Bayou. Here it was that the modern Charles de Moor developed his few noble traits; for to this man, who had come to destroy his life and all that was dear to him, he not only spared his life, but offered him that which would have made the honest soldier easy for the remainder of his days, which was indignantly refused. He then, with the approbation of his captor, returned to the city. This circumstance, and some concomitant events, proved that this band of pirates was not to be taken by land. Our naval force having always been small in that quarter, exertions for the destruction of this illicit establishment could not be expected from them until augmented; for an officer of the navy, with most of the gun-boats on that station, had to retreat from an overwhelming force of La Fitte's. So soon as the augmentation of the navy authorized an attack, one was made; the overthrow of this banditti has been the result; and, now this almost invulnerable point and key to New Orleans is clear of an enemy, it is to be hoped the government will hold it by a strong military force."—*From an American Newspaper.*

In Noble's continuation of "Granger's Biographical Dictionary," there is a singular passage in his account of Archbishop Blackbourne; and as in some measure connected with the profession of the hero of the foregoing poem, I cannot resist the temptation of extracting it:—

"There is something mysterious in the history and character of Dr. Blackbourne. The former is but imperfectly known; and report has even asserted he was a buccaneer; and that one of his brethren in that profession having asked, on his arrival in England, what had become of his old chum, Blackbourne, was answered, he is Archbishop of York. We are informed, that Blackbourne was installed sub-dean of Exeter in 1694, which office he resigned in 1702; but after his successor Lewis Barnet's death, in 1704, he regained it. In the following year he became dean; and, in 1714, held with it the archdeanery of Cornwall. He was consecrated Bishop of Exeter, February 24, 1716; and translated to York, November 28, 1724, as a reward, according to court scandal, for uniting George I. to the Duchess of Munster. This, however, appears to have been an unfounded calumny. As archbishop he behaved with great prudence, and was equally respectable as the guardian of the revenues of the see. Rumour whispered he retained the vices of his youth, and that a passion for the fair sex formed an item in the list of his weaknesses; but so far from being convicted by seventy witnesses, he does not appear to have been directly criminated by one. In short, I look upon these aspersions as the effects of mere malice. How is it possible a buccaneer should have been so good a scholar as Blackbourne certainly was? He who had so perfect a knowledge of the classics (particularly of the Greek tragedians), as to be able to read them with the same ease as he could Shakspeare, must have taken great pains to acquire the learned languages, and have had both leisure and good masters. But he was undoubtedly educated at Christ Church College, Oxford. He is allowed to have been a pleasant man: this, however, was turned against him, by its being said, 'he gained more hearts than souls.'"

"The only voice that could soothe the passions of the savage (Alphonso III.) was that of an amiable and virtuous wife, the sole object of his love; the voice of Donna Isabella, the daughter of the Duke of Savoy, and the granddaughter of Philip II., King of Spain. Her dying words sunk deep into his memory; his fierce spirit melted into tears; and after the last embrace, Alphonso retired into his chamber to bewail his irreparable loss, and to meditate on the vanity of human life."—*Miscellaneous Works of Gibbon*, New Edit., 8vo, vol. iii., p. 473.

LARA.[1]

CANTO THE FIRST.

I.

THE Serfs are glad through Lara's wide domain,[2]
And slavery half forgets her feudal chain;
He, their unhoped, but unforgotten lord—
The long self-exiled chieftain is restored:
There be bright faces in the busy hall,
Bowls on the board, and banners on the wall;
Far chequering o'er the pictured window, plays
The unwonted fagots' hospitable blaze;
And gay retainers gather round the hearth,
With tongues all loudness, and with eyes all mirth.

II.

The chief of Lara is return'd again:
And why had Lara cross'd the bounding main?
Left by his sire, too young such loss to know,
Lord of himself;—that heritage of woe,
That fearful empire which the human breast
But holds to rob the heart within of rest!—
With none to check, and few to point in time
The thousand paths that slope the way to crime;
Then, when he most required commandment, then
Had Lara's daring boyhood govern'd men.
It skills not, boots not step by step to trace
His youth through all the mazes of its race;
Short was the course his restlessness had run,
But long enough to leave him half undone.

III.

And Lara left in youth his father-land;
But from the hour he waved his parting hand
Each trace wax'd fainter of his course, till all
Had nearly ceased his memory to recall.
His sire was dust, his vassals could declare,
'T was all they knew, that Lara was not there;
Nor sent, nor came he, till conjecture grew
Cold in the many, anxious in the few.
His hall scarce echoes with his wonted name,
His portrait darkens in its fading frame,
Another chief consoled his destined bride,
The young forgot him, and the old had died;
"Yet doth he live!" exclaims the impatient heir,
And sighs for sables which he must not wear.
A hundred scutcheons deck with gloomy grace
The Laras' last and longest dwelling-place;
But one is absent from the mouldering file,
That now were welcome in that Gothic pile.

IV.

He comes at last in sudden loneliness,
And whence they know not, why they need not guess;
They more might marvel, when the greeting 's o'er,
Not that he came, but came not long before:
No train is his beyond a single page,
Of foreign aspect, and of tender age.
Years had roll'd on, and fast they speed away
To those that wander as to those that stay;
But lack of tidings from another clime
Had lent a flagging wing to weary Time.
They see, they recognise, yet almost deem
The present dubious, or the past a dream.

He lives, nor yet is past his manhood's prime,
Though sear'd by toil, and something touch'd by time;
His faults, whate'er they were, if scarce forgot,
Might be untaught him by his varied lot;
Nor good nor ill of late were known, his name
Might yet uphold his patrimonial fame.
His soul in youth was haughty, but his sins
No more than pleasure from the stripling wins;
And such, if not yet hardened in their course,
Might be redeem'd, nor ask a long remorse.

V.

And they indeed were changed—'t is quickly seen,
Whate'er he be, 't was not what he had been:
That brow in furrow'd lines had fix'd at last,
And spake of passions, but of passion past;
The pride, but not the fire, of early days,
Coldness of mien, and carelessness of praise;
A high demeanour, and a glance that took
Their thoughts from others by a single look;
And that sarcastic levity of tongue,
The stinging of a heart the world hath stung,
That darts in seeming playfulness around,
And makes those feel that will not own the wound;
All these seem'd his, and something more beneath
Than glance could well reveal, or accent breathe.
Ambition, glory, love, the common aim
That some can conquer, and that all would claim,
Within his breast appear'd no more to strive,
Yet seem'd as lately they had been alive;
And some deep feeling it were vain to trace
At moments lighten'd o'er his livid face.

VI.

Not much he loved long question of the past,
Nor told of wondrous wilds, and deserts vast,
In those far lands where he had wander'd lone,
And—as himself would have it seem—unknown:
Yet these in vain his eye could scarcely scan,
Nor glean experience from his fellow man;
But what he had beheld he shunn'd to show,
As hardly worth a stranger's care to know;
If still more prying such inquiry grew,
His brow fell darker, and his words more few.

VII.

Not unrejoiced to see him once again,
Warm was his welcome to the haunts of men;
Born of high lineage, link'd in high command,
He mingled with the magnates of his land;
Join'd the carousals of the great and gay,
And saw them smile or sigh their hours away;
But still he only saw, and did not share
The common pleasure or the general care;
He did not follow what they all pursued,
With hope still baffled, still to be renew'd;
Nor shadowy honour, nor substantial gain,
Nor beauty's preference, and the rival's pain:
Around him some mysterious circle thrown
Repell'd approach, and show'd him still alone;
Upon his eye sate something of reproof,
That kept at least frivolity aloof;
And things more timid that beheld him near,
In silence gazed, or whisper'd mutual fear;
And they the wiser, friendlier few confess'd
They deem'd him better than his air express'd.

VIII.

'T was strange—in youth all action and all life,
Burning for pleasure, not averse from strife;
Woman—the field—the ocean—all that gave
Promise of gladness, peril of a grave,
In turn he tried—he ransack'd all below,
And found his recompence in joy or woe,
No tame, trite medium; for his feelings sought
In that intenseness an escape from thought:
The tempest of his heart in scorn had gazed
On that the feebler elements hath raised;
The rapture of his heart had look'd on high,
And ask'd if greater dwelt beyond the sky:
Chain'd to excess, the slave of each extreme,
How woke he from the wildness of that dream?
Alas! he told not—but he did awake
To curse the wither'd heart that would not break.

IX.

Books, for his volume heretofore was Man,
With eye more curious he appear'd to scan,
And oft, in sudden mood, for many a day
From all communion he would start away:
And then, his rarely call'd attendants said,
Through night's long hours would sound his hurried tread
O'er the dark gallery, where his fathers frown'd
In rude but antique portraiture around.
They heard, but whisper'd—"*that* must not be known—
The sound of words less earthly than his own.
Yes, they who chose might smile, but some had seen
They scarce knew what, but more than should have been.
Why gazed he so upon the ghastly head
Which hands profane had gather'd from the dead,
That still beside his open'd volume lay,
As if to startle all save him away?
Why slept he not when others were at rest?
Why heard no music, and received no guest?
All was not well, they deem'd—but where the wrong?
Some knew perchance—but 't were a tale too long;
And such besides were too discreetly wise,
To more than hint their knowledge in surmise;
But if they would—they could"—around the board,
Thus Lara's vassals prattled of their lord.

X.

It was the night—and Lara's glassy stream
The stars are studding, each with imaged beam:
So calm, the waters scarcely seem to stray,
And yet they glide like happiness away;
Reflecting far and fairy-like from high
The immortal lights that live along the sky:
Its banks are fringed with many a goodly tree,
And flowers the fairest that may feast the bee;
Such in her chaplet infant Dian wove,
And Innocence would offer to her love.
These deck the shore; the waves their channel make
In windings bright and mazy like the snake.
All was so still, so soft in earth and air,
You scarce would start to meet a spirit there;
Secure that nought of evil could delight
To walk in such a scene, on such a night!
It was a moment only for the good:
So Lara deemed, nor longer there he stood,
But turned in silence to his castle-gate;
Such scene his soul no more could contemplate:
Such scene reminded him of other days,
Of skies more cloudless, moons of purer blaze,
Of nights more soft and frequent, hearts that now—
No—no—the storm may beat upon his brow,
Unfelt—unsparing—but a night like this,
A night of beauty mock'd such breast as his.

XI.

He turned within his solitary hall,
And his high shadow shot along the wall;
There were the painted forms of other times,
'T was all they left of virtues or of crimes,
Save vague tradition; and the gloomy vaults
That hid their dust, their foibles, and their faults;
And half a column of the pompous page,
That speeds the specious tale from age to age;
Where history's pen its praise or blame supplies,
And lies like truth, and still most truly lies.
He wandering mused, and as the moonbeam shone
Through the dim lattice o'er the floor of stone,
And the high fretted roof, and saints, that there
O'er Gothic windows knelt in pictured prayer,
Reflected in fantastic figures grew,
Like life, but not like mortal life, to view;
His bristling locks of sable, brow of gloom,
And the wide waving of his shaken plume,
Glanced like a spectre's attributes, and gave
His aspect all that terror gives the grave.

XII.

'T was midnight—all was slumber; the lone light
Dimm'd in the lamp, as loth to break the night.
Hark! there be murmurs heard in Lara's hall—
A sound—a voice—a shriek—a fearful call!
A long, loud shriek—and silence—did they hear
That frantic echo burst the sleeping ear?
They heard and rose, and tremulously brave
Rush where the sound invoked their aid to save;
They come with half-lit tapers in their hands,
And snatch'd in startled haste unbelted brands.

XIII.

Cold as the marble where his length was laid,
Pale as the beam that o'er his features played,
Was Lara stretch'd; his half-drawn sabre near,
Dropp'd it should seem in more than nature's fear;
Yet he was firm, or had been firm till now,
And still defiance knit his gathered brow;

Though mix'd with terror, senseless as he lay,
There lived upon his lip the wish to slay;
Some half-form'd threat in utterance there had died,
Some imprecation of despairing pride;
His eye was almost seal'd, but not forsook,
Even in its trance the gladiator's look,
That oft awake his aspect could disclose,
And now was fix'd in horrible repose.

They raise him, bear him: hush! he breathes, he speaks,
The swarthy blush recolours in his cheeks,
His lip resumes its red, his eye, though dim,
Rolls wide and wild, each slowly quivering limb
Recalls its function, but his words are strung
In terms that seem not of his native tongue;
Distinct but strange, enough they understand
To deem them accents of another land,

And such they were, and meant to meet an ear
That hears him not—alas! that cannot hear!

XIV.

His page approach'd, and he alone appear'd
To know the import of the words they heard;
And by the changes of his cheek and brow
They were not such as Lara should avow,
Nor he interpret, yet with less surprise
Than those around their chieftain's state he eyes,
But Lara's prostrate form he bent beside,
And in that tongue which seem'd his own replied,
And Lara heeds those tones that gently seem
To soothe away the horrors of his dream;
If dream it were, that thus could overthrow
A breast that needed not ideal woe.

XV.

Whate'er his phrenzy dream'd or eye beheld,
If yet remember'd ne'er to be reveal'd,
Rests at his heart: the custom'd morning came,
And breath'd new vigour in his shaking frame;
And solace sought he none from priest nor leech,
And soon the same in movement and in speech
As heretofore he fill'd the passing hours,
Nor less he smiles, nor more his forehead lours
Than these were wont; and if the coming night
Appear'd less welcome now to Lara's sight,
He to his marvelling vassals show'd it not,
Whose shuddering proved *their* fear was less forgot.
In trembling pairs (alone they dared not) crawl
The astonish'd slaves, and shun the fated hall;
The waving banner, and the clapping door;
The rustling tapestry, and the echoing floor;
The long dim shadows of surrounding trees,
The flapping bat, the night song of the breeze;
Aught they behold or hear their thought appals
As evening saddens o'er the dark gray walls.

XVI.

Vain thought! that hour of ne'er unravell'd gloom
Came not again, or Lara could assume
A seeming of forgetfulness that made
His vassals more amaz'd nor less afraid—
Had memory vanish'd then with sense restored?
Since word, nor look, nor gesture of their lord
Betrayed a feeling that recalled to these
That fevered moment of his mind's disease.
Was it a dream? was his the voice that spoke
Those strange wild accents; his the cry that broke
Their slumber? his the oppress'd o'er-laboured heart
That ceased to beat, the look that made them start?
Could he who thus had suffered, so forget
When such as saw that suffering shudder yet?
Or did that silence prove his memory fix'd
Too deep for words, indelible, unmix'd
In that corroding secrecy which gnaws
The heart to show the effect, but not the cause?
Not so in him; his breast had buried both,
Nor common gazers could discern the growth
Of thoughts that mortal lips must leave half told;
They choke the feeble words that would unfold.

XVII.

In him inexplicably mix'd appeared
Much to be loved and hated, sought and feared;
Opinion varying o'er his hidden lot,
In praise or railing ne'er his name forgot;
His silence formed a theme for others' prate—
They guess'd—they gazed—they fain would know his fate.
What had he been? what was he, thus unknown,
Who walked their world, his lineage only known?
A hater of his kind? yet some would say,
With them he could seem gay amidst the gay;
But own'd, that smile if oft observed and near,
Waned in its mirth and withered to a sneer;
That smile might reach his lip, but passed not by,
None e'er could trace its laughter to his eye:
Yet there was softness too in his regard,
At times, a heart as not by nature hard,
But once perceiv'd, his spirit seem'd to chide
Such weakness, as unworthy of its pride,
And steel'd itself, as scorning to redeem
One doubt from others' half withheld esteem
In self-inflicted penance of a breast
Which tenderness might once have wrung from rest;
In vigilance of grief that would compel
The soul to hate for having lov'd too well.

XVIII.

There was in him a vital scorn of all:
As if the worst had fall'n which could befall,
He stood a stranger in this breathing world,
An erring spirit from another hurled;
A thing of dark imaginings, that shaped
By choice the perils he by chance escaped;
But 'scaped in vain, for in their memory yet
His mind would half exult and half regret:
With more capacity for love than earth
Bestows on most of mortal mould and birth,
His early dreams of good outstripp'd the truth,
And troubled manhood followed baffled youth;
With thought of years in phantom chase mispent,
And wasted powers for better purpose lent;
And fiery passions that had poured their wrath
In hurried desolation o'er his path,
And left the better feelings all at strife
In wild reflection o'er his stormy life;
But haughty still, and loth himself to blame,
He called on Nature's self to share the shame,
And charged all faults upon the fleshly form
She gave to clog the soul, and feast the worm;
'Till he at last confounded good and ill,
And half mistook for fate the acts of will:

Too high for common selfishness, he could
At times resign his own for others' good,
But not in pity, not because he ought,
But in some strange perversity of thought,
That swayed him onward with a secret pride
To do what few or none would do beside;
And this same impulse would in tempting time
Mislead his spirit equally to crime;
So much he soared beyond, or sunk beneath
The men with whom he felt condemned to breathe,
And longed by good or ill to separate
Himself from all who shared his mortal state;
His mind abhorring this had fixed her throne
Far from the world, in regions of her own;
Thus coldly passing all that passed below,
His blood in temperate seeming now would flow:
Ah! happier if it ne'er with guilt had glowed,
But ever in that icy smoothness flowed!
'T is true, with other men their path he walked,
And like the rest in seeming did and talked,
Nor outraged Reason's rules by flaw nor start,
His madness was not of the head, but heart;
And rarely wandered in his speech, or drew
His thoughts so forth as to offend the view.

XIX.

With all that chilling mystery of mien,
And seeming gladness to remain unseen;
He had (if 't were not nature's boon) an art
Of fixing memory on another's heart:
It was not love, perchance—nor hate—nor aught
That words can image to express the thought;
But they who saw him did not see in vain,
And once beheld, would ask of him again:
And those to whom he spake remembered well,
And on the words, however light, would dwell:
None knew nor how, nor why, but he entwined
Himself perforce around the hearer's mind;
There he was stamp'd, in liking, or in hate,
If greeted once; however brief the date
That friendship, pity, or aversion knew,
Still there within the inmost thought he grew.
You could not penetrate his soul, but found,
Despite your wonder, to your own he wound;
His presence haunted still; and from the breast
He forced an all-unwilling interest;
Vain was the struggle in that mental net,
His spirit seemed to dare you to forget!

XX.

There is a festival, where knights and dames,
And aught that wealth or lofty lineage claims
Appear—a high-born and a welcomed guest
To Otho's hall came Lara with the rest.
The long carousal shakes the illumin'd hall,
Well speeds alike the banquet and the ball;
And the gay dance of bounding Beauty's train
Links grace and harmony in happiest chain:
Blest are the early hearts and gentle hands
That mingle there in well according bands;
It is a sight the careful brow might smoothe,
And make Age smile, and dream itself to youth,
And Youth forget such hour was past on earth,
So springs the exulting bosom to that mirth!

XXI.

And Lara gaz'd on these sedately glad,
His brow belied him if his soul was sad,
And his glance followed fast each fluttering fair,
Whose steps of lightness woke no echo there:
He lean'd against the lofty pillar nigh
With folded arms and long attentive eye,
Nor mark'd a glance so sternly fix'd on his,
Ill brook'd high Lara scrutiny like this:
At length he caught it, 't is a face unknown,
But seems as searching his, and his alone;
Prying and dark, a stranger's by his mien,
Who still till now had gaz'd on him unseen;
At length encountering meets the mutual gaze
Of keen inquiry, and of mute amaze;
On Lara's glance emotion gathering grew,
As if distrusting that the stranger threw;
Along the stranger's aspect fix'd and stern
Flash'd more than thence the vulgar eye could learn.

XXII.

"'T is he!" the stranger cried, and those that heard
Re-echoed fast and far the whisper'd word.
"'T is he!"—"'T is who?" they question far and near,
Till louder accents rung on Lara's ear;
So widely spread, few bosoms well could brook
The general marvel, or that single look;
But Lara stirr'd not, changed not, the surprise
That sprung at first to his arrested eyes
Seem'd now subsided, neither sunk nor rais'd
Glanced his eye round, though still the stranger gaz'd;
And drawing nigh, exclaim'd, with haughty sneer,
"'T is he!—how came he thence?—what doth he here?"

XXIII.

It were too much for Lara to pass by
Such question, so repeated fierce and high;
With look collected, but with accent cold,
More mildly firm than petulantly bold,
He turn'd, and met the inquisitorial tone—
"My name is Lara!—when thine own is known,
Doubt not my fitting answer to requite
The unlook'd for courtesy of such a knight.
'T is Lara!—further wouldst thou mark or ask?
I shun no question, and I wear no mask."
"Thou shun'st no question! Ponder—is there none
Thy heart must answer, though thine ear would shun?
And deem'st thou me unknown too? Gaze again!
At least thy memory was not given in vain.

Oh! never canst thou cancel half her debt,
Eternity forbids thee to forget."
With slow and searching glance upon his face
Grew Lara's eyes, but nothing there could trace
They knew, or chose to know—with dubious look
He deign'd no answer, but his head he shook,
And half contemptuous turn'd to pass away;
But the stern stranger motioned him to stay.
"A word!—I charge thee stay, and answer here
To one, who, wert thou noble, were thy peer,
But as thou wast and art—nay, frown not, lord,
If false, 't is easy to disprove the word—

But, as thou wast and art, on thee looks down,
Distrusts thy smiles, but shakes not at thy frown.
Art thou not he? whose deeds——"
"Whate'er I be,
Words wild as these, accusers like to thee
I list no further; those with whom they weigh
May hear the rest, nor venture to gainsay
The wondrous tale no doubt thy tongue can tell,
Which thus begins so courteously and well.
Let Otho cherish here his polish'd guest,
To him my thanks and thoughts shall be expressed."
And here their wondering host hath interposed—
"Whate'er there be between you undisclosed,

This is no time nor fitting place to mar
The mirthful meeting with a wordy war.
If thou, Sir Ezzelin, hast aught to show
Which it befits Count Lara's ear to know,
To-morrow, here, or elsewhere, as may best
Beseem your mutual judgment, speak the rest;
I pledge myself for thee, as not unknown,
Though like Count Lara now return'd alone
From other lands, almost a stranger grown;
And if from Lara's blood and gentle birth
I augur right of courage and of worth,
He will not that untainted line belie,
Nor aught that knighthood may accord deny."
"To-morrow be it," Ezzelin replied,
"And here our several worth and truth be tried;
I gage my life, my falchion to attest
My words, so may I mingle with the blest!"
What answers Lara? to its centre shrunk
His soul, in deep abstraction sudden sunk;
The words of many, and the eyes of all
That there were gather'd seem'd on him to fall;
But his were silent, his appear'd to stray
In far forgetfulness away—away—
Alas! that heedlessness of all around
Bespoke remembrance only too profound.

XXIV.

"To-morrow!—ay, to-morrow!" further word
Than those repeated none from Lara heard;
Upon his brow no outward passion spoke,
From his large eye no flashing anger broke;
Yet there was something fix'd in that low tone
Which show'd resolve, determined, though unknown.
He seiz'd his cloak—his head he slightly bow'd,
And passing Ezzelin he left the crowd;
And, as he pass'd him, smiling met the frown
With which that chieftain's brow would bear him down:
It was nor smile of mirth, nor struggling pride
That curbs to scorn the wrath it cannot hide;
But that of one in his own heart secure
Of all that he would do, or could endure.
Could this mean peace? the calmness of the good?
Or guilt grown old in desperate hardihood?
Alas! too like in confidence are each
For man to trust to mortal look or speech;
From deeds, and deeds alone, may he discern
Truths which it wrings the unpractised heart to learn.

XXV.

And Lara called his page, and went his way—
Well could that stripling word or sign obey:
His only follower from those climes afar
Where the soul glows beneath a brighter star;
For Lara left the shore from whence he sprung,
In duty patient, and sedate though young;
Silent as him he served, his fate appears
Above his station, and beyond his years.
Though not unknown the tongue of Lara's land,
In such from him he rarely heard command;
But fleet his step, and clear his tones would come,
When Lara's lip breathed forth the words of home:
Those accents, as his native mountains dear,
Awake their absent echoes in his ear,
Friends', kindreds', parents', wonted voice recall,
Now lost, abjured, for one—his friend, his all:
For him earth now disclosed no other guide;
What marvel then he rarely left his side?

XXVI.

Light was his form, and darkly delicate
That brow whereon his native sun had sate,
But had not marr'd, though in his beams he grew,
The cheek where oft the unbidden blush shone through;
Yet not such blush as mounts when health would show
All the heart's hue in that delighted glow;
But 't was a hectic tint of secret care
That for a burning moment fever'd there;
And the wild sparkle of his eye seemed caught
From high, and lightened with electric thought,
Though its black orb those long low lashes fringe,
Had tempered with a melancholy tinge;
Yet less of sorrow than of pride was there,
Or, if 't were grief, a grief that none should share:
And pleased not him the sports that please his age,
The tricks of youth, the frolics of the page;
For hours on Lara he would fix his glance,
As all-forgotten in that watchful trance;
And from his chief withdrawn, he wander'd lone,
Brief were his answers, and his questions none;
His walk the wood, his sport some foreign book;
His resting-place the bank that curbs the brook:
He seem'd, like him he served, to live apart
From all that lures the eye, and fills the heart;
To know no brotherhood, and take from earth
No gift beyond that bitter boon—our birth.

XXVII.

If aught he loved, 't was Lara; but was shown
His faith in reverence and in deeds alone;
In mute attention; and his care, which guess'd
Each wish, fulfilled it ere the tongue expressed.
Still there was haughtiness in all he did,
A spirit deep that brook'd not to be chid;
His zeal, though more than that of servile hands,
In act alone obeys, his air commands;
As if 't was Lara's less than *his* desire
That thus he served, but surely not for hire.
Slight were the tasks enjoined him by his lord,
To hold the stirrup, or to bear the sword;
To tune his lute, or, if he will'd it more,
On tomes of other times and tongues to pore;

But ne'er to mingle with the menial train,
To whom he show'd nor deference nor disdain,
But that well-worn reserve which proved he knew
No sympathy with that familiar crew:
His soul, whate'er his station or his stem,
Could bow to Lara, not descend to them.
Of higher birth he seem'd, and better days,
Nor mark of vulgar toil that hand betrays,
So femininely white it might bespeak
Another sex, when match'd with that smooth cheek,
But for his garb, and something in his gaze,
More wild and high than woman's eye betrays;
A latent fierceness that far more became
His fiery climate than his tender frame:
True, in his words it broke not from his breast,
But from his aspect might be more than guess'd.
Kaled his name, though rumour said he bore
Another ere he left his mountain shore;
For sometimes he would hear, however nigh,
That name repeated loud without reply,
As unfamiliar, or, if roused again,
Start to the sound, as but remember'd then;
Unless 't was Lara's wonted voice that spake,
For then, ear, eyes, and heart would all awake.

XXVIII.

He had look'd down upon the festive hall,
And mark'd that sudden strife so mark'd of all;
And when the crowd around and near him told
Their wonder at the calmness of the bold,
Their marvel how the high-born Lara bore
Such insult from a stranger, doubly sore,
The colour of young Kaled went and came,
The lip of ashes, and the cheek of flame;
And o'er his brow the dampening heart-drops threw
The sickening iciness of that cold dew
That rises as the busy bosom sinks
With heavy thoughts from which reflection shrinks.
Yes—there be things which we must dream and dare,
And execute ere thought be half aware:
Whate'er might Kaled's be, it was enow
To seal his lip, but agonise his brow.
He gazed on Ezzelin till Lara cast
That sidelong smile upon the knight he past;
When Kaled saw that smile his visage fell,
As if on something recognised right well:
His memory read in such a meaning more
Than Lara's aspect unto others wore.
Forward he sprung—a moment, both were gone,
And all within that hall seem'd left alone;
Each had so fix'd his eye on Lara's mien,
All had so mix'd their feelings with that scene,
That when his long dark shadow through the porch
No more relieves the glare of yon high torch,
Each pulse beats quicker, and all bosoms seem
To bound as doubting from too black a dream,
Such as we know is false, yet dread in sooth,
Because the worst is ever nearest truth.
And they are gone—but Ezzelin is there,
With thoughtful visage and imperious air;
But long remained not; ere an hour expired
He waved his hand to Otho, and retired.

XXIX.

The crowd are gone, the revellers at rest;
The courteous host, and all-approving guest,
Again to that accustom'd couch must creep
Where joy subsides, and sorrow sighs to sleep,
And man, o'erlabour'd with his being's strife,
Shrinks to that sweet forgetfulness of life:
There lie love's feverish hope, and cunning's guile,
Hate's working brain, and lull'd ambition's wile;
O'er each vain eye oblivion's pinions wave,
And quench'd existence crouches in a grave.
What better name may slumber's bed become?
Night's sepulchre, the universal home,
Where weakness, strength, vice, virtue, sunk supine,
Alike in naked helplessness recline;
Glad for awhile to heave unconscious breath,
Yet wake to wrestle with the dread of death,
And shun, though day but dawn on ills increased,
That sleep, the loveliest, since it dreams the least.

I.

Night wanes—the vapours round the mountains curl'd,
Melt into morn, and Light awakes the world.
Man has another day to swell the past,
And lead him near to little, but his last;
But mighty Nature bounds as from her birth,
The sun is in the heavens, and life on earth;
Flowers in the valley, splendour in the beam,
Health on the gale, and freshness in the stream.
Immortal man! behold her glories shine,
And cry, exulting inly, "They are thine!"
Gaze on, while yet thy gladden'd eye may see,
A morrow comes when they are not for thee;
And grieve what may above thy senseless bier,
Nor earth nor sky will yield a single tear;
Nor cloud shall gather more, nor leaf shall fall,
Nor gale breathe forth one sigh for thee, for all;
But creeping things shall revel in their spoil,
And fit thy clay to fertilise the soil.

II.

'T is morn—'t is noon—assembled in the hall,
The gather'd chieftains come to Otho's call;
'T is now the promised hour, that must proclaim
The life or death of Lara's future fame;
When Ezzelin his charge may here unfold,
And whatso'er the tale, it must be told.
His faith was pledged, and Lara's promise given,
To meet it in the eye of man and Heaven.
Why comes he not? Such truths to be divulged,
Methinks the accuser's rest is long indulged.

III.

The hour is past, and Lara too is there,
With self-confiding, coldly patient air;
Why comes not Ezzelin? The hour is past,
And murmurs rise, and Otho's brow's o'ercast.
"I know my friend! his faith I cannot fear,
If yet he be on earth, expect him here;

The roof that held him in the valley stands
Between my own and noble Lara's lands;
My halls from such a guest had honour gain'd,
Nor had Sir Ezzelin his host disdain'd,
But that some prèvious proof forbade his stay,
And urged him to prepare against to-day;
The word I pledged for his I pledge again,
Or will myself redeem his knighthood's stain."

He ceased—and Lara answer'd, "I am here
To lend at thy demand a listening ear,
To tales of evil from a stranger's tongue,
Whose words already might my heart have wrung,
But that I deem'd him scarcely less than mad,
Or, at the worst, a foe ignobly bad.
I know him not—but me it seems he knew
In lands where—but I must not trifle too:
Produce this babbler—or redeem the pledge;
Here in thy hold, and with thy falchion's edge."

Proud Otho on the instant, reddening, threw
His glove on earth, and forth his sabre flew.

"The last alternative befits me best,
And thus I answer for mine absent guest."

With cheek unchanging from its sallow gloom,
However near his own or other's tomb;
With hand, whose almost careless coolness spoke
Its grasp well-used to deal the sabre-stroke;
With eye, though calm, determined not to spare,
Did Lara too his willing weapon bare.
In vain the circling chieftains round them closed,
For Otho's frenzy would not be opposed;
And from his lip those words of insult fell—
His sword is good who can maintain them well.

IV.

Short was the conflict; furious, blindly rash,
Vain Otho gave his bosom to the gash:
He bled, and fell; but not with deadly wound,
Stretch'd by a dextrous sleight along the ground.
"Demand thy life!" He answer'd not: and then
From that red floor he ne'er had risen again,
For Lara's brow upon the moment grew
Almost to blackness in its demon hue;
And fiercer shook his angry falchion now
Than when his foe's was levell'd at his brow;
Then all was stern collectedness and art,
Now rose the unleaven'd hatred of his heart;
So little sparing to the foe he fell'd,
That when the approaching crowd his arm withheld,
He almost turn'd the thirsty point on those
Who thus for mercy dared to interpose;
But to a moment's thought that purpose bent;
Yet look'd he on him still with eye intent,
As if he loathed the ineffectual strife
That left a foe, howe'er o'erthrown, with life;
As if to search how far the wound he gave
Had sent its victim onward to his grave.

V.

They raised the bleeding Otho, and the Leech
Forbade all present question, sign, and speech;
The others met within a neighbouring hall,
And he, incensed and heedless of them all,
The cause and conqueror in this sudden fray,
In haughty silence slowly strode away;
He back'd his steed, his homeward path he took,
Nor cast on Otho's towers a single look.

VI.

But where was he? that meteor of a night,
Who menaced but to disappear with light.
Where was this Ezzelin? who came and went
To leave no other trace of his intent.
He left the dome of Otho long ere morn,
In darkness, yet so well the path was worn
He could not miss it: near his dwelling lay;
But there he was not, and with coming day
Came fast inquiry, which unfolded nought
Except the absence of the chief it sought.
A chamber tenantless, a steed at rest,
His host alarm'd, his murmuring squires distress'd:
Their search extends along, around the path,
In dread to meet the marks of prowlers' wrath:
But none are there, and not a brake hath borne
Nor gout of blood, nor shred of mantle torn;
Nor fall nor struggle hath defaced the grass,
Which still retains a mark where murder was;
Nor dabbling fingers left to tell the tale,
The bitter print of each convulsive nail,
When agonisèd hands that cease to guard,
Wound in that pang the smoothness of the sward.
Some such had been, if here a life was reft,
But these were not; and doubting hope is left;
And strange suspicion, whispering Lara's name,
Now daily mutters o'er his blacken'd fame;
Then sudden silent when his form appear'd,
Awaits the absence of the thing it fear'd;
Again its wonted wondering to renew,
And dye conjecture with a darker hue.

VII.

Days roll along, and Otho's wounds are heal'd,
But not his pride; and hate no more conceal'd:
He was a man of power, and Lara's foe,
The friend of all who sought to work him woe,
And from his country's justice now demands
Account of Ezzelin at Lara's hands.
Who else than Lara could have cause to fear
His presence? who had made him disappear,
If not the man on whom his menaced charge
Had sate too deeply were he left at large?
The general rumour ignorantly loud,
The mystery dearest to the curious crowd;
The seeming friendlessness of him who strove
To win no confidence, and wake no love;
The sweeping fierceness which his soul betray'd,
The skill with which he wielded his keen blade;
Where had his arm unwarlike caught that art?
Where had that fierceness grown upon his heart?
For it was not the blind capricious rage
A word can kindle and a word assuage;
But the deep working of a soul unmix'd
With aught of pity where its wrath had fix'd;
Such as long power and overgorged success
Concentrates into all that's merciless:
These, link'd with that desire which ever sways
Mankind, the rather to condemn than praise,
'Gainst Lara gathering raised at length a storm,
Such as himself might fear, and foes would form,
And he must answer for the absent head
Of one that haunts him still, alive or dead.

VIII.

Within that land was many a malcontent,
Who cursed the tyranny to which he bent;

That soil full many a wringing despot saw,
Who work'd his wantonness in form of law;
Long war without and frequent broil within
Had made a path for blood and giant sin,
That waited but a signal to begin
New havoc, such as civil discord blends,
Which knows no neuter, owns but foes or friends;
Fix'd in his feudal fortress each was lord,
In word and deed obey'd, in soul abhorr'd.
Thus Lara had inherited his lands,
And with them pining hearts and sluggish hands;
But that long absence from his native clime
Had left him stainless of oppression's crime,
And now, diverted by his milder sway,
All dread by slow degrees had worn away;
The menials felt their usual awe alone,
But more for him than them that fear was grown;
They deem'd him now unhappy, though at first
Their evil judgment augur'd of the worst,
And each long restless night, and silent mood,
Was traced to sickness, fed by solitude:
And though his lonely habits threw of late
Gloom o'er his chamber, cheerful was his gate;
For thence the wretched ne'er unsoothed withdrew,
For them, at least, his soul compassion knew.
Cold to the great, contemptuous to the high,
The humble pass'd not his unheeding eye;
Much he would speak not, but beneath his roof
They found asylum oft, and ne'er reproof.
And they who watch'd might mark that, day by day,
Some new retainers gather'd to his sway;
But most of late, since Ezzelin was lost,
He play'd the courteous lord and bounteous host:
Perchance his strife with Otho made him dread
Some snare prepared for his obnoxious head;
Whate'er his view, his favour more obtains
With these, the people, than his fellow thanes.
If this were policy, so far 't was sound,
The million judged but of him as they found;
From him by sterner chiefs to exile driven
They but required a shelter, and 't was given.
By him no peasant mourned his rifled cot,
And scarce the serf could murmur o'er his lot;
With him old avarice found its hoard secure,
With him contempt forbore to mock the poor;
Youth present cheer and promised recompense
Detain'd, till all too late to part from thence:
To hate he offer'd, with the coming change,
The deep reversion of delay'd revenge;
To love, long baffled by the unequal match,
The well-won charms success was sure to snatch.
All now was ripe, he waits but to proclaim
That slavery nothing which was still a name.
The moment came, the hour when Otho thought
Secure at last the vengeance which he sought:
His summons found the destined criminal
Begirt by thousands in his swarming hall,
Fresh from their feudal fetters newly riven,
Defying earth, and confident of heaven.
That morning he had freed the soil-bound slaves
Who dig no land for tyrants but their graves!
Such is their cry — some watchword for the fight
Must vindicate the wrong, and warp the right:
Religion—freedom—vengeance—what you will,
A word 's enough to raise mankind to kill;
Some factious phrase by cunning caught and spread,
That guilt may reign, and wolves and worms be fed!

IX.

Throughout that clime the feudal chiefs had gain'd
Such sway, their infant monarch hardly reign'd
Now was the hour for faction's rebel growth,
The serfs contemn'd the one, and hated both:
They waited but a leader, and they found
One to their cause inseparably bound;
By circumstance compell'd to plunge again,
In self-defence, amidst the strife of men.
Cut off by some mysterious fate from those
Whom birth and nature meant not for his foes,
Had Lara from that night, to him accurst,
Prepared to meet, but not alone, the worst:
Some reason urged, whate'er it was, to shun
Inquiry into deeds at distance done;
By mingling with his own the cause of all,
E'en if he fail'd, he still delay'd his fall.
The sullen calm that long his bosom kept,
The storm that once had spent itself and slept,
Roused by events that seem'd foredoom'd to urge
His gloomy fortunes to their utmost verge,
Burst forth, and made him all he once had been,
And is again; he only changed the scene.
Light care had he for life, and less for fame,
But not less fitted for the desperate game:
He deem'd himself mark'd out for others' hate,
And mock'd at ruin so they shared his fate.
What cared he for the freedom of the crowd?
He raised the humble but to bend the proud.
He had hoped quiet in his sullen lair,
But man and destiny beset him there:
Inured to hunters, he was found at bay;
And they must kill, they cannot snare the prey.
Stern, unambitious, silent, he had been
Henceforth a calm spectator of life's scene;
But dragg'd again upon the arena, stood
A leader not unequal to the feud;
In voice—mien—gesture—savage nature spoke,
And from his eye the gladiator broke.

X.

What boots the oft-repeated tale of strife,
The feast of vultures, and the waste of life?
The varying fortune of each separate field,
The fierce that vanquish, and the faint that yield?
The smoking ruin, and the crumbled wall?
In this the struggle was the same with all;
Save that distemper'd passions lent their force
In bitterness that banish'd all remorse.
None sued, for Mercy knew her cry was vain,
The captive died upon the battle-slain:
In either cause, one rage alone possess'd
The empire of the alternate victor's breast;
And they that smote for freedom or for sway,
Deem'd few were slain, while more remain'd to slay.
It was too late to check the wasting brand,
And Desolation reap'd the famish'd land;
The torch was lighted, and the flame was spread,
And Carnage smiled upon her daily bread.

XI.

Fresh with the nerve the new-born impulse strung,
The first success to Lara's numbers clung;
But that vain victory hath ruin'd all,
They form no longer to their leader's call;
In blind confusion on the foe they press,
And think to snatch is to secure success.
The lust of booty, and the thirst of hate,
Lure on the broken brigands to their fate:
In vain he doth whate'er a chief may do,
To check the headlong fury of that crew;
In vain their stubborn ardour he would tame,
The hand that kindles cannot quench the flame;
The wary foe alone hath turn'd their mood,
And shown their rashness to that erring brood:
The feign'd retreat, the nightly ambuscade,
The daily harass, and the fight delay'd,
The long privation of the hoped supply,
The tentless rest beneath the humid sky,
The stubborn wall that mocks the leaguer's art,
And palls the patience of his baffled heart,
Of these they had not deem'd: the battle-day
They could encounter as a veteran may;
But more preferr'd the fury of the strife,
And present death, to hourly suffering life:
And famine wrings, and fever sweeps away
His numbers melting fast from their array;
Intemperate triumph fades to discontent,
And Lara's soul alone seems still unbent:
But few remain to aid his voice and hand,
And thousands dwindled to a scanty band:
Desperate, though few, the last and best remain'd
To mourn the discipline they late disdain'd.
One hope survives, the frontier is not far,
And thence they may escape from native war;
And bear within them to the neighbouring state
An exile's sorrows, or an outlaw's hate:
Hard is the task their father-land to quit,
But harder still to perish or submit.

XII.

It is resolved—they march—consenting Night
Guides with her star their dim and torchless flight:
Already they perceive its tranquil beam
Sleep on the surface of the barrier stream;
Already they descry—Is yon the bank?
Away! 't is lined with many a hostile rank.
Return or fly!—What glitters in the rear?
'T is Otho's banner—the pursuer's spear!
Are those the shepherds' fires upon the height?
Alas! they blaze too widely for the flight:
Cut off from hope, and compass'd in the toil,
Less blood, perchance, hath bought a richer spoil!

XIII.

A moment's pause — 't is but to breathe their band,
Or shall they onward press, or here withstand?
It matters little—if they charge the foes
Who by their border-stream their march oppose,
Some few, perchance, may break and pass the line,
However link'd to baffle such design.
"The charge be ours! to wait for their assault
Were fate well worthy of a coward's halt."
Forth flies each sabre, rein'd is every steed,
And the next word shall scarce outstrip the deed:
In the next tone of Lara's gathering breath
How many shall but hear the voice of death!

XIV.

His blade is bared,—in him there is an air
As deep, but far too tranquil for despair;
A something of indifference more than then
Becomes the bravest, if they feel for men—
He turn'd his eye on Kaled, ever near,
And still too faithful to betray one fear;
Perchance 't was but the moon's dim twilight threw
Along his aspect an unwonted hue
Of mournful paleness, whose deep tint express'd
The truth, and not the terror of his breast.
This Lara mark'd, and laid his hand on his:
It trembled not in such an hour as this;
His lip was silent, scarcely beat his heart,
His eye alone proclaim'd—
"We will not part!
Thy band may perish, or thy friends may flee,
Farewell to life, but not adieu to thee!"

The word hath pass'd his lips, and onward driven,
Pours the link'd band through ranks asunder riven;
Well has each steed obey'd the armed heel,
And flash the scimitars, and rings the steel;
Outnumber'd, not outbraved, they still oppose
Despair to daring, and a front to foes;
And blood is mingled with the dashing stream,
Which runs all redly till the morning beam.

XV.

Commanding, aiding, animating all,
Where foe appeared to press, or friend to fall,
Cheers Lara's voice, and waves or strikes his steel,
Inspiring hope, himself had ceased to feel.
None fled, for well they knew that flight were vain,
But those that waver turn to smite again,
While yet they find the firmest of the foe
Recoil before their leader's look and blow;

Now girt with numbers, now almost alone,
He foils their ranks, or reunites his own;
Himself he spared not — once they seemed to fly—
Now was the time, he waved his hand on high,
And shook — why sudden droops that plumed crest?
The shaft is sped—the arrow's in his breast!
That fatal gesture left the unguarded side,
And Death hath stricken down yon arm of pride.
The word of triumph fainted from his tongue;
That hand, so raised, how droopingly it hung!
But yet the sword instinctively retains,
Though from its fellow shrink the falling reins;
These Kaled snatches: dizzy with the blow,
And senseless bending o'er his saddle-bow,
Perceives not Lara that his anxious page
Beguiles his charger from the combat's rage:
Meantime his followers charge, and charge again;
Too mix'd the slayers now to heed the slain!

XVI.

Day glimmers on the dying and the dead,
The cloven cuirass, and the helmless head;
The war-horse masterless is on the earth,
And that last gasp hath burst his bloody girth;
And near yet quivering with what life remain'd,
The heel that urg'd him and the hand that rein'd;
And some too near that rolling torrent lie,
Whose waters mock the lip of those that die;
That panting thirst which scorches in the breath
Of those that die the soldier's fiery death,
In vain impels the burning mouth to crave
One drop—the last—to cool it for the grave;
With feeble and convulsive effort swept
Their limbs along the crimson'd turf have crept;
The faint remains of life such struggles waste,
But yet they reach the stream, and bend to taste:
They feel its freshness, and almost partake—
Why pause? — No further thirst have they to slake—
It is unquench'd, and yet they feel it not
It was an agony—but now forgot!

XVII.

Beneath a lime, remoter from the scene,
Where but for him that strife had never been,
A breathing but devoted warrior lay:
'Twas Lara bleeding fast from life away.
His follower once, and now his only guide,
Kneels Kaled watchful o'er his welling side,
And with his scarf would staunch the tides that rush
With each convulsion in a blacker gush;
And then as his faint breathing waxes low,
In feebler, not less fatal tricklings flow:
He scarce can speak, but motions him 'tis vain,
And merely adds another throb to pain.
He clasps the hand that pang which would assuage,
And sadly smiles his thanks to that dark page,
Who nothing fears, nor feels, nor heeds, nor sees,
Save that damp brow which rests upon his knees;
Save that pale aspect, where the eye, though dim,
Held all the light that shone on earth for him.

XVIII.

The foe arrives, who long had search'd the field,
Their triumph nought till Lara too should yield;
They would remove him, but they see 'twere vain,
And he regards them with a calm disdain,
That rose to reconcile him with his fate,
And that escape to death from living hate:
And Otho comes, and leaping from his steed,
Looks on the bleeding foe that made him bleed,
And questions of his state; he answers not,
Scarce glances on him as on one forgot,
And turns to Kaled:—each remaining word,
They understood not, if distinctly heard;
His dying tones are in that other tongue,
To which some strange remembrance wildly clung.
They spake of other scenes, but what—is known
To Kaled, whom their meaning reach'd alone;
And he replied, though faintly, to their sound,
While gaz'd the rest in dumb amazement round:
They seem'd even then—that twain—unto the last
To half forget the present in the past;
To share between themselves some separate fate,
Whose darkness none beside should penetrate.

XIX.

Their words though faint were many — from the tone
Their import those who heard could judge alone;
From this, you might have deem'd young Kaled's death
More near than Lara's by his voice and breath,
So sad, so deep, and hesitating broke
The accents his scarce-moving pale lips spoke;
But Lara's voice, though low, at first was clear
And calm, till murmuring death gasp'd hoarsely near:
But from his visage little could we guess,
So unrepentant, dark, and passionless,
Save that when struggling nearer to his last,
Upon that page his eye was kindly cast;
And once as Kaled's answering accents ceas'd,
Rose Lara's hand, and pointed to the East:
Whether (as then the breaking sun from high
Roll'd back the clouds) the morrow caught his eye,
Or that 'twas chance, or some remember'd scene
That rais'd his arm to point where such had been,
Scarce Kaled seem'd to know, but turn'd away,
As if his heart abhorred that coming day,

And shrunk his glance before that morning light
To look on Lara's brow—where all grew night.
Yet sense seem'd left, though better were its loss;
For when one near display'd the absolving cross,
And proffered to his touch the holy bead
Of which his parting soul might own the need,
He look'd upon it with an eye profane,
And smiled—Heaven pardon! if 'twere with disdain;
And Kaled, though he spoke not, nor withdrew
From Lara's face his fix'd despairing view,
With brow repulsive, and with gesture swift,
Flung back the hand which held the sacred gift,
As if such but disturbed the expiring man,
Nor seem'd to know his life but *then* began,
The life immortal, infinite, secure,
To all for whom that cross hath made it sure!

XX.

But gasping heav'd the breath that Lara drew,
And dull the film along his dim eye grew;
His limbs stretch'd fluttering, and his head droop'd o'er
The weak yet still-untiring knee that bore;
He press'd the hand he held upon his heart—
It beats no more, but Kaled will not part
With the cold grasp, but feels, and feels in vain,
For that faint throb which answers not again.
"It beats!"—Away, thou dreamer! he is gone—
It once was Lara which thou look'st upon.

XXI.

He gaz'd, as if not yet had pass'd away
The haughty spirit of that humble clay;

And those around have rous'd him from his trance,
But cannot tear from thence his fixèd glance;
And when in raising him from where he bore
Within his arms the form that felt no more,
He saw the head his breast would still sustain,
Roll down like earth to earth upon the plain;
He did not dash himself thereby, nor tear
The glossy tendrils of his raven hair,
But strove to stand and gaze, but reel'd and fell,
Scarce breathing more than that he lov'd so well.
Than that *he* lov'd! Oh! never yet beneath
The breast of man such trusty love may breathe!
That trying moment hath at once reveal'd
The secret long and yet but half-conceal'd;
In baring to revive that lifeless breast,
Its grief seem'd ended, but the sex confest;
And life return'd, and Kaled felt no shame—
What now to her was Womanhood or Fame?

XXII.

And Lara sleeps not where his fathers sleep,
But where he died his grave was dug as deep;
Nor is his mortal slumber less profound,
Though priest nor bless'd, nor marble deck'd the mound;
And he was mourn'd by one whose quiet grief
Less loud, outlasts a people's for their chief.
Vain was all question ask'd her of the past,
And vain e'en menace—silent to the last;
She told nor whence nor why she left behind
Her all for one who seem'd but little kind.
Why did she love him? Curious fool!—be still—
Is human love the growth of human will?
To her he might be gentleness; the stern
Have deeper thoughts than your dull eyes discern,
And when they love, your smilers guess not how
Beats the strong heart, though less the lips avow.
They were not common links that form'd the chain
That bound to Lara Kaled's heart and brain;
But that wild tale she brook'd not to unfold,
And seal'd is now each lip that could have told.

XXIII.

They laid him in the earth, and on his breast,
Besides the wound that sent his soul to rest,
They found the scattered dints of many a scar
Which were not planted there in recent war:
Where'er had pass'd his summer years of life,
It seems they vanish'd in a land of strife;
But all unknown his glory or his guilt,
These only told that somewhere blood was spilt,
And Ezzelin, who might have spoke the past,
Return'd no more—that night appear'd his last.

XXIV.

Upon that night (a peasant's is the tale)
A serf that cross'd the intervening vale,
When Cynthia's light almost gave way to morn,
And nearly veil'd in mist her waning horn;
A serf, that rose betimes to thread the wood,
And hew the bough that bought his children's food,
Pass'd by the river that divides the plain
Of Otho's lands and Lara's broad domain:
He heard a tramp—a horse and horseman broke
From out the wood—before him was a cloak
Wrapt round some burthen at his saddle-bow,
Bent was his head, and hidden was his brow.
Rous'd by the sudden sight at such a time,
And some foreboding that it might be crime,
Himself unheeded watch'd the stranger's course,
Who reach'd the river, bounded from his horse,
And lifting thence the burthen which he bore,
Heav'd up the bank, and dash'd it from the shore,[3]
Then paus'd, and look'd, and turn'd, and seem'd to watch,
And still another hurried glance would snatch,
And follow with his step the stream that flow'd,
As if even yet too much its surface show'd:
At once he started, stoop'd, around him strown
The winter floods had scatter'd heaps of stone;
Of these the heaviest thence he gather'd there,
And slung them with a more than common care.
Meantime the serf had crept to where unseen
Himself might safely mark what this might mean;
He caught a glimpse, as of a floating breast,
And something glittered starlike on the vest,
But ere he well could mark the buoyant trunk,
A massy fragment smote it, and it sunk:
It rose again but indistinct to view,
And left the waters of a purple hue,
Then deeply disappear'd: the horseman gaz'd
Till ebbed the latest eddy it had rais'd;
Then turning, vaulted on his pawing steed,
And instant spurr'd him into panting speed.
His face was mask'd—the features of the dead,
If dead it were, escaped the observer's dread;
But if in sooth a star its bosom bore,
Such is the badge that knighthood ever wore,
And such 'tis known Sir Ezzelin had worn
Upon the night that led to such a morn.
If thus he perish'd, Heaven receive his soul!
His undiscover'd limbs to ocean roll;
And charity upon the hope would dwell
It was not Lara's hand by which he fell.

XXV.

And Kaled—Lara—Ezzelin, are gone,
Alike without their monumental stone!
The first, all efforts vainly strove to wean
From lingering where her chieftain's blood had been;
Grief had so tam'd a spirit once too proud,
Her tears were few, her wailing never loud;

But furious would you tear her from the spot
Where yet she scarce believ'd that he was not,
Her eye shot forth with all the living fire
That haunts the tigress in her whelpless ire;
But left to waste her weary moments there,
She talk'd all idly unto shapes of air,
Such as the busy brain of Sorrow paints,
And woos to listen to her fond complaints:
And she would sit beneath the very tree
Where lay his drooping head upon her knee;
And in that posture where she saw him fall,
His words, his looks, his dying grasp recall;
And she had shorn, but sav'd her raven hair,
And oft would snatch it from her bosom there,
And fold, and press it gently to the ground,
As if she staunch'd anew some phantom's wound.
Herself would question, and for him reply;
Then rising, start, and beckon him to fly
From some imagin'd spectre in pursuit;
Then seat her down upon some linden's root,
And hide her visage with her meagre hand,
Or trace strange characters along the sand.—
This could not last—she lies by him she lov'd;
Her tale untold—her truth too dearly prov'd.

NOTES TO LARA.

Note 1, page 31.

The reader of Lara may probably regard it as a sequel to a poem that recently appeared:* whether the cast of the hero's character, the turn of his adventures, and the general outline and colouring of the story, may not encourage such a supposition, shall be left to his determination.

Note 2, page 31.

The Serfs are glad through Lara's wide domain.

The reader is advertised that the name only of Lara being Spanish, and no circumstance of local or national description fixing the scene or hero of the poem to any country or age, the word "Serf," which could not be correctly applied to the lower classes in Spain, who were never vassals of the soil, has nevertheless been employed to designate the followers of our fictitious chieftain.

Note 3, page 48.

And lifting thence the burden which he bore,
Heaved up the bank, and dash'd it from the shore.

The event in this section was suggested by the description of the death, or rather burial, of the Duke of Gandia. The most interesting and particular account of it is given by Burchard, and is in substance as follows:—"On the eighth day of June, the Cardinal of Valenza and the Duke of Gandia, sons of the Pope, supped with their mother, Vanozza, near the church of *S. Pietro ad vincula;* several other persons being present at the entertainment. A late hour approaching, and the cardinal having reminded his brother, that it was time to return to the apostolic palace, they mounted their horses or mules, with only a few attendants, and proceeded together as far as the palace of Cardinal Ascanio Sforza, when the duke informed the cardinal that, before he returned home, he had to pay a visit of pleasure. Dismissing therefore all his attendants, excepting his *staffiero*, or footman, and a person in a mask, who had paid him a visit whilst at supper, and who, during the space of a month, or thereabouts, previous to this time, had called upon him almost daily at the apostolic palace, he took this person behind him on his mule, and proceeded to the street of the Jews, where he quitted his servant, directing him to remain there until a certain hour; when, if he did not return, he might repair to the palace. The duke then seated the person in the mask behind him, and rode, I know not whither; but in that night he was assassinated, and thrown into the river. The servant, after having been dismissed, was also assaulted and mortally wounded; and although he was attended with great care, yet such was his situation, that he could give no intelligible account of what had befallen his master. In the morning, the duke not having returned to the palace, his servants began to be alarmed; and one of them informed the pontiff of the evening excursion of his sons, and that the duke had not yet made his appearance. This gave the pope no small anxiety; but he conjectured that the duke had been attracted by some courtesan to pass the night with her, and, not choosing to quit the house in open day, had waited till the following evening to return home. When, however, the evening arrived, and he found himself disappointed in his expectations, he became deeply afflicted, and began to make inquiries from different persons, whom he ordered to attend him for that purpose. Amongst these was a man named Giorgio Schiavoni, who, having discharged some timber from a bark in the river, had remained on board the vessel to watch it; and being interrogated whether he had seen any one thrown into the river on the night preceding, he replied, that he saw two men on foot, who came down the street, and looked diligently about, to observe whether any person was passing. That seeing no one, they returned, and a short time afterwards two others came, and looked around in the same manner as the former: no person still appearing, they gave a sign to their companions, when a man came, mounted on a white horse, having behind him a dead body, the head and arms of which hung on one side, and the feet on the other side of the horse; the two persons on foot supporting the body, to prevent its falling. They thus proceeded towards that part, where the filth of the city is usually discharged into the river, and turning the horse, with his tail towards the water, the two persons took the dead body by the arms and feet, and with all their strength flung it into the river. The person on horseback then asked if they had thrown it in; to which they replied, 'Signor, si' (yes, Sir). He then looked towards the river, and seeing a mantle floating on the stream, he inquired what it was that appeared black, to which they answered, it was a mantle; and one of them threw stones upon it, in consequence of which it sunk. The attendants of the pontiff then inquired from Giorgio, why he had not revealed this to the governor of the city; to which he replied, that he had seen in his time a hundred dead bodies thrown into the river at the same place, without any inquiry being made respecting them; and that he had not, therefore, considered it as a matter of any importance. The fishermen and seamen were then collected, and ordered to search the river, where, on the following evening, they found the body of the duke, with his habit entire, and thirty ducats in his purse. He was pierced with nine wounds, one of which was in his throat, the others in his head, body, and limbs. No sooner was the pontiff informed of the death of his son, and that he had been thrown, like filth, into the river, than, giving way to his grief, he shut himself up in a chamber, and wept bitterly. The Cardinal of Segovia, and other attendants on the pope, went to the door, and after many hours spent in persuasions and exhortations, prevailed upon him to admit them. From the evening of Wednesday till the following Saturday the pope took no food; nor did he sleep from Thursday morning till the same hour on the ensuing day. At length, however, giving way to the entreaties of his attendants, he began to restrain his sorrow, and to consider the injury which his own health might sustain, by the further indulgence of his grief."—*Roscoe's Leo the Tenth*, vol. i., p. 265.

* *The Corsair.*

THE GIAOUR:

A FRAGMENT OF A TURKISH TALE.

"One fatal remembrance—one sorrow that throws
Its bleak shade alike o'er our joys and our woes—
To which Life nothing darker nor brighter can bring,
For which joy hath no balm—and affliction no sting."

MOORE.

TO

SAMUEL ROGERS, ESQ.,

AS A SLIGHT BUT MOST SINCERE TOKEN OF ADMIRATION FOR HIS GENIUS,
RESPECT FOR HIS CHARACTER, AND GRATITUDE FOR HIS FRIENDSHIP,

THIS PRODUCTION IS INSCRIBED

BY HIS OBLIGED AND AFFECTIONATE SERVANT,

LONDON, MAY, 1813. BYRON.

ADVERTISEMENT.

THE tale which these disjointed fragments present, is founded upon circumstances now less common in the East than formerly; either because the ladies are more circumspect than in the "olden time," or because the Christians have better fortune, or less enterprise. The story, when entire, contained the adventures of a female slave, who was thrown, in the Mussulman manner, into the sea for infidelity, and avenged by a young Venetian, her lover, at the time the Seven Islands were possessed by the Republic of Venice, and soon after the Arnauts were beaten back from the Morea, which they had ravaged for some time subsequent to the Russian invasion. The desertion of the Mainotes, on being refused the plunder of Misitra, led to the abandonment of that enterprise, and to the desolation of the Morea, during which the cruelty exercised on all sides was unparalleled even in the annals of the faithful.

THE GIAOUR.

No breath of air to break the wave
That rolls below the Athenian's grave,
That tomb which, gleaming o'er the cliff,[1]
First greets the homeward-veering skiff,
High o'er the land he saved in vain;
When shall such hero live again?

* * * * * *

Fair clime! where every season smiles
Benignant o'er those blessed isles,
Which, seen from far Colonna's height,
Make glad the heart that hails the sight,
And lend to loneliness delight.
There mildly dimpling, Ocean's cheek
Reflects the tints of many a peak
Caught by the laughing tides that lave
These Edens of the Eastern wave:
And if at times a transient breeze
Break the blue crystal of the seas,
Or sweep one blossom from the trees,

How welcome is each gentle air
That wakes and wafts the odours there!
For there—the Rose o'er crag or vale,
Sultana of the Nightingale,[2]
 The maid for whom his melody,
 His thousand songs are heard on high,
Blooms blushing to her lover's tale;
His queen, the garden queen, his Rose,
Unbent by winds, unchill'd by snows,
Far from the winters of the West,
By every breeze and season blest,
Returns the sweets by nature given
In softest incense back to heaven;
And grateful yields that smiling sky
Her fairest hue and fragrant sigh.
And many a summer flower is there,
And many a shade that love might share,
And many a grotto, meant for rest,
That holds the pirate for a guest;
Whose bark in sheltering cove below
Lurks for the passing peaceful prow,
Till the gay mariner's guitar[3]
Is heard, and seen the evening star;
Then stealing with the muffled oar,
Far shaded by the rocky shore,
Rush the night-prowlers on the prey,
And turn to groans his roundelay.
Strange—that where Nature loved to trace,
As if for Gods, a dwelling-place,
And every charm and grace hath mix'd
Within the paradise she fix'd,
There man, enamour'd of distress,
Should mar it into wilderness,
And trample, brute-like, o'er each flower
That tasks not one laborious hour;
Nor claims the culture of his hand
To bloom along the fairy land,
But springs as to preclude his care,
And sweetly woos him—but to spare!
Strange—that where all is peace beside,
There passion riots in her pride,
And lust and rapine wildly reign
To darken o'er the fair domain.
It is as though the fiends prevail'd
Against the seraphs they assail'd,
And, fix'd on heavenly thrones, should dwell
The freed inheritors of hell;
So soft the scene, so form'd for joy,
So curst the tyrants that destroy!

 He who hath bent him o'er the dead
Ere the first day of death is fled,
The first dark day of nothingness,
The last of danger and distress,
(Before Decay's effacing fingers
Have swept the lines where beauty lingers),
And mark'd the mild angelic air,
The rapture of repose that 's there,
The fix'd yet tender traits that streak
The langour of the placid cheek,
And—but for that sad shrouded eye,
 That fires not, wins not, weeps not now,
 And but for that chill, changeless brow,
Where cold Obstruction's apathy[4]
Appals the gazing mourner's heart,
As if to him it could impart
The doom he dreads, yet dwells upon;
Yes, but for these and these alone,
Some moments, ay, one treacherous hour,
He still might doubt the tyrant's power;
So fair, so calm, so softly seal'd,
The first, last look by death reveal'd![5]
Such is the aspect of this shore;
'T is Greece, but living Greece no more!
So coldly sweet, so deadly fair,
We start, for soul is wanting there.
Hers is the loveliness in death,
That parts not quite with parting breath;
But beauty with that fearful bloom,
That hue which haunts it to the tomb,
Expression's last receding ray,
A gilded halo hovering round decay,
The farewell beam of Feeling past away!
Spark of that flame, perchance of heavenly birth,
Which gleams, but warms no more its cherish'd
 earth!

 Clime of the unforgotten brave!
Whose land from plain to mountain-cave
Was Freedom's home, or Glory's grave!
Shrine of the mighty! can it be
That this is all remains of thee?
Approach, thou craven crouching slave:
 Say, is not this Thermopylæ?
These waters blue that round you lave,
 Oh servile offspring of the free—
Pronounce what sea, what shore is this?
The gulf, the rock of Salamis!
These scenes, their story not unknown,
Arise, and make again your own;
Snatch from the ashes of your sires
The embers of their former fires;
And he who in the strife expires
Will add to theirs a name of fear
That Tyranny shall quake to hear,
And leave his sons a hope, a fame,
They too will rather die than shame:
For Freedom's battle once begun,
Bequeath'd by bleeding Sire to Son,
Though baffled oft is ever won.
Bear witness, Greece, thy living page,
Attest it many a deathless age!
While kings, in dusty darkness hid,
Have left a nameless pyramid,
Thy heroes, though the general doom
Hath swept the column from their tomb,

A mightier monument command,
The mountains of their native land!
There points thy Muse to stranger's eye
The graves of those that cannot die!
'T were long to tell, and sad to trace,
Each step from splendour to disgrace:
Enough—no foreign foe could quell
Thy soul, till from itself it fell;
Yes! Self-abasement paved the way
To villain-bonds and despot sway.

What can he tell who treads thy shore?
No legend of thine olden time,
No theme on which the muse might soar,
High as thine own in days of yore,
When man was worthy of thy clime.
The hearts within thy valleys bred,
The fiery souls that might have led
Thy sons to deeds sublime,
Now crawl from cradle to the grave,
Slaves—nay, the bondsmen of a slave,[5]
And callous, save to crime;
Stain'd with each evil that pollutes
Mankind, where least above the brutes;
Without even savage virtue blest,
Without one free or valiant breast.
Still to the neighbouring ports they waft
Proverbial wiles, and ancient craft;
In this the subtle Greek is found,
For this, and this alone, renown'd.
In vain might Liberty invoke
The spirit to its bondage broke,
Or raise the neck that courts the yoke:
No more her sorrows I bewail,
Yet this will be a mournful tale,
And they who listen may believe,
Who heard it first had cause to grieve.

* * * * * *

Far, dark, along the blue sea glancing,
The shadows of the rocks advancing,
Start on the fisher's eye like boat
Of island-pirate or Mainote;
And fearful for his light caique,
He shuns the near but doubtful creek
Though worn and weary with his toil,
And cumber'd with his scaly spoil,
Slowly, yet strongly, plies the oar,
Till Port Leone's safer shore
Receives him by the lovely light
That best becomes an Eastern night.

* * * * * *

Who thundering comes on blackest steed,
With slacken'd bit and hoof of speed?
Beneath the clattering iron's sound
The cavern'd echoes wake around
In lash for lash, and bound for bound;
The foam that streaks the courser's side
Seems gather'd from the ocean-tide:
Though weary waves are sunk to rest,
There 's none within his rider's breast;
And though to-morrow's tempest lower,
'T is calmer than thy heart, young Giaour![7]
I know thee not, I loathe thy race,
But in thy lineaments I trace
What time shall strengthen, not efface:
Though young and pale, that sallow front
Is scathed by fiery passion's brunt;
Though bent on earth thine evil eye,
As meteor-like thou glidest by,
Right well I view and deem thee one
Whom Othman's sons should slay or shun.

On—on he hasten'd, and he drew
My gaze of wonder as he flew:
Though like a demon of the night
He pass'd, and vanish'd from my sight,
His aspect and his air impress'd
A troubled memory on my breast,
And long upon my startled ear
Rung his dark courser's hoofs of fear.
He spurs his steed; he nears the steep,
That, jutting, shadows o'er the deep;
He winds around; he hurries by;
The rock relieves him from mine eye;
For well I ween unwelcome he
Whose glance is fixed on those that flee;
And not a star but shines too bright
On him who takes such timeless flight.
He wound along; but ere he pass'd
One glance he snatch'd, as if his last,
A moment check'd his wheeling steed,
A moment breathed him from his speed,
A moment on his stirrup stood—
Why looks he o'er the olive wood?
The crescent glimmers on the hill,
The Mosque's high lamps are quivering still:
Though too remote for sound to wake
In echoes of the far tophaike,[6]
The flashes of each joyous peal
Are seen to prove the Moslem's zeal.
To-night, set Rhamazani's sun;
To-night, the Bairam feast's begun;
To-night—but who and what art thou
Of foreign garb and fearful brow?
And what are these to thine or thee,
That thou shouldst either pause or flee?

He stood—some dread was on his face,
Soon Hatred settled in its place:
It rose not with the reddening flush
Of transient Anger's hasty blush,
But pale as marble o'er the tomb,
Whose ghastly whiteness aids its gloom.
His brow was bent, his eye was glazed;
He raised his arm, and fiercely raised,
And sternly shook his hand on high,

As doubting to return or fly:
Impatient of his flight delay'd,
Here loud his raven charger neigh'd—
Down glanced that hand, and grasp'd his blade;
That sound had burst his waking dream,
As Slumber starts at owlet's scream.
The spur hath lanced his courser's sides;
Away, away, for life he rides:
Swift as the hurl'd on high jerreed[9]
Springs to the touch his startled steed;
The rock is doubled, and the shore
Shakes with the clattering tramp no more;
The crag is won, no more is seen
His Christian crest and haughty mien.
'T was but an instant he restrain'd
That fiery barb so sternly rein'd;
'T was but a moment that he stood,
Then sped as if by death pursued:
But in that instant o'er his soul
Winters of Memory seem'd to roll,
And gather in that drop of time
A life of pain, an age of crime.
O'er him who loves, or hates, or fears,
Such moment pours the grief of years:
What felt *he* then, at once opprest
By all that most distracts the breast?
That pause, which ponder'd o'er his fate,
Oh, who its dreary length shall date!
Though in Time's record nearly nought,
It was Eternity to Thought!
For infinite as boundless space
The thought that Conscience must embrace,
Which in itself can comprehend
Woe without name, or hope, or end

The hour is past, the Giaour is gone;
And did he fly or fall alone?
Woe to that hour he came or went!
The curse for Hassan's sin was sent
To turn a palace to a tomb:
He came, he went, like the Simoom,[10]
That harbinger of fate and gloom,
Beneath whose widely-wasting breath
The very cypress droops to death—

Dark tree, still sad when others' grief is fled,
The only constant mourner o'er the dead!

The steed is vanish'd from the stall;
No serf is seen in Hassan's hall;
The lonely Spider's thin gray pall
Waves slowly widening o'er the wall;
The Bat builds in his Haram bower,
And in the fortress of his power
The Owl usurps the beacon-tower;
The wild-dog howls o'er the fountain's brim,
With baffled thirst, and famine, grim;
For the stream has shrunk from its marble bed,
Where the weeds and the desolate dust are spread.
'T was sweet of yore to see it play
And chase the sultriness of day,
As springing high the silver dew
In whirls fantastically flew,
And flung luxurious coolness round
The air, and verdure o'er the ground.
'T was sweet, when cloudless stars were bright,
To view the wave of watery light,
And hear its melody by night.
And oft had Hassan's Childhood play'd
Around the verge of that cascade;
And oft upon his mother's breast
That sound had harmonized his rest;
And oft had Hassan's Youth along
Its bank been soothed by Beauty's song;
And softer seem'd each melting tone
Of Music mingled with its own.
But ne'er shall Hassan's Age repose
Along the brink at Twilight's close:
The stream that fill'd that font is fled—
The blood that warm'd his heart is shed!
And here no more shall human voice
Be heard to rage, regret, rejoice.
The last sad note that swell'd the gale
Was woman's wildest funeral wail:
That quench'd in silence, all is still,
But the lattice that flaps when the wind is shrill;
Though raves the gust, and floods the rain,
No hand shall close its clasp again.
On desert sands 't were joy to scan
The rudest steps of fellow man,
So here the very voice of Grief
Might wake an Echo like relief—
At least 't would say, "All are not gone;
There lingers Life, though but in one"—
For many a gilded chamber 's there,
Which Solitude might well forbear;
Within that dome as yet Decay
Hath slowly work'd her cankering way—
But gloom is gather'd o'er the gate,
Nor there the Fakir's self will wait;
Nor there will wandering Dervise stay,
For bounty cheers not his delay;
Nor there will weary stranger halt
To bless the sacred "bread and salt."[11]
Alike must Wealth and Poverty
Pass heedless and unheeded by,
For Courtesy and Pity died
With Hassan on the mountain side.
His roof, that refuge unto men,
Is Desolation's hungry den.
The guest flies the hall, and the vassal from labour,
Since his turban was cleft by the Infidel's sabre![12]

* * * * * *

I hear the sound of coming feet,
But not a voice mine ear to greet;
More near—each turban I can scan,
And silver-sheathed ataghan;[13]
The foremost of the band is seen
An Emir by his garb of green:[14]
"Ho! who art thou?"—"This low salam[15]
Replies of Moslem faith I am."
"The burthen ye so gently bear
Seems one that claims your utmost care,
And, doubtless, holds some precious freight,
My humble bark would gladly wait."

"Thou speakest sooth; thy skiff unmoor,
And waft us from the silent shore;
Nay, leave the sail still furl'd, and ply
The nearest oar that 's scattered by,
And midway to those rocks where sleep
The channel'd waters dark and deep.
Rest from your task—so—bravely done,
Our course has been right swiftly run·
Yet 't is the longest voyage, I trow
That one of——" * * *

* * * * * *

Sullen it plunged, and slowly sank,
The calm wave rippled to the bank;
I watch'd it as it sank: methought
Some motion from the current caught
Bestirr'd it more,—'t was but the beam
That checker'd o'er the living stream:
I gazed, till vanishing from view,
Like lessening pebble it withdrew;
Still less and less, a speck of white
That gemm'd the tide, then mock'd the sight;
And all its hidden secrets sleep,
Known but to Genii of the deep,
Which, trembling in their coral caves,
They dare not whisper to the waves.

* * * * * *

As rising on its purple wing
The insect-queen of eastern spring,[16]
O'er emerald meadows of Kashmeer
Invites the young pursuer near,
And leads him on from flower to flower
A weary chase and wasted hour,
Then leaves him, as it soars on high,
With panting heart and tearful eye:
So Beauty lures the full-grown child,

With hue as bright, and wing as wild;
A chase of idle hopes and fears,
Begun in folly, closed in tears.
If won, to equal ills betray'd,
Woe waits the insect and the maid;
A life of pain, the loss of peace,
From infant's play and man's caprice:
The lovely toy so fiercely sought
Hath lost its charm by being caught,
For every touch that woo'd its stay
Hath brushed its brightest hues away,
Till charm, and hue, and beauty gone,
'T is left to fly or fall alone.
With wounded wing or bleeding breast,
Ah! where shall either victim rest?
Can this with faded pinion soar
From rose to tulip as before?
Or Beauty, blighted in an hour,
Find joy within her broken bower?
No: gayer insects fluttering by
Ne'er droop the wing o'er those that die,
And lovelier things have mercy shown
To every failing but their own,
And every woe a tear can claim
Except an erring sister's shame.

* * * * * *

The Mind, that broods o'er guilty woes,
Is like the Scorpion girt by fire,
In circle narrowing as it glows,
The flames around their captive close,
Till inly search'd by thousand throes,
And maddening in her ire,
One sad and sole relief she knows,
The sting she nourish'd for her foes,
Whose venom never yet was vain,
Gives but one pang, and cures all pain,
And darts into her desperate brain:
So do the dark in soul expire,
Or live like Scorpion girt by fire;[17]
So writhes the mind Remorse hath riven,
Unfit for earth, undoom'd for heaven,
Darkness above, despair beneath,
Around it flame, within it death!

* * * * * *

Black Hassan from the Haram flies,
Nor bends on woman's form his eyes;
The unwonted chase each hour employs,
Yet shares he not the hunter's joys.
Not thus was Hassan wont to fly
When Leila dwelt in his Serai.
Doth Leila there no longer dwell?
That tale can only Hassan tell:
Strange rumours in our city say
Upon that eve she fled away
When Rhamazan's last sun was set,[18]
And flashing from each minaret
Millions of lamps proclaim'd the feast
Of Bairam through the boundless East.
'T was then she went as to the bath,
Which Hassan vainly search'd in wrath;
For she was flown her master's rage
In likeness of a Georgian page,
And far beyond the Moslem's power
Had wrong'd him with the faithless Giaour.
Somewhat of this had Hassan deem'd;
But still so fond, so fair she seem'd,
Too well he trusted to the slave
Whose treachery deserved a grave:
And on that eve had gone to mosque,
And thence to feast in his kiosk.
Such is the tale his Nubians tell,
Who did not watch their charge too well;
But others say, that on that night,
By pale Phingari's trembling light,[19]
The Giaour upon his jet black steed
Was seen, but seen alone, to speed
With bloody spur along the shore,
Nor maid nor page behind him bore.

* * * * * *

Her eye's dark charm 't were vain to tell,
But gaze on that of the Gazelle,
It will assist thy fancy well;
As large, as languishingly dark,
But Soul beam'd forth in every spark
That darted from beneath the lid,
Bright as the jewel of Giamschid.[20]
Yea, *Soul*, and should our Prophet say
That form was nought but breathing clay,
By Alla! I would answer nay;
Though on Al-Sirat's arch I stood,[21]
Which totters o'er the fiery flood,
With Paradise within my view,
And all his Houris beckoning through.
Oh! who young Leila's glance could read
And keep that portion of his creed,[22]
Which saith that woman is but dust,
A soulless toy for tyrant's lust?
On her might Muftis gaze, and own
That through her eye the Immortal shone;
On her fair cheek's unfading hue
The young pomegranate's blossoms strew[23]
Their bloom in blushes ever new;
Her hair in hyacinthine flow,[24]
When left to roll its folds below,
As midst her handmaids in the hall
She stood superior to them all,
Hath swept the marble where her feet
Gleam'd whiter than the mountain sleet,
Ere from the cloud that gave it birth
It fell, and caught one stain of earth.
The cygnet nobly walks the water;
So moved on earth Circassia's daughter,
The loveliest bird of Franguestan![25]
As rears her crest the ruffled Swan,
And spurns the wave with wings of pride,
When pass the steps of stranger man

Along the banks that bound her tide;
Thus rose fair Leila's whiter neck:—
Thus armed with beauty would she check
Intrusion's glance, till Folly's gaze
Shrunk from the charms it meant to praise:
Thus high and graceful was her gait;
Her heart as tender to her mate;
Her mate—stern Hassan, who was he?
Alas! that name was not for thee!

* * * * * *

Stern Hassan hath a journey ta en
With twenty vassals in his train,
Each arm'd, as best becomes a man,
With arquebuss and ataghan;
The chief before, as deck'd for war,
Bears in his belt the scimitar
Stain'd with the best of Arnaut blood,
When in the pass the rebels stood,
And few return'd to tell the tale
Of what befell in Parne's vale.
The pistols which his girdle bore
Were those that once a pacha wore,
Which still, though gemm'd and boss'd with gold,
Even robbers tremble to behold.
'T is said he goes to woo a bride
More true than her who left his side;
The faithless slave that broke her bower,
And, worse than faithless, for a Giaour!

* * * * * *

The sun's last rays are on the hill,
And sparkle in the fountain rill,
Whose welcome waters, cool and clear,
Draw blessings from the mountaineer;
Here may the loitering merchant Greek
Find that repose 't were vain to seek
In cities, lodged too near his lord,
And trembling for his secret hoard—
Here may he rest where none can see,
In crowds a slave, in deserts free;
And with forbidden wine may stain
The bowl a Moslem must not drain.

* * * * * *

The foremost Tartar 's in the gap,
Conspicuous by his yellow cap;
The rest in lengthening line the while
Wind slowly through the long defile:
Above, the mountain rears a peak,
Where vultures whet the thirsty beak;
And theirs may be a feast to-night,
Shall tempt them down ere morrow's light;
Beneath, a river's wintry stream
Has shrunk before the summer beam,
And left a channel bleak and bare,
Save shrubs that spring to perish there:
Each side the midway path there lay
Small broken crags of granite gray,
By time, or mountain lightning, riven
From summits clad in mists of heaven;
For where is he that hath beheld
The peak of Liakura unveil'd?

* * * * * *

They reach the grove of pine at last:
"Bismillah! now the peril 's past;[26]
For yonder view the opening plain,
And there we 'll prick our steeds amain:"
The Chiaus spake, and as he said,
A bullet whistled o'er his head;
The foremost Tartar bites the ground!
Scarce had they time to check the rein,
Swift from their steeds the riders bound;
But three shall never mount again:
Unseen the foes that gave the wound,
The dying ask revenge in vain.
With steel unsheath'd, and carbine bent,
Some o'er their courser's harness leant,
Half sheltered by the steed;
Some fly behind the nearest rock,
And there await the coming shock,
Nor tamely stand to bleed
Beneath the shaft of foes unseen,
Who dare not quit their craggy screen.
Stern Hassan only from his horse
Disdains to light, and keeps his course,
Till fiery flashes in the van
Proclaim too sure the robber-clan
Have well secured the only way
Could now avail the promised prey;
Then curl'd his very beard with ire,[27]
And glared his eye with fiercer fire:
"Though far and near the bullets hiss,
I 've 'scaped a bloodier hour than this."
And now the foe their covert quit,
And call his vassals to submit;
But Hassan's frown and furious word
Are dreaded more than hostile sword,
Nor of his little band a man
Resign'd carbine or ataghan,
Nor raised the craven cry, Amaun![28]
In fuller sight, more near and near,
The lately ambush'd foes appear,
And, issuing from the grove, advance
Some who on battle-charger prance.
Who leads them on with foreign brand,
Far flashing in his red right hand?
"'T is he! 't is he! I know him now;
I know him by his pallid brow;
I know him by the evil eye[29]
That aids his envious treachery;
I know him by his jet-black barb;
Though now array'd in Arnaut garb,
Apostate from his own vile faith,
It shall not save him from the death:
'T is he! well met in any hour,
Lost Leila's love, accursed Giaour!"

As rolls the river into ocean,
In sable torrent wildly streaming;
As the sea-tide's opposing motion,
In azure column proudly gleaming,
Beats back the current many a rood,
In curling foam and mingling flood,
While eddying whirl, and breaking wave,
Roused by the blasts of winter, rave;
Through sparkling spray, in thundering clash,
The lightnings of the waters flash
In awful whiteness o'er the shore,
That shines and shakes beneath the roar;
Thus—as the stream and ocean greet,
With waves that madden as they meet—
Thus join the bands, whom mutual wrong,
And fate, and fury, drive along.
The bickering sabres' shivering jar;
And, pealing wide or ringing near
Its echoes on the throbbing ear,
The deathshot hissing from afar;
The shock, the shout, the groan of war,
Reverberate along that vale,
More suited to the shepherd's tale:
Though few the numbers—theirs the strife,
That neither spares nor speaks for life!
Ah! fondly youthful hearts can press,
To seize and share the dear caress;
But Love itself could never pant
For all that Beauty sighs to grant,

With half the fervour Hate bestows
Upon the last embrace of foes,
When grappling in the fight they fold
Those arms that ne'er shall lose their hold:
Friends meet to part; Love laughs at faith;
True foes, once met, are join'd till death!

* * * * * *

With sabre shiver'd to the hilt,
Yet dripping with the blood he spilt;
Yet strain'd within the sever'd hand
Which quivers round that faithless brand;
His turban far behind him roll'd,
And cleft in twain its firmest fold;
His flowing robe by falchion torn,
And crimson as those clouds of morn
That, streak'd with dusky red, portend
The day shall have a stormy end;
A stain on every bush that bore
A fragment of his palampore,[30]
His breast with wounds unnumber'd riven,
His back to earth, his face to heaven,
Fall'n Hassan lies—his unclosed eye
Yet lowering on his enemy,
As if the hour that seal'd his fate
Surviving left his quenchless hate;

And o'er him bends that foe, with brow
As dark as his that bled below.—

* * * * * *

"Yes, Leila sleeps beneath the wave,
But his shall be a redder grave;
Her spirit pointed well the steel
Which taught that felon heart to feel.
He called the Prophet, but his power
Was vain against the vengeful Giaour:
He call'd on Alla—but the word
Arose unheeded or unheard.
Thou Paynim fool! could Leila's prayer
Be pass'd, and thine accorded there?
I watch'd my time, I leagued with these,
The traitor in his turn to seize;
My wrath is wreak'd, the deed is done,
And now I go—but go alone."

* * * * * *
* * * * * *

The browsing camels' bells are tinkling:
His Mother look'd from her lattice high—
She saw the dews of eve besprinkling
The pasture green beneath her eye,
She saw the planets faintly twinkling:
"'T is twilight—sure his train is nigh."
She could not rest in the garden-bower,
But gazed through the grate of his steepest tower:
"Why comes he not? his steeds are fleet,
Nor shrink they from the summer heat;
Why sends not the bridegroom his promised gift?
Is his heart more cold, or his barb less swift?
Oh, false reproach! yon Tartar now
Has gain'd our nearest mountain's brow,
And warily the steep descends,
And now within the valley bends;
And he bears the gift at his saddle bow—
How could I deem his courser slow?
Right well my largess shall repay
His welcome speed, and weary way."

The Tartar lighted at the gate,
But scarce upheld his fainting weight;
His swarthy visage spake distress,
But this might be from weariness;
His garb with sanguine spots was dyed,
But these might be from his courser's side:
He drew the token from his vest—
Angel of Death! 't is Hassan's cloven crest!
His calpac rent—his caftan red—[31]
"Lady, a fearful bride thy Son hath wed:
Me, not from mercy, did they spare,
But this empurpled pledge to bear.
Peace to the brave! whose blood is spilt:
Woe to the Giaour! for his the guilt."

* * * * * *

A turban carved in coarsest stone,[32]
A pillar with rank weeds o'ergrown,
Whereon can now be scarcely read
The Koran verse that mourns the dead,
Point out the spot where Hassan fell
A victim in that lonely dell.
There sleeps as true an Osmanlie
As e'er at Mecca bent the knee;
As ever scorn'd forbidden wine,
Or prayed with face towards the shrine,
In orisons resumed anew
At solemn sound of "Alla Hu!"[33]
Yet died he by a stranger's hand,
And stranger in his native land;
Yet died he as in arms he stood,
And unavenged, at least in blood.
But him the maids of Paradise
Impatient to their halls invite,
And the dark Heaven of Houris' eyes
On him shall glance for ever bright;
They come—their kerchiefs green they wave,[34]
And welcome with a kiss the brave!
Who falls in battle 'gainst a Giaour
Is worthiest an immortal bower.

* * * * * *

But thou, false Infidel! shalt writhe
Beneath avenging Monkir's scythe;[35]
And from its torments 'scape alone
To wander round lost Eblis' throne;[36]
And fire, unquench'd, unquenchable,
Around, within, thy heart shall dwell;
Nor ear can hear nor tongue can tell
The tortures of that inward hell!
But first, on earth as Vampire sent[37]
Thy corse shall from its tomb be rent:
Then ghastly haunt thy native place,
And suck the blood of all thy race;
There from thy daughter, sister, wife,
At midnight drain the stream of life;
Yet loath the banquet which perforce
Must feed thy livid living corse:
Thy victims, ere they yet expire
Shall know the demon for their sire,
As cursing thee, thou cursing them,
Thy flowers are wither'd on the stem.
But one that for thy crime must fall,
The youngest, most beloved of all,
Shall bless thee with a *father's* name—
That word shall wrap thy heart in flame!
Yet must thou end thy task, and mark
Her cheek's last tinge, her eye's last spark,
And the last glassy glance must view
Which freezes o'er its lifeless blue;
Then with unhallow'd hand shalt tear
The tresses of her yellow hair,
Of which in life a lock when shorn
Affection's fondest pledge was worn;
But now is borne away by thee,
Memorial of thine agony!
Wet with thine own best blood shall drip[38]

Thy gnashing tooth and haggard lip;
Then stalking to thy sullen grave,
Go—and with Gouls and Afrits rave;
Till these in horror shrink away
From spectre more accursed than they!

"How name ye yon lone Caloyer?
His features I have scann'd before
In mine own land: 't is many a year,
Since, dashing by the lonely shore,
I saw him urge as fleet a steed
As ever served a horseman's need.
But once I saw that face, yet then
It was so mark'd with inward pain,
I could not pass it by again;
It breathes the same dark spirit now,
As death were stamp'd upon his brow."
"'T is twice three years at summer tide
Since first among our frères he came;
And here it soothes him to abide
For some dark deed he will not name.
But never at our vesper prayer,
Nor e'er before confession chair
Kneels he, nor recks he when arise
Incense or anthem to the skies,
But broods within his cell alone,
His faith and race alike unknown.
The sea from Paynim land he crost,
And here ascended from the coast;
Yet seems he not of Othman race,
But only Christian in his face:
I'd judge him some stray renegade,
Repentant of the change he made,
Save that he shuns our holy shrine,
Nor tastes the sacred bread and wine.
Great largess to these walls he brought,
And thus our abbot's favour bought;
But were I prior, not a day
Should brook such stranger's further stay,
Or pent within our penance cell
Should doom him there for aye to dwell.
Much in his visions mutters he
Of maiden 'whelm'd beneath the sea;
Of sabres clashing, foemen flying,
Wrongs avenged, and Moslem dying.
On cliff he hath been known to stand,
And rave as to some bloody hand,
Fresh sever'd from its parent limb,
Invisible to all but him,
Which beckons onward to his grave,
And lures to leap into the wave."

* * * * * *

Dark and unearthly is the scowl
That glares beneath his dusky cowl:
The flash of that dilating eye
Reveals too much of times gone by;
Though varying, indistinct its hue,
Oft will his glance the gazer rue,
For in it lurks that nameless spell,
Which speaks, itself unspeakable,
A spirit yet unquell'd and high,
That claims and keeps ascendancy;
And like the bird whose pinions quake,
But cannot fly the gazing snake,
Will others quail beneath his look,
Nor 'scape the glance they scarce can brook.
From him the half-affrighted Friar
When met alone would fain retire,
As if that eye and bitter smile
Transferr'd to others fear and guile:
Not oft to smile descendeth he,
And when he doth 't is sad to see
That he but mocks at Misery.
How that pale lip will curl and quiver!
Then fix once more as if for ever;
As if his sorrow or disdain
Forbade him e'er to smile again.
Well were it so—such ghastly mirth
From joyaunce ne'er derived its birth.
But sadder still it were to trace
What once were feelings in that face;
Time hath not yet the features fix'd,
But brighter traits with evil mix'd;
And there are hues not always faded,
Which speak a mind not all degraded,
Even by the crimes through which it waded:
The common crowd but see the gloom
Of wayward deeds, and fitting doom;
The close observer can espy
A noble soul, and lineage high:
Alas! though both bestow'd in vain,
Which Grief could change, and Guilt could stain,
It was no vulgar tenement
To which such lofty gifts were lent,
And still with little less than dread
On such the sight is riveted.
The roofless cot, decay'd and rent,
Will scarce delay the passer by;
The tower by war or tempest bent,
While yet may frown one battlement,
Demands and daunts the stranger's eye;
Each ivied arch and pillar lone,
Pleads haughtily for glories gone!

"His floating robe around him folding,
Slow sweeps he through the column'd aisle,
With dread beheld, with gloom beholding
The rites that sanctify the pile.
But when the anthem shakes the choir,
And kneel the monks, his steps retire;
By yonder lone and wavering torch
His aspect glares within the porch;
There will he pause till all is done—
And hear the prayer, but utter none.
See—by the half-illumined wall
His hood fly back, his dark hair fall,

That pale brow wildly wreathing round,
As if the Gorgon there had bound
The sablest of the serpent-braid
That o'er her fearful forehead stray'd:
For he declines the convent oath,
And leaves those locks unhallow'd growth,
But wears our garb in all beside;
And, not from piety but pride,
Gives wealth to walls that never heard
Of his one holy vow nor word.
Lo!—mark ye, as the harmony
Peals louder praises to the sky,
That livid cheek, that stony air
Of mix'd defiance and despair!
Saint Francis, keep him from the shrine!
Else may we dread the wrath divine

Made manifest by awful sign.
If ever evil angel bore
The form of mortal, such he wore:
By all my hope of sins forgiven,
Such looks are not of earth nor heaven!"

To love the softest hearts are prone,
But such can ne'er be all his own;
Too timid in his woes to share,
Too meek to meet, or brave despair;
And sterner hearts alone may feel
The wound that time can never heal.
The rugged metal of the mine,
Must burn before its surface shine,
But plunged within the furnace-flame,
It bends and melts—though still the same;
Then temper'd to thy want, or will,
'T will serve thee to defend or kill;
A breast-plate for thine hour of need,
Or blade to bid thy foeman bleed;

But if a dagger's form it bear,
Let those who shape its edge, beware!
Thus passion's fire, and woman's art,
Can turn and tame the sterner heart;
From these its form and tone are ta'en,
And what they make it, must remain,
But break—before it bend again.

* * * * * *

If solitude succeed to grief,
Release from pain is slight relief;
The vacant bosom's wilderness
Might thank the pang that made it less.
We loathe what none are left to share:
Even bliss—'t were woe alone to bear;
The heart once left thus desolate
Must fly at last for ease—to hate.
It is as if the dead could feel
The icy worm around them steal,
And shudder, as the reptiles creep
To revel o'er their rotting sleep,
Without the power to scare away
The cold consumers of their clay!
It is as if the desert-bird,[39]
Whose beak unlocks her bosom's stream
To still her famish'd nestlings' scream,
Nor mourns a life to them transferr'd,
Should rend her rash devoted breast,
And find them flown her empty nest.
The keenest pangs the wretched find
Are rapture to the dreary void,
The leafless desert of the mind,
The waste of feelings unemploy'd.
Who would be doom'd to gaze upon
A sky without a cloud or sun?
Less hideous far the tempest's roar
Than ne'er to brave the billows more—
Thrown, when the war of winds is o'er,
A lonely wreck on fortune's shore,
'Mid sullen calm, and silent bay,
Unseen to drop by dull decay;—
Better to sink beneath the shock
Than moulder piecemeal on the rock!

* * * * * *

"Father! thy days have pass'd in peace,
'Mid counted beads, and countless prayer;
To bid the sins of others cease,
Thyself without a crime or care,
Save transient ills that all must bear,
Has been thy lot from youth to age;
And thou wilt bless thee from the rage
Of passions fierce, and uncontroll'd,
Such as thy penitents unfold,
Whose secret sins and sorrows rest
Within thy pure and pitying breast.
My days, though few, have pass'd below
In much of joy, but more of woe;
Yet still in hours of love or strife,
I've 'scaped the weariness of life:
Now leagued with friends, now girt by foes,
I loathed the langour of repose.
Now nothing left to love or hate,
No more with hope or pride elate,
I'd rather be the thing that crawls
Most noxious o'er a dungeon's walls,
Than pass my dull, unvarying days,
Condemn'd to meditate and gaze.
Yet, lurks a wish within my breast
For rest—but not to feel 't is rest.
Soon shall my fate that wish fulfil;
And I shall sleep without the dream
Of what I was, and would be still,
Dark as to thee my deeds may seem:
My memory now is but the tomb
Of joys long dead; my hope, their doom:
Though better to have died with those
Than bear a life of lingering woes.
My spirit shrunk not to sustain
The searching throes of ceaseless pain;
Nor sought the self-accorded grave
Of ancient fool and modern knave:
Yet death I have not fear'd to meet;
And in the field it had been sweet,
Had danger woo'd me on to move
The slave of glory, not of love.
I've braved it—not for honour's boast;
I smile at laurels won or lost;
To such let others carve their way,
For high renown, or hireling pay:
But place again before my eyes
Aught that I deem a worthy prize;
The maid I love, the man I hate,
And I will hunt the steps of fate,
To save or slay, as these require,
Through rending steel, and rolling fire:
Nor need'st thou doubt this speech from one
Who would but do—what he *hath* done.
Death is but what the haughty brave,
The weak must bear, the wretch must crave;
Then let Life go to Him who gave:
I have not quail'd to danger's brow
When high and happy—need I *now?*

* * * * * *

"I loved her, Friar! nay, adored—
But these are words that all can use—
I proved it more in deed than word;
There's blood upon that dinted sword,
A stain its steel can never lose:
'T was shed for her, who died for me,
It warm'd the heart of one abhorr'd:
Nay, start not—no—nor bend thy knee,
Nor midst my sins such act record;
Thou wilt absolve me from the deed,
For he was hostile to thy creed:
The very name of Nazarene
Was wormwood to his Paynim spleen.

Ungrateful fool! since but for brands
Well wielded in some hardy hands,
And wounds by Galileans given,
The surest pass to Turkish heaven,
For him his Houris still might wait
Impatient at the Prophet's gate.

I loved her—love will find its way
Through paths where wolves would fear to prey;
And if it dares enough, 't were hard
If passion met not some reward—
No matter how, or where, or why,
I did not vainly seek, nor sigh:

Yet sometimes, with remorse, in vain
I wish she had not loved again.
She died—I dare not tell thee how;
But look—'t is written on my brow!
There read of Cain the curse and crime,
In characters unworn by time:
Still, ere thou dost condemn me, pause;
Not mine the act, though I the cause.
Yet did he but what I had done

Had she been false to more than one.
Faithless to him, he gave the blow;
But true to me, I laid him low:
Howe'er deserved her doom might be,
Her treachery was truth to me;
To me she gave her heart, that all
Which tyranny can ne'er enthrall;
And I, alas! too late to save!
Yet all I then could give, I gave—

'T was some relief—our foe a grave.
His death sits lightly; but her fate
Has made me—what thou well may'st hate.
His doom was seal'd—he knew it well,
Warn'd by the voice of stern Taheer,
Deep in whose darkly boding ear [40]
The deathshot peal'd of murder near,
As filed the troop to where they fell!
He died too in the battle broil,
A time that heeds nor pain nor toil;
One cry to Mahomet for aid,
One prayer to Alla all he made:
He knew and cross'd me in the fray—
I gazed upon him where he lay,
And watch'd his spirit ebb away:
Though pierced like pard by hunters' steel,
He felt not half that now I feel.
I search'd, but vainly search'd, to find
The workings of a wounded mind;
Each feature of that sullen corse
Betray'd his rage, but no remorse.
Oh, what had Vengeance given to trace
Despair upon his dying face!
The late repentance of that hour,
When Penitence hath lost her power
To tear one terror from the grave,
And will not soothe, and cannot save.

* * * * * *

"The cold in clime are cold in blood,
Their love can scarce deserve the name;
But mine was like the lava flood
That boils in Ætna's breast of flame.
I cannot prate in puling strain
Of ladye-love, and beauty's chain:
If changing cheek, and scorching vein,
Lips taught to writhe, but not complain,
If bursting heart, and madd'ning brain,
And daring deed, and vengeful steel,
And all that I have felt, and feel,
Betoken love—that love was mine,
And shown by many a bitter sign.
'T is true, I could not whine nor sigh,
I knew but to obtain or die.
I die—but first, I have possess'd,
And come what may, I *have been* bless'd.
Shall I the doom I sought upbraid?
No—reft of all, yet undismay'd
But for the thought of Leila slain,
Give me the pleasure with the pain,
So would I live and love again.
I grieve, but not, my holy guide!
For him who dies, but her who died:
She sleeps beneath the wandering wave—
Ah! had she but an earthly grave,
This breaking heart and throbbing head
Should seek and share her narrow bed.
She was a form of life and light,
That, seen, became a part of sight;
And rose, where'er I turn'd mine eye,
The Morning-star of Memory!

"Yes, love indeed is light from heaven;
A spark of that immortal fire
With angels shared, by Alla given,
To lift from earth our low desire.
Devotion wafts the mind above,
But Heaven itself descends in love;
A feeling from the Godhead caught,
To wean from self each sordid thought;
A Ray of Him who form'd the whole;
A Glory circling round the soul!
I grant *my* love imperfect, all
That mortals by the name miscall;
Then deem it evil, what thou wilt;
But say, oh say, *hers* was not guilt!
She was my life's unerring light:
That quench'd, what beam shall break my night?
Oh! would it shone to lead me still,
Although to death or deadliest ill!
Why marvel ye, if they who lose
This present joy, this future hope,
No more with sorrow meekly cope;
In phrensy then their fate accuse:
In madness do those fearful deeds
That seem to add but guilt to woe?
Alas! the breast that inly bleeds
Hath nought to dread from outward blow:
Who falls from all he knows of bliss,
Cares little into what abyss.
Fierce as the gloomy vulture's now
To thee, old man, my deeds appear:
I read abhorrence on thy brow,
And this too was I born to bear!
'T is true, that like that bird of prey,
With havock have I mark'd my way:
But this was taught me by the dove,
To die—and know no second love.
This lesson yet hath man to learn,
Taught by the thing he dares to spurn:
The bird that sings within the brake,
The swan that swims upon the lake,
One mate, and one alone, will take.
And let the fool still prone to range,
And sneer on all who cannot change,
Partake his jest with boasting boys;
I envy not his varied joys,
But deem such feeble, heartless man,
Less than yon solitary swan;
Far, far beneath the shallow maid
He left believing and betray'd.
Such shame at least was never mine—
Leila! each thought was only thine!
My good, my guilt, my weal, my woe,
My hope on high—my all below.

Earth holds no other like to thee,
Or, if it doth, in vain for me:
For worlds I dare not view the dame
Resembling thee, yet not the same.
The very crimes that mar my youth,
This bed of death—attest my truth!
'T is all too late—thou wert, thou art
The cherish'd madness of my heart!

"And she was lost—and yet I breathed,
But not the breath of human life;
A serpent round my heart was wreathed,
And stung my every thought to strife.
Alike all time, abhorr'd all place,
Shuddering I shrunk from Nature's face,
Where every hue that charm'd before
The blackness of my bosom wore.
The rest thou dost already know,
And all my sins, and half my woe.
But talk no more of penitence;
Thou see'st I soon shall part from hence:
And if thy holy tale were true,
The deed that's done, canst *thou* undo?
Think me not thankless—but this grief
Looks not to priesthood for relief.[41]
My soul's estate in secret guess:
But would'st thou pity more, say less.
When thou canst bid my Leila live,
Then will I sue thee to forgive;
Then plead my cause in that high place
Where purchased masses proffer grace.
Go, when the hunter's hand hath wrung
From forest-cave her shrieking young,
And calm the lonely lioness:
But soothe not—mock not *my* distress!

"In earlier days, and calmer hours,
When heart with heart delights to blend,
Where bloom my native valley's bowers,
I had—Ah! have I now?—a friend!
To him this pledge I charge thee send,
Memorial of a youthful vow;
I would remind him of my end:
Though souls absorb'd like mine allow
Brief thought to distant friendship's claim,
Yet dear to him my blighted name.
'T is strange—he prophesied my doom,
And I have smiled—I then could smile—
When Prudence would his voice assume,
And warn—I reck'd not what—the while:
But now remembrance whispers o'er
Those accents scarcely mark'd before.
Say—that his bodings came to pass,
And he will start to hear their truth,
And wish his words had not been sooth:
Tell him, unheeding as I was,
Through many a busy bitter scene
Of all our golden youth had been,
In pain, my faltering tongue had tried
To bless his memory ere I died;
But Heaven in wrath would turn away,
If Guilt should for the guiltless pray.
I do not ask him not to blame,
Too gentle he to wound my name;
And what have I to do with fame?
I do not ask him not to mourn,
Such cold request might sound like scorn;
And what than friendship's manly tear
May better grace a brother's bier?
But bear this ring, his own of old,
And tell him—what thou dost behold!
The wither'd frame, the ruin'd mind,
The wrack by passion left behind,
A shriveled scroll, a scatter'd leaf,
Sear'd by the autumn blast of grief!

* * * * * *

"Tell me no more of fancy's gleam,
No, father, no, 't was not a dream;
Alas! the dreamer first must sleep,
I only watch'd, and wish'd to weep;
But could not, for my burning brow
Throbb'd to the very brain as now:
I wish'd but for a single tear,
As something welcome, new, and dear;
I wish'd it then, I wish it still;
Despair is stronger than my will.
Waste not thine orison, despair
Is mightier than thy pious prayer:
I would not, if I might, be blest;
I want no paradise, but rest.
'T was then, I tell thee, father! then
I saw her; yes, she lived again;
And shining in her white symar,[42]
As through yon pale gray cloud the star
Which now I gaze on, as on her,
Who look'd and looks far lovelier;
Dimly I view its trembling spark;
To-morrow's night shall be more dark;
And I, before its rays appear,
That lifeless thing the living fear.
I wander, father! for my soul
Is fleeting towards the final goal.
I saw her, friar! and I rose
Forgetful of our former woes;
And rushing from my couch, I dart,
And clasp her to my desperate heart;
I clasp—what is it that I clasp?
No breathing form within my grasp,
No heart that beats reply to mine,
Yet, Leila! yet the form is thine!
And art thou, dearest, changed so much
As meet my eye, yet mock my touch?
Ah! were thy beauties e'er so cold,
I care not; so my arms enfold
The all they ever wish'd to hold.
Alas! around a shadow prest,

They shrink upon my lonely breast;
Yet still 't is there! In silence stands,
And beckons with beseeching hands!
With braided hair, and bright-black eye—
I knew 't was false—she could not die!
But he is dead! within the dell
I saw him buried where he fell;
He comes not, for he cannot break
From earth; why then art thou awake?
They told me wild waves roll'd above
The face I view, the form I love:
They told me—'t was a hideous tale!
I'd tell it, but my tongue would fail:
If true, and from thine ocean-cave
Thou com'st to claim a calmer grave;
Oh! pass thy dewy fingers o'er
This brow that then will burn no more;
Or place them on my hopeless heart:
But, shape or shade! whate'er thou art,
In mercy ne'er again depart!
Or farther with thee bear my soul
Than winds can waft or waters roll!

* * * * * *

"Such is my name, and such my tale.
Confessor! to thy secret ear
I breathe the sorrows I bewail,
And thank thee for the generous tear
This glazing eye could never shed.
Then lay me with the humblest dead,
And, save the cross above my head,
Be neither name nor emblem spread,
By prying stranger to be read,
Or stay the passing pilgrim's tread."

He pass'd—nor of his name and race
Hath left a token or a trace,
Save what the father must not say
Who shrived him on his dying day:
This broken tale was all he knew
Of her he loved, or him he slew.[43]

NOTES TO THE GIAOUR.

Note 1, page 52.

That tomb, which, gleaming o'er the cliff.

A tomb above the rocks on the promontory, by some supposed the sepulchre of Themistocles.

Note 2, page 53.

Sultana of the Nightingale.

The attachment of the nightingale to the rose is a well-known Persian fable. If I mistake not, the "Bulbul of a thousand tales" is one of his appellations.

Note 3, page 53.

Till the gay mariner's guitar.

The guitar is the constant amusement of the Greek sailor by night: with a steady fair wind, and during a calm, it is accompanied always by the voice, and often by dancing.

Note 4, page 53.

Where cold Obstruction's apathy.

"Ay, but to die and go we know not where,
To lye in cold obstruction."—
Measure for Measure, Act iii. Sc. 2.

Note 5, page 53.

The first, last look by death reveal'd!

I trust that few of my readers have ever had an opportunity of witnessing what is here attempted in description; but those who have will probably retain a painful remembrance of that singular beauty which pervades, with few exceptions, the features of the dead, a few hours, and but for a few hours, after "the spirit is not there." It is to be remarked in cases of violent death by gun-shot wounds, the expression is always that of langour, whatever the natural energy of the sufferer's character: but in death from a stab, the countenance preserves its traits of feeling or ferocity, and the mind its bias, to the last.

Note 6, page 54.

Slaves—nay, the bondsmen of a slave.

Athens is the property of the Kislar Aga, (the slave of the seraglio and guardian of the women), who appoints the Waywode. A pander and eunuch—these are not polite yet true appellations—now *governs* the *governor* of Athens

Note 7, page 54.

'T is calmer than thy heart, young Giaour!

Infidel.

Note 8, page 54.

In echoes of the far tophaike.

"Tophaike," musket.—The Bairam is annonnced by the cannon at sunset; the illumination of the Mosques, and the firing of all kinds of small arms, loaded with *ball*, proclaims it during the night.

Note 9, page 55.

Swift as the hurl'd on high jerreed.

Jerreed, or Djerrid, a blunted Turkish javelin, which is darted from horseback with great force and precision. It is a favourite exercise of the Mussulmans; but I know not if it can be called a *manly* one, since the most expert in the art are the black eunuchs of Constantinople. I think, next to these, a Mamlouk at Smyrna was the most skilful that came within my observation.

Note 10, page 55.

He came, he went, like the Simoom.

The blast of the desert, fatal to every thing living, and often alluded to in eastern poetry.

Note 11, page 56.

To bless the sacred "bread and salt."

To partake of food, to break bread and salt with your host, ensures the safety of the guest: even though an enemy, his person from that moment is sacred.

Note 12, page 56.

Since his turban was cleft by the Infidel's sabre.

I need hardly observe, that Charity and Hospitality are the first duties enjoined by Mahomet; and to say truth, very generally practised by his disciples. The first praise that can be bestowed on a chief, is a panegyric on his bounty; the next, on his valour.

NOTE 13, page 56.

And silver-sheathèd ataghan.

The ataghan, a long dagger worn with pistols in the belt, in a metal scabbard, generally of silver; and, among the wealthier, gilt, or of gold.

NOTE 14, page 56.

An Emir by his garb of green.

Green is the privileged colour of the Prophet's numerous pretended descendants; with them, as here, faith (the family inheritance) is supposed to supersede the necessity of good works: they are the worst of a very indifferent brood.

NOTE 15, page 56.

"Ho! who art thou?"—"This low salam."

"Salam aleikoum! aleikoum salam!"—"Peace be with you; be with you peace"—the salutation reserved for the Faithful:—to a Christian, "Urlarula!"—"A good journey;" or, "Saban hiresem, saban serula"—"Good morn, good even;" and sometimes, "May your end be happy," are the usual salutes.

NOTE 16, page 56.

The insect-queen of eastern spring.

The blue-winged butterfly of Kashmeer, the most rare and beautiful of the species.

NOTE 17, page 57.

Or live like Scorpion girt by fire.

Alluding to the dubious suicide of the scorpion, so placed for experiment by gentle philosophers. Some maintain that the position of the sting, when turned towards the head, is merely a convulsive movement; but others have actually brought in the verdict, "Felo de se." The scorpions are surely interested in a speedy decision of the question; as, if once fairly established as insect Catos, they will probably be allowed to live as long as they think proper, without being martyred for the sake of an hypothesis.

NOTE 18, page 57.

When Rhamazan's last sun was set.

The cannon at sunset close the Rhamazan. See *ante*, note 8.

NOTE 19, page 57.

By pale Phingari's trembling light.

Phingari, the moon.

NOTE 20, page 57.

Bright as the jewel of Giamschid.

The celebrated fabulous ruby of Sultan Giamschid, the embellisher of Istakhar; from its splendour, named Schebgerag, "The Torch of Night;" also, the "Cup of the Sun," &c. In the first edition, "Giamschid" was written as a word of three syllables; so D'Herbelot has it; but I am told Richardson reduces it to a dissyllable, and writes "Jamshid." I have left in the text the orthography of the one with the pronunciation of the other.

NOTE 21, page 57.

Though on Al-Sirat's arch I stood.

Al-Sirat, the bridge of breadth, less than the thread of a famished spider, over which the Mussulmans must *skate* into Paradise, to which it is the only entrance; but this is not the worst, the river beneath being hell itself, into which, as may be expected, the unskilful and tender of foot contrive to tumble with a "facilis descensus Averni," not very pleasing in prospect to the next passenger. There is shorter cut downwards to the Jews and Christians.

NOTE 22, page 57.

A soulless toy for tyrant's lust.

A vulgar error: the Koran allots at least a third of Paradise to well-behaved women; but by far the greater number of Mussulmans interpret the text their own way, and exclude their moities from heaven. Being enemies to Platonics, they cannot discern "any fitness of things" in the souls of the other sex, conceiving them to be superseded by the Houris.

NOTE 23, page 57.

The young pomegranate's blossoms strew.

An oriental simile, which may, perhaps, though fairly stolen, be deemed "plus Arabe qu'en Arabie."

NOTE 24, page 57.

Her hair in hyacinthine flow.

Hyacinthine, in Arabic "Sunbul;" as common a thought in the eastern poets as it was among the Greeks.

NOTE 25, page 57.

The loveliest bird of Franguestan.

"Franguestan," Circassia.

NOTE 26, page 59.

"Bismillah! now the peril's past."

Bismillah—"in the name of God;" the commencement of all the chapters of the Koran but one, and of prayer and thanksgiving.

NOTE 27, page 59.

Then curl'd his very beard with ire.

A phenomenon not uncommon with an angry Mussulman. In 1809, the Capitan Pacha's whispers at a diplomatic audience were no less lively with indignation than a tiger cat's, to the horror of all the dragomans; the portentous mustachios twisted, they stood erect of their own accord, and were expected every moment to change their colour, but at last condescended to subside, which, probably, saved more heads than they contained hairs.

NOTE 28, page 59.

Nor raised the craven cry, Amaun!

"Amaun," quarter, pardon.

NOTE 29, page 59.

I know him by the evil eye.

The "evil eye," a common superstition in the Levant, and of which the imaginary effects are yet very singular on those who conceive themselves affected.

NOTE 30, page 60.

A fragment of his palampore.

The flowered shawls generally worn by persons of rank.

NOTE 31, page 61.

His calpac rent—his caftan red.

The calpac is the solid cap or centre part of the head-dress; the shawl is wound round it, and forms the turban.

NOTE 32, page 61.

A turban carved in coarsest stone.

The turban, pillar, and inscriptive verse, decorate the tombs of the Osmanlies, whether in the cemetery or the wilderness. In the mountains you frequently pass similar mementos; and on inquiry you are informed that they record some victim of rebellion, plunder, or revenge.

NOTE 33, page 61.

At solemn sound of "Alla Hu!"

"Alla Hu!" the concluding words of the Muezzin's call to prayer from the highest gallery on the exterior of the Minaret. On a still evening, when the Muezzin has a fine voice, which is frequently the case, the effect is solemn and beautiful beyond all the bells in Christendom.

NOTE 34, page 61.

They come—their kerchiefs green they wave.

The following is part of a battle song of the Turks:—"I see—I see a dark-eyed girl of Paradise, and she waves a handkerchief, a kerchief of green; and cries aloud, 'Come, kiss me, for I love thee,'" &c.

NOTE 35, page 61.

Beneath avenging Monkir's scythe.

Monkir and Nekir are the inquisitors of the dead, before whom the corpse undergoes a slight noviciate and preparatory training for damnation. If the answers are none of the clearest, he is hauled up with a scythe and thumped down with a red hot mace till properly seasoned, with a variety of subsidiary probations. The office of these angels is no sinecure; there are but two, and the number of orthodox deceased being in a small proportion to the remainder, their hands are always full.

NOTE 36, page 61.

To wander round lost Eblis' throne.

Eblis, the Oriental Prince of Darkness.

NOTE 37, page 61.

But first, on earth as Vampire sent.

The Vampire superstition is still general in the Levant. Honest Tournefort tells a long story, which Mr. Southey, in his notes on "Thalaba," quotes, about these "Vroncolochas," as he calls them. The Romaic term is "Vardoulacha." I recollect a whole family being terrified by the scream of a child, which they imagined must proceed from such a visitation. The Greeks never mention the word without horror. I find that "Broucolokas" is an old legitimate Hellenic appellation—at least is so applied to Arsenius, who, according to the Greeks, was after his death animated by the Devil.—The moderns, however, use the word I mention.

NOTE 38, page 61.

Wet with thine own best blood shall drip.

The freshness of the face, and the wetness of the lip with blood, are the never-failing signs of a Vampire. The stories told in Hungary and Greece of these foul feeders are singular, and some of them most *incredibly* attested.

NOTE 39, page 64.

It is as if the desert bird.

The pelican is, I believe, the bird so libelled by the imputation of feeding her chickens with her blood.

NOTE 40, page 66.

Deep in whose darkly boding ear.

This superstition of a second-hearing (for I never met with downright second-sight in the East) fell once under my own observation. On my third journey to Cape Colonna, early in 1811, as we passed through the defile that leads from the hamlet between Keratia and Colonna, I observed Dervish Tahiri riding rather out of the path, and leaning his head upon his hand, as if in pain. I rode up and inquired. "We are in peril," he answered. "What peril? we are not now in Albania, nor in the passes to Ephesus, Messalunghi, or Lepanto; there are plenty of us, well armed, and the Choriates have not courage to be thieves." —"True, Affendi, but nevertheless the shot is ringing in my ears."—"The shot! not a tophaike has been fired this morning." —"I hear it, notwithstanding—Bom—Bom—as plainly as I hear your voice."—"Psha!"—"As you please, Affendi; if it is written, so will it be."—I left this quick-eared predestinarian, and rode up to Basili, his Christian compatriot, whose ears, though not at all prophetic, by no means relished the intelligence. We all arrived at Colonna, remained some hours, and returned leisurely, saying a variety of brilliant things, in more languages than spoiled the building of Babel, upon the mistaken seer. Romaic, Arnaut, Turkish, Italian, and English were all exercised, in various conceits, upon the unfortunate Mussulman. While we were contemplating the beautiful prospect, Dervish was occupied about the columns. I thought he was deranged into an antiquarian, and asked him if he had become a "*Palao-castro*" man? "No," said he, "but these pillars will be useful in making a stand;" and added other remarks, which at least evinced his own belief in his troublesome faculty of *fore-hearing*. On our return to Athens we heard from Leoné (a prisoner set ashore some days after) of the intended attack of the Mainotes, mentioned, with the cause of its not taking place, in the notes to "Childe Harold," Canto II. I was at some pains to question the man, and he described the dresses, arms, and marks of the horses of our party so accurately, that, with other circumstances, we could not doubt of *his* being in "villanous company," and ourselves in a bad neighbourhood. Dervish became a soothsayer for life, and I daresay he is now hearing more musquetry than ever will be fired, to the great refreshment of the Arnauts of Berat, and his native mountains.—I shall mention one trait more of this singular race. In March, 1811, a remarkably stout and active Arnaut came (I believe the fiftieth on the same errand) to offer himself as an attendant, which was declined. "Well, Affendi," quoth he, "may you live!—you would have found me useful. I shall leave the town for the hills to-morrow; in the winter I return, perhaps you will then receive me."—Dervish, who was present, remarked as a thing of course, and of no consequence, "in the mean time, he will join the Klephtes" (robbers), which was true to the letter. If not cut off, they come down in the winter, and pass it unmolested in some town, where they are often as well known as their exploits.

NOTE 41, page 67.

Looks not to priesthood for relief.

The monk's sermon is omitted. It seems to have had so little effect upon the patient, that it could have no hopes from the reader. It may be sufficient to say, that it was of a customary length (as may be perceived from the interruptions and uneasiness of the penitent), and was delivered in the nasal tone of all orthodox preachers.

NOTE 42, page 67.

And shining in her white symar.

"Symar,"—Shroud.

NOTE 43, page 68.

Of her he loved, or him he slew.

The circumstance to which the above story relates, was not very uncommon in Turkey. A few years ago, the wife of Muchtar Pacha complained to his father of his son's supposed infidelity; he asked with whom, and she had the barbarity to give in a list of the twelve handsomest women in Yanina. They were seized, fastened up in sacks, and drowned in the lake the same night! One of the guards who was present informed me, that not one of the victims uttered a cry, or showed a symptom of terror, at so sudden a "wrench from all we know, from all we love." The fate of Phrosine, the fairest of this sacrifice, is the subject of many a Romaic and Arnaut ditty. The story in the text is one told of a young Venetian many years ago, and now nearly forgotten. I heard it by accident recited by one of the coffee-house story-tellers who abound in the Levant, and sing or recite their narratives. The additions and interpolations by the translator will be easily distinguished from the rest, by the want of Eastern imagery; and I regret that my memory has retained so few fragments of the original. For the contents of some of the notes, I am indebted partly to D'Herbelot, and partly to that most Eastern, and, as Mr. Webber justly entitles it, "sublime tale," the "Caliph Vathek." I do not know from what source the author of that singular volume may have drawn his materials; some of his incidents are to be found in the "Bibliothèque Orientale;" but for correctness of costume, beauty of description, and power of imagination, it far surpasses all European imitations; and bears such marks of originality, that those who have visited the East will find some difficulty in believing it to be more than a translation. As an Eastern tale, even Rasselas must bow before it; his "Happy Valley" will not bear a comparison with the "Hall of Eblis."

THE BRIDE OF ABYDOS:

A TURKISH TALE.

"Had we never loved so kindly,
Had we never loved so blindly,
Never met or never parted,
We had ne'er been broken-hearted."

BURNS.

TO

THE RIGHT HONOURABLE LORD HOLLAND,

THIS TALE IS INSCRIBED.

WITH EVERY SENTIMENT OF REGARD AND RESPECT,

BY HIS GRATEFULLY OBLIGED AND SINCERE FRIEND,

BYRON.

CANTO THE FIRST.

I.

KNOW ye the land where the cypress and myrtle
 Are emblems of deeds that are done in their clime,
Where the rage of the vulture, the love of the turtle,
 Now melt into sorrow, now madden to crime?
Know ye the land of the cedar and vine,
Where the flowers ever blossom, the beams ever shine;
Where the light wings of Zephyr, oppress'd with perfume,
Wax faint o'er the gardens of Gúl in her bloom;[1]
Where the citron and olive are fairest of fruit,
And the voice of the nightingale never is mute;
Where the tints of the earth, and the hues of the sky,
In colour though varied, in beauty may vie,
And the purple of Ocean is deepest in dye;
Where the virgins are soft as the roses they twine,
And all, save the spirit of man, is divine?

'T is the clime of the East; 't is the land of the Sun—
Can he smile on such deeds as his children have done?[2]
Oh! wild as the accents of lovers' farewell
Are the hearts which they bear, and the tales which they tell.

II.

Begirt with many a gallant slave,
Apparell'd as becomes the brave,
Awaiting each his lord's behest
To guide his steps, or guard his rest,
Old Giaffir sate in his Divan:
Deep thought was in his aged eye;
And though the face of Mussulman
Not oft betrays to standers by
The mind within, well skill'd to hide
All but unconquerable pride,
His pensive cheek and pondering brow
Did more than he was wont avow.

III.

"Let the chamber be clear'd."—The train disappear'd—
"Now call me the chief of the Haram guard."
With Giaffir is none but his only son,
And the Nubian awaiting the sire's award.
"Haroun—when all the crowd that wait
Are pass'd beyond the outer gate,
(Woe to the head whose eye beheld
My child Zuleika's face unveil'd!)
Hence, lead my daughter from her tower;
Her fate is fix'd this very hour:

Yet not to her repeat my thought;
By me alone be duty taught!"
"Pacha! to hear is to obey."
No more must slave to despot say—
Then to the tower had ta'en his way,
But here young Selim silence brake,
First lowly rendering reverence meet;
And downcast look'd, and gently spake,
Still standing at the Pacha's feet:
For son of Moslem must expire,
Ere dare to sit before his sire!

"Father! for fear that thou shouldst chide
My sister, or her sable guide,
Know—for the fault, if fault there be,
Was mine—then fall thy frowns on me—
So lovelily the morning shone,
That—let the old and weary sleep—
I could not; and to view alone
The fairest scenes of land and deep,
With none to listen and reply
To thoughts with which my heart beat high,
Were irksome—for whate'er my mood,
In sooth I love not solitude;
I on Zuleika's slumber broke,
And, as thou knowest that for me
Soon turns the Haram's grating key,
Before the guardian slaves awoke
We to the cypress groves had flown,
And made earth, main, and heaven our own!
There linger'd we, beguiled too long
With Mejnoun's tale, or Sadi's song,[3]
Till I, who heard the deep tambour[4]
Beat thy Divan's approaching hour,
To thee, and to my duty true,
Warn'd by the sound, to greet thee flew:
But there Zuleika wanders yet—
Nay, father, rage not—nor forget
That none can pierce that secret bower
But those who watch the women's tower."

IV.

"Son of a slave"—the Pacha said—
"From unbelieving mother bred,
Vain were a father's hope to see
Aught that beseems a man in thee.
Thou, when thine arm should bend the bow,
And hurl the dart, and curb the steed,
Thou, Greek in soul if not in creed,
Must pore where babbling waters flow,
And watch unfolding roses blow.
Would that yon orb, whose matin glow
Thy listless eyes so much admire,
Would lend thee something of his fire!
Thou, who would'st see this battlement
By Christian cannon piecemeal rent;
Nay, tamely view old Stambol's wall
Before the dogs of Moscow fall,
Nor strike one stroke for life and death
Against the curs of Nazareth!
Go—let thy less than woman's hand
Assume the distaff—not the brand.
But, Haroun!—to my daughter speed:
And hark—of thine own head take heed—
If thus Zuleika oft takes wing—
Thou see'st yon bow—it hath a string!"

V.

No sound from Selim's lip was heard,
At least that met old Giaffir's ear,
But every frown and every word
Pierced keener than a Christian's sword.
"Son of a slave!—reproach'd with fear!
Those gibes had cost another dear.
Son of a slave!—and *who* my sire?"
Thus held his thoughts their dark career;
And glances ev'n of more than ire
Flash forth, then faintly disappear.
Old Giaffir gazed upon his son
And started; for within his eye
He read how much his wrath had done;
He saw rebellion there begun:
"Come hither, boy—what, no reply?
I mark thee—and I know thee too;
But there be deeds thou dar'st not do:
But if thy beard had manlier length,
And if thy hand had skill and strength,
I'd joy to see thee break a lance,
Albeit against my own perchance."

As sneeringly these accents fell,
On Selim's eye he fiercely gazed:
That eye return'd him glance for glance,
And proudly to his sire's was raised,
Till Giaffir's quail'd and shrunk askance—
And why—he felt, but durst not tell.
"Much I misdoubt this wayward boy
Will one day work me more annoy:
I never loved him from his birth,
And—but his arm is little worth,
And scarcely in the chase could cope
With timid fawn or antelope,
Far less would venture into strife
Where man contends for fame and life—
I would not trust that look or tone:
No—nor the blood so near my own.
That blood—he hath not heard—no more—
I'll watch him closer than before.
He is an Arab to my sight,[5]
Or Christian crouching in the fight—
But hark!—I hear Zuleika's voice;
Like Houris' hymn it meets mine ear:
She is the offspring of my choice;
Oh! more than ev'n her mother dear,
With all to hope, and nought to fear—
My Peri!—ever welcome here!

Sweet, as the desert fountain's wave,
To lips just cool'd in time to save—
Such to my longing sight art thou;
Nor can they waft to Mecca's shrine
More thanks for life, than I for thine,
Who blest thy birth, and bless thee now."

VI.

Fair, as the first that fell of womankind,
When on that dread yet lovely serpent smiling,
Whose image then was stamped upon her mind—
But once beguiled—and ever more beguiling;
Dazzling, as that, oh! too transcendent vision
To Sorrow's phantom-peopled slumber given,
When heart meets heart again in dreams Elysian,
And paints the lost on Earth revived in Heaven;
Soft, as the memory of buried love;
Pure, as the prayer which Childhood wafts above;
Was she—the daughter of that rude old Chief,
Who met the maid with tears—but not of grief.

Who hath not proved how feebly words essay
To fix one spark of Beauty's heavenly ray?
Who doth not feel, until his failing sight
Faints into dimness with its own delight,
His changing cheek, his sinking heart confess
The might—the majesty of Loveliness?
Such was Zuleika—such around her shone
The nameless charms unmark'd by her alone;
The light of love, the purity of grace,
The mind, the Music breathing from her face,[6]
The heart whose softness harmonized the whole—
And, oh! that eye was in itself a Soul!

Her graceful arms in meekness bending
Across her gently-budding breast;
At one kind word those arms extending
To clasp the neck of him who blest
His child caressing and carest,
Zuleika came—and Giaffir felt
His purpose half within him melt:
Not that against her fancied weal
His heart though stern could ever feel;
Affection chain'd her to that heart;
Ambition tore the links apart.

VII.

"Zuleika! child of gentleness!
How dear this very day must tell,
When I forget my own distress,
In losing what I love so well,
To bid thee with another dwell:
Another! and a braver man
Was never seen in battle's van.
We Moslem reck not much of blood;
But yet the line of Carasman [7]
Unchanged, unchangeable, hath stood
First of the bold Timariot bands
That won and well can keep their lands.
Enough that he who comes to woo
Is kinsman of the Bey Oglou:
His years need scarce a thought employ:
I would not have thee wed a boy.
And thou shalt have a noble dower:
And his and my united power
Will laugh to scorn the death-firman,
Which others tremble but to scan,
And teach the messenger what fate
The bearer of such boon may wait.[8]
And now thou knowest thy father's will:
All that thy sex hath need to know:
'T was mine to teach obedience still—
The way to love, thy lord may show."

VIII.

In silence bow'd the virgin's head;
And if her eye was fill'd with tears
That stifled feeling dare not shed,
And changed her cheek from pale to red,
And red to pale, as through her ears
Those wingèd words like arrows sped,
What could such be but maiden fears?
So bright the tear in Beauty's eye,
Love half regrets to kiss it dry;
So sweet the blush of Bashfulness,
Even Pity scarce can wish it less!

Whate'er it was the sire forgot;
Or if remember'd, mark'd it not;
Thrice clapp'd his hands, and call'd his steed,[9]
Resign'd his gem-adorn'd chibouque,[10]
And mounting featly for the mead,
With Maugrabee and Mamaluke,[11]
His way amid his Delis took,[12]
To witness many an active deed
With sabre keen, or blunt jerreed.
The Kislar only and his Moors
Watch well the Haram's massy doors.

IX.

His head was leant upon his hand,
His eye look'd o'er the dark blue water
That swiftly glides and gently swells
Between the winding Dardanelles;
But yet he saw nor sea nor strand,
Nor even his Pacha's turban'd band
Mix in the game of mimic slaughter,
Careering cleave the folded felt[13]
With sabre stroke right sharply dealt;
Nor mark'd the javelin-darting crowd,
Nor heard their Ollahs wild and loud—[14]
He thought but of old Giaffir's daughter!

X.

No word from Selim's bosom broke;
One sigh Zuleika's thought bespoke:

Still gazed he through the lattice grate,
Pale, mute, and mournfully sedate.
To him Zuleika's eye was turn'd,
But little from his aspect learn'd:
Equal her grief, yet not the same;
Her heart confess'd a gentler flame:
But yet that heart, alarm'd or weak,
She knew not why, forbade to speak.
Yet speak she must—but when essay?
" How strange he thus should turn away!
Not thus we e'er before have met;
Not thus shall be our parting yet."

Thrice paced she slowly through the room,
And watch'd his eye—it still was fixed:
She snatch'd the urn wherein was mix'd
The Persian Atar-gul's perfume,[15]
And sprinkled all its odours o'er
The pictured roof and marble floor:[16]
The drops, that through his glittering vest
The playful girl's appeal address'd,
Unheeded o'er his bosom flew,
As if that breast were marble too.
" What, sullen yet? it must not be—
Oh! gentle Selim, this from thee!"

She saw in curious order set
 The fairest flowers of eastern land—
"He lov'd them once; may touch them yet
 If offer'd by Zuleika's hand."
The childish thought was hardly breathed
Before the Rose was pluck'd and wreathed;

The next fond moment saw her seat
Her fairy form at Selim's feet:
"This rose to calm my brother's cares
A message from the Bulbul bears; [17]
It says to-night he will prolong
For Selim's ear his sweetest song;
And though his note is somewhat sad,
He'll try for once a strain more glad,
With some faint hope his alter'd lay
May sing these gloomy thoughts away.

XI.

"What! not receive my foolish flower?
 Nay then I am indeed unblest:
On me can thus thy forehead lower?
 And know'st thou not who loves thee best?

Oh, Selim dear! oh, more than dearest!
Say, is it me thou hat'st or fearest?
Come, lay thy head upon my breast,
And I will kiss thee into rest,
Since words of mine, and songs must fail,
Ev'n from my fabled nightingale.
I knew our sire at times was stern,
But this from thee had yet to learn:
Too well I know he loves thee not;
But is Zuleika's love forgot?
Ah! deem I right? the Pacha's plan—
This kinsman Bey of Carasman
Perhaps may prove some foe of thine:
If so, I swear by Mecca's shrine,
If shrines that ne'er approach allow
To woman's step, admit her vow,
Without thy free consent, command,
The Sultan should not have my hand!
Think'st thou that I could bear to part
With thee, and learn to halve my heart?
Ah! were I sever'd from thy side,
Where were thy friend—and who my guide?
Years have not seen, Time shall not see
The hour that tears my soul from thee:
Even Azrael, from his deadly quiver [18]
 When flies that shaft, and fly it must,
That parts all else, shall doom for ever
 Our hearts to undivided dust!"

XII.

He lived—he breathed—he moved—he felt;
He raised the maid from where she knelt;
His trance was gone—his keen eye shone
With thoughts that long in darkness dwelt;
With thoughts that burn—in rays that melt.

As the stream late conceal'd
 By the fringe of its willows,
When it rushes reveal'd
 In the light of its billows;
As the bolt bursts on high
 From the black cloud that bound it,
Flash'd the soul of that eye
 Through the long lashes round it.
A war-horse at the trumpet's sound,
A lion rous'd by heedless hound,
A tyrant waked to sudden strife
By graze of ill-directed knife,
Starts not to more convulsive life
Than he, who heard that vow, display'd,
And all, before repress'd, betray'd:

"Now thou art mine, for ever mine,
With life to keep, and scarce with life resign;
Now thou art mine, that sacred oath,
Though sworn by one, hath bound us both.
Yes, fondly, wisely hast thou done;
That vow hath saved more heads than one:
But blench not thou—thy simplest tress
Claims more from me than tenderness;
I would not wrong the slenderest hair
That clusters round thy forehead fair,
For all the treasures buried far
Within the caves of Istakar.[19]
This morning clouds upon me lower'd,
Reproaches on my head were shower'd,
And Giaffir almost call'd me coward!
Now I have motive to be brave;
The son of his neglected slave,
Nay, start not, 'twas the term he gave,
May show, though little apt to vaunt,
A heart his words nor deeds can daunt.
His son, indeed!—yet, thanks to thee,
Perchance I am, at least shall be;
But let our plighted secret vow
Be only known to us as now.
I know the wretch who dares demand
From Giaffir thy reluctant hand;
More ill-got wealth, a meaner soul
Holds not a Musselim's control: [20]
Was he not bred in Egripo? [21]
A viler race let Israel show!
But let that pass—to none be told
Our oath; the rest let time unfold.
To me and mine leave Osman Bey;
I've partisans for peril's day:
Think not I am what I appear;
I've arms, and friends, and vengeance near."

XIII.

"Think not thou art what thou appearest!
 My Selim, thou art sadly changed:
This morn I saw thee gentlest, dearest;
 But now thou 'rt from thyself estranged.
My love thou surely knew'st before,
It ne'er was less, nor can be more.
To see thee, hear thee, near thee stay,
 And hate the night, I know not why,
Save that we meet not but by day;
 With thee to live, with thee to die,
 I dare not to my hope deny:
Thy cheek, thine eyes, thy lips to kiss,
Like this—and this—no more than this;
For, Alla! sure thy lips are flame:
 What fever in thy veins is flushing?
My own have nearly caught the same,
 At least I feel my cheek too blushing.
To soothe thy sickness, watch thy health,
Partake, but never waste thy wealth,
Or stand with smiles unmurmuring by,
And lighten half thy poverty;
Do all but close thy dying eye,
For that I could not live to try;
To these alone my thoughts aspire:
More can I do? or thou require?
But, Selim, thou must answer why

We need so much of mystery?
The cause I cannot dream nor tell,
But be it, since thou say'st 'tis well;
Yet what thou mean'st by 'arms' and 'friends,'
Beyond my weaker sense extends.
I meant that Giaffir should have heard
 The very vow I plighted thee;
His wrath would not revoke my word:
 But surely he would leave me free.
 Can this fond wish seem strange in me,
To be what I have ever been?
What other hath Zuleika seen
From simple childhood's earliest hour?
 What other can she seek to see
Than thee, companion of her bower,
 The partner of her infancy?
These cherished thoughts with life begun,
 Say, why must I no more avow?
What change is wrought to make me shun
 The truth; my pride, and thine till now?
To meet the gaze of strangers' eyes
Our law, our creed, our God denies;
Nor shall one wandering thought of mine
At such, our Prophet's will, repine:
No! happier made by that decree!
He left me all in leaving thee.
Deep were my anguish, thus compell'd
To wed with one I ne'er beheld:
This wherefore should I not reveal?
Why wilt thou urge me to conceal?
I know the Pacha's haughty mood
To thee hath never boded good;
And he so often storms at nought,
Alla! forbid that e'er he ought!
And why I know not, but within
My heart concealment weighs like sin.
If then such secrecy be crime,
 And such it feels while lurking here;
Oh, Selim! tell me yet in time,
 Nor leave me thus to thoughts of fear.
Ah! yonder see the Tchocadar,[22]
My father leaves the mimic war:
I tremble now to meet his eye—
Say, Selim, canst thou tell me why?"

XIV.

"Zuleika—to thy tower's retreat
Betake thee—Giaffir I can greet:
And now with him I fain must prate
Of firmans, imposts, levies, state.
There's fearful news from Danube's banks,
Our Vizier nobly thins his ranks,
For which the Giaour may give him thanks!
Our Sultan hath a shorter way
Such costly triumph to repay.
But, mark me, when the twilight drum
 Hath warn'd the troops to food and sleep,
Unto thy cell will Selim come:
 Then softly from the Haram creep
 Where we may wander by the deep:
 Our garden-battlements are steep;
Nor these will rash intruder climb
To list our words, or stint our time;
And if he doth, I want not steel
Which some have felt, and more may feel.
Then shalt thou learn of Selim more
Than thou hast heard or thought before:
Trust me, Zuleika—fear not me!
Thou know'st I hold a Haram key."

"Fear thee, my Selim! ne'er till now
Did word like this—"
 "Delay not thou;
I keep the key—and Haroun's guard
Have *some*, and hope of *more* reward.
To-night, Zuleika, thou shalt hear
My tale, my purpose, and my fear:
I am not, love! what I appear."

I.

THE winds are high on Helle's wave,
 As on that night of stormy water,
When Love, who sent, forgot to save
The young, the beautiful, the brave,
 The lonely hope of Sestos' daughter.
Oh! when alone along the sky
Her turret-torch was blazing high,
Though rising gale, and breaking foam,
And shrieking sea-birds warn'd him home;
And clouds aloft and tides below,
With signs and sounds, forbade to go,
He could not see, he would not hear,
Or sound or sign foreboding fear;
His eye but saw the light of love,
The only star it hail'd above;
His ear but rang with Hero's song,
"Ye waves, divide not lovers long!"—
That tale is old, but love anew
May nerve young hearts to prove as true.

II.

The winds are high, and Helle's tide
Rolls darkly heaving to the main;
And Night's descending shadows hide
That field with blood bedew'd in vain,
The desert of old Priam's pride;
The tombs, sole relics of his reign,
All—save immortal dreams that could beguile
The blind old man of Scio's rocky isle!

III.

Oh! yet—for there my steps have been;
These feet have press'd the sacred shore,
These limbs that buoyant wave hath borne—
Minstrel! with thee to muse, to mourn,
To trace again those fields of yore,
Believing every hillock green
Contains no fabled hero's ashes,
And that around the undoubted scene
Thine own "broad Hellespont" still dashes,[23]
Be long my lot! and cold were he
Who there could gaze denying thee!

IV.

The night hath closed on Helle's stream,
Nor yet hath risen on Ida's hill
That moon, which shone on his high theme:
No warrior chides her peaceful beam,
But conscious shepherds bless it still.
Their flocks are grazing on the mound
Of him who felt the Dardan's arrow:
That mighty heap of gather'd ground
Which Ammon's son ran proudly round,[24]
By nations rais'd, by monarchs crown'd,
Is now a lone and nameless barrow!
Within—thy dwelling-place how narrow!
Without—can only strangers breathe
The name of him that *was* beneath:
Dust long outlasts the storied stone;
But Thou—thy very dust is gone!

V.

Late, late to-night will Dian cheer
The swain, and chase the boatman's fear;
Till then—no beacon on the cliff
May shape the course of struggling skiff;
The scatter'd lights that skirt the bay,
All, one by one, have died away;
The only lamp of this lone hour
Is glimmering in Zuleika's tower.

Yes! there is light in that lone chamber,
And o'er her silken Ottoman
Are thrown the fragrant beads of amber,
O'er which her fairy fingers ran;[25]
Near these, with emerald rays beset,
(How could she thus that gem forget?)
Her mother's sainted amulet,[26]
Whereon engraved the Koorsee text,
Could smooth this life, and win the next;
And by her Comboloio lies[27]
A Koran of illumined dyes;
And many a bright emblazon'd rhyme
By Persian scribes redeem'd from time;
And o'er those scrolls, not oft so mute,
Reclines her now neglected lute;
And round her lamp of fretted gold
Bloom flowers in urns of China's mould;
The richest work of Iran's loom,
And Sheeraz' tribute of perfume;
All that can eye or sense delight
Are gather'd in that gorgeous room:
But yet it hath an air of gloom.
She, of this Peri cell the sprite,
What doth she hence, and on so rude a night?

VI.

Wrapt in the darkest sable vest,
Which none save noblest Moslem wear,
To guard from winds of heaven the breast
As heaven itself to Selim dear,
With cautious steps the thicket threading,
And starting oft, as through the glade
The gust its hollow moanings made;
Till on the smoother pathway treading,
More free her timid bosom beat,
The maid pursued her silent guide;
And though her terror urged retreat,
How could she quit her Selim's side?
How teach her tender lips to chide?

VII.

They reach'd at length a grotto, hewn
By nature, but enlarged by art,
Where oft her lute she wont to tune,
And oft her Koran conn'd apart:
And oft in youthful reverie
She dream'd what Paradise might be;
Where woman's parted soul shall go
Her Prophet had disdain'd to show;
But Selim's mansion was secure,
Nor deem'd she, could he long endure
His bower in other worlds of bliss,
Without *her*, most beloved in this!
Oh! who so dear with him could dwell?
What Houri soothe him half so well?

VIII.

Since last she visited the spot
Some change seem'd wrought within the grot:
It might be only that the night
Disguised things seen by better light:
That brazen lamp but dimly threw
A ray of no celestial hue;
But in a nook within the cell
Her eye on stranger objects fell.

There arms were piled, not such as wield
The turban'd Delis in the field;
But brands of foreign blade and hilt,
And one was red—perchance with guilt!
Ah! how without can blood be spilt?
A cup too on the board was set
That did not seem to hold sherbet.
What may this mean? she turn'd to see
Her Selim—"Oh! can this be he?"

IX.

His robe of pride was thrown aside,
His brow no high-crown'd turban bore,
But in its stead a shawl of red,
Wreathed lightly round, his temples wore:
That dagger, on whose hilt the gem
Were worthy of a diadem,
No longer glitter'd at his waist,
Where pistols unadorn'd were braced;
And from his belt a sabre swung,
And from his shoulder loosely hung
The cloak of white, the thin capote
That decks the wandering Candiote:
Beneath—his golden plated vest
Clung like a cuirass to his breast;
The greaves below his knee that wound
With silvery scales were sheathed and bound.
But were it not that high command
Spake in his eye, and tone, and hand,
All that a careless eye could see
In him was some young Galiongée.[28]

X.

"I said I was not what I seem'd;
And now thou seest my words were true:
I have a tale thou hast not dream'd,
If sooth—its truth must others rue.
My story now 'twere vain to hide,
I must not see thee Osman's bride:
But had not thine own lips declared
How much of that young heart I shared,
I could not, must not, yet have shown
The darker secret of my own.
In this I speak not now of love;
That, let time, truth, and peril prove:
But first—Oh! never wed another—
Zuleika! I am not thy brother!"

XI.

"Oh! not my brother!—yet unsay—
God! am I left alone on earth
To mourn—I dare not curse—the day
That saw my solitary birth?
Oh! thou wilt love me now no more!
My sinking heart foreboded ill;
But know *me* all I was before,
Thy sister—friend—Zuleika still.
Thou ledd'st me here perchance to kill;
If thou hast cause for vengeance, see
My breast is offer'd—take thy fill!
Far better with the dead to be
Than live thus nothing now to thee;
Perhaps far worse, for now I know
Why Giaffir always seem'd thy foe;
And I, alas! am Giaffir's child,
For whom thou wert contemn'd, reviled.
If not thy sister—would'st thou save
My life, oh! bid me be thy slave!"

XII.

"My slave, Zuleika!—nay, I'm thine:
But, gentle love, this transport calm,
Thy lot shall yet be link'd with mine;
I swear it by our Prophet's shrine,
And be that thought thy sorrow's balm.
So may the Koran verse display'd[29]
Upon its steel direct my blade,
In danger's hour to guard us both,
As I preserve that awful oath!
The name in which thy heart hath prided
Must change; but, my Zuleika, know,
That tie is widen'd, not divided,
Although thy Sire's my deadliest foe.
My father was to Giaffir all
That Selim late was deem'd to thee;
That brother wrought a brother's fall,
But spared, at least, my infancy;
And lull'd me with a vain deceit
That yet a like return may meet.
He rear'd me, not with tender help,
But like the nephew of a Cain;[30]
He watch'd me like a lion's whelp,
That gnaws and yet may break his chain.
My father's blood in every vein
Is boiling; but for thy dear sake
No present vengeance will I take;
Though here I must no more remain.
But first, beloved Zuleika! hear
How Giaffir wrought this deed of fear.

XIII.

"How first their strife to rancour grew,
If love or envy made them foes,
It matters little if I knew;
In fiery spirits, slights, though few
And thoughtless, will disturb repose.
In war Abdallah's arm was strong,
Remember'd yet in Bosniac song,
And Paswan's rebel hordes attest[31]
How little love they bore such guest:
His death is all I need relate,
The stern effect of Giaffir's hate;
And how my birth disclosed to me.
Whate'er beside it makes, hath made me free.

XIV.

"When Paswan, after years of strife,
At last for power, but first for life,

In Widdin's walls too proudly sate,
Our Pachas rallied round the state;
Nor last nor least in high command,
Each brother led a separate band;
They gave their horsetails to the wind,[32]
And mustering in Sophia's plain
Their tents were pitch'd, their posts assign'd;
To one, alas! assign'd in vain!
What need of words? the deadly bowl,
By Giaffir's order drugged and given,
With venom subtle as his soul,
Dismiss'd Abdallah's hence to heaven.
Reclined and feverish in the bath,
He, when the hunter's sport was up,
But little deem'd a brother's wrath
To quench his thirst had such a cup:
The bowl a bribed attendant bore;
He drank one draught, nor needed more![33]
If thou my tale, Zuleika, doubt,
Call Haroun—he can tell it out.

XV.

"The deed once done, and Paswan's feud
In part suppress'd, though ne'er subdued,
Abdallah's Pachalick was gain'd:—
Thou know'st not what in our Divan
Can wealth procure for worse than man—
Abdallah's honours were obtain'd
By him a brother's murder stain'd;
'T is true, the purchase nearly drain'd
His ill got treasure, soon replaced.
Would'st question whence? Survey the waste,
And ask the squalid peasant how
His gains repay his broiling brow!—
Why me the stern usurper spared,
Why thus with me his palace shared,
I know not. Shame, regret, remorse,
And little fear from infant's force;
Besides, adoption as a son
By him whom Heaven accorded none,
Or some unknown cabal, caprice,
Preserved me thus; but not in peace:
He cannot curb his haughty mood,
Nor I forgive a father's blood!

XVI.

"Within thy father's house are foes;
Not all who break his bread are true:
To these should I my birth disclose,
His days, his very hours, were few:
They only want a heart to lead,
A hand to point them to the deed.
But Haroun only knows—or knew—
This tale, whose close is almost nigh:
He in Abdallah's palace grew,
And held that post in his Serai
Which holds he here—he saw him die:
But what could single slavery do?
Avenge his lord? alas! too late;
Or save his son from such a fate?
He chose the last, and when elate
With foes subdued, or friends betray'd,
Proud Giaffir in high triumph sate,
He led me helpless to his gate,
And not in vain it seems essay'd
To save the life for which he pray'd.
The knowledge of my birth secured
From all and each, but most from me;
Thus Giaffir's safety was insured.
Removed he too from Roumelie
To this our Asiatic side,
Far from our seats by Danube's tide,
With none but Haroun, who retains
Such knowledge—and that Nubian feels
A tyrant's secrets are but chains,
From which the captive gladly steals,
And this and more to me reveals:
Such still to guilt just Alla sends—
Slaves, tools, accomplices—no friends!

XVII.

"All this, Zuleika, harshly sounds;
But harsher still my tale must be:
Howe'er my tongue thy softness wounds,
Yet I must prove all truth to thee.
I saw thee start this garb to see,
Yet is it one I oft have worn,
And long must wear: this Galiongée,
To whom thy plighted vow is sworn,
Is leader of those pirate hordes,
Whose laws and lives are on their swords;
To hear whose desolating tale
Would make thy waning cheek more pale:
Those arms thou seest my band have brought,
The hands that wield are not remote;
This cup too for the rugged knaves
Is fill'd—once quaff'd, they ne'er repine:
Our Prophet might forgive the slaves;
They 're only infidels in wine!

XVIII.

"What could I be? Proscribed at home,
And taunted to a wish to roam;
And listless left—for Giaffir's fear
Denied the courser and the spear—
Though oft—Oh, Mahomet! how oft!—
In full Divan the despot scoff'd,
As if *my* weak unwilling hand
Refused the bridle or the brand:
He ever went to war alone,
And pent me here untried—unknown;
To Haroun's care with women left,
By hope unblest, of fame bereft.
While thou—whose softness long endear'd,
Though it unmann'd me, still had cheer'd—

To Brusa's walls for safety sent,
Awaited'st there the field's event.
Haroun, who saw my spirit pining
 Beneath inaction's sluggish yoke,
His captive, though with dread, resigning,
 My thraldom for a season broke,
On promise to return before
The day when Giaffir's charge was o'er.

"'T is vain—my tongue can not impart
My almost drunkenness of heart,
When first this liberated eye
Survey'd Earth, Ocean, Sun, and Sky,
As if my spirit pierced them through,
And all their inmost wonders knew!
One word alone can paint to thee
That more than feeling—I was Free!
Ev'n for thy presence ceased to pine;
The World—nay—Heaven itself was mine!

XIX.

"The shallop of a trusty Moor
Convey'd me from this idle shore;
I long'd to see the isles that gem
Old Ocean's purple diadem:
I sought by turns, and saw them all;[34]
 But when and where I join'd the crew,
With whom I'm pledged to rise or fall,
 When all that we design to do
Is done, 't will then be time more meet
To tell thee, when the tale's complete.

XX.

"'T is true, they are a lawless brood,
But rough in form, nor mild in mood;
And every creed, and every race,
With them hath found—may find—a place:
But open speech, and ready hand,
Obedience to their chief's command;
A soul for every enterprise,
That never sees with terror's eyes;
Friendship for each, and faith to all,
And vengeance vow'd for those who fall,
Have made them fitting instruments
For more than ev'n my own intents.
And some—and I have studied all
 Distinguish'd from the vulgar rank,
But chiefly to my council call
 The wisdom of the cautious Frank—
And some to higher thoughts aspire,
 The last of Lambro's patriots there[35]
 Anticipated freedom share;
And oft around the cavern fire
On visionary schemes debate,
To snatch the Rayahs from their fate.[36]
So let them ease their hearts with prate
Of equal rights, which man ne'er knew:
I have a love for freedom too.
Ay! let me like the ocean-Patriarch roam,[37]
Or only know on land the Tartar's home![38]
My tent on shore, my galley on the sea,
Are more than cities and Serais to me:
Borne by my steed, or wafted by my sail,
Across the desert, or before the gale,
Bound where thou wilt, my barb! or glide, my prow
But be the star that guides the wanderer, Thou!
Thou, my Zuleika, share and bless my bark;
The Dove of peace and promise to mine ark!
Or, since that hope denied in worlds of strife,
Be thou the rainbow to the storms of life!
The evening beam that smiles the clouds away,
And tints to-morrow with prophetic ray!
Blest—as the Muezzin's strain from Mecca's wall
To pilgrims pure and prostrate at his call;
Soft—as the melody of youthful days,
That steals the trembling tear of speechless praise;
Dear—as his native song to Exile's ears,
Shall sound each tone thy long-loved voice endears.
For thee in those bright isles is built a bower
Blooming as Aden in its earliest hour.[39]
A thousand swords, with Selim's heart and hand,
Wait—wave—defend—destroy—at thy command!
Girt by my band, Zuleika at my side,
The spoil of nations shall bedeck my bride.
The Haram's languid years of listless ease
Are well resign'd for cares—for joys like these:
Not blind to fate, I see, where'er I rove,
Unnumber'd perils—but one only love!
Yet well my toils shall that fond breast repay,
Though fortune frown, or falser friends betray.
How dear the dream in darkest hours of ill,
Should all be changed, to find thee faithful still!
Be but thy soul, like Selim's, firmly shown;
To thee be Selim's tender as thine own;
To soothe each sorrow, share in each delight,
Blend every thought, do all—but disunite!
Once free, 't is mine our horde again to guide;
Friends to each other, foes to aught beside:
Yet there we follow but the bent assign'd
By fatal Nature to man's warring kind:
Mark! where his carnage and his conquests cease!
He makes a solitude, and calls it—peace!
I like the rest must use my skill or strength,
But ask no land beyond my sabre's length:
Power sways but by division—her resource
The blest alternative of fraud or force!
Ours be the last; in time deceit may come
When cities cage us in a social home:
There ev'n thy soul might err—how oft the heart
Corruption shakes which peril could not part!
And woman, more than man, when death or woe,
Or even Disgrace, would lay her lover low,
Sunk in the lap of Luxury will shame—
Away Suspicion!—*not* Zuleika's name!
But life is hazard at the best; and here
No more remains to win, and much to fear:

Yes, fear!—the doubt, the dread of losing thee,
By Osman's power, and Giaffir's stern decree.
That dread shall vanish with the favouring gale,
Which love to-night hath promised to my sail:
No danger daunts the pair his smile hath blest,
Their steps still roving, but their hearts at rest.
With thee all toils are sweet, each clime hath charms;
Earth—sea alike—our world within our arms!

Ay—let the loud winds whistle o'er the deck,
So that those arms cling closer round my neck:
The deepest murmur of this lip shall be
No sigh for safety, but a prayer for thee!
The war of elements no fears impart
To Love, whose deadliest bane is human Art:
There lie the only rocks our course can check;
Here moments menace—*there* are years of wreck!
But hence ye thoughts that rise in Horror's shape!
This hour bestows, or ever bars escape.
Few words remain of mine my tale to close:
Of thine but *one* to waft us from our foes;
Yea—foes—to me will Giaffir's hate decline?
And is not Osman, who would part us, thine?

XXI.

"His head and faith from doubt and death
Return'd in time my guard to save;
Few heard, none told, that o'er the wave
From isle to isle I roved the while:
And since, though parted from my band,
Too seldom now I leave the land,
No deed they've done, nor deed shall do,
Ere I have heard and doom'd it too:
I form the plan, decree the spoil,
'T is fit I oftener share the toil.
But now too long I've held thine ear;
Time presses, floats my bark, and here
We leave behind but hate and fear.
To-morrow Osman with his train
Arrives—to-night must break thy chain:
And would'st thou save that haughty Bey,
Perchance, *his* life who gave thee thine,
With me this hour away—away!
But yet, though thou art plighted mine,
Would'st thou recall thy willing vow,
Appall'd by truths imparted now,
Here rest I—not to see thee wed:
But be that peril on *my* head!"

XXII.

Zuleika, mute and motionless,
Stood like that statue of distress,
When, her last hope for ever gone,
The mother harden'd into stone;
All in the maid that eye could see
Was but a younger Niobé.
But ere her lip, or even her eye,
Essay'd to speak, or look reply,
Beneath the garden's wicket porch
Far flash'd on high a blazing torch!
Another—and another—and another—
"Oh! fly—no more—yet now my more than brother!"
Far, wide, through every thicket spread,
The fearful lights are gleaming red;
Nor these alone—for each right hand
Is ready with a sheathless brand.
They part, pursue, return, and wheel
With searching flambeau, shining steel;
And last of all, his sabre waving,
Stern Giaffir in his fury raving:
And now almost they touch the cave—
Oh! must that grot be Selim's grave?

XXIII.

Dauntless he stood—"'T is come—soon past—
One kiss, Zuleika—'t is my last:
But yet my band not far from shore
May hear this signal, see the flash;
Yet now too few—the attempt were rash:
No matter—yet one effort more."
Forth to the cavern mouth he stept;
His pistol's echo rang on high,
Zuleika started not, nor wept,
Despair benumb'd her breast and eye!—
"They hear me not, or if they ply
Their oars, 't is but to see me die;
That sound hath drawn my foes more nigh.
Then forth my father's scimitar,
Thou ne'er hast seen less equal war!
Farewell, Zuleika!—Sweet! retire:
Yet stay within—here linger safe,
At thee his rage will only chafe.
Stir not—lest even to thee perchance
Some erring blade or ball should glance.
Fear'st thou for him?—may I expire
If in this strife I seek thy sire!
No—though by him that poison pour'd:
No—though again he call me coward!
But tamely shall I meet their steel?
No—as each crest save *his* may feel!"

XXIV.

One bound he made, and gain'd the sand:
Already at his feet hath sunk
The foremost of the prying band,
A gasping head, a quivering trunk:
Another falls—but round him close
A swarming circle of his foes;
From right to left his path he cleft,
And almost met the meeting wave:
His boat appears—not five oars' length—
His comrades strain with desperate strength—
Oh! are they yet in time to save?
His feet the foremost breakers lave;
His band are plunging in the bay,
Their sabres glitter through the spray;
Wet—wild—unwearied to the strand
They struggle—now they touch the land!
They come—'t is but to add to slaughter—
His heart's best blood is on the water!

XXV.

Escaped from shot, unharm'd by steel,
Or scarcely grazed its force to feel,

Had Selim won, betray'd, beset,
To where the strand and billows met:
There as his last step left the land,
And the last death-blow dealt his hand—
Ah! wherefore did he turn to look
For her his eye but sought in vain?
That pause, that fatal gaze he took,
Hath doom'd his death, or fix'd his chain.
Sad proof, in peril and in pain,
How late will Lover's hope remain!
His back was to the dashing spray;
Behind, but close, his comrades lay,
When, at the instant, hiss'd the ball—
"So may the foes of Giaffir fall!"
Whose voice is heard? whose carbine rang?
Whose bullet through the night-air sang,
Too nearly, deadly aim'd to err?
'T is thine—Abdallah's Murderer!

The father slowly rued thy hate,
The son hath found a quicker fate:
Fast from his breast the blood is bubbling,
The whiteness of the sea-foam troubling—
If aught his lips essay'd to groan,
The rushing billows choked the tone!

XXVI.

Morn slowly rolls the clouds away;
Few trophies of the fight are there:
The shouts that shook the midnight-bay
Are silent; but some signs of fray
That strand of strife may bear,
And fragments of each shiver'd brand;
Steps stamp'd; and dash'd into the sand
The print of many a struggling hand
May there be mark'd; nor far remote
A broken torch, an oarless boat;
And tangled on the weeds that heap
The beach where shelving to the deep
There lies a white capote!
'T is rent in twain—one dark-red stain
The wave yet ripples o'er in vain:
But where is he who wore?
Ye! who would o'er his relics weep,
Go, seek them where the surges sweep
Their burthen round Sigæum's steep,
And cast on Lemnos' shore:
The sea-birds shriek above the prey,
O'er which their hungry beaks delay,
As shaken on his restless pillow,
His head heaves with the heaving billow;
That hand, whose motion is not life,
Yet feebly seems to menace strife,
Flung by the tossing tide on high,
Then levell'd with the wave—
What recks it, though that corse shall lie
Within a living grave?
The bird that tears that prostrate form
Hath only robb'd the meaner worm;
The only heart, the only eye
Had bled or wept to see him die,
Had seen those scatter'd limbs composed,
And mourn'd above his turban-stone,[40]
That heart hath burst—that eye was closed—
Yea—closed before his own!

XXVII.

By Helle's stream there is a voice of wail!
And woman's eye is wet—man's cheek is pale:
Zuleika! last of Giaffir's race,
Thy destined lord is come too late:
He sees not—ne'er shall see—thy face!
Can he not hear
The loud Wul-wulleh warn his distant ear?[41]
Thy handmaids weeping at the gate,
The Koran-chanters of the hymn of fate,
The silent slaves with folded arms that wait,
Sighs in the hall, and shrieks upon the gale.
Tell him thy tale!
Thou didst not view thy Selim fall!
That fearful moment when he left the cave
Thy heart grew chill:
He was thy hope—thy joy—thy love—thine all—
And that last thought on him thou could'st not save
Sufficed to kill;
Burst forth in one wild cry—and all was still.
Peace to thy broken heart, and virgin grave!
Ah! happy! but of life to lose the worst!
That grief—though deep—though fatal—was thy first!
Thrice happy! ne'er to feel nor fear the force
Of absence, shame, pride, hate, revenge, remorse!
And, oh! that pang where more than madness lies!
The worm that will not sleep—and never dies;
Thought of the gloomy day and ghastly night,
That dreads the darkness, and yet loathes the light,
That winds around, and tears the quivering heart!
Ah! wherefore not consume it—and depart!
Woe to thee, rash and unrelenting chief!
Vainly thou heap'st the dust upon thy head,
Vainly the sackcloth o'er thy limbs doth spread;
By that same hand Abdallah—Selim—bled.
Now let it tear thy beard in idle grief:
Thy pride of heart, thy bride for Osman's bed,
She, whom thy sultan had but seen to wed,
Thy Daughter's dead!
Hope of thine age, thy twilight's lonely beam,
The Star hath set that shone on Helle's stream.
What quench'd its ray?—the blood that thou hast shed!
Hark! to the hurried question of Despair:
"Where is my child?"—an Echo answers—"Where?"[42]

XXVIII.

Within the place of thousand tombs
That shine beneath, while dark above
The sad but living cypress glooms,
And withers not, though branch and leaf
Are stamp'd with an eternal grief,
Like early unrequited Love,
One spot exists, which ever blooms,
Ev'n in that deadly grove—
A single rose is shedding there
Its lonely lustre, meek and pale:
It looks as planted by Despair—
So white—so faint—the slightest gale
Might whirl the leaves on high;
And yet, though storms and blight assail,
And hands more rude than wintry sky
May wring it from the stem—in vain—
To-morrow sees it bloom again!
The stalk some spirit gently rears,
And waters with celestial tears;

For well may maids of Helle deem
That this can be no earthly flower,
Which mocks the tempest's withering hour,
And buds unshelter'd by a bower;
Nor droops, though spring refuse her shower,
Nor woos the summer beam:
To it the livelong night there sings
A bird unseen—but not remote:
Invisible his airy wings,
But soft as harp that Houri strings
His long entrancing note!
It were the Bulbul; but his throat,
Though mournful, pours not such a strain:
For they who listen cannot leave
The spot, but linger there and grieve,
As if they loved in vain!
And yet so sweet the tears they shed,
'T is sorrow so unmix'd with dread,
They scarce can bear the morn to break
That melancholy spell,
And longer yet would weep and wake,
He sings so wild and well!
But when the day-blush bursts from high
Expires that magic melody.
And some have been who could believe,
(So fondly youthful dreams deceive,
Yet harsh be they that blame,)
That note so piercing and profound
Will shape and syllable its sound
Into Zuleika's name. [43]
'Tis from her cypress' summit heard,
That melts in air the liquid word;
'T is from her lowly virgin earth
That white rose takes its tender birth.
There late was laid a marble stone;
Eve saw it placed—the Morrow gone!
It was no mortal arm that bore
That deep-fixed pillar to the shore;
For there, as Helle's legends tell,
Next morn 't was found where Selim fell;
Lash'd by the tumbling tide, whose wave
Denied his bones a holier grave:
And there by night, reclined, 't is said,
Is seen a ghastly turban'd head:
And hence extended by the billow,
'Tis named the "Pirate-phantom's pillow!"
Where first it lay that mourning flower
Hath flourish'd; flourisheth this hour,
Alone and dewy, coldly pure and pale;
As weeping Beauty's cheek at Sorrow's tale!

NOTES TO THE BRIDE OF ABYDOS.

NOTE 1, page 72.

Wax faint o'er the gardens of Gúl in her bloom.

"Gúl," the rose.

NOTE 2, page 73.

Can he smile on such deeds as his children have done?

"Souls made of fire, and children of the Sun,
With whom Revenge is Virtue."
YOUNG'S REVENGE.

NOTE 3, page 74.

With Mejnoun's tale, or Sadi's song.

Mejnoun and Leila, the Romeo and Juliet of the East. Sadi, the moral poet of Persia.

NOTE 4, page 74.

Till I, who heard the deep Tambour.

Tambour, Turkish drum, which sounds at sunrise, noon, and twilight.

NOTE 5, page 74.

He is an Arab to my sight.

The Turks abhor the Arabs (who return the compliment a hundred-fold) even more than they hate the Christians.

NOTE 6, page 75.

The mind, the Music breathing from her face.

This expression has met with objections. I will not refer to "Him who hath not Music in his soul," but merely request the reader to recollect, for ten seconds, the features of the woman whom he believes to be the most beautiful; and if he then does not comprehend fully what is feebly expressed in the above line, I shall be sorry for us both. For an eloquent passage in the latest work of the first female writer of this, perhaps, of any age, on the analogy (and the immediate comparison excited by that analogy) between "painting and music," see vol. iii. cap. 10, "De L'Allemagne." And is not this connection still stronger with the original than the copy? With the colouring of Nature than of Art? After all, this is rather to be felt than described; still, I think there are some who will understand it, at least they would have done had they beheld the countenance whose speaking harmony suggested the idea; for this passage is not drawn from imagination but memory, that mirror which Affliction dashes to the earth, and looking down upon the fragments, only beholds the reflection multiplied!

NOTE 7, page 75.

But yet the line of Carasman.

Carasman Oglou, or Kara Osman Oglou, is the principal landholder in Turkey; he governs Magnesia. Those who, by a kind of feudal tenure, possess land on condition of service, are called Timariots; they serve as Spahis, according to the extent of territory, and bring a certain number into the field, generally cavalry.

NOTE 8, page 75.

And teach the messenger what fate.

When a Pacha is sufficiently strong to resist, the single messenger, who is always the first bearer of the order for

his death, is strangled instead, and sometimes five or six, one after the other, on the same errand, by command of the refractory patient; if, on the contrary, he is weak or loyal, he bows, kisses the Sultan's respectable signature, and is bowstrung with great complacency. In 1810, several of "these presents" were exhibited in the niche of the Seraglio gate; among others, the head of the Pacha of Bagdat, a brave young man, cut off by treachery, after a desperate resistance.

NOTE 9, page 75.

Thrice clapp'd his hands, and call'd his steed.

Clapping of the hands calls the servants. The Turks hate a superfluous expenditure of voice, and they have no bells.

NOTE 10, page 75.

Resign'd his gem-adorned Chibouque.

Chibouque, the Turkish pipe, of which the amber mouth-piece, and sometimes the ball which contains the leaf, is adorned with precious stones, if in possession of the wealthier orders.

NOTE 11, page 75.

With Maugrabee and Mamaluke.

Maugrabee, Moorish Mercenaries.

NOTE 12, page 75.

His way amid his Delis took.

Deli, bravos who form the forlorn-hope of the cavalry, and always begin the action.

NOTE 13, page 75.

Careering cleave the folded felt.

A twisted fold of *felt* is used for scimitar practice by the Turks, and few but Mussulman arms can cut through it at a single stroke: sometimes a tough turban is used for the same purpose. The jerreed is a game of blunt javelins, animated and graceful.

NOTE 14, page 75.

Nor heard their Ollahs wild and loud.

"Ollahs," Alla il Allah, the "Leilies," as the Spanish poets call them; the sound is Ollah; a cry of which the Turks, for a silent people, are somewhat profuse, particularly during the jerreed, or in the chase, but mostly in battle. Their animation in the field, and gravity in the chamber, with their pipes and comboloios, form an amusing contrast.

NOTE 15, page 76.

The Persian Atar-gúl's perfume.

"Atar-gúl," ottar of roses. The Persian is the finest.

NOTE 16, page 76.

The pictured roof and marble floor.

The ceiling and wainscots, or rather walls, of the Mussulman apartments are generally painted, in great houses, with one eternal and highly-coloured view of Constantinople, wherein the principal feature is a noble contempt of perspective; below, arms, scimitars, &c., are in general fancifully and not inelegantly disposed.

NOTE 17, page 77.

A message from the Bulbul bears.

It has been much doubted whether the notes of this "Lover of the rose" are sad or merry; and Mr. Fox's remarks on the subject have provoked some learned controversy as to the opinions of the ancients on the subject. I dare not venture a conjecture on the point, though a little inclined to the "errare mallem," &c., *if* Mr. Fox *was* mistaken.

17

NOTE 18, page 78.

Even Azrael from his deadly quiver.

"Azrael," the angel of death.

NOTE 19, page 78.

Within the caves of Istakar.

The treasures of the Pre-adamite Sultans. See D'Herbelot, article *Istakar.*

NOTE 20, page 78.

Holds not a Musselim's control.

Musselim, a governor, the next in rank after a Pacha; a Waywode is the third; and then come the Agas.

NOTE 21, page 78.

Was he not bred in Egripo?

Egripo—the Negropont. According to the proverb, the Turks of Egripo, the Jews of Salonica, and the Greeks of Athens, are the worst of their respective races.

NOTE 22, page 79.

Ah! yonder see the Tchocadar.

"Tchocadar," one of the attendants who precedes a man of authority.

NOTE 23, page 80.

Thine own "broad Hellespont" still dashes.

The wrangling about this epithet, "the broad Hellespont," or the "boundless Hellespont," whether it means one or the other, or what it means at all, has been beyond all possibility of detail. I have even heard it disputed on the spot; and not foreseeing a speedy conclusion to the controversy, amused myself with swimming across it in the mean time, and probably may again, before the point is settled. Indeed, the question as to the truth of "the tale of Troy divine" still continues, much of it resting upon the talismanic word "απειρος:" probably Homer had the same notion of distance that a coquette has of time, and when he talks of boundless, means half a mile; as the latter, by a like figure, when she says *eternal* attachment, simply specifies three weeks.

NOTE 24, page 80.

Which Ammon's son ran proudly round.

Before his Persian invasion, and crowned the altar with laurel, &c. He was afterwards imitated by Caracalla in his race. It is believed that the last also poisoned a friend, named Festus, for the sake of new Patroclan games. I have seen the sheep feeding on the tombs of Æsietes and Antilochus: the first is in the centre of the plain.

NOTE 25, page 80.

O'er which her fairy fingers ran.

When rubbed, the amber is susceptible of a perfume, which is slight but not disagreeable.

NOTE 26, page 80.

Her mother's sainted amulet.

The belief in amulets engraved on gems, or enclosed in gold boxes, containing scraps from the Koran, worn round the neck, wrist, or arm, is still universal in the East. The Koorsee (throne) verse in the second cap. of the Koran describes the attributes of the Most High, and is engraved in this manner, and worn by the pious, as the most esteemed and sublime of all sentences.

NOTE 27, page 80.

And by her Comboloio lies.

"Comboloio"—a Turkish rosary. The MSS., particularly those of the Persians, are richly adorned and illuminated. The Greek females are kept in utter ignorance;

but many of the Turkish girls are highly accomplished, though not actually qualified for a Christian coterie. Perhaps some of our own "*blues*" might not be the worse for *bleaching*.

NOTE 28, page 81.

In him was some young Galiongée.

"Galiongée"—or Galiongi, a sailor, that is, a Turkish sailor; the Greeks navigate, the Turks work the guns. Their dress is picturesque; and I have seen the Capitan Pacha more than once wearing it as a kind of *incog.* Their legs, however, are generally naked. The buskins described in the text as sheathed behind with silver are those of an Arnaut robber, who was my host (he had quitted the profession) at his Pyrgo, near Gastouni in the Morea; they were plated in scales one over the other, like the back of an armadillo.

NOTE 29, page 81.

So may the Koran verse displayed.

The characters on all Turkish scimitars contain sometimes the name of the place of their manufacture, but more generally a text from the Koran, in letters of gold. Amongst those in my possession is one with a blade of singular construction; it is very broad, and the edge notched into serpentine curves like the ripple of water, or the wavering of flame. I asked the Armenian who sold it what possible use such a figure could add: he said, in Italian, that he did not know; but the Mussulmans had an idea that those of this form gave a severer wound; and liked it because it was "piu feroce." I did not much admire the reason, but bought it for its peculiarity.

NOTE 30, page 81.

But like the nephew of a Cain.

It is to be observed, that every allusion to any thing or personage in the Old Testament, such as the Ark, or Cain, is equally the privilege of Mussulman and Jew: indeed, the former profess to be much better acquainted with the lives, true and fabulous, of the patriarchs, than is warranted by our own sacred writ; and not content with Adam, they have a biography of Pre-Adamites. Solomon is the monarch of all necromancy, and Moses a prophet inferior only to Christ and Mahomet. Zuleika is the Persian name of Potiphar's wife; and her amour with Joseph constitutes one of the finest poems in their language. It is, therefore, no violation of costume to put the names of Cain, or Noah, into the mouth of a Moslem.

NOTE 31, page 81.

And Paswan's rebel hordes attest.

Paswan Oglou, the rebel of Widdin; who, for the last years of his life, set the whole power of the Porte at defiance.

NOTE 32, page 82.

They gave their horse-tails to the wind.

"Horse-tail," the standard of a Pacha.

NOTE 33, page 82.

He drank one draught, nor needed more.

Giaffir, Pacha of Argyro Castro, or Scutari, I am not sure which, was actually taken off by the Albanian Ali, in the manner described in the text. Ali Pacha, while I was in the country, married the daughter of his victim, some years after the event had taken place at a bath in Sophia, or Adrianople. The poison was mixed in the cup of coffee, which is presented before the sherbet by the bath-keeper, after dressing.

NOTE 34, page 83.

I sought by turns, and saw them all.

The Turkish notions of almost all islands are confined to the Archipelago, the sea alluded to

NOTE 35, page 83.

The last of Lambro's patriots there.

Lambro Canzani, a Greek, famous for his efforts in 1789-90, for the independence of his country. Abandoned by the Russians, he became a pirate, and the Archipelago was the scene of his enterprises. He is said to be still alive at Petersburg. He and Riga are the two most celebrated of the Greek revolutionists.

NOTE 36, page 83.

To snatch the Rayahs from their fate.

"Rayahs,"—all who pay the capitation tax, called the "Haratch."

NOTE 37, page 83.

Ay! let me like the ocean-Patriarch roam.

This first of voyages is one of the few with which the Mussulmans profess much acquaintance.

NOTE 38, page 83.

Or only know on land the Tartar's home.

The wandering life of the Arabs, Tartars, and Turkomans, will be found well detailed in any book of Eastern travels. That it possesses a charm peculiar to itself, cannot be denied. A young French renegado confessed to Chateaubriand, that he never found himself alone, galloping in the desert, without a sensation approaching to rapture, which was indescribable.

NOTE 39, page 83.

Blooming as Aden in its earliest hour.

"Jannat al Aden," the perpetual abode, the Mussulman paradise.

NOTE 40, page 87.

And mourn'd above his turban-stone.

A turban is carved in stone above the graves of *men* only.

NOTE 41, page 87.

The loud Wul-wulleh warn his distant ear.

The death-song of the Turkish women. The "silent slaves" are the men, whose notions of decorum forbid complaint in *public*.

NOTE 42, page 87.

"Where is my child?"—an Echo answers—"Where?"

"I came to the place of my birth and cried, 'The friends of my youth, where are they?' and an Echo answered, 'Where are they?'"—*From an Arabic MS.*

The above quotation (from which the idea in the text is taken) must be already familiar to every reader—it is given in the first annotation, p. 67, of "The Pleasures of Memory;" a poem so well known as to render a reference almost superfluous; but to whose pages all will be delighted to recur.

NOTE 43, page 88.

Into Zuleika's name.

"And airy tongues that *syllable* men's names." — MILTON.

For a belief that the souls of the dead inhabit the form of birds, we need not travel to the East. Lord Lyttleton's ghost story, the belief of the Duchess of Kendal, that George I. flew into her window in the shape of a raven (see Orford's "Reminiscences"), and many other instances, bring this superstition nearer home. The most singular was the whim of a Worcester lady, who, believing her daughter to exist in the shape of a singing bird, literally furnished her pew in the cathedral with cages-full of the kind; and as she was rich, and a benefactress in beautifying the church, no objection was made to her harmless folly.—For this anecdote, see Orford's "Letters."

THE SIEGE OF CORINTH.

TO

JOHN HOBHOUSE, ESQUIRE,

THIS POEM IS INSCRIBED,

BY HIS

FRIEND.

JANUARY 22, 1816.

ADVERTISEMENT.

"THE grand army of the Turks (in 1715), under the Prime Vizier, to open to themselves a way into the heart of the Morea, and to form the siege of Napoli di Romania, the most considerable place in all that country,[1] thought it best in the first place to attack Corinth, upon which they made several storms. The garrison being weakened, and the governor seeing it was impossible to hold out against so mighty a force, thought it fit to beat a parley: but while they were treating about the articles, one of the magazines in the Turkish army, wherein they had six hundred barrels of powder, blew up by accident, whereby six or seven hundred men were killed; which so enraged the infidels, that they would not grant any capitulation, but stormed the place with so much fury, that they took it, and put most of the garrison, with Signior Minotti, the governor, to the sword. The rest, with Antonio Bembo, proveditor extraordinary, were made prisoners of war."—*History of the Turks*, vol. iii., p. 151.

THE SIEGE OF CORINTH.

I.

MANY a vanish'd year and age,
And tempest's breath, and battle's rage,
Have swept o'er Corinth; yet she stands
A fortress form'd to Freedom's hands.
The whirlwind's wrath, the earthquake's shock
Have left untouch'd her hoary rock,
The keystone of a land, which still,
Though fall'n, looks proudly on that hill,
The landmark to the double tide
That purpling rolls on either side,
As if their waters chafed to meet,
Yet pause and crouch beneath her feet.
But could the blood before her shed
Since first Timoleon's brother bled,
Or baffled Persia's despot fled,
Arise from out the earth which drank
The stream of slaughter as it sank,
That sanguine ocean would o'erflow
Her isthmus idly spread below:
Or could the bones of all the slain,
Who perish'd there, be piled again,
That rival pyramid would rise
More mountain-like, through those clear skies,
Than yon tower-capp'd Acropolis,
Which seems the very clouds to kiss.

II.

On dun Cithæron's ridge appears
The gleam of twice ten thousand spears;
And downward to the Isthmian plain,
From shore to shore of either main,
The tent is pitch'd, the crescent shines
Along the Moslem's leaguering lines;
And the dusk Spahi's bands advance
Beneath each bearded pacha's glance;
And far and wide as eye can reach
The turban'd cohorts throng the beach;
And there the Arab's camel kneels,
And there his steed the Tartar wheels;
The Turcoman hath left his herd,[2]
The sabre round his loins to gird;
And there the volleying thunders pour,
Till waves grow smoother to the roar.
The trench is dug, the cannon's breath
Wings the far hissing globe of death;
Fast whirl the fragments from the wall,
Which crumbles with the ponderous ball;
And from that wall the foe replies,
O'er dusty plain and smoky skies,
With fires that answer fast and well
The summons of the Infidel.

III.

But near and nearest to the wall
Of those who wish and work its fall,
With deeper skill in war's black art
Than Othman's sons, and high of heart
As any chief that ever stood
Triumphant in the fields of blood;
From post to post, and deed to deed,
Fast spurring on his reeking steed,
Where sallying ranks the trench assail,
And make the foremost Moslem quail;
Or where the battery, guarded well,
Remains as yet impregnable,
Alighting cheerly to inspire
The soldier slackening in his fire;
The first and freshest of the host
Which Stamboul's sultan there can boast,
To guide the follower o'er the field,
To point the tube, the lance to wield,
Or whirl around the bickering blade;—
Was Alp, the Adrian renegade!

IV.

From Venice—once a race of worth
His gentle sires—he drew his birth;
But late an exile from her shore,
Against his countrymen he bore
The arms they taught to bear; and now
The turban girt his shaven brow.
Through many a change had Corinth pass'd
With Greece to Venice' rule at last;
And here, before her walls, with those
To Greece and Venice equal foes,
He stood a foe, with all the zeal
Which young and fiery converts feel,
Within whose heated bosom throngs
The memory of a thousand wrongs.
To him had Venice ceased to be
Her ancient civic boast—"the Free;"
And in the palace of St. Mark
Unnamed accusers in the dark
Within the "Lion's mouth" had placed
A charge against him uneffaced:
He fled in time, and saved his life,
To waste his future years in strife,
That taught his land how great her loss
In him who triumph'd o'er the Cross,
'Gainst which he rear'd the Crescent high,
And battled to avenge or die.

V.

Coumourgi—he whose closing scene[3]
Adorn'd the triumph of Eugene,
When on Carlowitz' bloody plain,
The last and mightiest of the slain,
He sank, regretting not to die,
But cursed the Christian's victory
Coumourgi—can his glory cease,
That latest conqueror of Greece,
Till Christian hands to Greece restore
The freedom Venice gave of yore?
A hundred years have roll'd away
Since he refix'd the Moslem's sway,
And now he led the Mussulman,
And gave the guidance of the van
To Alp, who well repaid the trust
By cities levell'd with the dust;
And proved, by many a deed of death,
How firm his heart in novel faith.

VI.

The walls grew weak; and fast and hot
Against them pour'd the ceaseless shot,
With unabating fury sent
From battery to battlement;
And thunder-like the pealing din
Rose from each heated culverin;
And here and there some crackling dome
Was fired before the exploding bomb:
And as the fabric sank beneath
The shattering shell's volcanic breath,
In red and wreathing columns flash'd
The flame, as loud the ruin crash'd,
Or into countless meteors driven,
Its earth-stars melted into heaven;
Whose clouds that day grew doubly dun,
Impervious to the hidden sun,
With volumed smoke that slowly grew
To one wide sky of sulphurous hue.

VII.

But not for vengeance, long delay'd,
Alone, did Alp, the renegade,
The Moslem warriors sternly teach
His skill to pierce the promised breach.
Within those walls a maid was pent
His hope would win, without consent
Of that inexorable sire,
Whose heart refused him in its ire,
When Alp, beneath his Christian name,
Her virgin hand aspired to claim.
In happier mood, and earlier time,
While unimpeach'd for traitorous crime,
Gayest in Gondola or hall,

He glitter'd through the Carnival;
And tuned the softest serenade
That e'er on Adria's waters play'd
At midnight to Italian maid.

VIII.

And many deem'd her heart was won;
For sought by numbers, given to none,
Had young Francesca's hand remain'd
Still by the church's bonds unchain'd:
And when the Adriatic bore
Lanciotto to the Paynim shore,
Her wonted smiles were seen to fail,
And pensive wax'd the maid and pale;
More constant at confessional,
More rare at masque and festival;
Or seen at such, with downcast eyes,
Which conquer'd hearts they ceased to prize:
With listless look she seems to gaze;
With humbler care her form arrays;
Her voice less lively in the song;
Her step, though light, less fleet among
The pairs, on whom the Morning's glance
Breaks, yet unsated with the dance.

IX.

Sent by the state to guard the land,
(Which, wrested from the Moslem's hand,
While Sobieski tamed his pride
By Buda's wall and Danube's side,
The chiefs of Venice wrung away
From Patra to Eubœa's bay,)
Minotti held in Corinth's towers
The Doge's delegated powers,
While yet the pitying eye of Peace
Smiled o'er her long-forgotten Greece:
And ere that faithless truce was broke
Which freed her from the unchristian yoke.
With him his gentle daughter came;
Nor there, since Menelaus' dame
Forsook her lord and land, to prove
What woes await on lawless love,
Had fairer form adorn'd the shore
Than she, the matchless stranger, bore.

X.

The wall is rent, the ruins yawn,
And, with to-morrow's earliest dawn,
O'er the disjointed mass shall vault
The foremost of the fierce assault.
The bands are rank'd; the chosen van
Of Tartar and of Mussulman,
The full of hope, misnamed "forlorn,"
Who hold the thought of death in scorn,
And win their way with falchion's force,
Or pave the path with many a corse,
O'er which the following brave may rise,
Their stepping-stone—the last who dies!

XI.

'T is midnight: on the mountains brown
The cold, round moon shines deeply down;
Blue roll the waters, blue the sky
Spreads like an ocean hung on high,
Bespangled with those isles of light,
So wildly, spiritually bright;
Who ever gazed upon them shining,
And turn'd to earth without repining,
Nor wish'd for wings to flee away,
And mix with their eternal ray?
The waves on either shore lay there
Calm, clear, and azure as the air;
And scarce their foam the pebbles shook,
But murmur'd meekly as the brook.
The winds were pillow'd on the waves;
The banners droop'd along their staves,
And, as they fell around them furling,
Above them shone the crescent curling;
And that deep silence was unbroke,
Save where the watch his signal spoke,
Save where the steed neigh'd oft and shrill,
And echo answer'd from the hill,
And the wide hum of that wild host
Rustled like leaves from coast to coast,
As rose the Muezzin's voice in air
In midnight call to wonted prayer;
It rose, that chanted mournful strain,
Like some lone spirit's o'er the plain:
'T was musical, but sadly sweet,
Such as when winds and harp-strings meet,
And take a long unmeasured tone,
To mortal minstrelsy unknown.
It seem'd to those within the wall
A cry prophetic of their fall:
It struck even the besieger's ear
With something ominous and drear,
An undefined and sudden thrill,
Which makes the heart a moment still,
Then beat with quicker pulse, ashamed
Of that strange sense its silence framed;
Such as a sudden passing-bell
Wakes, though but for a stranger's knell.

XII.

The tent of Alp was on the shore;
The sound was hush'd, the prayer was o'er;
The watch was set, the night-round made,
All mandates issued and obey'd:
'T is but another anxious night,
His pains the morrow may requite
With all revenge and love can pay,
In guerdon for their long delay.
Few hours remain, and he hath need
Of rest, to nerve for many a deed
Of slaughter; but within his soul
The thoughts like troubled waters roll.
He stood alone among the host;

Not his the loud fanatic boast
To plant the crescent o'er the cross,
Or risk a life with little loss,
Secure in Paradise to be
By Houris loved immortally:
Nor his, what burning patriots feel,
The stern exaltedness of zeal,
Profuse of blood, untired in toil,
When battling on the parent soil.
He stood alone—a renegade
Against the country he betray'd;
He stood alone amidst his band,
Without a trusted heart or hand:
They follow'd him, for he was brave,
And great the spoil he got and gave;
They crouch'd to him, for he had skill
To warp and wield the vulgar will:
But still his Christian origin
With them was little less than sin.
They envied even the faithless fame
He earn'd beneath a Moslem name;
Since he, their mightiest chief, had been
In youth a bitter Nazarene.
They did not know how pride can stoop,
When baffled feelings withering droop;
They did not know how hate can burn
In hearts once changed from soft to stern;
Nor all the false and fatal zeal
The convert of revenge can feel.
He ruled them—man may rule the worst,
By ever daring to be first:
So lions o'er the jackal sway;
The jackal points, he fells the prey,
Then on the vulgar yelling press,
To gorge the relics of success.

XIII.

His head grows fever'd, and his pulse
The quick successive throbs convulse;
In vain from side to side he throws
His form, in courtship of repose;
Or if he dozed, a sound, a start
Awoke him with a sunken heart.
The turban on his hot brow press'd,
The mail weigh'd lead-like on his breast,
Though oft and long beneath its weight
Upon his eyes had slumber sate,
Without or couch or canopy,
Except a rougher field and sky
Than now might yield a warrior's bed,
Than now along the heaven was spread.
He could not rest, he could not stay
Within his tent to wait for day,
But walk'd him forth along the sand,
Where thousand sleepers strew'd the strand.
What pillow'd them? and why should he
More wakeful than the humblest be?
Since more their peril, worse their toil,
And yet they fearless dream of spoil;
While he alone, where thousands pass'd
A night of sleep, perchance their last,
In sickly vigil wander'd on,
And envied all he gazed upon.

XIV.

He felt his soul become more light
Beneath the freshness of the night.
Cool was the silent sky, though calm,
And bathed his brow with airy balm:
Behind, the camp—before him lay,
In many a winding creek and bay,
Lepanto's gulf; and, on the brow
Of Delphi's hill, unshaken snow,
High and eternal, such as shone
Through thousand summers brightly gone,
Along the gulf, the mount, the clime;
It will not melt, like man, to time:
Tyrant and slave are swept away,
Less form'd to wear before the ray;
But that white veil, the lightest, frailest,
Which on the mighty mount thou hailest,
While tower and tree are torn and rent,
Shines o'er its craggy battlement;
In form a peak, in height a cloud,
In texture like a hovering shroud,
Thus high by parting Freedom spread,
As from her fond abode she fled,
And linger'd on the spot, where long
Her prophet spirit spake in song.
Oh! still her step at moments falters
O'er wither'd fields, and ruin'd altars,
And fain would wake, in souls too broken,
By pointing to each glorious token.
But vain her voice, till better days
Dawn in those yet remember'd rays,
Which shone upon the Persian flying,
And saw the Spartan smile in dying.

XV.

Not mindless of these mighty times
Was Alp, despite his flight and crimes;
And through this night, as on he wander'd,
And o'er the past and present ponder'd,
And thought upon the glorious dead
Who there in better cause had bled,
He felt how faint and feebly dim
The fame that could accrue to him,
Who cheer'd the band, and waved the sword,
A traitor in a turban'd horde;
And led them to the lawless siege,
Whose best success were sacrilege.
Not so had those his fancy number'd,
The chiefs whose dust around him slumber'd;
Their phalanx marshall'd on the plain,
Whose bulwarks were not then in vain.
They fell devoted, but undying;
The very gale their names seem'd sighing:

The waters murmur'd of their name;
The woods were peopled with their fame;
The silent pillar, lone and gray,
Claim'd kindred with their sacred clay;
Their spirits wrapt the dusky mountain,
Their memory sparkled o'er the fountain;
The meanest rill, the mightiest river,
Roll'd mingling with their fame for ever.
Despite of every yoke she bears,
That land is glory's still, and theirs!
'Tis still a watch-word to the earth:
When man would do a deed of worth
He points to Greece, and turns to tread,
So sanction'd, on the tyrant's head:
He looks to her, and rushes on
Where life is lost, or freedom won.

XVI.

Still by the shore Alp mutely mused,
And woo'd the freshness Night diffus'd.

There shrinks no ebb in that tideless sea,[4]
Which changeless rolls eternally;
So that wildest of waves, in their angriest mood,
Scarce break on the bounds of the land for a rood;
And the powerless moon beholds them flow,
Heedless if she come or go:
Calm or high, in main or bay,
On their course she hath no sway.
The rock unworn its base doth bare,
And looks o'er the surf, but it comes not there;
And the fringe of the foam may be seen below,
On the line that it left long ages ago:
A smooth short space of yellow sand
Between it and the greener land.

He wander'd on, along the beach,
Till within the range of a carbine's reach
Of the leaguer'd wall; but they saw him not,
Or how could he 'scape from the hostile shot?
Did traitors lurk in the Christians' hold?
Were their hands grown stiff, or their hearts wax'd cold?
I know not, in sooth; but from yonder wall
There flash'd no fire, and there hiss'd no ball,
Though he stood beneath the bastion's frown,
That flank'd the sea-ward gate of the town;
Though he heard the sound, and could almost tell
The sullen words of the sentinel,
As his measured step on the stone below
Clank'd, as he paced it to and fro;
And he saw the lean dogs beneath the wall
Hold o'er the dead their carnival,
Gorging and growling o'er carcass and limb;
They were too busy to bark at him!
From a Tartar's skull they had stripp'd the flesh,
As ye peel the fig when its fruit is fresh;
And their white tusks crunch'd o'er the whiter skull,[5]
As it slipp'd through their jaws, when their edge drew dull,
As they lazily mumbled the bones of the dead,
When they scarce could rise from the spot where they fed;
So well had they broken a lingering fast
With those who had fall'n for that night's repast.
And Alp knew, by the turbans that roll'd on the sand,
The foremost of these were the best of his band:
Crimson and green were the shawls of their wear,
And each scalp had a single long tuft of hair,[6]
All the rest were shaven and bare.
The scalps were in the wild dog's maw,
The hair was tangled round his jaw.
But close by the shore, on the edge of the gulf,
There sat a vulture flapping a wolf,
Who had stolen from the hills, but kept away,
Scared by the dogs, from the human prey;
But he seized on his share of a steed that lay,
Pick'd by the birds, on the sands of the bay.

XVII.

Alp turn'd him from the sickening sight:
Never had shaken his nerves in fight;
But he better could brook to behold the dying,
Deep in the tide of their warm blood lying,
Scorch'd with the death-thirst, and writhing in vain,
Than the perishing dead who are past all pain.
There is something of pride in the perilous hour,
Whate'er be the shape in which death may lower;
For Fame is there to say who bleeds,
And Honour's eye on daring deeds!
But when all is past, it is humbling to tread
O'er the weltering field of the tombless dead,
And see worms of the earth, and fowls of the air,
Beasts of the forest, all gathering there;
All regarding man as their prey,
All rejoicing in his decay.

XVIII.

There is a temple in ruin stands,
Fashion'd by long-forgotten hands;
Two or three columns, and many a stone,
Marble and granite, with grass o'ergrown!
Out upon Time! it will leave no more
Of the things to come than the things before!
Out upon Time! who for ever will leave
But enough of the past for the future to grieve
O'er that which hath been, and o'er that which must be:
What we have seen, our sons shall see;
Remnants of things that have pass'd away,
Fragments of stone, rear'd by creatures of clay!

XIX.

He sate him down at a pillar's base,
And pass'd his hand athwart his face;
Like one in dreary musing mood,
Declining was his attitude;
His head was drooping on his breast,
Fever'd, throbbing, and opprest;
And o'er his brow, so downward bent,
Oft his beating fingers went,
Hurriedly, as you may see
Your own run over the ivory key,
Ere the measured tone is taken
By the chords you would awaken.
There he sate all heavily,
As he heard the night-wind sigh.
Was it the wind, through some hollow stone,[7]
Sent that soft and tender moan?
He lifted his head, and he look'd on the sea,
But it was unrippled as glass may be;
He look'd on the long grass — it waved not a blade;
How was that gentle sound convey'd?
He look'd to the banners—each flag lay still,
So did the leaves on Cithæron's hill,

And he felt not a breath come over his cheek;
What did that sudden sound bespeak?
He turn'd to the left—is he sure of sight?
There sate a lady, youthful and bright!

XX.

He started up with more of fear
Than if an armèd foe were near.
"God of my fathers! what is here?
Who art thou, and wherefore sent
So near a hostile armament?"
His trembling hands refused to sign
The cross he deem'd no more divine:
He had resumed it in that hour,
But conscience wrung away the power.
He gazed—he saw: he knew the face
Of beauty, and the form of grace;
It was Francesca by his side,
The maid who might have been his bride!

The rose was yet upon her cheek,
But mellow'd with a tenderer streak:

Where was the play of her soft lips fled?
Gone was the smile that enliven'd their red.
The ocean's calm within their view,
Beside her eye had less of blue;
But like that cold wave it stood still,
And its glance, though clear, was chill.
Around her form a thin robe twining,
Nought conceal'd her bosom shining;
Through the parting of her hair,
Floating darkly downward there,
Her rounded arm show'd white and bare:
And ere yet she made reply,
Once she rais'd her hand on high;
It was so wan, and transparent of hue,
You might have seen the moon shine through.

XXI.

"I come from my rest to him I love best,
That I may be happy, and he may be blest.
I have pass'd the guards, the gate, the wall;
Sought thee in safety through foes and all.
'T is said the lion will turn and flee
From a maid in the pride of her purity;
And the Power on high, that can shield the good
Thus from the tyrant of the wood,
Hath extended its mercy to guard me as well
From the hands of the leaguering infidel.
I come—and if I come in vain,
Never, oh never, we meet again!
Thou hast done a fearful deed
In falling away from thy father's creed:
But dash that turban to earth, and sign
The sign of the cross, and for ever be mine;
Wring the black drop from thy heart,
And to-morrow unites us no more to part."

"And where should our bridal couch be spread?
In the midst of the dying and the dead?
For to-morrow we give to the slaughter and flame
The sons and the shrines of the Christian name.
None, save thou and thine, I've sworn,
Shall be left upon the morn:
But thee will I bear to a lovely spot,
Where our hands shall be join'd, and our sorrow forgot.
There thou yet shalt be my bride,
When once again I've quell'd the pride
Of Venice; and her hated race
Have felt the arm they would debase,
Scourge, with a whip of scorpions, those
Whom vice and envy made my foes."

Upon his hand she laid her own—
Light was the touch, but it thrill'd to the bone,
And shot a chillness to his heart,
Which fix'd him beyond the power to start.
Though slight was that grasp so mortal cold,
He could not loose him from its hold;
But never did clasp of one so dear
Strike on the pulse with such feeling of fear,
As those thin fingers, long and white,
Froze through his blood by their touch that night.
The feverish glow of his brow was gone,
And his heart sank so still that it felt like stone,
As he look'd on the face, and beheld its hue,
So deeply changed from what he knew:
Fair but faint—without the ray
Of mind, that made each feature play
Like sparkling waves on a sunny day;
And her motionless lips lay still as death,
And her words came forth without her breath,
And there rose not a heave o'er her bosom's swell,
And there seem'd not a pulse in her veins to dwell.
Though her eye shone out, yet the lids were fix'd,
And the glance that it gave was wild and unmix'd
With aught of change, as the eyes may seem
Of the restless who walk in a troubled dream;
Like the figures on arras, that gloomily glare,
Stirr'd by the breath of the wintry air,
So seen by the dying lamp's fitful light,
Lifeless, but life-like, and awful to sight;
As they seem, through the dimness, about to come down
From the shadowy wall where their images frown;
Fearfully flitting to and fro,
As the gusts on the tapestry come and go.

"If not for love of me be given
Thus much, then, for the love of heaven,—
Again I say—that turban tear
From off thy faithless brow, and swear
Thine injured country's sons to spare,
Or thou art lost; and never shalt see—
Not earth—that's past—but heaven or me
If this thou dost accord, albeit
A heavy doom 't is thine to meet,
That doom shall half absolve thy sin,
And mercy's gate may receive thee within:
But pause one moment more, and take
The curse of Him thou didst forsake;
And look once more to heaven, and see
Its love for ever shut from thee.
There is a light cloud by the moon—[8]
'T is passing, and will pass full soon—
If, by the time its vapoury sail
Hath ceased her shaded orb to veil,
Thy heart within thee is not changed,
Then God and man are both avenged;
Dark will thy doom be, darker still
Thine immortality of ill."

Alp look'd to heaven, and saw on high
The sign she spake of in the sky;
But his heart was swoll'n, and turn'd aside,
By deep interminable pride.
This first false passion of his breast
Roll'd like a torrent o'er the rest.

He sue for mercy! *He* dismay'd
By wild words of a timid maid!
He, wrong'd by Venice, vow to save
Her sons, devoted to the grave!
No—though that cloud were thunder's worst,
And charg'd to crush him—let it burst!

He look'd upon it earnestly,
Without an accent of reply;
He watch'd it passing; it is flown:
Full on his eye the clear moon shone,
And thus he spake—"Whate'er my fate,
I am no changeling—'tis too late:
The reed in storms may bow and quiver,
Then rise again; the tree must shiver.
What Venice made me, I must be,
Her foe in all, save love to thee:
But thou art safe: oh, fly with me!"
He turn'd, but she is gone!
Nothing is there but the column stone.
Hath she sunk in the earth, or melted in air?
He saw not—he knew not; but nothing is there.

XXII.

The night is past, and shines the sun
As if that morn were a jocund one.
Lightly and brightly breaks away
The Morning from her mantle gray,
And the Noon will look on a sultry day.
Hark to the trump, and the drum,
And the mournful sound of the barbarous horn,
And the flap of the banners, that flit as they 're borne,
And the neigh of the steed, and the multitude's hum,
And the clash, and the shout, "They come, they come!"
The horsetails are pluck'd from the ground, and the sword[9]
From its sheath; and they form, and but wait for the word.
Tartar, and Spahi, and Turcoman,
Strike your tents, and throng to the van;
Mount ye, spur ye, skirr the plain,
That the fugitive may flee in vain,
When he breaks from the town; and none escape,
Aged or young, in the Christian shape;
While your fellows on foot, in a fiery mass,
Bloodstain the breach through which they pass.
The steeds are all bridled, and snort to the rein;
Curved is each neck, and flowing each mane;
White is the foam of their champ on the bit:
The spears are uplifted; the matches are lit;
The cannon are pointed, and ready to roar,
And crush the wall they have crumbled before:
Forms in his phalanx each Janizar;
Alp at their head; his right arm is bare,
So is the blade of his scimitar;
The khan and the pachas are all at their post;
The vizier himself at the head of the host.
When the culverin's signal is fired, then on;
Leave not in Corinth a living one—
A priest at her altars, a chief in her halls,
A hearth in her mansions, a stone on her walls.
God and the prophet—Alla Hu!
Up to the skies with that wild halloo!

"There the breach lies for passage, the ladder to scale;
And your hands on your sabres, and how should ye fail?
He who first downs with the red cross may crave
His heart's dearest wish; let him ask it, and have!"

Thus utter'd Coumourgi, the dauntless vizier;
The reply was the brandish of sabre and spear,
And the shout of fierce thousands in joyous ire:—
Silence—hark to the signal—fire!

XXIII.

As the wolves, that headlong go
On the stately buffalo,
Though with fiery eyes, and angry roar,
And hoofs that stamp, and horns that gore,
He tramples on earth, or tosses on high
The foremost, who rush on his strength but to die
Thus against the wall they went,
Thus the first were backward bent;
Many a bosom, sheathed in brass,
Strew'd the earth like broken glass,
Shiver'd by the shot, that tore
The ground whereon they moved no more:
Even as they fell, in files they lay,
Like the mower's grass at the close of day,
When his work is done on the level'd plain;
Such was the fall of the foremost slain.

XXIV.

As the spring-tides, with heavy splash,
From the cliffs invading dash
Huge fragments, sapp'd by the ceaseless flow,
Till white and thundering down they go,
Like the avalanche's snow
On the Alpine vales below;
Thus at length, outbreathed and worn,
Corinth's sons were downward borne
By the long and oft-renew'd
Charge of the Moslem multitude.
In firmness they stood, and in masses they fell,
Heap'd, by the host of the infidel,
Hand to hand, and foot to foot:
Nothing there, save death, was mute;
Stroke, and thrust, and flash, and cry
For quarter, or for victory,
Mingle there with the volleying thunder,
Which makes the distant cities wonder
How the sounding battle goes,
If with them, or for their foes;
If they must mourn, or may rejoice
In that annihilating voice,
Which pierces the deep hills through and through
With an echo dread and new:
You might have heard it, on that day,
O'er Salamis and Megara;
(We have heard the hearers say,)
Even unto Piræus bay.

XXV.

From the point of encountering blades to the hilt,
Sabres and swords with blood were gilt;
But the rampart is won, and the spoil begun,
And all but the after carnage done.
Shriller shrieks now mingling come
From within the plunder'd dome:
Hark to the haste of flying feet,
That splash in the blood of the slippery street;

But here and there, where 'vantage ground
Against the foe may still be found,
Desperate groups, of twelve or ten,
Make a pause, and turn again—
With banded backs against the wall,
Fiercely stand, or fighting fall.

There stood an old man—his hairs were white,
But his veteran arm was full of might:
So gallantly bore he the brunt of the fray,
The dead before him, on that day,
In a semicircle lay;
Still he combated unwounded,
Though retreating, unsurrounded.
Many a scar of former fight
Lurk'd beneath his corselet bright;
But of every wound his body bore,
Each and all had been ta'en before:
Though aged, he was so iron of limb,
Few of our youth could cope with him;
And the foes, whom he singly kept at bay,
Outnumber'd his thin hairs of silver gray.
From right to left his sabre swept:
Many an Othman mother wept
Sons that were unborn, when dipp'd
His weapon first in Moslem gore,
Ere his years could count a score.
Of all he might have been the sire
Who fell that day beneath his ire:
For, sonless left long years ago,
His wrath made many a childless foe;
And since the day, when in the strait[10]
His only boy had met his fate,
His parent's iron hand did doom
More than a human hecatomb.
If shades by carnage be appeased,
Patroclus' spirit less was pleased
Than his, Minotti's son, who died
Where Asia's bounds and ours divide.
Buried he lay, where thousands before
For thousands of years were inhumed on the shore;
What of them is left, to tell
Where they lie, and how they fell?
Not a stone on their turf, nor a bone in their graves;
But they live in the verse that immortally saves.

XXVI.

Hark to the Allah shout! a band
Of the Mussulman bravest and best is at hand:
Their leader's nervous arm is bare,
Swifter to smite, and never to spare—
Unclothed to the shoulder it waves them on;
Thus in the fight is he ever known:
Others a gaudier garb may show,
To tempt the spoil of the greedy foe;
Many a hand 's on a richer hilt,
But none on a steel more ruddily gilt;
Many a loftier turban may wear,—
Alp is but known by the white arm bare;
Look through the thick of the fight, 't is there!
There is not a standard on that shore
So well advanced the ranks before;
There is not a banner in Moslem war
Will lure the Delis half so far;
It glances like a falling star!
Where'er that mighty arm is seen,
The bravest be, or late have been;
There the craven cries for quarter
Vainly to the vengeful Tartar;
Or the hero, silent lying,
Scorns to yield a groan in dying
Mustering his last feeble blow
'Gainst the nearest level'd foe,
Though faint beneath the mutual wound,
Grappling on the gory ground.

XXVII.

Still the old man stood erect,
And Alp's career a moment check'd.

"Yield thee, Minotti; quarter take,
For thine own, thy daughter's sake."

"Never, renegado, never!
Though the life of thy gift would last for ever."

"Francesca!---Oh, my promised bride!
Must she too perish by thy pride?"

"She is safe."—"Where? where?"—"In heaven:
From whence thy traitor soul is driven—
Far from thee, and undefiled."
Grimly then Minotti smiled,
As he saw Alp staggering bow
Before his words, as with a blow.

"Oh God! when died she?"—"Yesternight—
Nor weep I for her spirit's flight:
None of my pure race shall be
Slaves to Mahomet and thee—
Come on!"—That challenge is in vain—
Alp 's already with the slain!
While Minotti's words were wreaking
More revenge in bitter speaking
Than his falchion's point had found,
Had the time allow'd to wound,
From within the neighbouring porch
Of a long-defended church,
Where the last and desperate few
Would the failing fight renew,
The sharp shot dash'd Alp to the ground;
Ere an eye could view the wound
That crash'd through the brain of the infidel,
Round he spun, and down he fell;

A flash like fire within his eyes
Blazed, as he bent no more to rise,
And then eternal darkness sunk
Through all the palpitating trunk;
Nought of life left, save a quivering
Where his limbs were slightly shivering:
They turn'd him on his back; his breast
And brow were stain'd with gore and dust,

And through his lips the life-blood oozed,
From its deep veins lately loosed;
But in his pulse there was no throb,
Nor on his lips one dying sob;
Sigh, nor word, nor struggling breath
Heralded his way to death:
Ere his very thought could pray,
Unaneled he pass'd away,
Without a hope from mercy's aid,—
To the last—a Renegade.

XXVIII.

Fearfully the yell arose
Of his followers, and his foes;
These in joy, in fury those:
Then again in conflict mixing,
Clashing swords, and spears transfixing,
Interchanged the blow and thrust,
Hurling warriors in the dust.
Street by street, and foot by foot,
Still Minotti dares dispute
The latest portion of the land
Left beneath his high command;
With him, aiding heart and hand,
The remnant of his gallant band.
 Still the church is tenable,
Whence issued late the fated ball
That half avenged the city's fall,
 When Alp, her fierce assailant, fell:
Thither bending sternly back,
They leave before a bloody track;
And, with their faces to the foe,
Dealing wounds with every blow,
The chief, and his retreating train,
Join to those within the fane;
There they yet may breathe awhile,
Shelter'd by the massy pile.

XXIX.

Brief breathing-time! the turban'd host,
With added ranks and raging boast,
Press onwards with such strength and heat,
Their numbers balk their own retreat;
For narrow the way that led to the spot
Where still the Christians yielded not;
And the foremost, if fearful, may vainly try
Through the massy column to turn and fly;
They perforce must do or die.
They die; but ere their eyes could close,
Avengers o'er their bodies rose;
Fresh and furious, fast they fill
The ranks unthinn'd, though slaughter'd still;
And faint the weary Christians wax
Before the still renew'd attacks:
And now the Othmans gain the gate;
Still resists its iron weight,
And still, all deadly aim'd and hot,
From every crevice comes the shot;
From every shatter'd window pour
The volleys of the sulphurous shower:
But the portal wavering grows and weak—
The iron yields, the hinges creak—
It bends—it falls—and all is o'er;
Lost Corinth may resist no more!

XXX.

Darkly, sternly, and all alone,
Minotti stood o'er the altar stone:
Madonna's face upon him shone,
Painted in heavenly hues above,
With eyes of light and looks of love;
And placed upon that holy shrine
To fix our thoughts on things divine,
When pictured there, we kneeling see
Her, and the boy-God on her knee,
Smiling sweetly on each prayer
To heaven, as if to waft it there.
Still she smiled; even now she smiles,
Though slaughter streams along her aisles:
Minotti lifted his aged eye,
And made the sign of a cross with a sigh,
Then seized a torch which blazed thereby;
And still he stood, while, with steel and flame,
Inward and onward the Mussulman came.

XXXI.

The vaults beneath the mosaic stone
Contain'd the dead of ages gone;
Their names were on the graven floor,
But now illegible with gore;
The carvèd crests, and curious hues
The varied marble's veins diffuse,
Were smear'd, and slippery — stain'd, and strown
With broken swords, and helms o'erthrown:
There were dead above, and the dead below
Lay cold in many a coffin'd row;
You might see them piled in sable state,
By a pale light through a gloomy grate;
But War had enter'd their dark caves,
And stored along the vaulted graves
Her sulphurous treasures, thickly spread
In masses by the fleshless dead:
Here, throughout the siege, had been
The Christians' chiefest magazine;
To these a late-form'd train now led,
Minotti's last and stern resource,
Against the foe's o'erwhelming force.

XXXII.

The foe came on, and few remain
To strive, and those must strive in vain:
For lack of further lives, to slake
The thirst of vengeance now awake,
With barbarous blows they gash the dead,
And lop the already lifeless head,
And fell the statues from their niche,
And spoil the shrines of offerings rich,
And from each other's rude hands wrest
The silver vessels saints had bless'd.
To the high altar on they go;
Oh, but it made a glorious show!
On its table still behold
The cup of consecrated gold;
Massy and deep, a glittering prize,

Brightly it sparkles to plunderers' eyes:
That morn it held the holy wine,
Converted by Christ to His blood so divine,
Which His worshippers drank at the break of day,
To shrive their souls ere they join'd in the fray,
Still a few drops within it lay;
And round the sacred table glow
Twelve lofty lamps, in splendid row,
From the purest metal cast;
A spoil—the richest, and the last.

XXXIII.

So near they came, the nearest stretch'd
To grasp the spoil he almost reach'd,
When old Minotti's hand
Touch'd with a torch the train—
'T is fired!
Spire, vaults, and shrine, the spoil, the slain,
The turban'd victors, the Christian band,
All that of living or dead remain,
Hurl'd on high with the shiver'd fane,
In one wild roar expired!
The shatter'd town—the walls thrown down—
The waves a moment backward bent—
The hills that shake, although unrent,
As if an earthquake pass'd—
The thousand shapeless things all driven
In cloud and flame athwart the heaven,
By that tremendous blast—
Proclaim'd the desperate conflict o'er
On that too long afflicted shore:
Up to the sky like rockets go
All that mingled there below:
Many a tall and goodly man,
Scorch'd and shrivel'd to a span,
When he fell to earth again
Like a cinder strew'd the plain:
Down the ashes shower like rain;
Some fell in the gulf, which received the sprinkles
With a thousand circling wrinkles;
Some fell on the shore, but, far away,
Scatter'd o'er the isthmus lay;
Christian or Moslem, which be they?
Let their mothers see and say!
When in cradled rest they lay,
And each nursing mother smiled
On the sweet sleep of her child,
Little deem'd she such a day
Would rend those tender limbs away.
Not the matrons that them bore
Could discern their offspring more;
That one moment left no trace
More of human form or face
Save a scatter'd scalp or bone:
And down came blazing rafters, strown
Around, and many a falling stone,
Deeply dinted in the clay,
All blacken'd there and reeking lay.
All the living things that heard
That deadly earth-shock disappear'd:
The wild birds flew; the wild dogs fled,
And howling left the unburied dead;
The camels from their keepers broke;
The distant steer forsook the yoke—
The nearer steed plung'd o'er the plain,
And burst his girth, and tore his rein;
The bull-frog's note, from out the marsh,
Deep-mouth'd arose, and doubly harsh;
The wolves yell'd on the cavern'd hill
Where echo roll'd in thunder still;
The jackal's troop, in gather'd cry,[11]
Bay'd from afar complainingly,
With a mix'd and mournful sound,
Like crying babe, and beaten hound:
With sudden wing, and ruffled breast,
The eagle left his rocky nest,
And mounted nearer to the sun,
The clouds beneath him seem'd so dun;
Their smoke assail'd his startled beak,
And made him higher soar and shriek—
Thus was Corinth lost and won!

NOTES TO THE SIEGE OF CORINTH.

NOTE 1, page 91.

Napoli di Romania is not now the most considerable place in the Morea, but Tripolitza, where the Pacha resides, and maintains his government. Napoli is near Argos. I visited all three in 1810-11; and, in the course of journeying through the country from my first arrival in 1809, I crosed the Isthmus eight times in my way from Attica to the Morea, over the mountains, or in the other direction, when passing from the Gulf of Athens to that of Lepanto. Both the routes are picturesque and beautiful, though very different: that by sea has more sameness; but the voyage being always within sight of land, and often very near it, presents many attractive views of the islands Salamis, Ægina, Poro, &c., and the coast of the continent.

NOTE 2, page 93.

The Turcoman hath left his herd.

The life of the Turcomans is wandering and patriarchal: they dwell in tents.

NOTE 3, page 93.

Coumourgi—he whose closing scene.

Ali Coumourgi, the favourite of three sultans, and Grand Vizier to Achmet III., after recovering Peloponnesus from the Venetians in one campaign, was mortally wounded in the next, against the Germans, at the battle of Peterwaradin (in the plain of Carlowitz), in Hungary, endeavouring to rally his guards. He died of his wounds next day. His last order was the decapitation of General Breuner, and some other German prisoners; and his last words, "Oh that I could thus serve all the Christian dogs!" a speech and act not unlike one of Caligula. He was a young man of great ambition and unbounded presumption: on being told that Prince Eugene, then opposed to him, "was a great general," he said, "I shall become a greater, and at his expense."

NOTE 4, page 98

There shrinks no ebb in that tideless sea.

The reader need hardly be reminded that there are no perceptible tides in the Mediterranean.

NOTE 5, page 98.

And their white tusks crunch'd o'er the whiter skull.

This spectacle I have seen, such as described, beneath the wall of the Seraglio at Constantinople, in the little cavities worn by the Bosphorus in the rock, a narrow terrace of which projects between the wall and the water. I think the fact is also mentioned in Hobhouse's Travels. The bodies were probably those of some refractory Janizaries.

NOTE 6, page 98.

And each scalp had a single long tuft of hair.

This tuft, or long lock, is left from a superstition that Mahomet will draw them into Paradise by it.

NOTE 7, page 98.

Was it the wind, through some hollow stone.

I must here acknowledge a close, though unintentional, resemblance in these twelve lines to a passage in an unpublished poem of Mr. Coleridge, called "Christabel." It was not till after these lines were written that I heard that wild and singularly original and beautiful poem recited: and the MS. of that production I never saw till very recently, by the kindness of Mr. Coleridge himself, who, I hope, is convinced that I have not been a wilful plagiarist. The original idea undoubtedly pertains to Mr. Coleridge, whose poem has been composed above fourteen years. Let me conclude by a hope that he will not longer delay the publication of a production, of which I can only add my mite of approbation to the applause of far more competent judges.

NOTE 8, page 100.

There is a light cloud by the moon.

I have been told that the idea expressed from lines 598 to 603 has been admired by those whose approbation is valuable. I am glad of it: but it is not original—at least not mine; it may be found much better expressed in pages 182-3-4 of the English version of "Vathek" (I forget the precise page of the French), a work to which I have before referred; and never recur to, or read, without a renewal of gratification.

NOTE 9, page 102.

The horsetails are pluck'd from the ground, and the sword.

The horsetail, fixed upon a lance, a Pacha's standard.

NOTE 10, page 103.

And since the day, when in the strait.

In the naval battle at the mouth of the Dardanelles, between the Venetians and the Turks.

NOTE 10, page 106.

The jackal's troop, in gather'd cry.

I believe I have taken a poetical license to transplant the jackal from Asia. In Greece I never saw nor heard these animals; but among the ruins of Ephesus I have heard them by hundreds. They haunt ruins, and follow armies.

PARISINA.

TO

SCROPE BERDMORE DAVIES, ESQUIRE,

THE FOLLOWING POEM IS INSCRIBED,

BY ONE WHO HAS LONG ADMIRED HIS TALENTS AND VALUED HIS FRIENDSHIP.

ADVERTISEMENT.

THE following poem is grounded on a circumstance mentioned in Gibbon's "Antiquities of the House of Brunswick." I am aware, that in modern times the delicacy or fastidiousness of the reader may deem such subjects unfit for the purposes of poetry. The Greek dramatists, and some of the best of our old English writers, were of a different opinion: as Alfieri and Schiller have also been, more recently, upon the Continent. The following extract will explain the facts on which the story is founded. The name of *Azo* is substituted for Nicholas, as more metrical.

"Under the reign of Nicholas III. Ferrara was polluted with a domestic tragedy. By the testimony of an attendant, and his own observation, the Marquis of Este discovered the incestuous loves of his wife Parisina, and Hugo his bastard son, a beautiful and valiant youth. They were beheaded in the castle by the sentence of a father and husband, who published his shame, and survived their execution. He was unfortunate, if they were guilty; if they were innocent, he was still more unfortunate; nor is there any possible situation in which I can sincerely approve the last act of the justice of a parent."—*Gibbon's Miscellaneous Works*, vol. iii., p. 470.

FERRARA.

I.

It is the hour when from the boughs
The nightingale's high note is heard;
It is the hour when lovers' vows
Seem sweet in every whisper'd word
And gentle winds, and waters near,
Make music to the lonely ear.
Each flower the dews have lightly wet,
And in the sky the stars are met,
And on the wave is deeper blue,
And on the leaf a browner hue,
And in the heaven that clear obscure,
So softly dark, and darkly pure,
Which follows the decline of day,
As twilight melts beneath the moon away.

II.

But it is not to list to the waterfall
That Parisina leaves her hall,
And it is not to gaze on the heavenly light
That the lady walks in the shadow of night;
And if she sits in Este's bower,
'T is not for the sake of the full-blown flower—
She listens—but not for the nightingale—
Though her ear expects as soft a tale.
There glides a step through the foliage thick,
And her cheek grows pale—and her heart beats quick.
There whispers a voice through the rustling leaves,
And her blush returns, and her bosom heaves:
A moment more—and they shall meet—
'T is past—her lover's at her feet.

III.

And what unto them is the world beside,
With all its change of time and tide?
Its living things—its earth and sky—
Are nothing to their mind and eye.
And heedless as the dead are they
Of aught around, above, beneath.
As if all else had pass'd away,
They only for each other breathe
Their very sighs are full of joy
So deep, that did it not decay,
That happy madness would destroy
The hearts which feel its fiery sway:
Of guilt, of peril, do they deem
In that tumultuous tender dream?

Who that have felt that passion's power,
Or paus'd, or fear'd, in such an hour?
Or thought how brief such moments last?
But yet—they are already past
Alas! we must awake before
We know such vision comes no more.

IV.

With many a lingering look they leave
 The spot of guilty gladness past;
And though they hope, and vow, they grieve,
 As if that parting were the last.
The frequent sigh—the long embrace—
 The lip that there would cling for ever,
While gleams on Parisina's face
 The Heaven she fears will not forgive her,
As if each calmly conscious star
Beheld her frailty from afar—
The frequent sigh, the long embrace,
Yet binds them to their trysting-place.
But it must come, and they must part
In fearful heaviness of heart,
With all the deep and shuddering chill
Which follows fast the deeds of ill.

V.

And Hugo is gone to his lonely bed,
 To covet there another's bride;
But she must lay her conscious head
 A husband's trusting heart beside.
But fever'd in her sleep she seems,
And red her cheek with troubled dreams,
 And mutters she in her unrest
A name she dare not breathe by day,
 And clasps her lord unto the breast
Which pants for one away:
And he to that embrace awakes,
And, happy in the thought, mistakes
That dreaming sigh, and warm caress,
For such as he was wont to bless;
And could in very fondness weep
O'er her who loves him even in sleep.

VI.

He clasp'd her sleeping to his heart,
 And listen'd to each broken word:
He hears—Why doth Prince Azo start,
 As if the Archangel's voice he heard?
And well he may—a deeper doom
Could scarcely thunder o'er his tomb,
When he shall wake to sleep no more,
And stand the eternal throne before.
And well he may—his earthly peace
Upon that sound is doom'd to cease.
That sleeping whisper of a name
Bespeaks her guilt and Azo's shame.
And whose that name? that o'er his pillow
Sounds fearful as the breaking billow,
Which rolls the plank upon the shore,
 And dashes on the pointed rock
The wretch who sinks to rise no more,—
 So came upon his soul the shock.
And whose that name? 'tis Hugo's—his—
In sooth he had not deem'd of this!—
'Tis Hugo's—he, the child of one
He loved—his own all-evil son—
The offspring of his wayward youth,
When he betray'd Bianca's truth,
The maid whose folly could confide
In him who made her not his bride.

VII.

He pluck'd his poinard in its sheath,
 But sheath'd it ere the point was bare—
Howe'er unworthy now to breathe,
 He could not slay a thing so fair—
 At least, not smiling—sleeping—there—
Nay more:—he did not wake her then,
 But gazed upon her with a glance,
 Which, had she roused her from her trance,
Had frozen her sense to sleep again—
And o'er his brow the burning lamp
Gleam'd on the dew-drops big and damp.
She spake no more—but still she slumbered—
While, in his thought, her days are number'd.

VIII.

And with the morn he sought, and found,
In many a tale from those around,
The proof of all he fear'd to know.
Their present guilt, his future woe;
The long-conniving damsels seek
 To save themselves, and would transfer
 The guilt—the shame—the doom—to her
Concealment is no more—they speak
All circumstance which may compel
Full credence to the tale they tell:
And Azo's tortured heart and ear
Have nothing more to feel or hear.

IX.

He was not one who brook'd delay:
 Within the chamber of his state,
The chief of Este's ancient sway
 Upon his throne of judgment sate;
His nobles and his guards are there,—
Before him is the sinful pair;
Both young,—and *one* how passing fair!
With swordless belt, and fetter'd hand.
Oh, Christ! that thus a son should stand
 Before a father's face!
Yet thus must Hugo meet his sire,
And hear the sentence of his ire,
 The tale of his disgrace!
And yet he seems not overcome,
Although, as yet, his voice be dumb.

X.

And still, and pale, and silently
 Did Parisina wait her doom;

How changed since last her speaking eye
 Glanced gladness round the glittering room,
Where high-born men were proud to wait—
Where Beauty watch'd to imitate
 Her gentle voice—her lovely mien—
And gather from her air and gait
 The graces of its queen:
Then,—had her eye in sorrow wept,
A thousand warriors forth had leapt,
A thousand swords had sheathless shone,
And made her quarrel all their own.
Now,—what is she! and what are they?

Can she command, or these obey?
All silent and unheeding now,
With downcast eyes and knitting brow,
And folded arms, and freezing air,
And lips that scarce their scorn forbear,
Her knights and dames, her court—is there:
And he, the chosen one, whose lance
Had yet been couch'd before her glance,
Who—were his arm a moment free—
Had died or gain'd her liberty;
The minion of his father's bride,—
He, too, is fetter'd by her side:
Nor sees her swoln and full eyes swim
Less for her own despair than him:
Those lids—o'er which the violet vein
Wandering, leaves a tender stain,
Shining through the smoothest white
That e'er did softest kiss invite—
Now seem'd with hot and livid glow
To press, not shade, the orbs below;
Which glance so heavily, and fill,
As tear on tear grows gathering still.

XI.

And he for her had also wept,
 But for the eyes that on him gazed:
His sorrow, if he felt it, slept;
 Stern and erect his brow was raised.
Whate'er the grief his soul avow'd,
He would not shrink before the crowd;
But yet he dared not look on her:
Remembrance of the hours that were—
His guilt—his love—his present state—
His father's wrath—all good men's hate—
His earthly, his eternal fate—
And hers,—oh, hers! he dared not throw
One look upon that deathlike brow!
Else had his rising heart betray'd
Remorse for all the wreck it made.

XII.

And Azo spake:—"But yesterday
 I gloried in a wife and son;
That dream this morning pass'd away;
 Ere day declines, I shall have none.
My life must linger on alone;
Well,—let that pass,—there breathes not one
Who would not do as I have done:
Those ties are broken—not by me;
 Let that too pass;—the doom's prepared!
Hugo, the priest awaits on thee,
 And then—thy crime's reward!
Away! address thy prayers to Heaven,
 Before its evening stars are met—
Learn if thou there canst be forgiven;
 Its mercy may absolve thee yet.
But here, upon the earth beneath,
 There is no spot where thou and I
Together, for an hour, could breathe:
 Farewell! I will not see thee die—
But thou, frail thing! shalt view his head—
 Away! I cannot speak the rest:
 Go! woman of the wanton breast;
Not I, but thou, his blood dost shed:
Go! if that sight thou canst outlive,
And joy thee in the life I give."

XIII.

And here stern Azo hid his face—
 For on his brow the swelling vein
 Throbb'd as if back upon his brain
 The hot blood ebb'd and flow'd again;
And therefore bow'd he for a space,
And pass'd his shaking hand along
His eye, to veil it from the throng;
While Hugo raised his chainèd hands.
And for a brief delay demands
His father's ear: the silent sire
Forbids not what his words require.

"It is not that I dread the death—
For thou hast seen me by thy side
All redly through the battle ride,
And that not once a useless brand
Thy slaves have wrested from my hand,
Hath shed more blood in cause of thine,
Than e'er can stain the axe of mine;
 Thou gav'st, and may'st resume my breath,
A gift for which I thank thee not;
Nor are my mother's wrongs forgot,
Her slighted love and ruin'd name,
Her offspring's heritage of shame;
But she is in the grave, where he,
Her son, thy rival, soon shall be.
Her broken heart—my sever'd head—
Shall witness for thee from the dead
How trusty and how tender were
Thy youthful love—paternal care.
'Tis true that I have done thee wrong—
 But wrong for wrong:—this, deem'd thy bride,
 The other victim of thy pride,
Thou know'st for me was destined long.
Thou saw'st, and covetedst her charms—
 And with thy very crime—my birth,
 Thou tauntedst me—as little worth;
A match ignoble for her arms,
Because, forsooth, I could not claim
The lawful heirship of thy name,
Nor sit on Este's lineal throne:
 Yet, were a few short summers mine,
 My name should more than Este's shine
With honours all my own.
I had a sword—and have a breast
That should have won as haught a crest[3]
As ever waved along the line

Of all these sovereign sires of thine.
Not always knightly spurs are worn
The brightest by the better born;
And mine have lanced my courser's flank
Before proud chiefs of princely rank,
When charging to the cheering cry
Of 'Este and of Victory!'
I will not plead the cause of crime,
Nor sue thee to redeem from time
A few brief hours or days that must
At length roll o'er my reckless dust;—
Such maddening moments as my past,
They could not, and they did not, last.
Albeit my birth and name be base,
And thy nobility of race
Disdain'd to deck a thing like me—
Yet in my lineaments they trace
Some features of my father's face,
And in my spirit—all of thee.
From thee—this tamelessness of heart—
From thee—nay, wherefore dost thou start?—
From thee in all their vigour came
My arm of strength, my soul of flame—
Thou didst not give me life alone,
But all that made me more thine own.
See what thy guilty love hath done!
Repaid thee with too like a son!
I am no bastard in my soul,
For that, like thine, abhorr'd control:
And for my breath, that hasty boon
Thou gav'st, and wilt resume so soon,
I value it no more than thou,
When rose thy casque above thy brow,
And we, all side by side, have striven
And o'er the dead our coursers driven:
The past is nothing—and at last
The future can but be the past;
Yet would I that I then had died;
For though thou work'dst my mother's ill,
And made thy own my destined bride,
I feel thou art my father still;
And, harsh as sounds thy hard decree,
'Tis not unjust, although from thee.
Begot in sin, to die in shame,
My life begun and ends the same:
As err'd the sire, so err'd the son,
And thou must punish both in one.
My crime seems worst to human view,
But God must judge between us too!"

XIV.

He ceased—and stood with folded arms,
On which the circling fetters sounded;
And not an ear but felt as wounded,
Of all the chiefs that there were rank'd,
When those dull chains in meeting clank'd:
Till Parisina's fatal charms
Again attracted every eye—
Would she thus hear him doom'd to die!
She stood, I said, all pale and still,
The living cause of Hugo's ill:
Her eyes unmoved, but full and wide,
Not once had turn'd to either side—
Nor once did those sweet eyelids close,
Or shade the glance o'er which they rose,
But round their orbs of deepest blue
The circling white dilated grew—
And there with glassy gaze she stood
As ice were in her curdled blood;
But every now and then a tear
So large and slowly gather'd slid
From the long dark fringe of that fair lid,
It was a thing to see, not hear!
And those who saw, it did surprise,
Such drops could fall from human eyes.
To speak she thought—the imperfect note
Was choked within her swelling throat,
Yet seem'd in that low hollow groan
Her whole heart gushing in the tone.
It ceased—again she thought to speak,
Then burst her voice in one long shriek,
And to the earth she fell like stone
Or statue from its base o'erthrown,
More like a thing that ne'er had life,—
A monument of Azo's wife,—
Than her, that living guilty thing,
Whose every passion was a sting,
Which urged to guilt, but could not bear
That guilt's detection and despair.
But yet she lived—and all too soon
Recover'd from that death-like swoon—
But scarce to reason—every sense
Had been o'erstrung by pangs intense;
And each frail fibre of her brain
(As bowstrings, when relax'd by rain,
The erring arrow launch aside)
Sent forth her thoughts all wild and wide—
The past a blank, the future black,
With glimpses of a dreary track,
Like lightning on the desert path,
When midnight storms are mustering wrath
She fear'd—she felt that something ill
Lay on her soul, so deep and chill—
That there was sin and shame she knew;
That some one was to die—but who?
She had forgotten:—did she breathe?
Could this be still the earth beneath,
The sky above, and men around;
Or were they fiends who now so frown'd
On one, before whose eyes each eye
Till then had smiled in sympathy?
All was confused and undefined
To her all-jarr'd and wandering mind:
A chaos of wild hopes and fears:
And now in laughter, now in tears,

But madly still in each extreme,
She strove with that convulsive dream;
For so it seem'd on her to break:
Oh! vainly must she strive to wake!

XV.

The Convent bells are ringing,
 But mournfully and slow;
In the gray square turret swinging,
 With a deep sound, to and fro.
 Heavily to the heart they go!
Hark! the hymn is singing—
 The song for the dead below,
 Or the living who shortly shall be so!
For a departing being's soul
The death-hymn peals and the hollow bells knoll:
He is near his mortal goal;
Kneeling at the friar's knee;
Sad to hear—and piteous to see—
Kneeling on the bare cold ground,

With the block before and the guards around—
And the headsman with his bare arm ready,
That the blow may be both swift and steady,
Feels if the axe be sharp and true—
Since he set its edge anew:
While the crowd in speechless circle gather
To see the Son fall by the doom of the Father.

XVI.

It is a lovely hour as yet
Before the summer sun shall set,
Which rose upon that heavy day,
And mock'd it with his steadiest ray;
And his evening beams are shed
Full on Hugo's fated head,
As his last confession pouring
To the monk, his doom deploring
In penitential holiness,
He bends to hear his accents bless
With absolution such as may
Wipe our mortal stains away.
That high sun on his head did glisten
As he there did bow and listen—
And the rings of chestnut hair
Curl'd half down his neck so bare;
But brighter still the beam was thrown
Upon the axe which near him shone
With a clear and ghastly glitter.—
Oh! that parting hour was bitter!
Even the stern stood chill'd with awe:
Dark the crime, and just the law—
Yet they shudder'd as they saw.

XVII.

The parting prayers are said and over
Of that false son—and daring lover!
His beads and sins are all recounted,
His hours to their last minute mounted—
His mantling cloak before was stripp'd,
His bright brown locks must now be clipp'd;
'T is done—all closely are they shorn—
The vest which till this moment worn—
The scarf which Parisina gave—
Must not adorn him to the grave.
Even that must now be thrown aside,
And o'er his eyes the kerchief tied;
But no—that last indignity
Shall ne'er approach his haughty eye,
All feelings seemingly subdued,
In deep disdain were half renew'd,
When headman's hands prepared to bind
Those eyes which would not brook such blind:
As if they dared not look on death.
"No—yours my forfeit blood and breath—
These hands are chain'd, but let me die
At least with an unshackled eye—
Strike:"—and as the word he said,
Upon the block he bow'd his head;
These the last accents Hugo spoke:
"Strike:"—and flashing fell the stroke—
Roll'd the head—and, gushing, sunk
Back the stain'd and heaving trunk,
In the dust, which each deep vein
Slaked with its ensanguined rain;
His eyes and lips a moment quiver,
Convulsed and quick—then fix for ever.
He died, as erring man should die,
 Without display, without parade;
 Meekly had he bow'd and pray'd,
 As not disdaining priestly aid,
Nor desperate of all hope on high.
And while before the prior kneeling,
His heart was wean'd from earthly feeling;
His wrathful sire—his paramour—
What were they in such an hour?
No more reproach—no more despair;
No thought but heaven—no word but prayer—
Save the few which from him broke,
When, bared to meet the headsman's stroke,
He claim'd to die with eyes unbound,
His sole adieu to those around.

XVIII.

Still as the lips that closed in death,
Each gazer's bosom held his breath:
But yet, afar, from man to man,
A cold electric shiver ran,
As down the deadly blow descended
On him whose life and love thus ended;
And, with a hushing sound compress'd,
A sigh shrunk back on every breast;
But no more thrilling noise rose there,
 Beyond the blow that to the block
 Pierced through with forced and sullen shock,
Save one:—what cleaves the silent air
So madly shrill—so passing wild?
That, as a mother's o'er her child,
Done to death by sudden blow,
To the sky these accents go,
Like a soul's in endless woe.
Through Azo's palace-lattice driven,
That horrid voice ascends to heaven,
And every eye is turn'd thereon;
But sound and sight alike are gone!
It was a woman's shriek—and ne'er
In madlier accents rose despair;
And those who heard it, as it past,
In mercy wish'd it were the last.

XIX.

Hugo is fallen; and from that hour,
No more in palace, hall, or bower,
Was Parisina heard or seen:
Her name—as if she ne'er had been—

Was banish'd from each lip and ear,
Like words of wantonness or fear;
And from Prince Azo's voice, by none
Was mention heard of wife or son;
No tomb—no memory had they;
Theirs was unconsecrated clay;
At least the knight's who died that day.
But Parisina's fate lies hid
Like dust beneath the coffin lid:
Whether in convent she abode,
And won to heaven her dreary road,
By blighted and remorseful years
Of scourge and fast, and sleepless tears;
Or if she fell by bowl or steel,
For that dark love she dared to feel;
Or if, upon the moment smote,
She died by tortures less remote;
Like him she saw upon the block,
With heart that shared the headsman's shock,
In quicken'd brokenness that came,
In pity, o'er her shatter'd frame,
None knew—and none can ever know:
But whatsoe'er its end below,
Her life began and closed in woe!

XX.

And Azo found another bride,
And goodly sons grew by his side;
But none so lovely and so brave
As him who wither'd in the grave;
Or if they were—on his cold eye
Their growth but glanced unheeded by,
Or noticed with a smother'd sigh.
But never tear his cheek descended,
And never smile his brow unbended;
And o'er that fair broad brow were wrought
The intersected lines of thought;
Those furrows which the burning share
Of Sorrow ploughs untimely there;
Scars of the lacerating mind
Which the Soul's war doth leave behind.
He was past all mirth or woe:
Nothing more remain'd below
But sleepless nights and heavy days,
A mind all dead to scorn or praise,
A heart which shunn'd itself—and yet
That would not yield—nor could forget,
Which, when it least appear'd to melt,
Intently thought—intensely felt:
The deepest ice which ever froze
Can only o'er the surface close—
The living stream lies quick below,
And flows—and cannot cease to flow.
Still was his sealed-up bosom haunted
By thoughts which Nature hath implanted;
Too deeply rooted thence to vanish,
Howe'er our stifled fears we banish;
When, struggling as they rise to start,
We check those waters of the heart,
They are not dried—those tears unshed,
But flow back to the fountain head,
And resting in their spring more pure,
For ever in its depth endure,
Unseen, unwept, but uncongeal'd,
And cherish'd most where least reveal'd.
With inward starts of feeling left,
To throb o'er those of life bereft;
Without the power to fill again
The desert gap which made his pain;
Without the hope to meet them where
United souls shall gladness share,
With all the consciousness that he
Had only pass'd a just decree;
That they had wrought their doom of ill;
Yet Azo's age was wretched still.
The tainted branches of the tree,
 If lopp'd with care, a strength may give,
 By which the rest shall bloom and live
All greenly fresh and wildly free:
But if the lightning, in its wrath,
The waving boughs with fury scathe,
The massy trunk the ruin feels,
And never more a leaf reveals.

NOTES TO PARISINA.

NOTE 1, page 108.

The facts on which the present poem was grounded are thus given in Frizzi's History of Ferrara:—

"This turned out a calamitous year for the people of Ferrara; for there occurred a very tragical event in the court of their sovereign. Our annals, both printed and in manuscript, with the exception of the unpolished and negligent work of Sardi, and one other, have given the following relation of it,—from which, however, are rejected many details, and especially the narrative of Bandelli, who wrote a century afterwards, and who does not accord with the contemporary historians.

"By the above-mentioned Stella dell' Assassino, the Marquis, in the year 1405, had a son called Ugo, a beautiful and ingenius youth. Parisina Malatesta, second wife of Niccolo, like the generality of step-mothers, treated him with little kindness, to the infinite regret of the Marquis, who regarded him with fond partiality. One day she asked leave of her husband to undertake a certain journey, to which he consented, but upon condition that Ugo should bear her company; for he hoped by these means to induce her, in the end, to lay aside the obstinate aversion which she had conceived against him. And indeed his intent was accomplished but too well, since, during the journey, she not only divested herself of all her hatred, but fell into the opposite extreme. After their return, the Marquis had no longer any occasion to renew his former reproofs. It happened one day that a servant of the Marquis, named Zoese, or, as some call him, Giorgio, passing before the apartments of Parisina, saw going out from them one of her chamber-maids, all terrified and in tears. Asking the reason, she told him that her mistress, for some slight offence, had been beating her; and, giving vent to her rage, she added, that she could easily be revenged, if she chose to make known the criminal familiarity which subsisted between Parisina and her step-son. The servant took note of the words, and related them to his master. He was astounded thereat, but scarcely believing his ears, he assured himself of the fact—alas! too clearly—on the 18th of May, by looking through a hole made in the ceiling of his wife's chamber. Instantly he broke into a furious rage, and arrested both of them, together with Aldobrandino Rangoni, of Modena, her gentleman, and also, as some say, two of the women of her chamber, as abettors of this sinful act. He ordered them to be brought to a hasty trial, desiring the judges to pronounce sentence, in the accustomed forms, upon the culprits. This sentence was death. Some there were that bestirred themselves in favour of the delinquents, and amongst others, Ugoccion Contrario, who was all-powerful with Niccolo, and also his aged and much deserving minister, Alberto dal Sale. Both of these, their tears flowing down their checks, and upon their knees, implored him for mercy; adducing whatever reasons they could suggest for sparing the offenders, besides those motives of honour and decency which might persuade him to conceal from the public so scandalous a deed. But his rage made him inflexible, and, on the instant, he commanded that the sentence should be put in execution.

"It was, then, in the prisons of the castle, and exactly in those frightful dungeons which are seen at this day beneath the chamber called the Aurora, at the foot of the Lion's tower, at the top of the street Giovecca, that on the night of the 21st of May were beheaded, first, Ugo, and afterwards Parisina. Zoese, he that accused her, conducted the latter under his arm to the place of punishment. She, all along, fancied that she was to be thrown into a pit, and asked at every step, whether she was yet come to the spot? She was told that her punishment was the axe. She inquired what was become of Ugo, and received for answer, that he was already dead; at the which, sighing grievously, she exclaimed, 'Now, then, I wish not myself to live;' and being come to the block, she stripped herself with her own hands of all her ornaments, and wrapping a cloth round her head, submitted to the fatal stroke, which terminated the cruel scene. The same was done with Rangoni, who, together with the others, according to two calendars in the library of St. Francesco, was buried in the cemeteryof that convent. Nothing else is known respecting the women.

"The Marquis kept watch the whole of that dreadful night, and, as he was walking backwards and forwards, inquired of the captain of the castle if Ugo was dead yet? who answered him, Yes. He then gave himself up to the most desperate lamentations, exclaiming, 'Oh! that I too were dead, since I have been hurried on to resolve thus against my own Ugo!' And then gnawing with his teeth a cane which he had in his hand, he passed the rest of the night in sighs and in tears, calling frequently upon his own dear Ugo. On the following day, calling to mind that it would be necessary to make public his justification, seeing that the transaction could not be kept secret, he ordered the narrative to be drawn out upon paper, and sent it to all the courts of Italy.

"On receiving this advice, the Doge of Venice, Francesco Foscari, gave orders, but without publishing his reasons, that stop should be put to the preparations for a tournament, which, under the auspices of the Marquis, and at the expense of the city of Padua, was about to take place, in the square of St. Mark, in order to celebrate his advancement to the ducal chair."

"The Marquis, in addition to what he had already done, from some unaccountable burst of vengeance, commanded that as many of the married women as were well known to him to be faithless, like his Parisina, should, like her, be beheaded. Amongst others, Barberina, or, as some call her, Laodamia Romei, wife of the court judge, underwent this sentence, at the usual place of execution; that is to say, in the quarter of St. Giacoma, opposite the present fortress, beyond St. Paul's. It cannot be told how strange appeared this proceeding in a prince, who, considering his own disposition, should, as it seemed, have been in such cases most indulgent. Some, however, there were who did not fail to commend him."

NOTE 2, page 113.

Haught—haughty.—"Away *haught* man, thou art insulting me."—SHAKSPEARE.

THE PRISONER OF CHILLON.

ADVERTISEMENT.

When this poem was composed, I was not sufficiently aware of the history of Bonnivard, or I should have endeavoured to dignify the subject by an attempt to celebrate his courage and his virtues. Some account of his life will be found below, furnished me by the kindness of a citizen of that republic, which is still proud of the memory of a man worthy of the best age of ancient freedom:—

Francois de Bonnivard, son of Louis de Bonnivard, a native of Seysel, and Seigneur of Lunes, was born in 1496; he was educated at Turin. In 1510 his uncle, Jean-Reiné de Bonnivard, resigned to him the Priory of Saint-Victor, which adjoins the walls of Geneva, and which was a considerable living.

This great man—Bonnivard is deserving of this title from his greatness of soul, the uprightness of his heart, the nobility of his intentions, the wisdom of his counsels, the courage of his actions, the extent of his learning, and the brilliancy of his wit—this great man, who will ever excite the admiration of all those whom an heroic virtue can move, will always inspire the most lively gratitude in the hearts of those Genoese who love Geneva. Bonnivard was always one of its firmest supports; to protect the liberty of our republic, he never feared to lose his own; he forgot his ease, he despised his wealth; he neglected nothing to render certain the happiness of the country that he dignified by his adoption; from that moment he loved it as the most zealous of its citizens, he served it with the intrepidity of a hero, and he wrote its history with the simplicity of a philosopher, and the ardour of a patriot.

He says in the commencement of his "History of Geneva," that, "As soon as he commenced to read the histories of nations, he felt himself carried away by his love for republics, the interest of which he always advocated." It was, doubtless, this very love of liberty, that made him adopt Geneva as his country.

Bonnivard, while yet young, boldly stood forward as the defender of Geneva, against the Duke of Savoy and the Bishop.

In 1519, Bonnivard became the martyr of his country; the Duke of Savoy having entered Geneva with five hundred men, Bonnivard feared the resentment of the Duke; he wished to return to Flabourg to avoid the consequences; but he was betrayed by two men who accompanied him, and conducted by order of the prince to Grolée, where for two years he remained a prisoner.

Bonnivard was unfortunate in his travels. As his misfortunes had not slackened his zeal for Geneva, he was always a redoubtable enemy to those who threatened it, and accordingly was likely to be exposed to their violence. He was met in 1530 on the Jura, by thieves, who stripped him of everything, and placed him again in the hands of the Duke of Savoy. This prince caused him to be confined in the Chateau of Chillon, where he remained without being submitted to any interrogatory, until 1536; he was then delivered by the Bernois, who took possession of the Pays de Vaud.

Bonnivard, on leaving his captivity, had the pleasure of finding Geneva free and reformed. The Republic hastened to testify its gratitude to him, and to recompense him for the evils which he had suffered. It received him as a citizen of the town, in the month of June, 1536; it gave him the house formerly inhabited by the Vicar-General, and assigned to him a pension of two hundred gold crowns, as long as he should sojourn in Geneva. He was admitted into the council of Two Hundred in 1537.

Bonnivard did not now cease to be useful; after having laboured to make Geneva free, he succeeded in making it tolerant. Bonnivard prevailed upon the council to accord to the Calvinists and peasants a sufficient time for examining the propositions which were made to them; he succeeded by his meekness. Christianity is always preached with success, when it is preached with charity.

Bonnivard was learned. His manuscripts, which are in the public library, prove that he had diligently studied the Latin classics, and that he had penetrated the depths of theology and history. This great man loved the sciences, and thought they would constitute the glory of Geneva; accordingly he neglected nothing to establish them in this rising town. In 1551, he gave his library to the public; it was the commencement of our public library. And a portion of his books, are those rare and beautiful editions of the fifteenth century, which are seen in our collection. Finally, during the same year, this good patriot appointed the republic his heir, on condition that it would employ his wealth in supporting the college, the foundation of which was being projected.

It appears that Bonnivard died in 1570; but this cannot be certified, as an hiatus occurs in the Necrology, from the month of July, 1570, to 1571.

CASTLE OF CHILLON.

SONNET ON CHILLON.

ETERNAL Spirit of the chainless Mind!
 Brightest in dungeons, Liberty! thou art,
 For there thy habitation is the heart—
The heart which love of thee alone can bind;
And when thy sons to fetters are consigned—
 To fetters, and the damp vault's dayless gloom,
 Their country conquers with their martyrdom,
And Freedom's fame finds wings on every wind.
Chillon! thy prison is a holy place,
 And thy sad floor an altar—for 't was trod,
Until his very steps have left a trace
 Worn, as if thy cold pavement were a sod,
By Bonnivard!—May none those marks efface!
 For they appeal from tyranny to God.

THE PRISONER OF CHILLON.

I.

My hair is gray, but not with years,
Nor grew it white
In a single night,
As men's have grown from sudden fears:
My limbs are bow'd, though not with toil,
But rusted with a vile repose,
For they have been a dungeon's spoil,
And mine has been the fate of those
To whom the goodly earth and air
Are bann'd, and barr'd—forbidden fare;
But this was for my father's faith
I suffered chains and courted death;
That father perish'd at the stake
For tenets he would not forsake;
And for the same his lineal race
In darkness found a dwelling-place;
We were seven—who now are one,
Six in youth, and one in age,
Finish'd as they had begun,
Proud of Persecution's rage;
One in fire, and two in field,
Their belief with blood have seal'd;
Dying as their father died,
For the God their foes denied;
Three were in a dungeon cast,
Of whom this wreck is left the last.

II.

There are seven pillars of Gothic mould,
In Chillon's dungeons deep and old,
There are seven columns, massy and gray,
Dim with a dull imprison'd ray,
A sunbeam which hath lost its way,
And through the crevice and the cleft
Of the thick wall is fallen and left;
Creeping o'er the floor so damp,
Like a marsh's meteor lamp:
And in each pillar there is a ring,
And in each ring there is a chain;
That iron is a cankering thing,
For in these limbs its teeth remain,
With marks that will not wear away,
Till I have done with this new day,
Which now is painful to these eyes,
Which have not seen the sun so rise

For years—I cannot count them o'er,
I lost their long and heavy score
When my last brother droop'd and died,
And I lay living by his side.

III.

They chained us each to a column stone,
And we were three—yet, each alone:
We could not move a single pace,
We could not see each other's face,
But with that pale and livid light
That made us strangers in our sight;
And thus together—yet apart,
Fetter'd in hand, but pined in heart;
'T was still some solace in the dearth
Of the pure elements of earth,
To hearken to each other's speech,
And each turn comforter to each
With some new hope, or legend old,
Or song heroically bold;
But even these at length grew cold.
Our voices took a dreary tone,
An echo of the dungeon-stone,
 A grating sound—not full and free
 As they of yore were wont to be;
 It might be fancy—but to me
They never sounded like our own.

IV.

I was the eldest of the three,
 And to uphold and cheer the rest
 I ought to do—and did—my best,
And each did well in his degree.
 The youngest, whom my father loved,
Because our mother's brow was given
To him—with eyes as blue as heaven,
 For him my soul was sorely moved;
And truly might it be distrest
To see such bird in such a nest;
For he was beautiful as day—
 (When day was beautiful to me
 As to young eagles, being free)—
 A polar day, which will not see
A sunset till its summer's gone,
 Its sleepless summer of long light,
The snow-clad offspring of the sun:
 And thus he was as pure and bright,
And in his natural spirit gay,
With tears for nought but others' ills,
And then they flow'd like mountain rills,
Unless he could assuage the woe
Which he abhorr'd to view below.

V.

The other was as pure of mind,
But form'd to combat with his kind;
Strong in his frame, and of a mood
Which 'gainst the world in war had stood,
And perish'd in the foremost rank
 With joy:—but not in chains to pine:
His spirit wither'd with their clank,
 I saw it silently decline—
 And so perchance in sooth did mine;
But yet I forced it on to cheer
Those relics of a home so dear.
He was a hunter of the hills,
 Had follow'd there the deer and wolf;
 To him this dungeon was a gulf,
And fetter'd feet the worst of ills.

VI.

 Lake Leman lies by Chillon's walls:
A thousand feet in depth below
Its massy waters meet and flow;
Thus much the fathom-line was sent
From Chillon's snow-white battlement,[2]
 Which round about the wave enthralls:
A double dungeon wall and wave
Have made—and like a living grave.
Below the surface of the lake
The dark vault lies wherein we lay,
We heard it ripple night and day;
 Sounding o'er our heads it knock'd;
And I have felt the winter's spray
Wash through the bars when winds were high,
And wanton in the happy sky;
 And then the very rock hath rock'd,
 And I have felt it shake, unshock'd,
Because I could have smiled to see
The death that would have set me free.

VII.

I said my nearer brother pined,
I said his mighty heart declined,
He loathed and put away his food;
It was not that 't was coarse and rude,
For we were used to hunter's fare,
And for the like had little care:
The milk drawn from the mountain goat
Was changed for water from the moat,
Our bread was such as captive's tears
Have moisten'd many a thousand years,
Since man first pent his fellow-men
Like brutes within an iron den:
But what were these to us or him?
These wasted not his heart or limb;
My brother's soul was of that mould
Which in a palace had grown cold,
Had his free breathing been denied
The range of the steep mountain's side;
But why delay the truth?—he died.
I saw, and could not hold his head,
Nor reach his dying hand—nor dead,

Though hard I strove, but strove in vain,
To rend and gnash my bonds in twain.
He died—and they unlock'd his chain,
And scoop'd for him a shallow grave
Even from the cold earth of our cave.
I begg'd them, as a boon, to lay
His corse in dust whereon the day
Might shine—it was a foolish thought,
But then within my brain it wrought,
That even in death his freeborn breast
In such a dungeon could not rest.
I might have spared my idle prayer—
They coldly laugh'd—and laid him there:
The flat and turfless earth above
The being we so much did love;
His empty chain above it leant,
Such murder's fitting monument!

VIII.

But he, the favourite and the flower,
Most cherish'd since his natal hour,
His mother's image in fair face,
The infant love of all his race,
His martyr'd father's dearest thought,
My latest care, for whom I sought
To hoard my life, that his might be
Less wretched now, and one day free;
He, too, who yet had held untired
A spirit natural or inspired—
He, too, was struck, and day by day
Was wither'd on the stalk away.
Oh God! it is a fearful thing
To see the human soul take wing
In any shape, in any mood:—
I've seen it rushing forth in blood,
I've seen it on the breaking ocean
Strive with a swoln convulsive motion,
I've seen the sick and ghastly bed
Of Sin delirious with its dread:
But these were horrors—this was woe
Unmix'd with such—but sure and slow:
He faded, and so calm and meek,
So softly worn, so sweetly weak,
So tearless, yet so tender—kind,
And grieved for those he left behind;
With all the while a cheek whose bloom
Was as a mockery of the tomb,
Whose tints as gently sunk away
As a departing rainbow's ray—
An eye of most transparent light,
That almost made the dungeon bright,
And not a word of murmur—not
A groan o'er his untimely lot,—
A little talk of better days,
A little hope my own to raise,
For I was sunk in silence—lost
In this last loss, of all the most;
And then the sighs he would suppress
Of fainting nature's feebleness,
More slowly drawn, grew less and less:
I listen'd, but I could not hear—
I call'd, for I was wild with fear
I knew 't was hopeless, but my dread
Would not be thus admonished;
I call'd, and thought I heard a sound—
I burst my chain with one strong bound,
And rush'd to him:—I found him not,
I only stirr'd in this black spot,
I only lived—*I* only drew
The accursed breath of dungeon-dew;
The last—the sole—the dearest link
Between me and the eternal brink,
Which bound me to my failing race,
Was broken in this fatal place.
One on the earth, and one beneath—
My brothers—both had ceased to breathe:
I took that hand which lay so still,
Alas! my own was full as chill;
I had not strength to stir, or strive,
But felt that I was still alive—
A frantic feeling, when we know
That what we love shall ne'er be so.
I know not why
I could not die,
I had no earthly hope—but faith,
And that forbade a selfish death.

IX.

What next befell me then and there
I know not well—I never knew—
First came the loss of light, and air,
And then of darkness too:
I had no thought, no feeling—none—
Among the stones I stood a stone,
And was, scarce conscious what I wist,
As shrubless crags within the mist;
For all was blank, and bleak, and gray,
It was not night—it was not day,
It was not even the dungeon-light,
So hateful to my heavy sight,
But vacancy absorbing space,
And fixedness—without a place;
There were no stars—no earth—no time—
No check—no change—no good—no crime—
But silence, and a stirless breath
Which neither was of life nor death;
A sea of stagnant idleness,
Blind, boundless, mute, and motionless!

X.

A light broke in upon my brain,—
It was the carol of a bird;
It ceased, and then it came again,
The sweetest song ear ever heard,
And mine was thankful till my eyes
Ran over with the glad surprise,

And they that moment could not see
I was the mate of misery;
But then by dull degrees came back
My senses to their wonted track,
I saw the dungeon walls and floor
Close slowly round me as before,
I saw the glimmer of the sun
Creeping as it before had done,
But through the crevice where it came
That bird was perch'd, as fond and tame
 And tamer than upon the tree;
A lovely bird, with azure wings,
And song that said a thousand things,
 And seem'd to say them all for me!
I never saw its like before,
I ne'er shall see its likeness more:
It seem'd, like me, to want a mate,
But was not half so desolate,
And it was come to love me when
None lived to love me so again,
And cheering from my dungeon's brink,
Had brought me back to feel and think.
I know not if it late were free,
 Or broke its cage to perch on mine,
But knowing well captivity,
 Sweet bird! I could not wish for thine!
Or if it were, in wingèd guise,
A visitant from Paradise;
For — Heaven forgive that thought! the while
Which made me both to weep and smile—
I sometimes deem'd that it might be
My brother's soul come down to me;
But then at last away it flew,
And then 't was mortal—well I knew,
For he would never thus have flown,
And left me twice so doubly lone,—
Lone—as the corse within its shroud,
Lone—as a solitary cloud,
 A single cloud on a sunny day,
While all the rest of heaven is clear,
A frown upon the atmosphere,
That hath no business to appear
 When skies are blue, and earth is gay.

XI.

A kind of change came in my fate,
My keepers grew compassionate,
I know not what had made them so,
They were inured to sights of woe,
But so it was:—my broken chain
With links unfasten'd did remain,
And it was liberty to stride
Along my cell from side to side,
And up and down, and then athwart,
And tread it over every part;
And round the pillars one by one,
Returning where my walk begun,
Avoiding only, as I trod,
My brothers' graves without a sod;
For if I thought with heedless tread
My step profaned their lowly bed,
My breath came gaspingly and thick,
And my crush'd heart fell blind and sick.

XII.

I made a footing in the wall,
 It was not therefrom to escape,
For I had buried one and all,
 Who loved me in a human shape;
And the whole earth would henceforth be
A wider prison unto me:
No child—no sire—no kin had I,
No partner in my misery:
I thought of this, and I was glad,
For thought of them had made me mad:
But I was curious to ascend
To my barr'd windows, and to bend
Once more, upon the mountains high,
The quiet of a loving eye.

XIII.

I saw them—and they were the same,
They were not changed like me in frame;
I saw their thousand years of snow
On high—their wide long lake below,
And the blue Rhone in fullest flow;
I heard the torrents leap and gush
O'er channel'd rock and broken bush;
I saw the white-wall'd distant town,
And whiter sails go skimming down;
And then there was a little isle,[3]
Which in my very face did smile,
 The only one in view;
A small green isle, it seem'd no more,
Scarce broader than my dungeon floor,
But in it there were three tall trees,
And o'er it blew the mountain breeze,
And by it there were waters flowing,
And on it there were young flowers growing,
 Of gentle breath and hue.
The fish swam by the castle wall,
And they seem'd joyous each and all;
The eagle rode the rising blast,
Methought he never flew so fast
As then to me he seem'd to fly,
And then new tears came in my eye,
And I felt troubled—and would fain
I had not left my recent chain;
And when I did descend again,
The darkness of my dim abode
Fell on me as a heavy load;
It was as is a new-dug grave,
Closing o'er one we sought to save,
And yet my glance, too much opprest,
Had almost need of such a rest.

XIV.

It might be months, or years, or days,
I kept no count—I took no note,
I had no hope my eyes to raise,
And clear them of their dreary mote;
At last men came to set me free,
I ask'd not why, and reck'd not where,
It was at length the same to me,
Fetter'd or fetterless to be,
I learn'd to love despair.
And thus when they appear'd at last,
And all my bonds aside were cast,
These heavy walls to me had grown
A hermitage—and all my own!
And half I felt as they were come
To tear me from a second home:
With spiders I had friendship made,
And watch'd them in their sullen trade,
Had seen the mice by moonlight play,
And why should I feel less than they?
We were all inmates of one place,
And I, the monarch of each race,
Had power to kill—yet, strange to tell
In quiet we had learn'd to dwell—
My very chains and I grew friends,
So much a long communion tends
To make us what we are:—even I
Regain'd my freedom with a sigh.

THE DUNGEON OF CHILLON.

NOTES TO THE PRISONER OF CHILLON.

Note 1, page 121.

In a single night.

Ludovico Sforza, and others.—The same is asserted of Marie Antoinette's, the wife of Louis XVI., though not in quite so short a period. Grief is said to have the same effect: to such, and not to fear, this change in *hers* was to be attributed.

Note 2, page 122.

From Chillon's snow-white battlement.

The Chateau de Chillon is situated between Clarens and Villeneuve, which last is at one extremity of the Lake of Geneva. On its left are the entrances of the Rhone, and opposite are the heights of Meillerie and the range of Alps above Boveret and St. Gingo.

Near it, on a hill behind, is a torrent; below it, washing its walls, the lake has been fathomed to the depth of 800 feet (French measure); within it are a range of dungeons, in which the early reformers, and subsequently prisoners of state, were confined. Across one of the vaults is a beam black with age, on which we were informed that the condemned were formerly executed. In the cells are seven pillars, or, rather, eight, one being half merged in the wall; in some of these are rings for the fetters and the fettered: in the pavement the steps of Bonnivard have left their traces—he was confined here several years.

It is by this castle that Rousseau has fixed the catastrophe of his Heloise, in the rescue of one of her children by Julie from the water; the shock of which, and the illness produced by the immersion, is the cause of her death.

The chateau is large, and seen along the lake for a great distance. The walls are white.

Note 3, page 124.

And then there was a little isle.

Between the entrances of the Rhone and Villeneuve, not far from Chillon, is a very small island; the only one I could perceive, in my voyage round and over the lake, within its circumference. It contains a few trees (I think not above three), and from its singleness and diminutive size has a peculiar effect upon the view.

I.

OUR life is twofold: Sleep hath its own world,
A boundary between the things misnamed
Death and existence: Sleep hath its own world,
And a wide realm of wild reality,
And dreams in their development have breath,
And tears, and tortures, and the touch of joy;
They leave a weight upon our waking thoughts,
They take a weight from off our waking toils,
They do divide our being; they become
A portion of ourselves as of our time,
And look like heralds of eternity;
They pass like spirits of the past—they speak
Like sibyls of the future; they have power—
The tyranny of pleasure and of pain;
They make us what we were not—what they will,
And shake us with the vision that's gone by,
The dread of vanish'd shadows—Are they so?
Is not the past all shadow? What are they?
Creations of the mind?—The mind can make

Substance, and people planets of its own
With beings brighter than have been, and give
A breath to forms which can outlive all flesh.
I would recall a vision which I dream'd
Perchance in sleep—for in itself a thought,
A slumbering thought, is capable of years,
And curdles a long life into one hour.

II.

I saw two beings in the hues of youth
Standing upon a hill, a gentle hill,
Green and of mild declivity, the last
As 't were the cape of a long ridge of such,
Save that there was no sea to lave its base,
But a most living landscape, and the wave
Of woods and cornfields, and the abodes of men
Scatter'd at intervals, and wreathing smoke
Arising from such rustic roofs;—the hill
Was crown'd with a peculiar diadem
Of trees, in circular array, so fix'd,
Not by the sport of nature, but of man:
These two, a maiden and a youth, were there
Gazing—the one on all that was beneath
Fair as herself—but the boy gazed on her;
And both were young, and one was beautiful:
And both were young—yet not alike in youth.
As the sweet moon on the horizon's verge,
The maid was on the eve of womanhood;
The boy had fewer summers, but his heart
Had far outgrown his years, and to his eye
There was but one belovèd face on earth,
And that was shining on him; he had look'd
Upon it till it could not pass away;
He had no breath, no being, but in hers:
She was his voice; he did not speak to her,
But trembled on her words: she was his sight,
For his eye follow'd hers, and saw with hers,
Which colour'd all his objects:—he had ceased
To live within himself; she was his life,
The ocean to the river of his thoughts,
Which terminated all: upon a tone,
A touch of hers, his blood would ebb and flow,
And his cheek change tempestuously—his heart
Unknowing of its cause of agony.
But she in these fond feelings had no share:
Her sighs were not for him; to her he was
Even as a brother—but no more; 't was much,
For brotherless she was, save in the name
Her infant friendship had bestow'd on him;
Herself the solitary scion left
Of a time-honour'd race.—It was a name
Which pleased him, and yet pleased him not—and why?
Time taught him a deep answer—when she loved
Another; even *now* she loved another,
And on the summit of that hill she stood
Looking afar if yet her lover's steed
Kept pace with her expectancy, and flew.

III.

A change came o'er the spirit of my dream.
There was an ancient mansion, and before
Its walls there was a steed caparison'd:
Within an antique Oratory stood
The Boy of whom I spake;—he was alone,
And pale, and pacing to and fro: anon
He sate him down, and seized a pen, and traced
Words which I could not guess of; then he lean'd
His bow'd head on his hands, and shook as 't were
With a convulsion—then arose again,
And with his teeth and quivering hands did tear
What he had written, but he shed no tears.
And he did calm himself, and fix his brow
Into a kind of quiet: as he paused,
The Lady of his love re-enter'd there;
She was serene and smiling then, and yet
She knew she was by him beloved;—she knew—
For quickly comes such knowledge—that his heart
Was darken'd with her shadow, and she saw
That he was wretched, but she saw not all.
He rose, and with a cold and gentle grasp
He took her hand; a moment o'er his face
A tablet of unutterable thoughts
Was traced, and then it faded, as it came;
He dropp'd the hand he held, and with slow steps
Retired, but not as bidding her adieu,
For they did part with mutual smiles; he pass'd
From out the massy gate of that old Hall,
And mounting on his steed he went his way;
And ne'er repass'd that hoary threshold more.

IV.

A change came o'er the spirit of my dream.
The Boy was sprung to manhood: in the wilds
Of fiery climes he made himself a home,
And his Soul drank their sunbeams: he was girt
With strange and dusky aspects; he was not
Himself like what he had been; on the sea
And on the shore he was a wanderer;
There was a mass of many images
Crowded like waves upon me, but he was
A part of all; and in the last he lay
Reposing from the noontide sultriness,
Couch'd among fallen columns, in the shade
Of ruin'd walls that had survived the names
Of those who rear'd them; by his sleeping side
Stood camels grazing, and some goodly steeds
Were fasten'd near a fountain; and a man,
Clad in a flowing garb, did watch the while,
While many of his tribe slumber'd around:
And they were canopied by the blue sky,
So cloudless, clear, and purely beautiful,
That God alone was to be seen in heaven.

V.

A change came o'er the spirit of my dream.
The Lady of his love was wed with One

Who did not love her better:—in her home,
A thousand leagues from his,—her native home,
She dwelt, begirt with growing Infancy,
Daughters and sons of Beauty,—but behold!
Upon her face there was the tint of grief,
The settled shadow of an inward strife,
And an unquiet drooping of the eye,
As if its lid were charged with unshed tears,
What could her grief be?—she had all she loved,
And he who had so loved her was not there
To trouble with bad hopes, or evil wish,
Or ill-repress'd affliction, her pure thoughts.
What could her grief be?—she had loved him not,
Nor given him cause to deem himself beloved,
Nor could he be a part of that which prey'd
Upon her mind—a spectre of the past.

VI.

A change came o'er the spirit of my dream.
The Wanderer was return'd.—I saw him stand
Before an Altar—with a gentle bride;
Her face was fair, but was not that which made
The Starlight of his Boyhood;—as he stood
Even at the altar, o'er his brow there came
The selfsame aspect, and the quivering shock
That in the antique Oratory shook
His bosom in its solitude; and then—
As in that hour—a moment o'er his face
The tablet of unutterable thoughts
Was traced—and then it faded as it came,
And he stood calm and quiet, and he spoke
The fitting vows, but heard not his own words,
And all things reel'd around him; he could see
Not that which was, nor that which should have been—

But the old mansion, and the accustom'd hall,
And the remember'd chambers, and the place,
The day, the hour, the sunshine, and the shade,
All things pertaining to that place and hour,
And her who was his destiny, came back
And thrust themselves between him and the light:
What business had they there at such a time?

VII.

A change came o'er the spirit of my dream.
The Lady of his love;—Oh! she was changed,
As by the sickness of the soul; her mind
Had wander'd from its dwelling, and her eyes,
They had not their own lustre, but the look
Which is not of the earth; she was become
The queen of a fantastic realm; her thoughts
Were combinations of disjointed things;
And forms impalpable and unperceived
Of others' sight familiar were to hers.
And this the world calls phrenzy: but the wise
Have a far deeper madness, and the glance
Of melancholy is a fearful gift;
What is it but the telescope of truth?
Which strips the distance of its fantasies,
And brings life near in utter nakedness,
Making the cold reality too real!

VIII.

A change came o'er the spirit of my dream.
The Wanderer was alone as heretofore,
The beings which surrounded him were gone,
Or were at war with him; he was a mark
For blight and desolation, compass'd round
With Hatred and Contention; Pain was mix'd
In all which was served up to him, until,
Like to the Pontic monarch of old days,
He fed on poisons, and they had no power,
But were a kind of nutriment; he lived
Through that which had been death to many men,
And made him friends of mountains: with the stars
And the quick Spirit of the Universe
He held his dialogues: and they did teach
To him the magic of their mysteries;
To him the book of Night was open'd wide,
And voices from the deep abyss reveal'd
A marvel and a secret.—Be it so.

IX.

My dream is past; it had no further change.
It was of a strange order, that the doom
Of these two creatures should be thus traced out
Almost like a reality—the one
To end in madness—both in misery.

JULY, 1816.

THE LAMENT OF TASSO.

ADVERTISEMENT.

At Ferrara, in the Library, are preserved the original MSS. of Tasso's "Gierusalemme" and of Guarini's "Pastor Fido," with letters of Tasso, one from Titian to Ariosto, and the inkstand and chair, the tomb and house, of the latter. But, as misfortune has a greater interest for posterity, and little or none for the cotemporary, the cell where Tasso was confined in the hospital of St. Anna attracts a more fixed attention than the residence or monument of Ariosto—at least it had this effect on me. There are two inscriptions, one on the outer gate, the second over the cell itself, inviting, unnecessarily, the wonder and the indignation of the spectator. Ferrara is much decayed and depopulated: the castle still exists entire; and I saw the court where Parisina and Hugo were beheaded, according to the annal of Gibbon.

THE LAMENT OF TASSO.

I.

LONG years!—It tries the thrilling frame to bear
And eagle-spirit of a child of Song—
Long years of outrage, calumny, and wrong;
Imputed madness, prison'd solitude,
And the mind's canker in its savage mood,
When the impatient thirst of light and air
Parches the heart; and the abhorrèd grate,
Marring the sunbeams with its hideous shade,
Works through the throbbing eyeball to the brain,
With a hot sense of heaviness and pain;
And bare, at once, Captivity display'd
Stands scoffing through the never-open'd gate,
Which nothing through its bars admits, save day,
And tasteless food, which I have eat alone
Till its unsocial bitterness is gone;
And I can banquet like a beast of prey,
Sullen and lonely, couching in the cave
Which is my lair, and—it may be—my grave.
All this hath somewhat worn me, and may wear,
But must be borne. I stoop not to despair;
For I have battled with mine agony,
And made me wings wherewith to overfly
The narrow circus of my dungeon wall,
And freed the Holy Sepulchre from thrall;
And revell'd among men and things divine,
And pour'd my spirit over Palestine,
In honour of the sacred war for Him,
The God who was on earth and is in heaven,
For He has strengthen'd me in heart and limb.
That through this sufferance I might be forgiven,
I have employ'd my penance to record
How Salem's shrine was won and how adored.

II.

But this is o'er—my pleasant task is done:—
My long-sustaining friend of many years!
If I do blot thy final page with tears,
Know, that my sorrows have wrung from me none.
But thou, my young creation! my soul's child!
Which ever playing round me came and smiled,
And woo'd me from myself with thy sweet sight,
Thou too art gone—and so is my delight:
And therefore do I weep and inly bleed
With this last bruise upon a broken reed.
Thou too art ended—what is left me now?
For I have anguish yet to bear—and how?
I know not that—but in the innate force
Of my own spirit shall be found resource.
I have not sunk, for I had no remorse,
Nor cause for such: they call'd me mad—and why?
Oh Leonora! wilt not *thou* reply?
I was indeed delirious in my heart
To lift my love so lofty as thou art;
But still my frenzy was not of the mind;
I knew my fault, and feel my punishment
Not less because I suffer it unbent.
That thou wert beautiful, and I not blind,
Hath been the sin which shuts me from mankind;
But let them go, or torture as they will,
My heart can multiply thine image still;
Successful love may sate itself away,
The wretched are the faithful; 't is their fate
To have all feeling save the one decay
And every passion into one dilate,
As rapid rivers into ocean pour;
But ours is fathomless, and hath no shore.

III.

Above me, hark! the long and maniac cry
Of minds and bodies in captivity,
And hark! the lash and the increasing howl,
And the half-inarticulate blasphemy!
There be some here with worse than frenzy foul,
Some who do still goad on the o'er-labour'd mind,
And dim the little light that 's left behind
With needless torture, as their tyrant will
Is wound up to the lust of doing ill:
With these and with their victims am I class'd,
'Mid sounds and sights like these long years have pass'd:
'Mid sounds and sights like these my life may close:
So let it be—for then I shall repose.

IV.

I have been patient, let me be so yet;
I had forgotten half I would forget,
But it revives—Oh! would it were my lot
To be forgetful as I am forgot!—
Feel I not wroth with those who bade me dwell
In this vast lazar-house of many woes?
Where laughter is not mirth, nor thought the mind,
Nor words a language, nor ev'n men mankind;
Where cries reply to curses, shrieks to blows,
And each is tortured in his separate hell—
For we are crowded in our solitudes—
Many, but each divided by the wall,
Which echoes Madness in her babbling moods;—
While all can hear, none heed his neighbour's call—
None! save that One, the veriest wretch of all,
Who was not made to be the mate of these,
Nor bound between Distraction and Disease.

Feel I not wroth with those who placed me here?
Who have debased me in the minds of men,
Debarring me the usage of my own,
Blighting my life in best of its career,

Branding my thoughts as things to shun and fear?
Would I not pay them back these pangs again,
And teach them inward Sorrow's stifled groan?
The struggle to be calm, and cold distress,
Which undermines our Stoical success?
No!—still too proud to be vindictive—I
Have pardon'd princes' insults, and would die.
Yes, Sister of my Sovereign! for thy sake
I weed all bitterness from out my breast,
It hath no business where *thou* art a guest;
Thy brother hates—but I can not detest;
Thou pitiest not—but I can not forsake.

V.

Look on a love which knows not to despair,
But all unquench'd is still my better part,
Dwelling deep in my shut and silent heart,
As dwells the gather'd lightning in its cloud,
Encompass'd with its dark and rolling shroud,
Till struck,—forth flies the all ethereal dart!
And thus at the collision of thy name
The vivid thought still flashes through my frame,
And for a moment all things as they were
Flit by me;—they are gone—I am the same.
And yet my love without ambition grew;
I knew thy state, my station, and I knew
A Princess was no love-mate for a bard;
I told it not. I breathed it not, it was
Sufficient to itself, its own reward;
And if my eyes reveal'd it, they, alas!
Were punish'd by the silentness of thine,
And yet I did not venture to repine.
Thou wert to me a crystal-girded shrine
Worshipp'd at holy distance, and around
Hallow'd and meekly kiss'd the saintly ground;
Not for thou wert a princess, but that Love
Had robed thee with a glory, and array'd
Thy lineaments in a beauty that dismay'd—
Oh! not dismay'd—but awed, like One above!
And in that sweet severity there was
A something which all softness did surpass—
I know not how—thy genius master'd mine—
My star stood still before thee:—if it were
Presumptuous thus to love without design,
That sad fatality hath cost me dear;
But thou art dearest still, and I should be
Fit for this cell, which wrongs me—but for *thee*.
The very love which lock'd me to my chain
Hath lighten'd half its weight; and for the rest,
Though heavy, lent me vigour to sustain,
And look to thee with undivided breast,
And foil the ingenuity of Pain.

VI.

It is no marvel—from my very birth
My soul was drunk with love,—which did pervade
And mingle with whate'er I saw on earth;
Of objects all inanimate I made
Idols, and out of wild and lonely flowers,
And rocks, whereby they grew, a paradise.
Where I did lay me down within the shade
Of waving trees, and dream'd uncounted hours,
Though I was chid for wandering; and the Wise
Shook their white agèd heads o'er me, and said
Of such materials wretched men were made,
And such a truant boy would end in woe,
And that the only lesson was a blow;
And then they smote me, and I did not weep,
But cursed them in my heart, and to my haunt
Return'd and wept alone, and dream'd again
The visions which arise without a sleep.
And with my years my soul began to pant
With feelings of strange tumult and soft pain;
And the whole heart exhaled into One Want,
But undefined and wandering, till the day
I found the thing I sought—and that was thee;
And then I lost my being all to be
Absorb'd in thine—the world was past away—
Thou didst annihilate the earth to me!

VII.

I loved all Solitude—but little thought
To spend I know not what of life, remote
From all communion with existence, save
The maniac and his tyrant;—had I been
Their fellow, many years ere this had seen
My mind like theirs corrupted to its grave,
But who hath seen me writhe, or heard me rave?
Perchance in such a cell we suffer more
Than the wreck'd sailor on his desert shore:
The world is all before him—*mine* is *here*,
Scarce twice the space they must accord my bier.
What though *he* perish, he may lift his eye
And with a dying glance upbraid the sky—
I will not raise my own in such reproof,
Although 't is clouded by my dungeon roof.

VIII.

Yet do I feel at times my mind decline,
But with a sense of its decay:—I see
Unwonted lights along my prison shine,
And a strange demon, who is vexing me
With pilfering pranks and petty pains, below
The feeling of the healthful and the free;
But much to One, who long hath suffer'd so,
Sickness of heart, and narrowness of place,
And all that may be borne, or can debase.
I thought mine enemies had been but Man,
But spirits may be leagued with them—all Earth
Abandons—Heaven forgets me;—in the dearth
Of such defence the Powers of Evil can,
It may be, tempt me further,—and prevail
Against the outworn creature they assail.
Why in this furnace is my spirit proved
Like steel in tempering fire?—because I loved?
Because I loved what not to love, and see,
Was more or less than mortal, and than me.

IX.

I once was quick in feeling—that is o'er;—
My scars are callous, or I should have dash'd
My brain against these bars, as the sun flash'd
In mockery through them;—If I bear and bore
The much I have recounted, and the more
Which hath no words,—'tis that I would not die
And sanction with self-slaughter the dull lie
Which snared me here, and with the brand of shame
Stamp Madness deep into my memory,
And woo Compassion to a blighted name,
Sealing the sentence which my foes proclaim.
No—it shall be immortal!—and I make
A future temple of my present cell,
Which nations yet shall visit for my sake.
While thou, Ferrara! when no longer dwell
The ducal chiefs within thee, shalt fall down,
And crumbling piecemeal view thy hearthless halls,
A poet's wreath shall be thine only crown,—
A poet's dungeon thy most far renown,
While strangers wander o'er thy unpeopled walls!
And thou, Leonora!—thou—who wert ashamed
That such as I could love—who blush'd to hear
To less than monarchs that thou couldst be dear,
Go! tell thy brother, that my heart, untamed
By grief, years, weariness—and it may be
A taint of that he would impute to me—
From long infection of a den like this,
Where the mind rots congenial with the abyss,
Adores thee still;—and add—that when the towers
And battlements which guard his joyous hours
Of banquet, dance, and revel are forgot,
Or left untended in a dull repose,
This—this—shall be a consecrated spot!
But thou—when all that Birth and Beauty throws
Of magic round thee is extinct—shalt have
One half the laurel which o'ershades my grave.
No power in death can tear our names apart,
As none in life could rend thee from my heart.
Yes, Leonora! it shall be our fate
To be entwined for ever—but too late!

DON JUAN.

"Difficile est propriè communia dicere."—HOR.

"Dost thou think, because thou art virtuous, there shall be no more Cakes and Ale?—Yes, by St. Anne, and Ginger shall be hot i' the mouth, too!"—SHAKSPEARE, *Twelfth Night, or What You Will.*

I.

SOUTHEY! You're a poet—Poet-laureate,
And representative of all the race,
Although 't is true that you 're turn'd out a Tory at
Last,—yours has lately been a common case,—
And now, my Epic Renegade! what are ye at?
With all the Lakers, in and out of place?
A nest of tuneful persons, to my eye
Like "four-and-twenty Blackbirds in a pie;

II.

"Which pie being open'd, they began to sing"
(This old song and new simile holds good),
"A dainty dish to set before the King,"
Or Regent, who admires such kind of food;—
And Coleridge, too, has lately taken wing,
But like a hawk encumber'd with his hood,—
Explaining metaphysics to the nation—
I wish he would explain his Explanation.

III.

You, Bob! are rather insolent, you know,
At being disappointed in your wish
To supersede all warblers here below,
And be the only Blackbird in the dish;
And then you overstrain yourself, or so,
And tumble downward like the flying fish
Gasping on deck, because you soar too high, Bob,
And fall, for lack of moisture, quite a-dry, Bob!

IV.

And Wordsworth, in a rather long "Excursion"
(I think the quarto holds five hundred pages),
Has given a sample from the vasty version
Of his new system to perplex the sages;
'T is poetry—at least by his assertion,
And may appear so when the dog-star rages;
And he who understands it would be able
To add a storey to the Tower of Babel.

V.

You, Gentlemen! by dint of long seclusion
From better company, have kept your own
At Keswick, and, through still-continued fusion
Of one another's minds, at last have grown
To deem, as a most logical conclusion,
That Poesy has wreaths for you alone:
There is a narrowness in such a notion,
Which makes me wish you'd change your lakes for ocean.

VI.

I would not imitate the petty thought,
Nor coin my self-love to so base a vice,
For all the glory your conversion brought,
Since gold alone should not have been its price.

You have your salary: was 't for that you wrought?
 And Wordsworth has his place in the Excise.
You 're shabby fellows—true—but poets still,
And duly seated on the immortal hill.

VII.

Your bays may hide the baldness of your brows—
 Perhaps some virtuous blushes;—let them go—
To you I envy neither fruit nor boughs—
 And for the fame you would engross below,
The field is universal, and allows
 Scope to all such as feel the inherent glow;
Scott, Rogers, Campbell, Moore, and Crabbe, will try
'Gainst you the question with posterity.

VIII.

For me, who, wandering with pedestrian Muses,
 Contend not with you on the wingèd steed,
I wish your fate may yield ye, when she chooses,
 The fame you envy, and the skill you need;
And recollect a poet nothing loses
 In giving to his brethren their full meed
Of merit, and complaint of present days
Is not the certain path to future praise.

IX.

He that reserves his laurels for posterity
 (Who does not often claim the bright reversion)
Has generally no great crop to spare it, he
 Being only injured by his own assertion;
And although here and there some glorious rarity
 Arise like Titan from the sea's immersion,
The major part of such appellants go
To—God knows where—for no one else can know.

X.

If, fallen in evil days on evil tongues,
 Milton appeal'd to the Avenger, Time,
If Time, the Avenger, execrates his wrongs,
 And makes the word "Miltonic" mean "*sublime*,"
He deign'd not to belie his soul in songs,
 Nor turn his very talent to a crime;
He did not loathe the Sire to laud the Son,
But closed the tyrant-hater he begun.

XI.

Think'st thou, could he—the blind Old Man—arise
 Like Samuel from the grave, to freeze once more
The blood of monarchs with his prophecies,
 Or be alive again—again all hoar
With time and trials, and those helpless eyes,
 And heartless daughters—worn—and pale—and poor;
Would *he* adore a sultan? *he* obey
The intellectual eunuch Castlereagh?

XII.

Cold-blooded, smooth-faced, placid miscreant!
 Dabbling its sleek young hands in Erin's gore,
And thus for wider carnage taught to pant,
 Transferr'd to gorge upon a sister shore,
The vulgarest tool that Tyranny could want,
 With just enough of talent, and no more,
To lengthen fetters by another fix'd,
And offer poison long already mix'd.

XIII.

An orator of such set trash of phrase
 Ineffably—legitimately vile,
That even its grossest flatterers dare not praise,
 Nor foes—all nations—condescend to smile,—
Nor even a sprightly blunder's spark can blaze
 From that Ixion grindstone's ceaseless toil,
That turns and turns to give the world a notion
Of endless torments and perpetual motion.

XIV.

A bungler even in its disgusting trade,
 And botching, patching, leaving still behind
Something of which its masters are afraid,
 States to be curb'd, and thoughts to be confined,
Conspiracy or Congress to be made—
 Cobbling at manacles for all mankind—
A tinkering slave-maker, who mends old chains,
With God and man's abhorrence for its gains.

XV.

If we may judge of matter by the mind,
 Emasculated to the marrow *It*
Hath but two objects, how to serve, and bind,
 Deeming the chain it wears even men may fit,
Eutropius of its many masters,—blind
 To worth as freedom, wisdom as to wit,
Fearless—because *no* feeling dwells in ice,
Its very courage stagnates to a vice.

XVI.

Where shall I turn me not to *view* its bonds,
 For I will never *feel* them;—Italy!
Thy late reviving Roman soul desponds
 Beneath the lie this State-thing breathed o'er thee—
Thy clanking chain, and Erin's yet green wounds,
 Have voices—tongues to cry aloud for me.
Europe has slaves—allies—kings—armies still,
And Southey lives to sing them very ill.

XVII.

Meantime—Sir Laureate—I proceed to dedicate,
 In honest simple verse, this song to you.
And, if in flattering strains I do not predicate,
 'Tis that I still retain my "buff and blue;"
My politics as yet are all to educate:
 Apostasy's so fashionable, too,
To keep *one* creed's a task grown quite Herculean;
Is it not so, my Tory, ultra-Julian?

VENICE, Sept. 16, 1818.

CANTO THE FIRST.

I.

I WANT a hero: an uncommon want,
 When every year and month sends forth a new one,
Till, after cloying the gazettes with cant,
 The age discovers he is not the true one;
Of such as these I should not care to vaunt,
 I'll therefore take our ancient friend Don Juan—
We all have seen him, in the pantomime,
Sent to the devil somewhat ere his time.

II.

Vernon, the butcher Cumberland, Wolfe, Hawke,
Prince Ferdinand, Granby, Burgoyne, Keppel, Howe,
Evil and good, have had their tithe of talk,
And fill'd their sign-posts then, like Wellesley now;
Each in their turn like Banquo's monarchs stalk,
Followers of fame, "nine farrow" of that sow:
France, too, had Buonaparté and Dumourier
Recorded in the "Moniteur" and "Courier."

III.

Barnave, Brissot, Condorcet, Mirabeau,
Petion, Clootz, Danton, Marat, La Fayette,
Were French, and famous people, as we know;
And there were others, scarce forgotten yet,
Joubert, Hoche, Marceau, Lannes, Desaix, Moreau,
With many of the military set,
Exceedingly remarkable at times,
But not at all adapted to my rhymes.

IV.

Nelson was once Britannia's god of war,
And still should be so, but the tide is turn'd;
There 's no more to be said of Trafalgar,
'T is with our hero quietly inurn'd;
Because the army 's grown more popular,
At which the naval people are concern'd;
Besides, the Prince is all for the land-service,
Forgetting Duncan, Nelson, Howe, and Jervis.

V.

Brave men were living before Agamemnon,
And since, exceeding valorous and sage,
A good deal like him too, though quite the same none;
But then they shone not on the poet's page,
And so have been forgotten:—I condemn none,
But can't find any in the present age
Fit for my poem (that is for my new one);
So, as I said, I'll take my friend Don Juan.

VI.

Most epic poets plunge "in medias res"
(Horace makes this the heroic turnpike road),
And then your hero tells, whene'er you please,
What went before—by way of episode,
While seated after dinner at his ease,
Beside his mistress in some soft abode,
Palace, or garden, paradise, or cavern,
Which serves the happy couple for a tavern.

VII.

That is the usual method, but not mine—
My way is to begin with the beginning;
The regularity of my design
Forbids all wandering as the worst of sinning,
And therefore I shall open with a line
(Although it cost me half an hour in spinning)
Narrating somewhat of Don Juan's father,
And also of his mother, if you 'd rather.

VIII.

In Seville was he born, a pleasant city,
Famous for oranges and women—he
Who has not seen it will be much to pity,
So says the proverb—and I quite agree;
Of all the Spanish towns is none more pretty,
Cadiz perhaps—but that you soon may see;—
Don Juan's parents lived beside the river,
A noble stream, and called the Guadalquiver.

IX.

His father's name was Jóse—*Don*, of course,
A true Hidalgo, free from every stain
Of Moor or Hebrew blood, he traced his source
Through the most Gothic gentlemen of Spain;
A better cavalier ne'er mounted horse,
Or, being mounted, e'er got down again,
Than Jóse, who begot our hero, who
Begot—but that's to come——Well, to renew:

X.

His mother was a learnèd lady, famed
For every branch of every science known—
In every Christian language ever named,
With virtues equall'd by her wit alone
She made the cleverest people quite ashamed,
And even the good with inward envy groan,
Finding themselves so very much exceeded
In their own way by all the things that she did.

XI.

Her memory was a mine: she knew by heart
All Calderon and greater part of Lopé,
So that if any actor miss'd his part
She could have served him for the prompter's copy;
For her Feinagle's were an useless art,
And he himself obliged to shut up shop—he
Could never make a memory so fine as
That which adorn'd the brain of Donna Inez.

XII.

Her favourite science was the mathematical,
Her noblest virtue was her magnanimity,
Her wit (she sometimes tried at wit) was Attic all,
Her serious sayings darken'd to sublimity;
In short, in all things she was fairly what I call
A prodigy—her morning dress was dimity,
Her evening silk, or, in the summer, muslin,
And other stuffs,—with which I won't stay puzzling.

XIII.

She knew the Latin—that is, "The Lord's Prayer,"
And Greek—the alphabet—I'm nearly sure;
She read some French romances here and there,
Although her mode of speaking was not pure;
For native Spanish she had no great care,
At least her conversation was obscure;
Her thoughts were theorems, her words a problem,
As if she deem'd that mystery would ennoble 'em.

XIV.

She liked the English and the Hebrew tongue,
And said there was analogy between 'em;
She proved it somehow out of sacred song,
But I must leave the proofs to those who 've seen 'em,
But this I heard her say, and can't be wrong,
And all may think which way their judgments lean 'em,
"'T is strange—the Hebrew noun which means 'I am,'
The English always use to govern d——n."

XV.

* * * * * *
* * * * * *

XVI.

In short, she was a walking calculation,
Miss Edgeworth's novels stepping from their covers,
Or Mrs. Trimmer's books on education,
Or "Cœlebs' Wife" set out in quest of lovers,
Morality's prim personification,
In which not Envy's self a flaw discovers;
To others' share let "female errors fall,"
For she had not even one—the worst of all.

XVII.

Oh! she was perfect past all parallel—
Of any modern female saint's comparison;
So far, above the cunning powers of hell,
Her guardian angel had given up his garrison:
Even her minutest motions went as well
As those of the best time-piece made by Harrison:
In virtues nothing earthly could surpass her,
Save thine "incomparable oil," Macassar![2]

XVIII.

Perfect she was, but as perfection is
Insipid in this naughty world of ours,
Where our first parents never learn'd to kiss
Till they were exiled from their earlier bowers,
Where all was peace, and innocence, and bliss,
(I wonder how they got through the twelve hours),
Don Jóse, like a lineal son of Eve,
Went plucking various fruit without her leave.

XIX.

He was a mortal of the careless kind,
With no great love for learning, or the learn'd,
Who chose to go where'er he had a mind,
And never dream'd his lady was concern'd;
The world, as usual, wickedly inclined
To see a kingdom or a house o'erturn'd,
Whisper'd he had a mistress, some said *two*
But for domestic quarrels *one* will do.

XX.

Now Donna Inez had, with all her merit,
A great opinion of her own good qualities;
Neglect, indeed, requires a saint to bear it,
And such, indeed, she was in her moralities;
But then she had a devil of a spirit,
And sometimes mix'd up fancies with realities,
And let few opportunities escape
Of getting her liege lord into a scrape.

XXI.

This was an easy matter with a man
Oft in the wrong, and never on his guard;
And even the wisest, do the best they can,
Have moments, hours, and days, so unprepared,
That you might "brain them with their lady's fan;"
And sometimes ladies hit exceeding hard,
And fans turn into falchions in fair hands,
And why and wherefore no one understands

XXII.

'T is pity learnèd virgins ever wed
With persons of no sort of education,
Or gentlemen, who, though well born and bred,
Grow tired of scientific conversation:
I don't choose to say much upon this head,
I'm a plain man, and in a single station,
But—Oh! ye lords of ladies intellectual,
Inform us truly, have they not hen-peck'd you all?

XXIII.

Don Jóse and his lady quarrell'd—*why*,
Not any of the many could divine,
Though several thousand people chose to try,
'T was surely no concern of theirs nor mine;
I loathe that low vice—curiosity:
But if there's anything in which I shine,
'T is in arranging all my friends' affairs,
Not having, of my own, domestic cares

XXIV.

And so I interfered, and with the best
Intentions, but their treatment was not kind;
I think the foolish people were possess'd,
For neither of them could I ever find,

Although their porter afterwards confess'd—
But that's no matter, and the worst 's behind,
For little Juan o'er me threw, down stairs,
A pail of housemaid's water unawares.

XXV.

A little curly-headed, good-for-nothing,
And mischief-making monkey from his birth;
His parents ne'er agreed except in doting
Upon the most unquiet imp on earth;
Instead of quarrelling, had they been but both in
Their senses, they'd have sent young master forth
To school, or had him soundly whipp'd at home,
To teach him manners for the time to come.

XXVI.

Don Jóse and the Donna Inez led
For some time an unhappy sort of life,
Wishing each other, not divorced, but dead;
They lived respectably as man and wife,
Their conduct was exceedingly well-bred,
And gave no outward signs of inward strife,
Until at length the smother'd fire broke out,
And put the business past all kind of doubt.

XXVII.

For Inez call'd some druggists, and physicians,
And tried to prove her loving lord was *mad:*
But as he had some lucid intermissions,
She next decided he was only *bad;*
Yet when they asked her for her depositions,
No sort of explanation could be had,
Save that her duty both to man and God
Required this conduct—which seem'd very odd.

XXVIII.

She kept a journal, where his faults were noted,
And open'd certain trunks of books and letters,
All which might, if occasion served, be quoted;
And then she had all Seville for abettors,
Besides her good old grandmother (who doted);
The hearers of her case became repeaters,
Then advocates, inquisitors, and judges,
Some for amusement, others for old grudges.

XXIX.

And then this best and meekest woman bore
With such serenity her husband's woes,
Just as the Spartan ladies did of yore,
Who saw their spouses kill'd, and nobly chose
Never to say a word about them more—
Calmly she heard each calumny that rose,
And saw his agonies with such sublimity,
That all the world exclaim'd, "What magnanimity!"

XXX.

No doubt this patience, when the world is damning us,
Is philosophic in our former friends;
'T is also pleasant to be deem'd magnanimous,
The more so in obtaining our own ends;
And what the lawyers call a "*malus animus*"
Conduct like this by no means comprehends:
Revenge in person 's certainly no virtue,
But then 't is not *my* fault, if *others* hurt you.

XXXI.

And if our quarrels should rip up old stories,
And help them with a lie or two additional,
I 'm not to blame, as you well know—no more is
Any one else—they were become traditional;
Besides, their resurrection aids our glories
By contrast, which is what we just were wishing all:
And science profits by this resurrection—
Dead scandals form good subjects for dissection.

XXXII.

Their friends had tried at reconciliation,
Then their relations, who made matters worse.
('T were hard to tell upon a like occasion
To whom it may be best to have recourse—
I can't say much for friend or yet relation):
The lawyers did their utmost for divorce,
But scarce a fee was paid on either side
Before, unluckily, Don Jóse died.

XXXIII.

He died: and most unluckily, because
According to all hints I could collect
From counsel learnèd in those kinds of laws,
(Although their talk 's obscure and circumspect)
His death contriv'd to spoil a charming cause;
A thousand pities also with respect
To public feeling, which on this occasion
Was manifested in a great sensation.

XXXIV.

But ah! he died; and buried with him lay
The public feeling and the lawyers' fees:
His house was sold, his servants sent away,
A Jew took one of his two mistresses,
A priest the other—at least so they say:
I ask'd the doctors after his disease—
He died of the slow fever called the tertian,
And left his widow to her own aversion.

XXXV.

Yet Jóse was an honourable man,
That I must say, who knew him very well;
Therefore his frailties I'll no further scan,
Indeed there were not many more to tell:
And if his passions now and then outran
Discretion, and were not so peaceable
As Numa's (who was also named Pompilius)
He had been ill brought up, and was born bilious.

XXXVI.

Whate'er might be his worthlessness or worth,
Poor fellow! he had many things to wound him.
Let's own—since it can do no good on earth—
It was a trying moment that which found him
Standing alone beside his desolate hearth,
Where all his household gods lay shiver'd round him
No choice was left his feelings or his pride,
Save death or Doctors' Commons—so he died.

XXXVII.

Dying intestate, Juan was sole heir
To a chancery suit, and messuages, and lands,
Which, with a long minority and care,
Promised to turn out well in proper hands:
Inez became sole guardian, which was fair,
And answered but to nature's just demands;
An only son left with an only mother
Is brought up much more wisely than another.

XXXVIII.

Sagest of women, even of widows, she
Resolved that Juan should be quite a paragon,
And worthy of the noblest pedigree:
(His sire was of Castile, his dam from Aragon).

Then for accomplishments of chivalry,
 In case our lord the king should go to war again,
He learn'd the arts of riding, fencing, gunnery,
And how to scale a fortress—or a nunnery.

XXXIX.

But that which Donna Inez most desired,
 And saw into herself each day before all
The learned tutors whom for him she hired,
 Was, that his breeding should be strictly moral:
Much into all his studies she inquired,
 And so they were submitted first to her, all,
Arts, sciences, no branch was made a mystery
To Juan's eyes, excepting natural history.

XL.

The languages, especially the dead,
 The sciences, and most of all the abstruse,
The arts, at least all such as could be said,
 To be the most remote from common use,
In all these he was much and deeply read :
 But not a page of anything that's loose,
Or hints continuation of the species,
Was ever suffer'd, lest he should grow vicious.

XLI.

His classic studies made a little puzzle,
 Because of filthy loves of gods and goddesses,
Who in the earlier ages raised a bustle,
 But never put on pantaloons or bodices ;
His reverend tutors had at times a tussle,
 And for their Æneids, Iliads, and Odysseys,
Were forced to make an odd sort of apology,
For Donna Inez dreaded the Mythology.

XLII.

Ovid's a rake, as half his verses show him,
 Anacreon's morals are a still worse sample,
Catullus scarcely has a decent poem,
 I don't think Sappho's Ode a good example,
Although Longinus tells us there is no hymn [3]
 Where the sublime soars forth on wings more ample ;
But Virgil's songs are pure, except that horrid one
Beginning with "Formosum Pastor Corydon."

XLIII.

Lucretius' irreligion is too strong,
 For early stomachs, to prove wholesome food ;
I can't help thinking Juvenal was wrong,
 Although no doubt his real intent was good,
For speaking out so plainly in his song,
 So much indeed as to be downright rude ;
And then what proper person can be partial
To all those nauseous epigrams of Martial ?

XLIV.

Juan was taught from out the best edition,
 Expurgated by learnèd men, who place,
Judiciously, from out the schoolboy's vision,
 The grosser parts ; but, fearful to deface
Too much their modest bard by this omission,
 And pitying sore his multilated case,
They only add them all in an appendix, [4]
Which saves, in fact, the trouble of an index ;

XLV.

For there we have them all "at one fell swoop,"
 Instead of being scatter'd through the pages ;
They stand forth marshall'd in a handsome troop,
 To meet the ingenuous youth of future ages,
Till some less rigid editor shall stoop
 To call them back into their separate cages,
Instead of standing staring altogether,
Like garden gods—and not so decent either.

XLVI.

The Missal too (it was the family Missal)
 Was ornamented in a sort of way
Which ancient mass-books often are, and this all
 Kinds of grotesques illumined ; and how they,
Who saw those figures on the margin kiss all,
 Could turn their optics to the text and pray,
Is more than I know—but Don Juan's mother
Kept this herself, and gave her son another.

XLVII.

Sermons he read, and lectures he endured,
 And homilies, and lives of all the saints ;
To Jerome and to Chrysostom inured,
 He did not take such studies for restraints ;
But how faith is acquired, and then ensured,
 So well not one of the aforesaid paints
As Saint Augustine in his fine Confessions,
Which make the reader envy his trangressions.

XLVIII.

This, too, was a seal'd book to little Juan—
 I can't but say that his mamma was right,
If such an education was the true one.
 She scarcely trusted him from out her sight ;
Her maids were old, and if she took a new one,
 You might be sure she was a perfect fright :
She did this during even her husband's life—
I recommend as much to every wife.

XLIX.

Young Juan wax'd in goodliness and grace ;
 At six a charming child, and at eleven
With all the promise of as fine a face
 As e'er to man's maturer growth was given :
He studied steadily, and grew apace,
 And seem'd, at least, in the right road to heaven,
For half his days were pass'd at church, the other
Between his tutors, confessor, and mother.

L.

At six I said, he was a charming child,
 At twelve he was a fine, but quiet boy ;
Although in infancy a little wild,
 They tamed him down amongst them : to destroy
His natural spirit not in vain they toil'd.
 At least it seem'd so ; and his mother's joy
Was to declare how sage, and still, and steady,
Her young philosopher was grown already

LI.

I had my doubts, perhaps I have them still,
 But what I say is neither here nor there :

I knew his father well, and have some skill
 In character—but it would not be fair
From sire to son to augur good or ill:
 He and his wife were an ill-sorted pair—
But scandal's my aversion—I protest
Against all evil-speaking, even in jest.

LII.

For my part I say nothing—nothing—but
 This I will say—my reasons are my own—
That if I had an only son to put
 To school (as God be praised that I have none),
'T is not with Donna Inez I would shut
 Him up to learn his Catechism alone,
No—no—I'd send him out betimes to college,
For there it was I pick'd up my own knowledge.

LIII.

For there one learns— 'tis not for me to boast,
 Though I acquired—but I pass over *that*,
As well as all the Greek I since have lost:
 I say that there's the place—but "*Verbum sat*,"
I think I pick'd up too, as well as most,
 Knowledge of matters—but no matter *what*—
I never married—but, I think, I know
That sons should not be educated so.

LIV.

Young Juan now was sixteen years of age,
 Tall, handsome, slender, but well knit: he seem'd
Active, though not so sprightly, as a page;
 And everybody but his mother deem'd
Him almost man; but she flew in a rage
 And bit her lips (for else she might have scream'd)
If any said so, for to be precocious
Was in her eyes a thing the most atrocious.

LV.

Amongst her numerous acquaintance—all
 Selected for discretion and devotion—
There was the Donna Julia, whom to call
 Pretty were but to give a feeble notion
Of many charms in her as natural
 As sweetness to the flower, or salt to ocean,
Her zone to Venus, or his bow to Cupid,
(But this last simile is trite and stupid).

LVI.

The darkness of her Oriental eye
 Accorded with her Moorish origin;
(Her blood was not all Spanish, by-the-by;
 In Spain, you know, this is a sort of sin).
When proud Granada fell, and, forced to fly,
 Boabdil wept, of Donna Julia's kin
Some went to Africa, some stayed in Spain,
Her great-great-grandmamma chose to remain.

LVII.

She married (I forget the pedigree)
 With an Hidalgo, who transmitted down
His blood less noble than such blood should be;
 At such alliances his sires would frown,
In that point so precise in each degree
 That they bred *in and in*, as might be shown,
Marrying their cousins—nay, their aunts, and nieces,
Which always spoils the breed, if it increases.

LVIII.

This heathenish cross restored the breed again,
 Ruin'd its blood, but much improved its flesh;
For from a root the ugliest in Old Spain
 Sprung up a branch as beautiful as fresh;
The sons no more were short, the daughters plain:
 But there's a rumour which I fain would hush,
'T is said that Donna Julia's grandmamma
Produced her Don more heirs at love than law.

LIX.

However this might be, the race went on
 Improving still through every generation,
Until it centred in an only son,
 Who left an only daughter; my narration
May have suggested that this single one
 Could be but Julia (whom on this occasion
I shall have much to speak about), and she
Was married, charming, chaste, and twenty-three.

LX.

Her eye (I'm very fond of handsome eyes)
 Was large and dark, suppressing half its fire
Until she spoke, then through its soft disguise
 Flash'd an expression more of pride than ire,
And love than either; and there would arise
 A something in them which was not desire,
But would have been, perhaps, but for the soul
Which struggled through and chasten'd down the whole.

LXI.

Her glossy hair was cluster'd o'er a brow
 Bright with intelligence, and fair, and smooth;
Her eyebrow's shape was like the aërial bow,
 Her cheek all purple with the beam of youth,
Mounting, at times, to a transparent glow,
 As if her veins ran lightning; she, in sooth,
Possess'd an air and grace by no means common:
Her stature tall—I hate a dumpy woman.

LXII.

Wedded she was some years, and to a man
 Of fifty, and such husbands are in plenty;
And yet, I think, instead of such a ONE,
 'T were better to have two of five and twenty,

Especially in countries near the sun:
And now I think on 't, "*mi vien in mente*,"
Ladies even of the most uneasy virtue
Prefer a spouse whose age is short of thirty.

LXIII.

'T is a sad thing, I cannot choose but say,
And all the fault of that indecent sun,
Who cannot leave alone our helpless clay,
But will keep baking, broiling, burning on,
That howsoever people fast and pray,
The flesh is frail, and so the soul undone:
What men call gallantry, and gods adultery,
Is much more common where the climate's sultry.

LXIV.

Happy the nations of the moral North!
Where all is virtue, and the winter season
Sends sin, without a rag on, shivering forth
('T was snow that brought St. Anthony to reason);
Where juries cast up what a wife is worth,
By laying whate'er sum, in mulct, they please on
The lover, who must pay a handsome price,
Because it is a marketable vice.

LXV.

Alfonso was the name of Julia's lord,
A man well looking for his years, and who

Was neither much beloved nor yet abhorr'd:
They lived together as most people do,
Suffering each other's foibles by accord,
And not exactly either *one* or *two;*
Yet he was jealous, though he did not show it,
For jealousy dislikes the world to know it.

LXVI.

Julia was—yet I never could see why—
With Donna Inez quite a favourite friend;
Between their tastes there was small sympathy,
For not a line had Julia ever penn'd:
Some people whisper (but, no doubt, they lie,
For malice still imputes some private end)
That Inez had, ere Don Alfonso's marriage,
Forgot with him her very prudent carriage;

LXVII.

And that, still keeping up the old connection,
Which time had lately render'd much more chaste,
She took his lady also in affection,
And certainly this course was much the best:
She flatter'd Julia with her sage protection,
And complimented Don Alfonso's taste;
And if she could not (who can?) silence scandal,
At least she left it a more slender handle.

LXVIII.

I can't tell whether Julia saw the affair
With other people's eyes, or if her own
Discoveries made, but none could be aware
Of this, at least no symptom e'er was shown;
Perhaps she did not know, or did not care,
Indifferent from the first, or callous grown:
I'm really puzzled what to think or say,
She kept her counsel in so close a way.

LXIX.

Juan she saw, and, as a pretty child,
Caress'd him often—such a thing might be
Quite innocently done, and harmless styled,
When she had twenty years, and thirteen he;
But I am not so sure I should have smiled
When he was sixteen, Julia twenty-three;
These few short years make wondrous alterations,
Particularly amongst sun-burnt nations.

LXX.

Whate'er the cause might be, they had become
Changed; for the dame grew distant, the youth shy,
Their looks cast down, their greetings almost dumb,
And much embarrassment in either eye;
There surely will be little doubt with some
That Donna Julia knew the reason why,
But as for Juan, he had no more notion
Than he who never saw the sea of ocean.

LXXI.

Yet Julia's very coldness still was kind,
And tremulously gentle her small hand
Withdrew itself from his, but left behind
A little pressure, thrilling, and so bland
And slight, so very slight, that to the mind
'T was but a doubt; but ne'er magician's wand
Wrought change with all Armida's fairy art
Like what this light touch left on Juan's heart.

LXXII.

And if she met him, though she smiled no more,
She looked a sadness sweeter than her smile,
As if her heart had deeper thoughts in store
She must not own, but cherished more the while
For that compression in its burning core;
Even innocence itself has many a wile,
And will not dare to trust itself with truth,
And love is taught hypocrisy from youth.

LXXIII.

But passion most dissembles, yet betrays
Even by its darkness; as the blackest sky
Foretells the heaviest tempest, it displays
Its workings through the vainly guarded eye,
And in whatever aspect it arrays
Itself, 't is still the same hypocrisy;
Coldness or anger, even disdain or hate,
Are masks it often wears, and still too late.

LXXIV.

Then there were sighs, the deeper for suppression,
And stolen glances, sweeter for the theft,
And burning blushes, though for no transgression,
Tremblings when met, and restlessness when left;
All these are little preludes to possession,
Of which young passion cannot be bereft,
And merely tend to show how greatly love is
Embarrass'd at first starting with a novice.

LXXV.

Poor Julia's heart was in an awkward state;
She felt it going, and resolved to make
The noblest efforts for herself and mate,
For honour's, pride's, religion's, virtue's sake.
Her resolutions were most truly great,
And almost might have made a Tarquin quake
She pray'd the Virgin Mary for her grace,
As being the best judge of a lady's case.

LXXVI.

She vow'd she never would see Juan more,
And next day paid a visit to his mother,
And look'd extremely at the opening door,
Which, by the Virgin's grace, let in another;
Grateful she was, and yet a little sore—
Again it opens, it can be no other,

T is surely Juan now—No! I'm afraid
That night the Virgin was no further pray'd.

LXXVII.

She now determined that a virtuous woman
 Should rather face and overcome temptation,
That flight was base and dastardly, and no man
 Should ever give her heart the least sensation;
That is to say, a thought beyond the common
 Preference, that we must feel upon occasion,
For people who are pleasanter than others,
But then they only seem so many brothers.

LXXVIII.

And even if by chance—and who can tell?
 The devil 's so very sly—she should discover
That all within was not so very well,
 And, if still free, that such or such a lover
Might please perhaps, a virtuous wife can quell
 Such thoughts, and be the better when they're over,
And if the man should ask, 'tis but denial:
I recommend young ladies to make trial.

LXXIX.

And then there are such things as love divine,
 Bright and immaculate, unmix'd and pure,
Such as the angels think so very fine,
 And matrons, who would be no less secure,
Platonic, perfect, "just such love as mine;"
 Thus Julia said—and thought so, to be sure;
And so I'd have her think, were I the man
On whom her reveries celestial ran.

LXXX.

Such love is innocent, and may exist
 Between young persons without any danger.
A hand may first, and then a lip be kist;
 For my part, to such doings I'm a stranger,
But *hear* these freedoms form the utmost list
 Of all o'er which such love may be a ranger:
If people go beyond, 't is quite a crime,
But not my fault—I tell them all in time.

LXXXI.

Love, then, but love within its proper limits,
 Was Julia's innocent determination
In young Don Juan's favour, and to him its
 Exertion might be useful on occasion:
And, lighted at too pure a shrine to dim its
 Ethereal lustre, with what sweet persuasion
He might be taught, by love and her together—
I really don't know what, nor Julia either.

LXXXII.

Fraught with this fine intention, and well fenced
 In mail of proof—her purity of soul,
She, for the future of her strength convinced,
 And that her honour was a rock, or mole,
Exceeding sagely from that hour dispensed
 With any kind of troublesome control;
But whether Julia to the task was equal
Is that which must be mention'd in the sequel.

LXXXIII.

Her plan she deem'd both innocent and feasible,
 And, surely, with a stripling of sixteen
Not scandal's fangs could fix on much that 's seizable,
 Or if they did so, satisfied to mean
Nothing but what was good, her breast was peace-
 able—
 A quiet conscience makes one so serene!
Christians have burnt each other, quite persuaded
That all the Apostles would have done as they did.

LXXXIV.

And if in the meantime her husband died,
 But Heaven forbid that such a thought should
 cross
Her brain, though in a dream! (and then she
 sigh'd)
 Never could she survive that common loss;
But just suppose that moment should betide,
 I only say suppose it—*inter nos.*
(This should be *entre nous*, for Julia thought
 In French, but then the rhyme would go for
 nought.)

LXXXV.

I only say, suppose this supposition:
 Juan being then grown up to man's estate
Would fully suit a widow of condition,
 Even seven years hence it would not be too late;
And in the interim (to pursue this vision)
 The mischief, after all, could not be great,
For he would learn the rudiments of love,—
I mean the seraph way of those above.

LXXXVI.

So much for Julia. Now we'll turn to Juan.
 Poor little fellow! he had no idea
Of his own case, and never hit the true one;
 In feelings quick as Ovid's Miss Medea,
He puzzled over what he found a new one,
 But not as yet imagined it could be a
Thing quite in course, and not at all alarming,
Which, with a little patience, might grow charming.

LXXXVII.

Silent and pensive, idle, restless, slow,
 His home deserted for the lonely wood,
Tormented with a wound he could not know,
 His, like all deep grief, plunged in solitude:
I'm fond myself of solitude or so,
 But then, I beg it may be understood,
By solitude I mean a sultan's, not
A hermit's, with a haram for a grot.

LXXXVIII.

"Oh Love! in such a wilderness as this,
Where transport and security entwine,
Here is the empire of thy perfect bliss,
And here thou art a god indeed divine."
The bard I quote from does not sing amiss,[5]
With the exception of the second line,
For that same twining "transport and security"
Are twisted to a phrase of some obscurity.

LXXXIX.

The poet meant, no doubt, and thus appeals
To the good sense and senses of mankind,
The very thing which every body feels,
As all have found on trial, or may find,
That no one likes to be disturb'd at meals
Or love.—I won't say more about "entwined"
Or "transport," as we knew all that before,
But beg "Security" will bolt the door.

XC.

Young Juan wander'd by the glassy brooks,
Thinking unutterable things; he threw
Himself at length within the leafy nooks
Where the wild branch of the cork forest grew;
There poets find materials for their books,
And every now and then we read them through,
So that their plan and prosody are eligible,
Unless, like Wordsworth, they prove unintelligible.

XCI.

He (Juan, and not Wordsworth) so pursued
His self-communion with his own high soul,
Until his mighty heart, in its great mood,
Had mitigated part, though not the whole
Of its disease; he did the best he could
With things not very subject to control,
And turn'd, without perceiving his condition,
Like Coleridge, into a metaphysician.

XCII.

He thought about himself, and the whole earth,
Of man the wonderful, and of the stars,
And how the deuce they ever could have birth;
And then he thought of earthquakes, and of wars,
How many miles the moon might have in girth,
Of air-balloons, and of the many bars
To perfect knowledge of the boundless skies;—
And then he thought of Donna Julia's eyes.

XCIII.

In thoughts like these true wisdom may discern
Longings sublime, and aspirations high,
Which some are born with, but the most part learn
To plague themselves withal, they know not why:
'Twas strange that one so young should thus concern
His brain about the action of the sky;
If *you* think 't was philosophy that this did,
I can't help thinking puberty assisted.

XCIV.

He pored upon the leaves, and on the flowers,
And heard a voice in all the winds; and then
He thought of wood-nymphs and immortal bowers,
And how the goddesses came down to men:
He missed the pathway, he forgot the hours,
And when he looked upon his watch again,
He found how much old Time had been a winner—
He also found that he had lost his dinner.

XCV.

Sometimes he turn'd to gaze upon his book,
Boscan, or Garcilasso;—by the wind
Even as the page is rustled while we look,
So by the poesy of his own mind
Over the mystic leaf his soul was shook,
As if 't were one whereon magicians bind
Their spells, and give them to the passing gale,
According to some good old woman's tale.

XCVI.

Thus would he while his lonely hours away
Dissatisfied, nor knowing what he wanted;
Nor glowing reverie, nor poet's lay,
Could yield his spirit that for which it panted,
A bosom whereon he his head might lay,
And hear the heart beat with the love it granted,
With——several other things, which I forget,
Or which, at least, I need not mention yet.

XCVII.

Those lonely walks, and lengthening reveries,
Could not escape the gentle Julia's eyes;
She saw that Juan was not at his ease;
But that which chiefly may, and must surprise,
Is, that the Donna Inez did not tease
Her only son with question or surmise;
Whether it was she did not see, or would not,
Or, like all very clever people, could not.

XCVIII.

This may seem strange, but yet 't is very common;
For instance—gentlemen, whose ladies take
Leave to o'erstep the written rights of woman,
And break the——Which commandment is't they break?
(I have forgot the number, and think no man
Should rashly quote, for fear of a mistake).
I say, when these same gentlemen are jealous,
They make some blunder, which their ladies tell us.

XCIX.

A real husband always is suspicious,
But still no less suspects in the wrong place,
Jealous of some one who had no such wishes,
Or pandering blindly to his own disgrace,

By harbouring some dear friend extremely vicious;
 The last indeed's infallibly the case:
And when the spouse and friend are gone off wholly,
He wonders at their vice, and not his folly.

C.

Thus parents also are at times short-sighted:
 Though watchful as the lynx, they ne'er discover,
The while the wicked world beholds delighted,
 Young Hopeful's mistress, or Miss Fanny's lover,
Till some confounded escapade has blighted
 The plan of twenty years, and all is over;
And then the mother cries, the father swears,
And wonders why the devil he got heirs.

CI.

But Inez was so anxious and so clear
 Of sight, that I must think, on this occasion,
She had some other motive much more near
 For leaving Juan to this new temptation,
But what that motive was, I sha'n't say here;
 Perhaps to finish Juan's education,
Perhaps to open Don Alfonso's eyes,
In case he thought his wife too great prize.

CII.

It was upon a day, a summer's day;—
 Summer's indeed a very dangerous season,
And so is spring, about the end of May;
 The sun, no doubt, is the prevailing reason;
But whatsoe'er the cause is, one may say,
 And stand convicted of more truth than treason,
That there are months which nature grows more merry in,—
March has its hares, and May must have its heroine.

CIII.

'T was on a summer's day—the sixth of June:
 I like to be particular in dates,
Not only of the age, and year, but moon;
 They are a sort of post-house, where the Fates
Change horses, making history change its tune,
 Then spur away o'er empires and o'er states,
Leaving at last not much besides chronology,
Excepting the post-obits of theology.

CIV.

'Twas on the sixth of June, about the hour
 Of half-past six—perhaps still nearer seven—
When Julia sate within as pretty a bower
 As e'er held houri in that heathenish heaven
Described by Mahomet and Anacreon Moore,
 To whom the lyre and laurels have been given,
With all the trophies of triumphant song—
He won them well, and may he wear them long!

CV.

She sate, but not alone; I know not well
 How this same interview had taken place,
And even if I knew, I should not tell—
 People should hold their tongues in any case;
No matter how or why the thing befell,
 But there were she and Juan, face to face—
When two such faces are so, 't would be wise,
But very difficult, to shut their eyes.

CVI.

How beautiful she look'd! Her conscious heart
 Glow'd in her cheek, and yet she felt no wrong.
Oh Love! how perfect is thy mystic art,
 Strengthening the weak, and trampling on the strong,
How self-deceitful is the sagest part
 Of mortals whom thy lure hath led along—
The precipice she stood on was immense,
So was her creed in her own innocence.

CVII.

She thought of her own strength, and Juan's youth,
 And of the folly of all prudish fears,
Victorious virtue, and domestic truth,
 And then of Don Alfonso's fifty years:
I wish these last had not occurr'd, in sooth,
 Because that number rarely much endears;
And through all climes, the snowy and the sunny,
Sounds ill in love, whate'er it may in money.

CVIII.

When people say, "I've told you *fifty* times,"
 They mean to scold, and very often do;
When poets say, "I've written *fifty* rhymes,"
 They make you dread that they'll recite them too;
In gangs of *fifty*, thieves commit their crimes;
 At *fifty* love for love is rare, 't is true,
But then, no doubt, it equally as true is,
A good deal may be bought for *fifty* Louis.

CIX.

Julia had honour, virtue, truth, and love
 For Don Alfonso; and she inly swore,
By all the vows below to powers above,
 She never would disgrace the ring she wore,
Nor leave a wish which wisdom might reprove;
 And while she ponder'd this, besides much more,
One hand on Juan's carelessly was thrown,
Quite by mistake—she thought it was her own;

CX.

Unconsciously she lean'd upon the other,
 Which play'd within the tangles of her hair;
And to contend with thoughts she could not smother
 She seem'd, by the distraction of her air.

'T was surely very wrong in Juan's mother
 To leave together this imprudent pair,
She who for many years had watch'd her son so—
I'm very certain *mine* would not have done so.

CXI.

The hand which still held Juan's, by degrees
 Gently, but palpably confirm'd its grasp,

As if it said, "Detain me, if you please;"
 Yet there's no doubt she only meant to clasp
His fingers with a pure Platonic squeeze;
 She would have shrunk as from a toad, or asp,
Had she imagined such a thing could rouse
A feeling dangerous to a prudent spouse.

CXII.

I cannot know what Juan thought of this,
 But what he did, is much what you would do;
His young lip thank'd it with a grateful kiss,
 And then, abash'd at its own joy, withdrew
In deep despair, lest he had done amiss,—
 Love is so very timid when 't is new:
She blush'd, and frown'd not, but she strove to speak,
And held her tongue, her voice was grown so weak.

CXIII.

The sun set, and up rose the yellow moon:
 The devil's in the moon for mischief; they
Who call'd her CHASTE, methinks, began too soon
 Their nomenclature; there is not a day,
The longest, not the twenty-first of June,
 Sees half the business in a wicked way,
On which three single hours of moonshine smile—
And then she looks so modest all the while!

CXIV.

There is a dangerous silence in that hour,
 A stillness, which leaves room for the full soul
To open all itself, without the power
 Of calling wholly back its self-control;
The silver light which, hallowing tree and tower,
 Sheds beauty and deep softness o'er the whole,
Breathes also to the heart, and o'er it throws
A loving langour, which is not repose.

CXV.

And Julia sate with Juan, half embraced
 And half retiring from the glowing arm,
Which trembled like the bosom where 't was placed;
 Yet still she must have thought there was no harm,
Or else 't were easy to withdraw her waist;
 But then the situation had its charm,
And then——God knows what next—I can't go on;
I'm almost sorry that I e'er begun.

CXVI

Oh Plato! Plato! you have paved the way,
 With your confounded fantasies, to more
Immoral conduct by the fancied sway
 Your system feigns o'er the controlless core
Of human hearts, than all the long array
 Of poets and romancers:—You're a bore.
A charlatan, a coxcomb—and have been,
At best, no better than a go-between.

CXVII

And Julia's voice was lost, except in sighs,
 Until too late for useful conversation;
The tears were gushing from her gentle eyes,
 I wish, indeed, they had not had occasion;
But who, alas! can love, and then be wise?
 Not that remorse did not oppose temptation;
A little still she strove, and much repented,
And whispering "I will ne'er consent"—consented

CXVIII.

'T is said that Xerxes offered a reward
 To those who could invent him a new pleasure:
Methinks, the requisition's rather hard,
 And must have cost his majesty a treasure:
For my part, I'm a moderate-minded bard,
 Fond of a little love (which I call leisure);
I care not for new pleasures, as the old
Are quite enough for me, so they but hold.

CXIX.

Oh Pleasure! you are indeed a pleasant thing,
 Although one must be damn'd for you, no doubt:
I make a resolution every spring
 Of reformation, ere the year run out,
But somehow, this my vestal vow takes wing,
 Yet still, I trust, it may be kept throughout:
I'm very sorry, very much ashamed,
And mean, next winter, to be quite reclaim'd.

CXX.

Here my chaste Muse a liberty must take—
 Start not! still chaster reader—she'll be nice hence-
Forward, and there is no great cause to quake;
 This liberty is a poetic licence,
Which some irregularity may make
 In the design, and as I have a high sense
Of Aristotle and the Rules, 't is fit
To beg his pardon when I err a bit.

CXXI.

This licence is to hope the reader will
 Suppose from June the sixth (the fatal day,
Without whose epoch my poetic skill
 For want of facts would all be thrown away),
But keeping Julia and Don Juan still
 In sight, that several months have pass'd; we'll say
'T was in November, but I'm not so sure
About the day—the era's more obscure.

CXXII.

We'll talk of that anon.—'T is sweet to hear
 At midnight on the blue and moonlit deep
The song and oar of Adria's gondolier,
 By distance mellow'd, o'er the waters sweep,
'T is sweet to see the evening star appear;
 'T is sweet to listen as the night-winds creep

From leaf to leaf; 't is sweet to view on high
The rainbow, based on ocean, span the sky.

CXXIII.

'T is sweet to hear the watch-dog's honest bark
Bay deep-mouth'd welcome as we draw near home;
'T is sweet to know there is an eye will mark
Our coming, and look brighter when we come;
'T is sweet to be awaken'd by the lark,
Or lull'd by falling waters; sweet the hum
Of bees, the voice of girls, the song of birds,
The lisp of children, and their earliest words.

CXXIV.

Sweet is the vintage, when the showering grapes
In Bacchanal profusion reel to earth,
Purple and gushing: sweet are our escapes
From civic revelry to rural mirth;
Sweet to the miser are his glittering heaps,
Sweet to the father is his first-born's birth,
Sweet is revenge—especially to women,
Pillage to soldiers, prize-money to seamen.

CXXV.

Sweet is a legacy, and passing sweet
The unexpected death of some old lady,
Or gentleman of seventy years complete,
Who've made "us youth" wait too—too long already,
For an estate, or cash, or country seat,
Still breaking, but with stamina so steady,
That all the Israelites are fit to mob its
Next owner for their double-damn'd post-obits.

CXXVI.

'T is sweet to win, no matter how, one's laurels,
By blood or ink; 't is sweet to put an end
To strife; 't is sometimes sweet to have our quarrels,
Particularly with a tiresome friend:
Sweet is old wine in bottles, ale in barrels;
Dear is the helpless creature we defend
Against the world; and dear the schoolboy spot
We ne'er forget, though there we are forgot.

CXXVII.

But sweeter still than this, than these, than all,
Is first and passionate love—it stands alone,
Like Adam's recollection of his fall;
The tree of knowledge has been pluck'd—all 's known—
And life yields nothing further to recall
Worthy of this ambrosial sin, so shown,
No doubt in fable, as the unforgiven
Fire which Prometheus filch'd for us from heaven.

CXXVIII.

Man 's a strange animal, and makes strange use
Of his own nature, and the various arts,
And likes particularly to produce
Some new experiment to show his parts;
This is the age of oddities let loose,
Where different talents find their different marts;
You'd best begin with truth, and when you 've lost your
Labour, there 's a sure market for imposture.

CXXIX.

What opposite discoveries we have seen!
(Signs of true genius, and of empty pockets.)
One makes new noses, one a guillotine,
One breaks your bones, one sets them in their sockets;
But vaccination certainly has been
A kind antithesis to Congreve's rockets,

* * * * * *

CXXX.

Bread has been made (indifferent) from potatoes;
And galvanism has set some corpses grinning,
But has not answer'd like the apparatus
Of the Humane Society's beginning,
By which men are unsuffocated gratis;
What wondrous new machines have late been spinning!

* * * * * *

CXXXI.

* * * * * *
* * * * * *

CXXXII.

This is the patent age of new inventions
For killing bodies, and for saving souls,
All propagated with the best intentions;
Sir Humphrey Davy's lantern, by which coals
Are safely mined for in the mode he mentions;
Tombuctoo travels, voyages to the Poles
Are ways to benefit mankind, as true,
Perhaps, as shooting them at Waterloo.

CXXXIII.

Man' s a phenomenon, one knows not what,
And wonderful beyond all wondrous measure;
'T is pity though, in this sublime world, that
Pleasure 's a sin, and sometimes sin 's a pleasure;
Few mortals know what end they would be at,
But whether glory, power, or love, or treasure,
The path is through perplexing ways, and when
The goal is gain'd we die, you know—and then——

CXXXIV.

What then?—I do not know, no more do you—
And so good night.—Return we to our story:
'T was in November, when fine days are few,
And the far mountains wax a little hoary,

And clap a white cape on their mantles blue:
 And the sea dashes round the promontory,
And the loud breaker boils against the rock,
And sober suns must set at five o'clock.

CXXXV.

'T was, as the watchmen say, a cloudy night;
 No moon, no stars, the wind was low or loud
By gusts, and many a sparkling hearth was bright
 With the piled wood, round which the family crowd;
There 's something cheerful in that sort of light,
 Even as a summer sky 's without a cloud:
I 'm fond of fire, and crickets, and all that,
A lobster salad, and champagne, and chat.

CXXXVI.

'T was midnight—Donna Julia was in bed,
Sleeping, most probably,—when at her door
Arose a clatter might awake the dead,
If they had never been awoke before,
And that they have been so we all have read,
And are to be so, at the least, once more;—
The door was fasten'd, but with voice and fist
First knocks were heard, then "Madam—Madam—hist!

CXXXVII.

"For God's sake, Madam—Madam—here's my master,
With more than half the city at his back—
Was ever heard of such a curst disaster!
'T is not my fault—I kept good watch—Alack!
Do, pray, undo the bolt a little faster—
They 're on the stair just now, and in a crack
Will all be here; perhaps he yet may fly—
Surely the window 's not so *very* high!"

CXXXVIII.

By this time Don Alfonso was arrived,
With torches, friends, and servants in great number;
The major part of them had long been wived,
And therefore paused not to disturb the slumber
Of any wicked woman, who contrived
By stealth her husband's temples to encumber:
Examples of this kind are so contagious,
Were *one* not punish'd, *all* would be outrageous.

CXXXIX.

I can't tell how, or why, or what suspicion
Could enter into Don Alfonso's head;
But for a cavalier of his condition
It surely was exceedingly ill-bred,
Without a word of previous admonition,
To hold a levee round his lady's bed,
And summon lackeys, arm'd with fire and sword,
To prove himself the thing he most abhorr'd.

CXL.

Poor Donna Julia! starting as from sleep,
(Mind—that I do not say—she had not slept)
Began at once to scream, and yawn, and weep;
Her maid Antonia, who was an adept,
Contrived to fling the bed-clothes in a heap,
As if she had just now from out them crept:
I can't tell why she should take all this trouble
To prove her mistress had been sleeping double.

CXLI.

But Julia mistress, and Antonia maid,
Appear'd like two poor harmless women, who
Of goblins, but still more of men afraid,
Had thought one man might be deterr'd by two,
And therefore side by side were gently laid,
Until the hours of absence should run through,
And truant husband should return, and say,
"My dear, I was the first who came away."

CXLII.

Now Julia found at length a voice, and cried,
"In Heaven's name, Don Alfonso, what d' ye mean?
Has madness seized you? would that I had died
Ere such a monster's victim I had been!
What may this midnight violence betide,
A sudden fit of drunkenness or spleen?
Dare you suspect me, whom the thought would kill?
Search, then, the room!"—Alfonso said, "I will."

CXLIII.

He search'd, *they* search'd, and rummaged everywhere,
Closet and clothes' press, chest and window-seat,
And found much linen, lace, and several pair
Of stockings, slippers, brushes, combs, complete,
With other articles of ladies fair,
To keep them beautiful, or leave them neat:
Arras they prick'd and curtains with their swords,
And wounded several shutters, and some boards.

CXLIV.

Under the bed they search'd, and there they found—
No matter what—it was not that they sought:
They open'd windows, gazing if the ground
Had signs or footmarks, but the earth said nought;
And then they stared each others' faces round:
'T is odd, not one of all these seekers thought,
And seems to me almost a sort of blunder,
Of looking *in* the bed as well as under.

CXLV.

During this inquisition, Julia's tongue
Was not asleep—"Yes, search and search," she cried,
"Insult on insult heap, and wrong on wrong!
It was for this that I became a bride!
For this in silence I have suffer'd long
A husband like Alfonso at my side;
But now I'll bear no more, nor here remain,
If there be law or lawyers, in all Spain.

CXLVI.

"Yes, Don Alfonso! husband now no more,
If ever you indeed deserved the name,
Is 't worthy of your years?—you have threescore—
Fifty, or sixty, it is all the same—
Is 't wise or fitting, causeless to explore
For facts against a virtuous woman's fame?
Ungrateful, perjured, barbarous Don Alfonso,
How dare you think your lady would go on so?

CXLVII.

"Is it for this I have disdained to hold
The common privileges of my sex?
That I have chosen a confessor so old
And deaf, that any other it would vex,
And never once he has had cause to scold,
But found my very innocence perplex
So much, he always doubted I was married—
How sorry you will be when I've miscarried.

CXLVIII.

"Was it for this that no Cortejo e'er
I yet have chosen from out the youth of Seville?
Is it for this I scarce went any where,
Except to bull-fights, mass, play, rout, and revel?
Is it for this, whate'er my suitors were,
I favour'd none—nay, was almost uncivil?
Is it for this that General Count O'Reilly,
Who took Algiers, declares I used him vilely?[6]

CXLIX.

"Did not the Italian Musico Cazzani
Sing at my heart six months at least in vain?
Did not his countryman, Count Corniani,
Call me the only virtuous wife in Spain?
Were there not also Russians, English, many?
The Count Strongstroganoff I put in pain,
And Lord Mount Coffeehouse, the Irish peer,
Who kill'd himself for love (with wine) last year.

CL.

"Have I not had two bishops at my feet?
The Duke of Ichar, and Don Fernan Nunez;
And is it thus a faithful wife you treat?
I wonder in what quarter now the moon is;
I praise your vast forbearance not to beat
Me also, since the time so opportune is—
Oh, valiant man! with sword drawn and cock'd trigger,
Now, tell me, don't you cut a pretty figure?

CLI.

"Was it for this you took your sudden journey,
Under pretence of business indispensable
With that sublime of rascals your attorney,
Whom I see standing there, and looking sensible
Of having played the fool? Though both I spurn, he
Deserves the worst, his conduct's less defensible,
Because, no doubt, 't was for his dirty fee,
And not from any love to you nor me.

CLII.

"If he comes here to take a deposition,
By all means let the gentleman proceed;
You've made the apartment in a fit condition:—
There's pen and ink for you, sir, when you need—
Let everything be noted with precision,
I would not you for nothing should be fee'd—
But, as my maid's undrest, pray turn your spies out."
"Oh!" sobb'd Antonia, "I could tear their eyes out."

CLIII.

"There is the closet, there the toilet, there
The antechamber—search them under, over;
There is the sofa, there the great arm-chair,
The chimney—which would really hold a lover.
I wish to sleep, and beg you will take care
And make no further noise, till you discover
The secret cavern of this lurking treasure—
And when 't is found, let me, too, have that pleasure.

CLIV.

"And now, Hidalgo! now that you have thrown
Doubt upon me, confusion over all,
Pray have the courtesy to make it known
Who is the man you search for? how d'ye call
Him? what's his lineage? let him but be shown—
I hope he's young and handsome—is he tall?
Tell me—and be assured, that since you stain
My honour thus, it shall not be in vain.

CLV.

"At least, perhaps, he has not sixty years,
At that age he would be too old for slaughter,
Or for so young a husband's jealous fears—
(Antonia! let me have a glass of water).
I am ashamed of having shed these tears,
They are unworthy of my father's daughter;
My mother dream'd not in my natal hour,
That I should fall into a monster's power.

CLVI.

"Perhaps 't is of Antonia you are jealous,
You saw that she was sleeping by my side,
When you broke in upon us with your fellows:
Look where you please—we've nothing, sir, to hide;
Only another time, I trust, you'll tell us,
Or for the sake of decency abide
A moment at the door, that we may be
Drest to receive so much good company.

CLVII.

"And now, sir, I have done, and say no more;
The little I have said may serve to show
The guileless heart in silence may grieve o'er
The wrongs to whose exposure it is slow:—
I leave you to your conscience as before,
'T will one day ask you *why* you used me so?
God grant you feel not then the bitterest grief!—
Antonia! where's my pocket-handkerchief?"

CLVIII.

She ceased and turned upon her pillow; pale
She lay, her dark eyes flashing through their tears,

Like skies that rain and lighten ; as a veil,
 Waved and o'ershading her wan cheek, appears
Her streaming hair ; the black curls strive, but fail,
 To hide the glossy shoulder, which uprears
Its snow through all ;—her soft lips lie apart,
And louder than her breathing beats her heart.

CLIX.

The Senhor Don Alfonso stood confused;
Antonia bustled round the ransack'd room,
And, turning up her nose, with looks abused
Her master, and his myrmidons, of whom
Not one, except the attorney, was amused;
He, like Achates, faithful to the tomb,
So there were quarrels, cared not for the cause,
Knowing they must be settled by the laws.

CLX.

With prying snub-nose, and small eyes, he stood,
Following Antonia's motions here and there,
With much suspicion in his attitude;
For reputations he had little care;
So that a suit or action were made good,
Small pity had he for the young and fair,
And ne'er believed in negatives, till these
Were proved by competent false witnesses.

CLXI.

But Don Alfonso stood with downcast looks,
And, truth to say, he made a foolish figure;
When, after searching in five hundred nooks,
And treating a young wife with so much rigour,
He gain'd no point, except some self-rebukes,
Added to those his lady with such vigour
Had pour'd upon him for the last half-hour,
Quick, thick, and heavy—as a thunder-shower.

CLXII.

At first he tried to hammer an excuse,
To which the sole reply was tears, and sobs,
And indications of hysterics, whose
Prologue is always certain throes, and throbs,
Gasps, and whatever else the owners choose:
Alfonso saw his wife, and thought of Job's;
He saw, too, in perspective, her relations,
And then he tried to muster all his patience.

CLXIII.

He stood in act to speak, or rather stammer,
But sage Antonia cut him short before
The anvil of his speech received the hammer,
With "Pray, sir, leave the room, and say no more,
Or madam dies."--Alfonso mutter'd, "D——n her,"
But nothing else, the time of words was o'er;
He cast a rueful look or two, and did,
He knew not wherefore, that which he was bid.

CLXIV.

With him retired his "*posse comitatus*,"
The attorney last, who linger'd near the door
Reluctantly, still tarrying there as late as
Antonia let him—not a little sore
At this most strange and unexplain'd "*hiatus*"
In Don Alfonso's facts, which just now wore
An awkward look; as he revolved the case,
The door was fastened in his legal face.

CLXV.

No sooner was it bolted, than—O shame!
Oh sin! Oh sorrow! and Oh womankind!
How can you do such things and keep your fame,
Unless this world, and t' other too, be blind?
Nothing so dear as an unfilch'd good name!
But to proceed—for there is more behind:
With much heartfelt reluctance be it said,
Young Juan slipp'd, half-smother'd, from the bed.

CLXVI.

He had been hid—I don't pretend to say
How, nor can I indeed describe the where—
Young, slender, and pack'd easily, he lay,
No doubt, in little compass, round or square;
But pity him I neither must nor may
His suffocation by that pretty pair;
'T were better, sure, to die so, than be shut
With maudlin Clarence in his Malmsey butt.

CLXVII.

And, secondly, I pity not, because
He had no business to commit a sin,
Forbid by heavenly, fined by human laws,
At least 't was rather early to begin;
But at sixteen the conscience rarely gnaws
So much as when we call our old debts in
At sixty years, and draw the accompts of evil,
And find a deuced balance with the devil.

CLXVIII.

Of his position I can give no notion:
'T is written in the Hebrew Chronicle,
How the physicians, leaving pill and potion,
Prescribed, by way of blister, a young belle,
When old King David's blood grew dull in motion,
And that the medicine answer'd very well;
Perhaps 't was in a different way applied,
For David lived, but Juan nearly died.

CLXIX.

What 's to be done? Alfonso will be back
The moment he has sent his fools away.
Antonia's skill was put upon the rack,
But no device could be brought into play—
And how to parry the renew'd attack?
Besides, it wanted but few hours of day:
Antonia puzzled; Julia did not speak,
But press'd her bloodless lip to Juan's cheek.

CLXX.

He turn'd his lip to hers, and with his hand
Call'd back the tangles of her wandering hair;
Even then their love they could not all command,
And half forgot their danger and despair:

Antonia's patience now was at a stand—
 "Come, come, 'tis no time now for fooling there,"
She whisper'd, in great wrath—"I must deposit
This pretty gentleman within the closet:

CLXXI.

"Pray, keep your nonsense for some luckier night—
 Who can have put my master in this mood?
What will become on 't—I'm in such a fright;
 The devil's in the urchin, and no good—
Is this a time for giggling? this a plight?
 Why, don't you know that it may end in blood?
You'll lose your life, and I shall lose my place,
My mistress all, for that half-girlish face.

CLXXII.

"Had it but been for a stout cavalier
 Of twenty-five or thirty—(come, make haste)
But for a child, what piece of work is here!
 I really, madam, wonder at your taste—
(Come, sir, get in)—my master must be near:
 There, for the present, at the least, he's fast,
And if we can but till the morning keep
Our counsel—(Juan, mind, you must not sleep)."

CLXXIII.

Now, Don Alfonso entering, but alone,
 Closed the oration of the trusty maid:
She loiter'd, and he told her to be gone,
 An order somewhat sullenly obey'd;
However, present remedy was none,
 And no great good seem'd answer'd if she stay'd:
Regarding both with slow and sidelong view,
She snuff'd the candle, curtsied, and withdrew.

CLXXIV.

Alfonso paused a minute—then begun
 Some strange excuses for his late proceeding;
He would not justify what he had done,
 To say the best, it was extreme ill-breeding;
But there were ample reasons for it, none
 Of which he specified in this his pleading;
His speech was a fine sample, on the whole,
Of rhetoric, which the learn'd call "*rigmarole*."

CLXXV.

Julia said nought; though all the while there rose
 A ready answer, which at once enables
A matron, who her husband's foible knows,
 By a few timely words to turn the tables,
Which, if it does not silence, still must pose,—
 Even if it should comprise a pack of fables;
'T is to retort with firmness, and when he
Suspects with *one*, do you reproach with *three*.

CLXXVI.

Julia, in fact, had tolerable grounds,—
 Alfonso's loves with Inez were well known;
But whether 'twas that one's own guilt confounds—
 But that can't be, as has been often shown,
A lady with apologies abounds;—
 It might be that her silence sprang alone
From delicacy to Don Juan's ear,
To whom she knew his mother's fame was dear.

CLXXVII.

There might be one more motive, which makes two;
 Alfonso ne'er to Juan had alluded,—
Mention'd his jealousy, but never who
 Had been the happy lover, he concluded
Conceal'd amongst his premises; 't is true
 His mind the more o'er this its mystery brooded;
To speak of Inez now, were, one may say,
Like throwing Juan in Alfonso's way.

CLXXVIII.

A hint, in tender cases, is enough;
 Silence is best; besides, there is a *tact*—
(That modern phrase appears to me sad stuff,
 But it will serve to keep my verse compact)—
Which keeps, when push'd by questions rather rough,
 A lady always distant from the fact:
The charming creatures lie with such a grace,
There's nothing so becoming to the face.

CLXXIX.

They blush, and we believe them; at least I
 Have always done so; 'tis of no great use,
In any case, attempting a reply,
 For then their eloquence grows quite profuse;
And when at length they're out of breath, they sigh,
 And cast their languid eyes down, and let loose
A tear or two, and then we make it up;
And then—and then—and then—sit down and sup.

CLXXX.

Alfonso closed his speech, and begged her pardon,
 Which Julia half withheld, and then half granted,
And laid conditions he thought very hard on,
 Denying several little things he wanted:
He stood like Adam lingering near his garden,
 With useless penitence perplexed and haunted,
Beseeching she no further would refuse,
When, lo! he stumbled o'er a pair of shoes.

CLXXXI.

A pair of shoes!—what then? not much, if they
 Are such as fit with ladies' feet; but these
(No one can tell how much I grieve to say)
 Were masculine; to see them, and to seize,
Was but a moment's act.—Ah! well-a-day!
 My teeth begin to chatter, my veins freeze!
Alfonso first examined well their fashion,
And then flew out into another passion.

CLXXXII.

He left the room for his relinquish'd sword,
 And Julia instant to the closet flew.
" Fly, Juan, fly! for heaven's sake—not a word—
 The door is open—you may yet slip through
The passage you so often have explored—
 Here is the garden-key—Fly—fly—Adieu!
Haste—haste! I hear Alfonso's hurrying feet—
Day has not broke—there's no one in the street."

CLXXXIII.

None can say that this was not good advice,
 The only mischief was, it came too late;
Of all experience 'tis the usual price,
 A sort of income-tax laid on by fate:
Juan had reach'd the room-door in a trice,
 And might have done so by the garden-gate,
But met Alfonso in his dressing-gown,
Who threaten'd death—so Juan knock'd him down.

CLXXXIV.

Dire was the scuffle, and out went the light;
 Antonia cried out " Rape!" and Julia " Fire!"
But not a servant stirr'd to aid the fight.
 Alfonso, pommell'd to his heart's desire,
Swore lustily he'd be reveng'd this night;
 And Juan, too, blasphem'd an octave higher;
His blood was up: though young, he was a Tartar,
And not at all disposed to prove a martyr.

CLXXXV.

Alfonso's sword had dropp'd ere he could draw it,
 And they continued, battling hand to hand,
For Juan very luckily ne'er saw it;
 His temper not being under great command,
If at that moment he had chanced to claw it,
 Alfonso's days had not been in the land
Much longer.—Think of husbands', lovers' lives
And how ye may be doubly widows—wives.

CLXXXVI.

Alfonso grappled to detain the foe,
 And Juan throttled him to get away,
And blood ('t was from the nose) began to flow;
 At last, as they more faintly wrestling lay,
Juan contrived to give an awkward blow,
 And then his only garment quite gave way;
He fled, like Joseph, leaving it; but there,
I doubt, all likeness ends between the pair.

CLXXXVII.

Lights came at length, and men, and maids, who found
 An awkward spectacle their eyes before;
Antonia in hysterics, Julia swoon'd,
 Alfonso leaning, breathless, by the door;
Some half-torn drapery scatter'd on the ground,
 Some blood, and several footsteps, but no more:
Juan the gate gain'd, turn'd the key about,
And liking not the inside, lock'd the out.

CLXXXVIII.

Here ends this canto.—Need I sing or say,
 How Juan, naked, favour'd by the night,
Who favours what she should not, found his way,
 And reach'd his home in an unseemly plight?
The pleasant scandal which arose next day,
 The nine days' wonder which was brought to light,
And how Alfonso sued for a divorce,
Were in the English newspapers, of course.

CLXXXIX.

If you would like to see the whole proceedings,
 The depositions, and the cause at full,
The names of all the witnesses, the pleadings
 Of counsel to nonsuit, or to annul,
There 's more than one edition, and the readings
 Are various, but they none of them are dull:
The best is that in short-hand ta'en by Gurney,
Who to Madrid on purpose made a journey.

CXC.

But Donna Inez, to divert the train
 Of one of the most circulating scandals
That had for centuries been known in Spain,
 At least since the retirement of the Vandals,
First vow'd (and never had she vow'd in vain)
 To Virgin Mary several pounds of candles:
And then, by the advice of some old ladies,
She sent her son to be shipp'd off from Cadiz.

CXCI.

She half resolved that he should travel through
 All European climes, by land or sea,
To mend his former morals, and get new,
 Especially in France and Italy,
(At least this is the thing most people do).
 Julia was sent into a convent: she
Grieved, but, perhaps, her feelings may be better
Shown in the following copy of her Letter:—

CXCII.

"They tell me 't is decided; you depart:
 'T is wise—'t is well, but not the less a pain;
I have no further claim on your young heart,
 Mine is the victim, and would be again;
To love too much has been the only art
 I used;—I write in haste, and if a stain
Be on this sheet, 't is not what it appears;
My eyeballs burn and throb, but have no tears.

CXCIII.

"I loved, I love you, for this love have lost
 State, station, heaven, mankind's, my own esteem,
And yet cannot regret what it hath cost,
 So dear is still the memory of that dream;
Yet, if I name my guilt, 't is not to boast,
 None can deem harshlier of me than I deem:
I trace this scrawl because I cannot rest—
I 've nothing to reproach, or to request.

CXCIV

"Man's love is of man's life a thing apart,
 'T is woman's whole existence; man may range
The court, camp, church, the vessel, and the mart,
 Sword, gown, gain, glory, offer in exchange
Pride, fame, ambition, to fill up his heart,
 And few there are whom these can not estrange;
Men have all these resources, we but one,—
To love again, and be again undone.

CXCV.

"You will proceed in pleasure, and in pride,
 Beloved and loving many; all is o'er
For me on earth, except some years to hide
 My shame and sorrow deep in my heart's core!
These I could bear, but cannot cast aside
 The passion which still rages as before,—
And so farewell—forgive me, love me—No,
That word is idle now—but let it go.

CXCVI.

"My breast has been all weakness, is so yet;
 But still I think I can collect my mind;
My blood still rushes where my spirit's set,
 As roll the waves before the settled wind;
My heart is feminine, nor can forget—
 To all, except one image, madly blind;
So shakes the needle, and so stands the pole,
As vibrates my fond heart to my fix'd soul.

CXCVII.

" I have no more to say, but linger still,
 And dare not set my seal upon this sheet,
And yet I may as well the task fulfil,
 My misery can scarce be more complete;
I had not lived till now, could sorrow kill;
 Death shuns the wretch who fain the blow would meet,
And I must even survive this last adieu,
And bear with life, to love and pray for you!"

CXCVIII.

This note was written upon gilt-edged paper,
 With a neat little crowquill, slight and new;
Her small white hand could hardly reach the taper,
 It trembled as magnetic needles do,
And yet she did not let one tear escape her;
 The seal a sunflower; " *Elle vous suit partout,*"
The motto cut upon a white cornelian;
The wax was superfine, its hue vermilion.

CXCIX.

This was Don Juan's earliest scrape; but whether
 I shall proceed with his adventures is
Dependent on the public altogether;
 We 'll see, however, what they say to this,
Their favour in an author's cap 's a feather,
 And no great mischief 's done by their caprice;
And if their approbation we experience,
Perhaps they 'll have some more about a year hence.

CC.

My poem's epic, and is meant to be
 Divided in twelve books; each book containing,
With love, and war, a heavy gale at sea,
 A list of ships, and captains, and kings reigning,

New characters; the episodes are three:
 A panoramic view of hell's in training,
After the style of Virgil and of Homer,
So that my name of Epic's no misnomer.

CCI.

All these things will be specified in time,
 With strict regard to Aristotle's rules,
The *Vade Mecum* of the true sublime,
 Which makes so many poets, and some fools:
Prose poets like blank-verse, I'm fond of rhyme,
 Good workmen never quarrel with their tools;
I've got new mythological machinery,
And very handsome supernatural scenery.

CCII.

There's only one slight difference between
 Me and my epic brethren gone before,
And here the advantage is my own, I ween;
 (Not that I have not several merits more,
But this will more peculiarly be seen);
 They so embellish, that 't is quite a bore
Their labyrinth of fables to thread through,
Whereas this story's actually true.

CCIII.

If any person doubt it, I appeal
 To history, tradition, and to facts,
To newspapers, whose truth all know and feel,
 To plays in five, and operas in three acts;
All these confirm my statement a good deal,
 But that which more completely faith exacts
Is, that myself, and several now in Seville,
Saw Juan's last elopement with the devil.

CCIV.

If ever I should condescend to prose,
 I'll write poetical commandments, which
Shall supersede beyond all doubt all those
 That went before; in these I shall enrich
My text with many things that no one knows,
 And carry precept to the highest pitch:
I'll call the work "Longinus o'er a Bottle,
Or, Every Poet his own Aristotle."

CCV.

Thou shalt believe in Milton, Dryden, Pope;
 Thou shalt not set up Wordsworth, Coleridge, Southey;
Because the first is crazed beyond all hope,
 The second drunk, the third so quaint and mouthy;
With Crabbe it may be difficult to cope,
 And Campbell's Hippocrene is somewhat drouthy;
Thou shalt not steal from Samuel Rogers, nor
Commit—flirtation with the muse of Moore.

CCVI.

Thou shalt not covet Mr. Sotheby's Muse,
 His Pegasus, nor any thing that's his;
Thou shalt not bear false witness, like "the Blues"—
 (There's one, at least, is very fond of this);
Thou shalt not write, in short, but what I choose:
 This is true criticism, and you may kiss—
Exactly as you please, or not—the rod;
But if you don't, I'll lay it on, by G—d!

CCVII.

If any person should presume to assert
 This story is not moral, first, I pray,
That they will not cry out before they're hurt,
 Then that they'll read it o'er again, and say,
(But, doubtless, nobody will be so pert),
 That this is not a moral tale, though gay:
Besides, in Canto Twelfth, I mean to show
The very place where wicked people go.

CCVIII.

If, after all, there should be some so blind
 To their own good this warning to despise,
Led by some tortuosity of mind,
 Not to believe my verse and their own eyes,
And cry that they "the moral cannot find,
 I tell him, if a clergyman, he lies;
Should captains the remark, or critics make,
They also lie too—under a mistake.

CCIX.

The public approbation I expect,
 And beg they'll take my word about the moral,
Which I with their amusement will connect
 (So children cutting teeth receive a coral);
Meantime they'll doubtless please to recollect
 My epical pretensions to the laurel:
For fear some prudish readers should grow skittish,
I've bribed my grandmother's review—the British.

CCX.

I sent it in a letter to the Editor,
 Who thank'd me duly by return of post—
I'm for a handsome article his creditor;
 Yet, if my gentle Muse he please to roast,
And break a promise after having made it her,
 Denying the receipt of what it cost,
And smear his page with gall instead of honey,
All I can say is—that he had the money.

CCXI.

I think that with this holy new alliance
 I may ensure the public, and defy
All other magazines of art or science,
 Daily, or monthly, or three monthly; I
Have not essay'd to multiply their clients,
 Because they tell me 't were in vain to try,
And that the "Edinburgh Review" and "Quarterly"
Treat a dissenting author very martyrly.

CCXII.

'*Non ego hoc ferrem calida juventâ*
Consule Planco," Horace said, and so
Say I; by which quotation there is meant a
Hint that some six or seven good years ago
(Long ere I dreamt of dating from the Brenta)
I was most ready to return a blow,
And would not brook at all this sort of thing
In my hot youth—when George the Third was King.

CCXIII.

But now at thirty years my hair is gray—
(I wonder what it will be like at forty?
I thought of a peruke the other day—)
My heart is not much greener; and, in short, I
Have squander'd my whole summer while 't was May,
And feel no more the spirit to retort; I
Have spent my life, both interest and principal,
And deem not, what I deem'd, my soul invincible.

CCXIV.

No more—no more—Oh! never more on me
The freshness of the heart can fall like dew,
Which out of all the lovely things we see
Extracts emotions beautiful and new,
Hived in our bosoms like the bag o' the bee,
Think'st thou the honey with those objects grew?
Alas! 't was not in them, but in thy power
To double even the sweetness of a flower.

CCXV.

No more—no more—Oh! never more, my heart,
Canst thou be my sole world, my universe!
Once all in all, but now a thing apart,
Thou canst not be my blessing or my curse:
The illusion 's gone for ever, and thou art
Insensible, I trust, but none the worse,
And in thy stead I 've got a deal of judgment,
Though Heaven knows how it ever found a lodgment.

CCXVI.

My days of love are over; me no more
The charms of maid, wife, and still less of widow,
Can make the fool of which they made before,—
In short, I must not lead the life I did do;
The credulous hope of mutual minds is o'er,
The copious use of claret is forbid too,
So for a good old gentlemanly vice,
I think I must take up with avarice.

CCXVII.

Ambition was my idol, which was broken
Before the shrines of Sorrow, and of Pleasure;
And the two last have left me many a token,
O'er which reflection may be made at leisure:
Now, like Friar Bacon's brazen head, I 've spoken,
"Time is, Time was, Time 's past:"—a chymic treasure
Is glittering youth, which I have spent betimes—
My heart in passion, and my head on rhymes.

CCXVIII.

What is the end of Fame? 'T is but to fill
A certain portion of uncertain paper:
Some liken it to climbing up a hill,
Whose summit, like all hills, is lost in vapour;
For this men write, speak, preach, and heroes kill,
And bards burn what they call their "midnight taper,"
To have, when the original is dust,
A name, a wretched picture, and worse bust.

CCXIX.

What are the hopes of man? Old Egypt's King
Cheops erected the first pyramid
And largest, thinking it was just the thing
To keep his memory whole, and mummy hid;
But somebody or other rummaging
Burglariously broke his coffin's lid;
Let not a monument give you or me hopes,
Since not a pinch of dust remains of Cheops.

CCXX.

But I being fond of true philosophy,
Say very often to myself, "Alas!
All things that have been born were born to die,
And flesh (which Death mows down to hay) is grass;
You 've pass'd your youth not so unpleasantly,
And if you had it o'er again—'t would pass—
So thank your stars that matters are no worse,
And read your Bible, Sir, and mind your purse."

CCXXI.

But for the present, gentle reader! and
Still gentler purchaser! the bard—that 's I—
Must, with permission, shake you by the hand,
And so your humble servant, and good-b'ye!
We meet again, if we should understand
Each other; and if not, I shall not try
Your patience further than by this short sample—
'T were well if others follow'd my example.

CCXXII.

"Go, little book, from this my solitude!
I cast thee on the waters—go thy ways!
And if, as I believe, thy vein be good,
The world will find thee after many days."
When Southey 's read, and Wordsworth understood,
I can't help putting in my claim to praise—
The four first rhymes are Southey's every line:
For God's sake, reader! take them not for mine.

CANTO THE SECOND.

I.

Oh ye! who teach the ingenious youth of nations,
 Holland, France, England, Germany, or Spain,
 pray ye flog them upon all occasions,
 It mends their morals, never mind the pain;
The best of mothers and of educations
 In Juan's case were but employ'd in vain,
Since, in a way that's rather of the oddest, he
Became divested of his native modesty.

II.

Had he but been placed at a public school,
 In the third form, or even in the fourth,
His daily task had kept his fancy cool,
 At least, had he been nurtured in the north;
Spain may prove an exception to the rule,
 But then exceptions always prove its worth—
A lad of sixteen causing a divorce
Puzzled his tutors very much, of course.

III.

I can't say that it puzzles me at all,
 If all things be consider'd: first, there was
His lady-mother, mathematical,
 A—— never mind;—his tutor, an old ass;
A pretty woman—(that's quite natural,
 Or else the thing had hardly come to pass);
A husband rather old, not much in unity
With his young wife—a time, and opportunity.

IV.

Well—well, the world must turn upon its axis,
 And all mankind turn with it, heads or tails,
And live and die, make love and pay our taxes,
 And as the veering wind shifts, shift our sails;
The king commands us, and the doctor quacks us,
 The priest instructs, and so our life exhales,
A little breath, love, wine, ambition, fame,
Fighting, devotion, dust,—perhaps a name.

V.

I said, that Juan had been sent to Cadiz—
 A pretty town, I recollect it well—
'T is there the mart of the colonial trade is,
 (Or was, before Peru learn'd to rebel,)
And such sweet girls — I mean, such graceful ladies,
 Their very walk would make your bosom swell;
I can't describe it, though so much it strike,
Nor liken it—I never saw the like:

VI.

An Arab horse, a stately stag, a barb
New broke, a cameleopard, a gazelle,
No—none of these will do;—and then their garb!
Their veil and petticoat—Alas! to dwell
Upon such things would very near absorb
A canto—then their feet and ankles—well,
Thank Heaven I've got no metaphor quite ready,
(And so, my sober Muse—come, let's be steady—

VII.

Chaste Muse!—well, if you must, you must)—the veil
Thrown back a moment with the glancing hand,
While the o'erpowering eye, that turns you pale,
Flashes into the heart:—All sunny land
Of love, when I forget you, may I fail
To —— say my prayers—but never was there plann'd
A dress through which the eyes gave such a volley,
Excepting the Venetian Fazzioli.[8]

VIII.

But to our tale: the Donna Inez sent
Her son to Cadiz only to embark;
To stay there had not answer'd her intent,
But why?—we leave the reader in the dark—
'Twas for a voyage that the young man was meant,
As if a Spanish ship were Noah's ark,
To wean him from the wickedness of earth,
And send him like a dove of promise forth.

IX.

Don Juan bade his valet pack his things
According to direction, then received
A lecture and some money: for four springs
He was to travel; and though Inez grieved
(As every kind of parting has its stings),
She hoped he would improve—perhaps believed:
A letter, too, she gave (he never read it)
Of good advice—and two or three of credit.

X.

In the mean time, to pass her hours away,
Brave Inez now set up a Sunday school
For naughty children, who would rather play
(Like truant rogues) the devil, or the fool;
Infants of three years old were taught that day,
Dunces were whipt, or set upon a stool:
The great success of Juan's education,
Spurr'd her to teach another generation.

XI.

Juan embark'd—the ship got under way,
The wind was fair, the water passing rough;
A devil of a sea rolls in that bay,
As I, who've cross'd it oft, know well enough;
And standing upon the deck, the dashing spray
Flies in one's face, and makes it weather-tough
And there he stood to take, and take again,
His first—perhaps his last—farewell of Spain.

XII.

I can't but say it is an awkward sight
To see one's native land receding through
The growing waters; it unmans one quite,
Especially when life is rather new:
I recollect Great Britain's coast looks white,
But almost every other country's blue,
When gazing on them, mystified by distance,
We enter on our nautical existence.

XIII.

So Juan stood, bewilder'd, on the deck:
The wind sung, cordage strain'd, and sailors swore,
And the ship creak'd, the town became a speck,
From which away so fair and fast they bore;—
The best of remedies is a beef-steak
Against sea-sickness: try it, Sir, before
You sneer, and I assure you this is true,
For I have found it answer—so may you.

XIV.

Don Juan stood, and, gazing from the stern,
Beheld his native Spain receding far:
First partings form a lesson hard to learn,
Even nations feel this when they go to war
There is a sort of unexprest concern,
A kind of shock that sets one's heart ajar:
At leaving even the most unpleasant people
And places, one keeps looking at the steeple.

XV.

But Juan had got many things to leave—
His mother, and a mistress, and no wife,
So that he had much better cause to grieve,
Than many persons more advanced in life;
And if we now and then a sigh must heave
At quitting even those we quit in strife,
No doubt we weep for those the heart endears—
That is, till deeper griefs congeal our tears.

XVI.

So Juan wept, as wept the captive Jews
By Babel's waters, still remembering Sion:
I'd weep—but mine is not a weeping Muse,
And such light griefs are not a thing to die on;
Young men should travel, if but to amuse
Themselves; and the next time their servants tie on
Behind their carriages their new portmanteau
Perhaps it may be lined with this my canto.

XVII.

And Juan wept, and much he sigh'd and thought
While his salt tears dropp'd into the salt sea,

"Sweets to the sweet;" (I like so much to quote,
You must excuse this extract,—'t is where she,
The Queen of Denmark, for Ophelia brought
Flowers to the grave); and, sobbing often, he
Reflected on his present situation,
And seriously resolved on reformation.

XVIII.

"Farewell, my Spain! a long farewell!" he cried,
"Perhaps I may revisit thee no more,
But die, as many an exiled heart hath died,
Of its own thirst to see again thy shore:
Farewell, where Guadalquivir's waters glide,
Farewell, my mother! and, since all is o'er,
Farewell, too, dearest Julia!—(here he drew
Her letter out again, and read it through).

XIX.

"And oh! if e'er I should forget, I swear—
But that's impossible, and cannot be—
Sooner shall this blue ocean melt to air,
Sooner shall earth resolve itself to sea,
Than I resign thine image, oh, my fair!
Or think of anything excepting thee;
A mind diseased no remedy can physic—
(Here the ship gave a lurch, and he grew sea-sick).

XX.

"Sooner shall heaven kiss earth—(here he fell sicker)
Oh, Julia! what is every other woe?—
(For God's sake let me have a glass of liquor;
Pedro, Battista, help me down below).
Julia, my love!—(you rascal, Pedro, quicker)—
Oh Julia!—(this curst vessel pitches so)—
Beloved Julia, hear me still beseeching!"
(Here he grew inarticulate with retching).

XXI.

He felt that chilling heaviness of heart,
Or rather stomach, which, alas! attends,
Beyond the best apothecary's art,
The loss of love, the treachery of friends,
Or death of those we dote on, when a part
Of us dies with them as each fond hope ends:
No doubt he would have been much more pathetic,
But the sea acted as a strong emetic.

XXII.

Love's a capricious power: I've known it hold
Out through a fever caused by its own heat,
But be much puzzled by a cough and cold,
And find a quinsy very hard to treat;
Against all noble maladies he's bold,
But vulgar illnesses don't like to meet,
Nor that a sneeze should interrupt his sigh,
Nor inflammation redden his blind eye.

XXIII.

But worst of all is nausea, or a pain
About the lower region of the bowels;
Love, who heroically breathes a vein,
Shrinks from the application of hot towels,
And purgatives are dangerous to his reign,
Sea-sickness death: his love was perfect, how else
Could Juan's passion, while the billows roar,
Resist his stomach, ne'er at sea before?

XXIV.

The ship, call'd the most holy "Trinidada,"
Was steering duly for the port Leghorn;
For there the Spanish family Moncada
Were settled long ere Juan's sire was born:
They were relations, and for them he had a
Letter of introduction, which the morn
Of his departure had been sent him by
His Spanish friends for those in Italy.

XXV.

His suite consisted of three servants and
A tutor, the licentiate Pedrillo,
Who several languages did understand,
But now lay sick and speechless on his pillow,
And, rocking in his hammock, long'd for land,
His headache being increased by every billow;
And the waves oozing through the port-hole made
His berth a little damp, and him afraid.

XXVI.

'T was not without some reason, for the wind
Increased at night, until it blew a gale;
And though 't was not much to a naval mind,
Some landsmen would have look'd a little pale,
For sailors are, in fact, a different kind:
At sunset they began to take in sail,
For the sky show'd it would come on to blow,
And carry away, perhaps, a mast or so.

XXVII.

At one o'clock the wind with sudden shift
Threw the ship right into the trough of the sea,
Which struck her aft, and made an awkward rift,
Started the stern-post, also shatter'd the
Whole of her stern-frame, and, ere she could lift
Herself from out her present jeopardy,
The rudder tore away: 't was time to sound
The pumps, and there were four feet water found.

XXVIII.

One gang of people instantly was put
Upon the pumps, and the remainder set
To get up part of the cargo, and what not;
But they could not come at the leak as yet;
At last they did get at it really, but
Still their salvation was an even bet.

The water rush'd through in a way quite puzzling,
While they thrust sheets, shirts, jackets, bales of muslin,

XXIX.

Into the opening; but all such ingredients
Would have been vain, and they must have gone down,
Despite of all their efforts and expedients,
But for the pumps; I'm glad to make them known
To all the brother tars who may have need hence,
For fifty tons of water were upthrown
By them per hour, and they had all been undone,
But for the maker, Mr. Mann, of London.

XXX.

As day advanced the weather seem'd to abate,
And then the leak they reckon'd to reduce,
And keep the ship afloat, though three feet yet
Kept two hand and one chain pump still in use.
The wind blew fresh again: as it grew late
A squall came on, and while some guns broke loose,
A gust—which all descriptive power transcends—
Laid with one blast the ship on her beam ends.

XXXI.

There she lay, motionless, and seem'd upset;
The water left the hold, and wash'd the decks,
And made a scene men do not soon forget;
For they remember battles, fires, and wrecks,
Or any other thing that brings regret,
Or breaks their hopes, or hearts, or heads, or necks:
Thus drownings are much talk'd of by the divers,
And swimmers, who may chance to be survivors.

XXXII.

Immediately the masts were cut away,
Both main and mizen; first the mizen went,

The main-mast follow'd: but the ship still lay
Like a mere log, and baffled our intent.
Foremast and bowsprit were cut down, and they
Eased her at last (although we never meant
To part with all till every hope was blighted),
And then with violence the old ship righted.

XXXIII.

It may be easily supposed, while this
Was going on, some people were unquiet,
That passengers would find it much amiss
To lose their lives, as well as spoil their diet;
That even the able seaman, deeming his
Days nearly o'er, might be disposed to riot,
As upon such occasions tars will ask
For grog, and sometimes drink rum from the cask.

XXXIV.

There 's nought, no doubt, so much the spirit calms
As rum and true religion: thus it was,
Some plunder'd, some drank spirits, some sung psalms,
The high wind made the treble, and as bass
The hoarse harsh waves kept time; fright cured the qualms
Of all the luckless landsmen's sea-sick maws:
Strange sounds of wailing, blasphemy, devotion,
Clamour'd in chorus to the roaring ocean.

XXXV.

Perhaps more mischief had been done, but for
Our Juan, who, with sense beyond his years.
Got to the spirit-room, and stood before
It with a pair of pistols; and their fears.

As if Death were more dreadful by his door
 Of fire than water, spite of oaths and tears,
Kept still aloof the crew, who, ere they sunk,
Thought it would be becoming to die drunk.

XXXVI.

"Give us more grog," they cried, "for it will be
 All one an hour hence." Juan answer'd, "No!
'T is true that death awaits both you and me,
 But let us die like men, not sink below
Like brutes:"—and thus his dangerous post kept he,
 And none liked to anticipate the blow;
And even Pedrillo, his most reverend tutor,
Was for some rum a disappointed suitor.

XXXVII.

The good old gentleman was quite aghast,
 And made a loud and pious lamentation
Repented all his sins, and made a last
 Irrevocable vow of reformation;
Nothing should tempt him more (this peril past)
 To quit his academic occupation,
In cloisters of the classic Salamanca,
To follow Juan's wake, like Sancho Panca.

XXXVIII.

But now there came a flash of hope once more;
 Day broke, and the wind lull'd: the masts were gone,
The leak increased; shoals round her, but no shore,
 The vessel swam, yet still she held her own.
They tried the pumps again, and though before
 Their desperate efforts seem'd all useless grown,
A glimpse of sunshine set some hands to bale—
The stronger pump'd, the weaker thrumm'd a sail.

XXXIX.

Under the vessel's keel the sail was past,
 And for the moment it had some effect;
But with a leak, and not a stick of mast,
 Nor rag of canvas, what could they expect?
But still 't is best to struggle to the last,
 'T is never too late to be wholly wreck'd:
And though 't is true that man can only die once,
'T is not so pleasant in the Gulf of Lyons.

XL.

There winds and waves had hurl'd them, and from thence
 Without their will, they carried them away;
For they were forced with steering to dispense,
 And never had as yet a quiet day
On which they might repose, or even commence
 A jurymast or rudder, or could say
The ship would swim an hour, which, by good luck,
Still swam—though not exactly like a duck.

XLI.

The wind, in fact, perhaps, was rather less,
 But the ship labour'd so, they scarce could hope
To weather out much longer; the distress
 Was also great with which they had to cope
For want of water, and their solid mess
 Was scant enough: in vain the telescope
Was used—nor sail nor shore appear'd in sight,
Nought but the heavy sea, and coming night.

XLII.

Again the weather threaten'd,—again blew
 A gale, and in the fore and after hold
Water appear'd; yet, though the people knew
 All this, the most were patient, and some bold,
Until the chains and leathers were worn through
 Of all our pumps:—a wreck complete she roll'd,
At mercy of the waves, whose mercies are
Like human beings during civil war.

XLIII.

Then came the carpenter, at last, with tears
 In his rough eyes, and told the captain, he
Could do no more: he was a man in years,
 And long had voyaged through many a stormy sea,
And if he wept at length, they were not fears
 That made his eyelids as a woman's be,
But he, poor fellow, had a wife and children,—
Two things for dying people quite bewildering.

XLIV.

The ship was evidently settling now
 Fast by the head; and, all distinction gone,
Some went to prayers again, and made a vow
 Of candles to their saints—but there were none
To pay them with; and some look'd o'er the bow;
 Some hoisted out the boats; and there was one
That begg'd Pedrillo for an absolution,
Who told him to be damn'd—in his confusion.

XLV.

Some lash'd them in their hammocks; some put on
 Their best clothes, as if going to a fair;
Some cursed the day on which they saw the sun,
 And gnash'd their teeth, and, howling, tore their hair;
And others went on as they had begun,
 Getting the boats out, being well aware,
That a tight boat will live in a rough sea,
Unless with breakers close beneath her lee.

XLVI.

The worst of all was, that in their condition,
 Having been several days in great distress,
'T was difficult to get out such provision
 As now might render their long suffering less:

Men, even when dying, dislike inanition;
 Their stock was damaged by the weather's stress:
Two casks of biscuit, and a keg of butter,
Were all that could be thrown into the cutter.

XLVII.

But in the long-boat they contrived to stow
 Some pounds of bread, though injured by the wet;
Water, a twenty-gallon-cask or so;
 Six flasks of wine; and they contrived to get
A portion of their beef up from below,
 And with a piece of pork, moreover, met,
But scarce enough to serve them for a luncheon—
Then there was rum, eight gallons in a puncheon.

XLVIII.

The other boats, the yawl and pinnace, had
 Been stove in the beginning of the gale;
And the long boat's condition was but bad,
 As there were but two blankets for a sail,
And one oar for a mast, which a young lad
 Threw in by good luck, over the ship's rail;
And two boats could not hold, far less be stored,
To save one half the people then on board.

XLIX.

'T was twilight, and the sunless day went down
 Over the waste of waters; like a veil,
Which, if withdrawn, would but disclose the frown
 Of one whose hate is mask'd but to assail.
Thus to their hopeless eyes the night was shown,
 And grimly darkled o'er the faces pale,
And the dim desolate deep: twelve days had Fear
Been their familiar, and now Death was here.

L.

Some trial had been making at a raft,
 With little hope in such a rolling sea,
A sort of thing at which one would have laugh'd,
 If any laughter at such times could be,
Unless with people who too much have quaff'd,
 And have a kind of wild and horrid glee,
Half epileptical, and half hysterical:—
Their preservation would have been a miracle.

LI.

At half-past eight o'clock, booms, hencoops, spars,
 And all things, for a chance, had been cast loose,
That still could keep afloat the struggling tars,
 For yet they strove, although of no great use:
There was no light in heaven but a few stars,
 The boats put off o'ercrowded with their crews;
She gave a heel, and then a lurch to port,
And, going down head foremost—sunk, in short.

LII.

Then rose from sea to sky the wild farewell—
 Then shriek'd the timid, and stood still the brave,—
Then some leap'd overboard with dreadful yell,
 As eager to anticipate their grave;
And the sea yawn'd around her like a hell,
 And down she suck'd with her the whirling wave,
Like one who grapples with his enemy,
And strives to strangle him before he die.

LIII.

And first one universal shriek there rush'd,
 Louder than the loud ocean, like a crash
Of echoing thunder; and then all was hush'd,
 Save the wild wind and the remorseless dash
Of billows; but at intervals there gush'd,
 Accompanied with a convulsive splash,
A solitary shriek, the bubbling cry
Of some strong swimmer in his agony.

LIV.

The boats, as stated, had got off before,
 And in them crowded several of the crew;
And yet their present hope was hardly more
 Than what it had been, for so strong it blew,
There was slight chance of reaching any shore;
 And then they were too many, though so few—
Nine in the cutter, thirty in the boat,
Were counted in them when they got afloat.

LV.

All the rest perish'd; near two hundred souls
 Had left their bodies; and what 's worse, alas!
When over Catholics the ocean rolls,
 They must wait several weeks before a mass
Takes off one peck of purgatorial coals,
 Because, till people know what 's come to pass,
They won't lay out their money on the dead—
It costs three francs for every mass that 's said.

LVI.

Juan got into the long-boat, and there
 Contrived to help Pedrillo to a place;
It seem'd as if they had exchanged their care,
 For Juan wore the magisterial face
Which courage gives, while poor Pedrillo's pair
 Of eyes were crying for their owner's case:
Battista, though, (a name call'd shortly Tita)
Was lost by getting at some aqua-vita.

LVII.

Pedro, his valet, too, he tried to save,
 But the same cause, conducive to his loss,
Left him so drunk, he jump'd into the wave,
 As o'er the cutter's edge he tried to cross,
And so he found a wine-and-watery grave;
 They could not rescue him although so close,
Because the sea ran higher every minute,
And for the boat—the crew kept crowding in it.

LVIII.

A small old Spaniel,—which had been Don Jóse's,
His father's, whom he loved, as ye may think,
For on such things the memory reposes
With tenderness—stood howling on the brink.
Knowing, (dogs have such intellectual noses!)
No doubt, the vessel was about to sink;
And Juan caught him up, and ere he stepp'd
Off, threw him in, then after him he leap'd.

LIX.

He also stuff'd his money where he could
About his person, and Pedrillo's too,
Who let him do, in fact, whate'er he would,
Not knowing what himself to say, or do.
As every rising wave his dread renew'd;
But Juan, trusting they might still get through,
And deeming there were remedies for any ill,
Thus re-embark'd his tutor and his spaniel.

LX.

'T was a rough night, and blew so stiffly yet,
 That the sail was becalm'd between the seas,
Though on the wave's high top too much to set,
 They dared not take it in for all the breeze:
Each sea curl'd o'er the stern, and kept them wet,
 And made them bale without a moment's ease,
So that themselves as well as hopes were damp'd,
And the poor little cutter quickly swamp'd.

LXI.

Nine souls more went in her: the long-boat still
 Kept above water, with an oar for mast,
Two blankets stitch'd together, answering ill
 Instead of sail, were to the oar made fast;
Though every wave roll'd menacing to fill,
 And present peril all before surpass'd,
They grieved for those who perish'd with the cutter,
And also for the biscuit-casks and butter.

LXII.

The sun rose red and fiery, a sure sign
 Of the continuance of the gale: to run
Before the sea until it should grow fine,
 Was all that for the present could be done:
A few tea-spoonfuls of their rum and wine
 Were served out to the people, who begun
To faint, and damaged bread wet through the bags,
And most of them had little clothes but rags.

LXIII.

They counted thirty, crowded in a space
 Which left scarce room for motion or exertion;
They did their best to modify their case,
 One half sate up, though numb'd with the immersion,
While t'other half were laid down in their place,
 At watch and watch; thus, shivering like the tertian
Ague in its cold fit, they fill'd their boat,
With nothing but the sky for a great coat.

LXIV.

'T is very certain the desire of life
 Prolongs it: this is obvious to physicians,
When patients, neither plagued with friends nor wife,
 Survive through very desperate conditions,
Because they still can hope, nor shines the knife
 Nor shears of Atropos before their visions:
Despair of all recovery spoils longevity,
And makes men's miseries of alarming brevity.

LXV.

'T is said that persons living on annuities
 Are longer lived than others,—God knows why,
Unless to plague the grantors,—yet so true it is,
 That some I really think, *do* never die:
Of any creditors the worst a Jew it is,
 And *that*'s their mode of furnishing supply:
In my young days they lent me cash that way,
Which I found very troublesome to pay.

LXVI.

'T is thus with people in an open boat,
 They live upon the love of life, and bear
More than can be believed, or even thought,
 And stand like rocks the tempest's wear and tear;
And hardship still has been the sailor's lot,
 Since Noah's ark went cruising here and there;
She had a curious crew as well as cargo,
Like the first old Greek privateer, the Argo.

LXVII.

But man is a carnivorous production,
 And must have meals, at least one meal a day;
He cannot live, like woodcocks, upon suction,
 But, like the shark and tiger, must have prey;
Although his anatomical construction
 Bears vegetables, in a grumbling way,
Your labouring people think beyond all question,
Beef, veal, and mutton, better for digestion.

LXVIII.

And thus it was with this our hapless crew;
 For on the third day there came on a calm,
And though at first their strength it might renew,
 And, lying on their weariness like balm,
Lull'd them like turtles sleeping on the blue
 Of ocean, when they woke they felt a qualm,
And fell all ravenously on their provision,
Instead of hoarding it with due precision.

LXIX.

The consequence was easily foreseen—
 They ate up all they had, and drank their wine,
In spite of all remonstrances, and then
 On what, in fact, next day were they to dine?
They hoped the wind would rise, these foolish men!
 And carry them to shore; these hopes were fine,
But as they had but one oar, and that brittle,
It would have been more wise to save their victual.

LXX.

The fourth day came, but not a breath of air,
 And Ocean slumber'd like an unwean'd child:
The fifth day, and their boat lay floating there;
 The sea and sky were blue, and clear, and mild—
With their one oar (I wish they had had a pair)
 What could they do? and hunger's rage grew wild:
So Juan's spaniel, spite of his entreating,
Was kill'd, and portion'd out for present eating.

LXXI.

On the sixth day they fed upon his hide,
And Juan, who had still refused, because
The creature was his father's dog that died,
Now feeling all the vulture in his jaws,
With some remorse received (though first denied)
As a great favour one of the fore-paws,
Which he divided with Pedrillo, who
Devour'd it, longing for the other too.

LXXII.

The seventh day, and no wind—the burning sun
Blister'd and scorch'd, and, stagnant on the sea,
They lay like carcasses; and hope was none,
Save in the breeze that came not; savagely
They glared upon each other: all was done,
Water, and wine, and food,—and you might see
The longings of the cannibal arise
(Although they spoke not) in their wolfish eyes.

LXXIII.

At length one whisper'd his companion, who
Whisper'd another, and thus it went round,
And then into a hoarser murmur grew,
An ominous, and wild, and desperate sound;
And when his comrade's thought each sufferer knew,
'Twas but his own, suppress'd till now, he found:
And out they spoke of lots for flesh and blood,
And who should die to be his fellows' food.

LXXIV.

But ere they came to this, they that day shared
Some leathern caps, and what remain'd of shoes;
And then they look'd around them, and despair'd,
And none to be the sacrifice would choose;
At length the lots were torn up, and prepared,
But of materials that much shock the Muse—
Having no paper, for the want of better,
They took by force from Juan Julia's letter.

LXXV.

The lots were made, and mark'd, and mix'd, and handed,
In silent horror, and their distribution
Lull'd even the savage hunger which demanded,
Like the Promethean vulture, this pollution;
None in particular had sought or plann'd it,
'Twas nature gnaw'd them to this resolution,
By which none were permitted to be neuter—
And the lot fell on Juan's luckless tutor.

LXXVI.

He but requested to be bled to death:
The surgeon had his instruments, and bled
Pedrillo, and so gently ebb'd his breath,
You hardly could perceive when he was dead.
He died as born, a Catholic in faith,
Like most in the belief in which they're bred,
And first a little crucifix he kiss'd,
And then held out his jugular and wrist.

LXXVII.

The surgeon, as there was no other fee,
Had his first choice of morsels for his pains;
But being thirstiest at the moment, he
Preferr'd a draught from the fast-flowing veins:
Part was divided, part thrown in the sea,
And such things as the entrails and the brains
Regaled two sharks, who follow'd o'er the billow—
The sailors ate the rest of poor Pedrillo.

LXXVIII.

The sailors ate him, all save three or four,
Who were not quite so fond of animal food;
To these was added Juan, who, before
Refusing his own spaniel, hardly could
Feel now his appetite increased much more:
'Twas not to be expected that he should,
Even in extremity of their disaster,
Dine with them on his pastor and his master.

LXXIX.

'Twas better that he did not; for, in fact,
The consequence was awful in the extreme;
For they, who were most ravenous in the act,
Went raging mad—Lord! how they did blaspheme!
And foam and roll, with strange convulsions rack'd,
Drinking salt-water like a mountain stream,
Tearing, and grinning, howling, screeching, swearing
And, with hyæna-laughter, died despairing.

LXXX.

Their numbers were much thinn'd by this infliction,
And all the rest were thin enough, Heaven knows;
And some of them had lost their recollection,
Happier than they who still perceived their woes;
But others ponder'd on a new dissection,
As if not warn'd sufficiently by those
Who had already perish'd, suffering madly,
For having used their appetites so sadly.

LXXXI.

And next they thought upon the master's mate,
As fattest; but he saved himself, because
Besides being much averse from such a fate,
There were some other reasons: the first was,
He had been rather indisposed of late;
And that which chiefly proved his saving clause,
Was a small present made to him at Cadiz,
By general subscription of the ladies.

LXXXII.

Of poor Pedrillo something still remain'd,
 But was used sparingly,—some were afraid,
And others still their appetites constrain'd,
 Or but at times a little supper made;
All except Juan, who throughout abstain'd,
 Chewing a piece of bamboo, and some lead:
At length they caught two boobies, and a noddy,
And then they left off eating the dead body.

LXXXIII.

And if Pedrillo's fate should shocking be,
 Remember Ugolino condescends
To eat the head of his arch-enemy
 The moment after he politely ends
His tale: if foes be food in hell, at sea
 'T is surely fair to dine upon our friends,
When shipwreck's short allowance grows too scanty,
Without being much more horrible than Dante.

LXXXIV.

And the same night there fell a shower of rain,
 For which their mouths gaped, like the cracks of earth
When dried to summer dust; till taught by pain,
 Men really know not what good water 's worth;
If you had been in Turkey or in Spain,
 Or with a famish'd boat's-crew had your berth,
Or in the desert heard the camel's bell,
You 'd wish yourself where Truth is—in a well.

LXXXV.

It pour'd down torrents, but they were no richer
 Until they found a ragged piece of sheet,
Which served them as a sort of spongy pitcher,
 And when they deem'd its moisture was complete,
They wrung it out; and though a thirsty ditcher
 Might not have thought the scanty draught so sweet
As a full pot of porter, to their thinking
They ne'er till now had known the joys of drinking.

LXXXVI.

And their baked lips, with many a bloody crack,
 Suck'd in the moisture, which like nectar stream'd;
Their throats were ovens, their swoln tongues were black,
 As the rich man's in hell, who vainly scream'd
To beg the beggar, who could not rain back
 A drop of dew, when every drop had seem'd
To taste of heaven—If this be true, indeed,
Some Christians have a comfortable creed.

LXXXVII.

There were two fathers in this ghastly crew,
 And with them their two sons, of whom the one
Was more robust and hardy to the view,
 But he died early; and when he was gone,
His nearest messmate told his sire, who threw
 One glance at him, and said, "Heaven's will be done!
I can do nothing," and he saw him thrown
Into the deep without a tear or groan.

LXXXVIII.

The other father had a weaklier child,
 Of a soft cheek, and aspect delicate;
But the boy bore up long, and with a mild
 And patient spirit held aloof his fate;
Little he said, and now and then he smiled,
 As if to win a part from off the weight
He saw increasing on his father's heart,
With the deep deadly thought, that they must part.

LXXXIX.

And o'er him bent his sire, and never raised
 His eyes from off his face, but wiped the foam
From his pale lips, and ever on him gazed,
 And when the wish'd-for shower at length was come,
And the boy's eyes, which the dull film half glazed,
 Brighten'd, and for a moment seem'd to roam,
He squeezed from out a rag some drops of rain
Into his dying child's mouth—but in vain.

XC.

The boy expired—the father held the clay,
 And look'd upon it long, and when at last
Death left no doubt, and the dead burthen lay
 Stiff on his heart, and pulse and hope were past,
He watch'd it wistfully, until away
 'T was borne by the rude wave wherein 't was cast;
Then he himself sunk down all dumb and shivering,
And gave no sign of life, save his limbs quivering.

XCI.

Now overhead a rainbow, bursting through
 The scattering clouds, shone, spanning the dark sea,
Resting its bright base on the quivering blue;
 And all within its arch appear'd to be
Clearer than that without, and its wide hue
 Wax'd broad and waving, like a banner free,
Then changed like to a bow that 's bent, and then
Forsook the dim eyes of these shipwreck'd men.

XCII.

It changed, of course; a heavenly cameleon,
 The airy child of vapour and the sun,
Brought forth in purple, cradled in vermilion,
 Baptized in molten gold, and swathed in dun,
Glittering like crescents o'er a Turk's pavilion,
 And blending every colour into one,
Just like a black eye in a recent scuffle,
(For sometimes we must box without the muffle).

XCIII.

Our shipwreck'd seamen thought it a good omen—
 It is as well to think so, now and then;
'T was an old custom of the Greek and Roman,
 And may become of great advantage when
Folks are discouraged; and most surely no men
 Had greater need to nerve themselves again
Than these, and so this rainbow look'd like hope—
Quite a celestial kaleidoscope.

XCIV.

About this time a beautiful white bird,
Webfooted, not unlike a dove in size
And plumage (probably it might have err'd
Upon its course), pass'd oft before their eyes,
And tried to perch, although it saw and heard
The men within the boat, and in this guise
It came and went, and flutter'd round them till
Night fell:—this seem'd a better omen still.

XCV.

But in this case I also must remark,
'T was well this bird of promise did not perch,
Because the tackle of our shattered bark
Was not so safe for roosting as a church;
And had it been the dove from Noah's ark,
Returning there from her successful search,
Which in their way that moment chanced to fall,
They would have eat her, olive-branch and all.

XCVI.

With twilight it again came on to blow,
But not with violence; the stars shone out,
The boat made way; yet now they were so low,
They knew not where, nor what, they were about;
Some fancied they saw land, and some said "No!"
The frequent fog-banks gave them cause to doubt—
Some swore that they heard breakers, others guns,
And all mistook about the latter once.

XCVII.

As morning broke, the light wind died away,
When he who had the watch sung out and swore,
If 't was not land that rose with the sun's ray,
He wish'd that land he never might see more:
And the rest rubb'd their eyes and saw a bay,
Or thought they saw, and shaped their course for shore;
For shore it was, and gradually grew
Distinct, and high, and palpable to view.

XCVIII.

And then of these some part burst into tears,
And others, looking with a stupid stare,
Could not yet separate their hopes from fears,
And seem'd as if they had no further care;
While a few pray'd—(the first time for some years)—
And at the bottom of the boat three were
Asleep: they shook them by the hand and head,
And tried to awaken them, but found them dead.

XCIX.

The day before, fast sleeping on the water,
They found a turtle of the hawk's-bill kind,
And by good fortune, gliding softly, caught her,
Which yielded a day's life, and to their mind
Proved even still a more nutritious matter,
Because it left encouragement behind:
They thought that in such perils, more than chance
Had sent them this for their deliverance.

C.

The land appear'd a high and rocky coast,
And higher grew the mountains as they drew,
Set by a current, toward it: they were lost
In various conjectures, for none knew
To what part of the earth they had been tost,
So changeable had been the winds that blew;
Some thought it was Mount Ætna, some the highlands
Of Candia, Cyprus, Rhodes, or other islands.

CI.

Meantime the current, with a rising gale,
Still set them onwards to the welcome shore,
Like Charon's bark of spectres, dull and pale:
Their living freight was now reduced to four,
And three dead, whom their strength could not avail
To heave into the deep with those before,
Though the two sharks still follow'd them, and dash'd
The spray into their faces as they splash'd.

CII.

Famine, despair, cold, thirst, and heat, had done
Their work on them by turns, and thinn'd them to
Such things a mother had not known her son
Amidst the skeletons of that gaunt crew;
By night chill'd, by day scorch'd, thus one by one
They perish'd, until wither'd to these few,
But chiefly by a species of self-slaughter,
In washing down Pedrillo with salt water.

CIII.

As they drew nigh the land, which now was seen
Unequal in its aspect here and there,
They felt the freshness of its growing green,
That waved in forest tops, and smooth'd the air,
And fell upon their glazed eyes like a screen
From glistening waves, and skies so hot and bare—
Lovely seem'd any object that should sweep
Away the vast, salt, dread, eternal deep.

CIV.

The shore look'd wild, without a trace of man
And girt by formidable waves; but they

Were mad for land, and thus their course they ran,
 Though right ahead the roaring breakers lay:
A reef between them also now began
 To show its boiling surf and bounding spray,
But finding no place for their landing better,
They ran the boat ashore,—and overset her.

CV.

But in his native stream, the Guadalquivir,
 Juan to lave his youthful limbs was wont;
And having learnt to swim in that sweet river,
 Had often turn'd the art to some account:
A better swimmer you could scarce see ever,
 He could, perhaps, have pass'd the Hellespont,
As once (a feat on which ourselves we prided)
Leander, Mr. Ekenhead, and I did.

CVI.

So here, though faint, emaciated, and stark,
 He buoy'd his boyish limbs, and strove to ply
With the quick wave, and gain, ere it was dark,
 The beach which lay before him, high and dry:
The greatest danger here was from a shark,
 That carried off his neighbour by the thigh;
As for the other two, they could not swim,
So nobody arrived on shore but him.

CVII.

Nor yet had he arrived but for the oar,
 Which, providentially for him, was wash'd
Just as his feeble arms could strike no more,
 And the hard wave o'erwhelmed him as 't was dash'd
Within his grasp: he clung to it, and sore
 The waters beat while he thereto was lash'd;
At last, with swimming, wading, scrambling, he
Roll'd on the beach, half-senseless, from the sea:

CVIII.

There, breathless, with his digging nails he clung
 Fast to the sand, lest the returning wave,
From whose reluctant roar his life he wrung,
 Should suck him back to her insatiate grave:
And there he lay, full length, where he was flung,
 Before the entrance of a cliff-worn cave,
With just enough of life to feel its pain,
And deem that it was saved, perhaps, in vain.

CIX.

With slow and staggering effort he arose,
 But sunk again upon his bleeding knee
And quivering hand; and then he look'd for those
 Who long had been his mates upon the sea;
But none of them appear'd to share his woes,
 Save one, a corpse, from out the famish'd three,
Who died two days before, and now had found
An unknown barren beach for burial ground.

CX.

And as he gazed, his dizzy brain spun fast,
 And down he sunk; and as he sunk, the sand
Swam round and round, and all his senses pass'd:
 He fell upon his side, and his stretch'd hand
Droop'd dripping on the oar (their jury-mast),
 And, like a wither'd lily, on the land
His slender frame and pallid aspect lay
As fair a thing as e'er was form'd of clay.

CXI.

How long in his damp trance young Juan lay
 He knew not, for the earth was gone for him,
And Time had nothing more of night nor day
 For his congealing blood, and senses dim;
And how this heavy faintness pass'd away
 He knew not, till each painful pulse and limb,
And tingling vein, seem'd throbbing back to life,
For Death, though vanquish'd, still retir'd with strife.

CXII.

His eyes he open'd, shut, again unclosed,
 For all was doubt and dizziness; he thought
He still was in the boat, and had but dozed,
 And felt again with his despair o'erwrought,
And wish'd it death in which he had reposed,
 And then once more his feelings back were brought,
And slowly by his swimming eyes was seen
A lovely female face of seventeen.

CXIII.

'T was bending close o'er his, and the small mouth
 Seem'd almost prying into his for breath;
And chaffing him, the soft warm hand of youth
 Recall'd his answering spirits back from death;
And, bathing his chill temples, tried to soothe
 Each pulse to animation, till beneath
Its gentle touch and trembling care, a sigh
To these kind efforts made a low reply.

CXIV.

Then was the cordial pour'd, and mantle flung
 Around his scarce-clad limbs; and the fair arm
Rais'd higher the faint head which o'er it hung;
 And her transparent cheek, all pure and warm,
Pillow'd his death-like forehead; then she wrung
 His dewy curls, long drench'd by every storm;
And watch'd with eagerness each throb that drew
A sigh from his heaved bosom—and hers, too.

CXV.

And lifting him with care into the cave,
 The gentle girl, and her attendant,—one

Young, yet her elder, and of brow less grave,
 And more robust of figure,—then begun
To kindle fire, and as the new flames gave

 Light to the rocks that roof'd them, which the sun
Had never seen, the maid, or whatsoe'er
She was, appear'd distinct, and tall, and fair.

CXVI.

Her brow was overhung with coins of gold,
That sparkled o'er the auburn of her hair,
Her clustering hair, whose longer locks were roll'd
In braids behind; and though her stature were
Even of the highest for a female mould,
They nearly reach'd her heel; and in her air
There was a something which bespoke command,
As one who was a lady in the land.

CXVII.

Her hair, I said, was auburn; but her eyes
Were black as death, their lashes the same hue,
Of downcast length, in whose silk shadow lies
Deepest attraction; for when to the view
Forth from its raven fringe the full glance flies,
Ne'er with such force the swiftest arrow flew;
'T is as the snake late coil'd, who pours his length,
And hurls at once his venom and his strength.

CXVIII.

Her brow was white and low, her cheek's pure dye
Like twilight rosy still with the set sun;
Short upper lip—sweet lips! that make us sigh
Ever to have seen such; for she was one
Fit for the model of a statuary,
(A race of mere impostors, when all 's done—
I 've seen much finer women, ripe and real,
Than all the nonsense of their stone ideal).

CXIX.

I'll tell you why I say so, for 't is just
One should not rail without a decent cause:
There was an Irish lady, to whose bust
I ne'er saw justice done, and yet she was
A frequent model: and if e'er she must
Yield to stern Time and Nature's wrinkling laws,
They will destroy a face which mortal thought
Ne'er compass'd, nor less mortal chisel wrought.

CXX.

And such was she, the lady of the cave:
Her dress was very different from the Spanish,
Simpler, and yet of colours not so grave;
For, as you know, the Spanish women banish
Bright hues when out of doors, and yet, while wave
Around them (what I hope will never vanish)
The basquina and the mantilla, they
Seem at the same time mystical and gay.

CXXI.

But with our damsel this was not the case:
Her dress was many-coloured, finely spun;
Her locks curl'd negligently round her face,
But through them gold and gems profusely shone:
Her girdle sparkled, and the richest lace
Flow'd in her veil, and many a precious stone
Flash'd on her little hand; but, what was shocking,
Her small snow feet had slippers, but no stocking.

CXXII.

The other female's dress was not unlike,
But of inferior materials; she
Had not so many ornaments to strike,
Her hair had silver only, bound to be
Her dowry; and her veil, in form alike,
Was coarser; and her air, though firm, less free;
Her hair was thicker, but less long; her eyes
As black, but quicker, and of smaller size.

CXXIII.

And these two tended him, and cheer'd him both
With food and raiment, and those soft attentions
Which are—(as I must own)—of female growth,
And have ten thousand delicate inventions:
They made a most superior mess of broth,
A thing which poesy but seldom mentions,
But the best dish that e'er was cooked since Homer's
Achilles order'd dinner for new comers.

CXXIV.

I 'll tell you who they were, this female pair,
Lest they should seem princesses in disguise;
Besides, I hate all mystery, and that air
Of clap-trap, which your recent poets prize;
And so, in short, the girls they really were
They shall appear before your curious eyes,
Mistress and maid; the first was only daughter
Of an old man, who lived upon the water.

CXXV.

A fisherman he had been in his youth,
And still a sort of fisherman was he;
But other speculations were, in sooth,
Added to his connection with the sea,
Perhaps not so respectable, in truth:
A little smuggling, and some piracy,
Left him, at last, the sole of many masters
Of an ill-gotten million of piastres.

CXXVI.

A fisher, therefore, was he,—though of men,
Like Peter the Apostle,—and he fish'd
For wandering merchant-vessels, now and then,
And sometimes caught as many as he wish'd;
The cargoes he confiscated, and gain
He sought in the slave-market, too, and dish'd
Full many a morsel for that Turkish trade,
By which, no doubt, a good deal may be made.

CXXVII.

He was a Greek, and on his isle had built
(One of the wild and smaller Cyclades)
A very handsome house from out his guilt,
And there he lived exceedingly at ease;
Heaven knows what cash he got or blood he spilt,
A sad old fellow was he, if you please;
But this I know, it was a spacious building,
Full of barbaric carving, paint, and gilding.

CXXVIII.

He had an only daughter, call'd Haidée,
The greatest heiress of the Eastern Isles;
Besides, so very beautiful was she,
Her dowry was as nothing to her smiles:
Still in her teens, and like a lovely tree,
She grew to womanhood, and between whiles
Rejected several suitors, just to learn
How to accept a better in his turn.

CXXIX.

And walking out upon the beach, below
The cliff, towards sunset, on that day she found,
Insensible,—not dead, but nearly so,—
Don Juan, almost famish'd, and half drown'd;
But being naked, she was shock'd, you know,
Yet deem'd herself in common pity bound,
As far as in her lay, "to take him in,
A stranger" dying, with so white a skin.

CXXX.

But taking him into her father's house
Was not exactly the best way to save,
But like conveying to the cat the mouse,
Or people in a trance into their grave;
Because the good old man had so much "νους,"
Unlike the honest Arab thieves so brave,
He would have hospitably cured the stranger,
And sold him instantly when out of danger.

CXXXI.

And therefore, with her maid, she thought it best
(A virgin always on her maid relies)
To place him in the cave for present rest:
And when, at last, he open'd his black eyes,
Their charity increased about their guest;
And their compassion grew to such a size,
It open'd half the turnpike-gates to heaven—
(St. Paul says, 't is the toll which must be given).

CXXXII.

They made a fire,—but such a fire as they
Upon the moment could contrive with such
Materials as were cast up round the bay,—
Some broken planks, and oars, that to the touch
Were nearly tinder, since so long they lay
A mast was almost crumbled to a crutch;
But, by God's grace, here wrecks were in such plenty,
That there was fuel to have furnish'd twenty.

CXXXIII.

He had a bed of furs, and a pelisse,
For Haidée stripp'd her sables off to make
His couch; and, that he might be more at ease,
And warm, in case by chance he should awake,
They also gave a petticoat apiece,
She and her maid,—and promised by daybreak
To pay him a fresh visit, with a dish
For breakfast, of eggs, coffee, bread, and fish.

CXXXIV.

And thus they left him to his lone repose:
Juan slept like a top, or like the dead,
Who sleep at last, perhaps (God only knows),
Just for the present; and in his lull'd head
Not even a vision of his former woes
Throbb'd in accursèd dreams, which sometimes spread
Unwelcome visions of our former years,
'Till the eye, cheated, opens thick with tears.

CXXXV.

Young Juan slept all dreamless:—but the maid,
Who smooth'd his pillow, as she left the den
Look'd back upon him, and a moment stay'd,
And turn'd, believing that he call'd again.
He slumber'd; yet she thought, at least she said
(The heart will slip, even as the tongue and pen),
He had pronounced her name—but she forgot
That at this moment Juan knew it not.

CXXXVI.

And pensive to her father's house she went,
Enjoining silence strict to Zoe, who
Better than her knew what, in fact, she meant,
She being wiser by a year or two:
A year or two 's an age when rightly spent,
And Zoe spent hers, as most women do,
In gaining all that useful sort of knowledge,
Which is acquired in Nature's good old college.

CXXXVII.

The morn broke, and found Juan slumbering still
Fast in his cave, and nothing clash'd upon
His rest; the rushing of the neighbouring rill,
And the young beams of the excluded sun,
Troubled him not, and he might sleep his fill;
And need he had of slumber yet, for none
Had suffer'd more—his hardships were comparative
To those related in my grand-dad's "Narrative."

CXXXVIII.

Not so Haidée: she sadly toss'd and tumbled,
And started from her sleep, and, turning o'er,

Dream'd of a thousand wrecks, o'er which she stumbled,
And handsome corpses strew'd upon the shore;
And woke her maid so early that she grumbled,
And call'd her father's old slaves up, who swore
In several oaths—Armenian, Turk, and Greek—
They knew not what to think of such a freak.

CXXXIX.

But up she got, and up she made them get,
With some pretence about the sun, that makes
Sweet skies just when he rises, or is set;
And 't is, no doubt, a sight to see when breaks
Bright Phœbus, while the mountains still are wet
With mist, and every bird with him awakes,
And night is flung off like a mourning suit
Worn for a husband,—or some other brute.

CXL.

I say, the sun is a most glorious sight;
I've seen him rise full oft,—indeed of late
I have sat up on purpose all the night,
Which hastens, as physicians say, one's fate;
And so all ye, who would be in the right
In health and purse, begin your day to date
From daybreak, and when coffin'd at fourscore,
Engrave upon the plate, you rose at four.

CXLI.

And Haidée met the morning face to face;
Her own was freshest, though a feverish flush
Had dyed it with the headlong blood, whose race
From heart to cheek is curb'd into a blush,
Like to a torrent which a mountain's base,
That overpowers some Alpine river's rush,
Checks to a lake, whose waves in circles spread;
Or the Red Sea—but the sea is not red.

CXLII.

And down the cliff the island virgin came,
And near the cave her quick light footsteps drew,
While the sun smiled on her with his first flame,
And young Aurora kiss'd her lips with dew,
Taking her for a sister; just the same
Mistake you would have made on seeing the two,
Although the mortal, quite as fresh and fair,
Had all the advantage, too, of not being air.

CXLIII.

And when into the cavern Haidée stepp'd
All timidly, yet rapidly, she saw
That like an infant Juan sweetly slept;
And then she stopp'd, and stood as if in awe
(For sleep is awful), and on tiptoe crept
And wrapt him closer, lest the air, too raw,
Should reach his blood, then o'er him still as death
Bent, with hush'd lips, that drank his scarce-drawn breath.

CXLIV.

And thus like to an angel o'er the dying
Who die in righteousness, she lean'd; and there
All tranquilly the shipwreck'd boy was lying,
As o'er him lay the calm and stirless air:
But Zoe the meantime some eggs was frying,
Since, after all, no doubt the youthful pair
Must breakfast, and betimes—lest they should ask it—
She drew out her provision from the basket.

CXLV.

She knew that the best feelings must have victual,
And that a shipwreck'd youth would hungry be;
Besides, being less in love, she yawn'd a little,
And felt her veins chill'd by the neighbouring sea;
And so, she cook'd their breakfast to a tittle;
I can't say that she gave them any tea,
But there were eggs, fruit, coffee, bread, fish, honey,
With Scio wine,—and all for love, not money.

CXLVI.

And Zoe, when the eggs were ready, and
The coffee made, would fain have waken'd Juan;
But Haidée stopp'd her with her quick small hand,
And without word, a sign her finger drew on
Her lip, which Zoe needs must understand;
And, the first breakfast spoilt, prepared a new one,
Because her mistress would not let her break
That sleep which seem'd as it would ne'er awake.

CXLVII.

For still he lay, and on his thin worn cheek
A purple hectic play'd like dying day
On the snow-tops of distant hills; the streak
Of sufferance yet upon his forehead lay,
Where the blue veins look'd shadowy, shrunk, and weak;
And his black curls were dewy with the spray,
Which weigh'd upon them yet, all damp and salt,
Mix'd with the stony vapours of the vault.

CXLVIII.

And she bent o'er him, and he lay beneath,
Hush'd as the babe upon its mother's breast,
Droop'd as the willow when no winds can breathe,
Lull'd like the depth of ocean when at rest,
Fair as the crowning rose of the whole wreath,
Soft as the callow cygnet in its nest;
In short, he was a very pretty fellow,
Although his woes had turn'd him rather yellow.

CXLIX.

He woke and gazed, and would have slept again,
 But the fair face which met his eyes forbade
Those eyes to close, though weariness and pain
 Had further sleep a further pleasure made;
For woman's face was never form'd in vain
 For Juan, so that even when he pray'd
He turn'd from grisly saints, and martyrs hairy,
To the sweet portraits of the Virgin Mary.

CL.

And thus upon his elbow he arose,
 And look'd upon the lady, in whose cheek
The pale contended with the purple rose,
 As with an effort she began to speak;
Her eyes were eloquent, her words would pose,
 Although she told him, in good modern Greek,
With an Ionian accent, low and sweet,
That he was faint, and must not talk, but eat.

CLI.

Now Juan could not understand a word,
 Being no Grecian; but he had an ear,
And her voice was the warble of a bird,
 So soft, so sweet, so delicately clear,
That finer, simpler music ne'er was heard;
 The sort of sound we echo with a tear,
Without knowing why—an overpowering tone,
Whence Melody descends as from a throne.

CLII.

And Juan gazed as one who is awoke
 By a distant organ, doubting if he be
Not yet a dreamer, till the spell is broke
 By the watchman, or some such reality,
Or by one's early valet's cursèd knock;
 At least it is a heavy sound to me,
Who like a morning slumber—for the night
Shows stars and women in a better light.

CLIII.

And Juan, too, was help'd out from his dream,
 Or sleep, or whatso'er it was, by feeling
A most prodigious appetite: the steam
 Of Zoe's cookery no doubt was stealing
Upon his senses, and the kindling beam
 Of the new fire, which Zoe kept up, kneeling
To stir her viands, made him quite awake,
And long for food, but chiefly a beef-steak.

CLIV.

But beef is rare within these oxless isles;
 Goat's flesh there is, no doubt, and kid, and mutton;
And, when a holiday upon them smiles,
 A joint upon their barbarous spits they put on:
But this occurs but seldom, between whiles,
 For some of these are rocks with scarce a hut on,
Others are fair and fertile, among which
This, though not large, was one of the most rich

CLV.

I say that beef is rare, and can't help thinking
 That the old fable of the Minotaur—
From which our modern morals, rightly shrinking
 Condemn the royal lady's taste who wore
A cow's shape for a mask—was only (sinking
 The allegory) a mere type, no more,
That Pasiphae promoted breeding cattle,
To make the Cretans bloodier in battle.

CLVI.

For we all know that English people are
 Fed upon beef—I won't say much of beer,
Because 't is liquor only, and being far
 From this my subject, has no business here;
We know, too, they are very fond of war,
 A pleasure—like all pleasures—rather dear;
So were the Cretans—from which I infer,
That beef and battles both were owing to her.

CLVII.

But to resume. The languid Juan raised
 His head upon his elbow, and he saw
A sight on which he had not lately gazed,
 As all his latter meals had been quite raw,
Three or four things, for which the Lord he praised,
 And, feeling still the famish'd vulture gnaw,
He fell upon whate'er was offer'd, like
A priest, a shark, an alderman, or pike.

CLVIII.

He ate, and he was well supplied: and she,
 Who watch'd him like a mother, would have fed
Him past all bounds, because she smiled to see
 Such appetite in one she had deem'd dead:
But Zoe, being older than Haidée,
 Knew (by tradition, for she ne'er had read)
That famish'd people must be slowly nurst,
And fed by spoonfuls, else they always burst.

CLIX.

And so she took the liberty to state—
 Rather by deeds than words, because the case
Was urgent—that the gentleman, whose fate
 Had made her mistress quit her bed to trace
The sea-shore at this hour, must leave his plate,
 Unless he wish'd to die upon the place—
She snatch'd it, and refused another morsel,
Saying, he had gorged enough to make a horse ill.

CLX.

Next they—he being naked, save a tatter'd
Pair of scarce decent trousers—went to work,
And in the fire his recent rags they scatter'd,
And dress'd him, for the present, like a Turk,
Or Greek—that is, although it not much matter'd,
Omitting turban, slippers, pistols, dirk,—
They furnish'd him, entire, except some stitches,
With a clean shirt, and very spacious breeches.

CLXI.

And then fair Haidée tried her tongue at speaking,
But not a word could Juan comprehend,
Although he listen'd so that the young Greek in
Her earnestness would ne'er have made an end;
And, as he interrupted not, went eking
Her speech out to her protégé and friend,
Till pausing at the last her breath to take,
She saw he did not understand Romaic.

CLXII.

And then she had recourse to nods, and signs,
And smiles, and sparkles of the speaking eye,
And read (the only book she could) the lines
Of his fair face, and found, by sympathy,
The answer eloquent, where the soul shines
And darts in one quick glance a long reply;
And thus in every look she saw exprest
A world of words, and things at which she guess'd.

CLXIII.

And now, by dint of fingers and of eyes,
And words repeated after her, he took
A lesson in her tongue; but by surmise
No doubt, less of her language than her look;
As he who studies fervently the skies
Turns oftener to the stars than to his book:
Thus Juan learn'd his alpha beta better
From Haidée's glance than any graven letter.

CLXIV.

'T is pleasing to be school'd in a strange tongue
By female lips and eyes—that is, I mean,
When both the teacher and the taught are young,
As was the case, at least, where I have been;
They smile so when one 's right, and when one 's wrong
They smile still more, and then there intervene
Pressure of hands, perhaps even a chaste kiss;—
I learn'd the little that I know by this:

CLXV.

That is, some words of Spanish, Turk, and Greek,
Italian not at all, having no teachers;
Much English I cannot pretend to speak,
Learning that language chiefly from its preachers,
Barrow, South, Tillotson, whom every week
I study, also Blair, the highest reachers
Of eloquence in piety and prose—
I hate your poets, so read none of those.

CLXVI.

As for the ladies, I have nought to say,
A wanderer from the British world of fashion,
Where I, like other "dogs, have had my day,"
Like other men, too, may have had my passion—
But that, like other things, has pass'd away,
And all her fools whom I *could* lay the lash on:
Foes, friends, men, women, now are nought to me,
But dreams of what has been, no more to be.

CLXVII.

Return we to Don Juan. He begun
To hear new words, and to repeat them; but
Some feelings, universal as the sun,
Were such as could not in his breast be shut,
More than within the bosom of a nun:
He was in love,—as you would be, no doubt,
With a young benefactress,—so was she,
Just in the way we very often see.

CLXVIII.

And every day by daybreak—rather early
For Juan, who was somewhat fond of rest—
She came into the cave, but it was merely
To see her bird reposing in his nest;
And she would softly stir his locks so curly,
Without disturbing her yet slumbering guest,
Breathing all gently o'er his cheek and mouth,
As o'er a bed of roses the sweet south.

CLXIX.

And every morn his colour freshlier came,
And every day help'd on his convalescence;
'T was well, because health in the human frame
Is pleasant, besides being true love's essence,
For health and idleness to passion's flame
Are oil and gunpowder; and some good lessons
Are also learnt from Ceres and from Bacchus,
Without whom Venus will not long attack us.

CLXX.

While Venus fills the heart (without heart really
Love, though good always, is not quite so good,)
Ceres presents a plate of vermicelli,—
For love must be sustain'd like flesh and blood,—
While Bacchus pours out wine, or hands a jelly:
Eggs, oysters, too, are amatory food;
But who is their purveyor from above
Heaven knows,—it may be Neptune, Pan, or Jove.

CLXXI.

When Juan woke he found some good things ready,
 A bath, a breakfast, and the finest eyes
That ever made a youthful heart less steady,
 Besides her maid's, as pretty for their size;
But I have spoken of all this already—
 And repetition 's tiresome and unwise,—
Well—Juan, after bathing in the sea,
Came always back to coffee and Haidée.

CLXXII.

Both were so young, and one so innocent,
 That bathing pass'd for nothing; Juan seem'd
To her, as 't were, the kind of being sent,
 Of whom these two years she had nightly dream'd,
A something to be loved, a creature meant
 To be her happiness, and whom she deem'd
To render happy; all who joy would win
Must share it,—Happiness was born a twin.

CLXXIII.

It was such pleasure to behold him, such
 Enlargement of existence to partake
Nature with him, to thrill beneath his touch,
 To watch him slumbering, and to see him wake:
To live with him for ever were too much;
 But then the thought of parting made her quake:
He was her own, her ocean-treasure, cast
Like a rich wreck—her first love, and her last.

CLXXIV.

And thus a moon roll'd on, and fair Haidée
 Paid daily visits to her boy, and took
Such plentiful precautions, that still he
 Remained unknown within his craggy nook;
At last her father's prows put out to sea,
 For certain merchantmen upon the look,
Not as of yore to carry off an Io,
But three Ragusan vessels, bound for Scio.

CLXXV.

Then came her freedom, for she had no mother,
 So that, her father being at sea, she was
Free as a married woman, or such other
 Female, as where she likes may freely pass,
Without even the incumbrance of a brother,
 The freest she that ever gazed on glass;
I speak of Christian lands in this comparison,
Where wives, at least, are seldom kept in garrison.

CLXXVI.

Now she prolong'd her visits and her talk
 (For they must talk), and he had learnt to say
So much as to propose to take a walk,—
 For little had he wander'd since the day
On which, like a young flower snapp'd from the stalk,
 Drooping and dewy on the beach he lay,—
And thus they walk'd out in the afternoon,
And saw the sun set opposite the moon.

CLXXVII.

It was a wild and breaker-beaten coast,
 With cliffs above, and a broad-sandy shore,
Guarded by shoals and rocks as by an host,
 With here and there a creek, whose aspect wore
A better welcome to the tempest-tost;
 And rarely ceased the haughty billow's roar,
Save on the dead long summer days, which make
The outstretch'd ocean glitter like a lake.

CLXXVIII.

And the small ripple spilt upon the beach
 Scarcely o'erpass'd the cream of your champagne,
When o'er the brim the sparkling bumpers reach,
 That spring-dew of the spirit! the heart's rain!
Few things surpass old wine; and they may preach
 Who please,—the more because they preach in vain,—
Let us have wine and women, mirth and laughter,
Sermons and soda-water the day after.

CLXXIX.

Man, being reasonable, must get drunk;
 The best of life is but intoxication:
Glory, the grape, love, gold, in these are sunk
 The hopes of all men, and of every nation;
Without their sap, how branchless were the trunk
 Of life's strange tree, so fruitful on occasion:
But to return,—Get very drunk; and when
You wake with headache, you shall see what then.

CLXXX.

Ring for your valet—bid him quickly bring
 Some hock and soda-water, then you 'll know
A pleasure worthy Xerxes the great king;
 For not the blest sherbet, sublimed with snow,
Nor the first sparkle of the desert-spring,
 Nor Burgundy in all its sunset glow,
After long travel, ennui, love, or slaughter,
Vie with that draught of hock and soda-water.

CLXXXI.

The coast—I think it was the coast that I
 Was just describing—Yes, it *was* the coast—
Lay at this period quiet as the sky,
 The sands untumbled, the blue waves untost,
And all was stillness, save the sea-bird's cry,
 And dolphin's leap, and little billow crost
By some low rock or shelve, that made it fret
Against the boundary it scarcely wet.

CLXXXII.

And forth they wander'd, her sire being gone,
 As I have said, upon an expedition;
And mother, brother, guardian, she had none,
 Save Zoe, who, although with due precision
She waited on her lady with the sun,
 Thought daily service was her only mission,
Bringing warm water, wreathing her long tresses,
And asking now and then for cast-off dresses.

CLXXXIII.

It was the cooling hour, just when the rounded
 Red sun sinks down behind the azure hill,
Which then seems as if the whole earth it bounded,
 Circling all nature, hush'd, and dim, and still,
With the far mountain-crescent half surrounded
 On one side, and the deep sea calm and chill
Upon the other, and the rosy sky
With one star sparkling through it like an eye.

CLXXXIV.

And thus they wander'd forth, and hand in hand,
 Over the shining pebbles and the shells,
Glided along the smooth and harden'd sand,
 And in the worn and wild receptacles
Work'd by the storms, yet work'd as it were plann'd,
 In hollow halls, with sparry roofs and cells,
They turn'd to rest; and, each clasp'd by an arm,
Yielded to the deep twilight's purple charm.

CLXXXV.

They look'd up to the sky, whose floating glow
 Spread like a rosy ocean, vast and bright;
They gazed upon the glittering sea below,
 Whence the broad moon rose circling into sight;
They heard the waves' splash, and the wind so low,
 And saw each other's dark eyes darting light
Into each other—and, beholding this,
Their lips drew near, and clung into a kiss;

CLXXXVI.

A long, long kiss, a kiss of youth, and love,
 And beauty, all concentrating like rays
Into one focus, kindled from above.
 Such kisses as belong to early days,
Where heart, and soul, and sense, in concert move,
 And the blood 's lava, and the pulse a blaze,
Each kiss a heart-quake,—for a kiss's strength,
I think, it must be reckon'd by its length.

CLXXXVII.

By length I mean duration; theirs endured
 Heaven knows how long—no doubt they never reckon'd;
And if they had, they could not have secured
 The sum of their sensations to a second:
They had not spoken; but they felt allured,
 As if their souls and lips each other beckon'd,
Which, being join'd, like swarming bees they clung—
Their hearts the flowers from whence the honey sprung.

CLXXXVIII.

They were alone, but not alone as they
 Who shut in chambers think it loneliness;
The silent ocean, and the starlight bay,
 The twilight glow, which momently grew less,
The voiceless sands, and dropping caves, that lay
 Around them, made them to each other press,
As if there were no life beneath the sky
Save theirs, and that their life could never die.

CLXXXIX.

They fear'd no eyes nor ears on that lone beach,
 They felt no terrors from the night, they were
All in all to each other: though their speech
 Was broken words, they *thought* a language there,—
And all the burning tongues the passions teach,
 Found in one sigh the best interpreter
Of nature's oracle—first love,—that all
Which Eve has left her daughters since her fall.

CXC.

Haidée spoke not of scruples, ask'd no vows,
 Nor offer'd any; she had never heard
Of plight and promises to be a spouse,
 Or perils by a loving maid incurr'd;
She was all which pure ignorance allows,
 And flew to her young mate like a young bird;
And, never having dreamt of falsehood, she
Had not one word to say of constancy.

CXCI.

She loved, and was belovèd—she adored,
 And she was worshipp'd; after nature's fashion,
Their intense souls, into each other pour'd,
 If souls could die, had perish'd in that passion,—
But by degrees their senses were restored,
 Again to be o'ercome, again to dash on;
And, beating 'gainst *his* bosom, Haidée's heart
Felt as if never more to beat apart.

CXCII.

Alas! they were so young, so beautiful,
 So lonely, loving, helpless, and the hour
Was that in which the heart is always full,
 And, having o'er itself no further power,
Prompts deeds eternity can not annul,
 But pays off moments in an endless shower
Of hell-fire—all prepared for people giving
Pleasure or pain to one another living.

CXCIII.

Alas! for Juan and Haidée! they were
 So loving and so lovely—till then never,
Excepting our first parents, such a pair
 Had run the risk of being damned for ever:
And Haidée, being devout as well as fair,
 Had, doubtless, heard about the Stygian river,
And hell and purgatory—but forgot
Just in the very crisis she should not.

CXCIV.

They look upon each other, and their eyes
 Gleam in the moonlight; and her white arm clasps
Round Juan's head, and his around her lies
 Half buried in the tresses which it grasps;
She sits upon his knee, and drinks his sighs,
 He hers, until they end in broken gasps;
And thus they form a group that 's quite antique,
Half naked, loving, natural, and Greek.

CXCV.

And when those deep and burning moments pass'd,
And Juan sunk to sleep within her arms,
She slept not, but all tenderly, though fast,
Sustain'd his head upon her bosom's charms;
And now and then her eye to heaven is cast,
And then on the pale cheek her breast now warms,
Pillow'd on her o'erflowing heart, which pants
With all it granted, and with all it grants.

CXCVI.

An infant when it gazes on a light,
A child the moment when it drains the breast,
A devotee when soars the Host in sight,
An Arab with a stranger for a guest,
A sailor when the prize has struck in fight,
A miser filling his most hoarded chest,
Feel rapture; but not such true joy are reaping
As they who watch o'er what they love while sleeping.

CXCVII.

For there it lies so tranquil, so beloved,
All that it hath of life with us is living;
So gentle, stirless, helpless, and unmoved,
And all unconscious of the joy 't is giving;
All it hath felt, inflicted, pass'd, and proved,
Hush'd into depths beyond the watcher's diving;
There lies the thing we love with all its errors
And all its charms, like death without its terrors.

CXCVIII.

The lady watch'd her lover—and that hour
Of Love's, and Night's, and Ocean's solitude,
O'erflow'd her soul with their united power;
Amidst the barren sand and rocks so rude
She and her wave-worn love had made their bower,
Where nought upon their passion could intrude,
And all the stars that crowded the blue space
Saw nothing happier than her glowing face.

CXCIX.

Alas! the love of women! it is known
To be a lovely and a fearful thing;
For all of theirs upon that die is thrown,
And if 't is lost, life hath no more to bring
To them but mockeries of the past alone,
And their revenge is as the tiger's spring,
Deadly, and quick, and crushing; yet, as real
Torture is theirs, what they inflict they feel.

CC.

They are right; for man, to man so oft unjust,
Is always so to women; one sole bond
Awaits them, treachery is all their trust;
aught to conceal, their bursting hearts despond
Over their idol, till some wealthier lust
Buys them in marriage—and what rests beyond?
A thankless husband, next a faithless lover,
Then dressing, nursing, praying, and all's over.

CCI.

Some take a lover, some take drams or prayers,
Some mind their household, others dissipation,
Some run away, and but exchange their cares,
Losing the advantage of a virtuous station;
Few changes e'er can better their affairs,
Theirs being an unnatural situation,
From the dull palace to the dirty hovel:
Some play the devil, and then write a novel.

CCII.

Haidée was Nature's bride, and knew not this;
Haidée was Passion's child, born where the sun
Showers triple light, and scorches even the kiss
Of his gazelle-eyed daughters; she was one
Made but to love, to feel that she was his
Who was her chosen; what was said or done
Elsewhere was nothing.—She had nought to fear,
Hope, care, nor love, beyond, her heart beat *here*.

CCIII.

And oh! that quickening of the heart, that beat!
How much it costs us! yet each rising throb
Is in its cause as its effect so sweet,
That Wisdom, ever on the watch to rob
Joy of its alchemy, and to repeat
Fine truths; even Conscience, too, has a tough job
To make us understand each good old maxim,
So good—I wonder Castlereagh don't tax 'em.

CCIV.

And now 't was done—on the lone shore were plighted
Their hearts; the stars, their nuptial torches, shed
Beauty upon the beautiful they lighted:
Ocean their witness, and the cave their bed,
By their own feelings hallow'd and united,
Their priest was Solitude, and they were wed:
And they were happy, for to their young eyes
Each was an angel, and earth paradise.

CCV.

Oh, Love! of whom great Cæsar was the suitor,
Titus the master, Antony the slave,
Horace, Catullus, scholars, Ovid tutor,
Sappho the sage blue-stocking, in whose grave
All those may leap who rather would be neuter—
(Leucadia's rock still overlooks the wave)—
Oh, Love! thou art the very god of evil,
For, after all, we cannot call thee devil.

CCVI.

Thou mak'st the chaste connubial state precarious,
 And jestest with the brows of mightiest men:
Cæsar and Pompey, Mahomet, Belisarius,
 Have much employ'd the muse of history's pen:
Their lives and fortunes were extremely various,
 Such worthies Time will never see again;
Yet to these four in three things the same luck holds,
They were all heroes, conquerors, and cuckolds.

CCVII.

Thou mak'st philosophers; there's Epicurus
 And Aristippus, a material crew!
Who to immoral courses would allure us
 By theories quite practicable too;
If only from the devil they would insure us,
 How pleasant were the maxim (not quite new),
"Eat, drink, and love, what can the rest avail us?"
So said the royal sage Sardanapalus.

CCVIII.

But Juan! had he quite forgotten Julia?
 And should he have forgotten her so soon?
I can't but say it seems to me most truly a
 Perplexing question; but, no doubt, the moon
Does these things for us, and whenever newly a
 Palpitation rises, 't is her boon,
Else how the devil is it that fresh features
Have such a charm for us poor human creatures?

CCIX.

I hate inconstancy—I loathe, detest,
 Abhor, condemn, abjure the mortal made
Of such quicksilver clay that in his breast
 No permanent foundation can be laid;
Love, constant love, has been my constant guest,
 And yet, last night, being at a masquerade,
I saw the prettiest creature, fresh from Milan,
Which gave me some sensations like a villain.

CCX.

But soon Philosophy came to my aid
 And whisper'd, "Think of every sacred tie!"
"I will, my dear Philosophy!" I said,
 "But then her teeth, and then, oh, Heaven! her eye!
I'll just inquire if she be wife or maid,
 Or neither—out of curiosity."
"Stop!" cried Philosophy, with air so Grecian,
(Though she was masqued then as a fair Venetian);

CCXI.

"Stop!" so I stopp'd.—But to return: that which
 Men call inconstancy is nothing more
Than admiration due where nature's rich
 Profusion with young beauty covers o'er
Some favour'd object; and as in the niche
 A lovely statue we almost adore,
This sort of adoration of the real
Is but a heightening of the "beau ideal."

CCXII.

'T is the perception of the beautiful,
 A fine extension of the faculties,
Platonic, universal, wonderful,
 Drawn from the stars, and filter'd through the skies,
Without which life would be extremely dull;
 In short, it is the use of our own eyes,
With one or two small senses added, just
To hint that flesh is form'd of fiery dust.

CCXIII.

Yet 't is a painful feeling, and unwilling,
 For surely if we always could perceive
In the same object graces quite as killing
 As when she rose upon us like an Eve,
'T would save us many a heartache, many a shilling,
 (For we must get them anyhow, or grieve,)
Whereas if one sole lady pleased for ever,
How pleasant for the heart, as well as liver

CCXIV.

The heart is like the sky, a part of heaven,
 But changes night and day, too, like the sky;
Now o'er it clouds and thunder must be driven,
 And darkness and destruction as on high:
But when it hath been scorch'd, and pierced, and riven,
 Its storms expire in water-drops; the eye
Pours forth at last the heart's blood turn'd to tears,
Which make the English climate of our years.

CCXV.

The liver is the lazaret of bile,
 But very rarely executes its function,
For the first passion stays there such a while,
 That all the rest creep in and form a junction,
Like knots of vipers on a dung-hill's soil,
 Rage, fear, hate, jealousy, revenge, compunction,
So that all mischiefs spring up from this entrail,
Like earthquakes from the hidden fire called "central."

CCXVI.

In the mean time, without proceeding more
 In this anatomy, I've finished now
Two hundred and odd stanzas as before,
 That being about the number I'll allow
Each canto of the twelve, or twenty-four;
 And, laying down my pen, I make my bow,
Leaving Don Juan and Haidée to plead
For them and theirs with all who deign to read.

I.

Hail, Muse! *et cetera.*—We left Juan sleeping,
Pillow'd upon a fair and happy breast,
And watch'd by eyes that never yet knew weeping,
And loved by a young heart, too deeply blest
To feel the poison through her spirit creeping,
Or know who rested there, a foe to rest,
Had soil'd the current of her sinless years,
And turn'd her pure heart's purest blood to tears!

II.

Oh, Love! what is it in this world of ours
Which makes it fatal to be loved? Ah why
With cypress branches hast thou wreathed thy bowers,
And made thy best interpreter a sigh?
As those who dote on odours pluck the flowers,
And place them on their breast—but place to die—
Thus the frail beings we would fondly cherish
Are laid within our bosoms but to perish.

III.

In her first passion woman loves her lover,
In all the others all she loves is love,
Which grows a habit she can ne'er get over,
And fits her loosely—like an easy glove,
As you may find, whene'er you like to prove her:
One man alone at first her heart can move;
She then prefers him in the plural number,
Not finding that the additions much encumber.

IV.

I know not if the fault be men's or theirs;
But one thing's pretty sure: a woman planted
(Unless at once she plunge for life in prayers)—
After a decent time must be gallanted;
Although, no doubt, her first of love affairs
Is that to which her heart is wholly granted;
Yet there are some, they say, who have had *none*,
But those who have ne'er end with only *one*.

V.

'Tis melancholy, and a fearful sign
Of human frailty, folly, also crime,
That love and marriage rarely can combine,
Although they both are born in the same clime;
Marriage from love, like vinegar from wine—
A sad, sour, sober beverage—by time
Is sharpen'd from its high celestial flavour
Down to a very homely household savour.

VI.

There's something of antipathy, as 't were,
Between their present and their future state;
A kind of flattery, that's hardly fair,
Is used until the truth arrives too late—
Yet what can people do, except despair?
The same things change their names at such a rate;
For instance—passion in a lover's glorious,
But in a husband is pronounced uxorious.

VII.

Men grow ashamed of being so very fond;
They sometimes also get a little tired
(But that, of course, is rare), and then despond:
The same things cannot always be admired;
Yet 't is "so nominated in the bond,"
That both are tied till one shall have expired.
Sad thought! to lose the spouse that was adorning
Our days, and put one's servants into mourning.

VIII.

There's doubtless something in domestic doings
Which forms, in fact, true love's antithesis;
Romances paint at full length people's wooings,
But only give a bust of marriages;
For no one cares for matrimonial cooings,
There's nothing wrong in a connubial kiss:
Think you, if Laura had been Petrarch's wife,
He would have written sonnets all his life?

IX.

All tragedies are finish'd by a death,
All comedies are ended by a marriage;
The future states of both are left to faith,
For authors fear description might disparage
The worlds to come of both, or fall beneath,
And then both worlds would punish their miscarriage;
So leaving each their priest and prayer-book ready,
They say no more of Death, or of the Lady.

X.

The only two that in my recollection
Have sung of heaven and hell, or marriage, are
Dante and Milton, and of both the affection[9]
Was hapless in their nuptials, for some bar
Of fault or temper ruin'd the connection
(Such things, in fact, it don't ask much to mar);
But Dante's Beatrice and Milton's Eve
Were not drawn from their spouses, you conceive.

XI.

Some persons say that Dante meant theology
By Beatrice, and not a mistress—I,
Although my opinion may require apology,
Deem this a commentator's phantasy,
Unless indeed it was from his own knowledge he
Decided thus, and show'd good reason why;
I think that Dante's more abstruse ecstatics
Meant to personify the mathematics

XII.

Haidée and Juan were not married, but
The fault was theirs, not mine: it is not fair,
Chaste reader, then, in any way to put
The blame on me, unless you wish they were;
Then if you'd have them wedded, please to shut
The book which treats of this erroneous pair,
Before the consequences grow too awful;
'T is dangerous to read of loves unlawful.

XIII.

Yet they were happy,—happy in the illicit
Indulgence of their innocent desires;
But, more imprudent grown with every visit,
Haidée forgot the island was her sire's;

When we have what we like 't is hard to miss it,
At least in the beginning, ere one tires;
Thus she came often, not a moment losing,
Whilst her piratical papa was cruising.

XIV.

Let not his mode of raising cash seem strange,
Although he fleeced the flags of every nation,
For into a prime minister but change
His title, and 't is nothing but taxation;
But he, more modest, took an humbler range
Of life, and in an honester vocation
Pursued o'er the high seas his watery journey,
And merely practised as a sea-attorney.

XV.

The good old gentleman had been detain'd
By winds and waves, and some important captures;
And, in the hope of more, at sea remain'd,
Although a squall or two had damp'd his raptures,
By swamping one of the prizes; he had chain'd
His prisoners, dividing them like chapters,
In number'd lots; they all had cuffs and collars,
And averaged each from ten to a hundred dollars.

XVI.

Some he disposed of off Cape Matapan,
Among his friends the Mainots; some he sold
To his Tunis correspondents, save one man
Toss'd overboard unsaleable (being old);
The rest, save here and there some richer one,
Reserved for future ransom in the hold,
Were link'd alike; as for the common people, he
Had a large order from the Dey of Tripoli.

XVII.

The merchandise was served in the same way,
Pieced out for different marts in the Levant,
Except some certain portions of the prey,
Light classic articles of female want,
French stuffs, lace, tweezers, toothpicks, teapot, tray,
Guitars and castanets from Alicant,
All which selected from the spoil he gathers,
Robb'd for his daughter by the best of fathers.

XVIII.

A monkey, a Dutch mastiff, a mackaw,
Two parrots, with a Persian cat and kittens,
He chose from several animals he saw—
A terrier, too, which once had been a Briton's,
Who dying on the coast of Ithaca,
The peasants gave the poor dumb thing a pittance,
These to secure in this strong blowing weather,
He caged in one huge hamper altogether.

XIX.

Then having settled his marine affairs,
Despatching single cruisers here and there,
His vessel having need of some repairs,
He shaped his course to where his daughter fair
Continued still her hospitable cares;
But that part of the coast being shoal and bare,
And rough with reefs which ran out many a mile,
His port lay on the other side o' the isle.

XX.

And there he went ashore without delay,
Having no custom-house nor quarantine
To ask him awkward questions on the way,
About the time and place where he had been:
He left his ship to be hove down next day,
With orders to the people to careen;
So that all hands were busy beyond measure,
In getting out goods, ballast, guns, and treasure.

XXI.

Arriving at the summit of a hill,
Which overlook'd the white walls of his home,
He stopp'd.—What singular emotions fill
Their bosoms who have been induced to roam!
With fluttering doubts if all be well or ill—
With love for many, and with fears for some;
All feelings which o'erleap the years long lost,
And bring our hearts back to their starting-post.

XXII.

The approach of home to husbands and to sires,
After long travelling by land or water,
Most naturally some small doubt inspires—
A female family 's a serious matter;
(None trust the sex more, or so much admires—
But they hate flattery, so I never flatter;)
Wives in their husbands' absences grow subtler,
And daughters sometimes run off with the butler.

XXIII.

An honest gentleman at his return
May not have the good fortune of Ulysses;
Not all lone matrons for their husbands mourn,
Or show the same dislike to suitors' kisses;
The odds are that he finds a handsome urn
To his memory—and two or three young misses
Born to some friend—who holds his wife and riches—
And that *his* Argus bites him by—the breeches.

XXIV.

If single, probably his plighted fair
Has in his absence wedded some rich miser;
But all the better, for the happy pair
May quarrel, and the lady growing wiser,
He may resume his amatory care
As cavalier servente, or despise her;
And that his sorrow may not be a dumb one,
Write odes on the Inconstancy of Woman.

XXV.

And oh! ye gentlemen who have already
 Some chaste *liaison* of the kind—I mean
An honest friendship with a married lady—
 The only thing of this sort ever seen
To last—of all connections the most steady,
 And the true Hymen (the first's but a screen)—
Yet for all that keep not too long away,
I've known the absent wrong'd four times a day.

XXVI.

Lambro, our sea-solicitor, who had
 Much less experience of dry land than ocean,
On seeing his own chimney-smoke, felt glad;
 But not knowing metaphysics, had no notion
Of the true reason of his not being sad,
 Or that of any other strong emotion;
He loved his child, and would have wept the loss of her,
But knew the cause no more than a philosopher.

XXVII.

He saw his white walls shining in the sun,
 His garden trees all shadowy and green;
He heard his rivulet's light bubbling run,
 The distant dog-bark; and perceived between
The umbrage of the wood so cool and dun
 The moving figures, and the sparkling sheen
Of arms (in the East all arm)—and various dyes
Of colour'd garbs, as bright as butterflies.

XXVIII.

And as the spot where they appear he nears,
 Surprised at these unwonted signs of idling,
He hears—alas! no music of the spheres,
 But an unhallow'd, earthly sound of fiddling!
A melody which made him doubt his ears,
 The cause being past his guessing or unriddling;
A pipe, too, and a drum, and shortly after
A most unoriental roar of laughter.

XXIX.

And still more nearly to the place advancing,
 Descending rather quickly the declivity,
Through the waved branches, o'er the greensward glancing,
 'Midst other indications of festivity,
Seeing a troop of his domestics dancing
 Like dervises, who turn as on a pivot, he
Perceived it was the Pyrrhic dance so martial,
To which the Levantines are very partial.

XXX.

And further on a troop of Grecian girls,
 The first and tallest her white kerchief waving,
Were strung together like a row of pearls,
 Link'd hand in hand, and dancing; each, too, having
Down her white neck long floating auburn curls—
 (The least of which would set ten poets raving);
Their leader sang—and bounded to her song,
With choral step and voice, the virgin throng.

XXXI.

And here, assembled cross-legg'd round their trays,
 Small social parties just begun to dine;
Pilaus and meats of all sorts met the gaze,
 And flasks of Samian and of Chian wine,
And sherbet cooling in the porous vase;
 Above them their dessert grew on its vine;
The orange and pomegranate nodding o'er
Dropp'd in their laps, scarce pluck'd, their mellow store.

XXXII.

A band of children, round a snow-white ram,
 There wreathe his venerable horns with flowers;
While peaceful, as if still an unwean'd lamb,
 The patriarch of the flock all gently cowers
His sober head, majestically tame,
 Or eats from out the palm, or playful lowers
His brow, as if in act to butt, and then
Yielding to their small hands, draws back again.

XXXIII.

Their classical profiles, and glittering dresses,
 Their large black eyes, and soft seraphic cheeks,
Crimson as cleft pomegranates, their long tresses,
 The gesture which enchants, the eye that speaks,
The innocence which happy childhood blesses,
 Made quite a picture of these little Greeks;
So that the philosophical beholder
Sigh'd for their sakes—that they should e'er grow older.

XXXIV.

Afar, a dwarf buffoon stood telling tales
 To a sedate gray circle of old smokers,
Of secret treasures found in hidden vales,
 Of wonderful replies from Arab jokers,
Of charms to make good gold and cure bad ails,
 Of rocks bewitched that open to the knockers,
Of magic ladies who, by one sole act,
Transform'd their lords to beasts (but that's a fact).

XXXV.

Here was no lack of innocent diversion
 For the imagination or the senses,
Song, dance, wine, music, stories from the Persian,
 All pretty pastimes in which no offence is;
But Lambro saw all these things with aversion,
 Perceiving in his absence such expenses,
Dreading that climax of all human ills,
The inflammation of his weekly bills.

XXXVI.

Ah! what is man? what perils still environ
The happiest mortals even after dinner—
A day of gold from out an age of iron
Is all that life allows the luckiest sinner;
Pleasure (whene'er she sings, at least) 's a siren,
That lures, to flay alive, the young beginner;
Lambro's reception at his people's banquet
Was such as fire accords to a wet blanket.

XXXVII.

He—being a man who seldom used a word
Too much, and wishing gladly to surprise
(In general he surprised men with the sword)
His daughter—had not sent before to advise
Of his arrival, so that no one stirr'd;
And long he paused to re-assure his eyes,
In fact much more astonish'd than delighted,
To find so much good company invited.

XXXVIII.

He did not know (alas! how men will lie)
That a report (especially the Greeks)
Avouch'd his death (such people never die),
And put his house in mourning several weeks,—
But now their eyes and also lips were dry;
The bloom, too, had return'd to Haidée's cheeks,
Her tears, too, being return'd into their fount,
She now kept house upon her own account.

XXXIX.

Hence all this rice, meat, dancing, wine, and fiddling,
Which turn'd the isle into a place of pleasure;
The servants all were getting drunk or idling,
A life which made them happy beyond measure.
Her father's hospitality seem'd middling,
Compar'd with what Haidée did with his treasure;
'T was wonderful how things went on improving,
While she had not one hour to spare from loving.

XL.

Perhaps you think in stumbling on this feast
He flew into a passion, and in fact
There was no mighty reason to be pleased;
Perhaps you prophesy some sudden act,
The whip, the rack, or dungeon at the least,
To teach his people to be more exact,
And that, proceeding at a very high rate,
He showed the royal *penchants* of a pirate.

XLI.

You 're wrong.—He was the mildest manner'd man
That ever scuttled ship or cut a throat;
With such true breeding of a gentleman,
You never could divine his real thought;
No courtier could, and scarcely woman can
Gird more deceit within a petticoat;
Pity he loved adventurous life's variety,
He was so great a loss to good society.

XLII.

Advancing to the nearest dinner tray,
Tapping the shoulder of the nighest guest,
With a peculiar smile, which, by the way,
Boded no good, whatever it express'd,
He ask'd the meaning of this holiday;
The vinous Greek, to whom he had address'd
His question, much too merry to divine
The questioner, fill'd up a glass of wine,

XLIII.

And without turning his facetious head,
Over his shoulder, with a Bacchant air,
Presented the o'erflowing cup, and said,
"Talking 's dry work, I have no time to spare."
A second hiccup'd, "Our old master 's dead,
You 'd better ask our mistress who 's his heir."
"Our mistress!" quoth a third: "Our mistress!—pooh!—
You mean our master—not the old, but new."

XLIV.

These rascals, being new comers, knew not whom
They thus address'd—and Lambro's visage fell—
And o'er his eye a momentary gloom
Pass'd, but he strove quite courteously to quell
The expression, and endeavouring to resume
His smile, requested one of them to tell
The name and quality of his new patron,
Who seem'd to have turn'd Haidée into a matron.

XLV.

"I know not," quoth the fellow, "who or what
He is, nor whence he came—and little care;
But this I know, that this roast capon 's fat,
And that good wine ne'er wash'd down better fare;
And if you are not satisfied with that,
Direct your questions to my neighbour there;
He 'll answer all for better or for worse,
For none likes more to hear himself converse." [10]

XLVI.

I said that Lambro was a man of patience,
And certainly he show'd the best of breeding,
Which scarce even France, the paragon of nations,
E'er saw her most polite of sons exceeding;
He bore these sneers against his near relations,
His own anxiety, his heart, too, bleeding,
The insults, too, of every servile glutton,
Who all the time was eating up his mutton.

XLVII.

Now in a person used to much command—
To bid men come, and go, and come again—
To see his orders done, too, out of hand—
Whether the word was death, or but the chain—
It may seem strange to find his manners bland;
Yet such things are, which I can not explain,
Though doubtless he who can command himself
Is good to govern—almost as a Guelf.

XLVIII.

Not that he was not sometimes rash or so,
But never in his real and serious mood;
Then calm, concentrated, and still, and slow,
He lay coil'd like the boa in the wood;
With him it never was a word and blow,
His angry word once o'er, he shed no blood,
But in his silence there was much to rue,
And his *one* blow left little work for *two*.

XLIX.

He ask'd no further questions, and proceeded
On to the house, but by a private way,
So that the few who met him hardly heeded,
So little they expected him that day;
If love paternal in his bosom pleaded
For Haidée's sake, is more than I can say,
But certainly to one deem'd dead returning,
This revel seem'd a curious mode of mourning.

L.

If all the dead could now return to life,
(Which God forbid!) or some, or a great many,
For instance, if a husband or his wife
(Nuptial examples are as good as any),
No doubt whate'er might be their former strife,
The present weather would be much more rainy—
Tears shed into the grave of the connection
Would share most probably its resurrection.

LI.

He enter'd in the house no more his home,
A thing to human feelings the most trying,
And harder for the heart to overcome,
Perhaps, than even the mental pangs of dying;
To find our hearthstone turn'd into a tomb,
And round its once warm precincts palely lying
The ashes of our hopes, is a deep grief,
Beyond a single gentleman's belief.

LII.

He enter'd in the house—his home no more,
For without hearts there is no home;—and felt
The solitude of passing his own door
Without a welcome: *there* he long had dwelt,
There his few peaceful days Time had swept o'er,
There his worn bosom and keen eye would melt
Over the innocence of that sweet child,
His only shrine of feelings undefiled.

LIII.

He was a man of a strange temperament,
Of mild demeanour though of savage mood,
Moderate in all his habits, and content
With temperance in pleasure, as in food,
Quick to perceive, and strong to bear, and meant
For something better, if not wholly good;
His country's wrongs and his despair to save her
Had stung him from a slave to an enslaver.

LIV.

The love of power, and rapid gain of gold,
The hardness by long habitude produced,
The dangerous life in which he had grown old,
The mercy he had granted oft abused,
The sights he was accustom'd to behold,
The wild seas, and wild men with whom he cruised,
Had cost his enemies a long repentance,
And made him a good friend, but bad acquaintance.

LV.

But something of the spirit of old Greece
Flash'd o'er his soul a few heroic rays,
Such as lit onward to the Golden Fleece
His predecessors in the Colchian days;
'T is true he had no ardent love for peace—
Alas! his country show'd no path to praise:
Hate to the world and war with every nation
He waged, in vengeance of her degradation.

LVI.

Still o'er his mind the influence of the clime
Shed its Ionian elegance, which show'd
Its power unconsciously full many a time,—
A taste seen in the choice of his abode,
A love of music and of scenes sublime,
A pleasure in the gentle stream that flow'd
Past him in crystal, and a joy in flowers,
Bedew'd his spirit in his calmer hours.

LVII.

But whatsoe'er he had of love reposed
On that beloved daughter; she had been
The only thing which kept his heart unclosed
Amidst the savage deeds he had done and seen,
A lonely pure affection unopposed:
There wanted but the loss of this to ween
His feelings from all milk of human kindness,
And turn him, like the Cyclops, mad with blindness.

LVIII.

The cubless tigress in her jungle raging,
Is dreadful to the shepherd and the flock;
The ocean when its yeasty war is waging,
Is awful to the vessel near the rock;
But violent things will sooner bear assuaging,
Their fury being spent by its own shock,
Than the stern, single, deep, and wordless ire
Of a strong human heart, and in a sire.

LIX.

It is a hard, although a common case,
To find our children running restive—they
In whom our brightest days we would retrace,
Our little selves re-form'd in finer clay,

Just as old age is creeping on apace,
And clouds come o'er the sunset of our day,
They kindly leave us, though not quite alone,
But in good company—the gout or stone.

LX.

Yet a fine family is a fine thing
(Provided they don't come in after dinner);
'T is beautiful to see a matron bring
Her children up (if nursing them don't thin her);
Like cherubs round an altar-piece they cling
To the fire-side (a sight to touch a sinner).
A lady with her daughters or her nieces
Shine like a guinea and seven-shilling pieces.

LXI.

Old Lambro pass'd unseen a private gate,
And stood within his hall at eventide;
Meantime the lady and her lover sate
At wassail in their beauty and their pride:
An ivory inlaid table spread with state
Before them, and fair slaves on every side;
Gems, gold, and silver, form'd the service mostly,
Mother of pearl and coral the less costly.

LXII.

The dinner made about a hundred dishes;
Lamb and pistachio nuts—in short, all meats,
And saffron soups, and sweetbreads; and the fishes
Were of the finest that e'er flounced in nets,
Drest to a Sybarite's most pamper'd wishes;
The beverage was various sherbets
Of raisin, orange, and pomegranate juice,
Squeezed through the rind, which makes it best for use.

LXIII.

These were ranged round, each in its crystal ewer,
And fruits, and date-bread loaves closed the repast,
And Mocha's berry, from Arabia pure,
In small fine China cups, came in at last;
Gold cups of filigree made to secure
The hand from burning underneath them placed,
Cloves, cinnamon, and saffron too were boil'd
Up with the coffee, which (I think) they spoil'd.

LXIV.

The hangings of the room were tapestry, made
Of velvet panels, each of different hue,
And thick with damask flowers of silk inlaid;
And round them ran a yellow border too;
The upper border, richly wrought, display'd,
Embroider'd delicately o'er with blue,
Soft Persian sentences, in lilac letters,
From poets, or the moralists their betters.

LXV.

These Oriental writings on the wall,
Quite common in those countries are a kind
Of monitors adapted to recall,
Like skulls at Memphian banquets, to the mind
The words which shook Belshazzar in his hall,
And took his kingdom from him: You will find,
Though sages may pour out their wisdom's treasure
There is no sterner moralist than Pleasure.

LXVI.

A beauty at the season's close grown hectic,
A genius who has drunk himself to death,
A rake turn'd methodistic, or Eclectic—
(For that's the name they like to pray beneath)—
But most, an alderman struck apoplectic,
Are things that really take away the breath,—
And show that late hours, wine, and love, are able
To do not much less damage than the table.

LXVII.

Haidée and Juan carpeted their feet
On crimson satin, border'd with pale blue;
Their sofa occupied three parts complete
Of the apartment—and appear'd quite new;
The velvet cushions (for a throne more meet)
Were scarlet, from whose glowing centre grew
A sun emboss'd in gold, whose rays of tissue,
Meridian-like, were seen all light to issue.

LXVIII.

Crystal and marble, plate and porcelain,
Had done their work of splendour; Indian mats
And Persian carpets, which the heart bled to stain,
Over the floors were spread; gazelles and cats,
And dwarfs and blacks, and such like things, that gain
Their bread as ministers and favourites—(that's
To say, by degradation)—mingled there
As plentiful as in a court, or fair.

LXIX.

There was no want of lofty mirrors, and
The tables, most of ebony inlaid
With mother of pearl or ivory, stood at hand,
Or were of tortoise-shell or rare woods made,
Fretted with gold or silver:—by command,
The greater part of these were ready spread
With viands and sherbets in ice—and wine—
Kept for all comers, at all hours to dine.

LXX.

Of all the dresses I select Haidée's:
She wore two jelicks—one was of pale yellow;
Of azure, pink, and white was her chemise—
'Neath which her breast heaved like a little billow;
With buttons form'd of pearls as large as peas,
All gold and crimson shone her jelick's fellow,
And the striped white gauze baracan that bound her,
Like fleecy clouds about the moon, flow'd round her.

LXXI.

One large gold bracelet clasp'd each lovely arm,
 Lockless—so pliable from the pure gold
That the hand stretch'd and shut it without harm,
 The limb which it adorn'd its only mould;
So beautiful—its very shape would charm,
 And clinging as if loath to lose its hold,
The purest ore enclosed the whitest skin
That e'er by precious metal was held in.[11]

LXXII.

Around, as princess of her father's land,
 A like gold bar above her instep roll'd,[12]
Announced her rank; twelve rings were on her hand;
 Her hair was starr'd with gems; her veil's fine fold
Below her breast was fasten'd with a band
 Of lavish pearls, whose worth could scarce be told;
Her orange silk full Turkish trousers furl'd
Above the prettiest ankle in the world.

LXXIII.

Her hair's long auburn waves down to her heel
 Flow'd like an Alpine torrent which the sun
Dyes with his morning light,—and would conceal
 Her person if allow'd at large to run,[13]

And still they seem resentfully to feel
 The silken fillet's curb, and sought to shun
Their bonds whene'er some zephyr caught began
To offer his young pinion as her fan.

LXXIV.

Round her she made an atmosphere of life,
 The very air seem'd lighter from her eyes,
They were so soft and beautiful, and rife
 With all we can imagine of the skies,
And pure as Psyche ere she grew a wife—
 Too pure even for the purest human ties;
Her overpowering presence made you feel
It would not be idolatry to kneel.

LXXV.

Her eyelashes, though dark as night, were tinged
 (It is the country's custom), but in vain;
For those large black eyes were so blackly fringed,
 The glossy rebels mock'd the jetty stain,
And in their native beauty stood avenged:
 Her nails were touch'd with henna; but again
The power of art was turn'd to nothing, for
They could not look more rosy than before.

LXXVI.

The henna should be deeply dyed to make
 The skin relieved appear more fairly fair;
She had no need of this, day ne'er will break
 On mountain tops more heavenly white than her;
The eye might doubt if it were well awake,
 She was so like a vision; I might err,
But Shakspeare also says, 't is very silly
"To gild refined gold, or paint the lily."

LXXVII.

Juan had on a shawl of black and gold,
 But a white baracan, and so transparent
The sparkling gems beneath you might behold,
 Like small stars through the milky way apparent;
His turban, furl'd in many a graceful fold,
 An emerald aigrette with Haidée's hair in 't
Surmounted, as its clasp, a glowing crescent,
Whose rays shone ever trembling, but incessant.

LXXVIII.

And now they were diverted by their suite,
 Dwarfs, dancing girls, black eunuchs, and a poet,
Which made their new establishment complete;
 The last was of great fame, and liked to show it:
His verses rarely wanted their due feet—
 And for his theme—he seldom sung below it,
He being paid to satirise or flatter,
As the psalm says, "inditing a good matter."

LXXIX.

He praised the present, and abused the past,
 Reversing the good custom of old days,
An Eastern anti-jacobin at last
 He turn'd, preferring pudding to no praise—
For some few years his lot had been o'ercast
 By his seeming independent in his lays,
But now he sung the Sultan and the Pacha
With truth like Southey, and with verse like Crashaw.

LXXX.

He was a man who had seen many changes,
 And always changed as true as any needle;
His polar star being one which rather ranges,
 And not the fix'd—he knew the way to wheedle:
So vile he 'scaped the doom which oft avenges;
 And being fluent (save indeed when fee'd ill),
He lied with such a fervour of intention—
There was no doubt he earn'd his laureate pension.

LXXXI.

But he had genius,—when a turn-coat has it,
 The "Vates irritabilis" takes care
That without notice few full moons shall pass it;
 Even good men like to make the public stare:—
But to my subject—let me see—what was it?—
 Oh!—the third canto—and the pretty pair—
Their loves, and feasts, and house, and dress, and mode
Of living in their insular abode.

LXXXII.

Their poet, a sad trimmer, but no less
 In company a very pleasant fellow,
Had been the favourite of full many a mess
 Of men, and made them speeches when half mellow;
And though his meaning they could rarely guess,
 Yet still they deign'd to hiccup or to bellow
The glorious meed of popular applause,
Of which the first ne'er knows the second cause.

LXXXIII.

But now being lifted into high society,
 And having pick'd up several odds and ends
Of free thoughts in his travels, for variety
 He deem'd, being in a lone isle, among friends,
That without any danger of a riot, he
 Might for long lying make himself amends;
And singing as he sung in his warm youth,
Agree to a short armistice with truth.

LXXXIV.

He had travell'd 'mongst the Arabs, Turks, and Franks,
 And knew the self-loves of the different nations;
And having lived with people of all ranks,
 Had something ready upon most occasions—
Which got him a few presents and some thanks.
 He varied with some skill his adulations;

To "do at Rome as Romans do," a piece
Of conduct was which he observed in Greece.

LXXXV.

Thus, usually, when he was ask'd to sing,
He gave the different nations something national,
'T was all the same to him—"God save the king,"
Or "Ca ira," according to the fashion all:
His muse made increment of any thing,
From the high lyric down to the low rational;
If Pindar sang horse-races, what should hinder
Himself from being as pliable as Pindar?

LXXXVI.

In France, for instance, he would write a chanson;
In England, a six canto quarto tale;
In Spain, he 'd make a ballad or romance on
The last war—much the same in Portugal;
In Germany, the Pegasus he 'd prance on
Would be old Goethe's—(see what says De Staël);
In Italy, he 'd ape the "Trecentisti;"
In Greece, he 'd sing some sort of hymn like this t' ye:

1.

The isles of Greece, the isles of Greece!
Where burning Sappho loved and sung,
Where grew the arts of war and peace,—
Where Delos rose, and Phœbus sprung!
Eternal summer gilds them yet,
But all, except their sun, is set.

2.

The Scian and the Teian muse,
The hero's harp, the lover's lute,
Have found the fame your shores refuse;
Their place of birth alone is mute
To sounds which echo further west
Than your sires' "Islands of the Blest." [14]

3.

The mountains look on Marathon—
And Marathon looks on the sea;
And musing there an hour alone,
I dream'd that Greece might still be free;
For standing on the Persians' grave,
I could not deem myself a slave.

4.

A king sate on the rocky brow
Which looks o'er sea-born Salamis;
And ships, by thousands, lay below,
And men in nations;—all were his!
He counted them at break of day—
And when the sun set, where were they? [15]

5.

And where are they? and where art thou,
My country? On thy voiceless shore
The heroic lay is tuneless now—
The heroic bosom beats no more!
And must thy lyre, so long divine,
Degenerate into hands like mine?

6.

'T is something, in the dearth of fame,
Though link'd among a fetter'd race,
To feel at least a patriot's shame,
Even as I sing, suffuse my face;
For what is left the poet here?
For Greeks a blush—for Greece a tear.

7.

Must *we* but weep o'er days more blest?
Must *we* but blush?—Our fathers bled.
Earth! render back from out thy breast
A remnant of our Spartan dead!
Of the three hundred grant but three,
To make a new Thermopylæ!

8.

What, silent still? and silent all?
Ah! no;—the voices of the dead
Sound like a distant torrent's fall,
And answer, "Let one living head,
But one arise,—we come, we come!"
'T is but the living who are dumb.

9.

In vain—in vain; strike other chords;
Fill high the cup with Samian wine!
Leave battles to the Turkish hordes,
And shed the blood of Scio's vine!
Hark! rising to the ignoble call—
How answers each bold Bacchanal!

10.

You have the Pyrrhic dance as yet,
Where is the Pyrrhic phalanx gone?
Of two such lessons, why forget
The nobler and the manlier one?
You have the letters Cadmus gave—
Think ye he meant them for a slave?

11.

Fill high the bowl with Samian wine!
We will not think of themes like these!
It made Anacreon's song divine:
He served—but served Polycrates—
A tyrant; but our masters then
Were still, at least, our countrymen.

12.

The tyrant of the Chersonese
 Was freedom's best and bravest friend;
That tyrant was Miltiades!
 Oh! that the present hour would lend
Another despot of the kind!
 Such chains as his were sure to bind.

13.

Fill high the bowl with Samian wine!
On Suli's rock, and Parga's shore,
Exists the remnant of a line
Such as the Doric mothers bore;
And there, perhaps, some seed is sown,
The Heracleidan blood might own.

14.

Trust not for freedom to the Franks—
They have a king who buys and sells:
In native swords, and native ranks,
The only hope of courage dwells;
But Turkish force, and Latin fraud,
Would break your shield, however broad.

15.

Fill high the bowl with Samian wine!
Our virgins dance beneath the shade—
I see their glorious black eyes shine;
But gazing on each glowing maid,
My own the burning tear-drop laves,
To think such breasts must suckle slaves.

16.

Place me on Sunium's marbled steep,
Where nothing, save the waves and I,
May hear our mutual murmurs sweep;
There, swan-like, let me sing and die:
A land of slaves shall ne'er be mine—
Dash down yon cup of Samian wine!

LXXXVII.

Thus sung, or would, or could, or should have sung,
The modern Greek, in tolerable verse;
If not like Orpheus quite, when Greece was young,
Yet in these times he might have done much worse:
His strain display'd some feeling—right or wrong;
And feeling, in a poet, is the source
Of others' feeling; but they are such liars,
And take all colours—like the hands of dyers.

LXXXVIII.

But words are things, and a small drop of ink,
Falling like dew, upon a thought, produces
That which makes thousands, perhaps millions, think;
'T is strange, the shortest letter which man uses
Instead of speech, may form a lasting link
Of ages; to what straits old Time reduces
Frail man, when paper—even a rag like this,
Survives himself, his tomb, and all that 's his!

LXXXIX.

And when his bones are dust, his grave a blank,
His station, generation, even his nation,
Become a thing, or nothing, save to rank,
In chronological commemoration,
Some dull MS. oblivion long has sank,
Or graven stone found in a barrack's station,
In digging the foundation of a closet,
May turn his name up, as a rare deposit.

XC.

And glory long has made the sages smile;
'T is something, nothing, words, illusion, wind—
Depending more upon the historian's style
Than on the name a person leaves behind:
Troy owes to Homer what whist owes to Hoyle:
The present century was growing blind
To the great Marlborough's skill in giving knocks
Until his late Life by Archdeacon Coxe.

XCI.

Milton 's the prince of poets—so we say;
A little heavy, but no less divine:
An independent being in his day—
Learn'd, pious, temperate in love and wine;
But his life falling into Johnson's way,
We 're told this great high-priest of all the Nine
Was whipt at college—a harsh sire—odd spouse,
For the first Mrs. Milton left his house.[16]

XCII.

All these are, *certes*, entertaining facts,
Like Shakspeare's stealing deer, Lord Bacon's bribes;
Like Titus' youth, and Cæsar's earliest acts;
Like Burns (whom Dr. Currie well describes),
Like Cromwell's pranks;—but although truth exacts
These amiable descriptions from the scribes,
As most essential to their hero's story,
They do not much contribute to his glory.

XCIII.

All are not moralists, like Southey, when
He prated to the world of "Pantisocrasy;"
Or Wordsworth unexcised, unhired, who then
Season'd his pedlar poems with democracy;
Or Coleridge, long before his flighty pen
Let to the Morning Post its aristocrasy;
When he and Southey, following the same path,
Espoused two partners (milliners of Bath).

XCIV.

Such names at present cut a convict figure,
The very Botany Bay in moral geography;
Their loyal treason, renegado rigour,
Are good manure for their more bare biography;
Wordsworth's last quarto, by the way, is bigger
Than any since the birthday of typography;
A drowsy frowzy poem, call'd the "Excursion,"
Writ in a manner which is my aversion.

XCV.

He there builds up a formidable dyke
 Between his own and others' intellect;
But Wordsworth's poem, and his followers, like
 Johanna Southcote's Shiloh, and her sect,
Are things which in this century don't strike
 The public mind—so few are the elect;
And the new births of both their stale virginities
Have proved but dropsies, taken for divinities.

XCVI.

But let me to my story: I must own,
 If I have any fault, it is digression—
Leaving my people to proceed alone,
 While I soliloquise beyond expression;
But these are my addresses from the throne,
 Which put off business to the ensuing session:
Forgetting each omission is a loss to
The world, not quite so great as Ariosto.

XCVII.

I know that what our neighbours call "*longueurs*,"
 (We've not so good a *word*, but have the *thing*,
In that complete perfection which ensures
 An epic from Bob Southey every spring—)
Form not the true temptation which allures
 The reader; but 't would not be hard to bring
Some fine examples of the *epopée*,
To prove its grand ingredient is *ennui*.

XCVIII.

We learn from Horace, "Homer sometimes sleeps;"
 We feel without him, Wordsworth sometimes wakes,
To show with what complacency he creeps,
 With his dear "*Waggoners*," around his lakes.
He wishes for "a boat" to sail the deeps—
 Of ocean?—No, of air; and then he makes
Another outcry for "a little boat,"
And drivels seas to set it well afloat. [17]

XCIX.

If he must fain sweep o'er the ethereal plain,
 And Pegasus runs restive in his "Waggon,"
Could he not beg the loan of Charles's Wain?
 Or pray Medea for a single dragon?
Or if too classic for his vulgar brain,
 He fear'd his neck to venture such a nag on,
And he must needs mount nearer to the moon,
Could not the blockhead ask for a balloon?

C.

"Pedlars," and "Boats," and "Waggons!" Oh! ye shades
 Of Pope and Dryden, are we come to this?
That trash of such sort not alone evades
 Contempt, but from the bathos' vast abyss
Floats scumlike uppermost, and these Jack Cades
 Of sense and song above your graves may hiss—
The "little boatman" and his "Peter Bell"
Can sneer at him who drew "Achitophel!" [18]

CI.

T' our tale.—The feast was over, the slaves gone,
 The dwarfs and dancing girls had all retired;
The Arab lore and poet's song were done,
 And every sound of revelry expired;
The lady and her lover, left alone,
 The rosy flood of twilight's sky admired;—
Ave Maria! o'er the earth and sea,
That heavenliest hour of Heaven is worthiest thee!

CII.

Ave Maria! blessed be the hour,
 The time, the clime, the spot, where I so soft
Have felt that moment in its fullest power
 Sink o'er the earth so beautiful and soft,
While swung the deep bell in the distant tower,
 Or the faint dying day-hymn stole aloft,
And not a breath crept through the rosy air,
And yet the forest leaves seem stirr'd with prayer.

CIII.

Ave Maria! 't is the hour of prayer!
 Ave Maria! 't is the hour of love!
Ave Maria! may our spirits dare
 Look up to thine and to thy Son's above!
Ave Maria! oh that face so fair!
 Those downcast eyes beneath the Almighty dove—
What though 't is but a pictured image?—strike—
That painting is no idol,—'t is too like.

CIV.

Some kinder casuists are pleased to say,
 In nameless print—that I have no devotion;
But set those persons down with me to pray,
 And you shall see who has the properest notion
Of getting into heaven the shortest way;
 My altars are the mountains and the ocean,
Earth, air, stars—all that springs from the great Whole,
Who hath produced, and will receive the soul.

CV.

Sweet hour of twilight!—in the solitude
 Of the pine forest, and the silent shore
Which bounds Ravenna's immemorial wood,
 Rooted where once the Adrian wave flow'd o'er,
To where the last Cæsarean fortress stood,
 Evergreen forest! which Boccaccio's lore
And Dryden's lay made haunted ground to me,
How have I loved the twilight hour and thee!

CVI.

The shrill cicalas, people of the pine,
 Making their summer lives one ceaseless song,
Were the sole echoes, save my steed's and mine,
 And vesper bell's that rose the boughs along;
The spectre huntsman of Onesti's line,
 His hell-dogs, and their chase, and the fair throng

Which learn'd from this example not to fly
From a true lover—shadow'd my mind's eye.

CVII.

Oh, Hesperus! thou bringest all good things—[19]
 Home to the weary, to the hungry cheer,
To the young bird the parent's brooding wings,
 The welcome stall to the o'erlabour'd steer;
Whate'er of peace about our hearthstone clings,
 Whate'er our household gods protect of dear,
Are gather'd round us by thy look of rest;
Thou bring'st the child, too, to the mother's breast.

CVIII.

Soft hour! which wakes the wish and melts the heart
 Of those who sail the seas, on the first day
When they from their sweet friends are torn apart;
 Or fills with love the pilgrim on his way
As the far bell of vesper makes him start,
 Seeming to weep the dying day's decay;
Is this a fancy which our reason scorns?
Ah! surely nothing dies but something mourns![20]

CIX.

When Nero perish'd by the justest doom
 Which ever the destroyer yet destroy'd,
Amidst the roar of liberated Rome,
 Of nations freed, and the world overjoy'd,
Some hands unseen strew'd flowers upon his tomb
 Perhaps the weakness of a heart not void
Of feeling for some kindness done, when power
Had left the wretch an uncorrupted hour.

CX.

But I'm digressing; what on earth has Nero,
 Or any such like sovereign buffoons,
To do with the transactions of my hero,
 More than such madmen's fellow man—the moon's?
Sure my invention must be down at zero,
 And I grown one of many "wooden spoons"
Of verse (the name with which we Cantabs please
To dub the last of honours in degrees).

CXI.

I feel this tediousness will never do—
 'T is being *too* epic, and I must cut down
(In copying) this long canto into two;
 They 'll never find it out, unless I own
The fact, excepting some experienced few;
 And then as an improvement 't will be shown:
I 'll prove that such the opinion of the critic is
From Aristotle *passim*.—See Ποιητικης.

I.

NOTHING so difficult as a beginning
 In poesy, unless perhaps the end ;
For oftentimes when Pegasus seems winning
 The race, he sprains a wing, and down we tend,
Like Lucifer when hurl'd from heaven for sinning,
 Our sin the same, and hard as his to mend,
Being pride, which leads the mind to soar too far,
Till our own weakness shows us what we are

II.

But Time, which brings all beings to their level,
And sharp Adversity, will teach at last
Man,—and, as we would hope, perhaps the devil,—
That neither of their intellects are vast:
While youth's hot wishes in our red veins revel,
We know not this—the blood flows on too fast;
But as the torrent widens towards the ocean,
We ponder deeply on each past emotion.

III.

As boy, I thought myself a clever fellow,
And wish'd that others held the same opinion;
They took it up when my days grew more mellow,
And other minds acknowledged my dominion:
Now my sere fancy "falls into the yellow
Leaf," and Imagination droops her pinion,
And the sad truth which hovers o'er my desk
Turns what was once romantic to burlesque.

IV.

And if I laugh at any mortal thing,
'T is that I may not weep; and if I weep
'T is that our nature cannot always bring
Itself to apathy, for we must steep
Our hearts first in the depths of Lethe's spring,
Ere what we least wish to behold will sleep:
Thetis baptised her mortal son in Styx;
A mortal mother would on Lethe fix.

V.

Some have accused me of a strange design
Against the creed and morals of the land,
And trace it in this poem every line:
I don't pretend that I quite understand
My own meaning when I would be *very* fine;
But the fact is that I have nothing plann'd,
Unless it were to be a moment merry,
A novel word in my vocabulary.

VI.

To the kind reader of our sober clime
This way of writing will appear exotic;
Pulci was sire of the half-serious rhyme,
Who sang when chivalry was more Quixotic,
And revell'd in the fancies of the time,
True knights, chaste dames, huge giants, kings despotic;
But all these, save the last, being obsolete,
I chose a modern subject as more meet.

VII.

How I have treated it, I do not know;
Perhaps no better than they have treated me,
Who have imputed such designs as show
Not what they saw, but what they wish'd to see:
But if it gives them pleasure, be it so;
This is a liberal age, and thoughts are free
Meantime Apollo plucks me by the ear,
And tells me to resume my story here.

VIII.

Young Juan and his lady-love were left
To their own hearts' most sweet society;
Even Time the pitiless in sorrow cleft
With his rude scythe such gentle bosoms, he
Sigh'd to behold them of their hours bereft,
Though foe to love; and yet they could not be
Meant to grow old, but die in happy spring,
Before one charm or hope had taken wing.

IX.

Their faces were not made for wrinkles, their
Pure blood to stagnate, their great hearts to fail;
The blank gray was not made to blast their hair,
But, like the climes that know nor snow nor hail,
They were all summer: lightning might assail
And shiver them to ashes, but to trail
A long and snake-like life of dull decay
Was not for them—they had too little clay.

X.

They were alone once more; for them to be
Thus was another Eden; they were never
Weary, unless when separate: the tree
Cut from its forest root of years—the river
Damm'd from its fountain—the child from the knee
And breast maternal wean'd at once for ever,—
Would wither less than these two torn apart;
Alas! there is no instinct like the heart—

XI.

The heart—which may be broken: happy they!
Thrice fortunate! who of that fragile mould,
The precious porcelain of human clay,
Break with the first fall: they can ne'er behold
The long year link'd with heavy day on day,
And all which must be borne, and never told;
While life's strange principle will often lie
Deepest in those who long the most to die.

XII.

"Whom the gods love die young," was said of yore,[22]
And many deaths do they escape by this:
The death of friends, and that which slays even more—
The death of friendship, love, youth, all that is,
Except mere breath; and since the silent shore
Awaits at last even those who longest miss
The old archer's shafts, perhaps the early grave
Which men weep over may be meant to save.

XIII.

Haidée and Juan thought not of the dead.
The heavens, and earth, and air, seem'd made for them:

They found no fault with Time, save that he fled;
 They saw not in themselves aught to condemn:
Each was the other's mirror, and but read
 Joy sparkling in their dark eyes like a gem,
And knew such brightness was but the reflection
Of their exchanging glances of affection.

XIV.

The gentle pressure, and the thrilling touch,
 The least glance better understood than words,
Which still said all, and ne'er could say too much;
 A language, too, but like to that of birds,
Known but to them, at least appearing such
 As but to lovers a true sense affords;
Sweet playful phrases, which would seem absurd
To those who hath ceased to hear such, or ne'er heard:

XV.

All these were theirs, for they were children still,
 And children still they should have ever been;
They were not made in the real world to fill
 A busy character in the dull scene,
But like two beings born from out a rill,
 A nymph and her beloved, all unseen
To pass their lives in fountains and on flowers,
And never know the weight of human hours.

XVI.

Moons changing had roll'd on, and changeless found
 Those their bright rise had lighted to such joys
As rarely they beheld throughout their round;
 And these were not of the vain kind which cloys,
For theirs were buoyant spirits, never bound
 By the mere senses; and that which destroys
Most love, possession, unto them appear'd
A thing which each endearment more endear'd.

XVII.

Oh beautiful! and rare as beautiful!
 But theirs was love in which the mind delights
To lose itself, when the old world grows dull,
 And we are sick of its hack sounds and sights,
Intrigues, adventures of the common school,
 Its petty passions, marriages, and flights,
Where Hymen's torch but brands one strumpet more,
Whose husband only knows her not a wh—re.

XVIII.

Hard words; harsh truth; a truth which many know.
 Enough.—The faithful and the fairy pair,
Who never found a single hour too slow,
 What was it made them thus exempt from care?
Young innate feelings all have felt below,
 Which perish in the rest, but in them were
Inherent; what we mortals call romantic,
And always envy, though we deem it frantic.

XIX.

This is in others a factitious state,
 An opium dream of too much youth and reading,
But was in them their nature or their fate:
 No novels e'er had set their young hearts bleeding,
For Haidée's knowledge was by no means great,
 And Juan was a boy of saintly breeding;
So that there was no reason for their loves
More than for those of nightingales or doves.

XX.

They gazed upon the sunset; 't is an hour
 Dear unto all, but dearest to *their* eyes,
For it had made them what they were: the power
 Of love had first o'erwhelm'd them from such skies,
When happiness had been their only dower,
 And twilight saw them link'd in passion's ties;
Charm'd with each other, all things charm'd that brought
The past still welcome as the present thought.

XXI.

I know not why, but in that hour to-night,
 Even as they gazed, a sudden tremor came,
And swept, as 't were, across their hearts' delight,
 Like the wind o'er a harp-string, or a flame,
When one is shook in sound, and one in sight:
 And thus some boding flash'd through either frame,
And call'd from Juan's breast a faint low sigh,
While one new tear arose in Haidée's eye.

XXII.

That large black prophet eye seem'd to dilate
 And follow far the disappearing sun,
As if their last day of a happy date
 With his broad, bright, and dropping orb were gone;
Juan gazed on her as to ask his fate—
 He felt a grief, but knowing cause for none,
His glance inquired of hers for some excuse
For feelings causeless, or at least abstruse.

XXIII.

She turn'd to him, and smiled, but in that sort
 Which makes not others smile; then turn'd aside:
Whatever feeling shook her, it seem'd short,
 And master'd by her wisdom or her pride;
When Juan spoke, too—it might be in sport—
 Of this their mutual feeling, she replied—
"If it should be so,—but—it cannot be—
Or I at least shall not survive to see."

XXIV.

Juan would question further, but she press'd
 His lip to hers, and silenced him with this,
And then dismiss'd the omen from her breast,
 Defying augury with that fond kiss;

And no doubt of all methods 't is the best:
Some people prefer wine—'t is not amiss;
I have tried both; so those who would a part take,
May choose between the headache and the heart-ache.

XXV.

One of the two, according to your choice,
Woman or wine, you'll have to undergo;
Both maladies are taxes on our joys:
But which to choose, I really hardly know;
And if I had to give a casting voice,
For both sides I could many reasons show,
And then decide, without great wrong to either,
It were much better to have both than neither.

XXVI.

Juan and Haidée gazed upon each other
With swimming looks of speechless tenderness,
Which mix'd all feelings, friend, child, lover, brother,
All that the best can mingle and express
When two pure hearts are pour'd in one another,
And love too much, and yet can not love less;
But almost sanctify the sweet excess
By the immortal wish and power to bless.

XXVII.

Mix'd in each other's arms, and heart in heart,
Why did they not then die?—they had lived too long
Should an hour come to bid them breathe apart;
Years could but bring them cruel things or wrong;
The world was not for them, nor the world's art
For beings passionate as Sappho's song;
Love was born *with* them, *in* them, so intense,
It was their very spirit—not a sense.

XXVIII.

They should have lived together deep in woods,
Unseen as sings the nightingale; they were
Unfit to mix in these thick solitudes
Call'd social, haunts of Hate, and Vice, and Care:
How lonely every freeborn creature broods!
The sweetest song-birds nestle in a pair;
The eagle soars alone; the gull and crow
Flock o'er their carrion, just like men below.

XXIX.

Now pillow'd cheek to cheek, in loving sleep,
Haidée and Juan their siesta took,
A gentle slumber, but it was not deep,
For ever and anon a something shook
Juan, and shuddering o'er his frame would creep,
And Haidée's sweet lips murmur'd like a brook,
A wordless music, and her face so fair
Stirr'd with her dream, as rose leaves with the air;

XXX.

Or as the stirring of a deep clear stream
Within an Alpine hollow, when the wind
Walks o'er it, was she shaken by the dream,
The mystical usurper of the mind—
O'erpowering us to be whate'er may seem
Good to the soul which we no more can bind;
Strange state of being! (for 't is still to be)
Senseless to feel, and with seal'd eyes to see.

XXXI.

She dream'd of being alone on the sea-shore,
Chain'd to a rock; she knew not how, but stir
She could not from the spot, and the loud roar
Grew, and each wave rose roughly, threatening her;
And o'er her upper lip they seem'd to pour,
Until she sobb'd for breath, and soon they were
Foaming o'er her lone head, so fierce and high—
Each broke to drown her, yet she could not die.

XXXII.

Anon—she was released, and then she stray'd
O'er the sharp shingles with her bleeding feet,
And stumbled almost every step she made:
And something roll'd before her in a sheet,
Which she must still pursue howe'er afraid:
'T was white and indistinct, nor stopp'd to meet
Her glance nor grasp, for still she gazed and grasp'd,
And ran, but it escaped her as she clasp'd.

XXXIII.

The dream changed:—in a cave she stood, its walls
Were hung with marble icicles; the work
Of ages on its water-fretted halls,
Where waves might wash, and seals might breed and lurk;
Her hair was dripping, and the very balls
Of her black eyes seem'd turn'd to tears, and mirk
The sharp rocks look'd below each drop they caught,
Which froze to marble as it fell,—she thought.

XXXIV.

And wet, and cold, and lifeless at her feet,
Pale as the foam that frothed on his dead brow,
Which she essay'd in vain to clear, (how sweet
Were once her cares, how idle seem'd they now!)
Lay Juan, nor could aught renew the beat
Of his quench'd heart; and the sea dirges low
Rang in her sad ears like a mermaid's song,
And that brief dream appear'd a life too long.

XXXV.

And gazing on the dead, she thought his face
Faded, or alter'd into something new—
Like to her father's features, till each trace
More like and like to Lambro's aspect grew—

With all his keen worn look and Grecian grace;
And starting, she awoke, and what to view?
Oh! Powers of Heaven! what dark eye meets she there?
'T is—'t is her father's—fix'd upon the pair!

XXXVI.

Then shrieking, she arose, and shrieking fell,
With joy and sorrow, hope and fear, to see
Him whom she deem'd a habitant where dwell
The ocean-buried, risen from death, to be
Perchance the death of one she loved too well:
Dear as her father had been to Haidée,
It was a moment of that awful kind——
I have seen such—but must not call to mind.

XXXVII.

Up Juan sprung to Haidée's bitter shriek,
And caught her falling, and from off the wall
Snatch'd down his sabre, in hot haste to wreak
Vengeance on him who was the cause of all:
Then Lambro, who till now forbore to speak,
Smiled scornfully, and said, "Within my call
A thousand scimitars await the word;
Put up, young man, put up your silly sword."

XXXVIII.

And Haidée clung around him; "Juan, 't is—
'T is Lambro—'t is my father! Kneel with me—
He will forgive us—yes—it must be—yes.
Oh! dearest father, in this agony
Of pleasure and of pain—even while I kiss
Thy garment's hem with transport, can it be
That doubt should mingle with my filial joy?
Deal with me as thou wilt, but spare this boy."

XXXIX.

High and inscrutable the old man stood,
Calm in his voice, and calm within his eye—
Not always signs with him of calmest mood:
He look'd upon her, but gave no reply;
Then turn'd to Juan, in whose cheek the blood
Oft came and went, as there resolved to die;
In arms, at least, he stood, in act to spring
On the first foe whom Lambro's call might bring.

XL.

"Young man, your sword;" so Lambro once more said:
Juan replied, "Not while this arm is free."
The old man's cheek grew pale, but not with dread,
And drawing from his belt a pistol, he
Replied, "Your blood be then on your own head."
Then look'd close at the flint, as if to see
'T was fresh—for he had lately used the lock—
And next proceeded quietly to cock.

XLI.

It has a strange quick jar upon the ear,
That cocking of a pistol, when you know
A moment more will bring the sight to bear
Upon your person, twelve yards off, or so;
A gentlemanly distance, not too near,
If you have got a former friend for foe;
But after being fired at once or twice,
The ear becomes more Irish, and less nice.

XLII.

Lambro presented, and one instant more
Had stopp'd this Canto, and Don Juan's breath,
When Haidée threw herself her boy before;
Stern as her sire: "On me," she cried, "let death
Descend—the fault is mine; this fatal shore
He found—but sought not. I have pledged my faith;
I love him—I will die with him: I knew
Your nature's firmness—know your daughter's too."

XLIII.

A minute past, and she had been all tears,
And tenderness, and infancy; but now
She stood as one who champion'd human fears—
Pale, statue-like, and stern, she woo'd the blow
And tall beyond her sex, and their compeers,
She drew up to her height, as if to show
A fairer mark; and with a fix'd eye scann'd
Her father's face—but never stopp'd his hand.

XLIV.

He gazed on her, and she on him; 't was strange
How like they look'd! the expression was the same;
Serenely savage, with a little change
In the large dark eye's mutual-darted flame;
For she, too, was as one who could avenge
If cause should be—a lioness, though tame,
Her father's blood before her father's face
Boil'd up, and proved her truly of his race.

XLV.

I said they were alike, their features and
Their stature, differing but in sex and years;
Even to the delicacy of their hand
There was resemblance, such as true blood wears;
And now to see them, thus divided, stand
In fix'd ferocity, when joyous tears,
And sweet sensations, should have welcomed both,
Show what the passions are in their full growth.

XLVI.

The father paused a moment, then withdrew
His weapon, and replaced it; but stood still,
And looking on her, as to look her through,
"Not *I*," he said, "have sought this stranger's ill

Not *I* have made this desolation: few
 Would bear such outrage, and forbear to kill;
But I must do my duty—how thou hast
Done thine, the present vouches for the past.

XLVII.

"Let him disarm; or, by my father's head,
 His own shall roll before you like a ball!"
He raised his whistle, as the word he said,
 And blew, another answer'd to the call,
And rushing in disorderly, though led,
 And arm'd from boot to turban, one and all,
Some twenty of his train came, rank on rank:
He gave the word,—"Arrest or slay the Frank."

XLVIII.

Then, with a sudden movement, he withdrew
 His daughter; while compress'd within his clasp,
'Twixt her and Juan interposed the crew;
 In vain she struggled in her father's grasp—
His arms were like a serpent's coil: then flew
 Upon their prey, as darts an angry asp,
The file of pirates; save the foremost, who
Had fallen, with his right shoulder half cut through.

XLIX.

The second had his cheek laid open; but
 The third, a wary, cool old sworder, took
The blows upon his cutlass, and then put
 His own well in; so well, ere you could look
His man was floor'd, and helpless at his foot,
 With the blood running like a little brook
From two smart sabre gashes, deep and red—
One on the arm, the other on the head.

L.

And then they bound him where he fell, and bore
 Juan from the apartment: with a sign
Old Lambro bade them take him to the shore,
 Where lay some ships which were to sail at nine.
They laid him in a boat, and plied the oar
 Until they reach'd some galliots, placed in line;
On board of one of these, and under hatches,
They stow'd him, with strict orders to the watches.

LI.

The world is full of strange vicissitudes,
 And here was one exceedingly unpleasant:
A gentleman so rich in the world's goods,
 Handsome and young, enjoying all the present,
Just at the very time when he least broods
 On such a thing, is suddenly to sea sent,
Wounded and chain'd, so that he cannot move,
And all because a lady fell in love.

LII.

Here I must leave him, for I grow pathetic,
 Moved by the Chinese nymph of tears, green tea!
Than whom Cassandra was not more prophetic
 For if my pure libations exceed three,
I feel my heart become so sympathetic,
 That I must have recourse to Black Bohea:
'Tis pity wine should be so deleterious,
For tea and coffee leave us much more serious.

LIII.

Unless when qualified with thee, Cogniac
 Sweet Naïad of the Phlegethonic rill!
Ah! why the liver wilt thou thus attack,
 And make, like other nymphs, thy lovers ill?
I would take refuge in weak punch, but *rack*
 (In each sense of the word), whene'er I fill
My mild and midnight beakers to the brim,
Wakes me next morning with its synonym.

LIV.

I leave Don Juan for the present, safe—
 Not sound, poor fellow, but severely wounded;
Yet could his corporal pangs amount to half
 Of those with which his Haidée's bosom bounded!
She was not one to weep, and rave, and chafe,
 And then give way, subdued because surrounded;
Her mother was a Moorish maid, from Fez,
Where all is Eden, or a wilderness.

LV.

There the large olive rains its amber store
 In marble fonts; there grain, and flower, and fruit,
Gush from the earth until the land runs o'er;
 But there, too, many a poison-tree has root,
And midnight listens to the lion's roar,
 And long, long deserts scorch the camel's foot,
Or heaving whelm the helpless caravan;
And as the soil is, so the heart of man.

LVI.

Afric is all the sun's, and as her earth
 Her human clay is kindled; full of power
For good or evil, burning from its birth,
 The Moorish blood partakes the planet's hour,
And like the soil beneath it will bring forth:
 Beauty and love were Haidée's mother's dower;
But her large dark eye showed deep Passion's force,
Though sleeping like a lion near a source.

LVII.

Her daughter, temper'd with a milder ray,
 Like summer clouds all silvery, smooth, and fair,
Till slowly charged with thunder, they display
 Terror to earth, and tempest to the air,
Had held till now her soft and milky way;
 But overwrought with passion and despair,
The fire burst forth from her Numidian veins,
Even as the Simoom sweeps the blasted plains.

LVIII.

The last sight which she saw was Juan's gore,
 And he himself o'ermaster'd and cut down;
His blood was running on the very floor
 Where late he trod, her beautiful, her own;
Thus much she viewed an instant and no more,—
 Her struggles ceased with one convulsive groan;
On her sire's arm, which until now scarce held
Her writhing, fell she like a cedar fell'd.

LIX.

A vein had burst, and her sweet lips' pure dyes [23]
 Were dabbled with the deep blood which ran o'er;
And her head droop'd as when the lily lies
 O'ercharged with rain; her summon'd handmaids bore
Their lady to her couch with gushing eyes;
 Of herbs and cordials they produced their store,
But she defied all means they could employ,
Like one life could not hold, nor death destroy.

LX.

Days lay she in that state unchanged, though chill—
 With nothing livid, still her lips were red;
She had no pulse, but death seem'd absent still;
 No hideous sign proclaim'd her surely dead;
Corruption came not in each mind to kill
 All hope; to look upon her sweet face bred
New thoughts of life, for it seem'd full of soul—
She had so much, earth could not claim the whole.

LXI.

The ruling passion, such as marble shows
 When exquisitely chisell'd, still lay there,
But fix'd as marble's unchanged aspect throws
 O'er the fair Venus, but for ever fair;
O'er the Laocoon's all-eternal throes,
 And ever-dying Gladiator's air,
Their energy like life forms all their fame,
Yet looks not life, for they are still the same.—

LXII.

She woke at length, but not as sleepers wake,
 Rather the dead, for life seem'd something new,
A strange sensation which she must partake
 Perforce, since whatsoever met her view
Struck not her memory, though a heavy ache
 Lay at her heart, whose earliest beat still true
Brought back the sense of pain without the cause,
For, for a while, the furies made a pause.

LXIII.

She look'd on many a face with vacant eye,
 On many a token without knowing what;
She saw them watch her without asking why;
 And reck'd not who around her pillow sat;
Not speechless, though she spoke not; not a sigh
 Relieved her thoughts; dull silence and quick chat
Were tried in vain by those who served; she gave
No sign, save breath, of having left the grave.

LXIV.

Her handmaids tended, but she heeded not;
 Her father watch'd, she turn'd her eyes away;
She recognised no being, and no spot,
 However dear or cherish'd in their day;
They changed from room to room, but all forgot,
 Gentle, but without memory she lay;
At length those eyes, which they would fain be weaning
Back to old thoughts, wax'd full of fearful meaning.

LXV.

And then a slave bethought her of a harp;
 The harper came, and tuned his instrument;
At the first notes, irregular and sharp,
 On him her flashing eyes a moment bent,
Then to the wall she turn'd as if to warp
 Her thoughts from sorrow through her heart re-sent;
And he began a long low island song
Of ancient days, ere tyranny grew strong.

LXVI.

Anon her thin wan fingers beat the wall
 In time to his old tune; he changed the theme,
And sung of love; the fierce name struck through all
 Her recollection: on her flash'd the dream
Of what she was, and is, if ye could call
 To be so being; in a gushing stream
The tears rush'd forth from her o'erclouded brain,
Like mountain mists at length dissolved in rain.

LVII.

Short solace, vain relief!—thought came too quick,
 And whirl'd her brain to madness; she arose
As one who ne'er had dwelt among the sick,
 And flew at all she met, as on her foes;
But no one ever heard her speak or shriek,
 Although her paroxysm drew towards its close;—
Hers was a frenzy which disdain'd to rave,
Even when they smote her, in the hope to save.

LXVIII.

Yet she betray'd at times a gleam of sense;
 Nothing could make her meet her father's face,
Though on all other things with looks intense
 She gazed, but none she ever could retrace;
Food she refused, and raiment; no pretence
 Avail'd for either; neither change of place,
Nor time, nor skill, nor remedy, could give her
Senses to sleep—the power seem'd gone for ever.

LXIX.

Twelve days and nights she wither'd thus; at last,
 Without a groan, or sigh, or glance, to show
A parting pang, the spirit from her past:
 And they who watch'd her nearest could not know
The very instant, till the change that cast
 Her sweet face into shadow, dull and slow,
Glazed o'er her eyes—the beautiful, the black—
Oh! to possess such lustre—and then lack!

LXX.

She died, but not alone; she held within
 A second principle of life, which might
Have dawn'd a fair and sinless child of sin;
 But closed its little being without light,
And went down to the grave unborn, wherein
 Blossom and bough lie wither'd with one blight
In vain the dews of Heaven descend above
The bleeding flower and blasted fruit of love.

LXXI.

Thus liv'd—thus died she; never more on her
Shall sorrow light, or shame. She was not made
Through years or moons the inner weight to bear,
Which colder hearts endure till they are laid
By age in earth: her days and pleasures were
Brief, but delightful—such as had not stay'd
Long with her destiny; but she sleeps well
By the sea-shore, whereon she loved to dwell.

LXXII.

That isle is now all desolate and bare,
Its dwellings down, its tenants pass'd away;
None but her own and father's grave is there,
And nothing outward tells of human clay:
Ye could not know where lies a thing so fair,
No stone is there to show, no tongue to say
What was; no dirge, except the hollow sea's,
Mourns o'er the beauty of the Cyclades.

LXXIII.

But many a Greek maid in a loving song
Sighs o'er her name; and many an islander
With her sire's story makes the night less long;
Valour was his, and beauty dwelt with her:
If she loved rashly, her life paid for wrong—
A heavy price must all pay who thus err,
In some shape; let none think to fly the danger,
For soon or late Love is his own avenger.

LXXIV.

But let me change this theme, which grows too sad,
And lay this sheet of sorrows on the shelf;
I do n't much like describing people mad,
For fear of seeming rather touch'd myself—
Besides, I've no more on this head to add;
And as my Muse is a capricious elf,
We'll put about, and try another tack
With Juan, left half-kill'd some stanzas back.

LXXV.

Wounded and fetter'd, "cabin'd, cribb'd, confined,"
Some days and nights elapsed before that he
Could altogether call the past to mind;
And when he did, he found himself at sea,
Sailing six knots an hour before the wind;
The shores of Ilion lay beneath their lee—
Another time he might have liked to see 'em,
But now was not much pleased with Cape Sigæum.

LXXVI.

There, on the green and village-cotted hill, is
(Flank'd by the Hellespont, and by the sea)
Entomb'd the bravest of the brave, Achilles;
They say so—(Bryant says the contrary):
And further downward, tall and towering still, is
The tumulus—of whom? Heaven knows; 't may be
Patroclus, Ajax, or Protesilaus;
All heroes, who if living still would slay us.

LXXVII.

High barrows, without marble, or a name,
A vast, untill'd, and mountain-skirted plain,
And Ida in the distance, still the same,
And old Scamander, (if 't is he) remain;
The situation seems still form'd for fame—
A hundred thousand men might fight again
With ease; but where I sought for Ilion's walls
The quiet sheep feeds, and the tortoise crawls;

LXXVIII.

Troops of untended horses; here and there
Some little hamlets, with new names uncouth;
Some shepherds, (unlike Paris) led to stare
A moment at the European youth
Whom to the spot their school-boy feelings bear;
A Turk,—with beads in hand, and pipe in mouth,
Extremely taken with his own religion,
Are what I found there—but the devil a Phrygian.

LXXIX.

Don Juan, here permitted to emerge
From his dull cabin, found himself a slave;
Forlorn, and gazing on the deep blue surge,
O'ershadow'd there by many a hero's grave;
Weak still with loss of blood, he scarce could urge
A few brief questions; and the answers gave
No very satisfactory information
About his past or present situation.

LXXX.

He saw some fellow captives, who appear'd
To be Italians, as they were in fact;
From them, at least, *their* destiny he heard,
Which was an odd one; a troop going to act
In Sicily—all singers, duly rear'd
In their vocation; had not been attack'd
In sailing from Livorno by the pirate,
But sold by the impresario at no high rate.[24]

LXXXI.

By one of these, the buffo of the party,
Juan was told about their curious case;
For although destined to the Turkish mart, he
Still kept his spirits up—at least his face;
The little fellow really look'd quite hearty,
And bore him with some gaiety and grace,
Showing a much more reconciled demeanour
Than did the prima donna and the tenor.

LXXXII.

In a few words he told their hapless story,
 Saying, "Our Machiavelian impresario,
Making a signal off some promontory,
 Hail'd a strange brig; Corpo di Caio Mario!
We were transferr'd on board her in a hurry,
 Without a single scudo of salario;
But if the sultan has a taste for song,
We will revive our fortunes before long.

LXXXIII.

"The prima donna, though a little old,
 And haggard with a dissipated life,
And subject, when the house is thin, to cold,
 Has some good notes; and then the tenor's wife,
With no great voice, is pleasing to behold;
 Last carnival she made a deal of strife
By carrying off Count Cesare Cicogna
From an old Roman princess at Bologna.

LXXXIV.

"And then there are the dancers; there's the Nini,
With more than one profession gains by all;
Then there's that laughing slut the Pelegrini,
She, too, was fortunate last carnival,
And made at least five hundred good zecchini,
But spends so fast, she has not now a paul;
And then there's the Grotesca—such a dancer!
Where men have souls or bodies she must answer.

LXXXV.

"As for the figuranti, they are like
The rest of all that tribe; with here and there
A pretty person, which perhaps may strike,
The rest are hardly fitted for a fair;
There's one, though tall and stiffer than a pike,
Yet has a sentimental kind of air
Which might go far, but she don't dance with vigour;
The more's the pity, with her face and figure.

LXXXVI.

"As for the men, they are a middling set;
The musico is but a crack'd old basin,
But being qualified in one way yet,
May the seraglio do to set his face in,
And as a servant some preferment get;
His singing I no further trust can place in:
From all the Pope makes yearly 't would perplex [25]
To find three perfect pipes of the *third* sex.

LXXXVII.

"The tenor's voice is spoilt by affectation;
And for the bass, the beast can only bellow;
In fact, he had no singing education,
An ignorant, noteless, timeless, tuneless fellow.
But being the prima donna's near relation,
Who swore his voice was very rich and mellow,
They hired him, though to hear him you'd believe
An ass was practising recitative.

LXXXVIII.

"'T would not become myself to dwell upon
My own merits, and though young,—I see, Sir—you
Have got a travell'd air, which speaks you one
To whom the opera is by no means new:
You've heard of Raucocanti?—I'm the man;
The time may come when you may hear me too:
You was not last year at the fair of Lugo,
But next, when I'm engaged to sing there—do go.

LXXXIX.

"Our baritone I almost had forgot,
A pretty lad, but bursting with conceit:
With graceful action, science not a jot,
A voice of not great compass, and not sweet,
He always is complaining of his lot,
Forsooth, scarce fit for ballads in the street;
In lovers' parts his passion more to breathe,
Having no heart to show, he shows his teeth."

XC.

Here Raucocanti's eloquent recital
Was interrupted by the pirate crew,
Who came at stated moments to invite all
The captives back to their sad berths; each threw
A rueful glance upon the waves, (which bright all
From the blue skies derived a double blue,
Dancing all free and happy in the sun,)
And then went down the hatchway one by one.

XCI.

They heard next day—that in the Dardanelles,
Waiting for his Sublimity's firman,
The most imperative of sovereign spells,
Which every body does without who can,
More to secure them in their naval cells,
Lady to lady, well as man to man,
Were to be chain'd and lotted out per couple,
For the slave market of Constantinople.

XCII.

It seems when this allotment was made out,
There chanc'd to be an odd male, and odd female,
Who (after some discussion and some doubt,
If the soprano might be deem'd to be male,
They plac'd him o'er the woman as a scout)
Were link'd together, and it happen'd the male
Was Juan, who,—an awkward thing at his age,—
Pair'd off with a Bacchante blooming visage.

XCIII.

With Raucocanti lucklessly was chain'd
The tenor; these two hated with a hate
Found only on the stage, and each more pain'd
With this his tuneful neighbour than his fate;
Sad strife arose, for they were so cross-grain'd,
Instead of bearing up without debate,
That each pull'd different ways with many an oath,
"Arcades ambo," *id est*—blackguards both.

XCIV.

Juan's companion was a Romagnole,
But bred within the march of old Ancona,
With eyes that look'd into the very soul
(And other chief points of a "bella donna"),
Bright—and as black and burning as a coal;
And through her clear brunette complexion shone a
Great wish to please—a most attractive dower,
Especially when added to the power.

XCV.

But all that power was wasted upon him,
For sorrow o'er each sense held stern command;

Her eye might flash on his, but found it dim;
And though thus chain'd, as natural, her hand
Touch'd his, nor that—nor any handsome limb
(And she had some not easy to withstand)
Could stir his pulse, or make his faith feel brittle,
Perhaps his recent wounds might help a little.

XCVI.

No matter; we should ne'er too much inquire,
But facts are facts: no knight could be more true,
And firmer faith no ladye-love desire;
We will omit the proofs, save one or two:
'T is said no one in hand "can hold a fire
By thought of frosty Caucasus;" but few,
I really think; yet Juan's then ordeal
Was more triumphant, and not much less real.

XCVII.

Here I might enter on a chaste description,
Having withstood temptation in my youth,
But hear that several people take exception
At the first two books having too much truth;
Therefore I'll make Don Juan leave the ship soon,
Because the publisher declares, in sooth,
Through needles' eyes it easier for the camel is
To pass, than those two cantos into families.

XCVIII.

'T is all the same to me; I'm fond of yielding,
And therefore leave them to the purer page
Of Smollett, Prior, Ariosto, Fielding,
Who say strange things for so correct an age;
I once had great alacrity in wielding
My pen, and liked poetic war to wage,
And recollect the time when all this cant
Would have provoked remarks which now it shan't.

XCIX.

As boys love rows, my boyhood liked a squabble;
But at this hour I wish to part in peace,
Leaving such to the literary rabble,
Whether my verse's fame be doom'd to cease,
While the right hand which wrote it still is able,
Or of some centuries to take a lease;
The grass upon my grave will grow as long,
And sigh to midnight winds, but not to song.

C.

Of poets who come down to us through distance
Of time and tongues, the foster-babes of Fame,
Life seems the smallest portion of existence;
Where twenty ages gather o'er a name,
'T is as a snowball which derives assistance
From every flake, and yet rolls on the same,
Even till an iceberg it may chance to grow;
But, after all 't is nothing but cold snow.

CI.

And so great names are nothing more than nominal,
And love of glory 's but an airy lust,
Too often in its fury overcoming all
Who would as 't were identify their dust
From out the wide destruction, which, entombing all,
Leaves nothing till "the coming of the just"—
Save change: I've stood upon Achilles' tomb,
And heard Troy doubted; time will doubt of Rome.

CII.

The very generations of the dead
Are swept away, and tomb inherits tomb,
Until the memory of an age is fled,
And, buried, sinks beneath its offspring's doom:
Where are the epitaphs our fathers read?
Save a few glean'd from the sepulchral gloom
Which once-named myriads nameless lie beneath,
And lose their own in universal death.

CIII.

I canter by the spot each afternoon
Where perish'd in his fame the hero-boy,
Who lived too long for men, but died too soon
For human vanity, the young De Foix!
A broken pillar, not uncouthly hewn,
But which neglect is hastening to destroy,
Records Ravenna's carnage on its face,
While weeds and ordure rankle round the base.[26]

CIV.

I pass each day where Dante's bones are laid:
A little cupola, more neat than solemn,
Protects his dust, but reverence here is paid
To the bard's tomb, and not the warrior's column:
The time must come, when both alike decay'd,
The chieftain's trophy, and the poet's volume,
Will sink where lie the songs and wars of earth,
Before Pelides' death, or Homer's birth.

CV.

With human blood that column was cemented,
With human filth that column is defiled,
As if the peasant's coarse contempt were vented
To show his loathing of the spot he soil'd:
Thus is the trophy used, and thus lamented
Should ever be those bloodhounds, from whose wild
Instinct of gore and glory earth has known
Those sufferings Dante saw in hell alone.

CVI.

Yet there will still be bards: though fame is smoke,
Its fumes are frankincense to human thought;
And the unquiet feelings, which first woke
Song in the world, will seek what then they sought;

As on the beach the waves at last are broke,
 Thus to their extreme verge the passions brought
Dash into poetry, which is but passion,—
Or at least was so ere it grew a fashion.

CVII.

If in the course of such a life as was
 At once adventurous and contemplative,
Men who partake all passions as they pass,
 Acquire the deep and bitter power to give
Their images again as in a glass,
 An in such colours that they seem to live;
You may do right forbidding them to show 'em,
But spoil (I think) a very pretty poem.

CVIII.

Oh! ye, who make the fortunes of all books!
 Benign Ceruleans of the second sex!
Who advertise new poems by your looks,
 Your "imprimatur" will ye not annex?
What! must I go to the oblivious cooks?
 Those Cornish plunderers of Parnassian wrecks?
Ah! must I then the only minstrel be,
Proscribed from tasting your Castalian tea!

CIX.

What! can I prove "a lion" then no more?
 A ball-room bard, a foolscap, hot-press darling?
To bear the compliments of many a bore,
 And sigh, "I can't get out," like Yorick's starling;
Why, then, I'll swear, as poet Wordy swore
 (Because the world won't read him, always snarling),
That taste is gone, that fame is but a lottery
Drawn by the blue-coat misses of a coterie.

CX.

Oh! "darkly, deeply, beautifully blue,"
 As some one somewhere sings about the sky,
And I, ye learnèd ladies, say of you;
 They say your stockings are so (Heaven knows why,
I have examined few pair of that hue);
 Blue as the garters which serenely lie
Round the Patrician left-legs, which adorn
The festal midnight, and the levee morn.

CXI.

Yet some of you are most seraphic creatures—
 But times are alter'd since, a rhyming lover,
You read my stanzas, and I read your features:
 And—but no matter, all those things are over;
Still I have no dislike to learned natures,
 For sometimes such a world of virtues cover;
I knew one woman of that purple school,
The loveliest, chastest, best, but—quite a fool.

CXII.

Humboldt, "the first of travellers," but not
 The last, if late accounts be accurate,

Invented, by some name I have forgot,
 As well as the sublime discovery's date,
An airy instrument, with which he sought
 To ascertain the atmospheric state,
By measuring "the *intensity of blue:*"
Oh, Lady Daphne! let me measure you!

CXIII.

But to the narrative:—The vessel bound
 With slaves to sell off in the capital,
After the usual process, might be found
 At anchor under the seraglio wall;
Her cargo, from the plague being safe and sound,
 Were landed in the market, one and all,
And there with Georgians, Russians, and Circassians,
Bought up for different purposes and passions.

CXIV.

Some went off dearly; fifteen hundred dollars
 For one Circassian, a sweet girl, were given,
Warranted virgin; beauty's brightest colours
 Had deck'd her out in all the hues of heaven:
Her sale sent home some disappointed bawlers,
 Who bade on till the hundreds reach'd eleven;
But when the offer went beyond, they knew
'T was for the Sultan, and at once withdrew.

CXV.

Twelve negresses from Nubia brought a price
 Which the West Indian market scarce could bring;
Though Wilberforce, at last, has made it twice
 What 't was ere Abolition; and the thing
Need not seem very wonderful, for vice
 Is always much more splendid than a king:
The virtues, even the most exalted, Charity,
Are saving—vice spares nothing for a rarity.

CXVI.

But for the destiny of this young troop,
 How some were bought by pachas, some by Jews,
How some to burdens were obliged to stoop,
 And others rose to the command of crews
As renegadoes; while in hapless group,
 Hoping no very old vizier might choose,
The females stood, as one by one they pick'd 'em,
To make a mistress, or fourth wife, or victim:

CXVII.

All this must be reserved for further song;
 Also our hero's lot, howe'er unpleasant,
(Because this Canto has become too long),
 Must be postponed discreetly for the present;
I'm sensible redundancy is wrong,
 But could not for the muse of me put less in't:
And now delay the progress of Don Juan,
Till what is call'd in Ossian the fifth Duan.

CANTO V.

I.

WHEN amatory poets sing their loves
 In liquid lines mellifluously bland,
And pair their rhymes as Venus yokes her doves,
 They little think what mischief is in hand;
The greater their success the worse it proves,
 As Ovid's verse may give to understand;
Even Petrarch's self, if judged with due severity,
Is the Platonic pimp of all posterity.

II.

I therefore do denounce all amorous writing,
 Except in such a way as not to attract;
Plain—simple—short, and by no means inviting,
 But with a moral to each error tack'd,
Form'd rather for instructing than delighting,
 And with all passions in their turn attack'd;
Now, if my Pegasus should not be shod ill,
This poem will become a moral model.

III.

The European with the Asian shore
 Sprinkled with palaces; the ocean stream[27]
Here and there studded with a seventy-four;
 Sophia's cupola with golden gleam;
The cypress groves; Olympus high and hoar;
 The twelve isles, and the more than I could dream

Far less describe, present the very view
Which charm'd the charming Mary Montagu.

IV.

I have a passion for the name of "Mary,"
For once it was a magic sound to me;
And still it half calls up the realms of fairy,
Where I beheld what never was to be;
All feelings changed, but this was last to vary,
A spell from which even yet I am not quite free:
But I grow sad—and let a tale grow cold,
Which must not be pathetically told.

V.

The wind swept down the Euxine, and the wave
Broke foaming o'er the blue Symplegades;
'T is a grand sight from off "the Giant's Grave"[26]
To watch the progress of those rolling seas,
Between the Bosphorus, as they lash and lave
Europe and Asia, you being quite at ease;
There's not a sea the passenger e'er pukes in,
Turns up more dangerous breakers than the Euxine.

VI.

'T was a raw day of Autumn's bleak beginning,
When nights are equal, but not so the days;
The Parcæ then cut short the further spinning
Of seamen's fates, and the loud tempests raise
The waters, and repentance for past sinning
In all, who o'er the great deep take their ways:
They vow to amend their lives, and yet they don't;
Because if drown'd, they can't—if spared, they won't.

VII.

A crowd of shivering slaves of every nation,
And age, and sex, were in the market ranged;
Each bevy with the merchant in his station:
Poor creatures! their good looks were sadly changed.
All save the blacks seem'd jaded with vexation,
From friends, and home, and freedom far estranged;
The negroes more philosophy display'd,—
Used to it, no doubt, as eels are to be flay'd.

VIII.

Juan was juvenile, and thus was full,
As most at his age are, of hope, and health;
Yet I must own, he look'd a little dull,
And now and then a tear stole down by stealth;
Perhaps his recent loss of blood might pull
His spirit down; and then the loss of wealth,
A mistress, and such comfortable quarters,
To be put up for auction amongst Tartars,

IX.

Were things to shake a stoic; ne'ertheless,
Upon the whole his courage was serene:
His figure, and the splendour of his dress,
Of which some gilded remnants still were seen,
Drew all eyes on him, giving them to guess
He was above the vulgar by his mien;
And then, though pale, he was so very handsome;
And then—they calculated on his ransom.

X.

Like a backgammon board the place was dotted
With whites and blacks, in groups on show for sale,
Though rather more irregularly spotted:
Some bought the jet, while others chose the pale.
It chanced amongst the other people lotted,
A man of thirty, rather stout and hale,
With resolution in his dark gray eye,
Next Juan stood, till some might choose to buy.

XI.

He had an English look; that is, was square
In make, of a complexion white and ruddy,
Good teeth, with curling rather dark brown hair,
And, it might be from thought, or toil, or study,
An open brow, a little mark'd with care:
One arm had on a bandage rather bloody;
And there he stood with such *sang-froid*, that greater
Could scarce be shown even by a mere spectator.

XII.

But seeing at his elbow a mere lad,
Of a high spirit evidently, though
At present weigh'd down by a doom which had
O'erthrown even men, he soon began to show
A kind of blunt compassion for the sad
Lot of so young a partner in the woe,
Which for himself he seem'd to deem no worse
Than any other scrape, a thing of course.

XIII.

"My boy!"—said he, "amidst this motley crew
Of Georgians, Russians, Nubians, and what not,
All ragamuffins differing but in hue,
With whom it is our luck to cast our lot,
The only gentlemen seem I and you;
So let us be acquainted, as we ought:
If I could yield you any consolation,
'T would give me pleasure.—Pray, what is your nation?"

XIV.

When Juan answer'd—"Spanish!" he replied,
"I thought, in fact, you could not be a Greek;
Those servile dogs are not so proudly eyed:
Fortune has play'd you here a pretty freak,

But that's her way with all men, till they're
tried;
But never mind,—she'll turn, perhaps, next week;
She has served me also much the same as you,
Except that I have found it nothing new."

XV.

"Pray, sir," said Juan, "if I may presume,
What brought you here?"—"Oh! nothing very
rare,—
Six Tartars and a drag chain——" —"To this doom
But what conducted, if the question's fair,
Is that which I would learn."—"I served for some
Months with the Russian army here and there,
And taking lately, by Suwarrow's bidding,
A town, was ta'en myself instead of Widdin."

XVI.

"Have you no friends?"—"I had—but, by God's
blessing,
Have not been troubled with them lately. Now
I have answer'd all your questions without pressing,
And you an equal courtesy should show."
"Alas!" said Juan, "'t were a tale distressing,
And long besides."—"Oh! if 't is really so,
You're right on both accounts to hold your tongue;
A sad tale saddens doubly, when 't is long.

XVII.

"But droop not: Fortune at your time of life,
Although a female moderately fickle,
Will hardly leave you (as she's not your wife)
For any length of days in such a pickle.
To strive, too, with our fate were such a strife
As if the corn-sheaf should oppose the sickle:
Men are the sport of circumstances, when
The circumstances seem the sport of men."

XVIII.

"'T is not," said Juan, "for my present doom
I mourn, but for the past;—I loved a maid:"—
He paused, and his dark eye grew full of gloom;
A single tear upon his eyelash stay'd
A moment, and then dropp'd; "but to resume,
'T is not my present lot, as I have said,
Which I deplore so much; for I have borne
Hardships which have the hardiest overworn,

XIX.

"On the rough deep. But this last blow—" and
here
He stopp'd again, and turn'd away his face.
"Ay," quoth his friend, "I thought it would appear
That there had been a lady in the case;
And these are things which ask a tender tear,
Such as I, too, would shed if in your place:
I cried upon my first wife's dying day,
And also when my second ran away:

XX.

"My third——"—"Your third!" quoth Juan, turn-
ing round;
"You scarcely can be thirty: have you three?"
"No—only two at present abôve ground:
Surely 't is nothing wonderful to see
One person thrice in holy wedlock bound!"
"Well, then, your third," said Juan; "what did
she?
She did not run away, too,—did she, sir?"
"No, faith."—"What then?"—"I ran away from
her."

XXI.

"You take things coolly, sir," said Juan. "Why,"
Replied the other, "what can a man do?
There still are many rainbows in your sky,
But mine have vanish'd. All, when life is new,
Commence with feelings warm, and prospects
high;
But time strips our illusions of their hue,
And one by one in turn, some grand mistake
Casts off its bright skin yearly like the snake.

XXII.

"'T is true, it gets another bright and fresh,
Or fresher, brighter; but the year gone through,
This skin must go the way, too, of all flesh,
Or sometimes only wear a week or two;—
Love's the first net which spreads its deadly mesh;
Ambition, Avarice, Vengeance, Glory, glue
The glittering lime-twigs of our latter days,
Where still we flutter on for pence or praise."

XXIII.

"All this is very fine, and may be true,"
Said Juan; "but I really don't see how
It betters present times with me or you."
"No?" quoth the other; "yet you will allow
By setting things in their right point of view,
Knowledge, at least, is gained; for instance,
now,
We know what slavery is, and our disasters
May teach us better to behave when masters."

XXIV.

"Would we were masters now, if but to try
Their present lessons on our Pagan friends here,"
Said Juan,—swallowing a heart-burning sigh
"Heaven help the scholar whom his fortune sends
here!"
"Perhaps we shall be one day, by and by,"
Rejoin'd the other, "when our bad luck mends here;
Meantime (yon old black eunuch seems to eye us)
I wish to G—d that somebody would buy us.

XXV.

"But after all, what *is* our present state?
'T is bad, and may be better—all men's lot:

Most men are slaves, none more so than the great,
To their own whims and passions, and what not;
Society itself, which should create
Kindness, destroys what little we had got:
To feel for none is the true social art
Of the world's stoics—men without a heart."

XXVI.

Just now a black old neutral personage
Of the third sex stept up, and peering over
The captives seem'd to mark their looks and age,
And capabilities, as to discover
If they were fitted for the purposed cage:
No lady e'er is ogled by a lover,
Horse by a blackleg, broadcloth by a tailor,
Fee by a counsel, felon by a jailor,

XXVII.

As is a slave by his intended bidder.
'T is pleasant purchasing our fellow creatures;
And all are to be sold, if you consider
Their passions, and are dext'rous; some by features
Are bought up, others by a warlike leader,
Some by a place—as tend their years or natures;
The most by ready cash—but all have prices,
From crowns to kicks, according to their vices.

XXVIII.

The eunuch having eyed them o'er with care,
Turn'd to the merchant, and begun to bid
First but for one, and after for the pair;
They haggled, wrangled, swore, too—so they did!
As though they were in a mere Christian fair
Cheapening an ox, an ass, a lamb, or kid;
So that their bargain sounded like a battle
For this superior yoke of human cattle.

XXIX.

At last they settled into simple grumbling,
And pulling out reluctant purses, and
Turning each piece of silver o'er, and tumbling
Some down, and weighing others in their hand,
And by mistake sequins with paras jumbling,
Until the sum was accurately scann'd;
And then the merchant, giving change, and signing
Receipts in full, began to think of dining.

XXX.

I wonder if his appetite was good?
Or, if it were, if also his digestion?
Methinks at meals some odd thoughts might intrude,
And conscience ask a curious sort of question
About the right divine, how far we should
Sell flesh and blood. When dinner has oppress'd one,
I think it is, perhaps, the gloomiest hour
Which turns up out of the sad twenty-four.

XXXI.

Voltaire says "No:" he tells you that Candide
Found life most tolerable after meals;
He's wrong—unless man were a pig, indeed,
Repletion rather adds to what he feels,
Unless he's drunk, and then, no doubt, he's freed
From his own brain's oppression while it reels
Of food I think with Philip's son, or rather [29]
Ammon's (ill-pleased with one world and one father):

XXXII.

I think with Alexander, that the act
Of eating, with another act or two,
Makes us feel our mortality, in fact,
Redoubled; when a roast and a ragout,
And fish, and soup, by some side dishes back'd,
Can give us either pain or pleasure, who
Would pique himself on intellects, whose use
Depends so much upon the gastric juice?

XXXIII.

The other evening ('t was on Friday last)—
This is a fact, and no poetic fable—
Just as my great coat was about me cast,
My hat and gloves still lying on the table,
I heard a shot—'t was eight o'clock scarce past—
And, running out as fast as I was able, [30]
I found the military commandant
Stretch'd in the street, and able scarce to pant.

XXXIV.

Poor fellow! for some reason, surely bad,
They had slain him with five slugs; and left him there
To perish on the pavement: so I had
Him borne into the house and up the stair,
And stripp'd, and look'd to,—But why should I add
More circumstances? vain was every care;
The man was gone: in some Italian quarrel
Kill'd by five bullets from an old gun-barrel.

XXXV.

I gazed upon him, for I knew him well;
And though I have seen many corpses, never
Saw one, whom such an accident befell,
So calm; though pierced through stomach, heart, and liver,
He seem'd to sleep,—for you could scarcely tell
(As he bled inwardly, no hideous river

Of gore divulged the cause) that he was dead:
So as I gazed on him, I thought or said—

XXXVI.

"Can this be death? then what is life or death?
Speak!" but he spoke not: "wake!" but still he slept:—
"But yesterday, and who had mightier breath?
A thousand warriors by his word were kept
In awe: he said, as the centurion saith,
'Go,' and he goeth; 'come,' and forth he stepp'd.
The trump and bugle, till he spake, were dumb;
And now, nought left him but the muffled drum."

XXXVII.

And they who waited once and worshipp'd—they
With their rough faces throng'd about the bed
To gaze once more on the commanding clay,
Which for the last, though not the first, time bled:
And such an end! that he who many a day
Had faced Napoleon's foes until they fled,—
The foremost in the charge or in the sally,
Should now be butcher'd in a civic alley.

XXXVIII.

The scars of his old wounds were near his new,
Those honourable scars which brought him fame;
And horrid was the contrast to the view—
But let me quit the theme; as such things claim
Perhaps even more attention than is due
From me: I gazed (as oft I have gazed the same)
To try if I could wrench aught out of death
Which should confirm, or shake, or make a faith;

XXXIX.

But it was all a mystery. Here we are,
And there we go:—but *where?* five bits of lead,
Or three, or two, or one, send very far!
And is this blood, then, form'd but to be shed?
Can every element our elements mar?
And air—earth—water—fire live—and we dead?
We, whose minds comprehend all things? No more;
But let us to the story as before.

XL.

The purchaser of Juan and acquaintance
Bore off his bargains to a gilded boat,
Embark'd himself and them, and off they went thence
As fast as oars could pull and water float;
They look'd like persons being led to sentence,
Wondering what next, till the caïque was brought[31]
Up in a little creek below a wall
O'ertopp'd with cypresses, dark-green and tall.

XLI.

Here their conductor tapping at the wicket
Of a small iron door, 'twas open'd, and
He led them onward, first through a low thicket
Flank'd by large groves, which tower'd on either hand:
They almost lost their way, and had to pick it—
For night was closing ere they came to land.
The eunuch made a sign to those on board,
Who row'd off, leaving them without a word.

XLII.

As they were plodding on their winding way
Through orange bowers, and jasmine, and so forth:
(Of which I might have a good deal to say,
There being no such profusion in the North
Of oriental plants, "et cetera,"
But that of late your scribblers think it worth
Their while to rear whole hotbeds in *their* works,
Because one poet travell'd 'mongst the Turks):

XLIII.

As they were threading on their way, there came
Into Don Juan's head a thought, which he
Whisper'd to his companion:—'twas the same
Which might have then occurr'd to you or me.
"Methinks," said he, "it would be no great shame
If we should strike a stroke to set us free:
Let's knock that old black fellow on the head,
And march away—'twere easier done than said."

XLIV.

"Yes," said the other, "and when done, what then?
How get out? How the devil got we in?
And when we once were fairly out, and when
From Saint Bartholomew we have saved our skin,[32]
To-morrow 'd see us in some other den,
And worse off than we hitherto have been;
Besides, I 'm hungry, and just now would take
Like Esau, for my birthright a beef-steak.

XLV.

"We must be near some place of man's abode;—
For the old negro's confidence in creeping,
With his two captives, by so queer a road,
Shows that he thinks his friends have not been sleeping;
A single cry would bring them all abroad:
'T is therefore better looking before leaping—
And there, you see, this turn has brought us through,
By Jove, a noble palace!—lighted, too."

XLVI.

It was, indeed, a wide extensive building
Which open'd on their view, and o'er the front
There seem'd to be besprent a deal of gilding
And various hues, as is the Turkish wont,—
A gaudy taste; for they are little skill'd in
The arts of which these lands were once the font:

Each villa on the Bosphorus looks a screen
New painted, or a pretty opera-scene.

XLVII.

And nearer as they came, a genial savour
Of certain stews, and roast-meats, and pilaus,
Things which in hungry mortals' eyes find favour,
Made Juan in his harsh intentions pause,
And put himself upon his good behaviour:
His friend, too, adding a new saving clause,
Said, "In Heaven's name let's get some supper now
And then I'm with you, if you're for a row."

XLVIII.

Some talk of an appeal unto some passion,
Some to men's feelings, others to their reason;
The last of these was never much the fashion,
For reason thinks all reasoning out of season.
Some speakers whine, and others lay the lash on,
But more or less continue still to tease on,
With arguments according to their "forte;"
But no one ever dreams of being short.—

XLIX.

But I digress: of all appeals, although
I grant the power of pathos, and of gold,
Of beauty, flattery, threats, a shilling,—no
Method's more sure at moments to take hold
Of the best feelings of mankind, which grow
More tender, as we every day behold,
Than that all-softening, overpowering knell,
The tocsin of the soul—the dinner-bell.

L.

Turkey contains no bells, and yet men dine:
And Juan and his friend, albeit they heard
No Christian knoll to table, saw no line
Of lacqueys usher to the feast prepared,
Yet smelt roast-meat, beheld a huge fire shine,
And cooks in motion with their clean arms bared,
And gazed around them to the left and right,
With the prophetic eye of appetite.

LI.

And giving up all notions of resistance,
They follow'd close behind their sable guide,
Who little thought that his own crack'd existence
Was on the point of being set aside:
He motion'd them to stop at some small distance,
And knocking at the gate, 't was opened wide,
And a magnificent large hall display'd
The Asian pomp of Ottoman parade.

LII.

I won't describe; description is my forte,
But every fool describes in these bright days
His wondrous journey to some foreign court,
And spawns his quarto, and demands your praise—
Death to his publisher, to him 't is sport;
While Nature, tortured twenty thousand ways,
Resigns herself with exemplary patience
To guide-books, rhymes, tours, sketches, illustrations.

LIII.

Along this hall, and up and down, some, squatted
Upon their hams, were occupied at chess;
Others in monosyllable talk chatted,
And some seem'd much in love with their own dress,
And divers smoked superb pipes decorated
With amber mouths of greater price or less
And several strutted, others slept, and some
Prepared for supper with a glass of rum. [33]

LIV.

As the black eunuch enter'd with his brace
Of purchased Infidels, some raised their eyes
A moment without slackening from their pace;
But those who sate, ne'er stirr'd in any wise:
One or two stared the captives in the face,
Just as one views a horse to guess his price;
Some nodded to the negro from their station,
But no one troubled him with conversation.

LV.

He leads them through the hall, and, without stopping,
On through a farther range of goodly rooms,
Splendid, but silent, save in *one*, where, dropping, [34]
A marble fountain echoes through the glooms
Of night, which robe the chamber, or where popping
Some female head most curiously presumes
To thrust its black eyes through the door or lattice,
As wondering what the devil noise that is.

LVI.

Some faint lamps gleaming from the lofty walls
Gave light enough to hint their farther way,
But not enough to show the imperial halls
In all the flashing of their full array;
Perhaps there 's nothing—I 'll not say appals,
But saddens more by night as well as day,
Than an enormous room without a soul
To break the lifeless splendour of the whole.

LVII.

Two or three seem so little, *one* seems nothing:
In deserts, forests, crowds, or by the shore,
There solitude, we know, has her full growth in
The spots which were her realms for evermore;
But in a mighty hall or gallery, both in
More modern buildings and those built of yore,
A kind of death comes o'er us all alone,
Seeing what 's meant for many with but one.

LVIII.

A neat, snug study on a winter's night,
A book, friend, single lady, or a glass
Of claret, sandwich, and an appetite,
Are things which make an English evening pass;
Though *certes* by no means so grand a sight
As is a theatre lit up by gas.
I pass my evenings in long galleries solely;
And that 's the reason I'm so melancholy.

LIX.

Alas! man makes that great which makes him little:
I grant you in a church 't is very well:

What speaks of heaven should by no means be brittle,
But strong and lasting, till no tongue can tell
Their names who rear'd it; but huge houses fit ill—
And huge tombs worse—mankind, since Adam fell:
Methinks the story of the tower of Babel
Might teach them this much better than I'm able.

LX.

Babel was Nimrod's hunting-box, and then
A town of gardens, walls, and wealth amazing,
Where Nebuchadonosor, king of men,
Reign'd, till one summer's day he took to grazing,
And Daniel tamed the lions in their den,
The people's awe and admiration raising;
'T was famous, too, for Thisbe, and for Pyramus,
And the calumniated queen Semiramis.

LXI.

* * * * * *
* * * * * *

LXII.

But to resume,—should there be (what may not
Be in these days?) some infidels, who don't,
Because they can't find out the very spot
Of that same Babel, or because they won't
(Though Claudius Rich, Esquire, some bricks has got,
And written lately two memoirs upon't,)
Believe the Jews, those unbelievers, who
Must be believed, though they believe not you.

LXIII.

Yet let them think that Horace has exprest
Shortly and sweetly the masonic folly
Of those, forgetting the great place of rest,
Who give themselves to architecture wholly;
We know where things and men must end at best:
A moral (like all morals) melancholy,
And "Et sepulchri immemor struis domos"
Shows that we build when we should but entomb us.

LXIV.

At last they reach'd a quarter most retired,
Where echo woke as if from a long slumber;
Though full of all things which could be desired,
One wonder'd what to do with such a number
Of articles which nobody required;
Here wealth had done its utmost to encumber
With furniture an exquisite apartment,
Which puzzled Nature much to know what Art meant.

LXV.

It seem'd, however, but to open on
A range or suite of further chambers, which
Might lead to Heaven knows where; but in this one
The moveables were prodigally rich:

34

Sofas 't was half a sin to sit upon,
So costly were they; carpets every stitch
Of workmanship so rare, they made you wish
You could glide o'er them like a golden fish.

LXVI.

The black, however, without hardly deigning
A glance at that which wrapt the slaves in wonder,
Trampled what they scarce trod for fear of staining,
As if the milky way their feet was under
With all its stars; and with a stretch attaining
A certain press or cupboard niched in yonder—
In that remote recess which you may see—
Or if you don't the fault is not in me,—

LXVII.

I wish to be perspicuous; and the black,
I say, unlocking the recess, pull'd forth
A quantity of clothes fit for the back
Of any Mussulman, whate'er his worth;
And of variety there was no lack—
And yet, though I have said there was no dearth,—
He chose himself to point out what he thought
Most proper for the Christians he had bought.

LXVIII.

The suit he thought most suitable to each
Was, for the elder and the stouter, first
A Candiote cloak, which to the knee might reach,
And trousers not so tight that they would burst,
But such as fit an Asiatic breech;
A shawl, whose folds in Cashmire had been nurst,
Slippers of saffron, dagger rich and handy;
In short, all things which form a Turkish Dandy.

LXIX.

While he was dressing, Baba, their black friend,
Hinted the vast advantages which they
Might probably attain both in the end,
If they would but pursue the proper way
Which Fortune plainly seem'd to recommend;
And then he added, that he needs must say,
"'T would greatly tend to better their condition,
If they would condescend to circumcision.

LXX.

"For his own part, he really should rejoice
To see them true believers, but no less
Would leave his proposition to their choice."
The other, thanking him for this excess
Of goodness, in thus leaving them a voice
In such a trifle, scarcely could express
"Sufficiently" (he said) "his approbation
Of all the customs of this polish'd nation.

LXXI.

"For his own share—he saw but small objection
To so respectable an ancient rite;

And, after swallowing down a slight refection,
 For which he own'd a present appetite,
He doubted not a few hours of reflection
 Would reconcile him to the business quite."
"Will it?" said Juan, sharply: "Strike me dead,
But they as soon shall circumcise my head!

LXXII.

"Cut off a thousand heads, before——"—"Now, pray,"
 Replied the other, "do not interrupt:
You put me out in what I had to say.
 Sir!—as I said, as soon as I have supt,
I shall perpend if your proposal may
 Be such as I can properly accept;
Provided always your great goodness still
Remits the matter to our own free-will."

LXXIII.

Baba eyed Juan, and said, "Be so good
 As dress yourself—" and pointed out a suit
In which a princess with great pleasure would
 Array her limbs; but Juan standing mute,
As not being in a masquerading mood,
 Gave it a slight kick with his Christian foot;
And when the old negro told him to "Get ready,"
Replied, "Old gentleman, I'm not a lady."

LXXIV.

"What you may be, I neither know nor care,"
 Said Baba; "but pray do as I desire:
I have no more time nor many words to spare."
 "At least," said Juan, "sure I may inquire
The cause of this odd travesty?"—"Forbear,"
 Said Baba, "to be curious; 't will transpire,
No doubt, in proper place, and time, and season:
I have no authority to tell the reason."

LXXV.

"Then if I do," said Juan, "I'll be——"—"Hold!"
 Rejoin'd the negro, "pray be not provoking;
This spirit's well, but it may wax too bold,
 And you will find us not too fond of joking."
"What, sir!" said Juan, "shall it e'er be told
 That I unsex'd my dress?" But Baba stroking
The things down, said, "Incense me, and I call
Those who will leave you of no sex at all.

LXXVI.

"I offer you a handsome suit of clothes:
 A woman's, true; but then there is a cause
Why you should wear them."—"What, though my soul loathes
 The effeminate garb?"—thus, after a short pause,
Sigh'd Juan, muttering also some slight oaths,
 "What the devil shall I do with all this gauze?"
Thus he profanely term'd the finest lace
Which e'er set off a marriage-morning face.

LXXVII.

And then he swore; and, sighing, on he slipp'd
 A pair of trousers of flesh-colour'd silk;
Next with a virgin zone he was equipp'd,
 Which girt a slight chemise as white as milk;
But tugging on his petticoat, he tripp'd,
 Which—as we say—or, as the Scotch say, *whilk*,
(The rhyme obliges me to this; sometimes
Monarchs are less imperative than rhymes)—

LXXVIII.

Whilk, which (or what you please), was owing to
 His garment's novelty, and his being awkward:
And yet at last he managed to get through
 His toilet, though no doubt a little backward:
The negro Baba help'd a little too,
 When some untoward part of raiment stuck hard;
And, wrestling both his arms into a gown,
He paused, and took a survey up and down.

LXXIX.

One difficulty still remain'd—his hair
 Was hardly long enough; but Baba found
So many false long tresses all to spare,
 That soon his head was most completely crown'd,
After the manner then in fashion there;
 And this addition with such gems was bound
As suited the *ensemble* of his toilet,
While Baba made him comb his head and oil it.

LXXX.

And now being femininely all array'd,
 With some small aid from scissors, paint, and tweezers,
He look'd in almost all respects a maid,
 And Baba smilingly exclaim'd, "You see, sirs,
A perfect transformation here display'd;
 And now, then, you must come along with me, sirs,
That is—the Lady:"—clapping his hands twice,
Four blacks were at his elbow in a trice.

LXXXI.

"You, sir," said Baba, nodding to the one,
 "Will please to accompany those gentlemen
To supper; but you, worthy Christian nun,
 Will follow me: no trifling, sir; for when
I say a thing, it must at once be done.
 What fear you? think you this a lion's den?
Why, 't is a palace; where the truly wise
Anticipate the Prophet's paradise.

LXXXII.

"You fool! I tell you no one means you harm."
 "So much the better," Juan said, "for them;
Else they shall feel the weight of this my arm,
 Which is not quite so light as you may deem.

I yield thus far; but soon will break the charm
 If any take me for that which I seem:
So that I trust for every body's sake,
That this disguise may lead to no mistake."

LXXXIII.

"Blockhead! come on, and see," quoth Baba: while
 Don Juan, turning to his comrade, who
Though somewhat grieved, could scarce forbear a smile
 Upon the metamorphosis in view,—
"Farewell!" they mutually exclaim'd: "this soil
 Seems fertile in adventures strange and new;
One 's turn'd half Mussulman, and one a maid,
By this old black enchanter's unsought aid."

LXXXIV.

"Farewell!" said Juan, "should we meet no more,
 I wish you a good appetite." "Farewell!"
Replied the other; "though it grieves me sore;
 When we next meet, we 'll have a tale to tell:
We needs must follow when Fate puts from shore.
 Keep your good name; though Eve herself once fell."
"Nay," quoth the maid, the Sultan's self shan't carry me,
Unless his Highness promises to marry me."

LXXXV.

And thus they parted, each by separate doors;
 Baba led Juan onward room by room
Through glittering galleries, and o'er marble floors,
 Till a gigantic portal through the gloom,
Haughty and huge, along the distance lowers;
 And wafted far arose a rich perfume:
It seem'd as though they came upon a shrine,
For all was vast, still, fragrant, and divine.

LXXXVI.

The giant door was broad, and bright, and high,
 Of gilded bronze, and carved in curious guise;
Warriors thereon were battling furiously;
 Here stalks the victor, there the vanquish'd lies;
There captives led in triumph droop the eye,
 And in perspective many a squadron flies:
It seems the work of times before the line
Of Rome transplanted fell with Constantine.

LXXXVII.

This massy portal stood at the wide close
 Of a huge hall, and on its either side
Two little dwarfs, the least you could suppose,
 Were sate, like ugly imps, as if allied
In mockery to the enormous gate which rose
 O'er them in almost pyramidic pride:
The gate so splendid was in all its *features*,[35]
You never thought about those little creatures,

LXXXVIII.

Until you nearly trod on them, and then
 You started back in horror to survey
The wondrous hideousness of those small men,
 Whose colour was not black, nor white, nor gray
But an extraneous mixture, which no pen
 Can trace, although perhaps the pencil may;
They were mis-shapen pigmies, deaf and dumb—
Monsters, who cost a no less monstrous sum.

LXXXIX.

Their duty was—for they were strong, and though
 They look'd so little, did strong things at times—
To ope this door, which they could really do,
 The hinges being as smooth as Rogers' rhymes;
And now and then, with tough strings of the bow,
 As is the custom of those Eastern climes,
To give some rebel Pacha a cravat;
For mutes are generally used for that.

XC.

They spoke by signs—that is, not spoke at all;
 And looking like two incubi, they glared
As Baba with his fingers made them fall
 To heaving back the portal folds: it scared
Juan a moment, as this pair so small,
 With shrinking serpent optics on him stared;
It was as if their little looks could poison
Or fascinate whome'er they fix'd their eyes on.

XCI.

Before they enter'd, Baba paused to hint
 To Juan some slight lessons as his guide:
"If you could just contrive," he said, "to stint
 That somewhat manly majesty of stride,
'T would be as well, and,—(though there 's not much in 't)
 To swing a little less from side to side,
Which has at times an aspect of the oddest;—
And also could you look a little modest,

XCII.

"'T would be convenient, for these mutes have eyes
 Like needles, which may pierce those petticoats;
And if they should discover your disguise,
 You know how near us the deep Bosphorus floats;
And you and I may chance, ere morning rise,
 To find our way to Marmora without boats,
Stitch'd up in sacks—a mode of navigation
A good deal practised here upon occasion.[36]

XCIII.

With this encouragement, he led the way
 Into a room still nobler than the last;
A rich confusion form'd a disarray
 In such sort, that the eye along it cast

Could hardly carry any thing away,
 Object on object flash'd so bright and fast;
A dazzling mass of gems, and gold, and glitter,
Magnificently mingled in a litter.

XCIV.

Wealth had done wonders—taste not much; such things
 Occur in Orient palaces, and even
In the more chasten'd domes of Western kings
 (Of which I have also seen some six or seven)
Where I can't say or gold or diamond flings
 Great lustre, there is much to be forgiven;
Groups of bad statues, tables, chairs, and pictures,
On which I cannot pause to make my strictures.

XCV.

In this imperial hall, at distance lay
 Under a canopy, and there reclined
Quite in a confidential queenly way,
 A lady; Baba stopp'd, and kneeling, sign'd
To Juan, who though not much used to pray
 Knelt down by instinct, wondering in his mind
What all this meant: while Baba bowed and bended
His head, until the ceremony ended.

XCVI.

The lady rising up with such an air
 As Venus rose with from the wave, on them
Bent like an antelope a Paphian pair
 Of eyes, which put out each surrounding gem;
And raising up an arm as moonlight fair,
 She sign'd to Baba, who first kiss'd the hem
Of her deep purple robe, and speaking low,
Pointed to Juan, who remain'd below.

XCVII.

Her presence was as lofty as her state;
 Her beauty of that overpowering kind,
Whose force description only would abate:
 I'd rather leave it much to your own mind,
Than lessen it by what I could relate
 Of forms and features; it would strike you blind
Could I do justice to the full detail;
So, luckily for both, my phrases fail.

XCVIII.

Thus much, however, I may add,—her years
 Were ripe, they might make six-and-twenty springs,
But there are forms which Time to touch forbears,
 And turns aside his scythe to vulgar things,
Such as was Mary Queen of Scots; true—tears
 And love destroy; and sapping sorrow wrings
Charms from the charmer, yet some never grow
Ugly: for instance—Ninon de l'Enclos.

XCIX.

She spake some words to her attendants, who
 Composed a choir of girls, ten or a dozen,
And were all clad alike; like Juan, too,
 Who wore their uniform, by Baba chosen;
They form'd a very nymph-like looking crew,
 Which might have call'd Diana's chorus "cousin,"
As far as outward show may correspond;
I won't be bail for anything beyond.

C.

They bow'd obeisance and withdrew, retiring,
 But not by the same door through which came in
Baba and Juan, which last stood admiring,
 At some some small distance, all he saw within
This strange saloon, much fitted for inspiring
 Marvel and praise; for both or none things win;
And I must say, I ne'er could see the very
Great happiness of the "Nil Admirari."

CI.

"Not to admire is all the art I know
 (Plain truth, dear Murray, needs few flowers of speech)
To make men happy, or to keep them so;"
 (So take it in the very words of Creech).
Thus Horace wrote, we all know, long ago;
 And thus Pope quotes the precept to re-teach
From his translation; but had *none admired*,
Would Pope have sung, or Horace been inspired?

CII.

Baba, when all the damsels were withdrawn,
 Motion'd to Juan to approach, and then
A second time desired him to kneel down,
 And kiss the lady's foot; which maxim when
He heard repeated, Juan with a frown
 Drew himself up to his full height again,
And said, "It grieved him, but he could not stoop
To any shoe, unless it shod the Pope."

CIII.

Baba, indignant at this ill-timed pride,
 Made fierce remonstrances, and then a threat
He mutter'd (but the last was given aside)
 About a bow-string—quite in vain; not yet
Would Juan bend, though 't were to Mahomet's bride:
 There's nothing in the world like *etiquette*
In kingly chambers or imperial halls,
As also at the race and county balls.

CIV.

He stood like Atlas, with a world of words
 About his ears, and nathless would not bend;
The blood of all his line's Castilian lords
 Boil'd in his veins, and rather than descend
To stain his pedigree a thousand swords
 A thousand times of him had made an end;
At length perceiving the "*foot*" could not stand,
Baba proposed that he should kiss the hand.

CV.

Here was an honourable compromise,
 A half-way house of diplomatic rest

Where they might meet in much more peaceful guise;
 And Juan now his willingness exprest,
To use all fit and proper courtesies;
 Adding, that this was commonest and best,
For through the South, the custom still commands
The gentleman to kiss the lady's hands.

CVI.

And he advanced, though with but a bad grace,
 Though on more *thorough-bred* or fairer fingers [37]
No lips e'er left their transitory trace:
 On such as these the lip too fondly lingers,
And for one kiss would fain imprint a brace,
 As you will see, if she you love shall bring hers
In contact; and sometimes even a fair stranger's
An almost twelvemonth's constancy endangers.

CVII.

The lady eyed him o'er and o'er, and bade
 Baba retire, which he obey'd in style,
As if well used to the retreating trade;
 And, taking hints in good part all the while,
He whisper'd Juan not to be afraid;
 And looking on him with a sort of smile,
Took leave, with such a face of satisfaction,
As good men wear who have done a virtuous action.

CVIII.

When he was gone, there was a sudden change:
 I know not what might be the lady's thought,
But o'er her bright brow flash'd a tumult strange,
 And into her clear cheek the blood was brought,
Blood-red as sunset summer clouds which range
 The verge of heaven; and in her large eyes wrought
A mixture of sensations, might be scann'd,
Of half voluptuousness and half command.

CIX.

Her form had all the softness of her sex,
 Her features all the sweetness of the devil,
When he put on the cherub to perplex
 Eve, and paved (God knows how) the road to evil;
The sun himself was scarce more free from specks
 Than she from aught at which the eye could cavil;
Yet, somehow, there was something somewhere wanting,
As if she rather *order'd* than was *granting*.—

CX.

Something imperial, or imperious, threw
 A chain o'er all she did; that is, a chain
Was thrown as 't were about the neck of you—
 And rapture's self will seem almost a pain
With aught which looks like despotism in view:
 Our souls at least are free, and 't is in vain
We would against them make the flesh obey—
The spirit in the end will have its way.

CXI.

Her very smile was haughty, though so sweet;
 Her very nod was not an inclination;
There was a self-will even in her small feet,
 As though they were quite conscious of her station—
They trod as upon necks; and to complete
 Her state (it is the custom of her nation),
A poniard deck'd her girdle, as the sign
She was a sultan's bride (thank Heaven, not mine!)

CXII.

"To hear and to obey" had been from birth
 The law of all around her: to fulfil
All phantasies which yielded joy or mirth,
 Had been her slaves' chief pleasure, as her will;
Her blood was high, her beauty scarce of earth:
 Judge, then, if her caprices e'er stood still;
Had she but been a Christian, I've a notion
We should have found out the "perpetual motion."

CXIII.

Whate'er she saw and coveted was brought;
 Whate'er she did *not* see, if she supposed
It might be seen, with diligence was sought,
 And when 't was found straightway the bargain closed:
There was no end unto the things she bought,
 Nor to the trouble which her fancies caused;
Yet even her tyranny had such a grace,
The women pardon'd all except her face.

CXIV.

Juan, the latest of her whims, had caught,
 Her eye in passing on his way to sale;
She order'd him directly to be bought,
 And Baba, who had ne'er been known to fail
In any kind of mischief to be wrought,
 At all such auctions knew how to prevail:
She had no prudence, but he had; and this
Explains the garb which Juan took amiss.

CXV.

His youth and features favour'd the disguise,
 And, should you ask how she, a sultan's bride,
Could risk or compass such strange phantasies,
 This I must leave sultanas to decide:
Emperors are only husbands in wives' eyes,
 And kings and consorts oft are mystified,
As we may ascertain with due precision,
Some by experience, others by tradition.

CXVI.

But to the main point, where we have been tending:—
 She now conceived all difficulties past,
And deem'd herself extremely condescending

When, being made her property at last,
Without more preface, in her blue eyes blending
Passion and power, a glance on him she cast,
And merely saying, "Christian, can'st thou love?"
Conceived that phrase was quite enough to move.

CXVII.

And so it was, in proper time and place;
But Juan, who had still his mind o'erflowing
With Haidée's isle and soft Ionian face,
Felt the warm blood, which in his face was glowing,

Rush back upon his heart, which filled apace,
And left his cheeks as pale as snow-drops blowing:
These words went through his soul like Arab-spears,
So that he spoke not, but burst into tears.

CXVIII.

She was a good deal shock'd; not shock'd at tears,
For women shed and use them at their liking;
But there is something when man's eye appears
Wet, still more disagreeable and striking:

A woman's tear-drop melts, a man's half sears,
 Like molten lead, as if you thrust a pike in
His heart to force it out, for (to be shorter)
To them 't is a relief, to us a torture.

CXIX.

And she would have consoled, but knew not how:
 Having no equals, nothing which had e'er
Infected her with sympathy till now,
 And never having dreamt what 't was to bear
Aught of a serious, sorrowing kind, although
 There might arise some pouting petty care
To cross her brow, she wonder'd how so near
Her eye another's eyes could shed a tear.

CXX.

But nature teaches more than power can spoil,
 And, when a *strong* although a strange sensation
Moves—female hearts are such a genial soil
 For kinder feelings, whatsoe'er their nation,
They naturally pour the "wine and oil,"
 Samaritans in every situation;
And thus Gulbeyaz, though she knew not why,
Felt an odd glistening moisture in her eye.

CXXI.

But tears must stop like all things else; and soon
 Juan, who for an instant had been moved
To such a sorrow by the intrusive tone
 Of one who dared to ask if "he *had* loved,"
Call'd back the stoic to his eyes, which shone
 Bright with the very weakness he reproved;
And although sensitive to beauty, he
Felt most indignant still at not being free.

CXXII.

Gulbeyaz, for the first time in her days,
 Was much embarrass'd, never having met
In all her life with aught save prayers and praise;
 And as she also risk'd her life to get
Him whom she meant to tutor in love's ways
 Into a comfortable tête-à-tête,
To lose the hour would make her quite a martyr,
And they had wasted now almost a quarter.

CXXIII.

I also would suggest the fitting time,
 To gentlemen in any such like case,
That is to say—in a meridian clime,
 With us there is more law given to the chase,
But here a small delay forms a great crime:
 So recollect that the extremest grace
Is just two minutes for your declaration—
A moment more would hurt your reputation.

CXXIV.

Juan's was good; and might have been still better,
 But he had got Haidée into his head:
However strange, he could not yet forget her,
 Which made him seem exceedingly ill-bred.
Gulbeyaz, who look'd on him as her debtor
 For having had him to her palace led,
Began to blush up to the eyes, and then
Grow deadly pale, and then blush back again.

CXXV.

At length, in an imperial way, she laid
 Her hand on his, and bending on him eyes,
Which needed not an empire to persuade,
 Look'd into his for love, where none replies:
Her brow grew black, but she would not upbraid,
 That being the last thing a proud woman tries;
She rose, and pausing one chaste moment, threw
Herself upon his breast, and there she grew.

CXXVI.

This was an awkward test, as Juan found,
 But he was steel'd by sorrow, wrath, and pride:
With gentle force her white arms he unwound,
 And seated her all drooping by his side,
Then rising haughtily he glanced around,
 And looking coldly in her face, he cried,
"The prison'd eagle will not pair, nor I
Serve a sultana's sensual phantasy.

CXXVII.

"Thou ask'st, if I can love? be this the proof
 How much I *have* loved—that I love not *thee!*
In this vile garb, the distaff, web, and woof,
 Were fitter for me: Love is for the free!
I am not dazzled by this splendid roof;
 Whate'er thy power, and great it seems to be;
Heads bow, knees bend, eyes watch around a throne,
And hands obey—our hearts are still our own."

CXXVIII.

This was a truth to us extremely trite;
 Not so to her, who ne'er had heard such things:
She deem'd her least command must yield delight,
 Earth being only made for queens and kings.
If hearts lay on the left side or the right
 She hardly knew, to such perfection brings
Legitimacy its born votaries, when
Aware of their due royal rights o'er men.

CXXIX.

Besides, as has been said, she was so fair
 As even in a much humbler lot had made
A kingdom or confusion any where,
 And also, as may be presumed, she laid
Some stress on charms, which seldom are, if e'er,
 By their possessors thrown into the shade:
She thought hers gave a double "right divine;"
And half of that opinion's also mine.

CXXX.

Remember, or (if you can not) imagine,
 Ye who have kept your chastity when young,
While some more desperate dowager has been waging
 Love with you, and been in the dog-days stung
By your refusal, recollect her raging!
 Or recollect all that was said or sung
On such a subject; then suppose the face
Of a young downright beauty in this case.

CXXXI.

Suppose,—but you already have supposed,
 The spouse of Potiphar, the Lady Booby,
Phædra, and all which story has disclosed
 Of good examples; pity that so few by
Poets and private tutors are exposed,
 To educate—ye youth of Europe—you by!
But when you have supposed the few we know,
You can't suppose Gulbeyaz' angry brow.

CXXXII.

A tigress robb'd of young, a lioness
 Or any interesting beast of prey,
Are similes at hand for the distress
 Of ladies who can not have their own way;
But though my turn will not be served with less,
 These don't express one half what I should say:
For what is stealing young ones, few or many,
To cutting short their hopes of having any?

CXXXIII.

The love of offspring's nature's general law,
 From tigresses and cubs to ducks and ducklings;
There's nothing whets the beak, or arms the claw,
 Like an invasion of their babes and sucklings;
And all who have seen a human nursery, saw
 How mothers love their children's squalls and chucklings;
This strong extreme effect (to tire no longer
Your patience) shows the cause must still be stronger.

CXXXIV.

If I said fire flash'd from Gulbeyaz' eyes,
 'Twere nothing—for her eyes flash'd always fire;
Or said her cheeks assumed the deepest dyes,
 I should but bring disgrace upon the dyer,
So supernatural was her passion's rise;
 For ne'er till now she knew a check'd desire:
Even ye who know what a check'd woman is
(Enough, God knows!) would much fall short of this.

CXXXV.

Her rage was but a minute's, and 't was well—
 A moment's more had slain her; but the while
It lasted t' was like a short glimpse of hell:
 Nought's more sublime than energetic bile,
Though horrible to see yet grand to tell,
 Like ocean warring 'gainst a rocky isle;
And the deep passions flashing through her form,
Made her a beautiful embodied storm.

CXXXVI.

A vulgar tempest 't were to a typhoon
 To match a common fury with her rage,
And yet she did not want to reach the moon,
 Like moderate Hotspur on the immortal page;
Her anger pitch'd into a lower tune,
 Perhaps the fault of her soft sex and age—
Her wish was but to "kill, kill, kill," like Lear's,
And then her thirst of blood was quench'd in tears.

CXXXVII.

A storm it raged, and like the storm it pass'd,
 Pass'd without words—in fact she could not speak;
And then her sex's shame broke in at last,
 A sentiment till then in her but weak,
But now it flow'd in natural and fast,
 As water through an unexpected leak,
For she felt humbled—and humiliation
Is sometimes good for people in her station.

CXXXVIII.

It teaches them that they are flesh and blood,
 It also gently hints to them that others,
Although of clay, are yet not quite of mud;
 That urns and pipkins are but fragile brothers,
And works of the same pottery, bad or good,
 Though not all born of the same sires and mothers:
It teaches—Heaven knows only what it teaches,
But sometimes it may mend, and often reaches.

CXXXIX.

Her first thought was to cut off Juan's head;
 Her second, to cut only his—acquaintance;
Her third, to ask him where he had been bred;
 Her fourth, to rally him into repentance;
Her fifth, to call her maids and go to bed;
 Her sixth, to stab herself; her seventh, to sentence
The lash to Baba:—but her grand resource
Was to sit down again, and cry, of course.

CXL.

She thought to stab herself, but then she had
 The dagger close at hand, which made it awkward;
For Eastern stays are little made to pad,
 So that a poniard pierces if 't is stuck hard:
She thought of killing Juan—but, poor lad!
 Though he deserved it well for being so backward,
The cutting off his head was not the art
Most likely to attain her aim—his heart.

CXLI.

Juan was moved: he had made up his mind
 To be impaled, or quarter'd as a dish
For dogs, or to be slain with pangs refined,
 Or thrown to lions, or made baits for fish,
And thus heroically stood resign'd,
 Rather than sin—except to his own wish:
But all his great preparatives for dying
Dissolved like snow before a woman crying.

CXLII.

As through his palms Bob Acres' valour oozed,
 So Juan's virtue ebb'd, I know not how;
And first he wonder'd why he had refused;
 And then, if matters could be made up now;
And next his savage virtue he accused,
 Just as a friar may accuse his vow,
Or as a dame repents her of her oath,
Which mostly ends in some small breach of both.

CXLIII.

So he began to stammer some excuses;
 But words are not enough in such a matter,
Although you borrow'd all that e'er the muses
 Have sung, or even a Dandy's dandiest chatter,
Or all the figures Castlereagh abuses;
 Just as a languid smile began to flatter
His peace was making, but before he ventured
Further, old Baba rather briskly enter'd.

CXLIV.

"Bride of the Sun! and Sister of the Moon!"
 ('Twas thus he spake,) "and Empress of the Earth!
Whose frown would put the spheres all out of tune,
 Whose smile makes all the planets dance with mirth,
Your slave brings tidings—he hopes not too soon—
 Which your sublime attention may be worth:
The Sun himself has sent me like a ray,
To hint that he is coming up this way."

CXLV.

"Is it," exclaim'd Gulbeyaz, "as you say?
 I wish to Heaven he would not shine till morning!
But bid my women form the milky way.
 Hence, my old comet! give the stars due warning—
And, Christian! mingle with them as you may,
 And as you'd have me pardon your past scorning——"
Here they were interrupted by a humming
Sound, and then by a cry, "The Sultan's coming!"

CXLVI.

First came her damsels, a decorous file,
 And then his Highness' eunuchs, black and white;
The train might reach a quarter of a mile:
 His Majesty was always so polite
As to announce his visits a long while
 Before he came, especially at night;
For being the last wife of the Emperour,
She was of course the favourite of the four.

CXLVII.

His Highness was a man of solemn port,
 Shawl'd to the nose, and bearded to the eyes,
Snatch'd from a prison to preside at court,
 His lately bowstrung brother caused his rise,
He was as good a sovereign of the sort
 As any mention'd in the histories
Of Cantemir, or Knolles, where few shine
Save Solyman, the glory of their line.[38]

CXLVIII.

He went to mosque in state, and said his prayers
 With more than "Oriental scrupulosity;"
He left to his vizier all state affairs,
 And show'd but little royal curiosity;
I know not if he had domestic cares—
 No process proved connubial animosity;
Four wives, and twice five hundred maids, unseen,
Were ruled as calmly as a Christian queen.

CXLIX.

If now and then there happen'd a slight slip,
 Little was heard of criminal or crime;
The story scarcely pass'd a single lip—
 The sack and sea had settled all in time,
From which the secret nobody could rip:
 The public knew no more than does this rhyme;
No scandals made the daily press a curse—
Morals were better, and the fish no worse.

CL.

He saw with his own eyes the moon was round,
 Was also certain that the earth was square,
Because he had journey'd fifty miles, and found
 No sign that it was circular any where;
His empire also was without a bound:
 'T is true, a little troubled here and there,
By rebel pachas, and encroaching giaours,
But then they never came to "the Seven Towers;"

CLI.

Except in shape of envoys, who were sent
 To lodge there when a war broke out, according
To the true law of nations, which ne'er meant
 Those scoundrels, who have never had a sword in
Their dirty diplomatic hands, to vent
 Their spleen in making strife, and safely wording
Their lies, yclep'd despatches, without risk or
The singeing of a single inky whisker.

CLII.

He had fifty daughters and four dozen sons,
 Of whom all such as came of age were stow'd,
The former in a palace, where like nuns
 They lived till some bashaw was sent abroad,
When she, whose turn it was, was wed at once,
 Sometimes at six years old—though this seems odd,
'T is true; the reason is, that the bashaw
Must make a present to his sire-in-law.

CLIII.

His sons were kept in prison, till they grew
 Of years to fill a bowstring or the throne,
One or the other, but which of the two
 Could yet be known unto the fates alone;
Meantime the education they went through
 Was princely, as the proofs have always shown:
So that the heir-apparent still was found
No less deserving to be hang'd than crown'd.

CLIV.

His Majesty saluted his fourth spouse
 With all the ceremonies of his rank,
Who clear'd her sparkling eyes and smooth'd her brows,
 As suits a matron who has play'd a prank;
These must seem doubly mindful of their vows,
 To save the credit of their breaking bank:
To no men are such cordial greetings given,
As those whose wives have made them fit for heaven.

CLV.

His Highness cast around his great black eyes,
 And looking, as he always look'd, perceived
Juan amongst the damsels in disguise,
 At which he seem'd no whit surprised nor grieved,
But just remark'd with air sedate and wise,
 While still a fluttering sigh Gulbeyaz heaved,
"I see you've bought another girl; 'tis pity
That a mere Christian should be half so pretty."

CLVI.

This compliment, which drew all eyes upon
The new-bought virgin, made her blush and shake.
Her comrades, also, thought themselves undone:
Oh! Mahomet! that his Majesty should take
Such notice of a giaour, while scarce to one
Of them his lips imperial ever spake!
There was a general whisper, toss, and wriggle,
But etiquette forbade them all to giggle.

CLVII.

The Turks do well to shut—at least, sometimes—
The women up—because, in sad reality,
Their chastity in these unhappy climes
Is not a thing of that astringent quality,
Which, in the North, prevents precocious crimes,
And makes our snow less pure than our morality;
The sun, which yearly melts the polar ice,
Has quite the contrary effect on vice.

CLVIII.

Thus in the East they are extremely strict,
And wedlock and a padlock mean the same;
Excepting only when the former 's pick'd
It ne'er can be replaced in proper frame;
Spoilt, as a pipe of claret is when prick'd:
But then their own polygamy 's to blame;
Why don't they knead two virtuous souls for life
Into that moral centaur, man and wife?

CLIX.

Thus far our chronicle; and now we pause,
Though not for want of matter; but 't is time,
According to the ancient epic laws,
To slacken sail, and anchor with our rhyme.
Let this fifth canto meet with due applause,
The sixth shall have a touch of the sublime;
Meanwhile, as Homer sometimes sleeps, perhaps
You 'll pardon to my muse a few short naps.

PREFACE TO CANTOS VI. VII. AND VIII.

The details of the siege of Ismail in two of the following cantos (*i. e.* the seventh and eighth) are taken from a French work, entitled "Histoire de la Nouvelle Russie." Some of the incidents attributed to Don Juan really occurred, particularly the circumstance of his saving the infant, which was the actual case of the late Duc de Richelieu, then a young volunteer in the Russian service, and afterwards the founder and benefactor of Odessa, where his name and memory can never cease to be regarded with reverence.

In the course of these cantos a stanza or two will be found relative to the late Marquis of Londonderry, but written some time before his decease. Had that person's oligarchy died with him, they would have been suppressed; as it is, I am aware of nothing in the manner of his death or of his life to prevent the free expression of the opinions of all whom his whole existence was consumed in endeavouring to enslave. That he was an amiable man in *private* life, may or may not be true; but with this the public have nothing to do; and as to lamenting his death, it will be time enough when Ireland has ceased to mourn or his birth. As a minister, I, for one of millions, looked upon him as the most despotic in intention, and the weakest in intellect, that ever tyrannised over a country. It is the first time indeed, since the Normans, that England has been insulted by a *minister* (at least) who could not speak English, and that Parliament permitted itself to be dictated to in the language of Mrs. Malaprop.

Of the manner of his death little need be said, except that if a poor radical, such as Waddington or Watson, had cut his throat, he would have been buried in a cross-road, with the usual appurtenances of the stake and mallet. But the minister was an elegant lunatic—a sentimental suicide —he merely cut the "carotid artery," (blessings on their learning!) and lo! the pageant and the Abbey! and the "syllables of dolour yelled forth" by the newspapers—and the harangue of the Coroner in an eulogy over the bleeding body of the deceased—(an Anthony worthy of such a Cæsar)—and the nauseous and atrocious cant of a degraded crew of conspirators against all that is sincere and honourable. In his death he was necessarily one of two things by the *law*[39]—a felon or a madman—and in either case no great subject for panegyric. In his life he was—what the world knows, and half of it will feel for years to come, unless his death prove a "moral lesson" to the surviving Sejani of Europe.[40] It may at least serve as some consolation to the nations, that their oppressors are not happy, and in some instances judge so justly of their own actions, as to anticipate the sentence of mankind. Let us hear no more of this man; and let Ireland remove the ashes of her Grattan from the sanctuary of Westminster. Shall the patriot of humanity repose by the Werther of politics!!!

With regard to the objections which have been made on another score to the already published cantos of this poem, I shall content myself with two quotations from Voltaire: —"La pudeur s'est enfuite de cœurs, et s'est refugiée sur les lèvres." . . . "Plus les mœurs sont dépravés, plus les expressions deviennent mesurées; on croit regagner en langage ce qu'on a perdu en vertu."

This is the real fact, as applicable to the degraded and hypocritical mass which leavens the present English generation, and is the only answer they deserve. The hackneyed and lavished title of Blasphemer—which, with Radical, Liberal, Jacobin, Reformer, &c., are the changes which the hirelings are daily ringing in the ears of those who will listen—should be welcome to all who recollect on *whom* it was originally bestowed. Socrates and Jesus Christ were put to death publicly as *blasphemers*, and so have been, and may be, many who dare to oppose the most notorious abuses of the name of God and the mind of man. But persecution is not refutation, nor even triumph: the "wretched infidel," as he is called, is probably happier in his prison than the proudest of his assailants. With his opinions I have nothing to do—they may be right or wrong—but he has suffered for them, and that very suffering for conscience' sake will make more proselytes to deism than the example of heterodox[41] prelates to Christianity, suicide statesmen to oppression, or overpensioned homicides to the impious alliance which insults the world with the name of "Holy!" I have no wish to trample on the dishonoured or the dead; but it would be well if the adherents to the classes from whence those persons sprung, should abate a little of the *cant* which is the crying sin of this double-dealing and false-speaking time of selfish spoilers, and—but enough for the present.

CANTO VI.

I.

"There is a tide in the affairs of men
 Which,—taken at the flood,"—you know the
 rest,
And most of us have found it now and then:
 At least we think so, though but few have
 guess'd
The moment, till too late to come again.
 But no doubt everything is for the best—
Of which the surest sign is in the end:
When things are at the worst they sometimes
 mend.

II.

There is a tide in the affairs of women
 Which, taken at the flood, leads—God knows where:
Those navigators must be able seamen
 Whose charts lay down its current to a hair;
Not all the reveries of Jacob Behmen
 With its strange whirls and eddies can compare:
Men with their heads reflect on this and that—
But women with their hearts on Heaven knows what!

III.

And yet a headlong, headstrong, downright she,
 Young, beautiful, and daring—who would risk
A throne, the world, the universe, to be
 Beloved in her own way, and rather whisk
The stars from out the sky, than not be free
 As are the billows when the breeze is brisk—
Though such a she's a devil (if that there be one),
Yet she would make full many a Manichean.

IV.

Thrones, worlds, et cetera, are so oft upset
 By commonest ambition, that when passion
O'erthrows the same, we readily forget,
 Or at the least forgive, the loving rash one.
If Anthony be well remember'd yet,
 'T is not his conquests keep his name in fashion,
But Actium, lost for Cleopatra's eyes,
Out balances all Cæsar's victories.

V.

He died at fifty for a queen of forty;
 I wish their years had been fifteen and twenty,
For then wealth, kingdoms, worlds are but a sport.—I
 Remember when, though I had no great plenty
Of worlds to lose, yet still, to pay my court, I
 Gave what I had—a heart: as the world went, I
Gave what was worth a world; for worlds could never
Restore me those pure feelings, gone for ever.

VI.

'T was the boy's "mite," and like the "widow's," may
 Perhaps be weigh'd hereafter, if not now;
But whether such things do or do not weigh,
 All who have loved, or love, will still allow
Life has nought like it. God is love, they say,
 And Love 's a god, or was before the brow
Of earth was wrinkled by the sins and tears
Of—but Chronology best knows the years.

VII.

We left our hero and third heroine in
 A kind of state more awkward than uncommon,
For gentlemen must sometimes risk their skin
 For that sad tempter, a forbidden woman:
Sultans too much abhor this sort of sin,
 And don't agree at all with the wise Roman,
Heroic, stoic Cato, the sententious,
Who lent his lady to his friend Hortensius.[42]

VIII.

I know Gulbeyaz was extremely wrong;
 I own it, I deplore it, I condemn it;
But I detest all fiction even in song,
 And so must tell the truth, howe'er you blame it.
Her reason being weak, her passions strong,
 She thought that her lord's heart (even could she claim it)
Was scarce enough; for he had fifty-nine
Years, and a fifteen-hundredth concubine.

IX.

I am not, like Cassio, "an arithmetician,"
 But by "the bookish theoric" it appears,
If 't is summ'd up with feminine precision,
 That, adding to the account his Highness' years,
The fair Sultana err'd from inanition;
 For, were the Sultan just to all his dears,
She could but claim the fifteen-hundreth part
Of what should be monopoly—the heart.

X.

It is observed that ladies are litigious
 Upon all legal objects of possession,
And not the least so when they are religious,
 Which doubles what they think of the transgression;
With suits and prosecutions they besiege us,
 As the tribunals show through many a session,
When they suspect that any one goes shares
In that to which the law makes them sole heirs.

XI.

Now, if this holds good in a Christian land,
 The heathen also, though with lesser latitude,
Are apt to carry things with a high hand,
 And take, what kings call "an imposing attitude;"
And for their rights connubial make a stand,
 When their liege husbands treat them with ingratitude:
And as four wives must have quadruple claims,
The Tigris hath its jealousies like Thames.

XII.

Gulbeyaz was the fourth, and (as I said)
 The favourite; but what's favour amongst four?
Polygamy may well be held in dread,
 Not only as a sin, but as a *bore:*
Most wise men with *one* moderate woman wed,
 Will scarcely find philosophy for more;
And all (except Mahometans) forbear
To make the nuptial couch a "Bed of Ware."

XIII.

His Highness, the sublimest of mankind,—
So styled, according to the usual forms
Of every monarch, till they are consign'd
To those sad hungry jacobins the worms,[43]
Who on the very loftiest kings have dined,—
His Highness gazed upon Gulbeyaz' charms,
Expecting all the welcome of a lover
(A "Highland welcome" all the wide world over).[44]

XIV.

Now here we should distinguish; for howe'er
Kisses, sweet words, embraces, and all that,
May look like what is—neither here nor there,
They are put on as easily as a hat,
Or rather bonnet, which the fair sex wear,
Trimm'd either heads or hearts to decorate,
Which form an ornament, but no more part
Of heads, than their caresses of the heart.

XV.

A slight blush, a soft tremor, a calm kind
Of gentle feminine delight, and shown
More in the eyelids than the eyes, resign'd
Rather to hide what pleases most unknown,
Are the best tokens (to a modest mind)
Of love, when seated on his loveliest throne,
A sincere woman's breast,—for over-*warm*
Or over-*cold* annihilates the charm.

XVI.

For over-warmth, if false, is worse than truth;
If true, 't is no great lease of its own fire;
For no one, save in very early youth,
Would like (I think) to trust all to desire,
Which is but a precarious bond, in sooth,
And apt to be transferr'd to the first buyer
At a sad discount: while your over-chilly
Women, on t' other hand, seem somewhat silly.

XVII.

That is, we cannot pardon their bad taste,
For so it seems to lovers swift or slow,
Who fain would have a mutual flame confess'd,
And see a sentimental passion glow,
Even were St. Francis' paramour their guest,
In his monastic concubine of snow;—[45]
In short, the maxim for the amorous tribe is
Horatian, "Medio tu tutissimus ibis."

XVIII.

The "tu" 's *too* much,—but let it stand,—the verse
Requires it,—that 's to say, the English rhyme,
And not the pink of old hexameters;
But, after all, there 's neither tune or time
In the last line, which cannot well be worse,
And was thrust in to close the octave's chime:
I own no prosody can ever rate it
As a rule, but *truth* may, if you translate it.

XIX.

If fair Gulbeyaz overdid her part,
I know not—it succeeded, and success
Is much in most things, not less in the heart
Than other articles of female dress.
Self-love in man, too, beats all female art;
They lie, we lie, all lie, but love no less:
And no one virtue yet, except starvation,
Could stop that worst of vices—propagation.

XX.

We leave this royal couple to repose:
A bed is not a throne, and they may sleep,
Whate'er their dreams be, if of joys or woes:
Yet disappointed joys are woes as deep
As any man's clay mixture undergoes.
Our least of sorrows are such as we weep;
'T is the vile daily drop on drop which wears
The soul out (like the stone) with petty cares

XXI.

A scolding wife, a sullen son, a bill
To pay, unpaid, protested, or discounted
At a per-centage; a child cross, dog ill,
A favourite horse fallen lame just as he 's mounted,
A bad old woman making a worse will,
Which leaves you minus of the cash you counted
As certain;—these are paltry things, and yet
I 've rarely seen the man they did not fret.

XXII.

I 'm a philosopher; confound them all!
Bills, beasts, and men, and—no! *not* womankind!
With one good hearty curse I vent my gall,
And then my stoicism leaves nought behind
Which it can either pain or evil call,
And I can give my whole soul up to mind;
Though what *is* soul or mind, their birth or growth,
Is more than I know—the deuce take them both!

XXIII.

So now all things are d—n'd one feels at ease,
As after reading Athanasius' curse,
Which doth your true believer so much please:
I doubt if any now could make it worse
O'er his worst enemy when at his knees,
'T is so sententious, positive, and terse,
And decorates the book of Common Prayer,
As doth a rainbow the just clearing air.

XXIV.

Gulbeyaz and her lord were sleeping, or
At least one of them!—oh, the heavy night,
When wicked wives, who love some bachelor,
Lie down in dudgeon to sigh for the light

Of the gray morning, and look vainly for
 Its twinkle through the lattice dusky quite—
To toss, to tumble, doze, revive, and quake
Lest their too lawful bed-fellow should wake!

XXV.

These are beneath the canopy of heaven,
 Also beneath the canopy of beds,
Four-posted and silk-curtain'd, which are given
 For rich men and their brides to lay their heads
Upon, in sheets white as what bards call "driven
 Snow." Well! 't is all hap-hazard when one weds,
Gulbeyaz was an empress, but had been
Perhaps as wretched if a *peasant's quean*.

XXVI.

Don Juan in his feminine disguise,
 With all the damsels in their long array,
Had bow'd themselves before th' imperial eyes,
 And at the usual signal ta'en their way
Back to their chambers, those long galleries
 In the seraglio, where the ladies lay
Their delicate limbs; a thousand bosoms there
Beating for love, as the caged bird's for air.

XXVII.

I love the sex, and sometimes would reverse
 The tyrant's wish, "that mankind only had [46]
One neck, which he with one fell stroke might pierce:"
 My wish is quite as wide, but not so bad,
And much more tender on the whole than fierce;
 It being (not *now*, but only while a lad)
That womankind had but one rosy mouth,
To kiss them all at once from North to South.

XXVIII.

Oh, enviable Briareus; with thy hands
 And heads, if thou hadst all things multiplied
In such proportion!—But my Muse withstands
 The giant thought of being a Titan's bride,
Or travelling in Patagonian lands;
 So let us back to Lilliput, and guide
Our hero through the labyrinth of love
In which we left him several lines above.

XXIX.

He went forth with the lovely Odalisques, [47]
 At the given signal join'd to their array;
And though he certainly ran many risks,
 Yet he could not at times keep, by the way,
(Although the consequences of such frisks
 Are worse than the worst damages men pay
In moral England, where the thing 's a tax,)
From ogling all their charms from breasts to backs.

XXX.

Still he forgot not his disguise:—along
 The galleries from room to room they walk'd,
A virgin-like and edifying throng,
 By eunuchs flank'd; while at their head there stalk'd
A dame who kept up discipline among
 The female ranks, so that none stirr'd or talk'd,
Without her sanction, on their she-parades:
Her title was "the Mother of the Maids."

XXXI.

Whether she was a "mother," I know not,
 Or whether they were "maids" who call'd her mother;
But this is her seraglio title, got
 I know not how, but good as any other;
So Cantemir can tell you, or De Tott:
 Her office was to keep aloof or smother
All bad propensities in fifteen hundred
Young women, and correct them when they blunder'd.

XXXII.

A goodly sinecure, no doubt! but made
 More easy by the absence of all men—
Except his Majesty,—who, with her aid,
 And guards, and bolts, and walls, and now and then
A slight example, just to cast a shade
 Along the rest, contrived to keep this den
Of beauties cool as an Italian convent,
Where all the passions have, alas! but one vent.

XXXIII.

And what is that? Devotion, doubtless—how
 Could you ask such a question?—but we will
Continue. As I said, this goodly row
 Of ladies of all countries at the will
Of one good man, with stately march and slow,
 Like water-lilies floating down a rill—
Or rather lake—for *rills* do *not* run *slowly*,—
Paced on most maidenlike and melancholy.

XXXIV.

But when they reach'd their own apartments, there,
 Like birds, or boys, or bedlamites broke loose,
Waves at spring-tide, or women any where
 When freed from bonds (which are of no great use
After all), or like Irish at a fair,
 Their guards being gone, and as it were a truce
Establish'd between them and bondage, they
Began to sing, dance, chatter, smile, and play.

XXXV.

Their talk, of course, ran most on the new comer;
 Her shape, her hair her air, her everything:

Some thought her dress did not so much become her,
Or wonder'd at her ears without a ring;
Some said her years were getting nigh their summer
Others contended they were but in spring;
Some thought her rather masculine in height,
While others wish'd that she had been so quite.

XXXVI.

But no one doubted on the whole, that she
Was what her dress bespoke, a damsel fair,
And fresh, and "beautiful exceedingly,"
Who with the brightest Georgians might compare:[48]
They wonder'd how Gulbeyaz, too, could be
So silly as to buy slaves who might share
(If that his Highness wearied of his bride)
Her throne and power, and every thing beside.

XXXVII.

But what was strangest in this virgin crew,
Although her beauty was enough to vex,
After the first investigating view,
They all found out as few, or fewer, specks
In the fair form of their companion new,
Than is the custom of the gentle sex,
When they survey, with Christian eyes or Heathen,
In a new face, "the ugliest creature breathing."

XXXVIII.

And yet they had their little jealousies,
Like all the rest; but upon this occasion,
Whether there are such things as sympathies
Without our knowledge or our approbation,
Although they could not see through his disguise,
All felt a soft kind of concatenation,
Like magnetism, or devilism, or what
You please—we will not quarrel about that:

XXXIX.

But certain 't is they all felt for their new
Companion something newer still, as 't were
A sentimental friendship through and through,
Extremely pure, which made them all concur
In wishing her their sister, save a few
Who wish'd they had a brother just like her,
Whom, if they were at home in sweet Circassia,
They would prefer to Padisha or Pacha.[49]

XL.

Of those who had most genius for this sort
Of sentimental friendship, there were three,
Lolah, Katinka, and Dudù; in short,
(To save description) fair as fair can be
Were they, according to the best report,
Though differing in stature and degree,
And clime and time, and country and complexion;
They all alike admired their new connexion.

XLI.

Lolah was dusk as India, and as warm;
Katinka was a Georgian, white and red,
With great blue eyes, a lovely hand and arm,
And feet so small they scarce seem'd made to tread,
But rather skim the earth; while Dudù's form
Look'd more adapted to be put to bed,
Being somewhat large, and languishing, and lazy,
Yet of a beauty that would drive you crazy.

XLII.

A kind of sleepy Venus seem'd Dudù,
Yet very fit to "murder sleep" in those
Who gazed upon her cheek's transcendent hue,
Her attic forehead, and her Phidian nose:
Few angles were there in her form, 't is true,
Thinner she might have been, and yet scarce lose;
Yet, after all, 't would puzzle to say where
It would not spoil some separate charm to *pare*.

XLIII.

She was not violently lively, but
Stole on your spirit like a May-day breaking;
Her eyes were not too sparkling, yet, half-shut,
They put beholders in a tender taking;
She look'd (this simile 's quite new) just cut
From marble, like Pygmalion's statue waking,
The mortal and the marble still at strife,
And timidly expanding into life.

XLIV.

Lolah demanded the new damsel's name—
"Juanna."—Well, a pretty name enough.
Katinka ask'd her also whence she came—
"From Spain."—"But where *is* Spain?"—"Don't ask such stuff,
Nor show your Georgian ignorance—for shame!"
Said Lolah, with an accent rather rough,
To poor Katinka: "Spain 's an island near
Morocco, betwixt Egypt and Tangier."

XLV.

Dudù said nothing, but sat down beside
Juanna, playing with her veil or hair;
And looking at her steadfastly, she sigh'd,
As if she pitied her for being there,
A pretty stranger without friend or guide,
And all abash'd, too, at the general stare
Which welcomes hapless strangers in all places,
With kind remarks upon their mien and faces.

XLVI.

But here the Mother of the Maids drew near,
With, "Ladies, it is time to go to rest.
I'm puzzled what to do with you, my dear,"
She added to Juanna, their new guest

"Your coming has been unexpected here,
 And every couch is occupied; you had best
Partake of mine; but by to-morrow early
We will have all things settled for you fairly."

XLVII.

Here Lolah interposed—"Mamma, you know
 You don't sleep soundly, and I cannot bear
That anybody should disturb you so;
 I'll take Juanna; we're a slenderer pair
Than you would make the half of;—don't say no:
 And I of your young charge will take due care."
But here Katinka interfered, and said,
"She also had compassion and a bed."

XLVIII.

"Besides, I hate to sleep alone," quoth she.
 The matron frown'd: "Why so?"—"For fear of ghosts,"
Replied Katinka; "I am sure I see
 A phantom upon each of the four posts;
And then I have the worst dreams that can be,
 Of Guebres, Giaours, and Ginns, and Gouls in hosts."
The dame replied, "Between your dreams and you,
I fear Juanna's dreams would be but few.

XLIX.

"You, Lolah, must continue still to lie
 Alone, for reasons which don't matter; you
The same, Katinka, until by and by;
 And I shall place Juanna with Dudù,
Who's quiet, inoffensive, silent, shy,
 And will not toss and chatter the night through.
What say you, child?"—Dudù said nothing, as
Her talents were of the more silent class;

L.

But she rose up, and kiss'd the matron's brow
 Between the eyes, and Lolah on both cheeks,
Katinka, too; and with a gentle bow
 (Curt'sies are neither used by Turks nor Greeks)
She took Juanna by the hand to show
 Their place of rest, and left to both their piques,
The others pouting at the matron's preference
Of Dudù, though they held their tongues from deference.

LI.

It was a spacious chamber (Oda is
 The Turkish title), and ranged round the wall
Were couches, toilets—and much more than this
 I might describe, as I have seen it all,
But it suffices—little was amiss;
 'Twas on the whole a nobly furnish'd hall,
With all things ladies want, save one or two,
And even those were nearer than they knew.

LII.

Dudù, as has been said, was a sweet creature,
 Not very dashing, but extremely winning,
With the most regulated charms of feature
 Which painters cannot catch like faces sinning
Against proportion—the wild strokes of nature
 Which they hit off at once in the beginning,
Full of expression, right or wrong, that strike,
And pleasing, or unpleasing, still are like.

LIII.

But she was a soft landscape of mild earth,
 Where all was harmony, and calm, and quiet,
Luxuriant, budding; cheerful without mirth,
 Which, if not happiness, is much more nigh it
Than are your mighty passions and so forth,
 Which some call "the sublime:" I wish they'd try it:
I've seen your stormy seas and stormy women,
And pity lovers rather more than seamen.

LIV.

But she was pensive more than melancholy,
 And serious more than pensive, and serene
It may be, more than either—not unholy
 Her thoughts, at least till now, appear to have been.
The strangest thing was, beauteous, she was wholly
 Unconscious, albeit turn'd of quick seventeen,
That she was fair, or dark, or short, or tall;
She never thought about herself at all.

LV.

And therefore was she kind and gentle as
 The Age of Gold (when gold was yet unknown,
By which its nomenclature came to pass;
 Thus most appropriately has been shown
"Lucus à *non* lucendo," *not* what *was*,
 But *was not;* a sort of style that's grown
Extremely common in this age, whose metal
The devil may decompose, but never settle:

LVII

I think it may be of "Corinthian Brass,"
 Which was a mixture of all metals, but
The brazen uppermost). Kind reader! pass
 This long parenthesis: I could not shut
It sooner for the soul of me, and class
 My faults even with your own; which meaneth, Put
A kind construction upon them and me:
But *that* you won't—then don't—I am not less free.

LVII.

'Tis time we should return to plain narration,
 And thus my narrative proceeds:—Dudù,

With every kindness, short of ostentation,
 Show'd Juan, or Juanna, through and through
This labyrinth of females, and each station
 Described—what's strange—in words extremely few:
I have but one simile, and that's a blunder,
For wordless woman, which is *silent* thunder.

LVIII.

And next she gave her (I say *her*, because
 The gender still was epicene, at least
In outward show, which is a saving clause)
 An outline of the customs of the East,
With all their chaste integrity of laws,
 By which the more a harem is increased,
The stricter doubtless grow the vestal duties
Of any supernumerary beauties.

LIX.

And then she gave Juanna a chaste kiss:
 Dudù was fond of kissing—which I'm sure
That nobody can ever take amiss,
 Because 'tis pleasant, so that it be pure,
And between females means no more than this—
 That they have nothing better near, or newer,
"Kiss" rhymes to "bliss" in fact as well as verse—
I wish it never led to something worse.

LX.

In perfect innocence she then unmade
 Her toilet, which cost little, for she was
A child of Nature, carelessly array'd:
 If fond of a chance ogle at her glass,
'Twas like the fawn, which, in the lake display'd,
 Beholds her own shy, shadowy image pass,
When first she starts, and then returns to peep,
Admiring this new native of the deep.

LXI.

And one by one her articles of dress
 Were laid aside; but not before she offer'd
Her aid to fair Juanna, whose excess
 Of modesty declined the assistance proffer'd:
Which pass'd well off—as she could do no less;
 Though by this politesse she rather suffer'd,
Pricking her fingers with those cursèd pins,
Which surely were invented for our sins,—

LXII.

Making a woman like a porcupine,
 Not to be rashly touch'd. But still more dread,
Oh ye! whose fate it is, as once 'twas mine,
 In early youth, to turn a lady's maid;—
I did my very boyish best to shine
 In tricking her out for a masquerade:
The pins were placed sufficiently, but not
Stuck all exactly in the proper spot.

LXIII.

But these are foolish things to all the wise,
 And I love wisdom more than she loves me;
My tendency is to philosophise
 On most things, from a tyrant to a tree;
But still the spouseless virgin *Knowledge* flies.
 What are we? and whence came we? what shall be
Our *ultimate* existence? what's our present?
Are questions answerless, and yet incessant.

LXIV.

There was deep silence in the chamber: dim
 And distant from each other burn'd the lights,
And slumber hovered o'er each lovely limb
 Of the fair occupants: if there be sprites,
They should have walk'd there in their sprightliest trim,
 By way of change from their sepulchral sites,
And shown themselves as ghosts of better taste
Than haunting some old ruin or wild waste.

LXV.

Many and beautiful lay those around,
 Like flowers of different hue, and clime, and root,
In some exotic garden sometimes found,
 With cost, and care, and warmth induced to shoot.
One with her auburn tresses lightly bound,
 And fair brows gently drooping, as the fruit
Nods from the tree, was slumbering with soft breath,
And lips apart, which show'd the pearls beneath.

LXVI.

One with her flush'd cheek laid on her white arm,
 And raven ringlets gather'd in dark crowd
Above her brow, lay dreaming soft and warm;
 And smiling through her dream, as through a cloud
The moon breaks, half unveil'd each further charm,
 As, slightly stirring in her snowy shroud,
Her beauties seized the unconscious hour of night
All bashfully to struggle into light.

LXVII.

This is no bull, although it sounds so; for
 'Twas night, but there were lamps, as hath been said.
A third's all-pallid aspect offered more
 The traits of sleeping sorrow, and betray'd
Through the heaved breast the dream of some far shore
 Belovèd and deplored; while slowly stray'd
(As night-dew, on a cypress glittering, tinges
 The black bough) tear-drops through her eyes' dark fringes.

LXVIII.

A fourth as marble, statue-like, and still,
 Lay in a breathless, hush'd, and stony sleep
White, cold, and pure, as looks a frozen rill,
 Or the snow minaret on an Alpine steep,
Or Lot's wife done in salt,—or what you will ;—
 My similes are gather'd in a heap,
So pick and choose—perhaps you'll be content
With a carved lady on a monument.

LXIX.

And, lo! a fifth appears ;—and what is she?
 A lady of a "certain age," which means
Certainly agèd—what her years might be
 I know not, never counting past their teens ;

But there she slept, not quite so fair to see,
As ere that awful period intervenes
Which lays both men and women on the shelf,
To meditate upon their sins and self.

LXX.

But all this time how slept, or dream'd, Dudù?
With strict inquiry I could ne'er discover,
And scorn to add a syllable untrue;
But ere the middle watch was hardly over,
Just when the fading lamps waned dim and blue,
And phantoms hover'd, or might seem to hover,
To those who like their company, about
The apartment, on a sudden she scream'd out:

LXXI.

And that so loudly, that upstarted all
The Oda, in a general commotion:
Matron and maids, and those whom you may call
Neither, came crowding like the waves of ocean,
One on the other, throughout the whole hall,
All trembling, wondering, without the least notion
More than I have myself of what could make
The calm Dudù so turbulently wake.

LXXII.

But wide awake she was, and round her bed,
With floating draperies and with flying hair,
With eager eyes, and light but hurried tread,
And bosoms, arms, and ankles glancing bare,
And bright as any meteor ever bred
By the North Pole,—they sought her cause of care,
For she seem'd agitated, flush'd, and frighten'd,
Her eye dilated and her colour heighten'd.

LXXIII.

But what is strange—and a strong proof how great
A blessing is sound sleep—Juanna lay
As fast as ever husband by his mate
In holy matrimony snores away.
Not all the clamour broke her happy state
Of slumber, ere they shook her,—so they say,
At least,—and then she, too, unclosed her eyes,
And yawn'd a good deal with discreet surprise.

LXXIV.

And now commenced a strict investigation,
Which, as all spoke at once, and more than once
Conjecturing, wondering, asking a narration,
Alike might puzzle either wit or dunce
To answer in a very clear oration.
Dudù had never passed for wanting sense,
But, being "no orator as Brutus is,"
Could not at first expound what was amiss.

LXXV.

At length she said, that in a slumber sound
She dream'd a dream, of walking in a wood—
A "wood obscure," like that where Dante found[50]
Himself in at the age when all grow good;
Life's half-way house, where dames with virtue crown'd
Run much less risk of lovers turning rude;
And that this wood was full of pleasant fruits,
And trees of goodly growth and spreading roots;

LXXVI.

And in the midst a golden apple grew,—
A most prodigious pippin—but it hung
Rather too high and distant; that she threw
Her glances on it, and then, longing, flung
Stones, and whatever she could pick up, to
Bring down the fruit, which still perversely clung
To its own bough, and dangled yet in sight,
But always at a most provoking height;—

LXXVII.

That on a sudden, when she least had hope,
It fell down of its own accord before
Her feet; that her first movement was to stoop
And pick it up, and bite it to the core;
That just as her young lip began to ope
Upon the golden fruit the vision bore,
A bee flew out, and stung her to the heart,
And so—she awoke with a great scream and start.

LXXVIII.

All this she told with some confusion and
Dismay, the usual consequence of dreams
Of the unpleasant kind, with none at hand
To expound their vain and visionary gleams.
I've known some odd ones which seem'd really plann'd
Prophetically, or that which one deems
A "strange coincidence," to use a phrase
By which such things are settled now-a-days.

LXXIX.

The damsels, who had thoughts of some great harm,
Began, as is the consequence of fear,
To scold a little at the false alarm
That broke for nothing on their sleeping ear.
The matron, too, was wrath to leave her warm
Bed for the dream she had been obliged to hear,
And chafed at poor Dudù, who only sigh'd,
And said, that she was sorry she had cried.

LXXX.

"I've heard of stories of a cock and bull;
But visions of an apple and a bee,
To take us from our natural rest, and pull
The whole Oda from their beds at half-past three,
Would make us think the moon is at its full.
You surely are unwell, child! we must see,
To-morrow, what his Highness's physician
Will say to this hysteric of a vision.

LXXXI.

"And poor Juanna, too, the child's first night
Within these walls, to be broke in upon
With such a clamour—I had thought it right
That the young stranger should not lie alone.

And, as the quietest of all, she might
 With you, Dudù, a good night's rest have known;
But now I must transfer her to the charge
Of Lolah—though her couch is not so large."

LXXXII.

Lolah's eyes sparkled at the proposition;
 But poor Dudù, with large drops in her own,
Resulting from the scolding or the vision,
 Implored that present pardon might be shown
For this first fault, and that on no condition
 (She added in a soft and piteous tone)
Juanna should be taken from her, and
Her future dreams should all be kept in hand.

LXXXIII.

She promised never more to have a dream,
 At least to dream so loudly as just now;
She wonder'd at herself how she could scream—
 'T was foolish, nervous, as she must allow,
A fond hallucination, and a theme
 For laughter—but she felt her spirits low,
And begged they would excuse her; she'd get over
This weakness in a few hours, and recover.

LXXXIV.

And here Juanna kindly interposed,
 And said she felt herself extremely well
Where she then was, as her sound sleep disclosed,
 When all around rang like a tocsin bell;
She did not find herself the least disposed
 To quit her gentle partner, and to dwell
Apart from one who had no sin to show,
Save that of dreaming once "mal-à-propos."

LXXXV.

As thus Juanna spoke, Dudù turn'd round
 And hid her face within Juanna's breast;
Her neck alone was seen, but that was found
 The colour of a budding rose's crest,
I can't tell why she blush'd, nor can expound
 The mystery of this rupture of their rest;
All that I know is, that the facts I state
Are true as truth has ever been of late.

LXXXVI.

And so good night to them,—or, if you will,
 Good morrow—for the cock had crown, and light
Began to clothe each Asiatic hill,
 And the mosque crescent struggled into sight
Of the long caravan, which in the chill
 Of dewy dawn wound slowly round each height,
That stretches to the stony belt, which girds
Asia, where Kaff looks down upon the Kurds.

LXXXVII.

With the first ray, or rather gray of morn,
 Gulbeyaz rose from restlessness; and pale
As passion rises, with its bosom worn,
 Array'd herself with mantle, gem, and veil.
The nightingale that sings with the deep thorn,
 Which fable places in her breast of wail,
Is lighter far of heart and voice than those
Whose headlong passions form their proper woes.

LXXXVIII.

And that's the moral of this composition,
 If people would but see its real drift;
But *that* they will not do without suspicion,
 Because all gentle readers have the gift
Of closing 'gainst the light their orbs of vision;
 While gentle writers also love to lift
Their voices 'gainst each other, which is natural,
The numbers are too great for them to flatter all.

LXXXIX.

Rose the Sultana from a bed of splendour,
 Softer than the soft Sybarite's, who cried
Aloud because his feelings were too tender
 To brook a ruffled rose-leaf by his side,—
So beautiful that art could little mend her,
 Though pale with conflicts between love and pride;—
So agitated was she with her error,
She did not even look into the mirror.

XC.

Also arose about the self-same time,
 Perhaps a little later, her great lord,
Master of thirty kingdoms so sublime,
 And of a wife by whom he was abhorr'd;
A thing of much less import in that clime—
 At least to those of incomes which afford
The filling up their whole connubial cargo—
Than where two wives are under an embargo.

XCI.

He did not think much on the matter, nor
 Indeed on any other: as a man
He liked to have a handsome paramour
 At hand, as one may like to have a fan,
And therefore of Circassians had good store,
 As an amusement after the Divan;
Though an unusual fit of love, or duty,
Had made him lately bask in his bride's beauty.

XCII.

And now he rose; and after due ablutions
 Exacted by the customs of the East,
And prayers and other pious evolutions,
 He drank six cups of coffee at the least,
And then withdrew to hear about the Russians,
 Whose victories had recently increased
In Catherine's reign, whom glory still adores,
As greatest of all sovereigns and w——s.

XCIII.

But oh, thou grand legitimate Alexander!
 Her son's son, let not this last phrase offend
Thine ear, if it should reach—and now rhymes wander
 Almost as far as Petersburgh, and lend
A dreadful impulse to each loud meander
 Of murmuring Liberty's wide waves, which blend
Their roar even with the Baltic's—so you be
Your father's son, 't is quite enough for me.

XCIV.

To call men love-begotten, or proclaim
 Their mothers as the antipodes of Timon,
That hater of mankind, would be a shame,
 A libel, or whate'er you please to rhyme on:
But people's ancestors are history's game;
 And if one lady's slip could leave a crime on
All generations, I should like to know
What pedigree the best would have to show?

XCV.

Had Catherine and the Sultan understood
 Their own true interests, which kings rarely know,
Until 't is taught by lessons rather rude,
 There was a way to end their strife, although
Perhaps precarious, had they but thought good,
 Without the aid of prince or plenipo:
She to dismiss her guards and he his harem,
And for their other matters, meet and share 'em.

XCVI.

But as it was, his Highness had to hold
 His daily council upon ways and means
How to encounter with this martial scold,
 This modern Amazon and queen of queans;
And the perplexity could not be told
 Of all the pillars of the state, which leans
Sometimes a little heavy on the backs
Of those who cannot lay on a new tax.

XCVII.

Meantime Gulbeyaz, when her king was gone,
 Retired into her boudoir, a sweet place
For love or breakfast; private, pleasing, lone,
 And rich with all contrivances which grace
Those gay recesses:—many a precious stone
 Sparkled along its roof, and many a vase
Of porcelain held in the fetter'd flowers,
Those captive soothers of a captive's hours.

XCVIII.

Mother-of-pearl, and porphyry, and marble,
 Vied with each other on this costly spot;
And singing birds without were heard to warble;
 And the stain'd glass which lighted this fair grot
Varied each ray;—but all descriptions garble
 The true effect, and so we had better not
Be too minute; an outline is the best,—
A lively reader's fancy does the rest.

XCIX.

And here she summon'd Baba, and required
 Don Juan at his hands, and information
Of what had pass'd since all the slaves retired,
 And whether he had occupied their station;
If matters had been managed as desired,
 And his disguise with due consideration
Kept up; and, above all, the where and how
He had pass'd the night, was what she wish'd to know.

C.

Baba, with some embarrassment, replied
 To this long catechism of questions, ask'd
More easily than answer'd,—that he had tried
 His best to obey in what he had been task'd;
But there seem'd something that he wish'd to hide,
 Which hesitation more betray'd than mask'd;
He scratch'd his ear, the infallible resource
To which embarrass'd people have recourse.

CI.

Gulbeyaz was no model of true patience,
 Nor much disposed to wait in word or deed;
She liked quick answers in all conversations;
 And when she saw him stumbling like a steed
In his replies, she puzzled him for fresh ones;
 And as his speech grew still more broken-kneed,
Her cheek began to flush, her eyes to sparkle,
And her proud brow's blue veins to swell and darkle.

CII.

When Baba saw these symptoms, which he knew
 To bode him no great good, he deprecated
Her anger, and beseech'd she 'd hear him through—
 He could not help the thing which he related:
Then out it came at length, that to Dudù
 Juan was given in charge, as hath been stated;
But not by Baba's fault, he said, and swore on
The holy camel's hump, besides the Koran.

CIII.

The chief dame of the Oda, upon whom
 The discipline of the whole harem bore,
As soon as they re-entered their own room,
 For Baba's function stopt short at the door,
Had settled all, nor could he then presume
 (The aforesaid Baba) just then to do more,
Without exciting such suspicion as
Might make the matter still worse than it was.

CIV.

He hoped, indeed he thought he could be sure,
 Juan had not betray'd himself; in fact
'T was certain that his conduct had been pure,
 Because a foolish or imprudent act

Would not alone have made him insecure,
 But ended in his being found out and *sack'd*,
And thrown into the sea.—Thus Baba spoke
Of all save Dudù's dream, which was no joke.

CV.

This he discreetly kept in the back ground,
 And talk'd away, and might have talk'd till now,
For any further answer that he found,
 So deep an anguish wrung Gulbeyaz' brow:
Her cheek turn'd ashes, ears rung, brain whirl'd round,
 As if she had received a sudden blow,
And the heart's dew of pain sprang fast and chilly
O'er her fair front, like Morning's on a lily.

CVI.

Although she was not of the fainting sort,
 Baba thought she would faint, but there he err'd—
It was but a convulsion, which, though short,
 Can never be described; we all have heard,
And some of us have felt thus "*all amort*,"
 When things beyond the common have occurr'd;—
Gulbeyaz proved in that brief agony
What she could ne'er express—then how should I?

CVII.

She stood a moment as a Pythoness
 Stands on her tripod, agonised, and full
Of inspiration gather'd from distress,
 When all the heart-strings like wild horses pull
The heart asunder;—then, as more or less
 Their speed abated or their strength grew dull,
She sunk down on her seat by slow degrees,
And bow'd her throbbing head o'er trembling knees.

CVIII.

Her face declined and was unseen; her hair
 Fell in long tresses like the weeping willow,
Sweeping the marble underneath her chair,
 Or rather sofa, (for it was all pillow,
A low, soft ottoman,) and black despair
 Stirr'd up and down her bosom like a billow,
Which rushes to some shore whose shingles check
Its further course, but must receive its wreck.

CIX.

Her head hung down, and her long hair in stooping
 Conceal'd her features better than a veil;
And one hand o'er the ottoman lay drooping,
 White, waxen, and as alabaster pale:
Would that I were a painter! to be grouping
 All that a poet drags into detail!
Oh that my words were colours! but their tints
May serve perhaps as outlines or slight hints.

CX.

Baba, who knew by experience when to talk
 And when to hold his tongue, now held it till
This passion might blow o'er, nor dared to balk
 Gulbeyaz' taciturn or speaking will.
At length she rose up, and began to walk
 Slowly along the room, but silent still,
And her brow clear'd, but not her troubled eye;
The wind was down, but still the sea ran high.

CXI.

She stopp'd, and raised her head to speak—but paused,
 And then moved on again with rapid pace;
Then slacken'd it, which is the march most caused
 By deep emotion:—you may sometimes trace
A feeling in each footstep, as disclosed
 By Sallust in his Catiline, who, chased
By all the demons of all passions, show'd
Their work even by the way in which he trode.

CXII.

Gulbeyaz stopp'd and beckon'd Baba:—"Slave!
 Bring the two slaves!" she said in a low tone,
But one which Baba did not like to brave,
 And yet he shudder'd, and seem'd rather prone
To prove reluctant, and begg'd leave to crave
 (Though he well knew the meaning) to be shown
What slaves her Highness wish'd to indicate,
For fear of any error, like the late.

CXIII.

"The Georgian and her paramour," replied
 The imperial bride—and added, "Let the boat
Be ready by the secret portal's side:
 You know the rest." The words stuck in her throat
Despite her injured love and fiery pride;
 And of this Baba willingly took note,
And begg'd by every hair of Mahomet's beard,
She would revoke the order he had heard.

CXIV.

"To hear is to obey," he said; "but still—
 Sultana, think upon the consequence:
It is not that I shall not all fulfil
 Your orders, even in their severest sense;
But such precipitation may end ill,
 Even at your own imperative expense:
I do not mean destruction and exposure,
In case of any premature disclosure;

CXV.

"But your own feelings. Even should all the rest
 Be hidden by the rolling waves, which hide
Already many a once love-beaten breast
 Deep in the caverns of the deadly tide—
You love this boyish, new, seraglio guest,
 And if this violent remedy be tried—
Excuse my freedom, when I here assure you,
That killing him is not the way to cure you."

CXVI.

"What dost thou know of love or feeling?—Wretch!
 Begone!" she cried, with kindling eyes "and do
My bidding!" Baba vanish'd, for to stretch
 His own remonstrance further he well knew

Might end in acting as his own "Jack Ketch;"
And though he wish'd extremely to get through
This awkward business without harm to others,
He still preferr'd his own neck to another's.

CXVII.

Away he went then upon his commission,
Growling and grumbling in good Turkish phrase
Against all women of whate'er condition,
Especially sultanas and their ways;
Their obstinacy, pride, and indecision,
Their never knowing their own mind two days,
The trouble that they gave, their immorality,
Which made him daily bless his own neutrality.

CXVIII.

And then he call'd his brethren to his aid,
And sent one on a summons to the pair,
That they must instantly be well array'd,
And, above all, be comb'd even to a hair,
And brought before the Empress, who had made
Inquiries after them with kindest care:
At which Dudù look'd strange, and Juan silly;
But go they must at once, and will I—nill I.

CXIX.

And here I leave them at their preparation
For the imperial presence, wherein whether
Gulbeyaz show'd them both commiseration,
Or got rid of the parties altogether,
Like other angry ladies of her nation,—
Are things the turning of a hair or feather
May settle; but far be 't from me to anticipate
In what way feminine caprice may dissipate.

CXX.

I leave them for the present with good wishes,
Though doubts of their well doing, to arrange
Another part of history; for the dishes
Of this our banquet we must sometimes change;
And trusting Juan may escape the fishes,
Although his situation now seems strange,
And scarce secure, as such digressions *are* fair,
The Muse will take a little touch at warfare.

CANTO THE SEVENTH

I.

O LOVE! O Glory! what are ye who fly
 Around us ever, rarely to alight?
There's not a meteor in the polar sky
 Of such transcendent and more fleeting flight.
Chill, and chain'd to cold earth, we lift on high
 Our eyes in search of either lovely light;
A thousand and a thousand colours they
Assume, then leave us on our freezing way.

II.

And such as they are, such my present tale is,
 A non-descript and ever-varying rhyme,
A versified Aurora Borealis,
 Which flashes o'er a waste and icy clime.
When we know what all are, we must bewail us,
 But ne'ertheless, I hope it is no crime
To laugh at *all* things—for I wish to know
What, after *all*, are *all* things—but a *show?*

III.

They accuse me—*Me*—the present writer of
 The present poem—of—I know not what—
A tendency to under-rate and scoff
 At human power and virtue, and all that;
And this they say in language rather rough.
 Good God! I wonder what they would be at!
I say no more than hath been said in Danté's
Verse, and by Solomon and by Cervantes;

IV.

By Swift, by Machiavel, by Rochefoucault,
 By Fénélon, by Luther, and by Plato;
By Tillotson, and Wesley, and Rousseau,
 Who knew this life was not worth a potato.
'T is not their fault, nor mine, if this be so—
 For my part, I pretend not to be Cato,
Nor even Diogenes.—We live and die,
But which is best, you know no more than I.

V.

Socrates said, our only knowledge was
 "To know that nothing could be known;" a pleasant
Science enough, which levels to an ass
 Each man of wisdom, future, past, or present.
Newton (that proverb of the mind), alas!
 Declared, with all his grand discoveries recent,
That he himself felt only "like a youth
Picking up shells by the great ocean—Truth."

VII.

Ecclesiastes said, "that all is vanity"—
 Most modern preachers say the same, or show it
By their examples of true Christianity:
 In short, all know, or very soon may know it;
And in this scene of all-confess'd inanity,
 By saint, by sage, by preacher, and by poet,
Must I restrain me, through the fear of strife,
From holding up the nothingness of life?

VII.

Dogs, or men!—for I flatter you in saying
 That ye are dogs—your betters far—ye may
Read, or read not, what I am now essaying
 To show ye what ye are in every way.
As little as the moon stops for the baying
 Of wolves, will the bright muse withdraw one ray
From out her skies—then howl your idle wrath!
While she still silvers o'er your gloomy path.

VIII.

"Fierce loves and faithless wars"—I am not sure
 If this be the right reading—'t is no matter;
The fact 's about the same, I am secure;
 I sing them both, and am about to batter
A town which did a famous siege endure,
 And was beleaguer'd both by land and water
By Souvaroff, or Anglicè Suwarrow,
Who loved blood as an alderman loves marrow.

IX.

The fortress is call'd Ismail, and is placed
 Upon the Danube's left branch and left bank,
With buildings in the Oriental taste,
 But still a fortress of the foremost rank,
Or was at least, unless 't is since defaced,
 Which with your conquerors is a common prank:
It stands some eighty versts from the high sea,
And measures round of toises thousands three.

X.

Within the extent of this fortification
 A borough is compris'd along the height
Upon the left, which from its loftier station
 Commands the city, and upon its site
A Greek had raised around this elevation
 A quantity of palisades *upright*,
So placed as to *impede* the fire of those
Who held the place, and to *assist* the foe's.

XI.

This circumstance may serve to give a notion
 Of the high talents of this new Vauban:
But the town ditch below was deep as ocean,
 The rampart higher than you'd wish to hang:
But then there was a great want of precaution
 (Prithee, excuse this engineering slang),
Nor work advanced, nor cover'd way was there,
To hint at least "Here is no thoroughfare."

XII.

But a stone bastion, with a narrow gorge,
 And walls as thick as most skulls born as yet;
Two batteries, cap-à-pie, as our St. George,
 Case-mated one, and t'other "a barbette,"
Of Danube's bank took formidable charge;
 While two and twenty cannon duly set
Rose over the town's right side, in bristling tier,
Forty feet high, upon a cavalier.

XIII.

But from the river the town 's open quite,
 Because the Turks could never be persuaded

A Russian vessel e'er would heave in sight;
 And such their creed was, till they were invaded,
When it grew rather late to set things right.
 But as the Danube could not well be waded,
They look'd upon the Muscovite flotilla,
And only shouted, "Allah!" and "Bis Millah!"

XIV.

The Russians now were ready to attack;
 But oh, ye goddesses of war and glory!
How shall I spell the name of each Cossacque
 Who were immortal, could one tell their story?
Alas! what to their memory can lack?
 Achilles' self was not more grim and gory
Than thousands of this new and polish'd nation,
Whose names want nothing but—pronunciation.

XV.

Still I'll record a few, if but to increase
 Our euphony: there was Strongenoff, and Strokonoff,
Meknop, Serge Low, Arsniew of modern Greece,
 And Tschitsshakoff, and Roguenoff, and Chokenoff,
And others of twelve consonants a-piece;
 And more might be found out, if I could poke enough
Into gazettes; but Fame (capricious strumpet),
It seems, has got an ear as well as trumpet.

XVI.

And cannot tune those discords of narration,
 Which may be names at Moscow, into rhyme;
Yet there were several worth commemoration,
 As e'er was virgin of a nuptial chime;
Soft words, too, fitted for the peroration
 Of Londonderry drawling against time,
Ending in "ischskin," "ousckin," "iffskchy," "ouski,"
Of whom we can insert but Rousamouski,

XVII.

Scherematoff and Chrematoff, Koklophti,
 Koclobski, Kourakin, and Mouskin Pouskin,
All proper men of weapons, as e'er scoff'd high
 Against a foe, or ran a sabre through skin:
Little cared they for Mahomet or Mufti,
 Unless to make their kettle-drums a new skin
Out of their hides, if parchment had grown dear,
And no more handy substitute been near.

XVIII.

Then there were foreigners of much renown,
 Of various nations, and all volunteers;
Not fighting for their country or its crown,
 But wishing to be one day brigadiers:
Also to have the sacking of a town;
 A pleasant thing to young men at their years.
'Mongst them were several Englishmen of pith,
Sixteen called Thomson, and nineteen named Smith.

XIX.

Jack Thomson and Bill Thomson;—all the rest
 Had been called "*Jemmy*," after the great bard;
I don't know whether they had arms or crest,
 But such a godfather's as good a card.
Three of the Smiths were Peters; but the best
 Amongst them all, hard blows to inflict or ward,
Was *he*, since so renown'd "in country quarters
At Halifax;" but now he served the Tartars.

XX.

The rest were Jacks and Gills and Wills and Bills,
 But when I've added that the elder Jack Smith
Was born in Cumberland among the hills,
 And that his father was an honest blacksmith,
I've said all *I* know of a name that fills
 Three lines of the despatch in taking "Schmacksmith,"
A village of Moldavia's waste, wherein
He fell, immortal in a bulletin.

XXI.

I wonder (although Mars no doubt's a god I
 Praise) if a man's name in a *bulletin*
May make up for a *bullet in* his body?
 I hope this little question is no sin,
Because, though I am but a simple noddy,
 I think one Shakspeare puts the same thought in
The mouth of some one in his plays so doting,
Which many people pass for wits by quoting.

XXII.

Then there were Frenchmen, gallant, young, and gay:
 But I'm too great a patriot to record
Their Gallic names upon a glorious day;
 I'd rather tell ten lies than say a word
Of truth;—such truths are treason; they betray
 Their country; and as traitors are abhorr'd
Who name the French in English, save to show
How Peace should make John Bull the Frenchman's foe.

XXIII.

The Russians, having built two batteries on
 An isle near Ismail, had two ends in view:
The first was to bombard it, and knock down
 The public buildings and the private too,
No matter what poor souls might be undone.
 The city's shape suggested this, 't is true;
Form'd like an amphitheatre, each dwelling
Presented a fine mark to throw a shell in.

XXIV.

The second object was to profit by
The moment of the general consternation,
To attack the Turks' flotilla, which lay nigh,
Extremely tranquil, anchor'd at its station;
But a third motive was as probably
To frighten them into capitulation;
A phantasy which sometimes seizes warriors,
Unless they are game as bull-dogs and fox-terriers.

XXV.

A habit rather blameable, which is
That of despising those we combat with,
Common in many cases, was in this
The cause of killing Tchitchitzkoff and Smith,
One of the valorous "Smiths" whom we shall miss
Out of those nineteen who late rhymed to "pith;"
But 't is a name so spread o'er "Sir" and "Madam,"
That one would think the first who bore it "Adam."

XXVI.

The Russian batteries were incomplete,
Because they were constructed in a hurry;
Thus the same cause which makes a verse want feet,
And throws a cloud o'er Longman and John Murray,
When the sale of new books is not so fleet
As they who print them think is necessary,
May likewise put off for a time what story
Sometimes calls "murder," and at others "glory."

XXVII.

Whether it was their engineer's stupidity,
Their haste or waste, I neither know nor care,
Or come contractor's personal cupidity,
Saving his soul by cheating in the ware
Of homicide, but there was no solidity
In the new batteries erected there;
They either miss'd, or they were never miss'd,
And added greatly to the missing list.

XXVIII.

A sad miscalculation about distance
Made all their naval matters incorrect;
Three fireships lost their amiable existence
Before they reach'd a spot to take effect:
The match was lit too soon, and no assistance
Could remedy this lubberly defect;
They blew up in the middle of the river,
While, though t' was dawn, the Turks slept fast as ever.

XXIX.

At seven they rose, however, and survey'd
The Russ flotilla getting under way;
'T was nine, when still advancing undismay'd,
Within a cable's length their vessels lay
Off Ismail, and commenced a cannonade,
Which was return'd with interest, I may say,
And by a fire of musketry and grape,
And shells and shot of every size and shape.

XXX.

For six hours bore they without intermission
The Turkish fire, and, aided by their own
Land batteries, work'd their guns with great precision:
At length they found mere cannonade alone
By no means would produce the town's submission,
And made a signal to retreat at one.
One bark blew up, a second near the works
Running aground, was taken by the Turks.

XXXI.

The Moslem, too, had lost both ships and men;
But when they saw the enemy retire,
Their Delhis mann'd some boats, and sail'd again,
And gall'd the Russians with a heavy fire,
And tried to make a landing on the main;
But here the effect fell short of their desire:
Count Damas drove them back into the water
Pell-mell, and with a whole gazette of slaughter.

XXXII.

"If" (says the historian here) "I could report
All that the Russians did upon this day,
I think that several volumes would fall short,
And I should still have many things to say;"
And so he says no more—but pays his court
To some distinguish'd strangers in that fray;
The Prince de Ligne, and Langeron, and Damas,
Names great as any that the roll of Fame has.

XXXIII.

This being the case, may show us what Fame *is:*
For out of these three "*preux Chevaliers,*" how
Many of common readers give a guess
That such existed? (and they may live now
For aught we know). Renown 's all hit or miss;
There 's fortune even in fame, we must allow.
'T is true, the Memoirs of the Prince de Ligne
Have half withdrawn from *him* oblivion's screen.

XXXIV.

But here are men who fought in gallant actions
As gallantly as ever heroes fought,
But buried in the heap of such transactions
Their names are rarely found, nor often sought.
Thus even good fame may suffer sad contractions,
And is extinguish'd sooner than she ought:
Of all our modern battles, I will bet
You can't repeat nine names from each gazette.

XXXV.

In short, this last attack, though rich in glory,
Show'd that *somewhere, somehow*, there was a fault,
And Admiral Ribas (known in Russian story)
Most strongly recommended an assault;
In which he was opposed by young and hoary,
Which made a long debate; but I must halt,
For if I wrote down every warrior's speech,
I doubt few readers e'er would mount the breach.

XXXVI.

There was a man, if that he was a man,
Not that his manhood could be call'd in question,
For had he not been Hercules, his span
Had been as short in youth, as indigestion
Made his last illness, when, all worn and wan,
He died beneath a tree, as much unblest on
The soil of the green province he had wasted,
As e'er was locust on the land it blasted.

XXXVII.

This was Potemkin—a great thing in days
When homicide and harlotry made great;
If stars and titles could entail long praise,
His glory might half equal his estate.
This fellow, being six foot high, could raise
A kind of phantasy proportionate
In the then sovereign of the Russian people,
Who measured men as you would do a steeple.

XXXVIII.

While things were in abeyance, Ribas sent
A courier to the prince, and he succeeded
In ordering matters after his own bent;
I cannot tell the way in which he pleaded,
But shortly he had cause to be content.
In the mean time, the batteries proceeded,
And fourscore cannon on the Danube's border
Were briskly fired and answer'd in due order.

XXXIX.

But on the thirteenth, when already part
Of the troops were embark'd, the siege to raise,
A courier on the spur inspired new heart
Into all panters for newspaper praise,
As well as dilettanti in war's art,
By his despatches couch'd in pithy phrase;
Announcing the appointment of that lover of
Battles to the command, Field-Marshal Souvaroff.

XL.

The letter of the prince to the same marshal
Was worthy of a Spartan, had the cause
Been one to which a good heart could be partial—
Defence of freedom, country, or of laws;
But as it was mere lust of power to o'er-arch all
With its proud brow, it merits slight applause,
Save for its style, which said, all in a trice,
"You will take Ismail at whatever price."

XLI.

"Let there be light! said God, and there was light!"
"Let there be blood!" says man, and there's a sea!
The fiat of this spoil'd child of the Night
(For Day ne'er saw his merits) could decree
More evil in an hour, than thirty bright
Summers could renovate, though they should be
Lovely as those which ripen'd Eden's fruit;
For war cuts up not only branch, but root.

XLII.

Our friends the Turks, who with loud "Allahs" now
Began to signalise the Russ retreat,
Were damnably mistaken; few are slow
In thinking that their enemy is beat,
(Or *beaten*, if *you* insist on grammar, though
I never think about it in a heat,)
But here I say the Turks were much mistaken,
Who hating hogs, yet wish'd to save their bacon.

LXIII.

For, on the sixteenth, at full gallop, drew
In sight two horsemen, who were deem'd Cossacques
For some time, till they came in nearer view.
They had but little baggage at their backs,
For there were but *three* shirts between the two;
But on they rode upon two Ukraine hacks,
Till, in approaching, were at length descried
In this plain pair, Suwarrow and his guide.

XLIV.

"Great joy to London now!" says some great fool,
When London had a grand illumination,
Which to that bottle-conjuror, John Bull,
Is of all dreams the first hallucination;
So that the streets of colour'd lamps are full,
That Sage (*said* John) surrenders at discretion
His purse, his soul, his sense, and even his nonsense,
To gratify, like a huge moth, this *one* sense.

XLV.

'Tis strange that he should farther "damn his eyes,"
For they are damn'd; that once all-famous oath

38

Is to the devil now no farther prize,
 Since John has lately lost the use of both.
Debt he calls wealth, and taxes Paradise;
 And Famine, with her gaunt and bony growth,
Which stare him in the face, he won't examine,
Or swears that Ceres hath begotten Famine.

XLVI.

But to the tale;—great joy unto the camp!
 To Russian, Tartar, English, French, Cossacque,
O'er whom Suwarrow shone like a gas lamp,
 Presaging a most luminous attack;
Or like a wisp along the marsh so damp,
 Which leads beholders on a boggy walk,
He flitted to and fro a dancing light,
Which all who saw it follow'd, wrong or right.

XLVII.

But certes matters took a different face;
 There was enthusiasm and much applause,
The fleet and camp saluted with great grace,
 And all presaged good fortune to their cause.
Within a cannon-shot length of the place
 They drew, constructed ladders, repair'd flaws

In former works, made new, prepared fascines,
And all kinds of benevolent machines.

XLVIII.

'T is thus the spirit of a single mind
Makes that of multitudes take one direction,
As roll the waters to the breathing wind,
Or roams the herd beneath the bull's protection;
Or as a little dog will lead the blind,
Or a bell-wether form the flock's connection
By tinkling sounds, when they go forth to victual;
Such is the sway of your great men o'er little.

XLIX.

The whole camp rung with joy; you would have thought
That they were going to a marriage feast,
(This metaphor, I think, holds good as aught,
Since there is discord after both at least):
There was not now a luggage boy but sought
Danger and spoil with ardour much increased;
And why? Because a little—odd—old man,
Stript to his shirt, was come to lead the van.

L.

But so it was; and every preparation
Was made with all alacrity; the first
Detachment of three columns took its station,
And waited but the signal's voice to burst
Upon the foe: the second's ordination
Was also in three columns, with a thirst
For glory gaping o'er a sea of slaughter:
The third, in columns two, attack'd by water.

LI.

New batteries were erected, and was held
A general council, in which unanimity,
That stranger to most councils, here prevail'd,
As sometimes happens in a great extremity;
And every difficulty being dispell'd,
Glory began to dawn with due sublimity,
While Souvaroff, determined to obtain it,
Was teaching his recruits to use the bayonet.[51]

LII.

It is an actual fact, that he, commander
In chief, in proper person deign'd to drill
The awkward squad, and could afford to squander
His time, a corporal's duty to fulfil;
Just as you 'd break a sucking salamander
To swallow flame, and never take it ill:
He show'd them how to mount a ladder (which
Was not like Jacob's) or to cross a ditch.

LIII.

Also he dress'd up, for the nonce, fascines
Like men with turbans, scimitars, and dirks,
And made them charge with bayonet these machines,
By way of lesson against actual Turks;
And when well practised in these mimic scenes,
He judged them proper to assail the works;
At which your wise men sneer'd in phrases witty:
He made no answer; but he took the city.

LIV.

Most things were in this posture on the eve
Of the assault, and all the camp was in
A stern repose; which you would scarce conceive;
Yet men resolved to dash through thick and thin
Are very silent when they once believe
That all is settled:—there was little din,
For some were thinking of their home and friends,
And others of themselves and latter ends.

LV.

Suwarrow chiefly was on the alert,
Surveying, drilling, ordering, jesting, pondering:
For the man was, we safely may assert,
A thing to wonder at beyond most wondering;
Hero, buffoon, half-demon, and half-dirt,
Praying, instructing, desolating, plundering;
Now Mars, now Momus; and when bent to storm
A fortress, Harlequin in uniform.

LVI.

The day before the assault, while upon drill—
For this great conqueror play'd the corporal—
Some Cossacques, hov'ring like hawks round a hill,
Had met a party towards the twilight's fall,
One of whom spoke their tongue—or well or ill,
'T was much that he was understood at all;
But whether from his voice, or speech, or manner,
They found that he had fought beneath their banner.

LVII.

Whereon immediately at his request
They brought him and his comrades to head quarters;
Their dress was Moslem, but you might have guess'd
That these were merely masquerading Tartars,
And that beneath each Turkish-fashion'd vest
Lurk'd Christianity; which sometimes barters
Her inward grace for outward show, and makes
It difficult to shun some strange mistakes.

LVIII.

Suwarrow, who was standing in his shirt
Before a company of Calmucks, drilling,
Exclaiming, fooling, swearing at the inert,
And lecturing on the noble art of killing,—
For deeming human clay but common dirt,
This great philosopher was thus instilling
His maxims, which to martial comprehension
Proved death in battle equal to a pension;—

LIX.

Suwarrow, when he saw this company
Of Cossacques and their prey, turn'd round and cast
Upon them his slow brow and piercing eye:—
"Whence come ye?"—"From Constantinople last,
Captives just now escaped," was the reply.
"What are ye?"—"What you see us." Briefly pass'd
This dialogue; for he who answer'd knew
To whom he spoke, and made his words but few.

LX.

"Your names?"—"Mine's Johnson, and my comrade's Juan:
The other two are women, and the third
Is neither man nor woman." The chief threw on
The party a slight glance, then said, "I have heard
Your name before, the second is a new one:
To bring the other three here was absurd:
But let that pass:—I think I have heard your name
In the Nikolaiew regiment?"—"The same."

LXI.

"You served at Widdin?"—"Yes."—"You led the attack?"
"I did."—"What next?"—"I really hardly know."
"You were the first i' the breach?"—"I was not slack
At least to follow those who might be so."
"What follow'd?"—"A shot laid me on my back,
And I became a prisoner to the foe."
"You shall have vengeance, for the town surrounded
Is twice as strong as that where you were wounded

LXII.

"Where will you serve?"—"Where'er you please."—"I know
You like to be the hope of the forlorn,
And doubtless would be foremost on the foe
After the hardships you've already borne.
And this young fellow—say what can he do?
He with the beardless chin and garments torn?"
"Why, general, if he hath no greater fault
In war than love, he had better lead the assault."

LXIII.

"He shall, if that he dare." Here Juan bow'd
Low as the compliment deserved. Suwarrow
Continued: "Your old regiment's allow'd,
By special providence, to lead to-morrow,
Or it may be to-night, the assault: I have vow'd
To several saints, that shortly plough or harrow
Shall pass o'er what was Ismail, and its tusk
Be unimpeded by the proudest mosque.

LXIV.

"So now, my lads, for glory!"—Here he turn'd
And drill'd away in the most classic Russian,
Until each high, heroic bosom burn'd
For cash and conquest, as if from a cushion
A preacher had held forth (who nobly spurn'd
All earthly goods save tithes) and bade them push on
To slay the Pagans who resisted, battering
The armies of the Christian Empress Catherine.

LXV.

Johnson, who knew by this long colloquy
Himself a favourite, ventured to address
Suwarrow, though engaged with accents high
In his resumed amusement. "I confess
My debt in being thus allow'd to die
Among the foremost; but if you'd express
Explicitly our several posts, my friend
And self would know what duty to attend."

LXVI.

"Right! I was busy, and forgot. Why, you
Will join your former regiment, which should be
Now under arms. Ho! Katskoff, take him to—
(Here he call'd up a Polish orderly)
His post, I mean the regiment Nikolaiew:
The stranger stripling may remain with me;
He's a fine boy. The women may be sent
To the other baggage, or to the sick tent."

LXVII.

But here a sort of scene began to ensue:
The ladies,—who by no means had been bred
To be disposed of in a way so new,
Although their harem education led
Doubtless to that of doctrines the most true,
Passive obedience,—now raised up the head,
With flashing eyes and starting tears, and flung
Their arms, as hens their wings about their young,

LXVIII.

O'er the promoted couple of brave men,
 Who were thus honour'd by the greatest chief
That ever peopled hell with heroes slain,
 Or plunged a province or a realm in grief.
Oh, foolish mortals! Always taught in vain!
 Oh, glorious laurel! since for one sole leaf
Of thine imaginary deathless tree,
Of blood and tears must flow the unebbing sea.

LXIX.

Suwarrow, who had small regard for tears,
 And not much sympathy for blood, survey'd
The women with their hair about their ears,
 And natural agonies, with a slight shade
Of feeling: for however habit sears
 Men's hearts against whole millions, when their trade
Is butchery, sometimes a single sorrow
Will touch even heroes—and such was Suwarrow.

LXX.

He said,—and in the kindest Calmuck tone,—
 "Why, Johnson, what the devil do you mean
By bringing women here? They shall be shown
 All the attention possible, and seen
In safety to the waggons, where alone
 In fact they can be safe. You should have been
Aware this kind of baggage never thrives:
Save wed a year, I hate recruits with wives."

LXXI.

"May it please your excellency," thus replied
 Our British friend, "these are the wives of others,
And not our own. I am too qualified
 By service with my military brothers,
To break the rules by bringing one's own bride
 Into a camp: I know that nought so bothers
The hearts of the heroic on a charge,
As leaving a small family at large.

LXXII.

"But these are but two Turkish ladies, who
 With their attendant aided our escape,
And afterwards accompanied us through
 A thousand perils in this dubious shape.
To me this kind of life is not so new;
 To them, poor things, it is an awkward scrape.
I therefore, if you wish me to fight freely,
Request that they may both be used genteelly."

LXXIII.

Meantime these two poor girls, with swimming eyes,
 Look'd on as if in doubt if they could trust
Their own protectors; nor was their surprise
 Less than their grief (and truly not less just)
To see an old man, rather wild than wise
 In aspect, plainly clad, besmeared with dust,
Stript to his waistcoat, and that not too clean,
More fear'd than all the sultans ever seen.

LXXIV.

For every thing seem'd resting on his nod,
 As they could read in all eyes. Now to them,
Who were accustom'd, as a sort of god,
 To see the sultan, rich in many a gem,
Like an imperial peacock stalk abroad
 (That royal bird, whose tail 's a diadem,)
With all the pomp of power, it was a doubt
How power could condescend to do without.

LXXV.

John Johnson, seeing their extreme dismay,
 Though little versed in feelings oriental,
Suggested some slight comfort in his way:
 Don Juan, who was much more sentimental,
Swore they should see him by the dawn of day,
 Or that the Russian army should repent all:
And, strange to say, they found some consolation
In this—for females like exaggeration.

LXXVI.

And then with tears, and sighs, and some slight kisses,
 They parted for the present—these to await
According to the artillery's hits or misses,
 What sages call Chance, Providence, or Fate—
(Uncertainty is one of many blisses,
 A mortgage on Humanity's estate)—
While their belovèd friends began to arm,
To burn a town which never did them harm.

LXXVII.

Suwarrow,—who but saw things in the gross,
 Being much too gross to see them in detail,
Who calculated life as so much dross,
 And as the wind a widow'd nation's wail,
And cared as little for his army's loss
 (So that their efforts should at length prevail)
As wife and friends did for the boils of Job,—
What was 't to him to hear two women sob?

LXXVIII.

Nothing.—The work of glory still went on
 In preparations for a cannonade
As terrible as that of Ilion,
 If Homer had found mortars ready made;
But now, instead of slaying Priam's son,
 We only can but talk of escalade,
Bombs, drums, guns, bastions, batteries, bayonets, bullets;
Hard words, which stick in the soft Muses' gullets.

LXXIX.

Oh, thou eternal Homer! who couldst charm
All ears, though long; all ages, though so short,
By merely wielding with poetic arm
Arms to which men will never more resort,
Unless gunpowder should be found to harm
Much less than is the hope of every court,
Which now is leagued young Freedom to annoy;
But they will not find Liberty a Troy:—

LXXX.

Oh, thou eternal Homer! I have now
To paint a siege, wherein more men were slain,
With deadlier engines and a speedier blow,
Than in thy Greek gazette of that campaign;
And yet, like all men else, I must allow,
To vie with thee would be about as vain
As for a brook to cope with ocean's flood;
But still we moderns equal you in blood;

LXXXI.

If not in poetry, at least in fact;
And fact is truth, the grand desideratum!
Of which, howe'er the Muse describes each act,
There should be ne'ertheless a slight substratum.
But now the town is going to be attack'd;
Great deeds are doing—how shall I relate 'em?
Souls of immortal generals! Phœbus watches
To colour up his rays from your despatches.

LXXXII.

Oh, ye great bulletins of Bonaparte!
Oh, ye less grand long lists of kill'd and wounded!
Shade of Leonidas, who fought so hearty,
When my poor Greece was once, as now, surrounded!
Oh, Cæsar's Commentaries! now impart, ye
Shadows of glory! (lest I be confounded)
A portion of your fading twilight hues,
So beautiful, so fleeting, to the Muse.

LXXXIII.

When I call "fading" martial immortality,
I mean that every age and every year,
And almost every day, in sad reality,
Some sucking hero is compell'd to rear,
Who, when we come to sum up the totality
Of deeds to human happiness most dear,
Turns out to be a butcher in great business,
Afflicting young folks with a sort of dizziness.

LXXXIV.

Medals, rank, ribands, lace, embroidery, scarlet,
Are things immortal to immortal man,
As purple to the Babylonian harlot:
An uniform to boys is like a fan
To women; there is scarce a crimson varlet
But deems himself the first in Glory's van.
But Glory's glory; and if you would find
What that is—ask the pig who sees the wind!

LXXXV.

At least *he feels it*, and some say he *sees*,
Because he runs before it like a pig;
Or, if that simple sentence should displease,
Say, that he scuds before it like a brig,
A schooner, or—but it is time to ease
This Canto, ere my Muse perceives fatigue.
The next shall ring a peal to shake all people,
Like a bob-major from a village steeple.

LXXXVI.

Hark! through the silence of the cold, dull night,
The hum of armies gathering rank on rank!
Lo! dusky masses steal in dubious sight
Along the leaguer'd wall and bristling bank
Of the arm'd river, while with straggling light
The stars peep through the vapours dim and dank,
Which curl in curious wreaths:—how soon the smoke
Of Hell shall pall them in a deeper cloak.

LXXXVII.

Here pause we for the present—as even then
That awful pause, dividing life from death,
Struck for an instant on the hearts of men,
Thousands of whom were drawing their last breath!
A moment—and all will be life again!
The march! the charge! the shouts of either faith!
Hurra! and Allah! and—one moment more—
The death-cry drowning in the battle's roar.

CANTO THE EIGHTH.

I.

Oh blood and thunder! and oh blood and wounds!
These are but vulgar oaths, as you may deem
Too gentle reader! and most shocking sounds:
And so they are; yet thus is Glory's dream
Unriddled, and as my true Muse expounds
At present such things, since they are her theme,
So be they her inspirers! Call them Mars,
Bellona, what you will—they mean but wars.

II.

All was prepared—the fire, the sword, the men
To wield them in their terrible array.
The army, like a lion from his den,
March'd forth with nerve and sinews bent to slay—
A human Hydra, issuing from its fen
To breathe destruction on its winding way,
Whose heads were heroes, which cut off in vain,
Immediately in others grew again.

III.

History can only take things in the gross;
But could we know them in detail, perchance

In balancing the profit and the loss,
 War's merit it by no means might enhance,
To waste so much gold for a little dross,
 As hath been done, mere conquest to advance.
The drying up a single tear has more
Of honest fame, than shedding seas of gore.

IV.

And why? because it brings self-approbation;
 Whereas the other, after all its glare,
Shouts, bridges, arches, pensions from a nation,
 Which (it may be) has not much left to spare,
A higher title, or a loftier station,
 Though they may make Corruption gape or stare,
Yet, in the end, except in Freedom's battles,
Are nothing but a child of Murder's rattles.

V.

And such they are,—and such they will be found:
 Not so Leonidas and Washington,
Whose every battle-field is holy ground,
 Which breathes of nations saved, not worlds undone.
How sweetly on the ear such echoes sound!
 While the mere victor's may appal or stun
The servile and the vain, such names will be
A watchword till the future shall be free.

VI.

The night was dark, and the thick mist allow'd
 Nought to be seen save the artillery's flame,
Which arch'd the horizon like a fiery cloud,
 And in the Danube's waters shone the same—
A mirror'd hell! the volleying roar, and loud
 Long booming of each peal on peal, o'ercame
The ear far more than thunder; for Heaven's flashes
Spare, or smite rarely—man's make millions ashes!

VII.

The column order'd on the assault scarce pass'd
 Beyond the Russian batteries a few toises,
When up the bristling Moslem rose at last,
 Answering the Christian thunders with like voices:
Then one vast fire air, earth, and stream embraced,
 Which rock'd as 't were beneath the mighty noises;
While the whole rampart blazed like Etna, when
The restless Titan hiccups in his den.

VIII.

And one enormous shout of "Allah!" rose
 In the same moment, loud as even the roar
Of war's most mortal engines, to their foes
 Hurling defiance: city, stream, and shore
Resounded "Allah!" and the clouds which close
 With thickening canopy the conflict o'er,
Vibrate to the Eternal name. Hark! through
All sounds it pierceth—"Allah! Allah! Hu!"[52]

IX.

The columns were in movement one and all,
 But of the portion which attack'd by water,
Thicker than leaves the lives began to fall,
 Though led by Arsniew, that great son of slaughter,
As brave as ever faced both bomb and ball.
 "Carnage" (so Wordsworth tells you) "is God's daughter:"[53]
If *he* speak truth, she is Christ's sister, and
Just now behaved as in the Holy Land.

X.

The Prince de Ligne was wounded in the knee;
 Count Chapeau-Bras, too, had a ball between
His cap and head, which proves the head to be
 Aristocratic as was ever seen,
Because it then received no injury
 More than the cap; in fact, the ball could mean
No harm unto a right legitimate head:
"Ashes to ashes"—why not lead to lead?

XI.

Also the General Markow, Brigadier,
 Insisting on removal of *the prince*
Amidst some groaning thousands dying near,—
 All common fellows, who might writhe and wince,
And shriek for water into a deaf ear,—
 The General Markow, who could thus evince
His sympathy for rank, by the same token,
To teach him greater, had his own leg broken.

XII.

Three hundred cannon threw up their emetic,
 And thirty thousand muskets flung their pills
Like hail, to make a bloody diuretic.
 Mortality! thou hast thy monthly bills;
Thy plagues, thy famines, thy physicians, yet tick,
 Like the death-watch, within our ears the ills
Past, present, and to come;—but all may yield
To the true portrait of one battle-field.

XIII.

There the still varying pangs, which multiply
 Until their very number makes men hard
By the infinities of agony,
 Which meet the gaze, whate'er it may regard—
The groan, the roll in dust, the all-white eye
 Turn'd back within its socket,—these reward
Your rank and file by thousands, while the rest
May win perhaps a riband at the breast!

XIV.

Yet I love glory;—glory 's a great thing:—
 Think what it is to be in your old age
Maintain'd at the expense of your good king
 A moderate pension shakes full many a sage,

And heroes are but made for bards to sing,
Which is still better; thus in verse to wage
Your wars eternally, besides enjoying
Half-pay for life, make mankind worth destroying.

XV.

The troops, already disembark'd, push'd on
To take a battery on the right; the others,
Who landed lower down, their landing done,
Had set to work as briskly as their brothers:
Being grenadiers, they mounted one by one,
Cheerful as children climb the breasts of mothers,
O'er the entrenchment and the palisade,
Quite orderly, as if upon parade.

XVI.

And this was admirable; for so hot
The fire was, that were red Vesuvius loaded,
Besides its lava, with all sorts of shot
And shells or hells, it could not more have goaded.
Of officers a third fell on the spot,
A thing which victory by no means boded
To gentlemen engaged in the assault:
Hounds, when the huntsman tumbles, are at fault.

XVII.

But here I leave the general concern,
To track our hero on his path of fame:
He must his laurels separately earn;
For fifty thousand heroes, name by name,
Though all deserving equally to turn
A couplet, or an elegy to claim,
Would form a lengthy lexicon of glory,
And what is worse still, a much longer story:

XVIII.

And therefore we must give the greater number
To the Gazette—which doubtless fairly dealt
By the deceased, who lie in famous slumber
In ditches, fields, or where'er they felt
Their clay for the last time their souls encumber;—
Thrice happy he whose name has been well spelt
In the despatch: I knew a man whose loss
Was printed *Grove*, although his name was Grose.[54]

XIX.

Juan and Johnson joined a certain corps,
And fought away with might and main, not knowing
The way which they had never trod before,
And still less guessing where they might be going;
But on they march'd, dead bodies trampling o'er,
Firing, and thrusting, slashing, sweating, glowing,
But fighting thoughtlessly enough to win,
To their *two* selves, *one* whole bright bulletin.

39

XX.

Thus on they wallow'd in the bloody mire
Of dead and dying thousands,—sometimes gaining
A yard or two of ground, which brought them nigher
To some odd angle for which all were straining;
At other times, repulsed by the close fire,
Which really pour'd as if all hell were raining
Instead of heaven, they stumbled backwards o'er
A wounded comrade, sprawling in his gore.

XXI.

Though 't was Don Juan's first of fields, and though
The nightly muster and the silent march
In the chill dark, when courage does not glow
So much as under a triumphal arch,
Perhaps might make him shiver, yawn, or throw
A glance on the dull clouds (as thick as starch,
Which stiffen'd heaven) as if he wish'd for day;—
Yet for all this he did not run away.

XXII.

Indeed he could not. But what if he had?
There *have been* and *are* heroes who begun
With something not much better, or as bad:
Frederic the Great from Molwitz deign'd to run
For the first and last time; for, like a pad,
Or hawk, or bride, most mortals after one
Warm bout are broken into their new tricks,
And fight like fiends for pay or politics.

XXIII.

He was what Erin calls, in her sublime
Old Erse or Irish, or it may be *Punic*;—
(The antiquarians who can settle time,[55]
Which settles all things, Roman, Greek, or Runic,
Swear that Pat's language sprung from the same clime
With Hannibal, and wears the Tyrian tunic
Of Dido's alphabet; and this is rational
As any other notion, and not national);—

XXIV.

But Juan was quite "a broth of a boy,"
A thing of impulse and a child of song;
Now swimming in the sentiment of joy,
Or the *sensation* (if that phrase seem wrong),
And afterward, if he must needs destroy,
In such good company as always throng
To battles, sieges, and that kind of pleasure,
No less delighted to employ his leisure;

XXV.

But always without malice: if he warr'd
Or loved, it was with what we call "the best
Intentions," which form all mankind's *trump card*,
To be produced when brought up to the test.

The statesman, hero, harlot, lawyer—ward
 Off each attack, when people are in quest
Of their designs, by saying they *meant well;*
'T is pity "that such meaning should pave hell."[56]

XXVI.

I almost lately have begun to doubt,
 Whether hell's pavement—if it be so *paved*—
Must not have latterly been quite worn out,
 Not by the numbers good intent hath saved,
But by the mass who go below without
 Those ancient good intentions, which once shaved
And smooth'd the brimstone of that street of hell,
Which bears the greatest likeness to Pall Mall.

XXVII.

Juan, by some strange chance, which oft divides
 Warrior from warrior, in their grim career,
Like chastest wives from constant husbands' sides
 Just at the close of the first bridal year,
By one of those odd turns of Fortune's tides,
 Was on a sudden rather puzzled here,
When, after a good deal of heavy firing,
He found himself alone, and friends retiring.

XXVIII.

I do n't know how the thing occurr'd—it might
 Be that the greater part were kill'd or wounded,
And that the rest had faced unto the right
 About; a circumstance which has confounded
Cæsar himself, who, in the very sight
 Of his whole army, which so much abounded
In courage, was obliged to snatch a shield,
And rally back his Romans to the field.

XXIX.

Juan, who had no shield to snatch, and was
 No Cæsar, but a fine young lad, who fought
He knew not why, arriving at this pass,
 Stopp'd for a minute, as perhaps he ought
For a much longer time; then, like an ass—
 (Start not, kind reader, since great Homer thought
This simile enough for Ajax, Juan
Perhaps may find it better than a new one);—

XXX.

Then, like an ass, he went upon his way,
 And, what was stranger, never look'd behind;
But seeing, flashing forward, like the day
 Over the hills, a fire enough to blind
Those who dislike to look upon a fray,
 He stumbled on, to try if he could find
A path, to add his own slight arm and forces
To corps, the greater part of which were corses.

XXXI.

Perceiving then no more the commandant
 Of his own corps, nor even the corps, which had
Quite disappear'd—the gods know how! (I can't
 Account for every thing which may look bad
In history; but we at least may grant
 It was not marvellous that a mere lad,
In search of glory, should look on before,
Nor care a pinch of snuff about his corps:)—

XXXII.

Perceiving nor commander nor commanded,
 And left at large, like a young heir, to make
His way to—where he knew not—single handed;
 As travellers follow over bog and brake
An "ignis fatuus;" or as sailors stranded
 Unto the nearest hut themselves betake;
So Juan, following honour and his nose,
Rush'd where the thickest fire announced most foes.

XXXIII.

He knew not where he was, nor greatly cared,
 For he was dizzy, busy, and his veins
Fill'd as with lightning—for his spirit shared
 The hour, as is the case with lively brains;
And where the hottest fire was seen and heard,
 And the loud cannon peal'd his hoarsest strains,
He rush'd, while earth and air were sadly shaken
By thy humane discovery, Friar Bacon![57]

XXXIV.

And as he rush'd along, it came to pass he
 Fell in with what was late the second column,
Under the orders of the General Lascy,
 But now reduced, as is a bulky volume
Into an elegant extract (much less massy)
 Of heroism, and took his place with solemn
Air 'midst the rest, who kept their valiant faces
And levell'd weapons still against the glacis.

XXXV.

Just at this crisis up came Johnson too,
 Who had "retreated," as the phrase is when
Men run away much rather than go through
 Destruction's jaws into the devil's den;
But Johnson was a clever fellow, who
 Knew when and how "to cut and come again,"
And never ran away, except when running
Was nothing but a valorous kind of cunning.

XXXVI.

And so, when all his corps were dead or dying,
 Except Don Juan, a mere novice, whose
More virgin valour never dreamt of flying,
 From ignorance of danger, which indues
Its votaries, like innocence relying
 On its own strength, with careless nerves and thews,—
Johnson retired a little, just to rally
Those who catch cold in "shadows of Death's valley."

XXXVII.

And there, a little shelter'd from the shot,
Which rain'd from bastion, battery, parapet,
Rampart, wall, casement, house—for there was not
In this extensive city, sore beset
By Christian soldiery, a single spot
Which did not combat like the devil, as yet,—
He found a number of Chasseurs, all scatter'd
By the resistance of the chase they batter'd.

XXXVIII.

And these he call'd on; and, what 's strange, they came
Unto his call, unlike "the spirits from
The vasty deep," to whom you may exclaim,
Says Hotspur, long ere they will leave their home.
Their reasons were uncertainty, or shame
At shrinking from a bullet or a bomb,
And that odd impulse, which in wars or creeds
Makes men, like cattle, follow him who leads.

XXXIX.

By Jove! he was a noble fellow, Johnson,
And though his name, than Ajax or Achilles,
Sounds less harmonious, underneath the sun soon
We shall not see his likeness: he could kill his
Man quite as quietly as blows the monsoon
Her steady breath (which some months the same *still* is):
Seldom he varied feature, hue, or muscle,
And could be very busy without bustle;

XL.

And therefore, when he ran away, he did so
Upon reflection, knowing that behind
He would find others who would fain be rid so
Of idle apprehensions, which like wind
Trouble heroic stomachs. Though their lids so
Oft are soon closed, all heroes are not blind,
But when they light upon immediate death,
Retire a little, merely to take breath.

XLI.

But Johnson only ran off, to return
With many other warriors, as we said,
Unto that rather somewhat misty bourn,
Which Hamlet tells us is a pass of dread.
To Jack, howe'er, this gave but slight concern:
His soul (like galvanism upon the dead)
Acted upon the living as on wire,
And led them back into the heaviest fire.

XLII.

Egad! they found the second time what they
The first time thought quite terrible enough
To fly from, malgré all which people say
Of glory, and all that immortal stuff
Which fills a regiment (besides their pay,
That daily shilling which makes warriors tough)—
They found on their return the self-same welcome,
Which made some *think*, and others *know*, a *hell* come.

XLIII.

They fell as thick as harvests beneath hail,
Grass before scythes, or corn below the sickle,
Proving that trite old truth, that life 's as frail
As any other boon for which men stickle.
The Turkish batteries thrash'd them like a flail,
Or a good boxer, into a sad pickle
Putting the very bravest, who were knock'd
Upon the head, before their guns were cock'd.

XLIV.

The Turks behind the traverses and flanks
Of the next bastion, fired away like devils,
And swept, as gales sweep foam away, whole ranks:
However, Heaven knows how, the Fate who levels
Towns, nations, worlds, in her revolving pranks,
So order'd it, amidst these sulphury revels,
That Johnson and some few who had not scamper'd,
Reach'd the interior talus of the rampart

XLV.

First one or two, then five, six, and a dozen
Came mounting quickly up, for it was now
All neck or nothing, as, like pitch or rosin,
Flame was shower'd forth above, as well 's below,
So that you scarce could say who best had chosen,
The gentlemen that were the first to show
Their martial faces on the parapet,
Or those who thought it brave to wait as yet.

XLVI.

But those who scaled, found out that their advance
Was favour'd by an accident or blunder:
The Greek or Turkish Cohorn's ignorance
Had palisado'd in a way you'd wonder
To see in forts of Netherlands or France—
(Though these to our Gibraltar must knock under)—
Right in the middle of the parapet
Just named, these palisades were primly set:

XLVII.

So that on either side some nine or ten
Paces were left, whereon you could contrive
To march; a great convenience to our men,
At least to all those who were left alive,
Who thus could form a line and fight again;
And that which further aided them to strive
Was, that they could kick down the palisades,
Which scarcely rose much higher than grass blades.

XLVIII.

Among the first,—I will not say the *first*,
 For such precedence upon such occasions
Will oftentimes make deadly quarrels burst
 Out between friends as well as allied nations:
The Briton must be bold who really durst
 Put to such trial John Bull's partial patience,
As say that Wellington at Waterloo
Was beaten,—though the Prussians say so too;—

XLIX.

And that if Blucher, Bulow, and Gneisenau,
 And God knows who besides in "au" and "ow,"
Had not come up in time to cast an awe
 Into the hearts of those who fought till now
As tigers combat with an empty craw,
 The Duke of Wellington had ceased to show
His orders, also to receive his pensions;
Which are the heaviest that our history mentions.

L.

But never mind;—"God save the king!" and kings!
 For if *He* don't, I doubt if *men* will longer—
I think I hear a little bird, who sings
 The people by and by will be the stronger:
The veriest jade will wince whose harness wrings
 So much into the raw as quite to wrong her
Beyond the rules of posting,—and the mob
At last fall sick of imitating Job.

LI.

At first it grumbles, then it swears, and then,
 Like David, flings smooth pebbles 'gainst a giant;
At last it takes to weapons such as men
 Snatch when despair makes human hearts less pliant.
Then comes "the tug of war;"—'t will come again,
 I rather doubt; and I would fain say "fie on 't,"
If I had not perceived that revolution
Alone can save the earth from hell's pollution.

LII.

But to continue:—I say not *the* first,
 But of the first, our little friend Don Juan
Walk'd o'er the walls of Ismail, as if nursed
 Amidst such scenes—though this was quite a new one
To him, and I should hope to *most*. The thirst
 Of glory, which so pierces through and through one,
Pervaded him—although a generous creature,
As warm in heart as feminine in feature.

LIII.

And here he was—who upon woman's breast,
 Even from a child, felt like a child; howe'er
The man in all the rest might be confest,
 To him it was Elysium to be there;
And he could even withstand that awkward test
 Which Rousseau points out to the dubious fair,
"Observe your lover when he *leaves* your arms;"
But Juan never left them, while they had charms,

LIV.

Unless compell'd by fate, or wave, or wind,
 Or near relations, who are much the same.
But *here* he was!—where each tie that can bind
 Humanity must yield to steel and flame:
And *he* whose very body was all mind,
 Flung here by fate or circumstance, which tame
The loftiest, hurried by the time and place,
Dash'd on like a spurr'd blood-horse in a race.

LV.

So was his blood stirr'd while he found resistance,
 As is the hunter's at the five-bar gate,
Or double post and rail, where the existence
 Of Britain's youth depends upon their weight,
The lightest being the safest: at a distance
 He hated cruelty, as all men hate
Blood, until heated—and even then his own
At times would curdle o'er some heavy groan.

LVI.

The General Lascy, who had been hard press'd,
 Seeing arrive an aid so opportune
As were some hundred youngsters all abreast,
 Who came as if just dropp'd down from the moon,
To Juan, who was nearest him, address'd
 His thanks, and hopes to take the city soon,
Not reckoning him to be a "base Bezonian,"
(As Pistol calls it) but a young Livonian.

LVII.

Juan, to whom he spoke in German, knew
 As much of German as of Sanscrit, and
In answer made an inclination to
 The general who held him in command;
For seeing one with ribands, black and blue,
 Stars, medals, and a bloody sword in hand,
Addressing him in tones which seem'd to thank,
He recognised an officer of rank.

LVIII.

Short speeches pass between two men who speak
 No common language; and besides, in time
Of war and taking towns, when many a shriek
 Rings o'er the dialogue, and many a crime
Is perpetrated ere a word can break
 Upon the ear, and sounds of horror chime
In like church-bells, with sigh, howl, groan, yell, prayer,
There cannot be much conversation there.

LIX.

And therefore all we have related in
 Two long octaves, pass'd in a little minute;
But in the same small minute, every sin
 Contrived to get itself comprised within it.
The very cannon, deafened by the din,
 Grew dumb, for you might almost hear a linnet,
As soon as thunder, 'midst the general noise
Of human nature's agonising voice!

LX.

The town was enter'd. Oh eternity!—
 "God made the country, and man made the town,"
So Cowper says—and I begin to be
 Of his opinion, when I see cast down
Rome, Babylon, Tyre, Carthage, Nineveh,
 All walls men know, and many never known;
And pondering on the present and the past,
To deem the woods shall be our home at last:—

LXI.

Of all men, saving Sylla the man-slayer,
 Who passes for in life and death most lucky,
Of the great names which in our faces stare,
 The General Boon, back-woodsman of Kentucky,
Was happiest amongst mortals any where;
 For killing nothing but a bear or buck, he
Enjoy'd the lonely, vigorous, harmless days
Of his old age in wilds of deepest maze.

LXII.

Crime came not near him—she is not the child
 Of Solitude; Health shrank not from him—for
Her home is in the rarely trodden wild,
 Where if men seek her not, and death be more
Their choice than life, forgive them, as beguiled
 By habit to what their own hearts abhor—
In cities caged. The present case in point I
Cite is, that Boon lived hunting up to ninety;

LXIII.

And what's still stranger, left behind a name
 For which men vainly decimate the throng,
Not only famous, but of that *good* fame,
 Without which glory 's but a tavern song—
Simple, serene, the antipodes of shame,
 Which hate nor envy e'er could tinge with wrong;
An active hermit, even in age the child
Of Nature, or the Man of Ross run wild.

LXIV.

'Tis true he shrank from men even of his nation,
 When they built up unto his darling trees,—
He moved some hundred miles off, for a station
 Where there were fewer houses and more ease;
The inconvenience of civilisation
 Is, that you neither can be pleased nor please;
But where he met the individual man,
He show'd himself as kind as mortal can.

LXV.

He was not all alone: around him grew
 A sylvan tribe of children of the chase,
Whose young, unawaken'd world was ever new,
 Nor sword nor sorrow yet had left a trace
On her unwrinkled brow, nor could you view
 A frown on Nature's or on human face;—
The free-born forest found and kept them free,
And fresh as is a torrent, or a tree.

LXVI.

And tall, and strong, and swift of foot were they,
 Beyond the dwarfing city's pale abortions,
Because their thoughts had never been the prey
 Of care or gain; the green woods were their portions;
No sinking spirits told them they grew gray,
 No fashion made them apes of her distortions;
Simple they were, not savage; and their rifles,
Though very true, were not yet used for trifles.

LXVII.

Motion was in their days, rest in their slumbers,
 And cheerfulness the handmaid of their toil;
Nor yet too many nor too few their numbers;
 Corruption could not make their hearts her soil;
The lust which stings, the splendour which encumbers,
 With the free foresters divide no spoil;
Serene, not sullen, were the solitudes
Of this unsighing people of the woods.

LXVIII.

So much for Nature:—by way of variety,
 Now back to thy great joys, Civilisation!
And the sweet consequence of large society,
 War, pestilence, the despot's desolation,
The kingly scourge, the lust of notoriety,
 The millions slain by soldiers for their ration,
The scenes like Catherine's boudoir at threescore,
With Ismail's storm to soften it the more.

LXIX.

The town was enter'd: first one column made
 Its sanguinary way good—then another;
The reeking bayonet and the flashing blade
 Clash'd 'gainst the scimitar, and babe and mother
With distant shrieks were heard Heaven to upbraid:
 Still closer sulphury clouds began to smother
The breath of morn and man, where foot by foot
The madden'd Turks their city still dispute.

LXX.

Koutousow, he who afterward beat back
(With some assistance from the frost and snow)
Napoleon on his bold and bloody track,
It happen'd was himself beat back just now:
He was a jolly fellow, and could crack
His jest alike in face of friend or foe,
Though life, and death, and victory were at stake;
But here it seem'd his jokes had ceased to take:

LXXI.

For having thrown himself into a ditch,
Follow'd in haste by various grenadiers,
Whose blood the puddle greatly did enrich,
He climb'd to where the parapet appears;
But there his project reach'd its utmost pitch
('Mongst other deaths the General Ribaupierre's
Was much regretted), for the Moslem men
Threw them all down into the ditch again.

LXXII.

And had it not been for some stray troops landing
They knew not where, being carried by the stream
To some spot, where they lost their understanding,
And wander'd up and down as in a dream,
Until they reach'd, as daybreak was expanding,
That which a portal to their eyes did seem,—
The great and gay Koutousow might have lain
Where three parts of his column yet remain.

LXXIII.

And scrambling round the rampart, these same troops,
After the taking of the "Cavalier,"
Just as Koutousow's most "forlorn" of "hopes"
Took, like chameleons, some slight tinge of fear,
Open'd the gate call'd "Kilia," to the groups
Of baffled heroes, who stood shyly near,
Sliding knee-deep in lately frozen mud,
Now thaw'd into a marsh of human blood.

LXXIV.

The Kozacks, or, if so you please, Cossacques—
(I don't much pique myself upon orthography,
So that I do not grossly err in facts,
Statistics, tactics, politics, and geography)—
Having been used to serve on horses' backs,
And no great dilettanti in topography
Of fortresses, but fighting where it pleases
Their chiefs to order,—were all cut to pieces.

LXXV.

Their column, though the Turkish batteries thunder'd
Upon them, ne'ertheless had reach'd the rampart,
And naturally thought they could have plunder'd
The city, without being farther hamper'd;
But as it happens to brave men, they blunder'd—
The Turks at first pretended to have scamper'd,
Only to draw them 'twixt two bastion corners,
From whence they sallied on those Christian scorners.

LXXVI.

Then being taken by the tail—a taking
Fatal to bishops as to soldiers—these
Cossacques were all cut off as day was breaking,
And found their lives were let at a short lease—
But perish'd without shivering or shaking,
Leaving as ladders their heap'd carcasses,
O'er which Lieutenant-Colonel Yesouskoi
March'd with the brave battalion of Polouzki:—

LXXVII.

This valiant man kill'd all the Turks he met,
But could not eat them, being in his turn
Slain by some Mussulmans, who would not yet,
Without resistance, see their city burn.
The walls were won, but 't was an even bet
Which of the armies would have cause to mourn:
'T was blow for blow, disputing inch by inch,
For one would not retreat, nor 't other flinch.

LXXVIII.

Another column also suffer'd much:—
And here we may remark with the historian,
You should but give few cartridges to such
Troops as are meant to march with greatest glory on:
When matters must be carried by the touch
Of the bright bayonet, and they all should hurry on,
They sometimes, with a hankering for existence,
Keep merely firing at a foolish distance.

LXXIX.

A junction of the General Meknop's men
(Without the General, who had fallen some time
Before, being badly seconded just then)
Was made at length with those who dared to climb
The death-disgorging rampart once again;
And though the Turks' resistance was sublime,
They took the bastion, which the Seraskier
Defended at a price extremely dear.

LXXX.

Juan and Johnson, and some volunteers
Among the foremost, offer'd him good quarter,
A word which little suits with Seraskiers,
Or at least suited not this valiant Tartar.
He died, deserving well his country's tears,
A savage sort of military martyr.
An English naval officer, who wish'd
To make him prisoner, was also dish'd:

LXXXI.

For all the answer to his proposition
Was from a pistol-shot that laid him dead;
On which the rest, without more intermission,
Began to lay about with steel and lead—
The pious metals most in requisition
On such occasions: not a single head
Was spared;—three thousand Moslems perish'd here,
And sixteen bayonets pierced the Seraskier.

LXXXII.

The city 's taken—only part by part—
And Death is drunk with gore: there 's not a street
Where fights not to the last some desperate heart,
For those for whom it soon shall cease to beat.
Here war forgot his own destructive art
In more destroying Nature; and the heat
Of carnage, like the Nile's sun-sodden slime,
Engender'd monstrous shapes of every crime.

LXXXIII.

A Russian officer, in martial tread
Over a heap of bodies, felt his heel
Seized fast, as if 't were by the serpent's head
Whose fangs Eve taught her human seed to feel;
In vain he kick'd, and swore, and writhed, and bled,
And howl'd for help as wolves do for a meal—
The teeth still kept their gratifying hold,
As do the subtle snakes described of old.

LXXXIV.

A dying Moslem, who had felt the foot
Of a foe o'er him, snatch'd at it, and bit
The very tendon which is most acute—
(That which some ancient Muse or modern wit
Named after thee, Achilles) and quite through 't
He made the teeth meet, nor relinquish'd it
Even with his life—for (but they lie) 't is said
To the live leg still clung the sever'd head.

LXXXV.

However this may be, 't is pretty sure
The Russian officer for life was lamed,
For the Turk's teeth stuck faster than a skewer,
And left him 'midst the invalid and maim'd:
The regimental surgeon could not cure
His patient, and perhaps was to be blamed
More than the head of the inveterate foe,
Which was cut off, and scarce even then let go.

LXXXVI.

But then the fact 's a fact—and 't is the part
Of a true poet to escape from fiction
Whene'er he can; for there is little art
In leaving verse more free from the restriction
Of truth than prose, unless to suit the mart
For what is sometimes called poetic diction,
And that outrageous appetite for lies
Which Satan angles with for souls, like flies.

LXXXVII.

The city 's taken, but not render'd!—No!
There's not a Moslem that hath yielded swor
The blood may gush out, as the Danube's flow
Rolls by the city wall; but deed nor word
Acknowledge aught of dread of death or foe:
In vain the yell of victory is roar'd
By the advancing Muscovite—the groan
Of the last foe is echoed by his own.

LXXXVIII.

The bayonet pierces and the sabre cleaves,
And human lives are lavish'd every where,
As the year closing whirls the scarlet leaves,
When the stripp'd forest bows to the bleak air,
And groans; and thus the peopled city grieves,
Shorn of its best and loveliest, and left bare;
But still it falls in vast and awful splinters,
As oaks blown down with all their thousand winters.

LXXXIX.

It is an awful topic—but 't is not
My cue for any time to be terrific:
For checker'd as is seen our human lot
With good, and bad, and worse, alike prolific
Of melancholy merriment, to quote
Too much of one sort would be soporific;—
Without, or with, offence to friends or foes,
I sketch your world exactly as it goes.

XC.

And one good action in the midst of crimes
Is "quite refreshing," in the affected phrase
Of these ambrosial, Pharisaic times,
With all their pretty milk-and-water ways,
And may serve therefore to bedew these rhymes,
A little scorch'd at present with the blaze
Of conquest and its consequences, which
Make epic poesy so rare and rich.

XCI.

Upon a taken bastion, where there lay
Thousands of slaughter'd men, a yet warm group
Of murder'd women, who had found their way
To this vain refuge, made the good heart droop
And shudder;—while, as beautiful as May,
A female child of ten years tried to stoop
And hide her little palpitating breast
Amidst the bodies lull'd in bloody rest.

XCII.

Two villanous Cossacques pursued the child
With flashing eyes and weapons; match'd with them,
The rudest brute that roams Siberia's wild
Has feelings pure and polish'd as a gem,—
The bear is civilised, the wolf is mild;
And whom for this at last must we condemn?
Their natures? or their sovereigns, who employ
All arts to teach their subjects to destroy?

XCIII.

Their sabres glitter'd o'er her little head,
 Whence her fair hair rose twining with affright,
Her hidden face was plunged amidst the dead:
 When Juan caught a glimpse of this sad sight,
I shall not say exactly what he *said*
 Because it might not solace "ears polite;"
But what he *did*, was to lay on their backs,
The readiest way of reasoning with Cossacques.

XCIV.

One's hip he slash'd, and split the other's shoulder,
 And drove them with their brutal yells to seek,
If there might be chirurgeons who could solder
 The wounds they richly merited, and shriek
Their baffled rage and pain; while waxing colder
 As he turn'd o'er each pale and gory cheek,
Don Juan raised his little captive from
The heap a moment more had made her tomb.

XCV.

And she was chill as they, and on her face
 A slender streak of blood announced how near
Her fate had been to that of all her race;
 For the same blow which laid her mother here
Had scarr'd her brow, and left its crimson trace,
 As the last link with all she had held dear;
But else unhurt, she open'd her large eyes,
And gazed on Juan with a wild surprise.

XCVI.

Just at this instant, while their eyes were fix'd
 Upon each other, with dilated glance,
In Juan's look, pain, pleasure, hope, fear, mix'd
 With joy to save, and dread of some mischance
Unto his protégée; while her's, transfix'd
 With infant terrors, glared as from a trance,
A pure, transparent, pale, yet radiant face,
Like to a lighted alabaster vase;—

XCVII.

Up came John Johnson (I will not say "*Jack*,"
 For that were vulgar, cold, and common-place
On great occasions, such as an attack
 On cities, as hath been the present case):
Up Johnson came, with hundreds at his back,
 Exclaiming:—"Juan! Juan! On, boy! brace
Your arm, and I'll bet Moscow to a dollar,
That you and I will win St. George's collar.[58]

XCVIII.

"The Seraskier is knock'd upon the head,
 But the stone bastion still remains, wherein
The old Pacha sits among some hundreds dead,
 Smoking his pipe quite calmly 'midst the din
Of our artillery and his own: 't is said
 Our kill'd, already piled up to the chin,
Lie round the battery; but still it batters,
And grape in volleys, like a vineyard, scatters.

XCIX.

"Then up with me!"—But Juan answer'd, "Look
 Upon this child—I saved her—must not leave
Her life to chance; but point me out some nook
 Of safety, where she less may shrink and grieve,
And I am with you."—Whereon Johnson took
 A glance around—and shrugg'd—and twitch'd his sleeve
And black silk neckcloth—and replied, "You're right;
Poor thing! what's to be done? I'm puzzled quite."

C.

Said Juan—"Whatsoever is to be
 Done, I'll not quit her till she seems secure
Of present life a good deal more than we."—
 Quoth Johnson—"*Neither* will I quite ensure;
But at the least *you* may die gloriously."—
 Juan replied—"At least I will endure
Whate'er is to be borne—but not resign
This child, who is parentless, and therefore mine."

CI.

Johnson said—"Juan, we've no time to lose;
 The child's a pretty child—a very pretty—
I never saw such eyes—but hark! now choose
 Between your fame and feelings, pride and pity;—
Hark! how the roar increases!—no excuse
 Will serve when there is plunder in a city;—
I should be loath to march without you, but,
By God! we'll be too late for the first cut."

CII.

But Juan was immoveable; until
 Johnson, who really loved him in his way,
Pick'd out amongst his followers with some skill
 Such as he thought the least given up to prey;
And swearing if the infant came to ill
 That they should all be shot on the next day;
But if she were deliver'd safe and sound,
They should at least have fifty rubles round,

CIII.

And all allowances besides of plunder
 In fair proportion with their comrades;—then
Juan consented to march on through thunder,
 Which thinn'd at every step their ranks of men:
And yet the rest rush'd eagerly—no wonder,
 For they were heated by the hope of gain,
A thing which happens every where each day—
No hero trusteth wholly to half-pay.

CIV.

And such is victory, and such is man!
 At least nine tenths of what we call so;—God
May have another name for half we scan
 As human beings, or His ways are odd.
But to our subject: a brave Tartar khan—
 Or "sultan," as the author (to whose nod
In prose I bend my humble verse) doth call
This chieftain—somehow would not yield at all:

CV.

But flank'd by *five* brave sons (such is polygamy,
 That she spawns warriors by the score, where none
Are prosecuted for that false crime bigamy),
 He never would believe the city won
While courage clung but to a single twig.—Am I
 Describing Priam's, Peleus', or Jove's son?
Neither—but a good, plain, old, temperate man,
Who fought with his five children in the van.

CVI.

To *take* him was the point.—The truly brave,
 When they behold the brave oppress'd with odds,
Are touch'd with a desire to shield and save;—
 A mixture of wild beasts and demi-gods

Are they—now furious as the sweeping wave,
 Now moved with pity: even as sometimes nods
The rugged tree unto the summer wind,
Compassion breathes along the savage mind.

CVII.

But he would *not* be *taken*, and replied
 To all the propositions of surrender
By mowing Christians down on every side,
 As obstinate as Swedish Charles at Bender.
His five brave boys no less the foe defied;
 Whereon the Russian pathos grew less tender,
As being a virtue, like terrestrial patience,
Apt to wear out on trifling provocations.

CVIII.

And spite of Johnson and of Juan, who
 Expended all their Eastern phraseology
In begging him, for God's sake, just to show
 So much less fight as might form an apology
For *them* in saving such a desperate foe—
 He hew'd away, like doctors of theology—
When they dispute with sceptics; and with curses
Struck at his friends, as babies beat their nurses.

CIX.

Nay, he had wounded, though but slightly, both
 Juan and Johnson; whereupon they fell,
The first with sighs, the second with an oath,
 Upon his angry sultanship, pell-mell,
And all around were grown exceeding wroth
 At such a pertinacious infidel,
And pour'd upon him and his sons like rain,
Which they resisted like a sandy plain

CX.

That drinks and still is dry. At last they perish'd—
 His second son was levell'd by a shot;
His third was sabred; and the fourth, most cherish'd
 Of all the five, on bayonets met his lot;
The fifth, who, by a Christian mother nourish'd,
 Had been neglected, ill-used, and what not,
Because deform'd, yet died all game and bottom,
To save a sire who blush'd that he begot him.

CXI.

The eldest was a true and tameless Tartar,
 As great a scorner of the Nazarene
As ever Mahomet pick'd out for a martyr,
 Who only saw the black-eyed girls in green,
Who make the beds of those who won't take quarter
 On earth, in Paradise; and when once seen,
Those houris, like all other pretty creatures,
Do just whate'er they please, by dint of features.

CXII.

And what they pleased to do with the young khan
 In heaven I know not, nor pretend to guess;
But doubtless they prefer a fine young man
 To tough old heroes, and can do no less;
And that's the cause no doubt, why, if we scan
 A field of battle's ghastly wilderness,
For one rough, weather-beaten, veteran body,
You'll find ten thousand handsome coxcombs bloody.

CXIII.

Your houris also have a natural pleasure
 In lopping off your lately married men,
Before the bridal hours have danced their measure,
 And the sad, second moon grows dim again,
Or dull repentance hath had dreary leisure
 To wish him back a bachelor now and then.
And thus your houri (it may be) disputes
Of these brief blossoms the immediate fruits.

CXIV.

Thus the young khan, with houris in his sight,
 Thought not upon the charms of four young brides,
But bravely rush'd on his first heavenly night.
 In short, howe'er *our* better faith derides,
These black-eyed virgins make the Moslems fight,
 As though there were one heaven and none besides,
Whereas, if all be true we hear of heaven
And hell, there must at least be six or seven.

CXV.

So fully flash'd the phantom on his eyes
 That when the very lance was in his heart,
He shouted "Allah!" and saw Paradise
 With all its veil of mystery drawn apart,
And bright eternity without disguise
 On his soul, like a ceaseless sunrise, dart:—
With prophets, houris, angels, saints, descried
In one voluptuous blaze,—and then he died:

CXVI.

But with a heavenly rapture on his face,
 The good old khan, who long had ceased to see
Houris, or aught except his florid race
 Who grew like cedars round him gloriously—
When he beheld his latest hero grace
 The earth, which he became like a fell'd tree,
Paused for a moment from the fight, and cast
A glance on that slain son, his first and last.

CXVII.

The soldiers, who beheld him drop his point,
 Stopp'd as if once more willing to concede
Quarter, in case he bade them not "aroynt!"
 As he before had done. He did not heed
Their pause nor signs: his heart was out of joint,
 And shook (till now unshaken) like a reed,
As he look'd down upon his children gone,
And felt—though done with life—he was alone.

CXVIII.

But 't was a transient tremor:—with a spring
 Upon the Russian steel his breast he flung,

As carelessly as hurls the moth her wing
 Against the light wherein she dies: he clung
Closer, that all the deadlier they might wring,
 Unto the bayonets which had pierced his young;
And throwing back a dim look on his sons,
In one wide wound pour'd forth his soul at once.

CXIX.

'T is strange enough—the rough, tough soldiers, who
 Spared neither sex nor age in their career
Of carnage, when this old man was pierced through,
 And lay before them with his children near,
Touch'd by the heroism of him they slew,
 Were melted for a moment: though no tear
Flow'd from their bloodshot eyes, all red with strife,
They honour'd such determined scorn of life.

CXX.

But the stone bastion still kept up its fire,
 Where the chief pacha calmly held his post:
Some twenty times he made the Russ retire,
 And baffled the assaults of all their host:
At length he condescended to inquire
 If yet the city's rest were won or lost;
And being told the latter, sent a bey
To answer Ribas' summons to give way

CXXI.

In the mean time, cross-legg'd, with great sang-froid,
 Among the scorching ruins he sat smoking
Tobacco on a little carpet:—Troy
 Saw nothing like the scene around;—yet looking
With martial stoicism, nought seem'd to annoy
 His stern philosophy; but gently stroking
His beard, he puff'd his pipe's ambrosial gales,
As if he had three lives, as well as tails.

CXXII.

The town was taken—whether he might yield
 Himself or bastion, little matter'd now:
His stubborn valour was no future shield.
 Ismail's no more! The crescent's silver bow
Sunk, and the crimson cross glared o'er the field,
 But red with no *redeeming* gore: the glow
Of burning streets, like moonlight on the water,
Was imaged back in blood, the sea of slaughter.

CXXIII.

All that the mind would shrink from of excesses;
 All that the body perpetrates of bad;
All that we read, hear, dream, of man's distresses;
 All that the devil would do if run stark mad;
All that defies the worst which pen expresses;
 All by which hell is peopled, or as sad
As hell—mere mortals who their power abuse—
Was here (as heretofore and since) let loose.

CXXIV.

If here and there some transient trait of pity
 Was shown, and some more noble heart broke through
Its bloody bond, and saved, perhaps, some pretty
 Child, or an aged, helpless man or two—
What's this in one annihilated city,
 Where thousand loves, and ties, and duties grew?
Cockneys of London! Muscadins of Paris!
Just ponder what a pious pastime war is.

CXXV.

Think how the joys of reading a Gazette
 Are purchased by all agonies and crimes:
Or if these do not move you, do n't forget
 Such doom may be your own in after-times.
Meantime the Taxes, Castlereagh, and Debt,
 Are hints as good as sermons, or as rhymes.
Read your own hearts and Ireland's present story,
Then feed her famine fat with Wellesley's glory.

CXXVI.

But still there is unto a patriot nation,
 Which loves so well its country and its king,
A subject of sublimest exultation—
 Bear it, ye Muses, on your brightest wing!
Howe'er the mighty locust, Desolation,
 Strip your green fields, and to your harvests cling,
Gaunt famine never shall approach the throne—
Though Ireland starve, great George weighs twenty stone.

CXXVII.

But let me put an end unto my theme:
 There was an end of Ismail—hapless town!
Far flash'd her burning towers o'er Danube's stream,
 And redly ran his blushing waters down.
The horrid war-whoop and the shriller scream
 Rose still; but fainter were the thunders grown:
Of forty thousand who had mann'd the wall,
Some hundreds breathed—the rest were silent all!

CXXVIII.

In one thing ne'ertheless 't is fit to praise
 The Russian army upon this occasion,
A virtue much in fashion now-a-days,
 And therefore worthy of commemoration:
The topic's tender, so shall be my phrase—
 Perhaps the season's chill, and their long station
In winter's depth, or want of rest and victual,
Had made them chaste;—they ravish'd very little.

CXXIX.

Much did they slay, more plunder, and no less
 Might here and there occur some violation
In the other line;—but not to such excess
 As when the French, that dissipated nation,
Take towns by storm: no causes can I guess,
 Except cold weather and commiseration;
But all the ladies, save some twenty score,
Were almost as much virgins as before.

CXXX.

Some odd mistakes, too, happen'd in the dark,
 Which show'd a want of lanterns, or of taste—
Indeed the smoke was such they scarce could mark
 Their friends from foes,—besides, such things from haste
Occur, though rarely, when there is a spark
 Of light to save the venerably chaste:

But six old damsels, each of seventy years,
Were all deflower'd by different grenadiers.

CXXXI.

But on the whole their continence was great;
So that some disappointment there ensued
To those who had felt the inconvenient state
Of "single blessedness," and thought it good
(Since it was not their fault, but only fate,
To bear these crosses) for each waning prude
To make a Roman sort of Sabine wedding,
Without the expense and the suspense of bedding.

CXXXII.

Some voices of the buxom middle-aged
Were also heard to wonder in the din
(Widows of forty were these birds long caged)
"Wherefore the ravishing did not begin!"
But while the thirst for gore and plunder raged,
There was small leisure for superfluous sin:
But whether they escaped or no, lies hid
In darkness—I can only hope they did.

CXXXIII.

Suwarrow now was conqueror—a match
For Timour or for Zinghis in his trade.
While mosques and streets, beneath his eyes, like thatch
Blazed, and the cannon's roar was scarce allay'd,
With bloody hands he wrote his first despatch;
And here exactly follows what he said:—
"Glory to *God* and to the Empress!" (*Powers
Eternal! such names mingled!*) "Ismail 's ours."[59]

CXXXIV.

Methinks these are the most tremendous words
Since "Menè, Menè, Tekel," and "Upharsin,"
Which hands or pens have ever traced of swords.
Heaven help me! I'm but little of a parson:
What Daniel read was short-hand of the Lord's,
Severe, sublime; the prophet wrote no farce on
The fate of nations;—but this Russ so witty
Could rhyme, like Nero, o'er a burning city.

CXXXV.

He wrote this Polar melody, and set it,
Duly accompanied by shrieks and groans,
Which few will sing, I trust, but none forget it—
For I will teach, if possible, the stones
To rise against earth's tyrants. Never let it
Be said that we still truckle unto thrones;—
But ye—our children's children! think how we
Show'd *what things were* before the world was free!

CXXXVI.

That hour is not for us, but 't is for you·
And as, in the great joy of your millennium,
You hardly will believe such things were true
As now occur, I thought that I would pen you 'em;
But may their very memory perish too!—
Yet if perchance remember'd, still disdain you 'em
More than you scorn the savages of yore,
Who *painted* their *bare* limbs, but *not* with gore.

CXXXVII.

And when you hear historians talk of thrones,
And those that sate upon them, let it be
As we now gaze upon the mammoth's bones,
And wonder what old world such things could see,
Or hieroglyphics on Egyptian stones,
The pleasant riddles of futurity—
Guessing at what shall happily be hid,
As the real purpose of a pyramid.

CXXXVIII.

Reader! I have kept my word,—at least so far
As the first Canto promised. You have now
Had sketches of love, tempest, travel, war—
All very accurate, you must allow,
And *epic*, if plain truth should prove no bar;
For I have drawn much less with a long bow
Than my forerunners. Carelessly I sing,
But Phœbus lends me now and then a string,

CXXXIX.

With which I still can harp, and carp, and fiddle
What farther hath befallen or may befall
The hero of this grand poetic riddle,
I by and by may tell you, if at all:
But now I choose to break off in the middle,
Worn out with battering Ismail's stubborn wall,
While Juan is sent off with the despatch,
For which all Petersburgh is on the watch.

CXL.

This special honour was conferr'd, because
He had behaved with courage and humanity—
Which *last* men like, when they have time to pause
From their ferocities produced by vanity.
His little captive gain'd him some applause
For saving her amidst the wild insanity
Of carnage—and I think he was more glad in her
Safety, than his new order of St. Vladimir.

CXLI.

The Moslem orphan went with her protector.
For she was homeless, houseless, helpless; all
Her friends, like the sad family of Hector,
Had perish'd in the field or by the wall:
Her very place of birth was but a spectre
Of what it had been; there the Muezzin's call
To prayer was heard no more!—and Juan wept,
And made a vow to shield her, which he kept.

CANTO THE NINTH.

I.

Oh, Wellington! (or "Villainton"—for Fame
 Sounds the heroic syllables both ways;
France could not even conquer your great name,
 But punn'd it down to this facetious phrase—
Beating or beaten she will laugh the same),
 You have obtain'd great pensions and much praise:
Glory like yours should any dare gainsay,
Humanity would rise, and thunder "Nay!"[60]

II.

I don't think that you used Kinnaird quite well
 In Marinèt's affair—in fact, 'twas shabby,
And like some other things won't do to tell
 Upon your tomb in Westminster's old abbey.
Upon the rest 't is not worth while to dwell,
 Such tales being for the tea-hours of some tabby;
But though your years as *man* tend fast to zero,
In fact your grace is still but a *young hero*.

III.

Though Britain owes (and pays you too) so much,
Yet Europe doubtless owes you greatly more:
You have repair'd Legitimacy's crutch,
A prop not quite so certain as before:
The Spanish, and the French, as well as Dutch,
Have seen, and felt, how strongly you *restore;*
And Waterloo has made the world your debtor
(I wish your bards would sing it rather better).

IV.

You are "the best of cut-throats:"—do not start;
The phrase is Shakspeare's, and not misapplied:—
War 's a brain-spattering, windpipe-slitting art,
Unless her cause by right be sanctified.
If you have acted *once* a generous part,
The world, not the world's masters, will decide,
And I shall be delighted to learn who,
Save you and yours, have gain'd by Waterloo?

V.

I am no flatterer—you 've supp'd full of flattery:
They say you like it too—'t is no great wonder.
He whose whole life has been assault and battery,
At last may get a little tired of thunder;
And swallowing eulogy much more than satire, he
May like being praised for every lucky blunder,
Call'd "Saviour of the Nations"—not yet saved,
And "Europe's Liberator"—still enslaved.[61]

VI.

I've done. Now go and dine from off the plate
Presented by the Prince of the Brazils,
And send the sentinel before your gate
A slice or two from your luxurious meals:[62]
He fought, but has not fed so well of late.
Some hunger, too, they say the people feels:—
There is no doubt that you deserve your ration,
But pray give back a little to the nation.

VII.

I don't mean to reflect—a man so great as
You, my lord duke! is far above reflection:
The high Roman fashion, too, of Cincinnatus,
With modern history has but small connection:
Though as an Irishman you love potatoes,
You need not take them under your direction;
And half a million for your Sabine farm
Is rather dear!—I'm sure I mean no harm.

VIII.

Great men have always scorn'd great recompences:
Epaminondas saved his Thebes, and died,
Not leaving even his funeral expenses:
George Washington had thanks and nought beside
Except the all-cloudless glory (which few men's is)
To free his country: Pitt too had his pride,
And as a high soul'd minister of state is
Renown'd for ruining Great Britain gratis.

IX.

Never had mortal man such opportunity,
Except Napoleon, or abused it more:
You might have freed fallen Europe from the unity
Of tyrants, and been blest from shore to shore:
And *now*—what *is* your fame? Shall the Muse tune it ye?
Now—that the rabble's first vain shouts are o'er?
Go! hear it in your famish'd country's cries!
Behold the world! and curse your victories!

X.

As these new cantos touch on warlike feats,
To *you* the unflattering Muse deigns to inscribe
Truths, that you will not read in the Gazettes,
But which 't is time to teach the hireling tribe
Who fatten on their country's gore, and debts,
Must be recited, and—without a bribe.
You *did great* things; but not being *great* in mind,
Have left *undone* the *greatest*—and mankind.

XI.

Death laughs—Go ponder o'er the skeleton
With which men image out the unknown thing
That hides the past world, like to a set sun
Which still elsewhere may rouse a brighter spring—
Death laughs at all you weep for:—look upon
This hourly dread of all! whose *threaten'd sting*
Turns life to terror, even though in its sheath:
Mark! how its lipless mouth grins without breath!

XII.

Mark! how it laughs and scorns at all you are!
And yet *was* what you are: from *ear* to *ear*
It *laughs not*—there is now no fleshy bar
So call'd; the Antic long hath ceased to *hear*,
But still he *smiles;* and whether near or far,
He strips from man that mantle (far more dear
Than even the tailor's), his incarnate skin,
White, black, or copper—the dead bones will grin.

XIII.

And thus Death laughs,—it is sad merriment,
But still it *is* so; and with such example
Why should not Life be equally content
With his superior, in a smile to trample
Upon the nothings which are daily spent
Like bubbles on an ocean much less ample
Than the eternal deluge, which devours
Suns as rays—worlds like atoms—years like hours?

XIV.

"To be, or not to be? that is the question,"
Says Shakspeare, who just now is much in fashion.
I am neither Alexander nor Hephæstion,
Nor ever had for *abstract* fame much passion;
But would much rather have a sound digestion
Than Buonaparte's cancer:—could I dash on
Through fifty victories to shame or fame,
Without a stomach—what were a good name?

XV.

"Oh dura ilia messorum!"—"Oh
Ye rigid guts of reapers!" I translate
For the great benefit of those who know
What indigestion is—that inward fate
Which makes all Styx through one small liver flow.
A peasant's sweat is worth his lord's estate:
Let *this* one toil for bread—*that* rack for rent,
He who sleeps best may be the most content.

XVI.

"To be, or not to be?"—Ere I decide,
I should be glad to know that which *is being.*
'T is true we speculate both far and wide,
And deem, because we *see*, we are *all-seeing:*
For my part, I'll enlist on neither side,
Until I see both sides for once agreeing.
For me, I sometimes think that life is death,
Rather than life a mere affair of breath.

XVII.

"Que scais-je?" was the motto of Montaigne,
As also of the first academicians:
That all is dubious which man may attain,
Was one of their most favourite positions.
There's no such thing as certainty, that's plain,
As any of Mortality's conditions;
So little do we know what we 're about in
This world, I doubt if doubt itself be doubting.

XVIII.

It is a pleasant voyage perhaps to float,
Like Pyrrho, on a sea of speculation;
But what if carrying sail capsize the boat?
Your wise men don't know much of navigation;
And swimming long in the abyss of thought
Is apt to tire: a calm and shallow station
Well nigh the shore, where one stoops down and gathers
Some pretty shell, is best for moderate bathers.

XIX.

"But heaven," as Cassio says, "is above all—[63]
No more of this, then,—let us pray!" We have
Souls to save, since Eve's slip and Adam's fall,
Which tumbled all mankind into the grave,
Besides fish, beasts, and birds. "The sparrow's fall
Is special providence," though how it gave
Offence, we know not; probably it perch'd
Upon the tree which Eve so fondly search'd.

XX.

Oh! ye immortal Gods! what is theogony?
Oh! thou, too, mortal man! what is philanthropy?
Oh! world, which was and is, what is cosmogony?
Some people have accused me of misanthropy;
And yet I know no more than the mahogany
That forms this desk, of what they mean; *lykanthropy*
I comprehend, for without transformation
Men become wolves on any slight occasion.

XXI.

But I, the mildest, meekest of mankind,
Like Moses, or Melancthon, who have ne'er
Done anything exceedingly unkind,—
And (though I could not now and then forbear
Following the bent of body or of mind)
Have always had a tendency to spare,—
Why do they call me misanthrope? Because
They hate me, not I them:—and here we 'll pause.

XXII.

'T is time we should proceed with our good poem,—
For I maintain that it is really good,
Not only in the body but the proem,
However little both are understood
Just now,—but by and by the Truth will show 'em
Herself in her sublimest attitude:
And till she doth, I fain must be content
To share her beauty and her banishment.

XXIII.

Our hero (and, I trust, kind reader! yours—)
Was left upon his way to the chief city
Of the immortal Peter's polish'd boors,
Who still hath shown themselves more brave than witty.
I know its mighty empire now allures
Much flattery—even Voltaire's, and that 's a pity.
For me, I deem an absolute autocrat
Not a barbarian, but much worse than that.

XXIV.

And I will war, at least in words (and—should
My chance so happen—deeds), with all who war
With Thought;—and of Thought's foes by far most rude,
Tyrants and sycophants have been and are.
I know not who may conquer: if I could
Have such a prescience, it should be no bar
To this my plain, sworn, downright detestation
Of every despotism in every nation.

XXV.

It is not that I adulate the people:
Without *me*, there are demagogues enough,

And infidels, to pull down every steeple,
 And set up in their stead some proper stuff.
Whether they may sow scepticism to reap hell,
 As is the Christian dogma rather rough,
I do not know;—I wish men to be free
As much from mobs as kings—from you as me.

XXVI.

The consequence is, being of no party,
 I shall offend all parties:—never mind!
My words, at least, are more sincere and hearty
 Than if I sought to sail before the wind.
He who has nought to gain can have small art: he
 Who neither wishes to be bound nor bind,
May still expatiate freely, as will I,
Nor give my voice to slavery's jackall cry.

XXVII.

That's an appropriate simile, *that jackall*;—
 I've heard them in the Ephesian ruins howl[64]
By night, as do that mercenary pack all,
 Power's base purveyors, who for pickings prowl,
And scent the prey their masters would attack all.
 However, the poor jackalls are less foul
(As being the brave lion's keen providers)
Than human insects, catering for spiders.

XXVIII.

Raise but an arm! 't will brush their web away,
 And without *that*, their poison and their claws
Are useless. Mind, good people! what I say—
 (Or rather peoples)—*go on* without pause!
The web of these tarantulas each day
 Increases, till you shall make common cause:
None, save the Spanish Fly and Attic Bee,
As yet are strongly stinging to be free.

XXIX.

Don Juan, who had shone in the late slaughter,
 Was left upon his way with the despatch,
Where blood was talk'd of as we would of water;
 And carcasses that lay as thick as thatch
O'er silenced cities, merely served to flatter
 Fair Catherine's pastime—who look'd on the match
Between these nations as a main of cocks,
Wherein she liked her own to stand like rocks.

XXX.

And there in a *kibitka* he roll'd on
 (A cursed sort of carriage without springs,
Which on rough roads leaves scarcely a whole bone,)
 Pondering on glory, chivalry, and kings,
And orders, and on all that he had done—
 And wishing that post-horses had the wings
Of Pegasus, or at the least post-chaises
Had feathers, when a traveller on deep ways is.

XXXI.

At every jolt—and they were many—still
 He turn'd his eyes upon his little charge,
As if he wish'd that she should fare less ill
 Than he, in these sad highways left at large
To ruts, and flints, and lovely Nature's skill,
 Who is no paviour, nor admits a barge
On *her* canals, where God takes sea and land,
Fishery and farm, both into His own hand.

XXXII.

At least He pays no rent, and has best right
 To be the first of what we used to call
"Gentlemen farmers"—a race worn out quite,
 Since lately there have been no rents at all,
And "gentlemen" are in a piteous plight,
 And "farmers" can't raise Ceres from her fall:
She fell with Buonaparte—What strange thoughts
Arise, when we see emperors fall with oats!

XXXIII.

But Juan turn'd his eyes on the sweet child
 Whom he had saved from slaughter—what a trophy!
Oh! ye who build up monuments, defiled
 With gore, like Nadir Shah, that costive sophy,
Who, after leaving Hindostan a wild,
 And scarce to the Mogul a cup of coffee
To soothe his woes withal, was slain, the sinner!
Because he could no more digest his dinner;—[65]

XXXIV.

Oh ye! or we! or he! or she! reflect,
 That *one* life saved, especially if young
Or pretty, is a thing to recollect
 Far sweeter than the greenest laurels sprung
From the manure of human clay, though deck'd
 With all the praises ever said or sung:
Though hymn'd by every harp, unless within
Your heart joins chorus, Fame is but a din.

XXXV.

Oh! ye great authors luminous, voluminous!
 Ye twice ten hundred thousand daily scribes!
Whose pamphlets, volumes, newspapers, illumine us!
 Whether you're paid by government in bribes,
To prove the public debt is not consuming us—
 Or, roughly treading on the "courtier's kibes,"
With clownish heel, your popular circulation
Feeds you by printing half the realm's starvation;—

XXXVI.

Oh, ye great authors!—"Apropos des bottes."—
 I have forgotten what I meant to say,
As sometimes have been greater sages' lots;—
 'T was something calculated to allay
All wrath in barracks, palaces, or cots:
 Certes it would have been but thrown away,
And that's one comfort for my lost advice,
Although no doubt it was beyond all price.

XXXVII.

But let it go:—it will one day be found
 With other relics of a "former world,"

When this world shall be *former*, underground,
Thrown topsy-turvy, twisted, crisp'd, and curl'd,
Baked, fried, or burnt, turn'd inside-out, or drown'd,
Like all the worlds before, which have been hurl'd
First out of, and then back again to chaos,
The superstratum which will overlay us.

XXXVIII.

So Cuvier says;—and then shall come again
Unto the new creation, rising out
From our old crash, some mystic, ancient strain
Of things destroy'd and left in airy doubt;
Like to the notions we now entertain
Of Titans, giants, fellows of about

Some hundred feet in height, *not* to say *miles*,
And mammoths, and your wingèd crocodiles.

XXXIX.

Think if then George the Fourth should be dug up!
How the new worldlings of the then new East
Will wonder where such animals could sup;
(For they themselves will be but of the least:
Even worlds miscarry, when too oft they pup,
And every new creation hath decreased
In size, from overworking the material—
Men are but maggots of some huge Earth's burial).

XL.

How will—to these young people, just thrust out
From some fresh Paradise, and set to plough,
And dig, and sweat, and turn themselves about,
And plant, and reap, and spin, and grind, and sow,
Till all the arts at length are brought about,
Especially of war and taxing—how,
I say, will these great relics, when they see 'em,
Look like the monsters of a new museum?

XLI.

But I am apt to grow too metaphysical:
"The time is out of joint,"—and so am I;
I quite forget this poem's merely quizzical,
And deviate into matters rather dry.
I ne'er decide what I shall say, and this I call
Much too poetical: men should know why
They write, and for what end; but, note or text,
I never know the word which will come next.

XLII.

So on I ramble, now and then narrating,
Now pondering:—it is time we should narrate.
I left Don Juan, with his horses baiting—
Now we'll get o'er the ground at a great rate.
I shall not be particular in stating
His journey, we've so many tours of late:
Suppose him then at Petersburg; suppose
That pleasant capital of painted snows;

XLIII.

Suppose him in a handsome uniform;
A scarlet coat, black facings, a long plume,
Waving, like sails new shiver'd in a storm,
Over a cock'd hat in a crowded room,
And brilliant breeches, bright as a Cairn Gorme,
Of yellow casimire we may presume,
White stockings drawn uncurdled as new milk
O'er limbs whose symmetry set off the silk;

XLIV.

Suppose him sword by side, and hat in hand,
Made up by youth, fame, and an army tailor—
That great enchanter, at whose rod's command
Beauty springs forth, and Nature's self turns paler,
Seeing how Art can make her work more grand
(When she don't pin men's limbs in like a goaler),—
Behold him placed as if upon a pillar! He
Seems Love turn'd a lieutenant of artillery.

XLV.

His bandage slipp'd down into a cravat;
His wings subdued to epaulettes; his quiver
Shrunk to a scabbard, with his arrows at
His side as a small sword, but sharp as ever;
His bow converted into a cock'd hat;
But still so like, that Psyche were more clever
Than some wives (who make blunders no less stupid),
If she had not mistaken him for Cupid.

XLVI.

The courtiers stared, the ladies whisper'd, and
The Empress smil'd, the reigning favourite frown'd:
I quite forget which of them was in hand
Just then; as they are rather numerous found,
Who took by turns that difficult command,
Since first her Majesty was singly crown'd:
But they were mostly nervous six-foot fellows,
All fit to make a Patagonian jealous.

XLVII.

Juan was none of these, but slight and slim,
Blushing and beardless; and yet ne'ertheless
There was a something in his turn of limb,
And still more in his eye, which seem'd to express,
That though he look'd like one of the seraphim,
There lurk'd a man beneath the spirit's dress.
Besides, the Empress sometimes liked a boy,
And had just buried the fair-faced Lanskoi.[66]

XLVIII.

No wonder then that Yermoloff, or Momonoff,
Or Scherbatoff, or any other *off*
Or *on*, might dread her Majesty had not room enough
Within her bosom (which was not too tough)
For a new flame; a thought to cast of gloom enough
Along the aspect, whether smooth or rough,
Of him who, in the language of his station,
Then held that "high official situation."

XLIX.

O, gentle ladies! should you seek to know
The import of this diplomatic phrase,
Bid Ireland's Londonderry's Marquess show
His parts of speech; and in the strange displays
Of that odd string of words, all in a row,
Which none divine, and every one obeys,
Perhaps you may pick out some queer *no* meaning,
Of that weak wordy harvest the sole gleaning

L.

I think I can explain myself without
That sad inexplicable beast of prey—
That Sphinx, whose words would ever be a doubt,
Did not his deeds unriddle them each day—
That monstrous hieroglyphic—that long spout
Of blood and water, leaden Castlereagh!

And here I must an anecdote relate,
But luckily of no great length or weight.

LI.

An English lady ask'd of an Italian,
What were the actual and official duties
Of the strange thing, some women set a value on,
Which hovers oft about some married beauties,
Call'd "Cavalier servente?" a Pygmalion
Whose statues warm (I fear, alas! too true 't is)
Beneath his art. The dame, press'd to disclose them,
Said—"Lady, I beseech you to *suppose them*."

LII.

And thus I supplicate your supposition,
And mildest matron-like interpretation,
Of the imperial favourite's condition.
'T was a high place, the highest in the nation
In fact, if not in rank; and the supicion
Of any one's attaining to his station,
No doubt gave pain, where each new pair of shoulders,
If rather broad, made stocks rise and their holders.

LIII.

Juan, I said, was a most beauteous boy,
And had retain'd his boyish look beyond
The usual hirsute seasons which destroy,
With beards and whiskers, and the like, the fond
Parisian aspect, which upset old Troy
And founded Doctors' Commons:—I have conn'd
The history of divorces, which, though chequer'd,
Calls Ilion's the first damages on record.

LIV.

And Catherine, who lov'd all things, (save her lord,
Who was gone to his place,) and pass'd for much,
Admiring those (by dainty dames abhorr'd)
Gigantic gentlemen, yet had a touch
Of sentiment; and he she most adored
Was the lamented Lanskoi, who was such
A lover as had cost her many a tear,
And yet but made a middling grenadier.

LV.

Oh thou "teterrima causa" of all "belli"—[67]
Thou gate of life and death—thou nondescript!
Whence is our exit and our entrance,—well I
May pause in pondering how all souls are dipt
In thy perennial fountain:—how man *fell*, I
Know not, since knowledge saw her branches stript
Of her first fruit; but how he falls and rises
Since, thou hast settled beyond all surmises.

LVI.

Some call thee "the worst cause of war," but I
Maintain thou art the *best:* for after all
From thee we come, to thee we go, and why
To get at thee not batter down a wall,
Or waste a world? since no one can deny
Thou dost replenish worlds both great and small:
With, or without thee, all things at a stand
Are, or would be, thou sea of life's dry land!

LVII.

Catherine, who was the grand epitome
Of that great cause of war, or peace, or what
You please (it causes all the things which be,
So you may take your choice of this or that)—
Catherine, I say, was very glad to see
The handsome herald, on whose plumage sat
Victory; and, pausing as she saw him kneel
With his despatch, forgot to break the seal.

LVIII.

Then recollecting the whole empress, nor
Forgetting quite the woman (which composed
At least three parts of this great whole,) she tore
The letter open with an air which posed
The court, that watch'd each look her visage wore,
Until a royal smile at length disclosed
Fair weather for the day. Though rather spacious,
Her face was noble, her eyes fine, mouth gracious.

LIX.

Great joy was hers, or rather joys: the first
Was a ta'en city, thirty thousand slain.
Glory and triumph o'er her aspect burst,
As an East Indian sunrise on the main.
These quench'd a moment her ambition's thirst—
So Arab deserts drink in summer's rain;
In vain!—As fall the dews on quenchless sands,
Blood only serves to wash Ambition's hands!

LX.

Her next amusement was more fanciful;
She smiled at mad Suwarrow's rhymes, who threw
Into a Russian couplet rather dull
The whole gazette of thousands whom he slew.
Her third was feminine enough to annul
The shudder which runs naturally through
Our veins, when things call'd sovereigns think it best
To kill, and generals turn it into jest.

LXI.

The two first feelings ran their course complete,
And lighted first her eye, and then her mouth:
The whole court look'd immediately most sweet,
Like flowers well water'd after a long drouth:—
But when on the lieutenant at her feet
Her Majesty, who liked to gaze on youth
Almost as much as on a new despatch,
Glanced mildly, all the world was on the watch.

LXII.

Though somewhat large, exuberant, and truculent,
When *wroth*—while *pleased*, she was as fine a figure
As those who like things rosy, ripe, and succulent,
Would wish to look on, while they are in vigour.
She could repay each amatory look you lent
With interest, and in turn was wont with rigour

To exact of Cupid's bills the full amount
At sight, nor would permit you to discount.

LXIII.

With her the latter, though at times convenient,
Was not so necessary; for they tell
That she was handsome, and tho' fierce *look'd* lenient,
And always used her favourites too well.
If once beyond her boudoir's precincts in ye went
Your "fortune" was in a fair way "to swell
A man" (as Giles says);[68] for tho' she would widow all
Nations, she liked man as an individual.

LXIV.

What a strange thing is man! and what a stranger
 Is woman! What a whirlwind is her head,
And what a whirlpool full of depth and danger
 Is all the rest about her! Whether wed,
Or widow, maid, or mother, she can change her
 Mind like the wind: whatever she has said
Or done, is light to what she'll say or do;—
The oldest thing on record, and yet new!

LXV.

Oh Catherine! (for of all interjections,
 To thee both *oh!* and *ah!* belong of right
I love and war) how odd are the connections
 Of human thoughts, which jostle in their flight!
Just now *yours* were cut out in different sections:
 First Ismail's capture caught your fancy quite;
Next of new knights, the fresh and glorious batch;
And *thirdly* he who brought you the despatch!

LXVI.

Shakspeare talks of "the herald Mercury
 New lighted on a heaven-kissing hill;"
And some such visions cross'd her Majesty,
 While her young herald knelt before her still.
T is very true the hill seem'd rather high,
 For a lieutenant to climb up; but skill
Smooth'd even the Simplon's steep, and by God's blessing,
With youth and health all kisses are "heaven-kissing."

LXVII.

Her Majesty look'd down, the youth look'd up—
 And so they fell in love;—she with his face,
His grace, his God-knows-what: for Cupid's cup
 With the first draught intoxicates apace,
A quintessential laudanum or "black drop,"
 Which makes one drunk at once, without the base
Expedient of full bumpers; for the eye
In love drinks all life's fountains (save tears) dry.

LXVIII.

He, on the other hand, if not in love,
 Fell into that no less imperious passion,
Self-love—which, when some sort of thing above
 Ourselves, a singer, dancer, much in fashion,
Or duchess, princess, empress, "deigns to prove"
 ('T is Pope's phrase) a great longing, though a rash one,
For one especial person out of many,
Makes us believe ourselves as good as any.

LXIX.

Besides, he was of that delighted age
 Which makes all female ages equal—when
We don't much care with whom we may engage,
 As bold as Daniel in the lion's den,
So that we can our native sun assuage
 In the next ocean, which may flow just then,
To make a twilight in, just as Sol's heat is
Quench'd in the lap of the salt sea, or Thetis.

LXX.

And Catherine (we must say thus much for Catherine),
 Though bold and bloody, was the kind of thing
Whose temporary passion was quite flattering,
 Because each lover look'd a sort of king,
Made up upon an amatory pattern,
 A royal husband in all save the *ring*—
Which, being the damn'dest part of matrimony,
Seem'd taking out the sting to leave the honey.

LXXI.

And when you add to this, her womanhood
 In its meridian, her blue eyes or gray—
(The last, if they have soul, are quite as good,
 Or better, as the best examples say:
Napoleon's, Mary's (queen of Scotland), should
 Lend to that colour a transcendent ray;
And Pallas also sanctions the same hue,
Too wise to look through optics black or blue)—

LXXII.

Her sweet smile, and her, then, majestic figure,
 Her plumpness, her imperial condescension,
Her preference of a boy to men much bigger,
 (Fellows whom Messalina's self would pension),
Her prime of life, just now in juicy vigour,
 With other *extras*, which we need not mention,—
All these, or any one of these, explain
Enough to make a stripling very vain.

LXXIII.

And that's enough, for love is vanity,
 Selfish in its beginning as its end,
Except where 't is a mere insanity,
 A maddening spirit which would strive to blend
Itself with beauty's frail inanity,
 On which the passion's self seems to depend:
And hence some heathenish philosophers
Make love the main-spring of the universe.

LXXIV.

Besides Platonic love, besides the love
 Of God, the love of sentiment, the loving
Of faithful pairs—(I needs must rhyme with dove,
 That good old steam-boat which keeps verses moving
'Gainst reason—Reason ne'er was hand-and-glove
 With rhyme, but always lent less to improving
The sound than sense)—besides all these pretences
To love, there are those things which words name senses;

LXXV.

Those movements, those improvements in our bodies
 Which make all bodies anxious to get out
Of their own sand-pits, to mix with a goddess,
 For such all women are at first no doubt.
How beautiful that moment! and how odd is
 That fever which precedes the languid rout
Of our sensations! What a curious way
The whole thing is of clothing souls in clay!

LXXVI.

The noblest kind of love is love Platonical,
 To end or to begin with; the next grand
Is that which may be christen'd love canonical,
 Because the clergy take the thing in hand;
The third sort to be noted in our chronicle
 As flourishing in every Christian land,
Is, when chaste matrons to their other ties
Add what may be call'd *marriage in disguise.*

LXXVII.

Well, we won't analyse—our story must
 Tell for itself: the Sovereign was smitten,
Juan much flatter'd by her love, or lust;—
 I cannot stop to alter words once written,
And the two are so mix'd with human dust,
 That he who *names one,* both perchance may hit on:
But in such matters Russia's mighty Empress
Behaved no better than a common sempstress.

LXXVIII.

The whole court melted into one wide whisper,
 And all lips were applied unto all ears!
The elder ladies' wrinkles curl'd much crisper
 As they beheld; the younger cast some leers
On one another, and each lovely lisper
 Smil'd as she talk'd the matter o'er; but tears
Of rivalship rose in each clouded eye
Of all the standing army who stood by.

LXXIX.

All the Ambassadors of all the powers
 Inquired, Who was this very new young man,
Who promised to be great in some few hours?
 Which is full soon (though life is but a span).
Already they beheld the silver showers
 Of rubles rain, as fast as specie can,
Upon his cabinet, besides the presents
Of several ribands, and some thousand peasants.[69]

LXXX.

Catherine was generous,—all such ladies are:
 Love, that great opener of the heart and all
The ways that lead there, be they near or far,
 Above, below, by turnpikes great or small,—
Love—(though she had a cursèd taste for war,
 And was not the best wife, unless we call
Such Clytemnestra, though perhaps 'tis better
That one should die, than two drag on the fetter)—

LXXXI.

Love had made Catherine make each lover's fortune,
 Unlike our own half-chaste Elizabeth,
Whose avarice all disbursements did importune,
 If history, the grand liar, ever saith
The truth; and tho' grief her old age might shorten,
 Because she put a favourite to death,
Her vile, ambiguous method of flirtation,
And stinginess, disgrace her sex and station.

LXXXII.

But when the levee rose, and all was bustle
 In the dissolving circle, all the nations'
Ambassadors began as 't were to hustle
 Round the young man with their congratulations.
Also the softer silks were heard to rustle
 Of gentle dames, among whose recreations
It is to speculate on handsome faces,
Especially when such lead to high places.

LXXXIII.

Juan, who found himself, he knew not how,
 A general object of attention, made
His answers with a very graceful bow,
 As if born for the ministerial trade.
Though modest, on his unembarrass'd brow
 Nature had written "gentleman." He said
Little, but to the purpose; and his manner
Flung hovering graces o'er him like a banner.

LXXXIV.

An order from her Majesty consign'd
 Our young lieutenant to the genial care
Of those in office: all the world look'd kind,
 (As it will look sometimes with the first stare,
Which youth would not act ill to keep in mind,)
 As also did Miss Protasoff then there,
Named from her mystic office "l'Eprouveuse,"
A term inexplicable to the Muse.

LXXXV.

With *her* then, as in humble duty bound,
 Juan retired,—and so will I, until
My Pegasus shall tire of touching ground.
 We have just lit on a "heaven-kissing hill,"
So lofty that I feel my brain turn round,
 And all my fancies whirling like a mill;
Which is a signal to my nerves and brain,
To take a quiet ride in some green lane.

CANTO X.

I.

WHEN Newton saw an apple fall, he found
 In that slight startle from his contemplation—
'T is *said* (for I'll not answer above ground
 For any sage's creed or calculation)—
A mode of proving that the earth turn'd round
 In a most natural whirl, call'd "gravitation;"
And this is the sole mortal who could grapple,
Since Adam, with a fall, or with an apple.

II.

Man fell with apples, and with apples rose,
 If this be true; for we must deem the mode
In which Sir Isaac Newton could disclose
 Through the then unpaved stars the turnpike road,
A thing to counterbalance human woes:
 For ever since immortal man hath glow'd
With all kinds of mechanics, and full soon
Steam-engines will conduct him to the moon.

III.

And wherefore this exordium?—Why, just now,
 In taking up this paltry sheet of paper,
My bosom underwent a glorious glow,
 And my internal spirit cut a caper:
And though so much inferior, as I know,
 To those who, by the dint of glass and vapour,
Discover stars, and sail in the wind's eye,
I wish to do as much by poesy.

IV.

In the wind's eye I have sail'd, and sail; but for
The stars, I own my telescope is dim;
But at the least I have shunn'd the common shore,
And leaving land far out of sight, would skim
The ocean of eternity: the roar
Of breakers has not daunted my slight, trim,
But *still* sea-worthy skiff; and she may float
Where ships have founder'd, as doth many a boat.

V.

We left our hero, Juan, in the *bloom*
Of favouritism, but not yet in the *blush*;—
And far be it from my *Muses* to presume
(For I have more than one Muse at a push)
To follow him beyond the drawing-room:
It is enough that Fortune found him flush
Of youth, and vigour, beauty, and those things
Which for an instant clip enjoyment's wings.

VI.

But soon they grow again and leave their nest.
"Oh!" saith the Psalmist, "that I had a dove's
Pinions to flee away, and be at rest!"
And who that recollects young years and loves,—
Though hoary now, and with a withering breast,
And palsied fancy, which no longer roves
Beyond its dimm'd eye's sphere,—but would much rather
Sigh like his son, than cough like his grandfather?

VII.

But sighs subside, and tears (even widows') shrink,
Like Arno in the summer, to a shallow,
So narrow as to shame their wintry brink,
Which threatens inundations deep and yellow!
Such difference doth a few months make. You'd think
Grief a rich field which never would lie fallow;
No more it doth, its ploughs but change their boys,
Who furrow some new soil to sow for joys.

VIII.

But coughs will come when sighs depart—and now
And then before sighs cease; for oft the one
Will bring the other, ere the lake-like brow
Is ruffled by a wrinkle, or the sun
Of life reach'd ten o'clock: and while a glow,
Hectic and brief as summer's day nigh done,
O'erspreads the cheek which seems too pure for clay,
Thousands blaze, love, hope, die,—how happy they!—

IX.

But Juan was not meant to die so soon.
We left him in the focus of such glory
As may be won by favour of the moon
Or ladies' fancies—rather transitory
Perhaps; but who would scorn the month of June
Because December, with his breath so hoary,
Must come? Much rather should he court the ray,
To hoard up warmth against a wintry day.

X.

Besides, he had some qualities which fix
Middle-aged ladies even more than young:
The former know what's what; while new-fledged chicks
Know little more of love than what is sung
In rhymes, or dreamt (for fancy will play tricks)
In visions of those skies from whence love sprung.
Some reckon women by their suns or years,
I rather think the moon should date the dears.

XI.

And why? Because she's changeable and chaste.
I know no other reason, whatsoe'er
Suspicious people, who find fault in haste,
May choose to tax me with; which is not fair,
Nor flattering to "their temper or their taste,"
As my friend Jeffrey writes with such an air:
However, I forgive him, and I trust
He will forgive himself;—if not, I must.

XII.

Old enemies who have become new friends
Should so continue—'t is a point of honour,
And I know nothing which could make amends
For a return to hatred: I would shun her
Like garlic, howsoever she extends
Her hundred arms and legs, and fain outrun her
Old flames, new wives, become our bitterest foes—
Converted foes should scorn to join with those.

XIII.

This were the worst desertion:—renegadoes,
Even shuffling Southey, that incarnate lie,
Would scarcely join again the "reformadoes,"[70]
Whom he forsook to fill the laureate's sty;
And honest men from Iceland to Barbadoes,
Whether in Caledon or Italy,
Should not veer round with every breath, nor seize
To pain, the moment when you cease to please.

XIV.

The lawyer and the critic but behold
The baser sides of literature and life,
And nought remains unseen, but much untold,
By those who scour those double vales of strife.
While common men grow ignorantly old,
The lawyer's brief is like the surgeon's knife,
Dissecting the whole inside of a question,
And with it all the process of digestion.

XV.

A legal broom's a moral chimney-sweeper,
And that's the reason he himself's so dirty;
The endless soot bestows a tint far deeper
Than can be hid by altering his shirt; he
Retains the sable stains of the dark creeper,
At least some twenty-nine do out of thirty,
In all their habits;—not so *you*, I own;
As Cæsar wore his robe, you wear your gown.

XVI.

And all our little feuds, at least all *mine*,
 Dear Jeffrey, once my most redoubted foe
(As far as rhyme and criticism combine
 To make such puppets of us things below),
Are over: Here's a health to "Auld Lang Syne!"
 I do not know you, and may never know
Your face—but you have acted on the whole
Most nobly, and I own it from my soul.

XVII.

And when I use the phrase of "Auld Lang Syne!"
 'T is not address'd to you—the more 's the pity
For me, for I would rather take my wine
 With you, than aught (save Scott) in your proud city.
But somehow,—it may seem a schoolboy's whine,
 And yet I seek not to be grand nor witty,
But I am half a Scot by birth, and bred
A whole one, and my heart flies to my head,—

XVIII.

As "Auld Lang Syne" brings Scotland, one and all,
 Scotch plaids, Scotch snoods, the blue hills, and clear streams,
The Dee, the Don, Balgounie's brig's *black wall*,[71]
 All my boy feelings, all my gentler dreams
Of what I *then dreamt*, clothed in their own pall,
 Like Banquo's offspring;—floating past me seems
My childhood in this childishness of mine:
I care not—'t is a glimpse of "Auld Lang Syne."

XIX.

And though, as you remember, in a fit
 Of wrath and rhyme, when juvenile and curly,
I rail'd at Scots to show my wrath and wit,
 Which must be own'd was sensitive and surly,
Yet 't is in vain such sallies to permit,
 They cannot quench young feelings fresh and early:
I "*scotch'd*, not kill'd," the Scotchman in my blood,
And love the land of "mountain and of flood."

XX.

Don Juan, who was real, or ideal,—
 For both are much the same, since what men think
Exists when the once thinkers are less real
 Than what they thought, for mind can never sink,
And 'gainst the body makes a strong appeal;
 And yet 't is very puzzling on the brink
Of what is call'd eternity, to stare,
And know no more of what is here, than there;—

XXI.

Don Juan grew a very polish'd Russian—
 How we won't mention, *why* we need not say:
Few youthful minds can stand the strong concussion
 Of any slight temptation in their way;
But *his* just now were spread as is a cushion
 Smooth'd for a monarch's seat of honour: gay
Damsels, and dances, revels, ready money,
Made ice seem paradise, and winter sunny.

XXII.

The favour of the Empress was agreeable;
 And though the duty wax'd a little hard,
Young people at his time of life should be able
 To come off handsomely in that regard.
He was now growing up like a green tree, able
 For love, war, or ambition, which reward
Their luckier votaries, till old age's tedium
Make some prefer the circulating medium.

XXIII.

About this time, as might have been anticipated,
 Seduced by youth and dangerous examples,
Don Juan grew, I fear, a little dissipated;
 Which is a sad thing, and not only tramples
On our fresh feelings, but—as being participated
 With all kinds of incorrigible samples
Of frail humanity—must make us selfish,
And shut our souls up in us like a shell-fish.

XXIV.

This we pass over. We will also pass
 The usual progress of intrigues between
Unequal matches, such as are, alas!
 A young lieutenant's with a *not old* queen.
But one who is not so youthful as she was
 In all the royalty of sweet seventeen.
Sovereigns may sway materials, but not matter,
And wrinkles, the d——d democrats, won't flatter.

XXV.

And Death, the sovereign's sovereign, tho' the great
 Gracchus of all mortality, who levels,
With his *Agrarian* laws, the high estate[72]
 Of him who feasts, and fights, and roars, and revels,
To one small grass-grown patch (which must await
 Corruption for its crop) with the poor devils
Who never had a foot of land till now,—
Death 's a reformer, all men must allow.

XXVI.

He lived (not Death, but Juan) in a hurry
 Of waste, and haste, and glare, and gloss, and glitter,
In this gay clime of bear-skins black and furry,—
 Which (though I hate to say a thing that 's bitter)
Peep out sometimes, when things are in a flurry,
 Through all the "purple and fine linen," fitter
For Babylon 's than Russia's royal harlot—
And neutralise her outward show of scarlet.

XXVII.

And this same state we won't describe: we would
 Perhaps from hearsay, or from recollection;
But getting nigh grim Dante's "obscure wood,"[73]
 That horrid equinox, that hateful section
Of human years, that half-way house, that rude
 Hut, whence wise travellers drive with circumspection

Life's sad post-horses o'er the dreary frontier,
Of age, and looking back to youth, give *one* tear;—

XXVIII.

I won't describe,—that is, if I can help
 Description; and I won't reflect,—that is,
If I can stave off thought, which—as a whelp
 Clings to its teat—sticks to me through the abyss
Of this odd labyrinth; or as the kelp
 Holds by the rock; or as a lover's kiss
Drains its first draught of lips:—but, as I said,
I *won't* philosophise, and *will* be read.

XXIX.

Juan, instead of courting courts, was courted,—
 A thing which happens rarely: this he owed
Much to his youth, and much to his reported
 Valour; much also to the blood he show'd,
Like a race-horse; much to each dress he sported,
 Which set the beauty off in which he glow'd,
As purple clouds befringe the sun; but most
He owed to an old woman and his post.

XXX.

He wrote to Spain:—and all his near relations,
 Perceiving he was in a handsome way
Of getting on himself, and finding stations
 For cousins also, answer'd the same day.
Several prepared themselves for emigrations;
 And eating ices, were o'erheard to say,
That with the addition of a slight pelisse,
Madrid's and Moscow's climes were of a piece.

XXXI.

His mother, Donna Inez, finding, too,
 That in the lieu of drawing on his banker,
Where his assets were waxing rather few,
 He had brought his spending to a handsome anchor,
Replied, "that she was glad to see him through
 Those pleasures after which wild youth will hanker;
As the sole sign of man's being in his senses
Is, learning to reduce his past expenses.

XXXII.

"She also recommended him to God,
 And no less to God's Son, as well as Mother,
Warn'd him against Greek worship, which looks odd
 In Catholic eyes; but told him, too, to smother
Outward dislike, which don't look well abroad;
 Inform'd him that he had a little brother
Born in a second wedlock; and above
All, praised the Empress's *maternal* love.

XXXIII.

"She could not too much give her approbation
 Unto an empress, who preferr'd young men
Whose age, and what was better still, whose nation
 And climate, stopp'd all scandal (now and then:—)
At home it might have given her some vexation
 But where thermometers sunk down to ten,
Or five, or one, or zero, she could never
Believe that virtue thaw'd before the river."

XXXIV.

Oh for a *forty-parson power* to chant[74]
 Thy praise, Hypocrisy! Oh for a hymn
Loud as the virtues thou dost loudly vaunt,
 Not practise! Oh for trumps of cherubim!
Or the ear-trumpet of my good old aunt,
 Who, although her spectacles at last grew dim,
Drew quiet consolation through its hint,
When she no more could read the pious print.

XXXV.

She was no hypocrite at least, poor soul,
 But went to heaven in as sincere a way
As any body on the elected roll,
 Which portions out upon the judgment day
Heaven's freeholds, in a sort of doomsday scroll,
 Such as the conqueror William did repay
His knights with, lotting others' properties
Into some sixty thousand new knights' fees.

XXXVI.

I can't complain, whose ancestors are there,
 Erneis, Radulphus—eight-and-forty manors
(If that my memory doth not greatly err)
 Were their reward for following Billy's banners;
And though I can't help thinking 't was scarce fair
 To strip the Saxons of their *hydes*, like tanners;[75]
Yet as they founded churches with the produce,
You'll deem, no doubt, they put it to a good use.

XXXVII.

The gentle Juan flourish'd, though at times
 He felt like other plants call'd sensitive,
Which shrink from touch, as monarchs do from rhymes
 Save such as Southey can afford to give.
Perhaps he long'd in bitter frosts for climes
 In which the Neva's ice would cease to live
Before May-day: perhaps, despite his duty,
In royalty's vast arms he sigh'd for beauty:

XXXVIII.

Perhaps—but, sans perhaps, we need not seek
 For causes young or old: the canker-worm
Will feed upon the fairest, freshest cheek,
 As well as further drain the wither'd form:
Care, like a housekeeper, brings every week
 His bills in, and however we may storm,
They must be paid: though six days smoothly run,
The seventh will bring blue devils or a dun.

XXXIX.

I don't know how it was, but he grew sick:
 The Empress was alarm'd, and her physician

(The same who physick'd Peter) found the tick
Of his fierce pulse betoken a condition
Which augur'd of the dead, however *quick*
Itself, and show'd a feverish disposition;
At which the whole court was extremely troubled,
The Sovereign shock'd, and all his medicines doubled.

XL.

Low were the whispers, manifold the rumours:
Some said he had been poison'd by Potemkin;
Others talk'd learnèdly of certain tumours,
Exhaustion, or disorders of the same kin;
Some said 't was a concoction of the humours,
Which with the blood too readily will claim kin;
Others again were ready to maintain,
"'T was only the fatigue of last campaign."

XLI.

But here is one prescription out of many:
"Sodæ sulphat. ʒ vj. ʒ ss. Mannæ optim.
Aq. fervent. f. ℥iss. ʒ ij. tinct. Sennæ
Haustus" (And here the surgeon came and cupp'd him)
"℞. Pulv. Com. gr. iij. Ipecacuanhæ"
(With more besides if Juan had not stopp'd 'em),
"Bolus Potassæ Sulphuret. sumendus,
Et haustus ter in die capiendus."

XLII.

This is the way physicians mend or end us,
Secundum artem: but although we sneer
In health—when ill, we call them to attend us,
Without the least propensity to jeer:
While that "hiatus maxime deflendus"
To be fill'd up by spade or mattock 's near,
Instead of gliding graciously down Lethe,
We tease mild Baillie, or soft Abernethy.

XLIII.

Juan demurr'd at this first notice to
Quit; and though death had threaten'd an ejection,
His youth and constitution bore him through,
And sent the doctors in a new direction.
But still his state was delicate: the hue
Of health but flicker'd with a faint reflection
Along his wasted cheek, and seem'd to gravel
The faculty—who said that he must travel.

XLIV.

The climate was too cold, they said, for him,
Meridian-born, to bloom in. This opinion
Made the chaste Catherine look a little grim,
Who did not like at first to lose her minion:
But when she saw his dazzling eye wax dim,
And drooping like an eagle's with clipt pinion,
She then resolved to send him on a mission,
But in a style becoming his condition.

XLV.

There was just then a kind of a discussion,
A sort of treaty or negotiation,
Between the British cabinet and Russian,
Maintain'd with all the due prevarication
With which great states such things are apt to push on;
Something about the Baltic's navigation,
Hides, train-oil, tallow, and the rights of Thetis,
Which Britons deem their "uti possidetis."

XLVI.

So Catherine, who had a handsome way
Of fitting out her favourites, conferr'd
This secret charge on Juan, to display
At once her royal splendour, and reward
His services. He kiss'd hands the next day,
Received instructions how to play his card,
Was laden with all kinds of gifts and honours,
Which show'd what great discernment was the donor's.

XLVII.

But she was lucky, and luck 's all. Your queens
Are generally prosperous in reigning;
Which puzzles us to know what Fortune means.
But to continue: though her years were waning,
Her climacteric teased her like her teens;
And though her dignity brook'd no complaining,
So much did Juan's setting off distress her,
She could not find at first a fit successor.

XLVIII.

But time, the comforter, will come at last;
And four-and-twenty hours, and twice that number
Of candidates requesting to be placed,
Made Catherine taste next night a quiet slumber
Not that she meant to fix again in haste,
Nor did she find the quantity encumber,
But always choosing with deliberation,
Kept the place open for their emulation.

XLIX.

While this high post of honour 's in abeyance,
For one or two days, reader, we request
You'll mount with our young hero the conveyance
Which wafted him from Petersburg: the best
Barouche, which had the glory to display once
The fair Czarina's autocratic crest,
When, a new Iphigene, she went to Tauris,[76]
Was given to her favourite, and now *bore his*.

L.

A bull-dog, and a bullfinch, and an ermine,
All private favourites of Don Juan;—for
(Let deeper sages the true cause determine)
He had a kind of inclination, or
Weakness, for what most people deem mere vermin,
Live animals: an old maid of threescore

For cats and birds more penchant ne'er display'd,
Although he was not old, nor even a maid;—

LI.

The animals aforesaid occupied
 Their station: there were valets, secretaries,
In other vehicles; but at his side
 Sat little Leila, who survived the parries
He made 'gainst Cossacque sabres, in the wide
 Slaughter of Ismail. Though my wild Muse varies
Her note, she do n't forget the infant girl
Whom he preserved, a pure and living pearl.

LII.

Poor little thing! she was as fair as docile,
 And with that gentle, serious character,
As rare in living beings as a fossile
 Man, 'midst thy mouldy mammoths, "grand Cuvier!"
Ill fitted was her ignorance to jostle
 With this o'erwhelming world, where all must err:
But she was yet but ten years old, and therefore
Was tranquil, tho' she knew not why or wherefore.

LIII.

Don Juan loved her, and she loved him, as
 Nor brother, father, sister, daughter love.
I cannot tell exactly what it was;
 He was not yet quite old enough to prove
Parental feelings, and the other class,
 Call'd brotherly affections, could not move
His bosom—for he never had a sister:
Ah! if he had, how much he would have miss'd her!

LIV.

And still less was it sensual; for besides
 That he was not an ancient debauchee,
(Who like sour fruit, to stir their veins' salt tides,
 As acids rouse a dormant alkali,)
Although (*'t will* happen as our planet guides)
 His youth was not the chastest that might be,
There was the purest Platonism at bottom
Of all his feelings—only he forgot 'em.

LV.

Just now there was no peril of temptation;
 He loved the infant orphan he had saved,
As patriots (now and then) may love a nation;
 His pride, too, felt that she was not enslaved
Owing to him;—as also her salvation
 Thro' his means and the church's might be paved.
But one thing's odd, which here must be inserted,
The little Turk refused to be converted.

LVI.

T was strange enough she should retain the impression
 Through such a scene of change, and dread, and slaughter;
But though three bishops told her the transgression,
 She show'd a great dislike to holy water:
She also had no passion for confession;
 Perhaps she had nothing to confess:—no matter
Whate'er the cause, the church made little of it—
She still held out that Mahomet was a prophet.

LVII.

In fact, the only Christian she could bear
 Was Juan; whom she seem'd to have selected
In place of what her home and friends once *were*.
 He *naturally* loved what he protected:
And thus they form'd a rather curious pair,
 A guardian green in years, a ward connected
In neither clime, time, blood, with her defender;
And yet this want of ties made theirs more tender.

LVIII.

They journey'd on thro' Poland and thro' Warsaw,
 Famous for mines of salt and yokes of iron:
Through Courland also, which that famous farce saw
 Which gave her dukes the graceless name of "Biron."[77]
'Tis the same landscape which the modern Mars saw,
 Who march'd to Moscow, led by Fame, the siren!
To lose by one month's frost some twenty years
Of conquest, and his guard of grenadiers.

LIX.

Let this not seem an anti-climax:—"Oh!
 My guard! my old guard!" exclaim'd that god of clay.
Think of the Thunderer's falling down below
 Carotid-artery-cutting Castlereagh!
Alas! that glory should be chill'd by snow!
 But should we wish to warm us on our way
Through Poland, there is Kosciusko's name
Might scatter fire through ice, like Hecla's flame.

LX.

From Poland, they came on through Prussia Proper,
 And Königsberg the capital, whose vaunt,
Besides some veins of iron, lead, or copper,
 Has lately been the great Professor Kant.
Juan, who cared not a tobacco-stopper
 About philosophy, pursued his jaunt
To Germany, whose somewhat tardy millions
Have princes who spur more than their postilions.

LXI.

And thence through Berlin, Dresden, and the like,
 Until he reach'd the castellated Rhine:—
Ye glorious Gothic scenes! how much ye strike
 All phantasies, not even excepting mine;
A gray wall, a green ruin, rusty pike,
 Make my soul pass the equinoctial line
Between the present and past worlds, and hover
Upon their airy confine, half-seas over.

LXII.

But Juan posted on through Manheim, Bonn,
Which Drachenfels frowns over like a spectre
Of the good old feudal times for ever gone,
On which I have not time just now to lecture.
From thence he was drawn onwards to Cologne,
A city which presents to the inspector
Eleven thousand maidenheads of bone,
The greatest number flesh hath ever known.[78]

LXIII.

From thence to Holland's Hague and Helvoetsluys,
That water-land of Dutchmen and of ditches,
Where juniper expresses its best juice,
The poor man's sparkling substitute for riches.
Senates and sages have condemn'd its use—
But to deny the mob a cordial, which is
Too often all the clothing, meat, or fuel,
Good government has left them, seems but cruel.

LXIV.

Here he embark'd, and with a flowing sail
Went bounding for the island of the free,
Towards which the impatient wind blew half a gale;
High dash'd the spray, the bows dipp'd in the sea,
And sea-sick passengers turn'd somewhat pale;
But Juan, season'd, as he well might be,
By former voyages, stood to watch the skiffs
Which pass'd, or catch the first glimpse of the cliffs.

LXV.

At length they rose, like a white wall along
The blue sea's border: and Don Juan felt—
What even young strangers feel a little strong
At the first sight of Albion's chalky belt—
A kind of pride that he should be among
Those haughty shopkeepers, who sternly dealt
Their goods and edicts out from pole to pole,
And made the very billows pay them toll.

LXVI.

I've no great cause to love that spot of earth,
Which holds what *might have been* the noblest nation;
But though I owe it little but my birth,
I feel a mix'd regret and veneration
For its decaying fame and former worth.
Seven years (the usual term of transportation)
Of absence lay one's old resentments level,
When a man's country's going to the devil.

LXVII.

Alas! could she but fully, truly, know
How her great name is now throughout abhorr'd;
How eager all the earth is for the blow
Which shall lay bare her bosom to the sword;
How all the nations deem her their worst foe,
That worse than *worst of foes*, the once adored
False friend, who held out freedom to mankind,
And now would chain them, to the very mind;—

LXVIII.

Would she be proud, or boast herself the free,
Who is but first of slaves? The nations are
In prison,—but the gaoler, what is he?
No less a victim to the bolt and bar.
Is the poor privilege to turn the key
Upon the captive, freedom? He's as far
From the enjoyment of the earth and air
Who watches o'er the chain, as they who wear.

LXIX.

Don Juan now saw Albion's earliest beauties,
Thy cliffs, *dear* Dover! harbour, and hotel;
Thy custom-house, with all its delicate duties;
Thy waiters running mucks at every bell;
Thy packets, all whose passengers are booties
To those who upon land or water dwell;
And last, not least, to strangers uninstructed,
Thy long, long bills, whence nothing is deducted.

LXX.

Juan, though careless, young, and magnifique,
And rich in rubles, diamonds, cash, and credit,
Who did not limit much his bills per week,
Yet stared at this a little, though he paid it,—
(His Maggior Duomo, a smart, subtle Greek,
Before him summ'd the awful scroll and read it)
But doubtless as the air, though seldom sunny,
Is free, the respiration's worth the money.

LXXI.

On with the horses! Off to Canterbury!
Tramp, tramp o'er pebble, and splash, splash through puddle;
Hurrah! how swiftly speeds the post so merry!
Not like slow Germany, wherein they muddle
Along the road, as if they went to bury
Their fare; and also pause besides, to fuddle,
With "schnapps"—sad dogs! whom "Hundsfot," or "Verflucter,"
Affect no more than lightning a conductor.

LXXII.

Now there is nothing gives a man such spirits,
Leavening his blood as cayenne doth a curry,
As going at full speed—no matter where its
Direction be, so 't is but in a hurry,
And merely for the sake of its own merits;
For the less cause there is for all this flurry,
The greater is the pleasure in arriving
At the great *end* of travel—which is driving.

LXXIII.

They saw at Canterbury the cathedral;
Black Edward's helm, and Becket's bloody stone,

Were pointed out as usual by the bedral,
 In the same quaint, uninterested tone:—
There's glory again for you, gentle reader! All
 Ends in a rusty casque and dubious bone,
Half-solved into these sodas or magnesias,
Which form that bitter draught, the human species.

LXXIV.

The effect on Juan was of course sublime:
 He breathed a thousand Cressys, as he saw
That casque, which never stoop'd except to Time.
 Even the bold Churchman's tomb excited awe,
Who died in the then great attempt to climb
 O'er kings, who *now* at least *must talk* of law

Before they butcher. Little Leila gazed,
And asked why such a structure had been raised:

LXXV.

And being told it was "God's house," she said
He was well lodged, but only wonder'd how
He suffer'd Infidels in His homestead,
The cruel Nazarenes, who had laid low
His holy temples in the lands which bred
The true Believers;—and her infant brow
Was bent with grief that Mahomet should resign
A mosque so noble, flung like pearls to swine.

LXXVI.

On! on! through meadows, managed like a garden,
A paradise of hops and high production;
For after years of travel by a bard in
Countries of greater heat, but lesser suction,
A green field is a sight which makes him pardon
The absence of that more sublime construction;

Which mixes up vines, olives, precipices,
Glaciers, volcanoes, oranges, and ices.

LXXVII.

And when I think upon a pot of beer——
But I won't weep!—and so drive on, postilions!
As the smart boys spurr'd fast in their career,
Juan admired these highways of free millions;
A country in all senses the most dear
To foreigner or native, save some silly ones
Who "kick against the pricks" just at this juncture,
And for their pains get only a fresh puncture.

LXXVIII.

What a delightful thing 's a turnpike road
So smooth, so level, such a mode of shaving
The earth, as scarce the eagle in the broad
Air can accomplish, with his wide wings waving.
Had such been cut in Phaeton's time, the god
Had told his son to satisfy his craving
With the York mail;—but onward as we roll,
"Surgit amari aliquid"—the toll!

LXXIX.

Alas! how deeply painful is all payment!
Take lives, take wives, take aught except men's purses.
As Machiavel shows those in purple raiment,
Such is the shortest way to general curses.
They hate a murderer much less than a claimant
On that sweet ore which everybody nurses.—
Kill a man's family, and he may brook it,
But keep your hands out of his breeches' pocket:

LXXX.

So said the Florentine: ye monarchs, hearken
To your instructor. Juan now was borne,
Just as the day began to wane and darken,
O'er the high hill, which looks with pride or scorn
Toward the great city.—Ye who have a spark in
Your veins of Cockney spirit, smile or mourn
According as you take things well or ill;—
Bold Britons, we are now on Shooter's Hill!

LXXXI.

The sun went down, the smoke rose up, as from
A half-unquench'd volcano, o'er a space
Which well beseem'd the "Devil's drawing-room,"
As some have qualified that wondrous place;
But Juan felt, though not approaching *home*,
As one who, though he were not of the race,
Revered the soil, of those true sons the mother,
Who butcher'd half the earth, and bullied t' other.

LXXXII.

A mighty mass of brick, and smoke, and shipping,
Dirty and dusky, but as wide as eye
Could reach, with here and there a sail just skipping
In sight, then lost amidst the forestry
Of masts; a wilderness of steeples peeping
On tiptoe through their sea-coal canopy;
A huge, dun cupola, like a foolscap crown
On a fool's head—and there is London Town!

LXXXIII.

But Juan saw not this: each wreath of smoke
Appeared to him but as the magic vapour
Of some alchymic furnace, from whence broke
The wealth of worlds (a wealth of tax and paper):
The gloomy clouds, which o'er it as a yoke
Are bow'd, and put the sun out like a taper,
Were nothing but the natural atmosphere,
Extremely wholesome, though but rarely clear.

LXXXIV.

He paused—and so will I; as doth a crew
Before they give their broadside. By and by,
My gentle countrymen, we will renew
Our old acquaintance; and at least I'll try
To tell you truths *you* will not take as true,
Because they are so;—a male Mrs. Fry,
With a soft besom will I sweep your halls,
And brush a web or two from off the walls.

LXXXV.

Oh, Mrs. Fry! Why go to Newgate? Why
Preach to poor rogues? And wherefore not begin
With Carlton, or with other houses? Try
Your hand at harden'd and imperial sin.
To mend the people 's an absurdity,
A jargon, a mere philanthropic din,
Unless you make their betters better:—Fy!
I thought you had more religion, Mrs. Fry.

LXXXVI.

Teach them the decencies of good threescore;
Cure them of tours, hussar and highland dresses;
Tell them that youth once gone returns no more,
That hired hussars redeem no land's distresses;
Tell them Sir William Curtis is a bore,
Too dull even for the dullest of excesses,
The witless Falstaff of a hoary Hal,
A fool whose bells have ceased to ring at all.

LXXXVII.

Tell them, though it may be perhaps too late
On life's worn confine, jaded, bloated, sated,
To set up vain pretences of being great,
'T is not so to be good; and be it stated,
The worthiest kings have ever loved least state:
And tell them —— But you won't, and I have prated
Just now enough; but by and by I'll prattle
Like Roland's horn in Roncesvalles' battle.

CANTO THE ELEVENTH.

I.

WHEN Bishop Berkely said "there was no matter,"
And proved it—'t was no matter what he said:
They say his system 't is in vain to batter,
Too subtle for the airiest human head;
And yet who can believe it? I would shatter
Gladly all matters down to stone or lead,
Or adamant, to find the world a spirit,
And wear my head, denying that I wear it.

II.

What a sublime discovery 't was to make the
Universe universal egotism,
That all 's ideal—*all ourselves!* I'll stake the
World (be it what you will) that *that*'s no schism.
Oh Doubt!—if thou be'st Doubt, for which some take thee,
But which I doubt extremely—thou sole prism
Of the Truth's rays, spoil not my draught of spirit!
Heaven's brandy, though our brain can hardly bear it.

III.

For ever and anon comes Indigestion,
(Not the most "dainty Ariel") and perplexes
Our soarings with another sort of question:
And that which after all my spirit vexes,
Is, that I find no spot where man can rest eye on,
Without confusion of the sorts and sexes,
Of beings, stars, and this unriddled wonder,
The world, which at the worst 's a glorious blunder—

IV.

If it be chance; or if it be according
So the old text, still better:—lest it should
Turn out so, we'll say nothing 'gainst the wording,
As several people think such hazards rude.
They 're right; our days are too brief for affording
Space to dispute what *no one* ever could
Decide, and *everybody one day* will
Know very clearly—or at least lie still.

V.

And therefore will I leave off metaphysical
Discussion, which is neither here nor there:
If I agree that what is, is; then this I call
Being quite perspicuous and extremely fair;
The truth is, I've grown lately rather phthisical;
I don't know what the reason is—the air
Perhaps; but as I suffer from the shocks
Of illness, I grow much more orthodox.

VI.

The first attack at once proved the Divinity
(But *that* I never doubted, nor the Devil);
The next, the Virgin's mystical virginity;
The third, the usual Origin of Evil;
The fourth at once established the whole Trinity
On so uncontrovertible a level,
That I devoutly wish'd the three were four,
On purpose to believe so much the more.

VII.

To our theme.—The man who has stood on the Acropolis,
And look'd down over Attica; or he
Who has sail'd where picturesque Constantinople is,
Or seen Timbuctoo, or hath taken tea
In small-eyed China's crockery-ware metropolis,
Or sat amidst the bricks of Nineveh,
May not think much of London's first appearance—
But ask him what he thinks of it a year hence?

VIII.

Don Juan had got out on Shooter's Hill,
Sunset the time, the place the same declivity
Which looks along that vale of good and ill
Where London streets ferment in full activity;
While everything around was calm and still,
Except the creak of wheels, which on their pivot he
Heard,—and that bee-like, bubbling, busy hum
Of cities, that boil over with their scum:—

IX.

I say, Don Juan, wrapt in contemplation,
Walk'd on behind his carriage, o'er the summit,
And lost in wonder of so great a nation,
Gave way to 't, since he could not overcome it.
"And here," he cried, "is Freedom's chosen station;
Here peals the people's voice, nor can entomb it
Racks, prisons, inquisitions; resurrection
Awaits it, each new meeting or election.

X.

"Here are chaste wives, pure lives; here people pay
But what they please; and if that things be dear
'T is only that they love to throw away
Their cash, to show how much they have a-year.
Here laws are all inviolate; none lay
Traps for the traveller; every highway's clear:
Here—" he was interrupted by a knife,
With—"Damn your eyes! your money or your life!"—

XI.

These freeborn sounds proceeded from four pads
In ambush laid, who had perceived him loiter
Behind his carriage; and, like handy lads,
Had seized the lucky hour to reconnoître,
In which the heedless gentleman who gads
Upon the road, unless he prove a fighter,
May find himself within that isle of riches
Exposed to lose his life as well as breeches.

XII.

Juan, who did not understand a word
Of English, save their shibboleth, "God damn!"
And even that he had so rarely heard,
He sometimes thought 't was only their "Salam,"
Or "God be with you!"—and 't is not absurd
To think so: for half English as I am
(To my misfortune) never can I say
I heard them wish "God with you," save that way;—

XIII.

Juan yet quickly understood their gesture,
And being somewhat choleric and sudden,
Drew forth a pocket pistol from his vesture,
And fired it into one assailant's pudding—

Who fell, as rolls an ox o'er in his pasture,
And roar'd out, as he writhed his native mud in,
Unto his nearest follower or henchman,
"Oh Jack! I'm floor'd by that'ere bloody Frenchman!"

XIV.

On which Jack and his train set off at speed,
And Juan's suite, late scatter'd at a distance,
Came up, all marvelling at such a deed,
And offering, as usual, late assistance.
Juan, who saw the moon's late minion bleed
As if his veins would pour out his existence,
Stood calling out for bandages and lint,
And wish'd he had been less hasty with his flint.

XV.

"Perhaps," thought he, "it is the country's wont
To welcome foreigners in this way: now
I recollect some innkeepers who do n't
Differ, except in robbing with a bow,

In lieu of a bare blade and brazen front.
But what is to be done? I ca n't allow
The fellow to lie groaning on the road:
So take him up; I'll help you with the load."

XVI.

But ere they could perform this pious duty,
The dying man cried, "Hold! I've got my gruel!
Oh! for a glass of *max!* We 've miss'd our booty;
Let me die where I am!" And as the fuel
Of life shrunk in his heart, and thick and sooty
The drops fell from his death-wound, and he drew ill
His breath,—he from his swelling throat untied
A kerchief, crying, "Give Sal that!"—and died.

XVII.

The cravat stain'd with bloody drops fell down
Before Don Juan's feet: he could not tell
Exactly why it was before him thrown,
Nor what the meaning of the man's farewell.
Poor Tom was once a kiddy upon town,
A thorough varmint, and a *real* swell,
Full flash, all fancy, until fairly diddled,
His pockets first, and then his body riddled.

XVIII.

Don Juan, having done the best he could
In all the circumstances of the case,
As soon as "Crowner's quest" allow'd, pursued
His travels to the capital apace;—
Esteeming it a little hard he should
In twelve hours' time, and very little space,
Have been obliged to slay a freeborn native
In self-defence: this made him meditative.

XIX.

He from the world had cut off a great man,
Who in his time had made heroic bustle.
Who in a row like Tom could lead the van,
Booze in the ken, or at the spellken hustle?
Who queer a flat? Who (spite of Bow Street's ban)
On the high toby-spice so flash the muzzle?
Who on a lark, with black-eyed Sal (his blowing),
So prime, so swell, so nutty, and so knowing?[79]

XX.

But Tom 's no more—and so no more of Tom.
Heroes must die; and by God's blessing 't is
Not long before the most of them go home.
Hail! Thamis, hail! Upon thy verge it is
That Juan's chariot, rolling like a drum
In thunder, holds the way it ca n't well miss,
Through Kennington and all the other "tons,"
Which make us wish ourselves in town at once;—

XXI.

Through Groves, so call'd as being void of trees,
(Like *lucus* from *no* light); through prospects named
Mount Pleasant, as containing nought to please,
Nor much to climb; through little boxes framed
Of bricks, to let the dust in at your ease,
With "To be let," upon their doors proclaim'd;
Through "Rows" most modestly call'd "Paradise,"
Which Eve might quit without much sacrifice;—

XXII.

Through coaches, drays, choked turnpikes, and a whirl
Of wheels, and roar of voices, and confusion;
Here taverns wooing to a pint of "purl,"
There mails fast flying off like a delusion;
There barbers' blocks with periwigs in curl
In windows; here the lamplighter's infusion
Slowly distill'd into the glimmering glass
(For in those days we had not got to gas—);

XXIII.

Through this, and much, and more, is the approach
Of travellers to mighty Babylon:
Whether they come by horse, or chaise, or coach,
With slight exceptions, all the ways seem one.
I could say more, but do not choose to encroach
Upon the Guide-book's privilege. The sun
Had set some time, and night was on the ridge
Of twilight, as the party cross'd the bridge.

XXIV.

That 's rather fine, the gentle sound of Thamis—
Who vindicates a moment, too, his stream—
Tho' hardly heard through multifarious "damme's."
The lamps of Westminster's more regular gleam,
The breadth of pavement, and yon shrine where fame is
A spectral resident—whose pallid beam
In shape of moonshine hovers o'er the pile—
Make this a sacred part of Albion's isle.

XXV.

The Druids' groves are gone—so much the better:
Stone-Henge is not—but what the devil is it?—
But Bedlam still exists with its sage fetter,
That madmen may not bite you on a visit;
The Bench too seats or suits full many a debtor;
The Mansion House too (though some people quiz it)
To me appears a stiff yet grand erection;
But then the Abbey 's worth the whole collection.

XXVI.

The line of lights too up to Charing Cross,
Pall-Mall, and so forth, have a coruscation
Like gold as in comparison to dross,
Match'd with the Continent's illumination,
Whose cities Night by no means deigns to gloss.
The French were not yet a lamp-lighting nation,
And when they grew so — on their new-found lantern,
Instead of wicks, they made a wicked man turn.

XXVII.

A row of gentlemen along the streets
 Suspended may illuminate mankind,
As also bonfires made of country seats;
 But the old way is best for the purblind:
The other looks like phosphorus on sheets,
 A sort of ignis fatuus to the mind,
Which, though 't is certain to perplex and frighten,
Must burn more mildly ere it can enlighten.

XXVIII.

But London's so well lit, that if Diogenes
Could recommence to hunt his *honest man*,
And found him not amidst the various progenies
Of this enormous city's spreading spawn,
T were not for want of lamps to aid his dodging his
Yet undiscover'd treasure. What *I* can,
I've done to find the same throughout life's journey,
But see the world is only one attorney.

XXIX.

Over the stones still rattling, up Pall-Mall,
Through crowds and carriages, but waxing thinner
As thunder'd knockers broke the long seal'd spell
Of doors 'gainst duns, and to an early dinner
Admitted a small party as night fell,—
Don Juan, our young diplomatic sinner,
Pursued his path, and drove past some hotels,
St. James's Palace and St. James's "Hells."[80]

XXX.

They reach'd the hotel; forth stream'd from the front door
A tide of well-clad waiters, and around
The mob stood, and as usual several score
Of those pedestrian Paphians who abound
In decent London when the daylight's o'er;
Commodious, but immoral, they are found
Useful, like Malthus, in promoting marriage—
But Juan now is stepping from his carriage.

XXXI.

Into one of the sweetest of hotels,
Especially for foreigners—and mostly
For those whom favour or whom fortune swells,
And cannot find a bill's small items costly.
There many an envoy either dwelt or dwells
(The den of many a diplomatic lost lie),
Until to some conspicuous square they pass,
And blazen o'er their door their names in brass.

XXXII.

Juan, whose was a delicate commission,
Private, though publicly important, bore
No title to point out with due precision
The exact affair on which he was sent o'er.
'T was merely known, that on a secret mission
A foreigner of rank had graced our shore,
Young, handsome, and accomplish'd, who was said
(In whispers) to have turn'd his Sovereign's head.

XXXIII.

Some rumour also of some strange adventures
Had gone before him, and his wars and loves;
And as romantic heads are pretty painters,
And, above all, an Englishwoman's roves
Into the excursive, breaking the indentures
Of sober reason, wheresoe'er it moves,
He found himself extremely in the fashion,
Which serves our thinking people for a passion.

XXXIV.

I don't mean that they are passionless, but quite
The contrary; but then 'tis in the head;
Yet as the consequences are as bright
As if they acted with the heart instead,
What after all can signify the site
Of ladies' lucubrations? So they lead
In safety to the place for which you start,
What matters if the road be head or heart?

XXXV.

Juan presented in the proper place,
To proper placemen, every Russ credential;
And was received with all the due grimace,
By those who govern in the mood potential,
Who, seeing a handsome stripling with smooth face,
Thought (what in state affairs is most essential)
That they as easily might *do* the youngster,
As hawks may pounce upon a woodland songster.

XXXVI.

They err'd, as aged men will do; but by
And by we'll talk of that; and if we don't,
'T will be because our notion is not high
Of politicians and their double front,
Who live by lies, yet dare not boldly lie:—
Now what I love in women is, they won't
Or can't do otherwise than lie, but do it
So well, the very truth seems falsehood to it.

XXXVII.

And, after all, what is a lie? 'T is but
The truth in masquerade; and I defy
Historians, heroes, lawyers, priests, to put
A fact without some leaven of a lie.
The very shadow of true Truth would shut
Up annals, revelations, poesy,
And prophecy—except it should be dated
Some years before the incidents related.

XXXVIII.

Praised be all liars and all lies! Who now
Can tax my mild Muse with misanthropy?
She rings the world's "Te Deum," and her brow
Blushes for those who will not:—but to sigh
Is idle; let us like most others bow,
Kiss hands, feet, any part of majesty,
After the good example of "Green Erin,"
Whose shamrock now seems rather worse for wearing.

XXXIX.

Don Juan was presented, and his dress
And mien excited general admiration—
I don't know which was more admired or less:
One monstrous diamond drew much observation,

Which Catherine in a moment of "ivresse"
(In love or brandy's fervent fermentation)
Bestow'd upon him, as the public learn'd;
And, to say truth, it had been fairly earn'd.

XL.

Besides the ministers and underlings,
Who must be courteous to the accredited
Diplomatists of rather wavering kings,
Until their royal riddle's fully read,
The very clerks,—those somewhat dirty springs
Of office, or the house of office, fed
By foul corruption into streams,—even they
Were hardly rude enough to earn their pay:

XLI.

And insolence no doubt is what they are
Employ'd for, since it is their daily labour,
In the dear offices of peace or war;
And should you doubt, pray ask of your next neighbour,
When for a passport, or some other bar
To freedom, he applied (a grief and *a* bore),
If he found not this spawn of taxborn riches,
Like lap-dogs, the least civil sons of b——s.

XLII.

But Juan was received with much "empressement:"—
These phrases of refinement I must borrow
From our next neighbours' land, where, like a chessman,
There is a move set down for joy or sorrow,
Not only in mere talking, but the press. Man
In islands is, it seems, downright and thorough,
More than on continents—as if the sea
(See Billingsgate) made even the tongue more free.

XLIII.

And yet the British "Damme"'s rather Attic,
Your continental oaths are but incontinent,
And turn on things which no aristocratic
Spirit would name, and therefore even I won't anent [81]
This subject quote; as it would be schismatic
In politesse, and have a sound affronting in't:
But "Damme"'s quite ethereal, though too daring—
Platonic blasphemy, the soul of swearing.

XLIV.

For downright rudeness, ye may stay at home;
For true or false politeness (and scarce *that*
Now) you may cross the blue deep and white foam—
The first the emblem (rarely though) of what
You leave behind, the next of much you come
To meet. However, 't is no time to chat
On general topics: poems must confine
Themselves to unity, like this of mine.

44

XLV.

In the great world,—which, being interpreted,
Meaneth the west or worst end of a city,
And about twice two thousand people bred
By no means to be very wise or witty,
But to sit up while others lie in bed,
And look down on the universe with pity,—
Juan, as an inveterate patrician,
Was well received by persons of condition.

XLVI.

He was a bachelor, which is a matter
Of import both to virgin and to bride,
The former's hymeneal hopes to flatter;
And (should she not hold fast by love or pride)
'T is also of some moment to the latter:
A rib's a thorn in a wed gallant's side,
Requires decorum, and is apt to double
The horrid sin—and what's still worse, the trouble.

XLVII.

But Juan was a bachelor—of arts,
And parts, and hearts: he danced and sung, and had
An air as sentimental as Mozart's
Softest of melodies; and could be sad
Or cheerful, without any "flaws or starts,"
Just at the proper time; and though a lad,
Had seen the world—which is a curious sight,
And very much unlike what people write.

XLVIII.

Fair virgins blush'd upon him; wedded dames
Bloom'd also in less transitory hues;
For both commodities dwell by the Thames,
The painting and the painted; youth, ceruse,
Against his heart preferr'd their usual claims,
Such as no gentleman can quite refuse:
Daughters admired his dress, and pious mothers
Inquired his income, and if he had brothers.

XLIX.

The milliners who furnish "drapery Misses" [82]
Throughout the season, upon speculation
Of payment ere the honey-moon's last kisses
Have waned into a crescent's coruscation,
Thought such an opportunity as this is,
Of a rich foreigner's initiation,
Not to be overlook'd—and gave such credit,
That future bridegrooms swore, and sigh'd, and paid it.

L.

The Blues, that tender tribe, who sigh o'er sonnets,
And with the pages of the last Review
Line the interior of their heads or bonnets,
Advanced in all their azure's highest hue
They talk'd bad French or Spanish, and upon its
Late authors ask'd him for a hint or two;

And which was softest, Russian or Castilian?
And whether in his travels he saw Ilion?

LI.

Juan, who was a little superficial,
And not in literature a great Drawcansir,
Examined by this learned and especial
Jury of matrons, scarce knew what to answer:
His duties warlike, loving, or official,
His steady application as a dancer,
Had kept him from the brink of Hippocrene,
Which now he found was blue instead of green.

LII.

However, he replied at hazard, with
A modest confidence and calm assurance,
Which lent his learned lucubrations pith,
And pass'd for arguments of good endurance.
That prodigy, Miss Araminta Smith,
(Who at sixteen translated "Hercules Furens"
Into as furious English), with her best look,
Set down his sayings in her common-place book.

LIII.

Juan knew several languages—as well
He might—and brought them up with skill, in time
To save his fame with each accomplish'd belle,
Who still regretted that he did not rhyme.
There wanted but this requisite to swell
His qualities (with them) into sublime:
Lady Fitz-Frisky, and Miss Mævia Mannish,
Both long'd extremely to be sung in Spanish.

LIV.

However, he did pretty well, and was
Admitted as an aspirant to all
The coteries, and, as in Banquo's glass,
At great assemblies or in parties small,
He saw ten thousand living authors pass,
That being about their average numeral;
Also the eighty "greatest living poets,"
As every paltry magazine can show *it's*.

LV.

In twice five years the "greatest living poet,"
Like to the champion in the fisty ring,
Is call'd on to support his claim, or show it,
Although 't is an imaginary thing.
Even I—albeit I'm sure I did not know it,
Nor sought of foolscap subjects to be king,—
Was reckon'd a considerable time,
The grand Napoleon of the realms of rhyme.

LVI.

But Juan was my Moscow, and Faliero
My Leipsic, and my Mount Saint Jean seems Cain:
"La Belle Alliance" of dunces down at zero,
Now that the Lion 's fall'n, may rise again:
But I will fall at least as fell my hero;
Nor reign at all, or as a *monarch* reign;
Or to some lonely isle of gaolers go,
With turncoat Southey for my turnkey Lowe.

LVII.

Sir Walter reign'd before me; Moore and Campbell
Before and after; but now grown more holy,
The Muses upon Sion's hill must ramble
With poets almost Clergymen, or wholly;
And Pegasus has a psalmodic amble
Beneath the very Reverend Rowley Powley,
Who shoes the glorious animal with stilts,
A modern Ancient Pistol—by the hilts!

LVIII.

Still he excels that artificial hard
Labourer in the same vineyard, though the vine
Yields him but vinegar for his reward,—
That neutralised dull Dorus of the Nine;
That swarthy Sporus, neither man or bard:
That ox of verse, who *ploughs* for every line:—
Cambyses' roaring Romans beat at least
The howling Hebrews of Cybele's priest.

LIX.

Then there 's my gentle Euphues; who, they say,
Sets up for being a sort of *moral me;*
He 'll find it rather difficult some day
To turn out both, or either, it may be.
Some persons think that Coleridge hath the sway;
And Wordsworth has supporters, two or three;
And that deep-mouth'd Bœotian "Savage Landor"
Has taken for a swan rogue Southey's gander.

LX.

John Keats, who was kill'd off by one critique,
Just as he really promised something great,
If not intelligible, without Greek
Contrived to talk about the gods of late,
Much as they might have been supposed to speak.
Poor fellow! His was an untoward fate;
'T is strange the mind, that very fiery particle,[83]
Should let itself be snuff'd out by an article.

LXI.

The list grows long of live and dead pretenders
To that which none will gain — or none will know
The conqueror at least; who, ere Time renders
His last award, will have the long grass grow
Above his burnt-out brain, and sapless cinders.
If I might augur, I should rate but low

Their chances;—they 're too numerous, like the thirty
Mock tyrants, when Rome's annals wax'd but dirty.

LXII.

This is the literary *lower* empire,
Where the prætorian bands take up the matter;—
A "dreadful trade," like his who "gathers samphire,"
The insolent soldiery to soothe and flatter,
With the same feelings as you 'd coax a vampire.
Now, were I once at home, and in good satire,
I 'd try conclusions with those Janizaries,
And show them *what* an intellectual war is.

LXIII.

I think I know a trick or two, would turn
Their flanks;—but it is hardly worth my while,
With such small gear to give myself concern:
Indeed I 've not the necessary bile;
My natural temper's really aught but stern,
And even my Muse's worst reproof's a smile;
And then she drops a brief and modern curtsy,
And glides away, assured she never hurts ye.

LXIV.

My Juan, whom I left in deadly peril
Amongst live poets, and blue ladies, past
With some small profit through that field so sterile.
Being tired in time, and neither least nor last,
Left it before he had been treated very ill;
And henceforth found himself more gaily class'd
Amongst the higher spirits of the day,
The sun's true son, no vapour, but a ray.

LXV.

His morns he pass'd in business—which, dissected,
Was like all business, a laborious nothing
That leads to lassitude, the most infected
And Centaur Nessus garb of mortal clothing,[81]
And on our sofas makes us lie dejected,
And talk in tender horrors of our loathing
All kinds of toil, save for our country's good,—
Which grows no better, though 't is time it should.

LXVI.

His afternoons he pass'd in visits, luncheons,
Lounging, and boxing; and the twilight hour
In riding round those vegetable puncheons
Call'd "Parks," where there is neither fruit nor flower
Enough to gratify a bee's slight munchings;
But, after all, it is the only "bower,"
(In Moore's phrase) where the fashionable fair
Can form a slight acquaintance with fresh air.

LXVII.

Then dress, then dinner, then awakes the world!
Then glare the lamps, then whirl the wheels, then roar
Through street and square fast flashing chariots hurl'd
Like harness'd meteors; then along the floor
Chalk mimics painting; then festoons are twirl'd;
Then roll the brazen thunders of the door,
Which opens to the thousand happy few
An earthly paradise of "Or-Molu."

LXVIII.

There stands the noble hostess, nor shall sink
With the three-thousandth curtsy; there the waltz,
The only dance which teaches girls to think,
Makes one in love even with its very faults.
Saloon, room, hall, o'erflow beyond their brink,
And long the latest of arrivals halts,
'Midst royal dukes and dames condemn'd to climb,
And gain an inch of staircase at a time.

LXIX.

Thrice happy he, who, after a survey
Of the good company, can win a corner,
A door that 's *in* or boudoir *out* of the way,
Where he may fix himself like small "Jack Horner,"
And let the Babel round run as it may,
And look on as a mourner, or a scorner,
Or an approver, or a mere spectator,
Yawning a little as the night grows later.

LXX.

But this won't do, save by and by; and he
Who, like Don Juan, takes an active share,
Must steer with care through all that glittering sea
Of gems and plumes and pearls and silks, to where
He deems it is his proper place to be;
Dissolving in the waltz to some soft air,
Or proudlier prancing with mercurial skill,
Where Science marshals forth her own quadrille.

LXXI.

Or, if he dance not, but hath higher views
Upon an heiress or his neighbour's bride,
Let him take care that that which he pursues
Is not at once too palpably described.
Full many an eager gentleman oft rues
His haste: impatience is a blundering guide,
Amongst a people famous for reflection,
Who like to play the fool with circumspection.

LXXII.

But, if you can contrive, get next at supper;
Or if, forestall'd, get opposite and ogle:—

O, ye ambrosial moments! always upper
 In mind, a sort of sentimental bogle,[85]
Which sits for ever upon memory's crupper,
 The ghost of vanish'd pleasures once in vogue! Ill
Can tender souls relate the rise and fall
Of hopes and fears which shake a single ball.

LXXIII.

But these precautionary hints can touch
 Only the common run, who must pursue,
And watch, and ward; whose plans a word too much
 Or little overturns; and not the few
Or many (for the number 's sometimes such)
 Whom a good mien, especially if new,
Or fame, or name, for wit, war, sense, or nonsense,
Permits whate'er they please, or *did* not long since.

LXXIV.

Our hero, as a hero, young and handsome,
 Noble, rich, celebrated, and a stranger,
Like other slaves of course must pay his ransom,
 Before he can escape from so much danger
As will environ a conspicuous man. Some
 Talk about poetry, and "rack and manger,"
And ugliness, disease, as toil and trouble;—
I wish they knew the life of a young noble.

LXXV.

They are young, but know not youth—it is anticipated;
 Handsome but wasted, rich without a son;
Their vigour in a thousand arms is dissipated;
 Their cash comes *from*, their wealth goes *to* a Jew;
Both senates see their nightly votes participated
 Between the tyrant's and the tribunes' crew;
And having voted, dined, drank, gamed, and whored,
The family vault receives another lord.

LXXVI.

"Where is the world?" cries Young, at *eighty*—"Where
 The world in which a man was born?" Alas!
Where is the world of *eight* years past? *'Twas there*—
 I look for it—'tis gone, a globe of glass!
Crack'd, shiver'd, vanish'd, scarcely gazed on, ere
 A silent change dissolves the glittering mass.
Statesmen, chiefs, orators, queens, patriots, kings,
And dandies, all are gone on the wind's wings.

LXXVII.

Where is Napoleon the Grand? God knows:
 Where little Castlereagh? The devil can tell:
Where Grattan, Curran, Sheridan—all those
 Who bound the bar or senate in their spell?
Where is the unhappy Queen, with all her woes?
 And where the Daughter, whom the Isles loved well?
Where are those martyr'd saints, the Five per Cents?
And where—oh, where the devil are the Rents?

LXXVIII.

Where's Brummel? Dish'd. Where's Long Pole Wellesley? Diddled.
Where's Whitbread? Romilly? Where's George the Third?
Where is his will? (That's not so soon unriddled.)
 And where is "Fum" the Fourth, our "royal bird?"
Gone down, it seems, to Scotland to be fiddled
 Unto by Sawney's violin, we have heard:
"Caw me, caw thee"—for six months hath been hatching
This scene of royal itch and loyal scratching.

LXXIX.

Where is Lord This? And where my Lady That?
 The Honourable Mistresses and Misses?
Some laid aside like an old Opera hat,
 Married, unmarried, and remarried: (this is
An evolution oft performed of late).
 Where are the Dublin shouts—and London hisses?
Where are the Grenvilles? Turn'd as usual. Where
My friends the Whigs? Exactly where they were.

LXXX.

Where are the Lady Carolines and Franceses?
 Divorced or doing thereanent. Ye annals
So brilliant, where the list of routs and dances is,—
 Thou "Morning Post," sole record of the panels
Broken in carriages, and all the phantasies
 Of fashion,—say what streams now fill those channels?
Some die, some fly, some languish on the Continent,
Because the times have hardly left them *one* tenant.

LXXXI.

Some who once set their caps at cautious dukes,
 Have taken up at length with younger brothers:
Some heiresses have bit at sharpers' hooks:
 Some maids have been made wives, some merely mothers;
Others have lost their fresh and fairy looks:
 In short, the list of alterations bothers.
There's little strange in this, but something strange is
The unusual quickness of these common changes.

LXXXII.

Talk not of seventy years as age; in seven
 I have seen more changes, down from monarchs to
The humblest individual under heaven,
 That might suffice a moderate century through.

I knew that nought was lasting, but now even
 Change grows too changeable, without being new:
Nought's permanent among the human race,
Except the Whigs *not* getting into place.

LXXXIII.

I have seen Napoleon, who seem'd quite a Jupiter,
 Shrink to a Saturn. I have seen a Duke
(No matter which) turn politician stupider,
 If that can well be, than his wooden look.
But it is time that I should hoist my "Blue Peter,"
 And sail for a new theme:—I have seen—and shook
To see it—the king hiss'd, and then carest;
But don't pretend to settle which was best.

LXXXIV.

I have seen the Landholders without a rap—
 I have seen Joanna Southcote—I have seen
The House of Commons turn'd to a tax-trap—
 I have seen that sad affair of the late Queen—
I have seen crowns worn instead of a fool's cap—
 I have seen a Congress doing all that's mean—
I have seen some nations, like o'erloaded asses,
Kick off their burthens—meaning the high classes.

LXXXV.

I have seen small poets, and great prosers, and
 Interminable—*not eternal*—speakers—
I have seen the funds at war with house and land—
 I have seen the country gentlemen turn squeakers—
I have seen the people ridden o'er like sand
 By slaves on horseback—I have seen malt liquors
Exchanged for "thin potations" by John Bull—
I have seen John half detect himself a fool.—

LXXXVI.

But "carpe diem," Juan, "carpe, carpe!"
 To-morrow sees another race as gay
And transient, and devour'd by the same harpy.
 "Life's a poor player,"—then "play out the play,
Ye villains!" and, above all, keep a sharp eye
 Much less on what you do than what you say:
Be hypocritical, be cautious, be
Not what you *seem*, but always what you *see*.

LXXXVII.

But how shall I relate in other cantos
 Of what befell our hero in the land,
Which 'tis the common cry and lie to vaunt as
 A moral country? But I hold my hand—
For I disdain to write an Atalantus;
 But 'tis as well at once to understand
You are *not* a moral people, and you know it,
Without the aid of too sincere a poet.

LXXXVIII.

What Juan saw and underwent shall be
 My topic, with of course the due restriction
Which is required by proper courtesy;
 And recollect the work is only fiction,
And that I sing of neither mine nor me,
 Though every scribe, in some slight turn of diction,
Will hint allusions never *meant*. Ne'er doubt
This—when I speak, I *don't hint*, but *speak out*.

LXXXIX.

Whether he married with the third or fourth
 Offspring of some sage husband-hunting countess,
Or whether with some virgin of more worth
 (I mean in Fortune's matrimonial bounties)
He took to regularly peopling earth,
 Of which your lawful awful wedlock fount is,—
Or whether he was taken in for damages,
For being too excursive in his homages,—

XC.

Is yet within the unread events of time.
 Thus far, go forth, thou lay, which I will back
Against the same given quantity of rhyme,
 For being as much the subject of attack
As ever yet was any work sublime,
 By those who love to say that white is black.
So much the better!—I may stand alone,
But would not change my free thoughts for a throne.

CANTO XII.

I.

Of all the barbarous middle ages, that
 Which is most barbarous is the middle age
Of man: it is—I really scarce know what;
 But when we hover between fool and sage,
And do n't know justly what we would be at—
 A period something like a printed page,
Black letter upon foolscap, while our hair
Grows grizzled, and we are not what we were;—

II.

Too old for youth,—too young, at thirty-five,
 To herd with boys, or hoard with good threescore,—
I wonder people should be left alive;
 But since they are, that epoch is a bore:
Love lingers still, although 't were late to wive;
 And as for other love, the illusion 's o'er;
And money, that most pure imagination,
Gleams only through the dawn of its creation.

III.

O Gold! Why call we misers miserable?
 Theirs is the pleasure that can never pall;
Theirs is the best bower anchor, the chain cable
 Which holds fast other pleasures great and small.
Ye who but see the saving man at table,
 And scorn his temperate board, as none at all,
And wonder how the wealthy can be sparing,
Know not what visions spring from each cheese-paring.

IV.

Love or lust makes man sick, and wine much sicker;
 Ambition rends, and gaming gains a loss;
But making money, slowly first, then quicker,
 And adding still a little through each cross
(Which *will* come over things), beats love or liquor,
 The gamester's counter, or the statesman's *dross*.
O Gold! I still prefer thee unto paper,
Which makes bank credit like a bark of vapour.

V.

Who hold the balance of the world? Who reign
O'er congress, whether royalist or liberal?
Who rouse the shirtless patriots of Spain?[86] [all.)
(That make old Europe's journals squeak and gibber
Who keep the world, both old and new, in pain
Or pleasure? Who make politics run glibber all?
The shade of Buonaparte's noble daring?—
Jew Rothschild, and his fellow-Christian, Baring.

VI.

Those, and the truly liberal Lafitte,
Are the true lords of Europe. Every loan
Is not a merely speculative hit,
But seats a nation or upsets a throne.
Republics also get involved a bit;
Columbia's stock hath holders not unknown
On 'Change; and even thy silver soil, Peru,
Must get itself discounted by a Jew.

VII.

Why call the miser miserable? as
I said before: the frugal life is his,
Which in a saint or cynic ever was
The theme of praise: a hermit would not miss
Canonization for the self-same cause,—
And wherefore blame gaunt wealth's austerities?
Because, you'll say, nought calls for such a trial;—
Then there's more merit in his self-denial.

VIII.

He is your only poet;—passion, pure,
And sparkling on from heap to heap, displays,
Possess'd, the ore, of which *mere hopes* allure
Nations athwart the deep: the golden rays
Flash up in ingots from the mine obscure:
On him the diamond pours its brilliant blaze;
While the mild emerald's beam shades down the dies
Of other stones, to soothe the miser's eyes.

IX.

The lands on either side are his: the ship
From Ceylon, Inde, or far Cathay, unloads
For him the fragrant produce of each trip;
Beneath his cars of Ceres groan the roads,
And the vine blushes like Aurora's lip;
His very cellars might be kings' abodes;
While he, despising every sensual call,
Commands—the intellectual lord of all.

X.

Perhaps he hath great projects in his mind,
To build a college, or to found a race,
A hospital, a church,—and leave behind
Some dome surmounted by his meagre face.
Perhaps he fain would liberate mankind
Even with the very ore which makes them base;
Perhaps he would be wealthiest of his nation,
Or revel in the joys of calculation.

XI.

But whether all, or each, or none of these
May be the hoarder's principle of action,
The fool will call such mania a disease:—
What is his *own?* Go—look at each transaction,
Wars, revels, loves—do these bring men more ease
Than the mere plodding thro' each "vulgar frac-
Or do they benefit mankind? Lean miser! [tion?"
Let spendthrifts' heirs inquire of yours—who's wiser?

XII.

How beauteous are rouleaus! how charming chests
Containing ingots, bags of dollars, coins
(Not of old victors, all whose heads and crests
Weigh not the thin ore where their visage shines,
But) of fine unclipt gold, where dully rests
Some likeness, which the glittering cirque confines,
Of modern, reigning, sterling, stupid stamp:—
Yes! ready money *is* Aladdin's lamp.

XIII.

"Love rules the camp, the court, the grove,—for love
Is heaven, and heaven is love:"—so sings the bard;
Which it were rather difficult to prove,
(A thing with poetry in general hard).
Perhaps there may be something in "the grove,"
At least it rhymes to "love:" but I'm prepared
To doubt (no less than landlords of their rental)
If "courts" and "camps" be quite so sentimental.

XIV.

But if Love don't, *Cash* does, and Cash alone:
Cash rules the grove, and fells it too besides;
Without cash, camps were thin, and courts were none;
Without cash, Malthus tells you—"take no brides."
So Cash rules Love the ruler, on his own
High ground, as virgin Cynthia sways the tides:
And as for "Heaven being Love," why not say honey
Is wax? Heaven is not Love, 't is Matrimony.

XV.

Is not all love prohibited whatever,
Excepting marriage? Which is love, no doubt,
After a sort; but somehow people never [out:
With the same thought the two words have help'd
Love may exist *with* marriage, and *should* ever,
And marriage also may exist without;
But love *sans* banns is both a sin and shame,
And ought to go by quite another name.

XVI.

Now if the "court," and "camp," and "grove," be not
Recruited all with constant married men,
Who never coveted their neighbour's lot,
I say *that* line's a lapsus of the pen;—
Strange too in my "buon camerado" Scott,
So celebrated for his morals, when
My Jeffrey held him up as an example
To me;—of which these morals are a sample.

XVII.

Well, if I do n't succeed, I *have* succeeded,
And that 's enough; succeeded in my youth
The only time when much success is needed:
And my success produced what I, in sooth,
Cared most about; it need not now be pleaded—
Whate'er it was, 't was mine; I 've paid, in truth,
Of late, the penalty of such success,
But have not learn'd to wish it any less.

XVIII.

That suit in Chancery,—which some persons plead
In an appeal to the unborn, whom they,
In the faith of their procreative creed,
Baptize posterity, or future clay,—
To me seems but a dubious kind of reed
To lean on for support in any way;
Since odds are that posterity will know
No more of them, than they of her, I trow.

XIX.

Why, I 'm posterity—and so are you;
And whom do we remember? Not a hundred.
Were every memory written down all true,
The tenth or twentieth name would be but blunder'd;
Even Plutarch's Lives have but pick'd out a few,
And 'gainst those few your annalists have thunder'd;
And Mitford in the ninteenth century [87]
Gives, with Greek truth, the good old Greek the lie.

XX.

Good people all, of every degree,
Ye gentle readers and ungentle writers,
In this twelfth Canto 't is my wish to be
As serious as if I had for my inditers
Malthus and Wilberforce:—the last set free
The Negroes, and is worth a million fighters;
While Wellington has but enslaved the Whites,
And Malthus does the thing 'gainst which he writes.

XXI.

I 'm serious—so are all men upon paper;
And why should I not form my speculation,
And hold up to the sun my little taper?
Mankind just now seem wrapt in meditation
On constitutions and steam-boats of vapour;
While sages write against all procreation,
Unless a man can calculate his means
Of feeding brats the moment his wife weans.

XXII.

That 's noble! That 's romantic! For my part,
I think that "Philo-genitiveness" is—
(Now here 's a word quite after my own heart,
Though there's a shorter a good deal than this,
If that politeness set it not apart;
But I'm resolved to say nought that 's amiss)—
I say, methinks that "Philo-genitiveness"
Might meet from men a little more forgiveness.

XXIII.

And now to business.—O my gentle Juan!
Thou art in London—in that pleasant place,
Where every kind of mischief 's daily brewing,
Which can await warm youth in its wild race
'T is true, that thy career is not a new one;
Thou art no novice in the headlong chase
Of early life; but this is a new land,
Which foreigners can never understand.

XXIV.

What with a small diversity of climate,
Of hot or cold, mercurial or sedate,
I could send forth my mandate like a primate
Upon the rest of Europe's social state;
But thou art the most difficult to rhyme at,
Great Britain, which the Muse may penetrate.
All countries have their "Lions," but in thee
There is but one superb menagerie.

XXV.

But I am sick of politics. Begin,
"Paulo Majora." Juan, undecided
Amongst the paths of being "taken in,"
Above the ice had like a skater glided:
When tired of play, he flirted without sin
With some of those fair creatures who have prided
Themselves on innocent tantalisation,
And hate all vice except its reputation.

XXVI.

But these are few, and in the end they make
Some devilish escapade or stir, which shows
That even the purest people may mistake
Their way thro' virtue's primrose paths of snows;
And then men stare, as if a new ass spake
To Balaam, and from tongue to ear o'erflows
Quicksilver small talk, ending (if you note it)
With the kind world's amen—" Who would have thought it?"

XXVII.

The little Leila, with her orient eyes,
And taciturn Asiatic disposition,
(Which saw all western things with small surprise,
To the surprise of people of condition,
Who think that novelties are butterflies,
To be pursued as food for inanition,)
Her charming figure and romantic history
Became a kind of fashionable mystery.

XXVIII.

The women much divided—as is usual
Amongst the sex in little things or great.
Think not, fair creatures, that I mean to abuse you all
I have always liked you better than I state:
Since I've grown moral, still I must accuse you all
Of being apt to talk at a great rate,
And now there was a general sensation
Amongst you, about Leila's education.

XXIX.

In one point only were you settled—and
You had reason: 't was that a young child of grace,
As beautiful as her own native land,
And far away, the last bud of her race,
Howe'er our friend Don Juan might command
Himself for five, four, three, or two years' space,
Would be much better taught beneath the eye
Of peeresses whose follies had run dry.

XXX.

So first there was a generous emulation,
And then there was a general competition,
To undertake the orphan's education.
As Juan was a person of condition,
It had been an affront on this occasion
To talk of a subscription or petition;
But sixteen dowagers, ten unwed she sages,
Whose tale belongs to "Hallam's Middle Ages,"

XXXI.

And one or two sad, separate wives, without
A fruit to bloom upon their withering bough—
Begged to bring *up* the little girl, and "*out*,"—
For that's the phrase that settles all things now,
Meaning a virgin's first blush at a rout,
And all her points as thorough-bred to show:
And I assure you, that like virgin honey
Tastes their first season (mostly if they have money).

XXXII.

How all the needy honourable misters,
Each out-at-elbow peer, or desperate dandy,
The watchful mothers, and the careful sisters,
(Who, by the by, when clever, are more handy
At making matches, where "'t is gold that glisters,"
Than their *he* relatives,) like flies o'er candy
Buzz round "*the* Fortune" with their busy battery,
To turn her head with waltzing and with flattery!

XXXIII.

Each aunt, each cousin, hath her speculation;
Nay, married dames will now and then discover
Such pure disinterestedness of passion,
I've known them court an heiress for their lover.
"Tantæne!" Such the virtues of high station,
Even in the hopeful Isle, whose outlet's "Dover!"
While the poor rich wretch, object of these cares,
Has cause to wish her sire had had male heirs.

XXXIV.

Some are soon bagg'd, and some reject three dozen.
'T is fine to see them scattering refusals
And wild dismay o'er every angry cousin
(Friends of the party), who begin accusals,
Such as—"Unless Miss (Blank) meant to have chosen
Poor Frederick, why did she accord perusals
To his billets? *Why* waltz with him? Why, I pray,
Look *yes* last night, and yet say *no* to-day?

45

XXXV.

"Why?—Why?—Besides, Fred really was *attach'd*,
'T was not her fortune—he has enough without:
The time will come she'll wish that she had snatch'd
So good an opportunity, no doubt:—
But the old Marchioness some plan had hatch'd,
As I'll tell Aurea at to-morrow's rout:
And after all poor Frederick may do better—
Pray, did you see her answer to his letter?"

XXXVI.

Smart uniforms and sparkling coronets
Are spurn'd in turn, until her turn arrives,
After male loss of time, and hearts, and bets
Upon the sweepstakes for substantial wives;
And when at last the pretty creature gets
Some gentleman, who fights, or writes, or drives,
It soothes the awkward squad of the rejected,
To find how very badly she selected.

XXXVII.

For sometimes they accept some long pursuer,
Worn out with importunity; or fall
(But here perhaps the instances are fewer)
To the lot of him who scarce pursued at all.
A hazy widower turn'd of forty's sure[88]
(If 't is not vain examples to recall)
To draw a high prize: now, howe'er he got her, I
See nought more strange in this than 't other lottery.

XXXVIII.

I, for my part—(one "modern instance" more,
"True, 't is a pity—pity 't is, 't is true,")
Was chosen from out an amatory score,
Albeit my years were less discreet than few;
But though I also had reform'd before
Those became one who soon were to be two,
I'll not gainsay the generous public's voice,
That the young lady made a monstrous choice.

XXXIX.

Oh, pardon my digression—or at least
Peruse! 'T is always with a moral end
That I dissert, like grace before a feast:
For, like an aged aunt or tiresome friend,
A rigid guardian, or a zealous priest,
My Muse by exhortation means to mend
All people, at all times, and in most places,
Which puts my Pegasus to these grave paces.

XL.

But now I'm going to be immoral, now
I mean to show things really as they are,
Not as they ought to be: for I avow,
That till we see what's what, in fact, we're far
From much improvement with that virtuous plough
Which skims the surface, leaving scarce a scar
Upon the black loam long manured by Vice,
Only to keep its corn at the old price.

XLI.

But first of little Leila we'll dispose;
For, like a day-dawn, she was young and pure,
Or like the old comparison of snows,
Which are more pure than pleasant, to be sure.
Like many people every body knows,
Don Juan was delighted to secure
A goodly guardian for his infant charge,
Who might not profit much by being at large.

XLII.

Besides, he had found out he was no tutor
(I wish that others would find out the same);
And rather wish'd in such things to stand neuter,
For silly wards will bring their guardians blame:
So when he saw each ancient dame a suitor
To make his little wild Asiatic tame,
Consulting "the Society for Vice
Suppression," Lady Pinchbeck was his choice.

XLIII.

Olden she was—but had been very young;
Virtuous she was—and had been, I believe;
Although the world has such an evil tongue
That——But my chaster ear will not receive
An echo of a syllable that's wrong:
In fact, there's nothing makes me so much grieve,
As that abominable tittle-tattle,
Which is the cud eschew'd by human cattle.

XLIV.

Moreover, I've remark'd (and I was once
A slight observer in a modest way),
And so may every one except a dunce,
That ladies in their youth a little gay,
Besides their knowledge of the world, and sense
Of the sad consequence of going astray,
Are wiser in their warnings 'gainst the woe
Which the mere passionless can never know.

XLV.

While the harsh prude indemnifies her virtue
By railing at the unknown and envied passion,
Seeking far less to save you than to hurt you,
Or, what's still worse, to put you out of fashion,—
The kinder veteran with calm words will court you,
Entreating you to pause before you dash on;
Expounding and illustrating the riddle
Of epic Love's beginning, end, and middle.

XLVI.

Now whether it be thus, or that they are stricter,
As better knowing why they should be so,
I think you'll find from many a family picture,
That daughters of such mothers as may know
The world by experience rather than by lecture,
Turn out much better for the Smithfield Show
Of vestals brought into the marriage mart,
Than those bred up by prudes without a heart.

XLVII.

I said that Lady Pinchbeck had been talk'd about—
As who has not, if female, young, and pretty?
But now no more the ghost of Scandal stalk'd about;
She merely was deem'd amiable and witty,
And several of her best bon-mots were hawk'd about:
Then she was given to charity and pity,
And pass'd (at least the latter years of life)
For being a most exemplary wife.

XLVIII.

High in high circles, gentle in her own,
She was the mild reprover of the young,
Whenever—which means every day—they'd shown
An awkward inclination to go wrong.
The quantity of good she did's unknown,
Or, at the least, would lengthen out my song:
In brief, the little orphan of the East
Had raised an interest in her, which increased.

XLIX.

Juan, too, was a sort of favourite with her,
Because she thought him a good heart at bottom
A little spoil'd, but not so altogether;
Which was a wonder, if you think who got him,
And how he had been toss'd, he scarce knew whither:
Though this might ruin others, it did *not* him,
At least entirely—for he had seen too many
Changes in youth, to be surprised at any.

L.

And these vicissitudes tell best in youth;
For when they happen at a riper age,
People are apt to blame the Fates, forsooth,
And wonder Providence is not more sage.
Adversity is the first path to truth:
He who hath proved war, storm, or woman's rage,
Whether his winters be eighteen or eighty,
Hath won the experience which is deem'd so weighty.

LI.

How far it profits is another matter.—
Our hero gladly saw his little charge
Safe with a lady, whose last grown-up daughter
Being long married, and thus set at large,
Had left all the accomplishments she taught her
To be transmitted, like the Lord Mayor's barge,
To the next comer; or—as it will tell
More Muse-like—like to Cytherea's shell.

LII.

I call such things transmission—for there is
A floating balance of accomplishment,
Which forms a pedigree from Miss to Miss,
According as their minds or backs are bent.
Some waltz; some draw; some fathom the abyss
Of metaphysics; others are content
With music; the most moderate shine as wits;
While others have a genius turn'd for fits

LIII.

But whether fits, or wits, or harpsichords,
Theology, fine arts, or finer stays,
May be the baits for gentlemen or lords
With regular descent, in these our days,
The last year to the new transfers its hoards;
New vestals claim men's eyes with the same praise
Of "elegant," *et cætera*, in fresh batches—
All matchless creatures, and yet bent on matches.

LIV.

But now I will begin my poem. 'T is
Perhaps a little strange, if not quite new,
That from the first of Cantos up to this
I've not begun what we have to go through.
These first twelve books are merely flourishes,
Preludios, trying just a string or two
Upon my lyre, or making the pegs sure;
And when so, you shall have the overture.

LV.

My Muses do not care a pinch of rosin
About what's called success, or not succeeding:
Such thoughts are quite below the strain they have chosen;
'T is a "great moral lesson" they are reading.
I thought, at setting off, about two dozen
Cantos would do; but at Apollo's pleading,
If that my Pegasus should not be founder'd,
I think to canter gently through a hundred.

LVI.

Don Juan saw that microcosm on stilts,
Yclept the Great World; for it is the least,
Although the highest: but as swords have hilts
By which their power of mischief is increased,
When man in battle or in quarrel tilts,
Thus the low world, north, south, or west, or east,
Must still obey the high—which is their handle,
Their moon, their sun, their gas, their farthing candle.

LVII.

He had many friends who had many wives, and was
Well look'd upon by both, to that extent
Of friendship which you may accept or pass,
It does nor good nor harm; being merely meant
To keep the wheels going of the higher class,
And draw them nightly when a ticket's sent:
And what with masquerades, and fêtes, and balls,
For the first season such a life scarce palls.

LVIII.

A young unmarried man, with a good name
And fortune, has an awkward part to play;
For good society is but a game,
"The royal game of Goose," as I may say,
Where every body has some separate aim,
An end to answer, or a plan to lay—
The single ladies wishing to be double,
The married ones to save the virgins trouble.

LIX.

I do n't mean this as general, but particular
Examples may be found of such pursuits:
Though several also keep their perpendicular
Like poplars, with good principles for roots;
Yet many have a method more *reticular*—
"Fishers for men," like sirens with soft lutes
For talk six times with the same single lady,
And you may get the wedding dresses ready.

LX.

Perhaps you'll have a letter from the mother,
To say her daughter's feelings are trepann'd;
Perhaps you'll have a visit from the brother,
All strut, and stays, and whiskers, to demand
What "your intentions are?"—One way or other
It seems the virgin's heart expects your hand:
And between pity for her case and yours,
You'll add to Matrimony's list of cures.

LXI.

I've known a dozen weddings made even *thus*,
And some of them high names: I have also known
Young men who—though they hated to discuss
Pretensions which they never dream'd to have shown—
Yet neither frighten'd by a female fuss,
Nor by mustachios moved, were let alone,
And lived, as did the broken-hearted fair,
In happier plight than if they form'd a pair.

LXII.

There's also nightly, to the uninitiated,
A peril—not indeed like love or marriage,
But not the less for this to be depreciated:
It is—I meant and mean not to disparage
The show of virtue even in the vitiated—
It adds an outward grace unto their carriage—
But to denounce the amphibious sort of harlot,
"Couleur de rose," who's neither white nor scarlet.

LXIII.

Such is your cold coquette, who can't say "No,"
And won't say "Yes," and keeps you on and offing
On a lee-shore, till it begins to blow—
Then sees your heart wreck'd, with an inward scoffing.
This works a world of sentimental woe,
And sends new Werters yearly to their coffin;
But yet is merely innocent flirtation,
Not quite adultery, but adulteration.

LXIV.

"Ye gods, I grow a talker!" Let us prate
The next of perils, though I place it *stern*est,

Is when, without regard to "church or state,"
 A wife makes or takes love in upright earnest.
Abroad, such things decide few women's fate—
 (Such, early traveller! is the truth thou learnest)—
But in old England, when a young bride errs,
Poor thing! Eve's was a trifling case to hers.

LXV.

For 't is a low, newspaper, humdrum, lawsuit
 Country, where a young couple of the same ages
Ca n't form a friendship, but the world o'erawes it.
 Then there 's the vulgar trick of those d——d damages!
A verdict—grievous foe to those who cause it!—
 Forms a sad climax to romantic homages:
Besides those soothing speeches of the pleaders,
And evidences which regale all readers.

LXVI.

But they who blunder thus are raw beginners;
 A little genial sprinkling of hypocrisy
Has saved the fame of thousand splendid sinners,
 The loveliest oligarchs of our gynocrasy;
You may see such at all the balls and dinners,
 Among the proudest of our aristocrasy,
So gentle, charming, charitable, chaste—
And all by having *tact* as well as taste.

LXVII.

Juan, who did not stand in the predicament
 Of a mere novice, had one safeguard more;
For he was sick—no, 't was not the word *sick* I meant;
 But he had seen so much good love before,
That he was not in heart so very weak;—I meant
 But thus much, and no sneer against the shore
Of white cliffs, white necks, blue eyes, bluer stockings,
Tithes, taxes, duns, and doors with double knockings.

LXVIII.

But coming young from lands and scenes romantic,
 Where lives, not lawsuits, must be risk'd for Passion,
And Passion's self must have a spice of frantic,
 Into a country where 't is half a fashion,
Seem'd to him half commercial, half pedantic,
 Howe'er he might esteem this moral nation:
Besides (alas! his taste—forgive and pity!)
At first he did not think the women pretty.

LXIX.

I say at *first*—for he found out at *last*,
 But by degrees, that they were fairer far
Than the more glowing dames whose lot is cast
 Beneath the influence of the eastern star.
A further proof we should not judge in haste;
 Yet inexperience could not be his bar
To taste:—the truth is, if men would confess,
That novelties *please* less than they *impress*.

LXX.

Though travell'd, I have never had the luck to
 Trace up those shuffling negroes, Nile or Niger,
To that impracticable place, Timbuctoo,
 When Geography finds no one to oblige her
With such a chart as may be safely stuck to—
 For Europe ploughs in Afric like "bos piger:"
But if I *had been* at Timbuctoo, there
No doubt I should be told that black is fair.

LXXI.

It is. I will not swear that black is white;
 But I suspect in fact that white is black,
And the whole matter rests upon eye-sight.
 Ask a blind man, the best judge. You 'll attack
Perhaps this new position—but I 'm right;
 Or if I 'm wrong, I 'll not be ta'en aback:—
He hath no morn nor night, but all is dark
Within; and what seest thou? A dubious spark.

LXXII.

But I 'm relapsing into metaphysics,
 That labyrinth, whose clue is of the same
Construction as your cures for hectic phthisics,
 Those bright moths fluttering round a dying flame;
And this reflection brings me to plain physics,
 And to the beauties of a foreign dame,
Compared with those of our pure pearls of price,
Those polar summers, *all* sun, and some ice.

LXXIII.

Or say they are like virtuous mermaids, whose
 Beginnings are fair faces, ends mere fishes;—
Not that there 's not a quantity of those
 Who have a due respect for their own wishes.
Like Russians rushing from hot baths to snows [89]
 Are they, at bottom virtuous even when vicious:
They warm into a scrape, but keep of course,
As a reserve, a plunge into remorse.

LXXIV.

But this has nought to do with their outsides.
 I said that Juan did not think them pretty
At the first blush; for a fair Briton hides
 Half her attractions—probably from pity—
And rather calmly into the heart glides,
 Than storms it as a foe would take a city;
But once there (if you doubt this, prithee try)
She keeps it for you like a true ally.

LXXV.

She cannot step as does an Arab barb,
 Or Andalusian girl from mass returning,
Nor wear as gracefully as Gauls her garb,
 Nor in her eye Ausonia's glance is burning;
Her voice, though sweet, is not so fit to warb-
 Le those bravuras (which I still am learning
To like, though I have been seven years in Italy,
And have, or had, an ear that served me prettily)—

LXXVI.

She cannot do these things, nor one or two
 Others, in that off-hand and dashing style
Which takes so much—to give the devil his due;
 Nor is she quite so ready with her smile,
Nor settles all things in one interview,
 (A thing approved as saving time and toil):—
But though the soil may give you time and trouble,
Well cultivated, it will render double.

LXXVII.

And if in fact she takes to a "grande passion,"
It is a very serious thing indeed:
Nine times in ten 't is but caprice or fashion,
Coquetry, or a wish to take the lead,
The pride of a mere child with a new sash on,
Or wish to make a rival's bosom bleed:
But the tenth instance will be a tornado,
For there 's no saying what they will or may do.

LXXVIII.

The reason 's obvious; if there 's an éclat,
They lose their caste at once, as do the Parias;
And when the delicacies of the law
Have fill'd their papers with their comments various,
Society, that China without flaw,
(The hypocrite!) will banish them like Marius,
To sit amidst the ruins of their guilt:
For Fame 's a Carthage not so soon rebuilt.

LXXIX.

Perhaps this is as it should be :—it is
A comment on the Gospel's "Sin no more,
And be thy sins forgiven:"—but upon this
I leave the saints to settle their own score.
Abroad, though doubtless they do much amiss.
An erring woman finds an opener door
For her return to Virtue—as they call
That lady, who should be at home to all.

LXXX.

For me, I leave the matter where I find it,
Knowing that such uneasy virtue leads
People some ten times less in fact to mind it,
And care but for discoveries and not deeds.
And as for chastity, you 'll never bind it
By all the laws the strictest lawyer pleads,
But aggravate the crime you have not prevented,
By rendering desperate those who had else repented.

LXXXI.

But Juan was no casuist, nor had ponder'd
Upon the moral lessons of mankind:
Besides, he had not seen of several hundred
A lady altogether to his mind.
A little "blasé"—'t is not to be wonder'd
At, that his heart had got a tougher rind:
And though not vainer from his past success,
No doubt his sensibilities were less.

LXXXII.

He also had been busy seeing sights—
The Parliament and all the other houses;
Had sat beneath the gallery at nights,
To hear debates whose thunder *roused* (not *rouses*)
The world to gaze upon those northern lights,
Which flash'd as far as where the musk-bull browses;[90]
He had also stood at times behind the throne—
But Grey was not arrived, and Chatham gone.

LXXXIII.

He saw, however, at the closing session,
That noble sight, when *really* free the nation,
A king in constitutional possession
Of such a throne as is the proudest station,
Though despots know it not—till the progression
Of freedom shall complete their education.
'T is not mere splendour makes the show august
To eye or heart—it is the people's trust.

LXXXIV.

There, too, he saw (whate'er he may be now)
A Prince, the prince of princes at the time,
With fascination in his very bow,
And full of promise, as the spring of prime.
Though royalty was written on his brow,
He had *then* the grace, too, rare in every clime,
Of being, without alloy of fop or beau
A finished gentleman from top to toe.

LXXXV.

And Juan was received, as hath been said,
Into the best society: and there
Occurr'd what often happens, I'm afraid,
However disciplined and debonnaire:—
The talent and good humour he display'd,
Besides the mark'd distinction of his air,
Exposed him, as was natural, to temptation,
Even though himself avoided the occasion.

LXXXVI.

But what, and where, with whom, and when, and why,
Is not to be put hastily together;
And as my object is morality
(Whatever people say), I don't know whether
I'll leave a single reader's eyelid dry,
But harrow up his feelings, till they wither,
And hew out a huge monument of pathos,
As Philip's son proposed to do with Athos.[91]

LXXXVII.

Here the twelfth canto of our introduction
Ends. When the body of the book's begun,
You 'll find it of a different construction
From what some people say 't will be when done:
The plan at present 's simply in concoction.
I can't oblige you, reader, to read on;
That 's your affair, not mine: a real spirit
Should neither court neglect, nor dread to bear it.

LXXXVIII.

And if my thunderbolt not always rattles,
 Remember, reader! you have had before,
The worst of tempests and the best of battles,
 That e'er were brew'd from elements or gore,
Besides the most sublime of—Heaven knows what else:
 An usurer could scarce expect much more—
But my best canto, save one on astronomy,
Will turn upon "political economy."

LXXXIX.

That is your present theme for popularity:
 Now that the public hedge hath scarce a stake,
It grows an act of patriotic charity,
 To show the people the best way to break.
My plan (but I, if but for singularity,
 Reserve it) will be very sure to take.
Meantime, read all the national-debt sinkers,
And tell me what you think of our great thinkers.

I NOW mean to be serious;—it is time,
Since laughter now-a-days is deem'd too serious.
A jest at Vice by Virtue 's call'd a crime,
And critically held as deleterious:
Besides, the sad 's a source of the sublime,
Although when long a little apt to weary us;
And therefore shall my lay soar high and solemn,
As an old temple dwindled to a column.

II.

The Lady Adeline Amundeville
('T is an old Norman name, and to be found
In pedigrees, by those who wander still
Along the last fields of that Gothic ground)
Was high born, wealthy by her father's will,
And beauteous,—even where beauties most abound,
In Britain—which of course true patriots find
The goodliest soil of body and of mind.

III.

I'll not gainsay them; it is not my cue;
I'll leave them to their taste, no doubt the best:
An eye 's an eye, and whether black or blue,
Is no great matter, so 't is in request,

'T is nonsense to dispute about a hue—
The kindest may be taken as a test.
The fair sex should be always fair; and no man,
Till thirty, should perceive there's a plain woman.

IV.

And after that serene and somewhat dull
Epoch, that awkward corner turn'd for days
More quiet, when our moon's no more at full,
We may presume to criticise or praise;
Because indifference begins to lull
Our passions, and we walk in wisdom's ways;
Also, because the figure and the face
Hint, that 't is time to give the younger place.

V.

I know that some would fain postpone this era,
Reluctant as all placemen to resign
Their post; but theirs is merely a chimera,
For they have pass'd life's equinoctial line:
But then they have their claret and Madeira,
To irrigate the dryness of decline;
And county meetings, and the parliament,
And debt, and what not, for their solace sent.

VI.

And is there not religion, and reform,
Peace, war, the taxes, and what's called the "Nation?"
The struggle to be pilots in a storm?
The landed and the monied speculation?
The joys of mutual hate to keep them warm,
Instead of love, the mere hallucination?
Now hatred is by far the longest pleasure;
Men love in haste, but they detest at leisure.

VII.

Rough Johnson, the great moralist, profess'd,
Right honestly, "he liked an honest hater!"—
The only truth that yet has been confest
Within these latest thousand years, or later.
Perhaps the fine old fellow spoke in jest:—
For my part, I am but a mere spectator,
And gaze where'er the palace or the hovel is,
Much in the mode of Goethe's Mephistopheles;

VIII.

But neither love nor hate in much excess;
Though 't was not once so. If I sneer sometimes,
It is because I cannot well do less,
And now and then it also suits my rhymes.
I should be very willing to redress
Men's wrongs, and rather check than punish crimes,
Had not Cervantes, in that too true tale
Of Quixote, shown how all such efforts fail.

46

IX.

Of all tales 't is the saddest—and more sad,
Because it makes us smile: his hero 's right,
And still pursues the right;—to curb the bad
His only object, and 'gainst odds to fight
His guerdon: 't is his virtue makes him mad!
But his adventures form a sorry sight;—
A sorrier still is the great moral taught
By that real epic unto all who have thought.

X.

Redressing injury, revenging wrong,
To aid the damsel and destroy the caitiff;
Opposing singly the united strong,
From foreign yoke to free the helpless native:—
Alas! must noblest views, like an old song,
Be for mere fancy's sport a theme creative,
A jest, a riddle, Fame through thick and thin sought!
And Socrates himself but Wisdom's Quixote?

XI.

Cervantes smiled Spain's chivalry away;
A single laugh demolish'd the right arm
Of his own country;—seldom since that day
Has Spain had heroes. While Romance could charm,
The world gave ground before her bright array;
And therefore have his volumes done such harm,
That all their glory, as a composition,
Was dearly purchased by his land's perdition.

XII.

I'm "at my old lunes"—digression, and forget
The Lady Adeline Amundeville:
The fair most fatal Juan ever met,
Although she was not evil nor meant ill;
But Destiny and Passion spread the net
(Fate is a good excuse for our own will),
And caught them;—what do they *not* catch, methinks?
But I'm not Œdipus, and life 's a Sphinx.

XIII.

I tell the tale as it is told, nor dare
To venture a solution: "Davus sum!"
And now I will proceed upon the pair.
Sweet Adeline, amidst the gay world's hum,
Was the Queen-Bee, the glass of all that's fair;
Whose charms made all men speak, and women dumb.
The last 's a miracle, and such was reckon'd,
And since that time there has not been a second.

XIV.

Chaste was she, to detraction's desperation,
And wedded unto one she had loved well—

A man known in the councils of the nation,
 Cool, and quite English, imperturbable,
Though apt to act with fire upon occasion,
 Proud of himself and her: the world could tell
Nought against either, and both seem'd secure—
She in her virtue, he in his hauteur.

XV.

It chanced some diplomatical relations,
 Arising out of business, often brought
Himself and Juan in their mutual stations
 Into close contact. Though reserved, nor caught
By specious seeming, Juan's youth, and patience,
 And talent, on his haughty spirit wrought,
And form'd a basis of esteem, which ends
In making men what courtesy calls friends.

XVI.

And thus Lord Henry, who was cautious as
 Reserve and pride could make him, and full slow
In judging men—when once his judgment was
 Determined, right or wrong, on friend or foe,
Had all the pertinacity pride has,
 Which knows no ebb to its imperious flow,
And loves or hates, disdaining to be guided,
Because its own good pleasure hath decided.

XVII.

His friendships, therefore, and no less aversions,
 Though oft well founded, which confirm'd but more
His prepossessions, like the laws of Persians
 And Medes, would ne'er revoke what went before.
His feelings had not those strange fits, like tertians,
 Of common likings, which make some deplore
What they should laugh at—the mere ague still
Of men's regard, the fever or the chill.

XVIII.

"'Tis not in mortals to command success;
 But *do you more*, Sempronius—*do n't* deserve it,"
And take my word, you wo n't have any less.
 Be wary, watch the time, and always serve it;
Give gently way, when there's too great a press;
 And for your conscience, only learn to nerve it;
For, like a racer, or a boxer, training,
'T will make, if proved, vast efforts without paining.

XIX.

Lord Henry also liked to be superior,
 As most men do, the little or the great;
The very lowest find out an inferior,
 At least they think so, to exert their state
Upon: for there are very few things wearier
 Than solitary Pride's oppressive weight,
Which mortals generously would divide,
By bidding others carry while they ride.

XX.

In birth, in rank, in fortune likewise equal,
 O'er Juan he could no distinction claim;
In years he had the advantage of time's sequel;
 And, as he thought, in country much the same—
Because bold Britons have a tongue and free quill,
 At which all modern nations vainly aim;
And the Lord Henry was a great debater,
So that few members kept the house up later.

XXI.

These were advantages: and then he thought—
 It was his foible, but by no means sinister—
That few or none more than himself had caught
 Court mysteries, having been himself a minister:
He liked to teach that which he had been taught,
 And greatly shone whenever there had been a stir:
And reconciled all qualities which grace man,
Always a patriot, and sometimes a placeman.

XXII.

He liked the gentle Spaniard for his gravity;
 He almost honour'd him for his docility,
Because, though young, he acquiesced with suavity,
 Or contradicted but with proud humility.
He knew the world, and would not see depravity
 In faults which sometimes show the soil's fertility,
If that the weeds o'erlive not the first crop—
For then they are very difficult to stop.

XXIII.

And then he talk'd with him about Madrid,
 Constantinople, and such distant places;
Where people always did as they were bid,
 Or did what they should not with foreign graces.
Of coursers also spake they: Henry rid
 Well, like most Englishmen, and loved the races;
And Juan, like a true-born Andalusian,
Could back a horse, as despots ride a Russian.

XXIV.

And thus acquaintance grew, at noble routs,
 And diplomatic dinners, or at other—
For Juan stood well, both with Ins and Outs,
 As in freemasonry a higher brother.
Upon his talent Henry had no doubts;
 His manner show'd him sprung from a high mother;
And all men like to show their hospitality
To him whose breeding matches with his quality.

XXV.

At Blank-Blank Square;—for we will break no squares
 By naming streets: since men are so censorious,
And apt to sow an author's wheat with tares,
 Reaping allusions private and inglorious,

Where none were dreamt of, unto love's affairs,
 Which were, or are, or are to be notorious,
That therefore do I previously declare,
Lord Henry's mansion was in Blank-Blank Square,

XXVI.

Also there bin another pious reason[92]
 For making squares and streets anonymous;
Which is, that there is scarce a single season
 Which doth not shake some very splendid house
With some slight heart-quake of domestic treason—
 A topic scandal doth delight to rouse;
Such I might stumble over unawares,
Unless I knew the very chastest squares.

XXVII.

'T is true, I might have chosen Piccadilly,
 A place where peccadillos are unknown;
But I have motives, whether wise or silly,
 For letting that pure sanctuary alone.
Therefore I name not square, street, place, until I
 Find one where nothing naughty can be shown,
A vestal shrine of innocence of heart:
Such are——but I have lost the London chart.

XXVIII.

At Henry's mansion, then, in Blank-Blank Square,
 Was Juan a recherché, welcome guest,
As many other noble scions were;
 And some who had but talent for their crest;
Or wealth, which is a passport everywhere;
 Or even mere fashion, which indeed 's the best
Recommendation; and to be well drest
Will very often supersede the rest.

XXIX.

And since "there 's safety in a multitude
 Of counsellors," as Solomon has said,
Or some one for him, in some sage, grave mood;—
 Indeed we see the daily proof display'd
In senates, at the bar, in wordy feud,
 Where'er collective wisdom can parade,
Which is the only cause that we can guess
Of Britain's present wealth and happiness;—

XXX.

But as "there's safety" grafted in the number
 "Of counsellors," for men,—thus for the sex
A large acquaintance lets not Virtue slumber;
 Or should it shake, the choice will more perplex—
Variety itself will more encumber.
 'Midst many rocks we guard more against wrecks;
And thus with women: howsoe'er it shocks some's
Self-love, there's safety in a crowd of coxcombs.

XXXI.

But Adeline had not the least occasion
 For such a shield, which leaves but little merit
To virtue proper, or good education.
 Her chief resource was in her own high spirit,
Which judged mankind at their due estimation;
 And for coquetry, she disdain'd to wear it:
Secure of admiration, its impression
Was faint, as of an every-day possession.

XXXII.

To all she was polite, without parade;
 To some she show'd attention of that kind
Which flatters, but is flattery convey'd
 In such a sort as cannot leave behind
A trace unworthy either wife or maid;—
 A gentle, genial courtesy of mind,
To those who were, or pass'd for meritorious,
Just to console sad glory for being glorious;

XXXIII.

Which is in all respects, save now and then,
 A dull and desolate appendage. Gaze
Upon the shades of those distinguish'd men,
 Who were or are the puppet-shows of praise,
The praise of persecution. Gaze again
 On the most favour'd; and amidst the blaze
Of sunset halos o'er the laurel-brow'd,
What can ye recognise?—a gilded cloud.

XXXIV.

There also was of course in Adeline
 That calm patrician polish in the address,
Which ne'er can pass the equinoctial line
 Of any thing which nature would express;
Just as a mandarin finds nothing fine,—
 At least his manner suffers not to guess,
That any thing he views can greatly please.
Perhaps we have borrow'd this from the Chinese—

XXXV.

Perhaps from Horace: his "*Nil admirari*"
 Was what he call'd the "Art of Happiness;"
An art on which the artists greatly vary,
 And have not yet attain'd to much success.
However, 't is expedient to be wary:
 Indifference certes don't produce distress;
And rash enthusiasm in good society
Were nothing but a moral inebriety.

XXXVI.

But Adeline was not indifferent: for
 (*Now* for a common-place!) beneath the snow,
As a volcano holds the lava more
 Within—*et cætera*. Shall I go on?—No!
I hate to hunt down a tired metaphor,
 So let the often-used volcano go.
Poor thing! How frequently, by me and others,
It hath been stirr'd up till its smoke quite smothers

XXXVII.

I'll have another figure in a trice:—
 What say you to a bottle of champagne?
Frozen into a very vinous ice,
 Which leaves few drops of that immortal rain,
Yet in the very centre, past all price,
 About a liquid glassful will remain;
And this is stronger than the strongest grape
Could e'er express in its expanded shape:

XXXVIII.

'T is the whole spirit brought to a quintessence;
 And thus the chilliest aspects may concentre
A hidden nectar under a cold presence.
 And such are many—though I only meant her
From whom I now deduce these moral lessons,
 On which the muse has always sought to enter.
And your cold people are beyond all price,
When once you have broken their confounded ice.

XXXIX.

But after all they are a North-West Passage
 Unto the glowing India of the soul;
And as the good ships sent upon that message
 Have not exactly ascertain'd the Pole
(Though Parry's efforts look a lucky presage),
 Thus gentlemen may run upon a shoal;
For if the Pole's not open, but all frost
(A chance still), 't is a voyage or vessel lost.

XL.

And young beginners may as well commence
 With quiet cruising o'er the ocean, woman;
While those who are not beginners should have sense
 Enough to make for port, ere time shall summon
With his gray signal-flag; and the past tense,
 The dreary "*Fuimus*" of all things human,
Must be declined, while life's thin thread's spun out
Between the gaping heir and gnawing gout.

XLI.

But heaven must be diverted; its diversion
 Is sometimes truculent—but never mind:
The world upon the whole is worth the assertion
 (If but for comfort) that all things are kind:
And that same devilish doctrine of the Persian,
 Of the two principles, but leaves behind
As many doubts as any other doctrine
Has ever puzzled Faith withal, or yoked her in.

XLII.

The English winter—ending in July,
 To recommence in August—now was done.
'T is the postilion's paradise: wheels fly;
 On roads, east, south, north, west, there is a run.
But for post-horses who finds sympathy?
 Man's pity's for himself, or for his son,
Always premising that said son at college
Has not contracted much more debt than knowledge.

XLIII.

The London winter's ended in July—
 Sometimes a little later. I do n't err
In this: whatever other blunders lie
 Upon my shoulders, here I must aver
My Muse a glass of weatherology;
 For Parliament is our barometer:
Let radicals its other acts attack,
Its sessions form our only almanack.

XLIV

When its quicksilver's down at zero,—lo!
 Coach, chariot, luggage, baggage, equipage!
Wheels whirl from Carlton palace to Soho,
 And happiest they who horses can engage;
The turnpikes glow with dust; and Rotton Row
 Sleeps from the chivalry of this bright age;
And tradesmen, with long bills and longer faces,
Sigh—as the postboys fasten on the traces.

XLV.

They and their bills, "Arcadians both," are left[93]
 To the Greek kalends of another session.
Alas! to them, of ready cash bereft,
 What hope remains? Of *hope* the full possession,
Or generous draft, conceded as a gift,
 At a long date—till they can get a fresh one—
Hawk'd about at a discount, small or large;
Also the solace of an overcharge.

XLVI.

But these are trifles. Downward flies my lord,
 Nodding beside my lady, in his carriage.
Away! away! "Fresh horses!" are the word,
 And changed as quickly as hearts after marriage;
The obsequious landlord hath the change restored;
 The postboys have no reason to disparage
Their fee; but ere the water'd wheels may hiss hence,
The ostler pleads too for a reminiscence.

XLVII.

'T is granted; and the valet mounts the dickey—
 That gentleman of lords and gentlemen
Also my lady's gentlewomen, tricky,
 Trick'd out, but modest more than poet's pen
Can paint,—"*Cosi viaggino i Ricchi!*"
 (Excuse a foreign slipslop now and then,
If but to show I've travell'd; and what's travel,
Unless it teaches one to quote and cavil?)

XLVIII.

The London winter and the country summer
 Were well nigh over. 'T is perhaps a pity,
When nature wears the gown that doth become her,
 To lose those best months in a sweaty city

And wait until the nightingale grows dumber,
 Listening debates not very wise or witty,
Ere patriots their true *country* can remember,—
 But there 's no shooting (save grouse) till September.

XLIX.

I 've done with my tirade. The world was gone;
 The twice two thousand, for whom earth was made,
Were vanish'd to be what they call alone—
 That is, with thirty servants for parade.

As many guests, or more; before whom groan
 As many covers, duly, daily laid.
Let none accuse old England's hospitality—
Its quantity is but condensed to quality.

L.

Lord Henry and the Lady Adeline
 Departed like the rest of their compeers,
The peerage, to a mansion very fine;
 The Gothic Babel of a thousand years.
None than themselves could boast a longer line,
 Where time through heroes and through beauties steers;
And oaks as olden as their pedigree
Told of their sires, a tomb in every tree.

LI.

A paragraph in every paper told
 Of their departure. such is modern fame:
'T is pity that it takes no farther hold
 Than an advertisement, or much the same;
When, ere the ink be dry, the sound grows cold:
 The Morning Post was foremost to proclaim—
"Departure, for his country seat, to-day,
Lord H. Amundeville and Lady A.

LII.

"We understand the splendid host intends
 To entertain, this autumn, a select
And numerous party of his noble friends;
 Midst whom we have heard, from sources quite correct,
The Duke of D—— the shooting season spends,
 With many more by rank and fashion deck'd;
Also a foreigner of high condition,
The envoy of the secret Russian mission."

LIII.

And thus we see—who doubts the Morning Post?
 (Whose articles are like the "Thirty-nine,"
Which those most swear to who believe them most)—
 Our gay Russ-Spaniard was ordain'd to shine,
Deck'd by the rays reflected from his host,
 With those who, Pope says, "greatly daring dine."—
'T is odd, but true,—last war the news abounded
More with these dinners than the kill'd or wounded;—

LIV

As thus: "On Thursday there was a grand dinner;
 Present, Lords A.B.C."—Earls, dukes, by name
Announced with no less pomp than victory's winner:
 Then underneath, and in the very same
Column; date, "Falmouth. There has lately been here
 The Slap-dash regiment, so well known to fame;
Whose loss in the late action we regret:
The vacancies are fill'd up—see Gazette."

LV

To Norman Abbey whirl'd the noble pair,—
 An old, old monastery once, and now
Still older mansion,—of a rich and rare
 Mix'd Gothic, such as artists all allow
Few specimens yet left us can compare
 Withal: it lies perhaps a little low,
Because the monks preferr'd a hill behind,
To shelter their devotion from the wind.

LVI.

It stood embosom'd in a happy valley,
 Crown'd by high woodlands, where the Druid oak
Stood like Caractacus in act to rally
 His host, with broad arm 'gainst the thunder-stroke;
And from beneath his boughs were seen to sally
 The dappled foresters—as day awoke.
The branching stag swept down with all his herd,
To quaff a brook which murmur'd like a bird.

LVII.

Before the mansion lay a lucid lake,
 Broad as transparent, deep, and freshly fed
By a river, which its soften'd way did take
 In currents through the calmer water spread
Around: the wildfowl nestled in the brake
 And sedges, brooding in their liquid bed:
The woods sloped downwards to its brink, and stood
With their green faces fixed upon the flood.

LVIII.

Its outlet dash'd into a deep cascade,
 Sparkling with foam, until again subsiding,
Its shriller echoes—like an infant made
 Quiet—sank into softer ripples, gliding
Into a rivulet; and thus allay'd,
 Pursued its course, now gleaming, and now hiding
Its windings through the woods; now clear, now blue,
According as the skies their shadows threw.

LIX.

A glorious remnant of the Gothic pile
 (While yet the church was Rome's) stood half apart
In a grand arch, which once screen'd many an aisle.
 These last had disappear'd—a loss to art:
The first yet frown'd superbly o'er the soil,
 And kindled feelings in the roughest heart,
Which mourn'd the power of time's or tempest's march,
In gazing on that venerable arch

LX.

Within a niche, nigh to its pinnacle,
 Twelve saints had once stood sanctified in stone;
But these had fallen, not when the friars fell,
 But in the war which struck Charles from his throne,
When each house was a fortalice—as tell
 The annals of full many a line undone,—
The gallant cavaliers, who fought in vain
For those who knew not to resign or reign.

LXI.

But in a higher niche, alone, but crown'd,
The Virgin Mother of the God-born Child,
With her Son in her blessed arms, look'd round,
Spared by some chance when all beside was spoil'd;
She made the earth below seem holy ground.
This may be superstition, weak or wild,
But even the faintest relics of a shrine
Of any worship wake some thoughts divine.

LXII.

A mighty window, hollow in the centre,
Shorn of its glass of thousand colourings,
Through which the deepen'd glories once could enter,
Streaming from off the sun like seraph's wings,
Now yawns all desolate: now loud, now fainter,
The gale sweeps thro' its fretwork, and oft sings
The owl his anthem, where the silenced quire
Lie with their hallelujahs quench'd like fire.

LXIII.

But in the noontide of the moon, and when
The wind is winged from one point of heaven,
There moans a strange unearthly sound, which then
Is musical—a dying accent driven
Through the huge arch, which soars and sinks again,
Some deem it but the distant echo given

Back to the night wind by the waterfall,
And harmonised by the old choral wall:

LXIV.

Others, that some original shape, or form
Shaped by decay perchance, hath given the power
(Though less than that of Memnon's statue, warm
In Egypt's rays, to harp at a fix'd hour)
To this gray ruin, with a voice to charm
Sad, but serene, it sweeps over tree or tower;
The cause I know not, nor can solve; but such
The fact: I've heard it,—once, perhaps, too much.

LXV.

Amidst the court a Gothic fountain play'd,
Symmetrical, but deck'd with carvings quaint—
Strange faces, like to men in masquerade,
And here perhaps a monster, there a saint:
The spring gush'd through grim mouths of granite made,
And sparkled into basins, where it spent
Its little torrent in a thousand bubbles,
Like man's vain glory, and his vainer troubles.

LXVI.

The mansion's self was vast and venerable,
With more of the monastic than has been
Elsewhere preserved: the cloisters still were stable,
The cells, too, and refectory, I ween:
An exquisite small chapel had been able,
Still unimpair'd, to decorate the scene;
The rest had been reform'd, replac'd, or sunk,
And spoke more of the baron than the monk.

LXVII.

Huge halls, long galleries, spacious chambers, join'd
By no quite lawful marriage of the arts,
Might shock a connoisseur; but when combined,
Form'd a whole which, irregular in parts,
Yet left a grand impression on the mind,
At least of those whose eyes are in their hearts;
We gaze upon a giant for his stature,
Nor judge at first if all be true to nature.

LXVIII.

Steel barons, molten the next generation
To silken rows of gay and garter'd earls,
Glanced from the walls in goodly preservation:
And Lady Marys blooming into girls,
With fair long locks, had also kept their station:
And countesses mature in robes and pearls;
Also some beauties of Sir Peter Lely,
Whose drapery hints we may admire them freely.

LXIX.

Judges in very formidable ermine
Were there, with brows that did not much invite
The accused to think their lordships would determine
His cause by leaning much from might to right:
Bishops, who had not left a single sermon;
Attorneys-general, awful to the sight,
As hinting more (unless our judgments warp us)
Of the "Star Chamber" than of "Habeas Corpus."

LXX.

Generals, some all in armour, of the old
And iron time, ere lead had ta'en the lead;
Others in wigs of Marlborough's martial fold,
Huger than twelve of our degenerate breed:
Lordlings, with staves of white or keys of gold:
Nimrods, whose canvas scarce contain'd the steed;
And here and there some stern high patriot stood,
Who could not get the place for which he sued.

LXXI.

But ever and anon, to soothe your vision,
Fatigued with these hereditary glories,
There rose a Carlo Dolce or a Titian,
Or wilder group of savage Salvatore's:[94]
Here danced Albano's boys, and here the sea shone
In Vernet's ocean lights; and there the stories
Of martyrs awed, as Spagnoletto tainted
His brush with all the blood of all the sainted.

LXXII.

Here sweetly spread a landscape of Lorraine;
There Rembrandt made his darkness equal light,
Or gloomy Caravaggio's gloomier stain
Bronzed o'er some lean and stoic anchorite:—
But, lo! a Teniers woos, and not in vain,
Your eyes to revel in a livelier sight:
His bell-mouth'd goblet makes me feel quite Danish[95]
Or Dutch with thirst—What, ho! a flask of Rhenish.

LXXIII.

O reader! if that thou canst read,—and know,
'T is not enough to spell, or even to read,
To constitute a reader; there must go
Virtues of which both you and I have need.
Firstly, begin with the beginning—(though
That clause is hard); and secondly, proceed;
Thirdly, commence not with the end—or, sinning
In this sort, end at least with the beginning.

LXXIV.

But, reader, thou hast patient been of late,
While I, without remorse of rhyme, or fear

Have built and laid out ground at such a rate,
 Dan Phœbus takes me for an auctioneer.
That poets were so from their earliest date,
 By Homer's "catalogue of ships" is clear;
But a mere modern must be moderate—
I spare you then the furniture and plate.

LXXV.

The mellow autumn came, and with it came
 The promised party, to enjoy its sweets.
The corn is cut, the manor full of game;
 The pointer ranges, and the sportsman beats
In russet jacket:—lynx-like is his aim;

Full grows his bag, and wonder*ful* his feats.
Ah, nutbrown partridges! Ah, brilliant pheasants!
And ah, ye poachers!—'Tis no sport for peasants.

LXXVI.

An English autumn, though it hath no vines,
Blushing with Bacchant coronals along
The paths, o'er which the far festoon entwines
The red grape in the sunny lands of song,
Hath yet a purchased choice of choicest wines;
The claret light, and the Madeira strong.
If Britain mourn her bleakness, we can tell her,
The very best of vineyards is the cellar.

LXXVII.

Then, if she hath not that serene decline
Which makes the southern autumn's day appear
As if 't would to a second spring resign
The season, rather than to winter drear,—
Of in-door comforts still she hath a mine,—
The sea-coal fires, the "earliest of the year;"
Without doors, too, she may compete in mellow,
As what is lost in green is gain'd in yellow.

LXXVIII.

And for the effeminate *villeggiatura*—
Rife with more horns than hounds—she hath the chase,
So animated that it might allure a
Saint from his beads to join the jocund race;
Even Nimrod's self might leave the plains of Dura,[96]
And wear the Melton jacket for a space:
If she hath no wild boars, she hath a tame
Preserve of bores, who ought to be made game.

LXXIX.

The noble guests, assembled at the Abbey,
Consisted of—we give the sex the *pas*—
The Duchess of Fitz-Fulke; the Countess Crabby;
The Ladies Scilly, Busey;—Miss Eclat,
Miss Bombazeen, Miss Mackstay, Miss O'Tabby,
And Mrs. Rabbi, the rich banker's squaw:
Also the honourable Mrs. Sleep,
Who look'd a white lamb, yet was a black sheep:

LXXX.

With other Countesses of Blank—but rank;
At once the "lie" and the "élite" of crowds;
Who pass like water filter'd in a tank,
All purged and pious from their native clouds;
Or paper turned to money by the Bank:
No matter how or why, the passport shrouds
The "passée" and the past; for good society
Is no less famed for tolerance than piety,—

LXXXI.

That is, up to a certain point; which point
Forms the most difficult in punctuation.
Appearances appear to form the joint
On which it hinges in a higher station;
And so that no explosion cry "Aroint
Thee, witch!" or each Medea has her Jason;
Or (to the point with Horace and with Pulci)
"*Omne tulit punctum*, quæ *miscuit utile dulci*."

LXXXII.

I can't exactly trace their rule of right,
Which hath a little leaning to a lottery.
I've seen a virtuous woman put down quite
By the mere combination of a coterie;
Also a so-so matron boldly fight
Her way back to the world by dint of plottery,
And shine the very *Siria* of the spheres,[97]
Escaping with a few slight, scarless sneers.

LXXXIII.

I have seen more than I'll say:—but we will see
How our *villeggiatura* will get on.
The party might consist of thirty-three
Of highest caste—the Brahmins of the ton.
I have named a few, not foremost in degree,
But ta'en at hazard as the rhyme may run.
By way of sprinkling, scatter'd amongst these,
There also were some Irish absentees.

LXXXIV.

There was Parolles, too, the legal bully,
Who limits all his battles to the bar
And senate: when invited elsewhere, truly,
He shows more appetite for words than war.
There was the young bard Rackrhyme, who had newly
Come out and glimmer'd as a six weeks' star.
There was Lord Pyrrho, too, the great freethinker;
And Sir John Pottledeep, the mighty drinker.

LXXXV.

There was the Duke of Dash, who was a—duke,
"Ay, every inch a" duke; there were twelve peers
Like Charlemagne's—and all such peers in look
And intellect, that neither eyes nor ears
For commoners had ever them mistook.
There were the six Miss Rawbolds—pretty dears!
All song and sentiment; whose hearts were set
Less on a convent than a coronet.

LXXXVI.

There were four Honourable Misters, whose
Honour was more before their names than after

There was the preux Chevalier de la Ruse,
Whom France and Fortune lately deign'd to waft here,
Whose chiefly harmless talent was to amuse;
But the clubs found it rather serious laughter,
Because—such was his magic power to please—
The dice seem'd charm'd, too, with his repartees.

LXXXVII.

There was Dick Dubious, the metaphysician,
Who loved philosophy and a good dinner;
Angle, the soi-disant mathematician;
Sir Henry Silvercup, the great race-winner.
There was the Reverend Rodomont Precision,
Who did not hate so much the sin as sinner;
And Lord Augustus Fitz-Plantagenet,
Good at all things, but better at a bet.

LXXXVIII.

There was Jack Jargon, the gigantic guardsman;
And General Fireface, famous in the field,
A great tactician, and no less a swordsman,
Who ate—last war—more Yankees than he kill'd.
There was the waggish Welsh Judge, Jefferies Hardsman,
In his grave office so completely skill'd,
That when a culprit came for condemnation,
He had his judge's joke for consolation.

LXXXIX.

Good company's a chess-board—there are kings,
Queens, bishops, knights, rooks, pawns; the world's a game:
Save that the puppets pull at their own strings,
Methinks gay Punch hath something of the same.
My Muse, the butterfly hath but her wings,
Not stings, and flits through ether without aim,
Alighting rarely:—were she but a hornet,
Perhaps there might be vices which would mourn it.

XC.

I had forgotten—but must not forget—
An orator, the latest of the session,
Who had delivered well a very set
Smooth speech, his first and maidenly transgression
Upon debate: the papers echoed yet
With his debut, which made a strong impression,
And rank'd with what is every day display'd—
"The best first speech that ever yet was made."

XCI.

Proud of his "Hear hims!" proud, too, of his vote
And lost virginity of oratory,
Proud of his learning, (just enough to quote)
He revell'd in his Ciceronian glory:
With memory excellent to get by rote,
With wit to hatch a pun or tell a story,
Graced with some merit, and with more effrontery,
"His country's pride," he came down to the country.

XCII.

There also were two wits by acclamation,
Longbow from Ireland, Strongbow from the Tweed,
Both lawyers and both men of education,
But Strongbow's wit was of more polished breed:
Longbow was rich in an imagination
As beautiful and bounding as a steed,
But sometimes stumbling over a potato,—
While Strongbow's best things might have come from Cato.

XCIII.

Strongbow was like a new-tuned harpsichord;
But Longbow wild as an Æolian harp,
With which the winds of heaven can claim accord,
And make a music, whether flat or sharp.
Of Strongbow's talk you would not change a word:
At Longbow's phrases you might sometimes carp:
Both wits—one born so, and the other bred,
This by his heart, his rival by his head.

XCIV.

If all these seem an heterogeneous mass
To be assembled at a country seat,
Yet think, a specimen of every class
Is better than a humdrum tête-à-tête.
The days of Comedy are gone, alas!
When Congreve's fool could vie with Molière's *bête:*
Society is smooth'd to that excess,
That manners hardly differ more than dress.

XCV.

Our ridicules are kept in the back-ground—
Ridiculous enough, but also dull;
Professions, too, are no more to be found
Professional; and there is nought to cull
Of folly's fruit: for though your fools abound,
They're barren, and not worth the pains to pull.
Society is now one polish'd horde
Form'd of two mighty tribes, the *Bores* and *Bored*.

XCVI.

But from being farmers, we turn gleaners, gleaning
The scanty but right-well thresh'd ears of truth ;
And, gentle reader ! when you gather meaning,
You may be Boaz, and I—modest Ruth.

Farther I'd quote, but Scripture intervening
 Forbids. A great impression in my youth
Was made by Mrs. Adams, where she cries,
"That Scriptures out of church are blasphemies."[98]

XCVII.

But what we can we glean in this vile age
 Of chaff, although our gleanings be not grist.
I must not quite omit the talking sage,
 Kit-Cat, the famous Conversationist,
Who, in his common-place book, had a page
 Prepared each morn for evenings. "List, oh list!"—
"Alas, poor ghost!"—What unexpected woes
Await those who have studied their bon-mots!

XCVIII.

Firstly, they must allure the conversation,
 By many windings to their clever clinch;
And secondly, must let slip no occasion,
 Nor *bate* (abate) their hearers of an *inch*,
But take an ell—and make a great sensation,
 If possible; and thirdly, never flinch
When some smart talker puts them to the test,
But seize the last word, which no doubt's the best.

XCIX.

Lord Henry and his lady were the hosts;
 The party we have touched on were the guests.
Their table was a board to tempt even ghosts
 To pass the Styx for more substantial feasts.
I will not dwell upon ragoûts or roasts,
 Albeit all human history attests
That happiness for man—the hungry sinner!—
Since Eve ate apples, much depends on dinner.

C.

Witness the lands which "flow'd with milk and honey,"
 Held out unto the hungry Israelites:
To this we have added since, the love of money,
 The only sort of pleasure which requites.
Youth fades, and leaves our days no longer sunny;
 We tire of mistresses and parasites;
But oh, ambrosial cash! Ah! who would lose thee?
When we no more can use, or even abuse thee!

CI.

The gentlemen got up betimes to shoot,
 Or hunt: the young, because they liked the sport—
The first thing boys like, after play and fruit;
 The middle-aged, to make the day more short;
For *ennui* is a growth of English root,
 Though nameless in our language!—we retort
The fact for words, and let the French translate
That awful yawn which sleep can not abate.

CII.

The elderly walk'd through the library,
 And tumbled books, or criticised the pictures,
Or saunter'd through the gardens piteously,
 And made upon the hot-house several strictures,
Or rode a nag which trotted not too high,
 Or on the morning papers read their lectures,
Or on the watch their longing eyes would fix,
Longing at sixty for the hour of six.

CIII.

But none were "gêné:" the great hour of union
 Was rung by dinner's knell; till then all were
Masters of their own time—or in communion,
 Or solitary, as they chose to bear
The hours, which how to pass is but to few known.
 Each rose up at his own, and had to spare
What time he chose for dress, and broke his fast
When, where, and how he chose for that repast.

CIV.

The ladies—some rouged, some a little pale—
 Met the morn as they might. If fine, they rode,
Or walk'd; if foul, they read, or told a tale,
 Sung, or rehearsed the last dance from abroad;
Discuss'd the fashion which might next prevail,
 And settled bonnets by the newest code,
Or cramm'd twelve sheets into one little letter,
To make each correspondent a new debtor.

CV.

For some had absent lovers, all had friends.
 The earth has nothing like a she epistle,
And hardly heaven—because it never ends.
 I love the mystery of a female missal,
Which, like a creed, ne'er says all it intends,
 But full of cunning as Ulysses' whistle,
When he allured poor Dolon:—you had better
Take care what you reply to such a letter.

CVI.

Then there were billiards;—cards, too, but *no* dice;—
 Save in the clubs no man of honour plays;—
Boats when 't was water, skating when 't was ice,
 And the hard frost destroy'd the scenting days:
And angling, too, that solitary vice,
 Whatever Isaak Walton sings or says:
The quaint, old, cruel coxcomb, in his gullet
Should have a hook, and a small trout to pull it.[99]

CVII.

With evening came the banquet and the wine;
 The conversazione; the duet,
Attuned by voices more or less divine
 (My heart or head aches with the memory yet).

The four Miss Rawbolds in a glee would shine;
 But the two youngest loved more to be set
Down to the harp—because to music's charms
They added graceful necks, white hands and arms.

CVIII.

Sometimes a dance (though rarely on field days,
 For then the gentlemen were rather tired)
Display'd some sylph-like figures in its maze;
 Then there was small talk ready when required;
Flirtation—but decorous; the mere praise
 Of charms that should or should not be admired.
The hunters fought their fox-hunt o'er again,
And then retreated soberly—at ten.

CIX.

The politicians, in a nook apart,
 Discuss'd the world, and settled all the spheres:
The wits watch'd every loophole for their art,
 To introduce a bon-mot head and ears;
Small is the rest of those who would be smart,
 A moment's good thing may have cost them years,
Before they find an hour to introduce it;
And then, even *then*, some bore may make them lose it.

CX.

But all was gentle and aristocratic
 In this our party; polish'd, smooth, and cold,
As Phidian forms cut out of marble Attic.
 There now are no Squire Westerns as of old;
And our Sophias are not so emphatic,
 But fair as then, or fairer to behold.
We have no accomplish'd blackguards, like Tom Jones,
But gentlemen in stays, as stiff as stones.

CXI.

They separated at an early hour;
 That is, ere midnight—which is London's noon:
But in the country ladies seek their bower
 A little earlier than the waning moon.
Peace to the slumbers of each folded flower—
 May the rose call back its true colour soon!
Good hours of fair cheeks are the fairest tinters,
And lower the price of rouge—at least some winters

CANTO THE FOURTEENTH.

I.

If from great nature's or our own abyss
 Of thought we could but snatch a certainty,
Perhaps mankind might find the path they miss—
 But then 't would spoil much good philosophy.
One system eats another up, and this
 Much as old Saturn ate his progeny;
For when his pious consort gave him stones
In lieu of sons, of these he made no bones.

II.

But System doth reverse the Titan's breakfast,
And eats her parents, albeit the digestion
Is difficult. Pray, tell me, can you make fast,
After due search, your faith to any question?
Look back o'er ages, ere unto the stake fast
You bind yourself, and call some mode the best one.
Nothing more true than *not* to trust your senses;
And yet what are your other evidences?

III.

For me, I know nought; nothing I deny,
Admit, reject, contemn; and what know *you*,
Except perhaps that you were born to die?
And both may after all turn out untrue.
An age may come, Font of Eternity,
When nothing shall be either old or new.
Death, so call'd, is a thing which makes men weep,
And yet a third of life is pass'd in sleep.

IV.

A sleep without dreams, after a rough day
Of toil, is what we covet most; and yet
How clay shrinks back from more quiescent clay!
The very Suicide that pays his debt
At once without instalments (an old way
Of paying debts, which creditors regret)
Lets out impatiently his rushing breath,
Less from disgust of life than dread of death.

V.

'T is round him, near him, here, there, every where,
And there's a courage which grows out of fear,
Perhaps of all most desperate, which will dare
The worst to *know* it:—when the mountains rear
Their peaks beneath your human foot, and there
You look down o'er the precipice, and drear
The gulf of rock yawns,—you ca n't gaze a minute,
Without an awful wish to plunge within it.

VI.

'T is true, you do n't—but, pale and struck with terror,
Retire: but look into your past impression!
And you will find, though shuddering at the mirror
Of your own thoughts, in all their self-confession,
The lurking bias, be it truth or error,
To the *unknown*; a secret prepossession,
To plunge with all your fears—but where? You know not,
And that's the reason why you do—or do not.

VII.

But what's this to the purpose? you will say,
Gent. reader, nothing; a mere speculation,

For which my sole excuse is—'t is my way
Sometimes *with* and sometimes without occasion
I write what's uppermost, without delay;
This narrative is not meant for narration,
But a mere airy and fantastic basis,
To build up common things with common places.

VIII.

You know, or do n't know, that great Bacon saith,
"Fling up a straw, 't will show the way the wind blows;"
And such a straw, borne on by human breath,
Is poesy, according as the mind glows;
A paper kite which flies 'twixt life and death,
A shadow which the onward soul behind throws:
And mine's a bubble, not blown up for praise,
But just to play with, as an infant plays.

IX.

The world is all before me—or behind;
For I have seen a portion of that same,
And quite enough for me to keep in mind;—
Of passions, too, I have proved enough to blame,
To the great pleasure of our friends, mankind,
Who like to mix some slight alloy with fame;
For I was rather famous in my time,
Until I fairly knock'd it up with rhyme.

X.

I have brought this world about my ears, and eke
The other: that's to say, the clergy—who
Upon my head have bid their thunders break
In pious libels by no means a few.
And yet I ca n't help scribbling once a week,
Tiring old readers, nor discovering new.
In youth I wrote because my mind was full,
And now because I feel it growing dull.

XI.

But "why then publish?"—There are no rewards
Of fame or profit when the world grows weary.
I ask in turn,—Why do you play at cards?
Why drink? Why read?—To make some hour less dreary.
It occupies me to turn back regards
On what I've seen or ponder'd, sad or cheery;
And what I write I cast upon the stream,
To swim or sink—I have had at least my dream.

XII.

I think that were I *certain* of success,
I hardly could compose another line:
So long I've battled either more or less,
That no defeat can drive me from the Nine.
This feeling 't is not easy to express,
And yet 't is not affected, I opine.
In play, there are two pleasures for your choosing—
The one is winning, and the other losing.

XIII.

Besides, my Muse by no means deals in fiction:
 She gathers a repertory of facts,
Of course with some reserve and slight restriction,
 But mostly sings of human things and acts—
And that 's one cause she meets with contradiction;
 For too much truth, at first sight, ne'er attracts;
And were her object only what 's call'd glory,
With more ease too she 'd tell a different story.

XIV.

Love, war, a tempest—surely there 's variety;
 Also a seasoning slight of lucubration;
A bird's-eye view, too, of that wild, Society;
 A slight glance thrown on men of every station.
If you have nought else, here 's at least satiety,
 Both in performance and in preparation;
And though these lines should only line portmanteaus,
Trade will be all the better for these Cantos.

XV.

The portion of this world which I at present
 Have taken up to fill the following sermon,
Is one of which there 's no description recent;
 The reason why, is easy to determine:
Although it seems both prominent and pleasant,
 There is a sameness in its gems and ermine,
A dull and family likeness through all ages,
Of no great promise for poetic pages.

XVI.

With much to excite, there 's little to exalt;
 Nothing that speaks to all men and all times;
A sort of varnish over every fault;
 A kind of common-place, even in their crimes;
Factitious passions, wit without much salt,
 A want of that true nature which sublimes
Whate'er it shows with truth; a smooth monotony
Of character, in those at least who have got any.

XVII.

Sometimes, indeed, like soldiers off parade,
 They break their ranks and gladly leave the drill;
But then the roll-call draws them back afraid,
 And they must be or seem what they were: still
Doubtless it is a brilliant masquerade;
 But when of the first sight you have had your fill,
It palls—at least it did so upon me,
This paradise of pleasure and *ennui*.

XVIII.

When we have made our love, and gamed our gaming,
 Drest, voted, shone, and, may be, something more;
With dandies dined; heard senators declaiming;
 Seen beauties brought to market by the score,
Sad rakes to sadder husbands chastely taming;
 There 's little left but to be bored or bore.
Witness those "*ci-devant jeunes hommes*" who stem
The stream, nor leave the world which leaveth them.

XIX.

'T is said—indeed a general complaint—
 That no one has succeeded in describing
The monde, exactly as they ought to paint:
 Some say, that authors only snatch, by bribing
The porter, some slight scandals strange and quaint,
 To furnish matter for their moral gibing;
And that their books have but one style in common—
My lady's prattle, filter'd through her woman.

XX.

But this can't well be true, just now; for writers
 Are grown of the beau monde a part potential:
I 've seen them balance even the scale with fighters,
 Especially when young, for that 's essential.
Why do their sketches fail them as inditers
 Of what they deem themselves most consequential,
The *real* portrait of the highest tribe?
'T is that, in fact, there 's little to describe.

XXI.

"*Haud ignara loquor;*" these are *Nugæ*, "*quarum*
 Pars parva *fui*," but still art and part.
Now I could much more easily sketch a harem,
 A battle, wreck, or history of the heart,
Than these things; and besides, I wish to spare 'em
 For reasons which I choose to keep apart.
"*Vetabo Cereris sacrum qui vulgarit*"—
Which means that vulgar people must not share it.

XXII.

And therefore what I throw off is ideal—
 Lower'd, leaven'd, like a history of freemasons
Which bears the same relation to the real,
 As Captain Parry's voyage may do to Jason's.
The grand arcanum 's not for men to see all;
 My music has some mystic diapasons;
And there is much which could not be appreciated
In any manner by the uninitiated.

XXIII.

Alas! worlds fall—and woman, since she fell'd
 The world (as, since that history, less polite
Than true, hath been a creed so strictly held)
 Has not yet given up the practice quite.
Poor thing of usages! coerced, compell'd,
 Victim when wrong, and martyr oft when right,
Condemn'd to child-bed, as men for their sins
Have shaving too entail'd upon their chins,—

XXIV.

A daily plague, which in the aggregate
 May average on the whole with parturition.

But as to women, who can penetrate
 The real sufferings of their she condition?
Man's very sympathy with their estate
 Has much of selfishness, and more suspicion.
Their love, their virtue, beauty, education,
But form good housekeepers, to breed a nation.

XXV.

All this were very well, and can't be better;
 But even this is difficult, Heaven knows,
So many troubles from her birth beset her,
 Such small distinction between friends and foes,
The gilding wears so soon from off her fetter,
 That——but ask any woman if she'd choose
(Take her at thirty, that is) to have been
Female or male? a schoolboy or a queen?

XXVI.

"Petticoat influence" is a great reproach,
 Which even those who obey would fain be thought
To fly from, as from hungry pikes a roach;
 But since beneath it upon earth we are brought,
By various joltings of life's hackney coach,
 I for one venerate a petticoat—
A garment of a mystical sublimity,
No matter whether russet, silk, or dimity.

XXVII.

Much I respect, and much I have adored,
 In my young days, that chaste and goodly veil,
Which holds a treasure, like a miser's hoard,
 And more attracts by all it doth conceal—
A golden scabbard on a Damasque sword,
 A loving letter with a mystic seal,
A cure for grief—for what can ever rankle
Before a petticoat and peeping ankle?

XXVIII.

And when upon a silent, sullen day,
 With a sirocco, for example, blowing,
When even the sea looks dim with all its spray,
 And sulkily the river's ripple's flowing,
And the sky shows that very ancient gray,
 The sober, sad antithesis to glowing,—
'T is pleasant, if *then* any thing is pleasant,
To catch a glimpse even of a pretty peasant.

XXIX.

We left our heroes and our heroines
 In that fair clime which don't depend on climate,
Quite independent of the Zodiac's signs,
 Though certainly more difficult to rhyme at,
Because the sun, and stars, and aught that shines,
 Mountains, and all we can be most sublime at,
Are there oft dull and dreary as a *dun*—
Whether a sky's or tradesman's is all one.

XXX.

An in-door life is less poetical;
 And out of door hath showers, and mists, and sleet,
With which I could not brew a pastoral.
 But be it as it may, a bard must meet
All difficulties, whether great or small,
 To spoil his undertaking or complete,
And work away like spirit upon matter,
Embarrass'd somewhat both with fire and water.

XXXI.

Juan—in this respect, at least, like saints—
 Was all things unto people of all sorts,
And lived contentedly, without complaints,
 In camps, and ships, in cottages, or courts—
Born with that happy soul which seldom faints,
 And mingling modestly in toils or sports.
He likewise could be most things to all women,
Without the coxcombry of certain *she* men.

XXXII.

A fox-hunt to a foreigner is strange;
 'T is also subject to the double danger
Of tumbling first, and having in exchange
 Some pleasant jesting at the awkward stranger:
But Juan had been early taught to range
 The wilds, as doth an Arab turn'd avenger,
So that his horse, or charger, hunter, hack,
Knew that he had a rider on his back.

XXXIII.

And now in this new field, with some applause,
 He clear'd hedge, ditch, and double post, and rail,
And never *craned*, and made but few "*faux pas*,"[100]
 And only fretted when the scent 'gan fail.
He broke, 't is true, some statutes of the laws
 Of hunting—for the sagest youth is frail;
Rode o'er the hounds, it may be, now and then,
And once o'er several country gentlemen.

XXXIV.

But on the whole, to general admiration
 He acquitted both himself and horse: the squires
Marvell'd at merit of another nation;
 The boors cried "Dang it! who'd have thought it?"—Sires,
The Nestors of the sporting generation,
 Swore praises, and recall'd their former fires;
The huntsman's self relented to a grin,
And rated him almost a whipper-in.

XXXV.

Such were his trophies—not of spear and shield,
 But leaps, and bursts, and sometimes foxes' brushes;
Yet I must own,—although in this I yield
 To patriot sympathy a Briton's blushes,—

He thought at heart like courtly Chesterfield,
 Who, after a long chase o'er hills, dales, bushes,
And what not, though he rode beyond all price,
 Ask'd next day, "If men ever hunted *twice?*" [101]

XXXVI.

He also had a quality uncommon
To early risers after a long chase,
Who wake in winter ere the cock can summon
December's drowsy day to his dull race,—
A quality agreeable to woman,
When her soft, liquid words run on apace,
Who likes a listener, whether saint or sinner,—
He did not fall asleep just after dinner;

XXXVII.

But, light and airy, stood on the alert,
And shone in the best part of dialogue,
By humouring always what they might assert,
And listening to the topics most in vogue;
Now grave, now gay,—but never dull or pert;
And smiling but in secret—cunning rogue!
He ne'er presum'd to make an error clearer:—
In short, there never was a better hearer.

XXXVIII.

And then he danced;—all foreigners excel
The serious Angles in the eloquence
Of pantomime;—he danced, I say, right well,
With emphasis, and also with good sense—
A thing in footing indispensable;
He danced without theatrical pretence,
Not like a ballet-master in the van
Of his drill'd nymphs, but like a gentleman.

XXXIX.

Chaste were his steps, each kept within due bound,
And elegance was sprinkled o'er his figure;
Like swift Camilla, he scarce skimm'd the ground,
And rather held in than put forth his vigour;
And then he had an ear for music's sound,
Which might defy a crotchet critic's rigour.
Such classic pas— sans flaws—set off our hero,
He glanced like a personified Bolero;

XL.

Or like a flying Hour before Aurora,
In Guido's famous fresco, which alone
Is worth a tour to Rome, although no more a
Remnant were there of the old world's sole throne.
The "*tout ensemble*" of his movements wore a
Grace of the soft ideal, seldom shown,
And ne'er to be described; for to the dolour
Of bards and prosers, words are void of colour.

XLI.

No marvel then he was a favourite;
A full-grown Cupid, very much admired:
A little spoilt, but by no means so quite;
At least he kept his vanity retired.
Such was his tact, he could alike delight
The chaste, and those who are not so much inspired.
The Duchess of Fitz-Fulke, who loved "*tracasserie*,"
Began to treat him with some small "*agacerie*."

XLII.

She was a fine and somewhat full-blown blonde,
Desirable, distinguish'd, celebrated
For several winters in the grand, *grand monde.*
I'd rather not say what might be related
Of her exploits, for this were ticklish ground;
Besides there might be falsehood in what's stated
Her late performance had been a dead set
At Lord Augustus Fitz-Plantagenet.

XLIII.

This noble personage began to look
A little black upon this new flirtation;
But such small licences must lovers brook,
Mere freedoms of the female corporation.
Woe to the man who ventures a rebuke!
'T will but precipitate a situation
Extremely disagreeable, but common
To calculators, when they count on woman.

XLIV.

The circle smiled, then whisper'd, and then sneer'd;
The Misses bridled, and the matrons frown'd;
Some hoped things might not turn out as they fear'd;
Some would not deem such women could be found;
Some ne'er believed one half of what they heard;
Some look'd perplex'd, and others look'd profound;
And several pitied with sincere regret,
Poor Lord Augustus Fitz-Plantagenet.

XLV.

But what is odd, none ever named the Duke,
Who, one might think, was something in the affair:
True, he was absent, and, 't was rumour'd, took
But small concern about the when, or where,
Or what his consort did: if he could brook
Her gaieties, none had a right to stare:
Theirs was that best of unions, past all doubt,
Which never meets, and therefore ca n't fall out.

XLVI.

But, oh! that I should ever pen so sad a line!
Fired with an abstract love of virtue, she,
My Dian of the Ephesians, Lady Adeline,
Began to think the Duchess' conduct free;
Regretting much that she had chosen so bad a line,
And waxing chiller in her courtesy,
Look'd grave and pale to see her friend's fragility
For which most friends reserve their sensibility

XLVII.

There's nought in this bad world like sympathy:
'T is so becoming to the soul and face,
Sets to soft music the harmonious sigh,
And robes sweet friendship in a Brussels lace.
Without a friend, what were humanity,
To hunt our errors up with a good grace?
Consoling us with—"Would you had thought twice
Ah! if you had but followed my advice!"

XLVIII.

O Job! you had two friends: one 's quite enough,
 Especially when we are ill at ease;
They are but bad pilots when the weather's rough
 Doctors less famous for their cures than fees.
Let no man grumble when his friends fall off,
 As they will do like leaves at the first breeze:
When your affairs come round, one way or t' other,
Go to the coffee-house, and take another. [102]

XLIX.

But this is not my maxim: had it been,
 Some heart-aches had been spared me: yet I care
 not—
I would not be a tortoise in his screen
 Of stubborn shell, which waves and weather wear
 not.
'T is better on the whole to have felt and seen
 That which humanity may bear, or bear not:
'T will teach discernment to the sensitive,
And not to pour their ocean in a sieve.

L.

Of all the horrid, hideous notes of woe,
 Sadder than owl-songs or the midnight blast,
Is that portentous phrase, "I told you so,"
 Utter'd by friends, those prophets of the past,
Who, 'stead of saying what you now should do,
 Own they foresaw that you would fall at last,
And solace your slight lapse 'gainst "*bonos mores*,"
With a long memorandum of old stories.

LI.

The Lady Adeline's serene severity
 Was not confined to feeling for her friend,
Whose fame she rather doubted with posterity,
 Unless her habits should begin to mend:
But Juan also shared in her austerity,
 But mix'd with pity, pure as e'er was penn'd:
His inexperience moved her gentle ruth,
And (as her junior by six weeks) his youth.

LII.

These forty days' advantage of her years—
 And hers were those which can face calculation,
Boldly referring to the list of peers
 And noble births, nor dread the enumeration—
Gave her a right to have maternal fears
 For a young gentleman's fit education,
Though she was far from that leap year, whose leap,
In female dates, strikes Time all of a heap.

LIII.

This may be fix'd at somewhere before thirty—
 Say seven-and-twenty; for I never knew
The strictest in chronology and virtue
 Advance beyond, while they could pass for new.
O Time! why dost not pause? Thy scythe, so
 dirty
 With rust, should surely cease to hack and hew.
Reset it; shave more smoothly, also slower,
If but to keep thy credit as a mower.

LIV.

But Adeline was far from that ripe age,
 Whose ripeness is but bitter at the best:
'T was rather her experience made her sage,
 For she had seen the world and stood its test,
As I have said in—I forget what page;
 My Muse despises reference, as you have guess'd
By this time;—but strike six from seven-and-twenty
And you will find her sum of years in plenty.

LV.

At sixteen she came out; presented, vaunted,
 She put all coronets into commotion:
At seventeen, too, the world was still enchanted
 With the new Venus of their brilliant ocean:
At eighteen, though below her feet still panted
 A hecatomb of suitors with devotion,
She had consented to create again
That Adam, called "The happiest of men."

LVI.

Since then she had sparkled through three glowing
 winters,
 Admired, adored; but also so correct,
That she had puzzled all the acutest hinters,
 Without the apparel of being circumspect:
They could not even glean the slightest splinters
 From off the marble, which had no defect.
She had also snatch'd a moment since her marriage,
To bear a son and heir—and one miscarriage.

LVII.

Fondly the wheeling fire-flies flew around her,
 Those little glitterers of the London night;
But none of these possess'd a sting to wound her—
 She was a pitch beyond a coxcomb's flight.
Perhaps she wish'd an aspirant profounder;
 But whatsoe'er she wish'd, she acted right;
And whether coldness, pride, or virtue, dignify
A woman, so she 's good, what does it signify?

LVIII.

I hate a motive, like a lingering bottle
 Which with the landlord makes too long a
 stand,
Leaving all-claretless the unmoisten'd throttle,
 Especially with politics on hand;
I hate it, as I hate a drove of cattle,
 Who whirl the dust as simooms whirl the sand;
I hate it as I hate an argument,
A laureate's ode, or servile peer's "content."

LIX.

'T is sad to hack into the roots of things,
 They are so much intertwisted with the earth;
So that the branch a goodly verdure flings,
 I reck not if an acorn gave it birth.
To trace all actions to their secret springs
 Would make indeed some melancholy mirth;
But this is not at present my concern,
And I refer you to wise Oxenstiern.[103]

LX.

With the kind view of saving an éclat,
 Both to the Duchess and Diplomatist,
The Lady Adeline, as soon's she saw
 That Juan was unlikely to resist—
(For foreigners don't know that a *faux pas*
 In England ranks quite on a different list
From those of other lands unblest with juries,
Whose verdict for such sin a certain cure is;—)

LXI.

The Lady Adeline resolved to take
 Such measures as she thought might best impede
The farther progress of this sad mistake.
 She thought with some simplicity indeed;
But innocence is bold even at the stake,
 And simple in the world, and doth not need
Nor use those palisades by dames erected,
Whose virtue lies in never being detected.

LXII.

It was not that she fear'd the very worst:
 His Grace was an enduring, married man,
And was not likely all at once to burst
 Into a scene, and swell the clients' clan
Of Doctors' Commons; but she dreaded first
 The magic of her Grace's talisman,
And next a quarrel (as he seem'd to fret)
With Lord Augustus Fitz-Plantagenet.

LXIII.

Her Grace, too, pass'd for being an intrigante,
 And somewhat *mechante* in her amorous sphere;
One of those pretty, precious plagues, which haunt
 A lover with caprices soft and dear,
That like to *make* a quarrel, when they can't
 Find one, each day of the delightful year:
Bewitching, torturing, as they freeze or glow,
And—what is worst of all—won't let you go.

LXIV.

The sort of thing to turn a young man's head,
 Or make a Werter of him in the end.
No wonder then a purer soul should dread
 This sort of chaste *liaison* for a friend;
It were much better to be wed or dead,
 Than wear a heart a woman loves to rend.
'T is best to pause, and think, ere you rush on,
If that a "*bonne fortune*" be really "*bonne*."

LXV.

And first, in the overflowing of her heart,
 Which really knew or thought it knew no guile,
She call'd her husband now and then apart,
 And bade him counsel Juan. With a smile
Lord Henry heard her plans of artless art
 To wean Don Juan from the siren's wile;
And answer'd, like a statesman or a prophet,
In such guise that she could make nothing of it.

LXVI.

Firstly, he said, "he never interfered
 In anybody's business but the king's:"
Next, that "he never judged from what appear'd,
 Without strong reason, of those sort of things:"
Thirdly, that "Juan had more brain than beard,
 And was not to be held in leading strings:"
And fourthly, what need hardly be said twice,
"That good but rarely came from good advice."

LXVII.

And, therefore, doubtless to approve the truth
 Of the last axiom, he advised his spouse
To leave the parties to themselves, forsooth—
 At least as far as *bienséance* allows:
That time would temper Juan's faults of youth;
 That young men rarely made monastic vows;
That opposition only more attaches—
But here a messenger brought in despatches:

LXVIII.

And being of the council call'd "the Privy,"
 Lord Henry walk'd into his cabinet,
To furnish matter for some future Livy,
 To tell how he reduced the nation's debt;
And if their full contents I do not give ye,
 It is because I do not know them yet;
But I shall add them in a brief appendix,
To come between mine epic and its index.

LXIX.

But ere he went, he added a slight hint,
 Another gentle common-place or two,
Such as are coin'd in conversation's mint,
 And pass, for want of better, though not new:
Then broke his packet, to see what was in 't,
 And having casually glanced it through,
Retired; and, as he went out, calmly kiss'd her,
Less like a young wife than an aged sister.

LXX.

He was a cold, good, honourable man,
 Proud of his birth, and proud of every thing;
A goodly spirit for a state divan,
 A figure fit to walk before a king;

Tall, stately, form'd to lead the courtly van
 On birthdays, glorious with a star and string;
The very model of a chamberlain—
And such I mean to make him when I reign.

LXXI.

But there was something wanting on the whole—
 I do n't know what, and therefore cannot tell—
Which pretty women—the sweet souls!—call *soul.*
 Certes it was not body; he was well
Proportion'd, as a poplar or a pole,
 A handsome man, that human miracle;
And in each circumstance of love or war,
Had still preserved his perpendicular.

LXXII.

Still there was something wanting, as I've said—
 That undefinable "*Je ne sçais quoi,*"
Which, for what I know, may of yore have led
 To Homer's Iliad, since it drew to Troy
The Greek Eve, Helen, from the Spartan's bed;
 Though on the whole, no doubt, the Dardan boy
Was much inferior to King Menelaüs:—
But thus it is some women will betray us.

LXXIII.

There is an awkward thing which much perplexes,
 Unless like wise Tiresias we had proved
By turns the difference of the several sexes;
 Neither can show quite *how* they would be loved.
The sensual for a short time but connects us—
 The sentimental boasts to be unmoved;
But both together form a kind of centaur,
Upon whose back 't is better not to venture.

LXXIV.

A something all-sufficient for the *heart*
 Is that for which the sex are always seeking:
But how to fill up that same vacant part?
 There lies the rub—and this they are but weak in.
Frail mariners afloat without a chart,
 They run before the wind through high seas breaking;
And when they have made the shore through every shock,
'T is odd, or odds, it may turn out a rock.

LXXV.

There is a flower call'd "Love in Idleness,"
 For which see Shakspeare's ever-blooming garden;—
I will not make his great description less,
 And beg his British godship's humble pardon,
If in my extremity of rhyme's distress,
 I touch a single leaf where he is warden;—
But though the flower is different, with the French
Or Swiss Rousseau, cry "*Voilà la Pervenche!*"[104]

49

LXXVI.

Eureka! I have found it! What I mean
 To say is, not that love is idleness,
But that in love such idleness has been
 An accessory, as I have cause to guess.
Hard labour 's an indifferent go-between;
 Your men of business are not apt to express
Much passion, since the merchant-ship, the Argo,
Convey'd Medea as her supercargo.

LXXVII.

"*Beatus ille procul!*" from "*negotiis,*"[105]
 Saith Horace; the great little poet's wrong;
His other maxim, "*Noscitur à sociis,*"
 Is much more to the purpose of his song;
Though even that were sometimes too ferocious,
 Unless good company be kept too long;
But, in his teeth, whate'er their state or station,
Thrice happy they who *have* an occupation!

LXXVIII.

Adam exchanged his Paradise for ploughing,
 Eve made up millinery with fig leaves—
The earliest knowledge from the tree so knowing,
 As far as I know, that the church receives:
And since that time it need not cost much showing,
 That many of the ills o'er which man grieves,
And still more women, spring from not employing
Some hours to make the remnant worth enjoying.

LXXIX.

And hence high life is oft a dreary void,
 A rack of pleasures, where we must invent
A something wherewithal to be annoy'd.
 Bards may sing what they please about *Content*·
Contented, when translated, means but cloy'd;
 And hence arise the woes of sentiment,
Blue devils, and blue-stockings, and romances
Reduced to practice, and perform'd like dances.

LXXX.

I do declare, upon an affidavit,
 Romances I ne'er read like those I have seen;
Nor, if unto the world I ever gave it,
 Would some believe that such a tale had been:
But such intent I never had, nor have it;
 Some truths are better kept behind a screen,
Especially when they would look like lies;
I therefore deal in generalities.

LXXXI.

"An oyster may be cross'd in love,"—and why?
 Because he mopeth idly in his shell,
And heaves a lonely subterraqueous sigh,
 Much as a monk may do within his cell:
And *à-propos* of monks, their piety
 With sloth hath found it difficult to dwell;

Those vegetables of the Catholic creed
Are apt exceedingly to run to seed.

LXXXII.

O Wilberforce! thou man of black renown,
 Whose merit none enough can sing or say,
Thou hast struck one immense Colossus down,
 Thou moral Washington of Africa!
But there's another little thing, I own,
 Which you should perpetrate some summer's day,
And set the other half of earth to rights;
You have freed the *blacks*—now pray shut up the whites.

LXXXIII.

Shut up the bald-coot bully Alexander!
 Ship off the Holy Three to Senegal;
Teach them that "sauce for goose is sauce for gander,"
 And ask them how *they* like to be in thrall?
Shut up each high heroic salamander,
 Who eats fire gratis (since the pay's but small);
Shut up—no, *not* the King, but the Pavilion,
Or else 't will cost us all another million.

LXXXIV.

Shut up the world at large, let Bedlam out;
 And you will be perhaps surprised to find
All things pursue exactly the same route,
 As now with those of *soi-disant* sound mind.
This I could prove beyond a single doubt,
 Were there a jot of sense among mankind;
But till that *point d'appui* is found, alas!
Like Archimedes, I leave earth as 't was.

LXXXV.

Our gentle Adeline had one defect—
 Her heart was vacant, though a splendid mansion:
Her conduct had been perfectly correct,
 As she had seen nought claiming its expansion.
A wavering spirit may be easier wreck'd,
 Because 't is frailer, doubtless, than a stanch one;
But when the latter works its own undoing,
Its inner crash is like an earthquake's ruin.

LXXXVI.

She loved her lord, or thought so; but *that* love
 Cost her an effort, which is a sad toil,
The stone of Sysiphus, if once we move
 Our feelings 'gainst the nature of the soil.
She had nothing to complain of, or reprove,
 No bickerings, no connubial turmoil:
Their union was a model to behold,
Serene and noble,—conjugal, but cold.

LXXXVII.

There was no great disparity of years,
 Though much in temper; but they never clash'd:
They moved like stars united in their spheres,
 Or like the Rhone by Leman's waters wash'd
Where mingled and yet separate appears
 The river from the lake, all bluely dash'd
Through the serene and placid glassy deep,
Which fain would lull its river-child to sleep.

LXXXVIII.

Now when she once had ta'en an interest
 In any thing, however she might flatter
Herself that her intentions were the best,
 Intense intentions are a dangerous matter:
Impressions were much stronger than she guess'd,
 And gather'd as they ran like growing water
Upon her mind; the more so, as her breast
Was not at first too readily impress'd.

LXXXIX.

But when it was, she had that lurking demon
 Of double nature, and thus doubly named—
Firmness yclept in heroes, kings, and seamen,
 That is, when they succeed; but greatly blamed
As *obstinacy*, both in men and women,
 Whene'er their triumph pales, or star is tamed:—
And 't will perplex the casuist in morality
To fix the due bounds of this dangerous quality.

XC.

Had Buonaparte won at Waterloo,
 It had been firmness; now 't is pertinacity;
Must the event decide between the two?
 I leave it to your people of sagacity
To draw the line between the false and true;
 If such can e'er be drawn by man's capacity:
My business is with Lady Adeline,
Who in her way too was a heroine.

XCI.

She knew not her own heart; then how should I?
 I think not she was *then* in love with Juan:
If so, she would have had the strength to fly
 The wild sensation, unto her a new one:
She merely felt a common sympathy
 (I will not say it was a false or true one)
In him, because she thought he was in danger,—
Her husband's friend, her own, young, and a stranger.

XCII.

She was, or thought she was, his friend—and this
 Without the farce of friendship, or romance
Platonism, which leads so oft amiss
 Ladies who have studied friendship but in France,
Or Germany, where people *purely* kiss.
 To thus much Adeline would not advance;
But of such friendship as man's may to man be
She was as capable as woman can be.

XCIII.

No doubt the secret influence of the sex
 Will there, as also in the ties of blood,
An innocent predominance annex,
 And tune the concord to a finer mood.
If free from passion, which all friendship checks,
 And your true feelings fully understood,
No friend like to a woman earth discovers,
So that you have not been—nor will be—lovers.

XCIV.

Love bears within its breast the very germ
 Of change; and how should this be otherwise?
That violent things more quickly find a term
 Is shown through nature's whole analogies;
And how should the most fierce of all be firm?
 Would you have endless lightning in the skies?
Methinks Love's very title says enough:
How should "the *tender* passion" ere be *tough?*

XCV.

Alas! by all experience, seldom yet
 (I merely quote what I have heard from many)
Had lovers not some reason to regret
 The passion which made Solomon a zany.
I've also seen some wives (not to forget
 The marriage state, the best or worst of any)
Who were the very paragons of wives,
Yet made the misery of at least two lives.

XCVI.

I've also seen some female *friends* ('t is odd,
 But true—as, if expedient, I could prove)
That faithful were through thick and thin, abroad,
 At home, far more than ever yet was Love—
Who did not quit me when Oppression trod
 Upon me; whom no scandal could remove;
Who fought, and fight—in absence, too—my battles,
Despite the snake Society's loud rattles.

XCVII.

Whether Don Juan and chaste Adeline
 Grew friends in this or any other sense,
Will be discuss'd hereafter, I opine:
 At present I am glad of a pretence
To leave them hovering, as the effect is fine,
 And keeps the atrocious reader in *suspense* ·
The surest way for ladies and for books
To bait their tender or their tenter hooks.

XCVIII.

Whether they rode, or walk'd, or studied Spanish,
 To read Don Quixote in the original,
A pleasure before which all others vanish;
 Whether their talk was of the kind call'd "small,"
Or serious, are the topics I must banish
 To the next Canto; where perhaps I shall
Say something to the purpose, and display
Considerable talent in my way.

XCIX.

Above all, I beg all men to forbear
 Anticipating aught about the matter:
They'll only make mistakes about the fair,
 And Juan too, especially the latter.
And I shall take a much more serious air,
 Than I have yet done, in this epic satire.
It is not clear that Adeline and Juan
Will fall; but if they do, 't will be their ruin.

C.

But great things spring from little: Would you think,
 That in our youth, as dangerous a passion
As e'er brought man and woman to the brink
 Of ruin, rose from such a slight occasion,
As few would ever dream could form the link
 Of such a sentimental situation?
You'll never guess, I'll bet you millions, milliards—
It all sprung from a harmless game at billiards.

CI.

'T is strange, but true; for truth is always strange;
 Stranger than fiction: if it could be told,
How much would novels gain by the exchange!
 How differently the world would men behold!
How oft would vice and virtue places change!
 The new world would be nothing to the old,
If some Columbus of the moral seas
Would show mankind their souls' antipodes.

CII.

What "antres vast and deserts idle" then
 Would be discover'd in the human soul!
What icebergs in the hearts of mighty men,
 With self-love in the centre as their pole!
What Anthropophagi are nine of ten
 Of those who hold the kingdoms in control!
Were things but only call'd by their right name,
Cæsar himself would be ashamed of fame.

CANTO THE FIFTEENTH.

I.

Ah!—What should follow slips from my reflection;
 Whatever follows ne'ertheless may be
As à-propos of hope or retrospection,
 As though the lurking thought had follow'd free.
All present life is but an interjection,
 An "Oh!" or "Ah!" of joy or misery,
Or a "Ha! ha!" or "Bah!"—a yawn, or "Pooh!"
Of which perhaps the latter is most true.

II.

But, more or less, the whole 's a syncopé
 Or a singultus—emblems of emotion,
The grand antithesis to great ennui,
 Wherewith we break our bubbles on the ocean,
That watery outline of eternity,
 Or miniature at least, as is my notion,
Which ministers unto the soul's delight,
In seeing matters which are out of sight.

III.

But all are better than the sigh suppres,
 Corroding in the cavern of the heart;
Making the countenance a masque of rest,
 And turning human nature to an art.
Few men dare show their thoughts of worst or best;
 Dissimulation always sets apart
A corner for herself; and therefore fiction
Is that which passes with least contradiction.

IV.

Ah! who can tell? Or rather, who can not
 Remember, without telling, passion's errors?
The drainer of oblivion, even the sot
 Hath got blue devils for his morning mirrors:
What though on Lethe's stream he seem to float,
 He cannot sink his tremors or his terrors;
The ruby glass that shakes within his hand
Leaves a sad sediment of Time's worst sand.

V.

And as for love—O love!——We will proceed.
 The Lady Adeline Amundeville,
A pretty name as one would wish to read,
 Must perch harmonious on my tuneful quill.
There 's music in the sighing of a reed;
 There 's music in the gushing of a rill;
There 's music in all things, if men had ears:
Their earth is but an echo of the spheres.

VI.

The Lady Adeline, right honourable,
 And honour'd, ran a risk of growing less so;
For few of the soft sex are very stable
 In their resolves—alas! that I should say so!
They differ as wine differs from its label,
 When once decanted;—I presume to guess so,
But will not swear: yet both upon occasion,
Till old, may undergo adulteration.

VII.

But Adeline was of the purest vintage,
 The unmingled essence of the grape; and yet
Bright as a new Napoleon from its mintage,
 Or glorious as a diamond richly set;
A page where Time should hesitate to print age,
 And for which Nature might forego her debt—
Sole creditor whose process doth involve in 't
The luck of finding every body solvent.

VIII.

O Death! thou dunnest of all duns! thou daily
 Knockest at doors, at first with modest tap,
Like a meek tradesman, when, approaching palely
 Some splendid debtor he would take by sap:
But oft denied, as patience 'gins to fail, he
 Advances with exasperated rap,
And (if let in) insists, in terms unhandsome,
On ready money, or "a draft on Ransom."

IX.

Whate'er thou takest, spare a while poor Beauty!
 She is so rare, and thou hast so much prey.
What though she now and then may slip from duty,
 The more 's the reason why you ought to stay.
Gaunt Gourmand! with whole nations for your booty,
 You should be civil in a modest way:
Suppress, then, some slight feminine diseases,
And take as many heroes as Heaven pleases.

X.

Fair Adeline, the more ingenuous
 Where she was interested (as was said),
Because she was not apt, like some of us,
 To like too readily, or too high bred
To show it—(points we need not now discuss)—
 Would give up artlessly both heart and head
Unto such feelings as seem'd innocent,
For objects worthy of the sentiment.

XI.

Some parts of Juan's history, which Rumour,
 That live gazette, had scatter'd to disfigure,
She had heard; but women hear with more good humour
 Such aberrations than we men of rigour:
Besides, his conduct, since in England, grew more
 Strict, and his mind assumed a manlier vigour;
Because he had, like Alcibiades,
The art of living in all climes with ease.

XII.

His manner was perhaps the more seductive,
 Because he ne'er seem'd anxious to seduce;
Nothing affected, studied, or constructive
 Of coxcombry or conquest: no abuse
Of his attractions marr'd the fair perspective,
 To indicate a Cupidon broke loose,
And seem to say, "Resist us if you can"—
Which makes a dandy while it spoils a man.

XIII.

They are wrong—that's not the way to set about
it;
As, if they told the truth, could well be shown.
But, right or wrong, Don Juan was without it;
In fact, his manner was his own alone;
Sincere he was—at least you could not doubt it,
In listening merely to his voice's tone.
The devil hath not in all his quiver's choice
An arrow for the heart like a sweet voice.

XIV.

By nature soft, his whole address held off
Suspicion: though not timid, his regard
Was such as rather seem'd to keep aloof,
To shield himself than put you on your guard:
Perhaps 't was hardly quite assured enough,
But modesty 's at times its own reward,
Like virtue; and the absence of pretension
Will go much farther than there 's need to mention.

XV.

Serene, accomplish'd, cheerful but not loud;
Insinuating without insinuation;
Observant of the foibles of the crowd,
Yet ne'er betraying this in conversation;
Proud with the proud, yet courteously proud,
So as to make them feel he knew his station
And theirs:—without a struggle for priority,
He neither brook'd nor claim'd superiority.

XVI

That is, with men: with women he was what
They please to make or take him for; and their
Imagination 's quite enough for that:
So that the outline 's tolerably fair,
They fill the canvas up—and "verbum sat."
If once their phantasies be brought to bear
Upon an object, whether sad or playful,
They can transfigure brighter than a Raphael.

XVII.

Adeline, no deep judge of character,
Was apt to add a colouring from her own:
'T is thus the good will amiably err,
And eke the wise, as has been often shown.
Experience is the chief philosopher,
But saddest when his science is well known:
And persecuted sages teach the schools
Their folly in forgetting there are fools.

XVIII.

Was it not so, great Locke? and greater Bacon?
Great Socrates? And Thou, Diviner still,[106]
Whose lot it is by man to be mistaken,
And Thy pure creed made sanction of all ill?
Redeeming worlds to be by bigots shaken,
How was Thy toil rewarded? We might fill
Volumes with similar sad illustrations,
But leave them to the conscience of the nations.

XIX.

I perch upon an humbler promontory,
Amidst life 's infinite variety:
With no great care for what is nicknamed glory,
But speculating as I cast mine eye
On what may suit or may not suit my story,
And never straining hard to versify,
I rattle on exactly as I'd talk
With any body in a ride or walk.

XX.

I do n't know that there may be much ability
Shown in this sort of desultory rhyme;
But there 's a conversational facility,
Which may round off an hour upon a time.
Of this I'm sure at least, there 's no servility,
In mine irregularity of chime,
Which rings what 's uppermost of new or hoary,
Just as I feel the "Improvisatore."

XXI.

"Omnia vult *belle* Matho dicere—dic aliquando
Et *bene*, dic *neutrum*, dic aliquando *male*."
The first is rather more than mortal can do;
The second may be sadly done or gaily;
The third is still more difficult to stand to;
The fourth we hear, and see, and say too, daily:
The whole together is what I could wish
To serve in this conundrum of a dish.

XXII.

A modest hope—but modesty 's my forte,
And pride my feeble:—let us ramble on.
I meant to make this poem very short,
But now I can't tell where it may not run
No doubt, if I had wish'd to pay my court
To critics, or to hail the *setting* sun
Of tyranny of all kinds, my concision
Were more;—but I was born for opposition.

XXIII.

But then 't is mostly on the weaker side;
So that I verily believe if they
Who now are basking in their full-blown pride
Were shaken down, and "dogs had had their
day,"
Though at the first I might perchance deride
Their tumble, I should turn the other way,
And wax an ultra-royalist in loyalty,
Because I hate even democratic royalty.

XXIV.

I think I should have made a decent spouse,
 If I had never proved the soft condition;
I think I should have made monastic vows,
 But for my own peculiar superstition:
'Gainst rhyme I never should have knocked my brows,
 Nor broken my own head, nor that of Priscian,
Nor worn the motley mantle of a poet,
If some one had not told me to forego it.

XXV.

But "laissez aller"—knights and dames I sing,
 Such as the times may furnish. 'T is a flight
Which seems at first to need no lofty wing,
 Plumed by Longinus or the Stagyrite:
The difficulty lies in colouring
 (Keeping the due proportions still in sight)
With nature manners which are artificial,
And rend'ring general that which is especial.

XXVI.

The difference is, that in the days of old
 Men made the manners;—manners now make men—
Pinn'd like a flock, and fleeced too in their fold,
 At least nine, and a ninth beside of ten.
Now this at all events must render cold
 Your writers, who must either draw again
Days better drawn before, or else assume
The present, with their common place costume.

XXVII.

We'll do our best to make the best on't:—March!
 March, my Muse! If you cannot fly, yet flutter;
And when you may not be sublime, be arch,
 Or starch, as are the edicts statesmen utter.
We surely may find something worth research:
 Columbus found a new world in a cutter,
Or brigantine, or pink, of no great tonnage,
While yet America was in her non-age.

XXVIII.

When Adeline, in all her growing sense
 Of Juan's merits and his situation,
Felt on the whole an interest intense,—
 Partly perhaps because a fresh sensation,
Or that he had an air of innocence,
 Which is for innocence a sad temptation,—
As women hate half measures, on the whole,
She 'gan to ponder how to save his soul.

XXIX.

She had a good opinion of advice,
 Like all who give and eke receive it gratis,
For which small thanks are still the market price,
 Even where the article at highest rate is:
She thought upon the subject twice or thrice,
 And morally decided, the best state is
For morals, marriage; and this question carried,
She seriously advised him to get married.

XXX.

Juan replied, with all becoming deference,
 He had a predilection for that tie;
But that, at present, with immediate reference
 To his own circumstances, there might lie
Some difficulties, as in his own preference,
 Or that of her to whom he might apply:
That still he 'd wed with such or such a lady,
If that they were not married all already.

XXXI.

Next to the making matches for herself,
 And daughters, brothers, sisters, kith or kin,
Arranging them like books on the same shelf,
 There 's nothing women love to dabble in
More (like a stock-holder in growing pelf)
 Than match-making in general: 't is no sin,
Certes, but a preventative, and therefore
That is, no doubt, the only reason wherefore.

XXXII.

But never yet (except of course a miss
 Unwed, or mistress never to be wed,
Or wed already, who object to this)
 Was there chaste dame who had not in her head
Some drama of the marriage unities,
 Observed as strictly both at board and bed
As those of Aristotle, though sometimes
They turn out melodrames or pantomimes.

XXXIII.

They generally have some only son,
 Some heir to a large property, some friend
Of an old family, some gay Sir John,
 Or grave Lord George, with whom perhaps might end
A line, and leave posterity undone,
 Unless a marriage was applied to mend
The prospect and their morals; and besides,
They have at hand a blooming glut of brides.

XXXIV.

From these they will be careful to select,
 For this an heiress, and for that a beauty;
For one a songstress who hath no defect,
 For t' other one who promises much duty;
For this a lady no one can reject,
 Whose sole accomplishments were quite a booty
A second for her excellent connections;
A third, because there can be no objections.

XXXV.

When Rapp the Harmonist embargo'd marriage[107]
 In his harmonious settlement—(which flourishes
Strangely enough as yet without miscarriage,
 Because it breeds no more mouths than it nourishes,
Without those sad expenses which disparage
 What Nature naturally most encourages)—
Why call'd he "Harmony" a state sans wedlock?
Now here I've got the preacher at a dead lock.

XXXVI.

Because he either meant to sneer at harmony
 Or marriage, by divorcing them thus oddly.
But whether reverend Rapp learn'd this in Germany
 Or no, 't is said his sect is rich and godly,
Pious and pure, beyond what I can term any
 Of ours, although they propagate more broadly.
My objection 's to his title, not his ritual,
Although I wonder how it grew habitual.

XXXVII.

But Rapp is the reverse of zealous matrons,
 Who favour, malgré Malthus, generation—
Professors of that genial art, and patrons
 Of all the modest part of propagation;
Which after all at such a desperate rate runs,
 That half its produce tends to emigration,
That sad result of passions and potatoes—
Two weeds which pose our economic Catos.

XXXVIII.

Had Adeline read Malthus? I can't tell;
 I wish she had; his book 's the eleventh commandment,
Which says, "Thou shalt not marry," unless *well:*
 This he (as far as I can understand) meant.
'T is not my purpose on his views to dwell,
 Nor canvass what "so eminent a hand" meant;[108]
But certes it conducts to lives ascetic,
Or turning marriage into arithmetic.

XXXIX.

But Adeline, who probably presumed
 That Juan had enough of maintenance,
Or *separate* maintenance, in case 't was doom'd—
 As on the whole it is an even chance
That bridegrooms, after they are fairly *groom'd*,
 May retrograde a little in the dance
Of marriage—(which might form a painter's fame,
Like Holbein's "Dance of Death"—but 't is the same);—

XL.

But Adeline determined Juan's wedding
 In her own mind, and that's enough for woman:
But then, with whom? There was the sage Miss Reading,
 Miss Raw, Miss Flaw, Miss Showman, and Miss Knowman,
And the two fair co-heiresses Giltbedding.
 She deem'd his merits something more than common:
All these were unobjectionable matches,
And might go on, if well wound up, like watches.

XLI.

There was Miss Millpond, smooth as summer's sea,
 That usual paragon, an only daughter,
Who seem'd the cream of equanimity,
 Till skimm'd—and then there was some milk and water,
With a slight shade of blue too, it might be,
 Beneath the surface; but what did it matter?
Love 's riotous, but marriage should have quiet,
And being consumptive, live on a milk diet.

XLII.

And then there was the Miss Audacia Shoestring,
 A dashing demoiselle of good estate,
Whose heart was fix'd upon a star or blue string;
 But whether English dukes grew rare of late,
Or that she had not harp'd upon the true string,
 By which such sirens can attract our great,
She took up with some foreign younger brother,
A Russ or Turk—the one 's as good as t' other.

XLIII.

And then there was—but why should I go on,
 Unless the ladies should go off?—there was
Indeed a certain fair and fairy one,
 Of the best class, and better than her class,—
Aurora Raby, a young star who shone
 O'er life, too sweet an image for such glass,
A lovely being, scarcely form'd or moulded,
A rose with all its sweetest leaves yet folded;

XLIV.

Rich, noble, but an orphan; left an only
 Child to the care of guardians good and kind;
But still her aspect had an air so lonely!
 Blood is not water; and where shall we find
Feelings of youth like those which overthrown lie
 By death, when we are left, alas! behind,
To feel, in friendless palaces, a home
Is wanting, and our best ties in the tomb?

XLV.

Early in years, and yet more infantine
 In figure, she had something of sublime
In eyes which sadly shone, as seraphs' shine.
 All youth—but with an aspect beyond time;

Radiant and grave—as pitying man's decline;
 Mournful—but mournful of another's crime,
She look'd as if she sat by Eden's door,
And grieved for those who could return no more.

XLVI.

She was a Catholic, too, sincere, austere,
 As far as her own gentle heart allow'd,
And deem'd that fallen worship far more dear
 Perhaps because 't was fallen: her sires were proud
Of deeds and days when they had fill'd the ear
 Of nations, and had never bent or bow'd
To novel power; and as she was the last,
She held their old faith and old feelings fast.

XLVII.

She gazed upon a world she scarcely knew
 As seeking not to know it; silent, lone,
As grows a flower, thus quietly she grew,
 And kept her heart serene within its zone.
There was awe in the homage which she drew;
 Her spirit seem'd as seated on a throne
Apart from the surrounding world, and strong
In its own strength—most strange in one so young!

XLVIII.

Now it so happen'd, in the catalogue
 Of Adeline, Aurora was omitted,
Although her birth and wealth had given her vogue,
 Beyond the charmers we have already cited;
Her beauty also seem'd to form no clog
 Against her being mention'd as well fitted,
By many virtues, to be worth the trouble
Of single gentlemen who would be double.

XLIX.

And this omission, like that of the bust
 Of Brutus at the pageant of Tiberius,[109]
Made Juan wonder, as no doubt he must.
 This he express'd half smiling and half serious;
When Adeline replied with some disgust,
 And with an air, to say the least, imperious,
She marvell'd "what he saw in such a baby
As that prim, silent, cold Aurora Raby?"

L.

Juan rejoin'd—"She was a Catholic,
 And therefore fittest, as of his persuasion;
Since he was sure his mother would fall sick,
 And the Pope thunder excommunication,
If——." But here Adeline, who seem'd to pique
 Herself extremely on the inoculation
Of others with her own opinions, stated—
As usual—the same reason which she late did.

50

LI.

And wherefore not? A reasonable reason,
 If good, is none the worse for repetition;
If bad, the best way's certainly to tease on,
 And amplify: you lose much by concision,
Whereas insisting in or out of season
 Convinces all men, even a politician;
Or—what is just the same—it wearies out.
So the end's gain'd, what signifies the route?

LII.

Why Adeline had this slight prejudice—
 For prejudice it was—against a creature
As pure as sanctity itself from vice,
 With all the added charm of form and feature,
For me appears a question far too nice,
 Since Adeline was liberal by nature;
But nature's nature, and has more caprices
Than I have time, or will, to take to pieces.

LIII.

Perhaps she did not like the quiet way
 With which Aurora on those baubles look'd,
Which charm most people in their earlier day:
 For there are few things by mankind less brook'd,
And womankind too, if we so may say,
 Than finding thus their genius stand rebuked,
Like "Anthony's by Cæsar," by the few
Who look upon them as they ought to do.

LIV.

It was not envy—Adeline had none;
 Her place was far beyond it, and her mind.
It was not scorn—which could not light on one
 Whose greatest *fault* was leaving few to find.
It was not jealousy, I think: but shun
 Following the "ignes fatui" of mankind.
It was not——but 't is easier far, alas!
To say what it was not than what it was.

LV.

Little Aurora deem'd she was the theme
 Of such discussion. She was there a guest;
A beauteous ripple of the brilliant stream
 Of rank and youth, though purer than the rest,
Which flow'd on for a moment in the beam
 Time sheds a moment o'er each sparkling crest.
Had she known this, she would have calmly smiled—
She had so much, or little, of the child.

LVI.

The dashing and proud air of Adeline
 Imposed not upon her: she saw her blaze
Much as she would have seen a glow-worm shine,
 Then turn'd unto the stars for loftier rays.
Juan was something she could not divine,
 Being no sibyl in the new world's ways;

Yet she was nothing dazzled by the meteor,
Because she did not pin her faith on feature.

LVII.

His fame too,—for he had that kind of fame
Which sometimes plays the deuce with woman-kind,
A heterogeneous mass of glorious blame,
Half virtues and whole vices being combined;
Faults which attract because they are not tame;
Follies trick'd out so brightly that they blind:—
These seals upon her wax made no impression,
Such was her coldness or her self-possession.

LVIII.

Juan knew nought of such a character—
High, yet resembling not his lost Haidée;
Yet each was radiant in her proper sphere:
The island girl, bred up by the lone sea,
More warm, as lovely, and not less sincere,
Was Nature's all: Aurora could not be,
Nor would be thus:—the difference in them
Was such as lies between a flower and gem.

LIX.

Having wound up with this sublime comparison,
Methinks we may proceed upon our narrative,
And, as my friend Scott says, "I sound my warison;"
Scott, the superlative of my comparative—
Scott, who can paint your Christian knight or Saracen,
Serf, lord, man, with such skill as none would share it, if
There had not been one Shakspeare and Voltaire,
Of one or both of whom he seems the heir.

LX.

I say, in my slight way I may proceed
To play upon the surface of humanity.
I write the world, nor care if the world read,
At least for this I cannot spare its vanity.
My Muse hath bred, and still perhaps may breed,
More foes by this same scroll: when I began it, I
Thought that it might turn out so—*now* I *know* it,
But still I am, or was, a pretty poet.

LXI.

The conference or congress (for it ended
As congresses of late do) of the Lady
Adeline and Don Juan rather blended
Some acids with the sweets—for she was heady;
But, ere the matter could be marr'd or mended,
The silvery bell rang, not for "dinner ready,"
But for that hour, call'd *half-hour*, given to dress,
Though ladies' robes seem scant enough for less.

LXII.

Great things were now to be achieved at table,
With massy plate for armour, knives and forks
For weapons; but what Muse since Homer's able
(His feasts are not the worst part of his works)
To draw up in array a single day-bill
Of modern dinners? where more mystery lurks
In soups or sauces, or a sole ragoût,
Than witches, b—ches, or physicians, brew.

LXIII.

There was a goodly "soupe à la *bonne femme*,"
Though God knows whence it came from; there was, too,
A turbot for relief of those who cram,
Relieved with "dindon à la Parigeux;"
There also was——the sinner that I am!
How shall I get this gourmand stanza through?—
"Soupe à la Beauveau," whose relief was dory,
Relieved itself by pork, for greater glory.

LXIV.

But I must crowd all into one grand mess
Or mass, for should I stretch into detail,
My Muse would run much more into excess,
Than when some squeamish people deem her frail;
But though a "bonne vivante," I must confess
Her stomach's not her peccant part; this tale
However doth require some slight refection,
Just to relieve her spirits from dejection.

LXV.

Fowls "à la Condé," slices eke of salmon,
With "sauces Génévoises," and haunch of venison;
Wines, too, which might again have slain young Ammon—
A man like whom I hope we sha n't see many soon;
They also set a glazed Westphalian ham on,
Whereon Apicius would bestow his benison;
And then there was champagne with foaming whirls,
As white as Cleopatra's melted pearls.

LXVI.

Then there was God knows what "à l'Allemande,"
"A l'Espagnole," "timballe," and "salpicon,"—
With things I ca n't withstand or understand,
Though swallow'd with much zest upon the whole;
And "entremets" to piddle with at hand,
Gently to lull down the subsiding soul;
While great Lucullus' *Robe triumphal* muffles—[110]
(*There's fame!*)—young partridge fillets, deck'd with truffles.

LXVII.

What are the *fillets* on the victor's brow
To these? They are rags or dust. Where is the arch

Which nodded to the nation's spoils below
 Where the triumphal chariots' haughty march?
Gone to where victories must like dinners go.
 Farther I shall not follow the research:
But oh! ye modern heroes with your cartridges,
When will your names lend lustre e'en to partridges?

LXVIII.

Those truffles too are no bad accessories,
 Follow'd by "petits puits d'amour"—a dish
Of which perhaps the cookery rather varies,
 So every one may dress it to his wish,
According to the best of dictionaries,
 Which encyclopedize both flesh and fish;
But even sans "confitures," it no less true is,
There's pretty picking in those "petits puits."[111]

LXIX.

The mind is lost in mighty contemplation
 Of intellect expended on two courses;
And indigestion's grand multiplication
 Requires arithmetic beyond my forces.
Who would suppose, from Adam's simple ration,
 That cookery could have call'd forth such resources,
As form a science and a nomenclature
From out the commonest demands of nature?

LXX.

The glasses jingled, and the palates tingled;
 The diners of celebrity dined well;
The ladies with more moderation mingled
 In the feast, pecking less than I can tell;
Also the younger men too: for a springald
 Can't, like ripe age, in gormandize excel,
But thinks less of good eating than the whisper
(When seated next him) of some pretty lisper.

LXXI.

Alas! I must leave undescribed the gibier,
 The salmi, the consommé, the purée,
All which I use to make my rhymes run glibber
 Than could roast beef in our rough John Bull way:
I must not introduce even a spare rib here,
 "Bubble and squeak" would spoil my liquid lay,
But I have dined, and must forego, alas!
The chaste description even of a "bécasse;"

LXXII.

And fruits, and ice, and all that art refines
 From nature for the service of the goût—
Taste or the *gout*,—pronounce it as inclines
 Your stomach! Ere you dine, the French will do;
But *after*, there are sometimes certain signs
 Which prove plain English truer of the two.
Hast ever *had* the *gout?* I have not had it—
But I may have, and you too, reader, dread it.

LXXIII.

The simple olives, best allies of wine,
 Must I pass over in my bill of fare?
I must, although a favourite "plat" of mine
 In Spain, and Lucca, Athens, everywhere:
On them and bread 't was oft my luck to dine,
 The grass my table-cloth, in open air,
On Sunium or Hymettus, like Diogenes,
Of whom half my philosophy the progeny is.

LXXIV.

Amidst this tumult of fish, flesh, and fowl,
 And vegetables, all in masquerade,
The guests were placed according to their roll,
 But various as the various meats display'd;
Don Juan sat next an "à l'Espagnole"—
 No damsel, but a dish, as hath been said;
But so far like a lady, that 't was drest
Superbly, and contain'd a world of zest.

LXXV.

By some odd chance, too, he was placed between
 Aurora and the Lady Adeline—
A situation difficult, I ween,
 For man therein, with eyes and heart, to dine.
Also the conference which we have seen
 Was not such as to encourage him to shine,
For Adeline, addressing few words to him,
With two transcendent eyes seem'd to look through him.

LXXVI.

I sometimes almost think that eyes have ears:
 This much is sure, that, out of earshot, things
Are somehow echoed to the pretty dears,
 Of which I can't tell whence their knowledge springs.
Like that same mystic music of the spheres,
 Which no one hears, so loudly though it rings,
'T is wonderful how oft the sex have heard
Long dialogues—which pass'd without a word!

LXXVII.

Aurora sat with that indifference
 Which piques a preux chevalier—as it ought:
Of all offences that's the worst offence,
 Which seems to hint you are not worth a thought.
Now Juan, though no coxcomb in pretence,
 Was not exactly pleased to be so caught;
Like a good ship entangled among ice,
And after so much excellent advice.

LXXVIII.

To his gay nothings, nothing was replied,
 Or something which was nothing, as urbanity
Required. Aurora scarcely look'd aside,
 Nor even smiled enough for any vanity.
The devil was in the girl! Could it be pride?
 Or modesty, or absence, or inanity?
Heaven knows! But Adeline's malicious eyes
Sparkled with her successful prophecies,

LXXIX.

And look'd as much as if to say, "I said it ;"
 A kind of triumph I'll not recommend,
Because it sometimes, as I have seen or read it,
 Both in the case of lover and of friend,

Will pique a gentleman, for his own credit,
 To bring what was a jest to a serious end:
For all men prophesy what *is* or *was*,
And hate those who won't let them come to pass.

LXXX.

Juan was drawn thus into some attentions,
 Slight but select, and just enough to express,
To females of perspicuous comprehensions,
 That he would rather make them more than less.
Aurora at the last (so history mentions,
 Though probably much less a fact than guess)
So far relax'd her thoughts from their sweet prison,
As once or twice to smile, if not to listen.

LXXXI.

From answering she began to question: this
 With her was rare; and Adeline, who as yet
Thought her predictions went not much amiss,
 Began to dread she'd thaw to a coquette—
So very difficult, they say, it is
 To keep extremes from meeting, when once set
In motion; but she here too much refined—
Aurora's spirit was not of that kind.

LXXXII.

But Juan had a sort of winning way,
 A proud humility, if such there be,
Which show'd such deference to what females say,
 As if each charming word were a decree.
His tact, too, temper'd him from grave to gay,
 And taught him when to be reserved or free:
He had the art of drawing people out,
Without their seeing what he was about.

LXXXIII.

Aurora, who in her indifference
 Confounded him in common with the crowd
Of flatterers, though she deem'd he had more sense
 Than whispering foplings, or than witlings loud—
Commenced (from such slight things will great commence)
 To feel that flattery which attracts the proud,
Rather by deference than compliment,
And wins even by a delicate dissent.

LXXXIV.

And then he had good looks;—that point was carried
 Nem. con. amongst the women, which I grieve
To say leads oft to *crim. con.* with the married—
 A case which to the juries we may leave,
Since with digressions we too long have tarried.
 Now though we know of old that looks deceive,
And always have done, somehow these good looks
Make more impression than the best of books.

LXXXV.

Aurora, who look'd more on books than faces,
 Was very young, although so very sage,
Admiring more Minerva than the Graces,
 Especially upon a printed page.
But Virtue's self, with all her tightest laces,
 Has not the natural stays of strict old age;
And Socrates, that model of all duty,
Own'd to a penchant, though discreet, for beauty.

LXXXVI.

And girls of sixteen are thus far Socratic,
 But innocently so, as Socrates;
And really, if the sage sublime and Attic
 At seventy years had phantasies like these,
Which Plato in his dialogues dramatic
 Has shown, I know not why they should displease
In virgins—always in a modest way,
Observe; for that with me's a "sine quâ."[112]

LXXXVII.

Also observe, that, like the great Lord Coke
 (See Littleton), whene'er I have express'd
Opinions two, which at first sight may look
 Twin opposites, the second is the best.
Perhaps I have a third too, in a nook,
 Or none at all—which seems a sorry jest:
But if a writer should be quite consistent,
How could he possibly show things existent?

LXXXVIII.

If people contradict themselves, can I
 Help contradicting them, and everybody,
Even my veracious self?—But that's a lie:
 I never did so, never will—how should I?
He who doubts all things nothing can deny:
 Truth's fountains may be clear—her streams are muddy,
And cut through such canals of contradiction,
That she must often navigate o'er fiction.

LXXXIX.

Apologue, fable, poesy, and parable,
 Are false, but may be render'd also true,
By those who sow them in a land that's arable.
 'Tis wonderful what fable will not do!
'Tis said it makes reality more bearable:
 But what's reality? Who has its clue?
Philosophy? No: she too much rejects.
Religion? *Yes;* but which of all her sects?

XC.

Some millions must be wrong, that's pretty clear;
 Perhaps it may turn out that all were right.
God help us! Since we have need on our career
 To keep our holy beacons always bright,

T is time that some new prophet should appear,
 Or old indulge man with a second sight.
Opinions wear out in some thousand years,
Without a small refreshment from the spheres.

XCI.

But here again, why will I thus entangle
 Myself with metaphysics? None can hate
So much as I do any kind of wrangle;
 And yet, such is my folly, or my fate,
I always knock my head against some angle
 About the present, past, or future state:
Yet I wish well to Trojan and to Tyrian,
For I was bred a moderate Presbyterian.

XCII.

But though I am a temperate theologian,
 And also meek as a metaphysician,
Impartial between Tyrian and Trojan
 As Eldon on a lunatic commission,—
In politics my duty is to show John
 Bull something of the lower world's condition.
It makes my blood boil line the springs of Hecla,[113]
To see men let these scoundrel sovereigns break law.

XCIII.

But politics, and policy, and piety,
 Are topics which I sometimes introduce,
Not only for the sake of their variety,
 But as subservient to a moral use;
Because my business is to *dress* society,
 And stuff with *sage* that very verdant goose.
And now, that we may furnish with some matter all
Tastes, we are going to try the supernatural.

XCIV.

And now I will give up all argument;
 And positively henceforth no temptation
Shall "fool me to the top up of my bent:"[114]
 Yes, I'll begin a thorough reformation.
Indeed, I never knew what people meant
 By deeming that my Muse's conversation
Was dangerous;—I think she is as harmless
As some who labour more and yet may charm less.

XCV.

Grim reader! did you ever see a ghost?
 No; but you have heard—I understand—be dumb!
And do n't regret the time you may have lost,
 For you have got that pleasure still to come;
And do not think I mean to sneer at most
 Of these things, or by ridicule benumb
That source of the sublime and the mysterious:—
For certain reasons, my belief is serious.

XCVI.

Serious? You laugh;—you may: that will not,
 My smiles must be sincere or not at all.
I say I do believe a haunted spot
 Exists—and where? That shall I not recall,
Because I'd rather it should be forgot,
 "Shadows the soul of Richard" may appal.
In short, upon that subject I've some qualms very
Like those of the philosopher of Malmsbury.[115]

XCVII.

The night—(I sing by night—sometimes an owl,
 And now and then a nightingale)—is dim,
And the loud shriek of sage Minerva's fowl
 Rattles around me her discordant hymn:
Old portraits from old walls upon me scowl—
 I wish to heaven they would not look so grim;
The dying embers dwindle in the grate—
I think too that I have sate up too late:

XCVIII.

And therefore, though 't is by no means my way
 To rhyme at noon—when I have other things
To think of, if I ever think—I say
 I feel some chilly midnight shudderings,
And prudently postpone, until mid-day,
 Treating a topic which, alas! but brings
Shadows;—but you must be in my condition,
Before you learn to call this superstition.

XCIX.

Between two worlds life hovers like a star,
 'Twixt night and morn, upon the horizon's verge
How little do we know that which we are!
 How less what we may be! The eternal surge
On time and tide rolls on and bears afar
 Our bubbles; as the old burst, new emerge,
Lash'd from the foam of ages; while the graves
Of empires heave but like some passing waves.

I.

The antique Persians taught three useful things,
 To draw the bow, to ride, and speak the truth.[116]
This was the mode of Cyrus, best of kings—
 A mode adopted since by modern youth.
Bows have they, generally with two strings;
 Horses they ride without remorse or ruth;
At speaking truth perhaps they are less clever,
But draw the long bow better now than ever.

II.

The cause of this effect, or this defect,—
 "For this effect defective comes by cause,"—[117]
Is what I have not leisure to inspect;
 But this I must say in my own applause,
Of all the muses that I recollect,
 Whate'er may be her follies or her flaws
In some things, mine's beyond all contradiction
The most sincere that ever dealt in fiction.

III.

And as she treats all things, and ne'er retreats
 From anything, this epic will contain
A wilderness of the most rare conceits,
 Which you might elsewhere hope to find in vain.
'T is true there be some bitters with the sweets,
 Yet mix'd so slightly, that you can't complain,
But wonder they so few are, since my tale is,
"De rebus cunctis et quibusdam aliis."

IV.

But of all truths which she has told, the most
 True is that which she is about to tell.
I said it was a story of a ghost—
 What then? I only know it so befell.
Have you explored the limits of the coast,
 Where all the dwellers of the earth must dwell?
'T is time to strike such puny doubters dumb as
The sceptics who would not believe Columbus.

V.

Some people would impose now with authority,
Turpin's or Monmouth Geoffrey's Chronicle;
Men whose historical superiority
Is always greatest at a miracle.
But Saint Augustine has the great priority,
Who bids all men believe the impossible,
Because 't is so. Who nibble, scribble, quibble, he
Quiets at once with "*quia* impossibile."

VI.

And therefore, mortals, cavil not at all;
Believe:—if 't is improbable, you *must*,
And if it is impossible, you *shall:*
'T is always best to take things upon trust.
I do not speak profanely, to recall
Those holier mysteries which the wise and just
Receive as gospel, and which grow more rooted,
As all truths must, the more they are disputed:

VII.

I merely mean to say what Johnson said,
That in the course of some six thousand years,
All nations have believed that from the dead
A visitant at intervals appears;
And what is strangest upon this strange head,
Is, that whatever bar the reason rears
'Gainst such belief, there 's something stronger still
In its behalf, let those deny who will.

VIII.

The dinner and the soirée too were done,
The supper too discuss'd, the dames admired,
The banqueteers had dropp'd off one by one—
The song was silent, and the dance expired:
The last thin petticoats were vanish'd, gone
Like fleecy clouds into the sky retired,
And nothing brighter gleam'd through the saloon
Than dying tapers—and the peeping moon.

IX.

The evaporation of a joyous day
Is like the last glass of champagne, without
The foam which made its virgin bumper gay;
Or like a system coupled with a doubt;
Or like a soda bottle when its spray
Has sparkled and let half its spirit out;
Or like a billow left by storms behind,
Without the animation of the wind;

X.

Or like an opiate, which brings troubled rest,
Or none; or like—like nothing that I know
Except itself;—such is the human breast;
A thing, of which similitudes can show
No real likeness,—like the old Tyrian vest
Dyed purple, none at present can tell how,
If from a shell fish or from cochineal.[118]
So perish every tyrant's robe piece-meal!

XI.

But next to dressing for a rout or ball,
Undressing is a woe; our robe de chambre
May sit like that of Nessus, and recall
Thoughts quite as yellow, but less clear than amber.
Titus exclaim'd, "I've lost a day!" Of all
The nights and days most people can remember,
(I have had of both, some not to be disdained,)
I wish they 'd state how many they have gain'd.

XII.

And Juan, on retiring for the night,
Felt restless, and perplex'd, and compromis'd:
He thought Aurora Raby's eyes more bright
Than Adeline (such is advice) advised;
If he had known exactly his own plight,
He probably would have philosophised:
A great resource to all, and ne'er denied
Till wanted; therefore Juan only sigh'd.

XIII.

He sigh'd;—the next resource is the full moon,
Where all sighs are deposited; and now
It happen'd luckily, the chaste orb shone
As clear as such a climate will allow;
And Juan's mind was in the proper tone
To hail her with the apostrophe—"O thou!"
Of amatory egotism the *Tuism*,
Which further to explain would be a truism.

XIV.

But lover, poet, or astronomer,
Shepherd, or swain, whoever may behold,
Feel some abstraction when they gaze on her:
Great thoughts we catch from thence, (besides a cold
Sometimes, unless my feelings rather err);
Deep secrets to her rolling light are told;
The ocean's tides and mortals' brains she sways,
And also hearts, if there be truth in lays.

XV.

Juan felt somewhat pensive, and disposed
For contemplation rather than his pillow:
The Gothic chamber, where he was enclosed,
Let in the rippling sound of the lake's billow,
With all the mystery by midnight caused:
Below his window waved (of course) a willow;
And he stood gazing out on the cascade
That flash'd and after darken'd in the shade.

XVI.

Upon his table or his toilet,—*which*
Of these is not exactly ascertain'd,—

(I state this, for I am cautious to a pitch
 Of nicety, where a fact is to be gain'd,)
A lamp burn'd high, while he leant from a niche,
 Where many a Gothic ornament remain'd,
In chisell'd stone and painted glass, and all
That time has left our fathers of their hall.

XVII.

Then, as the night was clear though cold, he threw
 His chamber door wide open—and went forth
Into a gallery, of a sombre hue,
 Long, furnish'd with old pictures of great worth,
Of knights and dames heroic and chaste too,
 As doubtless should be people of high birth.
But by dim lights the portraits of the dead
Have something ghastly, desolate, and dread.

XVIII.

The forms of the grim knight and pictured saint
 Look living in the moon; and as you turn
Backward and forward to the echoes faint
 Of your own footsteps—voices from the urn
Appear to wake, and shadows wild and quaint
 Start from the frames which fence their aspects stern,
As if to ask how you can dare to keep
A vigil there, where all but death should sleep.

XIX.

And the pale smile of beauties in the grave,
 The charms of other days, in starlight gleams,
Glimmer on high; their buried locks still wave
 Along the canvas; their eyes glance like dreams
On ours, or spars within some dusky cave,
 But death is imaged in their shadowy beams.
A picture is the past; even ere its frame
Be gilt, who sate hath ceased to be the same.

XX.

As Juan mused on mutability,
 Or on his mistress—terms synonymous—
No sound except the echo of his sigh
 Or step ran sadly through that antique house;
When suddenly he heard, or thought so, nigh,
 A supernatural agent—or a mouse,
Whose little nibbling rustle will embarrass
Most people, as it plays along the arras.

XXI.

It was no mouse, but lo! a monk, array'd
 In cowl and beads, and dusky garb, appear'd,
Now in the moonlight, and now lapsed in shade,
 With steps that trod as heavy, yet unheard;
His garments only a slight murmur made;
 He moved as shadowy as the sisters weird,
But slowly; and as he passed Juan by,
Glanced, without pausing, on him a bright eye.

XXII.

Juan was petrified; he had heard a hint
 Of such a spirit in these halls of old,
But thought, like most men, there was nothing in 't
 Beyond the rumour which such spots unfold,
Coin'd from surviving superstition's mint,
 Which passes ghosts in currency like gold,
But rarely seen, like gold compared with paper.
And did he see this? or was it a vapour?

XXIII.

Once, twice, thrice pass'd, repass'd—the thing of air,
 Or earth beneath, or heaven, or t' other place:
And Juan gazed upon it with a stare,
 Yet could not speak or move; but, on its base
As stands a statue, stood: he felt his hair
 Twine like a knot of snakes around his face;
He tax'd his tongue for words, which were not granted,
To ask the reverend person what he wanted.

XXIV.

The third time, after a still longer pause,
 The shadow pass'd away—but where? The hall
Was long, and thus far there was no great cause
 To think his vanishing unnatural:
Doors there were many, through which, by the laws
 Of physics, bodies whether short or tall
Might come or go; but Juan could not state
Through which the spectre seem'd to evaporate.

XXV.

He stood—how long he knew not, but it seem'd
 An age—expectant, powerless, with his eyes
Strain'd on the spot where first the figure gleam'd,
 Then by degrees recall'd his energies,
And would have pass'd the whole off as a dream,
 But could not wake; he was, he did surmise,
Waking already, and return'd at length
Back to his chamber, shorn of half his strength.

XXVI.

All there was as he left it: still his taper
 Burnt, and not *blue*, as modest tapers use,
Receiving sprites with sympathetic vapour;
 He rubb'd his eyes, and they did not refuse
Their office: he took up an old newspaper;
 The paper was right easy to peruse;
He read an article the king attacking,
And a long eulogy of "patent blacking."

XXVII.

This savour'd of this world; but his hand shook:
 He shut his door, and after having read
A paragraph, I think about Horne Tooke,
 Undrest, and rather slowly went to bed.

There, couch'd all snugly on his pillow's nook,
 With what he had seen his phantasy he fed;
And though it was no opiate, slumber crept
Upon him by degrees, and so he slept.

XXVIII.

He woke betimes; and, as may be supposed,
 Ponder'd upon his visitant or vision,
And whether it ought not to be disclosed,
 At risk of being quizz'd for superstition.
The more he thought, the more his mind was posed:
 In the mean time, his valet, whose precision
Was great, because his master brook'd no less,
Knock'd to inform him it was time to dress.

XXIX.

He dress'd; and like young people he was wont
 To take some trouble with his toilet, but
This morning rather spent less time upon't;
 Aside his very mirror soon was put;
His curls fell negligently o'er his front,
 His clothes were not curb'd to their usual cut,
His very neckcloth's Gordian knot was tied
Almost an hair's breadth too much on one side.

XXX.

And when he walk'd down into the saloon,
 He sate him pensive o'er a dish of tea,
Which he perhaps had not discover'd soon,
 Had it not happen'd scalding hot to be,
Which made him have recourse unto his spoon;
 So much distrait he was, that all could see
That something was the matter—Adeline
The first—but *what* she could not well divine.

XXXI.

She look'd, and saw him pale, and turn'd as pale
 Herself; then hastily look'd down, and mutter'd
Something, but what's not stated in my tale.
 Lord Henry said, his muffin was ill butter'd;
The Duchess of Fitz-Fulke play'd with her veil,
 And look'd at Juan hard, but nothing utter'd.
Aurora Raby with her large dark eyes
Survey'd him with a kind of calm surprise.

XXXII.

But seeing him all cold and silent still,
 And every body wondering more or less,
Fair Adeline inquired, "If he were ill?"
 He started, and said, "Yes — no — rather — yes."
The family physician had great skill,
 And being present, now began to express
His readiness to feel his purse and tell
The cause, but Juan said, "He was quite well."

XXXIII.

"Quite well; yes,—no."—These answers were mysterious,
 And yet his looks appear'd to sanction both,
However they might savour of delirious;
 Something like illness of a sudden growth
Weigh'd on his spirit, though by no means serious:
 But for the rest, as he himself seem'd loath
To state the case, it might be ta'en for granted,
It was not the physician that he wanted.

XXXIV.

Lord Henry, who had now discuss'd his chocolate,
 Also the muffin whereof he complain'd,
Said, Juan had not got his usual look elate,
 At which he marvell'd, since it had not rain'd;
Then ask'd her Grace what news were of the Duke of late?
 Her Grace replied, *his* Grace was rather pain'd
With some slight, light, hereditary twinges
Of gout, which rusts aristocratic hinges.

XXXV.

Then Henry turn'd to Juan, and address'd
 A few words of condolence on his state:
"You look," quoth he, "as if you had had your rest
 Broke in upon by the Black Friar of late"
"What friar?" said Juan; and he did his best
 To put the question with an air sedate,
Or careless; but the effort was not valid
To hinder him from growing still more pallid.

XXXVI.

"Oh! have you never heard of the Black Friar?
 The spirit of these walls?"—"In truth not I."
"Why Fame—but Fame you know's sometimes a liar—
 Tells an odd story, of which by and by:
Whether with time the spectre has grown shyer,
 Or that our sires had a more gifted eye
For such sights, though the tale is half believed,
The friar of late has not been oft perceived.

XXXVII.

"The last time was——"—"I pray," said Adeline—
 (Who watch'd the changes of Don Juan's brow,
And from its context thought she could divine
 Connections stronger than he chose to avow
With this same legend)—"if you but design
 To jest, you'll choose some other theme just now
Because the present tale has oft been told,
And is not much improved by growing old."

XXXVIII.

"Jest!" quoth Milor; "why, Adeline, you know
 That we ourselves—'t was in the honey moon—

Saw——"—"Well, no matter, 't was so long ago;
But, come, I'll set your story to a tune."
Graceful as Dian, when she draws her bow,
She seized her harp, whose strings were kindled soon
As touch'd, and plaintively began to play
The air of "'T was a Friar of Orders Gray."

XXXIX.

"But add the words," cried Henry, "which you made;
For Adeline is half a poetess,"
Turning round to the rest, he smiling said.
Of course the others could not but express
In courtesy their wish to see display'd
By one *three* talents, for there were no less—
The voice, the words, the harper's skill, at once
Could hardly be united by a dunce.

XL.

After some fascinating hesitation,—
The charming of these charmers, who seem bound,
I can't tell why, to this dissimulation,—
Fair Adeline, with eyes fixed on the ground
At first, then kindling into animation,
Added her sweet voice to the lyric sound,
And sang with much simplicity,—a merit
Not the less precious, that we seldom hear it.

1.

Beware! beware! of the Black Friar,
Who sitteth by Norman stone,
For he mutters his prayer in the midnight air,
And his mass of the days that are gone.
When the Lord of the Hill, Amundeville,
Made Norman Church his prey,
And expell'd the friars, one friar still
Would not be driven away.

2.

Though he came in his might, with King Henry's right,
To turn church lands to lay,
With sword in hand, and torch to light
Their walls, if they said nay;
A monk remain'd, unchased, unchain'd,
And he did not seem form'd of clay,
For he's seen in the porch, and he's seen in the church,
Though he is not seen by day.

3.

And whether for good, or whether for ill,
It is not mine to say;
But still with the house of Amundeville
He abideth night and day.
By the marriage-bed of their lords, 't is said,
He flits on the bridal eve;
And 't is held as faith, to their bed of death
He comes—but not to grieve.

4.

When an heir is born, he's heard to mourn,
And when aught is to befall

That ancient line, in the pale moonshine
He walks from hall to hall.
His form you may trace, but not his face,
'T is shadow'd by his cowl:
But his eyes may be seen from the folds between,
And they seem of a parted soul.

5.

But beware! beware! of the Black Friar,
He still retains his sway,
For he is yet the church's heir
Whoever may be the lay.
Amundeville is lord by day,
But the monk is lord by night;
Nor wine nor wassail could raise a vassal,
To question that friar's right.

6.

Say nought to him as he walks the hall,
And he'll say nought to you;
He sweeps along in his dusky pall,
As o'er the grass the dew.
Then grammarcy! for the Black Friar;
Heaven sain him! fair or foul,
And whatso'er may be his prayer,
Let ours be for his soul.

XLI.

The lady's voice ceased, and the thrilling wires
Died from the touch that kindled them to sound;
And the pause follow'd, which, when song expires,
Pervades a moment those who listen round;
And then of course the circle much admires,
Nor less applauds, as in politeness bound,
The tone, the feeling, and the execution,
To the performer's diffident confusion.

XLII.

Fair Adeline, though in a careless way,
As if she rated such accomplishment
As the mere pastime of an idle day,
Pursued an instant for her own content,
Would now and then, as 't were *without* display,
Yet *with* display in fact, at times relent
To such performances with haughty smile,
To show she *could*, if it were worth her while.

XLIII.

Now this (but we will whisper it aside)
Was—pardon the pedantic illustration—
Trampling on Plato's pride with greater pride,
As did the Cynic on some like occasion;
Deeming the sage would be much mortified,
Or thrown into a philosophic passion,
For a spoilt carpet—but the "Attic Bee"
Was much consoled by his own repartee.[119]

XLIV.

Thus Adeline would throw into the shade
(By doing easily, whene'er she chose,
What dilettanti do with vast parade)
Their sort of *half profession;* for it grows
To something like this when too oft display'd;
And that it is so, every body knows,
Who have heard Miss That or This, or Lady T'other
Show off—to please their company or mother.

XLV.

Oh! the long evenings of duets and trios!
The admirations and the speculations;
The "Mamma Mia's!" and the "Amor Mio's!"
The "Tanti palpiti's" on such occasions:
The "Lasciami's," and quavering "Addio's!"
Amongst our own most musical of nations:
With "Tu mi chama's" from Portingale,
To soothe our ears, lest Italy should fail.[120]

XLVI.

In Babylon's bravuras—as the home
Heart-ballads of Green Erin or Gray Highlands,
That bring Lochaber back to eyes that roam
O'er far Atlantic continents or islands,
The calentures of music which o'ercome
All mountaineers with dreams that they are nigh lands,
No more to be beheld but in such visions—
Was Adeline well versed, as compositions.

XLVII.

She also had a twilight tinge of "*Blue*,"
Could write rhymes, and compose more than she wrote,
Made epigrams occasionally too
Upon her friends, as every body ought.
But still from that sublimer azure hue,
So much the present dye, she was remote;
Was weak enough to deem Pope a great poet,
And what was worse, was not ashamed to show it.

XLVIII.

Aurora—since we are touching upon taste,
Which now-a-days is the thermometer
By whose degrees all characters are class'd—
Was more Shakspearian, if I do not err.
The worlds beyond this world's perplexing waste
Had more of her existence, for in her
There was a depth of feeling to embrace
Thoughts, boundless, deep, but silent too as Space.

XLIX.

Not so her gracious, graceful, graceless Grace,
The full-grown Hebe of Fitz-Fulke, whose mind,
If she had any, was upon her face,
And that was of a fascinating kind.

A little turn for mischief you might trace
 Also thereon,—but that 's not much; we find
Few females without some such gentle leaven,
For fear we should suppose us quite in heaven.

L.

I have not heard she was at all poetic,
 Though once she was seen reading the "Bath Guide,"
And "Hayley's Triumphs," which she deem'd pathetic,
 Because she said her *temper* had been tried
So much, the bard had really been prophetic
 Of what she had gone through with — since a bride.
But of all verse, what most ensured her praise
Were sonnets to herself, or "bouts rimés."

LI.

'T were difficult to say what was the object
 Of Adeline, in bringing this same lay
To bear on what appear'd to her the subject
 Of Juan's nervous feelings on that day.
Perhaps she merely had the simple project
 To laugh him out of his supposed dismay;
Perhaps she might wish to confirm him in it,
Though why I cannot say—at least this minute.

LII.

But so far the immediate effect
 Was to restore him to his self-propriety,
A thing quite necessary to the elect,
 Who wish to take the tone of their society;
In which you cannot be too circumspect,
 Whether the mode be persiflage or piety,
But wear the newest mantle of hypocrisy,
On pain of much displeasing the gynocracy.

LIII.

And therefore Juan now began to rally
 His spirits, and without more explanation
To jest upon such themes in many a sally.
 Her Grace, too, also seized the same occasion,
With various similar remarks to tally,
 But wish'd for a still more detail'd narration
Of this same mystic friar's curious doings,
About the present family's deaths and wooings.

LIV.

Of these few could say more than has been said;
 They pass'd, as such things do, for superstition
With some, while others, who had more in dread
 The theme, half credited the strange tradition;
And much was talk'd on all sides on that head:
 But Juan, when cross-question'd on the vision,
Which some supposed (though he had not avowed it)
Had stirr'd him, answer'd in a way to cloud it.

LV.

And then, the mid-day having worn to one,
 The company prepared to separate;
Some to their several pastimes, or to none,
 Some wondering 't was so early, some so late.
There was a goodly match too, to be run
 Between some grayhounds on my lord's estate,
And a young race-horse of old pedigree,
Match'd for the spring, whom several went to see.

LVI.

There was a picture-dealer, who had brought
 A special Titian, warranted original,
So precious that it was not to be bought,
 Though princes the possessor were besieging all.
The king himself had cheapen'd it, but thought
 The civil list he deigns to accept (obliging all
His subjects by his gracious acceptation)—
Too scanty, in these times of low taxation.

LVII.

But as Lord Henry was a connoisseur,—
 The friend of artists, if not arts,—the owner,
With motives the most classical and pure,
 So that he would have been the very donor,
Rather than seller, had his wants been fewer,
 So much he deem'd his patronage an honour,
Had brought the capo d'opera, not for sale,
But for his judgment—never known to fail.

LVIII.

There was a modern Goth, I mean a Gothic
 Bricklayer of Babel, call'd an architect,
Brought to survey these gray walls, which, though so thick,
 Might have from time acquired some slight defect;
Who after rummaging the Abbey through thick
 And thin, produced a plan whereby to erect
New buildings of correctest conformation,
And throw down old, which he call'd *restoration*.

LIX.

The cost would be a trifle—an "old song,"
 Set to some thousands ('t is the usual burden
Of that same tune, when people hum it long)—
 The price would speedily repay its worth in
An edifice no less sublime than strong,
 By which Lord Henry's good taste would go forth in
Its glory, through all ages shining sunny,
For Gothic daring shown in English money.[121]

LX.

There were two lawyers busy on a mortgage
 Lord Henry wish'd to raise for a new purchase;
Also a lawsuit upon tenures burgage,
 And one on tithes, which sure are Discord's torches,
Kindling Religion till she throws down *her* gage,
 "Untying" squires to "fight against the churches;"[122]

There was a prize ox, a prize pig, and ploughman,
For Henry was a sort of Sabine showman.

LXI.

There were two poachers caught in a steel trap,
Ready for gaol, their place of convalescence;
There was a country girl in a close cap
And scarlet cloak (I hate the sight to see, since—
Since—since—in youth I had the sad mishap—
But luckily I have paid few parish fees since):
That scarlet cloak, alas! unclosed with rigour,
Presents the problem of a double figure.

LXII.

A reel within a bottle is a mystery,
One can't tell how it e'er got in or out;
Therefore the present piece of natural history
I leave to those who are fond of solving doubt;
And merely state, though not for the consistory,
Lord Henry was a justice, and that Scout
The Constable, beneath a warrant's banner,
Had bagg'd this poacher upon Nature's manor.

LXIII.

Now justices of peace must judge all pieces
 Of mischief of all kinds, and keep the game
And morals of the country from caprices
 Of those who have not a licence for the same;
And of all things, excepting tithes and leases,
 Perhaps these are most difficult to tame:
Preserving partridges and pretty wenches
Are puzzles to the most precautious benches.

LXIV.

The present culprit was extremely pale,
 Pale as if painted so; her cheek being red
By nature, as in higher dames less hale
 'T is white, at least when they just rise from bed.
Perhaps she was ashamed of seeming frail,
 Poor soul! for she was country born and bred,
And knew no better in her immorality
Than to wax white—for blushes are for quality.

LXV.

Her black, bright, downcast, yet espiègle eye,
 Had gather'd a large tear into its corner,
Which the poor thing at times essay'd to dry,
 For she was not a sentimental mourner
Parading all her sensibility,
 Nor insolent enough to scorn the scorner,
But stood in trembling, patient tribulation,
To be call'd up for her examination.

LXVI.

Of course these groups were scatter'd here and there,
 Not nigh the gay saloon of ladies gent.
The lawyers in the study; and in air
 The prize pig, ploughman, poachers; the men sent
From town, viz. architect and dealer, were
 Both busy (as a general in his tent
Writing despatches) in their several stations,
Exulting in their brilliant lucubrations.

LXVII.

But this poor girl was left in the great hall,
 While Scout, the parish guardian of the frail,
Discuss'd (he hated beer yclept the "small,")
 A mighty mug of *moral* double ale.
She waited until Justice could recall
 Its kind attentions to their proper pale,
To name a thing in nomenclature rather
Perplexing for most virgins—a child's father.

LXVIII.

You see here was enough of occupation
 For the Lord Henry, link'd with dogs and horses.
There was much bustle too, and preparation
 Below stairs on the score of second courses;
Because, as suits their rank and situation,
 Those who in counties have great land resources
Have "public days," when all men may carouse,
Though not exactly what 's called "open house."

LXIX.

But once a week or fortnight, *un*invited,
 (Thus we translate a *general invitation*)
All country gentlemen, esquired or knighted,
 May drop in without cards, and take their station
At the full board, and sit alike delighted
 With fashionable wines and conversation;
And, as the isthmus of the grand connection,
Talk o'er themselves the past and next election.

LXX.

Lord Henry was a great electioneerer,
 Burrowing for boroughs like a rat or rabbit;
But county contests cost him rather dearer,
 Because the neighbouring Scotch Earl of Giftgabbit
Had English influence, in the self-same sphere here;
 His son, the Honourable Dick Dicedrabbit,
Was member for the "other interest" (meaning
The self-same interest, with a different leaning).

LXXI.

Courteous and cautious therefore in his county,
 He was all things to all men, and dispensed
To some civility, to others bounty,
 And promises to all—which last commenced
To gather to a somewhat large amount, he
 Not calculating how much they condensed;
But what with keeping some, and breaking others,
His word had the same value as another's.

LXXII.

A friend to freedom and freeholders—yet
 No less a friend to government—he held,
That he exactly the just medium hit
 'Twixt place and patriotism—albeit compell'd,
Such was his sovereign's pleasure, (though unfit,
 He added modestly, when rebels rail'd,)
To hold some sinecures he wish'd abolish'd,
But that with them all law would be demolished.

LXXIII.

He was "free to confess"—(whence comes this phrase?
 Is 't English? No—'t is only parliamentary)
That innovation's spirit now-a-days
 Had made more progress than for the last century.
He would not tread a factious path to praise,
 Though for the public weal disposed to venture high;
As for his place, he could but say this of it,
That the fatigue was greater than the profit.

LXXIV.

Heaven, and his friends, knew that a private life
 Had ever been his sole and whole ambition;
But could he quit his king in times of strife,
 Which threaten'd the whole country with perdition?

When demagogues would with a butcher's knife
 Cut through and through (oh! damnable incision!)
The Gordian or the Geordi-an knot, whose strings
Have tied together commons, lords, and kings.

LXXV.

Sooner "come place into the civil list
 And champion him to the utmost"[123]—he would keep it,
Till duly disappointed or dismiss'd:
 Profit he cared not for, let others reap it;
But should the day come when place ceased to exist,
 The country would have far more cause to weep it:
For how could it go on? Explain who can!
He gloried in the name of Englishman.

LXXVI.

He was as independent—ay, much more—
 Than those who were not paid for independence,
As common soldiers, or a common——shore,
 Have in their several arts or parts ascendance
O'er the irregulars in lust or gore,
 Who do not give professional attendance.
Thus on the mob all statesmen are as eager
To prove their pride, as footmen to a beggar.

LXXVII.

All this (save the last stanza) Henry said,
 And thought. I say no more—I've said too much;
For all of us have either heard or read—
 Off—or *upon* the hustings—some slight such
Hints from the independent heart or head
 Of the official candidate. I'll touch
No more on this—the dinner-bell hath rung,
And grace is said; the grace I *should* have *sung*—

LXXVIII.

But I'm too late, and therefore must make play.
 'T was a great banquet, such as Albion old
Was wont to boast—as if a glutton's tray
 Were something very glorious to behold.
But 't was a public feast and public day,—
 Quite full, right dull, guests hot, and dishes cold,
Great plenty, much formality, small cheer,
And every body out of their own sphere.

LXXIX.

The squires familiarly formal, and
 My lords and ladies proudly condescending;
The very servants puzzling how to hand
 Their plates—without it might be too much bending
From their high places by the sideboard's stand—
 Yet, like their masters, fearful of offending,
For any deviation from the graces
Might cost both man and master too—their *places*.

LXXX.

There were some hunters bold, and coursers keen,
 Whose hounds ne'er err'd, nor grayhounds deign'd to lurch;
Some deadly shots too, Septembrizers, seen
 Earliest to rise, and last to quit the search
Of the poor partridge through his stubble screen.
 There were some massy members of the church,
Takers of tithes, and makers of good matches,
And several who sung fewer psalms than catches.

LXXXI.

There were some country wags too—and, alas!
 Some exiles from the town, who had been driven
To gaze, instead of pavement, upon grass,
 And rise at nine in lieu of long eleven.
And lo! upon that day it came to pass,
 I sate next that o'erwhelming son of heaven,
The very powerful parson, Peter Pith,
The loudest wit I e'er was deafen'd with.

LXXXII.

I knew him in his livelier London days,
 A brilliant diner out, though but a curate;
And not a joke he cut but earn'd its praise,
 Until preferment, coming at a sure rate,
(O Providence! how wondrous are thy ways!
 Who would suppose thy gifts sometimes obdurate?)
Gave him, to lay the devil who looks o'er Lincoln,
A fat fen vicarage, and nought to think on.

LXXXIII.

His jokes were sermons, and his sermons jokes;
 But both were thrown away amongst the fens;
For wit hath no great friend in aguish folks.
 No longer ready ears and short-hand pens
Imbibed the gay bon-mot, or happy hoax:
 The poor priest was reduced to common sense,
Or to coarse efforts very loud and long,
To hammer a hoarse laugh from the thick throng.

LXXXIV.

There *is* a difference, says the song, "between
 A beggar and a queen," or *was* (of late
The latter worse used of the two we've seen—
 But we'll say nothing of affairs of state)
A difference "'twixt a bishop and a dean,"
 A difference between crockery ware and plate,
As between English beef and Spartan broth—
And yet great heroes have been bred by both.

LXXXV

But of all nature's discrepancies, none
 Upon the whole is greater than the difference
Beheld between the country and the town,
 Of which the latter merits every preference

From those who have few resources of their own,
 And only think, or act, or feel, with reference
To some small plan of interest or ambition—
Both which are limited to no condition.

LXXXVI.

But "en evant!" The light loves languish o'er
 Long banquets and too many guests, although
A slight repast makes people love much more,
 Bacchus and Ceres being, as we know,
Even from our grammar upwards, friends of yore
 With vivifying Venus, who doth owe
To these the invention of champagne and truffles:
Temperance delights her, but long fasting ruffles.

LXXXVII.

Dully past o'er the dinner of the day;
 And Juan took his place, he knew not where,
Confused, in the confusion, and distrait,
 And sitting as if nail'd upon his chair:
Though knives and forks clank'd round as in a fray,
 He seem'd unconscious of all passing there,
Till some one, with a groan, exprest a wish
(Unheeded twice) to have a fin of fish.

LXXXVIII.

On which, at the *third* asking of the bans,
 He started; and perceiving smiles around
Broadening to grins, he colour'd more than once,
 And hastily—as nothing can confound
A wise man more than laughter from a dunce—
 Inflicted on the dish a deadly wound,
And with such hurry, that ere he could curb it,
He had paid his neighbour's prayer with half a turbot.

LXXXIX.

This was no bad mistake, as it occurr'd,
 The supplicator being an amateur;
But others, who were left with scarce a third,
 Were angry—as they well might, to be sure.
They wonder'd how a young man so absurd
 Lord Henry at his table should endure;
And this, and his not knowing how much oats
Had fallen last market, cost his host three votes.

XC.

They little knew, or might have sympathised,
 That he the night before had seen a ghost,
A prologue which but slightly harmonised
 With the substantial company engross'd
By matter, and so much materialised,
 That one scarce knew at what to marvel most
Of two things—how (the question rather odd is)
Such bodies could have souls, or souls such bodies.

52

XCI.

But what confused him more than smile or stare,
 From all the squires and squiresses around,
Who wonder'd at the abstraction of his air,
 Especially as he had been renown'd
For some vivacity among the fair,
 Even in the country circle's narrow bound—
(For little things upon my lord's estate
Were good small talk for others still less great)—

XCII.

Was, that he caught Aurora's eye on his,
 And something like a smile upon her cheek.
Now this he really rather took amiss:
 In those who rarely smile, their smile bespeaks
A strong external motive; and in this
 Smile of Aurora's there was nought to pique
Or hope, or love, with any of the wiles
Which some pretend to trace in ladies' smiles.

XCIII.

'T was a mere quiet smile of contemplation,
 Indicative of some surprise and pity;
And Juan grew carnation with vexation,
 Which was not very wise, and still less witty,
Since he had gain'd at least her observation,
 A most important outwork of the city—
As Juan should have known, had not his senses
By last night's ghost been driven from their defences.

XCIV.

But what was bad, she did not blush in turn,
 Nor seem embarrass'd—quite the contrary;
Her aspect was as usual, still—*not* stern—
 And she withdrew, but cast not down, her eye,
Yet grew a little pale—with what? concern?
 I know not; but her colour ne'er was high—
Though sometimes faintly flush'd—and always clear,
As deep seas in a sunny atmosphere.

XCV.

But Adeline was occupied by fame
 This day; and watching, witching, condescending
To the consumers of fish, fowl, and game,
 And dignity with courtesy so blending,
As all must blend whose part it is to aim
 (Especially as the sixth year is ending)
At their lord's, son's, or similar connection's
Safe conduct through the rocks of re-elections.

XCVI.

Though this was most expedient on the whole,
 And usual—Juan, when he cast a glance
On Adeline while playing her grand rôle,
 Which she went through as though it were a dance,

Betraying only now and then her soul
 By a look scarce perceptibly askance
(Of weariness or scorn), began to feel
Some doubt how much of Adeline was *real;*

XCVII.

So well she acted all and every part
 By turns—with that vivacious versatility,
Which many people take for want of heart.
 They err—'t is merely what is call'd mobility,[124]
A thing of temperament and not of art,
 Though seeming so, from its supposed facility;
And false — though true; for surely they're sincerest
Who are strongly acted on by what is nearest.

XCVIII.

This makes your actors, artists, and romancers,
 Heroes sometimes, though seldom—sages never:
But speakers, bards, diplomatists, and dancers,
 Little that's great, but much of what is clever;
Most orators, but very few financiers,
 Though all Exchequer chancellors endeavour,
Of late years, to dispense with Cocker's rigours,
And grow quite figurative with their figures.

XCIX.

The poets of arithmetic are they,
 Who, though they prove not two and two to be
Five, as they might do in a modest way,
 Have plainly made it out that four are three,
Judging by what they take, and what they pay.
 The Sinking Fund's unfathomable sea,
That most unliquidating liquid, leaves
The debt unsunk, yet sinks all it receives.

C.

While Adeline dispensed her airs and graces,
 The fair Fitz-Fulke seem'd very much at ease;
Though too well bred to quiz men to their faces,
 Her laughing blue eyes with a glance could seize
The ridicules of people in all places—
 That honey of your fashionable bees—
And store it up for mischievous enjoyment;
And this at present was her kind employment.

CI.

However, the day closed, as days must close;
 The evening also waned—and coffee came.
Each carriage was announced, and ladies rose,
 And curtsying off, as curtsies country dame,
Retired: with most unfashionable bows
 Their docile esquires also did the same,
Delighted with their dinner and their host,
But with the Lady Adeline the most.

CII.

Some praised her beauty: others her great grace;
 The warmth of her politeness, whose sincerity
Was obvious in each feature of her face,
 Whose traits were radiant with the rays of verity.
Yes; *she* was truly worthy *her* high place!
 No one could envy her deserved prosperity.
And then her dress—what beautiful simplicity
Draperied her form with curious felicity![125]

CIII.

Meanwhile sweet Adeline deserved their praises,
 By an impartial indemnification
For all her past exertion and soft phrases,
 In a most edifying conversation,
Which turn'd upon their late guests' miens and faces,
 And families, even to the last relation;
Their hideous wives, their horrid selves and dresses,
And truculent distortion of their tresses.

CIV.

True, *she* said little—'t was the rest that broke
 Forth into universal epigram;
But then 't was to the purpose what she spoke:
 Like Addison's "faint praise," so wont to damn,
Her own but served to set off every joke,
 As music chimes in with a melodrame.
How sweet the task to shield an absent friend!
I ask but this of mine, to——*not* defend.

CV.

There were but two exceptions to this keen
 Skirmish of wits o'er the departed; one
Aurora, with her pure and placid mien;
 And Juan, too, in general behind none
In gay remark on what he had heard or seen,
 Sate silent now, his usual spirits gone:
In vain he heard the others rail or rally,
He would not join them in a single sally.

CVI.

'T is true he saw Aurora look as though
 She approved his silence; she perhaps mistook
Its motive for that charity we owe
 But seldom pay the absent, nor would look
Farther; it might or it might not be so.
 But Juan, sitting silent in his nook,
Observing little in his reverie,
Yet saw this much, which he was glad to see.

CVII.

The ghost at least had done him this much good,
 In making him as silent as a ghost,
If in the circumstances which ensued
 He gain'd esteem where it was worth the most.
And certainly Aurora had renew'd
 In him some feelings he had lately lost,

Or harden d; feelings which, perhaps ideal,
Are so divine, that I must deem them real:—

CVIII.

The love of higher things and better days;
 The unbounded hope, and heavenly ignorance
Of what is call'd the world, and the world's ways;
 The moments when we gather from a glance
More joy than from all future pride or praise,
 Which kindle manhood, but can ne'er entrance
The heart in an existence of its own,
Of which another's bosom is the zone.

CIX.

Who would not sigh Αι αι ταν Κυθερειαν
 That *hath* a memory, or that *had* a heart?
Alas! *her* star must fade like that of Dian:
 Ray fades on ray, as years on years depart.
Anacreon only had the soul to tie an
 Unwithering myrtle round the unblunted dart
Of Eros: but though thou hast play'd us many tricks,
Still we respect thee, "Alma Venus Genetrix!"

CX.

And full of sentiments, sublime as billows
 Heaving between this world and worlds beyond,
Don Juan, when the midnight hour of pillows
 Arrived, retired to his; but to despond
Rather than rest. Instead of poppies, willows
 Waved o'er his couch; he meditated, fond
Of those sweet bitter thoughts which banish sleep,
And make the worldling sneer, the youngling weep.

CXI.

The night was as before: he was undrest,
 Saving his night-gown, which is an undress;
Completely "sans culotte," and without vest;
 In short, he hardly could be clothed with less:
But apprehensive of his spectral guest,
 He sate with feelings awkward to express
(By those who have not had such visitations),
Expectant of the ghost's fresh operations.

CXII.

And not in vain he listen'd;—Hush! what's that?
 I see—I see—Ah, no!—'tis not—yet 'tis—
Ye powers! it is the—the—the—Pooh! the cat!
 The devil may take that stealthy pace of his!
So like a spiritual pit-a-pat,
 Or tiptoe of an amatory Miss,
Gliding the first time to a rendezvous,
And dreading the chaste echoes of her shoe.

CXIII.

Again—what is't? The wind? No, no,—this time
 It is the sable friar as before,
With awful footeps regular as rhyme,
 Or (as rhymes may be in these days) much more.
Again through shadows of the night sublime,
 When deep sleep fell on men, and the world wore
The starry darkness round her like a girdle
Spangled with gems—the monk made his blood curdle.

CXIV.

A noise like to wet fingers drawn on glass,[126]
 Which sets the teeth on edge; and a slight clatter,
Like showers which on the midnight gusts will pass,
 Sounding like very supernatural water,
Came over Juan's ear, which throbb'd, alas!
 For immaterialism's a serious matter;
So that even those whose faith is the most great
In souls immortal, shun them tête-à-tête.

CXV.

Were his eyes open?—Yes! and his mouth too.
 Surprise has this effect—to make one dumb,
Yet leave the gate which eloquence slips through
 As wide as if a long speech were to come.
Nigh and more nigh the awful echoes drew,
 Tremendous to a mortal tympanum:
His eyes were open, and (as was before
Stated) his mouth. What open'd next?—the door.

CXVI.

It open'd with a most infernal creak,
 Like that of hell. "Lasciate ogni speranza
Voi che entrate!" The hinge seemed to speak,
 Dreadful as Dante's rhima, or this stanza;
Or—but all words upon such themes are weak:
 A single shade's sufficient to entrance a
Hero—for what is substance to a spirit?
Or how is't *matter* trembles to come near it?

CXVII.

The door flew wide, not swiftly,—but, as fly
 The sea-gulls, with a steady, sober flight—
And then swung back; nor close—but stood awry,
 Half letting in long shadows on the light,
Which still in Juan's candlesticks burn'd high,
 For he had two, both tolerably bright,
And in the door-way, darkening darkness, stood
The sable friar in his solemn hood.

CXVIII.

Don Juan shook, as erst he had been shaken
 The night before; but being sick of shaking,
He first inclined to think he had been mistaken;
 And then to be ashamed of such mistaking;
His own internal ghost began to awaken
 Within him, and to quell his corporal quaking—
Hinting that soul and body on the whole
Were odds against a disembodied soul.

CXIX.

And then his dread grew wrath, and his wrath fierce,
And he arose, advanced—the shade retreated;
But Juan, eager now the truth to pierce,
Follow'd, his veins no longer cold, but heated,
Resolved to thrust the mystery carte and tierce,
At whatsoever risk of being defeated;
The ghost stopp'd, menaced, then retired, until
He reach'd the ancient wall, then stood stone still.

CXX.

Juan put forth one arm—Eternal powers!
It touch'd no soul, no body, but the wall,
On which the moonbeams fell in silvery showers,
Chequer'd with all the tracery of the hall;
He shudder'd, as no doubt the bravest cowers
When he can't tell what 'tis that doth appal.
How odd, a single hobgoblin's non-entity
Should cause more fear than a whole host's identity.

CXXI.

But still the shade remain'd: the blue eyes glared,
And rather variably for stony death;
Yet one thing rather good the grave had spared,
The ghost had a remarkably sweet breath:
A straggling curl show'd he had been fair-hair'd;
A red lip, with two rows of pearls beneath,
Gleam'd forth, as through the casement's ivy shroud
The moon peep'd, just escaped from a gray cloud.

CXXII.

And Juan, puzzled, but still curious, thrust
His other arm forth—Wonder upon wonder!
It press'd upon a hard but glowing bust,
Which beat as if there was a warm heart under.
He found, as people on most trials must,
That he had made at first a silly blunder,
And that in his confusion he had caught
Only the wall, instead of what he sought.

CXXIII.

The ghost, if ghost it were, seem'd a sweet soul
As ever lurk'd beneath a holy hood:
A dimpled chin, a neck of ivory, stole
Forth into something much like flesh and blood;
Back fell the sable frock and dreary cowl,
And they reveal'd—alas! that e'er they should!
In full, voluptuous, but *not o'er*grown bulk,
The phantom of her frolic Grace—Fitz-Fulke!

NOTES TO DON JUAN.

NOTE 1, page 138.

Brave men were living before Agamemnon.

"Vixere fortes ante Agamemnona," &c.—HOR.

NOTE 2, page 139.

Save thine "incomparable oil," Macassar!

"Description des *vertus incomparables* de l'Huile de Macassar." See the Advertisement.

NOTE 3, page 143.

Although Longinus tells us there is no hymn.

See Longinus, Section 10.

NOTE 4, page 143.

They only add them all in an appendix.

Fact! There is, or was, such an edition, with all the obnoxious epigrams of Martial placed by themselves at the end.

NOTE 5, page 148.

The bard I quote from does not sing amiss.

Campbell's "Gertrude of Wyoming"—(I think)—the opening of Canto Second—but quote from memory.

NOTE 6, page 155.

Is it for this that General Count O'Reilly,
Who took Algiers, declares I used him vilely!

Donna Julia here made a mistake. Count O'Reilly did not take Algiers—but Algiers very nearly took him: he and his army and fleet retreated with great loss, and not much credit, from before that city, in the year 1775.

NOTE 7, page 163.

My days of love are over; me no more.

"Me nec femina, nec puer
Jam, nec spes animi credula mutui,
Nec certare juvat mero;
Nec vincire novis tempora floribus."—HOR.

NOTE 8, page 166.

Excepting the Venetian Fazzioli.

Fazzioli—literally, little handkerchiefs—the veils most availing of St. Mark.

NOTE 9, page 191.

Dante and Milton, and of both the affection.

Milton's first wife ran away from him within the first month. If she had not, what would John Milton have done?

NOTE 10, page 194.

For none likes more to hear himself converse.

"Rispone allor' Margutte, a dir tel tosto,
Io non credo piu al nero ch' all' azzurro;
Ma nel cappone, o lesso, o vuogli arrosto,
E credo alcuna volta anco nel burro;
Nella cervigia, e quando io n' ho nel mosto,
E molto piu nell' espro che il mangurro;

Ma sopra tutto nel buon vino o fede,
E credo che sia salvo chi gli crede."
PULCI, *Morgante Maggiore*, ca. 18. st. 151.

NOTE 11, page 198.

That e'er by precious metal was held in.

This dress is Moorish, and the bracelets and bar are worn in the manner described. The reader will perceive hereafter, that as the mother of Haidée was of Fez, her daughter wore the garb of the country.

NOTE 12, page 198.

A like gold bar above her instep roll'd.

The bar of gold above the instep is a mark of sovereign rank in the women of the families of the deys, and is worn as such by their female relatives.

NOTE 13, page 198.

Her person if allow'd at large to run.

This is no exaggeration: there were four women whom I remember to have seen, who possessed their hair in this profusion; of these, three were English, the other was a Levantine. Their hair was of that length and quantity, that, when let down, it almost entirely shaded the person, so as nearly to render dress a superfluity. Of these, only one had dark hair; the Oriental's had, perhaps, the lightest colour of the four.

NOTE 14, page 200.

Than your sires' "Islands of the Blest."

The νησοι μακαρων of the Greek poets were supposed to have been the Cape de Verd Islands or the Canaries.

NOTE 15, page 200.

And when the sun set, where were they?

"Deep were the groans of Xerxes, when he saw
This havoc; for his seat, a lofty mound
Commanding the wide sea, o'erlook'd the hosts.
With rueful cries he rent his royal robes,
And through his troops embattled on the shore
Gave signal of retreat; then started wild
And fled disordered."—ÆSCHYLUS.

NOTE 16, page 202.

For the first Mrs. Milton left his house.

See Johnson's Life of Milton.

NOTE 17, page 203.

And drivels seas to set it well afloat.

"There's something in a flying horse,
There's something in a huge balloon;
But through the clouds I'll never float
Until I have a little boat," &c.
WORDSWORTH'S *Peter Bell.*

NOTE 18, page 203.

Can sneer at him who drew "Achitophel!"

"The verses of Dryden, once highly celebrated, are forgotten."—Mr. W. WORDSWORTH'S *Preface.*

NOTE 19, page 204.

Oh, Hesperus! thou bringest all good things.

See Fragment of Sappho.

NOTE 20, page 204.

Ah! surely nothing dies but something mourns!

"Era gia l' ora che volge 'l disio,
A' naviganti, e 'ntenerisce il cuore;
Lo di ch' han detto a' dolci amici a dio;
E che lo nuovo peregrin' d' amore
Punge, se ode Squilla di lontano,
Che paia 'l giorno pianger che si muore."
DANTE'S *Purgatory*, canto viii.

This last line is the first of Gray's Elegy, taken by him without acknowledgment.

NOTE 21, page 204.

Some hands unseen strew'd flowers upon his tomb.

See Suetonius for this fact.

NOTE 22, page 206.

"Whom the Gods love die young," was said of yore.

See Herodotus.

NOTE 23, page 211.

A vein had burst, and her sweet lips' pure dyes.

This is no very uncommon effect of the violence of conflicting and different passions. The Doge Francis Foscari, on his deposition in 1457, hearing the bells of St. Mark announce the election of his successor, "mourut subitement d'une hémorragie causée par une veine qui s'éclata dans sa poitrine," (see Sismondi and Daru, vols. i. and ii.) at the age of eighty years, when "*Who would have thought the old man had so much blood in him?*" Before I was sixteen years of age, I was witness to a melancholy instance of the same effect of mixed passions upon a young person, who, however, did not die in consequence, at that time, but fell a victim some years afterwards to a seizure of the same kind, arising from causes intimately connected with agitation of mind.

NOTE 24, page 213.

But sold by the impresario at no high rate.

This is a fact. A few years ago a man engaged a company for some foreign theatre, embarked them at an Italian port, and carrrying them to Algiers, sold them all. One of the women, returned from her captivity, I heard sing, by a strange coincidence, in Rossini's opera of "L'Italiana in Algieri," at Venice, in the beginning of 1817.

NOTE 25, page 215.

From all the Pope makes yearly, 't would perplex.

It is strange that it should be the Pope and the Sultan, who are the chief encouragers of this branch of trade—women being prohibited as singers at St. Peter's, and not deemed trust-worthy as guardians of the harem.

NOTE 26, page 216.

While weeds and ordure rankle round the base.

The pillar which records the battle of Ravenna is about two miles from the city, on the opposite side of the river to the road towards Forli. Gaston de Foix, who gained the battle, was killed in it: there fell on both sides twenty thousand men. The present state of the pillar and its site is described in the text.

NOTE 27, page 218.

Sprinkled with palaces; the ocean stream.

The expression of Homer has been much criticised. It hardly answers to our Atlantic ideas of the ocean, but is sufficiently applicable to the Hellespont, and the Bosphorus, with the Ægean intersected with islands.

NOTE 28, page 219.

'Tis a grand sight from off "The Giant's Grave."

The "Giant's Grave" is a height on the Asiatic shore of the Bosphorus, much freqented by holiday parties; like Harrow and Highgate.

NOTE 29, page 221.

Of food I think with Philip's son, or rather.

See Plutarch in Alex., Q. Curt. Hist. Alexand., and Sir Richard Clayton's "Critical inquiry into the Life of Alexander the Great."

NOTE 30, page 221.

And, running out as fast as I was able.

The assassination alluded to took place on the 8th of December, 1820, in the streets of Ravenna, not a hundred paces from the residence of the writer. The circumstances were as described.

Note 31, page 222.

Wondering what next, till the caïque was brought.

The light and elegant wherries plying about the quays of Constantinople are so called.

Note 32, page 222.

From Saint Bartholomew we have saved our skin.

Saint Bartholomew is said to have been flayed alive.

Note 33, page 224.

Prepared for supper with a glass of rum.

In Turkey nothing is more common than for the Mussulmans to take several glasses of strong spirits by way of appetiser. I have seen them take as many as six of raki before dinner, and swear that they dined the better for it: I tried the experiment, but fared like the Scotchman, who, having heard that the birds called kittiwakes were admirable whets, ate six of them, and complained that "he was no hungrier than when he began."

Note 34, page 224.

Splendid but silent, save in one, *where, dropping.*

A common furniture. I recollect being received by Ali Pacha, in a large room, paved with marble, containing a marble basin, and a fountain playing in the centre, &c., &c.

Note 35, page 227.

The gate so splendid was in all its features.

Features of a gate—a ministerial metaphor: "the *feature* upon which this question *hinges.*" See the "Fudge Family," or hear Castlereagh.

Note 36, page 227.

A good deal practised here upon occasion.

A few years ago the wife of Muchtar Pacha complained to his father of his son's supposed infidelity; he asked with whom, and she had the barbarity to give in a list of the twelve handsomest women in Yanina. They were seized, fastened up in sacks, and drowned in the lake the same night. One of the guards who was present informed me, that not one of the victims uttered a cry, or showed a symptom of terror at so sudden a "wrench from all we know, from all we love."

Note 37, page 230.

Though on more thorough-bred *or fairer fingers.*

There is nothing, perhaps, more distinctive of birth than the hand. It is almost the only sign of blood which aristocracy can generate.

Note 38, page 235.

Save Solyman, the glory of their line.

It may not be unworthy of remark, that Bacon, in his essay on "Empire," hints that Solyman was the last of his line; on what authority, I know not. These are his words:—"The destruction of Mustapha was so fatal to Solyman's line; as the succession of the Turks from Solyman until this day is suspected to be untrue, and of strange blood; for that Selymus the Second was thought to be supposititious." But Bacon, in his historical authorities, is often inaccurate. I could give half a dozen instances from his Apophthegms only.

Note 39, page 237.

In his death he was necessarily one of two things by the law.

I say by the *law* of the *land*—the laws of humanity judge more gently; but as the legitimates have always the *law* in their mouths, let them here make the most of it.

Note 40, page 237.

Prove a "moral lesson" to the surviving Sejani of Europe.

From this number must be excepted Canning. Canning is a genius, almost a universal one, an orator, a wit, a poet, a statesman; and no man of talent can long pursue the path of his late predecessor, Lord C. If ever man saved his country, Canning *can*, but *will* he? I, for one, hope so.

Note 41, page 237.

Than the example of heterodox Prelates to Christianity.

When Lord Sandwich said "he did not know the difference between orthodoxy and heterodoxy," Warburton, the bishop, replied, "Orthodoxy, my lord, is *my doxy*, and heterodoxy is *another man's* doxy." A prelate of the present day has discovered, it seems, a *third* kind of doxy, which has not greatly exalted in the eyes of the elect that which Bentham calls "Church-of-Englandism."

Note 42, page 239.

Who lent his lady to his friend Hortensius.

Cato gave up his wife Martia to his friend Hortensius; but, on the death of the latter, took her back again. This conduct was ridiculed by the Romans, who observed, that Martia entered the house of Hortensius very poor, but returned to the bed of Cato loaded with treasures.—Plutarch.

Note 43, page 240.

To those sad hungry jacobins, the worms.

"Your worm is your only emperor for diet: we fat all creatures else, to fat us; and we fat ourselves for maggots. Your fat king, and your lean beggar, is but variable service: two dishes but to one table: that's the end."—*Hamlet.*

Note 44, page 240.

A "Highland welcome" all the wide world over.

See "Waverley."

Note 45, page 240.

In his monastic concubine of snow.

"The blessed Francis, being strongly solicited one day by the emotions of the flesh, pulled off his clothes and scourged himself soundly: being after this inflamed with a wonderful fervour of mind, he plunged his naked body into a great heap of snow. The devil, being overcome, retired immediately, and the holy man returned victorious into his cell."—See Butler's *Lives of the Saints.*

Note 46, page 241.

The tyrant's wish, "that mankind only had."

Caligula—see Suetonius. "Being in a rage at the people, for favouring a party in the Circensian games in opposition to him, he cried out, 'I wish the Roman people had but one neck.'"

Note 47, page 241.

He went forth with the lovely Odalisques.

The ladies of the seraglio.

Note 48, page 242.

Who with the brightest Georgians might compare.

"It is in the adjacent climates of Georgia, Mingrelia, and Circassia, that nature has placed, at least to our eyes, the model of beauty, in the shape of the limbs, the colour of the skin, the symmetry of the features, and the expression of the countenance: the men are formed for action, the women for love."—Gibbon.

Note 49, page 242.

They would prefer to Padisha or Pacha.

Padisha is the Turkish title of the Grand Signior.

Note 50, page 247.

A "wood obscure," like that where Dante found.

Nell' mezzo del' cammin' di nostra vita
Mi ritrovai per una selva oscura," &c.—*Inferno.*

Note 51, page 259.

Was teaching his recruits to use the bayonet.

Fact: Suwaroff did this in person.

Note 52, page 264.

All sounds it pierceth, "Allah! Allah! Hu!"

Allah Hu! is properly the war cry of the Mussulmans, and they dwell on the last syllable, which gives it a wild and peculiar effect.

Note, 53, page 264.

"Carnage," (so Wordsworth tells you) "is God's daughter."

"But *Thy* * most dreaded instrument
In working out a pure intent,
Is man array'd for mutual slaughter;
Yea, *Carnage is thy daughter!*"
Wordsworth's *Thanksgiving Ode.*

Note 54, page 265.

Was printed Grove, *although his name was Grose.*

A fact: see the Waterloo Gazettes. I recollect remarking at the time to a friend:—"*There* is *fame!* a man is killed, his name is Grose, and they print it Grove." I was at college with the deceased, who was a very amiable and clever man, and his society in great request for his wit, gaiety, and "Chansons à boire."

Note 55, page 265.

The antiquarians who can settle time.

See General Valancey and Sir Lawrence Parsons.

Note 56, page 266.

'Tis pity "that such meaning should pave hell."

The Portuguese proverb says that "hell is paved with good intentions."

Note 57, page 266.

By thy humane discovery, Friar Bacon!

Gunpowder is said to have been discovered by this friar.

Note 58, page 274.

That you and I will win St. George's collar.

A Russian military order.

Note 59, page 278.

"*Glory to* God *and to the Empress!*" (Powers
Eternal! such names mingled!) "*Ismail's ours.*"

In the original Russian:—

"Slava bogu! slava vam!
Krepost Vzala y ïä tam;"

a kind of couplet; for he was a poet.

Note 60, page 279.

Humanity would rise, and thunder "Nay!"

Query, *Ney!*—Printer's Devil.

Note 61, page 280.

And "Europe's Liberator"—still enslaved.

Vide Speeches in Parliament, after the battle of Waterloo.

Note 62, page 280.

A slice or two from your luxurious meals.

"I at this time got a post, being for fatigue, with four others. We were sent to break biscuit, and make a mess for Lord Wellington's hounds. I was very hungry, and thought it a good job at the time, as we got our own fill while we broke the biscuit,—a thing I had not got for some days. When thus engaged, the Prodigal Son was never once out of my mind; and I sighed, as I fed the dogs, over my humble situation and my ruined hopes."—*Journal of a Soldier of the 71st Regiment during the War in Spain.*

Note 63, page 281.

"But Heaven," as Cassio says, "is above all."

See Othello.

Note 64, page 282.

That's *an appropriate simile,* that jackall.

In Greece I never saw or heard these animals; but among the ruins of Ephesus I have heard them by hundreds.

Note 65, page 282.

Because he could no more digest his dinner.

He was killed in a conspiracy, after his temper had been exasperated by his extreme costivity to a degree of insanity.

Note 66, page 284.

And had just buried the fair-faced Lanskoi.

He was the grande passion of the grande Catherine. See her Lives, under the head of "Lanskoi."

Note 67, page 285.

Oh thou "teterrima causa" of all "belli."

Hor. Sat. lib. i. sat. iii.

Note 68, page 286.

*Your "fortune" was in a fair way "to swell
A man" (as Giles says).*

"His fortune swells him, it is rank, he's married."—*Sir Giles Overreach;* Massinger's *New Way to pay Old Debts.*

Note 69, page 288.

Of several ribands, and some thousand peasants.

A Russian estate is always valued by the number of the slaves upon it.

Note 70, page 290.

*Even shuffling Southey, that incarnate lie,
Would scarcely join again the "reformadoes."*

"Reformers," or rather "Reformed." The Baron Bradwardine in "Waverley" is authority for the word.

Note 71, page 291.

The Dee, the Don, Balgounie's brig's black wall.

The brig of Don, near the "auld toun" of Aberdeen, with its one arch, and its black deep salmon stream below, is in my memory as yesterday. I still remember, though perhaps I may misquote, the awful proverb which made me pause to cross it, and yet lean over it with a childish delight, being an only son, at least by the mother's side. The saying as recollected by me was this, but I have never heard or seen it since I was nine years of age:—

"Brig of Balgounie, *black's* your *wa',*
Wi' a wife's *ae son,* and a mear's *ae foal,*
Doun ye shall fa'!"

Note 72, page 291.

With his Agrarian *laws, the high estate.*

Tiberius Gracchus, being tribune of the people, demanded in their name the execution of the Agrarian law; by which all persons possessing above a certain number of acres were to be deprived of the surplus for the benefit of the poor citizens.

Note 73, page 291.

But getting nigh grim Dante's "obscure wood."

"Mi retrovai per un selva oscura."—*Inferno,* Canto i.

* To wit, the Deity's: this is perhaps as pretty a pedigree for murder as ever was found out by Garter-King-at-Arms.—What would have been said, had any free-spoken people discovered such a lineage?

NOTE 74, page 292.

Oh for a forty-parson power *to chant.*

A metaphor taken from the "forty-horse power" of a steam-engine. That mad wag, the Reverend Sydney Smith, sitting by a brother clergyman at dinner, observed afterwards that his dull neighbour had a "*twelve-parson power*" of conversation.

NOTE 75, page 292.

To strip the Saxons of their hydes, *like tanners.*

"Hyde."—I believe a hyde of land to be a legitimate word, and, as such, subject to the tax of a quibble.

NOTE 76, page 293.

When, a new Iphigene, she went to Tauris.

The Empress went to the Crimea, accompanied by the Emperor Joseph, in the year—I forget which.

NOTE 77, page 294.

Which gave her dukes the graceless name of "Biron."

In the Empress Anne's time, Biren, her favourite, assumed the name and arms of the "Birons" of France; which families are yet extant with that of England. There are still the daughters of Courland of that name; one of them I remember seeing in England, in the blessed year of the Allies (1814)—the Duchess of S.—to whom the English Duchess of Somerset presented me as a namesake.

NOTE 78, page 295.

Eleven thousand maidenheads of bone,
The greatest number flesh hath ever known.

St. Ursula and her eleven thousand virgins were still extant in 1816, and may be so yet, as much as ever.

NOTE 79, page 302.

So prime, so swell, so nutty, and so knowing?

The advance of science and of language has rendered it unnecessary to translate the above good and true English, spoken in its original purity by the select mobility and their patrons. The following is a stanza of a song which was very popular, at least in my early days:—

"On the high toby-spice flash the muzzle,
In spite of each gallows old scout;
If you at the spellken can't hustle,
You'll be hobbled in making a Clout.

"Then your Blowing will wax gallows haughty,
When she hears of your scaly mistake,
She'll surely turn snitch for the forty—
That her Jack may be regular weight."

If there be any gemman so ignorant as to require a traduction, I refer him to my old friend and corporeal pastor and master, John Jackson, Esq., Professor of Pugilism; who, I trust, still retains the strength and symmetry of his model of a form, together with his good humour, and athletic as well as mental accomplishments.

NOTE 80, page 304.

St. James Palace and St. James's "Hells."

"Hells," gaming-houses. What their number may now be in this life, I know not. Before I was of age I knew them pretty accurately, both "gold" and "silver." I was once nearly called out by an acquaintance, because when he asked me where I thought that his soul would be found hereafter, I answered, "In silver Hell.'

NOTE 81, page 305.

Spirit would name, and therefore even I *won't anent.*

"Anent" was a Scotch phrase meaning "concerning"—"with regard to:" it has been made English by the Scotch novels; and, as the Frenchman said, "If it *be not*, *ought to be* English."

NOTE 82, page 305.

The milliners who furnish "drapery Misses.

"Drapery Misses."—This term is any thing now but a *mystery*. It was, however, almost so to me when I first returned from the East in 1811—1812. It means a pretty, a high-born, a fashionable young female, well instructed by her friends, and furnished by her milliner with a wardrobe upon credit, to be repaid, when married, by the *husband*. The riddle was first read to me by a young and pretty heiress, on my praising the "drapery" of the "*untochered*" but "pretty virginities" (like Mrs. Anne Page) of the *then* day, which has now been some years yesterday: she assured me that the thing was common in London; and as her own thousands, and blooming looks, and rich simplicity of array, put any suspicion in her own case out of the question, I confess I gave some credit to the allegation. If necessary, authorities might be cited; in which case I could quote both "drapery" and the wearers. Let us hope, however, that it is now obsolete.

NOTE 83, page 306.

'T is strange the mind, that very fiery particle.

"Divinæ particulum auræ."

NOTE 84, page 307.

And Centaur Nessus garb of mortal clothing.

"Illita Nesseo tibi texta veneno."—OVID, Epist. ix.

NOTE 85, page 308.

In mind, a sort of sentimental bogle.

Scotch for goblin.

NOTE 86, page 311.

Who rouse the shirtless patriots of Spain?

The Descamisados.

NOTE 87, page 312.

And Mitford in the nineteenth century.

See Mitford's Greece. "Græcia *Verax*." His great pleasure consists in praising tyrants, abusing Plutarch, spelling oddly, and writing quaintly; and what is strange after all, *his* is the best modern history of Greece in any language, and he is perhaps the best of all modern historians whatsoever. Having named his sins, it is but fair to state his virtues—learning, labour, research, wrath, and partiality. I call the latter virtues in a writer, because they make him write in earnest.

NOTE 88, page 313.

A hazy widower turn'd of forty's sure.

This line may puzzle the commentators more than the present generation.

NOTE 89, page 316.

Like Russians rushing from hot baths to snows.

The Russians, as is well known, run out from their hot baths to plunge into the Neva; a pleasant practical antithesis, which it seems does them no harm.

NOTE 90, page 318.

Which flash'd as far as where the musk-bull browses.

For a description and print of this inhabitant of the polar region and native country of the Auroræ Boreales, see Parry's Voyage in search of a North-west Passage.

NOTE 91, page 318.

As Philip's son proposed to do with Athos.

A sculptor projected to hew Mount Athos into a statue of Alexander, with a city in one hand, and, I believe, a river in his pocket, with various other similar devices. But Alexander's gone, and Athos remains, I trust ere long to look over a nation of freemen.

NOTE 92, page 323.

Also there bin another pious reason.

"With every thing that pretty *bin*,
My lady sweet, arise."—SHAKSPEARE.

NOTE 93, page 324.

They and their bills, "*Arcadians both,*" *are left.*

"Arcades ambo."

NOTE 94, page 329.

Or wilder group of savage Salvatore's.

Salvator Rosa.

NOTE 95, page 329.

His bell-mouth'd goblet makes me feel quite Danish.

If I err not, "your Dane" is one of Iago's catalogue of nations "exquisite in their drinking."

NOTE 96, page 331.

Even Nimrod's self might leave the plains of Dura.

In Assyria.

NOTE 97, page 331.

And shine the very Siria *of the spheres.*

Siria, *i.e*, bitch-star.

NOTE 98, page 334.

"*That Scriptures out of church are blasphemies.*"

"Mrs. Adams answered Mr. Adams, that it was blasphemous to talk of Scripture out of church." This dogma was broached to her husband—the best Christian in any book.—See *Joseph Andrews.*

NOTE 99, page 334.

Should have a hook, and a small trout to pull it.

It would have taught him humanity at least. This sentimental savage, whom it is a mode to quote (amongst the novelists) to show their sympathy for innocent sports and old songs, teaches how to sew up frogs, and break their legs by way of experiment, in addition to the art of angling,—the cruelest, the coldest, and the stupidest of pretended sports. They may talk about the beauties of nature, but the angler merely thinks of his dish of fish; he has no leisure to take his eyes from off the streams, and a single *bite* is worth to him more than all the scenery around. Besides, some fish bite best on a rainy day. The whale, the shark, and the tunny fishery have somewhat of noble and perilous in them; even net fishing, trawling, &c., are more humane and useful. But angling!—no angler can be a good man.

"One of the best men I ever knew—as humane, delicate-minded, generous, and excellent a creature as any in the world,—was an angler: true, he angled with painted files, and would have been incapable of the extravagances of I. Walton."

The above addition was made by a friend in reading over the M.S.—"Audi alteram partem."—I leave it to counterbalance my own observation.

NOTE 100, page 339.

And never craned, *and made but few* "faux pas."

Craning.—"To *crane*" is, or was, an expression used to denote a gentleman's stretching out his neck over a hedge, "to look before he leaped;"—a pause in his "vaulting ambition," which in the field doth occasion some delay and execration in those who may be immediately behind the equestrian sceptic. "Sir, if you don't choose to take the leap, let me!"—was a phrase which generally sent the aspirant on again; and to good purpose: for though "the horse and rider" might fall, they made a gap through which, and over him and his steed, the field might follow.

NOTE 101, page 340.

Ask'd next day, "*If men ever hunted* twice?"

See his Letters to his Son.

NOTE 102, page 343.

Go to the coffee-house, and take another.

In Swift's or Horace Walpole's letters I think it is mentioned that somebody, regretting the loss of a friend, was answered by an universal Pylades: "When I lose one, I go to the Saint James's Coffee-house, and take another." I recollect having heard an anecdote of the same kind.—Sir W. D. was a great gamester. Coming in one day to the Club of which he was a member, he was observed to look melancholy. "What is the matter, Sir William?" cried Hare, of facetious memory. "Ah!" replied Sir W., "I have just *lost* poor Lady D."—"*Lost!* What at? *Quinze* or *Hazard?*" was the consolatory rejoinder of the querist.

NOTE 103, page 344.

And I refer you to wise Oxenstiern.

The famous Chancellor Oxenstiern said to his son, on the latter expressing his surprise upon the great effects arising from petty causes in the presumed mystery of politics: "You see by this, my son, with how little wisdom the kingdoms of the world are governed."

NOTE 104, page 345.

Or Swiss Rousseau, cry "Voilà la Pervenche!"

See "La Nouvelle Héloise."

NOTE 105, page 345.

"Beatus ille procul!" *from* "negotiis."

Hor. Epod. Od. ii.

NOTE 106, page 350.

Great Socrates? and Thou, Diviner still.

As it is necessary in these times to avoid ambiguity, I say that I mean, by "Diviner still," CHRIST. If ever God was man—or man God—He was *both.* I never arraigned His creed, but the use—or abuse—made of it. Mr. Canning one day quoted Christianity to sanction negro slavery, and Mr. Wilberforce had little to say in reply. And was Christ crucified, that black men might be scourged? If so, He had better been born a Mulatto, to give both colours an equal chance of freedom, or at least salvation.

NOTE 107, page 352.

When Rapp the Harmonist embargo'd marriage.

This extraordinary and flourishing German colony in America does not entirely exclude matrimony, as the "Shakers" do; but lays such restrictions upon it as prevents more than a certain quantum of births within a certain number of years; which births (as Mr. Hulme observes) generally arrive "in a little flock like those of a farmer's lambs, all within the same month perhaps." These Harmonists (so called from the name of their settlement) are represented as a remarkably flourishing, pious, and quiet people. See the various recent writers on America.

NOTE 108, page 352.

Nor canvass what "*so eminent a hand*" *meant.*

Jacob Tonson, according to Mr. Pope, was accustomed to call his writers "able pens," "persons of honour," and especially "eminent hands." *Vide* Correspondence, &c. &c.

NOTE 109, page 353.

Of Brutus at the pageant of Tiberius.

See Tacitus, b. vi.

Note 110, page 354.

While great Lucullus' Robe triumphal muffles.

A dish "à la Lucullus." This hero, who conquered the East, has left his more extended celebrity to the transplantation of cherries (which he first brought into Europe), and the nomenclature of some very good dishes;—and I am not sure that (barring indigestion) he has not done more service to makind by his cookery than by his conquests. A cherry-tree may weigh against a bloody laurel; besides, he has contrived to earn celebrity from both.

Note 111, page 355.

There's pretty picking in those "petits puits."

"Petits puits d'amour garnis des confitures."—a classical and well known dish for part of the flank of a second course.

Note 112, page 357.

Observe; for that with me's a "sine quâ"

Subauditer "*non;*" omitted for the sake of euphony.

Note 113, page 358.

It makes my blood boil like the springs of Hecla.

Hecla is a famous hot-spring in Iceland.

Note 114, page 358.

"Shall fool me to the top up of my bent."

Hamlet, Act III. sc. ii.

Note 115, page 358.

Like those of the philosopher of Malmsbury.

Hobbes: who, doubting of his own soul, paid that compliment to the souls of other people as to decline their visits, of which he had some apprehension.

Note 116, page 359.

To draw the bow, to ride, and speak the truth.

Xenophon, Cyrop.

Note 117, page 359.

"For this effect defective comes by cause."

Hamlet, Act II. sc. ii.

Note 118, page 360.

If from a shell-fish or from cochineal.

The composition of the old Tyrian purple—whether from a shell-fish, or from cochineal, or from kermes, is still an article of dispute; and even its colour—some say purple, others scarlet: I say nothing.

Note 119, page 364.

Was much consoled by his own repartee.

I think that it *was* a *carpet* on which Diogenes trod, with—"Thus I trample on the pride of Plato!"—"With greater pride," as the other replied. But as *carpets* are *meant* to be trodden upon, my memory probably misgives me, and it might be a robe, or tapestry, or a table-cloth, or some other expensive and uncynical piece of furniture.

Note 120, page 364.

To soothe our ears, lest Italy should fail.

I remember that the mayoress of a provincial town, somewhat surfeited with a similar display from foreign parts, did rather indecorously break through the applauses of an intelligent audience—intelligent, I mean, as to music—for the words, besides being in recondite languages (it was some years before the peace, ere all the world had travelled, and while I was a collegian), were sorely disguised by the performers:—this mayoress, I say, broke out with, "Rot your Italianos! for my part, I loves a simple ballad!" Rossini will go a good way to bring most people to the same opinion some day. Who would imagine that he was to be the successor of Mozart? However, I state this with diffidence, as a liege and loyal admirer of Italian music in general, and of much of Rossini's; but we may say, as the connoisseur did of painting in "The Vicar of Wakefield," that "the picture would be better painted if the painter had taken more pains."

Note 121, page 365.

For Gothic daring shown in English money.

"Ausu Romano, ære Veneto" is the inscription (and well inscribed in this instance) on the sea walls between the Adriatic and Venice. The walls were a republican work of the Venetians; the inscription, I believe, Imperial; and inscribed by Napoleon the *First*. It is time to continue to him that title—there will be a second by and by, "Spes altera mundi," *if he live;* let him not defeat it like his father. But in any case, he will be preferable to Imbéciles. There is a glorious field for him, if he know how to cultivate it.

Note 122, page 365.

"Untying" squires "to fight against the churches;"

"I conjure you, by that which you profess,
(Howe'er you come to know it) answer me:
Though ye *untie* the winds, and let them fight
Against the *churches*."—*Macbeth.*

Note 123, page 368.

"And champion him to the utmost—" he would keep it.

"Rather than so, come, fate, into the list,
And champion me to the utterance."—*Macbeth.*

Note 124, page 370.

They err, 't is merely what is call'd mobility.

In French "*mobilité*." I am not sure that mobility is English; but it is expressive of a quality which rather belongs to other climates, though it is sometimes seen to a great extent in our own. It may be defined as an excessive susceptibility of immediate impressions—at the same time without *losing* the past: and is, though sometimes apparently useful to the possessor, a most painful and unhappy attribute.

Note 125, page 370.

Draperied her form with curious felicity!

"Curiosa felicitas."—Petronius Arbiter.

Note 126, page 371.

A noise like to wet fingers drawn on glass.

See the account of the ghost of the uncle of Prince Charles of Saxony, raised by Schroepfer—"Karl—Karl—was wollst du mit mich?"

A DRAMATIC POEM.

"There are more things in heaven and earth, Horatio,
Than are dreamt of in your philosophy."

Dramatis Personæ.

MANFRED.
CHAMOIS HUNTER.
ABBOT OF ST. MAURICE.
MANUEL.
HERMAN.

WITCH OF THE ALPS.
ARIMANES.
NEMESIS.
THE DESTINIES.
SPIRITS, &c.

The scene of the Drama is amongst the Higher Alps —partly in the Castle of Manfred, and partly in the Mountains.

MANFRED.

ACT I.

SCENE I.

MANFRED *alone.—Scene, a Gothic Gallery.—Time, Midnight.*

Man. THE lamp must be replenish'd, but even then
It will not burn so long as I must watch:
My slumbers—if I slumber—are not sleep,
But a continuance of enduring thought,
Which then I can resist not: in my heart
There is a vigil, and these eyes but close
To look within; and yet I live, and bear
The aspect and the form of breathing men.
But grief should be the instructor of the wise;
Sorrow is knowledge: they who know the most
Must mourn the deepest o'er the fatal truth,
The Tree of Knowledge is not that of Life.
Philosophy and science, and the springs
Of wonder, and the wisdom of the world,
I have essay'd, and in my mind there is
A power to make these subject to itself—
But they avail not: I have done men good,
And I have met with good even among men—
But this avail'd not: I have had my foes,
And none have baffled, many fallen before me—
But this avail'd not:—Good, or evil, life,
Powers, passions, all I see in other beings,
Have been to me as rain unto the sands,
Since that all-nameless hour. I have no dread,
And feel the curse to have no natural fear,
Nor fluttering throb, that beats with hopes or wishes,
Or lurking love of something on the earth.—
Now to my task.—
Mysterious Agency!
Ye spirits of the unbounded Universe!
Whom I have sought in darkness and in light—
Ye, who do compass earth about, and dwell
In subtler essence—ye, to whom the tops
Of mountains inaccessible are haunts,
And earth's and ocean's caves familiar things—
I call upon ye by the written charm
Which gives me power upon you——Rise! appear!
[*A pause.*
They come not yet.—Now by the voice of him
Who is the first among you—by this sign,
Which makes you tremble—by the claims of him
Who is undying,—Rise! appear!——Appear!
[*A pause.*
If it be so.—Spirits of earth and air,
Ye shall not thus elude me: by a power,
Deeper than all yet urged, a tyrant-spell,
Which had its birthplace in a star condemn'd,
The burning wreck of a demolish'd world,
A wandering hell in the eternal space;
By the strong curse which is upon my soul,
The thought which is within me and around me,
I do compel ye to my will.—Appear!
[*A star is seen at the darker end of the gallery: it is stationary; and a voice is heard singing.*

FIRST SPIRIT.

Mortal! to thy bidding bow'd,
From my mansion in the cloud,
Which the breath of twilight builds,
And the summer's sunlight gilds
With the azure and vermilion,
Which is mix'd for my pavilion;
Though thy quest may be forbidden,
On a star-beam I have ridden;
To thine adjuration bow'd,
Mortal! be thy wish avow'd!

Voice of the SECOND SPIRIT.

Mont Blanc is the monarch of mountains:
They crown'd him long ago
On a throne of rocks, in a robe of clouds,
With a diadem of snow.
Around his waist are forests braced,
The Avalanche in his hand;
But ere it fall, that thundering ball
Must pause for my command.
The Glacier's cold and restless mass
Moves onward day by day;
But I am he who bids it pass,
Or with its ice delay.
I am the spirit of the place,
Could make the mountain bow
And quiver to his cavern'd base—
And what with me wouldst *Thou*?

Voice of the THIRD SPIRIT.

In the blue depth of the waters,
Where the wave hath no strife,
Where the wind is a stranger,
And the sea-snake hath life,
Where the Mermaid is decking
Her green hair with shells;
Like the storm on the surface
Came the sound of thy spells;
O'er my calm Hall of Coral
The deep echo roll'd—
To the Spirit of Ocean
Thy wishes unfold!

FOURTH SPIRIT.

Where the slumbering earthquake
Lies pillow'd on fire,

And the lakes of bitumen
 Rise boilingly higher;
Where the roots of the Andes
 Strike deep in the earth,
As their summits to heaven
 Shoot soaringly forth;
I have quitted my birthplace,
 Thy bidding to bide—
Thy spell hath subdued me,
 Thy will be my guide!

FIFTH SPIRIT.

I am the Rider of the wind,
 The Stirrer of the storm;
The hurricane I left behind
 Is yet with lightning warm;
To speed to thee, o'er shore and sea
 I swept upon the blast:
The fleet I met sail'd well, and yet
 'T will sink ere night be past.

SIXTH SPIRIT.

My dwelling is the shadow of the night,
Why doth thy magic torture me with light?

SEVENTH SPIRIT.

The star which rules thy destiny
Was ruled, ere earth began, by me:
It was a world as fresh and fair
As e'er revolved round sun in air;
Its course was free and regular,
Space bosom'd not a lovelier star.
The hour arrived—and it became
A wandering mass of shapeless flame,
A pathless comet, and a curse,
The menace of the universe;
Still rolling on with innate force,
Without a sphere, without a course,
A bright deformity on high,
The monster of the upper sky!
And thou! beneath its influence born—
Thou worm! whom I obey and scorn—
Forced by a power (which is not thine,
And lent thee but to make thee mine)
For this brief moment to descend,
Where these weak spirits round thee bend
And parley with a thing like thee—
What wouldst thou, Child of Clay! with me?

The SEVEN SPIRITS.

Earth, ocean, air, night, mountains, winds, thy star,
 Are at thy beck and bidding, Child of Clay!
Before thee at thy quest their spirits are—
 What wouldst thou with us, son of mortals—say?

Man. Forgetfulness——
First Spirit. Of what—of whom—and why?
Man. Of that which is within me; read it there—
Ye know it, and I cannot utter it.
Spirit. We can but give thee that which we possess:
Ask of us subjects, sovereignty, the power
O'er earth, the whole, or portion, or a sign
Which shall control the elements, whereof
We are the dominators, each and all,
These shall be thine.
Man. Oblivion, self-oblivion—
Can ye not wring from out the hidden realms
Ye offer so profusely what I ask?
Spirit. It is not in our essence, in our skill;
But—thou may'st die.
Man. Will death bestow it on me?
Spirit. We are immortal, and do not forget;
We are eternal; and to us the past
Is, as the future, present. Art thou answer'd?
Man. Ye mock me—but the power which brought ye here
Hath made you mine. Slaves, scoff not at my will!
The mind, the spirit, the Promethean spark,
The lightning of my being, is as bright,
Pervading, and far-darting as your own,
And shall not yield to yours, though coop'd in clay!
Answer, or I will teach you what I am.
Spirit. We answer as we answer'd; our reply
Is even in thine own words.
Man. Why say ye so?
Spirit. If, as thou say'st, thine essence be as ours,
We have replied in telling thee, the thing
Mortals call death hath nought to do with us.
Man. I then have call'd ye from your realms in vain;
Ye cannot, or ye will not, aid me.
Spirit. Say;
What we possess we offer; it is thine:
Bethink ere thou dismiss us, ask again—
Kingdom, and sway, and strength, and length of days——
Man. Accursed! what have I to do with days?
They are too long already.—Hence—begone!
Spirit. Yet pause: being here, our will would do thee service;
Bethink thee, is there then no other gift
Which we can make not worthless in thine eyes?
Man. No, none; yet stay—one moment, ere we part—
I would behold ye face to face. I hear
Your voices, sweet and melancholy sounds,
As music on the waters; and I see
The steady aspect of a clear large star;
But nothing more. Approach me as ye are,
Or one, or all, in your accustom'd forms.
Spirit. We have no forms beyond the elements
Of which we are the mind and principle:
But choose a form—in that we will appear.
Man. I have no choice; there is no form on earth
Hideous or beautiful to me. Let him,
Who is most powerful of ye, take such aspect
As unto him may seem most fitting—Come!

Seventh Spirit. (*Appearing in the shape of a beautiful female figure.*) Behold!

Man. Oh God! if it be thus, and *thou*
Are not a madness and a mockery,
I yet might be most happy. I will clasp thee,
And we again will be—— [*The figure vanishes*
My heart is crush'd.
[MANFRED *falls senseless*

A Voice is heard in the Incantation which follows.)

When the moon is on the wave,
And the glow-worm in the grass,
And the meteor on the grave,
And the wisp on the morass;
When the falling stars are shooting,
And the answer'd owls are hooting,
And the silent leaves are still
In the shadow of the hill,
Shall my soul be upon thine,
With a power and with a sign.

Though thy slumber may be deep,
Yet thy spirit shall not sleep;
There are shades which will not vanish,
There are thoughts thou canst not banish;
By a power to thee unknown,
Thou canst never be alone;
Thou art wrapt as with a shroud,
Thou art gather'd in a cloud;
And for ever shalt thou dwell
In the spirit of this spell.
Though thou seest me not pass by
Thou shalt feel me with thine eye
As a thing that, though unseen,
Must be near thee, and hath been;
And when in that secret dread
Thou hast turn'd around thy head,
Thou shalt marvel I am not
As thy shadow on the spot,
And the power which thou dost feel
Shall be what thou must conceal.

And a magic voice and verse
Hath baptized thee with a curse;
And a spirit of the air
Hath begirt thee with a snare;
In the wind there is a voice
Shall forbid thee to rejoice;
And to thee shall Night deny
All the quiet of her sky;
And the day shall have a sun,
Which shall make thee wish it done.

From thy false tears I did distil
An essence which hath strength to kill;
From thy own heart I then did wring
The black blood in its blackest spring;
From thy own smile I snatch'd the snake,
For there it coil'd as in a brake;
From thy own lip I drew the charm
Which gave all these their chiefest harm;
In proving every poison known,
I found the strongest was thine own.

By thy cold breast and serpent smile,
By thy unfathom'd gulfs of guile,
By that most seeming virtuous eye,
By thy shut soul's hypocrisy;
By the perfection of thine art
Which pass'd for human thine own heart;
By thy delight in others' pain,
And by thy brotherhood of Cain,
I call upon thee! and compel
Thyself to be thy proper Hell!

And on thy head I pour the vial
Which doth devote thee to this trial;
Nor to slumber, nor to die,
Shall be in thy destiny;
Though thy death shall still seem near
To thy wish, but as a fear;
Lo! the spell now works around thee,
And the clankless chain hath bound thee;
O'er thy heart and brain together
Hath the word been pass'd—now wither!

SCENE II.

The Mountain of the Jungfrau.—Time, Morning.—
MANFRED *alone upon the Cliffs.*

Man. The spirits I have raised abandon me—
The spells which I have studied baffle me—
The remedy I reck'd of tortured me;
I lean no more on superhuman aid,
It hath no power upon the past, and for
The future, till the past be gulf'd in darkness,
It is not of my search.—My mother Earth!
And thou fresh breaking Day, and you, ye Mountains,
Why are ye beautiful? I cannot love ye.
And thou, the bright eye of the universe,
That openest over all, and unto all
Art a delight—thou shin'st not on my heart.
And you, ye crags, upon whose extreme edge
I stand, and on the torrent's brink beneath
Behold the tall pines dwindled as to shrubs
In dizziness of distance; when a leap,
A stir, a motion, even a breath, would bring
My breast upon its rocky bosom's bed
To rest for ever—wherefore do I pause?
I feel the impulse—yet I do not plunge;
I see the peril—yet do not recede;
And my brain reels—and yet my foot is firm:
There is a power upon me which withholds,
And makes it my fatality to live;
If it be life to wear within myself
This barrenness of spirit, and to be
My own soul's sepulchre, for I have ceased
To justify my deeds unto myself—
The last infirmity of evil. Ay,
Thou wingèd and cloud-cleaving minister,
[*An eagle passes*
Whose happy flight is highest into heaven,
Well may'st thou swoop so near me—I should be
Thy prey, and gorge thine eaglets; thou art gone
Where the eye cannot follow thee; but thine
Yet pierces downward, onward, or above,

With a pervading vision.—Beautiful!
How beautiful is all this visible world!
How glorious in its action and itself!
But we, who name ourselves its sovereigns, we,
Half dust, half deity, alike unfit
To sink or soar, with our mix'd essence, make
A conflict of its elements, and breathe
The breath of degradation and of pride,
Contending with low wants and lofty will,
Till our mortality predominates,
And men are—what they name not to themselves,
And trust not to each other. Hark! the note,
[*The Shepherd's pipe in the distance is heard.*
The natural music of the mountain reed—
For here the patriarchal days are not
A pastoral fable—pipes in the liberal air,
Mix'd with the sweet bells of the sauntering herd;
My soul would drink those echoes.—Oh, that I were
The viewless spirit of a lovely sound,
A living voice, a breathing harmony,
A bodiless enjoyment—born and dying
With the blest tone which made me!

Enter from below a CHAMOIS HUNTER.

Chamois Hunter. Even so
This way the chamois leapt: her nimble feet
Have baffled me; my gains to-day will scarce
Repay my break-neck travail.—What is here?
Who seems not of my trade, and yet hath reach'd
A height which none even of our mountaineers,
Save our best hunters, may attain: his garb
Is goodly, his mien manly, and his air
Proud as a freeborn peasant's, at this distance—
I will approach him nearer.

Man. (not perceiving the other). To be thus—
Gray-hair'd with anguish, like these blasted pines,
Wrecks of a single winter, barkless, branchless,
A blighted trunk upon a cursed root,
Which but supplies a feeling to decay—
And to be thus, eternally but thus,
Having been otherwise! Now furrow'd o'er
With wrinkles, plough'd by moments, not by years
And hours—all tortured into ages—hours
Which I outlive!—Ye toppling crags of ice!
Ye avalanches, whom a breath draws down
In mountainous o'erwhelming, come and crush me!
I hear ye momently above, beneath,
Crash with a frequent conflict; but ye pass,
And only fall on things that still would live;
On the young flourishing forest, or the hut
And hamlet of the harmless villager.

C. Hun. The mists begin to rise from up the valley;
I'll warn him to descend, or he may chance
To lose at once his way and life together.

Man. The mists boil up around the glaciers; clouds
Rise curling fast beneath me, white and sulphury,
Like foam from the roused ocean of deep Hell,
Whose every wave breaks on a living shore,
Heap'd with the damn'd like pebbles.—I am giddy.

C. Hun. I must approach him cautiously; if near,
A sudden step will startle him, and he
Seems tottering already.

Man. Mountains have fallen,
Leaving a gap in the clouds, and with the shock
Rocking their Alpine brethren; filling up
The ripe green valleys with destruction's splinters;
Damming the rivers with a sudden dash,
Which crush'd the waters into mist, and made
Their fountains find another channel—Thus,
Thus, in its old age, did Mount Rosenberg—
Why stood I not beneath it?

C. Hun. Friend! have a care,
Your next step may be fatal!—for the love
Of Him who made you, stand not on that brink!

Man. (not hearing him). Such would have been for me a fitting tomb;
My bones had then been quiet in their depth:
They had not then been strewn upon the rocks
For the wind's pastime—as thus—thus they shall be—
In this one plunge.—Farewell, ye opening heavens!
Look not upon me thus reproachfully—
You were not meant for me—Earth! take these atoms!

[*As* MANFRED *is in act to spring from the cliff, the* CHAMOIS HUNTER *seizes and retains him with a sudden grasp.*]

C. Hun. Hold, madman!—though aweary of thy life,
Stain not our pure vales with thy guilty blood—
Away with me——I will not quit my hold.

Man. I am most sick at heart—nay, grasp me not—
I am all feebleness—the mountains whirl
Spinning around me——I grow blind——What art thou?

C. Hun. I'll answer that anon.—Away with me——
The clouds grow thicker——there—now lean on me—
Place your foot here—here, take this staff, and cling
A moment to that shrub—now give me your hand,
And hold fast by my girdle—softly—well—
The Chalet will be gain'd within an hour—
Come on, we'll quickly find a surer footing,

And something like a pathway, which the torrent
Hath wash'd since winter.—Come, 'tis bravely done—
You should have been a hunter.—Follow me.
[*As they descend the rocks with difficulty, the scene closes.*]

ACT II.

SCENE I.

A Cottage amongst the Bernese Alps.

MANFRED *and the* CHAMOIS HUNTER.

C. Hun. No, no—yet pause—thou must not yet go forth:
Thy mind and body are alike unfit
To trust each other, for some hours, at least;
When thou art better, I will be thy guide—
But whither?
Man. It imports not: I do know
My route full well, and need no further guidance.
C. Hun. Thy garb and gait bespeak thee of high lineage—
One of the many chiefs, whose castled crags
Look o'er the lower valleys—which of these
May call thee lord? I only know their portals;
My way of life leads me but rarely down
To bask by the huge hearths of those old halls,
Carousing with the vassals; but the paths,
Which step from out our mountains to their doors,
I know from childhood—which of these is thine?
Man. No matter

C. Hun. Well, sir, pardon me the question,
And be of better cheer. Come, taste my wine;
T is of an ancient vintage: many a day
'T has thaw'd my veins among our glaciers, now
Let it do thus for thine—Come pledge me fairly.

Man. Away, away! there 's blood upon the brim!
Will it then never—never sink in the earth?

C. Hun. What dost thou mean? thy senses wander from thee.

Man. I say 't is blood—my blood! the pure warm stream
Which ran in the veins of my fathers, and in ours
When we were in our youth, and had one heart,
And loved each other as we should not love,
And this was shed: but still it rises up,
Colouring the clouds, that shut me out from heaven,
Where thou art not—and I shall never be.

C. Hun. Man of strange words, and some half-maddening sin,
Which makes thee people vacancy, whate'er
Thy dread and sufferance be, there 's comfort yet—
The aid of holy men, and heavenly patience——

Man. Patience and patience! Hence—that word was made
For brutes of burthen, not for birds of prey;
Preach it to mortals of a dust like thine,—
I am not of thine order.

C. Hun. Thanks to Heaven!
I would not be of thine for the free fame
Of William Tell: but whatsoe'er thine ill,
It must be borne, and these wild starts are useless.

Man. Do I not bear it?—Look on me—I live.

C. Hun. This is convulsion, and no healthful life.

Man. I tell thee, man! I have lived many years,
Many long years, but they are nothing now
To those which I must number: ages—ages—
Space and eternity—and consciousness,
With the fierce thirst of death—and still unslaked!

C. Hun. Why, on thy brow the seal of middle age
Hath scarce been set, I am thine elder far.

Man. Think'st thou existence doth depend on time?
It doth; but actions are our epochs: mine
Have made my days and nights imperishable,
Endless, and all alike, as sands on the shore,
Innumerable atoms; and one desert,
Barren and cold, on which the wild waves break,
But nothing rests, save carcasses and wrecks,
Rocks, and the salt-surf weeds of bitterness.

C. Hun. Alas! he 's mad—but yet I must not leave him.

Man. I would I were—for then the things I see
Would be but a distemper'd dream.

C. Hun. What is it
That thou dost see, or think thou look'st upon?

Man. Myself, and thee—a peasant of the Alps—
Thy humble virtues, hospitable home,
And spirit patient, pious, proud, and free;
Thy self respect, grafted on innocent thoughts;
Thy days of health, and nights of sleep; thy toils,
By danger dignified, yet guiltless; hopes
Of cheerful old age and a quiet grave,
With cross and garland over its green turf,
And thy grandchildren's love for epitaph;
This do I see—and then I look within—
It matters not—my soul was scorch'd already!

C. Hun. And would'st thou then exchange thy lot for mine?

Man. No, friend! I would not wrong thee, nor exchange
My lot with living being: I can bear—
However wretchedly, 't is still to bear—
In life what others could not brook to dream,
But perish in their slumber.

C. Hun. And with this—
This cautious feeling for another's pain,
Canst thou be black with evil?—say not so.
Can one of gentle thoughts have wreak'd revenge
Upon his enemies?

Man. Oh! no, no, no!
My injuries came down on those who loved me—
On those whom I best loved: I never quell'd
An enemy, save in my just defence—
But my embrace was fatal!

C. Hun. Heaven give thee rest!
And penitence restore thee to thyself;
My prayers shall be for thee.

Man. I need them not,
But can endure thy pity. I depart—
'T is time—farewell!—Here 's gold, and thanks for thee—
No words—it is thy due.—Follow me not,
I know my path—the mountain peril 's past:—
And once again, I charge thee, follow not!

[*Exit* MANFRED.

SCENE II.

A lower Valley in the Alps.—A Cataract.

Enter MANFRED.

It is not noon—the sunbows rays still arch [1]
The torrent with the many hues of heaven,
And roll the sheeted silver's waving column
O'er the crag's headlong perpendicular,
And fling its lines of foaming light along,
And to and fro, like the pale courser's tail,
The Giant steed, to be bestrode by Death,
As told in the Apocalypse. No eyes
But mine now drink this sight of loveliness;
I should be sole in this sweet solitude,
And with the Spirit of the place divide
The homage of these waters.—I will call her.

[MANFRED *takes some of the water into the palm of his hand, and flings it in the air, muttering the adjuration. After a pause, the* WITCH OF THE ALPS *rises beneath the arch of the sunbow of the torrent.*

Beautiful Spirit! with thy hair of light,
And dazzling eyes of glory, in whose form
The charms of earth's least mortal daughters grow
To an unearthly stature, in an essence
Of purer elements; while the hues of youth,—

Carnation'd like a sleeping infant's cheek,
Rock'd by the beating of her mother's heart,
Or the rose tints, which summer's twilight leaves
Upon the lofty glacier's virgin snow,
The blush of earth, embracing with her heaven,—
Tinge thy celestial aspect, and make tame

The beauties of the sunbow which bends o'er thee.
Beautiful Spirit! in thy calm clear brow,
Wherein is glass'd serenity of soul,
Which of itself shows immortality,
I read that thou wilt pardon to a Son
Of Earth, whom the abstruser powers permit
At times to commune with them—if that he
Avail him of his spells—to call thee thus,
And gaze on thee a moment.

Witch. Son of Earth!
I know thee, and the powers which give thee power;
I know thee for a man of many thoughts,
And deeds of good and ill, extreme in both,
Fatal and fated in thy sufferings.
I have expected this—what would'st thou with me?

Man. To look upon thy beauty—nothing further.
The face of the earth hath madden'd me, and I
Take refuge in her mysteries, and pierce
To the abodes of those who govern her—
But they can nothing aid me. I have sought
From them what they could not bestow, and now
I search no further.

Witch. What could be the quest
Which is not in the power of the most powerful,
The rulers of the invisible?

Man. A boon;
But why should I repeat it? 't were in vain.

Witch. I know not that; let thy lips utter it.

Man. Well, though it torture me, 't is but the same;
My pang shall find a voice. From my youth upwards
My spirit walk'd not with the souls of men,
Nor look'd upon the earth with human eyes;
The thirst of their ambition was not mine,
The aim of their existence was not mine;
My joys, my griefs, my passions, and my powers,
Made me a stranger; though I wore the form,
I had no sympathy with breathing flesh,
Nor midst the creatures of clay that girded me
Was there but one who——but of her anon.
I said, with men, and with the thoughts of men,
I held but slight communion; but instead,
My joy was in the Wilderness, to breathe
The difficult air of the iced mountain's top,
Where the birds dare not build, nor insects wing
Flit o'er the herbless granite; or to plunge
Into the torrent, and to roll along
On the swift whirl of the new breaking wave
Of river-stream, or ocean, in their flow.
In these my early strength exulted; or
To follow through the night the moving moon,
The stars and their development; or catch
The dazzling lightnings till my eyes grew dim;
Or to look, list'ning, on the scatter'd leaves,
While Autumn winds were at their evening song.
These were my pastimes, and to be alone;
For if the beings, of whom I was one,—
Hating to be so,—crossed me in my path,
I felt myself degraded back to them,
And was all clay again. And then I dived,
In my lone wanderings, to the caves of death,
Searching its cause in its effect; and drew
From wither'd bones, and skulls, and heap'd up dust,
Conclusions most forbidden. Then I pass'd
The nights of years in sciences untaught,
Save in the old time; and with time and toil,
And terrible ordeal, and such penance
As in itself hath power upon the air,
And spirits that do compass air and earth,
Space, and the peopled infinite, I made
Mine eyes familiar with Eternity,
Such as, before me, did the Magi, and
He who from out their fountain dwellings raised
Eros and Anteros,[2] at Gadara,
As I do thee;—and with my knowledge grew
The thirst of knowledge, and the power and joy
Of this most bright intelligence, until——

Witch. Proceed.

Man. Oh! I but thus prolong my words
Boasting these idle attributes, because
As I approach the core of my heart's grief—
But to my task. I have not named to thee
Father or mother, mistress, friend, or being,
With whom I wore the chain of human ties;
If I had such, they seem'd not such to me—
Yet there was one——

Witch. Spare not thyself—proceed.

Man. She was like me in lineaments—her eyes,
Her hair, her features, all, to the very tone
Even of her voice, they said were like to mine;
But soften'd all, and temper'd into beauty:
She had the same lone thoughts and wanderings,
The quest of hidden knowledge, and a mind
To comprehend the universe: nor these
Alone, but with them gentler powers than mine,
Pity, and smiles, and tears—which I had not;
And tenderness—but that I had for her;
Humility—and that I never had.
Her faults were mine—her virtues were her own—
I loved her, and destroy'd her!

Witch. With thy hand?

Man. Not with my hand, but heart—which broke her heart—
It gazed on mine, and wither'd. I have shed
Blood, but not hers—and yet her blood was shed—
I saw—and could not stanch it.

Witch. And for this—
A being of the race thou dost despise,
The order which thine own would rise above,

Mingling with us and ours, thou dost forego
The gifts of our great knowledge, and shrink'st back
To recreant mortality——Away!

Man. Daughter of Air! I tell thee, since that hour—
But words are breath—look on me in my sleep,
Or watch my watchings—Come and sit by me!
My solitude is solitude no more,
But peopled with the Furies;—I have gnash'd
My teeth in darkness till returning morn,
Then cursed myself till sunset;—I have pray'd
For madness as a blessing—'tis denied me.
I have affronted death—but in the war
Of elements the waters shrunk from me,
And fatal things pass'd harmless—the cold hand
Of an all-pitiless demon held me back,
Back by a single hair, which would not break.
In fantasy, imagination, all
The affluence of my soul—which one day was
A Crœsus in creation—I plunged deep,
But, like an ebbing wave, it dash'd me back
Into the gulf of my unfathom'd thought.
I plunged amidst mankind—Forgetfulness
I sought in all, save where 't is to be found,
And that I have to learn—my sciences,
My long pursued and superhuman art,
Is mortal here—I dwell in my despair—
And live—and live for ever.

Witch. It may be
That I can aid thee.

Man. To do this thy power
Must wake the dead, or lay me low with them.
Do so—in any shape—in any hour—
With any torture—so it be the last.

Witch. That is not in my province; but if thou
Wilt swear obedience to my will, and do
My bidding, it may help thee to thy wishes.

Man. I will not swear—Obey! and whom? the spirits
Whose presence I command, and be the slave
Of those who served me—Never!

Witch. Is this all?
Has thou no gentler answer?—Yet bethink thee,
And pause ere thou rejectest.

Man. I have said it.

Witch. Enough!—I may retire then—say!

Man. Retire!

[*The* WITCH *disappears.*

Man. (alone). We are the fools of time and terror: Days
Steal on us and steal from us; yet we live,
Loathing our life, and dreading still to die.
In all the days of this detested yoke—
This vital weight upon the struggling heart,
Which sinks with sorrow, or beats quick with pain,
Or joy that ends in agony or faintness—
In all the days of past and future, for
In life there is no present, we can number
How few—how less than few—wherein the soul
Forbears to pant for death, and yet draws back
As from a stream in winter, though the chill
Be but a moment's. I have one resource
Still in my science—I can call the dead,
And ask them what it is we dread to be:
The sternest answer can but be the Grave,
And that is nothing—if they answer not—
The buried Prophet answer'd to the Hag
Of Endor; and the Spartan Monarch drew
From the Byzantine maid's unsleeping spirit
An answer and his destiny—he slew
That which he loved, unknowing what he slew,
And died unpardon'd—though he call'd in aid
The Phyxian Jove, and in Phigalia roused
The Arcadian Evocators to compel
The indignant shadow to depose her wrath,
Or fix her term of vengeance—she replied
In words of dubious import, but fulfill'd.[3]
If I had never lived, that which I love
Had still been living; had I never loved,
That which I love would still be beautiful—
Happy and giving happiness. What is she?
What is she now?—a sufferer for my sins—
A thing I dare not think upon—or nothing.
Within few hours I shall not call in vain—
Yet in this hour I dread the thing I dare:
Until this hour I never shrunk to gaze
On spirit, good or evil—now I tremble,
And feel a strange cold thaw upon my heart.
But I can act even what I most abhor,
And champion human fears.—The night approaches.

[*Exit.*

SCENE III.

The Summit of the Jungfrau Mountain.

Enter FIRST DESTINY.

The moon is rising broad, and round, and bright;
And here on snows, where never human foot
Of common mortal trod, we nightly tread,
And leave no traces; o'er the savage sea,
The glassy ocean of the mountain ice,
We skim its rugged breakers, which put on
The aspect of a tumbling tempest's foam,
Frozen in a moment—a dead whirlpool's image:
And this most steep fantastic pinnacle,
The fretwork of some earthquake—where the clouds
Pause to repose themselves in passing by—
Is sacred to our revels, or our vigils;
Here do I wait my sisters, on our way
To the Hall of Arimanes, for to-night
Is our great festival—'t is strange they come not.

A Voice without, singing.

The Captive Usurper,
Hurl'd down from the throne,
Lay buried in torpor,
Forgotten and lone;
I broke through his slumbers,
I shiver'd his chain,
I leagued him with numbers—
He's Tyrant again!
With the blood of a million he'll answer my care,
With a nation's destruction—his flight and despair.

Second Voice, without.

The ship sail'd on, the ship sail'd fast,
But I left not a sail, and I left not a mast;
There is not a plank of the hull or the deck,
And there is not a wretch to lament o'er his wreck;
Save one, whom I held, as he swam, by the hair,
And he was a subject well worthy my care;
A traitor on land, and a pirate at sea—
But I saved him to wreak further havoc for me!

FIRST DESTINY, *answering.*

The city lies sleeping;
The morn, to deplore it,
May dawn on it weeping:
Sullenly, slowly,
The black plague flew o'er it—
Thousands lie lowly;
Tens of thousands shall perish—
The living shall fly from
The sick they shall cherish;
But nothing can vanquish
The touch that they die from.
Sorrow and anguish,
And evil and dread,
Envelope a nation—
The blest are the dead,
Who see not the sight
Of their own desolation—
This work of a night—
This wreck of a realm—this deed of my doing—
For ages I've done, and shall still be renewing!

Enter the SECOND *and* THIRD DESTINIES.

The Three.

Our hands contain the hearts of men,
Our footsteps are their graves;
We only give to take again
The spirits of our slaves!

First Des. Welcome!—Where's Nemesis?
Second Des. At some great work;
But what I know not, for my hands were full.
Third Des. Behold she cometh.

Enter NEMESIS.

First Des. Say, where hast thou been?
My sisters and thyself are slow to-night.
Nem. I was detain'd repairing shatter'd thrones,
Marrying fools, restoring dynasties,
Avenging men upon their enemies,
And making them repent their own revenge;
Goading the wise to madness; from the dull
Shaping out oracles to rule the world
Afresh, for they were waxing out of date,
And mortals dared to ponder for themselves,
To weigh kings in the balance, and to speak
Of freedom, the forbidden fruit.—Away!
We have outstay'd the hour—mount we our clouds!
[*Exeunt.*

SCENE IV.

The Hall of Arimanes—Arimanes on his Throne, a Globe of Fire, surrounded by the Spirits.

Hymn of the SPIRITS.

Hail to our Master!—Prince of Earth and Air!
Who walks the clouds and waters—in his hand
The sceptre of the elements, which tear
Themselves to chaos at his high command!
He breatheth—and a tempest shakes the sea;
He speaketh—and the clouds reply in thunder;
He gazeth—from his glance the sunbeams flee;
He moveth—earthquakes rend the world asunder.
Beneath his footsteps the volcanoes rise;
His shadow is the Pestilence; his path
The comets herald through the crackling skies;
And planets turn to ashes at his wrath.
To him War offers daily sacrifice;
To him Death pays his tribute; Life is his,
With all its infinite of agonies—
And his the spirit of whatever is!

Enter the DESTINIES *and* NEMESIS.

First Des. Glory to Arimanes! on the earth
His power increaseth—both my sisters did
His bidding, nor did I neglect my duty!
Second Des. Glory to Arimanes! we who bow
The necks of men, bow down before his throne!
Third Des. Glory to Arimanes! we await
His nod!
Nem. Sovereign of Sovereigns! we are thine,
And all that liveth, more or less, is ours,
And most things wholly so; still to increase
Our power, increasing thine, demands our care,
And we are vigilant—Thy late commands
Have been fulfill'd to the utmost.

Enter MANFRED.

A Spirit. What is here?
A mortal!—Thou most rash and fatal wretch,
Bow down and worship!
Second Spirit. I do know the man—
A Magian of great power, and fearful skill!
Third Spirit. Bow down, and worship, slave!—
What, know'st thou not
Thine and our Sovereign?—Tremble and obey!

All the Spirits. Prostrate thyself, and thy condemned clay,
Child of the Earth! or dread the worst.
Man. I know it;
And yet ye see I kneel not.
Fourth Spirit. 'Twill be taught thee.
Man. 'Tis taught already;—many a night on the earth,
On the bare ground, have I bow'd down my face,
And strew'd my head with ashes; I have known
The fulness of humiliation, for
I sunk before my vain despair, and knelt
To my own desolation.
Fifth Spirit. Dost thou dare
Refuse to Arimanes on his throne
What the whole earth accords, beholding not
The terror of his Glory?—Crouch! I say.
Man. Bid *him* bow down to that which is above him,
The overruling Infinite—the Maker
Who made him not for worship—let him kneel,
And we will kneel together.
The Spirits. Crush the worm!
Tear him in pieces!—
First Des. Hence! Avaunt!—he's mine,
Prince of the Powers invisible! This man
Is of no common order, as his port
And presence here denote; his sufferings
Have been of an immortal nature, like
Our own; his knowledge, and his powers and will,
As far as is compatible with clay,
Which clogs the ethereal essence, have been such
As clay hath seldom borne; his aspirations
Have been beyond the dwellers of the earth,
And they have only taught him what we know—
That knowledge is not happiness, and science
But an exchange of ignorance for that
Which is another kind of ignorance.
This is not all—the passions, attributes
Of earth and heaven, from which no power, nor being,
Nor breath from the worm upwards, is exempt,
Have pierced his heart; and in their consequence
Made him a thing, which I, who pity not,
Yet pardon those who pity. He is mine,
And thine, it may be—be it so, or not,
No other Spirit in this region hath
A soul like his—or power upon his soul.
Nem. What doth he here then?
First Des. Let him answer that.
Man. Ye know what I have known; and without power
I could not be amongst ye: but there are
Powers deeper still beyond—I come in quest
Of such, to answer unto what I seek.
Nem. What would'st thou?
Man. Thou canst not reply to me.
Call up the dead—my question is for them.
Nem. Great Arimanes, doth thy will avouch
The wishes of this mortal?
Ari. Yea.
Nem. Whom would'st thou
Uncharnel?
Man. One without a tomb—call up
Astarte.

NEMESIS.

Shadow! or Spirit!
Whatever thou art,
Which still doth inherit
The whole or a part
Of the form of thy birth,
Of the mould of thy clay,
Which return'd to the earth,
Re-appear to the day!
Bear what thou borest,
The heart and the form,
And the aspect thou worest
Redeem from the worm.
Appear!—Appear!—Appear!
Who sent thee there requires thee here!

[*The Phantom of* ASTARTE *rises and stands in the midst.*

Man. Can this be death? there's bloom upon her cheek;
But now I see it is no living hue,
But a strange hectic—like the unnatural red
Which Autumn plants upon the perish'd leaf.
It is the same! Oh, God! that I should dread
To look upon the same—Astarte!—No,
I cannot speak to her—but bid her speak—
Forgive me or condemn me.

NEMESIS.

By the power which hath broken
The grave which enthrall'd thee,
Speak to him who hath spoken,
Or those who have call'd thee!

Man. She is silent,
And in that silence I am more than answer'd.
Nem. My power extends no further. Prince of Air!
It rests with thee alone—command her voice.
Ari. Spirit—obey this sceptre!
Nem. Silent still!
She is not of our order, but belongs
To the other powers. Mortal! thy quest is vain,
And we are baffled also.
Man. Hear me, hear me—
Astarte! my beloved! speak to me:
I have so much endured—so much endure—

Look on me! the grave hath not changed thee more
Than I am changed for thee. Thou lovedst me
Too much, as I loved thee: we were not made
To torture thus each other, though it were
The deadliest sin to love as we have loved.
Say that thou loath'st me not—that I do bear
This punishment for both—that thou wilt be
One of the blessed—and that I shall die;
For hitherto all hateful things conspire
To bind me in existence—in a life
Which makes me shrink from immortality—
A future like the past. I cannot rest.
I know not what I ask, nor what I seek:
I feel but what thou art—and what I am;
And I would hear yet once before I perish
The voice which was my music—Speak to me

For I have call'd on thee in the still night,
Startled the slumbering birds from the hush'd boughs,
And woke the mountain wolves, and made the caves

Acquainted with thy vainly echoed name,
Which answer'd me—many things answer'd me—
Spirits and men—but thou wert silent all.
Yet speak to me! I have outwatch'd the stars,
And gazed o'er heaven in vain in search of thee.
Speak to me! I have wander'd o'er the earth,
And never found thy likeness—Speak to me!
Look on the fiends around—they feel for me:
I fear them not, and feel for thee alone—
Speak to me! though it be in wrath;—but say—
I reck not what—but let me hear thee once—
This once—once more!

Phantom of Astarte. Manfred!

Man. Say on, say on—
I live but in the sound—it is thy voice!

Phan. Manfred! To-morrow ends thine earthly ills.
Farewell!

Man. Yet one word more—am I forgiven?

Phan. Farewell!

Man. Say, shall we meet again?

Phan. Farewell!

Man. One word for mercy! Say, thou lovest me.

Phan. Manfred!

[*The Spirit of* ASTARTE *disappears.*

Nem. She's gone, and will not be recall'd;
Her words will be fulfill'd. Return to the earth.

A Spirit. He is convulsed—This is to be a mortal,
And seek the things beyond mortality.

Another Spirit. Yet, see, he mastereth himself, and makes
His torture tributary to his will.
Had he been one of us, he would have made
An awful spirit.

Nem. Hast thou further question
Of our great sovereign, or his worshippers?

Man. None.

Nem. Then for a time farewell.

Man. We meet then! Where? On the earth?—
Even as thou wilt: and for the grace accorded
I now depart a debtor. Fare ye well!

[*Exit* MANFRED.

(*Scene closes.*)

ACT III.

SCENE I.

A Hall in the Castle of Manfred.

MANFRED *and* HERMAN.

Man. What is the hour?

Her. It wants but one till sunset,
And promises a lovely twilight.

Man. Say,
Are all things so disposed of in the tower
As I directed?

Her. All, my lord, are ready:
Here is the key and casket.

Man. It is well:
Thou may'st retire. [*Exit* HERMAN.

Man. (*alone*). There is a calm upon me—
Inexplicable stillness! which till now
Did not belong to what I knew of life.
If that I did not know philosophy
To be of all our vanities the motleyest,
The merest word that ever fool'd the ear
From out the schoolman's jargon, I should deem
The golden secret, the sought "Kalon," found,
And seated in my soul. It will not last,
But it is well to have known it, though but once:
It hath enlarged my thoughts with a new sense,
And I within my tablets would note down
That there is such a feeling. Who is there?

Re-enter HERMAN.

Her. My lord, the Abbot of St. Maurice craves
To greet your presence.

Enter the ABBOT OF ST. MAURICE.

Abbot. Peace be with Count Manfred.

Man. Thanks, holy father! welcome to these walls;
Thy presence honours them, and blesseth those
Who dwell within them.

Abbot. Would it were so, Count!—
But I would fain confer with thee alone.

Man. Herman, retire.—What would my reverend guest?

Abbot. Thus, without prelude:—Age and zeal, my office,
And good intent, must plead my privilege;
Our near, though not acquainted neighbourhood
May also be my herald. Rumours strange,
And of unholy nature, are abroad,
And busy with thy name; a noble name
For centuries: may he who bears it now
Transmit it unimpair'd!

Man. Proceed,—I listen.

Abbot. 'Tis said thou holdest converse with the things
Which are forbidden to the search of man;
That with the dwellers of the dark abodes,
The many evil and unheavenly spirits
Which walk the valley of the shade of death,
Thou communest. I know that with mankind,
Thy fellows in creation, thou dost rarely
Exchange thy thoughts, and that thy solitude
Is as an anchorite's, were it but holy.

Man. And what are they who do avouch these things?

Abbot. My pious brethren—the scared peasantry—
Even thy own vassals—who do look on thee
With most unquiet eyes. Thy life's in peril.

Man. Take it.
Abbot. I come to save, and not destroy—
I would not pry into thy secret soul;
But if these things be sooth, there still is time
For penitence and pity: reconcile thee
With the true church, and through the church to Heaven.
Man. I hear thee. This is my reply: whate'er
I may have been, or am, doth rest between
Heaven and myself.—I shall not choose a mortal
To be my mediator. Have I sinn'd
Against your ordinances? prove and punish!
Abbot. My son! I did not speak of punishment,
But penitence and pardon;—with thyself
The choice of such remains—and for the last,
Our institutions and our strong belief
Have given me power to smooth the path from sin
To higher hope and better thoughts; the first
I leave to Heaven,—"Vengeance is Mine alone!"
So saith the Lord, and with all humbleness
His servant echoes back the awful word.
Man. Old man! there is no power in holy men,
Nor charm in prayer—nor purifying form
Of penitence—nor outward look—nor fast—
Nor agony—nor, greater than all these,
The innate tortures of that deep despair,
Which is remorse without the fear of hell,
But all in all sufficient to itself
Would make a hell of heaven—can exorcise
From out the unbounded spirit, the quick sense
Of its own sins, wrongs, sufferance, and revenge
Upon itself; there is no future pang
Can deal that justice on the self-condemn'd
He deals on his own soul.
Abbot. All this is well;
For this will pass away, and be succeeded
By an auspicious hope, which shall look up
With calm assurance to that blessed place,
Which all who seek may win, whatever be
Their earthly errors, so they be atoned:
And the commencement of atonement is
The sense of its necessity.—Say on—
And all our church can teach thee shall be taught;
And all we can absolve thee shall be pardon'd.
Man. When Rome's sixth emperor was near his last,
The victim of a self-inflicted wound,
To shun the torments of a public death
From senates once his slaves, a certain soldier,
With show of loyal pity, would have stanch'd
The gushing throat with his officious robe;
The dying Roman thrust him back, and said—
Some empire still in his expiring glance,
"It is too late—is this fidelity?"
Abbot. And what of this?
Man. I answer with the Roman—
"It is too late!"
Abbot. It never can be so,
To reconcile thyself with thy own soul,
And thy own soul with Heaven. Hast thou no hope?
'T is strange—even those who do despair above,
Yet shape themselves some fantasy on earth,
To which frail twig they cling, like drowning men.
Man. Ay—father! I have had those earthly visions
And noble aspirations in my youth,
To make my own the mind of other men,
The enlightener of nations; and to rise
I knew not whither—it might be to fall;
But fall, even as the mountain-cataract,
Which having leapt from its more dazzling height,
Even in the foaming strength of its abyss,
(Which casts up misty columns that become
Clouds raining from the re-ascended skies,)
Lies low but mighty still.—But this is past,
My thoughts mistook themselves.
Abbot. And wherefore so?
Man. I could not tame my nature down; for he
Must serve who fain would sway—and soothe—and sue—
And watch all time—and pry into all place—
And be a living lie—who would become
A mighty thing amongst the mean, and such
The mass are; I disdain'd to mingle with
A herd, though to be leader—and of wolves.
The lion is alone, and so am I.
Abbot. And why not live and act with other men?
Man. Because my nature was averse from life;
And yet not cruel; for I would not make,
But find a desolation:—like the wind,
The red-hot breath of the most lone simoom,
Which dwells but in the desert, and sweeps o'er
The barren sands which bear no shrubs to blast,
And revels o'er their wild and arid waves,
And seeketh not, so that it is not sought,
But being met is deadly; such hath been
The course of my existence; but there came
Things in my path which are no more.
Abbot. Alas!
I 'gin to fear that thou art past all aid
From me and from my calling; yet so young,
I still would——
Man. Look on me! there is an order
Of mortals on the earth, who do become
Old in their youth, and die ere middle age,
Without the violence of warlike death;
Some perishing of pleasure—some of study—
Some worn with toil—some of mere weariness—
Some of disease—and some insanity—
And some of wither'd, or of broken hearts;
For this last is a malady which slays
More than are number'd in the lists of Fate,
Taking all shapes, and bearing many names.
Look upon me! for even of all these things
Have I partaken; and of all these things,
One were enough; then wonder not that I

Am what I am, but that I ever was,
Or having been, that I am still on earth.
Abbot. Yet, hear me still——
Man. Old man! I do respect
Thine order, and revere thine years; I deem
The purpose pious, but it is in vain:
Think me not churlish; I would spare thyself,
Far more than me, in shunning at this time
All further colloquy—and so—farewell.
[*Exit* MANFRED.
Abbot. This should have been a noble creature; he
Hath all the energy which would have made
A goodly frame of glorious elements,
Had they been wisely mingled; as it is,
It is an awful chaos—light and darkness—
And mind and dust—and passions and pure thoughts,
Mix'd, and contending without end or order,
All dormant or destructive; he will perish,
And yet he must not; I will try once more,
For such are worth redemption; and my duty
Is to dare all things for a righteous end.
I'll follow him—but cautiously, though surely.
[*Exit* ABBOT.

SCENE II.

Another Chamber.

MANFRED *and* HERMAN.

Her. My lord, you bade me wait on you at sunset:
He sinks behind the mountain.
Man. Doth he so?
I will look on him.
[MANFRED *advances to the Window of the Hall.*
Glorious Orb! the idol
Of early nature, and the vigorous race
Of undiseased mankind, the giant sons[4]
Of the embrace of angels, with a sex
More beautiful than they, which did draw down
The erring spirits, who can ne'er return.—
Most glorious orb! that wert a worship, ere
The mystery of thy making was reveal'd!
Thou earliest minister of the Almighty,
Which gladden'd, on their mountain tops, the hearts
Of the Chaldean shepherds, till they pour'd
Themselves in orisons! Thou material God!
And representative of the Unknown—
Who chose thee for His shadow! Thou chief star!
Centre of many stars! which mak'st our earth
Endurable, and temperest the hues
And hearts of all who walk within thy rays!
Sire of the seasons! Monarch of the climes,
And those who dwell in them! for near or far,
Our inborn spirits have a tint of thee,
Even as our outward aspects;—thou dost rise,
And shine, and set in glory. Fare thee well!
I ne'er shall see thee more. As my first glance
Of love and wonder was for thee, then take
My latest look: thou wilt not beam on one
To whom the gifts of life and warmth have been
Of a more fatal nature. He is gone:
I follow. [*Exit* MANFRED.

SCENE III.

The Mountains—The Castle of Manfred at some distance—A Terrace before a Tower.—Time, Twilight.

HERMAN, MANUEL, *and other Dependants of* MANFRED.

Her. 'T is strange enough; night after night, for years,
He hath pursued long vigils in this tower,
Without a witness. I have been within it,—
So have we all been oft-times: but from it,
Or its contents, it were impossible
To draw conclusions absolute, of aught
His studies tend to. To be sure, there is
One chamber where none enter: I would give
The fee of what I have to come these three years,
To pore upon its mysteries.
Manuel. 'T were dangerous;
Content thyself with what thou know'st already.
Her. Ah! Manuel! thou art elderly and wise,
And couldst say much; thou hast dwelt within the castle—
How many years is't?
Manuel. Ere Count Manfred's birth,
I served his father, whom he nought resembles.
Her. There be more sons in like predicament.
But wherein do they differ?
Manuel. I speak not
Of features or of form, but mind and habits;
Count Sigismund was proud,—but gay and free,—
A warrior and a reveller; he dwelt not
With books and solitude, nor made the night
A gloomy vigil, but a festal time,
Merrier than day; he did not walk the rocks
And forests like a wolf, nor turn aside
From men and their delights.
Her. Beshrew the hour,
But those were jocund times! I would that such
Would visit the old walls again; they look
As if they had forgotten them.
Manuel. These walls
Must change their chieftain first. Oh! I have seen
Some strange things in them, Herman.
Her. Come, be friendly;
Relate me some to while away our watch:
I've heard thee darkly speak of an event
Which happen'd hereabouts, by this same tower.
Manuel. That was a night indeed! I do remember
'T was twilight, as it may be now, and such
Another evening;—yon red cloud, which rests
On Eigher's pinnacle, so rested then,—
So like that it might be the same; the wind

Was faint and gusty, and the mountain snows
Began to glitter with the climbing moon;
Count Manfred was, as now, within his tower,—
How occupied, we knew not, but with him
The sole companion of his wanderings
And watchings—her, whom of all earthly things
That liv'd, the only thing he seem'd to love,—
As he, indeed, by blood was bound to do,
The Lady Astarte, his——
Hush! who comes here?

Enter the ABBOT.

Abbot. Where is your master?
Her. Yonder, in the tower.
Abbot. I must speak with him.
Manuel. 'Tis impossible;
He is most private, and must not be thus
Intruded on.
Abbot. Upon myself I take
The forfeit of my fault, if fault there be—
But I must see him.
Her. Thou hast seen him once
This eve already.
Abbot. Herman! I command thee,
Knock, and apprize the Count of my approach.
Her. We dare not.
Abbot. Then it seems I must be herald
Of my own purpose.
Manuel. Reverend father, stop—
I pray you pause.
Abbot. Why so?
Manuel. But step this way,
And I will tell you further. [*Exeunt.*

SCENE IV.

Interior of the Tower.

MANFRED *alone.*

The stars are forth, the moon above the tops
Of the snow-shining mountains.—Beautiful!
I linger yet with Nature, for the night
Hath been to me a more familiar face
Than that of man; and in her starry shade
Of dim and solitary loveliness,
I learn'd the language of another world.
I do remember me, that in my youth,
When I was wandering,—upon such a night
I stood within the Coliseum's wall,
Midst the chief relics of almighty Rome;
The trees which grew along the broken arches
Waved dark in the blue midnight, and the stars
Shone through the rents of ruin; from afar
The watchdog bay'd beyond the Tiber; and
More near from out the Cæsars' palace came
The owl's long cry, and, interruptedly,
Of distant sentinels the fitful song
Begun and died upon the gentle wind.
Some cypresses beyond the time-worn breach
Appear'd to skirt the horizon, yet they stood
Within a bowshot—where the Cæsars dwelt,
And dwell the tuneless birds of night, amidst
A grove which springs through levell'd battlements,
And twines its roots with the imperial hearths,
Ivy usurps the laurel's place of growth;—
But the gladiators' bloody Circus stands,
A noble wreck in ruinous perfection!
While Cæsar's chambers, and the Augustan halls,
Grovel on earth in indistinct decay.—
And thou didst shine, thou rolling moon, upon
All this, and cast a wide and tender light,
Which soften'd down the hoar austerity
Of rugged desolation, and fill'd up,
As 't were anew, the gaps of centuries;
Leaving that beautiful which still was so,
And making that which was not, till the place
Became religion, and the heart ran o'er
With silent worship of the great of old!—
The dead, but sceptred sovereigns, who still rule
Our spirits from their urns.—
'Twas such a night!
'Tis strange that I recall it at this time;
But I have found our thoughts take wildest flight
Even at the moment when they should array
Themselves in pensive order.

Enter the ABBOT.

Abbot. My good lord,
I crave a second grace for this approach;
But yet let not my humble zeal offend
By its abruptness—all it hath of ill
Recoils on me; its good in the effect
May light upon your head—could I say *heart*—
Could I touch *that*, with words or prayers, I should
Recall a noble spirit which hath wander'd,
But is not yet all lost.
Man. Thou know'st me not!
My days are number'd, and my deeds recorded:
Retire, or 't will be dangerous—Away!
Abbot. Thou dost not mean to menace me?
Man. Not I;
I simply tell thee peril is at hand,
And would preserve thee.
Abbot. What dost mean?
Man. Look there!
What dost thou see?
Abbot. Nothing.
Man. Look there, I say,
And steadfastly;—now tell me what thou seest.
Abbot. That which should shake me,—but I fear it not—
I see a dusk and awful figure rise,
Like an infernal god, from out the earth;
His face wrapt in a mantle, and his form
Robed as with angry clouds; he stands between
Thyself and me—but I do fear him not.

Man. Thou hast no cause—he shall not harm thee—but
His sight may shock thine old limbs into palsy.
I say to thee—Retire!
Abbot. And I reply—
Never—till I have battled with this fiend:—
What doth he here?—
Man. Why—ay—what doth he here?—
I did not send for him,—he is unbidden.

Abbot. Alas! lost mortal! what with guests like these
Hast thou to do? I tremble for thy sake:
Why doth he gaze on thee, and thou on him?
Ah! he unveils his aspect: on his brow
The thunder-scars are graven; from his eye
Glares forth the immortality of hell—
Avaunt!
Man. Pronounce—what is thy mission?

Spirit. Come!
Abbot. What art thou, unknown being? answer!—speak!
Spirit. The genius of this mortal.—Come! 'tis time.
Man. I am prepared for all things, but deny
The power which summons me. Who sent thee here?
Spirit. Thou'lt know anon—come! come!
Man. I have commanded
Things of an essence greater far than thine,
And striven with thy masters. Get thee hence!
Spirit. Mortal! thine hour is come—Away! I say.
Man. I knew, and know my hour is come, but not
To render up my soul to such as thee:
Away! I'll die as I have lived—alone.
Spirit. Then I must summon up my brethren.—
Rise! [*Other Spirits rise up.*
Abbot. Avaunt! ye evil ones!—Avaunt! I say,—
Ye have no power where piety hath power,
And I do charge thee in the name——
Spirit. Old man!
We know ourselves, our mission, and thine order;
Waste not thy holy words on idle uses,
It were in vain: this man is forfeited.
Once more I summon him—Away! away!
Man. I do defy ye,—though I feel my soul
Is ebbing from me, yet I do defy ye;
Nor will I hence, while I have earthly breath
To breathe my scorn upon ye—earthly strength
To wrestle, though with spirits; what ye take
Shall be ta'en limb by limb.
Spirit. Reluctant mortal!
Is this the magian who would so pervade
The world invisible, and make himself
Almost our equal?—Can it be that thou
Art thus in love with life? the very life
Which made thee wretched!
Man. Thou false fiend, thou liest!
My life is in its last hour;—*that* I know,
Nor would redeem a moment of that hour;
I do not combat against death, but thee
And thy surrounding angels; my past power
Was purchased by no compact with thy crew,
But by superior science—penance—daring—
And length of watching—strength of mind—and skill
In knowledge of our fathers—when the earth
Saw men and spirits walking side by side,
And gave ye no supremacy: I stand
Upon my strength—I do defy—deny—
Spurn back, and scorn ye!—
Spirit. But thy many crimes
Have made thee——
Man. What are they to such as thee?
Must crimes be punish'd but by other crimes,
And greater criminals?—Back to thy hell!
Thou hast no power upon me, *that* I feel;
Thou never shalt possess me, *that* I know:
What I have done is done; I bear within
A torture which could nothing gain from thine:
The mind which is immortal makes itself
Requital for its good or evil thoughts—
Is its own origin of ill and end—
And its own place and time—its innate sense,
When stripp'd of this mortality, derives
No colour from the fleeting things without;
But is absorb'd in sufferance or in joy,
Born from the knowledge of its own desert.
Thou didst not tempt me, and thou couldst not tempt me;
I have not been thy dupe, nor am thy prey—
But was my own destroyer, and will be
My own hereafter.—Back, ye baffled fiends!
The hand of death is on me—but not yours!
[*The Demons disappear.*
Abbot. Alas! how pale thou art—thy lips are white;
And thy breast heaves—and in thy gasping throat
The accents rattle—Give thy prayers to Heaven—
Pray—albeit but in thought,—but die not thus.
Man. 'T is over—my dull eyes can fix thee not;
But all things swim around me, and the earth
Heaves as it were beneath me. Fare thee well—
Give me thy hand.
Abbot. Cold—cold—even to the heart—
But yet one prayer—Alas! how fares it with thee?
Man. Old man! 't is not so difficult to die.
[Manfred *expires.*
Abbot. He 's gone—his soul hath ta'en his earthless flight—
Whither? I dread to think—but he is gone.

NOTES TO MANFRED.

Note 1, page 386.
It is not noon—the sunbow's rays still arch.

This iris is formed by the rays of the sun over the lower part of the Alpine torrents: it is exactly like a rainbow come down to pay a visit, and so close that you may walk into it: this effect lasts till noon.

Note 2, page 388.
Eros and Anteros.

The philosopher Jamblicus. The story of the raising of Eros and Anteros may be found in his life by Eunapius. It is well told.

Note 3, page 389.
In words of dubious import, but fulfill'd.

The story of Pausanias, king of Sparta (who commanded the Greeks at the battle of Platea, and afterwards perished for an attempt to betray the Lacedæmonians), and Cleonice, is told in Plutarch's Life of Cimon; and in the Laconics of Pausanias the sophist, in his description of Greece.

Note 4, page 395.
Of undiseased mankind, the giant sons.

"And it came to pass, that the *Sons of God* saw the daughters of men, that they were fair," &c.—"There were giants in the earth in those days; and also after that, when the *Sons of God* came in unto the daughters of men, and they bare children to them, the same became mighty men which were of old, men of renown."—*Genesis*, ch. vi. verses 2 and 4.

HEAVEN AND EARTH:

A MYSTERY,

FOUNDED ON THE FOLLOWING PASSAGE IN GENESIS,

CHAP. VI.

"And it came to pass that the sons of God saw the daughters of men that they were fair; and they took them wives of all which they chose."

"And woman wailing for her demon lover."—*Coleridge.*

Dramatis Personæ.

ANGELS.

SAMIASA.
AZAZIEL.
RAPHAEL, the Archangel.

MEN

NOAH and his SONS—IRAD and JAPHET.

WOMEN.

ANAH.
AHOLIBAMAH.

Chorus of Spirits of the Earth—Chorus of Mortals.

PART I.

SCENE I.

A woody and mountainous district near Mount Ararat. Time, Midnight.

Enter ANAH *and* AHOLIBAMAH.

Anah. Our father sleeps: it is the hour when they
Who love us are accustom'd to descend
Through the deep clouds o'er rocky Ararat:
How my heart beats!

Aho. Let us proceed upon
Our invocation.
Anah. But the stars are hidden.
I tremble.
Aho. So do I, but not with fear
Of aught save their delay.
Anah. My sister, though
I love Azaziel more than——oh, too much!—
What was I going to say? my heart grows impious.
Aho. And where is the impiety of loving
Celestial natures?
Anah. But, Aholibamah,
I love our God less since His angel loved me:
This cannot be of good; and though I know not
That I do wrong, I feel a thousand fears
Which are not ominous of right.
Aho. Then wed thee
Unto some son of clay, and toil and spin!
There's Japhet loves thee well, hath loved thee long;
Marry, and bring forth dust!
Anah. I should have loved
Azaziel not less, were he mortal; yet
I am glad he is not. I can not outlive him.
And when I think that his immortal wings
Will one day hover o'er the sepulchre
Of the poor child of clay which so adored him,
As he adores the Highest, death becomes
Less terrible: but yet I pity him;
His grief will be of ages, or at least
Mine would be such for him, were I the Seraph,
And he the perishable.
Aho. Rather say,
That he will single forth some other daughter
Of Earth, and love her as he once loved Anah.
Anah. And if it should be so, and she loved him,
Better thus than that he should weep for me.
Aho. If I thought thus of Samiasa's love,
All Seraph as he is, I'd spurn him from me.—
But to our invocation! 'Tis the hour.
Anah. Seraph!
From thy sphere!
Whatever star contain thy glory;
In the eternal depths of heaven
Albeit thou watchest with "the seven,"[1]
Though through space infinite and hoary
Before thy bright wings worlds be driven,
Yet hear!
Oh! think of her who holds thee dear!
And though she nothing is to thee,
Yet think that thou art all to her.
Thou canst not tell—and never be
Such pangs decreed to aught save me—
The bitterness of tears.
Eternity is in thine years,
Unborn, undying beauty in thine eyes;
With me thou canst not sympathise,
Except in love, and there thou must
Acknowledge that more loving dust
Ne'er wept beneath the skies.
Thou walk'st thy many worlds, thou see'st
The face of Him who made thee great,
As He hath made me of the least
Of those cast out from Eden's gate:
Yet, Seraph dear!
Oh hear!
For thou hast loved me, and I would not die
Until I know, what I must die in knowing,
That thou forgett'st in thine eternity
Her whose heart death could not keep from o'erflowing
For thee, immortal essence as thou art!
Great is their love who love in sin and fear;
And such, I feel, are waging in my heart
A war unworthy: to an Adamite
Forgive, my Seraph! that such thoughts appear,
For sorrow is our element;
Delight
An Eden kept afar from sight,
Though sometimes with our visions blent.
The hour is near
Which tells me we are not abandon'd quite—
Appear! appear!
Seraph!
My own Azaziel! be but here,
And leave the stars to their own light.
Aho. Samiasa!
Wheresoe'er
Thou rulest in the upper air—
Or warring with the spirits who may dare
Dispute with Him
Who made all empires, empire; or recalling
Some wandering star, which shoots through the abyss
Whose tenants dying, while their world is falling,
Share the dim destiny of clay in this;
Or joining with the inferior cherubim,
Thou deignest to partake their hymn—
Samiasa!
I call thee, I await thee, and I love thee.
Many may worship thee, that will I not:
If that thy spirit down to mine may move thee,
Descend and share my lot!
Though I be form'd of clay,
And thou of beams
More bright than those of day
On Eden's streams,
Thine immortality can not repay
With love more warm than mine,
My love. There is a ray
In me, which, though forbidden yet to shine,
I feel was lighted at thy God's and thine.
It may be hidden long: death and decay
Our mother Eve bequeath'd us—but my heart
Defies it: though this life must pass away,
Is *that* a cause for thee and me to part?

Thou art immortal—so am I: I feel—
I feel my immortality o'ersweep
All pains, all tears, all time, all fears, and peal,
Like the eternal thunders of the deep,
Into my ears this truth—"Thou liv'st for ever!"
But if it be in joy
I know not, nor would know;
That secret rests with the Almighty Giver,
Who folds in clouds the fonts of bliss and woe.
But thee and me He never can destroy:
Change us He may, but not o'erwhelm; we are
Of as eternal essence, and must war
With Him if He will war with us: with *thee*
I can share all things, even immortal sorrow;
For thou hast ventured to share life with *me*,
And shall *I* shrink from thine eternity?
No! though the serpent's sting should pierce me thorough,
And thou thyself wert like the serpent, coil
Around me still! and I will smile,
And curse thee not; but hold
Thee in as warm a fold
As——But descend, and prove
A mortal's love
For an immortal. If the skies contain
More joy than thou canst give and take, remain!
Anah. Sister! sister! I view them winging
Their bright way through the parted night.
Aho. The clouds from off their pinions flinging,
As though they bore to-morrow's light.
Anah. But if our father see the sight!
Aho. He would but deem it was the moon
Rising unto some sorcerer's tune
An hour too soon.
Anah. They come! *he* comes!—Azaziel!
Aho. Haste
To meet them! Oh, for wings to bear
My spirit, while they hover there,
To Samiasa's breast!
Anah. Lo! they have kindled all the west,
Like a returning sunset;—lo!
On Ararat's late secret crest
A mild and many-colour'd bow,
The remnant of their flashing path,
Now shines! and now, behold! it hath
Return'd to night, as rippling foam,
Which the leviathan hath lash'd
From his unfathomable home,
When sporting on the face of the calm deep,
Subsides soon after he again hath dashed
Down, down, to where the ocean's fountains sleep.
Aho. They have touch'd earth!—Samiasa!
Anah. My Azaziel!

[*Exeunt.*

SCENE II.

Enter IRAD *and* JAPHET.

Irad. Despond not: wherefore wilt thou wander thus
To add thy silence to the silent night,
And lift thy tearful eye unto the stars?
They cannot aid thee.
Japh. But they soothe me—now
Perhaps she looks upon them as I look.
Methinks a being that is beautiful
Becometh more so as it looks on beauty,
The eternal beauty of undying things.
Oh, Anah!
Irad. But she loves thee not.
Japh. Alas!
Irad. And proud Aholibamah spurns me also.
Japh. I feel for thee too.
Irad. Let her keep her pride,
Mine hath enabled me to bear her scorn:
It may be, time too will avenge it.
Japh. Canst thou
Find joy in such a thought?
Irad. Nor joy, nor sorrow.
I loved her well; I would have loved her better,
Had love been met with love; as 'tis, I leave her
To brighter destinies, if so she deems them.
Japh. What destinies?
Irad. I have some cause to think
She loves another.
Japh. Anah?
Irad. No; her sister.
Japh. What other?
Irad. That I know not; but her air,
If not her words, tells me she loves another.
Japh. Ay, but not Anah; she but loves her God.
Irad. Whate'er she loveth, so she loves thee not,
What can it profit thee?
Japh. True, nothing; but
I love.
Irad. And so did I.
Japh. And now thou lov'st not,
Or think'st thou lov'st not, art thou happier?
Irad. Yes.
Japh. I pity thee.
Irad. Me! Why?
Japh. For being happy,
Deprived of that which makes my misery.
Irad. I take thy taunt as part of thy distemper,
And would not feel as thou dost, for more shekels
Than all our father's herds would bring if weigh'd
Against the metal of the sons of Cain—
The yellow dust they try to barter with us,
As if such useless and discolour'd trash,
The refuse of the earth, could be received
For milk, and wool, and flesh, and fruits, and all
Our flocks and wilderness afford.—Go, Japhet,

Sigh to the stars, as wolves howl to the moon—
I must back to my rest.
Japh. And so would I,
If I could rest.
Irad. Thou wilt not to our tents then?
Japh. No, Irad; I will to the cavern, whose
Mouth, they say, opens from the internal world,
To let the inner spirits of the earth
Forth when they walk its surface.
Irad. Wherfeore so?
What wouldst thou there?
Japh. Soothe further my sad spirit
With gloom as sad: it is a hopeless spot,
And I am hopeless.
Irad. But 'tis dangerous;

Strange sounds and sights have peopled it with terrors.
I must go with thee.
Japh. Irad, no; believe me
I feel no evil thought, and fear no evil.
Irad. But evil things will be thy foe the more,
As not being of them: turn thy steps aside,
Or let mine be with thine.
Japh. No; neither, Irad;
I must proceed alone.
Irad. Then peace be with thee!
[*Exit* IRAD.

Japh. (*solus.*) Peace! I have sought it where it should be found,
In love—with love, too, which perhaps deserved it;
And, in its stead, a heaviness of heart—
A weakness of the spirit—listless days,
And nights inexorable to sweet sleep—
Have come upon me. Peace! what peace? the calm
Of desolation, and the stillness of
The untrodden forest, only broken by
The sweeping tempest through its groaning boughs;
Such is the sullen or the fitful state
Of my mind overworn. The earth's grown wicked,
And many signs and portents have proclaim'd
A change at hand, and an o'erwhelming doom
To perishable beings. Oh, my Anah!
When the dread hour denounced shall open wide
The fountains of the deep, how mightest thou
Have lain within this bosom, folded from
The elements—this bosom, which in vain
Hath beat for thee, and then will beat more vainly,
While thine——Oh, God! at least remit to her
Thy wrath! for she is pure amidst the failing,
As a star in the clouds, which cannot quench,
Although they obscure it for an hour. My Anah!
How would I have adored thee, but thou wouldst not;
And still would I redeem thee—see thee live
When Ocean is Earth's grave, and, unopposed
By rock or shallow, the leviathan,
Lord of the shoreless sea and watery world,
Shall wonder at his boundlessness of realm.
[*Exit* JAPHET.

Enter NOAH *and* SHEM.

Noah. Where is thy brother Japhet?
Shem. He went forth,
According to his wont, to meet with Irad,
He said; but, as I fear, to bend his steps
Towards Anah's tents, round which he hovers nightly,
Like a dove round and round its pillaged nest;
Or else he walks the wild up to the cavern
Which opens to the heart of Ararat.
Noah. What doth he there? It is an evil spot,
Upon an earth all evil; for things worse
Than even wicked men resort there: he
Still loves this daughter of a fated race,
Although he could not wed her if she loved him,
And that she doth not. Oh, the unhappy hearts
Of men! that one of my blood, knowing well
The destiny, and evil of these days,
And that the hour approacheth, should indulge
In such forbidden yearnings! Lead the way;
He must be sought for!
Shem. Go not forward, father;
I will seek Japhet.
Noah. Do not fear for me:
All evil things are powerless on the man
Selected by Jehovah.—Let us on.
Shem. To the tents of the father of the sisters?
Noah. No; to the cavern of the Caucasus.
[*Exeunt* NOAH *and* SHEM.

SCENE III.

The mountains.—A cavern, and the rocks of Caucasus.

Japh. (*solus.*) Ye wilds, that look eternal! and thou cave,
Which seem'st unfathomable! and ye mountains,
So varied and so terrible in beauty!
Here, in your rugged majesty of rocks,
And toppling trees that twine their roots with stone
In perpendicular places, where the foot
Of man would tremble, could he reach them—yes,
Ye look eternal! Yet, in a few days,
Perhaps even hours, ye will be changed, rent, hurl'd
Before the mass of waters; and yon cave,
Which seems to lead into a lower world,
Shall have its depths search'd by the sweeping wave,
And dolphins gambol in the lion's den!
And man——Oh, men! my fellow beings! Who
Shall weep above your universal grave,
Save I? Who shall be left to weep?—My kinsmen,
Alas! what am I better than ye are,
That I must live beyond ye? Where shall be
The pleasant places where I thought of Anah
While I had hope; or the more savage haunts,
Scarce less beloved, where I despair'd for her?
And can it be!—Shall yon exulting peak,
Whose glittering top is like a distant star,
Lie low beneath the boiling of the deep?
No more to have the morning sun break forth,

And scatter back the mists in floating folds
From its tremendous brow? no more to have
Day's broad orb drop behind its head at even,
Leaving it with a crown of many hues?
No more to be the beacon of the world,
For angels to alight on, as the spot
Nearest the stars? And can those words "*no more*"
Be meant for thee, for all things, save for us,
And the predestined creeping things reserved
By my sire to Jehovah's bidding? May
He preserve *them*, and *I not* have the power
So snatch the loveliest of earth's daughters from
A doom which even some serpent, with his mate,
Shall 'scape, to save his kind to be prolong'd,
To hiss and sting through some emerging world,

Reeking and dank from out the slime, whose ooze
Shall slumber o'er the wreck of this until
The salt morass subside into a sphere
Beneath the sun, and be the monument,
The sole and undistinguish'd sepulchre,
Of yet quick myriads of all life? How much
Breath will be still'd at once! All beauteous world!
So young, so mark'd out for destruction, I
With a cleft heart look on thee day by day,
And night by night, thy number'd days and nights.
I cannot save thee, cannot save even her
Whose love had made me love thee more; but as
A portion of thy dust, I cannot think
Upon thy coming doom without a feeling
Such as—Oh God! and canst Thou—— [*He pauses.*

A rushing sound from the cavern is heard, and shouts of laughter—afterwards a Spirit passes.

Japh. In the name
Of the Most High, what art thou?
Spirit (laughs). Ha! ha! ha!
Japh. By all that earth holds holiest, speak!
Spirit (laughs). Ha! ha!
Japh. By the approaching deluge! by the earth
Which will be strangled by the ocean! by
The deep which will lay open all her fountains!
The heaven which will convert her clouds to seas,
And the Omnipotent who makes and crushes!
Thou unknown, terrible, and indistinct,
Yet awful Thing of Shadows, speak to me!
Why dost thou laugh that horrid laugh?
Spirit. Why weep'st thou?
Japh. For earth and all her children.
Spirit. Ha! ha! ha!
[*Spirit vanishes.*
Japh. How the fiend mocks the tortures of a world,
The coming desolation of an orb,
On which the sun shall rise and warm no life!
How the earth sleeps! and all that in it is
Sleep too upon the very eve of death!
Why should they wake to meet it?—What is here,
Which looks like death in life, and speak like things
Born ere this dying world? They come like clouds!
[*Various Spirits pass from the cavern.*
Spirit. Rejoice!
The abhorred race
Which could not keep in Eden their high place,
But listen'd to the voice
Of knowledge without power,
Are nigh the hour
Of death!
Not slow, not single, not by sword, nor sorrow,
Nor years, nor heart-break, nor time's sapping motion,
Shall they drop off. Behold their last to-morrow!
Earth shall be ocean!
And no breath,
Save of the winds, be on the unbounded wave!
Angels shall tire their wings, but find no spot:
Not even a rock from out the liquid grave
Shall lift its point to save,
Or show the place where strong Despair hath died,
After long looking o'er the ocean wide
For the expected ebb which cometh not:
All shall be void,
Destroy'd!
Another element shall be the lord
Of life, and the abhorr'd
Children of dust be quench'd; and of each hue
Of earth nought left but the unbroken blue;
And of the variegated mountain
Shall nought remain
Unchanged, or of the level plain;
Cedar and pine shall lift their tops in vain:
All merged within the universal fountain,
Man, earth, and fire, shall die,
And sea and sky
Look vast and lifeless in the Eternal eye.
Upon the foam
Who shall erect a home?
Japh. (coming forward.) My sire!
Earth's seed shall not expire;
Only the evil shall be put away
From day.
Avaunt! ye exulting demons of the waste!
Who howl your hideous joy
When God destroys whom you dare not destroy;
Hence! haste!
Back to your inner caves!
Until the waves
Shall search you in your secret place,
And drive your sullen race
Forth, to be roll'd upon the tossing winds
In restless wretchedness along all space!
Spirit. Son of the saved!
When thou and thine have braved
The wide and warring element;
When the great barrier of the deep is rent,
Shall thou and thine be good or happy?—No;
Thy new world and new race shall be of woe—
Less goodly in their aspect, in their years
Less than the glorious giants, who
Yet walk the world in pride,
The Sons of Heaven by many a mortal bride.
Thine shall be nothing of the past, save tears.
And art thou not asham'd
Thus to survive,
And eat, drink, and wive?
With a base heart so far subdued and tamed,
As even to hear this wide destruction named,
Without such grief and courage, as should rather
Bid thee await the world-dissolving wave,

Than seek a shelter with thy favour'd father,
And build thy city o'er the drown'd earth's grave?
Who would outlive their kind,
Except the base and blind?
Mine
Hateth thine,
As of a different order in the sphere,
But not our own.
There is not one who hath not left a throne
Vacant in heaven, to dwell in darkness here,
Rather than see his mates endure alone.
Go, wretch! and give
A life like thine to other wretches—live!
And when the annihilating waters roar
Above what they have done,
Envy the Giant Patriarchs then no more,
And scorn thy sire as the surviving one!
Thyself for being his son!

Chorus of Spirits issuing from the cavern.

Rejoice!
No more the human voice
Shall vex our joys in middle air
With prayer;
No more
Shall they adore;
And we, who ne'er for ages have adored
The prayer-exacting Lord,
To whom the omission of a sacrifice
Is vice;—
We, we shall view the deep's salt sources pour'd
Until one element shall do the work
Of all in chaos; until they,
The creatures proud of their poor clay,
Shall perish, and their bleached bones shall lurk
In caves, in dens, in clefts of mountains, where
The deep shall follow to their latest lair;
Where even the brutes, in their despair,
Shall cease to prey on man and on each other,
And the striped tiger shall lie down to die
Beside the lamb, as though he were his brother;
Till all things shall be as they were,
Silent and uncreated, save the sky;
While a brief truce
Is made with Death, who shall forbear
The little remnant of the past creation,
To generate new nations for his use;
This remnant, floating o'er the undulation
Of the subduing deluge, from its slime,
When the hot sun hath baked the reeking soil
Into a world, shall give again to Time
New beings—years—diseases—sorrow—crime—
With all companionship of hate and toil,
Until———

Japh. (interrupting them.) The Eternal Will
Shall deign to expound this dream
Of good and evil; and redeem
Unto Himself all times, all things;
And, gather'd under His almighty wings,
Abolish hell!
And to the expiated Earth
Restore the beauty of her birth,
Her Eden, in an endless paradise,
Where man no more can fall as once he fell,
And even the very demons shall do well!

Spirits. And when shall take effect this wond'rous spell?—

Japh. When the Redeemer cometh; first in pain,
And then in glory.

Spirit. Meantime still struggle in the mortal chain,—
Till earth wax hoary;
War with yourselves, and hell, and heaven, in vain,—
Until the clouds look gory
With the blood reeking from each battle-plain;
New times, new climes, new arts, new men: but still
The same old tears, old crimes, and oldest ill,
Shall be amongst your race in different forms;
But the same moral storms
Shall oversweep the future, as the waves
In a few hours the glorious Giants' graves.[2]

Chorus of Spirits.

Brethren, rejoice!
Mortal, farewell!
Hark! hark! already we can hear the voice
Of growing ocean's gloomy swell;
The winds, too, plume their piercing wings;
The clouds have nearly fill'd their springs;
The fountains of the great deep shall be broken,
And heaven set wide her windows;[3] while mankind
View, unacknowledged, each tremendous token—
Still, as they were from the beginning, blind.
We hear the sound they cannot hear,
The mustering thunders of the threat'ning sphere;
Yet a few hours their coming is delay'd;
Their flashing banners, folded still on high,
Yet undisplay'd,
Save to the Spirits' all-pervading eye.
Howl, howl, oh Earth!
Thy death is nearer than thy recent birth:
Tremble, ye mountains, soon to shrink below
The ocean's overflow!
The wave shall break upon your cliffs; and shells,
The little shells, of ocean's least things be
Deposed where now the eagle's offspring dwells—
How shall he shriek o'er the remorseless sea!
And call his nestlings up with fruitless yell,
Unanswer'd, save by the encroaching swell;—
While man shall long in vain for his broad wings,
The wings which could not save:—

Where could he rest them while the whole space brings
Nought to his eye beyond the deep, his grave?
Brethren, rejoice!
And loudly lift each superhuman voice—
All die,—
Save the slight remnant of Seth's seed—
The seed of Seth,
Exempt for future Sorrow's sake from death.
But of the sons of Cain
None shall remain;
And all his goodly daughters
Must lie beneath the desolating waters—
Or, floating upward, with their long hair laid
Along the wave, the cruel Heaven upbraid,
Which would not spare
Beings even in death so fair.
It is decreed,
All die!
And to the universal human cry
The universal silence shall succeed!
Fly, brethren, fly!
But still rejoice!
We fell!
They fall!
So perish all
These petty foes of Heaven who shrink from Hell!

[*The Spirits disappear, soaring upwards.*

Japh. (*solus.*) God hath proclaim'd the destiny of earth;
My father's ark of safety hath announced it;
The very demons shriek it from their caves;
The scroll of Enoch prophesied it long[4]
In silent books, which, in their silence, say
More to the mind than thunder to the ear:
And yet men listen'd not, nor listen; but
Walk darkling to their doom; which, though so nigh
Shakes them no more in their dim disbelief,
Than their last cries shall shake the Almighty purpose,
Or deaf obedient Ocean, which fulfils it.
No sign yet hangs its banner in the air;
The clouds are few, and of their wonted texture;
The sun will rise upon the earth's last day
As on the fourth day of creation, when
God said unto him "Shine!" and he broke forth
Into the dawn, which lighted not the yet
Unform'd forefather of mankind—but roused
Before the human orison the earlier
Made and far sweeter voices of the birds,
Which in the open firmament of heaven
Have wings like angels, and like them salute
Heaven first each day before the Adamites!
Their matins now draw nigh—the East is kindling,
And they will sing! and day will break! both near,
So near, the awful close! For these must drop
Their outworn pinions on the deep; and Day,
After the bright course of a few brief morrows,—
Ay, day will rise—but upon what? a chaos,
Which was ere day; and which, renew'd, makes time
Nothing! for, without life, what are the hours?
No more to dust than is eternity
Unto Jehovah, who created both.
Without Him, even Eternity would be
A void: without man, Time, as made for man,
Dies with man, and is swallowed in that deep
Which has no fountain; as his race will be
Devour'd by that which drowns his infant world.—
What have we here? Shapes of both earth and air?
No—*all* of heaven, they are so beautiful.
I cannot trace their features; but their forms,
How lovelily they move along the side
Of the gray mountain, scattering its mist!
And after the swart savage spirits, whose
Infernal immortality pour'd forth
Their impious hymn of triumph, they shall be
Welcome as Eden. It may be, they come
To tell me the reprieve of our young world,
For which I have so often pray'd—They come!
Anah! oh, God! and with her——

Enter SAMIASA, AZAZIEL, ANAH, *and* AHOLIBAMAH.

Anah. Japhet!
Sam. Lo!
A son of Adam!
Aza. What doth the earth-born here,
While all his race are slumbering?
Japh. Angel! what
Dost thou on earth when thou should'st be on high?
Aza. Know'st thou not, or forgett'st thou, that a part
Of our great function is to guard thine earth?
Japh. But all good angels have forsaken earth,
Which is condemn'd; nay, even the evil fly
The approaching Chaos. Anah! Anah! my
In vain, and long, and still to be beloved!
Why walk'st thou with this Spirit, in those hours
When no good spirit longer lights below?
Anah. Japhet, I cannot answer thee; yet, yet
Forgive me——
Japh. May the Heaven, which soon no more
Will pardon, do so! for thou art greatly tempted.
Aho. Back to thy tents, insulting son of Noah!
We know thee not.
Japh. The hour may come when thou
May'st know me better; and thy sister know
Me still the same which I have ever been.
Sam. Son of the Patriarch, who hath ever been
Upright before his God, whate'er thy griefs,
And thy words seem of sorrow, mix'd with wrath,
How have Azaziel, or myself, brought on thee
Wrong?

Japh. Wrong! the greatest of all wrongs; but thou
Say'st well, though she be dust, I did not, could not,
Deserve her. Farewell, Anah! I have said
That word so often! but now say it, ne'er
To be repeated. Angel! or whate'er
Thou art, or must be soon, hast thou the power
To save this beautiful—*these* beautiful—
Children of Cain?
Aza. From what?
Japh. And is it so,
That ye too know not? Angels! angels! ye
Have shared man's sin, and, it may be, now must

Partake his punishment; or, at the least,
My sorrow.
Sam. Sorrow! I ne'er thought till now
To hear an Adamite speak riddles to me.
Japh. And hath not the Most High expounded them?
Then ye are lost, as they are lost.
Aho. So be it!
If they love as they are loved, they will not shrink
More to be mortal, than I would to dare
An immortality of agonies
With Samiasa!
Anah. Sister! sister! speak not
Thus.
Aza. Fearest thou, my Anah?
Anah. Yes, for thee:
I would resign the greater remnant of
This little life of mine, before one hour
Of thine eternity should know a pang.
Japh. It is for *him*, then! for the Seraph thou
Hast left me! That is nothing, if thou hast not
Left thy God too! for unions like to these,
Between a mortal and an immortal, cannot
Be happy or be hallow'd. We are sent
Upon the earth to toil and die; and they
Are made to minister on high unto
The Highest; but if he can *save* thee, soon
The hour will come in which celestial aid
Alone can do so.
Anah. Ah! he speaks of death.
Sam. Of death to *us!* and those who are with us!
But that the man seems full of sorrow, I
Could smile.
Japh. I grieve not for myself, nor fear;
I am safe, not for my own deserts, but those
Of a well-doing sire, who hath been found
Righteous enough to save his children. Would
His power was greater of redemption! or
That by exchanging my own life for hers,
Who could alone have made mine happy, she,
The last and loveliest of Cain's race, could share
The ark which shall receive a remnant of
The seed of Seth!
Aho. And dost thou think that we,
With Cain's, the eldest-born of Adam's, blood
Warm in our veins—srtong Cain! who was begotten
In Paradise—would mingle with Seth's children?
Seth, the last offspring of old Adam's dotage?
No, not to save all earth, were earth in peril!
Our race hath always dwelt apart from thine
From the beginning, and shall do so ever.
Japh. I did not speak to thee, Aholibamah!
Too much of the forefather, whom thou vauntest,
Has come down in that haughty blood which springs
From him who shed the first, and that a brother's!
But thou, my Anah!—let me call thee mine,
Albeit thou art not; 'tis a word I cannot
Part with, although I must from thee: my Anah
Thou who dost rather make me dream that Abel
Had left a daughter, whose pure pious race
Survived in thee, so much unlike thou art
The rest of the stern Cainites, save in beauty,
For all of them are fairest in their favour——
Aho. (interrupting him.) And would'st thou have her like our father's foe
In mind, in soul? If *I* partook thy thought,
And dream'd that aught of *Abel* was in *her!*—
Get thee hence, son of Noah; thou mak'st strife.
Japh. Offspring of Cain, thy father did so!
Aho. But
He slew not Seth: and what hast thou to do
With other deeds between his God and him?
Japh. Thou speakest well: his God hath judged him, and
I had not named his deed, but that thyself
Didst seem to glory in him, nor to shrink
From what he had done.
Aho. He was our fathers' father;
The eldest born of man, the strongest, bravest,
And most enduring:—Shall I blush for him,
From whom we had our being? Look upon
Our race; behold their stature and their beauty,
Their courage, strength, and length of days——
Japh. They are number'd.
Aho. Be it so! but while yet their hours endure,
I glory in my brethren and our fathers!
Japh. My sire and race but glory in their God,
Anah! and thou?——
Anah. Whate'er our God decrees,
The God of Seth as Cain, I must obey,
And will endeavour patiently to obey.
But could I dare to pray in this dread hour
Of universal vengeance (if such should be),
It would not be to live, alone exempt
Of all my house. My sister! oh, my sister!
What were the world, or other worlds, or all
The brightest future, without the sweet past—
Thy love—my father's—all the life, and all
The things which sprang up with me, like the stars,
Making my dim existence radiant with
Soft lights which were not mine? Aholibamah!
Oh! if there should be mercy—seek it, find it:
I abhor death, because that thou must die.
Aho. What! hath this dreamer, with his father's ark,
The bugbear he hath built to scare the world,
Shaken *my* sister? Are *we* not the loved
Of seraphs? and if we were not, must we
Cling to a son of Noah for our lives?
Rather than thus——But the enthusiast dreams
The worst of dreams, the phantasies engender'd
By hopeless love and heated vigils. Who
Shall shake these solid mountains, this firm earth,
And bid those clouds and waters take a shape
Distinct from that which we and all our sires

Have seen them wear on their eternal way?
Who shall do this?
Japh. He whose one word produced them.
Aho. Who *heard* that word?
Japh. The Universe, which leap'd
To life before it. Ah! smil'st thou still in scorn?
Turn to thy seraphs: if they attest it not,
They are none.
Sam. Aholibamah, own thy God!
Aho. I have ever hail'd our Maker, Samiasá,
As thine, and mine; a God of love, not sorrow.
Japh. Alas! what else is love but sorrow? Even
He who made earth in love, had soon to grieve
Above its first and best inhabitants.
Aho. 'Tis said so.
Japh. It is even so.

Enter NOAH *and* SHEM.

Noah. Japhet! What
Dost thou here with these children of the wicked?
Dread'st thou not to partake their coming doom?
Japh. Father, it cannot be a sin to seek
To save an earth-born being; and behold,
These are not of the sinful, since they have
The fellowship of angels.
Noah. These are they, then,
Who leave the throne of God, to take them wives
From out the race of Cain; the sons of heaven,
Who seek earth's daughters for their beauty?
Aza. Patriarch!
Thou hast said it.
Noah. Wo, wo, wo to such communion!
Has not God made a barrier between earth
And heaven, and limited each, kind to kind?
Sam. Was not man made in high Jehovah's image?
Did God not love what He had made? And what
Do we but imitate and emulate
His love unto created love?
Noah. I am
But man, and was not made to judge mankind,
Far less the sons of God; but as our God
Has deign'd to commune with me, and reveal
His judgments, I reply, that the descent
Of seraphs from their everlasting seat
Unto a perishable and perishing,
Even on the very *eve* of *perishing*, world,
Cannot be good.
Aza. What! though it were to save?
Noah. Not ye in all your glory can redeem
What He who made you glorious hath condemn'd.
Were your immortal mission safety, 'twould
Be general, not for two, though beautiful;
And beautiful they are, but not the less
Condemn'd.
Japh. Oh, father! say it not.
Noah. Son! son!
If that thou wouldst avoid their doom, forget
That they exist: they soon shall cease to be;
While thou shalt be the sire of a new world,
And better.
Japh. Let me die with *this*, and *them!*
Noah. Thou *shouldst* for such a thought, but shalt not; He
Who *can*, redeems thee.
Sam. And why him and thee,
More than what he, thy son, prefers to both?
Noah. Ask Him who made thee greater than myself
And mine, but not less subject to His own
Almightiness. And lo! his mildest and
Least to be tempted messenger appears!

Enter RAPHAEL *the Archangel.*

Raph. Spirits!
Whose seat is near the throne,
What do ye here?
Is thus a seraph's duty to be shown,
Now that the hour is near
When earth must be alone?
Return!
Adore and burn
In glorious homage with the elected "seven,"
Your place is heaven.
Sam. Raphael!
The first and fairest of the sons of God,
How long hath this been law,
That earth by angels must be left untrod?
Earth! which oft saw
Jehovah's footsteps not disdain her sod!
The world He loved, and made
For love; and oft have we obey'd
His frequent mission with delighted pinions;
Adoring Him in His least works display'd;
Watching this youngest star of His dominions:
And as the latest birth of His great word,
Eager to keep it worthy of our Lord.
Why is thy brow severe?
And wherefore speak'st thou of destruction near?
Raph. Had Samiasa and Azaziel been
In their true place, with the angelic choir,
Written in fire
They would have seen
Jehovah's late decree,
And not inquired their Maker's breath of me:
But ignorance must ever be
A part of sin;
And even the spirits' knowledge shall grow less
As they wax proud within:
For Blindness is the first-born of Excess.
When all good angels left the world, ye stay'd,
Stung with strange passions, and debased
By mortal feelings for a mortal maid;
But ye are pardon'd thus far, and replaced
With your pure equals. Hence! away! away!
Or stay,
And lose eternity by that delay!

Aza. And thou; if earth be thus forbidden
In the decree
To us until this moment hidden,
Dost thou not err, as we,
In being here?
Raph. I came to call ye back to your fit sphere,
In the great name and at the word of God!
Dear, dearest in themselves, and scarce less dear
That which I came to do: till now we trod
Together the eternal space, together
Let us still walk the stars. True, earth must die!
Her race, return'd into her womb, must wither,
And much which she inherits: but oh! why
Cannot this earth be made, or be destroy'd,
Without involving ever some vast void
In the immortal ranks? immortal still
In their immeasurable forfeiture.
Our brother Satan fell; his burning will
Rather than longer worship dared endure!
But ye who still are pure!
Seraphs! less mighty than that mightiest one,
Think how he was undone!
And think if tempting man can compensate
For heaven desired too late?
Long have I warred,
Long must I war
With him who deem'd it hard
To be created, and to acknowledge Him
Who, 'midst the cherubim
Made him as suns to a dependent star,
Leaving the archangels at his right hand dim.
I loved him—beautiful he was; oh, heaven!
Save *His* who made, what beauty and what power
Was ever like to Satan's! Would the hour
In which he fell could ever be forgiven!
The wish is impious: but, oh ye!
Yet undestroyed, be warn'd! Eternity
With him, or with his God, is in your choice!
He hath not tempted you, he cannot tempt
The angels, from his further snares exempt:
But man hath listen'd to his voice,
And ye to woman's—beautiful she is,
The serpent's voice less subtle than her kiss.
The snake but vanquish'd dust: but she will draw
A second host from heaven, to break heaven's law.
Yet, yet, oh fly!
Ye cannot die,
But they
Shall pass away,
While ye shall fill with shrieks the upper sky
For perishable clay,
Whose memory in your immortality
Shall long outlast the sun which gave them day.
Think how your essence differeth from theirs
In all but suffering! Why partake
The agony to which they must be heirs—
Born to be plough'd with years, and sown with cares,
And reap'd by Death, lord of the human soil?
Even had their days been left to toil their path
Through time to dust, unshorten'd by God's wrath,
Still they are Evil's prey, and Sorrow's spoil.
Aho. Let them fly!
I hear the voice which says that all must die,
Sooner than our white-bearded Patriarchs died;
And that on high
An ocean is prepared,
While from below
The deep shall rise to meet heaven's overflow.
Few shall be spared,
It seems; and, of that few, the race of Cain
Must lift their eyes to Adam's God in vain.
Sister! since it is so,
And the eternal Lord
In vain would be implored
For the remission of one hour of woe,
Let us resign even what we have adored,
And meet the wave, as we would meet the sword,
If not unmoved, yet undismay'd,
And wailing less for us than those who shall
Survive in mortal or immortal thrall,
And, when the fatal waters are allay'd,
Weep for the myriads who can weep no more.
Fly, Seraphs! to your own eternal shore,
Where winds nor howl nor waters roar.
Our portion is to die,
And yours to live for ever:
But which is best, a dead eternity,
Or living, is but known to the great Giver.
Obey Him, as we shall obey;
I would not keep this life of mine of clay
An hour beyond His will;
Nor see ye lose a portion of His grace,
For all the mercy which Seth's race
Find still.
Fly!
And as your pinions bear ye back to heaven,
Think that my love still mounts with thee on high,
Samiasa!
And if I look up with a tearless eye,
'Tis that an angel's bride disdains to weep
Farewell! Now rise, inexorable Deep!
Anah. And must we die?
And must I lose thee too,
Azaziel?
Oh, my heart! my heart!
Thy prophecies were true,
And yet thou wert so happy too!
The blow, though not unlook'd for, falls as new:
But yet depart!
Ah, why?
Yet let me not retain thee—fly!
My pangs can be but brief; but thine would be
Eternal, if repulsed from heaven for me.

Too much already hast thou deign'd
To one of Adam's race!
Our doom is sorrow; not to us alone,
But to the spirits who have not disdain'd
To love us, cometh anguish with disgrace.
The first who taught us knowledge hath been hurl'd
From his once archangelic throne
Into some unknown world:
And thou, Azaziel! No—
Thou shalt not suffer woe
For me. Away! nor weep!
Thou canst not weep; but yet
May'st suffer more, not weeping: then forget
Her, whom the surges of the all-strangling Deep
Can bring no pang like this. Fly! fly!
Being gone, 't will be less difficult to die.
Japh. Oh, say not so!
Father! and thou, Archangel, thou!
Surely celestial Mercy lurks below
That pure severe serenity of brow:
Let them not meet this sea without a shore,
Save in our ark, or let me be no more!
Noah. Peace, child of passion, peace!
If not within thy heart, yet with thy tongue
Do God no wrong!
Live as He wills it—die, when He ordains,
A righteous death, unlike the seed of Cain's.
Cease, or be sorrowful in silence; cease
To weary Heaven's ear with thy selfish plaint.
Would'st thou have God commit a sin for thee?
Such would it be
To alter His intent
For a mere mortal sorrow. Be a man!
And bear what Adam's race must bear, and can.
Japh. Ay, father! but when they are gone,
And we are all alone,
Floating upon the azure desert, and
The depth beneath us hides our own dear land,
And dearer, silent friends and brethren, all
Buried in its immeasurable breast,
Who, who, our tears, our shrieks, shall then command?
Can we in desolation's peace have rest?
Oh God! be Thou a God, and spare
Yet while 'tis time!
Renew not Adam's fall:
Mankind were then but twain,
But they are numerous now as are the waves
And the tremendous rain,
Whose drops shall be less thick than would their graves,
Were graves permitted to the seed of Cain.
Noah. Silence, vain boy! each word of thine's a crime!
Angel! forgive this stripling's fond despair.
Raph. Seraphs! these mortals speak in passion: Ye,
Who are, or should be, passionless and pure,
May now return with me.
Sam. It may not be:
We have chosen, and will endure.
Raph. Say'st thou?
Aza. He hath said it, and I say, Amen!
Raph. Again!
Then from this hour,
Shorn as ye are of all celestial power,
And aliens from your God,
Farewell!
Japh. Alas! where shall they dwell?
Hark, hark! Deep sounds, and deeper still,
Are howling from the mountain's bosom:
There's not a breath of wind upon the hill,
Yet quivers every leaf, and drops each blossom:
Earth groans as if beneath a heavy load.
Noah. Hark, hark! the sea-birds cry!
In clouds they overspread the lurid sky,
And hover round the mountain, where before
Never a white wing, wetted by the wave,
Yet dared to soar,
Even when the waters wax'd too fierce to brave.
Soon it shall be their only shore
And then, no more!
Japh. The sun! the sun!
He riseth, but his better light is gone,
And a black circle, bound
His glaring disk around,
Proclaims Earth's last of summer days hath shone!
The clouds return into the hues of night,
Save where their brazen-coloured edges streak
The verge where brighter morns were wont to break.
Noah. And lo! yon flash of light,
The distant thunder's harbinger, appears!
It cometh! hence, away!
Leave to the elements their evil prey!
Hence to where our all-hallowed ark uprears
Its safe and wreckless sides.
Japh. Oh, father, stay!
Leave not my Anah to the swallowing tides!
Noah. Must we not leave all life to such? Begone!
Japh. Not I.
Noah. Then die
With them!
How darest thou look on that prophetic sky,
And seek to save what all things now condemn,
In overwhelming unison
With just Jehovah's wrath?
Japh. Can rage and justice join in the same path?
Noah. Blasphemer! darest thou murmur even now?
Raph. Patriarch, be still a father! smoothe thy brow:
Thy son, despite his folly, shall not sink:

He knows not what he says, yet shall not drink
With sobs the salt foam of the swelling waters;
But be, when Passion passeth, good as thou,
Nor perish like Heaven's children with Man's daughters.

Aho. The tempest cometh; Heaven and Earth unite
For the annihilation of all life.
Unequal is the strife
Between our strength and the Eternal Might!

Sam. But ours is with thee: we will bear ye far
To some untroubled star,
Where thou and Anah shall partake our lot:
And if thou dost not weep for thy lost earth,
Our forfeit heaven shall also be forgot.

Anah. Oh! my dear father's tents, my place of birth!
And mountains, land, and woods! when ye are not,
Who shall dry up my tears?

Aza. Thy Spirit-lord.
Fear not; though we are shut from heaven,
Yet much is ours, whence we cannot be driven.

Raph. Rebel! thy words are wicked, as thy deeds
Shall henceforth be but weak: the flaming sword,
Which chased the first-born out of Paradise,
Still flashes in the angelic hands.

Aza. It cannot slay us: threaten dust with death,
And talk of weapons unto that which bleeds!
What are thy swords in our immortal eyes?

Raph. The moment cometh to approve thy strength;
And learn at length
How vain to war with what thy God commands.
Thy former force was in thy faith.

Enter MORTALS, *flying for refuge.*

Chorus of MORTALS.

The heavens and earth are mingling—God! oh God!
What have we done? Yet spare!
Hark! even the forest beasts howl forth their pray'r!
The dragon crawls from out his den,
To herd, in terror, innocent with men!
And the birds scream their agony through air.
Yet, yet, Jehovah! yet withdraw Thy rod
Of wrath, and pity Thine own world's despair!
Hear not man only but all Nature plead!

Raph. Farewell, thou earth! Ye wretched sons of clay,
I cannot, must not, aid you. 'Tis decreed!
[*Exit* RAPHAEL.

Japh. Some clouds sweep on as vultures for their prey,
While others, fix'd as rocks, await the word
At which their wrathful vials shall be pour'd.
No azure more shall robe the firmament,
Nor spangled stars be glorious: Death hath risen:
In the Sun's place, a pale and ghastly glare
Hath wound itself around the dying air.

Aza. Come, Anah! quit this chaos-founded prison,
To which the elements again repair,
To turn it into what it was: beneath
The shelter of these wings thou shalt be safe,
As was the eagle's nestling once within
Its mother's.—Let the coming chaos chafe
With all its elements! heed not their din!
A brighter world than this, where thou shalt breathe
Ethereal life, will we explore:
These darken'd clouds are not the only skies.

[AZAZIEL *and* SAMIASA *fly off, and disappear with* ANAH *and* AHOLIBAMAH.

Japh. They are gone! They have disappear'd amidst the roar
Of the forsaken world; and never more,
Whether they live, or die with all earth's life,
Now near its last, can aught restore
Anah unto these eyes.

Chorus of MORTALS.

Oh son of Noah! mercy on thy kind!
What, wilt thou leave us all—all—*all* behind?
While safe amidst the elemental strife,
Thou sitt'st within thy guarded ark?

A mother (*offering her infant to* JAPHET.) Oh, let this child embark!
I brought him forth in woe,
But thought it joy
To see him to my bosom clinging so.
Why was he born?
What hath he done—
My unwean'd son—
To move Jehovah's wrath or scorn?
What is there in this milk of mine, that Death
Should stir all heaven and earth up to destroy
My boy,
And roll the waters o'er his placid breath?
Save him, thou seed of Seth!
Or cursed be—with Him who made
Thee and thy race, for which we are betray'd!

Japh. Peace! 'tis no hour for curses, but for pray'r!

Chorus of MORTALS.

For prayer!!!
And where
Shall prayer ascend
When the swoln clouds unto the mountains bend
And burst,
And gushing oceans every barrier rend,
Until the very deserts know no thirst?
Accurst
Be He, who made thee and thy sire!
We deem our curses vain; we must expire;
But as we know the worst,
Why should our hymn be raised, our knees be bent
Before the implacable Omnipotent,

Since we must fall the same?
If He hath made earth, let it be His shame,
To make a world for torture.—Lo! they come,
 The loathsome waters, in their rage!
And with their roar make wholesome Nature dumb!
 The forest's trees (cöeval with the hour
When Paradise upsprung,
 Ere Eve gave Adam knowledge for her dower,
Or Adam his first hymn of slavery sung),
 So massy, vast, yet green in their old age,
 Are overtopt,
Their summer blossoms by the surges lopp'd,
Which rise, and rise, and rise.
Vainly we look up to the low'ring skies—
 They meet the seas,
And shut out God from our beseeching eyes.
 Fly, son of Noah, fly! and take thine ease
In thine allotted ocean-tent;
And view, all floating o'er the element,
The corpses of the world of thy young days:
 Then to Jehovah raise
 Thy song of praise!

A Mortal. Blessed are the dead
 Who die in the Lord!

And though the waters be o'er earth outspread,
Yet, as *His* word,
Be the decree adored!
He gave me life—He taketh but
The breath which is His own:
And though these eyes should be for ever shut,
Nor longer this weak voice before His throne
Be heard in supplicating tone,
Still blessed be the Lord,
For what is past,
For that which is:
For all are His,
From first to last—
Time—space—eternity—life—death—
The vast known and immeasurable unknown.
He made, and can unmake;
And shall *I*, for a little gasp of breath,
Blaspheme and groan?
No; let me die, as I have lived, in faith,
Nor quiver, though the universe may quake!

Chorus of MORTALS.

Where shall we fly?
Not to the mountains high;
For now their torrents rush, with double roar,
To meet the ocean, which, advancing still,
Already grasps each drowning hill,
Nor leaves an unsearch'd cave.

Enter a WOMAN.

Woman. Oh, save me, save!
Our valley is no more:
My father and my father's tent,
My brethren and my brethren's herds,
The pleasant trees that o'er our noonday bent
And sent forth evening songs from sweetest birds,
The little rivulet which freshen'd all
Our pastures green,
No more are to be seen.
When to the mountain cliff I climb'd this morn,
I turn'd to bless the spot,
And not a leaf appear'd about to fall;—
And now they are not!
Why was I born?

Japh. To die! in youth to die!
And happier in that doom,
Than to behold the universal tomb
Which I
Am thus condemn'd to weep above in vain.
Why, when all perish, why must I remain?

[*The Waters rise; Men fly in every direction; many are overtaken by the waves. The Chorus of Mortals disperses in search of safety up the Mountains;* JAPHET *remains upon a rock, while the ark floats towards him in the distance.*

NOTES TO HEAVEN AND EARTH.

NOTE 1, page 400.

Albeit thou watchest with "the seven."

The archangels, said to be seven in number, and to occupy the eighth rank in the celestial hierarchy.

NOTE 2, page 406.

In a few hours the glorious giants' graves.

"And there were giants in the earth in those days, and after; mighty men, which were of old, men of renown." —*Genesis.*

NOTE 3, page 406.

And heaven set wide her windows.

"The same day were all the fountains of the great deep broken up; and the windows of heaven were opened."—*Genesis.*

NOTE 4, page 407.

The scroll of Enoch prophesied it long.

The book of Enoch, preserved by the Ethiopians, is said by them to be anterior to the flood.

CAIN:
A MYSTERY.

"Now the Serpent was more subtil than any beast of the field which the Lord God had made."—*Gen.* ch. iii. ver 1.

TO

SIR WALTER SCOTT, Bart.,

THIS MYSTERY OF CAIN IS INSCRIBED,

BY HIS OBLIGED FRIEND, AND FAITHFUL SERVANT,

THE AUTHOR.

PREFACE.

The following scenes are entitled "A Mystery," in conformity with the ancient title annexed to dramas upon similar subjects, which were styled "Myteries, or Moralities." The author has by no means taken the same liberties with his subject which were common formerly, as may be seen by any reader curious enough to refer to those very profane productions, whether in English, French, Italian, or Spanish. The author has endeavoured to preserve the language adapted to his characters; and where it is (and this is but rarely) taken from actual *Scripture*, he has made as little alteration, even of words, as the rhythm would permit. The reader will recollect that the book of Genesis does not state that Eve was tempted by a demon, but by "the Serpent;" and that only because he was "the most subtil of all the beasts of the field." Whatever interpretation the Rabbins and the Fathers may have put upon this, I take the words as I find them, and reply, with Bishop Watson upon similar occasions, when the Fathers were quoted to him, as Moderator in the schools of Cambridge, "Behold the Book!"—holding up the Scripture. It is to be recollected that my present subject has nothing to do with the *New Testament*, to which no reference can be here made without anachronism. With the poems upon similar topics I have not been recently familiar. Since I was twenty, I have never read Milton; but I had read him so frequently before, that this may make little difference. Gesner's "Death of Abel" I have never read since I was eight years of age, at Aberdeen. The general impression of my recollection is delight; but of the contents I remember only that Cain's wife was called Mahala, and Abel's Thirza: in the following pages I have called them "Adah" and "Zillah," the earliest female names which occur in Genesis; they were those of Lamech's wives: those of Cain and Abel are not called by their names. Whether, then, a coincidence of subject may have caused the same in expression, I know nothing, and care as little.

The reader will please to bear in mind (what few choose to recollect), that there is no allusion to a future state in any of the books of Moses, nor indeed in the Old Testament. For a reason for this extraordinary omission, he may consult Warburton's "Divine Legation;" whether satisfactory or not, no better has yet been assigned. I have therefore supposed it new to Cain, without, I hope, any perversion of Holy Writ.

With regard to the language of Lucifer, it was difficult for me to make him talk like a clergyman upon the same subjects; but I have done what I could to restrain him within the bounds of spiritual politeness.

If he disclaims having tempted Eve in the shape of the Serpent, it is only because the book of Genesis has not the most distant allusion to anything of the kind, but merely to the Serpent in his serpentine capacity.

Note.—The reader will perceive that the author has partly adopted in this poem the notion of Cuvier, that the world had been destroyed several times before the creation of man. This speculation, derived from the different strata and the bones of enormous and unknown animals found in them, is not contrary to the Mosaic account, but rather confirms it; as no human bones have yet been discovered in those strata, although those of many known animals are found near the remains of the unknown. The assertion of Lucifer, that the pre-Adamite world was also peopled by rational beings much more intelligent than man, and proportionably powerful to the mammoth, &c. &c., is, of course, a poetical fiction to help him to make out his case.

I ought to add, that there is a "tramelogedia" of Alfieri, called "Abele."—I have never read that, nor any other of the posthumous works of the writer, except his Life.

Dramatis Personæ.

MEN.	SPIRITS.	WOMEN.
ADAM.	ANGEL OF THE LORD.	EVE.
CAIN.	LUCIFER.	ADAH.
ABEL.		ZILLAH.

ACT I.

SCENE I.

The Land without Paradise.—Time, Sunrise.

ADAM, EVE, CAIN, ABEL, ADAH, ZILLAH, *offering a Sacrifice.*

Adam. God, the Eternal! Infinite! Allwise!—
Who out of darkness on the deep didst make
Light on the waters with a word—all hail!
Jehovah, with returning light, all hail!
Eve. God! who didst name the day, and separate
Morning from night, till then divided never—
Who didst divide the wave from wave, and call
Part of Thy work the firmament—all hail!
Abel. God! who didst call the elements into
Earth—ocean—air—and fire, and with the day
And night, and worlds, which these illuminate,

Or shadow, madest beings to enjoy them,
And love both them and Thee—all hail! all hail!

Adah. God, the Eternal! Parent of all things!
Who didst create these best and beauteous beings,
To be beloved, more than all, save Thee—
Let me love Thee and them:—All hail! all hail!

Zillah. Oh, God! who loving, making, blessing all,
Yet didst permit the Serpent to creep in,
And drive my father forth from Paradise,
Keep us from further evil:—Hail! all hail!

Adam. Son Cain, my first-born, wherefore art thou silent?

Cain. Why should I speak?

Adam. To pray.

Cain. Have ye not pray'd?

Adam. We have, most fervently.

Cain. And loudly: I
Have heard you.

Adam. So will God, I trust.

Abel. Amen!

Adam. But thou, my eldest born, art silent still.

Cain. 'Tis better I should be so.

Adam. Wherefore so?

Cain. I have nought to ask.

Adam. Nor aught to thank for?

Cain. No.

Adam. Dost thou not live?

Cain. Must I not die?

Eve. Alas!
The fruit of our forbidden tree begins
To fall.

Adam. And we must gather it again.
Oh, God! why didst Thou plant the tree of knowledge?

Cain. And wherefore pluck'd ye not the tree of life?
Ye might have then defied Him.

Adam. Oh! my son,
Blaspheme not: these are serpents' words.

Cain. Why not?
The snake spoke *truth;* it *was* the tree of knowledge;
It *was* the tree of life: knowledge is good,
And life is good; and how can both be evil?

Eve. My boy! thou speakest as I spoke, in sin,
Before thy birth: let me not see renew'd
My misery in thine. I have repented.
Let me not see my offspring fall into
The snares beyond the walls of Paradise,
Which e'en in Paradise destroy'd his parents.
Content thee with what *is.* Had we been so,
Thou now hadst been contented.—Oh, my son!

Adam. Our orisons completed, let us hence,
Each to his task of toil—not heavy, though
Needful: the earth is young, and yields us kindly
Her fruits with little labour.

Eve. Cain, my son,
Behold thy father cheerful and resign'd,
And do as he doth.

[*Exeunt* ADAM *and* EVE.

Zillah. Wilt thou not, my brother?

Abel. Why wilt thou wear this gloom upon thy brow,
Which can avail thee nothing, save to rouse
The Eternal anger?

Adah. My beloved Cain,
Wilt thou frown even on me?

Cain. No, Adah! no;
I fain would be alone a little while.
Abel, I'm sick at heart; but it will pass.
Precede me, brother—I will follow shortly.
And you, too, sisters, tarry not behind;
Your gentleness must not be harshly met:
I'll follow you anon.

Adah. If not, I will
Return to seek you here.

Abel. The peace of God
Be on your spirit, brother!

[*Exeunt* ABEL, ZILLAH, *and* ADAH.

Cain (solus). And this is
Life!—Toil! and wherefore should I toil?—because
My father could not keep his place in Eden.
What had *I* done in this?—I was unborn:
I sought not to be born; nor love the state
To which that birth has brought me. Why did he
Yield to the serpent and the woman? or,
Yielding, why suffer? What was there in this?
The tree was planted, and why not for him?
If not, why place him near it, where it grew,
The fairest in the centre? They have but
One answer to all questions, "'Twas *His* will,
And *He* is good." How know I that? Because
He is all-powerful, must all-good, too, follow?
I judge but by the fruits—and they are bitter—
Which I must feed on for a fault not mine.
Whom have we here?—A shape like to the angels,
Yet of a sterner and a sadder aspect
Of spiritual essence: why do I quake?
Why should I fear him more than other spirits,
Whom I see daily wave their fiery swords
Before the gates round which I linger oft,
In twilight's hour, to catch a glimpse of those
Gardens which are my just inheritance,
Ere the night closes o'er the inhibited walls
And the immortal trees which overtop
The cherubim-defended battlements?
If I shrink not from these, the fire-arm'd angels,
Why should I quail from him who now approaches?

Yet he seems mightier far than them, nor less
Beauteous, and yet not all as beautiful
As he hath been, and might be: sorrow seems
Half of his immortality. And is it
So? and can aught grieve save humanity?
He cometh.

Enter LUCIFER.

Lucifer. Mortal!
Cain. Spirit, who art thou?
Lucifer. Master of spirits.
Cain. And being so, canst thou
Leave them, and walk with dust?
Lucifer. I know the thoughts
Of dust, and feel for it, and with you.
Cain. How!
You know my thoughts?
Lucifer. They are thoughts of all
Worthy of thought;—'tis your immortal part
Which speaks within you.
Cain. What immortal part?
This has not been reveal'd: the tree of life
Was withheld from us by my father's folly,
While that of knowledge, by my mother's haste,
Was pluck'd too soon; and all the fruit is death!
Lucifer. They have deceived thee; thou shalt live.
Cain. I live,
But live to die: and, living, see nothing
To make death hateful, save an inmate clinging,
A loathsome, and yet all invincible
Instinct of life, which I abhor, as I
Despise myself, yet cannot overcome—
And so I live. Would I had never lived!
Lucifer. Thou livest, and must live for ever: think not
The earth, which is thine outward cov'ring, is
Existence—it will cease, and thou wilt be
No less than thou art now.
Cain. No *less!* and why
No more?
Lucifer. It may be thou shalt be as we.
Cain. And ye?
Lucifer. Are everlasting.
Cain. Are ye happy?
Lucifer. We are mighty.
Cain. Are ye happy?
Lucifer. No: art thou?
Cain. How should I be so? Look on me!
Lucifer. Poor clay!
And thou pretendest to be wretched! Thou!
Cain. I am:—and thou, with all thy might, what art thou?
Lucifer. One who aspired to be what made thee, and
Would not have made thee what thou art.
Cain. Ah!
Thou look'st almost a god; and——
Lucifer. I am none:
And having fail'd to be one, would be nought
Save what I am. He conquer'd; let Him reign!
Cain. Who?
Lucifer. Thy sire's Maker, and the earth's.
Cain. And heaven's,
And all that in them is. So I have heard
His seraphs sing; and so my father saith.
Lucifer. They say—what they must sing and say, on pain
Of being that which I am—and thou art—
Of spirits and of men.
Cain. And what is that?
Lucifer. Souls who dare use their immortality—
Souls who dare look the Omnipotent tyrant in
His everlasting face, and tell Him, that
His evil is not good! If He has made,
As He saith—which I know not, nor believe—
But, if He made us—He cannot unmake:
We are immortal!—nay, He'd *have* us so,
That He may torture:—let Him! He is great—
But, in His greatness, is no happier than
We in our conflict! Goodness would not make
Evil; and what else hath He made? But let Him
Sit on His vast and solitary throne,
Creating worlds, to make eternity
Less burthensome to His immense existence
And unparticipated solitude!
Let Him crowd orb on orb: He is alone
Indefinite, indissoluble tyrant!
Could He but crush Himself, 'twere the best boon
He ever granted: but, let Him reign on,
And multiply Himself in misery!
Spirits and men, at least we sympathise—
And, suffering in concert, make our pangs,
Innumerable, more endurable,
By the unbounded sympathy of all—
With all! But *He!* so wretched in His height,
So restless in His wretchedness, must still
Create, and re-create——
Cain. Thou speak'st to me of things which long have swum
In visions through my thought: I never could
Reconcile what I saw with what I heard.
My father and my mother talk to me
Of serpents, and of fruits and trees: I see
The gates of what they call their Paradise
Guarded by fiery-sworded cherubim,
Which shut them out, and me: I feel the weight
Of daily toil and constant thought: I look
Around a world where I seem nothing, with
Thoughts which arise within me, as if they
Could master all things:—but I thought alone

This misery was *mine.*—My father is
Tamed down; my mother has forgot the mind
Which made her thirst for knowledge at the risk
Of an eternal curse; my brother is
A watching shepherd boy, who offers up
The firstlings of the flock to Him who bids
The earth yield nothing to us without sweat;
My sister Zillah sings an earlier hymn
Than the birds' matins; and my Adah, my
Own and beloved, she, too, understands not
The mind which overwhelms me: never till
Now met I aught to sympathise with me.
'T is well—I rather would consort with spirits.

Lucifer. And hadst thou not been fit by thine own soul
For such companionship, I would not now
Have stood before thee as I am: a serpent
Had been enough to charm ye, as before.

Cain. Ah! didst *thou* tempt my mother?

Lucifer. I tempt none,
Save with the truth: was not the tree, the tree
Of knowledge? and was not the tree of life
Still fruitful? Did *I* bid her pluck them not?
Did *I* plant things prohibited within
The reach of beings innocent, and curious
By their own innocence? I would have made ye
Gods; and even He who thrust ye forth, so thrust ye
Because "ye should not eat the fruits of life,
And become gods as We." Were those His words?

Cain. They were, as I have heard from those who heard them,
In thunder.

Lucifer. Then who was the demon? He
Who would not let ye live, or he who would
Have made ye live for ever in the joy
And power of knowledge?

Cain. Would they had snatch'd both
The fruits, or neither!

Lucifer. One is yours already;
The other may be still.

Cain. How so?

Lucifer. By being
Yourselves, in your resistance. Nothing can
Quench the mind, if the mind will be itself
And centre of surrounding things—'tis made
To sway.

Cain. But didst thou tempt my parents?

Lucifer. I?
Poor clay! what should I tempt them for, or how?

Cain. They say the serpent was a spirit.

Lucifer. Who
Saith that? It is not written so on high:
The proud One will not so far falsify,
Though man's vast fears and little vanity
Would make him cast upon the spiritual nature
His own low failing. The snake *was* the snake—
No more: and yet not less than those he tempted,
In nature being earth also—*more* in *wisdom,*
Since he could overcome them, and foreknew
The knowledge fatal to their narrow joys.
Think'st thou I'd take the shape of things that die?

Cain. But the thing had a demon?

Lucifer. He but woke one
In those he spake to with his forky tongue.
I tell thee that the serpent was no more
Than a mere serpent: ask the cherubim
Who guard the tempting tree. When thousand ages
Have roll'd o'er your dead ashes, and your seed's,
The seed of the then world may thus array
Their earliest fault in fable, and attribute
To me a shape I scorn, as I scorn all
That bows to Him, who made things but to bend
Before His sullen, sole eternity;
But we, who see the truth, must speak it. Thy
Fond parents listen'd to a creeping thing,
And fell. For what should spirits tempt them? What
Was there to envy in the narrow bounds
Of Paradise, that spirits who pervade
Space——but I speak to thee of what thou know'st not,
With all thy tree of knowledge.

Cain. But thou canst not
Speak aught of knowledge which I would not know,
And do not thirst to know, and bear a mind
To know.

Lucifer. And heart to look on?

Cain. Be it proved.

Lucifer. Darest thou to look on Death?

Cain. He has not yet
Been seen.

Lucifer. But must be undergone.

Cain. My father
Says he is something dreadful, and my mother
Weeps when he is named; and Abel lifts his eyes
To heaven, and Zillah casts hers to the earth,
And sighs a prayer; and Adah looks on me,
And speaks not.

Lucifer. And thou?

Cain. Thoughts unspeakable
Crowd in my breast to burning, when I hear
Of this almighty Death, who is, it seems,
Inevitable. Could I wrestle with him?
I wrestled with the lion, when a boy,
In play, till he ran roaring from my gripe.

Lucifer. It has no shape; but will absorb all things
That bear the form of earth-born being.

Cain. Ah!
I thought it was a being: who could do
Such evil things to beings save a being?
Lucifer. Ask the Destroyer.
Cain. Who?
Lucifer. The Maker—call Him
Which name thou wilt; He makes but to destroy.
Cain. I knew not that, yet thought it, since I heard
Of death: although I know not what it is,
Yet it seems horrible. I have look'd out
In the vast desolate night in search of him;
And when I saw gigantic shadows in
The umbrage of the walls of Eden, chequer'd
By the far-flashing of the cherubs' swords,
I watch'd for what I thought his coming; for
With fear rose longing in my heart to know
What 't was which shook us all—but nothing came.
And then I turn'd my weary eyes from off
Our native and forbidden Paradise,
Up to the lights above us, in the azure,
Which are so beautiful: shall they, too, die?
Lucifer. Perhaps—but long outlive both thine and thee.
Cain. I'm glad of that: I would not have them die—
They are so lovely. What is death? I fear,
I feel, it is a dreadful thing; but what,
I cannot compass: 'tis denounced against us,
Both them who sinn'd and sinn'd not, as an ill—
What ill?
Lucifer. To be resolved into the earth.
Cain. But shall I know it?
Lucifer. As I know not death,
I cannot answer.
Cain. Were I quiet earth,
That were no evil: would I ne'er had been
Aught else but dust!
Lucifer. That is a grovelling wish,
Less than thy father's, for he wish'd to know.
Cain. But not to live, or wherefore pluck'd he not
The life tree?
Lucifer. He was hinder'd.
Cain. Deadly error!
Not to snatch first that fruit:—but ere he pluck'd
The knowledge, he was ignorant of death.
Alas! I scarcely now know what it is,
And yet I fear it—fear I know not what!
Lucifer. And I, who know all things, fear nothing: see
What is true knowledge.
Cain. Wilt thou teach me all?
Lucifer. Ay, upon one condition.
Cain. Name it.
Lucifer. That
Thou dost fall down and worship me—thy Lord.
Cain. Thou art not the Lord my father worships.
Lucifer. No.
Cain. His equal?
Lucifer. No:—I have nought in common with Him!
Nor would: I would be aught above—beneath—
Aught save a sharer or a servant of
His power. I dwell apart; but I am great:—
Many there are who worship me, and more
Who shall—be thou amongst the first.
Cain. I never
As yet have bow'd unto my father's God,
Although my brother Abel oft implores
That I would join with him in sacrifice:—
Why should I bow to thee?
Lucifer. Hast thou ne'er bow'd
To Him?
Cain. Have I not said it?—need I say it?
Could not thy mighty knowledge teach thee that?
Lucifer. He who bows not to Him has bow'd to me!
Cain. But I will bend to neither.
Lucifer. Ne'er the less,
Thou art my worshipper: not worshipping
Him makes thee mine the same.
Cain. And what is that?
Lucifer. Thou'lt know here—and hereafter.
Cain. Let me but
Be taught the mystery of my being.
Lucifer. Follow
Where I will lead thee.
Cain. But I must retire
To till the earth—for I had promised——
Lucifer. What?
Cain. To cull some first-fruits.
Lucifer. Why?
Cain. To offer up
With Abel on an altar.
Lucifer. Saidst thou not
Thou ne'er hadst bent to Him who made thee?
Cain. Yes—
But Abel's earnest prayer has wrought upon me;
The offering is more his than mine—and Adah——
Lucifer. Why dost thou hesitate?
Cain. She is my sister,
Born on the same day, of the same womb: and
She wrung from me, with tears, this promise;
Rather than see her weep, I would, methinks,
Bear all—and worship aught.
Lucifer. Then follow me!
Cain. I will.

Enter ADAH.

Adah. My brother, I have come for thee;
It is our hour of rest and joy—and we
Have less without thee. Thou hast labour'd not
This morn; but I have done thy task: the fruits
Are ripe, and glowing as the light which ripens:
Come away.

Cain. See'st thou not?

Adah. I see an angel;
We have seen many: will he share our hour
Of rest?—he is welcome.

Cain. But he is not like
The angels we have seen.

Adah. Are there, then, others?
But he is welcome, as they were: they deign'd
To be our guests—will he?

Cain (to Lucifer). Wilt thou?

Lucifer. I ask
Thee to be mine.

Cain. I must away with him.

Adah. And leave us?

Cain. Ay.

Adah. And *me?*

Cain. Beloved Adah!

Adah. Let me go with thee.

Lucifer. No, she must not.

Adah. Who
Art thou that steppest between heart and heart?

Cain. He is a god.

Adah. How know'st thou?

Cain. He speaks like
A god.

Adah. So did the serpent, and it lied.

Lucifer. Thou errest, Adah!—was not the tree that
Of knowledge?

Adah. Ay—to our eternal sorrow.

Lucifer. And yet that grief is knowledge—so he lied not:
And if he did betray you, 'twas with truth;
And truth in its own essence cannot be
But good.

Adah. But all we know of it has gather'd
Evil on ill: expulsion from our home,
And dread, and toil, and sweat, and heaviness;
Remorse of that which was—and hope of that
Which cometh not. Cain! walk not with this spirit.
Bear with what we have borne, and love me—I
Love thee.

Lucifer. More than thy mother, and thy sire?

Adah. I do. Is that a sin, too?

Lucifer. No, not yet:
It one day will be in your children.

Adah. What!
Must not my daughter love her brother Enoch?

Lucifer. Not as thou lovest Cain.

Adah. Oh, my God!
Shall they not love and bring forth things that love
Out of their love? have they not drawn their milk
Out of this bosom? was not he, their father,
Born of the same sole womb, in the same hour
With me? did we not love each other? and
In multiplying our being multiply
Things which will love each other as we love
Them?—And as I love thee, my Cain! go not
Forth with this spirit; he is not of ours.

Lucifer. The sin I speak of is not of my making,
And cannot be a sin in you—whate'er
It seem in those who will replace ye in
Mortality.

Adah. What is the sin which is not
Sin in itself? Can circumstance make sin
Or virtue?—if it doth, we are the slaves
Of——

Lucifer. Higher things than ye are slaves: and higher
Than them or ye would be so, did they not
Prefer an independency of torture
To the smooth agonies of adulation,
In hymns and harpings, and self-seeking prayers,
To that which is omnipotent, because
It is omnipotent, and not from love,
But terror and self-hope.

Adah. Omnipotence
Must be all goodness.

Lucifer. Was it so in Eden?

Adah. Fiend! tempt me not with beauty; thou art fairer
Than was the serpent, and as false.

Lucifer. As true.
Ask Eve, your mother: bears she not the knowledge
Of good and evil?

Adah. Oh, my mother! thou
Hast pluck'd a fruit more fatal to thine offspring
Than to thyself; thou at the least hast pass'd
Thy youth in Paradise, in innocent
And happy intercourse with happy spirits:
But we, thy children, ignorant of Eden,
Are girt about by demons, who assume
The words of God, and tempt us with our own
Dissatisfied and curious thoughts—as thou
Wert work'd on by the snake, in thy most flush'd
And heedless, harmless wantonness of bliss.
I cannot answer this immortal thing
Which stands before me; I can not abhor him;
I look upon him with a pleasing fear,
And yet I fly not from him: in his eye
There is a fastening attraction which
Fixes my fluttering eyes on his; my heart
Beats quick; he awes me, and yet draws me near,
Nearer, and nearer:—Cain—Cain—save me from him!

Cain. What dreads my Adah? This is no ill spirit.
Adah. He is not God—nor God's: I have beheld
The cherubs and the seraphs; he looks not
Like them.
Cain. But there are spirits loftier still—
The archangels.
Lucifer. And still loftier than the archangels.
Adah. Ay—but not blessed.
Lucifer. If the blessedness
Consists in slavery—no.
Adah. I have heard it said,
The seraphs *love most*—cherubim *know most*—
And this should be a cherub—since he loves not.
Lucifer. And if the higher knowledge quenches love,
What must *he be* you cannot love when known?
Since the all-knowing cherubim love least,
The seraphs' love can be but ignorance:
That they are not compatible, the doom
Of thy fond parents, for their daring, proves.
Choose betwixt love and knowledge—since there is
No other choice: your sire hath chosen already;
His worship is but fear.
Adah. Oh, Cain! choose love.
Cain. For thee, my Adah, I choose not—it was
Born with me—but I love nought else.
Adah. Our parents?
Cain. Did they love us when they snatch'd from the tree
That which hath driven us all from Paradise?
Adah. We were not born then—and if we had been,
Should we not love them and our children, Cain?
Cain. My little Enoch! and his lisping sister!
Could I but deem them happy, I would half
Forget——but it can never be forgotten
Through thrice a thousand generations! never
Shall men love the remembrance of the man
Who sow'd the seed of evil and mankind
In the same hour! They pluck'd the tree of science
And sin—and, not content with their own sorrow,
Begot *me*—*thee*—and all the few that are,
And all the unnumber'd and innumerable
Multitudes, millions, myriads, which may be,
To inherit agonies accumulated
By ages!—and *I* must be sire of such things!
Thy beauty and thy love—my love and joy,
The rapturous moment and the placid hour,
All we love in our children and each other,
But lead them and ourselves through many years
Of sin and pain—or few, but still of sorrow,
Intercheck'd with an instant of brief pleasure,
To Death—the unknown! Methinks the tree of knowledge
Hath not fulfill'd its promise:—if they sinn'd,
At least they ought to have known all things that are
Of knowledge—and the mystery of death.
What do they know?—that they are miserable.
What need of snakes and fruits to teach us that?
Adah. I am not wretched, Cain, and if thou
Wert happy——
Cain. Be thou happy, then, alone—
I will have nought to do with happiness,
Which humbles me and mine.
Adah. Alone I could not,
Nor *would* be happy: but with those around us,
I think I could be so, despite of death,
Which, as I know it not, I dread not, though
It seems an awful shadow—if I may
Judge from what I have heard.
Lucifer. And thou couldst not
Alone, thou say'st, be happy?
Adah. Alone! Oh, my God!
Who could be happy and alone, or good?
To me my solitude seems sin; unless
When I think how soon I shall see my brother,
His brother, and our children, and our parents.
Lucifer. Yet thy God is alone; and is He happy?
Lonely, and good?
Adah. He is not so; He hath
The angels and the mortals to make happy,
And thus becomes so in diffusing joy!
What else can joy be, but the spreading joy?
Lucifer. Ask of your sire, the exile fresh from Eden;
Or of his first-born son: ask your own heart;
It is not tranquil.
Adah. Alas! no! and you—
Are you of heaven?
Lucifer. If I am not, inquire
The cause of this all-spreading happiness
(Which you proclaim) of the all-great and good
Maker of life and living things; it is
His secret, and He keeps it. *We* must bear,
And some of us resist, and both in vain,
His seraphs say; but it is worth the trial,
Since better may not be without: there is
A wisdom in the spirit, which directs
To right, as in the dim blue air the eye
Of you, young mortals, lights at once upon
The star which watches, welcoming the morn.
Adah. It is a beautiful star; I love it for
Its beauty.
Lucifer. And why not adore?
Adah. Our father
Adores the Invisible only.
Lucifer. But the symbols
Of the Invisible are the loveliest
Of what is visible; and yon bright star
Is leader of the host of heaven.

Adah. Our father
Saith that he has beheld the God Himself
Who made him and our mother.
Lucifer. Hast *thou* seen Him?
Adah. Yes—in His works.
Lucifer. But in His being?
Adah. No—
Save in my father, who is God's own image;
Or in His angels, who are like to thee—
And brighter, yet less beautiful and powerful
In seeming: as the silent sunny noon,
All light they look upon us; but thou seem'st
Like an ethereal night, where long white clouds
Streak the deep purple, and unnumber'd stars
Spangle the wonderful mysterious vault
With things that look as if they would be suns;
So beautiful, unnumber'd, and endearing,
Not dazzling, and yet drawing us to them,
They fill my eyes with tears, and so dost thou.
Thou seem'st unhappy: do not make us so,
And I will weep for thee.
Lucifer. Alas! those tears!
Could'st thou but know what oceans will be shed——
Adah. By me?
Lucifer. By all.
Adah. What all?
Lucifer. The million millions—
The myriad myriads—the all-peopled earth—
The unpeopled earth—and the o'er-peopled hell,
Of which thy bosom is the germ.
Adah. O, Cain!
This spirit curseth us.
Cain. Let him say on;
Him will I follow.
Adah. Whither?
Lucifer. To a place
Whence he shall come back to thee in an hour;
But in that hour see things of many days.
Adah. How can that be?
Lucifer. Did not your Maker make
Out of old worlds this new one in few days?
And cannot I, who aided in this work,
Show in an hour what He hath made in many,
Or hath destroyed in few?
Cain. Lead on.
Adah. Will he,
In sooth, return within an hour?
Lucifer. He shall.
With us acts are exempt from time, and we
Can crowd eternity into an hour,
Or stretch an hour into eternity:
We breathe not by a mortal measurement—
But that's a mystery. Cain, come on with me.
Adah. Will he return?
Lucifer. Ay, woman! he alone
Of mortals from that place (the first and last
Who shall return, save ONE),—shall come back to thee,
To make that silent and expectant world
As populous as this: at present there
Are few inhabitants.
Adah. Where dwellest thou?
Lucifer. Throughout all space. Where should I dwell? Where are
Thy God or Gods—there am I: all things are
Divided with me; life and death—and time—
Eternity—and heaven and earth—and that
Which is not heaven nor earth, but peopled with
Those who once peopled or shall people both—
These are my realms! So that I do divide
His, and possess a kingdom which is not
His. If I were not that which I have said,
Could I stand here? His angels are within
Your vision.
Adah. So they were when the fair serpent
Spoke with our mother first.
Lucifer. Cain! thou hast heard.
If thou dost long for knowledge, I can satiate
That thirst; nor ask thee to partake of fruits
Which shall deprive thee of a single good
The Conqueror has left thee. Follow me.
Cain. Spirit, I have said it.

[*Exeunt* LUCIFER *and* CAIN.

Adah. (*follows, exclaiming*). Cain! my brother! Cain!

ACT II.

SCENE I

The Abyss of Space.

Cain. I tread on air, and sink not; yet I fear
To sink.
Lucifer. Have faith in me, and thou shalt be
Borne on the air, of which I am the prince.
Cain. Can I do so without impiety?
Lucifer. Believe—and sink not! doubt—and perish! thus
Would run the edict of the other God,
Who names me demon to His angels; they
Echo the sound to miserable things,
Which, knowing nought beyond their shallow senses,
Worship the word which strikes their ear, and deem
Evil or good what is proclaim'd to them
In their abasement. I will have none such:

Worship or worship not, thou shalt behold
The worlds beyond thy little world, nor be
Amerced for doubts beyond thy little life,
With torture of *my* dooming. There will come
An hour, when, toss'd upon some water-drops,
A man shall say to a man, "Believe in me,
And walk the waters;" and the man shall walk
The billows and be safe. *I* will not say,
Believe in *me*, as a conditional creed
To save thee; but fly with me o'er the gulf
Of space an equal flight, and I will show
What thou dar'st not deny,—the history
Of past, and present, and of future worlds.
Cain. Oh, god, or demon, or whate'er thou art,
Is yon our earth?
Lucifer. Dost thou not recognise
The dust which form'd your father?
Cain. Can it be?
Yon small blue circle, swinging in far ether,
With an inferior circlet near it still,
Which looks like that which lit our earthly night?
Is this our Paradise? Where are its walls,
And they who guard them?
Lucifer. Point me out the site
Of Paradise.
Cain. How should I? As we move
Like sunbeams onward, it grows small and smaller,
And as it waxes little, and then less,
Gathers a halo round it, like the light
Which shone the roundest of the stars, when I
Beheld them from the skirts of Paradise:
Methinks they both, as we recede from them,
Appear to join the innumerable stars
Which are around us; and, as we move on,
Increase their myriads.
Lucifer. And if there should be
Worlds greater than thine own, inhabited
By greater things, and they themselves far more
In number than the dust of thy dull earth,
Though multiplied to animated atoms,
All living, and all doom'd to death, and wretched,
What would'st thou think?
Cain. I should be proud of thought
Which knew such things.
Lucifer. But if that high thought were
Link'd to a servile mass of matter, and,
Knowing such things, aspiring to such things,
And science still beyond them, were chain'd down
To the most gross and petty paltry wants,
All foul and fulsome, and the very best
Of thine enjoyments a sweet degradation,
A most enervating and filthy cheat
To lure thee on to the renewal of
Fresh souls and bodies, all foredoom'd to be
As frail, and few so happy——
Cain. Spirit! I
Know nought of death, save as a dreadful thing
Of which I have heard my parents speak, as of
A hideous heritage I owe to them
No less than life; a heritage not happy,
If I may judge, till now. But, spirit! if
It be as thou hast said (and I within
Feel the prophetic torture of its truth),
Here let me die: for to give birth to those
Who can but suffer many years, and die,
Methinks is merely propagating death,
And multiplying murder.
Lucifer. Thou canst not
All die—there is what must survive.
Cain. The Other
Spake not of this unto my father, when
He shut him forth from Paradise, with death
Written upon his forehead. But at least
Let what is mortal of me perish, that
I may be in the rest as angels are.
Lucifer. I am angelic: wouldst thou be as I am?
Cain. I know not what thou art: I see thy power,
And see thou show'st me things beyond *my* power,
Beyond all power of my born faculties,
Although inferior still to my desires
And my conceptions.
Lucifer. What are they which dwell
So humbly in their pride, as to sojourn
With worms in clay?
Cain. And what art thou who dwellest
So haughtily in spirit, and canst range
Nature and immortality—and yet
Seem'st sorrowful?
Lucifer. I seem that which I am;
And therefore do I ask of thee, if thou
Wouldst be immortal?
Cain. Thou hast said, I must be
Immortal in despite of me. I knew not
This until lately—but since it must be,
Let me, or happy or unhappy, learn
To anticipate my immortality.
Lucifer. Thou didst before I came upon thee.
Cain. How?
Lucifer. By suffering.
Cain. And must torture be immortal?
Lucifer. We and thy sons will try. But now, behold!
Is it not glorious?
Cain. Oh, thou beautiful
And unimaginable ether! and
Ye multiplying masses of increased
And still increasing lights! what are ye? what
Is this blue wilderness of interminable
Air, where ye roll along, as I have seen
The leaves along the limpid streams of Eden?
Is your course measured for ye? Or do ye
Sweep on in your unbounded revelry
Through an aërial universe of endless
Expansion—at which my soul aches to think—
Intoxicated with eternity?
Oh God! Oh Gods! or whatsoe'er ye are!

How beautiful ye are! how beautiful
Your works, or accidents, or whatsoe'er
They may be! Let me die, as atoms die,
(If that they die) or know ye in your might
And knowledge! My thoughts are not in this hour
Unworthy what I see, though my dust is;
Spirit! let me expire, or see them nearer.

Lucifer. Art thou not nearer? look back to thine earth!

Cain. Where is it? I see nothing save a mass
Of most innumerable lights.

Lucifer. Look there!

Cain. I cannot see it.

Lucifer. Yet it sparkles still.

Cain. That!—yonder!

Lucifer. Yea.

Cain. And wilt thou tell me so?
Why, I have seen the fire-flies and fire-worms
Sprinkle the dusky groves and the green banks
In the dim twilight, brighter than yon world
Which bears them.

Lucifer. Thou hast seen both worms and worlds,
Each bright and sparkling—what dost think of them?

Cain. That they are beautiful in their own sphere,
And that the night, which makes both beautiful,
The little shining fire-fly in its flight,
And the immortal star in its great course,
Must both be guided.

Lucifer. But by whom or what?

Cain. Show me.

Lucifer. Dar'st thou behold?

Cain. How know I what
I *dare* behold? As yet, thou hast shown nought
I dare not gaze on further.

Lucifer. On, then, with me.
Wouldst thou behold things mortal or immortal?

Cain. Why, what are things?

Lucifer. *Both* partly: but what doth
Sit next thy heart?

Cain. The things I see.

Lucifer. But what
Sate nearest it!

Cain. The things I have not seen,
Nor ever shall—the mysteries of death.

Lucifer. What, if I show to thee things which have died,
As I have shown thee much which cannot die?

Cain. Do so.

Lucifer. Away, then! on our mighty wings.

Cain. Oh! how we cleave the blue! The stars fade from us!
The earth! where is my earth? Let me look on it,
For I was made of it.

Lucifer. 'Tis now beyond thee,
Less, in the universe, than thou in it;
Yet deem not that thou canst escape it: thou
Shalt soon return to earth, and all its dust:
'Tis part of thy eternity, and mine.

Cain. Where dost thou lead me?

Lucifer. To what was before thee!
The phantasm of the world; of which thy world
Is but the wreck.

Cain. What! is it not then new?

Lucifer. No more than life is; and that was ere thou
Or *I* were, or the things which seem to us
Greater than either: many things will have
No end; and some, which would pretend to have
Had no beginning, have had one as mean
As thou; and mightier things have been extinct
To make way for much meaner than we can
Surmise; for *moments* only and the *space*
Have been and must be all *unchangeable.*
But changes make not death, except to clay;
But thou art clay,—and canst but comprehend
That which was clay, and such thou shalt behold.

Cain. Clay, spirit! what thou wilt, I can survey.

Lucifer. Away, then!

Cain. But the lights fade from me fast,
And some till now grew larger as we approach'd,
And wore the look of worlds.

Lucifer. And such they are.

Cain. And Edens in them?

Lucifer. It may be.

Cain. And men?

Lucifer. Yea, or things higher.

Cain. Ay? and serpents too?

Lucifer. Wouldst thou have men without them? must no reptiles
Breathe save the erect ones?

Cain. How the lights recede;
Where fly we?

Lucifer. To the world of phantoms, which
Are beings past, and shadows still to come.

Cain. But it grows dark and dark—the stars are gone!

Lucifer. And yet thou seest.

Cain. 'Tis a fearful light!
No sun, no moon, no lights innumerable.
The very blue of the empurpled night
Fades to a dreary twilight, yet I see
Huge dusky masses: but unlike the worlds
We were approaching, which, begirt with light,
Seem'd full of life even when their atmosphere
Of light gave way, and show'd them taking shapes
Unequal, of deep valleys and vast mountains;
And some emitting sparks, and some displaying
Enormous liquid plains, and some begirt
With luminous belts, and floating moons, which took,
Like them, the features of fair earth:—instead,
All here seems dark and dreadful.

Lucifer. But distinct
Thou seekest to behold death, and dead things?

Cain. I seek it not: but as I know there are
Such, and that my sire's sin makes him and me,
And all that we inherit, liable
To such, I would behold at once, what I
Must one day see perforce.

Lucifer. Behold!

Cain. 'Tis darkness.

Lucifer. And so it shall be ever; but we will
Unfold its gates!

Cain. Enormous vapours roll
Apart—what's this?

Lucifer. Enter!

Cain. Can I return?

Lucifer. Return? be sure: how else should death be peopled?
Its present realm is thin to what it will be,
Through thee and thine.

Cain. The clouds still open wide
And wider, and make widening circles round us.

Lucifer. Advance!

Cain. And thou!

Lucifer. Fear not—without me thou
Couldst not have gone beyond thy world. On! on!

[*They disappear through the clouds.*

SCENE II.

Hades.

Enter LUCIFER *and* CAIN.

Cain. How silent and how vast are these dim worlds!
For they seem more than one, and yet more peopled
Than the huge brilliant luminous orbs which swung
So thickly in the upper air, that I
Had deem'd them rather the bright populace
Of some all unimaginable heaven,
Than things to be inhabited themselves,
But that on drawing near them I beheld
Their swelling into palpable immensity
Of matter, which seem'd made for life to dwell on,
Rather than life itself. But here, all is
So shadowy and so full of twilight, that
It speaks of a day past.

Lucifer. It is the realm
Of death.—Wouldst have it present?

Cain. 'Till I know
That which it really is, I cannot answer.
But if it be as I have heard my father
Deal out in his long homilies, 'tis a thing—
Oh God! I dare not think on't! Cursed be
He who invented life that leads to death!
Or the dull mass of life, that, being life,
Could not retain, but needs must forfeit it—
Even for the innocent!

Lucifer. Dost thou curse thy father?

Cain. Cursed he not me in giving me my birth?
Cursed he not me before my birth, in daring
To pluck the fruit forbidden?

Lucifer. Thou say'st well:
The curse is mutual 'twixt thy sire and thee—
But for thy sons and brother?

Cain. Let them share it
With me, their sire and brother? What else is
Bequeath'd to me? I leave them my inheritance.
Oh, ye interminable gloomy realms
Of swimming shadows and enormous shapes,
Some fully shown, some indistinct, and all
Mighty and melancholy—what are ye?
Live ye, or have ye lived?

Lucifer. Somewhat of both.

Cain. Then what is death?

Lucifer. What? Hath not He who made ye
Said 'tis another life?

Cain. Till now He hath
Said nothing, save that all shall die.

Lucifer. Perhaps
He one day will unfold that further secret.

Cain. Happy the day!

Lucifer. Yes; happy! when unfolded
Through agonies unspeakable, and clogg'd
With agonies eternal, to innumerable
Yet unborn myriads of unconscious atoms,
All to be animated for this only!

Cain. What are these mighty phantoms which I see
Floating around me?—They wear not the form
Of the intelligences I have seen
Round our regretted and unenter'd Eden,
Nor wear the form of man as I have view'd it
In Adam's, and in Abel's, and in mine,
Nor in my sister-bride's, nor in my children's:
And yet they have an aspect, which, though not
Of men nor angels, looks like something, which
If not the last, rose higher than the first,
Haughty, and high, and beautiful, and full
Of seeming strength, but of inexplicable
Shape; for I never saw such. They bear not
The wing of seraph, nor the face of man,
Nor form of mightiest brute, nor aught that is
Now breathing; mighty yet and beautiful
As the most beautiful and mighty which
Live, and yet so unlike them, that I scarce
Can call them living.

Lucifer. Yet they lived.

Cain. Where?

Lucifer. Where
Thou livest.

Cain. When?

Lucifer. On what thou callest earth
They did inhabit.

Cain. Adam is the first.

Lucifer. Of thine, I grant thee—but too mean to be
The last of these.

Cain. And what are they?

Lucifer. That which
Thou shalt be.

Cain. But what *were* they?

Lucifer. Living, high,
Intelligent, good, great, and glorious things,
As much superior unto all thy sire,
Adam, could e'er have been in Eden, as
The sixty-thousandth generation shall be,
In its dull damp degeneracy, to
Thee and thy son;—and how weak they are, judge
By thy own flesh.

Cain. Ah me! and did *they* perish?

Lucifer. Yes, from their earth, as thou wilt fade from thine.

Cain. But was *mine* theirs?

Lucifer. It was.

Cain. But not as now.
It is too little and too lowly to
Sustain such creatures.

Lucifer. True, it was more glorious.

Cain. And wherefore did it fall?

Lucifer. Ask Him who fells.

Cain. But how?

Lucifer. By a most crushing and inexorable
Destruction and disorder of the elements,
Which struck a world to chaos, as a chaos

Subsiding has struck out a world: such things,
Though rare in time, are frequent in eternity.—
Pass on, and gaze upon the past.

Cain. 'Tis awful!

Lucifer. And true. Behold these phantoms! they were once
Material as thou art.

Cain. And must I be
Like them?

Lucifer. Let He who made thee answer that.
I show thee what thy predecessors are,
And what they *were* thou feelest, in degree
Inferior as thy petty feelings and
Thy pettier portion of the immortal part
Of high intelligence and earthly strength.
What ye in common have with what they had
Is life, and what ye *shall* have — death: the rest
Of your poor attributes is such as suits
Reptiles engender'd out of the subsiding
Slime of a mighty universe, crush'd into
A scarcely-yet shaped planet, peopled with
Things whose enjoyment was to be in blindness—
A Paradise of Ignorance, from which
Knowledge was barr'd as poison. But behold
What these superior beings are or were;
Or, if it irk thee, turn thee back and till
The earth, thy task—I'll waft thee there in safety.

Cain. No: I'll stay here.

Lucifer. How long?

Cain. For ever! Since
I must one day return here from the earth,
I rather would remain; I am sick of all
That dust has shown me—let me dwell in shadows.

Lucifer. It cannot be: thou now beholdest as
A vision that which is reality.
To make thyself fit for this dwelling, thou
Must pass through what the things thou see'st have pass'd—
The gates of death.

Cain. By what gate have we enter'd
Even now?

Lucifer. By mine! But, plighted to return,
My spirit buoys thee up to breathe in regions
Where all is breathless save thyself. Gaze on;
But do not think to dwell here till thine hour
Is come.

Cain. And these, too; can they ne'er repass
To earth again?

Lucifer. *Their* earth is gone for ever—
So changed by its convulsion, they would not
Be conscious to a single present spot
Of its new scarcely harden'd surface—'twas—
Oh, what a beautiful world it *was!*

Cain. And is.
It is not with the earth, though I must till it,
I feel at war, but that I may not profit
By what it bears of beautiful untoiling,
Nor gratify my thousand swelling thoughts
With knowledge, nor allay my thousand fears
Of death and life.

Lucifer. What thy world is, thou see'st,
But canst not comprehend the shadow of
That which it was.

Cain. And those enormous creatures,
Phantoms inferior in intelligence
(At least so seeming) to the things we have pass'd,
Resembling somewhat the wild habitants
Of the deep woods of earth, the hugest which
Roar nightly in the forest, but tenfold
In magnitude and terror; taller than
The cherub-guarded walls of Eden, with
Eyes flashing like the fiery swords which fence them,
And tusks projecting like the trees stripp'd of
Their bark and branches—what were they?

Lucifer. That which
The Mammoth is in thy world;—but these lie
By myriads underneath its surface.

Cain. But
None on it?

Lucifer. No: for thy frail race to war
With them would render the curse on it useless—
'Twould be destroyed so early.

Cain. But why *war?*

Lucifer. You have forgotten the denunciation
Which drove your race from Eden—war with all things,
And death to all things, and disease to most things,
And pangs, and bitterness; these were the fruits
Of the forbidden tree.

Cain. But animals—
Did they, too, eat of it, that they must die?

Lucifer. Your Maker told ye, *they* were made for you,
As you for Him.—You would not have their doom
Superior to your own? Had Adam not
Fallen, all had stood.

Cain. Alas! the hopeless wretches!
They too must share my sire's fate, like his sons;
Like them, too, without having shared the apple;
Like them, too, without the so dear-bought *knowledge!*
It was a lying tree—for we *know* nothing.
At least it *promised knowledge* at the *price*
Of death—but *knowledge* still; but what *knows* man?

Lucifer. It may be death leads to the *highest* knowledge;
And being of all things the sole thing certain,
At least leads to the *surest* science: therefore
The tree was true, though deadly.

Cain. These dim realms!
I see them, but I know them not.

Lucifer. Because
Thy hour is yet afar, and matter cannot
Comprehend spirit wholly—but 'tis something
To know there are such realms.

Cain. We knew already
That there was death.
Lucifer. But not what was beyond it.
Cain. Nor know I now.
Lucifer. Thou knowest that there is
A state, and many states beyond thine own—
And this thou knewest not this morn.
Cain. But all
Seems dim and shadowy.
Lucifer. Be content; it will
Seem clearer to thine immortality.
Cain. And yon immeasurable liquid space
Of glorious azure which floats on beyond us,
Which looks like water, and which I should deem
The river which flows out of Paradise
Past my own dwelling, but that it is bankless
And boundless, and of an ethereal hue—
What is it?
Lucifer. There is still some such on earth,
Although inferior, and thy children shall
Dwell near it—'t is the phantasm of an ocean.
Cain. 'T is like another world; a liquid sun—
And those inordinate creatures sporting o'er
Its shining surface?
Lucifer. Are its inhabitants;
The past leviathäns.
Cain. And yon immense
Serpent, which rears its dripping mane and vasty
Head ten times higher than the haughtiest cedar
Forth from the abyss, looking as he could coil
Himself around the orbs we lately look'd on—
Is he not of the kind which bask'd beneath
The tree in Eden?
Lucifer. Eve, thy mother, best
Can tell what shape of serpent tempted her.
Cain. This seems too terrible. No doubt the other
Had more of beauty.
Lucifer. Hast thou ne'er beheld him?
Cain. Many of the same kind (at least so call'd),
But never that precisely which persuaded
The fatal fruit, nor even of the same aspect.
Lucifer. Your father saw him not?
Cain. No: 't was my mother
Who tempted him—she tempted by the serpent.
Lucifer. Good man! whene'er thy wife, or thy sons' wives,
Tempt thee or them to aught that 's new or strange,
Be sure thou see' st first who hath tempted *them.*
Cain. Thy precept comes too late: there is no more
For serpents to tempt woman to.
Lucifer. But there
Are some things still which woman may tempt man to,
And man tempt woman:—let thy sons look to it!
My counsel is a kind one: for 't is even
Given chiefly at my own expense: 't is true,
'T will not be follow'd, so there 's little lost.
Cain. I understand not this.
Lucifer. The happier thou!—
Thy world and thou are still too young! Thou thinkest
Thyself most wicked and unhappy: is it
Not so?
Cain. For crime, I know not; but for pain,
I have felt much.
Lucifer. First-born of the first man!
Thy present state of sin—and thou art evil,
Of sorrow—and thou sufferest, are both Eden
In all its innocence compared to what
Thou shortly may'st be; and that state again
In its redoubled wretchedness, a Paradise
To what thy sons' sons' sons, accumulating
In generations like to dust (which they
In fact but add to), shall endure and do.—
Now let us back to earth!
Cain. And wherefore did'st thou
Lead me here only to inform me this?
Lucifer. Was not thy quest for knowledge?
Cain. Yes; as being
The road to happiness.
Lucifer. If truth be so,
Thou hast it.
Cain. Then my father's God did well
When He prohibited the fatal tree.
Lucifer. But had done better in not planting it.
But ignorance of evil doth not save
From evil; it must still roll on the same.
A part of all things.
Cain. Not of all things. No:
I 'll not believe it—for I thirst for good.
Lucifer. And who and what doth not? *Who* covets evil
For its own bitter sake?—*None*—nothing! 't is
The leaven of all life, and lifelessness.
Cain. Within those glorious orbs which we behold,
Distant, and dazzling, and innumerable,
Ere we came down into this phantom realm,
Ill cannot come: they are too beautiful.
Lucifer. Thou hast seen them from afar—
Cain. And what of that?
Distance can but diminish glory—they,
When nearer, must be more ineffable.
Lucifer. Approach the things of earth most beautiful,
And judge their beauty near.
Cain. I have done this—
The loveliest thing I know is loveliest nearest.
Lucifer. Then there must be delusion.—What is that,
Which being nearest to thine eyes is still
More beautiful than beauteous things remote?
Cain. My sister Adah.—All the stars of heaven,
The deep blue noon of night, lit by an orb
Which looks a spirit, or a spirit's world—
The hues of twilight—the sun's gorgeous coming—

His setting indescribable, which fills
My eyes with pleasant tears as I behold
Him sink, and feel my heart float softly with him
Along that western paradise of clouds—
The forest shade—the green bough—the bird's voice—
The vesper bird's, which seems to sing of love,
And mingles with the song of cherubim,
As the day closes over Eden's walls;—
All these are nothing, to my eyes and heart,
Like Adah's face: I turn from earth and heaven
To gaze on it.

Lucifer. 'T is fair as frail mortality,
In the first dawn and bloom of young creation,
And earliest embraces of earth's parents,
Can make its offspring; still it is delusion.

Cain. You think so, being not her brother.

Lucifer. Mortal!
My brotherhood 's with those who have no children.

Cain. Then thou canst have no fellowship with us.

Lucifer. It may be that thine own shall be for me.
But if thou dost possess a beautiful
Being beyond all beauty in thine eyes,
Why art thou wretched?

Cain. Why do I exist?
Why art *thou* wretched? why are all things so?
Ev'n He who made us must be, as the maker
Of things unhappy! To produce destruction
Can surely never be the task of joy,
And yet my sire says He 's omnipotent:
Then why is evil—He being good? I ask'd
This question of my father; and he said,
Because this evil only was the path
To good. Strange good, that must arise from out
Its deadly opposite. I lately saw
A lamb stung by a reptile: the poor suckling
Lay foaming on the earth, beneath the vain
And piteous bleating of its restless dam;
My father pluck'd some herbs, and laid them to
The wound; and by degrees the helpless wretch
Resumed its careless life, and rose to drain
The mother's milk, who o'er it tremulous
Stood licking its reviving limbs with joy.
Behold, my son! said Adam, how from evil
Springs good!

Lucifer. What didst thou answer?

Cain. Nothing; for
He is my father: but I thought, that 't were
A better portion for the animal
Never to have been *stung at all*, than to
Purchase renewal of its little life
With agonies unutterable, though
Dispell'd by antidotes.

Lucifer. But as thou said'st
Of all beloved things thou lovest her
Who shared thy mother's milk, and giveth hers
Unto thy children——

Cain. Most assuredly:
What should I be without her?

Lucifer. What am I?

Cain. Dost thou love nothing?

Lucifer. What does thy God love?

Cain. All things, my father says; but I confess
I see it not in their allotment here.

Lucifer. And, therefore, thou canst not see if *I* love
Or no, except some vast and general purpose,
To which particular things must melt like snows.

Cain. Snows! what are they?

Lucifer. Be happier in not knowing
What thy remoter offspring must encounter;
But bask beneath the clime which knows no winter!

Cain. But dost thou not love something like thyself?

Lucifer. And dost thou love *thyself?*

Cain. Yes, but love more
What makes my feelings more endurable,
And is more than myself, because I love it.

Lucifer. Thou lovest it, because 't is beautiful,
As was the apple in thy mother's eye;
And when it ceases to be so, thy love
Will cease, like any other appetite.

Cain. Cease to be beautiful! how can that be?

Lucifer. With time.

Cain. But time has past, and hitherto
Even Adam and my mother both are fair:
Not fair like Adah and the seraphim—
But very fair.

Lucifer. All that must pass away
In them and her.

Cain. I 'm sorry for it; but
Cannot conceive my love for her the less.
And when her beauty disappears, methinks
He who creates all beauty will lose more
Than me in seeing perish such a work.

Lucifer. I pity thee who lovest what must perish.

Cain. And I thee, who lov'st nothing.

Lucifer. And thy brother—
Sits he not near thy heart?

Cain. Why should he not?

Lucifer. Thy father loves him well—so does thy God.

Cain. And so do I.

Lucifer. 'T is well and meekly done.

Cain. Meekly!

Lucifer. He is the second born of flesh,
And is his mother's favourite.

Cain. Let him keep
Her favour, since the serpent was the first
To win it.

Lucifer. And his father's?

Cain. What is that
To me? should I not love that which all love?

Lucifer. And the Jehovah—the indulgent Lord,
And bounteous planter of barr'd Paradise—
He, too, looks smilingly on Abel.

Cain. I
Ne'er saw Him, and I know not if He smiles.
Lucifer. But you have seen His angels.
Cain. Rarely.
Lucifer. But
Sufficiently to see they love your brother:
His sacrifices are acceptable.
Cain. So be they! wherefore speak to me of this?
Lucifer. Because thou hast thought of this ere now.
Cain. And if
I *have* thought, why recall a thought that——(*he pauses, as agitated*)—Spirit!
Here we are in *thy* world: speak not of *mine.*
Thou hast shown me wonders; thou hast shown me those
Mighty pre-Adamites who walk'd the earth
Of which ours is the wreck; thou hast pointed out
Myriads of starry worlds, of which our own
Is the dim and remote companion, in
Infinity of life: thou hast shown me shadows
Of that existence with the dreaded name
Which my sire brought us—Death; thou hast shown me much—
But not all: show me where Jehovah dwells,
In his especial Paradise,—or *thine:*
Where is it?
Lucifer. *Here*, and o'er all space.
Cain. But ye
Have some allotted dwelling—as all things;
Clay has its earth, and other worlds their tenants;
All temporary breathing creatures their
Peculiar element; and things which have
Long ceased to breathe *our* breath, have theirs, thou say'st;
And the Jehovah and thyself have thine—
Ye do not dwell together?
Lucifer. No, we reign
Together; but our dwellings are asunder.
Cain. Would there were only one of ye! Perchance
An unity of purpose might make union
In elements which seem now jarr'd in storms.
How came ye, being spirits, wise and infinite,
To separate? Are ye not as brethren in
Your essence, and your nature, and your glory?
Lucifer. Art thou not Abel's brother?
Cain. We are brethren,
And so we shall remain; but were it not so,
Is spirit like to flesh? can it fall out?
Infinity with Immortality?
Jarring and turning space to misery—
For what?
Lucifer. To reign.
Cain. Did ye not tell me that
Ye are both eternal?
Lucifer. Yea!
Cain. And what I have seen,
Yon blue immensity, is boundless?
Lucifer. Ay.
Cain. And cannot ye both *reign* then?—is there not
Enough?—why should ye differ?
Lucifer. We *both* reign.
Cain. But one of you makes evil.
Lucifer. Which?
Cain. Thou! for
If thou canst do man good, why dost thou not?
Lucifer. And why not He who made? *I* made ye not:
Ye are *His* creatures, and not mine.
Cain. Then leave us,
His creatures, as thou say'st we are, or show me
Thy dwelling, or His dwelling.
Lucifer. I could show thee
Both; but the time will come thou shalt see one
Of them for evermore.
Cain. And why not now?
Lucifer. Thy human mind hath scarcely grasp to gather
The little I have shown thee into calm
And clear thought; and thou wouldst go on aspiring
To the great double Mysteries! the *two Principles!*
And gaze upon them on their secret thrones!
Dust! limit thy ambition; for to see
Either of these, would be for thee to perish!
Cain. And let me perish, so I see them!
Lucifer. There
The son of her who snatch'd the apple spake!
But thou wouldst only perish, and not see them;
That sight is for the other state.
Cain. Of death?
Lucifer. That is the prelude.
Cain. Then I dread it less,
Now that I know it leads to something definite.
Lucifer. And now I will convey thee to thy world,
Where thou shalt multiply the race of Adam,
Eat, drink, toil, tremble, laugh, weep, sleep, and die.
Cain. And to what end have I beheld these things
Which thou hast shown me?
Lucifer. Didst thou not require
Knowledge? And have I not, in what I show'd,
Taught thee to know thyself?
Cain. Alas! I seem
Nothing.
Lucifer. And this should be the human sum
Of knowledge, to know mortal nature's nothingness:
Bequeath that science to thy children, and
'T will spare them many tortures.
Cain. Haughty spirit!
Thou speak'st it proudly; but thyself, though proud,
Hast a superior.
Lucifer. No! by heaven, which He
Holds, and the abyss, and the immensity
Of worlds and life, which I hold with Him—No!

I have a victor—true ; but no superior.
Homage He has from all—but none from me :
I battle it against Him, as I battled
In highest heaven. Through all eternity,
And the unfathomable gulfs of Hades,
And the interminable realms of space,
And the infinity of the endless ages,
All, all, will I dispute! And world by world,
And star by star, and universe by universe,
Shall tremble in the balance, till the great
Conflict shall cease, if ever it shall cease,
Which it ne'er shall, till He or I be quench'd!
And what can quench our immortality,
Or mutual and irrevocable hate?
He as a conqueror will call the conquer'd
Evil ; but what will be the *good* He gives?
Were I the victor, *His* works would be deem'd
The only evil ones. And you, ye new
And scarce-born mortals, what have been His gifts
To you already, in your little world?

Cain. But few! and some of those but bitter.

Lucifer. Back
With me, then, to thine earth, and try the rest
Of His celestial boons to you and yours.
Evil and good are things in their own essence,
And not made good or evil by the giver ;
But if He gives you good—so call Him ; if
Evil springs from *Him*, do not name it *mine*,
Till ye know better its true fount ; and judge
Not by words, though of spirits, but the fruits
Of your existence, such as it must be.
One good gift has the fatal apple given—
Your *reason* :—let it not be over-sway'd
By tyrannous threats to force you into faith
'Gainst all external sense and inward feeling.
Think and endure,—and form an inner world
In your own bosom—where the outward fails;
So shall you nearer be the spiritual
Nature, and war triumphant with your own.

[*They disappear.*

ACT III.

SCENE I.

The Earth near Eden, as in Act I.

Enter CAIN *and* ADAH.

Adah. Hush! tread softly, Cain.

Cain. I will; but wherefore?

Adah. Our little Enoch sleeps upon yon bed
Of leaves, beneath the cypress.

Cain. Cypress! 't is
A gloomy tree, which looks as if it mourn'd
O'er what it shadows ; wherefore didst thou choose it
For our child's canopy?

Adah. Because its branches
Shut out the sun like night, and therefore seem'd
Fitting to shadow slumber.

Cain. Ay, the last—
And longest; but no matter—lead me to him.

[*They go up to the child.*

How lovely he appears! his little cheeks,
In their pure incarnation, vying with
The rose leaves strewn beneath them.

Adah. And his lips, too,
How beautifully parted! No; you shall not
Kiss him, at least not now: he will awake soon—
His hour of mid-day rest is nearly over;
But it were pity to disturb him till
'T is closed.

Cain. You have said well; I will contain
My heart till then. He smiles, and sleeps!—Sleep on
And smile, thou little, young inheritor
Of a world scarce less young: sleep on, and smile!
Thine are the hours and days when both are cheering
And innocent! *thou* hast not pluck'd the fruit—
Thou know'st not thou art naked! Must the time
Come thou shalt be amerced for sins unknown,
Which were not mine nor thine? But now sleep on.
His cheeks are reddening into deeper smiles,
And shining lids are trembling o'er his long
Lashes, dark as the cypress which waves o'er them ;
Half open, from beneath them the clear blue
Laughs out, although in slumber. He must dream—
Of what? Of Paradise!—Ay! dream of it,
My disinherited boy! 'T is but a dream ;
For never more thyself, thy sons, nor fathers,
Shall walk in that forbidden place of joy!

Adah. Dear Cain! Nay, do not whisper o'er our son
Such melancholy yearnings o'er the past:
Why wilt thou always mourn for Paradise?
Can we not make another?

Cain. Where?

Adah. Here, or
Where'er thou wilt: where'er thou art, I feel not
The want of this so much regretted Eden.
Have I not thee, our boy, our sire, and brother,
And Zillah—our sweet sister, and our Eve,
To whom we owe so much besides our birth?

Cain. Yes—death, too, is amongst the debts we owe her.

Adah. Cain! that proud spirit, who withdrew thee hence,
Hath sadden'd thine still deeper. I had hoped
The promised wonders which thou hast beheld,
Visions, thou say'st, of past and present words,
Would have composed thy mind into the calm
Of a contented knowledge; but I see
Thy guide hath done thee evil: still I thank him,
And can forgive him all, that he so soon
Hath given thee back to us.

Cain. So soon?

Adah 'T is scarcely

Two hours since ye departed: two *long* hours
To *me*, but only *hours* upon the sun.
Cain. And yet I have approach'd that sun, and seen
Worlds which he once shone on, and never more
Shall light; and worlds he never lit: methought
Years had roll'd o'er my absence.
Adah. Hardly hours.
Cain. The mind then hath capacity of time,
And measures it by that which it beholds,
Pleasing or painful; little or almighty.
I had beheld the immemorial works
Of endless beings; skirr'd extinguish'd worlds;
And, gazing on eternity, methought
I had borrow'd more by a few drops of ages
From its immensity; but now I feel
My littleness again. Well said the spirit,
That I was nothing!
Adah. Wherefore said he so?
Jehovah said not that.
Cain. No: *He* contents Him
With making us the *nothing* which we are;
And after flattering dust with glimpses of
Eden and Immortality, resolves
It back to dust again—for what?
Adah. Thou know'st—
Even for our parents' error.
Cain. What is that
To us! they sinn'd, then *let them* die!
Adah. Thou has not spoken well, nor is that thought
Thy own, but of the spirit who was with thee.
Would *I* could die for them, so *they* might live!
Cain. Why, so say I—provided that one victim
Might satiate the insatiable of life,
And that our little rosy sleeper there
Might never taste of death nor human sorrow,
Nor hand it down to those who spring from him.
Adah. How know we that some such atonement one day
May not redeem our race?
Cain. By sacrificing
The harmless for the guilty? what atonement
Were there? why, *we* are innocent: what have we
Done, that we must be victims for a deed
Before our birth, or need have victims to
Atone for this mysterious, nameless sin—
If it be such a sin to seek for knowledge?
Adah. Alas! thou sinnest now, my Cain: thy words
Sound impious in mine ears.
Cain. Then leave me!
Adah. Never,
Though thy God left thee.
Cain. Say, what have we here?
Adah. Two altars, which our brother Abel made
During thine absence, whereupon to offer
A sacrifice to God on thy return.
Cain. And how knew *he*, that *I* would be so ready
With the burnt offerings, which he daily brings
With a meek brow, whose base humility
Shows more of fear than worship, as a bribe
To the Creator?
Adah. Surely, 't is well done.
Cain. One altar may suffice; *I* have no offering.
Adah. The fruits of the earth, the early, beautiful
Blossom and bud, and bloom of flowers and fruits,
These are a goodly offering to the Lord,
Given with a gentle and a contrite spirit.
Cain. I have toil'd, and till'd, and sweaten in the sun
According to the curse:—must I do more?
For what should I be gentle? for a war
With all the elements ere they will yield
The bread we eat? For what must I be grateful?
For being dust, and grovelling in the dust,
Till I return to dust? If I am nothing—
For nothing shall I be an hypocrite,
And seem well-pleased with pain? For what should I
Be contrite? for my father's sin, already
Expiate with what we all have undergone,
And to be more than expiated by
The ages prophesied, upon our seed.
Little deems our young blooming sleeper, there,
The germs of an eternal misery
To myriads is within him! better 't were
I snatch'd him in his sleep, and dash'd him 'gainst
The rocks, than let him live to——
Adah. Oh, my God!
Touch not the child—my child! *thy* child! Oh Cain
Cain. Fear not! for all the stars, and all the power
Which sways them, I would not accost yon infant
With ruder greeting than a father's kiss.
Adah. Then, why so awful in thy speech?
Cain. I said,
'T were better that he ceased to live, than give
Life to so much of sorrow as he must
Endure, and, harder still, bequeath; but since
That saying jars you, let us only say—
'T were better that he never had been born.
Adah. Oh, do not say so! Where were then the joys,
The mother's joys of watching, nourishing,
And loving him? Soft! he awakes. Sweet Enoch!
[*She goes to the child.*
Oh Cain! look on him; see how full of life,
Of strength, of bloom, of beauty, and of joy,
How like to me—how like to thee, when gentle,
For *then* we are *all* alike; is 't not so, Cain?
Mother, and sire, and son, our features are
Reflected in each other; as they are
In the clear waters, when *they* are *gentle*, and
When *thou* art *gentle*. Love us, then, my Cain!
And love thyself for our sakes, for we love thee.
Look! how he laughs and stretches out his arms,
And opens wide his blue eyes upon thine,
To hail his father; while his little form
Flutters as wing'd with joy. Talk not of pain!
The childless cherubs well might envy thee
The pleasures of a parent! Bless him, Cain!

As yet he hath no words to thank thee, but
His heart will, and thine own too.
Cain. Bless thee, boy!
If that a mortal blessing may avail thee,
To save thee from the serpent's curse!
Adah. It shall.
Surely a father's blessing may avert
A reptile's subtlety.
Cain. Of that I doubt;
But bless him ne'er the less.
Adah. Our brother comes.
Cain. Thy brother Abel.

Enter ABEL.

Abel. Welcome, Cain! My brother,
The peace of God be on thee!
Cain. Abel, hail!
Abel. Our sister tells me thou hast been wandering,
In high communion with a spirit, far
Beyond our wonted range. Was he of those
We have seen and spoken with, like to our father?
Cain. No.
Abel. Why then commune with him? he may be
A foe to the Most High.
Cain. And friend to man.
Has the Most High been so—if so you term Him?
Abel. *Term Him!* your words are strange to-day, [my brother.
My sister Adah, leave us for awhile—
We mean to sacrifice.
Adah. Farewell, my Cain;
But first embrace thy son. May his soft spirit,
And Abel's pious ministry, recall thee
To peace and holiness! [*Exit* ADAH, *with her child.*
Abel. Where hast thou been?
Cain. I know not.
Abel. Nor what thou hast seen?
Cain. The dead,
The immortal, the unbounded, the omnipotent,
The overpowering mysteries of space—
The innumerable worlds that were and are—
A whirlwind of such overwhelming things, [spheres
Suns, moons, and earths, upon their loud-voiced
Singing in thunder round me, as have made me
Unfit for mortal converse: leave me, Abel.
Abel. Thine eyes are flashing with unnatural light,
Thy cheek is flush'd with an unnatural hue,
Thy words are fraught with an unnatural sound—
What may this mean?
Cain. It means——I pray thee, leave me. [gether.
Abel. Not till we have pray'd and sacrificed to-
Cain. Abel, I pray thee, sacrifice alone—
Jehovah loves thee well.
Abel. *Both* well, I hope.
Cain. But thee the better: I care not for that;
Thou art fitter for His worship than I am;
Revere Him, then—but let it be alone—
At least, without me.
Abel. Brother, I should ill
Deserve the name of our great father's son,
If, as my elder, I revered thee not,
And in the worship of our God call'd not
On thee to join me, and precede me in
Our priesthood—'tis thy place.
Cain. But I have ne'er
Asserted it.
Abel. The more my grief; I pray thee
To do so now: thy soul seems labouring in
Some strong delusion; it will calm thee.
Cain. No;
Nothing can calm me more. *Calm!* say I? Never
Knew I what calm was in the soul, although
I have seen the elements still'd. My Abel, leave me!
Or let me leave thee to thy pious purpose.
Abel. Neither: we must perform our task together.
Spurn me not.
Cain. If it must be so——well, then,
What shall I do?
Abel. Choose one of those two altars.
Cain. Choose for me: they to me are so much turf
And stone.
Abel. Choose thou!
Cain. I have chosen.
Abel. 'T is the highest,
And suits thee, as the elder. Now prepare
Thine offerings.
Cain. Where are thine?
Abel. Behold them here—
The firstlings of the flock, and fat thereof—
A shepherd's humble offering.
Cain. I have no flocks;
I am a tiller of the ground, and must
Yield what it yieldeth to my toil—its fruit:
[*He gathers fruits.*
Behold them in their various bloom and ripeness.
[*They dress their altars, and kindle a flame upon them.*
Abel. My brother, as the elder, offer first
Thy prayer and thanksgiving with sacrifice.
Cain. No—I am new to this; lead thou the way
And I will follow—as I may.
Abel. (*kneeling*). Oh God!
Who made us, and who breathed the breath of life
Within our nostrils, who hath blessed us,
And spared, despite our father's sin, to make
His children all lost, as they might have been,
Had not Thy justice been so temper'd with
The mercy which is Thy delight, as to
Accord a pardon like a Paradise,
Compared with our great crimes:—Sole Lord of light!
Of good, and glory, and eternity;
Without whom all were evil, and with whom
Nothing can err, except to some good end
Of Thine omnipotent benevolence—
Inscrutable, but still to be fulfill'd—
Accept from out thy humble first of shepherd's
First of the first-born flocks—an offering,
In itself nothing—as what offering can be

Aught unto Thee?—but yet accept it for
The thanksgiving of him who spreads it in
The face of Thy high heaven, bowing his own
Even to the dust, of which he is, in honour
Of Thee, and of Thy name, for evermore!
Cain (*standing erect during this speech*). Spirit!
whate'er or whosoe'er Thou art,
Omnipotent, it may be—and, if good,
Shown in the exemption of Thy deeds from evil;
Jehovah upon earth! and God in heaven!
And it may be with other names, because
Thine attributes seem many, as Thy works:—
If Thou must be propitiated with prayers,
Take them! If Thou must be induced with altars,
And soften'd with a sacrifice, receive them!
Two beings here erect them unto Thee. [smokes
If Thou lov'st blood, the shepherd's shrine, which
On my right hand, hath shed it for Thy service
In the first of his flock, whose limbs now reek
In sanguinary incense to Thy skies;
Or if the sweet and blooming fruits of earth,
And milder seasons, which the unstain'd turf
I spread them on now offers in the face
Of the broad sun which ripen'd them, may seem
Good to Thee, inasmuch as they have not
Suffer'd in limb or life, and rather form
A sample of Thy works, than supplication
To look on ours! If a shrine without victim,
And altar without gore, may win Thy favour,
Look on it! And for him who dresseth it,
He is—such as Thou mad'st him; and seeks nothing
Which must be won by kneeling: if he 's evil,
Strike him! Thou art omnipotent, and may'st—
For what can he oppose? If he be good,
Strike him, or spare him, as Thou wilt! since all
Rests upon Thee; and good and evil seem
To have no power themselves, save in Thy will;
And whether that be good or ill I know not,
Not being omnipotent, nor fit to judge
Omnipotence, but merely to endure
Its mandate; which thus far I have endured.

[*The fire upon the altar of* ABEL *kindles into a column of the brightest flame, and ascends to heaven; while a whirlwind throws down the altar of* CAIN, *and scatters the fruits abroad upon the earth.*

Abel. (*kneeling*). Oh, brother, pray! Jehovah 's
Cain. Why so? [wroth with thee.
Abel. Thy fruits are scatter'd on the earth. [turn;
Cain. From earth they came, to earth let them re-
Their seed will bear fresh fruit there ere the summer:
Thy burnt flesh-off'ring prospers better; see
How heav'n licks up the flames, when thick with blood!
Abel. Think not upon my offering's acceptance,
But make another of thine own before
It is too late.
Cain. I will build no more altars,
Nor suffer any.—
Abel (*rising*). Cain! what meanest thou?
Cain. To cast down yon vile flatterer of the clouds
The smoky harbinger of thy dull pray'rs—
Thine altar, with its blood of lambs and kids,
Which fed on milk, to be destroy'd in blood.
Abel (*opposing him*). Thou shalt not:—add not
impious works to impious
Words! let that altar stand—'t is hallowed now
By the immortal pleasure of Jehovah,
In His acceptance of the victims.
Cain. *His!*
His pleasure! what was His high pleasure in
The fumes of scorching flesh and smoking blood,
To the pain of the bleating mothers, which
Still yearn for their dead offspring? or the pangs
Of the sad ignorant victims underneath
Thy pious knife? Give way! this bloody record
Shall not stand in the sun, to shame creation!
Abel. Brother, give back! thou shalt not touch my
With violence: if that thou wilt adopt it, [altar
To try another sacrifice, 't is thine.
Cain. Another sacrifice! Give way, or else
That sacrifice may be——
Abel. What mean'st thou?
Cain. Give—
Give way!—thy God loves blood!—then look to it:—
Give way, ere He hath *more!*
Abel. In *His* great name,
I stand between thee and the shrine which hath
Had His acceptance.
Cain. If thou lov'st thyself,
Stand back till I have strew'd this turf along
Its native soil:—else——
Abel (*opposing him*). I love God far more
Than life.
Cain. (*striking him with a brand, on the temples, which he snatches from the altar*).
Then take thy life unto thy God,
Since He loves lives.
Abel (*falls*). What hast thou done, my brother?
Cain. Brother!
Abel. Oh, God! receive Thy servant, and
Forgive his slayer, for he knew not what
He did—Cain, give me—give me thy hand; and tell
Poor Zillah——
Cain (*after a moment's stupefaction*). *My* hand!
't is all red, and with—
What?

[*A long pause.—Looking slowly round.*

Where am I? alone! Where 's Abel? where
Cain? Can it be that I am he? My brother,
Awake!—why liest thou so on the green earth?
'T is not the hour of slumber;—why so pale?
What, hast thou!——thou wert full of life this morn!
Abel! I pray thee, mock me not! I smote
Too fiercely, but not fatally. Ah, why
Wouldst thou oppose me? This is mockery;
And only done to daunt me:—'t was a blow—
And but a blow. Stir—stir—nay, only stir!

Why, so—that's well!—thou breath'st! breathe upon
Oh, God! oh, God! [me!

Abel (*very faintly*). What's he who speaks of God?

Cain. Thy murderer.

Abel. Then may God forgive him! Cain,
Comfort poor Zillah:—she has but one brother
Now. [ABEL *dies.*

Cain. And I none!—Who makes me brotherless?
His eyes are open! then he is not dead!
Death is like sleep; and sleep shuts down our lids.
His lips, too, are apart; why then he breathes!
And yet I feel it not.—His heart!—his heart!—
Let me see, doth it beat? methinks——No!—no!
This is a vision, else I am become
The native of another and worse world.
The earth swims round me:—what is this?—'t is wet;

[*Puts his hand to his brow, and then looks at it.*

And yet there are no dews! 'T is blood—my blood—
My brother's and my own! and shed by me!
Then what have I further to do with life,
Since I have taken life from my own flesh?
But he can not be dead!—Is silence death?
No; he will wake: then let me watch by him.
Life cannot be so slight, as to be quench'd
Thus quickly!—he hath spoken to me since—
What shall I say to him?—My brother!—No:
He will not answer to that name; for brethren
Smite not each other. Yet—yet—speak to me.
Oh! for a word more of that gentle voice,
That I may bear to hear my own again!

Enter ZILLAH.

Zillah. I heard a heavy sound; what can it be?
'T is Cain; and watching by my husband. What
Dost thou there, brother? Doth he sleep? Oh, heav'n!
What means this paleness, and yon stream?—No, no!
It is not blood; for who would shed his blood? [not;
Abel! what's this?—who hath done this? He moves
He breathes not: and his hands drop down from mine
With stony lifelessness! Ah! cruel Cain!
Why cam'st thou not in time to save him from
This violence? Whatever hath assail'd him,
Thou wert the stronger, and should'st have stepp'd in

Between him and aggression! Father!—Eve!—
Adah!—come hither! Death is in the world!
[*Exit* ZILLAH, *calling on her Parents, &c.*
Cain. (*solus*). And who hath brought him there?
—I—who abhor
The name of Death so deeply, that the thought
Empoison'd all my life, before I knew
His aspect—I have led him here, and giv'n
My brother to his cold and still embrace,
As if he would not have asserted his
Inexorable claim without my aid.
I am awake at last—a dreary dream
Had madden'd me;—but *he* shall ne'er awake.

Enter ADAM, EVE, ADAH, *and* ZILLAH.

Adam. A voice of woe from Zillah brings me here.—
What do I see?—'T is true!—My son!—my son!
Woman, behold the serpent's work, and thine!
[*To* EVE.
Eve. Oh! speak not of it now: the serpent's fangs
Are in my heart. My best beloved, Abel!
Jehovah! this is punishment beyond
A mother's sin, to take *him* from me!
Adam. Who,
Or what hath done this deed?—speak, Cain, since thou
Wert present; was it some more hostile angel,
Who walks not with Jehovah? or some wild
Brute of the forest?
Eve. Ah! a livid light
Breaks through, as from a thunder-cloud! yon brand,
Massy and bloody! snatch'd from off the altar,
And black with smoke, and red with——
Adam. Speak, my son!
Speak, and assure us, wretched as we are,
That we are not more miserable still.
Adah. Speak, Cain! and say it was not *thou!*
Eve. It was. I see it now: he hangs his guilty head,
And covers his ferocious eye with hands
Incarnadine.
Adah. Mother, thou dost him wrong—
Cain! clear thee from this horrible accusal,
Which grief wrings from our parent.
Eve. Hear, Jehovah!
May the eternal serpent's curse be on him!
For he was fitter for his seed than ours.
May all his days be desolate. May——
Adah. Hold!
Curse him not, mother, for he is thy son—
Curse him not, mother, for he is my brother,
And my betroth'd.
Eve. He hath left thee no brother—
Zillah no husband—me *no son!*—for thus
I curse him from my sight for evermore!
All bonds I break between us! as he broke
That of his nature, in yon——Oh death! death!
Why didst thou not take *me*, who first incurr'd thee?
Why dost thou not so now?
Adam. Eve! let not this,
Thy natural grief, lead to impiety!
A heavy doom was long forespoken to us;
And now that it begins, let it be borne
In such sort as may show our God, that we
Are faithful servants to His holy will.
Eve (*pointing to Cain*). *His will?* the will of yon incarnate spirit
Of death, whom I have brought upon the earth
To strew it with the dead. May all the curses
Of life be on him! and his agonies
Drive him forth o'er the wilderness, like us
From Eden, till his children do by him
As he did by his brother! May the swords
And wings of fiery cherubim pursue him
By day and night—snakes spring up in his path—
Earth's fruits be ashes in his mouth—the leaves
On which he lays his head to sleep be strew'd
With scorpions! May his dreams be of his victim!
His waking a continual dread of death!
May the clear rivers turn to blood, as he
Stoops down to stain them with his raging lip!
May every element shun or change to him!
May he live in the pangs which others die with!
And death itself wax something worse than death
To him who first acquainted him with man!
Hence, fratricide! henceforth that word is *Cain*,
Through all the coming myriads of mankind,
Who shall abhor thee, though thou wert their sire!
May the grass wither from thy feet! the woods
Deny thee shelter! earth a home! the dust
A grave! the sun his light! and heaven her God!
[*Exit* EVE.
Adam. Cain! get thee forth: we dwell no more together.
Depart! and leave the dead to me——I am
Henceforth alone—we never must meet more.
Adah. Oh, part not with him thus, my father: do not
Add thy deep curse to Eve's upon his head!
Adam. I curse him not: his spirit be his curse
Come, Zillah!
Zillah. I must watch my husband's corse.
Adam. We will return again, when he is gone
Who hath provided for us this dread office.
Come, Zillah!
Zillah. Yet one kiss on yon pale clay,
And those lips once so warm—my heart! my heart!
[*Exeunt* ADAM *and* ZILLAH, *weeping.*
Adah. Cain! thou hast heard, we must go forth.
I am ready,
So shall our children be. I will bear Enoch,
And you his sister. Ere the sun declines
Let us depart, nor walk the wilderness
Under the cloud of night. Nay, speak to me.
To *me—thine own.*
Cain. Leave me!
Adah. Why, all have left thee.
Cain. And wherefore lingerest thou? Dost thou not fear.
To dwell with one who hath done this?
Adah. I fear
Nothing except to leave thee, much as I
Shrink from the deed which leaves thee brotherless.

I must not speak of this—it is between thee
And the great God.

A voice from within exclaims, Cain! Cain!

Adah. Hear'st thou that voice?

The voice within. Cain! Cain!

Adah. It soundeth like an angel's tone.

Enter the ANGEL *of the Lord.*

Angel. Where is thy brother Abel?

Cain. Am I then
My brother's keeper?

Angel. Cain! what hast thou done?
The voice of thy slain brother's blood cries out,
Even from the ground, unto the Lord!—Now art thou
Cursed from the earth, which open'd late her mouth
To drink thy brother's blood from thy rash hand.
Henceforth, when thou shalt till the ground, it shall not
Yield thee her strength: a fugitive shalt thou
Be from this day, and vagabond on earth!

Adah. This punishment is more than he can bear.
Behold, thou drivest him from the face of earth,
And from the face of God shall he be hid.
A fugitive and vagabond on earth,
'T will come pass, that whoso findeth him
Shall slay him.

Cain. Would they could! but who are they
Shall slay me? Where are these on the lone earth
As yet unpeopled?

Angel. Thou hast slain thy brother,
And who shall warrant thee against thy son?

Adah. Angel of Light! be merciful, nor say
That this poor aching breast now nourishes
A murderer in my boy, and of his father.

Angel. Then he would but be what his father is.
Did not the milk of Eve give nutriment
To him thou now see'st so besmear'd with blood?
The fratricide might well engender parricides.—
But it shall not be so—the Lord thy God
And mine commandeth me to set His seal
On Cain, so that he may go forth in safety.
Who slayeth Cain, a sevenfold vengeance shall
Be taken on his head. Come hither!

Cain. What
Wouldst thou with me?

Angel. To mark upon thy brow
Exemption from such deeds as thou hast done.

Cain. No, let me die!

Angel. It must not be.

[*The* ANGEL *sets the mark on* CAIN'S *brow.*

Cain. It burns
My brow, but nought to that which is within it.
Is there more? let me meet it as I may.

Angel. Stern hast thou been and stubborn from the [womb,
As the ground thou must henceforth till; but he
Thou slew'st was gentle as the flocks he tended.

Cain. After the fall too soon was I begotten;
Ere yet my mother's mind subsided from
The serpent, and my sire still mourn'd for Eden.
That which I am, I am; I did not seek
For life, nor did I make myself; but could I
With my own death redeem him from the dust—
And why not so? let him return to day,
And I lie ghastly! so shall he restored
By God the life to him He loved; and taken
From me a being I ne'er loved to bear.

Angel. Who shall heal murder? what is done is [done;
Go forth! fulfil thy days! and be thy deeds
Unlike the last! [*The* ANGEL *disappears.*

Adah. He 's gone, let us go forth;
I hear our little Enoch cry within our bower.

Cain. Ah! little knows he what he weeps for!
And I who have shed blood cannot shed tears!
But the four rivers would not cleanse my soul.
Think'st thou my boy will bear to look on me?

Adah. If I thought that he would not, I would—

Cain (*interrupting her*). No,
No more of threats: we have had too many of them:
Go to our children; I will follow thee!

Adah. I will not leave thee lonely with the dead;
Let us depart together.

Cain. Oh! thou dead
And everlasting witness! whose unsinking
Blood darkens earth and heaven! what thou *now* art
I know not! but if *thou* see'st what *I* am,
I think thou wilt forgive him, whom his God
Can ne'er forgive, nor his own soul.—Farewell!
I must not, dare not touch what I have made thee.
I, who sprung from the same womb with thee, drain'd
The same breast, clasp'd thee often to my own,
In fondness brotherly and boyish, I
Can never meet thee more, nor even dare
To do that for thee, which thou shouldst have done
For me—compose thy limbs into their grave—
The first grave yet dug for mortality.
But who hath dug that grave? Oh, earth! Oh, earth!
For all the fruits thou hast render'd to me, I
Give thee back this.—Now for the wilderness.

[ADAH *stoops down and kisses the body of* ABEL.

Adah. A dreary, and an early doom, my brother,
Has been thy lot! Of all who mourn for thee,
I alone must not weep. My office is
Henceforth to dry up tears, and not to shed them:
But yet, of all who mourn, none mourn like me,
Not only for thyself, but him who slew thee.
Now, Cain! I will divide thy burden with thee.

Cain. Eastward from Eden will we take our way:
'T is the most desolate, and suits my steps.

Adah. Lead! thou shalt be my guide, and may our [God
Be thine! Now let us carry forth our children.

Cain. And *he* who lieth there was childless. I
Have dried the fountain of a gentle race,
Which might have graced his recent marriage couch,
And might have temper'd this stern blood of mine,
Uniting with our children Abel's offspring!
O Abel!

Adah. Peace be with him!

Cain. But with *me!*

HEBREW MELODIES.

ADVERTISEMENT.

The subsequent poems were written at the request of my friend, the Hon. Douglas Kinnaird, for a selection of Hebrew Melodies, and have been published, with the music, arranged by Mr. Braham and Mr. Nathan.

SHE WALKS IN BEAUTY.

SHE walks in beauty, like the night
 Of cloudless climes and starry skies:
And all that's best of dark and bright
 Meet in her aspect and her eyes:
Thus mellow'd to that tender light
 Which Heaven to gaudy day denies

One shade the more, one ray the less,
 Had half impair'd the nameless grace,
Which waves in every raven tress,
 Or softly lightens o'er her face;
Where thoughts serenely sweet express,
 How pure, how dear their dwelling-place.

And on that cheek, and o'er that brow
So soft, so calm, yet eloquent,
The smiles that win, the tints that glow,
But tell of days in goodness spent,
A mind at peace with all below,
A heart whose love is innocent!

THE HARP THE MONARCH MINSTREL SWEPT.

The harp the monarch minstrel swept,
The King of men, the loved of Heaven,
Which Music hallow'd while she wept
O'er tones her heart of hearts had given,
Redoubled be her tears, its chords are riven!
It soften'd men of iron mould,
It gave them virtues not their own;
No ear so dull, no soul so cold,
That felt not, fired not to the tone,
Till David's lyre grew mightier than his throne!

It told the triumphs of our King,
It wafted glory to our God;
It made our gladden'd valleys ring,
The cedars bow, the mountains nod;
Its sound aspired to heaven and there abode!
Since then, though heard on earth no more,
Devotion and her daughter Love,
Still bid the bursting spirit soar
To sounds that seem as from above,
In dreams that day's broad light can not remove.

IF THAT HIGH WORLD.

If that high world, which lies beyond
Our own, surviving Love endears;
If there the cherish'd heart be fond,
The eye the same, except in tears—
How welcome those untrodden spheres!
How sweet this very hour to die!
To soar from earth and find all fears,
Lost in thy light—Eternity!

It must be so: 'tis not for self
That we so tremble on the brink;
And striving to o'erleap the gulf,
Yet cling to Being's severing link.
Oh! in that future let us think
To hold each heart the heart that shares,
With them the immortal waters drink,
And soul in soul grow deathless theirs!

THE WILD GAZELLE.

The wild gazelle on Judah's hills
Exulting yet may bound,
And drink from all the living rills
That gush on holy ground;

Its airy step and glorious eye
May glance in tameless transport by:—

A step as fleet, an eye more bright,
Hath Judah witnessed there;
And o'er her scenes of lost delight
Inhabitants more fair.
The cedars wave on Lebanon,
But Judah's statelier maids are gone!

More blest each palm that shades those plains
Than Israel's scatter'd race;
For, taking root, it there remain
In solitary grace:
It cannot quit its place of birth,
It will not live in other earth.

But we must wander witheringly,
In other lands to die;
And where our fathers' ashes be,
Our own may never lie:
Our temple hath not left a stone,
And Mockery sits on Salem's throne.

OH! WEEP FOR THOSE.

Oh! weep for those that wept by Babel's stream,
Whose shrines are desolate, whose land a dream;
Weep for the harp of Judah's broken shell;
Mourn—where their God hath dwelt the Godless dwell!

And where shall Israel lave her bleeding feet?
And when shall Zion's songs again seem sweet?
And Judah's melody once more rejoice
The hearts that leap'd before its heavenly voice?

Tribes of the wandering foot and weary breast,
How shall ye flee away and be at rest!
The wild-dove hath her nest, the fox his cave,
Mankind their country—Israel but the grave!

ON JORDAN'S BANKS.

On Jordan's banks the Arab's camels stray,
On Sion's hill the False One's votaries pray,
The Baal-adorer bows on Sinai's steep—
Yet there—even there—Oh God! Thy thunders sleep:

There—where Thy finger scorch'd the tablet stone!
There—where Thy shadow to Thy people shone!
Thy glory shrouded in its garb of fire:
Thyself—none living see and not expire!

Oh! in the lightning let Thy glance appear;
Sweep from his shiver'd hand the oppressor's spear:
How long by tyrants shall Thy land be trod!
How long Thy temple worshipless, Oh God!

JEPHTHA'S DAUGHTER.

Since our Country, our God—Oh, my sire
Demand that thy daughter expire;
Since thy triumph was bought by thy vow—
Strike the bosom that's bared for thee now!

And the voice of my mourning is o'er,
And the mountains behold me no more:
If the hand that I love lay me low,
There cannot be pain in the blow!

And of this, oh, my father! be sure—
That the blood of thy child is as pure
As the blessing I beg ere it flow,
And the last thought that soothes me below.

Though the virgins of Salem lament,
Be the judge and the hero unbent!
I have won the great battle for thee,
And my father and country are free!

When this blood of thy giving hath gush'd,
When the voice that thou lovest is hush'd,
Let my memory still be thy pride,
And forget not I smiled as I died!

OH! SNATCH'D AWAY IN BEAUTY'S BLOOM.

Oh! snatch'd away in beauty's bloom,
On thee shall press no ponderous tomb;
But on thy turf shall roses rear
Their leaves, the earliest of the year;
And the wild cypress wave in tender gloom:

And oft by yon blue gushing stream
Shall Sorrow lean her drooping head,
And feed deep thought with many a dream,
And lingering pause and lightly tread;
Fond wretch! as if her step disturb'd the dead!

Away! ye know that tears are vain,
That death nor heeds nor hears distress:
Will this unteach us to complain?
Or make one mourner weep the less?
And thou—who tell'st me to forget,
Thy looks are wan, thine eyes are wet.

MY SOUL IS DARK.

My soul is dark—Oh! quickly string
The harp I yet can brook to hear;
And let thy gentle fingers fling
Its melting murmurs o'er mine ear.
If in this heart a hope be dear,
That sound shall charm it forth again:
If in these eyes there lurk a tear,
'T will flow, and cease to burn my brain.

But bid the strain be wild and deep,
Nor let thy notes of joy be first:
I tell thee, minstrel, I must weep,
Or else this heavy heart will burst;
For it hath been by sorrow nursed,
And ached in sleepless silence long;
And now 't is doom'd to know the worst,
And break at once—or yield to song.

I SAW THEE WEEP.

I saw thee weep—the big bright tear
Came o'er that eye of blue;
And then methought it did appear
A violet dropping dew:
I saw thee smile—the sapphire's blaze
Beside thee ceased to shine;
It could not match the living rays
That fill'd that glance of thine.

As clouds from yonder sun receive
A deep and mellow dye,
Which scarce the shade of coming eve
Can banish from the sky,
Those smiles unto the moodiest mind
Their own pure joy impart;
Their sunshine leaves a glow behind
That lightens o'er the heart.

THY DAYS ARE DONE.

Thy days are done, thy fame begun;
Thy country's strains record
The triumphs of her chosen Son,
The slaughters of his sword;
The deeds he did, the fields he won,
The freedom he restored!

Though thou art fall'n, while we are free
Thou shalt not taste of death!
The generous blood that flow'd from thee
Disdain'd to sink beneath:
Within our veins its currents be,
Thy spirit on our breath!

Thy name, our charging hosts along,
Shall be the battle-word!
Thy fall, the theme of choral song
From virgin voices pour'd!
To weep would do thy glory wrong;
Thou shalt not be deplored.

SONG OF SAUL BEFORE HIS LAST BATTLE.

Warriors and chiefs! should the shaft or the sword
Pierce me in leading the host of the Lord,
Heed not the corse, though a king's, in your path:
Bury your steel in the bosoms of Gath!

Thou who art bearing my buckler and bow,
Should the soldiers of Saul look away from the foe,
Stretch me that moment in blood at thy feet!
Mine be the doom which they dared not to meet.

Farewell to others, but never we part,
Heir to my royalty, son of my heart!
Bright is the diadem, boundless the sway,
Or kingly the death, which awaits us to-day.

SAUL.

Thou whose spell can raise the dead,
Bid the prophet's form appear.
"Samuel, raise thy buried head!
King, behold the phantom seer!"

Earth yawn'd; he stood the centre of a cloud:
Light changed its hue, retiring from his shroud.
Death stood all glassy in his fixèd eye;
His hand was wither'd, and his veins were dry;
His foot, in bony whiteness, glitter'd there,
Shrunken and sinewless, and ghastly bare;
From lips that moved not, and unbreathing frame,
Like cavern'd winds, the hollow accents came.
Saul saw, and fell to earth, as falls the oak,
At once, and blasted by the thunder-stroke.

"Why is my sleep disquieted?
Who is he that calls the dead?
Is it thou, O King? Behold,
Bloodless are these limbs, and cold:
Such are mine; and such shall be
Thine to-morrow, when with me:
Ere the coming day is done,
Such shalt thou be, such thy son.
Fare thee well, but for a day,
Then we mix our mouldering clay.
Thou, thy race, lie pale and low,
Pierced by shafts of many a bow;
And the falchion by thy side
To thy heart thy hand shall guide:
Crownless, breathless, headless fall,
Son and sire, the house of Saul."

"ALL IS VANITY, SAITH THE PREACHER."

FAME, wisdom, love, and power were mine,
And health and youth possess'd me;
My goblets blush'd from every vine,
And lovely forms caress'd me;
I sunn'd my heart in beauty's eyes,
And felt my soul grow tender;
All earth can give, or mortal prize,
Was mine of regal splendour.

I strive to number o'er what days
Remembrance can discover,
Which all that life or earth displays
Would lure me to live over.
There rose no day, there roll'd no hour
Of pleasure unembitter'd;
And not a trapping deck'd my power,
That gall'd not while it glitter'd.

The serpent of the field, by art
And spells, is won from harming;
But that which coils around the heart,
Oh! who hath power of charming?
It will not list to wisdom's lore,
Nor music's voice can lure it;
But there it stings for evermore
The soul that must endure it.

WHEN COLDNESS WRAPS THIS SUFFERING CLAY.

WHEN coldness wraps this suffering clay,
Ah! whither strays the immortal mind?
It cannot die, it cannot stray,
But leaves its darken'd dust behind.
Then, unembodied, doth it trace
By steps each planet's heavenly way?
Or fill at once the realms of space,
A thing of eyes, that all survey?

Eternal, boundless, undecay'd,
A thought unseen, but seeing all,
All, all in earth, or skies display'd,
Shall it survey, shall it recall:
Each fainter trace that memory holds
So darkly of departed years,
In one broad glance the soul beholds,
And all, that was, at once appears.

Before Creation peopled earth,
Its eye shall roll through chaos back;
And where the furthest heaven had birth,
The spirit trace its rising track,
And where the future mars or makes,
Its glance dilate o'er all to be,
While sun is quench'd or system breaks,
Fix'd in its own eternity.

Above or Love, Hope, Hate, or Fear,
It lives all passionless and pure:
An age shall fleet like earthly year;
Its years as moments shall endure.
Away, away, without a wing,
O'er all, through all, its thought shall fly;
A nameless and eternal thing,
Forgetting what it was to die.

VISION OF BELSHAZZAR.

THE King was on his throne,
The Satraps throng'd the hall;
A thousand bright lamps shone
O'er that high festival.
A thousand cups of gold,
In Judah deem'd divine—
Jehovah's vessels hold
The godless heathen's wine.

In that same hour and hall,
The fingers of a hand
Came forth against the wall,
And wrote as if on sand:
The fingers of a man;—
A solitary hand
Along the letters ran,
And traced them like a wand.

The monarch saw, and shook,
And bade no more rejoice ;
All bloodless wax'd his look,
And tremulous his voice.

"Let the men of lore appear,
The wisest of the earth,
And expound the words of fear,
Which mar our royal mirth."

Chaldea's seers are good,
But here they have no skill;
And the unknown letters stood
Untold and awful still.
And Babel's men of age
Are wise and deep in lore;
But now they were not sage,
They saw—but knew no more.

A captive in the land,
A stranger and a youth,
He heard the king's command,
He saw that writing's truth,
The lamps around were bright,
The prophecy in view;
He read it on that night,—
The morrow proved it true.

"Belshazzar's grave is made
His kingdom pass'd away,
He, in the balance weigh'd,
Is light and worthless clay.
The shroud, his robe of state,
His canopy the stone:
The Mede is at his gate!
The Persian on his throne!"

SUN OF THE SLEEPLESS.

Sun of the sleepless! melancholy star!
Whose tearful beam glows tremulously far,
That show'st the darkness thou canst not dispel,
How like art thou to joy remember'd well!
So gleams the past, the light of other days,
Which shines, but warms not with its powerless rays;
A night-beam Sorrow watcheth to behold,
Distinct, but distant—clear—but oh, how cold!

WERE MY BOSOM AS FALSE AS THOU DEEM'ST IT TO BE.

Were my bosom as false as thou deem'st it to be,
I need not have wander'd from far Galilee;
It was but abjuring my creed to efface
The curse which, thou say'st, is the crime of my race:

If the bad never triumph, then God is with thee!
If the slave only sin, thou art spotless and free!
If the Exile on earth is an outcast on high,
Live on in thy faith, but in mine I will die.

I have lost for that faith more than thou canst bestow,
As the God who permits thee to prosper doth know;
In His hand is my heart and my hope—and in thine
The land and the life which for Him I resign.

HEROD'S LAMENT FOR MARIAMNE.

Oh, Mariamne! now for thee
The heart for which thou bled'st is bleeding:
Revenge is lost in agony,
And wild remorse to rage succeeding.
Oh, Mariamne! where thou art?
Thou canst not hear my bitter pleading.
Ah! couldst thou—thou wouldst pardon now,
Though Heaven were to my prayer unheeding.

And is she dead?—and did they dare
Obey my frenzy's jealous raving?
My wrath but doom'd my own despair:
The sword that smote her's o'er me waving.—
But thou art cold, my murdered love!
And this dark heart is vainly craving
For her who soars alone above,
And leaves my soul unworthy saving.

She's gone, who shared my diadem;
She sunk, with her my joys entombing;
I swept that flower from Judah's stem,
Whose leaves for me alone were blooming;
And mine 's the guilt, and mine the hell,
This bosom's desolation dooming;
And I have earn'd those tortures well,
Which unconsumed are still consuming!

ON THE DAY OF THE DESTRUCTION OF JERUSALEM BY TITUS.

From the last hill that looks on thy once holy dome
I beheld thee, oh Sion! when render'd to Rome:
'Twas thy last sun went down, and the flames of thy fall
Flash'd back on the last glance I gave to thy wall.

I look'd for thy temple, I look'd for my home,
And forgot for a moment my bondage to come;
I beheld but the death-fire that fed on thy fane,
And the fast-fetter'd hands that made vengeance in vain.

On many an eve, the high spot whence I gazed
Had reflected the last beam of day as it blazed:
While I stood on the height, and beheld the decline
Of the rays from the mountain that shone on thy shrine.

And now on that mountain I stood on that day,
But I mark'd not the twilight beam melting away;
Oh! would that the lightning had glared in its stead,
And the thunderbolt burst on the conqueror's head!

But the gods of the pagan shall never profane
The shrine where Jehovah disdain'd not to reign;
And scatter'd and scorn'd as Thy people may be,
Our worship, oh Father, is only for Thee.

BY THE RIVERS OF BABYLON WE SAT DOWN AND WEPT.

We sate down and wept by the waters
Of Babel, and thought of the day
When our foe, in the hue of his slaughters,
Made Salem's high places his prey;
And ye, oh her desolate daughters!
Were scatter'd all weeping away.

While sadly we gazed on the river
Which roll'd on in freedom below,
They demanded the song; but, oh never
That triumph the stranger shall know!
May this right hand be wither'd for ever,
Ere it string our high harp for the foe!

On the willow that harp is suspended,
Oh Salem! its sound should be free;
And the hour when thy glories were ended
But left me that token of thee:
And ne'er shall its soft tones be blended
With the voice of the spoiler by me!

THE DESTRUCTION OF SENNACHERIB.

The Assyrian came down like the wolf on the fold,
And his cohorts were gleaming in purple and gold;
And the sheen of their spears was like stars on the sea,
When the blue wave rolls nightly on deep Galilee.

Like the leaves of the forest when Summer is green,
That host with their banners at sunset were seen:
Like the leaves of the forest when Autumn hath blown,
That host on the morrow lay wither'd and strown.

For the Angel of Death spread his wings on the blast,
And breathed in the face of the foe as he pass'd;
And the eyes of the sleepers wax'd deadly and chill,
And their hearts but once heav'd, and for ever grew still!

And there lay the steed with his nostrils all wide,
But through it there roll'd not the breath of his pride:
And the foam of his gasping lay white on the turf,
And cold as the spray of the rock-beating surf.

And there lay the rider distorted and pale,
With the dew on his brow and the rust on his mail;
And the tents were all silent, the banners alone,
The lances unlifted, the trumpet unblown.

And the widows of Ashur are loud in their wail,
And the idols are broke in the temple of Baal;
And the might of the Gentile, unsmote by the sword,
Hath melted like snow in the glance of the Lord!

A SPIRIT PASSED BEFORE ME.

FROM JOB.

A spirit pass'd before me: I beheld
The face of immortality unveil'd—
Deep sleep came down on every eye save mine—
And there it stood,—all formless—but divine:
Along my bones the creeping flesh did quake;
And as my damp hair stiffen'd, thus it spake:

"Is man more just than God? Is man more pure
Than He who deems even Seraphs insecure?
Creatures of clay—vain dwellers in the dust!
The moth survives you, and are ye more just?
Things of a day! you wither ere the night,
Heedless and blind to Wisdom's wasted light!"

HOURS OF IDLENESS:

A SERIES OF POEMS, ORIGINAL AND TRANSLATED.

Virginibus puerisque canto.—HORACE, lib. iii. Ode 1.
Μήτ' ἄρ με μάλ' αἴνεε, μήτε τι νείκει.—HOMER, *Iliad*, x. 249.
He whistled as he went, for want of thought.—DRYDEN.

TO

THE RIGHT HONOURABLE FREDERICK, EARL OF CARLISLE,

KNIGHT OF THE GARTER, ETC., ETC.,

THE SECOND EDITION OF THESE POEMS IS INSCRIBED,

BY HIS OBLIGED WARD AND AFFECTIONATE KINSMAN,

THE AUTHOR.

PREFACE.

In submitting to the public eye the following collection, I have not only to combat the difficulties that writers of verse generally encounter, but may incur the charge of presumption for obtruding myself on the world, when, without doubt, I might be, at my age, more usefully employed.

These productions are the fruits of the lighter hours of a young man who has lately completed his nineteenth year. As they bear the internal evidence of a boyish mind, this is, perhaps, unnecessary information. Some few were written during the disadvantages of illness and depression of spirits: under the former influence, "Childish Recollections," in particular, were composed. This consideration, though it cannot excite the voice of praise, may at least arrest the arm of censure. A considerable portion of these poems has been privately printed, at the request and for the perusal of my friends. I am sensible that the partial and frequently injudicious admiration of a social circle is not the criterion by which poetical genius is to be estimated, yet, "to do greatly," we must "dare greatly;" and I have hazarded my reputation and feelings in publishing this volume. "I have passed the Rubicon," and must stand or fall by the "cast of the die." In the latter event, I shall submit without a murmur; for, though not without solicitude for the fate of these effusions, my expectations are by no means sanguine. It is probable that I may have dared much and done little; for, in the words of Cowper, "it is one thing to write what may please our friends, who, because they are such, are apt to be a little biased in our favour, and another to write what may please everybody; because they who have no connection, or even knowledge of the author will be sure to find fault if they can." To the truth of this, however, I do not wholly subscribe; on the contrary, I feel convinced that these trifles will not be treated with injustice. Their merit, if they possess any, will be liberally allowed; their numerous faults, on the other hand, cannot expect that favour which has been denied to others of maturer years, decided character, and far greater ability.

I have not aimed at exclusive originality, still less have I studied any particular model for imitation: some translations are given, of which many are paraphrastic. In the original pieces, there may appear a casual coincidence with authors whose works I have been accustomed to read; but I have not been guilty of intentional plagiarism. To produce anything entirely new, in an age so fertile in rhyme, would be a Herculean task, as every subject has already been treated to its utmost extent. Poetry, however, is not my primary vocation; to divert the dull moments of indisposition, or the monotony of a vacant hour, urged me "to this sin:" little can be expected from so unpromising a muse. My wreath, scanty as it must be, is all I shall derive from these productions; and I shall never attempt to replace its fading leaves, or pluck a single additional sprig from groves where I am, at best, an intruder. Though accustomed, in my younger days, to rove a a careless mountaineer on the Highlands of Scotland, I have not, of late years, had the benefit of such pure air, or so elevated a residence, as might enable me to enter the lists with genuine bards, who have enjoyed both these advantages. But they derive considerable fame, and a few not less profit, from their productions; while I shall expiate my rashness as an interloper, certainly without the latter and in all probability with a very slight share of the former. I leave to others "virum volitare per ora." I look to the few who will hear with patience "dulce est desipere in loco." To the former worthies I resign, without repining, the hope of immortality, and content myself with the not very magnificent prospect of ranking amongst "the mob of gentlemen who write;"—my readers must determine whether I dare say "with ease," or the honour of a posthumous page in "The Catalogue of Royal and Noble Authors,"—a work to which the Peerage is under infinite obligations, inasmuch as many names of considerable length, sound, and antiquity, are thereby rescued from the obscurity which unluckily overshadows several voluminous productions of their illustrious bearers.

With slight hopes, and some fears, I publish this first and last attempt. To the dictates of young ambition may be ascribed many actions more criminal and equally absurd. To a few of my own age, the contents may afford amusement: I trust they will, at least, be found harmless. It is highly improbable, from my situation and pursuits hereafter, that I should ever obtrude myself a second time on the public; nor, even in the very doubtful event of present indulgence, shall I be tempted to commit a future trespass of the same nature. The opinion of Dr. Johnson on the Poems of a noble relation of mine,[1] "That when a man of rank appeared in the character of an author, he deserved to have his merit handsomely allowed," can have little weight with verbal, and still less with periodical censors; but were it otherwise, I should be loath to avail myself of the privilege, and would rather incur the bitterest censure of anonymous criticism, than triumph in honours granted solely to a title.

HOURS OF IDLENESS.

ON THE DEATH OF A YOUNG LADY,[2]

COUSIN TO THE AUTHOR, AND VERY DEAR TO HIM.

Hush'd are the winds, and still the evening gloom,
Not e'en a zephyr wanders through the grove,
Whilst I return, to view my Margaret's tomb,
And scatter flowers on the dust I love.

Within this narrow cell reclines her clay,
That clay, where once such animation beam'd,
The King of Terrors seized her as his prey;
Not worth, nor beauty, have her life redeem'd.

Oh! could that King of Terrors pity feel,
Or Heaven reverse the dread decrees of fate!
Not here the mourner would his grief reveal,
Not here the muse her virtues would relate.

But wherefore weep? Her matchless spirit soars
Beyond where splendid shines the orb of day;
And weeping angels lead her to those bowers
Where endless pleasures virtue's deeds repay.

And shall presumptuous mortals Heaven arraign,
And, madly, godlike Providence accuse?
Ah! no, far fly from me attempts so vain;—
I'll ne'er submission to my God refuse.

Yet is remembrance of those virtues dear,
Yet fresh the memory of that beauteous face;
Still they call forth my warm affection's tear,
Still in my heart retain their wonted place.

1802.

TO E——.

Let Folly smile, to view the names
Of thee and me in friendship twined;
Yet Virtue will have greater claims
To love, than rank with vice combined.

And though unequal is thy fate,
Since title deck'd my higher birth!
Yet envy not this gaudy state;
Thine is the pride of modest worth.

Our souls at least congenial meet,
Nor can thy lot my rank disgrace;
Our intercourse is not less sweet,
Since worth of rank supplies the place.

November, 1802

TO D——.

In thee, I fondly hoped to clasp
A friend, whom death alone could sever;
Till envy, with malignant grasp,
Detach'd thee from my breast for ever.

True, she has forced thee from my breast,
Yet, in my heart thou keep'st thy seat;
There, there thine image still must rest,
Until that heart shall cease to beat.

And, when the grave restores her dead,
When life again to dust is given,
On thy dear breast I'll lay my head—
Without thee, where would be my heaven?

February, 1803.

EPITAPH ON A FRIEND.

'Αστὴρ πρὶν μὲν ἔλαμπες ἐνὶ ζωοῖσιν ἑῷος.—Laertius.

Oh, Friend! for ever loved, for ever dear!
What fruitless tears have bathed thy honour'd bier!
What sighs re-echo'd to thy parting breath,
Whilst thou wast struggling in the pangs of death!
Could tears retard the tyrant in his course;
Could sighs avert his dart's relentless force,
Could youth and virtue claim a short delay,
Or beauty charm the spectre from his prey;
Thou still hadst lived to bless my aching sight,
Thy comrade's honour and thy friend's delight.
If yet thy gentle spirit hover nigh
The spot where now thy mouldering ashes lie,
Here wilt thou read, recorded on my heart,
A grief too deep to trust the sculptor's art.
No marble marks thy couch of lowly sleep,
But living statues there are seen to weep;
Affliction's semblance bends not o'er thy tomb,
Affliction's self deplores thy youthful doom.

What though thy sire lament his failing line,
A father's sorrows cannot equal mine!
Though none, like thee, his dying hour will cheer,
Yet other offspring soothe his anguish here:
But, who with me shall hold thy former place?
Thine image, what new friendship can efface?
Ah! none!—a father's tears will cease to flow,
Time will assuage an infant brother's woe;
To all, save one, is consolation known,
While solitary friendship sighs alone.

1803.

A FRAGMENT.

When, to their airy hall, my fathers' voice
Shall call my spirit, joyful in their choice;
When, poised upon the gale, my form shall ride,
Or, dark in mist, descend the mountain's side;
Oh! may my shade behold no sculptured urns
To mark the spot where earth to earth returns!
No lengthen'd scroll, no praise encumber'd stone;
My epitaph shall be my name alone;
If *that* with honour fail to crown my clay,
Oh! may no other fame my deeds repay!
That, only *that*, shall single out the spot;
By that remember'd, or with that forgot.

1803.

ON LEAVING NEWSTEAD ABBEY.

"Why dost thou build the hall, son of the winged days? Thou lookest from thy tower to-day: yet a few years, and the blast of the desert comes, it howls in thy empty court."—Ossian.

Through thy battlements, Newstead, the hollow winds whistle;
Thou, the hall of my fathers, art gone to decay:
In thy once smiling garden, the hemlock and thistle
Have choked up the rose which late bloom'd in the way.

Of the mail-cover'd Barons, who proudly to battle
Led their vassals from Europe to Palestine's plain,
The escutcheon and shield, which with every blast rattle,
Are the only sad vestiges now that remain.

No more doth old Robert, with harp-stringing numbers,
Raise a flame in the breast for the war-laurell'd wreath;
Near Askalon's towers, John of Horistan slumbers;
Unnerved is the hand of his minstrel by death.

Paul and Hubert, too, sleep in the valley of Cressy;
For the safety of Edward and England they fell:
My fathers! the tears of your country redress ye;
How you fought, how you died, still her annals can tell.

On Marston, with Rupert, 'gainst traitors contending,[3]
Four brothers enrich'd with their blood the bleak field;
For the rights of a monarch their country defending,
Till death their attachment to royalty seal'd.

Shades of heroes, farewell! your descendant, departing
From the seat of his ancestors, bids you adieu!
Abroad, or at home, your remembrance imparting
New courage, he 'll think upon glory and you.

Though a tear dim his eye at this sad separation,
'Tis nature, not fear, that excites his regret;
Far distant he goes, with the same emulation,
The fame of his fathers he ne'er can forget.

That fame, and that memory, still will he cherish;
He vows that he ne'er will disgrace your renown:
Like you will he live, or like you will he perish:
When decay'd, may he mingle his dust with your own!

1803.

LINES

WRITTEN IN "LETTERS TO AN ITALIAN NUN AND AN ENGLISH GENTLEMAN: BY J. J. ROUSSEAU: FOUNDED ON FACTS."

"Away, away, your flattering arts
May now betray some simple hearts;
And you will smile at their believing,
And they shall weep at your deceiving."

ANSWER TO THE FOREGOING, ADDRESSED TO MISS ——.

Dear, simple girl, those flattering arts,
From which thou'dst guard frail female hearts,
Exist but in imagination,—
Mere phantoms of thine own creation;
For he who views that witching grace,
That perfect form, that lovely face,
With eyes admiring, oh! believe me,
He never wishes to deceive thee:
Once in thy polish'd mirror glance,
Thou'lt there descry that elegance
Which from our sex demands such praises,
But envy in the other raises:
Then he who tells thee of thy beauty,
Believe me, only does his duty:
Ah! fly not from the candid youth;
It is not flattery,—'t is truth.

July, 1804.

ADRIAN'S ADDRESS TO HIS SOUL WHEN DYING.

Ah! gentle, fleeting, wav'ring sprite,
Friend and associate of this clay!
To what unknown region borne,

Wilt thou now wing thy distant flight?
No more with wonted humour gay,
But pallid, cheerless, and forlorn.

TRANSLATION FROM CATULLUS.

AD LESBIAM.

EQUAL to Jove that youth must be—
Greater than Jove he seems to me—
Who, free from Jealousy's alarms,
Securely views thy matchless charms,
That cheek, which ever dimpling glows,
That mouth, from whence such music flows,
To him, alike, are always known,
Reserved for him, and him alone.
Ah! Lesbia! though 'tis death to me,
I cannot choose but look on thee;
But, at the sight, my senses fly;
I needs must gaze, but, gazing, die;
Whilst trembling with a thousand fears,
Parch'd to the throat my tongue adheres,
My pulse beats quick, my breath heaves short,
My limbs deny their slight support,
Cold dews my pallid face o'erspread,
With deadly languor droops my head,
My ears with tingling echoes ring,
And life itself is on the wing;
My eyes refuse the cheering light,
Their orbs are veil'd in starless night:
Such pangs my nature sinks beneath,
And feels a temporary death.

TRANSLATION OF THE EPITAPH ON VIRGIL AND TIBULLUS.

BY DOMITIUS MARSUS.

HE who sublime in epic numbers roll'd,
And he who struck the softer lyre of love,
By Death's unequal hand alike controll'd,[4]
Fit comrades in Elysian regions move!

IMITATION OF TIBULLUS.

"Sulpicia ad Cerinthum."—*Lib.* 4.

CRUEL Cerinthus! does the fell disease
Which racks my breast your fickle bosom please?
Alas! I wish'd but to o'ercome the pain,
That I might live for love and you again:
But now I scarcely shall bewail my fate;
By death alone I can avoid your hate.

TRANSLATION FROM CATULLUS.

YE Cupids, droop each little head,
Nor let your wings with joy be spread,
My Lesbia's favourite bird is dead,
Whom dearer than her eyes she loved:
For he was gentle, and so true,
Obedient to her call he flew,
No fear, no wild alarm he knew,
But lightly o'er her bosom moved:

And softly fluttering here and there,
He never sought to cleave the air,
But chirupp'd oft, and, free from care,
Tuned to her ear his grateful strain.
Now having pass'd the gloomy bourne
From whence he never can return,
His death and Lesbia's grief I mourn,
Who sighs, alas! but sighs in vain.

Oh! curst be thou, devouring grave!
Whose jaws eternal victims crave,
From whom no earthly power can save,
For thou hast ta'en the bird away:
From thee, my Lesbia's eyes o'erflow,
Her swollen cheeks with weeping glow;
Thou art the cause of all her woe,
Receptacle of life's decay.

IMITATED FROM CATULLUS.

TO ELLEN.

OH! might I kiss those eyes of fire,
A million scarce would quench desire:
Still would I steep my lips in bliss,
And dwell an age on every kiss:
Nor then my soul should sated be;
Still would I kiss and cling to thee:
Nought should my kiss from thine dissever;
Still would we kiss, and kiss for ever;
E'en though the numbers did exceed
The yellow harvest's countless seed.
To part would be a vain endeavour:
Could I desist?—ah! never—never!

TRANSLATION FROM HORACE.

THE man of firm and noble soul
No factious clamours can control;
No threat'ning tyrant's darkling brow
Can swerve him from his just intent:
Gales the warring waves which plough,
By Auster on the billows spent,
To curb the Adriatic main,
Would awe his fix'd determined mind in vain.

Ay, and the red right arm of Jove,
Hurtling his lightnings from above,
With all his terrors there unfurl'd,
He would, unmoved, unawed behold.
The flames of an expiring world,
Again in crashing chaos roll'd,
In vast promiscuous ruin hurl'd,
Might light his glorious funeral pile:
Still dauntless 'midst the wreck of earth he'd smile.

FROM ANACREON.

I WISH to tune my quivering lyre
To deeds of fame and notes of fire;
To echo, from its rising swell,
How heroes fought and nations fell,
When Atreus' sons advanced to war,
Or Tyrian Cadmus roved afar;
But still, to martial strains unknown,
My lyre recurs to love alone:
Fired with the hope of future fame,
I seek some nobler hero's name:
The dying chords are strung anew,
To war, to war, my harp is due:
With glowing strings, the epic strain
To Jove's great son I raise again;
Alcides and his glorious deeds,
Beneath whose arm the Hydra bleeds.
All, all in vain; my wayward lyre
Wakes silver notes of soft desire.
Adieu, ye chiefs renown'd in arms!
Adieu the clang of war's alarms!
To other deeds my soul is strung,
And sweeter notes shall now be sung;
My harp shall all its powers reveal,
To tell the tale my heart must feel:
Love, Love alone, my lyre shall claim,
In songs of bliss and sighs of flame.

FROM ANACREON.

'TWAS now the hour when Night had driven
Her car half round yon sable heaven;
Boötes, only, seem'd to roll
His arctic charge around the pole;

While mortals, lost in gentle sleep,
Forgot to smile, or ceased to weep:
At this lone hour, the Paphian boy,
Descending from the realms of joy,
Quick to my gate directs his course,
And knocks with all his little force.
My visions fled, alarm'd I rose,—
"What stranger breaks my blest repose?"
"Alas!" replies the wily child,
In faltering accents sweetly mild,
"A hapless infant here I roam,
Far from my dear maternal home.
Oh! shield me from the wintry blast!
The nightly storm is pouring fast.
No prowling robber lingers here,
A wandering baby who can fear?"
I heard his seeming artless tale,
I heard his sighs upon the gale:
My breast was never pity's foe,
But felt for all the baby's woe.
I drew the bar, and by the light,
Young Love, the infant, met my sight;
His bow across his shoulders flung,
And thence his fatal quiver hung
(Ah! little did I think the dart
Would rankle soon within my heart).
With care I tend my weary guest,
His little fingers chill my breast;
His glossy curls, his azure wing,
Which droop with nightly showers, I wring;
His shivering limbs the embers warm;
And now reviving from the storm,
Scarce had he felt his wonted glow,
Than swift he seized his slender bow:—
"I fain would know, my gentle host,"
He cried, "if this its strength has lost;
I fear, relax'd with midnight dews,
The strings their former aid refuse."
With poison tipt, his arrow flies,
Deep in my tortured heart it lies;
Then loud the joyous urchin laugh'd:—
"My bow can still impel the shaft:
'Tis firmly fix'd, thy sighs reveal it;
Say, courteous host, canst thou not feel it?"

FROM THE PROMETHEUS VINCTUS OF ÆSCHYLUS.

Great Jove, to whose almighty throne
Both gods and mortals homage pay,
Ne'er may my soul thy power disown,
Thy dread behests ne'er disobey.
Oft shall the sacred victim fall
In sea-girt Ocean's mossy hall;
My voice shall raise no impious strain,
'Gainst him who rules the sky and azure main.

How different now thy joyless fate,
Since first Hesione thy bride,
When placed aloft in godlike state,
The blushing beauty by thy side,
Thou sat'st, while reverend Ocean smiled,
And mirthful strains the hours beguiled,
The Nymphs and Tritons danced around,
Nor yet thy doom was fix'd, nor Jove relentless frown'd.

Harrow, Dec. 1, 1804.

TO EMMA.

Since now the hour is come at last,
When you must quit your anxious lover;
Since now our dream of bliss is past,
One pang, my girl, and all is over.

Alas! that pang will be severe,
Which bids us part to meet no more;
Which tears me far from one so dear,
Departing for a distant shore.

Well! we have pass'd some happy hours,
And joy will mingle with our tears;
When thinking on these ancient towers,
The shelter of our infant years;

Where from this Gothic casement's height,
We view'd the lake, the park, the dell;
And still, though tears obstruct our sight,
We lingering look a last farewell,

O'er fields through which we used run,
And spend the hours in childish play;
O'er shades where, when our race was done,
Reposing on my breast you lay;

Whilst I, admiring, too remiss,
Forgot to scare the hovering flies,
Yet envied every fly the kiss
It dared to give your slumbering eyes:

See still the little painted bark,
In which I row'd you o'er the lake;
See there, high waving o'er the park,
The elm I clamber'd for your sake.

These times are past—our joys are gone,
You leave me, leave this happy vale;
These scenes I must retrace alone:
Without thee, what will they avail?

Who can conceive, who has not proved,
The anguish of a last embrace?
When, torn from all you fondly loved,
You bid a long adieu to peace.

This is the deepest of our woes,
 For this these tears our cheeks bedew;
This is of love the final close,
 Oh, God! the fondest, last adieu!

TO M. S. G.

WHENE'ER I view those lips of thine,
 Their hue invites my fervent kiss;
Yet I forego that bliss divine,
 Alas! it were unhallow'd bliss.

Whene'er I dream of that pure breast,
 How could I dwell upon its snows!
Yet is the daring wish represt;
 For that,—would banish its repose.

A glance from thy soul-searching eye
 Can raise with hope, depress with fear;
Yet I conceal my love,—and why?
 I would not force a painful tear.

I ne'er have told my love, yet thou
 Hast seen my ardent flame too well;
And shall I plead my passion now,
 To make thy bosom's heaven a hell?

No! for thou never canst be mine,
 United by the priest's decree:
By any ties but those divine,
 Mine, my beloved, thou ne'er shalt be.

Then let the secret fire consume,
 Let it consume, thou shalt not know:
With joy I court a certain doom,
 Rather than spread its guilty glow.

I will not ease my tortured heart,
 By driving dove-eyed peace from thine;
Rather than such a sting impart,
 Each thought presumptuous I resign.

Yes! yield those lips, for which I'd brave
 More than I here shall dare to tell;
Thy innocence and mine to save,—
 I bid thee now a last farewell.

Yes! yield that breast, to seek despair,
 And hope no more thy soft embrace;
Which to obtain my soul would dare,
 All, all reproach—but thy disgrace.

At least from guilt shalt thou be free,
 No matron shall thy shame reprove;
Though cureless pangs may prey on me,
 No martyr shalt thou be to love.

TO CAROLINE.

THINK'ST thou I saw thy beauteous eyes,
 Suffused in tears, implore to stay;
And heard unmoved thy plenteous sighs,
 Which said far more than words can say?

Though keen the grief thy tears exprest,
 When love and hope lay both o'erthrown;
Yet still, my girl, this bleeding breast
 Throbb'd with deep sorrow as thine own.

But when our cheeks with anguish glow'd,
 When thy sweet lips were join'd to mine,
The tears that from my eyelids flow'd
 Were lost in those which fell from thine.

Thou could'st not feel my burning cheek,
 Thy gushing tears had quench'd its flame;
And as thy tongue essay'd to speak,
 In sighs alone it breathed my name.

And yet, my girl, we weep in vain,
 In vain our fate in sighs deplore;
Remembrance only can remain,—
 But that will make us weep the more.

Again, thou best beloved, adieu!
 Ah! if thou canst, o'ercome regret;
Nor let thy mind past joys review,—
 Our only hope is to forget!

TO CAROLINE.

WHEN I hear you express an affection so warm,
 Ne'er think, my beloved, that I do not believe;
For your lip would the soul of suspicion disarm,
 And your eye beams a ray which can never deceive.

Yet, still, this fond bosom regrets, while adoring,
 That love, like the leaf, must fall into the sear;
That age will come on, when remembrance, deploring,
 Contemplates the scenes of her youth with a tear;

That the time must arrive, when, no longer retaining
 Their auburn, those locks must wave thin to the breeze,
When a few silver hairs of those tresses remaining,
 Prove nature a prey to decay and disease.

'Tis this, my beloved, which spreads gloom o'er my features,
 Though I ne'er shall presume to arraign the decree,
Which God has proclaim'd as the fate of His creatures,
 In the death which one day will deprive you of me.

Mistake not, sweet sceptic, the cause of emotion,
No doubt can the mind of your lover invade;
He worships each look with such faithful devotion,
A smile can enchant, or a tear can dissuade.

But as death, my beloved, soon or late shall o'ertake us,
And our breasts, which alive with such sympathy glow,
Will sleep in the grave till the blast shall awake us,
When calling the dead, in earth's bosom laid low.

Oh! then let us drain, while we may, draughts of pleasure,
Which from passion like ours may unceasingly flow:
Let us pass round the cup of love's bliss in full measure,
And quaff the contents as our nectar below.

1805.

TO CAROLINE.

Oh! when shall the grave hide for ever my sorrows?
Oh! when shall my soul wing her flight from this clay?
The present is hell, and the coming to-morrow
But brings, with new torture, the curse of to-day.

From my eye flows no tear, from my lips flow no curses,
I blast not the fiends who have hurl'd me from bliss:
For poor is the soul which bewailing rehearses
Its querulous grief, when in anguish like this.

Was my eye, 'stead of tears, with red fury flakes bright'ning,
Would my lips breathe a flame which no stream could assuage,
On our foes should my glance launch in vengeance its lightning,
With transport my tongue give a loose to its rage.

But now tears and curses, alike unavailing,
Would add to the souls of our tyrants delight;
Could they view us our sad separation bewailing,
Their merciless hearts would rejoice at the sight.

Yet still, though we bend with a feign'd resignation,
Life beams not for us with one ray that can cheer,
Love and hope upon earth bring no more consolation!
In the grave is our hope, for in life is our fear.

Oh! when, my adored, in the tomb will they place me,
Since, in life, love and friendship for ever are fled?
If again in the mansion of death I embrace thee,
Perhaps they will leave unmolested the dead.

1805.

STANZAS TO A LADY.

WITH THE POEMS OF CAMOENS.

This votive pledge of fond esteem,
Perhaps, dear girl! for me thou'lt prize;
It sings of Love's enchanting dream,
A theme we never can despise.

Who blames it but the envious fool,
The old and disappointed maid;
Or pupil of the prudish school,
In single sorrow doom'd to fade?

Then read, dear girl! with feeling read,
For thou wilt ne'er be one of those;
To thee in vain I shall not plead
In pity for the poet's woes.

He was in sooth a genuine bard:
His was no faint, fictitious flame:
Like his, may love be thy reward,
But not thy hapless fate the same.

THE FIRST KISS OF LOVE.

'Α Βαρβιτος δε χορδαῖς
'Ερωτα μουνον ἠχεῖ.—Anacreon.

Away with your fictions of flimsy romance;
Those tissues of falsehood which folly has wove!
Give me the mild beam of the soul-breathing glance
Or the rapture which dwells on the first kiss of love.

Ye rhymers, whose bosoms with phantasy glow,
Whose pastoral passions are made for the grove;
From what blest inspiration your sonnets would flow,
Could you ever have tasted the first kiss of love!

If Apollo should e'er his assistance refuse,
Or the Nine be disposed from your service to rove,
Invoke them no more, bid adieu to the muse,
And try the effect of the first kiss of love!

I hate you, ye cold compositions of art!
Tho' prudes may condemn me, and bigots reprove,
I court the effusions that spring from the heart
Which throbs with delight to the first kiss of love.

Your shepherds, your flocks, those fantastical themes,
Perhaps may amuse, yet they never can move.
Arcadia displays but a region of dreams:
What are visions like these to the first kiss of love?

Oh! cease to affirm that man, since his birth,
From Adam till now, has with wretchedness strove,
Some portion of paradise still is on earth,
And Eden revives in the first kiss of love.

When age chills the blood, when our pleasures are past,
For years fleet away with the wings of the dove,
The dearest remembrance will still be the last,
Our sweetest memorial the first kiss of love.

ON A CHANGE OF MASTERS AT A GREAT PUBLIC SCHOOL.

WHERE are those honours, Ida! once your own,
When Probus filled your magisterial throne?
As ancient Rome, fast falling to disgrace,
Hail'd a barbarian in her Cæsar's place,
So you, degenerate, share as hard a fate,
And seat Pomposus where your Probus sate.

Of narrow brain, yet of a narrower soul,
Pomposus holds you in his harsh control;
Pomposus, by no social virtue sway'd,
With florid jargon, and with vain parade;
With noisy nonsense, and new-fangled rules,
Such as were ne'er before enforced in schools.

Mistaking pedantry for learning's laws,
He governs, sanction'd but by self-applause;
With him the same dire fate attending Rome,
Ill-fated Ida! soon must stamp your doom:
Like her o'erthrown, for ever lost to fame,
No trace of science left you, but the name.

July, 1805.

TO THE DUKE OF DORSET.[6]

Dorset! whose early steps with mine have stray'd,
Exploring every path of Ida's glade;
Whom still affection taught me to defend,
And made me less a tyrant than a friend,
Though the harsh custom of our youthful ban
Bade *thee* obey, and gave *me* to command;[7]
Thee, on whose head a few short years will shower
The gift of riches, and the pride of power;
E'en now a name illustrious is thine own,
Renown'd in rank, not far beneath the throne.
Yet, Dorset, let not this seduce thy soul
To shun fair science, or evade control,
Though passive tutors, fearful to dispraise[8]
The titled child, whose future breath may raise,
View ducal errors with indulgent eyes,
And wink at faults they tremble to chastise.

When youthful parasites, who bend the knee
To wealth, their golden idol, not to thee,—
And even in simple boyhood's opening dawn
Some slaves are found to flatter and to fawn,—
When these declare, "that pomp alone should wait
On one by birth predestined to be great;
That books were only meant for drudging fools,
That gallant spirits scorn the common rules;"
Believe them not;—they point the path to shame,
And seek to blast the honours of thy name.
Turn to the few in Ida's early throng,
Whose souls disdain not to condemn the wrong;
Or if, amidst the comrades of thy youth,
None dare to raise the sterner voice of truth,
Ask thine own heart; 't will bid thee, boy, forbear;
For *well* I know that virtue lingers there.

Yes! I have mark'd thee many a passing day,
But now new scenes invite me far away;
Yes! I have mark'd within that generous mind
A soul, if well matured, to bless mankind.
Ah! though myself, by nature haughty, wild,
Whom Indiscretion hail'd her favourite child;
Though every error stamps me for her own,
And dooms my fall, I fain would fall alone;
Though my proud heart no precept now can tame,
I love the virtues which I cannot claim.

'T is not enough, with other sons of power,
To gleam the lambent meteor of an hour;
To swell some peerage page in feeble pride,
With long-drawn names that grace no page beside;
Then share with titled crowds the common lot—
In life just gazed at, in the grave forgot;
While nought divides thee from the vulgar dead,
Except the dull cold stone that hides thy head,
The mouldering 'scutcheon, or the herald's roll,
That well-emblazon'd but neglected scroll,
Where lords, unhonour'd, in the tomb may find
One spot, to leave a worthless name behind.
There sleep, unnoticed as the gloomy vaults
That veil their dust, their follies, and their faults,
A race, with old armorial lists o'erspread,
In records destined never to be read.
Fain would I view thee, with prophetic eyes,
Exalted more among the good and wise,
A glorious and a long career pursue,
As first in rank, the first in talent too:
Spurn every vice, each little meanness shun;
Not Fortune's minion, but her noblest son.

Turn to the annals of a former day;
Bright are the deeds thine earlier sires display.
One, though a courtier, lived a man of worth,
And call'd, proud boast! the British drama forth.
Another view, not less renown'd for wit;
Alike for courts, and camps, or senates fit;
Bold in the field, and favour'd by the Nine;
In every splendid part ordain'd to shine;
Far, far distinguish'd from the glittering throng,
The pride of princes, and the boast of song.
Such were thy fathers; thus preserve their name;
Not heir to titles only, but to fame.
The hour draws nigh, a few brief days will close
To me, this little scene of joys and woes;
Each knell of Time now warns me to resign
Shades where Hope, Peace, and Friendship all were mine:
Hope, that could vary like the rainbow's hue,
And gild their pinions as the moments flew;
Peace, that reflection never frown'd away,
By dreams of ill to cloud some future day;
Friendship, whose truth let childhood only tell;
Alas! they love not long, who love so well.
To these adieu! nor let me linger o'er
Scenes hail'd, as exiles hail their native shore,
Receding slowly through the dark-blue deep,
Beheld by eyes that mourn, yet cannot weep.

Dorset, farewell! I will not ask one part
Of sad remembrance in so young a heart;
The coming morrow from thy youthful mind
Will sweep my name, nor leave a trace behind.
And yet, perhaps, in some maturer year,
Since chance has thrown us in the self-same sphere,
Since the same senate, nay, the same debate,
May one day claim our suffrage for the state,
We hence may meet, and pass each other by,
With faint regard, or cold and distant eye.

For me, in future, neither friend nor foe,
A stranger to thyself, thy weal or woe,
With thee no more again I hope to trace
The recollection of our early race;

No more, as once, in social hours rejoice,
Or hear, unless in crowds, thy well-known voice:
Still, if the wishes of a heart untaught
To veil those feelings which perchance it ought—
If these,—but let me cease the lengthen'd strain,—
Oh! if these wishes are not breathed in vain,
The guardian seraph who directs thy fate
Will leave thee glorious, as he found thee great.

1805.

FRAGMENT,

WRITTEN SHORTLY AFTER THE MARRIAGE OF MISS CHAWORTH.

Hills of Annesley! bleak and barren,
 Where my thoughtless childhood stray'd,
How the northern tempests, warring,
 Howl above thy tufted shade!

Now no more, the hours beguiling,
 Former favourite haunts I see;
Now no more my Mary smiling
 Makes ye seem a heaven to me.

1805.

GRANTA. A Medley.

'Αργυρέαις λόγχαισι μάχου καὶ πάντα Κρατήσαις.

Oh! could Le Sage's demon's gift[9]
 Be realised at my desire,
This night my trembling form he'd lift
 To place it on St. Mary's spire.

Then would, unroof'd, old Granta's halls
 Pedantic inmates full display;
Fellows who dream on lawn or stalls,
 The price of venal votes to pay.

Then would I view each rival wight,
 Petty and Palmerston survey;
Who canvass there with all their might,
 Against the next elective day.

Lo! candidates and voters lie
 All lull'd in sleep, a goodly number:
A race renown'd for piety,
 Whose conscience won't disturb their slumber.

Lord H——, indeed, may not demur;
 Fellows are sage reflecting men:
They know preferment can occur
 But very seldom,—now and then.

They know the Chancellor has got
 Some pretty livings in disposal:
Each hopes that one may be his lot,
 And therefore smiles on his proposal.

Now from the soporific scene
 I'll turn mine eye, as night grows later,
To view, unheeded and unseen,
 The studious sons of Alma Mater.

There, in apartments small and damp,
 The candidate for college prizes
Sits poring by the midnight lamp;
 Goes late to bed, yet early rises.

He surely well deserves to gain them,
 With all the honours of his college,
Who, striving hardly to obtain them,
 Thus seeks unprofitable knowledge:

Who sacrifices hours of rest
 To scan precisely metres Attic;
Or agitates his anxious breast
 In solving problems mathematic:

Who reads false quantities in Seale,[10]
 Or puzzles o'er the deep triangle;
Deprived of many a wholesome meal;
 In barbarous Latin doom'd to wrangle:[11]

Renouncing every pleasing page
 From authors of historic use;
Preferring to the letter'd sage,
 The square of the hypothenuse.[12]

Still, harmless are these occupations,
 That hurt none but the hapless student,
Compared with other recreations,
 Which bring together the imprudent;

Whose daring revels shock the sight,
 When vice and infamy combine,
When drunkenness and dice invite,
 As every sense is steep'd in wine.

Not so the methodistic crew,
 Who plans of reformation lay:
In humble attitude they sue,
 And for the sins of others pray:

Forgetting that their pride of spirit,
 Their exultation in their trial,
Detracts most largely from the merit
 Of all their boasted self-denial.

'Tis morn:—from these I turn my sight.
 What scene is this which meets the eye?
A numerous crowd, array'd in white,
 Across the green in numbers fly.

Loud rings in air the chapel bell;
 'Tis hush'd—what sounds are these I hear?
The organ's soft celestial swell
 Rolls deeply on the list'ning ear.

To this is join'd the sacred song,
 The royal minstrel's hallow'd strain;
Though he who hears the music long
 Will never wish to hear again.

Our choir would scarcely be excused,
 Even as a band of raw beginners;
All mercy now must be refused
 To such a set of croaking sinners.

If David, when his toils were ended,
 Had heard these blockheads sing before him,
To us his psalms had ne'er descended,—
 In furious mood he would have tore 'em

The luckless Israelites, when taken
 By some inhuman tyrant's order,
Were asked to sing, by joy forsaken,
 On Babylonian river's border.

Oh! had they sung in notes like these,
 Inspired by stratagem or fear,
They might have set their hearts at ease,
 The devil a soul had stay'd to hear.

But if I scribble longer now,
 The deuce a soul will stay to read:
My pen is blunt, my ink is low;
 'T is almost time to stop, indeed.

Therefore, farewell, old Granta's spires:
 No more, like Cleofas, I fly;
No more thy theme my muse inspires:
 The reader 's tired, and so am I.

1806.

ON A DISTANT VIEW OF THE VILLAGE AND SCHOOL OF HARROW-ON-THE-HILL.

"Oh! mihi præteritos referat si Jupiter annos."—Virgil.

Ye scenes of my childhood, whose loved recollection
 Embitters the present, compared with the past;
Where science first dawn'd on the powers of reflection,
 And friendships were form'd, too romantic to last

Where fancy yet joys to trace the resemblance
Of comrades, in friendship and mischief allied,
How welcome to me your ne'er fading remembrance,
Which rests in the bosom, though hope is denied!

Again I revisit the hills where we sported,
The streams where we swam, and the fields where we fought;
The school, where, loud warn'd by the bell, we resorted,
To pore o'er the precepts by pedagogues taught.

Again I behold where for hours I have ponder'd,
As reclining, at eve, on yon tombstone I lay;
Or round the steep brow of the churchyard I wander'd,
To catch the last gleam of the sun's setting ray.

I once more view the room, with spectators surrounded,
Where, as Zanga, I trod on Alonzo o'erthrown;
While, to swell my young pride, such applauses resounded,
I fancied that Mossop himself was outshone.[13]

Or, as Lear, I pour'd forth the deep imprecation,
By my daughters, of kingdom and reason deprived;
Till, fired by loud plaudits and self-adulation,
I regarded myself as a Garrick revived.

Ye dreams of my boyhood, how much I regret you!
Unfaded your memory dwells in my breast;
Though sad and deserted, I ne'er can forget you:
Your pleasures may still be in fancy possest.

To Ida full oft may remembrance restore me,
While fate shall the shades of the future unroll!
Since darkness o'ershadows the prospect before me,
More dear is the beam of the past to my soul.

But if, through the course of the years which await me,
Some new scene of pleasure should open to view,
I will say, while with rapture the thought shall elate me,
"Oh! such were the days which my infancy knew!"

1806.

TO M——.

Oh! did those eyes, instead of fire,
With bright but mild affection shine,
Though they might kindle less desire,
Love, more than mortal, would be thine.

For thou art form'd so heavenly fair,
Howe'er those orbs may wildly beam,
We must admire, but still despair;
That fatal glance forbids esteem.

When Nature stamp'd thy beauteous birth,
So much perfection in thee shone,
She fear'd that, too divine for earth,
The skies might claim thee for their own:

Therefore, to guard her dearest work,
Lest angels might dispute the prize,
She bade a secret lightning lurk
Within those once celestial eyes.

These might the boldest sylph appal,
When gleaming with meridian blaze;
Thy beauty must enrapture all;
But who can dare thine ardent gaze?

'T is said that Berenice's hair
In stars adorns the vault of heaven;
But they would ne'er permit thee there,
Thou wouldst so far outshine the seven.

For did those eyes as planets roll,
Thy sister-lights would scarce appear:
E'en suns, which systems now control,
Would twinkle dimly through their sphere.[1]

1806.

TO WOMAN.

Woman! experience might have told me,
That all must love thee who behold thee:
Surely experience might have taught
Thy firmest promises are nought:
But, placed in all thy charms before me,
All I forget, but to adore thee.
Oh memory! thou choicest blessing
When join'd with hope, when still possessing;
But how much cursed by every lover
When hope is fled, and passion 's over.
Woman, that fair and fond deceiver,
How prompt are striplings to believe her!
How throbs the pulse when first we view
The eye that rolls in glossy blue,
Or sparkles black, or mildly throws
A beam from under hazel brows!
How quick we credit every oath,
And hear her plight the willing troth
Fondly we hope 't will last for aye,
When lo! she changes in a day.
This record will for ever stand,
"Woman! thy vows are traced in sand."[15]

TO M. S. G.

When I dream that you love me, you 'll surely forgive;
Extend not your anger to sleep;
For in visions alone your affection can live,—
I rise, and it leaves me to weep.

Then, Morpheus! envelope my faculties fast,
Shed o'er me your languor benign;
Should the dream of to-night but resemble the last,
What rapture celestial is mine!

They tell us that slumber, the sister of death,
Mortality's emblem is given:
To fate how I long to resign my frail breath,
If this be a foretaste of heaven!

Ah! frown not, sweet lady, unbend your soft brow,
Nor deem me too happy in this;
If I sin in my dream, I atone for it now,
Thus doom'd but to gaze upon bliss.

Though in visions, sweet lady, perhaps you may smile,
Oh! think not my penance deficient!
When dreams of your presence my slumbers beguile,
To awake will be torture sufficient.

TO MARY.

ON RECEIVING HER PICTURE.

THIS faint resemblance of thy charms,
Though strong as mortal art could give,
My constant heart of fear disarms,
Revives my hopes, and bids me live.

Here I can trace the locks of gold
Which round thy snowy forehead wave,
The cheeks which sprung from beauty's mould,
The lips which made me beauty's slave.

Here I can trace—ah, no! that eye,
Whose azure floats in liquid fire,
Must all the painter's art defy,
And bid him from the task retire.

Here I behold its beauteous hue;
But where 's the beam so sweetly straying,
Which gave a lustre to its blue,
Like Luna o'er the ocean playing?

Sweet copy! far more dear to me,
Lifeless, unfeeling as thou art,
Than all the living forms could be,
Save her who placed thee next my heart.

She placed it, sad, with needless fear,
Lest time might shake my wavering soul,
Unconscious that her image there
Held every sense in fast control.

Through hours, through years, through time, 't will cheer;
My hope, in gloomy moments raise;
In life's last conflict 't will appear,
And meet my fond expiring gaze.

TO LESBIA.

LESBIA! since far from you I've ranged,
Our souls with fond affection glow not;
You say 't is I, not you, have changed,
I'd tell you why,—but yet I know not.

Your polished brow no cares have crost;
And, Lesbia! we are not much older
Since, trembling, first my heart I lost,
Or told my love, with hope grown bolder.

Sixteen was then our utmost age,
Two years have lingering past away, love!
And now new thoughts our minds engage,
At least I feel disposed to stray, love!

'T is I that am alone to blame,
I, that am guilty of love's treason;
Since your sweet breast is still the same,
Caprice must be my only reason.

I do not, love! suspect your truth,
With jealous doubt my bosom heaves not;
Warm was the passion of my youth,
One trace of dark deceit it leaves not.

No, no, my flame was not pretended;
For, oh! I loved you most sincerely;
And—though our dream at last is ended—
My bosom still esteems you dearly.

No more we meet in yonder bowers;
Absence has made me prone to roving;
But older, firmer hearts than ours,
Have found monotony in loving.

Your cheek's soft bloom is unimpair'd,
New beauties still are daily bright'ning,
Your eye for conquest beams prepared,
The forge of love's resistless lightning.

Arm'd thus, to make their bosoms bleed,
Many will throng to sigh like me, love!
More constant they may prove, indeed;
Fonder, alas! they ne'er can be, love!

LINES ADDRESSED TO A YOUNG LADY,

WHO HAD BEEN ALARMED BY A BULLET FIRED BY THE AUTHOR WHILE DISCHARGING HIS PISTOLS IN A GARDEN.

DOUBTLESS, sweet girl! the hissing lead,
Wafting destruction o'er thy charms,
And hurtling o'er thy lovely head,[16]
Has fill'd that breast with fond alarms.

Surely some envious demon's force,
Vex'd to behold such beauty here,
Impell'd the bullet's viewless course,
Diverted from its first career.

Yes! in that nearly fatal hour
The ball obeyed some hell-born guide;
But Heaven, with interposing power,
In pity turn'd the death aside.

Yet, as perchance one trembling tear
Upon that thrilling bosom fell;
Which I, th' unconscious cause of fear,
Extracted from its glistening cell:

Say, what dire penance can atone
For such an outrage done to thee?
Arraign'd before thy beauty's throne,
What punishment wilt thou decree?

Might I perform the judge's part,
The sentence I should scarce deplore;
It only would restore a heart
Which but belong'd to thee before.

The least atonement I can make
Is to become no longer free;
Henceforth I breathe but for thy sake,
Thou shalt be all in all to me.

But thou, perhaps, may'st now reject
Such expiation of my guilt:
Come, then, some other mode elect;
Let it be death, or what thou wilt.

Choose then, relentless! and I swear
Nought shall thy dread decree prevent;
Yet hold—one little word forbear!
Let it be aught but banishment.

LOVE'S LAST ADIEU.

Αει, δ' αει με φευγει.—Anacreon.

The roses of love glad the garden of life,
Though nurtur'd 'mid weeds dropping pestilent dew,
Till time crops the leaves with unmerciful knife,
Or prunes them for ever, in love's last adieu.

In vain with endearments we soothe the sad heart,
In vain do we vow for an age to be true;
The chance of an hour may command us to part,
Or death disunite us in love's last adieu!

Still Hope, breathing peace through the grief-swollen breast,
Will whisper, "Our meeting we yet may renew:"
With this dream of deceit half our sorrow's represt,
Nor taste we the poison of love's last adieu!

Oh! mark you yon pair: in the sunshine of youth
Love twined round their childhood his flow'rs as they grew;
They flourish awhile in the season of truth,
Till chill'd by the winter of love's last adieu!

Sweet lady! why thus doth a tear steal its way
Down a cheek which outrivals thy bosom in hue?
Yet why do I ask?—to distraction a prey,
Thy reason has perish'd with love's last adieu!

Oh! who is yon misanthrope, shunning mankind?
From cities to caves of the forest he flew:
There, raving, he howls his complaint to the wind;
The mountains reverberate love's last adieu!

Now hate rules a heart which in love's easy chains
Once passion's tumultuous blandishments knew,
Despair now inflames the dark tide of his veins;
He ponders in frenzy on love's last adieu!

How he envies the wretch with a soul wrapt in steel!
His pleasures are scarce, yet his troubles are few,
Who laughs at the pang that he never can feel,
And dreads not the anguish of love's last adieu!

Youth flies, life decays, even hope is o'ercast;
No more with love's former devotion we sue:
He spreads his young wing, he retires with the blast;
The shroud of affection is love's last adieu!

In this life of probation for rapture divine,
Astrea declares that some penance is due;
From him who has worshipp'd at love's gentle shrine,
The atonement is ample in love's last adieu!

Who kneels to the god, on his altar of light
Must myrtle and cypress alternately strew:
His myrtle, an emblem of purest delight;
His cypress the garland of love's last adieu!

DAMÆTAS.

In law an infant, and in years a boy,[17]
In mind a slave to every vicious joy;
From every sense of shame and virtue wean'd;
In lies an adept, in deceit a fiend;
Versed in hypocrisy, while yet a child;
Fickle as wind, of inclinations wild;
Woman his dupe, his heedless friend a tool;
Old in the world, though scarcely broke from school;
Damætas ran through all the maze of sin,
And found the goal when others just begin:
Even still conflicting passions shake his soul,
And bid him drain the dregs of pleasure's bowl;
But, pall'd with vice, he breaks his former chain,
And what was once his bliss appears his bane.

TO MARION.

Marion! why that pensive brow?
What disgust to life hast thou?
Change that discontented air;
Frowns become not one so fair.
'Tis not love disturbs thy rest,
Love's a stranger to thy breast;
He in dimpling smiles appears,
Or mourns in sweetly timid tears,
Or bends the languid eyelid down,
But shuns the cold forbidding frown.
Then resume thy former fire,
Some will love, and all admire;
While that icy aspect chills us,
Nought but cool indifference thrills us.
Wouldst thou wandering hearts beguile,
Smile at least, or seem to smile.
Eyes like thine were never meant
To hide their orbs in dark restraint;
Spite of all thou fain wouldst say,
Still in truant beams they play.
Thy lips—but here my modest Muse
Her impulse chaste must needs refuse:
She blushes, curt'sies, frowns—in short she
Dreads lest the subject should transport me;
And flying off in search of reason,
Brings prudence back in proper season,
All I shall therefore say (whate'er
I think, is neither here nor there)
Is, that such lips, of looks endearing,
Were form'd for better things than sneering:
Of smoothing compliments divested,
Advice at least's disinterested;
Such is my artless song to thee,
From all the flow of flattery free;
Counsel like mine is like a brother's.
My heart is given to some others;
That is to say, unskill'd to cozen,
It shares itself among a dozen.
Marion, adieu! oh, prythee slight not
This warning, though it may delight not;
And, lest my precepts be displeasing
To those who think remonstrance teasing
At once I'll tell thee our opinion
Concerning woman's soft dominion:
Howe'er we gaze with admiration
On eyes of blue or lips carnation,
Howe'er the flowing locks attract us,
Howe'er those beauties may distract us
Still fickle, we are prone to rove,
These cannot fix our souls to love:
It is not too severe a stricture
To say they form a pretty picture;
But wouldst thou see the secret chain
Which binds us in your humble train,
To hail you queens of all creation,
Know, in a word, 'tis Animation.

TO A LADY,

WHO PRESENTED TO THE AUTHOR A LOCK OF HAIR BRAIDED WITH HIS OWN, AND APPOINTED A NIGHT IN DECEMBER TO MEET HIM IN THE GARDEN.

These locks, which fondly thus entwine,
In firmer chains our hearts confine,
Than all th' unmeaning protestations
Which swell with nonsense love orations.
Our love is fix'd, I think we've proved it,
Nor time, nor place, nor art have moved it;
Then wherefore should we sigh and whine,
With groundless jealousy repine,
With silly whims, and fancies frantic,
Merely to make our love romantic?
Why should you weep like Lydia Languish,
And fret with self-created anguish?
Or doom the lover you have chosen,
On winter nights to sigh half frozen;
In leafless shades to sue for pardon,
Only because the scene's a garden?
For gardens seem, by one consent,
Since Shakspeare set the precedent,
Since Juliet first declared her passion,
To form the place of assignation.[18]
Oh! would some modern muse inspire,
And seat her by a sea-coal fire;
Or had the bard at Christmas written
And laid the scene of love in Britain,
He surely, in commiseration,
Had changed the place of declaration.
In Italy I've no objection:
Warm nights are proper for reflection
But here our climate is so rigid,
That love itself is rather frigid:
Think on our chilly situation,
And curb this rage for imitation;
Then let us meet, as oft we've done,
Beneath the influence of the sun;
Or, if at midnight I must meet you,
Within your mansion let me greet you:
There we can love for hours together,
Much better, in such snowy weather,
Than placed in all th' Arcadian groves
That ever witness'd rural loves;
Then, if my passion fail to please,
Next night I'll be content to freeze;
No more I'll give a loose to laughter,
But curse my fate for ever after.[19]

OSCAR OF ALVA.[20]

A TALE.

How sweetly shines through azure skies,
The lamp of heaven on Lora's shore;
Where Alva's hoary turrets rise,
And hear the din of arms no more.

But often has yon rolling moon
On Alva's casques of silver play'd;
And view'd, at midnight's silent noon,
Her chiefs in gleaming mail array'd:

And on the crimson'd rocks beneath,
Which scowl o'er ocean's sullen flow,
Pale in the scatter'd ranks of death,
She saw the gasping warrior low;

While many an eye which ne'er again
Could mark the rising orb of day,
Turn'd feebly from the gory plain,
Beheld in death her fading ray.

Once to those eyes the lamp of Love,
They blest her dear propitious light;
But now she glimmer'd from above,
A sad, funereal torch of night.

Faded is Alva's noble race,
And gray her towers are seen afar;
No more her heroes urge the chase,
Or roll the crimson tide of war.

But who was last of Alva's clan?
Why grows the moss on Alva's stone?
Her towers resound no steps of man,
They echo to the gale alone.

And when that gale is fierce and high,
A sound is heard in yonder hall;
It rises hoarsely through the sky,
And vibrates o'er the mouldering wall.

Yes, when the eddying tempest sighs,
It shakes the shield of Oscar brave;
But there no more his banners rise,
No more his plumes of sable wave.

Fair shone the sun on Oscar's birth,
When Angus hail'd his eldest born;
The vassals round their chieftain's hearth
Crowd to applaud the happy morn.

They feast upon the mountain deer,
The pibroch raised its piercing note:
To gladden more their highland cheer,
The strains in martial numbers float:

And they who heard the war-notes wild,
Hoped that one day the pibroch's strain,
Should play before the hero's child
While he should lead the tartan train.

Another year is quickly past,
And Angus hails another son;
His natal day is like the last,
Nor soon the jocund feast was done.

Taught by their sire to bend the bow,
On Alva's dusky hills of wind,
The boys in childhood chased the roe,
And left their hounds in speed behind.

But ere their years of youth are o'er,
They mingle in the ranks of war;
They lightly wheel the bright claymore,
And send the whistling arrow far.

Dark was the flow of Oscar's hair,
Wildly it stream'd along the gale;
But Allan's locks were bright and fair,
And pensive seem'd his cheek, and pale.

But Oscar own'd a hero's soul,
His dark eye shone through beams of truth;
Allan had early learn'd control,
And smooth his words had been from youth.

Both, both were brave: the Saxon spear
Was shivered oft beneath their steel;
And Oscar's bosom scorn'd to fear,
But Oscar's bosom knew to feel;

While Allan's soul belied his form,
Unworthy with such charms to dwell:
Keen as the lightning of the storm,
On foes his deadly vengeance fell.

From high Southannon's distant tower
Arrived a young and noble dame;
With Kenneth's lands to form her dower,
Glenalvon's blue-eyed daughter came;

And Oscar claim'd the beauteous bride,
And Angus on his Oscar smiled;
It soothed the father's feudal pride
Thus to obtain Glenalvon's child.

Hark to the pibroch's pleasing note!
Hark to the swelling nuptial song!
In joyous strains the voices float,
And still the choral peal prolong.

See how the heroes' blood-red plumes
Assembled wave in Alva's hall;
Each youth his varied plaid assumes,
Attending on their chieftain's call.

It is not war their aid demands,
The pibroch plays the song of peace;
To Oscar's nuptials throng the bands,
Nor yet the sounds of pleasure cease.

But where is Oscar? sure 'tis late:
Is this a bridegroom's ardent flame?
While thronging guests and ladies wait,
Nor Oscar nor his brother came.

At length young Allan join'd the bride:
"Why comes not Oscar?" Angus said;
"Is he not here?" the youth replied;
"With me he roved not o'er the glade.

"Perchance, forgetful of the day,
'T is his to chase the bounding roe;
Or ocean's waves prolong his stay;
Yet Oscar's bark is seldom slow."

"Oh, no!" the anguish'd sire rejoined,
"Nor chase nor wave my boy delay;
Would he to Mora seem unkind?
Would aught to her impede his way?

"Oh, search, ye chiefs! oh, search around!
Allan, with these through Alva fly;
Till Oscar, till my son is found,
Haste, haste, nor dare attempt reply."

All is confusion—through tne vale
The name of Oscar hoarsely rings,
It rises on the murmuring gale,
Till night expands her dusky wings;

It breaks the stillness of the night,
But echoes through her shades in vain,
It sounds through morning's misty light,
But Oscar comes not o'er the plain.

Three days, three sleepless nights, the Chief
For Oscar search'd each mountain cave!
Then hope is lost; in boundless grief,
His locks in gray-torn ringlets wave.

"Oscar! my son!—thou God of heav'n
Restore the prop of sinking age!
Or if that hope no more is given,
Yield his assassin to my rage.

"Yes, on some desert rocky shore
My Oscar's whitened bones must lie;
Then grant, thou God! I ask no more,
With him his frantic sire may die!

"Yet he may live—away, despair!
Be calm, my soul! he yet may live;
T' arraign my fate, my voice forbear!
O God! my impious prayer forgive.

"What, if he live for me no more,
I sink forgotten in the dust,
The hope of Alva's age is o'er;
Alas! can pangs like these be just?"

Thus did the hapless parent mourn,
Till Time, which soothes severest woe,
Had bade serenity return,
And made the tear-drop cease to flow.

For still some latent hope survived
That Oscar might once more appear;
His hope now droop'd and now revived,
Till Time had told a tedious year.

Days roll'd along, the orb of light
Again had run his destined race;
No Oscar bless'd his father's sight,
And sorrow left a fainter trace.

For youthful Allan still remain'd,
And now his father's only joy:
And Mora's heart was quickly gain'd,
For beauty crown'd the fair-hair'd boy.

She thought that Oscar low was laid,
And Allan's face was wondrous fair;
If Oscar lived, some other maid
Had claim'd his faithless bosom's care.

And Angus said, if one year more
In fruitless hope was pass'd away,
His fondest scruples should be o'er,
And he would name their nuptial day.

Slow roll'd the moons, but blest at last
Arrived the dearly destined morn;
The year of anxious trembling past,
What smiles the lovers' cheeks adorn!

Hark to the pibroch's pleasing note!
Hark to the swelling nuptial song!
In joyous strains the voices float,
And still the choral peal prolong.

Again the clan, in festive crowd,
Throng through the gate of Alva's hall;
The sounds of mirth re-echo loud,
And all their former joy recall.

But who is he, whose darken'd brow,
Glooms in the midst of general mirth?
Before his eyes' far fiercer glow
The blue flames curdle o'er the hearth.

Dark is the robe which wraps his form,
And tall his plume of gory red;
His voice is like the rising storm,
But light and trackless is his tread.

'Tis noon of night, the pledge goes round,
The bridegroom's health is deeply quaff'd;
With shouts the vaulted roofs resound,
And all combine to hail the draught.

Sudden the stranger-chief arose,
And all the clamorous crowd are hush'd;
And Angus' cheek with wonder glows,
And Mora's tender bosom blush'd.

"Old man!" he cried, "this pledge is done
Thou saw'st 't was duly drank by me:
It hail'd the nuptials of thy son:
Now will I claim a pledge from thee.

"While all around is mirth and joy,
To bless thy Allan's happy lot,
Say, had'st thou ne'er another boy?
Say, why should Oscar be forgot?"

"Alas!" the helpless sire replied,
The big tear starting as he spoke,
"When Oscar left my hall, or died,
This aged heart was almost broke.

"Thrice has the earth revolved her course
Since Oscar's form has bless'd my sight;
And Allan is my last resource,
Since martial Oscar's death or flight."

"'Tis well," replied the stranger stern,
And fiercely flash'd his rolling eye:
"Thy Oscar's fate I fain would learn:
Perhaps the hero did not die.

"Perchance, if those whom most he loved
Would call, thy Oscar might return;
Perchance the chief has only roved;
For him thy beltane yet may burn.[21]

"Fill high the bowl the table round,
We will not claim the pledge by stealth;
With wine let every cup be crown'd;
Pledge me departed Oscar's health."

"With all my soul," old Angus said,
And fill'd his goblet to the brim;
"Here 's to my boy! alive or dead,
I ne'er shall find a son like him."

"Bravely, old man, this health has sped;
But why does trembling Allan stand?
Come, drink remembrance of the dead,
And raise thy cup with firmer hand."

The crimson glow of Allan's face
Was turn'd at once to ghastly hue;
The drops of death each other chase
Adown in agonising dew.

Thrice did he raise the goblet high,
And thrice his lips refused to taste;
For thrice he caught the stranger's eye
On his with deadly fury placed.

"And is it thus a brother hails
A brother's fond remembrance here?
If thus affection's strength prevails,
What might we not expect from fear?"

Roused by the sneer, he raised the bowl,
"Would Oscar now could share our mirth!"
Internal fear appall'd his soul;
He said, and dash'd the cup to earth.

"'Tis he! I hear my murderer's voice!"
Loud shrieks a darkly gleaming form;
"A murderer's voice!" the roof replies,
And deeply swells the bursting storm.

The tapers wink, the chieftains shrink,
The stranger's gone—amidst the crew
A form was seen in tartan green,
And tall the shade terrific grew.

His waist was bound with a broad belt round,
His plume of sable stream'd on high;
But his breast was bare, with the red wounds there,
And fix'd was the glare of his glassy eye.

And thrice he smiled, with his eye so wild,
On Angus bending low the knee;
And thrice he frown'd on a chief on the ground,
Whom shivering crowds with horror see.

The bolts loud roll, from pole to pole
The thunders through the welkin ring,
And the gleaming form, thro' the mist of the storm,
Was borne on high by the whirlwind's wing.

Cold was the feast, the revel ceased,
Who lies upon the stony floor?
Oblivion press'd old Angus' breast,
At length his life-pulse throbs once more.

"Away! away! let the leech essay
To pour the light on Allan's eyes:"
His sand is done,—his race is run;
Oh! never more shall Allan rise!

But Oscar's breast is cold as clay,
His locks are lifted by the gale:
And Allan's barbèd arrow lay
With him in dark Glentanar's vale.

And whence the dreadful stranger came,
Or who, no mortal wight can tell;
But no one doubts the form of flame,
For Alva's sons knew Oscar well.

Ambition nerved young Allan's hand,
Exulting demons wing'd his dart;
While Envy waved her burning brand,
And pour'd her venom round his heart.

Swift is the shaft from Allan's bow;
Whose streaming life-blood stains his side?
Dark Oscar's sable crest is low,
The dart has drunk his vital tide.

And Mora's eye could Allan move,
She bade his wounded pride rebel;
Alas! that eyes which beam'd with love
Should urge the soul to deeds of hell.

Lo! seest thou not a lonely tomb
Which rises o'er a warrior dead?
It glimmers through the twilight gloom;
Oh! that is Allan's nuptial bed.

Far, distant far, the noble grave
Which held his clan's great ashes stood;
And o'er his corse no banners wave,
For they were stain'd with kindred blood.

What minstrel gray, what hoary bard,
Shall Allan's deeds on harp-strings raise?
The song is glory's chief reward,
But who can strike a murderer's praise?

Unstrung, untouch'd, the harp must stand,
No minstrel dare the theme awake;
Guilt would benumb his palsied hand,
His harp in shuddering chords would break.

No lyre of fame, no hallow'd verse,
Shall sound his glories high in air:
A dying father's bitter curse,
A brother's death-groan echoes there.

THE EPISODE OF NISUS AND EURYALUS.

A PARAPHRASE FROM THE ÆNEID, LIB. IX.

Nisus, the guardian of the portal, stood,
Eager to gild his arms with hostile blood;
Well skill'd in fight the quivering lance to wield,
Or pour his arrows through th' embattled field:
From Ida torn, he left his sylvan cave,
And sought a foreign home, a distant grave.
To watch the movements of the Daunian host,
With him Euryalus sustains the post;
No lovelier mien adorn'd the ranks of Troy,
And beardless bloom yet graced the gallant boy;
Though few the seasons of his youthful life,
As yet a novice in the martial strife,
'T was his, with beauty, valour's gifts to share—
A soul heroic, as his form was fair:
These burn with one pure flame of generous love;
In peace, in war, united still they move;
Friendship and glory form their joint reward;
And now combined they hold their nightly guard.

"What god," exclaim'd the first, "instils this fire?
Or, in itself a god, what great desire?
My labouring soul, with anxious thought oppress'd,
Abhors this station of inglorious rest;
The love of fame with this can ill accord,
Be't mine to seek for glory with my sword.
Seest thou yon camp, with torches twinkling dim,
Where drunken slumbers wrap each lazy limb?
Where confidence and ease the watch disdain,
And drowsy Silence holds her sable reign?
Then hear my thought:—In deep and sullen grief
Our troops and leaders mourn their absent chief:
Now could the gifts and promised prize be thine
(The deed, the danger, and the fame be mine),
Were this decreed, beneath yon rising mound,
Methinks, an easy path perchance were found:
Which past, I speed my way to Pallas' walls,
And lead Æneas from Evander's halls."

With equal ardour fired, and warlike joy,
His glowing friend address'd the Dardan boy:—
"These deeds, my Nisus, shalt thou dare alone?
Must all the fame, the peril, be thine own?
Am I by thee despised, and left afar,
As one unfit to share the toils of war?
Not thus his son the great Opheltes taught;
Not thus my sire in Argive combats fought;
Not thus, when Ilion fell by heavenly hate,
I track'd Æneas through the walks of fate:
Thou know'st my deeds, my breast devoid of fear,
And hostile life-drops dim my gory spear.
Here is a soul with hope immortal burns,
And life, ignoble life, for *glory* spurns.
Fame, fame is cheaply earn'd by fleeting breath:
The price of honour is the sleep of death."

Then Nisus,—"Calm thy bosom's fond alarms,
Thy heart beats fiercely to the din of arms.
More dear thy worth and valour than my own,
I swear by him who fills Olympus' throne!
So may I triumph, as I speak the truth,
And clasp again the comrade of my youth!

But should I fall,—and he who dares advance
Through hostile legions must abide by chance,—
If some Rutulian arm, with adverse blow,
Should lay the friend who ever loved thee low,
Live thou, such beauties I would fain preserve,
Thy budding years a lengthen'd term deserve.
When humbled in the dust, let some one be
Whose gentle eyes will shed one tear for me;
Whose manly arm may snatch me back by force,
Or wealth redeem from foes my captive corse;
Or, if my destiny these last deny,
If in the spoiler's power my ashes lie,
Thy pious care may raise a simple tomb,
To mark thy love, and signalise my doom.
Why should thy doting wretched mother weep
Her only boy, reclined in endless sleep?
Who, for thy sake, the tempest's fury dared,
Who, for thy sake, war's deadly peril shared;
Who braved what woman never braved before,
And left her native for the Latian shore."
"In vain you damp the ardour of my soul,"
Replied Euryalus: "it scorns control!
Hence, let us haste!"—their brother guards arose,
Roused by their call, nor court again repose;
The pair, buoy'd up on Hope's exulting wing,
Their stations leave, and speed to seek the king.

Now o'er the earth a solemn stillness ran,
And lull'd alike the cares of brute and man;
Save where the Dardan leaders nightly hold
Alternate converse, and their plans unfold.
On one great point the council are agreed,
An instant message to their prince decreed;
Each lean'd upon the lance he well could wield,
And poised with easy arm his ancient shield;
When Nisus and his friend their leave request
To offer something to their high behest.
With anxious tremors, yet unawed by fear,
The faithful pair before the throne appear:
Iulus greets them; at his kind command,
The elder first address'd the hoary band.

"With patience" (thus Hyrtacides began)
"Attend, nor judge from youth our humble plan.
Where yonder beacons half expiring beam,
Our slumbering foes of future conquest dream,
Nor heed that we a secret path have traced,
Between the ocean and the portal placed.
Beneath the covert of the blackening smoke,
Whose shade securely our design will cloak;
If you, ye chiefs, and fortune will allow,
We'll bend our course to yonder mountain's brow,
Where Pallas' walls at distance meet the sight,
Seen o'er the glade, when not obscured by night:
Then shall Æneas in his pride return,
While hostile matrons raise their offspring's urn;
And Latian spoils and purpled heaps of dead
Shall mark the havoc of our hero's tread.
Such is our purpose, not unknown the way
Where yonder torrent's devious waters stray
Oft have we seen, when hunting by the stream,
The distant spires above the valleys gleam."

Mature in years, for sober wisdom famed,
Moved by the speech, Alethes here exclaim'd,—
"Ye parent gods! who rule the fate of Troy,
Still dwells the Dardan spirit in the boy;
When minds like these in striplings thus ye raise,
Yours is the godlike act, be yours the praise;
In gallant youth, my fainting hopes revive,
And Ilion's wonted glories still survive."
Then in his warm embrace the boys he press'd,
And, quivering, strain'd them to his aged breast;
With tears the burning cheek of each bedew'd,
And, sobbing, thus his first discourse renew'd:
"What gift, my countrymen, what martial prize
Can we bestow, which you may not despise?
Our deities the first best boon have given—
Internal virtues are the gift of Heaven.
What poor rewards can bless your deeds on earth,
Doubtless await such young, exalted worth.
Æneas and Ascanius shall combine
To yield applause far, far surpassing mine."
Iulus then:—"By all the powers above!
By those Penates who my country love!
By hoary Vesta's sacred fane, I swear,
My hopes are all in you, ye generous pair!
Restore my father to my grateful sight,
And all my sorrows yield to one delight.
Nisus! two silver goblets are thine own,
Saved from Arisba's stately domes o'erthrown;
My sire secured them on that fatal day,
Nor left such bowls an Argive robber's prey:
Two massy tripods, also, shall be thine;
Two talents polish'd from the glittering mine;
An ancient cup, which Tyrian Dido gave,
While yet our vessels press'd the Punic wave:
But when the hostile chiefs at length bow down,
When great Æneas wears Hesperia's crown,
The casque, the buckler, and the fiery steed
Which Turnus guides with more than mortal speed,
Are thine; no envious lot shall then be cast,
I pledge my word, irrevocably past:
Nay, more, twelve slaves, and twice six captive dames,
To soothe thy softer hours with amorous flames,
And all the realms which now the Latins sway,
The labours of to-night shall well repay.
But thou, my generous youth, whose tender years
Are near my own, whose worth my heart reveres,
Henceforth affection, sweetly thus begun,
Shall join our bosoms and our souls in one;
Without thy aid, no glory shall be mine;
Without thy dear advice, no great design;

Alike through life esteem'd, thou godlike boy,
In war my bulwark, and in peace my joy."

To him Euryalus:—"No day shall shame
The rising glories which from this I claim.
Fortune may favour, or the skies may frown,
But valour, spite of fate, obtains renown.
Yet, ere from hence our eager steps depart,
One boon I beg, the nearest to my heart:
My mother, sprung from Priam's royal line,
Line thine ennobled, hardly less divine,
Nor Troy nor king Acestes' realms restrain
Her feeble age from dangers of the main;
Alone she came, all selfish fears above,
A bright example of maternal love.
Unknown the secret enterprise I brave,
Lest grief should bend my parent to the grave;
From this alone no fond adieus I seek,
No fainting mother's lips have press'd my cheek;
By gloomy night and thy right hand I vow
Her parting tears would shake my purpose now:
Do thou, my prince, her failing age sustain,
In thee her much loved child may live again;
Her dying hours with pious conduct bless,
Assist her wants, relieve her fond distress:
So dear a hope must all my soul inflame,
To rise in glory, or to fall in fame."
Struck with a filial care so deeply felt,
In tears at once the Trojan warriors melt:
Faster than all, Iulus' eyes o'erflow;
Such love was his, and such had been his woe.
"All thou hast asked, receive," the prince replied;
"Nor this alone, but many a gift beside,
To cheer thy mother's years, shall be my aim,
Creusa's style but wanting to the dame.[22]
Fortune an adverse wayward course may run,
But bless'd thy mother in so dear a son.
Now, by my life!—my sire's most sacred oath—
To thee I pledge my full, my firmest troth,
All the rewards which once to thee were vow'd,
If thou should'st fall, on her shall be bestow'd."
Thus spoke the weeping prince, then forth to view
A gleaming falchion from the sheath he drew;
Lycaon's utmost skill had graced the steel,
For friends to envy and for foes to feel:
A tawny hide, the Moorish lion's spoil,
Slain 'midst the forest, in the hunter's toil,
Mnestheus to guard the elder youth bestows,
And old Alethes' casque defends his brows.
Arm'd, thence they go, while all th' assembled train,
To aid their cause, implore the gods in vain.
More than a boy, in wisdom and in grace,
Iulus holds amidst the chiefs his place:
His prayer he sends; but what can prayers avail,
Lost in the murmurs of the sighing gale!

The trench is passed, and, favour'd by the night,
Through sleeping foes they wheel their wary flight.
When shall the sleep of many a foe be o'er?
Alas! some slumber who shall wake no more!
Chariots and bridles, mix'd with arms, are seen;
And flowing flasks, and scatter'd troops between:
Bacchus and Mars to rule the camp combine;
A mingled chaos this of war and wine.
"Now," cries the first, "for deeds of blood prepare,
With me the conquest and the labour share:
Here lies our path; lest any hand arise,
Watch thou, while many a dreaming chieftain dies:
I'll carve our passage through the heedless foe,
And clear thy road with many a deadly blow."
His whispering accents then the youth repress'd,
And pierced proud Rhamnes through his panting breast:
Stretch'd at his ease, th' incautious king reposed;
Debauch, and not fatigue, his eyes had closed:
To Turnus dear, a prophet and a prince,
His omens more than augur's skill evince;
But he, who thus foretold the fate of all,
Could not avert his own untimely fall.
Next Remus' armour-bearer, hapless, fell,
And three unhappy slaves the carnage swell;
The charioteer along his courser's sides
Expires, the steel his sever'd neck divides;
And, last, his lord is number'd with the dead:
Bounding convulsive, flies the gasping head;
From the swoll'n veins the blackening torrents pour;
Stain'd is the couch and earth with clotting gore.
Young Lamyrus and Lamus next expire,
And gay Seranus, fill'd with youthful fire;
Half the long night in childish games was pass'd,
Lull'd by the potent grape, he slept at last:
Ah! happier far had he the morn survey'd,
And till Aurora's dawn his skill display'd.

In slaughter'd fold, the keepers lost in sleep,
His hungry fangs a lion thus may steep;
'Mid the sad flock, at dead of night he prowls,
With murder glutted, and in carnage rolls:
Insatiate still, through teeming herds he roams.
In seas of gore the lordly tyrant foams.

Nor less the other's deadly vengeance came,
But falls on feeble crowds without a name;
His wound unconscious Fadus scarce can feel,
Yet wakeful Rhæsus sees the threatening steel;
His coward breast behind a jar he hides,
And vainly in the weak defence confides;
Full in his heart, the falchion searched his veins,
The reeking weapon bears alternate stains;
Through wine and blood, commingling as they flow,
One feeble spirit seeks the shades below.

Now where Messapus dwelt they bend their way,
Whose fires emit a faint and trembling ray;
There, unconfined, behold each grazing steed,
Unwatch'd, unheeded, on the herbage feed:
Brave Nisus here arrests his comrade's arm,
Too flush'd with carnage, and with conquest warm:
"Hence let us haste, the dangerous path is pass'd;
Full foes enough to-night have breathed their last:
Soon will the day those eastern clouds adorn;
Now let us speed, nor tempt the rising morn."

With silver arms, with various art emboss'd,
What bowls and mantles in confusion toss'd,
They leave regardless! yet one glittering prize
Attracts the younger hero's wandering eyes;
The gilded harness Rhamnes' coursers felt,
The gems which stud the monarch's golden belt:
This from the pallid corse was quickly torn,
Once by a line of former chieftains worn.
Th' exulting boy the studded girdle wears,
Messapus' helm his head in triumph bears;
Then from the tents their cautious steps they bend,
To seek the vale where safer paths extend.

Just at this hour, a band of Latian horse
To Turnus' camp pursue their destined course:
While the slow foot their tardy march delay,
The knights, impatient, spur along the way:
Three hundred mail-clad men, by Volscens led,
To Turnus with their master's promise sped;
Now they approach the trench, and view the walls,
When, on the left, a light reflection falls;
The plunder'd helmet, through the waning night,
Sheds forth a silver radiance, glancing bright.
Volscens with question loud the pair alarms:—
"Stand, stragglers! stand! why early thus in arms?
From whence, to whom?"—He meets with no reply!
Trusting the covert of the night, they fly:
The thicket's depth with hurried pace they tread,
While round the wood the hostile squadron spread.

With brakes entangled, scarce a path between,
Dreary and dark appears the sylvan scene:
Euryalus his heavy spoils impede,
The boughs and winding turns his steps mislead;
But Nisus scours along the forest's maze
To where Latinus' steeds in safety graze,
Then backward o'er the plain his eyes extend,
On every side they seek his absent friend.
"Oh God! my boy," he cries, "of me bereft,
In what impending perils art thou left!"
Listening he runs—above the waving trees,
Tumultuous voices swell the passing breeze;
The war-cry rises, thundering hoofs around
Wake the dark echoes of the trembling ground.
Again he turns, of footsteps hears the noise;
The sound elates, the sight his hope destroys:
The hapless boy a ruffian train surround,
While lengthening shades his weary way confound;
Him with loud shouts the furious knights pursue,
Struggling in vain, a captive to the crew.
What can his friend 'gainst thronging numbers dare?
Ah! must he rush, his comrade's fate to share?
What force, what aid, what stratagem essay,
Back to redeem the Latian spoiler's prey?
His life a votive ransom nobly give,
Or die with him for whom he wish'd to live?
Poising with strength his lifted lance on high,
On Luna's orb he cast his frenzied eye:—
"Goddess serene, transcending every star!
Queen of the sky, whose beams are seen afar!
By night heaven owns thy sway, by day the grove,
When, as chaste Dian, here thou deign'st to rove:
If e'er myself, or sire, have sought to grace
Thine altars with the produce of the chase,
Speed, speed my dart to pierce yon vaunting crowd,
To free my friend, and scatter far the proud."
Thus having said, the hissing dart he flung;
Through parted shades the hurtling weapon sung;
The thirsty point in Sulmo's entrails lay,
Transfix'd his heart, and stretch'd him on the clay:
He sobs, he dies,—the troop in wild amaze,
Unconscious whence the death, with horror gaze.
While pale they stare, through Tagus' temples riven,
A second shaft with equal force is driven.
Fierce Volscens rolls around his lowering eyes;
Veil'd by the night, secure the Trojan lies.
Burning with wrath, he view'd his soldiers fall:
"Thou youth accurst, thy life shall pay for all!"
Quick from the sheath his flaming glaive he drew,
And, raging, on the boy defenceless flew.
Nisus no more the blackening shape conceals,
Forth, forth he starts, and all his love reveals;
Aghast, confused, his fears to madness rise,
And pour these accents, shrieking as he flies:
"Me, me,—your vengeance hurl on me alone;
Here sheathe the steel, my blood is all your own.
Ye starry spheres! thou conscious Heaven! attest!
He could not—durst not—lo! the guile confest!
All, all was mine,—his early fate suspend;
He only loved too well his hapless friend:
Spare, spare, ye chiefs! from him your rage remove;
His fault was friendship, all his crime was love."
He pray'd in vain; the dark assassin's sword
Pierced the fair side, the snowy bosom gored;
Lowly to earth inclines his plume-clad crest,
And sanguine torrents mantle o'er his breast:
As some young rose, whose blossom scents the air,
Languid in death, expires beneath the share;

Or crimson poppy, sinking with the shower,
Declining gently, falls a fading flower:
Thus, sweetly drooping, bends his lovely head,
And lingering beauty hovers round the dead.

But fiery Nisus stems the battle's tide,
Revenge his leader and despair his guide:
Volscens he seeks amidst the gathering host,
Volscens must soon appease his comrade's ghost
Steel, flashing, pours on steel, foe crowds on foe;
Rage nerves his arm, fate gleams in every blow;
In vain beneath unnumber'd wounds he bleeds,
Nor wounds, nor death, distracted Nisus heeds;
In viewless circles wheel'd, his falchion flies,
Nor quits the hero's grasp till Volscens dies;
Deep in his throat its end the weapon found,
The tyrant's soul fled groaning through the wound.
Thus Nisus all his fond affection proved—
Dying, revenged the fate of him he loved;
Then on his bosom sought his wonted place,
And death was heavenly in his friend's embrace.

Celestial pair! if aught my verse can claim,
Wafted on Time's broad pinion, yours is fame!
Ages on ages shall your fate admire,
No future day shall see your names expire,
While stands the Capitol, immortal dome!
And vanquish'd millions hail their empress, Rome!

TRANSLATION FROM THE MEDEA OF EURIPIDES.

When fierce conflicting passions urge
The breast where love is wont to glow,
What mind can stem the stormy surge
Which rolls the tide of human woe?
The hope of praise, the dread of shame,
Can rouse the tortured breast no more;
The wild desire, the guilty flame,
Absorbs each wish it felt before.

But if affection gently thrills
The soul by purer dreams possest,
The pleasing balm of mortal ills
In love can soothe the aching breast:
If thus thou comest in disguise,
Fair Venus! from thy native heaven,
What heart unfeeling would despise
The sweetest boon the gods have given?

But never from thy golden bow
May I beneath the shaft expire!
Whose creeping venom, sure and slow,
Awakes an all-consuming fire:
Ye racking doubts! ye jealous fears!
With others wage internal war;
Repentance, source of future tears,
From me be ever distant far!

May no distracting thoughts destroy
The holy calm of sacred love!
May all the hours be wing'd with joy,
Which hover faithful hearts above!
Fair Venus! on thy myrtle shrine
May I with some fond lover sigh,
Whose heart may mingle pure with mine—
With me to live, with me to die.

My native soil! beloved before,
Now dearer as my peaceful home,
Ne'er may I quit thy rocky shore,
A hapless banish'd wretch to roam!
This very day, this very hour,
May I resign this fleeting breath!
Nor quit my silent humble bower;
A doom to me far worse than death.

Have I not heard the exile's sigh?
And seen the exile's silent tear,
Through distant climes condemn'd to fly,
A pensive weary wanderer here?
Ah! hapless dame! no sire bewails,[23]
No friend thy wretched fate deplores,
No kindred voice with rapture hails
Thy steps within a stranger's doors.

Perish the fiend whose iron heart,
To fair affection's truth unknown,
Bids her he fondly loved depart,
Unpitied, helpless, and alone;
Who ne'er unlocks with silver key[24]
The milder treasures of his soul,—
May such a friend be far from me,
And ocean's storms between us roll.

THOUGHTS SUGGESTED BY A COLLEGE EXAMINATION.

High in the midst, surrounded by his peers,
Magnus his ample front sublime uprears:[25]
Placed on his chair of state, he seems a god,
While Sophs and Freshmen tremble at his nod.
As all around sit wrapt in speechless gloom,
His voice in thunder shakes the sounding dome;
Denouncing dire reproach to luckless fools,
Unskill'd to plod in mathematic rules.

Happy the youth in Euclid's axioms tried,
Though little versed in any art beside;
Who, scarcely skill'd an English line to pen,
Scans Attic metres with a critic's ken.
What, though he knows not how his fathers bled,
When civil discord piled the fields with dead,
When Edward bade his conquering bands advance.
Or Henry trampled on the crest of France:

Though marvelling at the name of Magna Charta,
Yet well he recollects the law of Sparta:
Can tell what edicts sage Lycurgus made,
While Blackstone's on the shelf neglected laid;
Of Grecian dramas vaunts the deathless fame,
Of Avon's bard remembering scarce the name.

Such is the youth whose scientific pate
Class-honours, medals, fellowships, await;
Or even, perhaps, the declamation prize,
If to such glorious height he lifts his eyes.
But lo! no common orator can hope
The envied silver cup within his scope.
Not that our heads much eloquence require,
Th' Athenian's glowing style, or Tully's fire. [26]
A manner clear or warm is useless, since
We do not try by speaking to convince.
Be other orators of pleasing proud:
We speak to please ourselves, not move the crowd:
Our gravity prefers the muttering tone,
A proper mixture of the squeak and groan:
No borrow'd grace of action must be seen,
The slightest motion would displease the Dean;
Whilst every staring graduate would prate
Against what he could never imitate.

The man who hopes t' obtain the promised cup
Must in one posture stand, and ne'er look up,
Nor stop, but rattle over every word—
No matter what, so it can *not* be heard.
Thus let him hurry on, nor think to rest:
Who speaks the fastest 's sure to speak the best;
Who utters most within the shortest space
May safely hope to win the wordy race.

The sons of science these, who, thus repaid,
Linger in ease in Granta's sluggish shade;
Where on Cam's sedgy bank supine they lie
Unknown, unhonour'd live, unwept for die:
Dull as the pictures which adorn their halls,
They think all learning fix'd within their walls;
In manners rude, in foolish forms precise,
All modern arts affecting to despise;
Yet prizing Bentley's, Brunck's, or Porson's note, [27]
More than the verse on which the critic wrote;
Vain as their honours, heavy as their ale,
Sad as their wit, and tedious as their tale;
To friendship dead, though not untaught to feel
When Self and Church demand a bigot zeal.
With eager haste they court the lord of power,
Whether 't is Pitt or Petty rules the hour; [28]
To him, with suppliant smiles, they bend the head,
While distant mitres to their eyes are spread.
But should a storm o'erwhelm him with disgrace,
They 'd fly to seek the next who fill'd his place.
Such are the men who learning's treasures guard!
Such is their practice, such is their reward!
This much, at least we may presume to say—
The premium can't exceed the price they pay.

1806.

TO A BEAUTIFUL QUAKER.

Sweet girl! though only once we met,
That meeting I shall ne'er forget;
And though we ne'er may meet again,
Remembrance will thy form retain.
I would not say, "I love," but still
My senses struggle with my will:
In vain, to drive thee from my breast,
My thoughts are more and more represt;
In vain I check the rising sighs,
Another to the last replies:
Perhaps this is not love, but yet
Our meeting I can ne'er forget.
What though we never silence broke,
Our eyes a sweeter language spoke;
The tongue in flattering falsehood deals,
And tells a tale it never feels:
Deceit the guilty lips impart;
And hush the mandates of the heart;
But soul's interpreters, the eyes,
Spurn such restraint, and scorn disguise.
As thus our glances oft conversed,
And all our bosoms felt rehearsed,
No spirit, from within, reproved us,
Say rather, "'t was the spirit moved us."
Though what they utter'd I repress,
Yet I conceive thou 'lt partly guess;
For as on thee my memory ponders,
Perchance to me thine also wanders.
This for myself, at least, I 'll say,
Thy form appears through night, through day:
Awake, with it my fancy teems;
In sleep, it smiles in fleeting dreams:
The vision charms the hours away,
And bids me curse Aurora's ray,
For breaking slumbers of delight,
Which make me wish for endless night.
Since, oh! whate'er my future fate,
Shall joy or woe my steps await,
Tempted by love, by storms beset,
Thine image I can ne'er forget.
Alas! again no more we meet,
No more our former looks repeat;
Then let me breathe this parting prayer,
The dictate of my bosom's care:
"May Heaven so guard my lovely quaker,
That anguish never can o'ertake her;
That peace and virtue ne'er forsake her,
But bliss be aye her heart's partaker!
Oh! may the happy mortal, fated
To be, by dearest ties, related,
For her each hour new joys discover,
And lose the husband in the lover!
May that fair bosom never know
What 't is to feel the restless woe,
Which stings the soul with vain regret
Of him who never can forget!"

THE CORNELIAN.

No specious splendour of this stone
 Endears it to my memory ever;
With lustre only once it shone,
 And blushes modest as the giver.

Some, who can sneer at friendship's ties,
 Have, for my weakness, oft reproved me;
Yet still the simple gift I prize,—
 For I am sure the giver loved me.

He offer'd it with downcast look,
 As fearful that I might refuse it;
I told him when the gift I took,
 My only fear should be to lose it.

This pledge attentively I view'd,
 And sparkling as I held it near,
Methought one drop the stone bedew'd,
 And ever since I've loved a tear.

Still, to adorn his humble youth,
 Nor wealth, nor birth their treasures yield;
But he who seeks the flowers of truth,
 Must quit the garden for the field.

'Tis not the plant uprear'd in sloth,
 Which beauty shows, and sheds perfume;
The flowers which yield the most of both
 In Nature's wild luxuriance bloom.

Had Fortune aided Nature's care,
 For once forgetting to be blind,
His would have been an ample share,
 If well proportion'd to his mind.

But had the goddess clearly seen,
 His form had fix'd her fickle breast;
Her countless hoards would his have been,
 And none remain'd to give thee rest.

AN OCCASIONAL PROLOGUE,

DELIVERED PREVIOUS TO THE PERFORMANCE OF "THE WHEEL OF FORTUNE" AT A PRIVATE THEATRE.

SINCE the refinement of this polish'd age
Has swept immoral raillery from the stage;
Since taste has now expunged licentious wit,
Which stamp'd disgrace on all an author writ;
Since now to please with purer scenes we seek,
Nor dare to call the blush from Beauty's cheek,
Oh! let the modest Muse some pity claim,
And meet indulgence, though she find not fame.
Still, not for her alone we wish respect,
Others appear more conscious of defect:
To-night no veteran Roscii you behold
In all the arts of scenic action old;
No Cooke, no Kemble, can salute you here,
No Siddons draw the sympathetic tear;
To-night you throng to witness the *début*
Of embryo actors, to the Drama new:
Here, then, our almost unfledged wings we try;
Clip not our pinions ere the birds can fly:
Failing in this our first attempt to soar,
Drooping, alas! we fall to rise no more.
Not one poor trembler only fear betrays,
Who hopes, yet almost dreads, to meet your praise;
But all our dramatis personæ wait
In fond suspense this crisis of their fate.
No venal views our progress can retard,
Your generous plaudits are our sole reward:
For these, each Hero all his power displays,
Each timid Heroine shrinks before your gaze.
Surely the last will some protection find;
None to the softer sex can prove unkind:
While Youth and Beauty form the female shield,
The sternest censor to the fair must yield.
Yet, should our feeble efforts nought avail,
Should, after all, our best endeavours fail,
Still let some mercy in your bosoms live,
And, if you can't applaud, at least forgive.

ON THE DEATH OF MR. FOX.

THE FOLLOWING ILLIBERAL IMPROMPTU APPEARED IN A MORNING PAPER.

"Our nation's foes lament on Fox's death,
But bless the hour when Pitt resign'd his breath:
These feelings wide, let sense and truth unclue,
We give the palm where Justice points its due."

TO WHICH THE AUTHOR OF THESE PIECES SENT THE FOLLOWING REPLY.

OH factious viper! whose envenom'd tooth
Would mangle still the dead, perverting truth;
What though our "nation's foes" lament the fate,
With generous feeling, of the good and great,
Shall dastard tongues essay to blast the name
Of him whose meed exists in endless fame?
When Pitt expired in plenitude of power,
Though ill success obscured his dying hour,
Pity her dewy wings before him spread,
For noble spirits "war not with the dead:"
His friends, in tears, a last sad requiem gave,
As all his errors slumber'd in the grave;
He sunk, an Atlas bending 'neath the weight
Of cares o'erwhelming our conflicting state:
When, lo! a Hercules in Fox appear'd,
Who for a time the ruin'd fabric rear'd:
He, too, is fall'n, who Britain's loss supplied,
With him our fast-reviving hopes have died;
Not one great people only raise his urn,
All Europe's far-extended regions mourn.

"These feelings wide, let sense and truth unclue,
To give the palm where Justice points its due:"
Yet let not canker'd Calumny assail,
Or round our statesman wind her gloomy veil.
Fox! o'er whose corse a mourning world must weep,
Whose dear remains in honour'd marble sleep;
For whom, at last, e'en hostile nations groan,
While friends and foes alike his talents own;
Fox shall in Britain's future annals shine,
Nor e'en to Pitt the patriot's palm resign;
Which Envy, wearing Candour's sacred mask,
For Pitt, and Pitt alone, has dared to ask.

THE TEAR.

"O lachrymarum fons, tenero sacros
Ducentium ortus ex animo; quater
Felix! in imo qui scatentem
Pectore te, pia Nympha, sensit."—*Gray.*

When Friendship or Love our sympathies move,
When Truth in a glance should appear,
The lips may beguile with a dimple or smile,
But the test of affection's a Tear.

Too oft is a smile but the hypocrite's wile,
To mask detestation or fear;
Give me the soft sigh, whilst the soul-telling eye
Is dimm'd for a time with a Tear.

Mild Charity's glow, to us mortals below,
Shows the soul from barbarity clear;
Compassion will melt where this virtue is felt,
And its dew is diffused in a Tear.

The man doom'd to sail with the blast of the gale,
Through billows Atlantic to steer,
As he bends o'er the wave which may soon be his grave,
The green sparkles bright with a Tear.

The soldier braves death for a fanciful wreath
In Glory's romantic career:
But he raises the foe when in battle laid down,
And bathes every wound with a Tear.

If with high-bounding pride he return to his bride,
Renouncing the gore-crimson'd spear,
All his tolls are repaid, when, embracing the maid,
From her eyelid he kisses the Tear.

Sweet scene of my youth! seat of Friendship and Truth,[29]
Where love chased each fast-fleeting year,
Loath to leave thee, I mourn'd, for a last look I turned,
But thy spire was scarce seen through a Tear.

Though my vows I can pour to my Mary no more,
My Mary to love once so dear;
In the shade of her bower I remember the hour
She rewarded those vows with a Tear.

By another possest, may she live ever blest!
Her name still my heart must revere:
With a sigh I resign what I once thought was mine,
And forgive her deceit with a Tear.

Ye friends of my heart, ere from you I depart,
This hope to my breast is most near:
If again we shall meet in this rural retreat,
May we meet, as we part, with a Tear

When my soul wings her flight to the regions of night,
And my corse shall recline on its bier,
As ye pass by the tomb where my ashes consume,
Oh! moisten their dust with a Tear.

May no marble bestow the splendour of woe,
Which the children of vanity rear;
No fiction of fame shall blazon my name;
All I ask—all I wish—is a Tear.

October 26th, 1806.

REPLY TO SOME VERSES

OF J. M. B. PIGOT, ESQ., ON THE CRUELTY OF HIS MISTRESS.

Why, Pigot, complain of this damsel's disdain,
Why thus in despair do you fret?
For months you may try, yet, believe me, a sigh
Will never obtain a coquette.

Would you teach her to love? for a time seem to rove;
At first she may frown in a pet;
But leave her awhile, she shortly will smile,
And then you may kiss your coquette.

For such are the airs of these fanciful fairs,
They think all our homage a debt:
Yet a partial neglect soon takes an effect,
And humbles the proudest coquette.

Dissemble your pain, and lengthen your chain,
And seem her hauteur to regret;
If again you shall sigh, she no more will deny
That yours is the rosy coquette.

If still, from false pride, your pangs she deride,
This whimsical virgin forget;
Some other admire, who will melt with your fire,
And laugh at the little coquette.

For me, I adore some twenty or more,
And love them most dearly; but yet
Though my heart they enthral, I'd abandon them all,
Did they act like your blooming coquette.

No longer repine, adopt this design,
And break through her slight-woven net;
Away with despair, no longer forbear
To fly from the captious coquette.

Then quit her, my friend! your bosom defend,
Ere quite with her snares you're beset:
Lest your deep-wounded heart, when incensed by the smart,
Should lead you to curse the coquette.

October 27th, 1806.

TO THE SIGHING STREPHON.

Your pardon, my friend, if my rhymes did offend,
Your pardon, a thousand times o'er:
From friendship I strove your pangs to remove,
But I swear I will do so no more.

Since your beautiful maid your flame has repaid,
No more I your folly regret;
She's now most divine, and I bow at the shrine
Of this quickly reformed coquette.

Yet still, I must own, I should never have known
From your verses, what else she deserved;
Your pain seem'd so great, I pitied your fate,
As your fair was so devilish reserved.

Since the balm-breathing kiss of this magical miss
Can such wonderful transports produce;
Since the "world you forget, when your lips once have met,"
My counsel will get but abuse.

You say, when "I rove, I know nothing of love;"
'T is true, I am given to range:
If I rightly remember, I've loved a good number,
Yet there's pleasure, at least, in a change.

I will not advance, by the rules of romance,
To humour a whimsical fair;
Though a smile may delight, yet a frown won't affright,
Or drive me to dreadful despair.

While my blood is thus warm, I ne'er shall reform,
To mix in the Platonists' school;
Of this I am sure, was my passion so pure,
Thy mistress would think me a fool.

And if I should shun every woman for one,
Whose image must fill my whole breast—
Whom I must prefer, and sigh but for her—
What an insult 't would be to the rest!

Now, Strephon, good-bye; I cannot deny
Your passion appears most absurd;
Such love as you plead is pure love indeed,
For it only consists in the word.

TO ELIZA.

Eliza, what fools are the Mussulman sect,
Who to women deny the soul's future existence;
Could they see thee, Eliza, they'd own their defect,
And this doctrine would meet with a general resistance.

Had their prophet possess'd half an atom of sense,
He ne'er would have women from paradise driven;
Instead of his houris, a flimsy pretence,
With women alone he had peopled his heaven.

Yet still, to increase your calamities more,
Not content with depriving your bodies of spirit,
He allots one poor husband to share amongst four!—
With souls you'd dispense; but this last who could bear it?

His religion to please neither party is made;
On husbands 't is hard, to the wives most uncivil;
Still I can't contradict, what so oft has been said,
"Though women are angels, yet wedlock's the devil."

LACHIN Y GAIR.[31]

Away, ye gay landscapes, ye gardens of roses!
In you let the minions of luxury rove;
Restore me the rocks, where the snow-flake reposes,
Though still they are sacred to freedom and love:
Yet, Caledonia, beloved are thy mountains,
Round their white summits though elements war;
Though cataracts foam 'stead of smooth-flowing fountains,
I sigh for the valley of dark Loch na Garr.

Ah! there my young footsteps in infancy wander'd;
My cap was the bonnet, my cloak was the plaid;[31]
On chieftains long perish'd my memory ponder'd,
As daily I strode through the pine-covered glade.
I sought not my home till the day's dying glory
Gave place to the rays of the bright polar star;
For fancy was cheer'd by traditional story,
Disclosed by the natives of dark Loch na Garr.

"Shades of the dead! have I not heard your voices
Rise on the night-rolling breath of the gale?"
Surely the soul of the hero rejoices,
And rides on the wind, o'er his own highland vale

Round Loch na Garr while the stormy mist gathers,
Winter presides in his cold icy car:
Clouds there encircle the forms of my fathers;
They dwell in the tempests of dark Loch na Garr.

"Ill-starr'd, though brave, did no visions foreboding[32]
Tell you that fate had forsaken your cause?"
Ah! were you destined to die at Culloden,[33]
Victory crown'd not your fall with applause:
Still were you happy in death's earthy slumber,
You rest with your clan in the caves of Braemar;[34]
The pibroch resounds, to the piper's loud number,
Your deeds on the echoes of dark Loch na Garr.

Years have roll'd on, Loch na Garr, since I left you,
Years must elapse ere I tread you again;
Nature of verdure and flowers has bereft you,
Yet still are you dearer than Albion's plain.
England! thy beauties are tame and domestic
To one who has roved o'er the mountains afar:
Oh for the crags that are wild and majestic!
The steep frowning glories of dark Loch na Garr.

TO ROMANCE.

Parent of golden dreams, Romance!
Auspicious queen of childish joys,
Who lead'st along, in airy dance,
Thy votive train of girls and boys;
At length, in spells no longer bound,
I break the fetters of my youth;
No more I tread thy mystic round,
But leave thy realms for those of Truth.

And yet 'tis hard to quit the dreams
Which haunt the unsuspicious soul,
Where every nymph a goddess seems,
Whose eyes through rays immortal roll;

While Fancy holds her boundless reign,
 And all assume a varied hue;
When virgins seem no longer vain,
 And even woman's smiles are true.

And must we own thee but a name,
 And from thy hall of clouds descend?
Nor find a sylph in every dame,
 A Pylades in every friend?[35]
But leave at once thy realms of air
 To mingling bands of fairy elves:
Confess that woman 's false as fair,
 And friends have feeling for—themselves!

With shame I own I've felt thy sway
 Repentant, now thy reign is o'er:
No more thy precepts I obey,
 No more on fancied pinions soar.
Fond fool! to love a sparkling eye,
 And think that eye to truth was dear;
To trust a passing wanton's sigh,
 And melt beneath a wanton's tear!

Romance! disgusted with deceit,
 Far from thy motley court I fly,
Where Affectation holds her seat,
 And sickly Sensibility;
Whose silly tears can never flow
 For any pangs excepting thine;
Who turns aside from real woe,
 To steep in dew thy gaudy shrine.

Now join with sable Sympathy,
 With cypress crown'd, array'd in weeds,
Who heaves with thee her simple sigh,
 Whose breast for every bosom bleeds;
And call thy sylvan female choir,
 To mourn a swain for ever gone,
Who once could glow with equal fire,
 But bends not now before thy throne.

Ye genial nymphs, whose ready tears,
 On all occasions swiftly flow;
Whose bosoms heave with fancied fears,
 With fancied flames and phrenzy glow;
Say, will you mourn my absent name,
 Apostate from your gentle train?
An infant bard at least may claim
 From you a sympathetic strain.

Adieu, fond race! a long adieu!
 The hour of fate is hovering nigh;
E'en now the gulph appears in view,
 Where unlamented you must lie:
Oblivion's blackening lake is seen,
 Convulsed by gales you cannot weather;
Where you, and eke your gentle queen,
 Alas! must perish altogether.

ANSWER TO SOME ELEGANT VERSES,

SENT BY A FRIEND TO THE AUTHOR, COMPLAINING THAT ONE OF HIS DESCRIPTIONS WAS RATHER TOO WARMLY DRAWN.

"But if any old lady, knight, priest, or physician,
Should condemn me for printing a second edition;
If good Madam Squintum my work should abuse,
May I venture to give her a smack of my muse?"

New Bath Guide.

CANDOUR compels me, Becher! to commend
The verse which blends the censor with the friend.
Your strong yet just reproof extorts applause
From me, the heedless and imprudent cause.
For this wild error which pervades my strain,
I sue for pardon,—must I sue in vain?
The wise sometimes from Wisdom's ways depart:
Can youth then hush the dictates of the heart?
Precepts of prudence curb, but can't control,
The fierce emotions of the flowing soul.
When Love's delirium haunts the glowing mind,
Limping Decorum lingers far behind:
Vainly the dotard mends her prudish pace,
Outstript and vanquish'd in the mental chase.
The young, the old, have worn the chains of love:
Let those they ne'er confin'd my lay reprove:
Let those whose souls contemn the pleasing power,
Their censures on the hapless victim shower.

Oh! how I hate the nerveless, frigid song,
The ceaseless echo of the rhyming throng,
Whose labour'd lines in chilling numbers flow,
To paint a pang the author ne'er can know!
The artless Helicon I boast is youth;—
My lyre, the heart; my muse, the simple truth.
Far be 't from me the "virgin's mind" to "taint:"
Seduction's dread is here no slight restraint.
The maid whose virgin breast is void of guile,
Whose wishes dimple in a modest smile,
Whose downcast eye disdains the wanton leer,
Firm in her virtue's strength, yet not severe—
She whom a conscious grace shall thus refine,
Will ne'er be "tainted" by a strain of mine.
But for the nymph whose premature desires
Torment her bosom with unholy fires,
No net to snare her willing heart is spread;
She would have fallen, though she ne'er had read.
For me, I fain would please the chosen few,
Whose souls, to feeling and to nature true,
Will spare the childish verse, and not destroy
The light effusions of a heedless boy.
I seek not glory from the senseless crowd;
Of fancied laurels I shall ne'er be proud:
Their warmest plaudits I would scarcely prize,
Their sneers or censures I alike despise.

November 26, 1806.

ELEGY ON NEWSTEAD ABBEY.

"It is the voice of years that are gone! they roll before me with all their deeds."—OSSIAN.

NEWSTEAD! fast-falling, once-resplendent dome!
Religion's shrine! repentant Henry's pride![37]
Of warriors, monks, and dames the cloister'd tomb,
Whose pensive shades around thy ruins glide.

Hail to thy pile! more honour'd in thy fall,
Than modern mansions in their pillar'd state;
Proudly majestic frowns thy vaulted hall,
Scowling defiance on the blasts of fate.

No mail-clad serfs, obedient to their lord,[38]
In grim array the crimson cross demand;[39]
Or gay assemble round the festive board
Their chief's retainers, an immortal band:

Else might inspiring Fancy's magic eye
Retrace their progress through the lapse of time,
Marking each ardent youth, ordain'd to die,
A votive pilgrim in Judea's clime.

But not from thee, dark pile! departs the chief;
His feudal realm in other regions lay:
In thee the wounded conscience courts relief,
Retiring from the garish blaze of day.

Yes! in thy gloomy cells and shades profound,
The monk abjur'd a world he ne'er could view;
Or blood-stain'd guilt repenting solace found,
Or innocence from stern oppression flew.

A monarch bade thee from that wild arise,
Where Sherwood's outlaws once were wont to prowl;
And Superstition's crimes, of various dyes,
Sought shelter in the priest's protecting cowl.

Where now the grass exhales a murky dew,
The humid pall of life-extinguish'd clay,
In sainted fame the sacred fathers grew,
Nor raised their pious voices but to pray.

Where now the bats their wavering wings extend,
Soon as the gloaming spreads her waning shade,[40]
The choir did oft their mingling vespers blend,
Or matin orisons to Mary paid.[41]

Years roll on years; to ages, ages yield;
Abbots to abbots, in a line, succeed;
Religion's charter their protecting shield,
Till royal sacrilege their doom decreed.

One holy Henry rear'd the gothic walls,
And bade the pious inmates rest in peace;
Another Henry the kind gift recalls,[42]
And bids devotion's hallow'd echoes cease.

Vain is each threat or supplicating prayer;
He drives them exiles from their blest abode,
To roam a dreary world in deep despair—
No friend, no home, no refuge but their God.

Hark how the hall, resounding to the strain,
Shakes with the martial music's novel din!
The heralds of a warrior's haughty reign,
High crested banners wave thy walls within.

Of changing sentinels the distant hum,
The mirth of feasts, the clang of burnish'd arms,
The braying trumpet and the hoarser drum,
Unite in concert with increased alarms.

An abbey once, a regal fortress now,
Encircled by insulting rebel powers,
War's dread machines o'erhang thy threatening brow,
And dart destruction in sulphureous showers.

Ah, vain defence! the hostile traitor's siege,
Though oft repulsed, by guile o'ercomes the brave;
His thronging foes oppress the faithful liege,
Rebellion's reeking standards o'er him wave.

Not unavenged the raging baron yields;
The blood of traitors smears the purple plain;
Unconquer'd still, his falchion there he wields,
And days of glory yet for him remain.

Still in that hour the warrior wish'd to strew
Self-gather'd laurels on a self-sought grave:
But Charles' protecting genius hither flew,
The monarch's friend, the monarch's hope, to save.

Trembling, she snatch'd him from the unequal strife,[43]
In other fields the torrent to repel;
For nobler combats, here, reserv'd his life,
To lead the band where godlike Falkland fell.[44]

From thee, poor pile! to lawless plunder given,
While dying groans their painful requiem sound,
Far different incense now ascends to heaven,
Such victims wallow on the gory ground.

There many a pale and ruthless robber's corse,
Noisome and ghast, defiles thy sacred sod;
O'er mingling man, and horse commix'd with horse,
Corruption's heap, the savage spoilers trod.

Graves, long with rank and sighing weeds o'erspread,
Ransack'd, resign perforce their mortal mould;
From ruffian fangs escape not e'en the dead,
Raked from repose in search for buried gold.

Hush'd is the harp, unstrung the warlike lyre,
The minstrel's palsied hand reclines in death;
No more he strikes the quivering chords with fire,
Or sings the glories of the martial wreath.

At length the sated murderers, gorged with prey,
 Retire; the clamour of the fight is o'er;
Silence again resumes her awful sway,
 And sable Horror guards the massy door

Here Desolation holds her dreary court:
 What satellites declare her dismal reign!
Shrieking their dirge, ill-omen'd birds resort,
 To flit their vigils in the hoary fane.

Soon a new morn's restoring beams dispel
 The clouds of anarchy from Britain's skies;
The fierce usurper seeks his native hell,
 And Nature triumphs as the tyrant dies.

With storms she welcomes his expiring groans;
 Whirlwinds, responsive, greet his labouring breath
Earth shudders as her caves receive his bones,
 Loathing the offering of so dark a death.[45]

The legal ruler now resumes the helm,[46]
 He guides through gentle seas the prow of state;
Hope cheers, with wonted smiles, the peaceful realm,
 And heals the bleeding wounds of wearied hate.

The gloomy tenants, Newstead! of thy cells,
 Howling, resign their violated nest;
Again the master on his tenure dwells,
 Enjoy'd, from absence, with enraptured zest.

Vassals, within thy hospitable pale,
 Loudly carousing, bless their lord's return;
Culture again adorns the gladdening vale,
 And matrons, once lamenting, cease to mourn.

A thousand songs on tuneful echo float,
Unwonted foliage mantles o'er the trees:
And hark! the horns proclaim a mellow note,
The hunter's cry hangs lengthening on the breeze.

Beneath their coursers' hoofs the valleys shake:
What fears, what anxious hopes, attend the chase!
The dying stag seeks refuge in the Lake;
Exulting shouts announce the finish'd race.

Ah happy days! too happy to endure!
Such simple sports our plain forefathers knew:
No splendid vices glitter'd to allure;
Their joys were many, as their cares were few.

From these descending, sons to sires succeed;
Time steals along, and Death uprears his dart;
Another chief impels the foaming steed,
Another crowd pursue the panting hart.

Newstead! what saddening change of scene is thine!
Thy yawning arch betokens slow decay!
The last and youngest of a noble line
Now holds thy mouldering turrets in his sway.

Deserted now, he scans thy gray worn towers;
Thy vaults, where dead of feudal ages sleep;
Thy cloisters, pervious to the wintry showers;
These, these he views, and views them but to weep.

Yet are his tears no emblem of regret:
Cherish'd affection only bids them flow.
Pride, hope, and love forbid him to forget,
But warm his bosom with impassion'd glow.

Yet he prefers thee to the gilded domes
Or gewgaw grottoes of the vainly great;
Yet lingers 'mid thy damp and mossy tombs,
Nor breathes a murmur 'gainst the will of fate.

Haply thy sun, emerging, yet may shine,
Thee to irradiate with meridian ray;
Hours splendid as the past may still be thine,
And bless thy future as thy former day.

CHILDISH RECOLLECTIONS.

"I cannot but remember such things were,
And were most dear to me."

When slow Disease, with all her host of pains,
Chills the warm tide which flows along the veins;
When Health, affrighted, spreads her rosy wing,
And flies with every changing gale of spring;
Not to the aching frame alone confined,
Unyielding pangs assail the drooping mind:
What grisly forms, the spectre-train of woe,
Bid shuddering Nature shrink beneath the blow,
With Resignation wage relentless strife,
While Hope retires appall'd, and clings to life.
Yet less the pang, when, through the tedious hour,
Remembrance sheds around her genial power,
Calls back the vanish'd days to rapture given,
When love was bliss, and beauty form'd our heaven;
Or, dear to youth, portrays each childish scene,
Those fairy bowers, where all in turn have been.
As when through clouds that pour the summer storm
The orb of day unveils his distant form,
Gilds with faint beams the crystal dews of rain,
And dimly twinkles o'er the watery plain;
Thus, while the future dark and cheerless gleams,
The sun of memory, glowing through my dreams,
Though sunk the radiance of his former blaze,
To scenes far distant points his paler rays:
Still rules my senses with unbounded sway,
The past confounding with the present day.

Oft does my heart indulge the rising thought,
Which still recurs, unlook'd for and unsought;
My soul to fancy's fond suggestion yields,
And roams romantic o'er her airy fields:
Scenes of my youth, developed, crowd to view,
To which I long have bade a last adieu!
Seats of delight, inspiring youthful themes;
Friends lost to me for aye, except in dreams;
Some who in marble prematurely sleep,
Whose forms I now remember but to weep;
Some who yet urge the same scholastic course
Of early science, future fame the source;
Who, still contending in the studious race,
In quick rotation fill the senior place.
These with a thousand visions now unite,
To dazzle, though they please, my aching sight.
Ida! blest spot, where Science holds her reign,
How joyous once I join'd thy youthful train!
Bright in idea gleams thy lofty spire,
Again I mingle with thy playful quire;
Our tricks of mischief, every childish game,
Unchanged by time or distance, seem the same;
Through winding paths along the glade, I trace
The social smile of every welcome face;
My wonted haunts, my scenes of joy and woe,
Each early boyish friend, or youthful foe,
Our feuds dissolved, but not my friendship past:—
I bless the former, and forgive the last.
Hours of my youth! when, nurtured in my breast,
To love a stranger, friendship made me blest;—
Friendship, the dear peculiar bond of youth,
When every artless bosom throbs with truth;
Untaught by wordly wisdom how to feign,
And check each impulse with prudential rein;
When all we feel, our honest souls disclose—
In love to friends, in open hate to foes;
No varnish'd tales the lips of youth repeat,
No dear-bought knowledge purchased by deceit.

Hypocrisy, the gift of lengthen'd years,
Matured by age, the garb of prudence wears.
When now the boy is ripen'd into man,
His careful sire chalks forth some wary plan;
Instructs his son from candour's path to shrink,
Smoothly to speak, and cautiously to think;
Still to assent, and never to deny—
A patron's praise can well reward the lie:
And who, when Fortune's warning voice is heard,
Would lose his opening prospects for a word?
Although against that word his heart rebel,
And truth indignant all his bosom swell.

Away with themes like this! not mine the task
From flattering fiends to tear the hateful mask;
Let keener bards delight in satire's sting;
My fancy soars not on Detraction's wing:
Once, and but once, she aim'd a deadly blow,
To hurl defiance on a secret foe;
But when that foe, from feeling or from shame,
The cause unknown, yet still to me the same,
Warn'd by some friendly hint, perchance, retired,
With this submission all her rage expired.
From dreaded pangs that feeble foe to save,
She hush'd her young resentment, and forgave;
Or, if my muse a pedant's portrait drew,
Pomposus' virtues are but known to few:
I never fear'd the young usurper's nod,
And he who wields must sometimes feel the rod.
If since on Granta's failings, known to all
Who share the converse of a college hall,
She sometimes trifled in a lighter strain,
'Tis past, and thus she will not sin again,
Soon must her early song for ever cease,
And all may rail when I shall rest in peace.

Here first remember'd be the joyous band,
Who hail'd me chief, obedient to command;
Who join'd with me in every boyish sport—
Their first adviser, and their last resort;
Nor shrunk beneath the upstart pedant's frown,
Or all the sable glories of his gown;
Who, thus transplanted from his father's school
Unfit to govern, ignorant of rule—
Succeeded him, whom all unite to praise,
The dear preceptor of my early days;
Probus, the pride of science, and the boast,[47]
To Ida now, alas! for ever lost.
With him, for years, we search'd the classic page,
And fear'd the master, though we loved the sage:
Retired at last, his small yet peaceful seat,
From learning's labour is the blest retreat.
Pomposus fills his magisterial chair;
Pomposus governs,—but, my muse, forbear:
Contempt, in silence, be the pedant's lot;
His name and precepts be alike forgot!
No more his mention shall my verse degrade,—
To him my tribute is already paid.

High, thro' those elms, with hoary branches crown
Fair Ida's bower adorns the landscape round;
There Science, from her favour'd seat, surveys
The vale where rural Nature claims her praise;
To her awhile resigns her youthful train,
Who move in joy, and dance along the plain;
In scatter'd groups, each favour'd haunt pursue;
Repeat old pastimes, and discover new;
Flush'd with his rays, beneath the noontide sun,
In rival bands, between the wickets run,
Drive o'er the sward the ball with active force,
Or chase with nimble feet its rapid course.
But these with slower steps direct their way,
Where Brent's cool waves in limpid currents stray;
While yonder few search out some green retreat,
And arbours shade them from the summer heat:
Others again, a pert and lively crew,
Some rough and thoughtless stranger placed in view,
With frolic quaint their antic jests expose,
And tease the grumbling rustic as he goes;
Nor rest with this, but many a passing fray
Tradition treasures for a future day:
"'T was here the gather'd swains for vengeance fought,
And here we earn'd the conquest dearly bought;
Here have we fled before superior might,
And here renew'd the wild tumultuous fight."
While thus our souls with early passions swell,
In lingering tones resounds the distant bell;
Th' allotted hour of daily sport is o'er,
And Learning beckons from her temple's door.
No splendid tablets grace her simple hall,
But ruder records fill the dusky wall;
There, deeply carved, behold! each tyro's name
Secures its owner's academic fame;
Here mingling view the names of sire and son,
The one long graved, the other just begun:
These shall survive alike when son and sire
Beneath one common stroke of fate expire:
Perhaps their last memorial these alone,
Denied in death a monumental stone,
Whilst to the gale in mournful cadence wave
The sighing weeds that hide their nameless grave.
And here my name, and many an early friend's,
Along the wall in lengthen'd line extends.
Though still our deeds amuse the youthful race,
Who tread our steps, and fill our former place,
Who young obey'd their lords in silent awe,
Whose nod commanded, and whose voice was law
And now, in turn, possess the reins of power,
To rule the little tyrants of an hour;—
Though sometimes, with the tales of ancient day
They pass the dreary winter's eve away—
"And thus our former rulers stemm'd the tide,
And thus they dealt the combat side by side;
Just in this place the mouldering walls they scaled,
Nor bolts nor bars against their strength avail'd;

Here Probus came, the rising fray to quell,
And here he falter'd forth his last farewell;
And here one night abroad they dared to roam,
While bold Pomposus bravely stayed at home;"—
While thus they speak, the hour must soon arrive,
When names of these, like ours, alone survive:
Yet a few years, one general wreck will whelm
The faint remembrance of our fairy realm.

Dear honest race! though now we meet no more,
One last long look on what we were before—
Our first kind greetings, and our last adieu—
Drew tears from eyes unused to weep with you.
Through splendid circles, fashion's gaudy world,
Where folly's glaring standard waves unfurl'd,
I plunged to drown in noise my fond regret,
And all I sought or hoped was to forget.
Vain wish! if chance some well-remember'd face,
Some old companion of my early race,
Advanced to claim his friend with honest joy,
My eyes, my heart, proclaim'd me still a boy;
The glittering scene, the fluttering groups around,
Were quite forgotten when my friend was found;
The smiles of beauty—(for, alas! I've known
What 'tis to bend before Love's mighty throne)—
The smiles of beauty, though those smiles were dear,
Could hardly charm me, when that friend was near:
My thoughts bewilder'd in the fond surprise,
The woods of Ida danced before my eyes;
I saw the sprightly wand'rers pour along,
I saw and join'd again the joyous throng;
Panting, again I traced her lofty grove,
And friendship's feelings triumph'd over love.

Yet, why should I alone with such delight,
Retrace the circuit of my former flight?
Is there no cause beyond the common claim
Endear'd to all in childhood's very name?
Ah! sure some stronger impulse vibrates here,
Which whispers friendship will be doubly dear,
To one who thus for kindred hearts must roam,
And seek abroad the love denied at home.
Those hearts, dear Ida, have I found in thee—
A home, a world, a paradise to me.
Stern Death forbade my orphan youth to share
The tender guidance of a father's care.
Can rank, or e'en a guardian's name, supply
The love which glistens in a father's eye?
For this can wealth or title's sound atone,
Made, by a parent's early loss, my own?
What brother springs a brother's love to seek?
What sister's gentle kiss has prest my cheek?
For me how dull the vacant moments rise,
To no fond bosom link'd by kindred ties!
Oft in the progress of some fleeting dream
Fraternal smiles collected round me seem;
While still the visions to my heart are prest,
The voice of love will murmur in my rest:
I hear—I wake—and in the sound rejoice;
I hear again,— but ah! no brother's voice.
A hermit, 'midst of crowds, I fain must stray
Alone, though thousand pilgrims fill the way;
While these a thousand kindred wreaths entwine,
I cannot call one single blossom mine:
What then remains? in solitude to groan,
To mix in friendship, or to sigh alone.
Thus must I cling to some endearing hand,
And none more dear than Ida's social band.

Alonzo! best and dearest of my friends,
Thy name ennobles him who thus commends:
From this fond tribute thou canst gain no praise:
The praise is his who now that tribute pays.
Oh! in the promise of thy early youth,
If hope anticipate the words of truth,
Some loftier bard shall sing thy glorious name,
To build his own upon thy deathless fame.
Friend of my heart, and foremost of the list
Of those with whom I lived supremely blest,
Oft have we drain'd the font of ancient lore;
Though drinking deeply, thirsting still the more.
Yet, when confinement's lingering hour was done,
Our sports, our studies, and our souls were one:
Together we impell'd the flying ball;
Together waited in our tutor's hall:
Together join'd in cricket's manly toil,
Or shared the produce of the river's spoil;
Or, plunging from the green declining shore,
Our pliant limbs the buoyant billows bore;
In every element, unchanged, the same,
All, all that brothers should be, but the name.

Nor yet are you forgot, my jocund boy!
Davus, the harbinger of childish joy;
For ever foremost in the ranks of fun,
The laughing herald of the harmless pun;
Yet with a breast of such materials made—
Anxious to please, of pleasing half afraid;
Candid and liberal, with a heart of steel
In danger's path, though not untaught to feel.
Still I remember, in the factious strife,
The rustic's musket aim'd against my life:
High poised in air the massy weapon hung,
A cry of horror burst from every tongue;
Whilst I, in combat with another foe,
Fought on, unconscious of th' impending blow;
Your arm, brave boy, arrested his career—
Forward you sprung, insensible to fear;
Disarm'd and baffled by your conquering hand,
The grovelling savage roll'd upon the sand:
An act like this, can simple thanks repay?
Or all the labours of a grateful lay?
Oh no! whene'er my breast forgets the deed,
That instant, Davus, it deserves to bleed.

Lycus! on me thy claims are justly great:
Thy milder virtues could my muse relate,
To thee alone, unrivall'd, would belong
The feeble efforts of my lengthen'd song.
Well canst thou boast, to lead in senates fit,
A Spartan firmness with Athenian wit:
Though yet in embryo these perfections shine,
Lycus! thy father's fame will soon be thine.
Where learning nurtures the superior mind,
What may we hope from genius thus refined!
When time at length matures thy growing years,
How wilt thou tower above thy fellow peers!
Prudence and sense, a spirit bold and free,
With honour's soul, united beam in thee.

Shall fair Euryalus pass by unsung?
From ancient lineage, not unworthy, sprung:
What though one sad dissension bade us part,
That name is yet embalm'd within my heart;
Yet at the mention does that heart rebound,
And palpitate, responsive to the sound.
Envy dissolved our ties, and not our will:
We once were friends, — I'll think we are so still.
A form unmatch'd in nature's partial mould,
A heart untainted, we in thee behold:
Yet not the senate's thunder thou shalt wield,
Nor seek for glory in the tented field;
To minds of ruder texture these be given—
Thy soul shall nearer soar its native heaven.
Haply, in polish'd courts might be thy seat,
But that thy tongue could never forge deceit:
The courtier's supple bow and sneering smile,
The flow of compliment, the slippery wile,
Would make that breast with indignation burn,
And all the glittering snares to tempt thee spurn.
Domestic happiness will stamp thy fate;
Sacred to love, unclouded e'er by hate;
The world admire thee, and thy friends adore;—
Ambition's slave alone would toil for more.

Now last, but nearest, of the social band,
See honest, open, generous Cleon stand;
With scarce one speck to cloud the pleasing scene,
No vice degrades that purest soul serene.
On the same day our studious race begun,
On the same day our studious race was run;
Thus side by side we pass'd our first career,
Thus side by side we strove for many a year;
At last concluded our scholastic life,
We neither conquer'd in the classic strife:
As speakers each supports an equal name,[48]
And crowds allow to both a partial fame:
To soothe a youthful rival's early pride,
Though Cleon's candour would the palm divide,
Yet candour's self compels me now to own,
Justice awards it to my friend alone.

Oh! friends regretted, scenes for ever dear,
Remembrance hails you with her warmest tear!
Drooping, she bends o'er pensive Fancy's urn,
To trace the hours which never can return;
Yet with the retrospection loves to dwell,
And soothe the sorrows of her last farewell!
Yet greets the triumph of my boyish mind,
As infant laurels round my head were twined,
When Probus' praise repaid my lyric song,
Or placed me higher in the studious throng;
Or when my first harangue received applause,
His sage instruction the primeval cause,
What gratitude to him my soul possest,
While hope of dawning honours fill'd my breast!
For all my humble fame, to him alone
The praise is due, who made that fame my own.
Oh! could I soar above these feeble lays,
These young effusions of my early days,
To him my muse her noblest strain would give:
The song might perish, but the theme might live.
Yet why for him the needless verse essay?
His honour'd name requires no vain display:
By every son of grateful Ida blest,
It finds an echo in each youthful breast;
A fame beyond the glories of the proud,
Or all the plaudits of the venal crowd.

Ida! not yet exhausted is the theme,
Nor closed the progress of my youthful dream.
How many a friend deserves the grateful strain!
What scenes of childhood still unsung remain!
Yet let me hush this echo of the past,
This parting song, the dearest and the last;
And brood in secret o'er those hours of joy,
To me a silent and a sweet employ,
While future hope and fear alike unknown,
I think with pleasure on the past alone;
Yes, to the past alone my heart confine,
And chase the phantom of what once was mine.

Ida! still o'er thy hills in joy preside,
And proudly steer through time's eventful tide;
Still may thy blooming sons thy name revere,
Smile in thy bower, but quit thee with a tear;—
That tear, perhaps, the fondest which will flow,
O'er their last scene of happiness below.
Tell me, ye hoary few, who glide along,
The feeble veterans of some former throng,
Whose friends, like autumn leaves by tempests whirl'd
Are swept for ever from this busy world;
Revolve the fleeting moments of your youth,
While Care as yet withheld her venom'd tooth;
Say if remembrance days like this endears
Beyond the rapture of succeeding years?
Say, can ambition's fever'd dream bestow
So sweet a balm to soothe your hours of woe?
Can treasures, hoarded for some thankless son,
Can royal smiles, or wreaths by slaughter won,

Can stars or ermine, man's maturer toys,
(For glittering baubles are not left to boys)
Recall one scene so much beloved to view,
As those where Youth her garland twined for you?
Ah, no! amidst the gloomy calm of age
You turn with faltering hand life's varied page;
Peruse the record of your days on earth,
Unsullied only where it marks your birth;
Still lingering pause above each chequer'd leaf,
And blot with tears the sable lines of grief;
Where Passion o'er the theme her mantle threw,
Or weeping Virtue sigh'd a faint adieu;
But bless the scroll which fairer words adorn,
Traced by the rosy finger of the morn;
When Friendship bow'd before the shrine of truth,
And Love, without his pinion, smiled on youth.[49]

ANSWER TO A BEAUTIFUL POEM,

ENTITLED "THE COMMON LOT."[50]

MONTGOMERY! true, the common lot
 Of mortals lies in Lethe's wave;
Yet some shall never be forgot—
 Some shall exist beyond the grave.

"Unknown the region of his birth,"
 The hero rolls the tide of war;[51]
Yet not unknown his martial worth,
 Which glares a meteor from afar.

His joy or grief, his weal or woe,
 Perchance may 'scape the page of fame;
Yet nations now unborn will know
 The record of his deathless name.

The patriot's and the poet's frame
 Must share the common tomb of all:
Their glory will not sleep the same;
 That will arise, though empires fall.

The lustre of a beauty's eye
 Assumes the ghastly stare of death;
The fair, the brave, the good must die,
 And sink the yawning grave beneath.

Once more the speaking eye revives,
 Still beaming through the lover's strain;
For Petrarch's Laura still survives:
 She died, but ne'er will die again.

The rolling seasons pass away,
 And Time, untiring, waves his wing;
Whilst honour's laurels ne'er decay,
 But bloom in fresh, unfading spring.

All, all must sleep in grim repose,
 Collected in the silent tomb;
The old and young, with friends and foes,
 Festering alike in shrouds, consume.

The mouldering marble lasts its day,
 Yet falls at length an useless fane;
To ruin's ruthless fangs a prey,
 The wrecks of pillar'd pride remain.

What, though the sculpture be destroy'd,
 From dark oblivion meant to guard;
A bright renown shall be enjoy'd
 By those whose virtues claim reward.

Then do not say the common lot
 Of all lies deep in Lethe's wave;
Some few who ne'er will be forgot
 Shall burst the bondage of the grave.

1806.

LINES

ADDRESSED TO THE REV. J. T. BECHER, ON HIS ADVISING THE AUTHOR TO MIX MORE WITH SOCIETY.

DEAR BECHER, you tell me to mix with mankind;—
 I cannot deny such a precept is wise;
But retirement accords with the tone of my mind:
 I will not descend to a world I despise.

Did the senate or camp my exertions require,
 Ambition might prompt me, at once, to go forth;
When infancy's years of probation expire,
 Perchance I may strive to distinguish my birth.

The fire in the cavern of Etna conceal'd,
 Still mantles unseen in its secret recess;—
At length, in a volume terrific reveal'd,
 No torrent can quench it, no bounds can repress.

Oh! thus, the desire in my bosom for fame
 Bids me live but to hope for posterity's praise.
Could I soar with the phœnix on pinions of flame,
 With him I would wish to expire in the blaze.

For the life of a Fox, of a Chatham the death,
 What censure, what danger, what woe would I brave!
Their lives did not end when they yielded their breath!
 Their glory illumines the gloom of their grave.

Yet why should I mingle in Fashion's full herd?
 Why crouch to her leaders, or cringe to her rules?
Why bend to the proud, or applaud the absurd?
 Why search for delight in the friendship of fools?

I have tasted the sweets and the bitters of love;
 In friendship I early was taught to believe;
My passion the matrons of prudence reprove;
 I have found that a friend may profess, yet deceive.

To me what is wealth?—it may pass in an hour,
 If tyrants prevail, or if Fortune should frown;
To me what is title?—the phantom of power;
 To me what is fashion?—I seek but renown.

Deceit is a stranger as yet to my soul;
 I still am unpractised to varnish the truth:
Then why should I live in a hateful control?
 Why waste upon folly the days of my youth?

1806.

THE DEATH OF CALMAR AND ORLA.

AN IMITATION OF MACPHERSON'S OSSIAN.[52]

DEAR are the days of youth! Age dwells on their remembrance through the mist of time. In the twilight he recalls the sunny hours of morn. He lifts his spear with trembling hand. "Not thus feebly did I raise the steel before my fathers!" Past is the race of heroes! But their fame rises on the harp; their souls ride on the wings of the wind; they hear the sound through the sighs of the storm, and rejoice in their hall of clouds! Such is Calmar. The gray stone marks his narrow house. He looks down from eddying tempests: he rolls his form in the whirlwind, and hovers on the blast of the mountain.

In Morven dwelt the chief; a beam of war to Fingal. His steps in the field were marked in blood. Lochlin's sons had fled before his angry spear; but mild was the eye of Calmar; soft was the flow of his yellow locks, they streamed like the meteor of the night. No maid was the sigh of his soul: his thoughts were given to friendship,—to dark-haired Orla, destroyer of heroes! Equal were their swords in battle; but fierce was the pride of Orla:—gentle alone to Calmar. Together they dwelt in the cave of Oithona.

From Lochlin, Swaran bounded o'er the blue waves. Erin's sons fell beneath his might. Fingal roused his chiefs to combat. Their ships cover the ocean. Their hosts throng on the green hills. They come to the aid of Erin.

Night rose in clouds. Darkness veils the armies: but the blazing oaks gleam through the valley. The sons of Lochlin slept: their dreams were of blood. They lift the spear in thought, and Fingal flies. Not so the host of Morven. To watch was the post of Orla. Calmar stood by his side. Their spears were in their hands. Fingal called his chiefs: they stood around. The king was in the midst. Gray were his locks, but strong was the arm of the king. Age withered not his powers. "Sons of Morven," said the hero, "to-morrow we meet the foe. But where is Cuthullin, the shield of Erin? He rests in the halls of Tura; he knows not of our coming. Who will speed through Lochlin to the hero, and call the chief to arms? The path is by the swords of foes; but many are my heroes. They are thunderbolts of war. Speak, ye chiefs! Who will arise?"

"Son of Trenmor! mine be the deed," said dark-haired Orla, "and mine alone. What is death to me? I love the sleep of the mighty, but little is the danger. The sons of Lochlin dream. I will seek car-borne Cuthullin. If I fall, raise the song of bards; and lay me by the stream of Lubar."—"And shalt thou fall alone?" said fair-haired Calmar. "Wilt thou leave thy friend afar? Chief of Oithona! not feeble is my arm in fight. Could I see thee die, and not lift the spear? No, Orla! ours has been the chase of the roebuck, and the feast of shells; ours be the path of danger: ours has been the cave of Oithona; ours be the narrow dwelling on the banks of Lubar." "Calmar," said the chief of Oithona, "why should thy yellow locks be darkened in the dust of Erin? Let me fall alone. My father dwells in his hall of air: he will rejoice in his boy; but the blue-eyed Mora spreads the feast for her son in Morven. She listens to the steps of the hunter on the heath, and thinks it is the tread of Calmar. Let him not say, 'Calmar has fallen by the steel of Lochlin: he died with gloomy Orla, the chief of the dark brow.' Why should tears dim the azure eye of Mora? Why should her voice curse Orla, the destroyer of Calmar? Live, Calmar! Live to raise my stone of moss; live to revenge me in the blood of Lochlin. Join the song of bards above my grave. Sweet will be the song of death to Orla, from the voice of Calmar. My ghost shall smile on the notes of praise." "Orla," said the son of Mora, "could I raise the song of death to my friend? Could I give his fame to the winds? No, my heart would speak in sighs: faint and broken are the sounds of sorrow. Orla! our souls shall hear the song together. One cloud shall be ours on high: the bards will mingle the names of Orla and Calmar."

They quit the circle of the chiefs. Their steps are to the host of Lochlin. The dying blaze of oak dim twinkles through the night. The northern star points the path to Tura. Swaran, the king, rests on his lonely hill. Here the troops are mixed: they frown in sleep! their shields beneath their heads. Their swords gleam at distance in heaps. The fires are faint; their embers fail in smoke. All is hush'd; but the gale sighs on the rocks above. Lightly wheel the heroes through the slumbering band. Half the journey is past, when Mathon, resting on his shield, meets the eye of Orla. It rolls in flame, and glistens through the shade. His spear is raised on high. "Why dost thou bend thy brow, chief of Oithona?" said fair-haired Calmar: "we are in the midst of foes. Is this a time for delay?" "It is a time for vengeance," said Orla of the gloomy brow. "Mathon of Lochlin sleeps: see'st thou his spear? Its point is dim with the gore of my father. The blood of Mathon shall reek on mine; but shall I slay him sleeping, son of Mora? No! he shall feel his wound: my fame shall not soar on the blood of slumber. Rise, Mathon, rise! The son of Conna calls; thy life is his; rise to combat." Mathon starts

from sleep; but did he rise alone? No: the gathering chiefs bound on the plain. "Fly! Calmar, fly!" said dark-haired Orla. "Mathon is mine: I shall die in joy: but Lochlin crowds around. Fly through the shade of night." Orla turns. The helm of Mathon is cleft: his shield falls from his arm: he shudders in his blood. He rolls by the side of the blazing oak. Strumon sees him fall: his wrath rises: his weapon glitters on the head of Orla: but a spear pierced his eye. His brain gushes through the wound, and foams on the spear of Calmar. As roll the waves of the Ocean on two mighty barks of the north, so pour the men of Lochlin on the chiefs. As, breaking the surge in foam, proudly steer the barks of the north, so rise the chiefs of Morven on the scattered crests of Lochlin. The din of arms came to the ear of Fingal. He strikes his shield; his sons throng around; the people pour along the heath. Ryno bounds in joy. Ossian stalks in his arms. Oscar shakes the spear. The eagle wing of Fillan floats on the wind. Dreadful is the clang of death! many are the widows of Lochlin! Morven prevails in its strength.

Morn glimmers on the hills: no living foe is seen; but the sleepers are many; grim they lie on Erin. The breeze of ocean lifts their locks; yet they do not awake. The hawks scream above their prey.

Whose yellow locks wave o'er the breast of a chief? Bright as the gold of the stranger, they mingle with the dark hair of his friend. 'Tis Calmar: he lies on the bosom of Orla. Theirs is one stream of blood. Fierce is the look of the gloomy Orla. He breathes not; but his eye is still a flame. It glares in death unclosed. His hand is grasped in Calmar's; but Calmar lives! he lives, though low. "Rise," said the king, "rise, son of Mora: 'tis mine to heal the wounds of heroes. Calmar may yet bound on the hills of Morven."

"Never more shall Calmar chase the deer of Morven with Orla," said the hero. "What were the chase to me alone? Who should share the spoils of battle with Calmar? Orla is at rest! Rough was thy soul, Orla! yet soft to me as the dew of morn. It glared on others in lightning: to me a silver beam of night. Bear my sword to blue-eyed Mora; let it hang in my empty hall. It is not pure from blood: but it could not save Orla. Lay me with my friend. Raise the song when I am dark!"

They are laid by the stream of Lubar. Four gray stones mark the dwelling of Orla and Calmar. When Swaran was bound, our sails rose on the blue waves. The winds gave our barks to Morven:—the bards raised the song.

"What form rises on the roar of clouds? Whose dark ghost gleams on the red streams of tempests? His voice rolls on the thunder. 'T is Orla, the brown chief of Oithona. He was unmatched in war. Peace to thy soul, Orla; thy fame will not perish. Nor thine, Calmar! Lovely wast thou, son of blue-eyed Mora; but not harmless was thy sword. It hangs in thy cave. The ghosts of Lochlin shriek around its steel. Hear thy praise, Calmar! It dwells on the voice of the mighty. Thy name shakes on the echoes of Morven. Then raise thy fair locks, son of Mora. Spread them on the arch of the rainbow; and smile through the tears of the storm."[3]

TO EDWARD NOEL LONG, Esq.

"Nil ego contulerim jocundo sanus amico."—HORACE.

Dear Long, in this sequester'd scene,
 While all around in slumber lie,
The joyous days which ours have been
 Come rolling fresh on Fancy's eye;
Thus if amidst the gathering storm,
While clouds the darken'd noon deform,
Yon heaven assumes a varied glow,
I hail the sky's celestial bow,
Which spreads the sign of future peace,
And bids the war of tempests cease.
Ah! though the present brings but pain,
I think those days may come again;
Or if, in melancholy mood,
Some lurking envious fear intrude,
To check my bosom's fondest thought,
 And interrupt the golden dream,
I crush the fiend with malice fraught,
 And still indulge my wonted theme.
Although we ne'er again can trace,
 In Granta's vale, the pedant's lore;
Nor through the groves of Ida chase
 Our raptured visions as before,
Though Youth has flown on rosy pinion,
And manhood claims his stern dominion—
Age will not every hope destroy,
But yield some hours of sober joy.

Yes, I will hope that Time's broad wing
Will shed around some dews of spring:
But if his scythe must sweep the flowers
Which bloom among the fairy bowers,
Where smiling Youth delights to dwell,
And hearts with early rapture swell;
If frowning Age, with cold control,
Confines the current of the soul,
Congeals the tear of Pity's eye,
Or checks the sympathetic sigh,
Or hears unmoved misfortune's groan,
And bids me feel for self alone;
Oh may my bosom never learn
 To soothe its wonted heedless flow;
Still, still despise the censor stern,
 But ne'er forget another's woe.

Yes, as you knew me in the days
O'er which Remembrance yet delays,
Still may I rove, untutor'd, wild,
And even in age at heart a child.

Though now on airy visions borne,
 To you my soul is still the same.
Oft has it been my fate to mourn,
 And all my former joys are tame.
But, hence! ye hours of sable hue!
 Your frowns are gone, my sorrows o'er:
By every bliss my childhood knew,
 I'll think upon your shade no more.
Thus, when the whirlwind's rage is past,
 And caves their sullen roar enclose,
We heed no more the wintry blast,
 When lull'd by zephyr to repose.

Full often has my infant Muse
 Attuned to love her languid lyre;
But now without a theme to choose,
 The strains in stolen sighs expire.
My youthful nymphs, alas! are flown:
 E—— is a wife, and C—— a mother,
And Carolina sighs alone,
 And Mary's given to another;
And Cora's eye, which roll'd on me,
 Can now no more my love recall:
In truth, dear Long, 't was time to flee;
 For Cora's eye will shine on all.
And though the sun, with genial rays,
His beam alike to all displays,
And every lady's eye 's a *sun*,
These last should be confined to one.
The soul's meridian do n't become her,
Whose sun displays a general *summer!*
Thus faint is every former flame,
And passion's self is now a name.
As, when the ebbing flames are low,
 The aid which once improved their light,
And bade them burn with fiercer glow,
 Now quenches all their sparks in night;
Thus has it been with passion's fires,
 As many a boy and girl remembers,
While all the force of love expires,
 Extinguish'd with the dying embers.

But now, dear Long, 't is midnight's noon,
And clouds obscure the watery moon,
Whose beauties I shall not rehearse,
Described in every stripling's verse;
For why should I the path go o'er,
Which every bard has trod before?
Yet ere yon silver lamp of night
 Has thrice perform'd her stated round,
Has thrice retraced her path of light,
 And chased away the gloom profound,
I trust that we, my gentle friend,
Shall see her rolling orbit wend
Above the dear-loved peaceful seat
Which once contain'd our youth's retreat;
And then with those our childhood knew,
We'll mingle in the festive crew;
While many a tale of former day
Shall wing the laughing hours away;
And all the flow of soul shall pour
The sacred intellectual shower,
Nor cease till Luna's waning horn
Scarce glimmers through the mist of morn.

TO A LADY.

Oh! had my fate been join'd with thine,
 As once this pledge appear'd a token,
These follies had not then been mine,
 For then my peace had not been broken.

To thee these early faults I owe,
 To thee, the wise and old reproving:
They know my sins, but do not know
 'T was thine to break the bonds of loving.

For once my soul, like thine, was pure,
 And all its rising fires could smother;
But now thy vows no more endure,
 Bestow'd by thee upon another.

Perhaps his peace I could destroy,
 And spoil the blisses that await him;
Yet let my rival smile in joy,
 For thy dear sake I cannot hate him.

Ah! since thy angel form is gone,
 My heart no more can rest with any;
But what it sought in thee alone,
 Attempts, alas! to find in many.

Then fare thee well, deceitful maid!
 'T were vain and fruitless to regret thee;
Nor Hope, nor Memory yield their aid,
 But Pride may teach me to forget thee.

Yet all this giddy waste of years,
 This tiresome round of palling pleasures;
These varied loves, these matron's fears,
 These thoughtless strains to passion's measures—

If thou wert mine, had all been hush'd:—
 This cheek now pale from early riot,
With passion's hectic ne'er had flush'd,
 But bloom'd in calm domestic quiet.

Yes, once the rural scene was sweet,
 For Nature seem'd to smile before thee;
And once my breast abhorr'd deceit,—
 For then it beat but to adore thee.

But now I seek for other joys:
 To think would drive my soul to madness;
In thoughtless throngs and empty noise,
 I conquer half my bosom's sadness.

Yet, even in these a thought will steal,
In spite of every vain endeavour,—
And fiends might pity what I feel,—
To know that thou art lost for ever.

I WOULD I WERE A CARELESS CHILD.

I WOULD I were a careless child,
Still dwelling in my Highland cave,
Or roaming through the dusky wild,
Or bounding o'er the dark blue wave;
The cumbrous pomp of Saxon pride[54]
Accords not with the freeborn soul,
Which loves the mountain's craggy side,
And seeks the rocks where billows roll.

Fortune! take back these cultured lands,
Take back this name of splendid sound!
I hate the touch of servile hands,
I hate the slaves that cringe around.
Place me along the rocks I love,
Which sound to Ocean's wildest roar·
I ask but this—again to rove
Through scenes my youth hath known before.

Few are my years, and yet I feel
The world was ne'er design'd for me:
Ah! why do dark'ning shades conceal
The hour when man must cease to be?
Once I beheld a splendid dream,
A visionary scene of bliss:
Truth!—wherefore did thy hated beam
Awake me to a world like this?

I loved—but those I loved are gone;
Had friends—my early friends are fled:
How cheerless feels the heart alone
When all its former hopes are dead!
Though gay companions o'er the bowl
Dispel awhile the sense of ill;
Though pleasure stirs the maddening soul,
The heart—the heart—is lonely still.

How dull! to hear the voice of those
Whom rank or chance, whom wealth or power,
Have made, though neither friends nor foes,
Associates of the festive hour.
Give me again a faithful few,
In years and feelings still the same,
And I will fly the midnight crew,
Where boist'rous joy is but a name.

And woman, lovely woman! thou,
My hope, my comforter, my all!
How cold must be my bosom now,
When e'en thy smiles begin to pall!

Without a sigh would I resign
This busy scene of splendid woe,
To make that calm contentment mine,
Which virtue knows, or seems to know.

Fain would I fly the haunts of men—
I seek to shun, not hate mankind;
My breast requires the sullen glen,
Whose gloom may suit a darken'd mind.
Oh! that to me the wings were given
Which bears the turtle to her nest!
Then would I cleave the vault of heaven,
To flee away, and be at rest.[55]

WHEN I ROVED A YOUNG HIGHLANDER.

WHEN I roved a young Highlander o'er the dark heath,
And climb'd thy steep summit, oh Morven of snow![56]
To gaze on the torrent that thunder'd beneath,
Or the mist of the tempest that gather'd below,[57]
Untutor'd by science, a stranger to fear,
And rude as the rocks where my infancy grew,
No feeling, save one, to my bosom was dear;
Need I say, my sweet Mary, 'twas center'd in you?

Yet it could not be love, for I knew not the name,—
What passion can dwell in the heart of a child?
But still I perceive an emotion the same
As I felt, when a boy, on the crag-cover'd wild:
One image alone on my bosom impress'd,
I loved my bleak regions, nor panted for new;
And few were my wants, for my wishes were bless'd,
And pure were my thoughts, for my soul was with you.

I arose with the dawn; with my dog as my guide,
From mountain to mountain I bounded along;
I breasted the billows of Dee's rushing tide,[58]
And heard at a distance the Highlander's song:
At eve, on my heath-cover'd couch of repose,
No dreams, save of Mary, were spread to my view;
And warm to the skies my devotions arose,
For the first of my prayers was a blessing on you.

I left my bleak home, and my visions are gone;
The mountains are vanish'd, my youth is no more;
As the last of my race, I must wither alone,
And delight but in days I have witness'd before:
Ah! splendour has raised, but embitter'd, my lot;
More dear were the scenes which my infancy knew;
Though my hopes may have fail'd, yet they are not forgot;
Though cold is my heart, still it lingers with you.

When I see some dark hill point its crest to the sky,
I think of the rocks that o'ershadow Colbleen;[59]
When I see the soft blue of a love-speaking eye,
I think of those eyes that endear'd the rude scene;

When, haply, some light-waving locks I behold,
That faintly resemble my Mary's in hue,
I think on the long flowing ringlets of gold,
The locks that were sacred to beauty, and you.

Yet the day may arrive when the mountains once more
Shall rise to my sight in their mantles of snow:
But while these soar above me, unchanged as before,
Will Mary be there to receive me!—ah, no!
Adieu, then, ye hills, where my childhood was bred!
Thou sweet flowing Dee, to thy waters adieu!
No home in the forest shall shelter my head,—
Ah! Mary, what home could be mine but with you?

TO GEORGE, EARL DELAWARR.

Oh! yes, I will own we were dear to each other;
The friendships of childhood, though fleeting, are true;
The love which you felt was the love of a brother,
Nor less the affection I cherish'd for you.

But Friendship can vary her gentle dominion;
The attachment of years in a moment expires;
Like Love, too, she moves on a swift-waving pinion,
But glows not, like Love, with unquenchable fires.

Full oft have we wander'd through Ida together,
And blest were the scenes of our youth, I allow:
In the spring of our life, how serene is the weather!
But winter's rude tempests are gathering now.

No more with affection shall memory blending,
The wonted delights of our childhood retrace:
When pride steels the bosom, the heart is unbending,
And what would be justice appears a disgrace.

However, dear George, for I still must esteem you—
The few whom I love I can never upbraid—
The chance which has lost may in future redeem you,
Repentance will cancel the vow you have made.

I will not complain, and though chill'd is affection,
With me no corroding resentment shall live:
My bosom is calm'd by the simple reflection,
That both may be wrong, and that both should forgive.

You knew that my soul, that my heart, my existence,
If danger demanded, were wholly your own;
You knew me unalter'd by years or by distance,
Devoted to love and to friendship alone.

You knew,—but away with the vain retrospection!
The bond of affection no longer endures;
Too late you may droop o'er the fond recollection,
And sigh for the friend who was formerly yours.

For the present, we part,—I will hope not for ever;
For time and regret will restore you at last:
To forget our dissension we both should endeavour,
I ask no atonement, but days like the past.

TO THE EARL OF CLARE.

"Tu semper amoris
Sis memor et cari comitis ne abscedat imago."
Val. Flag

Friend of my youth! when young we roved,
Like striplings, mutually beloved,
With friendship's purest glow,
The bliss which wing'd those rosy hours
Was such as pleasure seldom showers
On mortals here below.

The recollection seems alone
Dearer than all the joys I've known,
When distant far from you:
Though pain, 'tis still a pleasing pain,
To trace those days and hours again,
And sigh again, adieu!

My pensive memory lingers o'er
Those scenes to be enjoy'd no more,
Those scenes regretted ever;
The measure of our youth is full,
Life's evening dream is dark and dull,
And we may meet—ah! never!

As when one parent spring supplies
Two streams which from one fountain rise,
Together join'd in vain;
How soon, diverging from their source,
Each, murmuring, seeks another course,
Till mingled in the main!

Our vital streams of weal or woe,
Though near, alas! distinctly flow,
 Nor mingle as before:
Now swift or slow, now black or clear,
Till death's unfathom'd gulf appear,
 And both shall quit the shore.

Our souls, my friend! which once supplied
One wish, nor breathed a thought beside,
 Now flow in different channels:
Disdaining humbler rural sports,
'Tis yours to mix in polish'd courts,
 And shine in fashion's annals;

'Tis mine to waste on love my time,
Or vent my reveries in rhyme,
 Without the aid of reason;
For sense and reason (critics know it)
Have quitted every amorous poet,
 Nor left a thought to seize on.

Poor Little! sweet, melodious bard!
Of late esteem'd it monstrous hard,
 That he, who sang before all,—
He who the lore of love expanded,—
By dire reviewers should be branded,
 As void of wit and moral.[60]

And yet, while Beauty's praise is thine,
Harmonious favourite of the Nine!
 Repine not at thy lot.
Thy soothing lays may still be read,
When Persecution's arm is dead,
 And critics are forgot.

Still I must yield those worthies merit,
Who chasten, with unsparing spirit,
 Bad rhymes, and those who write them:
And though myself may be the next
By critic sarcasm to be vext,
 I really will not fight them.[61]

Perhaps they would do quite as well
To break the rudely sounding shell
 Of such a young beginner.
He who offends at pert nineteen,
Ere thirty may become, I ween,
 A very harden'd sinner.

Now, Clare, I must return to you;
And, sure, apologies are due:
 Accept, then, my concession
In truth, dear Clare, in fancy's flight
I soar along from left to right!
 My muse admires digression.

I think I said 'twould be your fate
To add one star to royal state;—
 May regal smiles attend you!
And should a noble monarch reign,
You will not seek his smiles in vain,
 If worth can recommend you.

Yet since in danger courts abound,
Where specious rivals glitter round,
 From snares may saints preserve you;
And grant your love or friendship ne'er
From any claim a kindred care,
 But those who best deserve you!

Not for a moment may you stray
From truth's secure, unerring way:
 May no delights decoy!
O'er roses may your footsteps move
Your smiles be ever smiles of love,
 Your tears be tears of joy!

Oh! if you wish that happiness
Your coming days and years may bless,
 And virtues crown your brow;
Be still as you were wont to be,
Spotless as you 've been known to me,—
 Be still as you are now.

And though some trifling share of praise,
To cheer my last declining days,
 To me were doubly dear;
Whilst blessing your beloved name,
I'd waive at once a *poet's* fame,
 To prove a *prophet* here.

LINES WRITTEN BENEATH AN ELM IN THE CHURCHYARD OF HARROW.

Spot of my youth! whose hoary branches sigh,
Swept by the breeze that fans thy cloudless sky;
Where now alone I muse, who oft have trod,
With those I loved, the soft and verdant sod;
With those who, scatter'd far, perchance deplore.
Like me, the happy scenes they knew before:
Oh! as I trace again thy winding hill,
Mine eyes admire, my heart adores thee still,
Thou drooping elm! beneath whose boughs I lay,
And frequent mused the twilight hours away;
Where, as they once were wont, my limbs recline,
But, ah! without the thoughts which then were mine:
How do thy branches, moaning to the blast,
Invite the bosom to recall the past,
And seem to whisper, as they gently swell,
"Take, while thou canst, a lingering, last farewell!"

When fate shall chill, at length, this fever'd breast,
And calm its cares and passions into rest,
Oft have I thought, 'twould soothe my dying hour,—
If aught may soothe when life resigns her power,—
To know some humbler grave, some narrow cell,
Would hide my bosom where it loved to dwell.

With this fond dream, methinks, 't were sweet to
die—
And here it linger'd, here my heart might lie;
Here might I sleep where all my hopes arose;
Scene of my youth, and couch of my repose;
For ever stretch'd beneath this mantling shade,
Press'd by the turf where once my childhood play'd,
Wrapt by the soil that veils the spot I loved,
Mix'd with the earth o'er which my footsteps moved:
Blest by the tongues that charm'd my youthful ear,
Mourn'd by the few my soul acknowledged here;
Deplored by those in early days allied,
And unremember'd by the world beside.

September 2, 1807.

NOTES TO HOURS OF IDLENESS.

NOTE 1, page 449.

The Earl of Carlisle, whose works have long received the meed of public applause, to which, by their intrinsic worth, they were well entitled.

NOTE 2, page 450.

The author claims the indulgence of the reader more for this piece, than, perhaps, any other in the collection; but as it was written at an earlier period than the rest (being

composed at the age of fourteen), and his first essay, he preferred submitting it to the indulgence of his friends in its present state, to making either addition or alteration.

NOTE 3, page 451.

On Marston, with Rupert, 'gainst traitors contending.

The battle of Marston Moor, where the adherents of Charles I. were defeated. Rupert, son of the Elector Palatine, and nephew to Charles I. He afterwards commanded the fleet in the reign of Charles II.

NOTE 4, page 452.

By Death's unequal hand alike controll'd.

The hand of Death is said to be unjust or unequal, as Virgil was considerably older than Tibullus at his decease.

NOTE 5, page 452.

Adrian's address to his soul when dying.

Animula ! vagula, blandula,
Hospes comesque corporis,
Quæ nunc abibis in loca—
Pallidula, rigida, nudula,
Nec, ut soles, dabis jocos ?

NOTE 6, page 458.

In looking over my papers to select a few additional poems for this second edition, I found the above lines, which I had totally forgotten, composed in the summer of 1805, a short time previous to my departure from Harrow. They were addressed to a young schoolfellow of high rank, who had been my frequent companion in some rambles through the neighbouring country : however, he never saw the lines, and most probably never will. As, on a re-perusal, I found them not worse than some other pieces in the collection, I have now published them, for the first time, after a slight revision.

NOTE 7, page 458.

Bade thee obey, and gave me to command.

At every public school the junior boys are completely subservient to the upper forms till they attain a seat in the higher classes. From this state of probation, very properly, no rank is exempt, but after a certain period, they command in turn those who succeed.

NOTE 8, page 458.

Though passive tutors, fearful to dispraise.

Allow me to disclaim any personal allusions, even the most distant : I merely mention generally what is too often the weakness of preceptors.

NOTE 9, page 459.

Oh, could Le Sage's demon's gift.

The Diable Boiteux of Le Sage, where Asmodeus, the demon, places Don Cleofas on an elevated situation, and unroofs the houses for inspection.

NOTE 10, page 459.

Who reads false quantities in Seale.

Seale's publication on Greek metres displays considerable talent and ingenuity, but, as might be expected in so difficult a work, is not remarkable for accuracy.

NOTE 11, page 459.

In barbarous Latin doom'd to wrangle.

The Latin of the schools is of the *canine species* and not very intelligible.

NOTE 12, page 459.

The square of the hypothenuse.

The discovery of Pythagoras, that the square of the hypothenuse is equal to the squares of the other two sides of a right-angled triangle.

NOTE 13, page 461.

I fancied that Mossop himself was outshone.

Mossop, a contemporary of Garrick, famous for his performance of Zanga.

NOTE 14, page 461.

Would twinkle dimly through their sphere.

"Two of the fairest stars in all the heaven,
Having some business, do entreat her eyes,
To twinkle in their spheres till they return."—SHAKS.

NOTE 15, page 461.

"Woman, thy vows are traced in sand."

This line is almost a literal translation from a Spanish proverb.

NOTE 16, page 462.

And hurtling o'er thy lovely head.

This word is used by Gray, in his poem to the Fatal Sisters.

"Iron sleet of arrowy shower
Hurtles through the darken'd air."

NOTE 17, page 463.

In law an infant, and in years a boy.

In law every person is an infant who has not attained the age of twenty-one.

NOTE 18, page 464.

To form the place of assignation.

In the above little piece, the author has been accused by some *candid readers* of introducing the name of a lady from whom he was some hundred miles distant at the time this was written ; and poor Juliet, who has slept so long in "the tomb of all the Capulets," has been converted, with a trifling alteration of her name, into an English damsel, walking in a garden of their own creation, during the month of *December*, in a village where the author never passed a winter. Such has been the candour of some ingenious critics. We would advise these *liberal* commentators on taste and arbiters of decorum to read *Shakspeare.*

NOTE 19, page 464.

But curse my fate for ever after.

Having heard that a very severe and indelicate censure has been passed on the above poem, I beg leave to reply in a quotation from an admired work, "Carr's Stranger in France."—"As we were contemplating a painting on a large scale, in which, among other figures, is the uncovered whole length of a warrior, a prudish-looking lady, who seemed to have touched the age of desperation, after having attentively surveyed it through her glass, observed to her party, that there was a great deal of indecorum in that picture. Madame S. shrewdly whispered in my ear, that the indecorum was in the remark."

NOTE 20, page 464.

The catastrophe of this tale was suggested by the story of "Jeronyme and Lorenzo," in the first volume of Schiller's "Armenian, or the Ghost-Seer." It also bears some resemblance to a scene in the third act of "Macbeth."

Note 21, page 467.

For him thy beltane yet may burn.

Beltane Tree, a Highland festival on the first of May, held near fires lighted for the occasion.

Note 22, page 471.

Creusa's style but wanting to the dame.

The mother of Iulus, lost on the night when Troy was taken.

Note 23, page 473.

Ah! hapless dame! no sire bewails.

Medea, who accompanied Jason to Corinth, was deserted by him for the daughter of Creon, king of that city. The chorus from which this is taken here addresses Medea; though a considerable liberty is taken with the original, by expanding the idea, as also in some other parts of the translation.

Note 24, page 473.

Who ne'er unlocks with silver key.

The original means literally, "disclosing the bright key of the mind."

Note 25, page 473.

Magnus his ample front sublime uprears.

No reflection is here intended against the person mentioned under the name of Magnus. He is merely represented as performing an unavoidable function of his office. Indeed, such an attempt could only recoil upon myself; as that gentleman is now as much distinguished by his eloquence, and the dignified propriety with which he fills his situation, as he was in his younger days for wit and conviviality.

Note 26, page 474.

Th' Athenian's glowing style, or Tully's fire.

Demosthenes.

Note 27, page 474.

Yet prizing Bentley's, Brunck's, or Porson's note.

Porson, Greek professor of Trinity College, Cambridge; a man whose powers of mind and writings may, perhaps, justify their preference.

Note 28, page 474.

Whether 'tis Pitt or Petty rules the hour.

Since this was written, Lord Henry Petty has lost his place, and subsequently (I had almost said consequently) the honour of representing the University. A fact so glaring requires no comment.

Note 29, page 476.

Sweet scene of my youth! seat of Friendship and Truth.

Harrow.

Note 30, page 477.

Lachin y Gair, or, as it is pronounced in the Erse, *Loch na Garr*, towers proudly pre-eminent in the Northern Highlands near Invercauld. One of our modern tourists mentions it as the highest mountain, perhaps, in Great Britain. Be this as it may, it is certainly one of the most sublime and picturesque amongst our "Caledonian Alps." Its appearance is of a dusky hue, but the summit is the seat of eternal snows. Near Lachin y Gair I spent some of the early part of my life, the recollection of which has given birth to these stanzas.

Note 31, page 477.

My cap was the bonnet, my cloak was the plaid.

This word is erroneously pronounced *plad*: the proper pronunciation (according to the Scotch) is shown by the orthography.

Note 32, page 478.

Ill-starr'd, though brave, did no visions foreboding.

I allude here to my maternal ancestors, "the *Gordons*," many of whom fought for the unfortunate Prince Charles, better known by the name of the Pretender. This branch was nearly allied by blood, as well as attachment, to the Stuarts. George, the second Earl of Huntley, married the Princess Annabella Stuart, daughter of James the First of Scotland. By her he left four sons: the third, Sir William Gordon, I have the honour to claim as one of my progenitors.

Note 33, page 478.

Ah! were you destined to die at Culloden?

Whether any perished in the battle of Culloden, I am not certain; but, as many fell in the insurrection, I have used the name of the principal action, "*pars pro toto.*"

Note 34, page 478.

You rest with your clan in the caves of Braemar.

A tract of the Highlands so called. There is also a Castle of Braemar.

Note 35, page 479.

A Pylades in every friend.

It is hardly necessary to add, that Pylades was the companion of Orestes, and a partner in one of those friendships which, with those of Achilles and Patroclus, Nisus and Euryalus, Damon and Pythias, have been handed down to posterity as remarkable instances of attachments, which in all probability never existed beyond the imagination of the poet, or the page of an historian, or modern novelist.

Note 36, page 480.

As one poem on this subject is already printed, the author had, originally, no intention of inserting this piece. It is now added at the particular request of some friends.

Note 37, page 480.

Religion's shrine! repentant Henry's pride.

Henry II. founded Newstead soon after the murder of Thomas à Becket.

Note 38, page 480.

No mail-clad serfs, obedient to their lord.

This word is used by Walter Scott, in his poem, "The Wild Huntsman;" synonymous with vassal.

Note 39, page 480.

In grim array the crimson cross demand.

The red cross was the badge of the crusaders.

Note 40, page 480.

Soon as the gloaming spreads her waning shade.

As "gloaming," the Scottish word for twilight, is far more poetical, and has been recommended by many eminent literary men, particularly by Dr. Moore in his Letters to Burns, I have ventured to use it on account of its harmony.

Note 41, page 480.

Or matin orisons to Mary paid.

The priory was dedicated to the Virgin.

Note 42, page 480.

Another Henry the kind gift recalls.

At the dissolution of the monasteries, Henry VIII. bestowed Newstead Abbey on Sir John Byron.

NOTE 43, page 480.

Trembling, she snatch'd him from th' unequal strife.

Lord Byron, and his brother Sir William, held high commands in the royal army. The former was general in chief in Ireland, lieutenant of the Tower, and governor to James, Duke of York, afterwards the unhappy James II.; the latter had a principal share in many actions.

NOTE 44, page 480.

To lead the band where godlike Falkland fell.

Lucius Cary, Lord Viscount Falkland, the most accomplished man of his age, was killed at the battle of Newbury, charging in the ranks of Lord Byron's regiment of cavalry.

NOTE 45, page 481.

Loathing the offering of so dark a death.

This is an historical fact. A violent tempest occurred immediately subsequent to the death or interment of Cromwell, which occasioned many disputes between his partisans and the cavaliers: both interpreted the circumstance into divine interposition; but whether as approbation or condemnation, we leave for the casuists of that age to decide. I have made such use of the occurrence as suited the subject of my poem.

NOTE 46, page 481.

The legal ruler now resumes the helm.

Charles II.

NOTE 47, page 483.

Probus, the pride of science, and the boast.

Dr. Drury. This most able and excellent man retired from his situation in March, 1805, after having resided thirty-five years at Harrow; the last twenty as head-master; an office he held with equal honour to himself and advantage to the very extensive school over which he presided. Panegyric would here be superfluous: it would be useless to enumerate qualifications which were never doubted. A considerable contest took place between three rival candidates for his vacant chair: of this I can only say,

Si mea cum vestris valuissent vota, Pelasgi!
Non foret ambiguus tanti certaminis hæres.

NOTE 48, page 485.

As speakers each supports an equal name.

This alludes to the public speeches delivered at the school where the author was educated.

NOTE 49, page 486.

And Love, without his pinion, smiled on youth.

"L'Amitié est l'Amour sans ailes," is a French proverb.

NOTE 50, page 486.

Written by James Montgomery, author of "The Wanderer in Switzerland," &c.

NOTE 51, page 486.

The hero rolls the tide of war.

No particular hero is here alluded to. The exploits of Bayard, Nemours, Edward the Black Prince, and in more modern times the fame of Marlborough, Frederick the Great, Count Saxe, Charles of Sweden, &c., are familiar to every historical reader, but the exact places of their birth are known to a very small proportion of their admirers.

NOTE, 52, page 487.

It may be necessary to observe, that the story, though considerably varied in the catastrophe, is taken from "Nisus and Euryalus," of which episode a translation is already given in the present volume.

NOTE 53, page 488.

I fear Laing's late edition has completely overthrown every hope that Macpherson's Ossian might prove the translation of a series of poems complete in themselves; but, while the imposture is discovered, the merit of the work remains undisputed, though not without faults—particularly, in some parts, turgid and bombastic diction. The present humble imitation will be pardoned by the admirers of the original as an attempt, however inferior, which evinces an attachment to their favourite author.

NOTE 54, page 490.

The cumbrous pomp of Saxon pride.

Sassenach, or Saxon, a Gaelic word, signifying either Lowland or English.

NOTE 55, page 490.

To flee away, and be at rest.

"And I said, Oh! that I had wings like a dove; for then would I fly away, and be at rest."—*Psalm* lv. 6 This verse also constitutes a part of the most beautiful anthem in our language.

NOTE 56, page 490.

And climb'd thy steep summit, oh Morven of snow.

Morven, a lofty mountain in Aberdeenshire. "Gormal of snow," is an expression frequently to be found in Ossian.

NOTE 57, page 490.

Or the mist of the tempest that gather'd below.

This will not appear extraordinary to those who have been accustomed to the mountains. It is by no means uncommon, on attaining the top of Ben-e-vis, Ben-y-Bourd, &c., to perceive, between the summit and the valley, clouds pouring down rain, and occasionally accompanied by lightning, while the spectator literally looks down upon the storm, perfectly secure from its effects.

NOTE 58, page 490.

I breasted the billows of Dee's rushing tide.

"Breasting the lofty surge."—SHAKSPEARE. The Dee is a beautiful river, which rises near Mar Lodge, and falls into the sea at New Aberdeen.

NOTE 59, page 490.

I think of the rocks that o'ershadow Colbleen.

Colbleen is a mountain near the verge of the Highlands, not far from the ruins of Dee Castle.

NOTE 60, page 492.

As void of wit and moral.

These stanzas were written soon after the appearance of a severe critique, in a northern review, on a new publication of the British Anacreon.

NOTE 61, page 492.

I really will not fight them.

A bard (horresco referens) defied his reviewer to mortal combat. If this example becomes prevalent, our periodical censors must be dipped in the river Styx: for what else can secure them from the numerous host of their enraged assailants?

ENGLISH BARDS AND SCOTCH REVIEWERS:

A SATIRE.

> "I had rather be a kitten, and cry mew!
> Than one of these same metre ballad-mongers."—SHAKSPEARE.

> "Such shameless bards we have; and yet 't is true,
> There are as mad, abandon'd critics too."—POPE.

PREFACE TO THE THIRD EDITION.

ALL my friends, learned and unlearned, have urged me not to publish this Satire with my name. If I were to be "turn'd from the career of my humour by quibbles quick, and paper bullets of the brain," I should have complied with their counsel; but I am not to be terrified by abuse, or bullied by reviewers, with or without arms. I can safely say that I have attacked none *personally* who did not commence on the offensive. An author's works are public property: he who purchases may judge, and publish his opinion if he pleases; and the authors I have endeavoured to commemorate may do by me as I have done by them: I dare say they will succeed better in condemning my scribblings, than in mending their own. But my object is not to prove that I can write well, but, *if possible*, to make others write better.

As the poem has met with far more success than I expected, I have endeavoured in this edition to make some additions and alterations to render it more worthy of public perusal.

In the First Edition of this Satire, published anonymously, fourteen lines on the subject of Bowles's Pope were written and inserted at the request of an ingenious friend of mine, who has now in the press a volume of poetry. In the present edition they are erased, and some of my own substituted in their stead; my only reason for this being, that, which I conceive would operate with any other person in the same manner—a determination not to publish with my name any production which was not entirely and exclusively my own composition.

With regard to the real talents of many of the poetical persons whose performances are mentioned, or alluded to, in the following pages, it is presumed by the author that there can be little difference of opinion in the public at large; though, like other sectaries, each has his separate tabernacle of proselytes, by whom his abilities are overrated, his faults overlooked, and his metrical canons received without scruple and without consideration. But the unquestionable possession of considerable genius by several of the writers here censured, renders their mental prostitution more to be regretted. Imbecilty may be pitied, or, at worst, laughed at and forgotten; perverted powers demand the most decided reprehension. No one can wish more than the author, that some known and able writer had undertaken their exposure; but Mr. Gifford has devoted himself to Massinger, and in the absence of the regular physician, a country practitioner may, in cases of absolute necessity, be allowed to prescribe his nostrum to prevent the extension of so deplorable an epidemic, provided there be no quackery in his treatment of the malady. A caustic is here offered, as it is to be feared nothing short of actual cautery can recover the numerous patients afflicted with the present prevalent and distressing *rabies* for rhyming.

As to the Edinburgh Reviewers, it would, indeed, require a Hercules to crush the Hydra; but if the author succeeds in merely "bruising one of the heads of the serpent," though his own hand should suffer in the encounter, he will be amply satisfied.

ENGLISH BARDS AND SCOTCH REVIEWERS:
A SATIRE.

STILL must I hear?—shall hoarse Fitzgerald bawl
His creaking couplets in a tavern hall,

And I not sing, lest, haply, Scotch reviews
Should dub me scribbler, and denounce my muse?
Prepare for rhyme—I'll publish, right or wrong;
Fools are my theme, let satire be my song.

Oh! nature's noblest gift—my gray goose-quill!
Slave of my thoughts, obedient to my will,
Torn from thy parent bird to form a pen,
That mighty instrument of little men!
The pen! foredoomed to aid the mental throes
Of brains that labour, big with verse or prose.
Though nymphs forsake, and critics may deride,
The lover's solace, and the author's pride.
What wits, what poets, dost thou daily raise
How frequent is thy use, how small thy praise!
Condemn'd at length to be forgotten quite,
With all the pages which 't was thine to write.
But thou, at least, mine own especial pen!
Once laid aside, but now assumed again,
Our task complete, like Hamet's shall be free;[2]
Though spurn'd by others, yet beloved by me.
Then let us soar to-day, no common theme,
No eastern vision, no distemper'd dream
Inspires—our path, though full of thorns, is plain;
Smooth be verse, and easy be the strain.

When vice triumphant holds her sov'reign sway
And men through life her willing slaves obey;
When folly, frequent harbinger of crime,
Unfolds her motley store to suit the time;
When knaves and fools combined o'er all prevail,
When justice halts, and right begins to fail;
E'en then the boldest start from public sneers,
Afraid of shame, unknown to other fears,
More darkly sin, by satire kept in awe,
And shrink from ridicule, though not from law.

Such is the force of wit! but not belong
To me the arrows of satiric song;
The royal vices of our age demand
A keener weapon, and a mightier hand.
Still there are follies, e'en for me to chase,
And yield at least amusement in the race:
Laugh when I laugh, I seek no other fame;
The cry is up, and scribblers are my game.
Speed, Pegasus!—ye strains of great and small,
Ode, epic, elegy, have at you all!
I, too, can scrawl, and once upon a time
I pour'd along the town a flood of rhyme.
A schoolboy freak, unworthy praise or blame;
I printed—older children do the same.
'Tis pleasant, sure, to see one's name in print;
A book's a book, although there's nothing in't.
Not that a title's sounding charm can save
Or scrawl or scribbler from an equal grave:
This Lambe must own, since his patrician name
Fail'd to preserve the spurious farce from shame.[3]
No matter, George continues still to write,[4]
Though now the name is veil'd from public sight
Moved by the great example, I pursue
The self-same road, but make my own review;
Not seek great Jeffrey's, yet like him will be
Self-constituted judge of poesy.

A man must serve his time to every trade
Save censure—critics all are ready made.
Take hackney'd jokes from Miller, got by rote,
With just enough of learning to misquote;
A mind well skill'd to find or forge a fault;
A turn for punning, call it Attic salt;

To Jeffrey go; be silent and discreet,
His pay is just ten sterling pounds per sheet.
Fear not to lie, 't will seem a lucky hit;
Shrink not from blasphemy, 't will pass for wit;
Care not for feeling—pass your proper jest,
And stand a critic, hated yet caressed.

And shall we own such judgment? no—as soon
Seek roses in December—ice in June;
Hope constancy in wind, or corn in chaff;
Believe a woman, or an epitaph,
Or any other thing that 's false, before
You trust in critics, who themselves are sore;
Or yield one single thought to be misled
By Jeffrey's heart, or Lambe's Bœotian head.[5]
To these young tyrants, by themselves misplaced,
Combined usurpers on the throne of taste;
To these, when authors bend in humble awe,[6]
And hail their voice as truth, their word as law—
While these are censors, 't would be sin to spare;
While such are critics, why should I forbear?
But yet, so near all modern worthies run,
'T is doubtful whom to seek, or whom to shun;
Nor know we when to spare, or where to strike,
Our bards and censors are so much alike.

Then should you ask me, why I venture o'er[7]
The path that Pope and Gifford trod before;
If not yet sicken'd, you can still proceed:
Go on; my rhyme will tell you as you read.

Time was, e'er yet in these degenerate days
Ignoble themes obtain'd mistaken praise,
When sense and wit with poesy allied,
No fabled graces, flourish'd side by side,
From the same fount their inspiration drew,
And, rear'd by taste, bloom'd fairer as they grew.
Then, in this happy isle, a Pope's pure strain
Sought the rapt soul to charm, nor sought in vain;
A polish'd nation's praise aspired to claim,
And raised the people's, as the poet's fame.
Like him great Dryden pour'd the tide of song,
In stream less smooth, indeed, yet doubly strong.
Then Congreve's scenes could cheer, or Otway's melt;
For nature then an English audience felt.
But why these names, or greater still, retrace,
When all to feebler bards resign their place?
Yet to such times our lingering looks are cast,
When taste and reason with those times are past.
Now look around, and turn each trifling page,
Survey the precious works that please the age;
This truth at least let satire's self allow,
No dearth of bards can be complained of now:
The loaded press beneath her labour groans,
And printers' devils shake their weary bones;
While Southey's epics cram the creaking shelves,
And Little's lyrics shine in hot-pressed twelves.

Thus saith the preacher: "Nought beneath the sun[8]
Is new;" yet still from change to change we run;
What varied wonders tempt us as they pass!
The cow-pox, tractors, galvanism, and gas,
In turns appear, to make the vulgar stare,
Till the swoln bubble bursts—and all is air!
Nor less new schools of poetry arise,
Where dull pretenders grapple for the prize:
O'er taste awhile these pseudo-bards prevail:
Each country book-club bows the knee to Baal,
And, hurling lawful genius from the throne,
Erects a shrine and idol of its own;
Some leaden calf—but whom it matters not,
From soaring Southey down to grovelling Stott.[9]

Behold! in various throngs the scribbling crew,
For notice eager, pass in long review:
Each spurs his jaded Pegasus apace,
And rhyme and blank maintain an equal race;
Sonnets on sonnets crowd, and ode on ode;
And tales of terror jostle on the road;
Immeasurable measures move along,
For simpering folly loves a varied song,
To strange mysterious dulness still the friend,
Admires the strain she cannot comprehend.

Thus Lays of Minstrels—may they be the last!—[10]
On half-strung harps whine mournful to the blast;

SIR WALTER SCOTT

While mountain spirits prate to river sprites,
That dames may listen to the sound at nights;

And goblin brats, of Gilpin Horner's brood,
Decoy young border nobles through the wood,
And skip at every step, Lord knows how high,
And frighten foolish babes, the Lord knows why;
While high-born ladies in their magic cell,
Forbidding knights to read who cannot spell,
Despatch a courier to a wizard's grave,
And fight with honest men to shield a knave.

Next view in state, proud prancing on his roan,
The golden-crested haughty Marmion,
Now forging scrolls, now foremost in the fight,
Not quite a felon, yet but half a knight,
The gibbet or the field prepared to grace;
A mighty mixture of the great and base.
And think'st thou, Scott! by vain conceit perchance,
On public taste to foist thy stale romance?
Though Murray with his Miller may combine
To yield thy muse just half-a-crown per line?
No! when the sons of song descend to trade,
Their bays are sear, their former laurels fade.
Let such forego the poet's sacred name,
Who rack their brains for lucre, not for fame;
Low may they sink to merited contempt,
And scorn remunerate the mean attempt!
Such be their meed, such still the just reward
Of prostituted muse and hireling bard!
For this we spurn Apollo's venal son,
And bid a long "good night to Marmion."[11]

These are the themes that claim our plaudits now;
These are the bards to whom the muse must bow:
While Milton, Dryden, Pope, alike forgot,
Resign their hallowed bays to Walter Scott.

The time has been, when yet the muse was young,
When Homer swept the lyre, and Maro sung,
An epic scarce ten centuries could claim,
While awe-struck nations hail'd the magic name;
The work of each immortal bard appears
The single wonder of a thousand years.[12]
Empires have moulder'd from the face of earth,
Tongues have expired with those who gave them birth,
Without the glory such a strain can give,
As even in ruin bids the language live.
Not so with us, though minor bards content,
On one great work a life of labour spent:
With eagle pinion soaring to the skies,
Behold the ballad-monger Southey rise!
To him let Camoëns, Milton, Tasso yield,
Whose annual strains, like armies, take the field.

First in the ranks see Joan of Arc advance,
The scourge of England, and the boast of France!
Though burnt by wicked Bedford for a witch,
Behold her statue placed in glory's niche;
Her fetters burst, and just released from prison,
A virgin phœnix from her ashes risen.
Next see tremendous Thalaba come on,[13]
Arabia's monstrous, wild, and wond'rous son;
Domdaniel's dread destroyer, who o'erthrew
More mad magicians than the world e'er knew.
Immortal hero! all thy foes o'ercome,
For ever reign—the rival of Tom Thumb!
Since startled metre fled before thy face,
Well wert thou doom'd the last of all thy race!
Well might triumphant genii bear thee hence,
Illustrious conqueror of common sense!
Now, last and greatest, Madoc spreads his sails,
Cacique in Mexico, and Prince in Wales;
Tells us strange tales, as other travellers do,
More old than Mandeville's, and not so true.
Oh! Southey, Southey, cease thy varied song![14]
A bard may chant too often and too long;

As thou art strong in verse, in mercy spare!
A fourth, alas! were more than we could bear.
But if, in spite of all the world can say,
Thou still wilt verseward plod thy weary way;
If still in Berkley ballads most uncivil,
Thou wilt devote old women to the devil,[15]
The babe unborn thy dread intent may rue:
"God help thee," Southey, and thy readers too.[16]

Next comes the dull disciple of thy school,
That mild apostate from poetic rule,
The simple Wordsworth, framer of a lay
As soft as evening in his favourite May,
Who warns his friend "to shake off toil and trouble,
And quit his books, for fear of growing double;"[17]
Who, both by precept and example, shows
That prose is verse, and verse is merely prose;
Convincing all, by demonstration plain,
Poetic souls delight in prose insane;
And Christmas stories tortured into rhyme,
Contain the essence of the true sublime.
Thus, when he tells the tale of Betty Foy,
The idiot mother of "an idiot boy,"
A moon-struck, silly lad, who lost his way,
And, like his bard, confounded night with day;[18]

So close on each pathetic part he dwells,
And each adventure so sublimely tells,
That all who view "the idiot in his glory,"
Conceive the bard the hero of the story.

Shall gentle Coleridge pass unnoticed here,
To turgid ode and tumid stanza dear?
Though themes of innocence amuse him best,
Yet still obscurity's a welcome guest.
If Inspiration should her aid refuse
To him who takes a pixy for a muse,[19]
Yet none in lofty numbers can surpass
The bard who soars to elegise an ass.
How well the subject suits his noble mind
"A fellow-feeling makes us wond'rous kind.

Oh! wonder-working Lewis! monk, or bard,
Who fain would make Parnassus a churchyard!

Lo! wreaths of yew, not laurel, bind thy brow,
Thy muse a sprite, Apollo's sexton thou!
Whether on ancient tombs thou tak'st thy stand,
By gibb'ring spectres hail'd, thy kindred band;
Or tracest chaste descriptions on thy page,
To please the females of our modest age;
All hail, M.P.! from whose infernal brain [20]
Thin sheeted phantoms glide, a grisly train;
At whose command "grim women" throng in crowds,
And kings of fire, of water, and of clouds,
With "small gray men," "wild yagers," and what not,
To crown with honour thee, and Walter Scott!
Again all hail! if tales like thine may please,
St. Luke alone can vanquish the disease:
Even Satan's self with thee might dread to dwell,
And in thy skull discern a deeper hell.

Who in soft guise, surrounded by a choir,
Of virgins melting, not to Vesta's fire,
With sparkling eyes, and cheek by passion flush'd,
Strikes his wild lyre, whilst listening dames are hush'd?
'T is Little! young Catullus of his day,
As sweet, but as immoral, in his lay!
Grieved to condemn, the muse must still be just,
Nor spare melodious advocates of lust.
Pure is the flame which o'er her altar burns;
From grosser incense with disgust she turns:
Yet, kind to youth, this expiation o'er,
She bids thee "mend thy line, and sin no more."

For thee, translator of the tinsel song,
To whom such glittering ornaments belong,
Hibernian Strangford! with thine eyes of blue, [21]
And boasted locks of red, or auburn hue,
Whose plaintive strain each love-sick miss admires,
And o'er harmonious fustian half expires,
Learn, if thou canst, to yield thine author's sense,
Nor vend thy sonnets on a false pretence.
Think'st thou to gain thy verse a higher place,
By dressing Camoens in a suit of lace?
Mend, Strangford! mend thy morals and thy taste;
Be warm, but pure; be amorous, but be chaste:
Cease to deceive; thy pilfer'd harp restore,
Nor teach the Lusian bard to copy Moore.

In many marble-cover'd volumes view
Hayley, in vain attempting something new;
Whether he spin his comedies in rhyme,
Or scrawl, as Wood and Barclay walk, 'gainst time,
His style in youth or age is still the same,
For ever feeble and for ever tame.
Triumphant first see "Temper's Triumphs" shine!
At least I'm sure they triumphed over mine.
Of "Music's Triumphs," all who read may swear,
That luckless music never triumphed there.[22]

Moravians, rise! bestow some meet reward
On dull devotion—Lo! the Sabbath bard,
Sepulchral Grahame, pours his notes sublime,
In mangled prose, nor e'en aspires to rhyme,
Breaks into blank the Gospel of St. Luke,
And boldly pilfers from the Pentateuch;
And, undisturbed by conscientious qualms,
Perverts the Prophets, and purloins the Psalms.[23]

Hail, Sympathy! thy soft idea brings
A thousand visions of a thousand things,
And shows, dissolved in thine own melting tears,
The maudlin prince of mournful sonneteers.
And art thou not their prince, harmonious Bowles!
Thou first, great oracle of tender souls?
Whether in sighing winds thou seek'st relief,
Or consolation in a yellow leaf;
Whether thy muse most lamentably tells
What merry sounds proceed from Oxford bells,[24]
Or, still in bells delighting, finds a friend
In every chime that jingled from Ostend;
Ah! how much juster were thy muse's hap,
If to thy bells thou would'st but add a cap!
Delightful Bowles! still blessing and still blest,
All love thy strain, but children like it best.
'T is thine, with gentle Little's moral song,
To soothe the mania of the amorous throng!
With thee our nursery damsels shed their tears,
Ere miss, as yet, completes her infant years;
But in her teens thy whining powers are vain;
She quits poor Bowles, for Little's purer strain.
Now to soft themes thou scornest to confine
The lofty numbers of a harp like thine;
"Awake a louder and a loftier strain," [25]
Such as none heard before, or will again;
Where all discoveries jumbled from the flood,
Since first the leaky ark reposed in mud,
By more or less, are sung in every book,
From Captain Noah down to Captain Cook.
Nor this alone; but, pausing on the road,
The bard sighs forth a gentle episode; [26]
And gravely tells—attend, each beauteous miss!
When first Madeira trembled to a kiss.
Bowles! in thy memory let this precept dwell,
Stick to thy sonnets, man!—at least they sell.
But if some new-born whim, or larger bribe,
Prompt thy crude brain, and claim thee for a scribe,
If chance some bard, though once by dunces feared,
Now, prone in dust, can only be revered;
If Pope, whose fame and genius from the first,
Have foil'd the best of critics, needs the worst,
Do thou essay; each fault, each failing scan:
The first of poets was, alas! but man.
Rake from each ancient dunghill ev'ry pearl,
Consult Lord Fanny, and confide in Curll; [27]
Let all the scandals of a former age
Perch on thy pen, and flutter o'er thy page;

Affect a candour which thou canst not feel,
Clothe envy in the garb of honest zeal;
Write, as if St. John's soul could still inspire,
And do from hate, what Mallet did for hire.[28]
Oh! hadst thou lived in that congenial time,
To rave with Dennis, and with Ralph to rhyme;[29]
Throng'd with the rest around his living head,
Not raised thy hoof against the lion dead,
A meet reward had crown'd thy glorious gains,
And link'd thee to the Dunciad for thy pains.[30]

Another epic! who inflicts again
More books of blank upon the sons of men?
Bœotian Cottle, rich Bristowa's boast,
Imports old stories from the Cambrian coast,

AMOS COTTLE

And sends his goods to market—all alive!
Lines forty thousand, cantos twenty-five!
Fresh fish from Helicon! who'll buy? who'll buy?
The precious bargain's cheap—in faith, not I.
Too much in turtle Bristol's sons delight,
Too much o'er bowls of rack prolong the night!
If commerce fills the purse, she clogs the brain,
And Amos Cottle strikes the lyre in vain.
In him an author's luckless lot behold,
Condemn'd to make the books which once he sold.
Oh, Amos Cottle!—Phœbus! what a name,
To fill the speaking trump of future fame!—
Oh, Amos Cottle! for a moment think
What meagre profits spring from pen and ink!
When thus devoted to poetic dreams,
Who will peruse thy prostituted reams?
Oh, pen perverted! paper misapplied!
Had Cottle still adorn'd the counter's side,[31]
Bent o'er the desk, or, born to useful toils,
Been taught to make the paper which he soils,
Plough'd, delved, or plied the oar with lusty limb,
He had not sung of Wales, nor I of him.

As Sisyphus against the infernal steep,
Rolls the huge rock, whose motions ne'er may sleep,
So up thy hill, ambrosial Richmond! heaves
Dull Maurice all his granite weight of leaves:[32]
Smooth, solid monuments of mental pain!
The petrifactions of a plodding brain,
That ere they reach the top fall lumbering back again.

With broken lyre, and cheek serenely pale,
Lo! sad Alcæus wanders down the vale;
Though fair they rose, and might have bloom'd at last,
His hopes have perish'd by the northern blast:
Nipp'd in the bud by Caledonian gales,
His blossoms wither as the blast prevails!
O'er his lost works let *classic* Sheffield weep;
May no rude hand disturb their early sleep![33]

Yet, say! why should the bard at once resign
His claim to favour from the sacred Nine?
For ever startled by the mingled howl
Of northern wolves, that still in darkness prowl;
A coward brood, which mangle as they prey,
By hellish instinct, all that cross their way;
Aged or young, the living or the dead,
No mercy find—these harpies must be fed.
Why do the injured unresisting yield
The calm possession of their native field?
Why tamely thus before their fangs retreat,
Nor hunt the bloodhounds back to Arthur's Seat?[34]

Health to immortal Jeffrey! once, in name,
England could boast a judge almost the same;
In soul so like, so merciful, yet just,
Some think that Satan has resign'd his trust,
And given the spirit to the world again,
To sentence letters, as he sentenced men.
With hand less mighty, but with heart as black,
With voice as willing to decree the rack;
Bred in the courts betimes, though all that law
As yet hath taught him is to find a flaw.
Since well instructed in the patriot school
To rail at party, though a party tool,
Who knows, if chance his patrons should restore
Back to the sway they forfeited before,
His scribbling toils some recompense may meet,
And raise this Daniel to the judgment-seat.
Let Jeffries' shade indulge the pious hope,
And greeting thus, present him with a rope:
"Heir to my virtues! man of equal mind!
Skill'd to condemn as to traduce mankind,

This cord receive, for thee reserved with care,
To wield in judgment, and at length to wear."

Health to great Jeffrey! Heaven preserve his life,
To flourish on the fertile shores of Fife,
And guard it sacred in his future wars,
Since authors sometimes seek the field of Mars!
Can none remember that eventful day,
That ever glorious, almost fatal fray,
When Little's leadless pistol met his eye,
And Bow Street myrmidons stood laughing by? [35]
Oh, day disastrous! on her firm-set rock,
Dunedin's castle felt a secret shock:
Dark roll'd the sympathetic waves of Forth,
Low groan'd the startled whirlwinds of the north;
Tweed ruffled half his waves to form a tear,
The other half pursued its calm career; [36]
Arthur's steep summit nodded to its base,
The surly Tolbooth scarcely kept her place;
The Tolbooth felt—for marble sometimes can,
On such occasions, feel as much as man—
The Tolbooth felt defrauded of his charms,
If Jeffrey died, except within her arms: [37]
Nay, last, not least, on that portentous morn,
The sixteenth storey where himself was born,
His patrimonial garret, fell to ground,
And pale Edina shudder'd at the sound:
Strew'd were the streets around with milk-white reams,
Flow'd all the Canongate with inky streams;
This of his candour seem'd the sable dew,
That of his valour show'd the bloodless hue;
And all with justice deem'd the two combined
The mingled emblems of his mighty mind.
But Caledonia's goddess hover'd o'er
The field, and saved him from the wrath of Moore;
From either pistol snatch'd the vengeful lead,
And straight restored it to her favourite's head;
That head, with greater than magnetic pow'r,
Caught it, as Danæ caught the golden show'r,
And, though the thickening dross will scarce refine,
Augments its ore, and is itself a mine.
"My son," she cried, "ne'er thirst for gore again,
Resign the pistol, and resume the pen;
O'er politics and poesy preside,
Boast of thy country, and Britannia's guide!
For long as Albion's heedless sons submit,
Or Scottish taste decides on English wit,
So long shall last thine unmolested reign,
Nor any dare to take thy name in vain.
Behold, a chosen band shall aid thy plan,
And own thee chieftain of the critic clan.
First in the ranks illustrious shall be seen
The travell'd thane, Athenian Aberdeen. [38]
Herbert shall wield Thor's hammer, and sometimes, [39]
In gratitude, thou'lt praise his rugged rhymes.
Smug Sydney too thy bitter page shall seek, [40]
And classic Hallam, much renown'd for Greek; [41]
Scott may perchance his name and influence lend,
And paltry Pillans shall traduce his friend; [42]
While gay Thalia's luckless votary, Lambe, [43]
As he himself was damn'd, shall try to damn.
Known be thy name, unbounded be thy sway!
Thy Holland's banquets shall each toil repay;
While grateful Britain yields the praise she owes,
To Holland's hirelings, and to learning's foes.
Yet mark one caution, ere thy next review
Spread its light wings of saffron and of blue,
Beware lest blundering Brougham destroy the sale, [44]
Turn beef to bannocks, cauliflowers to kail."
Thus having said, the kilted goddess kist
Her son, and vanish'd in a Scottish mist. [45]

Illustrious Holland! hard would be his lot,
His hirelings mentioned, and himself forgot!
Holland, with Henry Petty at his back,
The whipper-in and huntsman of the pack.
Blest be the banquets spread at Holland House,
Where Scotchmen feed, and critics may carouse!
Long, long beneath that hospitable roof,
Shall Grub Street dine, while duns are kept aloof.
See honest Hallam lay aside his fork,
Resume his pen, review his Lordship's work,
And, grateful to the founder of the feast,
Declare his landlord can translate at least! [46]

Dunedin! view thy children with delight,
They write for food—and feed because they write:
And lest, when heated with the unusual grape,
Some glowing thoughts should to the press escape,
And tinge with red the female reader's cheek,
My lady skims the cream of each critique;
Breathes o'er the page her purity of soul,
Reforms each error, and refines the whole.[47]

Now to the Drama turn—Oh! motley sight,
What precious scenes the wondering eyes invite!
Puns, and a prince within a barrel pent,[48]
And Dibdin's nonsense, yield complete content.
Though now, thank Heaven! the Rosciomania's o'er,
And full-grown actors are endured once more;
Yet what avail their vain attempts to please,
While British critics suffer scenes like these?
While Reynolds vents his "Dammes!" "Poohs!" and "Zounds!"[49]
And common place and common sense confounds?
While Kenney's "World" just suffered to proceed,
Proclaims the audience very kind indeed!
And Beaumont's pilfer'd Caratach affords
A tragedy complete in all but words?[50]
Who but must mourn, while these are all the rage,
The degradation of our vaunted stage?
Heavens! is all sense of shame, and talent gone?
Have we no living bard of merit?—none?
Awake, George Colman! Cumberland, awake!
Ring the alarum bell! let folly quake!
Oh, Sheridan! if aught can move thy pen,
Let Comedy resume her throne again;
Abjure the mummery of German schools,
Leave new Pizarros to translating fools;
Give, as thy last memorial to the age,
One classic drama, and reform the stage.
Gods! o'er those boards shall Folly rear her head,
Where Garrick trod, and Kemble lives to tread?
On those shall Farce display Buffoon'ry's mask,
And Hook conceal his heroes in a cask?
Shall sapient managers new scenes produce
From Cherry, Skeffington, and Mother Goose?
While Shakspeare, Otway, Massinger, forgot,
On stalls must moulder, or in closets rot?
Lo! with what pomp the daily prints proclaim
The rival candidates for Attic fame!
In grim array though Lewis' spectres rise,
Still Skeffington and Goose divide the prize.
And sure *great* Skeffington must claim our praise,
For skirtless coats and skeletons of plays
Renown'd alike; whose genius ne'er confines
Her flight to garnish Greenwood's gay designs;[51]
Nor sleeps with "Sleeping Beauties," but anon
In five facetious acts comes thundering on,[52]
While poor John Bull, bewilder'd with the scene,
Stares, wondering what the devil it can mean;
But as some hands applaud—a venal few—
Rather than sleep, why John applauds it too.

Such are we now. Ah! wherefore should we turn
To what our fathers were, unless to mourn?
Degenerate Britons! are ye dead to shame,
Or, kind to dulness, do you fear to blame?
Well may the nobles of our present race
Watch each distortion of a Naldi's face;
Well may they smile on Italy's buffoons,
And worship Catalani's pantaloons,[53]
Since their own drama yields no fairer trace
Of wit than puns, of humour than grimace.

Then let Ausonia, skill'd in every art
To soften manners, but corrupt the heart,
Pour her exotic follies o'er the town,
To sanction vice, and hunt decorum down:
Let wedded strumpets languish o'er Deshayes,
And bless the promise which his form displays:
While Gayton bounds before th'enraptured looks
Of hoary marquises and stripling dukes;
Let high-born lechers eye the lively Presle
Twirl her light limbs, that spurn the needless veil;
Let Angiolini bare her breast of snow,
Wave the white arm, and point the pliant toe;
Collini trill her love-inspiring song,
Strain her fair neck, and charm the listening throng
Raise not your scythe, suppressors of our vice!
Reforming saints! too delicately nice!
By whose decrees, our sinful souls to save,
No Sunday tankards foam, no barbers shave;
And beer undrawn, and beards unmown, display
Your holy reverence for the Sabbath-day.

Or, hail at once the patron and the pile
Of vice and folly, Greville and Argyle![54]
Where yon proud palace, fashion's hallow'd fane,
Spreads wide her portals for the motley train,
Behold the new Petronius of the day,[55]
The arbiter of pleasure and of play!
There the hired eunuch, the Hesperian choir,
The melting lute, the soft lascivious lyre,
The song from Italy, the step from France,
The midnight orgy, and the mazy dance,
The smile of beauty, and the flush of wine,
For fops, fools, gamesters, knaves, and lords combine.
Each to his humour—Comus all allows
Champaign, dice, music, or your neighbour's spouse.
Talk not to us, ye starving sons of trade!
Of piteous ruin, which ourselves have made;
In Plenty's sunshine Fortune's minions bask,
Nor think of poverty, except "en masque,"
When for the night some lately titled ass
Appears the beggar which his grandsire was.
The curtain dropp'd, the gay burletta o'er,
The audience take their turn upon the floor;
Now round the room the circling dow'gers sweep,
Now in loose waltz the thin-clad daughters leap
The first in lengthen'd line majestic swim,
The last display the free, unfetter'd limb!

Those for Hibernia's lusty sons repair
With art the charms which nature could not spare;
These after husbands wing their eager flight,
Nor leave much mystery for the nuptial night

Oh! blest retreats of infamy and ease,
Where, all forgotten but the power to please,
Each maid may give aloose to genial thought,
Each swain may teach new systems, or be taught:
There the blithe youngster, just returned from Spain,
Cuts the light pack, or calls the rattling main,
The jovial caster's set, and seven's the nick,
Or—done!—a thousand on the coming trick!
If, mad with loss, existence 'gins to tire,
And all your hope or wish is to expire,
Here 's Powell's pistol ready for your life,
And, kinder still, a Paget for your wife:
Fit consummation of an earthly race,
Begun in folly, ended in disgrace,
While none but menials o'er the bed of death,
Wash thy red wounds, or watch thy wavering breath;
Traduced by liars, and forgot by all,
The mangled victim of a drunken brawl,
To live like Clodius, and like Falkland fall.[56]

Truth! rouse some genuine bard, and guide his hand,
To drive this pestilence from out the land.
E'en I—least thinking of a thoughtless throng,
Just skill'd to know the right and choose the wrong,
Freed at that age when reason's shield is lost,
To fight my course through passion's countless host,
Whom every path of pleasure's flow'ry way
Has lured in turn, and all have led astray—
E'en I must raise my voice, e'en I must feel
Such scenes, such men, destroy the public weal:
Although some kind, censorious friend will say,
"What art thou better, meddling fool, than they?"
And every brother rake will smile to see
That miracle, a moralist in me.
No matter: when some bard in virtue strong,—
Gifford perchance—shall raise the chastening song,
Then sleep my pen for ever! and my voice
Be only heard to hail him, and rejoice;
Rejoice, and yield my feeble praise, though I
May feel the lash that Virtue must apply.

As for the smaller fry, who swarm in shoals
From silly Hafiz up to simple Bowles,[57]
Why should we call them from their dark abode,
In broad St. Giles's or in Tottenham-road?
Or (since some men of fashion nobly dare
To scrawl in verse) from Bond Street or the Square?
If things of ton their harmless lays indite,
Most wisely doom'd to shun the public sight,
What harm? In spite of every critic elf,
Sir T. may read his stanzas to himself;
Miles Andrews still his strength in couplets try,
And live in prologues, though his dramas die.
Lords too are bards, such shings at times befall,
And 'tis some praise in peers to write at all.
Yet, did or taste or reason sway the times,
Ah! who would take their titles with their rhymes?
Roscommon! Sheffield! with your spirits fled,
No future laurels deck a noble head;
No muse will cheer, with renovating smile,
The paralytic puling of Carlisle:
The puny schoolboy and his early lay
Men pardon, if his follies pass away:
But who forgives the senior's ceaseless verse,
Whose hairs grow hoary as his rhymes grow worse?
What heterogeneous honours deck the peer!
Lord, rhymester, petit-maître, pamphleteer![58]
So dull in youth, so drivelling in his age,
His scenes alone had damn'd our sinking stage;
But managers for once cried, "Hold, enough!"
Nor drugg'd their audience with the tragic stuff.
Yet at their judgment let his Lordship laugh,
And case his volumes in congenial calf:
Yes! doff that covering, where morocco shines,
And hang a calf-skin on those recreant lines.[59]

With you, ye Druids! rich in native lead,
Who daily scribble for your daily bread,
With you I war not: Gifford's heavy hand
Has crash'd, without remorse, your numerous band.

W. GIFFORD

On "all the talents" vent your venal spleen;
Want is your plea, let pity be your screen.
Let monodies on Fox regale your crew,
And Melville's Mantle prove a blanket too.
One common Lethe waits each hapless bard,
And, peace be with you! 'tis your best reward.
Such damning fame as Dunciads only give,
Could bid your lines beyond a morning live;
But now at once your fleeting labours close,
With names of greater note in blest repose.
Far be 't from me unkindly to upbraid
The lovely Rosa's prose in masquerade,
Whose strains, the faithful echoes of her mind,
Leave wondering comprehension far behind.[60]
Though Bell has lost his nightingales and owls,
Matilda snivels still, and Hafiz howls;
And Crusca's spirit, rising from the dead,
Revives in Laura, Quiz, and X.Y.Z.[61]

When some brisk youth, the tenant of a stall,
Employs a pen less pointed than his awl,
Leaves his snug shop, forsakes his store of shoes,
St. Crispin quits, and cobbles for the muse,
Heavens! how the vulgar stare! how crowds applaud!
How ladies read, and literati laud!
If chance some wicked wag should pass his jest,
'Tis sheer ill-nature—don't the world know best?
Genius must guide when wits admire the rhyme,
And Capel Lofft declares 'tis quite sublime.[62]
Hear, then, ye happy sons of needless trade!
Swains! quit the plough, resign the useless spade!
Lo! Burns and Bloomfield, nay, a greater far,
Gifford was born beneath an adverse star,
Forsook the labours of a servile state,
Stemm'd the rude storm, and triumph'd over fate:
Then why no more? if Phœbus smiled on you,
Bloomfield! why not on brother Nathan too?
Him too the mania, not the muse, has seized;
Not inspiration, but a mind diseased:
And now no boor can seek his last abode,
No common be enclosed, without an ode.[63]
Oh! since increased refinement deigns to smile
On Britain's sons, and bless our genial isle,
Let poesy go forth, pervade the whole,
Alike the rustic, and mechanic soul.
Ye tuneful cobblers! still your notes prolong,
Compose at once a slipper and a song;
So shall the fair your handywork peruse,
Your sonnets sure shall please—perhaps your shoes.
May moorland weavers boast Pindaric skill,[64]
And tailors' lays be longer than their bill!
While punctual beaux reward the grateful notes,
And pay for poems—when they pay for coats.

To the famed throng now paid the tribute due,
Neglected genius! let me turn to you.

Come forth, oh Campbell! give thy talents scope;[65]
Who dares aspire if thou must cease to hope?
And thou, melodious Rogers! rise at last,
Recall the pleasing memory of the past;
Arise! let blest remembrance still inspire,
And strike to wonted tones thy hallow'd lyre;
Restore Apollo to his vacant throne,
Assert thy country's honour and thine own.
What! must deserted poesy still weep
Where her last hopes with pious Cowper sleep?
Unless, perchance, from his cold bier she turns
To deck the turf that wraps her minstrel, Burns!
No! though contempt hath mark'd the spurious brood,
The race who rhyme from folly, or for food,
Yet still some genuine sons 'tis her's to boast,
Who, least affecting, still affect the most:
Feel as they write, and write but as they feel—
Bear witness Gifford, Sotheby, Macneil.[66]

"Why slumbers Gifford?" once was ask'd in vain![67]
Why slumbers Gifford? let us ask again.
Are there no follies for his pen to purge?
Are there no fools whose backs demand the scourge?
Are there no sins for satire's bard to greet?
Stalks not gigantic Vice in every street?
Shall peers or princes tread pollution's path,
And 'scape alike the law's and muse's wrath?
Nor blaze with guilty glare through future time,
Eternal beacons of consummate crime?

Arouse thee, Gifford! be thy promise claim'd,
Make bad men better, or at least ashamed.

Unhappy White! while life was in its spring,[68]
And thy young muse just waved her joyous wing,

The spoiler came; and all thy promise fair,
Has sought the grave, to sleep for ever there.
Oh! what a noble heart was here undone,
When Science' self destroy'd her favourite son!
Yes, she too much indulged thy fond pursuit,
She sow'd the seeds, but death has reap'd the fruit.
'Twas thine own genius gave the final blow,
And help'd to plant the wound that laid thee low:
So the struck eagle, stretch'd upon the plain,
No more through rolling clouds to soar again,
View'd his own feather on the fatal dart,
And wing'd the shaft that quiver'd in his heart;
Keen were his pangs, but keener far to feel,
He nursed the pinion which impell'd the steel;
While the same plumage that had warm'd his nest
Drank the last life-drop of his bleeding breast.

There be, who say, in these enlighten'd days,
That splendid lies are all the poet's praise;
That strain'd invention, ever on the wing,
Alone impels the modern bard to sing:
'Tis true, that all who rhyme—nay, all who write,
Shrink from that fatal word to genius—trite;
Yet truth will sometimes lend her noblest fires,
And decorate the verse herself inspires:

This fact in Virtue's name let Crabbe attest;
Though nature's sternest painter, yet the best.

And here let Shee and genius find a place,[69]
Whose pen and pencil yield an equal grace:
To guide whose hands the sister arts combine,
And trace the poet's or the painter's line;
Whose magic touch can bid the canvas glow,
Or pour the easy rhyme's harmonious flow,
While honours, doubly merited, attend
The poet's rival, but the painter's friend.

Blest is the man who dares approach the bower
Where dwelt the muses at their natal hour;
Whose steps have press'd, whose eye has mark'd afar,
The clime that nursed the sons of song and war,
The scenes which glory still must hover o'er,
Her place of birth, her own Achaian shore.
But doubly blest is he, whose heart expands
With hallow'd feelings for those classic lands;
Who rends the veil of ages long gone by,
And views their remnants with a poet's eye.
Wright! 'twas thy happy lot at once to view[70]
Those shores of glory, and to sing them too;
And sure no common muse inspired thy pen
To hail the land of gods and godlike men.

And you, associate bards! who snatch'd to light[71]
Those gems too long withheld from modern sight;
Whose mingling taste combined to cull the wreath
Where Attic flowers Aonian odours breathe,
And all their renovated fragrance flung,
To grace the beauties of your native tongue;

Now let those minds, that nobly could transfuse
The glorious spirit of the Grecian muse,
Though soft the echo, scorn a borrow'd tone:
Resign Achaia's lyre, and strike your own.

Let these, or such as these, with just applause,
Restore the muse's violated laws;
But not in flimsy Darwin's pompous chime,
That mighty master of unmeaning rhyme;
Whose gilded cymbals, more adorn'd than clear,
The eye delighted, but fatigued the ear;
In show the simple lyre could once surpass,
But now, worn down, appear in native brass;
While all his train of hovering sylphs around
Evaporate in similes and sound:
Him let them shun, with him let tinsel die:
False glare attracts, but more offends the eye.[72]

Yet let them not to vulgar Wordsworth stoop,
The meanest object of the lowly group,
Whose verse, of all but childish prattle void,
Seems blessed harmony to Lambe and Lloyd:[73]
Let them—but hold, my muse, nor dare to teach
A strain, far, far beyond thy humble reach:
The native genius with their being given
Will point the path, and peal their notes to heaven.

And thou, too, Scott, resign to minstrels rude[74]
The wilder slogan of a border feud:
Let others spin their meagre lines for hire;
Enough for genius, if itself inspire!
Let Southey sing, although his teeming muse,
Prolific every spring, be too profuse;
Let simple Wordsworth chime his childish verse,
And brother Coleridge lull the babe at nurse;
Let spectre-mongering Lewis aim, at most,
To rouse the galleries, or to raise a ghost;
Let Moore be lewd: let Strangford steal from Moore,
And swear that Camoëns sang such notes of yore;
Let Hayley hobble on; Montgomery rave;
And godly Grahame chant a stupid stave;
Let sonneteering Bowles his strains refine,
And whine and whimper to the fourteenth line;
Let Stott, Carlisle, Matilda, and the rest[75]
Of Grub Street, and of Grosvenor Place the best,
Scrawl on, till death release us from the strain,
Or Common Sense assert her rights again.
But thou, with powers that mock the aid of praise,
Shouldst leave to humbler bards ignoble lays:
Thy country's voice, the voice of all the nine,
Demand a hallow'd harp—that harp is thine.
Say! will not Caledonia's annals yield
The glorious record of some nobler field,
Than the wild foray of a plundering clan,
Whose proudest deeds disgrace the name of man?
Or Marmion's acts of darkness, fitter food
For outlaw'd Sherwood's tales of Robin Hood?
Scotland! still proudly claim thy native bard,
And be thy praise his first, his best reward!
Yet not with thee alone his name should live,
But own the vast renown a world can give;
Be known, perchance, when Albion is no more,
And tell the tale of what she was before;
To future times her faded fame recall,
And save her glory, though his country fall.

Yet what avails the sanguine poet's hope,
To conquer ages, and with time to cope?
New eras spread their wings, new nations rise,
And other victors fill the applauding skies;[76]
A few brief generations fleet along,
Whose sons forget the poet and his song:
E'en now, what once-loved minstrels scarce may clain
The transient mention of a dubious name!
When fame's loud trump hath blown its noblest blast
Though long the sound, the echo sleeps at last;
And glory, like the phœnix 'midst her fires,
Exhales her odours, blazes, and expires.

Shall hoary Granta call her sable sons,
Expert in science, more expert at puns?
Shall these approach the muse? ah, no! she flies,
And even spurns the great Seatonian prize;
Though printers condescend the press to soil
With rhyme by Hoare, and epic blank by Hoyle:
Not him whose page, if still upheld by whist,
Requires no sacred theme to bid us list,[77]
Ye! who in Granta's honours would surpass,
Must mount her Pegasus, a full-grown ass;
A foal well worthy of her ancient dam,
Whose Helicon is duller than her Cam.

There Clarke, still striving piteously "to please,"
Forgetting doggrel leads not to degrees,
A would-be satirist, a hired buffoon,
A monthly scribbler of some low lampoon,
Condemn'd to drudge, the meanest of the mean,
And furbish falsehoods for a magazine,
Devotes to scandal his congenial mind;
Himself a living libel on mankind.[78]

Oh! dark asylum of a Vandal race![79]
At once the boast of learning, and disgrace;
So sunk in dulness, and so lost to shame,
That Smythe and Hodgson scarce redeem thy fame!
But where fair Isis rolls her purer wave,
The partial muse delighted loves to lave;
On her green banks a greener wreath is wove,
To crown the bards that haunt her classic grove;
Where Richards wakes a genuine poet's fires,
And modern Britons justly praise their sires.[81]

For me, who, thus unask'd, have dared to tell
My country, what her sons should know too well,
Zeal for her honour bade me here engage
The host of idiots that infest her age;
No just applause her honour'd name shall lose,
As first in freedom, dearest to the muse.

Oh. would thy bards but emulate thy fame,
And rise more worthy, Albion, of thy name!
What Athens was in science, Rome in power,
What Tyre appear'd in her meridian hour,
'Tis thine at once, fair Albion! to have been—
Earth's chief dictatress, ocean's mighty queen:
But Rome decay'd, and Athens strew'd the plain,
And Tyre's proud piers lie shatter'd in the main:
Like these, thy strength may sink, in ruin hurl'd,
And Britain fall, the bulwark of the world.
But let me cease, and dread Cassandra's fate,
With warning ever scoff'd at, till too late;
To themes less lofty still my lay confine,
And urge thy bards to gain a name like thine.

Then, hapless Britain! be thy rulers blest,
The senate's oracles, thy peoples' jest,
Still hear thy motley orators dispense
The flowers of rhetoric, though not of sense,
While Canning's colleagues hate him for his wit,
And old dame Portland fills the place of Pitt.[62]

Yet once again, adieu! ere this the sail
That wafts me hence is shivering in the gale;
And Afric's coast and Calpe's adverse height,[63]
And Stamboul's minarets must greet my sight:[64]
Thence shall I stray through beauty's native clime,[65]
Where Kaff is clad in rocks, and crown'd with snows sublime.[66]
But should I back return, no lettered rage
Shall drag my common-place book on the stage.
Let vain Valentia rival luckless Carr,[67]
And equal him whose work he sought to mar;
Let Aberdeen and Elgin still pursue[68]
The shade of fame through regions of virtu;
Waste useless thousands on their Phidian freaks,
Misshapen monuments and maim'd antiques;
And make their grand saloons a general mart
For all the mutilated blocks of art.
Of Dardan tours let dilettanti tell,
I leave topography to classic Gell;[59]
And, quite content, no more shall interpose
To stun mankind with poesy or prose.

Thus far I've held my undisturbed career,
Prepared for rancour, steel'd 'gainst selfish fear
This thing of rhyme I ne'er disdain'd to own—
Though not obtrusive, yet not quite unknown,
My voice was heard again, though not so loud,
My page, though nameless, never disavow'd;
And now at once I tear the veil away:—
Cheer on the pack—the quarry stands at bay,
Unscared by all the din of Melbourne house,
By Lambe's resentment, or by Holland's spouse,
By Jeffrey's harmless pistol, Hallam's rage,
Edina's brawny sons and brimstone page.
Our men in buckram shall have blows enough,
And feel they too "are penetrable stuff:"
And though I hope not hence unscathed to go,
Who conquers me shall find a stubborn foe.
The time hath been, when no harsh sound would fall
From lips that now may seem imbued with gall;
Nor fools nor follies tempt me to despise
The meanest thing that crawl'd beneath my eyes;
But now, so callous grown, so changed since youth,
I've learn'd to think, and sternly speak the truth;
Learn'd to deride the critic's starch decree,
And break him on the wheel he meant for me·
To spurn the rod a scribbler bids me kiss,
Nor care if courts and crowds applaud or hiss:
Nay more, though all my rival rhymesters frown,
I, too, can hunt a poetaster down;
And, arm'd in proof, the gauntlet cast at once
To Scotch marauder, and to southern dunce.
Thus much I've dared to do; how far my lay
Hath wrong'd these righteous times, let others say:
This, let the world, which knows not how to spare,
Yet rarely blames unjustly, now declare.

POSTSCRIPT.

I HAVE been informed, since the present edition went to the press, that my trusty and well-beloved cousins, the Edinburgh Reviewers, are preparing a most vehement critique on my poor, gentle, *unresisting* Muse, whom they have already so bedeviled with their ungodly ribaldry:

"Tantæne animis cœlestibus Iræ!"

I suppose I must say of Jeffrey as Sir Andrew Aguecheek saith, "an I had known he was so cunning of fence, I had seen him dammed ere I had fought him." What a pity it is that I shall be beyond the Bosphorus, before the next number has passed the Tweed. But I yet hope to light my pipe with it in Persia.

My Northern friends have accused me, with justice, of personality towards their great literary Anthropophagus, Jeffrey; but what else was to be done with him and his dirty pack, who feed by "lying and slandering," and slake their thirst by "evil speaking!" I have adduced facts already well-known, and of Jeffrey's mind I have stated my free opinion, nor has he thence sustained any injury;—what scavenger was ever soiled by being pelted with mud? It may be said that I quit England because I have censured there "persons of honour and wit about town," but I am coming back again, and their vengeance will keep hot till my return. Those who know me can testify that my motives for leaving England are very different from fears, literary or personal; those who do not, may one day be convinced. Since the publication of this thing, my name has not been concealed; I have been mostly in London, ready to answer for my transgressions, and in daily expectation of sundry cartels; but, alas! "the age of chivalry is over," or in the vulgar tongue, there is no spirit now-a-days.

There is a youth yclept Hewson Clarke (Subaudi Esquire), a Sizer of Emanuel College, and I believe a denizen of Berwick-upon-Tweed, whom I have introduced in these pages to much better company than he has been accustomed to meet; he is, notwithstanding, a very sad dog, and for no reason that I can discover, except a personal quarrel with a bear, kept by me at Cambridge to sit for a fellowship, and whom the jealousy of his Trinity contemporaries prevented from success, has been abusing me, and what is worse, the defenceless innocent above-mentioned, in the "Satirist," for one year and some months. I am utterly unconscious of having given him any provocation; indeed, I am guiltless of having heard his name till coupled with the "Satirist." He has therefore no reason to complain, and I dare say that, like Sir Fretful Plagiary, he is rather *pleased* than otherwise. I have now mentioned all who have done me the honour to notice me and mine, that is, my Bear and my Book, except the Editor of the "Satirist," who, it seems, is a gentleman, God wot! I wish he could impart a little of his gentility to his subordinate scribblers. I hear that Mr. Jerningham is about to take up the cudgels for his Mæcenas, Lord Carlisle; I hope not: he was one of the few, in the very short intercourse I had with him, treated me with kindness when a boy, and whatever he may say or do, "pour on, I will endure." I have nothing further to add, save a general note of thanksgiving to readers, purchasers, and publisher; and in the words of Scott, I wish

"To all and each a fair good night,
And rosy dreams and slumbers light."

NOTES TO ENGLISH BARDS AND SCOTCH REVIEWERS.

Note 1, page 498.

Still must I hear?—Shall hoarse Fitzgerald bawl?

Imitation:

Semper ego auditor tantum? nunquamne reponam
Vexatus toties rauci Theseide Codri?

Juvenal, *Satire* 1.

Mr. Fitzgerald, facetiously termed by Cobbett the "Small Beer Poet," inflicts his annual tribute of verse on the "Literary Fund;" not content with writing, he spouts in person after the company have imbibed a reasonable quantity of bad port, to enable them to sustain the operation.

Note 2, page 498.

Our task complete, like Hamet's shall be free.

Cid Hamet Benengeli promises repose to his pen in the ast chapter of "Don Quixote." Oh! that our voluminous gentry would follow the example of Cid Hamet Benengeli.

Note 3, page 498.

Fail'd to preserve the spurious farce from shame.

This ingenious youth is mentioned more particularly, with his production, in another place.

Note 4, page 498.

No matter, George continues still to write.

In the "Edinburgh Review."

Note 5, page 499.

By Jeffrey's heart or Lambe's Bœotian head.

Messrs. Jeffrey and Lambe are the Alpha and Omega, the first and last, of the "Edinburgh Review;" the others are mentioned hereafter.

Note 6, page 499.

To these young tyrants, by themselves misplaced.

Imitation:

Stulta est Clementia, cum tot ubique
——— occurras perituræ chartæ.

Juvenal, *Satire* 1.

Note 7, page 499.

Then should you ask me, why I venture o'er.

Imitation:

Cur tamen hoc libeat potius decurrere campo
Per quem magnus equos Auruncæ flexit alumnus.
Si vacat, et placidi rationem admittitis, edam.

Juvenal, *Satire* 1.

Note 8, page 499.

Thus saith the preacher: "Nought beneath the sun."

Ecclesiastes, Cap. 1.

Note 9, page 499.

From soaring Southey down to grovelling Stott.

Stott, better known in the "Morning Post" by the name of Hafiz. This person is at present the most profound explorer of the bathos. I remember, when the reigning family left Portugal, a special ode of Master Stott's, beginning thus:

(Stott loquitur quoad Hibernia.)
"Princely offspring of Braganza,
Erin greets thee with a stanza," &c., &c.

Also a sonnet to Rats, well worthy of the subject, and a most thundering ode, commencing as follows:

"O! for a lay! loud as the surge
That lashes Lapland's sounding shore."

Lord have mercy on us! the "Lay of the Last Minstrel" was nothing to this.

Note 10, page 499.

Thus Lays of Minstrels—may they be the last!—

See the "Lay of the Last Minstrel," *passim*. Never was any plan so incongruous and absurd as the groundwork of this production. The entrance of Thunder and Lightning prologuising to Bayes' Tragedy, unfortunately takes away the merit of originality from the dialogue between Messieurs the Spirits of Flood and Fell in the first canto. Then we have the amiable William of Deloraine, "a stark mosstrooper," *videlicet*, a happy compound of poacher, sheep-stealer, and highwayman. The propriety of his magical lady's injunction not to read can only be equalled by his candid acknowledgment of his independence of the trammels of spelling, although, to use his own elegant phrase, "'twas his neck-verse at hairibee," *i. e.* the gallows.

The biography of Gilpin Horner, and the marvellous pedestrian page, who travelled twice as fast as his master's horse, without the aid of seven-leagued boots, are *chef-d'œuvres* in the improvement of taste. For incident we have the invisible, but by no means sparing, box on the ear, bestowed on the page, and the entrance of a knight and charger into the castle, under the very natural disguise of a wain of hay. Marmion, the hero of the latter romance, is exactly what William of Deloraine would have been, had he been able to read and write. The poem was manufactured for Messrs. Constable, Murray, and Miller.

worshipful booksellers, in consideration of the receipt of a sum of money, and truly, considering the inspiration, it is a very creditable production. If Mr. Scott will write for hire, let him do his best for his paymasters, but not disgrace his genius, which is undoubtedly great, by a repetition of black letter ballad imitations.

NOTE 11, page 500.

And bid a long, "good night to Marmion."

"Good night to Marmion"—the pathetic and also prophetic exclamation of Henry Blount, Esquire, on the death of honest Marmion.

NOTE 12, page 500.

The single wonder of a thousand years.

As the "Odyssey" is so closely connected with the story of the "Iliad," they may almost be classed as one grand historical poem. In alluding to Milton and Tasso, we consider the "Paradise Lost," and "Gierusalemme Liberata," as their standard efforts, since neither the "Jerusalem Conquered" of the Italian, nor the "Paradise Regained" of the English bard, obtained a proportionate celebrity to their former poems. Query: Which of Mr. Southey's will survive?

NOTE 13, page 500.

Next see tremendous Thalaba come on.

Thalaba, Mr. Southey's second poem, is written in open defiance of precedent and poetry. Mr. S. wished to produce something novel, and succeeded to a miracle. Joan of Arc was marvellous enough, but Thalaba was one of those poems "which," in the words of Porson, "will be read when Homer and Virgil are forgotten, but—*not till then.*"

NOTE 14, page 500.

Oh Southey, Southey! cease thy varied song.

We beg Mr. Southey's pardon; "Madoc disdains the degraded title of epic." See his preface. Why is Epic degraded? and by whom? Certainly the late Romaunts of Masters Cottle, Laureat Pye, Ogilvy, Hole, and gentle Mistress Cowley, have not exalted the Epic Muse; but as Mr. Southey's poem "disdains the appellation," allow us to ask—has he substituted anything better in its stead? or must he be content to rival Sir Richard Blackmore, in the quantity as well as quality of his verse?

NOTE 15, page 500.

Thou wilt devote old women to the devil.

See, "The Old Woman of Berkley," a ballad by Mr. Southey, wherein an aged gentlewoman is carried away by Beelzebub, on a "high trotting horse."

NOTE 16, page 500.

"God help thee," Southey, and thy readers too.

The last line, "God help thee," is an evident plagiarism from the "Anti-Jacobin" to Mr. Southey, on his Dactylics. "God help thee, silly one."—Poetry of the "Anti-Jacobin," page 23.

NOTE 17, page 501.

And quit his books for fear of growing double.

"Lyrical Ballads," page 4,—"The tables turned." Stanza 1.

"Up, up, my friend, and clear your looks,
Why all this toil and trouble?
Up, up, my friend and quit your books,
Or surely you'll grow double."

NOTE 18, page 501.

And, like his bard, confounded night with day.

Mr. W. in his preface labours hard to prove, that prose and verse are much the same, and certainly his precepts and practice are strictly conformable.

"And thus to Betty's question he
Made answer, like a traveller bold,
The cock did crow to-whoo, to-whoo,
And the sun did shine so cold," &c., &c.
Lyrical Ballads, page 129.

NOTE 19, page 501.

To him who takes a Pixy for a Muse.

Coleridge's Poems, page 11, "Songs of the Pixies," *i.e.* Devonshire Fairies; p. 42, we have, "Lines to a Young Lady," and p. 52, "Lines to a Young Ass."

NOTE 20, page 502.

All hail, M.P.! from whose infernal brain.

"For every one knows little Matt's an M.P."—See a Poem to Mr. Lewis, in the "Statesman," supposed to be written by Mr. Jekyll.

NOTE 21, page 502.

Hibernian Strangford! with thine eyes of blue.

The reader who may wish for an explanation of this, may refer to "Strangford's Camoëns," p. 127, note to page 56, or to the last page of the Edinburgh review of Strangford's Camoëns.

It is also to be remarked, that the things given to the public as Poems of Camoëns, are no more to be found in the original Portuguese, than in the Song of Solomon.

NOTE 22, page 502.

That luckless music never triumphed there.

Hayley's two most notorious verse productions, are "Triumphs of Temper," and "Triumphs of Music." He has also written much Comedy in rhyme, Epistles, &c. &c. As he is rather an elegant writer of notes and biography, let us recommend Pope's advice to Wycherley, to Mr. H.'s consideration: viz. "to convert his poetry into prose," which may easily be done by taking away the final syllable of each couplet.

NOTE 23, page 502.

Perverts the Prophets, and purloins the Psalms.

Mr. Grahame has poured forth two volumes of cant, under the name of "Sabbath Walks," and "Biblical Pictures."

NOTE 24, page 502.

What merry sounds proceed from Oxford bells.

See Bowles's Sonnets, &c.—"Sonnet to Oxford," and "Stanzas on hearing the Bells of Ostend."

NOTE 25, page 502.

"Awake a louder and a loftier strain."

"Awake a louder," &c. &c., is the first line in Bowles's "Spirit of Discovery," a very spirited and pretty dwarf Epic. Among other exquisite lines we have the following:—

"A kiss
Stole on the list'ning silence, never yet
Here heard; they trembled even as if the power," &c.

That is, the woods of Madeira trembled to a kiss, very much astonished, as well they might be, at a such phenomenon.

NOTE 26, page 502.

The bard sighs forth a gentle episode.

The Episode here alluded to, is the story of "Robert a Machin," and "Anna d'Arfet," a pair of constant lovers, who performed the kiss before mentioned, that startled the woods of Madeira.

NOTE 27, page 502.

Consult Lord Fanny, and confide in Curll.

Curll is one of the heroes of the Dunciad, and was a bookseller. Lord Fanny is the poetical name of Lord Hervey, author of "Lines to the Imitator of Horace."

NOTE 28, page 503.

And do from hate, what Mallet did for hire.

Lord Bolingbroke hired Mallet to traduce Pope after his decease, because the Poet had retained some copies of a work by Lord Bolingbroke, (the "Patriot King") which that splendid, but malignant genius, had ordered to be destroyed.

NOTE 29, page 503.

To rave with Dennis, and with Ralph to rhyme.

Dennis, the critic, and Ralph, the rhymester.

"Silence, ye wolves! while Ralph to Cynthia howls,
Making night hideous; answer him, ye owls!"
Dunciad.

NOTE 30, page 503.

And linked thee to the Dunciad for thy pains.

See Bowles's late edition of Pope's works, for which he received 300 pounds: thus Mr. B. has experienced how much easier it is to profit by the reputation of another, than to elevate his own.

NOTE 31, page 503.

Had Cottle still adorned the counter's side.

Mr Cottle, Amos, Joseph, I don't know which, but one or both, once sellers of books they did not write, and now writers of books that do not sell, have published a pair of Epics. "Alfred," (poor Alfred! Pye has been at him too!) "Alfred" and the "Fall of Cambria."

NOTE 32, page 503.

Dull Maurice all his granite weight of leaves.

Mr. Maurice hath manufactured the component parts of a ponderous quarto, upon the "Beauties of Richmond Hill," and the like;—it also takes in a charming view of Turnham Green, Hammersmith, Brentford, Old and New, nd the parts adjacent.

NOTE 33, page 503.

May no rude hand disturb their early sleep.

Poor Montgomery! though praised by every English Review, has been bitterly reviled by the Edinburgh. After all, the bard of Sheffield is a man of considerable genius; his "Wanderer of Switzerland" is worth a thousand "Lyrical Ballads," and at least fifty "Degraded Epics."

NOTE 34, page 503.

Nor hunt the bloodhounds back to Arthur's seat.

Arthur's seat; the hill which overhangs Edinburgh.

NOTE 35, page 504.

And Bow Street Myrmidons stood laughing by.

In 1806, Messrs. Jeffrey and Moore met at Chalk Farm. The duel was prevented by the interference of the magistracy; and, on examination, the balls of the pistols, like the courage of the combatants, were found to have evaporated. This incident gave occasion to much waggery in the Daily Prints.

NOTE 36, page 504.

The other half pursued its calm career.

The Tweed here behaved with proper decorum; it would have been highly reprehensible in the English half of the river to have shown the smallest symptom of apprehension.

NOTE 37, page 504.

If Jeffrey died, except within her arms.

This display of sympathy on the part of the Tolbooth, (the principal prison in Edinburgh) which truly seems to have been most affected on this occasion, is much to be commended. It was to be apprehended, that the many unhappy criminals executed in the front, might have rendered the edifice more callous. She is said to be of the softer sex, because her delicacy of feeling on this day was truly feminine, though, like most feminine impulses, perhaps a little selfish.

NOTE 38, page 504.

The travelled Thane! Athenian Aberdeen.

His Lordship has been much abroad, is a member of the Athenian Society, and Reviewer of "Gell's Topography of Troy."

NOTE 39, page 504.

Herbert shall wield Thor's hammer, and sometimes.

Mr. Herbert is a translator of Icelandic and other poetry. One of the principal pieces is a "Song on the Recovery of Thor's Hammer:" the translation is a pleasant chant in the vulgar tongue, and endeth thus:—

"Instead of money and rings, I wot,
The hammer's bruises were her lot:
Thus Odin's son his hammer got."

NOTE 40, page 504.

Smug Sydney too thy bitter page shall seek.

The Reverend Sydney Smith, the reputed author of "Peter Plymley's Letters," and sundry criticisms.

NOTE 41, page 504.

And classic Hallam, much renowned for Greek.

Mr. Hallam reviewed Payne Knight's "Taste," and was exceedingly severe on some Greek verses therein: it was not discovered that the lines were Pindar's till the press rendered it impossible to cancel the critique, which still stands an everlasting monument of Hallam's ingenuity.

The said Hallam is incensed, because he is falsely accused, seeing that he never dineth at Holland House. If this be true, I am sorry—not for having said so, but on his account, as I understand his Lordship's feasts are preferable to his compositions. If he did not review Lord Holland's performance, I am glad, because it must have been painful to read, and irksome to praise it. If Mr. Hallam will tell me who did review it, the real name shall find a place in the text; provided, nevertheless, the said name be of two orthodox musical syllables, and will come into the verse; till then, Hallam must stand for want of a better.

NOTE 42, page 504.

And paltry Pillans shall traduce his friend.

Pillans was a tutor at Eton; and subsequently rector of the High School, and a professor in the University, of Edinburgh.

NOTE 43, page 504.

While gay Thalia's luckless votary, Lambe.

The Honourable G. Lambe reviewed "Beresford's Miseries," and is moreover author of a farce enacted with much

applause at the Priory, Stanmore; and damned with great expedition at the late Theatre, Covent Garden. It was entitled "Whistle for It."

NOTE 44, page 504.

Beware lest blundering Brougham destroy the sale.

Mr. Brougham, in No. XXV. of the Edinburgh Review, throughout the article concerning Don Pedro de Cevallos, has displayed more politics than policy; many of the worthy burgesses of Edinburgh being so incensed at the infamous principles it evinces, as to have withdrawn their subscriptions.

It seems that Mr. Brougham is not a Pict, as I supposed, but a Borderer, and his name is pronounced Broom, from Trent to Tay:—So be it.

NOTE 45, page 504.

Her son, and vanished in a Scottish mist.

I ought to apologise to the worthy Deities for introducing a new Goddess with short petticoats to their notice: but alas! what was to be done? I could not say Caledonia's Genius, it being well known there is no Genius to be found from Clackmannan to Caithness; yet without supernatural agency, how was Jeffrey to be saved? The national "Kelpies," &c., are too unpoetical, and the "Brownies" and "gude neighbours," (spirits of a good disposition) refused to extricate him. A Goddess therefore has been called for the purpose, and great ought to be the gratitude of Jeffrey, seeing it is the only communication he ever held, or is likely to hold, with any thing heavenly.

NOTE 46, page 504.

Declare his landlord can translate at least.

Lord H. has translated some specimens of Lope de Vega, inserted in his life of the Author: both are bepraised by his *disinterested* guests.

NOTE 47, page 505.

Reforms each error and refines the whole.

Certain it is, her Ladyship is suspected of having displayed her matchless wit in the "Edinburgh Review:" however that may be, we know from good authority, that the manuscripts are submitted to her perusal—no doubt for correction.

NOTE 48, page 505.

Puns, and a Prince within a barrel pent.

In the melo-drama of Tekeli, that heroic prince is clapt into a barrel on the stage: a new asylum for distressed heroes.

NOTE 49, page 505.

While Reynolds vents his "Dammes," "Poohs," and "Zounds."

All these are favourite expressions of Mr. R., and prominent in his Comedies, living and defunct.

NOTE 50, page 505.

A tragedy complete in all but words.

Mr. T. Sheridan, the new manager of Drury Lane Theatre, stripped the tragedy of "Bonduca" of the dialogue, and exhibited the scenes as the spectacle of Caractacus. Was this worthy of his sire? or of himself?

NOTE 51, page 505.

Her flight to garnish Greenwood's gay designs.

Mr. Greenwood is, we believe, Scene-Painter to Drury Lane Theatre—as such, Mr. S. is much indebted to him.

NOTE 52, page 505.

In five facetious acts comes thundering on.

Mr. S. is the illustrious author of the "Sleeping Beauty;" and some Comedies, particularly "Maids and Bachelors:" Baculaurii baculo magis quam lauro digni.

NOTE 53, page 505.

And worship Catalani's pantaloons.

Naldi and Catalani require little notice,—for the visage of the one, and the salary of the other, will enable us long to recollect these amusing vagabonds; besides we are still black and blue from the squeeze on the first night of the Lady's appearance in trousers.

NOTE 54, page 505.

Of vice and folly, Greville and Argyle.

To prevent any blunder, such as mistaking a street for a man, I beg leave to state, that it is the Institution, and not the Duke of that name, which is here alluded to.

A gentleman, with whom I am slightly acquainted, lost in the Argyle Rooms several thousand pounds at Backgammon; it is but justice to the manager in this instance to say, that some degree of disapprobation was manifested, but why are the implements of gaming allowed in a place devoted to the society of both sexes? A pleasant thing for the wives and daughters of those who are blest or curst with such connections, to hear the billiard-tables rattling in one room, and the dice in another! That this is the case, I myself can testify, as a late unworthy member of an Institution which materially affects the morals of the higher orders, while the lower may not even move to the sound of a tabor and fiddle without the chance of indictment for riotous behaviour.

NOTE 55, page 505.

Behold the new Petronius of the day.

Petronius, "Arbiter elegantiarum" to Nero, "and a very pretty fellow in his day," as Mr. Congreve's Old Bachelor saith.

NOTE 56, page 506.

To live like Clodius: and like Falkland fall.

Mutato nomine de te
Fabula narratur.

I knew the late Lord Falkland well. On Sunday night I beheld him presiding at his own table, in all the honest pride of hospitality; on Wednesday morning, at three o'clock, I saw stretched before me all that remained of courage, feeling, and a host of passions. He was a gallant and successful officer: his faults were the faults of a sailor; as such, Britons will forgive them. He died like a brave man in a better cause; for had he fallen in like manner on the deck of the frigate to which he was just appointed, his last moments would have been held up by his countrymen as an example to succeeding heroes.

NOTE 57, page 506.

From silly Hafiz up to simple Bowles.

What would be the sentiments of the Persian Anacreon, Hafiz, could he rise from his splendid sepulchre at Sheeraz, where he reposes with Ferdousi and Sadi, the Oriental Homer and Catullus, and behold his name assumed by one Stott of Dromore, the most impudent and execrable of literary poachers for the Daily Prints.

NOTE 58, page 506.

Lord, rhymester, petit-maitre, pamphleteer.

The Earl of Carlisle has lately published an eighteen-

penny pamphlet on the state of the stage, and offers his plan for building a new theatre: it is to be hoped his Lordship will be permitted to bring forward any thing for the stage, except his own tragedies.

NOTE 59, page 506.

And hang a calf-skin on those recreant lines.

" Doff that lion's hide,
And hang a calf-skin on those recreant limbs."
SHAK.: *King John.*

Lord C.'s works, most resplendently bound, form a conspicuous ornament to his book-shelves:

" The rest is all but leather and prunella."

NOTE 60, page 507.

Leave wondering comprehension far behind.

This lively little Jessica, the daughter of the noted Jew K——, seems to be a follower of the Della Crusca School, and has published two volumes of very respectable absurdities in rhyme, as times go; besides sundry novels in the style of the first edition of the Monk.

NOTE 61, page 507.

Revives in Laura, Quiz, and X. Y. Z.

These are the signatures of various worthies who figure in the poetical departments of the newspapers.

NOTE 62, page 507.

And Capel Lofft declares 'tis quite sublime.

Capel Lofft, Esq., the Mæcenas of shoemakers, and Preface-writer-General to distressed versemen; a kind of gratis Accoucheur to those who wish to be delivered of rhyme, but do not know how to bring forth.

NOTE 63, page 507.

No common be enclosed, without an ode.

See Nathaniel Bloomfield's ode, elegy, or whatever he or any one else chooses to call it, on the enclosure of " Honington Green."

NOTE 64, page 507.

May moorland weavers boast Pindaric skill.

Vide "Recollections of a Weaver in the Moorlands of Staffordshire."

NOTE 65, page 507.

Come forth, oh Campbell! give thy talents scope.

It would be superfluous to recall to the mind of the reader the authors of "The Pleasures of Memory" and "The Pleasures of Hope," the most beautiful didactic poems in our language, if we except Pope's "Essay on Man:" but so many poetasters have started up, that even the names of Campbell and Rogers become strange.

NOTE 66, page 507.

Bear witness Gifford, Sotheby, Macneil.

Gifford, author of the "Baviad and Mæviad," the first satires of the day, and translator of Juvenal.

Sotheby, translator of Wieland's "Oberon," and Virgil's " Georgics," and author of " Saul," an epic poem.

Macneil, whose poems are deservedly popular; particularly "Scotland's Scaith, or the Waes of War," of which ten thousand copies were sold in one month.

NOTE 67, page 508.

" Why slumbers Gifford?" once was asked in vain.

Mr. Gifford promised publicly that the "Baviad and Mæviad" should not be his last original works; let him remember " Mox in reluctantes Dracones."

NOTE 68, page 508.

Unhappy White, while life was in its spring.

Henry Kirke White died at Cambridge, in October, 1806, in consequence of too much exertion in the pursuit of studies that would have matured a mind which disease and poverty could not impair, and which death itself destroyed rather than subdued. His poems abound in such beauties as must impress the reader with the liveliest regret that so short a period was allotted to talents, which would have dignified even the sacred functions he was destined to assume.

NOTE 69, page 508.

And here let Shee and Genius find a place.

Mr. Shee, author of " Rhymes on Art," and "Elements of Art."

NOTE 70, page 508.

Wright, 'twas thy happy lot at once to view.

Mr. Wright, late Consul-General for the Seven Islands, is author of a very beautiful poem just published: it is entitled " Horæ Ionicæ," and is descriptive of the Isles and adjacent coast of Greece.

NOTE 71, page 508.

And you, associate Bards, who snatched to light.

The translators of the "Anthology" have since published separate poems, which evince genius that only requires opportunity to attain eminence.

NOTE 72, page 509.

False glare attracts, but more offends the eye.

The neglect of the "Botanic Garden," is some proof of returning taste: the scenery is its sole recommendation.

NOTE 73, page 509.

Seems blessed harmony to Lambe and Lloyd.

Messrs. Lambe and Lloyd, the most ignoble followers of Southey and Co.

NOTE 74, page 509.

And thou, too, Scott, resign to minstrels rude.

By-the-bye, I hope that in Mr. Scott's next poem, his hero or heroine will be less addicted to " Gramarye," and more to Grammar, than the Lady of the Lay, and her Bravo William of Deloraine.

NOTE 75, page 509.

Let Stott, Carlisle, Matilda, and the rest.

It may be asked why I have censured the Earl of Carlisle, my guardian and relative, to whom I dedicated a volume of puerile poems a few years ago. The guardianship was nominal, at least as far as I have been able to discover; the relationship I cannot help, and am very sorry for it; but as his Lordship seemed to forget it on a very essential occasion to me, I shall not burden my memory with the recollection. I do not think that personal differences sanction the unjust condemnation of a brother scribbler; but I see no reason why they should act as a preventive, when the author, noble or ignoble, has for a series of years, beguiled a "discerning public" (as the advertisements have it) with divers reams of most orthodox, imperial nonsense. Besides, I do not step aside to vituperate the Earl;

no—his works come fairly in review with those of other patrician literati. If, before I escaped from my teens, I said any thing in favour of his Lordship's paper books, it was in the way of dutiful dedication, and more from the advice of others than my own judgment, and I seize the first opportunity of pronouncing my sincere recantation. I have heard that some persons conceive me to be under obligations to Lord Carlisle; if so, I shall be most particularly happy to learn what they are, and when conferred, that they may be duly appreciated, and publicly acknowledged. What I have humbly advanced as an opinion on his printed things, I am prepared to support, if necessary, by quotations from Elegies, Eulogies, Odes, Episodes, and certain facetious and dainty tragedies bearing his name and mark:

"What can ennoble knaves, or *fools*, or cowards,
Alas! not all the blood of all the Howards!"

So says Pope. Amen!

NOTE 76, page 509.

And other Victors fill the applauding skies.

"Tollere humo, victorque virum volitare per ora."
VIRGIL.

NOTE 77, page 509.

Requires no sacred theme to bid us list.

The "Games of Hoyle," well known to the votaries of Whist, Chess, &c., are not to be superseded by the vagaries of his poetical namesake, whose poem comprised, as expressly stated in the advertisement, all the "Plagues of Egypt."

NOTE 78, page 509.

Himself a living libel on mankind.

This person, who has lately betrayed the most rapid symptoms of confirmed authorship, is writer of a poem denominated the "Art of Pleasing," as "Lucus a non lucendo," containing little pleasantry, and less poetry. He also acts as monthly stipendiary and collector of calumnies for the "Satirist." If this unfortunate young man would exchange the magazines for the mathematics, and endeavour to take a decent degree in his university, it might eventually prove more serviceable than his present salary.

NOTE 79, page 509.

Oh, dark asylum of a Vandal race.

"Into Cambridgeshire the Emperor Probus transported a considerable body of Vandals."—GIBBON'S "Decline and Fall," page 83, vol. 2. There is no reason to doubt the truth of this assertion; the breed is still in high perfection.

NOTE 80, page 509.

That Smythe and Hodgson scarce redeem thy fame.

Mr. Hodgson's name requires no praise; the man who in translation displays unquestionable genius, may well be expected to excel in original composition, of which it is to be hoped we shall soon see a splendid specimen.

NOTE 81, page 510.

And modern Britons justly praise their Sires.

The "Aboriginal Britons," an excellent poem by Richards.

NOTE 82, page 510.

And old dame Portland fills the place of Pitt.

A friend of mine being asked why his Grace of P. was likened to an old woman? replied, "he supposed it was because he was past bearing."

NOTE 83, page 510.

And Afric's coast and Calpe's adverse height.

Calpe is the ancient name of Gibraltar.

NOTE 84, page 510.

And Stamboul's minarets must greet my sight.

Stamboul is the Turkish word for Constantinople.

NOTE 85, page 510.

Thence shall I stray through beauty's native clime.

Georgia, remarkable for the beauty of its inhabitants.

NOTE 86, page 510.

Where Kaff is clad in rocks, and crowned with snows sublime.

Mount Caucasus.

NOTE 87, page 510.

Let vain Valentia rival luckless Carr.

Lord Valentia (whose tremendous travels are forthcoming with due decorations, graphical, topographical, and typographical) deposed, on Sir John Carr's unlucky suit, that Dubois's satire prevented his purchase of the "Stranger in Ireland."—Oh fie, my Lord! has your Lordship no more feeling for a fellow-tourist? "But two of a trade," they say, &c.

NOTE 88, page 510.

Let Aberdeen and Elgin still pursue.

Lord Elgin would fain persuade us that all the figures, with and without noses, in his stone-shop, are the work of Phidias; "Credat Judæus!"

NOTE 89, page 510.

I leave topography to classic Gell.

Mr. Gell's "Topography of Troy and Ithaca" cannot fail to ensure the approbation of every man possessed of classical taste, as well for the information Mr. G. conveys to the mind of the reader, as for the ability and research the respective works display.

THE WALTZ.

AN APOSTROPHIC HYMN.

"Qualis in Eurotæ ripis, aut per juga Cynthi,
Exercet Diana choros."
VIRGIL.

"Such on Eurotas' banks, or Cynthia's height,
Diana seems: and so she charms the sight,
When in the dance the graceful goddess leads
The quire of nymphs, and overtops their heads."
DRYDEN'S *Virgil*.

TO THE PUBLISHER.

SIR,—I am a country gentleman of a midland county. I might have been a parliament-man for a certain borough; having had the offer of as many votes as General T. at the general election in 1812.[1] But I was all for domestic happiness; as, fifteen years ago, on a visit to London, I married a middle-aged maid of honour. We lived happily at Hornem Hall till last season, when my wife and I were invited by the Countess of Waltzaway (a distant relation of my spouse) to pass the winter in town. Thinking no harm, and our girls being come to a marriageable (or, as they call it, *marketable*) age, and having besides a Chancery suit inveterately entailed upon the family estate, we came up in our old chariot,—of which, by-the-bye, my wife grew so much ashamed in less than a wek, that I was obliged to buy a second-hand barouche, of which I might mount the box, Mrs. H. says, if I could drive, but never see the inside —that place being reserved for the Honourable Augustus Tiptoe, her partner-general and opera-knight. Hearing great praises of Mrs. H.'s dancing (she was famous for birthnight minuets in the latter end of the last century), I unbooted, and went to a ball at the Countess's, expecting to see a country dance, or, at most, cotillions, reels, and all the old paces to the newest tunes. But, judge of my surprise, on arriving, to see poor dear Mrs. Hornem with her arms half round the loins of a huge hussar-looking gentleman I never set eyes on before: and his, to say truth, rather more than half round her waist, turning round, and round, and round, to a d——d see-saw up-and-down sort of tune, that reminded me of the "Black joke," only more "*affetuoso*," till it made me quite giddy with wondering they were not so. By and by they stopped a bit, and I thought they would sit or fall down:—but no; with Mrs. H.'s hand on his shoulder, "*quam familiariter*"[2] (as Terence said when I was at school), they walked about a minte, and then at it again, like two cockchafers spitted upon the same bodkin. I asked what all this meant, when, with a loud laugh, a child no older than our Wilhelmina (a name I never heard but in the Vicar of Wakefield, though her mother would call her after the Princess of Swappenbach,) said, "Lord! Mr. Hornem, can't you see they are valtzing!" or waltzing (I forget which); and then up she got, and her mother and sister, and away they went, and round-abouted it till supper time. Now, that I know what it is, I like it of all things, and so does Mrs. H. (though I have broken my shins, and four times overturned Mrs. Hornem's maid, in practising the preliminary steps in a morning). Indeed, so much do I like it, that having a turn for rhyme, tastily displayed in some election ballads and songs in honour of all the victories (but till lately I have had little practice in that way) I sat down, and with the aid of William Fitzgerald, Esq., and a few hints from Dr. Busby, (whose recitations I attend, and am monstrous fond of Master Busby's manner of delivering his father's late successful "Drury Lane Address,") I composed the following hymn, wherewithal to make my sentiments known to the public; whom, nevertheless, I heartily despise, as well as the critics.

I am, Sir, yours, &c., &c.

HORACE HORNEM.

THE WALTZ.

Muse of the many-twinkling feet! whose charms,[3]
Are now extended up from legs to arms;
Terpsichore!—too long misdeem'd a maid—
Reproachful term—bestow'd but to upbraid—
Henceforth in all the bronze of brightness shine,
The least a vestal of the virgin Nine.
Far be from thee and thine the name of prude;
Mock'd, yet triumphant; sneer'd at, unsubdued;
Thy legs must move to conquer as they fly,
If but thy coats are reasonably high;
Thy breast—if bare enough—requires no shield;
Dance forth,—*sans armour* thou shalt take the field,

And own—impregnable to *most* assaults,
Thy not too lawfully begotten "Waltz."'

Hail, nimble nymph! to whom the young hussar,
The whisker'd votary of waltz and war,
His night devotes, despite of spur and boots;
A sight unmatch'd since Orpheus and his brutes:
Hail, spirit-stirring Waltz!—beneath whose banners
A modern hero fought for modish manners;
On Hounslow's heath to rival Wellesley's fame,[4]
Cock'd—fired—and miss'd his man—but gain'd his aim;
Hail, moving Muse! to whom the fair one's breast
Gives all it can, and bids us take the rest.
Oh! for the flow of Busby, or of Fitz,
The latter's loyalty, the former's wits,
To "energise the object I pursue,"
And give both Belial and his dance their due!

Imperial Waltz! imported from the Rhine
(Famed for the growth of pedigrees and wine),
Long be thine import from all duty free,
And hock itself be less esteem'd than thee:
In some few qualities alike—for hock
Improves our cellar—*thou* our living stock.
The head to hock belongs—thy subtler art
Intoxicates alone the heedless heart:
Through the full veins thy gentler poison swims,
And wakes to wantonness the willing limbs.

Oh, Germany! how much to thee we owe,
As heaven-born Pitt can testify below,
Ere cursed confederation made thee France's,
And only left us thy d—d debts and dances!
Of subsidies and Hanover bereft,
We bless thee still—for George the Third is left!
Of kings the best—and last, not least in worth,
For graciously begetting George the Fourth.
To Germany, and highnesses serene,
Who owe us millions—don't we owe the Queen?
To Germany, what owe we not besides?
So oft bestowing Brunswickers and brides;
Who paid for vulgar, with her royal blood,
Drawn from the stem of each Teutonic stud;
Who sent us—so be pardon'd all her faults—
A dozen dukes, some kings, a queen—and Waltz.

But peace to her—her emperor and diet,
Though now transferr'd to Buonaparte's "fiat!"
Back to my theme—O Muse of Motion! say,
How first to Albion found thy Waltz her way?

Borne on the breath of hyperborean gales,
From Hamburg's port (while Hamburg yet had *mails*)
Ere yet unlucky fame—compelled to creep
To snowy Gottenburg—was chill'd to sleep;
Or, starting from her slumbers, deign'd arise,
Heligoland, to stock thy mart with lies;
While unburnt Moscow yet had news to send,[5]
Nor owed her fiery exit to a friend,
She came—Waltz came—and with her certain sets
Of true despatches, and as true gazettes:
Then flamed of Austerlitz the blest despatch,
Which Moniteur nor Morning Post can match;
And—almost crush'd beneath the glorious news—
Ten plays, and forty tales of Kotzebue's:
One envoy's letters, six composers' airs,
And loads from Frankfort and from Leipsic fairs;
Meiner's four volumes upon womankind,
Like Lapland witches to ensure a wind;
Brunck's heaviest tome for ballast, and, to back it,
Of Heyné, such as should not sink the packet.

Fraught with this cargo—and her fairest freight
Delightful Waltz, on tiptoe for a mate,
The welcome vessel reach'd the genial strand,
And round her flock'd the daughters of the land.
Not decent David, when, before the ark,
His grand pas-seul excited some remark;
Not love-lorn Quixote, when his Sancho thought
The knight's fandango friskier than it ought:
Not soft Herodias, when, with winning tread,
Her nimble feet danced off another's head;
Not Cleopatra on her galley's deck,
Display'd so much of *leg*, or more of *neck*,
Than thou, ambrosial Waltz, when first the moon
Beheld thee twirling to a Saxon tune!

To you, ye husbands of ten years! whose brows
Ache with the annual tributes of a spouse;
To you of nine years less, who only bear
The budding sprouts of those that you *shall* wear,
With added ornaments around them roll'd
Of native brass, or law-awarded gold;
To you, ye matrons, ever on the watch
To mar a son's, or make a daughter's, match;
To you, ye children of—whom chance accords—
Always the ladies, and *sometimes* their lords;
To you, ye single gentlemen, who seek
Torments for life, or pleasures for a week;
As Love or Hymen your endeavours guide,
To gain your own, or snatch another's bride;—
To one and all the lovely stranger came,
And every ball-room echoes with her name.

Endearing Waltz!—to thy more melting tune
Bow Irish Jig, and ancient Jigadoon.
Scotch Reels, avaunt! and Country-dance, forego
Your future claims to each fantastic toe!
Waltz—Waltz alone—both legs and arms demands,
Liberal of feet, and lavish of her hands;
Hands which may freely range in public sight
Where ne'er before—but—pray "put out the light."
Methinks the glare of yonder chandelier
Shines much too far—or I am much too near;
And true, tho' strange—Waltz whispers this remark
"My slippery steps are safest in the dark!"

But here the Muse with due decorum halts,
And lends her longest petticoat to Waltz.

Observant travellers of every time!
Ye quartos publish'd upon every clime!
Oh, say, shall dull Romaika's heavy round,
Fandango's wriggle, or Bolero's bound;
Can Egypt's Almas—tantalising group—[6]
Columbia's caperers to the warlike whoop—
Can aught from cold Kamschatka to Cape Horn
With Waltz compare, or after Waltz be borne?
Ah, no! from Morier's pages down to Galt's,
Each tourist pens a paragraph for "Waltz."

Shades of those belles whose reign began of yore,
With George the Third's and ended long before!—
Though in your daughters' daughters yet you thrive,
Burst from your lead, and be yourselves alive!
Back to the ball-room speed your spectred host;
Fool's Paradise is dull to that you lost.
No treacherous powder bids conjecture quake;
No stiff-starch'd stays make meddling fingers ache;
(Transferr'd to those ambiguous things that ape
Goats in their visage, women in their shape;)[7]
No damsel faints when rather closely press'd,
But more caressing seems when most caress'd;
Superfluous hartshorn, and reviving salts,
Both banish'd by the sovereign cordial "Waltz."

Seductive Waltz!—though on thy native shore
Even Werter's self proclaim'd thee half a whore;
Werter—to decent vice though much inclined,
Yet warm, not wanton; dazzled, but not blind—
Though gentle Genlis, in her strife with Staël,
Would even proscribe thee from a Paris ball;
The fashion hails—from countesses to queens,
And maids and valets waltz behind the scenes;
Wide and more wide thy witching circle spreads,
And turns—if nothing else—at least our *heads;*
With thee even clumsy cits attempt to bounce,
And cockneys practise what they can't pronounce.
God! how the glorious theme my strain exalts,
And rhyme finds partner rhyme in praise of Waltz!

Blest was the time Waltz chose for her *debût;*
The court, the Regent, like herself were new;[8]
New face for friends, for foes some new rewards;
New ornaments for black and royal guards;
New laws to hang the rogues that roar'd for bread;
New coins (most new) to follow those that fled;[9]
New victories—nor can we prize them less,
Though Jenky wonders at his own success;
New wars, because the old succeed so well,
That most survivors envy those who fell;
New mistresses—no, old—and yet 't is true,
Though they be *old,* the *thing* is something new;
Each new, quite new—(except some ancient tricks),[10]
New white-sticks, gold-sticks, broom-sticks, all new sticks!

With vests or ribbons, deck'd alike in hue,
New troopers strut, new turncoats blush in blue
So saith the muse: my——, what say you?[11]
Such was the time when Waltz might best maintain
Her new preferments in this novel reign;
Such was the time, nor ever yet was such;
Hoops are *no more,* and petticoats *not much;*
Morals and minuets, virtue and her stays,
And tell-tale powder—all have had their days.
The ball begins—the honours of the house
First duly done by daughter or by spouse,
Some potentate—or royal or serene—
With Kent's gay grace, or sapient Gloster's mien,
Leads forth the ready dame, whose rising flush
Might once have been mistaken for a blush.
From where the garb just leaves the bosom free,
That spot where hearts were once supposed to be;[12]
Round all the confines of the yielded waist,
The stranger's hand may wander undisplaced;
The lady's in return may grasp as much
As princely paunches offer to her touch.
Pleased round the chalky floor how well they trip,
One hand reposing on the royal hip;
The other to the shoulder no less royal
Ascending with affection truly loyal!
Thus front to front the partners move or stand,
The foot may rest, but none withdraw the hand;
And all in turn may follow in their rank,
The Earl of—Asterisk—and Lady—Blank;
Sir—Such-a-one—with those of fashion's host,
For whose blest surnames—*vide* "Morning Post"
(Or if for that impartial print too late,
Search Doctors' Commons six months from my date).
Thus all and each, in movements swift or slow,
The genial contact gently undergo;
Till some might marvel, with the modest Turk,
If "nothing follows all this palming work?"[13]
True, honest Mirza!—you may trust my rhyme—
Something does follow at a fitter time;
The breast thus publicly resign'd to man
In private may resist him——if it can.

O ye who loved our grandmothers of yore,
Fitzpatrick, Sheridan, and many more!
And thou, my Prince! whose sovereign taste and will
It is to love the lovely beldames still!
Thou ghost of Queensbury! whose judging sprite
Satan may spare to peep a single night,
Pronounce—if ever in your days of bliss
Asmodeus struck so bright a stroke as this?
To teach the young ideas how to rise,
Flush in the cheek, and languish in the eyes;
Rush to the heart, and lighten through the frame,
With half-told wish and ill-dissembled flame:
For prurient nature still will storm the breast—
Who, tempted thus, can answer for the rest?

But ye—who never felt a single thought
For what our morals are to be, or ought;
Who wisely wish the charms you view to reap,
Say—would you make those beauties quite so cheap?
Hot from the hands promiscuously applied,
Round the slight waist, or down the glowing side,
Where were the rapture then to clasp the form
From this lewd grasp and lawless contact warm?
At once love's most endearing thought resign,
To press the hand so press'd by none but thine;
To gaze upon that eye which never met
Another's ardent look without regret;
Approach the lip which all, without restraint,
Come near enough—if not to touch—to taint;
If such thou lovest—love her then no more,
Or give—like her—caresses to a score;
Her mind with these is gone, and with it go
The little left behind it to bestow.

Voluptuous Waltz! and dare I thus blaspheme?
Thy bard forgot thy praises were his theme.
Terpsichore, forgive!—at every ball
My wife *now* waltzes and my daughters *shall*,
My son—(or stop—'t is needless to inquire—
These little accidents should ne'er transpire;
Some ages hence our genealogic tree
Will wear as green a bough for him as me)—
Waltzing shall rear, to make our name amends,
Grandsons for me—in heirs to all his friends.

NOTES TO THE WALTZ.

NOTE 1, page 517.

State of the poll (last day), 5.

NOTE 2, page 517.

"Quam familiariter."

My Latin is all forgotten, if a man can be said to have forgotten what he never remembered; but I bought my title-page motto of a Catholic priest for a three-shilling bank token, after much haggling for the *even* sixpence. I grudged the money to a papist, being all for the memory of Perceval and "No popery," and quite regretting the downfall of the pope, because we can't burn him any more.

NOTE 3, page 518.

Muse of the many-twinkling feet! whose charms.

"Glance their many-twinkling feet."—GRAY.

NOTE 4, page 519.

On Hounslow's heath to rival Wellesley's fame.

To rival Lord Wellesley's, or his nephew's, as the reader pleases:—the one gained a pretty woman, whom he deserved, by fighting for; and the other, has been fighting in the Peninsula many a long day, "by Shrewsbury clock," without gaining anything in *that* country but the title of "the Great Lord;" and "the Lord;" which savours of profanation, having been hitherto applied only to that Being to whom "*Te Deums*" for carnage are the rankest blasphemy. It is to be presumed that the general will one day return to his Sabine farm; there

"To tame the genius of the stubborn plain,
Almost as quickly as he conquer'd Spain!"

The Lord Peterborough conquered continents in a summer; we do more—we contrive both to conquer and lose them in a shorter season. If the "great Lord's" *Cincinnatian* progress in agriculture be no speedier than the proportional average of time in Pope's couplet, it will, according to the farmers' proverb, be "ploughing with dogs."

By-the-bye—one of this illustrious person's new titles is forgotten—it is, however, worth remembering—"*Salvador del mundo!*" *credite posteri!* If this be the appellation annexed by the inhabitants of the Peninsula to the name of a *man* who has not yet saved them—query—are they worth saving, even in this world? for, according to the mildest modifications of any Christian creed, those three words make the odds much against them in the next. "Saviour of the world," quotha!—it were to be wished that he, or any one else, could save a corner of it—his country. Yet this stupid misnomer, although it shows the near connection between superstition and impiety, so far has its use, that it proves there can be little to dread from those Catholics (inquisitorial Catholics too) who can confer such an appellation on a *Protestant.* I suppose next year he will be entitled the "Virgin Mary;" if so, Lord George Gordon himself would have nothing to object to such liberal bastards of our Lady of Babylon.

NOTE 5, page 519.

While unburnt Moscow yet had news to send.

The patriotic arson of our amiable allies cannot be sufficiently commended—nor subscribed for. Amongst other details omitted in the various despatches of our eloquent ambassador, he did not state (being too much occupied with the exploits of Colonel C——, in swimming rivers frozen, and galloping over roads impassable,) that one entire province perished by famine in the most melancholy manner, as follows:—In General Rostopchin's consummate conflagration, the consumption of tallow and train oil was so great, that the market was inadequate to the demand; and thus one hundred and thirty-three thousand persons were starved to death, by being reduced to wholesome diet. The lamplighters of London have since subscribed a pint (of oil) a piece, and the tallow-chandlers have unanimously voted a quantity of the best moulds (four to the pound), to the relief of the surviving Scythians;—the scarcity will soon, by such exertions, and a proper attention to the *quality* rather than the quantity of provision, be totally alleviated. It is said, in return, that the untouched Ukraine has subscribed sixty thousand beeves for a day's meal to our suffering manufacturers.

NOTE 6, page 520.

Can Egypt's Almas—tantalising group.

Dancing girls—who do for hire what Waltz doth gratis.

NOTE 7, page 520.

Goats in their visage, women in their shape.

It cannot be complained now, as in the Lady Baussiere's time, of the "Sieur de la Croix," that there be "no whiskers;" but how far these are indications of valour in the field, or elsewhere, may *still* be questionable. Much may be, and hath been, avouched on both sides. In the olden time philosophers had whiskers, and soldiers none—Scipio himself was shaven—Hannibal thought his one eye handsome enough without a beard; but Adrian, the emperor, wore a beard (having warts on his chin, which neither the empress Sabina nor even the courtiers could abide)—Turenne had whiskers, Marlborough none—Buonaparte is unwhiskered, the Regent whiskered; "*argal*" greatness of mind and whiskers may or may not go together; but certainly the different occurrences, since the growth of the last mentioned, go further in behalf of whiskers than the anathema of Anselm did *against* long hair in the reign of Henry I. Formerly, *red* was a favourite colour. See Lodowick Barry's comedy of Ram Alley, 1661 · Act i. Sc. 1.

"*Taffeta* Now for a wager—What coloured beard comes next by the window?

"*Adriana.* A black man's, I think.

"*Taffeta.* I think not so: I think a *red*, for that is most in fashion."

There is "nothing new under the sun;" but *red*, then a *favourite*, has now subsided into a *favourite's* colour.

NOTE 8, page 520.

The court, the Regent, like herself, were new.

An anachronism—Waltz and the battle of Austerlitz are before said to have opened the ball together; the bard means (if he means any thing), Waltz was not so much in vogue till the Regent attained the acmé of his popularity. Waltz, the comet, whiskers, and the new government, illuminated heaven and earth, in all their glory, much about the same time; of these the comet only has disappeared; the other three continue to astonish us still.—*Printer's Devil.*

NOTE 9, page 520.

New coins (most new) to follow those that fled.

Amongst others a new ninepence—a creditable coin now forthcoming, worth a pound, in paper, a the fairest calculation.

NOTE 10, page 520

Each new, quite new—(except some ancient tricks.)

"Oh that *right* should thus overcome *might!*" Who does not remember the "delicate investigation" in the "Merry Wives of Windsor?"—

"*Ford.* Pray you, come near· if I suspect without cause, why then make sport at me: then let me be your jest; I deserve it. How now? whither bear you this?

"*Mrs. Ford.* What have you to do whither they bear it?—you were best meddle with buck-washing."

NOTE 11, page 520.

So saith the muse: my ——, what say you.

The gentle, or ferocious, reader may fill up the blank as he pleases—there are several dissyllabic names at his service (being already in the Regent's); it would not be fair to back any peculiar initial against the alphabet, as every month will add to the list now entered for the sweepstakes:—a distinguished consonant is said to be the favourite, much against the wishes of the *knowing ones.*

NOTE 12, page 520.

That spot where hearts were once supposed to be.

"We have changed all that," says the Mock Doctor—'t is all gone—Asmodeus knows where. After all, it is of no great importance how women's hearts are disposed of; they have nature's privilege to distribute them as absurdly as possible. But there are also some men with hearts so thoroughly bad, as to remind us of those phenomena often mentioned in natural history; viz. a mass of solid stone—only to be opened by force—and when divided, you find a *toad* in the centre, lively, and with the reputation of being venomous.

NOTE 13, page 520.

If "nothing follows all this palming work."

In Turkey a pertinent, here an impertinent and superfluous, question—literally put, as in the text, by a Persian to Morier, on seeing a waltz in Pera.—*Vide* Morier's Travels.

POEMS ON NAPOLEON.

ODE TO NAPOLEON.

"Expende Annibalem:—quot libras in duce summo
Invenies?" JUVENAL, *Sat.* X.

"The Emperor Nepos was acknowledged by the Senate, by the Italians, and by the Provincials of Gaul; his moral virtues, and military talents, were loudly celebrated; and those who derived any private benefit from his government announced in prophetic strains the restoration of public felicity.

* * * * * * * * * * * * * * * *

By this shameful abdication, he protracted his life a few years, in a very ambiguous state, between an Emperor and an Exile, till ——."—GIBBON'S *Decline and Fall*, vol. vi. p. 220.

'T IS done—but yesterday a King!
And arm'd with Kings to strive—
And now thou art a nameless thing;
So abject—yet alive!
Is this the man of thousand thrones,
Who strew'd our earth with hostile bones,
And can he thus survive?
Since he, miscall'd the Morning Star,
Nor man nor fiend hath fallen so far.

Ill-minded man! why scourge thy kind
Who bow'd so low the knee?

By gazing on thyself grown blind,
Thou taught'st the rest to see.
With might unquestion'd—power to save,—
Thine only gift hath been the grave,
To those that worshipp'd thee;
Nor till thy fall could mortals guess
Ambition's less than littleness!

Thanks for that lesson—it will teach
To after-warriors more,
Than high Philosophy can preach,
And vainly preach'd before.
That spell upon the minds of men
Breaks never to unite again,
That led them to adore
Those Pagod things of sabre sway,
With fronts of brass, and feet of clay.

The triumph, and the vanity,
The rapture of the strife—[1]
The earthquake voice of Victory,
To thee the breath of life;
The sword, the sceptre, and that sway
Which man seem'd made but to obey,
Wherewith renown was rife—
All quell'd!—Dark Spirit! what must be
The madness of thy memory!

The Desolator desolate!
The Victor overthrown!
The arbiter of others' fate
A suppliant for his own!
Is it some yet imperial hope,
That with such change can calmly cope?
Or dread of death alone?
To die a prince—or live a slave—
Thy choice is most ignobly brave!

He who of old would rend the oak,
Dream'd not of the rebound;
Chain'd by the trunk he vainly broke—
Alone—how look'd he round?
Thou, in the sternness of thy strength,
An equal deed hast done at length.
And darker fate hast found:
He fell the forest prowlers' prey;
But thou must eat thy heart away!

The Roman, when his burning heart
Was slaked with blood of Rome,
Threw down the dagger—dared depart,
In savage grandeur, home—
He dared depart in utter scorn
Of men that such a yoke had borne,
Yet left him such a doom!
His only glory was that hour
Of self-upheld abandon'd power.

The Spaniard, when the lust of sway
Had lost its quickening spell,
Cast crowns for rosaries away,
An empire for a cell;
A strict accountant of his beads,
A subtle disputant on creeds,
His dotage trifled well:
Yet better had he neither known
A bigot's shrine, nor despot's throne.

But thou—from thy reluctant hand
The thunderbolt is wrung—
Too late thou leav'st the high command
To which thy weakness clung;
All Evil Spirit as thou art,
It is enough to grieve the heart
To see thine own unstrung;
To think that God's fair world hath been
The footstool of a thing so mean!

And Earth hath spilt her blood for him,
Who thus can hoard his own!
And Monarchs bow'd the trembling limb,
And thank'd him for a throne!
Fair Freedom! may we hold thee dear,
When thus thy mightiest foes their fear
In humblest guise have shown.
Oh! ne'er may tyrant leave behind
A brighter name to lure mankind!

Thine evil deeds are writ in gore,
Nor written thus in vain—
Thy triumphs tell of fame no more,
Or deepen every stain:
If thou had'st died as honour dies,
Some new Napoleon might arise,
To shame the world again—
But who would soar the solar height,
To set in such a starless night?

Weigh'd in the balance, hero dust
Is vile as vulgar clay;
Thy scales, Mortality! are just
To all that pass away:
But yet methought the living great
Some higher sparks should animate,
To dazzle and dismay;
Nor deem'd Contempt could thus make mirth
Of these, the Conquerors of the earth.

And she, proud Austria's mournful flower,
Thy still imperial bride;
How bears her breast the torturing hour?
Still clings she to thy side?
Must she, too, bend,—must she, too, share,
Thy late repentance, long despair,
Thou throneless Homicide?

If still she loves thee, hoard that gem ;)
'Tis worth thy vanish'd diadem !

Then haste thee to thy sullen Isle,
And gaze upon the sea ;
That element may meet thy smile—
It ne'er was ruled by thee !
Or trace with thine all idle hand,
In loitering mood upon the sand,
That Earth is now as free !

That Corinth's pedagogue hath now
Transferr'd his by-word to thy brow.

Thou Timour ! in his captive's cage
What thoughts will there be thine,
While brooding in thy prison'd rage ?
But one—"The world *was* mine !"
Unless, like he of Babylon,
All sense is with thy sceptre gone,
Life will not long confine

That spirit pour'd so widely forth—
So long obey'd—so little worth!

Or, like the thief of fire from heaven,
 Wilt thou withstand the shock?
And share with him, the unforgiven,
 His vulture and his rock!
Foredoom'd by God—by man accurst,
And that last act, though not thy worst,
 The very Fiend's arch mock;
He, in his fall preserved his pride,
And, if a mortal, had as proudly died!

ODE FROM THE FRENCH.

I.

We do not curse thee, Waterloo!
Though Freedom's blood thy plain bedew:
There 't was shed, but is not sunk—
Rising from each gory trunk,
Like the water-spout from ocean,
With a strong and growing motion—
It soars, and mingles in the air,
With that of lost Labedoyère—
With that of him whose honour'd grave
Contains the "bravest of the brave."
A crimson cloud it spreads and glows,
But shall return to whence it rose;
When 't is full 't will burst asunder—
Never yet was heard such thunder,
As then shall shake the world with wonder—
Never yet was seen such lightning
As o'er heaven shall then be bright'ning!
Like the Wormwood Star foretold
By the sainted Seer of old,
Show'ring down a fiery flood,
Turning rivers into blood.[2]

II.

The chief has fallen! but not by you,
Vanquishers of Waterloo!
When the soldier-citizen
Sway'd not o'er his fellow-men—
Save in deeds that led them on
Where Glory smil'd on Freedom's son—
Who, of all the despots banded,
 With that youthful chief competed?
 Who could boast o'er France defeated,
Till lone tyranny commanded?
Till, goaded by ambition's sting,
The hero sunk into the King?
Then he fell:—so perish all,
Who would men by man enthrall!

III.

And thou, too, of the snow-white plume!
Whose realm refused thee e'en a tomb;
Better hadst thou still been leading
France o'er hosts of hirelings bleeding,
Than sold thyself to death and shame
For a meanly royal name;
Such as he of Naples wears,
Who thy blood-bought title bears.
Little didst thou deem, when dashing
 On thy war-horse through the ranks
 Like a stream which bursts its banks,
While helmets cleft, and sabres clashing,
Shone and shiver'd fast around thee—
Of the fate at last which found thee!
Was that haughty plume laid low
By a slave's dishonest blow?
Once—as the Moon sways o'er the tide,
It roll'd in air, the warrior's guide;
Through the smoke-created night
Of the black and sulphurous fight,
The soldier raised his seeking eye
To catch that crest's ascendancy—
And as it onward rolling rose,
So moved his heart upon our foes.
There, where death's brief pang was quickest,
And the battle's wreck lay thickest,
Strew'd beneath the advancing banner
 Of the eagle's burning crest—
(There with thunder-clouds to fan her,
Who could then her wing arrest—
 Victory beaming from her breast?)
While the broken line enlarging
 Fell, or fled along the plain;
There be sure was Murat charging!
 There he ne'er shall charge again!

IV.

O'er glories gone the invaders march,
Weep Triumph o'er each levell'd arch—
But let Freedom rejoice,
With her heart in her voice;
But her hand on her sword,
Doubly shall she be adored;
France hath twice too well been taught
The "moral lesson" dearly bought—
Her safety sits not on a throne,
With Capet or Napoleon!
But in equal rights and laws,
Hearts and hands in one great cause—
Freedom, such as God hath given
Unto all beneath His heaven,
With their breath, and from their birth,
Though Guilt would sweep it from the earth;
With a fierce and lavish hand
Scattering nations' wealth like sand;
Pouring nations' blood like water,
In imperial seas of slaughter!

V.

But the heart and the mind,
And the voice of mankind,
Shall arise in communion—
And who shall resist that proud union?
The time is past when swords subdued—
Man may die—the soul's renewed:
Even in this low world of care
Freedom ne'er shall want an heir;
Millions breathe but to inherit
Her for ever bounding spirit—
When once more her hosts assemble,
Tyrants shall believe and tremble—
Smile they at this idle threat?
Crimson tears will follow yet.

TO NAPOLEON.

FROM THE FRENCH.

Must thou go, my glorious Chief,[3]
 Sever'd from thy faithful few?
Who can tell thy warriors' grief,
 Maddening o'er that long adieu?
Woman's love, and friendship's zeal,
 Dear as both have been to me—
What are they to all I feel,
 With a soldier's faith for thee?

Idol of the soldier's soul!
 First in fight, but mightiest now!
Many could a world control;
 Thee alone no doom can bow.
By thy side for years I dared
 Death; and envied those who fell,
When their dying shout was heard,
 Blessing him they served so well.[4]

Would that I were cold with those,
 Since this hour I live to see;
When the doubts of coward foes
 Scarce dare trust a man with thee.
Dreading each should set thee free!
 Oh! although in dungeons pent,
All their chains were light to me,
 Gazing on thy soul unbent.

Would the sycophants of him
 Now so deaf to duty's prayer,
Were his borrow'd glories dim,
 In his native darkness share?
Were that world this hour his own,
 All thou calmly dost resign,
Could he purchase with that throne
 Hearts like those which still are thine?

My chief, my king, my friend, adieu!
Never did I droop before;
Never to my sovereign sue,
As his foes I now implore:

All I ask is to divide
Every peril he must brave;
Sharing by the hero's side
His fall, his exile, and his grave.

NAPOLEON'S FAREWELL.

FROM THE FRENCH.

Farewell to the Land, where the gloom of my Glory
Arose and o'ershadow'd the earth with her name—
She abandons me now—but the page of her story,
The brightest or blackest, is fill'd with my fame.
I have warr'd with a world which vanquish'd me only
When the meteor of conquest allured me too far:

I have coped with the nations which dread me thus lonely,
The last single Captive to millions in war.

Farewell to thee, France! when thy diadem crown'd me,
I made thee the gem and the wonder of earth,—
But thy weakness decrees I should leave as I found thee,
Decay'd in thy glory, and sunk in thy worth.
Oh! for the veteran hearts that were wasted
In strife with the storm, when their battles were won—
Then the Eagle, whose gaze in that moment was blasted,
Had still soar'd with eyes fix'd on victory's sun!

Farewell to thee, France!—but when Liberty rallies
Once more in thy regions, remember me then—
The violet still grows in the depth of thy valleys;
Though wither'd, thy tears will unfold it again—
Yet, yet I may baffle the hosts that surround us,
And yet may thy heart leap awake to my voice—
There are links which must break in the chain that has bound us,
Then turn thee and call on the Chief of thy choice!

ON THE STAR OF "THE LEGION OF HONOUR."

FROM THE FRENCH.

STAR of the brave!—whose beam hath shed
Such glory o'er the quick and dead—
Thou radiant and adored deceit!
Which millions rush'd in arms to greet,—
Wild meteor of immortal birth!
Why rise in heaven to set on Earth!

Souls of slain heroes form'd thy rays;
Eternity flash'd through thy blaze
The music of thy martial sphere
Was fame on high and honour here;
And thy light broke on human eyes,
Like a volcano of the skies.

Like lava roll'd thy stream of blood,
And swept down empires with its flood;
Earth rock'd beneath thee to her base,
As thou did'st lighten through all space;
And the shorn Sun grew dim in air,
And set while thou wert dwelling there.

Before thee rose, and with thee grew,
A rainbow of the loveliest hue
Of three bright colours, each divine,[5]
And fit for that celestial sign;
For Freedom's hand had blended them,
Like tints in an immortal gem.

One tint was of the sunbeam's dyes;
One, the blue depth of Seraph's eyes:
One, the pure Spirit's veil of white
Had robed in radiance of its light:
The three so mingled did beseem
The texture of a heavenly dream.

Star of the brave! thy ray is pale,
And darkness must again prevail!
But, oh thou Rainbow of the free!
Our tears and blood must flow for thee.
When thy bright promise fades away,
Our life is but a load of clay.

And Freedom hallows with her tread
The silent cities of the dead;
For beautiful in death are they
Who proudly fall in her array;
And soon, oh Goddess! may we be
For evermore with them or thee!

NOTES TO POEMS ON NAPOLEON.

NOTE 1, page 524.

The rapture of the strife.

"Certaminis *gaudia*"—the expression of Attila in his harangue to his army, previous to the battle of Chonsal, given in Cassiodorus.

NOTE 2, page 527.

Turning rivers into blood.

See Rev. chap. viii. v. 7, &c. "The first angel sounded, and there followed hail and fire mingled with blood," &c. v. 8. "And the second angel sounded, and as it were a great mountain burning with fire was cast into the sea; and the third part of the sea became blood," &c. v. 10. "And the third angel sounded, and there fell a great star from heaven, burning as it were a lamp; and it fell upon the third part of the rivers, and upon the fountains of waters." v. 11. "And the name of the star is called *Wormwood;* and the third part of the waters became *wormwood;* and many men died of the waters, because they were made bitter."

NOTE 3, page 528.

Must thou go, my glorious Chief?

"All wept, but particularly Savary, and a Polish officer who had been exalted from the ranks by Buonaparte. He clung to his master's knees; wrote a letter to Lord Keith, entreating permission to accompany him, even in the most menial capacity, which could not be admitted."

NOTE 4, page 528.

Blessing him they served so well.

"At Waterloo, one man was seen, whose left arm was shattered by a cannon ball, to wrench it off with the other, and throwing it up in the air, exclaimed to his comrades, 'Vive l'Empereur, jusqu'à la mort!' There were many other instances of the like: this, however, you may depend on as true."—*Private Letter from Brussels.*

NOTE 5, page 530.

Of three bright colours, each divine.

The tricolour.

MONODY

ON THE DEATH OF THE RIGHT HON. R. B. SHERIDAN,

SPOKEN AT DRURY-LANE THEATRE.

WHEN the last sunshine of expiring day
In summer's twilight weeps itself away,
Who hath not felt the softness of the hour
Sink on the heart, as dew along the flower?
With a pure feeling which absorbs and awes
While Nature makes that melancholy pause,
Her breathing moment on the bridge where Time
Of light and darkness forms an arch sublime,
Who hath not shared that calm so still and deep,
The voiceless thought which would not speak but weep,
A holy concord—and a bright regret,
A glorious sympathy with suns that set?
'Tis not harsh sorrow—but a tenderer woe.
Nameless, but dear to gentle hearts below,
Felt without bitterness—but full and clear,
A sweet dejection—a transparent tear,
Unmix'd with worldly grief or selfish stain,
Shed without shame—and secret without pain.

Even as the tenderness that hour instils
When summer's day declines along the hills

So feels the fulness of our heart and eyes,
When all of Genius which can perish dies.
A mighty Spirit is eclipsed—a Power
Hath passed from day to darkness—to whose hour
Of light no likeness is bequeath'd—no name,
Focus at once of all the rays of Fame!
The flash of Wit—the bright Intelligence,
The beam of Song—the blaze of Eloquence,
Set with their Sun—but still have left behind
The enduring produce of immortal Mind;
Fruits of a genial morn, and glorious noon,
A deathless part of him who died too soon.
But small that portion of the wondrous whole,
These sparkling segments of that circling soul,
Which all embraced—and lighten'd over all,
To cheer—to pierce—to please—or to appal.
From the charm'd council to the festive board,
Of human feelings the unbounded lord;
In whose acclaim the loftiest voices vied,
The praised—the proud—who made his praise their pride.
When the loud cry of trampled Hindostan
Arose to Heaven in her appeal from man,
His was the thunder—his the avenging rod,
The wrath—the delegated voice of God!
Which shook the nations through his lips—and blazed
Till vanquish'd senates trembled as they praised.

And here, oh! here, where yet all young and warm,
The gay creations of his spirit charm,
The matchless dialogue—the deathless wit,
Which knew not what it was to intermit;
The glowing portraits, fresh from life, that bring
Home to our hearts the truth from which they spring;
These wondrous beings of his Fancy, wrought
To fulness by the fiat of his thought,
Here in their first abode you still may meet,
Bright with the hues of his Promethean heat:
A halo of the light of other days,
Which still the splendour of its orb betrays.

But should there be to whom the fatal blight
Of failing Wisdom yields a base delight,
Men who exult when minds of heavenly tone
Jar in the music which was born their own,
Still let them pause—ah! little do they know
That what to them seem'd Vice might be but Woe.
Hard is his fate on whom the public gaze
Is fix'd for ever to detract or praise;
Repose denies her requiem to his name,
And Folly loves the martyrdom of Fame.
The secret enemy whose sleepless eye
Stands sentinel—accuser—judge—and spy,
The foe—the fool—the jealous—and the vain,
The envious who but breathe in others' pain,
Behold the host! delighting to deprave,
Who track the steps of glory to the grave,
Watch every fault that daring Genius owes
Half to the ardour which its birth bestows,
Distort the truth, accumulate the lie,
And pile the pyramid of Calumny!
These are his portion—but if joined to these
Gaunt Poverty should league with deep Disease,
If the high Spirit must forget to soar,
And stoop to strive with Misery at the door,
To soothe Indignity—and face to face
Meet sordid Rage—and wrestle with Disgrace,
To find in Hope but the renew'd caress,
The serpent-fold of further Faithlessness:—
If such may be the ills which men assail,
What marvel if at last the mightiest fail?
Breasts to whom all the strength of feeling given
Bear hearts electric—charged with fire from heaven,
Black with the rude collision, inly torn,
By clouds surrounded, and on whirlwinds borne,
Driven o'er the lowering atmosphere that nurst
Thoughts which have turn'd to thunder—scorch—and burst.

But far from us and from our mimic scene
Such things should be—if such have ever been;
Ours be the gentler wish, the kinder task,
To give the tribute Glory need not ask,
To mourn the vanish'd beam—and add our mite
Of praise in payment of a long delight.
Ye Orators! whom yet our councils yield,
Mourn for the veteran Hero of your field!
The worthy rival of the wondrous *Three!*
Whose words were sparks of Immortality!
Ye Bards! to whom the Drama's Muse is dear,
He was your Master—emulate him *here!*
Ye men of wit and social eloquence!
He was your brother—bear his ashes hence!
While Powers of mind almost of boundless range
Complete in kind—as various in their change,
While Eloquence—Wit—Poesy—and Mirth,
That humbler Harmonist of care on Earth,
Survive within our souls—while lives our sense
Of pride in Merit's proud pre-eminence,
Long shall we seek his likeness—long in vain,
And turn to all of him which may remain,
Sighing that Nature form'd but one such man,
And broke the die—in moulding Sheridan.

Diodati, July 17, 1816.

ADDRESS,

SPOKEN AT THE OPENING OF DRURY-LANE THEATRE, SATURDAY, OCTOBEER 10, 1812.

In one dread night our city saw, and sigh'd,
Bow'd to the dust, the Drama's tower of pride;
In one short hour beheld the blazing fane,
Apollo sink, and Shakspeare cease to reign.

Ye who beheld (oh! sight admired and mourn'd,
Whose radiance mock'd the ruin it adorn'd!
Through clouds of fire the massive fragments riven,
Like Israel's pillar, chase the night from heaven;
Saw the long column of revolving flames
Shake its red shadow o'er the startled Thames,
While thousands, throng'd around the burning dome,
Shrank back appall'd, and trembled for their home,
As glared the volumned blaze, and ghastly shone
The skies, with lightnings awful as their own,
Till blackening ashes and the lonely wall
Usurp'd the Muse's realm, and mark'd her fall;
Say—shall this new, nor less aspiring pile,
Rear'd where once rose the mightiest in our isle,
Know the same favour which the former knew,
A shrine for Shakspeare—worthy him and *you?*

Yes—it shall be—the magic of that name
Defies the scythe of time, the torch of flame;
On the same spot still consecrates the scene,
And bids the Drama *be* where she hath *been:*
This fabric's birth attests the potent spell—
Indulge our honest pride, and say, *How well!*

As soars this fane to emulate the last,
Oh! might we draw our omens from the past,
Some hour propitious to our prayers may boast
Names such as hallow still the dome we lost.
On Drury first your Siddons' thrilling art
O'erwhelm'd the gentlest, storm'd the sternest heart.
On Drury, Garrick's latest laurels grew;
Here your last tears retiring Roscius drew:
Sigh'd his last thanks, and wept his last adieu;
But still for living wit the wreaths may bloom,
That only waste their odours o'er the tomb.
Such Drury claim'd and claims—nor you refuse
One tribute to revive his slumbering muse;
With garlands deck your own Menander's head!
Nor hoard your honours idly for the dead!

Dear are the days which made our annals bright,
Ere Garrick fled, or Brinsley ceased to write.
Heirs to their labours, like all high-born heirs,
Vain of *our* ancestry as they of *theirs;*
While thus Remembrance borrows Banquo's glass
To claim the sceptred shadows as they pass,
And we the mirror hold, where imaged shine
Immortal names, emblazon'd on our line,
Pause—ere their feebler offspring you condemn,
Reflect how hard the task to rival them!

Friends of the stage! to whom both Players and Plays
Must sue alike for pardon or for praise,
Whose judging voice and eye alone direct
The boundless power to cherish or reject;
If e'er frivolity has led to fame,
And made us blush that you forbore to blame;
If e'er the sinking stage could condescend
To soothe the sickly taste it dare not mend,
All past reproach may present scenes refute,
And censure, wisely loud, be justly mute!
Oh! since your fiat stamps the Drama's laws,
Forbear to mock us with misplaced applause;
So pride shall doubly nerve the actor's powers,
And reason's voice be echo'd back by ours!

This greeting o'er, the ancient rule obey'd,
The Drama's homage by her herald paid,
Receive *our* welcome too, whose every tone
Springs from our hearts, and fain would win your own.
The curtain rises—may our stage unfold
Scenes not unworthy Drury's days of old!
Britons our judges, Nature for our guide,
Still may *we* please—long, long may *you* preside!

POEMS TO THYRZA.

TO THYRZA.

WITHOUT a stone to mark the spot,
 And say, what Truth might well have said,
By all, save one, perchance forgot,
 Ah! wherefore art thou lowly laid?

By many a shore and many a sea
 Divided, yet beloved in vain!
The past, the future fled to thee,
 To bid us meet—no—ne'er again!

Could this have been—a word, a look,
 That softly said, "We part in peace,"
Had taught my bosom how to brook,
 With fainter sighs, thy soul's release.

And didst thou not, since Death for thee
 Prepared a light and pangless dart,
Once long for him thou ne'er shalt see,
 Who held, and holds thee in his heart?

Oh! who like him had watch'd thee here?
 Or sadly mark'd thy glazing eye,
In that dread hour ere death appear,
 When silent sorrow fears to sigh.

Till all was past! But when no more
 'T was thine to reck of human woe,
Affection's heart-drops, gushing o'er,
 Had flow'd as fast—as now they flow.

Shall they not flow, when many a day
 In these, to me, deserted towers,
Ere call'd but for a time away,
 Affection's mingling tears were ours?

Ours too the glance none saw beside;
 The smile none else might understand;
The whisper'd thought of hearts allied,
 The pressure of the thrilling hand;

The kiss, so guiltless and refined,
 That Love each warmer wish forbore;
Those eyes proclaim'd so pure a mind,
 Even passion blush'd to plead for more.

The tone, that taught me to rejoice,
 When prone, unlike thee, to repine;
The song, celestial from thy voice,
 But sweet to me from none but thine;

The pledge we wore—I wear it still,
 But where is thine?—Ah! where art thou?
Oft have I borne the weight of ill,
 But never bent beneath till now!

Well hast thou left in life's best bloom
 The cup of woe for me to drain.
If rest alone be in the tomb,
 I would not wish thee here again;

But if in worlds more blest than this
 Thy virtues seek a fitter sphere,
Impart some portion of thy bliss,
 To wean me from mine anguish here.

Teach me—too early taught by thee!
 To bear, forgiving and forgiven:
On earth thy love was such to me;
 It fain would form my hope in heaven!

October 11, 1811.

AWAY, AWAY, YE NOTES OF WOE.

AWAY, away, ye notes of woe!
 Be silent, thou once soothing strain,
Or I must flee from hence—for, oh!
 I dare not trust those sounds again.
To me they speak of brighter days—
 But lull the chords, for now, alas!
I must not think, I may not gaze,
 On what I am—on what I was.

The voice that made those sounds more sweet
 Is hush'd, and all their charms are fled;
And now their softest notes repeat
 A dirge, an anthem o'er the dead!
Yes, Thyrza! yes, they breathe of thee,
 Beloved dust! since dust thou art;
And all that once was harmony
 Is worse than discord to my heart.

'T is silent all!—but on my ear
 The well remember'd echoes thrill,
I hear a voice I would not hear,
 A voice that now might well be still.
Yet oft my doubting soul 't will shake;
 Even slumber owns its gentle tone,
Till consciousness will vainly wake
 To listen, though the dream be flown.

Sweet Thyrza! waking as in sleep,
 Thou art but now a lovely dream;
A star that trembled o'er the deep,
 Then turn'd from earth its tender beam.
But he who through life's dreary way
 Must pass, when heaven is veil'd in wrath,
Will long lament the vanish'd ray
 That scatter'd gladness o'er his path.

December 6, 1811.

ONE STRUGGLE MORE, AND I AM FREE.

ONE struggle more, and I am free
 From pangs that rend my heart in twain;
One last long sigh to love and thee,
 Then back to busy life again.

It sutis me well to mingle now
With things that never pleas'd before:
Though every joy is fled below,
What future grief can touch me more?

Then bring me wine, the banquet bring!
Man was not form'd to live alone:
I'll be that light, unmeaning thing,
That smiles with all, and weeps with none.
It was not thus in days more dear,
It never would have been, but thou
Hast fled, and left me lonely here;
Thou'rt nothing—all are nothing now.

In vain my lyre would lightly breathe!
The smile that sorrow fain would wear
But mocks the woe that lurks beneath,
Like roses o'er a sepulchre.
Though gay companions o'er the bowl
Dispel awhile the sense of ill;
Though pleasure fires the maddening soul,
The heart—the heart is lonely still!

On many a lone and lovely night
It soothed to gaze upon the sky;
For then I deem'd the heavenly light
Shone sweetly on thy pensive eye:
And oft I thought at Cynthia's noon,
When sailing o'er the Ægean wave,
"Now Thyrza gazes on that moon—"
Alas, it gleam'd upon her grave!

When stretch'd on fever's sleepless bed,
And sickness shrunk my throbbing veins,
"'Tis comfort still," I faintly said,
"That Thyrza cannot know my pains:"
Like freedom to the time-worn slave,
A boon 'tis idle then to give,
Relenting Nature vainly gave
My life, when Thyrza ceased to live!

My Thyrza's pledge in better days,
When love and life alike were new!
How different now thou meet'st my gaze!
How tinged by time with sorrow's hue!
The heart that gave itself with thee
Is silent—ah, were mine as still!
Though cold as e'en the dead can be,
It feels, it sickens with the chill.

Thou bitter pledge! thou mournful token!
Though painful, welcome to my breast!
Still, still, preserve that love unbroken,
Or break the heart to which thou'rt press'd!
Time tempers love, but not removes,
More hallow'd when its hope is fled:
Oh! what are thousand living loves
To that which cannot quit the dead?

EUTHANASIA.

When Time, or soon or late, shall bring
The dreamless sleep that lulls the dead,
Oblivion! may thy languid wing
Wave gently o'er my dying bed!

No band of friends or heirs be there,
To weep or wish the coming blow:
No maiden, with dishevell'd hair,
To feel, or feign, decorous woe.

But silent let me sink to earth,
With no officious mourners near;
I would not mar one hour of mirth,
Nor startle friendship with a tear.

Yet Love, if Love in such an hour
Could nobly check its useless sighs,
Might then exert its latest power
In her who lives and him who dies.

'Twere sweet, my Psyche! to the last
Thy features still serene to see:
Forgetful of its struggles past,
E'en Pain itself should smile on thee.

But vain the wish—for Beauty still
Will shrink, as shrinks the ebbing breath;
And woman's tears, produced at will,
Deceive in life, unman in death.

Then lonely be my latest hour,
Without regret, without a groan;
For thousands Death hath ceased to lower,
And pain been transient or unknown.

"Ay, but to die, and go," alas!
Where all have gone, and all must go!
To be the nothing that I was
Ere born to life and living woe.

Count o'er the joys thine hours have seen,
Count o'er thy days from anguish free,
And know, whatever thou hast been,
'Tis something better not to be.

AND THOU ART DEAD, AS YOUNG AS FAIR.

"Heu, quanto minus est cum reliquis versari quam tui meminisse!"

And thou art dead, as young and fair,
As aught of mortal birth:
And form so soft, and charms so rare,
Too soon return'd to Earth!
Though Earth received them in her bed,
And o'er the spot the crowd may tread
In carelessness or mirth,
There is an eye which could not brook
A moment on that grave to look.

I will not ask where thou liest low,
Nor gaze upon the spot;
There flowers or weeds at will may grow,
So I behold them not:
It is enough for me to prove
That what I loved, and long must love,
Like common earth can rot;
To me there needs no stone to tell,
'T is Nothing that I loved so well.

Yet did I love thee to the last
As fervently as thou,
Who didst not change through all the past,
And canst not alter now.
The love where Death has set his seal,
Nor age can chill, nor rival steal,
Nor falsehood disavow:
And, what were worse, thou canst not see
Or wrong, or change, or fault in me.

The better days of life were ours
The worst can be but mine:
The sun that cheers, the storm that lowers,
Shall never more be thine.
The silence of that dreamless sleep
I envy now too much to weep;
Nor need I to repine
That all those charms have pass'd away;
I might have watch'd through long decay.

The flower in ripen'd bloom unmatched
Must fall the earliest prey;
Though by no hand untimely snatch'd,
The leaves must drop away:
And yet it were a greater grief
To watch it withering, leaf by leaf,
Than see it pluck'd today;
Since earthly eye but ill but bear
To trace the change to foul from fair.

I know not if I could have borne
To see thy beauties fade;
The night that followed such a morn
Had worn a deeper shade:
Thy day without a cloud hath pass'd,
And thou wert levely t• the last:
Extinguish'd, not decay'd;
As stars that shoot along the sky
Shine brightest as they fall from high.

As •nce I wept, if I could weep,
My tears might well be shed,
To think I was not near to keep
One vigil o'er thy bed;
To gaze, how fondly! on thy face,
To fold thee in a faint embrace,
Uphold thy drooping head;
And show that love, however vain,
Nor thou nor I can feel again.

Yet how much less it were to gain,
Though thou hast left me free,
The loveliest things that still remain,
Than thus remember thee!
The all of thine that cannot die
Through dark and dread Eternity
Returns again to me,
And more thy buried love endears
Than aught, except its living years.

February, 1812.

IF SOMETIMES IN THE HAUNTS OF MEN.

If sometimes in the haunts of men
Thine image from my breast may fade,
The lonely hour presents again
The semblance of thy gentle shade
And now that sad and silent hour
Thus much of thee can still restore,
And sorrow unobserved may pour
The plaint she dare not speak before.

Oh, pardon that in crowds awhile
I waste one thought I owe to thee,
And, self-condemn'd, appear to smile,
Unfaithful to thy memory!
Nor deem that memory less dear,
That then I seem not to repine
I would not fools should overhear
One sigh that should be wholly *thine.*

If not the goblet pass unquaff'd,
It is not drain'd to banish care;
The cup must hold a deadlier draught,
That brings a Lethe for despair.
And could Oblivion set my soul
From all her troubled visions free,
I'd dash to earth the sweetest bowl
That drown'd a single thought of thee.

For wert thou vanish'd from my mind,
Where could my vacant bosom turn?
And who would then remain behind
To honour thine abandon'd Urn?
No, no—it is my sorrow's pride
That last dear duty to fulfil;
Though all the world forget beside,
'T is meet that I remember still.

For well I know, that such had been
Thy gentle care for him, who now
Unmourn'd shall quit this mortal scene,
Where none regarded him, but thou:
And, oh! I feel in *that* was given
A blessing never meant for me;
Thou wert too like a dream of heaven,
For earthly Love to merit thee.

March 14, 1812.

LADY BYRON.

DOMESTIC PIECES.

FARE THEE WELL.

> "Alas! they have been friends in youth;
> But whispering tongues can poison truth;
> And constancy lives in realms above;
> And life is thorny, and youth is vain:
> And to be wroth with one we love,
> Doth work like madness in the brain;
> * * * * * * *
> But never either found another
> To free the hollow heart from paining—
> They stood aloof, the scars remaining,
> Like cliffs, which had been rent asunder;
> A dreary sea now flows between,
> But neither heat, nor frost, nor thunder,
> Shall wholly do away, I ween,
> The marks of that which once hath been."
>
> COLERIDGE'S *Christabel.*

FARE thee well! and if for ever,
Still for ever, fare *thee well;*
Even though unforgiving, never
'Gainst thee shall my heart rebel.

Would that breast were bared before thee,
Where thy head so oft hath lain,
While that placid sleep came o'er thee
Which thou ne'er canst know again:

Would that breast, by thee glanced over,
Every inmost thought could show!
Then thou would'st at last discover
'Twas not well to spurn it so.

Though the world for this commend thee—
Though it smile upon the blow,
Even its praises must offend thee,
Founded on another's woe:

Though my many faults defaced me,
Could no other arm be found,
Than the one which once embraced me,
To inflict a cureless wound?

Yet, oh yet, thyself deceive not:
Love may sink by slow decay,
But by sudden wrench, believe not
Hearts can thus be torn away;

Still thine own its life retaineth—
Still must mine, though bleeding, beat;
And the undying thought which paineth
Is—that we no more may meet.

These are words of deeper sorrow
Than the wail above the dead;
Both shall live, but every morrow
Wake us from a widow'd bed.

And when thou would solace gather,
When our child's first accents flow,
Wilt thou teach her to say "Father!"
Though his care she must forego?

When her little hands shall press thee,
When her lip to thine is press'd,
Think of him whose prayer shall bless thee,
Think of him thy love had bless'd!

Should her lineaments resemble
Those thou never more may'st see,
Then thy heart will softly tremble
With a pulse yet true to me.

All my faults perchance thou knowest,
All my madness none can know;
All my hopes, where'er thou goest,
Wither, yet with *thee* they go.

Every feeling hath been shaken;
Pride, which not a world could bow,
Bows to thee—by thee forsaken,
Even my soul forsakes me now:

But 't is done—all words are idle—
Words from me are vainer still;
But the thoughts we cannot bridle
Force their way without the will.

Fare thee well!—thus disunited,
Torn from every nearer tie,
Sear'd in heart, and lone, and blighted,
More than this I scarce can die.

March 17, 1826.

(A SKETCH.)

"Honest—honest Iago!
If that thou be'st a devil, I cannot kill thee."
SHAKSPEARE.

BORN in the garret, in the kitchen bred,
Promoted thence to deck her mistress' head;
Next—for some gracious service unexpress'd,
And from its wages only to be guess'd—
Raised from the toilette to the table,—where
Her wondering betters wait behind her chair.
With eye unmoved, and forehead unabash'd,
She dines from off the plate she lately wash'd.
Quick with the tale, and ready with the lie—
The genial confidante, and general spy—
Who could, ye gods! her next employment guess—
An only infant's earliest governess!
She taught the child to read, and taught so well,
That she herself, by teaching, learn'd to spell.
An adept next in penmanship she grows,
As many a nameless slander deftly shows:
What she had made the pupil of her art,
None know—but that high Soul secured the heart,
And panted for the truth it could not hear,
With longing breast and undeluded ear.
Foil'd was perversion by that youthful mind,
Which Flattery fool'd not—Baseness could not blind,
Deceit infect not—near Contagion soil—
Indulgence weaken—nor Example spoil—
Nor master'd Science tempt her to look down
On humbler talents with a pitying frown—
Nor Genius swell—nor Beauty render vain—
Nor Envy ruffle to retaliate pain—
Nor Fortune change—Pride raise—nor Passion bow,
Nor Virtue teach austerity—till now.
Serenely purest of her sex that live,
But wanting one sweet weakness—to forgive,
Too shock'd at faults her soul can never know,
She deems that all could be like her below:
Foe to all vice, yet hardly Virtue's friend,
For Virtue pardons those she would amend.

But to the theme:—now laid aside too long,
The baleful Burthen of this honest song—
Though all her former functions are no more,
She rules the circle which she served before.
If mothers—none know why—before her quake;
If daughters dread her for the mothers' sake;
If early habits—those false links, which bind
At times the loftiest to the meanest mind—
Have given her power too deeply to instil
The angry essence of her deadly will;
If like a snake she steal within your walls,
Till the black slime betray her as she crawls;
If like a viper to the heart she wind,
And leave the venom there she did not find;
What marvel that this hag of hatred works
Eternal evil latent as she lurks,
To make a Pandemonium where she dwells,
And reign the Hecate of domestic hells?
Skill'd by a touch to deepen scandal's tints
With all the kind mendacity of hints,
While mingling truth with falsehood—sneers with smiles—
A thread of candour with a web of wiles;
A plain blunt show of briefly-spoken seeming,
To hide her bloodless heart's soul-harden'd scheming;
A lip of lies—a face form'd to conceal;
And, without feeling, mock at all who feel:
With a vile mask the Gorgon would disown;
A cheek of parchment—and an eye of stone.
Mark, how the channels of her yellow blood
Ooze to her skin, and stagnate there to mud,
Cased like the centipede in saffron mail,
Or darker greenness of the scorpion's scale—
(For drawn from reptiles only may we trace
Congenial colours in that soul or face)—
Look on her features! and behold her mind
As in a mirror of itself defined:
Look on the picture! deem it not o'ercharged—
There is no trait which might not be enlarged:
Yet true to "Nature's journeymen," who made
This monster when their mistress left off trade—
This female dog-star of her little sky,
Where all beneath her influence droop or die.

Oh! wretch without a tear—without a thought,
Save joy above the ruin thou hast wrought—

The time shall come, nor long remote, when thou
Shall feel far more than thou inflictest now;
Feel for thy vile self-loving self in vain,
And turn thee howling in unpitied pain.
May the strong curse of crush'd affections light
Back on thy bosom with reflected blight!
And make thee in thy leprosy of mind
As loathesome to thyself as to mankind!
Till all thy self-thoughts curdle into hate,
Black—as thy will for others would create:
Till thy hard heart be calcined into dust,
And thy soul welter in its hideous crust.
Oh, may thy grave be sleepless as the bed,—
The widow'd couch of fire, that thou hast spread!
Then, when thou fain would'st weary Heaven with prayer,
Look on thine earthly victims—and despair!
Down to the dust!—and, as thou rott'st away,
Even worms shall perish on thy poisonous clay.
But for the love I bore, and still must bear,
To her thy malice from all ties would tear—
Thy name—thy human name—to every eye
The climax of all scorn should hang on high,
Exalted o'er thy less abhorr'd compeers—
And festering in the infamy of years.

March 29, 1816.

STANZAS TO AUGUSTA.

WHEN all around grew drear and dark,
 And reason half withheld her ray—
And hope but shed a dying spark
 Which more misled my lonely way;

In that deep midnight of the mind,
 And that internal strife of heart,
When dreading to be deem'd too kind,
 The weak despair—the cold depart;

When fortune changed—and love fled far,
 And hatred's shafts flew thick and fast,
Thou wert the solitary star
 Which rose, and set not to the last.

Oh! blest be thine unbroken light!
 That watch'd me as a seraph's eye,
And stood between me and the night,
 For ever shining sweetly nigh.

And when the cloud upon us came,
 Which strove to blacken o'er thy ray—
Then purer spread its gentle flame,
 And dash'd the darkness all away.

Still may thy spirit dwell on mine,
 And teach it what to brave or brook—
There's more in one soft word of thine
 Than in the world's defied rebuke.

Thou stood'st, as stands a lovely tree,
 That still unbroke, though gently bent,
Still waves with fond fidelity
 Its boughs above a monument.

The winds might rend—the skies might pour,
 But there thou wert—and still wouldst be
Devoted in the stormiest hour
 To shed thy weeping leaves o'er me.

But thou and thine shall know no blight,
 Whatever fate on me may fall;
For heaven in sunshine will requite
 The kind—and thee the most of all.

Then let the ties of baffled love
 Be broken—thine will never break;
Thy heart can feel—but will not move;
 Thy soul, though soft, will never shake.

And these, when all was lost beside,
 Were found, and still are fix'd in thee;—
And bearing still a breast so tried,
 Earth is no desert—ev'n to me.

STANZAS TO AUGUSTA.

THOUGH the day of my destiny 's over,
 And the star of my fate hath declined,
Thy soft heart refused to discover
 The faults which so many could find;
Though thy soul with my grief was acquainted,
 It shrunk not to share it with me,
And the love which my spirit hath painted
 It never hath found but in *thee.*

Then when nature around me is smiling,
 The last smile which answers to mine,
I do not believe it beguiling,
 Because it reminds me of thine;
And when winds are at war with the ocean,
 As the breasts I believed in with me,
If their billows excite an emotion,
 It is that they bear me from *thee.*

Though the rock of my last hope is shiver'd,
 And its fragments are sunk in the wave,
Though I feel that my soul is deliver'd
 To pain—it shall not be its slave.
There is many a pang to pursue me:
 They may crush, but they shall not contemn—
They may torture, but shall not subdue me—
 'T is of *thee* that I think—not of them.

Though human, thou didst not deceive me,
 Though woman, thou didst not forsake,
Though loved, thou forborest to grieve me,
 Though slandered, thou never couldst shake,—
Though trusted, thou didst not disclaim me,
 Though parted, it was not to fly,
Though watchful, 't was not to defame me,
 Nor, mute, that the world might belie.

Yet I blame not the world, nor despise it,
Nor the war of the many with one—
If my soul was not fitted to prize it,
'T was folly not sooner to shun:
And if dearly that error hath cost me,
And more than I once could foresee,
I have found that, whatever it lost me,
It could not deprive me of *thee.*

From the wreck of the past, which hath perish'd,
Thus much I at least may recall,
It hath taught me that what I most cherish'd
Deserved to be dearest of all:
In the desert a fountain is springing,
In the wide waste there still is a tree,
And a bird in the solitude singing,
Which speaks to my spirit of *thee.*

July 24, 1816.

EPISTLE TO AUGUSTA.

My sister! my sweet sister! if a name
Dearer and purer were, it should be thine,
Mountains and seas divide us, but I claim
No tears, but tenderness to answer mine:
Go where I will, to me thou art the same—
A loved regret which I would not resign.
There yet are two things in my destiny,—
A world to roam through, and a home with thee.

The first were nothing—had I still the last,
It were the haven of my happiness;
But other claims and other ties thou hast,
And mine is not the wish to make them less.
A strange doom is thy father's son's, and past
Recalling, as it lies beyond redress;
Reversed for him our grandsire's fate of yore,—
He had no rest at sea, nor I on shore.

If my inheritance of storms hath been
In other elements, and on the rocks
Of perils, overlook'd or unforeseen,
I have sustained my share of worldly shocks,
The fault was mine; nor do I seek to screen
My errors with defensive paradox;
I have been cunning in mine overthrow,
The careful pilot of my proper woe.

Mine were my faults, and mine be their reward,
My whole life was a contest, since the day
That gave me being, gave me that which marr'd
The gift,—a fate, or will, that walk'd astray;
And I at times have found the struggle hard,
And thought of shaking off my bonds of clay:
But now I fain would for a time survive,
If but to see what next can well arrive.

Kingdoms and empires in my little day
I have outlived, and yet I am not old;
And when I look on this, the petty spray
Of my own years of trouble, which have roll'd
Like a wild bay of breakers, melts away:
Something—I know not what—does still uphold
A spirit of slight patience;—not in vain,
Even for its own sake, do we purchase pain.

Perhaps the workings of defiance stir
Within me,—or perhaps a cold despair,
Brought on when ills habitually recur,—
Perhaps a kinder clime, or purer air,
(For even to this may change of soul refer,
And with light armour we may learn to bear,)
Have taught me a strange quiet, which was not
The chief companion of a calmer lot.

I feel almost at times as I have felt
In happy childhood; trees, and flowers, and brooks,
Which do remember me of where I dwelt,
Ere my young mind was sacrificed to books,
Come as of yore upon me, and can melt
My heart with recognition of their looks;
And even at moments I could think I see
Some living thing to love—but none like thee.

Here are the Alpine landscapes which create
A fund for contemplation;—to admire
Is a brief feeling of a trivial date;
But something worthier do such scenes inspire.
Here to be lonely is not desolate,
For much I view which I could most desire,
And, above all, a lake I can behold
Lovelier, not dearer, than our own of old.

Oh, that thou wert but with me!—but I grow
The fool of my own wishes, and forget
The solitude which I have vaunted so
Has lost its praise in this but one regret;
There may be others which I less may show;—
I am not of the plaintive mood, and yet
I feel an ebb in my philosophy,
And the tide rising in my alter'd eye.

I did remind thee of our own dear Lake,
By the old Hall which may be mine no more.
Leman's is fair; but think not I forsake
The sweet remembrance of a dearer shore:
Sad havoc Time must with my memory make,
Ere *that* or *thou* can fade these eyes before;
Though, like all things which I have loved, they are
Resign'd for ever, or divided far.

The world is all before me; I but ask
Of Nature that with which she will comply—
It is but in her summer's sun to bask,
To mingle with the quiet of her sky,
To see her gentle face without a mask,
And never gaze on it with apathy.

She was my early friend, and now shall be
My sister—till I look again on thee.

I can reduce all feelings but this one;
 And that I would not;—for at length I see
Such scenes as those wherein my life begun.
 The earliest—even the only paths for me—
Had I but sooner learnt the crowd to shun,
 I had been better than I now can be;
The passions which have torn me would have slept;
I had not suffer'd, and *thou* hadst not wept.

With false Ambition what I had to do?
 Little with Love, and least of all with Fame;
And yet they came unsought, and with me grew,
 And made me all which they can make—a name.
Yet this was not the end I did pursue;
 Surely I once beheld a nobler aim.
But all is over—I am one the more
To baffled millions which have gone before.

And for the future, this world's future may
 From me demand but little of my care;
I have outlived myself by many a day;
 Having survived so many things that were;
My years have been no slumber, but the prey
 Of ceaseless vigils; for I had the share
Of life which might have fill'd a century,
Before its fourth in time had pass'd me by.

And for the remnant which may be to come,
 I am content; and for the past I feel
Not thankless,—for within the crowded sum
 Of struggles, happiness at times would steal,
And for the present, I would not benumb
 My feelings farther.—Nor shall I conceal
That with all this I still can look around,
And worship Nature with a thought profound.

For thee, my own sweet sister, in thy heart
 I know myself secure, as thou in mine;
We were and are—I am, even as thou art—
 Beings who ne'er each other can resign;
It is the same, together or apart,
 From life's commencement to its slow decline
We are entwined—let death come slow or fast,
The tie which bound the first endures the last!

LINES

ON HEARING THAT LADY BYRON WAS ILL.

And thou wert sad—yet I was not with thee!
 And thou wert sick, and yet I was not near;
Methought that joy and health alone could be
 Where I was *not*—and pain and sorrow here.
And is it thus?—it is as I foretold,
 And shall be more so; for the mind recoils
Upon itself, and the wreck'd heart lies cold,
 While heaviness collects the shatter'd spoils.
It is not in the storm nor in the strife
 We feel benumb'd, and wish to be no more,
 But in the after-silence on the shore
When all is lost, except a little life.

I am too well avenged!—but 't was my right;
 Whate'er my sins might be, *thou* wert not sent
To be the Nemesis who should requite—
 Nor did Heaven choose so near an instrument.
Mercy is for the merciful!—if thou
Hast been of such, 't will be accorded now.
Thy nights are banish'd from the realms of sleep!—
 Yes! they may flatter thee, but thou shalt feel
 A hollow agony which will not heal,
For thou art pillow'd on a curse too deep;
Thou hast sown in my sorrow, and must reap
 The bitter harvest in a woe as real!
I have had many foes, but none like thee;
 For 'gainst the rest myself I could defend,
 And be avenged, or turn them into friend;
But thou in safe implacability
Hadst nought to dread—in thy own weakness shielded,
And in my love, which hath but too much yielded,
 And spared, for thy sake, some I should not spare—
And thus upon the world—trust in thy truth—
And the wild fame of my ungovern'd youth—
 On things that were not, and on things that are—
Even upon such a basis hast thou built
A monument, whose cement hath been guilt!
The moral Clytemnestra of thy lord,
And hew'd down, with an unsuspected sword,
Fame, peace, and hope—and all the better life
 Which, but for this cold treason of thy heart,
Might still have risen from out the grave of strife,
And found a nobler duty than to part.
But of thy virtues didst thou make a vice,
 Trafficking with them in a purpose cold,
 For present anger, and for future gold—
And buying other's grief at any price.
And thus once enter'd into crooked ways,
The early truth, which was thy proper praise,
Did not still walk beside thee—but at times,
And with a breast unknowing its own crimes,
Deceit, averments incompatible,
Equivocations, and the thoughts which dwell
 In Janus-spirits—the significant eye
Which learns to lie with silence—the pretext
Of Prudence, with advantages annex'd—
The acquiescence in all things which tend,
No matter how, to the desirèd end—
 All found a place in thy philosophy.
The means were worthy, and the end is won—
I would not do by thee as thou hast done!

September, 1816.

MISS CHAWORTH.

WELL! THOU ART HAPPY.

WELL! thou art happy, and I feel
That I should thus be happy too;
For still my heart regards thy weal
Warmly, as it was wont to do.

Thy husband's blest—and 't will impart
Some pangs to view his happier lot:
But let them pass—Oh! how my heart
Would hate him if he loved thee not!

When late I saw thy favourite child,
I thought my jealous heart would break;
But when the unconscious infant smiled,
I kiss'd it for its mother's sake.

I kiss'd it,—and repress'd my sighs,
Its father in its face to see;
But then it had its mother's eyes,
And they were all to love and me.

Mary, adieu! I must away:
While thou art blest I'll not repine;
But near thee I can never stay;
My heart would soon again be thine.

I deem'd that time, I deem'd that pride
Had quench'd at length my boyish flame;
Nor knew, till seated by thy side,
My heart in all—save hope—the same.

Yet was I calm: I knew the time
My breast would thrill before thy look;
But now to tremble were a crime—
We met,—and not a nerve was shook.

I saw thee gaze upon my face,
Yet meet with no confusion there;
One only feeling could'st thou trace—
The sullen calmness of despair.

Away! away! my early dream
Remembrance never must awake:
Oh! where is Lethe's fabled stream?
My foolish heart, be still, or break.

November 2, 1808.

THE VISION OF JUDGMENT.

BY QUEVEDO REDIVIVUS.

SUGGESTED BY THE COMPOSITION SO ENTITLED BY THE AUTHOR OF "WAT TYLER."

"A Daniel come to judgment! yea, a Daniel!
I thank thee, Jew, for teaching me that word."

PREFACE.

It hath been wisely said, that "One fool makes many," and it hath been poetically observed,

"That fools rush in where angels fear to tread."—*Pope.*

If Mr. Southey had not rushed in where he had no business, and where he never was before, and never will be again, the following poem would not have been written. It is not impossible that it may be as good as his own, seeing that it cannot, by any species of stupidity, natural or acquired, be *worse.* The gross flattery, the dull impudence, the renegado intolerance and impious cant, of the poem by the author of "Wat Tyler," are something so stupendous as to form the sublime of himself—containing the quintessence of his own attributes.

So much for his poem—a word on his preface. In this preface it has pleased the magnanimous Laureate to draw the picture of a supposed "Satanic School," the which he doth recommend to the notice of the legislature; thereby adding to his other laurels the ambition of those of an informer. If there exists any where, excepting in his imagination, such a School, is he not sufficiently armed against it by his own intense vanity? The truth is, that there are certain writers whom Mr. S. imagines, like Scrub, to have "talked of *him;* for they laughed consumedly."

I think I know enough of most of the writers to whom he is supposed to allude, to assert, that they, in their individual capacities, have done more good, in the charities of life, to their fellow-creatures in any one year, than Mr. Southey has done harm to himself by his absurdities in his whole life; and this is saying a great deal. But I have a few questions to ask.

1stly, Is Mr. Southey the author of "Wat Tyler"?

2ndly, Was he not refused a remedy at law by the highest judge of his beloved England, because it was a blasphemous and seditious publication?

3rdly, Was he not entitled by William Smith, in full Parliament, "a rancorous renegado"?

4thly, Is he not poet laureate, with his own lines on Martin the regicide staring him in the face?

And, 5thly, Putting the four preceding items together, with what conscience dare *he* call the attention of the laws to the publications of others, be they what they may?

I say nothing of the cowardice of such a proceeding; its meanness speaks for itself; but I wish to touch upon the *motive,* which is neither more nor less than that Mr. S. has been laughed at a little in some recent publications, as he was of yore in the "Anti-Jacobin" by his present patrons. Hence all this "skimble-scamble stuff" about "Satanic," and so forth. However, it is worthy of him—"*qualis ab incepto.*"

If there is anything obnoxious to the political opinions of a portion of the public in the following poem, they may thank Mr. Southey. He might have written hexameters, as he has written every thing else, for aught that the writer cared—had they been upon another subject. But to attempt to canonise a monarch, who, whatever were his household virtues, was neither a successful nor a patriot king,—inasmuch as several years of his reign passed in war with America and Ireland, to say nothing of the aggression upon France,—like all other exaggeration, necessarily begets opposition. In whatever manner he may be spoken of in this new "Vision," his *public* career will not be more favourably transmitted by history. Of his private virtues (although a little expensive to the nation) there can be no doubt.

With regard to the supernatural personages treated of, I can only say that I know as much about them, and (as an honest man) have a better right to talk of them, than Robert Southey. I have also treated them more tolerantly. The way in which that poor insane creature, the Laureate, deals about his judgments in the next world, is like his own judgment in this. If it was not completely ludicrous, it would be something worse. I don't think that there is much more to say at present.

QUEVEDO REDIVIVUS.

P.S.—It is possible that some readers may object, in these objectionable times, to the freedom with which saints, angels, and spiritual persons discourse in this "Vision." But, for precedents upon such points, I must refer them to Fielding's "Journey from this World to the next," and of the Visions of myself, the said Quevedo, in Spanish or translated. The reader is also requested to observe, that no doctrinal tenets are insisted upon or discussed; that the person of the Deity is carefully withheld from sight, which is more than can be said for the Laureate, who hath thought proper to make Him talk, not "like a school divine," but like the unscholarlike Mr. Southey. The whole action passes on the outside of heaven; and Chaucer's "Wife of Bath," Pulci's "Morgante Maggiore," Swift's "Tale of a Tub," and the other works above referred to, are cases in point of the freedom with which saints, &c. may be permitted to converse in works not intended to be serious. Q. R.

*** Mr. Southey, being, as he says, a good Christian and vindictive, threatens, I understand, a reply to this our answer. It is to be hoped that his visionary faculties will in the mean time have acquired a little more judgment, properly so called: otherwise he will get himself into new dilemmas. These apostate Jacobins furnish rich rejoinders. Let him take a specimen. Mr. Southey laudeth grievously "one Mr. Landor," who cultivates much private renown in the shape of Latin verses; and not long ago, the Poet Laureate dedicated to him, it appeareth, one of his fugitive lyrics upon the strength of a poem called *Gebir.* Who

could suppose, that in this same *Gebir* the aforesaid Savage Landor (for such is his grim cognomen) putteth into the infernal regions no less a person than the hero of his friend Mr. Southey's heaven,—yea, even George the Third! See also how personal Savage becometh, when he hath a mind. The following is his portrait of our late gracious sovereign:

(Prince Gebir having descended into the infernal regions, the shades of his royal ancestors are, at his request, called up to his view; and he exclaims to his ghostly guide)—

"Aroar, what wretch that nearest us? what wretch
Is that with eyebrows white and slanting brow?
Listen! him yonder, who, bound down supine,
Shrinks yelling from that sword there, engine-hung!
He too amongst my ancestors? I hate
The despot, but the dastard I despise.
Was he our countryman?"

"Alas, O king!
Iberia bore him, but the breed accurst
Inclement winds blew blighting from north-east."
"He was a warrior then, nor fear'd the gods?"
"Gebir, he fear'd the demons, not the gods,
Though them indeed his daily face adored;
And was no warrior, yet the thousand lives
Squander'd, as stones to exercise a sling,
And the tame cruelty and cold caprice—
Oh madness of mankind! address'd, adored!"—

Gebir, p. 28.

I omit noticing some edifying Ithyphallics of Savagius, wishing to keep the proper veil over them, if his grave but somewhat indiscreet worshipper will suffer it; but certainly these teachers of "great moral lessons" are apt to be found in strange company.

THE VISION OF JUDGMENT.

I.

Saint Peter sat by the celestial gate:
His keys were rusty, and the lock was dull,
So little trouble had been given of late;
Not that the place by any means was full,
But since the Gallic era "eighty-eight,"
The devils had ta'en a longer, stronger pull,
And "a pull altogether," as they say
At sea—which drew most souls another way.

II.

The angels all were singing out of tune,
And hoarse with having little else to do,
Excepting to wind up the sun and moon,
Or curb a runaway young star or two,
Or wild colt of a comet, which too soon
Broke out of bounds o'er the ethereal blue,
Splitting some planet with its playful tail,
As boats are sometimes by a wanton whale.

III.

The guardian seraphs had retired on high,
Finding their charges past all care below;
Terrestrial business fill'd nought in the sky
Save the recording angel's black bureau;
Who found, indeed, the facts to multiply
With such rapidity of vice and woe,
That he had stripp'd off both his wings in quills,
And yet was in arrear of human ills.

IV.

His business so augmented of late years,
That he was forced, against his will no doubt,
(Just like those cherubs, earthly ministers,)
For some resource to turn himself about,
And claim the help of his celestial peers,
To aid him ere he should be quite worn out,
By the increased demand for his remarks;
Six angels and twelve saints were named his clerks.

V.

This was a handsome board—at least for heaven;
And yet they had even then enough to do,
So many conquerors' cars were daily driven,
So many kingdoms fitted up anew;
Each day too slew its thousands six or seven,
Till at the crowning carnage, Waterloo,
They threw their pens down in divine disgust—
The page was so besmear'd with blood and dust.

VI.

This by the way! 't is not mine to record
What angels shrink from: even the very devil
On this occasion his own work abhorr'd,
So surfeited with the infernal revel:
Though he himself had sharpen'd every sword,
It almost quench'd his innate thirst of evil.
(Here Satan's sole good work deserves insertion—
'T is, that he has both generals in reversion.)

VII.

Let's skip a few short years of hollow peace,
Which peopled earth no better, hell as wont,
And heaven none—they form the tyrant's lease,
With nothing but new names subscribed upon't:
'T will one day finish: meantime they increase,
"With seven heads and ten horns," and all in front,
Like Saint John's foretold beast; but ours are born
Less formidable in the head than horn.

VIII.

In the first year of freedom's second dawn
Died George the Third; although no tyrant, one
Who shielded tyrants, till each sense withdrawn
Left him nor mental nor external sun:
A better farmer ne'er brush'd dew from lawn,
A worse king never left a realm undone!
He died—but left his subjects still behind,
One half as mad—and t'other no less blind.

IX.

He died!—his death made no great stir on earth;
His burial made some pomp; there was profusion
Of velvet, gilding, brass, and no great dearth
Of aught but tears—save those shed by collusion.
For these things may be bought at their true worth;
Of elegy there was the due infusion—
Bought also; and the torches, cloaks, and banners,
Heralds, and relics of old Gothic manners,

X.

Form'd a sepulchral melodrame. Of all
The fools who flock'd to swell or see the show,
Who cared about the corpse? The funeral
Made the attraction, and the black the wo.
There throbb'd not there a thought which pierced the pall;
And when the gorgeous coffin was laid low,
It seem'd the mockery of hell to fold
The rottenness of eighty years in gold.

XI.

So mix his body with the dust! It might
Return to what it *must* far sooner, were
The natural compound left alone to fight
Its way back into earth, and fire, and air;
But the unnatural balsams merely blight
What nature made him at his birth, as bare
As the mere million's base unmummied clay—
Yet all his spices but prolong decay.

XII.

He's dead—and upper earth with him has done;
He's buried; save the undertaker's bill,
Or lapidary scrawl, the world is gone
For him, unless he left a German will;
But where's the proctor who will ask his son?
In whom his qualities are reigning still,
Except that household virtue, most uncommon,
Of constancy to a bad, ugly woman.

XIII.

"God save the king!" It is a large economy
In God to save the like; but if He will
Be saving, all the better; for not one am I
Of those who think damnation better still:
I hardly know too if not quite alone am I
In this small hope of bettering future ill
By circumscribing, with some slight restriction,
The eternity of hell's hot jurisdiction.

XIV.

I know this is unpopular; I know
'T is blasphemous; I know one may be damn'd
For hoping no one else may e'er be so;
I know my catechism; I know we are cramm'd
With the best doctrines till we quite o'erflow;
I know that all save England's church have shamm'd,
And that the other twice two hundred churches
And synagogues have made a *damn'd* bad purchase.

XV.

God help us all! God help me too! I am,
God knows, as helpless as the devil can wish,
And not a whit more difficult to damn,
Than is to bring to land a late hook'd fish,
Or to the butcher to purvey the lamb;
Not that I'm fit for such a noble dish,
As one day will be that immortal fry
Of almost every body born to die.

XVI.

Saint Peter sat by the celestial gate,
And nodded o'er his keys; when, lo! there came
A wondrous noise he had not heard of late—
A rushing sound of wind, and stream, and flame;
In short, a roar of things extremely great,
Which would have made aught save a saint exclaim;
But he, with first a start and then a wink,
Said, "There's another star gone out, I think!"

XVII.

But ere he could return to his repose,
A cherub flapp'd his right wing o'er his eyes—
At which Saint Peter yawn'd, and rubb'd his nose:
"Saint Porter," said the Angel, "prithee rise!"
Waving a goodly wing, which glow'd, as glows
An earthly peacock's tail, with heavenly dyes;
To which the Saint replied, "Well, what's the matter?
Is Lucifer come back with all this clatter?"

XVIII.

"No," quoth the Cherub; "George the Third is dead."
"And who *is* George the Third?" replied the Apostle:
"*What George? what Third?*" "The king of England," said
The Angel. "Well! he won't find kings to jostle
Him on his way; but does he wear his head?
Because the last we saw here had a tustle,
And ne'er would have got into heaven's good graces,
Had he not flung his head in all our faces.

XIX.

"He was, if I remember, king of France;
That head of his, which could not keep a crown
On earth, yet ventured in my face to advance
A claim to those of martyrs—like my own:
If I had had my sword, as I had once
When I cut ears off, I had cut him down;
But having but my *keys*, and not my brand,
I only knock'd his head from out his hand.

XX.

"And then he set up such a headless howl,
That all the saints came out and took him in;
And there he sits by St. Paul, cheek by jowl;
That fellow Paul—the parvenù! The skin

Of Saint Bartholomew, which makes his cowl
 In heaven, and upon earth redeem'd his sin,
So as to make a martyr, never sped
Better than did this weak and wooden head.

XXI.

"But had it come up here upon its shoulders,
 There would have been a different tale to tell;
The fellow-feeling in the saints beholders
 Seems to have acted on them like a spell;
And so this very foolish head heaven solders
 Back on its trunk: it may be very well,
And seems the custom here to overthrow
Whatever has been wisely done below."

XXII.

The Angel answer'd, "Peter! do not pout:
 The king who comes has head and all entire,
And never knew much what it was about—
 He did as doth the puppet—by its wire,
And will be judged like all the rest, no doubt:
 My business and your own is not to inquire
Into such matters, but to mind our cue—
Which is to act as we are bid to do."

XXIII.

While thus they spake, the angelic caravan,
 Arriving like a rush of mighty wind,
Cleaving the fields of space, as doth the swan
 Some silver stream (say Ganges, Nile, or Inde,
Or Thames, or Tweed), and 'midst them an old man
 With an old soul, and both extremely blind,
Halted before the gate, and in his shroud
Seated their fellow-traveller on a cloud.

XXIV.

But cringing up the rear of this bright host,
 A Spirit of a different aspect waved
His wings, like thunder-clouds above some coast
 Whose barren beach with frequent wrecks is paved;
His brow was like the deep when tempest-toss'd;
 Fierce and unfathomable thoughts engraved
Eternal wrath on his immortal face,
And *where* he gazed a gloom pervaded space.

XXV.

As he drew near, he gazed upon the gate
 Ne'er to be enter'd more by him or Sin,
With such a glance of supernatural hate,
 As made St. Peter wish himself within;
He patter'd with his keys at a great rate,
 And sweated through his apostolic skin:
Of course his perspiration was but ichor,
Or some such other spiritual liquor.

XXVI.

The very cherubs huddled all together,
 Like birds when soars the falcon; and they felt
A tingling to the tip of every feather,
 And form'd a circle like Orion's belt
Around their poor old charge: who scarce knew whither
 His guards had led him, though they gently dealt
With royal manes (for by many stories,
And true, we learn the angels are all Tories).

XXVII.

As things were in this posture, the gate flew
 Asunder, and the flashing of its hinges
Flung over space an universal hue
 Of many-colour'd flame, until its tinges
Reach'd even our speck of earth, and made a new
 Aurora borealis spread its fringes
O'er the North Pole; the same seen, when ice-bound,
By Captain Parry's crew, in "Melville's Sound."

XXVIII.

And from the gate thrown open issued beaming
 A beautiful and mighty Thing of Light,
Radiant with glory, like a banner streaming
 Victorious from some world-o'erthrowing fight:
My poor comparisons must needs be teeming
 With earthly likenesses, for here the night
Of clay obscures our best conceptions, saving
Johanna Southcote, or Bob Southey raving.

XXIX.

'T was the archangel Michael: all men know
 The make of angels and archangels, since
There's scarce a scribbler has not one to show,
 From the fiends' leader to the angels' prince.
There also are some altar-pieces, though
 I really can't say that they much evince
One's inner notions of immortal spirits;
But let the connoisseurs explain *their* merits.

XXX.

Michael flew forth in glory and in good;
 A goodly work of Him from whom all glory
And good arise; the portal past—he stood;
 Before him the young cherubs and saints hoary—
(I say *young*, begging to be understood
 By looks, not years; and should be very sorry
To state, they were not older than St. Peter,
But merely that they seem'd a little sweeter).

XXXI.

The cherubs and the saints bow'd down before
 That arch-angelic hierarch, the first
Of essences angelical, who wore
 The aspect of a god; but this ne'er nursed
Pride in his heavenly bosom, in whose core
 No thought, save for his Maker's service, durst
Intrude, however glorified and high;
He knew him but the viceroy of the sky.

XXXII.

He and the sombre silent Spirit met—
 They knew each other both for good and ill;

Such was their power, that neither could forget
His former friend and future foe; but still
There was a high, immortal, proud regret
In either's eye, as if 'twere less their will
Than destiny to make the eternal years
Their date of war, and their "champ clos" the spheres.

XXXIII.

But here they were in neutral space: we know
From Job, that Satan hath the power to pay
A heavenly visit thrice a year or so;
And that "the sons of God," like those of clay,
Must keep him company; and we might show
From the same book, in how polite a way
The dialogue is held between the Powers
Of God and Evil—but 'twould take up hours.

XXXIV.

And this is not a theologic tract,
To prove with Hebrew and with Arabic,
If Job be allegory or a fact,
But a true narrative; and thus I pick
From out the whole but such and such an act,
As sets aside the slightest thought of trick.
'T is every tittle true, beyond suspicion,
And accurate as any other vision.

XXXV.

The spirits were in neutral space, before
The gate of heaven; like eastern thresholds is
The place where Death's grand cause is argued o'er,
And souls despatch'd to that world or to this;
And therefore Michael and the other wore
A civil aspect: though they did not kiss,
Yet still between his Darkness and his Brightness
There pass'd a mutual glance of great politeness.

XXXVI.

The Archangel bow'd, not like a modern beau,
But with a graceful oriental bend,
Pressing one radiant arm just where below
The heart in good men is supposed to tend.
He turn'd as to an equal, not too low,
But kindly; Satan met his ancient friend
With more hauteur, as might an old Castilian
Poor noble meet a mushroom rich civilian.

XXXVII.

He merely bent his diabolic brow
An instant; and then raising it, he stood
In act to assert his right or wrong, and show
Cause why King George by no means could or should
Make out a case to be exempt from woe
Eternal, more than other kings, endued
With better sense and hearts, whom history mentions,
Who long have "paved hell with their good intentions."[1]

XXXVIII.

Michael began: "What wouldst thou with this man,
Now dead, and brought before the Lord? What ill
Hath he wrought since his mortal race began,
That thou canst claim him? Speak! and do thy will,
If it be just: if in this earthly span
He hath been greatly failing to fulfil
His duties as a king and mortal, say,
And he is thine; if not, let him have way."

XXXIX.

"Michael!" replied the Prince of Air, "even here,
Before the gate of Him thou servest, must
I claim my subject: and will make appear
That as he was my worshipper in dust,
So shall he be in spirit, although dear
To thee and thine, because nor wine nor lust
Were of his weaknesses, yet on the throne
He reign'd o'er millions to serve me alone.

XL.

"Look to *our* earth, or rather *mine;* it was,
Once, more thy Master's: but I triumph not
In this poor planet's conquest; nor, alas!
Need He thou servest envy me my lot:
With all the myriads of bright worlds which pass
In worship round Him, He may have forgot
Yon weak creation of such paltry things:
I think few worth damnation save their kings,—

XLI.

"And these but as kind of quit-rent, to
Assert my right as lord; and even had
I such an inclination, 'twere (as you
Well know) superfluous; they are grown so bad,
That hell has nothing better left to do
Than leave them to themselves: so much more mad
And evil by their own internal curse,
Heaven cannot make them better, nor I worse.

XLII.

"Look to the earth, I said, and say again:
When this old, blind, mad, helpless, weak, poor worm
Began in youth's first bloom and flush to reign,
The world and he both wore a different form,
And much of earth and all the watery plain
Of ocean call'd him king: through many a storm
His isles had floated on the abyss of time;
For the rough virtues chose them for their clime.

XLIII.

"He came to his sceptre young; he leaves it old:
Look to the state in which he found his realm,
And left it; and his annals too behold,
How to a minion first he gave the helm;

How grew upon his heart a thirst for gold,
The beggar's vice, which can but overwhelm
The meanest hearts ; and for the rest, but glance
Thine eye along America and France.

XLIV.

"'Tis true, he was a tool from first to last
(I have the workmen safe) ; but as a tool
So let him be consumed. From out the past
Of ages, since mankind have known the rule
Of monarchs—from the bloody rolls amass'd
Of sin and slaughter—from the Cæsars' school,
Take the worst pupil; and produce a reign
More drench'd with gore, more cumber'd with the slain.

XLV.

"He ever warr'd with freedom and the free:
Nations as men, home subjects, foreign foes,
So that they utter'd the word 'Liberty!'
Found George the Third their first opponent. Whose
History was ever stain'd as his will be
With national and individual woes?
I grant his household abstinence; I grant
His neutral virtues, which most monarchs want;

XLVI.

"I know he was a constant consort; own
He was a decent sire, and middling lord.
All this is much, and most upon a throne;
As temperance, if at Apicius' board,
Is more than at an anchorite's supper shown.
I grant him all the kindest can accord;
And this was well for him, but not for those
Millions who found him what oppression chose.

XLVII.

"The New World shook him off; the Old yet groans
Beneath what he and his prepared, if not
Completed: he leaves heirs on many thrones
To all his vices, without what begot
Compassion for him—his tame virtues; drones
Who sleep, or despots who have now forgot
A lesson which shall be re-taught them, wake
Upon the thrones of earth ; but let them quake!

XLVIII.

"Five millions of the primitive, who hold
The faith which makes ye great on earth, implored
A *part* of that vast *all* they held of old,—
Freedom to worship—not alone your Lord,
Michael, but you, and you, Saint Peter! Cold
Must be your souls, if you have not abhorr'd
The foe to Catholic participation
In all the license of a Christian nation.

XLIX.

"True! he allow'd them to pray God : but as
A consequence of prayer, refused the law
Which would have placed them upon the same base
With those who did not hold the saints in awe."
But here Saint Peter started from his place,
And cried, "You may the prisoner withdraw ;
Ere heaven shall ope her portals to this Guelph,
While I am guard, may I be damn'd myself!

L.

"Sooner will I with Cerberus exchange
My office (and *his* is no sinecure)
Than see this royal Bedlam bigot range
The azure fields of heaven, of that be sure!"
"Saint!" replied Satan, "you do well to avenge
The wrongs he made your satellites endure ;
And if to this exchange you should be given,
I'll try to coax *our* Cerberus up to heaven."

LI.

Here Michael interposed: "Good saint! and devil!
Pray, not so fast; you both outrun discretion.
Saint Peter! you were wont to be more civil:
Satan! excuse this warmth of his expression,
And condescension to the vulgar's level :
Even saints sometimes forget themselves in session.
Have you got more to say?"—"No."—"If you please
I'll trouble you to call your witnesses."

LII.

Then Satan turn'd and waved his swarthy hand,
Which stirr'd with its electric qualities
Clouds farther off than we can understand,
Although we find him sometimes in our skies ;
Infernal thunder shook both sea and land
In all the planets, and hell's batteries
Let off the artillery, which Milton mentions
As one of Satan's most sublime inventions.

LIII.

This was a signal unto such damn'd souls
As have the privilege of their damnation
Extended far beyond the mere controls
Of worlds past, present, or to come ; no station
Is theirs particularly in the rolls
Of hell assign'd; but where their inclination
Or business carries them in search of game,
They may range freely—being damn'd the same.

LIV.

They are proud of this—as very well they may,
It being a sort of knighthood, or gilt key
Stuck in their loins ; or like to an "entré"
Up the back stairs, or such free-masonry.
I borrow my comparisons from clay,
Being clay myself. Let not those spirits be
Offended with such base low likenesses;
We know their posts are nobler far than these.

LV.

When the great signal ran from heaven to hell—
About ten million times the distance reckon'd

From our sun to its earth, as we can tell
How much time it takes up, even to a second,
For every ray that travels to dispel
The fogs of London, through which, dimly beacon'd
The weathercocks are gilt some thrice a year,
If that the *summer* is not too severe.

LVI.

I say that I can tell—'t was half a minute:
I know the solar beams take up more time
Ere, pack'd up for their journey, they begin it;
But then their telegraph is less sublime,
And if they ran a race, they would not win it
'Gainst Satan's couriers bound for their own clime.
The sun takes up some years for every ray
To reach its goal—the devil not half a day.

LVII.

Upon the verge of space, about the size
Of half-a-crown, a little speck appear'd
(I've seen a something like it in the skies
In the Ægean, ere a squall); it near'd,
And, growing bigger, took another guise;
Like an aërial ship, it tack'd and steer'd,
Or *was* steer'd (I am doubtful of the grammar
Of the last phrase, which makes the stanza stammer;—

LVIII.

But take your choice); and then it grew a cloud;
And so it was—a cloud of witnesses.
But such a cloud! No land e'er saw a crowd
Of locusts numerous as the heavens saw these;
They shadow'd with their myriads space; their loud
And varied cries were like those of wild geese
(If nations may be liken'd to a goose),
And realised the phrase of "hell broke loose."

LIX.

Here crash'd a sturdy oath of stout John Bull,
Who damn'd away his eyes as heretofore:
There Paddy brogued "By Jasus!"—"What's your wull?"
The temperate Scot exclaim'd: the French ghost swore
In certain terms I sha'n't translate in full,
As the first coachman will; and 'midst the war,
The voice of Jonathan was heard to express,
"*Our* president is going to war, I guess."

LX.

Besides, there were the Spaniard, Dutch, and Dane;
In short, an universal shoal of shades,
From Otaheite's isle to Salisbury Plain,
Of all climes and professions, years and trades,
Ready to swear against the good king's reign,
Bitter as clubs in cards are against spades:
All summon'd by this grand "subpœna," to
Try if kings may n't be damn'd like me or you.

LXI.

When Michael saw this host, he first grew pale,
As angels can; next, like Italian twilight,
He turn'd all colours—as a peacock's tail,
Or sunset streaming through a Gothic skylight
In some old abbey, or a trout not stale,
Or distant lightning on the horizon *by* night,
Or a fresh rainbow, or a grand review
Of thirty regiments in red, green, and blue.

LXII.

Then he address'd himself to Satan: "Why,
My good old friend—for such I deem you, though
Our different parties make us fight so shy,
I ne'er mistake you for a *personal* foe;
Our difference is *political*, and I
Trust that, whatever may occur below,
You know my great respect for you: and this
Makes me regret whate'er you do amiss—

LXIII.

"Why, my dear Lucifer, would you abuse
My call for witnesses? I did not mean
That you should half of earth and hell produce;
'T is even superfluous, since two honest, clean,
True testimonies are enough: we lose
Our time, nay, our eternity, between
The accusation and defence: if we
Hear both, 't will stretch our immortality."

LXIV.

Satan replied, "To me the matter is
Indifferent, in a personal point of view:
I can have fifty better souls than this
With far less trouble than we have gone through
Already; and I merely argued his
Late majesty of Britain's case with you
Upon a point of form: you may dispose
Of him; I've kings enough below, God knows!"

LXV.

Thus spoke the Demon (late call'd "multifaced"
By multo-scribbling Southey). "Then we'll call
One or two persons of the myriads placed
Around our congress, and dispense with all
The rest," quoth Michael: "Who may be so graced
As to speak first? there's choice enough—who shall
It be?" Then Satan answer'd, "There are many;
But you may choose Jack Wilkes as well as any."

LXVI.

A merry, cock-eyed, curious-looking sprite
Upon the instant started from the throng,
Dress'd in a fashion now forgotten quite;
For all the fashions of the flesh stick long
By people in the next world; where unite
All the costumes since Adam's, right or wrong,
From Eve's fig-leaf down to the petticoat,
Almost as scanty, of days less remote.

LXVII.

The spirit look'd around upon the crowds
 Assembled, and exclaim'd, "My friends of all
The spheres, we shall catch cold amongst these clouds:
 So let's to business: why this general call?
If those are freeholders I see in shrouds,
 And 'tis for an election that they bawl,
Behold a candidate with unturn'd coat!
Saint Peter, may I count upon your vote?"

LXVIII.

Sir," replied Michael, "you mistake; these things
 Are of a former life, and what we do
Above is more august; to judge of kings
 Is the tribunal met: so now you know."
"Then I presume those gentlemen with wings,"
 Said Wilkes, "are cherubs; and that soul below
Looks much like George the Third, but to my mind
A good deal older—Bless me! is he blind?"

LXIX.

"He is what you behold him, and his doom
 Depends upon his deeds," the Angel said.
"If you have aught to arraign in him, the tomb
 Gives license to the humblest beggar's head
To lift itself against the loftiest."—"Some,"
 Said Wilkes, "don't wait to see them laid in lead
For such a liberty—and I, for one,
Have told them what I thought beneath the sun."

LXX.

"*Above* the sun repeat, then, what thou hast
 To urge against him," said the Archangel. "Why,"
Replied the Spirit, "since old scores are past,
 Must I turn evidence? In faith, not I.
Besides, I beat him hollow at the last,
 With all his Lords and Commons: in the sky
I don't like ripping up old stories, since
His conduct was but natural in a prince.

LXXI.

"Foolish, no doubt, and wicked, to oppress
 A poor unlucky devil without a shilling;
But then I blame the man himself much less
 Than Bute and Grafton, and shall be unwilling
To see him punish'd here for their excess,
 Since they were both damn'd long ago, and still in
Their place below: for me, I have forgiven,
And vote his 'habeas corpus' into heaven."

LXXII.

"Wilkes," said the Devil, "I understand all this;
 You turn'd to half a courtier ere you died,
And seem to think it would not be amiss
 To grow a whole one on the other side
Of Charon's ferry; you forget that *his*
 Reign is concluded; whatsoe'er betide,
He won't be sovereign more: you've lost your labour,
For at the best he will but be your neighbour.

LXXIII.

"However, I knew what to think of it,
 When I beheld you in your jesting way,
Flitting and whispering round about the spit
 Where Belial, upon duty for the day,
With Fox's lard was basting William Pitt,
 His pupil; I knew what to think, I say:
That fellow even in hell breeds farther ills;
I'll have him *gagg'd*—'t was one of his own bills.

LXXIV.

"Call Junius!" From the crowd a shadow stalk'd,
 And at the name there was a general squeeze,
So that the very ghosts no longer walk'd
 In comfort at their own aërial ease,
But were all ramm'd, and jamm'd (but to be balk'd,
 As we shall see), and jostled hands and knees,
Like wind compress'd and pent within a bladder,
Or like a human colic, which is sadder.

LXXV.

The shadow came—a tall, thin, gray-hair'd figure,
 That look'd as it had been a shade on earth;
Quick in its motions, with an air of vigour,
 But nought to mark its breeding or its birth:
Now it wax'd little, then again grew bigger,
 With now an air of gloom, or savage mirth;
But as you gazed upon its features, they
Changed every instant—to *what*, none could say.

LXXVI.

The more intently the ghosts gazed, the less
 Could they distinguish whose the features were,
The Devil himself seem'd puzzled even to guess;
 They varied like a dream—now here, now there;
And several people swore from out the press,
 They knew him perfectly; and one could swear
He was his father: upon which another
Was sure he was his mother's cousin's brother:

LXXVII.

Another, that he was a duke, or knight,
 An orator, a lawyer, or a priest,
A nabob, a man-midwife: but the wight
 Mysterious changed his countenance at least
As oft as they their minds: though in full sight
 He stood, the puzzle only was increased;
The man was a phantasmagoria in
Himself;—he was so volatile and thin.

LXXVIII.

The moment that you had pronounced him *one*,
 Presto! his face changed, and he was another;
And when that change was hardly well put on,
 It varied, till I don't think his own mother
(If that he had a mother) would her son
 Have known, he shifted so from one to t' other;
Till guessing from a pleasure grew a task,
At this epistolary "Iron Mask."

LXXIX.

For sometimes he like Cerberus would seem—
 "Three gentlemen at once" (as sagely says
Good Mrs. Malaprop); then you might deem
 That he was not even *one;* now many rays
Were flashing round him: and now a thick steam
 Hid him from sight—like fogs on London days:
Now Burke, now Tooke, he grew to people's fancies,
And certes often like Sir Philip Francis.

LXXX.

I've an hypothesis—'t is quite my own;
 I never let it out till now, for fear
Of doing people harm about the throne,
 And injuring some minister or peer,
On whom the stigma might perhaps be blown:
 It is—my gentle public, lend thine ear!
'Tis that what Junius we are wont to call
Was *really, truly,* nobody at all.

LXXXI.

I don't see wherefore letters should not be
 Written without hands, since we daily view
Them written without heads; and books, we see,
 Are fill'd as well without the latter too:
And really till we fix on somebody
 For certain sure to claim them as his due,
Their author, like the Niger's mouth, will bother
The world to say if *there* be mouth or author.

LXXXII.

"And who and what art thou?" the Archangel said.
 "For *that* you may consult my title-page,"
Replied this mighty shadow of a shade:
 "If I have kept my secret half an age,
I scarce shall tell it now." "Canst thou upbraid,"
 Continued Michael, "George Rex, or allege
Aught farthur?" Junius answer'd, "You had better
First ask him for *his* answer to my letter:

LXXXIII.

"My charges upon record will outlast
 The brass of both his epitaph and tomb."
"Repent'st thou not," said Michael, "of some past
 Exaggeration? something which may doom
Thyself if false, as him if true? Thou wast
 Too bitter—is it not so?—in thy gloom
Of passion?"—"Passion!" cried the phantom dim,
"I loved my country, and I hated him.

LXXXIV.

"What I have written, I have written: let
 The rest be on his head or mine!" So spoke
Old "Nominis Umbra;" and while speaking yet,
 Away he melted in celestial smoke.
Then Satan said to Michael, "Don't forget
 To call George Washington, and John Horne Tooke,
And Franklin;"—but at this time there was heard
A cry for room, though not a phantom stirr'd.

LXXXV.

At length with jostling, elbowing, and the aid
 Of cherubim appointed to that post,
The devil Asmodeus to the circle made
 His way, and look'd as if his journey cost
Some trouble. When his burden down he laid,
 "What's this?" cried Michael; "why, 't is not a ghost!"
"I know it," quoth the incubus; "but he
Shall be one, if you leave the affair to me.

LXXXVI.

"Confound the renegado! I have sprain'd
 My left wing, he's so heavy; one would think
Some of his works about his neck were chain'd.
 But to the point: while hovering o'er the brink
Of Skiddaw (where as usual it still rain'd),
 I saw a taper, far below me, wink,
And stooping, caught this fellow at a libel—
No less on history than the Holy Bible.

LXXXVII.

"The former is the devil's scripture, and
 The latter yours, good Michael; so the affair
Belongs to all of us, you understand.
 I snatch'd him up just as you see him there,
And brought him off for sentence out of hand:
 I've scarcely been ten minutes in the air—
At least a quarter it can hardly be:
I dare say that his wife is still at tea."

LXXXVIII.

Here Satan said, "I know this man of old,
 And have expected him for some time here;
A sillier fellow you will scarce behold,
 Or more conceited in his petty sphere:
But surely it was not worth while to fold
 Such trash below your wing, Asmodeus dear:
We had the poor wretch safe (without being bored
With carriage) coming of his own accord.

LXXXIX.

"But since he's here, let's see what he has done."
 "Done!" cried Asmodeus, "he anticipates
The very business you are now upon,
 And scribbles as if head clerk to the Fates.
Who knows to what his ribaldry may run,
 When such an ass as this, like Balaam's, prates?"
"Let's hear," quoth Michael, "what he has to say;
You know we're bound to that in every way."

XC.

Now the bard, glad to get an audience, which
 By no means often was his case below,
Began to cough, and hawk, and hem, and pitch
 His voice into that awful note of woe

To all unhappy hearers within reach
Of poets when the tide of rhyme's in flow;
But stuck fast with his first hexameter,
Not one of all whose gouty feet would stir.

XCI.

But ere the spavin'd dactyls could be spurr'd
Into recitative, in great dismay,
Both cherubim and seraphim were heard
To murmur loudly through their long array;
And Michael rose ere he could get a word
Of all his founder'd verses under way,
And cried, "For God's sake stop, my friend; 't were best—
Non Di, non homines—you know the rest."

XCII.

A general bustle spread throughout the throng,
Which seem'd to hold all verse in detestation;
The angels had of course enough of song
When upon service; and the generation
Of ghosts had heard too much in life, not long
Before, to profit by a new occasion:
The monarch, mute till then, exclaim'd, "What! what!
Pye come again? No more—no more of that!"

XCIII.

The tumult grew; an universal cough
Convulsed the skies, as during a debate,
When Castlereagh has been up long enough
(Before he was first minister of state,
I mean—the *slaves hear now*); some cried "Off, off!"
As at a farce; till, grown quite desperate,
The bard Saint Peter pray'd to interpose
(Himself an author) only for his prose.

XCIV.

The varlet was not an ill-favour'd knave;
A good deal like a vulture in the face,
With a hook nose and a hawk's eye, which gave
A smart and sharper-looking sort of grace
To his whole aspect, which, though rather grave,
Was by no means so ugly as his case;
But that indeed was hopeless as can be,
Quite a poetic felony "*de se*."

XCV.

Then Michael blew his trump, and still'd the noise
With one still greater, as is yet the mode
On earth besides; except some grumbling voice,
Which now and then will make a slight inroad
Upon decorous silence, few will twice
Lift up their lungs when fairly overcrow'd;
And now the bard could plead his own bad cause,
With all the attitudes of self-applause.

XCVI.

He said—(I only give the heads)—he said,
He meant no harm in scribbling; 't was his way
Upon all topics; 't was, besides, his bread,
Of which he butter'd both sides; 't would delay
Too long the assembly (he was pleased to dread),
And take up rather more time than a day,
To name his works—he would but cite a few—
"Wat Tyler"—"Rhymes on Blenheim"—"Waterloo."

XCVII.

He had written praises of a regicide;
He had written praises of all kings whatever;
He had written for republics far and wide,
And then against them bitterer than ever;
For pantisocracy he once had cried
Aloud, a scheme less moral than 't was clever;
Then grew a hearty anti-jacobin—
Had turn'd his coat—and would have turn'd his skin.

XCVIII.

He had sung against all battles, and again
In their high praise and glory; he had call'd
Reviewing "the ungentle craft," and then [2]
Become as base a critic as e'er crawl'd—
Fed, paid, and pamper'd by the very men
By whom his muse and morals had been maul'd:
He had written much blank verse, and blanker prose,
And more of both than any body knows.

XCIX.

He had written Wesley's life;—here turning round
To Satan, "Sir, I'm ready to write yours,
In two octavo volumes, nicely bound,
With notes and preface, all that most allures
The pious purchaser; and there's no ground
For fear, for I can choose my own reviewers:
So let me have the proper documents
That I may add you to my other saints."

C.

Satan bow'd, and was silent. "Well, if you,
With amiable modesty, decline
My offer, what says Michael? There are few
Whose memoirs could be render'd more divine.
Mine is a pen of all work: not so new
As it was once, but I would make you shine
Like your own trumpet. By the way, my own
Has more of brass in it, and is as well blown.

CI.

"But talking about trumpets, here's my vision!
Now you shall judge, all people; yes, you shall
Judge with my judgment, and by my decision
Be guided who shall enter heaven or fall.
I settle all these things by intuition,
Times present, past, to come, heaven, hell, and all,
Like king Alfonso. When I thus see double, [3]
I save the Deity some worlds of trouble."

CII.

He ceased, and drew forth an MS.; and no
Persuasion on the part of devils, or saints,
Or angels, now could stop the torrent; so
He read the first three lines of the contents;
But at the fourth, the whole spiritual show
Had vanish'd, with variety of scents,
Ambrosial and sulphureous, as they sprang,
Like lightning, off from his "melodious twang."[4]

CIII.

Those grand heroics acted as a spell;
The angels stopp'd their ears and plied their pinions;
The devils ran howling, deafen'd, down to hell;
The ghosts fled, gibbering, for their own dominions—
(For 't is not yet decided where they dwell,
And I leave every man to his opinions);
Michael took refuge in his trump—but, lo!
His teeth were set on edge, he could not blow!

CIV.

Saint Peter, who has hitherto been known
For an impetuous saint, upraised his keys,
And at the fifth line knock'd the poet down;
Who fell like Phæton, but more at ease,
Into his lake, for there he did not drown;
A different web being by the Destinies
Woven for the Laureate's final wreath, whene'er
Reform shall happen either here or there.

CV.

He first sank to the bottom—like his works,
But soon rose to the surface—like himself;
For all corrupted things are buoy'd like corks,[5]
By their own rottenness, light as an elf,
Or wisp that flits o'er a morass; he lurks,
It may be, still, like dull books on a shelf,
In his own den, to scrawl some "Life" or "Vision,"
As Welborn says—"the devil turn'd precisian."

CVI.

As for the rest, to come to the conclusion
Of this true dream, the telescope is gone
Which kept my optics free from all delusion,
And show'd me what I in my turn have shown;
All I saw farther, in the last confusion,
Was, that King George slipp'd into heaven for one
And when the tumult dwindled to a calm,
I left him practising the hundreth psalm.

NOTES TO VISION OF JUDGMENT.

NOTE 1, page 547.

Who long have "paved hell with their good intentions."

"No saint in the course of his religious warfare was more sensible of the unhappy failure of pious resolves than Dr. Johnson: he said one day, talking to an acquaintance on this subject, "Sir, hell is paved with good intentions."

NOTE 2, page 552.

He had call'd reviewing "the ungentle craft."

See "Life of Henry Kirke White."

NOTE 3, page 552.

Like king Alfonso. When I thus see double.

Alfonso, speaking of the Ptolomean system, said, that "had he been consulted at the creation of the world, he would have spared the Maker some absurdities."

NOTE 4, page 553.

Like lightning, off from his "melodious twang."

See Aubrey's account of the apparition which disappeared "with a curious perfume and a *most melodious twang;*" or see the *Antiquary*, vol. i. p. 225.

NOTE 5, page 553.

For all corrupted things are buoy'd like corks.

A drowned body lies at the bottom till rotten; it then floats, as most people know.

MISCELLANEOUS POEMS.

MAID OF ATHENS, ERE WE PART.

Ζώη μοῦ, σάς ἀγαπῶ.

Maid of Athens, ere we part,
Give, oh, give back my heart!
Or, since that has left my breast.
Keep it now, and take the rest!
Hear my vow before I go,
Ζώη μοῦ, σάς ἀγαπῶ.

By those tresses unconfined,
Woo'd by each Ægean wind;
By those lids whose jetty fringe
Kiss thy soft cheeks' blooming tinge;
By those wild eyes like the roe,
Ζώη μοῦ, σάς ἀγαπῶ.

By that lip I long to taste;
By that zone-encircled waist;

By all the token-flowers that tell
What words can never speak so well;
By love's alternate joy and woe,
Ζώη μοῦ, σάς ἀγαπῶ.

Maid of Athens! I am gone:
Think of me, sweet! when alone.
Though I fly to Istambol,
Athens holds my heart and soul:
Can I cease to love thee? No!
Ζώη μοῦ, σάς ἀγαπῶ.

Athens, 1810.

FAREWELL! IF EVER FONDEST PRAYER.

Farewell! if ever fondest prayer
For others' weal avail'd on high,
Mine will not all be lost in air,
But waft thy name beyond the sky.
'Twere vain to speak, to weep, to sigh:
Oh! more than tears of blood can tell,
When wrung from guilt's expiring eye,
Are in that word—Farewell!—Farewell!

These lips are mute, these eyes are dry;
But in my breast and in my brain,
Awake the pangs that pass not by,
The thought that ne'er shall sleep again.
My soul nor deigns nor dares complain,
Though grief and passion there rebel:
I only know we loved in vain—
I only feel—Farewell!—Farewell!

1808.

BRIGHT BE THE PLACE OF THY SOUL.

Bright be the place of thy soul!
No lovelier spirit than thine
E'er burst from it mortal control,
In the orbs of the blessed to shine.

On earth thou wert all but divine,
As thy soul shall immortally be;
And our sorrow may cease to repine,
When we know that thy God is with thee.

Light be the turf of thy tomb!
May its verdure like emeralds be:
There should not be the shadow of gloom
In aught that reminds us of thee.

Young flowers and an evergreen tree
May spring from the spot of thy rest:
But nor cypress nor yew let us see;
For why should we mourn for the blest?

1808.

REMIND ME NOT, REMIND ME NOT.

Remind me not, remind me not,
Of those beloved, those vanish'd hours,
When all my soul was given to thee;
Hours that may never be forgot,
Till time unnerves our vital powers,
And thou and I shall cease to be.

Can I forget—canst thou forget,
When playing with thy golden hair,
How quick thy fluttering heart did move?
Oh! by my soul, I see thee yet,
With eyes so languid, breast so fair,
And lips, though silent, breathing love.

When thus reclining on my breast,
Those eyes threw back a glance so sweet,
As half reproach'd yet raised desire,
And still we near and nearer prest,
And still our glowing lips would meet,
As if in kisses to expire.

And then those pensive eyes would close,
And bid their lids each other seek,
Veiling the azure orbs below;
While their long lashes' darken'd gloss
Seem'd stealing o'er thy brilliant cheek,
Like raven's plumage smooth'd on snow.

I dreamt last night our love return'd,
And, sooth to say, that very dream
Was sweeter in its phantasy,
Than if for other hearts I burn'd,
For eyes that ne'er like thine could beam
In rapture's wild reality.

Then tell me not, remind me not,
Of hours which, though for ever gone,
Can still a pleasing dream restore,
Till thou and I shall be forgot,
And senseless as the mouldering stone
Which tells that we shall be no more.

THERE WAS A TIME, I NEED NOT NAME.

There was a time, I need not name,
Since it will ne'er forgotten be,
When all our feelings were the same
As still my soul hath been to thee.

And from that hour when first thy tongue
Confest'd a love which equall'd mine,
Though many a grief my heart hath wrung,
Unknown and thus unfelt by thine,

None, none hath sunk so deep as this—
To think how all that love hath flown;
Transient as every faithless kiss,
But transient in thy breast alone.

And yet my heart some solace knew,
When late I heard thy lips declare,
In accents once imagined true,
Remembrance of the days that were.

Yes! my adored, yet most unkind!
Though thou wilt never love again,
To me 't is doubly sweet to find
Remembrance of that love remain.

Yes! 't is a glorious thought to me,
Nor longer shall my soul repine,
Whate'er thou art or e'er shalt be,
Thou hast been dearly, solely mine.

AND WILT THOU WEEP WHEN I AM LOW?

AND wilt thou weep when I am low?
Sweet lady! speak those words again:
Yet if they grieve thee, say not so—
I would not give that bosom pain.

My heart is sad, my hopes are gone,
My blood runs coldly through my breast;
And when I perish, thou alone
Wilt sigh above my place of rest.

And yet, methinks, a gleam of peace
Doth through my cloud of anguish shine;
And for a while my sorrows cease,
To know thy heart hath felt for mine.

O lady! blessed be that tear—
It falls for one who cannot weep:
Such precious drops are doubly dear
To those whose eyes no tear may steep.

Sweet lady! once my heart was warm
With every feeling soft as thine;
But Beauty's self hath ceased to charm
A wretch created to repine.

Yet wilt thou weep when I am low?
Sweet lady! speak those words again;
Yet if they grieve thee, say not so—
I would not give that bosom pain.

ON PARTING.

THE kiss, dear maid! thy lip has left
Shall never part from mine,
Till happier hours restore the gift
Untainted back to thine.

Thy parting glance, which fondly beams,
An equal love may see:
The tear that from thine eyelid streams
Can weep no change in me.

I ask no pledge to make me blest
In gazing when alone;
Nor one memorial for a breast,
Whose thoughts are all thine own.

Nor need I write—to tell the tale
My pen were doubly weak:
Oh! what can idle words avail,
Unless the heart could speak?

By day or night, in weal or woe,
That heart, no longer free,
Must bear the love it cannot show,
And silent, ache for thee.

March, 1811.

THOU ART NOT FALSE, BUT THOU ART FICKLE.

THOU art not false, but thou art fickle,
To those thyself so fondly sought;
The tears that thou hast forced to trickle
Are doubly bitter from that thought:
'T is this which breaks the heart thou grievest,
Too well thou lov'st—too soon thou leavest.

The wholly false the heart despises,
And spurns deceiver and deceit;
But she who not a thought disguises,
Whose love is as sincere as sweet,—
When she can change who loved so truly,
It feels what mine has felt so newly.

To dream of joy and wake to sorrow,
Is doom'd to all who love or live;
And if, when conscious on the morrow,
We scarce our fancy can forgive,
That cheated us in slumber only,
To leave the waking soul more lonely.

What must they feel whom no false vision,
But truest, tenderest passion warm'd?
Sincere, but swift in sad transition;
As if a dream alone had charm'd?
Ah! sure such grief is fancy's scheming,
And all thy change can be but dreaming!

REMEMBER HIM, WHOM PASSION'S POWER.

REMEMBER him, whom passion's power
Severely, deeply, vainly proved:
Remember thou that dangerous hour
When neither fell, though both were loved.

That yielding breast, that melting eye,
Too much invited to be bless'd;
That gentle prayer, that pleading sigh,
The wilder wish reproved, repress'd.

Oh! let me feel that all I lost
 But saved thee all that conscience fears;
And blush for every pang it cost
 To spare the vain remorse of years.

Yet think of this when many a tongue,
 Whose busy accents whisper blame,
Would do the heart that loved thee wrong,
 And brand a nearly blighted name.

Think that, whate'er to others, thou
 Hast seen each selfish thought subdued:
I bless thy purer soul even now,
 Even now, in midnight solitude.

Oh, God! that we had met in time,
 Our hearts as fond, thy hand more free;
When thou hadst loved without a crime,
 And I been less unworthy thee.

Far may thy days, as heretofore,
 From this our gaudy world be past!
And that too bitter moment o'er,
 Oh! may such trial be thy last!

This heart, alas! perverted long,
 Itself destroy'd might thee destroy;
To meet thee in the glittering throng,
 Would wake Presumption's hope of joy.

Then to the things whose bliss or woe,
 Like mine, is wild and worthless all,
That world resign—such scenes forego,
 Where those who feel must surely fall.

Thy youth, thy charms, thy tenderness,
 Thy soul from long seclusion pure;
From what even here hath pass'd, may guess
 What there thy bosom must endure.

Oh! pardon that imploring tear,
 Since not by Virtue shed in vain,
My frenzy drew from eyes so dear;
 For me they shall not weep again.

Though long and mournful must it be,
 The thought that we no more may meet;
Yet I deserve the stern decree,
 And almost deem the sentence sweet.

Still, had I loved thee less, my heart
 Had then less sacrificed to thine;
It felt not half so much to part,
 As if its guilt had made thee mine.

1813.

LINES WRITTEN BENEATH A PICTURE.

Dear object of defeated care!
 Though now of Love and thee bereft,
To reconcile me with despair,
 Thine image and my tears are left.

'T is said with Sorrow Time can cope;
 But this I feel can ne'er be true:
For by the death-blow of my Hope
 My Memory immortal grew.

STANZAS FOR MUSIC.

There be none of Beauty's daughters
 With a magic like thee;
And like music on the waters
 Is thy sweet voice to me:
When, as if its sound were causing
The charmed ocean's pausing,
The waves lie still and gleaming,
And the lull'd winds seem dreaming.

And the midnight moon is weaving
 Her bright chain o'er the deep;
Whose breast is gently heaving,
 As an infant's asleep:
So the spirit bows before thee,
To listen and adore thee;
With a full but soft emotion,
Like the swell of Summer's ocean.

THE CHAIN I GAVE.

FROM THE TURKISH.

The chain I gave was fair to view,
 The lute I added sweet in sound;
The heart that offer'd both was true,
 And ill deserved the fate it found.

These gifts were charm'd by secret spell,
 Thy truth in absence to divine;
And they have done their duty well,—
 Alas! they could not teach thee thine.

That chain was firm in every link,
 But not to bear a stranger's touch;
That lute was sweet—till thou could'st think
 In other hands its notes were such.

Let him, who from thy neck unbound
 The chain which shiver'd in his grasp,
Who saw that lute refuse to sound,
 Restring the chords, renew the clasp.

When thou wert changed, they alter'd too;
 The chain is broke, the music mute.
'T is past—to them and thee adieu—
 False heart, frail chain, and silent lute.

TRANSLATION OF THE ROMAIC SONG,

" Μπενω μες 'τσ' πέριβόλι.
'Ωραιότατη Χάηδή," &c.

I enter thy garden of roses,
 Beloved and fair Haidée,
Each morning where Flora reposes,
 For surely I see her in thee.

Oh, Lovely! thus low I implore thee,
Receive this fond truth from my tongue,
Which utters its song to adore thee,
Yet trembles for what it has sung;
As the branch at the bidding of Nature,
Adds fragrance and fruit to the tree,
Through her eyes, through her every feature,
Shines the soul of the young Haidée.

But the loveliest garden grows hateful
When Love has abandon'd the bowers;
Bring me hemlock—since mine is ungrateful,
That herb is more fragrant than flowers.

The poison, when pour'd from the chalice,
Will deeply embitter the bowl;
But when drunk to escape from thy malice,
The draught shall be sweet to my soul.
Too cruel! in vain I implore thee
My heart from these horrors to save:
Will nought to my bosom restore thee?
Then open the gates of the grave.

As the chief who to combat advances
Secure of his conquest before,
Thus thou, with those eyes for thy lances,
Hast pierced through my heart to its core.

Ah, tell me, my soul! must I perish
 By pangs which a smile would dispel?
Would the hope, which thou once bad'st me cherish,
 For torture repay me too well?
Now sad is the garden of roses,
 Beloved but false Haidée?
There Flora all wither'd reposes
 And mourns o'er thine absence with me.

TRANSLATION OF A ROMAIC LOVE SONG.

AH! Love was never yet without
The pang, the agony, the doubt,
Which rends my heart with ceaseless sigh,
While day and night roll darkling by.

Without one friend to hear my woe,
I faint, I die beneath the blow.
That Love had arrows, well I knew;
Alas! I find them poison'd too.

Birds, yet in freedom, shun the net
Which Love around your haunts hath set;
Or, circled by his fatal fire,
Your hearts shall burn, your hopes expire.

A bird of free and careless wing
Was I, through many a smiling spring;
But caught within the subtle snare,
I burn, and feebly flutter there.

Who ne'er have loved, and loved in vain,
Can neither feel nor pity pain,
The cold repulse, the look askance,
The lightning of Love's angry glance.

In flattering dreams I deem'd thee mine;
Now hope, and he who hoped, decline;
Like melting wax, or withering flower,
I feel my passion, and thy power.
My light of life! ah, tell me why
That pouting lip, and alter'd eye?
My bird of love! my beauteous mate!
And art thou changed, and canst thou hate?

Mine eyes like wintry streams o'erflow:
What wretch with me would barter woe?
My bird! relent! one note could give
A charm, to bid thy lover live.

My curdling blood, my madd'ning brain,
In silent anguish I sustain;
And still thy heart, without partaking
One pang, exults—while mine is breaking.

Pour me the poison; fear not thou!
Thou canst not murder more than now:
I 've lived to curse my natal day,
And Love, that thus can lingering slay.

My wounded soul, my bleeding breast,
Can patience preach thee into rest?
Alas! too late, I dearly know
That joy is harbinger of woe.

FROM THE PORTUGUESE.

"TU MI CHAMAS."

IN moments to delight devoted,
 "My life!" with tenderest tone, you cry!
Dear words! on which my heart had doted,
 If youth could neither fade nor die.

To death even hours like these must roll,
 Ah! then repeat those accents never;
Or change "my life!" into "my soul!"
 Which, like my love, exists for ever.

ANOTHER VERSION.

You call me still your *life*.—Oh! change the word—
 Life is as transient as the inconstant sigh;
Say rather I' m your soul; more just that name;
 For, like the soul, my love can never die.

SONNETS.

TO GENEVRA.

I.

THINE eyes' blue tenderness, thy long fair hair,
 And the wan lustre of thy features—caught
 From contemplation—where serenely wrought,
Seems Sorrow's softness charm'd from its despair—
Have thrown such speaking sadness in thine air,
 That—but I know thy blessed bosom fraught
 With mines of unalloy'd and stainless thought—
I should have deem'd thee doom'd to earthly care.
With such an aspect, by his colours blent,
 When from his beauty-breathing pencil born,
(Except that *thou* hast nothing to repent)
 The Magdalen of Guido saw the morn—
Such seem'st thou—but how much more excellent!
 With nought Remorse can claim—nor Virtue scorn.

December 17, 1813.

II.

THY cheek is pale with thought, but not from woe,
And yet so lovely, that if Mirth could flush
Its rose of whiteness with the brightest blush,
My heart would wish away that ruder glow:
And dazzle not thy deep-blue eyes—but, oh!
While gazing on them sterner eyes will gush,
And into mine my mother's weakness rush,
Soft as the last drops round heaven's airy bow.
For, through thy long dark lashes low depending,
The soul of melancholy Gentleness
Gleams like a seraph from the sky descending,
Above all pain, yet pitying all distress;
At once such majesty with sweetness blending,
I worship more, but cannot love thee less.

TO LAKE LEMAN.

ROUSSEAU—Voltaire—Our Gibbon—and De Staël—
Leman! these names are worthy of thy shore,
Thy shore of names like these! wert thou no more,
Their memory thy remembrance would recall:
To them thy banks were lovely as to all,
But they have made them lovelier, for the lore
Of mighty minds doth hallow in the core
Of human hearts the ruin of a wall
Where dwelt the wise and wondrous; but by *thee*,
How much more, Lake of Beauty! do we feel,
In sweetly gliding o'er thy crystal sea,
The wild glow of that not ungentle zeal,
Which of the heirs of immortality
Is proud, and makes the breath of glory real!

DARKNESS.

I HAD a dream, which was not all a dream.
The bright sun was extinguish'd, and the stars
Did wander darkling in the eternal space,
Rayless, and pathless, and the icy earth
Swung blind and blackening in the moonless air;
Morn came and went—and came, and brought no day,
And men forgot their passions in the dread
Of this their desolation; and all hearts
Were chill'd into a selfish prayer for light:
And they did live by watchfires—and the thrones,
The palaces of crownèd kings—the huts,
The habitations of all things which dwell,
Were burnt for beacons; cities were consumed,
And men were gather'd round their blazing homes
To look once more into each others' face;
Happy were those who dwelt within the eye
Of the volcanos, and their mountain-torch:
A fearful hope was all the world contain'd;
Forests were set on fire—but hour by hour
They fell and faded—and the crackling trunks
Extinguish'd with a crash—and all was black.
The brows of men by the despairing light
Wore an unearthly aspect, as by fits
The flashes fell upon them; some lay down
And hid their eyes and wept; and some did rest
Their chins upon their clenched hands, and smiled;
And others hurried to and fro, and fed
Their funeral piles with fuel, and look'd up
With mad disquietude on the dull sky,
The pall of a past world; and then again
With curses cast them down upon the dust,
And gnash'd their teeth and howl'd: the wild birds shriek'd,
And, terrified, did flutter on the ground,
And flap their useless wings; the wildest brutes
Came tame and tremulous; and vipers crawl'd
And twined themselves among the multitude,
Hissing, but stingless—they were slain for food:
And War, which for a moment was no more,
Did glut himself again;—a meal was bought
With blood, and each sate sullenly apart
Gorging himself in gloom: no love was left;
All earth was but one thought—and that was death,
Immediate and inglorious; and the pang
Of famine fed upon all entrails—men
Died, and their bones were tombless as their flesh;
The meagre by the meagre were devour'd,
Even dogs assail'd their masters, all save one,
And he was faithful to a corse, and kept
The birds and beasts and famish'd men at bay,
Till hunger clung them, or the dropping dead
Lured their lank jaws; himself sought out no food,
But with a piteous and perpetual moan,
And a quick desolate cry, licking the hand
Which answer'd not with a caress—he died.
The crowd was famish'd by degrees; but two
Of an enormous city did survive,
And they were enemies: they met beside
The dying embers of an altar-place
Where had been heap'd a mass of holy things
For an unholy usage; they raked up,
And shivering scraped with their cold skeleton hands
The feeble ashes, and their feeble breath
Blew for a little life, and made a flame
Which was a mockery; then they lifted up
Their eyes as it grew lighter, and beheld
Each other's aspects—saw, and shriek'd, and died—
Even of their mutual hideousness they died,
Unknowing who he was upon whose brow
Famine had written Fiend. The world was void,
The populous and the powerful was a lump,
Seasonless, herbless, treeless, manless, lifeless—
A lump of death—a chaos of hard clay.
The rivers, lakes, and ocean all stood still,
And nothing stirr'd within their silent depths;
Ships sailorless lay rotting on the sea,
And their masts fell down piecemeal; as they dropp'd
They slept on the abyss without a surge—
The waves were dead; the tides were in their grave,
The Moon, their mistress, had expired before;
The winds were wither'd in the stagnant air,
And the clouds perish'd! Darkness had no need
Of aid from them—She was the Universe!

Diodati, July, 1816.

CHURCHILL'S GRAVE.

A FACT LITERALLY RENDERED.

I STOOD beside the grave of him who blazed
The comet of a season, and I saw
The humblest of all sepulchres, and gazed
With not the less of sorrow and of awe
On that neglected turf and quiet stone,
With name no clearer than the names unknown,
Which lay unread around it; and I ask'd
The Gardener of that ground, why it might be
That for this plant strangers his memory task'd
Through the thick deaths of half a century?
And thus he answer'd—"Well, I do not know
Why frequent travellers turn to pilgrims so;
He died before my day of Sextonship,
And I had not the digging of this grave."
And is this all? I thought,—and do we rip
The veil of Immortality? and crave
I know not what of honour and of light
Through unborn ages, to endure this blight?
So soon, and so successless? As I said,
The Architect of all on which we tread,
For Earth is but a tombstone, did essay

To extricate remembrance from the clay,
Whose minglings might confuse a Newton's thought,
Were it not that all life must end in one,
Of which we are but dreamers;—as he caught
As 'twere the twilight of a former Sun,
Thus spoke he,—"I believe the man of whom
You wot, who lies in this selected tomb,
Was a most famous writer in his day,
And therefore travellers step from out their way
To pay him honour,—and myself whate'er
Your honour pleases,"—then most pleased I shook
From out my pocket's avaricious nook
Some certain coins of silver, which as 'twere
Perforce I gave this man, though I could spare
So much but inconveniently:—Ye smile,
I see ye, ye profane ones! all the while,
Because my homely phrase the truth would tell.
You are the fools, not I—for I did dwell
With a deep thought, and with a soften'd eye,
On that Old Sexton's natural homily,
In which there was Obscurity and Fame,—
The Glory and the Nothing of a Name.

Diodati. 1816.

TO A YOUTHFUL FRIEND.

Few years have pass'd since thou and I
Were firmest friends, at least in name,
And childhood's gay sincerity
Preserved our feelings long the same.

But now, like me, too well thou know'st
What trifles oft the heart recall;
And those who once have loved the most
Too soon forget they loved at all.

And such the change the heart displays,
So frail is early friendship's reign,
A month's brief lapse, perhaps a day's,
Will view thy mind estranged again.

If so, it never shall be mine
To mourn the loss of such a heart;
The fault was Nature's fault, not thine,
Which made thee fickle as thou art.

As rolls the ocean's changing tide,
So human feelings ebb and flow;
And who would in a breast confide,
Where stormy passions ever glow?

It boots not that, together bred,
Our childish days were days of joy:
My spring of life has quickly fled;
Thou, too, hast ceased to be a boy.

And when we bid adieu to youth,
Slaves to the specious world's control,
We sigh a long farewell to truth;
That world corrupts the noblest soul.

Ah, joyous season! when the mind
Dares all things boldly but to lie;
When thought ere spoke is unconfined,
And sparkles in the placid eye.

Not so in Man's maturer years,
When Man himself is but a tool;
When interest sways our hopes and fears,
And all must love and hate by rule.

With fools in kindred vice the same,
We learn at length our faults to blend,
And those, and those alone, may claim
The prostituted name of friend.

Such is the common lot of man:
Can we then 'scape from folly free?
Can we reverse the general plan,
Nor be what all in turn must be.

No; for myself, so dark my fate
Through every turn of life hath been;
Man and the world I so much hate,
I care not when I quit the scene.

But thou, with spirit frail and light,
Wilt shine awhile, and pass away;
As glow-worms sparkle through the night,
But dare not stand the test of day.

Alas! whenever folly calls
Where parasites and princes meet,
(For cherish'd first in royal halls,
The welcome vices kindly greet)

Ev'n now thou 'rt nightly seen to add
One insect to the fluttering crowd;
And still thy trifling heart is glad
To join the vain, and court the proud.

There dost thou glide from fair to fair,
Still simpering on with eager haste,
As flies along the gay parterre
That taint the flowers they scarcely taste.

But say, what nymph will prize the flame
Which seems, as marshy vapours move,
To flit along from dame to dame,
An ignis-fatuus gleam of love?

What friend for thee, howe'er inclined,
Will deign to own a kindred care?
Who will debase his manly mind,
For friendship every fool may share?

In time forbear; amidst the throng
No more so base a thing be seen;
No more so idly pass along:
Be something, any thing, but—mean.

1808.

INSCRIPTION ON THE MONUMENT OF A NEWFOUNDLAND DOG.

WHEN some proud son of man returns to earth,
Unknown to glory, but upheld by birth,
The sculptor's art exhausts the pomp of woe,
And storied urns record who rests below;
When all is done, upon the tomb is seen,
Not what he was, but what he should have been:
But the poor dog, in life the firmest friend,
The first to welcome, foremost to defend,
Whose honest heart is still his master's own,
Who labours, fights, lives, breathes for him alone,
Unhonour'd falls, unnoticed all his worth,
Denied in heaven the soul he held on earth:
While man, vain insect! hopes to be forgiven,
And claims himself a sole exclusive heaven.
Oh man! thou feeble tenant of an hour,
Debased by slavery, or corrupt by power,
Who knows thee well must quit thee with disgust,
Degraded mass of animated dust!
Thy love is lust, thy friendship all a cheat,
Thy smiles hypocrisy, thy words deceit!
By nature vile, ennobled but by name,
Each kindred brute might bid thee blush for shame.
Ye! who perchance behold this simple urn,
Pass on—it honours none you wish to mourn:
To mark a friend's remains these stones arise;
I never knew but one,—and here he lies.

Newstead Abbey, November 30, 1808.

TO TIME.

TIME! on whose arbitrary wing
The varying hours must flag or fly,
Whose tardy winter, fleeting spring,
But drag or drive us on to die—

Hail thou! who on my birth bestow'd
Those boons to all that know thee known;
Yet better I sustain thy load,
For now I bear the weight alone.

I would not one fond heart should share
The bitter moments thou hast given;
And pardon thee, since thou couldst spare
All that I loved, to peace or heaven.

To them be joy or rest, on me
Thy future ills shall press in vain:
I nothing owe but years to thee,
A debt already paid in pain.

Yet even that pain was some relief;
It felt, but still forgot thy power:
The active agony of grief
Retards, but never counts the hour.

In joy I ve sigh'd to think thy flight
Would soon subside from swift to slow;
Thy cloud could overcast the light,
But could not add a night to woe;

For then, however drear and dark
My soul was suited to thy sky;
One star alone shot forth a spark
To prove thee not—Eternity.

That beam hath sunk, and now thou art
A blank; a thing to count and curse,
Through each dull tedious trifling part,
Which all regret, yet all rehearse.

One scene even thou canst not deform;
The limit of thy sloth or speed
When future wanderers bear the storm
Which we shall sleep too sound to heed:

And I can smile to think how weak
Thine efforts shortly shall be shown,
When all the vengeance thou canst wreak
Must fall upon—a nameless stone.

LINES INSCRIBED UPON A CUP FORMED FROM A SKULL.

START not—nor deem my spirit fled:
In me behold the only skull,
From which, unlike a living head,
Whatever flows is never dull.

I lived, I loved, I quaff'd, like thee:
I died: let earth my bones resign:
Fill up—thou canst not injure me;
The worm hath fouler lips than thine.

Better to hold the sparkling grape,
Than nurse the earth-worm's slimy brood;
And circle in the goblet's shape
The drink of gods, than reptile's food.

Where once my wit, perchance, hath shone,
In aid of others' let me shine;
And when, alas! our brains are gone,
What nobler substitute than wine?

Quaff while thou canst: another race,
When thou and thine, like me, are sped,
May rescue thee from earth's embrace,
And rhyme and revel with the dead.

Why not—since through life's little day
Our heads such sad effects produce?
Redeem'd from worms and wasting clay,
This chance is theirs, to be of use.

Newstead Abbey, 1808.

PROMETHEUS.

TITAN! to whose immortal eyes
The sufferings of mortality,
Seen in their sad reality,
Were not as things that gods despise;
What was thy pity's recompense?
A silent suffering, and intense;
The rock, the vulture, and the chain,
All that the proud can feel of pain,
The agony they do not show
The suffocating sense of woe,
Which speaks but in its loneliness,
And then is jealous lest the sky
Should have a listener, nor will sigh
Until its voice is echoless.

Titan! to thee the strife was given
Between the suffering and the will,
Which torture where they cannot kill;
And the inexorable Heaven,
And the deaf tyranny of Fate,
The ruling principle of Hate,
Which for its pleasure doth create
The things it may annihilate,
Refused thee even the boon to die;
The wretched gift eternity
Was thine—and thou hast borne it well.
All that the Thunderer wrung from thee
Was but the menace which flung back
On him the torments of thy rack;
The fate thou didst so well foresee,

But would not to appease him tell;
And in thy Silence was his Sentence,
And in his Soul a vain repentance,
And evil dread so ill dissembled,
That in his hand the lightnings trembled.

Thy Godlike crime was to be kind,
To render with thy precept less
The sum of human wretchedness,
And strengthen Man with his own mind;
But baffled as thou wert from high,
Still in thy patient energy,
In the endurance, and repulse
Of thine impenetrable Spirit,
Which Earth and Heaven could not convulse,
A mighty lesson we inherit:
Thou art a symbol and a sign
To Mortals of their fate and force;
Like thee, Man is in part divine,
A troubled stream from a pure source;
And Man in portions can foresee
His own funereal destiny;
His wretchedness, and his resistance,
And his sad unallied existence:
To which his Spirit may oppose
Itself—and equal to all woes,
And a firm will, and a deep sense,
Which even in torture can descry
Its own concenter'd recompense,
Triumphant where it dares defy,
And making Death a Victory!

Diodati, July, 1816.

LINES WRITTEN IN THE TRAVELLERS' BOOK AT ORCHOMENUS.

IN THIS BOOK A TRAVELLER HAD WRITTEN:—

"Fair Albion, smiling, sees her son depart,
To trace the birth and nursery of art:
Noble his object, glorious is his aim;
He comes to Athens, and he writes his name!"

BENEATH WHICH LORD BYRON INSERTED THE FOLLOWING:

The modest bard, like many a bard unknown,
Rhymes on our names, but wisely hides his own;
But yet, whoe'er he be, to say no worse,
His name would bring more credit than his verse.

LINES WRITTEN IN AN ALBUM, AT MALTA.

As o'er the cold sepulchral stone
Some name arrests the passer-by;
Thus, when thou view'st this page alone,
May mine attract thy pensive eye!

And when by thee that name is read,
Perchance in some succeeding year,
Reflect on me as on the dead,
And think my heart is buried here.

September 14, 1809.

WRITTEN AFTER SWIMMING FROM SESTOS TO ABYDOS.[6]

If, in the month of dark December,
Leander, who was nightly wont
(What maid will not the tale remember?)
To cross thy stream, broad Hellespont!

If, when the wintry tempest roar'd,
He sped to Hero, nothing loath,
And thus of old thy current pour'd,
Fair Venus! how I pity both!

For *me*, degenerate modern wretch,
Though in the genial month of May,
My dripping limbs I faintly stretch,
And think I've done a feat to-day.

But since he cross'd the rapid tide,
According to the doubtful story,
To woo—and—Lord knows what beside,
And swam for Love, as I for Glory;

'Twere hard to say who fared the best:
Sad mortals! thus the Gods still plague you!
He lost his labour, I my jest;
For he was drown'd, and I've the ague.

May 9, 1810.

TRANSLATION OF THE FAMOUS GREEK WAR SONG,

"Δεύτε παῖδες τῶν 'Ελλήνων."[7]

Sons of the Greeks, arise!
The glorious hour's gone forth,
And, worthy of such ties,
Display who gave us birth.

CHORUS.

Sons of Greeks! let us go
In arms against the foe,
Till their hated blood shall flow
In a river past our feet.

Then manfully despising
The Turkish tyrant's yoke,
Let your country see you rising,
And all her chains are broke.
Brave shades of chiefs and sages,
Behold the coming strife!
Hellênes of past ages,
Oh, start again to life!
At the sound of my trumpet, breaking
Your sleep, oh, join with me!
And the seven-hill'd city seeking,[8]
Fight, conquer, till we're free.
Sons of Greeks, &c.

Sparta, Sparta, why in slumbers
 Lethargic dost thou lie?
Awake, and join thy numbers
 With Athens, old ally!
Leonidas recalling,
 That chief of ancient song,
Who saved ye once from falling,
 The terrible! the strong!
Who made that bold diversion
 In old Thermopylæ,
And warring with the Persian
 To keep his country free;
With his three hundred waging
 The battle, long he stood,
And like a lion raging,
 Expired in seas of blood.
 Sons of Greeks, &c.

THE SPELL IS BROKE, THE CHARM IS FLOWN!

WRITTEN AT ATHENS, JANUARY 16, 1810.

The spell is broke, the charm is flown!
 Thus is it with life's fitful fever:
We madly smile when we should groan;
 Delirium is our best deceiver.

Each lucid interval of thought
 Recalls the woes of Nature's charter,
And he that acts as wise men ought,
 But lives, as saints have died, a martyr.

STANZAS

WRITTEN ON PASSING THE AMBRACIAN GULF.[9]

Through cloudless skies, in silvery sheen,
 Full beams the moon on Actium's coast;
And on these waves, for Egypt's queen,
 The ancient world was won and lost.

And now upon the scene I look,
 The azure grave of many a Roman;
Where stern Ambition once forsook
 His wavering crown to follow woman.

Florence! whom I will love as well
 As ever yet was said or sung,
(Since Orpheus sang his spouse from hell)
 Whilst thou art fair and I am young;

Sweet Florence! those were pleasant times,
 When worlds were staked for ladies' eyes:
Had bards as many realms as rhymes,
 Thy charms might raise new Antonies.

Though Fate forbids such things to be,
 Yet, by thine eyes and ringlets curl'd!
I cannot lose a world for thee,
 But would not lose thee for a world.

November 14, 1809.

TO FLORENCE.

Oh Lady! when I left the shore,
 The distant shore which gave me birth,
I hardly thought to grieve once more,
 To quit another spot on earth:

Yet here, amidst this barren isle,
 Where panting Nature droops the head,
Where only thou art seen to smile,
 I view my parting hour with dread.

Though far from Albin's craggy shore,
 Divided by the dark blue main;
A few, brief, rolling, seasons o'er,
 Perchance I view her cliffs again:

But wheresoe'er I now may roam,
 Through scorching clime, and varied sea,
Though Time restore me to my home,
 I ne'er shall bend mine eyes on thee:

On thee, in whom at once conspire
 All charms, which heedless hearts can move,
Whom but to see is to admire,
 And, oh! forgive the word—to love.

Forgive the word, in one who ne'er
 With such a word can more offend;
And since thy heart I cannot share,
 Believe me, what I am, thy friend.

And who so cold as look on thee,
 Thou lovely wand'rer, and be less?
Nor be, what man should ever be,
 The friend of Beauty in distress?

Ah! who would think that form had past
 Through Danger's most destructive path,
Had brav'd the death-wing'd tempest's blast,
 And 'scaped a tyrant's fiercer wrath?

Lady! when I shall view the walls
 Where free Byzantium once arose,
And Stamboul's Oriental halls
 The Turkish tyrants now enclose;

Though mightiest in the lists of fame,
 That glorious city still shall be;
On me 't will hold a dearer claim,
 As spot of thy nativity:

And though I bid thee now farewell,
 When I behold that wondrous scene,
Since where thou art I may not dwell,
 'T will soothe to be, where thou hast been.

September, 1809.

STANZAS

COMPOSED DURING A THUNDER-STORM, AND WHILE BEWILDERED NEAR MOUNT PINDUS IN ALBANIA.

Chill and mirk is the nightly blast,
 Where Pindus' mountains rise,
And angry clouds are pouring fast
 The vengeance of the skies.

Our guides are gone, our hope is lost,
 And lightnings, as they play,
But show where rocks our path have crost,
 Or gild the torrent's spray.

Is yon a cot I saw, though low?
 When lightning broke the gloom—
How welcome were its shade!—ah, no!
 'T is but a Turkish tomb.

Through sounds of foaming waterfalls,
 I hear a voice exclaim—
My way-worn countryman, who calls
 On distant England's name.

A shot is fired—by foe or friend?
 Another—'t is to tell
The mountain-peasants to descend,
 And lead us where they dwell.

Oh! who in such a night will dare
 To tempt the wilderness?
And who 'mid thunder peals can hear
 Our signal of distress?

And who that heard our shouts would rise,
 To try the dubious road?
Nor rather deem from nightly cries
 That outlaws were abroad.

Clouds burst, skies flash, oh, dreadful hour!
 More fiercely pours the storm!
Yet here one thought has still the power
 To keep my bosom warm.

While wand'ring through each broken path,
 O'er brake and craggy brow;
While elements exhaust their wrath,
 Sweet Florence, where art thou?

Not on the sea, not on the sea,
 Thy bark hath long been gone:
Oh, may the storm that pours on me,
 Bow down my head alone!

Full swiftly blew the swift Siroc,
 When last I press'd thy lip;
And long ere now, with foaming shock,
 Impell'd thy gallant ship.

Now thou art safe; nay, long ere now
 Hast trod the shore of Spain;
'T were hard if aught so fair as thou
 Should linger on the main.

And since I now remember thee
 In darkness and in dread,
As in those hours of revelry
 Which mirth and music sped;

Do thou, amid the fair white walls,
 If Cadiz yet be free,
At times, from out her latticed halls,
 Look o'er the dark blue sea;

Then think upon Calypso's isles,
 Endear'd by days gone by;
To others give a thousand smiles,
 To me a single sigh.

And when the admiring circle mark
 The paleness of thy face,
A half-form'd tear, a transient spark
 Of melancholy grace,

Again thou'lt smile, and blushing shun
 Some coxcomb's raillery;
Nor own for once thou thought'st on one,
 Who ever thinks on thee.

Though smile and sigh alike are vain,
 When sever'd hearts repine,
My spirit flies o'er mount and main,
 And mourns in search of thine.

ON BEING ASKED WHAT WAS THE "ORIGIN OF LOVE."

The "Origin of Love!"—Ah, why
 That cruel question ask of me,
When thou may'st read in many an eye
 He starts to life on seeing thee?

And shouldst thou seek his *end* to know:
 My heart forebodes, my fears foresee,
He'll linger long in silent woe;
 But live—until I cease to be.

IMPROMPTU, IN REPLY TO A FRIEND.

When, from the heart where Sorrow sits,
 Her dusky shadow mounts too high,
And o'er the changing aspect flits,
 And clouds the brow, or fills the eye;
Heed not that gloom, which soon shall sink:
 My thoughts their dungeon know too well—
Back to my breast the wanderers shrink
 And droop within their silent cell.

September, 1813.

TO SAMUEL ROGERS, ESQ.

Absent or present, still to thee,
 My friend, what magic spells belong!
As all can tell, who share, like me,
 In turn thy converse, and thy song.

But when the dreaded hour shall come,
 By Friendship ever deem'd too nigh,
And "Memory" o'er her Druid's tomb
 Shall weep that aught of thee can die

How fondly will she then repay
 Thy homage offer'd at her shrine,
And blend, while ages roll away,
 Her name immortally with *thine!*

April 19, 1813.

CONDOLATORY ADDRESS

TO SARAH, COUNTESS OF JERSEY, ON THE PRINCE REGENT'S RETURNING HER PICTURE TO MRS. MEE.

When the vain triumph of the imperial lord,
Whom servile Rome obey'd, and yet abhorr'd,
Gave to the vulgar gaze each glorious bust,
That left a likeness of the brave, or just;
What most admired each scrutinising eye
Of all that deck'd that passing pageantry?
What spread from face to face that wondering air?
The thought of Brutus—for his was not there!
That absence proved his worth,—that absence fix'd
His memory on the longing mind, unmix'd;
And more decreed his glory to endure,
Than all a gold Colossus could secure.

If thus, fair Jersey, our desiring gaze
Search for thy form, in vain and mute amaze,
Amidst those pictured charms, whose loveliness,
Bright though they be, thine own had render'd less
If he, that vain old man, whom truth admits
Heir of his father's crown, and of his wits,
If his corrupted eye, and wither'd heart,
Could with thy gentle image bear depart;
That tasteless shame be *his*, and ours the grief
To gaze on Beauty's band without its chief:
Yet comfort still one selfish thought imparts,
We lose the portrait, but preserve our hearts

What can his vaulted gallery now disclose?
A garden with all flowers—except the rose;—
A fount that only wants its living stream;—
A night, with every star, save Dian's beam.
Lost to our eyes the present forms shall be,
That turn from tracing them to dream of thee;
And more on that recall'd resemblance pause,
Than all he *shall* not force on our applause.
Long may thy yet meridian lustre shine,
With all that Virtue asks of Homage thine:
The symmetry of youth—the grace of mien—
The eye that gladdens—and the brow serene;
The glossy darkness of that clustering hair,
Which shades, yet shows that forehead more than fair!
Each glance that wins us, and the life that throws
A spell which will not let our looks repose,
But turn to gaze again, and find anew
Some charm that well rewards another view.
These are not lessen'd, these are still as bright,
Albeit too dazzling for a dotard's sight;
And those must wait till ev'ry charm is gone,
To please the paltry heart that pleases none:—
That dull cold sensualist, whose sickly eye
In envious dimness pass'd thy portrait by;
Who rack'd his little spirit to combine
Its hate of *Freedom's* loveliness, and *thine*.

August, 1814.

STANZAS TO A LADY ON LEAVING ENGLAND.[19]

'Tis done—and shivering in the gale
The bark unfurls her snowy sail;
And whistling o'er the bending mast,
Loud sings on high the fresh'ning blast;
And I must from this land be gone,
Because I cannot love but one.

But could I be what I have been,
And could I see what I have seen—
Could I repose upon the breast
Which once my warmest wishes blest—
I should not seek another zone
Because I cannot love but one.

'T is long since I beheld that eye
Which gave me bless or misery;
And I have striven, but in vain,
Never to think of it again;
For though I fly from Albion,
I still can only love but one.

As some lone bird, without a mate,
My weary heart is desolate;
I look around, and cannot trace
One friendly smile, or welcome face,
And ev'n in crowds am still alone,
Because I cannot love but one.

77

And I will cross the whitening foam,
And I will seek a foreign home;
Till I forget a false fair face,
I ne'er shall find a resting-place;
My own dark thoughts I cannot shun,
But ever love, and love but one.

The poorest, veriest, wretch on earth
Still finds some hospitable hearth,
Where friendship's or love's softer glow
May smile in joy or soothe in woe;
But friend or lover I have none,
Because I cannot love but one.

I go—but wheresoe'er I flee,
There 's not an eye will weep for me;
There 's not a kind congenial heart,
Where I can claim the meanest part;
Nor thou, who hast my hopes undone
Wilt sigh, although I love but one.

To think of every early scene,
Of what we are, and what we 've been,
Would whelm some softer hearts with woe—
But mine, alas! has stood the blow;
Yet still beats on as it begun,
And never truly loves but one.

And who that dear loved one may be
Is not for vulgar eyes to see,
And why that early love was crost,
Thou know'st the best, I feel the most;
But few that dwell beneath the sun
Have loved so long, and loved but one.

I 've tried another's fetters too,
With charms perchance as fair to view;
And I would fain have loved as well,
But some unconquerable spell
Forbade my bleeding breast to own
A kindred care for aught but one.

'T would soothe to take one lingering view,
And bless thee in my last adieu;
Yet wish I not those eyes to weep
For him that wanders o'er the deep;
Though wheresoe'er my bark may run,
I love but thee, I love but one.

1809.

THE FAREWELL.

TO A LADY.

When Man, expell'd from Eden's bowers,
A moment linger'd near the gate,
Each scene recall'd the vanish'd hours,
And bade him curse his future fate.

But, wandering on through distant climes,
He learnt to bear his load of grief;

Just gave a sigh to other times,
And found in busier scenes relief.

Thus, lady! will it be with me,
And I must view thy charms no more;
For, whilst I linger near to thee,
I sigh for all I knew before.

In flight I shall be surely wise,
Escaping from temptation's snare;
I cannot view my paradise
Without a wish to enter there.

December 2, 1808.

WHEN WE TWO PARTED.

When we two parted
In silence and tears,
Half broken-hearted
To sever for years,
Pale grew thy cheek and cold,
Colder thy kiss;
Truly that hour foretold
Sorrow to this.

The dew of the morning
Sunk chill on my brow—
It felt like the warning
Of what I feel now.
Thy vows are all broken,
And light is thy fame;
I hear thy name spoken,
And share in its shame.

They name thee before me,
A knell to mine ear;
A shudder comes o'er me—
Why wert thou so dear?
They know not I knew thee,
Who knew thee too well:—
Long, long shall I rue thee,
Too deeply to tell.

In secret we met—
In silence I grieve,
That thy heart could forget,
Thy spirit deceive.
If I should meet thee
After long years,
How should I greet thee?—
With silence and tears.

1808.

LINES TO A LADY WEEPING.[11]

Weep, daughter of a royal line,
A Sire's disgrace, a realm's decay;
Ah! happy if each tear of thine
Could wash a father's fault away!

Weep—for thy tears are Virtue's tears—
Auspicious to these suffering isles;
And be each drop in future years
Repaid thee by thy people's smiles!

March, 1812.

WINDSOR POETICS.

Lines composed on the occasion of his Royal Highness the Prince Regent being seen standing between the coffins of Henry VIII. and Charles I., in the royal vault at Windsor.

Famed for contemptuous breach of sacred ties,
By headless Charles see heartless Henry lies;
Between them stands another sceptered thing—
It moves, it reigns—in all but name, a king:
Charles to his people, Henry to his wife,
—In him the double tyrant starts to life:
Justice and death have mix'd their dust in vain,
Each royal vampire wakes to life again.
Ah, what can tombs avail!—since these disgorge
The blood and dust of both—to mould a George.

ELEGIAC STANZAS

ON THE DEATH OF SIR PETER PARKER, BART.

There is a tear for all that die,
A mourner o'er the humblest grave;
But nations swell the funeral cry,
And Triumph weeps above the brave.

For them is Sorrow's purest sigh
O'er Ocean's heaving bosom sent:
In vain their bones unburied lie,
All earth becomes their monument!

A tomb is theirs on every page,
An epitaph on every tongue:
The present hours, the future age,
For them bewail, to them belong.

For them the voice of festal mirth
Grows hush'd, *their name* the only sound;
While deep Remembrance pours to Worth
The goblet's tributary round.

A theme to crowds that knew them not,
Lamented by admiring foes,
Who would not share their glorious lot?
Who would not die the death they chose?

And, gallant Parker! thus enshrined
Thy life, thy fall, thy fame shall be;
And early valour, glowing, find
A model in thy memory.

But there are breasts that bleed with thee
In woe, that glory cannot quell;
And shuddering hear of victory,
Where one so dear, so dauntless, fell.

Where shall they turn to mourn thee less?
 When cease to hear thy cherish'd name?
Time cannot teach forgetfulness,
 While Grief's full heart is fed by Fame.

Alas! for them, though not for thee,
 They cannot choose but weep the more;
Deep for the dead the grief must be,
 Who ne'er gave cause to mourn before.

A FRAGMENT.

Could I remount the river of my years
To the first fountain of our smiles and tears,
I would not trace again the stream of hours
Between their outworn banks of wither'd flowers,
But bid it flow as now—until it glides
Into the number of the nameless tides. . . .

What is this Death?—a quiet of the heart?
The whole of that of which we are a part?
For life is but a vision—what I see
Of all which lives alone is life to me,
And being so—the absent are the dead,
Who haunt us from tranquillity, and spread
A dreary shroud around us, and invest
With sad remembrancers our hours of rest.

The absent are the dead, for they are cold,
And ne'er can be what once we did behold;
And they are changed, and cheerless,—or if yet
The unforgotten do not all forget,
Since thus divided—equal must it be
If the deep barrier be of earth, or sea;
It may be both—but one day end it must
In the dark union of insensate dust.

The under-earth inhabitants—are they
But mingled millions decomposed to clay?
The ashes of a thousand ages spread
Wherever man has trodden or shall tread?
Or do they in their silent cities dwell
Each in his incommunicative cell?
Or have they their own language? and a sense
Of breathless being?—darken'd and intense
As midnight in her solitude?—Oh Earth!
Where are the past?—and wherefore had they birth?
The dead are thy inheritors—and we
But bubbles on thy surface; and the key
Of thy profundity is in the grave,
The ebon portal of thy peopled cave,
Where I would walk in spirit, and behold
Our elements resolved to things untold,
And fathom hidden wonders, and explore
The essence of great bosoms now no more. . . .

Diodati, July, 1816.

STANZAS FOR MUSIC.

"O Lachrymarum fons, tenero sacros
Ducentium ortus ex animo: quater
Felix! in imo qui scatentem
Pectore te, pia Nympha, sensit."
GRAY'S "Poemata."

THERE'S not a joy the world can give like that it takes away,
When the glow of early thought declines in feeling's dull decay;
'T is not on youth's smooth cheek the blush alone, which fades so fast,
But the tender bloom of heart is gone, ere youth itself be past.

Then the few whose spirits float above the wreck of happiness
Are driven o'er the shoals of guilt or ocean of excess:
The magnet of their course is gone, or only points in vain
The shore to which their shiver'd sail shall never stretch again.

Then the mortal coldness of the soul like death itself comes down;
It cannot feel for others' woes, it dare not dream its own;
That heavy chill has frozen o'er the fountain of our tears,
And though the eye may sparkle still, 't is where the ice appears.

Though wit may flash from fluent lips, and mirth distract the breast,
Through midnight hours that yield no more their former hope of rest;
'T is but as ivy-leaves around the ruin'd turret wreath,
All green and wildly fresh without, but worn and gray beneath.

Oh! could I feel as I have felt,—or be what I have been,
Or weep as I could once have wept, o'er many a vanish'd scene;
As springs in deserts found seem sweet, all brackish though they be,
So midst the wither'd waste of life, those tears would flow to me.

March, 1815.

FILL THE GOBLET AGAIN.

A SONG.

FILL the goblet again! for I never before
Felt the glow which now gladdens my heart to its core;
Let us drink!—who would not?—since, through life's varied round,
In the goblet alone no deception is found.

I have tried in its turn all that life can supply:
I have bask'd in the beam of a dark rolling eye;
I have loved!—who has not?—but what heart can declare,
That pleasure existed while passion was there?

In the days of my youth, when the heart's in its spring,
And dreams that affection can never take wing,
I had friends!—who has not?—but what tongue will avow
That friends, rosy wine! are so faithful as thou?

The heart of a mistress some boy may estrange,
Friendship shifts with the sunbeam—thou never canst change:
Thou grow'st old—who does not?—but on earth what appears,
Whose virtues, like thine, still increase with its years?

Yet if blest to the utmost that love can bestow,
Should a rival bow down to our idol below,
We are jealous!—who's not?—thou hast no such alloy;
For the more that enjoy thee, the more we enjoy.

Then the season of youth and its vanities past,
For refuge we fly to the goblet at last;
There we find—do we not?—in the flow of the soul,
That truth, as of yore, is confined to the bowl.

When the box of Pandora was open'd on earth,
And Misery's triumph commenced over Mirth,
Hope was left,—was she not?—but the goblet we kiss,
And care not for Hope, who are certain of bliss.

Long life to the grape! for when summer is flown,
The age of our nectar shall gladden our own:
We must die—who shall not?—May our sins be forgiven,
And Hebe shall never be idle in heaven.

REMEMBER THEE! REMEMBER THEE!

REMEMBER thee! remember thee!
Till Lethe quench life's burning stream
Remorse and shame shall cling to thee,
And haunt thee like a feverish dream!

Remember thee! Ay, doubt it not.
Thy husband too shall think of thee:
By neither shalt thou be forgot,
Thou *false* to him, thou *fiend* to me!

ON A CORNELIAN HEART WHICH WAS BROKEN.

ILL-FATED Heart! and can it be,
That thou shouldst thus be rent in twain?
Have years of care for thine and thee
Alike been all employ'd in vain?

Yet precious seems each shatter'd part,
And every fragment dearer grown,
Since he who wears thee feels thou art
A fitter emblem of *his own*.

NOTES TO MISCELLANEOUS POEMS.

NOTE 1, page 554.

Romaic expression of tenderness: if I translate it, I shall affront the gentlemen, as it may seem that I supposed they could not; and if I do not, I may affront the ladies. For fear of any misconstruction on the part of the latter, I shall do so, begging pardon of the learned. It means, "My life, I love you!" which sounds very prettily in all languages, and is as much in fashion in Greece at this day, as, Juvenal tells us, the two first words were amongst the Roman ladies, whose erotic expressions were all Hellenised.

NOTE 2, page 555.

By all the token-flowers that tell.

In the East (where ladies are not taught to write, lest they should scribble assignations) flowers, cinders, pebbles, &c., convey the sentiments of the parties, by that universal deputy of Mercury—an old woman. A cinder says, "I burn for thee;" a bunch of flowers tied with hair, "Take me and fly;" but a pebble declares—what nothing else can.

NOTE 3, page 555.

Though I fly to Istambol.

Constantinople.

NOTE 4, page 557.

The song from which this is taken is a great favourite with the young girls of Athens of all classes. Their manner of singing it is by verses in rotation, the whole number present joining in the chorus. The air is plaintive and pretty.

NOTE 5, page 560.

Leman! these names are worthy of thy shore.

Geneva, Ferney, Copet, Lausanne.

NOTE 6, page 565.

On the 3rd of May, 1810, while the "Salsette" (Captain Bathurst) was lying in the Dardanelles, Lieutenant Ekenhead of that frigate and the writer of these rhymes swam from the European shore to the Asiatic—by-the-bye, from Abydos to Sestos would have been more correct. The whole distance from the place whence we started to our landing on the other side, including the length we were carried by the current, was computed by those on board the frigate at upwards of four English miles; though the actual breadth is barely one. The rapidity of the current is such that no boat can row directly across, and it may, in some measure, be estimated from the circumstance of the whole distance being accomplished by one of the parties in an hour and five, and by the other in an hour and ten minutes. The water was extremely cold, from the melting of the mountain snows. About three weeks before, in April, we had made an attempt; but having ridden all the way from the Troad the same morning, and the water being of an icy chillness, we found it necessary to postpone the completion till the frigate anchored below the castles, when we swam the straits, as just stated; entering a considerable way above the European, and landing below the Asiatic, fort. Chevalier says that a young Jew swam the same distance for his mistress; and Oliver mentions its having been done by a Neapolitan; but our consul, Tarragona, remembered neither of these circumstances, and tried to dissuade us from the attempt. A number of the "Salsette's" crew were known to have accomplished a greater distance; and the only thing that surprised me was, that, as doubts had been entertained of the truth of Leander's story, no traveller had ever endeavoured to ascertain its practicability.

NOTE 7, page 565.

The song was written by Riga, who perished in the attempt to revolutionise Greece. This translation is as literal as the author could make it in verse. It is of the same measure as that of the original.

NOTE 8, page 565.

And the seven-hill'd city seeking.

Constantinople.

NOTE 9, page 566.

The lady referred to in this and the two following pieces—the wife of Mr Spencer Smith, and daughter of Baron Herbert, Austrian Ambassador at Constantinople, where she was born—was a very remarkable person, and experienced a variety of striking adventures. She was unhappy in her marriage, yet of unblemished reputation; had engaged in some plots against Bonaparte, which excited his vengeance; was made prisoner, but subsequently escaped; afterwards suffered shipwreck—and all before she was 25 years of age. The poet met her at Malta, on her way to England to join her husband; and these poems, and a reference to her in "Childe Harold," are memorials of their brief acquaintance.

NOTE 10, page 569.

Mrs. Musters, formerly Mary Chaworth.

NOTE 11, page 570.

The Princess Charlotte.

CHILDE HAROLD'S PILGRIMAGE.

L'univers est une espèce de livre, dont on n'a lu que la première page quand on n'a vu que son pays. J'en ai feuilleté un assez grand nombre, que j'ai trouvé également mauvaises. Cet examen ne m'a point été infructueux. Je haïssais ma patrie. Toutes les impertinences des peuples divers, parmi lesquels j'ai vécu, m'ont reconcilié avec elle. Quand je n'aurais tiré d'autre bénéfice de mes voyages que celui-là, je n'en regretterais ni les frais ni les fatigues.—LE COSMOPOLITE.

PREFACE.

[TO THE FIRST AND SECOND CANTOS.]

THE following poem was written, for the most part, amidst the scenes which it attempts to describe. It was begun in Albania; and the parts relative to Spain and Portugal were composed from the author's observations in these countries. Thus much it may be necessary to state for the correctness of the descriptions. The scenes attempted to be sketched are in Spain, Portugal, Epirus, Acarnania, and Greece. There, for the present, the poem stops: its reception will determine whether the author may venture to conduct his readers to the capital of the East, through Ionia and Phrygia: these two Cantos are merely experimental.

A fictitious character is introduced for the sake of giving some connection to the piece; which, however, makes no pretensions to regularity. It has been suggested to me by friends, on whose opinions I set a high value, that in this fictitious character, "Childe Harold," I may incur the suspicion of having intended some real personage: this I beg leave, once for all, to disclaim—Harold is the child of imagination, for the purpose I have stated. In some very trivial particulars, and those merely local, there might be grounds for such a notion; but in the main points, I should hope, none whatever.

It is almost superfluous to mention that the appellation "Childe," as "Childe Waters," "Childe Childers," &c., is used as more consonant with the old structure of versification which I have adopted. The "Good Night," in the beginning of the first canto, was suggested by "Lord Maxwell's Good Night," in the Border Minstrelsy, edited by Mr. Scott.

With the different poems which have been published on Spanish subjects, there may be found some slight coincidence in the first part which treats of the Peninsula, but it can only be casual; as, with the exception of a few concluding stanzas, the whole of this poem was written in the Levant.

The stanza of Spenser, according to one of our most successful poets, admits of every variety. Dr. Beattie makes the following observation:—"Not long ago, I began a poem in the style and stanza of Spenser, in which I propose to give full scope to my inclination, and be either droll or pathetic, descriptive or sentimental, tender or satirical, as the humour strikes me; for, if I mistake not, the measure which I have adopted admits equally of all these kinds of composition." Strengthened in my opinion by such authority, and by the example of some in the highest order of Italian poets, I shall make no apology for attempts at similar variations in the following composition; satisfied that, if they are unsuccessful, their failure must be in the execution, rather than in the design, sanctioned by the practice of Ariosto, Thomson, and Beattie.

London, February, 1812.

ADDITION TO THE PREFACE.

I HAVE now waited till almost all our periodical journals have distributed their usual portion of criticism. To the justice of the generality of their criticisms I have nothing to object: it would ill become me to quarrel with their very slight degree of censure, when, perhaps, if they had been less kind, they had been more candid. Returning, therefore, to all and each my best thanks for their liberality, on one point alone shall I venture an observation. Amongst the many objections justly urged to the very indifferent character of the "vagrant Childe" (whom, notwithstanding many hints to the contrary, I still maintain to be a fictitious personage), it has been stated, that, besides the anachronism, he is very *unknightly*, as the times of the Knights were times of Love, Honour, and so forth. Now, it so happens that the good old times, when "l'amour du bon vieux tems, l'amour antique" flourished, were the most profligate of all possible centuries. Those who have any doubts on this subject may consult Sainte-Palaye, *passim*, and more particularly vol. ii. p. 69. The vows of chivalry were no better kept than any other vows whatsoever; and the songs of the Troubadours were not more decent, and certainly were much less refined, than those of Ovid. The "Cours d'amour, parlemens d'amour, ou de courtésie et de gentilesse," had much more of love than of courtesy or gentleness. See Roland on the same subject with Sainte-Palaye. Whatever other objection may be urged to that most unamiable personage, Childe Harold, he was so far perfectly knightly in his attributes—"No waiter, but a knight templar."[1] By-the-bye, I fear that Sir Tristrem and Sir Lancelot were no better than they should be, although very poetical personages and true knights, "sans peur," though not "sans reproche." If the story of the institution of the "Garter" be not a fable, the knights of that order have for several centuries borne the badge of a Countess of Salisbury, of indifferent memory. So much for chivalry. Burke need not have regretted that its days are over, though Marie-Antoinette was quite as chaste as most of those in whose honours lances were shivered, and knights unhorsed.

Before the days of Bayard, and down to those of Sir Joseph Banks (the most chaste and celebrated of ancient and modern times), few exceptions will be found to this statement; and I fear a little investigation will teach us not to regret these monstrous mummeries of the middle ages.

I now leave "Childe Harold" to live his day, such as he is; it had been more agreeable, and certainly more easy, to have drawn an amiable character. It had been easy to varnish over his faults, to make him do more and express less; but he never was intended as an example, further than to show, that early perversion of mind and morals leads to satiety of past pleasures and disappointment in new ones, and that even the beauties of nature, and the stimulus of travel (except ambition, the most powerful of all excitements), are lost on a soul so constituted, or rather misdirected. Had I proceeded with the poem, this character would have deepened as he drew to the close; for the outline which I once meant to fill up for him was, with some exceptions, the sketch of a modern Timon, perhaps a poetical Zeluco.

London, 1813.

TO IANTHE

Not in those climes where I have late been straying,
Though Beauty long hath there been matchless deem'd;
Not in those visions to the heart displaying
Forms which it sighs but to have only dream'd,
Hath aught like thee in truth or fancy seem'd:
Nor, having seen thee, shall I vainly seek
To paint those charms which varied as they beam'd;
To such as see thee not my words were weak;
To those who gaze on thee what language could they speak?

Ah! may'st thou ever be what now thou art,
Nor unbeseem the promise of thy spring,
As fair in form, as warm yet pure in heart,
Love's image upon earth without his wing,
And guileless beyond Hope's imagining!
And surely she who now so fondly rears
Thy youth, in thee, thus hourly brightening,
Beholds the rainbow of her future years,
Before whose heavenly hues all sorrow disappears.

Young Peri of the West!—'t is well for me
My years already doubly number thine;
My loveless eye unmoved may gaze on thee,
And safely view thy ripening beauties shine;
Happy, I ne'er shall see them in decline;
Happier, that while all younger hearts shall bleed,
Mine shall escape the doom thine eyes assign
To those whose admiration shall succeed,
But mix'd with pangs to Love's even loveliest hours decreed.

Oh! let that eye, which, wild as the gazelle's,
Now brightly bold or beautifully shy,
Wins as it wanders, dazzles where it dwells,
Glance o'er this page, nor to my verse deny
That smile for which my breast might vainly sigh,
Could I to thee be ever more than friend:
This much, dear maid, accord; nor question why
To one so young my strain I would commend,
But bid me with my wreath one matchless lily blend.

Such is thy name with this my verse entwined;
And long as kinder eyes a look shall cast
On Harold's page, Ianthe's here enshrined
Shall thus be first beheld, forgotten last:
My days once number'd, should this homage past
Attract thy fairy fingers near the lyre
Of him who hail'd thee, loveliest as thou wast,
Such is the most my memory may desire;
Though more than Hope can claim, could Friendship less require?

CHILDE HAROLD'S PILGRIMAGE.

A ROMAUNT.

CANTO THE FIRST.

I.

OH, thou! in Hellas deem'd of heavenly birth,
Muse! form'd or fabled at the minstrel's will!
Since shamed full oft by later lyres on earth,
Mine dares not call thee from thy sacred hill:
Yet there I've wander'd by thy vaunted rill;
Yes! sigh'd o'er Delphi's long-deserted shrine,
Where, save that feeble fountain, all is still;
Nor mote my shell awake the weary Nine
To grace so plain a tale—this lowly lay of mine.

II.

Whilome in Albion's isle there dwelt a youth,
Who ne in virtue's ways did take delight;
But spent his days in riot most uncouth,
And vex'd with mirth the drowsy ear of Night.
Ah, me! in sooth he was a shameless wight,
Sore given to revel and ungodly glee;
Few earthly things found favour in his sight
Save concubines and carnal companie,
And flaunting wassailers of high and low degree.

III.

Childe Harold was he hight:—but whence his name
And lineage long, it suits me not to say;
Suffice it, that perchance they were of fame,
And had been glorious in another day:
But one sad losel soils a name for aye,

However mighty in the olden time;
Nor all that heralds rake from coffin'd clay,
Nor florid prose, nor honied lies of rhyme,
Can blazon evil deeds, or consecrate a crime.

IV.

Childe Harold bask'd him in the noontide sun,
Disporting there like any other fly,
Nor deem'd before his little day was done
One blast might chill him into misery.
But long ere scarce a third of his pass'd by,
Worse than adversity the Childe befell;
He felt the fulness of satiety:
Then loathed he in his native land to dwell,
Which seem'd to him more lone than 'Eremite's sad cell.

V.

For he through Sin's long labyrinth had run,
Nor made atonement when he did amiss,
Had sigh'd to many though he lov'd but one,
And that loved one, alas! could ne'er be his.
Ah, happy she! to 'scape from him whose kiss
Had been pollution unto aught so chaste;
Who soon had left her charms for vulgar bliss,
And spoil'd her goodly lands to gild his waste,
Nor calm domestic peace had ever deign'd to taste.

VI.

And now Childe Harold was sore sick at heart,
And from his fellow bacchanals would flee;
'Tis said, at times the sullen tear would start,
But Pride congeal'd the drop within his e'e:
Apart he stalk'd in joyless reverie,
And from his native land resolved to go,
And visit scorching climes beyond the sea;
With pleasure drugg'd, he almost long'd for woe,
And e'en for change of scene would seek the shades below.

VII.

The Childe departed from his father's hall;
It was a vast and venerable pile;
So old, it seemèd only not to fall,
Yet strength was pillar'd in each massy aisle.
Monastic dome! condemn'd to uses vile!
Where Superstition once had made her den
Now Paphian girls were known to sing and smile;
And monks might deem their time was come agen,
If ancient tales say true, nor wrong these holy men.

VIII.

Yet oft-times in his maddest mirthful mood
Strange pangs would flash along Childe Harold's brow,
As if the memory of some deadly feud
Or disappointed passion lurk'd below:
But this none knew, nor haply cared to know:
For his was not that open, artless soul
That feels relief by bidding sorrow flow,
Nor sought he friend to counsel or condole,
Whate'er this grief mote be, which he could not control.

IX.

And none did love him—though to hall and bower
He gather'd revellers from far and near,
He knew them flatt'rers of the festal hour;
The heartless parasites of present cheer.
Yea! none did love him—not his lemans dear—
But pomp and power alone are woman's care,
And where these are light Eros finds a feere;
Maidens, like moths, are ever caught by glare,
And Mammon wins his way where Seraphs might despair.

X.

Childe Harold had a mother—not forgot,
Though parting from that mother he did shun;
A sister whom he loved, but saw her not
Before his weary pilgrimage begun:
If friends he had, he bade adieu to none.
Yet deem not thence his breast a breast of steel:
Ye, who have known what 't is to dote upon
A few dear objects, will in sadness feel
Such partings break the heart they fondly hope to heal.

XI.

His house, his home, his heritage, his lands,
The laughing dames in whom he did delight,
Whose large blue eyes, fair locks, and snowy hands,
Might shake the saintship of an anchorite,
And long had fed his youthful appetite;
His goblets brimm'd with every costly wine,
And all that mote to luxury invite,
Without a sigh he left to cross the brine,
And traverse Paynim shores, and pass Earth's central line.

XII.

The sails were fill'd, and fair the light winds blew,
As glad to waft him from his native home;
And fast the white rocks faded from his view,
And soon were lost in circumambient foam:
And then, it may be, of his wish to roam
Repented he, but in his bosom slept
The silent thought, nor from his lips did come
One word of wail, whilst others sate and wept,
And to the reckless gales unmanly moaning kept.

XIII.

But when the sun was sinking in the sea
He seized his harp, which he at times could string,
And strike, albeit with untaught melody,
When deem'd he no strange ear was listening:
And now his fingers o'er it he did fling,

And tuned his farewell in the dim twilight,
While flew the vessel on her snowy wing,
And fleeting shores receded from his sight,
Thus to the elements he pour'd his last "Good Night."

"Adieu, adieu! my native shore
Fades o'er the waters blue;
The Night-winds sigh, the breakers roar,
And shrieks the wild sea-mew.
Yon Sun that sets upon the sea
We follow in his flight:
Farewell awhile to him and thee,
My native Land—Good Night!

"A few short hours, and he will rise
To give the morrow birth;
And I shall hail the main and skies,
But not my mother earth.
Deserted is my own good hall,
Its hearth is desolate;
Wild weeds are gathering on the wall;
My dog howls at the gate.

"Come hither, hither, my little page
Why dost thou weep and wail?
Or dost thou dread the billow's rage,
Or tremble at the gale?
But dash the tear-drop from thine eye;
Our ship is swift and strong:
Our fleetest falcon scarce can fly
More merrily along."

'Let winds be shrill, let waves roll high,
I fear not wave nor wind:
Yet marvel not, Sir Childe, that I
Am sorrowful in mind;
For I have from my father gone,
A mother whom I love,
And have no friend, save these alone,
But thee—and One above.

'My father bless'd me fervently,
Yet did not much complain;
But sorely will my mother sigh
Till I come back again.'—
"Enough, enough, my little lad!
Such tears become thine eye;
If I thy guileless bosom had,
Mine own would not be dry.

"Come hither, hither, my staunch yeoman,
Why dost thou look so pale?
Or dost thou dread a French foeman?
Or shiver at the gale?"—
'Deem'st thou I tremble for my life?
Sir Childe, I'm not so weak;
But thinking on an absent wife
Will blanch a faithful cheek.

'My spouse and boys dwell near thy hall,
Along the bordering lake,
And when they on their father call,
What answer shall she make?'—
"Enough, enough, my yeoman good,
Thy grief let none gainsay;
But I, who am of lighter mood,
Will laugh to flee away.

"For who would trust the seeming sighs
Of wife or paramour?
Fresh feres will dry the bright blue eyes
We late saw streaming o'er.
For pleasures past I do not grieve,
Nor perils gathering near;
My greatest grief is that I leave
No thing that claims a tear.

"And now I'm in the world alone,
Upon the wide, wide sea:
But why should I for others groan,
When none will sigh for me?
Perchance my dog will whine in vain,
Till fed by stranger hands;
But long ere I come back again
He'd tear me where he stands.

"With thee, my bark, I'll swiftly go
Athwart the foaming brine;
Nor care what land thou bear'st me to,
So not again to mine.
Welcome, welcome, ye dark blue waves!
And when you fail my sight,
Welcome, ye deserts, and ye caves!
My native land—Good Night!"

XIV.

On, on the vessel flies, the land is gone,
And winds are rude, in Biscay's sleepless bay.
Four days are sped, but with the fifth, anon,
New shores descried make every bosom gay;
And Cintra's mountain greets them on their way,
And Tagus dashing onward to the deep,
His fabled golden tribute bent to pay;
And soon on board the Lusian pilots leap,
And steer 'twixt fertile shores where yet few rustics reap.

XV.

Oh, Christ! it is a goodly sight to see
What Heaven hath done for this delicious land!
What fruits of fragrance blush on every tree!
What goodly prospects o'er the hills expand!
But man would mar them with an impious hand:

And when the Almighty lifts His fiercest scourge
'Gainst those who most transgress His high command,
With treble vengeance will His hot shafts urge
Gaul's locust host, and earth from fellest foemen purge.

XVI.

What beauties doth Lisboa first unfold!
Her image floating on that noble tide,
Which poets vainly pave with sands of gold,
But now whereon a thousand keels did ride
Of mighty strength, since Albion was allied,
And to the Lusians did her aid afford:
A nation swol'n with ignorance and pride
Who lick yet loathe the hand that waves the sword
To save them from the wrath of Gaul's unsparing lord.

XVII.

But whoso entereth within this town,
That, sheening far, celestial seems to be,
Disconsolate will wander up and down,
'Mid many things unsightly to strange e'e;
For hut and palace show like filthily:
The dingy denizens are rear'd in dirt;
Ne personage of high or mean degree
Doth care for cleanness of surtout or shirt,
Tho' shent with Egypt's plague, unkempt, unwash'd; unhurt.

XVIII.

Poor, paltry slaves! yet born 'midst noblest scenes—
Why, Nature, waste thy wonders on such men?
Lo! Cintra's glorious Eden intervenes
In variegated maze of mount and glen.
Ah, me! what hand can pencil guide, or pen,
To follow half on which the eye dilates
Through views more dazzling unto mortal ken
Than those whereof such things the bard relates,
Who to the awe-struck world unlock'd Elysium's gates?

XIX.

The horrid crags, by toppling convent crown'd,
The cork-trees hoar that clothe the shaggy steep,
The mountain-moss by scorching skies imbrown'd,
The sunken glen, whose sunless shrubs must weep,
The tender azure of the unruffled deep,
The orange tints that gild the greenest bough,
The torrents that from cliff to valley leap,
The vine on high, the willow branch below,
Mix'd in one mighty scene, with varied beauty glow.

XX.

Then slowly climb the many-winding way,
And frequent turn to linger as you go,
From loftier rocks new loveliness survey,
And rest ye at "Our Lady's house of woe;"[3]
Where frugal monks their little relics show,
And sundry legends to the stranger tell:
Here impious men have punish'd been, and lo!
Deep in yon cave Honorius long did dwell,
In hope to merit Heaven by making earth a Hell.

XXI.

And here and there, as up the crags you spring,
Mark many rude-carved crosses near the path:
Yet deem not these devotion's offering—
These are memorials frail of murderous wrath:
For wheresoe'er the shrieking victim hath
Pour'd forth his blood beneath the assassin's knife,
Some hand erects a cross of mouldering lath;
And grove and glen with thousand such are rife
Throughout this purple land, where law secures not life![4]

XXII.

On sloping mounds, or in the vale beneath,
Are domes where whilome kings did make repair;
But now the wild flowers round them only breathe;
Yet ruin'd splendour still is lingering there,
And yonder towers the Prince's palace fair;
There thou too, Vathek! England's wealthiest son,
Once form'd thy Paradise, as not aware
When wanton Wealth her mightiest deeds hath done,
Meek Peace voluptuous lures was ever wont to shun.

XXIII.

Here didst thou dwell, here schemes of pleasure plan,
Beneath yon mountain's ever beauteous brow,
But now, as if a thing unblest by Man,
Thy fairy dwelling is as lone as thou!
Here giant weeds a passage scarce allow
To halls deserted, portals gaping wide;
Fresh lessons to the thinking bosom, how
Vain are the pleasaunces on earth supplied;
Swept into wrecks anon by Time's ungentle tide.

XXIV.

Behold the hall where chiefs were late convened![5]
Oh! dome displeasing unto British eye!
With diadem hight foolscap, lo! a fiend,
A little fiend that scoffs incessantly,
There sits in parchment robe array'd, and by
His side is hung a seal and sable scroll,
Where blazon'd glare names known to chivalry,
And sundry signatures adorn the roll,
Whereat the Urchin points, and laugh with all his soul.

XXV.

Convention is the dwarfish demon styled
That foil'd the knights in Marialva's dome:
Of brains (if brains they had) he them beguiled,
And turn'd a nation's shallow joy to gloom.
Here Folly dash'd to earth the victor's plume,
And Policy regain'd what arms had lost:
For chiefs like ours in vain may laurels bloom!
Woe to the conqu'ring, not the conquer'd host,
Since baffl'd Triumph droops on Lusitania's coast.

XXVI.

And ever since that martial synod met,
Britannia sickens, Cintra! at thy name;
And folks in office at the mention fret,
And fain would blush, if blush they could, for shame.
How will posterity the deed proclaim!
Will not our own and fellow-nations sneer,
To view these champions cheated of their fame,
By foes in fight o'erthrown, yet victors here,
Where Scorn her finger points through many a coming year?

XXVII.

So deem'd the Childe, as o'er the mountains he
Did take his way in solitary guise:
Sweet was the scene, yet soon he thought to flee,
More restless than the swallow in the skies:
Though here awhile he learn'd to moralize,
For Meditation fix'd at times on him,
And conscious Reason whisper'd to despise
His early youth misspent in maddest whim;
But as he gazed on truth his aching eyes grew dim.

XXVIII.

To horse! to horse! he quits, for ever quits
A scene of peace, though soothing to his soul:
Again he rouses from his moping fits,
But seeks not now the harlot and the bowl.
Onward he flies, nor fix'd as yet the goal
Where he shall rest him on his pilgrimage;
And o'er him many changing scenes must roll
Ere toil his thirst for travel can assuage,
Or he shall calm his breast, or learn experience sage.

XXIX.

Yet Mafra shall one moment claim delay,
Where dwelt of yore the Lusians' luckless queen;
And church and court did mingle their array,
And mass and revel were alternate seen
Lordlings and freres—ill-sorted fry I ween!
But here the Babylonian whore hath built
A dome, where flaunts she in such glorious sheen,
That men forget the blood which she hath spilt,
And bow the knee to Pomp that loves to varnish guilt.

XXX.

O'er vales that teem with fruits, romantic hills,
(Oh, that such hills upheld a freeborn race!)
Whereon to gaze the eye with joyaunce fills,
Childe Harold wends thro' many a pleasant place.
Though sluggards deem it but a foolish chase,
And marvel men should quit their easy chair,
The toilsome way, and long, long league to trace,
Oh! there is sweetness in the mountain air,
And life, that bloated Ease can never hope to share.

XXXI.

More bleak to view the hills at length recede,
And, less luxuriant, smoother vales extend;
Immense horizon-bounded plains succeed!
Far as the eye discerns, withouten end,
Spain's realms appear whereon her shepherds tend
Flocks, whose rich fleece right well the trader knows—
Now must the pastor's arm his lambs defend:
For Spain is compass'd by unyielding foes,
And all must shield their all, or share Subjection's woes.

XXXII.

Where Lusitania and her Sister meet,
Deem ye what bounds the rival realms divide?
Or ere the jealous queens of nations greet,
Doth Tayo interpose his mighty tide?
Or dark sierras rise in craggy pride?
Or fence of art, like China's vasty wall?—
Ne barrier wall, ne river deep and wide,
Ne horrid crags, nor mountains dark and tall,
Rise like the rocks that part Hispania's land from Gaul:

XXXIII.

But these between a silver streamlet glides,
And scarce a name distinguisheth the brook,
Though rival kingdoms press its verdant sides.
Here leans the idle shepherd on his crook,
And vacant on the rippling waves doth look,
That peaceful still 'twixt bitterest foemen flow;
For proud each peasant as the noblest duke:
Well doth the Spanish hind the difference know
'Twixt him and Lusian slave, the lowest of the low.[7]

XXXIV.

But ere the mingling bounds have far been pass'd,
Dark Guadiana rolls his power along
In sullen billows, murmuring and vast,
So noted ancient roundelays among.
Whilome upon his banks did legions throng
Of Moor and Knight, in mailèd splendour drest:
Here ceased the swift their race, here sunk the strong;
The Paynim turban and the Christian crest
Mix'd on the bleeding stream, by floating hosts oppress'd.

XXXV.

Oh, lovely Spain! renown'd, romantic land!
Where is that standard which Pelagio bore,
When Cava's traitor-sire first call'd the band
That dyed thy mountain-streams with Gothic gore?[8]
Where are those bloody banners which of yore
Waved o'er thy sons, victorious to the gale,
And drove at last the spoilers to their shore?
Red gleam'd the cross, and waned the crescent pale,
While Afric's echoes thrill'd with Moorish matrons' wail.

XXXVI.

Teems not each ditty with the glorious tale?
Ah! such, alas! the hero's amplest fate!
When granite moulders and when records fail,
A peasant's plaint prolongs his dubious date.
Pride! bend thine eye from heaven to thine estate,
See how the mighty shrink into a song!
Can Volume, Pillar, Pile, preserve thee great?
Or must thou trust Tradition's simple tongue,
When Flattery sleeps with thee, and History does thee wrong?

XXXVII.

Awake, ye sons of Spain! awake! advance!
Lo! Chivalry, your ancient goddess, cries;
But wields not, as of old, her thirsty lance,
Nor shakes her crimson plumage in the skies:
Now on the smoke of blazing bolts she flies,
And speaks in thunder through yon engine's roar!
In every peal she calls—"Awake! arise!"
Say, is her voice more feeble than of yore,
When her war-song was heard on Andalusia's shore?

XXXVIII.

Hark! heard you not those hoofs of dreadful note?
Sounds not the clang of conflict on the heath?
Saw ye not whom the reeking sabre smote;
Nor saved your brethren ere they sank beneath
Tyrants and tyrants' slaves?—the fires of death,
The bale-fires flash on high:—from rock to rock
Each volley tells that thousands cease to breathe;
Death rides upon the sulphury Siroc,
Red Battle stamps his foot, and nations feel the shock.

XXXIX.

Lo! where the Giant on the mountain stands,
His blood-red tresses deep'ning in the sun,
With death-shot glowing in his fiery hands,
And eye that scorcheth all it glares upon;
Restless it rolls, now fix'd, and now anon
Flashing afar,—and at his iron feet
Destruction cowers, to mark what deeds are done;
For on this morn three potent nations meet,
To shed before his shrine the blood he deems most sweet.

XL.

By Heaven! it is a splendid sight to see
(For one who hath no friend, no brother there,)
Their rival scarfs of mix'd embroidery,
Their various arms that glitter in the air!
What gallant war-hounds rouse them from their lair,
And gnash their fangs, loud yelling for the prey!
All join the chase, but few the triumph share;
The Grave shall bear the chiefest prize away,
And Havoc scarce for joy can number their array.

XLI.

Three hosts combine to offer sacrifice;
Three tongues prefer strange orisons on high;
Three gaudy standards flout the pale blue sky;
The shouts are France, Spain, Albion, Victory!
The foe, the victim, and the fond ally
That fights for all, but ever fights in vain,
Are met—as if at home they could not die—
To feed the crow on Talavera's plain,
And fertilize the field that each pretends to gain.

XLII.

There shall they rot—Ambition's honour'd fools!
Yes, Honour decks the turf that wraps their clay!
Vain Sophistry! in these behold the tools,
The broken tools, that tyrants cast away
By myriads, when they dare to pave their way
With human hearts—to what?—a dream alone.
Can despots compass aught that hails their sway?
Or call with truth one span of earth their own,
Save that wherein at last they crumble bone by bone?

XLIII.

Oh, Albuera, glorious field of grief!
As o'er thy plain the Pilgrim prick'd his steed,
Who could foresee thee, in a space so brief,
A scene where mingling foes should boast and bleed!
Peace to the perish'd! may the warrior's meed
And tears of triumph their reward prolong!
Till others fall where other chieftains lead,
Thy name shall circle round the gaping throng,
And shine in worthless lays, the theme of transient song.

XLIV.

Enough of Battle's minions! let them play
Their game of lives, and barter breath for fame:
Fame that will scarce re-animate their clay,
Though thousands fall to deck some single name.
In sooth 't were sad to thwart their noble aim
Who strike, blest hirelings! for their country's good,
And die, that living might have proved her shame;
Perish'd, perchance, in some domestic feud,
Or in a narrower sphere wild Rapine's path pursued.

XLV.

Full swiftly Harold wends his lonely way
Where proud Sevilla triumphs unsubdued:
Yet is she free—the spoiler's wished-for prey
Soon, soon shall Conquest's fiery foot intrude,
Blackening her lovely domes, with traces rude.
Inevitable hour! 'Gainst fate to strive
Where Desolation plants her famish'd brood
Is vain, or Ilion, Tyre, might yet survive,
And Virtue vanquish all, and Murder cease to thrive.

XLVI.

But all unconscious of the coming doom
The feast, the song, the revel here abounds;
Strange modes of merriment the hours consume,
Nor bleed these patriots with their country's wounds:
Nor here War's clarion, but Love's rebek sounds;
Here Folly still his votaries inthralls;
And young-eyed Lewdness walks her midnight rounds:
Girt with the silent crimes of capitals,
Still to the last kind Vice cling to the tott'ring walls.

XLVII.

Not so the rustic—with his trembling mate
He lurks, nor casts his heavy eye afar,
Lest he should view his vineyard desolate,
Blasted below the dun hot breath of war.
No more beneath soft Eve's consenting star
Fandango twirls his jocund castanet:
Ah, monarchs! could ye taste the mirth ye mar,
Not in the toils of Glory would ye fret;
The hoarse dull drum would sleep, and Man be happy yet.

XLVIII.

How carols now the lusty muleteer?
Of love, romance, devotion is his lay,
As whilome he was wont the leagues to cheer,
His quick bells wildly jingling on the way?
No! as he speeds, he chants "Viva el Rey?"[9]
And checks his song to execrate Godoy,
The royal wittol Charles, and curse the day
When first Spain's queen beheld the black-eyed boy,
And gore-faced Treason sprung from her adulterate joy.

XLIX.

On yon long, level plain, at distance crown'd
With crags, whereon those Moorish turrets rest,
Wide scatter'd hoof-marks dint the wounded ground;
And, scath'd by fire, the greensward's darken'd vest,
Tells that the foe was Andalusia's guest:
Here was the camp, the watch-flame, and the host,
Here the bold peasant storm'd the dragon's nest;
Still does he mark it with triumphant boast,
And points to yonder cliffs, which oft were won and lost.

L.

And whomsoe'er along the path you meet
Bears in his cap the badge of crimson hue,[10]
Which tells you whom to shun and whom to greet:
Woe to the man that walks in public view
Without of loyalty this token true:
Sharp is the knife, and sudden is the stroke;
And sorely would the Gallic foeman rue,
If subtle poinards, wrapt beneath the cloke,
Could blunt the sabre's edge, or clear the cannon's smoke.

LI.

At every turn Morena's dusky height
Sustains aloft the battery's iron load;
And, far as mortal eye can compass sight,
The mountain-howitzer, the broken road,
The bristling palisade, the fosse o'erflow'd,
The station'd bands, the never-vacant watch,
The magazine in rocky durance stow'd,
The holster'd steed beneath the shed of thatch,
The ball-piled pyramid, the ever-blazing match,[11]

LII.

Portend the deeds to come:—but he whose nod
Has tumbled feebler despots from their sway,
A moment pauseth ere he lifts the rod;
A little moment deigneth to delay:
Soon will his legions sweep through these their way;
The West must own the Scourger of the world.
Ah! Spain! how sad will be thy reckoning-day,
When soars Gaul's Vulture, with his wings unfurl'd,
And thou shalt view thy sons in crowds to Hadés hurl'd.

LIII.

And must they fall? the young, the proud, the
brave,
To swell one bloated chief's unwholesome reign?
No step between submission and a grave?
The rise of rapine and the fall of Spain?
And doth the Power that man adores ordain
Their doom, nor heed the suppliant's appeal?
Is all that desperate Valour acts in vain?
And Counsel sage, and patriotic Zeal,
The Veteran's skill, Youth's fire, and Manhood's heart
of steel?

LIV.

Is it for this the Spanish maid, aroused
Hangs on the willow her unstrung guitar,
And, all unsex'd, the anlace hath espoused,
Sung the loud song, and dared the deed of
war?
And she, whom once the semblance of a scar
Appall'd, an owlet's larum chill'd with dread,
Now views the column-scatt'ring bay'net jar,
The falchion flash, and o'er the yet warm dead
Stalks with Minerva's step where Mars might quake
to tread.

LV.

Ye who shall marvel when you hear her tale,
Oh! had you known her in her softer hour,
Mark'd her black eye that mocks her coal-black veil,
Heard her light, lively tones in lady's bower,
Seen her long locks that foil the painter's power
Her fairy form, with more than female grace,
Scarce would you deem that Saragoza's tower
Beheld her smile in Danger's Gorgon face,
Thin the closed ranks, and lead in Glory's fearful chase.

LVI.

Her lover sinks—she sheds no ill-timed tear;
Her chief is slain—she fills his fatal post;
Her fellows flee—she checks their base career;
The foe retires—she heads the sallying host:
Who can appease like her a lover's ghost?
Who can avenge so well a leader's fall?
What maid retrieve when man's flush'd hope is lost?
Who hang so fiercely on the flying Gaul,
Foil'd by a woman's hand, before a batter'd wall?[12]

LVII.

Yet are Spain's maids no race of Amazons,
But form'd for all the witching arts of love:
Though thus in arms they emulate her sons,
And in the horrid phalanx dare to move,
'T is but the tender fierceness of the dove,
Pecking the hand that hovers o'er her mate:
In softness as in firmness far above
Remoter females, famed for sickening prate;
Her mind is nobler sure, her charms perchance as great.

LVIII.

The seal Love's dimpling finger hath impress'd
Denotes how soft that chin which bears his touch:[13]
Her lips, whose kisses pout to leave their nest,
Bid man be valiant ere he merit such:
Her glance, how wildly beautiful! how much
Hath Phœbus woo'd in vain to spoil her cheek,
Which glows yet smoother from his amorous clutch!
Who round the North for paler dames would seek?
How poor their forms appear! how languid, wan, and weak!

LIX.

Match me, ye climes! which poets love to laud;
Match me, ye harams of the land! where now
I strike my strain, far distant, to applaud
Beauties that ev'n a cynic must avow!
Match me those houris, whom ye scarce allow
To taste the gale lest Love should ride the wind,
With Spain's dark-glancing daughters—deign to know,
There your wise Prophet's paradise we find,
His black-eyed maids of Heaven, angelically kind.

LX.

Oh thou, Parnassus! whom I now survey,
Not in the phrensy of a dreamer's eye,
Not in the fabled landscape of a lay,
But soaring snow-clad through thy native sky,
In the wild pomp of mountain majesty!
What marvel if I thus essay to sing?
The humblest of thy pilgrims passing by
Would gladly woo thine Echoes with his string,
Though from thy heights no more one Muse will wave her wing.

LXI.

Oft have I dream'd of thee! whose glorious name
Who knows not, knows not man's divinest lore:
And now I view thee, 't is, alas! with shame
That I in feeblest accents must adore.
When I recount thy worshippers of yore
I tremble, and can only bend the knee;
Nor raise my voice, nor vainly dare to soar,
But gaze beneath thy cloudy canopy
In silent joy to think at last I look on thee!

LXII.

Happier in this than mightiest bards have been,
Whose fate to distant homes confined their lot,
Shall I unmoved behold the hallow'd scene,
Which others rave of, though they know it not?
Though here no more Apollo haunts his grot,
And thou, the Muses' seat, art now their grave,
Some gentle spirit still pervades the spot,
Sighs in the gale, keeps silence in the cave,
And glides with glassy foot o'er yon melodious wave.

LXIII.

Of thee hereafter.—Ev'n amidst my strain
I turn'd aside to pay my homage here;
Forgot the land, the sons, the maids of Spain;
Her fate, to every freeborn bosom dear;
And hail'd thee, not perchance without a tear.
Now to my theme—but from thy holy haunt
Let me some remnant—some memorial bear;
Yield me one leaf of Daphné's deathless plant,
Nor let thy votary's hope be deem'd an idle vaunt.

LXIV.

But ne'er didst thou, fair Mount! when Greece was young,
See round thy giant base a brighter choir,
Nor e'er did Delphi, when her priestess sung
The Pythian hymn with more than mortal fire,
Behold a train more fitting to inspire
The song of love than Andalusia's maids,
Nurst in the glowing lap of soft desire:
Ah! that to these were given such peaceful shades
As Greece can still bestow, though Glory fly her glades.

LXV.

Fair is proud Seville; let her country boast
Her strength, her wealth, her site of ancient days;
But Cadiz, rising on the distant coast,
Calls forth a sweeter, though ignoble praise.
Ah, Vice! how soft are thy voluptuous ways!
While boyish blood is mantling, who can 'scape
The fascination of thy magic gaze?
A Cherub-hydra round us dost thou gape,
And mould to every taste thy dear delusive shape.

LXVI.

When Paphos fell by Time—accurs'd Time!
The Queen who conquers all must yield to thee—
The Pleasures fled, but sought as warm a clime;
And Venus, constant to her native sea,
To nought else constant, hither deign'd to flee;
And fix'd her shrine within these walls of white;
Though not to one dome circumscribeth she
Her worship, but, devoted to her rite,
A thousand altars rise, for ever blazing bright.

LXVII.

From morn till night, from night till startled Morn,
Peeps blushing on the revel's laughing crew,
The song is heard, the rosy garland worn;
Devices quaint, and frolics ever new,
Tread on each other's kibes. A long adieu
He bids to sober joy that here sojourns:
Nought interrupts the riot, though in lieu
Of true devotion monkish incense burns,
And love and prayer unite, or rule the hour by turns.

LXVIII.

The Sabbath comes, a day of blessed rest;
What hallows it upon this Christian shore?
Lo! it is sacred to a solemn feast:
Hark! heard you not the forest monarch's roar?
Crashing the lance, he snuffs the spouting gore
Of man and steed, o'erthrown beneath his horn;
The throng'd arena shakes with shouts for more;
Yells the mad crowd o'er entrails freshly torn,
Nor shrinks the female eye, nor ev'n affects to mourn.

LXIX.

The seventh day this; the jubilee of man.
London! right well thou know'st the day of prayer:
Then thy spruce citizen, wash'd artisan,
And smug apprentice gulp their weekly air:
Thy coach of hackney, whiskey, one-horse chair,
And humblest gig through sundry suburbs whirl;
To Hampstead, Brentford, Harrow, make repair;
Till the tired jade the wheel forgets to hurl,
Provoking envious gibe from each pedestrian churl.

LXX.

Some o'er thy Thamis row the ribbon'd fair,
Others along the safer turnpike fly;
Some Richmond-hill ascend, some scud to Ware,
And many to the steep of Highgate hie.
Ask ye, Bœotian shades! the reason why?
'T is to the worship of the solemn Horn,
Grasp'd in the holy hand of Mystery,
In whose dread name both men and maids are sworn,
And consecrate the oath with draught, and dance till morn.

LXXI.

All have their fooleries—not alike are thine,
Fair Cadiz, rising o'er the dark blue sea!
Soon as the matin bell proclaimeth nine,
Thy saint adorers count the rosary:
Much is the VIRGIN teased to shrive them free
(Well do I ween the only virgin there)
From crimes as numerous as her beadsmen be;
Then to the crowded circus forth they fare:
Young, old, high, low, at once the same diversion share.

LXXII.

The lists are oped, the spacious area clear'd,
Thousands on thousands piled are seated round;
Long ere the first loud trumpet's note is heard,
Ne vacant space for lated wight is found:
Here dons, grandees, but chiefly dames abound,
Skill'd in the ogle of a roguish eye,
Yet ever well inclined to heal the wound;
None through their cold disdain are doom'd to die,
As moon-struck bards complain, by Love's sad archery.

LXXIII.

Hush'd is the din of tongues—on gallant steeds,
With milk-white crest, gold spur, and light-pois'd lance,
Four cavaliers prepare for venturous deeds,
And lowly bending to the lists advance;
Rich are their scarfs, their chargers featly prance:
If in the dangerous game they shine to-day,
The crowd's loud shout and ladies' lovely glance,
Best prize of better acts, they bear away,
And all that kings or chiefs e'er gain their toils repay.

LXXIV.

In costly sheen and gaudy cloak array'd,
But all afoot, the light-limb'd Matadore
Stands in the centre, eager to invade
The lord of lowing herds; but not before
The ground, with cautious tread, is traversed o'er,
Lest aught unseen should lurk to thwart his speed:
His arms a dart, he fights aloof, nor more
Can man achieve without the friendly steed—
Alas! too oft condemn'd for him to bear and bleed.

LXXV.

Thrice sounds the clarion; lo! the signal falls,
The den expands, and Expectation mute
Gapes round the silent circle's peopled walls.
Bounds with one lashing spring the mighty brute,
And, wildly staring, spurns, with sounding foot,
The sand, nor blindly rushes on his foe:
Here, there, he points his threatening front, to suit
His first attack, wide waving to and fro
His angry tail; red rolls his eye's dilated glow.

LXXVI.

Sudden he stops; his eye is fix'd: away,
Away, thou heedless boy! prepare the spear:
Now is thy time, to perish, or display
The skill that yet may check his mad career.
With well-timed croupe the nimble coursers veer;
On foams the bull, but not unscathed he goes;
Streams from his flank the crimson torrent clear:
He flies, he wheels, distracted with his throes:
Dart follows dart; lance, lance; loud bellowings speak his woes.

LXXVII.

Again he comes; nor dart nor lance avail,
Nor the wild plunging of the tortured horse;
Though man and man's avenging arms assail,
Vain are his weapons, vainer is his force,
One gallant steed is stretch'd a mangled corse;
Another, hideous sight! unseam'd appears,
His gory chest unveils life's panting source;
Though death-struck, still his feeble frame he rears;
Staggering, but stemming all, his lord unharm'd he bears.

LXXVIII.

Foil'd, bleeding, breathless, furious to the last,
Full in the centre stands the bull at bay,
Mid wounds, and clinging darts, and lances brast,
And foes disabled in the brutal fray:
And now the Matadores around him play,
Shake the red cloak, and poise the ready brand:
Once more through all he bursts his thundering way—
Vain rage! the mantle quits the conynge hand,
Wraps his fierce eye—'t is past—he sinks upon the sand!

LXXIX.

Where his vast neck just mingles with the spine,
Sheathed in his form the deadly weapon lies.
He stops—he starts—disdaining to decline:
Slowly he falls, amidst triumphant cries,
Without a groan, without a struggle dies.
The decorated car appears—on high
The corse is piled—sweet sight for vulgar eyes—
Four steeds that spurn the rein, as swift as shy,
Hurl the dark bulk along, scarce seen in dashing by.

LXXX.

Such the ungentle sport that oft invites
The Spanish maid, and cheers the Spanish swain.
Nurtured in blood betimes, his heart delights
In vengeance, gloating on another's pain.
What private feuds the troubled village stain!
Though now one phalanx'd host should meet the foe,
Enough, alas! in humble homes remain,
To meditate 'gainst friends the secret blow,
For some slight cause of wrath, whence life's warm stream must flow.

LXXXI.

But Jealousy has fled: his bars, his bolts,
His wither'd sentinel, Duenna sage!
And all whereat the generous soul revolts,
Which the stern dotard deem'd he could encage,
Have pass'd to darkness with the vanished age.
Who late so free as Spanish girls were seen,
(Ere War uprose in his volcanic rage,)
With braided tresses bounding o'er the green,
While on the gay dance shone Night's lover-loving Queen?

LXXXII.

Oh! many a time and oft, had Harold loved,
Or dream'd he loved, since rapture is a dream;
But now his wayward bosom was unmoved,
For not yet had he drunk of Lethe's stream:
And lately had he learn'd with truth to deem
Love has no gift so grateful as his wings:
How fair, how young, how soft soe'er he seem,
Full from the font of Joy's delicious springs[14]
Some bitter o'er the flowers its bubbling venom flings.

LXXXIII.

Yet to the beauteous form he was not blind,
Though now it moved him as it moves the wise.
Not that Philosophy on such a mind
E'er deign'd to bend her chastely-awful eyes:
But Passion raves itself to rest, or flies;
And Vice, that digs her own voluptuous tomb,
Had buried long his hopes, no more to rise:
Pleasure's pall'd victim! life-abhorring gloom
Wrote on his faded brow curst Cain's unresting doom.

LXXXIV.

Still he beheld, nor mingled with the throng;
But view'd them not with misanthropic hate:
Fain would he now have join'd the dance, the song;
But who may smile that sinks beneath his fate?
Nought that he saw his sadness could abate:
Yet once he struggled 'gainst the demon's sway,
And as in Beauty's bower he pensive sate,
Pour'd forth this unpremeditated lay,
To charms as fair as those that soothed his happier day.

TO INEZ.

1.

Nay, smile not at my sullen brow;
Alas! I cannot smile again:
Yet Heaven avert that ever thou
Shouldst weep, and haply weep in vain.

2.

And dost thou ask, what secret woe
I bear, corroding joy and youth?
And wilt thou vainly seek to know
A pang, ev'n thou must fail to soothe?

3.

It is not love, it is not hate,
 Nor low Ambition's honours lost,
That bids me loathe my present state,
 And fly from all I prized the most:

4.

It is that weariness which springs
 From all I meet, or hear, or see:
To me no pleasure Beauty brings;
 Thine eyes have scarce a charm for me.

5.

It is that settled, ceaseless gloom
 The fabled Hebrew wanderer bore:
That will not look beyond the tomb,
 But cannot hope for rest before.

6.

What Exile from himself can flee?
 To zones, though more and more remote,
Still, still pursues, where'er I be,
 The blight of life—the demon Thought.

7.

Yet others rapt in pleasure seem,
 And taste of all that I forsake;
Oh! may they still of transport dream,
 And ne'er, at least like me, awake!

8.

Through many a clime 'tis mine to go,
 With many a retrospection curst;
And all my solace is to know,
 Whate'er betides, I've known the worst.

9.

What is that worst? Nay do not ask—
 In pity from the search forbear:
Smile on—nor venture to unmask
 Man's heart, and view the Hell that's there.

LXXXV.

Adieu, fair Cadiz! yea, a long adieu!
Who may forget how well thy walls have stood?
When all were changing thou alone wert true,
First to be free and last to be subdued:
And if amidst a scene, a shock so rude,
Some native blood was seen thy streets to dye;
A traitor only fell beneath the feud:[15]
Here all were noble, save Nobility;
None hugg'd a conqueror's chain, save fallen Chivalry!

LXXXVI.

Such be the sons of Spain, and strange her fate!
They fight for freedom, who were never free;
A kingless people for a nerveless state,
Her vassals combat when their chieftains flee,
True to the veriest slaves of Treachery;
Fond of a land which gave them nought but life,
Pride points the path that leads to liberty;
Back to the struggle, baffled in the strife;
War, was is still the cry, "War even to the knife!"[16]

LXXXVII.

Ye, who would more of Spain and Spaniards know,
Go, read whate'er is writ of bloodiest strife:
Whate'er keen Vengeance urged on foreign foe
Can act, is acting there against man's life:
From flashing scimitar to secret knife,
War mouldeth there each weapon to his need—
So may he guard the sister and the wife,
So may he make each curst oppressor bleed,
So may such foes deserve the most remorseless deed!

LXXXVIII.

Flows there a tear of pity for the dead?
Look o'er the ravage of the reeking plain:
Look on the hands with female slaughter red;
Then to the dogs resign the unburied slain,
Then to the vulture let each corse remain;
Albeit unworthy of the prey-bird's maw,
Let their bleach'd bones, and blood's unbleaching stain,
Long mark the battle-field with hideous awe:
Thus only may our sons conceive the scenes we saw!

LXXXIX.

Nor yet, alas! the dreadful work is done;
Fresh legions pour adown the Pyrenees:
It deepens still, the work is scarce begun,
Nor mortal eye the distant end foresees.
Fall'n nations gaze on Spain; if freed, she frees
More than her fell Pizarros once enchain'd:
Strange retribution! now Columbia's ease
Repairs the wrongs that Quito's sons sustain'd,
While o'er the parent clime prowls Murder unrestrain'd.

XC.

Not all the blood at Talavera shed,
Not all the marvels of Barossa's fight,
Not Albuera lavish of the dead,
Have won for Spain her well asserted right.
When shall her Olive-Branch be free from blight?
When shall she breathe her from the blushing toil?
How many a doubtful day shall sink in night,
Ere the Frank robber turn him from his spoil,
And Freedom's stranger-tree grow native of the soil!

XCI.

And thou, my friend!—since unavailing woe
Bursts from my heart, and mingles with the strain—
Had the sword laid thee with the mighty low,
Pride might forbid e'en Friendship to complain:
But thus unlaurel'd to descend in vain,
By all forgotten, save the lonely breast,
And mix unbleeding with the boasted slain,
While Glory crowns so many a meaner crest!
What hadst thou done to sink so peacefully to rest?

XCII.

Oh, known the earliest, and esteem'd the most!
Dear to a heart where nought was left so dear!
Though to my hopeless days for ever lost,
In dreams deny me not to see thee here!
And Morn in secret shall renew the tear
Of Consciousness awaking to her woes,
And Fancy hover o'er thy bloodless bier,
Till my frail frame return to whence it rose,
And mourn'd and mourner lie united in repose.

XCIII.

Here is one fytte of Harold's pilgrimage:
Ye who of him may further seek to know,
Shall find some tidings in a future page,
If he that rhymeth now may scribble moe.
Is this too much? stern Critic! say not so:
Patience! and ye shall hear what he beheld
In other lands, where he was doomed to go:
Lands that contain the monuments of Eld,
Ere Greece and Grecian arts by barbarous hands were quell'd

NOTES TO CANTO THE FIRST.

NOTE 1, page 575.

No Waiter, but a Knight Templar.

The Rovers, or the Double Arrangement.

NOTE 2, page 577.

Yes! sigh'd o'er Delphi's long deserted shrine.

The little village of Castri stands partly on the site of Delphi. Along the path of the mountain, from Chrysso, are the remains of sepulchres hewn in and from the rock. "One," said the guide, "of a king who broke his neck hunting." His majesty had certainly chosen the fittest spot for such an achievement. A little above Castri is a cave, supposed the Pythian, of immense depth; the upper part of it is paved, and now a cow-house. On the other side of Castri stands a Greek monastery; some way above which is the cleft in the rock, with a range of caverns difficult of ascent, and apparently leading to the interior of the mountain; probably to the Corycian Cavern mentioned by Pausanias. From this part descend the fountain and the "Dews of Castalie."

NOTE 3, page 582.

And rest ye at "Our Lady's house of woe."

The convent of "Our Lady of Punishment," *Nossa Senora de Pena*, on the summit of the rock. Below, at some distance, is the Cork Convent, where St. Honorius dug his den, over which is his epitaph. From the hills, the sea adds to the beauty of the view

NOTE 4, page 582.

Throughout this purple land, where law secures not life.

It is a well known fact, that in the year 1809, the assassinations in the streets of Lisbon and its vicinity were not confined by the Portuguese to their countrymen; but that Englishmen were daily butchered: and so far from redress being obtained, we were requested not to interfere if we perceived any compatriot defending himself against his allies. I was once stopped in the way to the theatre at eight o'clock in the evening, when the streets were not more empty than they generally are at that hour, opposite to an open shop, and in a carriage with a friend: had we not fortunately been armed, I have not the least doubt that we should have "adorned a tale" instead of telling one. The crime of assassination is not confined to Portugal: in Sicily and Malta we are knocked on the head at a handsome average nightly, and not a Sicilian or Maltese is ever punished!

NOTE 5, page 582.

Behold the hall where chiefs were late convened.

The Convention of Cintra was signed in the palace of the Marchese Marialva.

NOTE 6, page 582.

Where dwelt of yore the Lusians' luckless queen.

Her luckless Majesty went subsequently mad: and Dr. Willis, who so dexterously cudgelled kingly pericraniums, could make nothing of hers.

NOTE 7, page 583.

'Twixt him and Lusian slave, the lowest of the low.

As I found the Portuguese, so I have characterised them. That they are since improved, at least in courage, is evident. The late exploits of Lord Wellington have effaced the follies of Cintra. He has, indeed, done wonders: he has, perhaps, changed the character of a nation, reconciled rival superstitions, and baffled an enemy who never retreated before his predecessors.—1812.

NOTE 8, page 583.

That dyed thy mountain streams with Gothic gore.

Count Julian's daughter, the Helen of Spain. Pelagius preserved his independence in the fastnesses of the Asturias, and the descendants of his followers, after some centuries, completed their struggle by the conquest of Grenada.

NOTE 9, page 584.

No! as he speeds, he chants "Viva el Rey!"

"Viva el Rey Fernando!" Long live King Ferdinand! is the chorus of most of the Spanish patriotic songs. They are chiefly in dispraise of the old King Charles, the Queen, and the Prince of Peace. I have heard many of them: some of the airs are beautiful. Don Manuel Godoy, the *Principe de la Paz*, of an ancient but decayed family, was born at Badajoz, on the frontiers of Portugal, and was originally in the ranks of the Spanish guards; till his person attracted the queen's eyes, and raised him to the dukedom of Alcudia, &c. &c. It is to this man that the Spaniards universally impute the ruin of their country.

NOTE 10, page 585.

Bears in his cap the badge of crimson hue.

The red cockade, with "Fernando VII.," in the centre.

NOTE 11, page 585.

The ball-piled pyramid, the ever-blazing match.

All who have seen a battery will recollect the pyramidal form in which shot and shells are piled. The Sierra Morena was fortified in every defile through which I passed in my way to Seville.

NOTE 12, page 588.

Foil'd by a woman's hand, before a batter'd wall.

Such were the exploits of the Maid of Saragoza, who by her valour elevated herself to the highest rank of heroines. When the author was at Seville, she walked daily on the Prado, decorated with medals and orders, by command of the Junta.

NOTE 13, page 588.

Denotes how soft that chin which bears his touch.

"Sigilla in mento impressa Amoris digitulo
Vestigio demonstrant mollitudinem."—AUL. GEL.

NOTE 14, page 590.

Full from the fount of Joy's delicious springs.

"————Medio de fonte leporum,
Surgit amari aliquid quod in ipsis floribus angat."—
LUC.

NOTE 15, page 591.

A traitor only fell beneath the feud.

Alluding to the conduct and death of Solano, the governor of Cadiz, in May, 1809.

NOTE 16, page 591.

War, war is still the cry, "War even to the knife!"

"War to the knife." Palafox's answer to the French general at the siege of Saragoza.

CANTO THE SECOND.

I.

Come, blue-eyed maid of heaven.—but thou, alas!
Didst never yet one mortal song inspire—
Goddess of Wisdom! here thy temple was,
And is, despite of war and wasting fire,[1]
And years, that bade thy worship to expire:
But worse than steel, and flame, and ages slow,
Is the dread sceptre and dominion dire
Of men who never felt the sacred glow
That thoughts of thee and thine on polish'd breasts bestow.

II.

Ancient of days! august Athena! where,[2]
Where are thy men of might? thy grand in soul?
Gone—glimmering through the dream of things that were:
First in the race that led to Glory's goal,
They won, and pass'd away—is this the whole?
A schoolboy's tale, the wonder of an hour!
The warrior's weapon and the sophist's stole
Are sought in vain, and o'er each mouldering tower,
Dim with the mist of years, gray flits the shade of power.

III.

Son of the morning, rise! approach you here!
Come—but molest not yon defenceless urn:
Look on this spot—a nation's sepulchre!
Abode of gods, whose shrines no longer burn.
Even gods must yield—religions take their turn:
'T was Jove's—'t is Mahomet's—and other creeds
Will rise with other years, till man shall learn
Vainly his incense soars, his victim bleeds;
Poor child of Doubt and Death, whose hope is built on reeds.

IV.

Bound to the earth, he lifts his eye to heaven—
Is 't not enough, unhappy thing! to know
Thou art? Is this a boon so kindly given,
That being, thou would'st be again, and go,
Thou know'st not, reck'st not to what region, so
On earth no more, but mingled with the skies?
Still wilt thou dream on future joy and woe?
Regard and weigh yon dust before it flies:
That little urn saith more than thousand homilies.

V.

Or burst the vanish'd Hero's lofty mound;
Far on the solitary shore he sleeps:[3]
He fell, and falling nations mourn'd around;
But now not one of saddening thousands weeps,
Nor warlike worshipper his vigil keeps
Where demi-gods appear'd, as records tell.
Remove yon skull from out the scatter'd heaps:
Is that a temple where a God may dwell?
Why ev'n the worm at last disdains her shatter'd cell!

VI.

Look on its broken arch, its ruin'd wall,
Its chambers desolate, and portals foul:
Yes, this was once Ambition's airy hall,
The dome of Thought, the palace of the Soul:
Behold through each lack-lustre, eyeless hole,
The gay recess of Wisdom and of Wit,
And Passion's host, that never brook'd control:
Can all saint, sage, or sophist ever writ,
People this lonely tower, this tenement refit?

VII.

Well didst thou speak, Athena's wisest son!
"All that we know is, nothing can be known."
Why should we shrink from what we cannot shun?
Each hath his pang, but feeble sufferers groan
With brain-born dreams of evil all their own.
Pursue what Chance or Fate proclaimeth best;
Peace waits us on the shores of Acheron:
There no forced banquet claims the sated guest,
But Silence spreads the couch of ever welcome rest.

VIII.

Yet if, as holiest men have deem'd, there be
A land of souls beyond that sable shore,
To shame the doctrine of the Sadducee
And sophists, madly vain of dubious lore;
How sweet it were in concert to adore
With those who made our mortal labours light!
To hear each voice we fear'd to hear no more!
Behold each mighty shade reveal'd to sight,
The Bactrian, Samian rage, and all who taught the right!

IX.

There, thou!—whose love and life together fled,
Have left me here to love and live in vain—
Twined with my heart, and can I deem thee dead,
When busy memory flashes on my brain?
Well—I will dream that we may meet again,
And woo the vision to my vacant breast:
If aught of young Remembrance then remain,
Be as it may Futurity's behest,
For me 't were bliss enough to know thy spirit blest!

X.

Here let me sit upon this massy stone,
The marble column's yet unshaken base;
Here, son of Saturn! was thy fav'rite throne:[4]
Mightiest of many such! Hence let me trace
The latent grandeur of thy dwelling-place.
It may not be: nor ev'n can Fancy's eye
Restore what Time hath labour'd to deface.
Yet these proud pillars claim no passing sigh;
Unmoved the Moslem sits, the light Greek carols by.

XI.

But who, of all the plunderers of yon fane
On high, where Pallas linger'd loath to flee
The latest relic of her ancient reign;
The last, the worst, dull spoiler, who was he?
Blush, Caledonia! such thy son could be!
England! I joy no child he was of thine:
Thy free-born men should spare what once was free;
Yet they could violate each saddening shrine,
And bear these altars o'er the long reluctant brine.

XII.

But most the modern Pict's ignoble boast,
To rive what Goth, and Turk, and Time hath spared:
Cold as the crags upon his native coast,
His mind as barren and his heart as hard,
Is he whose head conceived, whose hand prepared,
Aught to displace Athena's poor remains:
Her sons too weak the sacred shrine to guard,
Yet felt some portion of their mother's pains,
And never knew, till then, the weight of Despot's chains.

XIII.

What! shall it e'er be said by British tongue,
Albion was happy in Athena's tears?
Though in thy name the slaves her bosom wrung,
Tell not the deed to blushing Europe's ears;
The ocean queen, the free Britannia, bears
The last poor plunder from a bleeding land:
Yes, she, whose gen'rous aid her name endears,
Tore down those remnants with a harpy's hand,
Which envious Eld forebore, and tyrants left to stand.

XIV.

Where was thine Ægis, Pallas! that appall'd
Stern Alaric and Havoc on their way?[5]
Where Peleus' son? whom Hell in vain enthrall'd,
His shade from Hades upon that dread day
Bursting to light in terrible array!
What! could not Pluto spare the chief once more,
To scare a second robber from his prey?
Idly he wander'd on the Stygian shore,
Nor now preserved the walls he loved to shield before.

XV.

Cold is the heart, fair Greece! that looks on thee,
Nor feels as lovers o'er the dust they loved;
Dull is the eye that will not weep to see
Thy walls defaced, thy mouldering shrines removed
By British hands, which it had best behoved
To guard those relics ne'er to be restored.
Curst be the hour when from their isle they roved,
And once again thy hapless bosom gored,
And snatch'd thy shrinking Gods to northern climes abhorr'd!

XVI.

But where is Harold? shall I then forget
To urge the gloomy wanderer o'er the wave?
Little reck'd he of all that men regret;
No loved-one now in feign'd lament could rave;
No friend the parting hand extended gave,
Ere the cold stranger pass'd to other climes:
Hard is his heart whom charms may not enslave;
But Harold felt not as in other times,
And left without a sigh the land of war and crimes.

XVII.

He that has sail'd upon the dark blue sea,
Has view'd at times, I ween, a full fair sight;
When the fresh breeze is fair as breeze may be,
The white sail set, the gallant frigate tight;
Masts, spires, and strand retiring to the right.
The glorious main expanding o'er the bow,
The convoy spread like wild swans in their flight,
The dullest sailor wearing bravely now,
So gaily curl the waves before each dashing prow.

XVIII.

And oh, the little warlike world within!
The well-reeved guns, the netted canopy,[6]
The hoarse command, the busy humming din,
When, at a word, the tops are mann'd on high:
Hark, to the Boatswain's call, the cheering cry!
While through the seaman's hand the tackle glides;
Or schoolboy Midshipman that, standing by,
Strains his shrill pipe as good or ill betides,
And well the docile crew that skilful urchin guides.

XIX.

White is the glassy deck, without a stain,
Where on the watch the staid Lieutenant walks:
Look on that part which sacred doth remain
For the lone Chieftain, who majestic stalks,
Silent and fear'd by all—not oft he talks
With aught beneath him, if he would preserve
That strict restraint, which broken, ever balks
Conquest and Fame: but Britons rarely swerve
From law, however stern, which tends their strength to nerve.

XX.

Blow! swiftly blow, thou keel-compelling gale!
Till the broad sun withdraws his lessening ray,
Then must the pennant-bearer slacken sail,
That lagging barks may make their lazy way.
Ah! grievance sore, and listless dull delay,
To waste on sluggish hulks the sweetest breeze!
What leagues are lost, before the dawn of day,
Thus loitering pensive on the willing seas,
The flapping sail haul'd down to halt for logs like these!

XXI.

The moon is up; by Heaven a lovely eve!
Long streams of light o'er dancing waves expand;
Now lads on shore may sigh, and maids believe:
Such be our fate when we return to land!
Meantime some rude Arion's restless hand
Wakes the brisk harmony that sailors love;
A circle there of merry listeners stand,
Or to some well-known measure featly move,
Thoughtless, as if on shore they still were free to rove.

XXII.

Through Calpe's straits survey the steepy shore;
Europe and Afric on each other gaze!
Lands of the dark-eyed Maid and dusky Moor
Alike beheld beneath pale Hecate's blaze:
How softly on the Spanish shore she plays,
Disclosing rock, and slope, and forest brown,
Distinct, though darkening with her waning phase;
But Mauritania's giant-shadows frown,
From mountain-cliff to coast descending sombre down.

XXIII.

'Tis night, when Meditation bids us feel
We once have loved, though love is at an end:
The Heart, lone mourner of its baffled zeal,
Though friendless now, will dream it had a friend.
Who with the weight of years would wish to bend,
When Youth itself survives young Love and joy?
Alas! when mingling souls forget to blend,
Death hath but little left him to destroy!
Ah! happy years! once more who would not be a boy?

XXIV.

Thus bending o'er the vessel's laving side,
To gaze on Dian's wave-reflected sphere,
The soul forgets her schemes of Hope and Pride,
And flies unconscious o'er each backward year.
None are so desolate but something dear,
Dearer than self, possesses or possess'd
A thought, and claims the homage of a tear;
A flashing pang! of which the weary breast
Would still, albeit in vain, the heavy heart divest.

XXV.

To sit on rocks, to muse o'er flood and fell,
To slowly trace the forest's shady scene,
Where things that own not man's dominion dwell,
And mortal foot hath ne'er or rarely been;
To climb the trackless mountain all unseen,
With the wild flock that never needs a fold;
Alone o'er steps and foaming falls to lean;
This is not solitude; 't is but to hold
Converse with Nature's charms, and view her stores unroll'd.

XXVI.

But 'midst the crowd, the hum, the shock of men,
To hear, to see, to feel, and to possess,
And roam along, the world's tired denizen,
With none who bless us, none whom we can bless;
Minions of splendour shrinking from distress!
None that, with kindred consciousness endued,
If we were not, would seem to smile the less
Of all that flatter'd, follow'd, sought, and sued;
This is to be alone; this, this is solitude!

XXVII.

More blest the life of godly eremite,
Such as on lonely Athos may be seen,
Watching at eve upon the giant height,
Which looks o'er waves so blue, skies so serene,
That he who there at such an hour hath been
Will wistful linger on that hallow'd spot;
Then slowly tear him from the 'witching scene,
Sigh forth one wish that such had been his lot,
Then turn to hate a world he had almost forgot.

XXVIII.

Pass we the long, unvarying course, the track
Oft trod, that never leaves a trace behind;
Pass we the calm, the gale, the change, the tack,
And each well known caprice of wave and wind;
Pass we the joys and sorrows sailors find,
Coop'd in their wingèd sea-girt citadel,
The foul, the fair, the contrary, the kind,
As breezes rise and fall and billows swell,
Till on some jocund morn—lo, land! and all is well.

XXIX.

But not in silence pass Calypso's isles,[7]
The sister tenants of the middle deep;
There for the weary still a haven smiles,
Though the fair goddess long hath ceased to weep,
And o'er her cliffs a fruitless watch to keep
For him who dared prefer a mortal bride:
Here, too, his boy essay'd the dreadful leap
Stern Mentor urged from high to yonder tide;
While thus of both bereft, the nymph-queen doubly sigh'd.

XXX.

Her reign is past, her gentle glories gone:
But trust not this; too easy youth, beware!
A mortal sovereign holds her dangerous throne,
And thou may'st find a new Calypso there.
Sweet Florence! could another ever share
This wayward, loveless heart, it would be thine:
But check'd by every tie, I may not dare
To cast a worthless offering at thy shrine,
Nor ask so dear a breast to feel one pang for mine.

XXXI.

Thus Harold deem'd, as on that lady's eye
He look'd, and met its beam without a thought,
Save Admiration glancing harmless by:
Love kept aloof, albeit not far remote,
Who knew his votary often lost and caught,
But knew him as his worshipper no more,
And ne'er again the boy his bosom sought:
Since now he vainly urged him to adore,
Well deem'd the little God his ancient sway was o'er.

XXXII.

Fair Florence, found, in sooth with some amaze,
One who, 't was said, still sigh'd to all he saw,
Withstand, unmoved, the lustre of her gaze,
Which others hail'd with real or mimic awe,
Their hope, their doom, their punishment, their law;
All that gay Beauty from her bondsmen claims:
And much she marvelled that a youth so raw
Nor felt, nor feign'd at least, the oft-told flames,
Which, though sometimes they frown, yet rarely anger dames.

XXXIII.

Little knew she that seeming marble heart,
Now mask'd in silence or withheld by pride,
Was not unskilful in the spoiler's art,
And spread its snares licentious far and wide;
Nor from the base pursuit had turn'd aside,
As long as aught was worthy to pursue:
But Harold on such arts no more relied;
And had he doted on those eyes so blue,
Yet never would he join the lover's whining crew.

XXXIV.

Not much he kens, I ween, of woman's breast,
Who thinks that wanton thing is won by sighs;
What careth she for hearts when once possess'd?
Do proper homage to thine idol's eyes;
But not too humbly, or she will despise
Thee and thy suit, though told in moving tropes;
Disguise ev'n tenderness, if thou art wise;
Brisk Confidence still best with woman copes;
Pique her and soothe in turn, soon Passion crowns thy hopes.

XXXV.

'T is an old lesson; Time approves it true,
And those who know it best, deplore it most;
When all is won that all desire to woo,
The paltry prize is hardly worth the cost:
Youth wasted, minds degraded, honour lost,
These are thy fruits, successful Passion! these!
If, kindly cruel, early Hope is crost,
Still to the last it rankles, a disease,
Not to be cured when Love itself forgets to please.

XXXVI.

Away! nor let me loiter in my song,
For we have many a mountain-path to tread,
And many a varied shore to sail along,
By pensive Sadness, not by Fiction, led—
Climes, fair withal as ever mortal head
Imagined in its little schemes of thought;
Or e'er in new Utopias were ared,
To teach man what he might be, or he ought;
If that corrupted thing could ever such be taught.

XXXVII.

Dear Nature is the kindest mother still,
Though alway changing, in her aspect mild;
From her bare bosom let me take my fill,
Her never-wean'd, though not her favour'd child.
Oh! she is fairest in her features wild,
Where nothing polish'd dares pollute her path:
To me by day or night she ever smiled,
Though I have mark'd her when none other hath,
And sought her more and more, and loved her best in wrath.

XXXVIII.

Land of Albania! where Iskander rose!
Theme of the young, and beacon of the wise,
And he his namesake, whose oft-baffled foes
Shrunk from his deeds of chivalrous emprize:
Land of Albania! let me bend mine eyes
On thee, thou rugged nurse of savage men!
The cross descends, thy minarets arise,
And the pale crescent sparkles in the glen,
Through many a cypress grove within each city's ken.

XXXIX.

Childe Harold sail'd, and pass'd the barren spot,
Where sad Penelope o'erlook'd the wave;[8]
And onward view'd the mount, not yet forgot,
The lover's refuge, and the Lesbian's grave.
Dark Sappho! could not verse immortal save
That breast imbued with such immortal fire?
Could she not live who life eternal gave?
If life eternal may await the lyre,
That only Heaven to which Earth's children may aspire.

XL.

'Twas on a Grecian autumn's gentle eve
Childe Harold hail'd Leucadia's cape afar;[9]
A spot he longed to see, nor cared to leave:
Oft did he mark the scenes of vanish'd war,
Actium, Lepanto, fatal Trafalgar:[10]
Mark them unmoved, for he would not delight
(Born beneath some remote inglorious star)
In themes of bloody fray, or gallant fight,
But loathed the bravo's trade, and laugh'd at martial wight.

XLI.

But when he saw the evening star above
Leucadia's far-projecting rock of woe,
And hail'd the last resort of fruitless love,
He felt, or deem'd he felt, no common glow:
And as the stately vessel glided slow
Beneath the shadow of that ancient mount,
He watch'd the billows' melancholy flow,
And, sunk albeit in thought as he was wont,
More placid seem'd his eye, and smooth his pallid front.

XLII.

Morn dawns; and with it stern Albania's hills,
Dark Suli's rocks, and Pindus' inland peak,
Robed half in mist, bedew'd with snowy rills,
Array'd in many a dun and purple streak,
Arise; and, as the clouds along them break,
Disclose the dwelling of the mountaineer:
Here roams the wolf, the eagle whets his beak,
Birds, beasts of prey, and wilder men appear,
And gathering storms around convulse the closing year.

XLIII.

Now Harold felt himself at length alone,
And bade to Christian tongues a long adieu;
Now he adventured on a shore unknown,
Which all admire, but many dread to view:
His breast was arm'd 'gainst fate, his wants were few;
Peril he sought not, but ne'er shrank to meet:
The scene was savage, but the scene was new;
This made the ceaseless toil of travel sweet,
Beat back keen winter's blast, and welcomed summer's heat.

XLIV.

Here the red cross, for still the cross is here,
Though sadly scoff'd at by the circumcised,
Forgets that pride to pamper'd priesthood dear;
Churchman and votary alike despised.
Foul Superstition! howsoe'er disguised,
Idol, saint, virgin, prophet, crescent, cross,
For whatsoever symbol thou art prized,
Thou sacerdotal gain, but general loss!
Who from true worship's gold can separate thy dross?

XLV.

Ambracia's gulf behold, where once was lost
A world for woman, lovely, harmless thing!
In yonder rippling bay, their naval host,
Did many a Roman chief and Asian king[11]
To doubtful conflict, certain slaughter bring:
Look where the second Cæsar's trophies rose![12]
Now, like the hands that rear'd them, withering;
Imperial anarchs, doubling human woes!
GOD! was Thy globe ordain'd for such to win and lose?

XLVI.

From the dark barriers of that rugged clime,
Ev'n to the centre of Illyria's vales,
Childe Harold pass'd o'er many a mount sublime,
Through lands scarce noticed in historic tales;
Yet in famed Attica such lovely dales
Are rarely seen; nor can fair Tempe boast
A charm they know not; loved Parnassus fails,
Though classic ground and consecrated most,
To match some spots that lurk within this lowering coast.

XLVII.

He pass'd bleak Pindus, Acherusia's lake,[13]
And left the primal city of the land,
And onwards did his further journey take
To greet Albania's chief, whose dread command[14]
Is lawless law; for with a bloody hand
He sways a nation, turbulent and bold:
Yet here and there some daring mountain-band
Disdain his power, and from their rocky hold
Hurl their defiance far, nor yield, unless to gold.[15]

XLVIII.

Monastic Zitza from thy shady brow,[16]
Thou small, but favour'd spot of holy ground!
Where'er we gaze, around, above, below,
What rainbow tints, what magic charms are found!
Rock, river, forest, mountain, all abound,
And bluest skies that harmonise the whole:
Beneath, the distant torrent's rushing sound
Tells where the volumed cataract doth roll
Between those hanging rocks, that shock yet please the soul.

LXIX.

Amidst the grove that crowns yon tufted hill,
Which, were it not for many a mountain nigh
Rising in lofty ranks, and loftier still,
Might well itself be deem'd of dignity,
The convent's white walls glisten fair on high:
Here dwells the caloyer, nor rude is he,[17]
Nor niggard of his cheer; the passer by
Is welcome still; nor heedless will he flee
From hence, if he delight kind Nature's sheen to see.

L.

Here in the sultriest season let him rest,
Fresh is the green beneath those aged trees;
Here winds of gentlest wing will fan his breast,
From heaven itself he may inhale the breeze:
The plain is far beneath—oh! let him seize
Pure pleasure while he can; the scorching ray
Here pierceth not, impregnate with disease:
Then let his length the loitering pilgrim lay,
And gaze, untired, the morn, the noon, the eve away.

LI.

Dusky and huge, enlarging on the sight,
Nature's volcanic amphitheatre,[18]
Chimæra's alps extend from left to right:
Beneath, a living valley seems to stir;
Flocks play, trees wave, streams flow, the mountain fir
Nodding above; behold black Acheron![19]
Once consecrated to the sepulchre.
Pluto! if this be hell I look upon,
Close shamed Elysium's gates, my shade shall seek for none.

LII.

Ne city's towers pollute the lovely view;
Unseen is Yanina, though not remote,
Veil'd by the screen of hills: here men are few,
Scanty the hamlet, rare the lonely cot;
But, peering down each precipice, the goat
Browseth; and, pensive o'er his scatter'd flock,
The little shepherd in his white capote[20]
Doth lean his boyish form along the rock,
Or in his cave awaits the tempest's short-lived shock.

LIII.

Oh! where, Dodona! is thine aged grove,
Prophetic fount, and oracle divine?
What valley echoed the response of Jove?
What trace remaineth of the Thunderer's shrine?
All, all forgotten—and shall man repine
That his frail bonds to fleeting life are broke?
Cease, fool! the fate of gods may well be thine:
Wouldst thou survive the marble or the oak?
When nations, tongues, and worlds must sink beneath the stroke!

LIV.

Epirus' bounds recede, and mountains fail;
Tired of up-gazing still, the wearied eye
Reposes gladly on as smooth a vale
As ever Spring yclad in grassy die:
Ev'n on a plain no humble beauties lie,
Where some bold river breaks the long expanse,
And woods along the banks are waving high,
Whose shadows in the glassy waters dance,
Or with the moonbeam sleep in midnight's solemn trance.

LV.

The sun had sunk behind vast Tomerit,[21]
The Laos wide and fierce came roaring by;[22]
The shades of wonted night were gathering yet,
When, down the steep banks winding warily
Childe Harold saw, like meteors in the sky
The glittering minarets of Tepalen,
Whose walls o'erlook the stream; and drawing nigh,
He heard the busy hum of warrior-men
Swelling the breeze that sigh'd along the lengthening glen.

LVI.

He pass'd the sacred Haram's silent tower,
And underneath the wide o'erarching gate
Survey'd the dwelling of this chief of power,
Where all around proclaim'd his high estate.
Amidst no common pomp the despot sate,
While busy preparation shook the court,
Slaves, eunuchs, soldiers, guests, and santons wait;
Within, a palace, and without, a fort:
Here men of every clime appear to make resort.

LVII.

Richly caparison'd, a ready row
Of armèd horse, and many a warlike store,
Circled the wide-extending court below;
Above, strange groups adorn'd the corridore;
And oft-times through the area's echoing door,
Some high-capp'd Tartar spurr'd his steed away:
The Turk, the Greek, the Albanian, and the Moor,
Here mingled in their many-hued array,
While the deep war-drum's sound announced the close of day.

LVIII.

The wild Albanian kirtled to his knee,
With shawl-girt head and ornamented gun,
And gold embroider'd garments, fair to see:
The crimson-scarfèd men of Macedon;
The Delhi with his cap of terror on,
And crooked glaive; the lively, supple Greek;
And swarthy Nubia's mutilated son;
The bearded Turk, that rarely deigns to speak,
Master of all around, too potent to be meek,

LIX.

Are mix'd conspicuous: some recline in groups,
Scanning the motley scene that varies round;
There some grave Moslem to devotion stoops,
And some that smoke, and some that play, are found;
Here the Albanian proudly treads the ground;
Half-whispering there the Greek is heard to prate;
Hark! from the mosque the nightly solemn sound,
The Muezzin's call doth shake the minaret,
"There is no god but God!—to prayer—lo! God is great!"

LX.

Just at this season Ramazani's fast
Through the long day its penance did maintain.
But when the lingering twilight hour was past,
Revel and feast assumed the rule again
Now all was bustle, and the menial train
Prepared and spread the plenteous board within;
The vacant gallery now seem'd made in vain,
But from the chambers came the mingling din,
As page and slave anon were passing out and in.

LXI.

Here woman's voice is never heard ; apart,
And scarce permitted, guarded, veil'd, to move,
She yields to one her person and her heart,
Tamed to her cage, nor feels a wish to rove:
For, not unhappy in her master's love.
And joyful in a mother's gentlest cares,
Blest cares ! all other feelings far above !
Herself more sweetly rears the babe she bears,
Who never quits the breast, no meaner passion shares

LXII.

In marble-paved pavilion, where a spring
Of living water from the centre rose,
Whose bubbling did a genial freshness fling,
And soft voluptuous couches breathed repose,
Ali reclined, a man of war and woes:
Yet in his lineaments ye cannot trace,
While Gentleness her milder radiance throws
Along that aged venerable face,
The deeds that lurk beneath, and stain him with disgrace.

LXIII.

It is not that yon hoary lengthening beard
Ill suits the passions which belong to youth:
Love conquers age—so Hafiz hath averr'd,
So sings the Teian, and he sings in sooth—
But crimes that scorn the tender voice of ruth,
Beseeming all men ill, but most the man
In years, have mark'd him with a tiger's tooth:
Blood follows blood, and through their mortal span,
In bloodier acts conclude those who with blood began.

LXIV.

'Mid many things most new to ear and eye
The pilgrim rested here his weary feet,
And gazed around on Moslem luxury,
Till quickly wearied with that spacious seat
Of Wealth and Wantonness, the choice retreat
Of sated Grandeur from the city's noise:
And were it humbler, it in sooth were sweet;
But Peace abhorreth artificial joys,
And Pleasure, leagued with Pomp, the zest of both destroys.

LXV.

Fierce are Albania's children, yet they lack
Not virtues, were those virtues more mature.
Where is the foe that ever saw their back?
Who can so well the toil of war endure?
Their native fastnesses not more secure
Than they in doubtful time of troublous need:
Their wrath how deadly! but their friendship sure,
When Gratitude or Valour bids them bleed,
Unshaken rushing on where'er their chief may lead.

LXVI.

Childe Harold saw them in their chieftain s tower,
Thronging to war in splendour and success;
And after view'd them, when, within their power,
Himself awhile the victim of distress;
That saddening hour when bad men hotlier press:
But these did shelter him beneath their roof,
When less barbarians would have cheer'd him less,
And fellow-countrymen have stood aloof—[23]
In aught that tries the heart how few withstand the proof!

LXVII.

It chanced that adverse winds once drove his bark
Full on the coast of Suli's shaggy shore,
When all around was desolate and dark;
To land was perilous, to sojourn more;
Yet for awhile the mariners forbore,
Dubious to trust where treachery might lurk:
At length they ventured forth, though doubting sore
That those who loathe alike the Frank and Turk
Might once again renew their ancient butcher-work

LXVIII.

Vain fear! the Suliotes stretch'd the welcome hand,
Led them o'er rocks and past the dangerous swamp,
Kinder than polish'd slaves though not so bland,
And piled the hearth, and wrung their garments damp,
And fill'd the bowl, and trimm'd the cheerful lamp,
And spread their fare: though homely, all they had:
Such conduct bears Philanthropy's rare stamp—
To rest the weary and to soothe the sad,
Doth lesson happier men. and shames at least the bad.

LXIX.

It came to pass, that when he did address
Himself to quit at length this mountain-land,
Combined marauders half-way barr'd egress,
And wasted far and near with glaive and brand;
And therefore did he take a trusty band
To traverse Acarnania's forest wide,
In war well season'd, and with labours tann'd,
Till he did greet white Achelous' tide,
And from his further bank Ætolia's wolds espied.

LXX.

Where lone Utraikey forms its circling cove,
And weary waves retire to gleam at rest,
How brown the foliage of the green hill's grove,
Nodding at midnight o'er the calm bay's breast,
As winds come whispering lightly from the west,
Kissing, not ruffling, the blue deep's serene:
Here Harold was received a welcome guest;
Nor did he pass unmoved the gentle scene,
For many a joy could he from Night's soft presence glean.

LXXI.

On the smooth shore the night-fires brightly blazed,
The feast was done, the red wine circling fast,[24]
And he that unawares had there ygazed
With gaping wonderment had stared aghast;
For ere night's midmost, stillest hour was past,
The native revels of the troop began;
Each Palikar his sabre from him cast,[25]
And bounding hand in hand, man link'd to man,
Yelling their uncouth dirge, long daunced the kirtled clan.

LXXII.

Childe Harold at a little distance stood,
And view'd, but not displeased, the revelrie,
Nor hated harmless mirth, however rude:
In sooth, it was no vulgar sight to see
Their barbarous, yet their not indecent, glee;
And, as the flames along their faces gleam'd,
Their gestures nimble, dark eyes flashing free,
The long wild locks that to their girdles stream'd,
While thus in concert they this lay half sang, half scream'd:—

1.

TAMBOURGI! Tambourgi! thy larum afar[26]
Gives hope to the valiant, and promise of war;
All the sons of the mountains arise at the note,
Chimariot, Illyrian, and dark Suliote![27]

2.

Oh! who is more brave than a dark Suliote,
In his snowy camese and his shaggy capote?
To the wolf and the vulture he leaves his wild flock,
And descends to the plain like the stream from the rock.

3.

Shall the sons of Chimari, who never forgive
The fault of a friend, bid an enemy live?
Let those guns so unerring such vengeance forego?
What mark is so fair as the breast of a foe?

4.

Macedonia sends forth her invincible race;
For a time they abandon the cave and the chase:
But those scarfs of blood-red shall be redder, before
The sabre is sheathed and the battle is o'er.

5.

Then the pirates of Parga that dwell by the waves,
And teach the pale Franks what it is to be slaves,
Shall leave on the beach the long galley and oar,
And track to his covert the captive on shore.

6.

I ask not the pleasures that riches supply,
My sabre shall win what the feeble must buy;
Shall win the young bride with her long flowing hair,
And many a maid from her mother shall tear.

7.

I love the fair face of the maid in her youth,
Her caresses shall lull me, her music shall soothe;
Let her bring from her chamber the many-toned lyre,
And sing us a song on the fall of her sire.

8.

Remember the moment when Previsa fell,[28]
The shrieks of the conquer'd, the conquerors' yell;
The roofs that we fired, and the plunder we shared,
The wealthy we slaughter'd, the lovely we spared.

9.

I talk not of mercy, I talk not of fear;
He neither must know who would serve the Vizier:
Since the days of our prophet the Crescent ne'er saw
A chief ever glorious like Ali Pashaw.

10.

Dark Muchtar his son to the Danube is sped,
Let the yellow-hair'd[29] Giaours[30] view his horse-tail[31] with dread,
When his Delhis come dashing in blood o'er the banks,[32]
How few shall escape from the Muscovite ranks!

11.

Selictar! unsheathe then our chief's scimitar:[33]
Tambourgi! thy larum gives promise of war.
Ye mountains, that see us descend to the shore,
Shall view us as victors, or view us no more!

LXXIII.

Fair Greece! sad relic of departed worth!
Immortal, though no more; though fallen, great!
Who now shall lead thy scatter'd children forth,
And long accustom'd bondage uncreate?
Not such thy sons who whilome did await,
The hopeless warriors of a willing doom,
In bleak Thermopylæ's sepulchral strait—
Oh! who that gallant spirit shall resume,
Leap from Eurotas' banks, and call thee from the tomb?

LXXIV.

Spirit of Freedom! when on Phyle's brow[34]
Thou sat'st with Thrasybulus and his train,
Couldst thou forebode the dismal hour which now
Dims the green beauties of thine Attic plain?
Not thirty tyrants now enforce the chain,
But every carle can lord it o'er thy land;
Nor rise thy sons, but idly rail in vain,
Trembling beneath the scourge of Turkish hand,
From birth till death enslaved; in word, in deed, unmann'd.

LXXV.

In all save form alone, how changed! and who
That marks the fire still sparkling in each eye,
Who but would deem their bosoms burn'd anew
With thy unquenchèd beam, lost Liberty!
And many dream withal the hour is nigh

That gives them back their fathers' heritage:
For foreign arms and aid they fondly sigh,
Nor solely dare encounter hostile rage,
Or tear their name defiled from Slavery's mournful page.

LXXVI.

Hereditary bondsmen! know ye not
Who would be free themselves must strike the blow?
By their right arms the conquest must be wrought?
Will Gaul or Muscovite redress ye? no!
True, they may lay your proud despoilers low,
But not for you will Freedom's altars flame.
Shades of the Helots! triumph o'er your foe!
Greece! change thy lords, thy state is still the same;
Thy glorious day is o'er, but not thine years of shame.

LXXVII.

The city won for Allah from the Giaour,
The Giaour from Othman's race again may wrest;
And the Serai's impenetrable tower
Receive the fiery Frank, her former guest;[35]
Or Wahab's rebel brood, who dared divest
The prophet's tomb of all its pious spoil,[36]
May wind their path of blood along the West;
But ne'er will freedom seek this fated soil,
But slave succeed to slave through years of endless toil.

LXXVIII.

Yet mark their mirth—ere lenten days begin,
That penance which their holy rites prepare
To shrive from man his weight of mortal sin,
By daily abstinence and nightly prayer;
But ere his sackcloth garb Repentance wear,
Some days of joyaunce are decreed to all,
To take of pleasaunce each his secret share,
In motley robe to dance at masking hall,
And join the mimic train of merry Carnival.

LXXIX.

And whose more rife with merriment than thine,
Oh Stamboul! once the empress of their reign?
Though turbans now pollute Sophia's shrine,
And Greece her very altars eyes in vain:
(Alas! her woes will still pervade my strain!)
Gay were her minstrels once, for free her throng,
All felt the common joy they now must feign,
Nor oft I've seen such sight, nor heard such song,
As woo'd the eye, and thrill'd the Bosphorus along.

LXXX.

Loud was the lightsome tumult on the shore,
Oft Music changed, but never ceased her tone,
And timely echo'd back the measured oar,
And rippling waters made a pleasant moan:
The Queen of tides on high consenting shone,
And when a transient breeze swept o'er the wave,
'T was, as if darting from her heavenly throne,
A brighter glance her form reflected gave,
Till sparkling billows seem'd to light the banks they lave.

LXXXI.

Glanced many a light caique along the foam,
Danced on the shore the daughters of the land,
Ne thought had man or maid of rest or home,
While many a languid eye and thrilling hand
Exchanged the look few bosoms may withstand,
Or gently prest, return'd the pressure still:
Oh Love! young Love! bound in thy rosy band,
Let sage or cynic prattle as he will,
These hours, and only these, redeem Life's years of ill!

LXXXII.

But, midst the throng in merry masquerade,
Lurk there no hearts that throb with secret pain,
Even through the closest searment half betray'd?
To such the gentle murmurs of the main
Seem to re-echo all they mourn in vain;
To such the gladness of the gamesome crowd
Is source of wayward thought and stern disdain:
How do they loathe the laughter idly loud,
And long to change the robe of revel for the shroud!

LXXXIII.

This must he feel, the true-born son of Greece,
If Greece one true-born patriot still can boast:
Not such as prate of war, but skulk in peace,
The bondsman's peace, who sighs for all he lost,
Yet with smoothe smile his tyrant can accost,
And wield the slavish sickle, not the sword:
Ah! Greece! they love thee least who owe thee most;
Their birth, their blood, and that sublime record
Of hero sires, who shame thy now degenerate horde!

LXXXIV.

When riseth Lacedæmon's hardihood,
When Thebes Epaminondas rears again,
When Athens' children are with hearts endued,
When Grecian mothers shall give birth to men,
Then may'st thou be restored; but not till then.
A thousand years scarce serve to form a state;
An hour may lay it in the dust: and when
Can man its shatter'd splendour renovate,
Recall its virtues back, and vanquish Time and Fate?

LXXXV.

And yet how lovely in thine age of woe,
Land of lost gods and godlike men—art thou!
Thy vales of evergreen, thy hills of snow,
Proclaim thee nature's varied favourite now;[37]
Thy fanes, thy temples to thy surface bow,
Commingling slowly with heroic earth,
Broke by the share of every rustic plough:
So perish monuments of mortal birth,
So perish all in turn, save well-recorded Worth;

LXXXVI.

Save where some solitary column mourns
Above its prostrate brethren of the cave;[38]
Save where Tritonia's airy shrine adorns
Colonna's cliff, and gleams along the wave;[39]
Save o'er some warrior's half forgotten grave,
Where the gray stones and unmolested grass
Ages, but not oblivion, feebly brave,
While strangers only not regardless pass,
Lingering like me, perchance, to gaze, and sigh "Alas!"

LXXXVII.

Yet are thy skies as blue, thy crags as wild:
Sweet are thy groves, and verdant are thy fields,
Thine olive ripe as when Minerva smiled,
And still his honied wealth Hymettus yields;
There the blithe bee his fragrant fortress builds,
The freeborn wanderer of thy mountain-air;
Apollo still thy long, long summer gilds,
Still in his beam Mendeli's marbles glare;
Art, Glory, Freedom fail, but Nature still is fair.

LXXXVIII.

Where'er we tread 'tis haunted, holy ground;
No earth of thine is lost in vulgar mould,
But one vast realm of wonder spreads around,
And all the Muse's tales seem truly told,
Till the sense aches with gazing to behold
The scenes our earliest dreams have dwelt upon:
Each hill and dale, each deepening glen and wold
Defies the power which crush'd thy temples gone:
Age shakes Athena's tower, but spares gray Marathon.

LXXXIX.

The sun, the soil, but not the slave, the same;
Unchanged in all except its foreign lord—
Preserves alike its bounds and boundless fame;
The Battle-field, where Persia's victim horde
First bow'd beneath the brunt of Hellas' sword,
As on the morn to distant Glory dear,
When Marathon became a magic word;[40]
Which utter'd, to the hearer's eye appear
The camp, the host, the fight, the conqueror's career,

XC.

The flying Mede, his shaftless broken bow;
The fiery Greek, his red pursuing spear;
Mountains above, Earth's, Ocean's plain below;
Death in the front, Destruction in the rear!
Such was the scene—what now remaineth here?
What sacred trophy marks the hallow'd ground,
Recording Freedom's smile and Asia's tear?
The rifled urn, the violated mound,
The dust thy courser's hoof, rude stranger! spurns around.

XCI.

Yet to the remnants of thy splendour past
Shall pilgrims, pensive, but unwearied, throng;
Long shall the voyager, with th' Ionian blast,
Hail the bright clime of battle and of song;
Long shall thine annals and immortal tongue
Fill with thy fame the youth of many a shore:
Boast of the aged! lesson of the young!
Which sages venerate and bards adore,
As Pallas and the Muse unveil their awful lore.

XCII.

The parted bosom clings to wonted home,
If aught that's kindred cheer the welcome hearth;
He that is lonely, hither let him roam,
And gaze complacent on congenial earth.
Greece is no lightsome land of social mirth;
But he whom Sadness sootheth may abide,
And scarce regret the region of his birth,
When wandering slow by Delphi's sacred side,
Or gazing o'er the plains where Greek and Persian died.

XCIII.

Let such approach this consecrated land,
And pass in peace along the magic waste:
But spare its relics—let no busy hand
Deface the scenes, already how defaced!
Not for such purpose were these altars placed.
Revere the remnants nations once revered:
So may our country's name be undisgraced,
So may'st thou prosper where thy youth was rear'd,
By every honest joy of love and life endeared!

XCIV.

For thee, who thus in too protracted song
Hast soothed thine idlesse with inglorious lays,
Soon shall thy voice be lost amid the throng
Of louder minstrels in these later days:
To such resign the strife for fading bays—
Ill may such contest now the spirit move
Which heeds nor keen reproach nor partial praise,
Since cold each kinder heart that might approve,
And none are left to please when none are left to love.

XCV.

Thou too art gone, thou loved and lovely one!
Whom youth and youth's affections bound to me;
Who did for me what none beside have done,
Nor shrank from one albeit unworthy thee.
What is my being? thou hast ceased to be!
Nor staid to welcome here thy wanderer home,
Who mourns o'er hours which we no more shall see—
Would they had never been, or were to come!
Would he had ne'er return'd to find fresh cause to roam!

XCVI.

Oh! ever loving, lovely, and beloved!
How selfish Sorrow ponders on the past,
And clings to thoughts now better far removed!
But Time shall tear thy shadow from me last.
All thou couldst have of mine, stern Death! thou hast:
The parent, friend, and now the more than friend;
Ne'er yet for one thine arrows flew so fast,
And grief with grief continuing still to blend,
Hath snatch'd the little joy that life had yet to lend

XCVII.

Then must I plunge again into the crowd,
And follow all that Peace disdains to seek?
Where Revel calls, and Laughter, vainly loud,
False to the heart, distorts the hollow cheek,
To leave the flagging spirit doubly weak!
Still o'er the features, which perforce they cheer,
To feign the pleasure or conceal the pique;
Smiles form the channel of a future tear,
Or raise the writhing lip with ill-dissembled sneer.

XCVIII.

What is the worst of woes that wait on age?
What stamps the wrinkle deeper on the brow?
To view each loved one blotted from life's page,
And be alone on earth, as I am now.
Before the Chastener humbly let me bow,
O'er hearts divided and o'er hopes destroy'd:
Roll on, vain days! full reckless may ye flow,
Since Time hath reft whate'er my soul enjoy'd,
And with the ills of Eld mine earlier years alloy'd.

NOTES TO CANTO THE SECOND.

NOTE 1, page 594.

And is, despite of war and wasting fire.

Part of the Acropolis was destroyed by the explosion of a magazine during the Venetian siege.

NOTE 2, page 594.

Ancient of days! august Athena! where.

We can all feel, or imagine, the regret with which the ruins of cities, once the capitals of empires, are beheld; the reflections suggested by such objects are too trite to require recapitulation. But never did the littleness of man, and the vanity of his very best virtues—of patriotism to exalt, and of valour to defend his country—appear more conspicuous than in the record of what Athens was, and the certainty of what she now is. This theatre of contention between mighty factions, of the struggles of orators, the exaltation and deposition of tyrants, the triumph and punishment of generals, is now become a scene of petty intrigue and perpetual disturbance, between the bickering agents of certain British nobility and gentry. "The wild foxes, the owls and serpents in the ruins of Babylon," were surely less degrading than such inhabitants. The Turks have the plea of conquest for their tyranny, and the Greeks have only suffered the fortune of war, incidental to the bravest; but how are the mighty fallen, when two painters contest the privilege of plundering the Parthenon, and triumph in turn, according to the tenor of each succeeding firman! Sylla could but punish, Philip subdue, and Xerxes burn Athens; but it remained for the paltry antiquarian, and his despicable agents, to render her contemptible as himself and his pursuits. The Parthenon, before its destruction in part, by fire during the Venetian siege, had been a temple, a church, and a mosque. In each point of view it is an object of regard: it changed its worshippers; but still it was a place of worship thrice sacred to devotion: its violation is a triple sacrifice. But—

"Man, proud man,
Drest in a little brief authority,
Plays such fantastic tricks before high Heaven
As make the angels weep."

82

NOTE 3, page 595.

Far on the solitary shore he sleeps.

It was not always the custom of the Greeks to burn their dead; the greater Ajax, in particular, was interred entire. Almost all the chiefs became gods after their decease; and he was indeed neglected, who had not annual games near his tomb, or festivals in honour of his memory by his countrymen, as Achilles, Brasidas, &c., and at last even Antinous, whose death was as heroic as his life was infamous.

NOTE 4, page 595.

Here, son of Saturn! was thy fav'rite throne.

The temple of Jupiter Olympius, of which sixteen columns, entirely of marble, yet survive: originally there were one hundred and fifty. These columns, however, are by many supposed to have belonged to the Pantheon.

NOTE 5, page 596.

Stern Alaric and Havoc on their way.

According to Zosimus, Minerva and Achilles frightened Alaric from the Acropolis; but others relate that the Gothic king was nearly as mischievous as the Scottish peer.—See CHANDLER.

NOTE 6, page 597.

The well-reeved guns, the netted canopy.

To prevent blocks or splinters from falling on deck during action.

NOTE 7, page 598.

But not in silence pass Calypso's isles.

Goza is said to have been the island of Calypso.

NOTE 8, page 599.

Where sad Penelope o'erlook'd the wave.

Ithaca.

NOTE 9, page 599.

Childe Harold hail'd Leucadia's cape afar.

Leucadia, now Santa Maura. From the promontory (the Lover's Leap) Sappho is said to have thrown herself.

NOTE 10, page 599.

Actium, Lepanto, fatal Trafalgar.

Actium and Trafalgar need no further mention. The battle of Lepanto, equally bloody and considerable, but less known, was fought in the Gulf of Patras. Here the author of Don Quixote lost his left hand.

NOTE 11, page 600.

Did many a Roman chief and Asian king.

It is said that, on the day previous to the battle of Actium, Anthony had thirteen kings at his levee.

NOTE 12, page 600.

Look where the second Cæsar's trophies rose.

Nicopolis, whose ruins are most extensive, is at some distance from Actium, where the wall of the Hippodrome survives in a few fragments. These ruins are large masses of brickwork, the bricks of which are joined by interstices of mortar, as large as the bricks themselves, and equally durable.

NOTE 13, page 600.

He pass'd bleak Pindus, Acherusia's lake.

According to Pouqueville, the lake of Yanina: but Pouqueville is always out.

NOTE 14, page 600.

To greet Albania's chief, whose dread command.

The celebrated Ali Pacha. Of this extraordinary man, there is an incorrect account in Pouqueville's Travels.

NOTE 15, page 600.

Hurl their defiance far, nor yield, unless to gold.

Five thousand Suliotes, among the rocks and in the castle of Suli, withstood thirty thousand Albanians for eighteen years; the castle at last was taken by bribery. In this contest there were several acts performed not unworthy of the better days of Greece.

NOTE 16, page 600.

Monastic Zitza! from thy shady brow.

The convent and village of Zitza are four hours' journey from Joannina, or Yanina, the capital of the Pachalick. In the valley the river Kalamas (once the Acheron) flows, and, not far from Zitza, forms a fine cataract. The situation is perhaps the finest in Greece, though the approach to Delvinachi and parts of Acarnania and Ætolia may contest the palm. Delphi, Parnassus, and, in Attica, even Cape Colonna and Port Raphti, are very inferior; as also every scene in Ionia, or the Troad: I am almost inclined to add the approach to Constantinople; but, from the different features of the last, a comparison can hardly be made.

NOTE 17, page 600.

Here dwells the caloyer, nor rude is he.

The Greek Monks are so called.

NOTE 18, page 601.

Nature's volcanic amphitheatre.

The Chimariot mountains appear to have been volcanic.

NOTE 19, page 601.

Nodding above, behold black Acheron.

Now called Kalamas.

NOTE 20, page 601.

The little shepherd in his white capote.

Albanese cloak.

NOTE 21, page 601.

The sun had sunk behind vast Tomerit.

Anciently Mount Tomarus.

NOTE 22, page 601.

And Laos wide and fierce came roaring by.

The river Laos was full at the time the author passed it; and, immediately above Tepaleen, was to the eye as wide as the Thames at Westminster; at least in the opinion of the author and his fellow-traveller. In the summer it must be much narrower. It certainly is the finest river in the Levant; neither Achelous, Alpheus, Acheron, Scamander, nor Cayster, approached it in breadth or beauty.

NOTE 23, page 604.

And fellow-countrymen have stood aloof.

Alluding to the wreckers of Cornwall.

NOTE 24, page 604.

The feast was done, the red wine circling fast.

The Albanian Mussulmans do not abstain from wine, and, indeed, very few of the others.

NOTE 25, page 604.

Each Palikar his sabre from him cast.

Palikar, a general name for a soldier amongst the Greeks and Albanese who speak Romaic: it means, properly, "a lad."

NOTE 26, page 605.

Tambourgi! Tambourg! thy larum afar.

Drummer.

NOTE 27, page 605.

Chimariot, Illyrian, and dark Suliote!

These stanzas are partly taken from different Albanese songs, as far as I was able to make them out by the exposition of the Albanese in Romaic and Italian.

NOTE 28, page 605.

Remember the moment when Previsa fell.

It was taken by storm from the French.

NOTES 29, 30, and 31, page 605.

Let the yellow-hair'd Giaours view his horse-tail with dread.

Yellow is the epithet given to the Russians. Giaour:

Note 32, page 605.

When his Delhis come dashing in blood o'er the banks.

Horsemen, answering to our forlorn hope.

Note 33, page 605.

Selictar! unsheathe then our chief's scimitar.

Selictar: Swordbearer.

Note 34, page 605.

Spirit of Freedom! when on Phyle's brow.

Phyle, which commands a beautiful view of Athens, has still considerable remains: it was seized by Thrasybulus, previous to the expulsion of the Thirty.

Note 35, page 606.

Receive the fiery Frank, her former guest.

When taken by the Latins, and retained for several years.

Note 36, page 606.

The prophet's tomb of all its pious spoil.

Mecca and Medina were taken some time ago by the Wahabees, a sect yearly increasing.

Note 37, page 607.

Thy vales of evergreen, thy hills of snow.

On many of the mountains, particularly Liakura, the snow never is entirely melted, notwithstanding the intense heat of the summer; but I never saw it lie on the plains, even in winter.

Note 38, page 607.

Above its prostrate brethren of the cave.

Of Mount Pentelicus, from whence the marble was dug that constructed the public edifices of Athens. The modern name is Mount Mendeli. An immense cave, formed by the quarries, still remains, and will till the end of time.

Note 39, page 607.

Colonna's cliff, and gleams along the wave.

In all Attica, if we except Athens itself and Marathon, there is no scene more interesting than Cape Colonna. To the antiquary and artist, sixteen columns are an inexhaustible source of observation and design; to the philosopher, the supposed scene of some of Plato's conversations will not be unwelcome; and the traveller will be struck with the beauty of the prospect over "Isles that crown the Ægean deep:" but, for an Englishman, Colonna has yet an additional interest, as the actual spot of Falconer's Shipwreck. Pallas and Plato are forgotten, in the recollection of Falconer and Campbell:—

"Here in the dead of night by Lonna's steep,
The seaman's cry was heard along the deep."

This temple of Minerva may be seen at sea from a great distance. In two journeys which I made, and one voyage to Cape Colonna, the view from either side, by land, was more striking than the approach from the isles. In our second land excursion, we had a narrow escape from a party of Mainotes, concealed in the caverns beneath. We were told afterwards, by one of their prisoners, subsequently ransomed, that they were deterred from attacking us by the appearance of my two Albanians: conjecturing very sagaciously, but falsely, that we had a complete guard of these Arnaouts at hand, they remained stationary, and thus saved our party, which was too small to have opposed any effectual resistance. Colonna is no less a resort of painters than of pirates; there

"The hireling artist plants his paltry desk,
And makes degraded nature picturesque."
(See Hodgson's *Lady Jane Grey*, &c.)

But there Nature, with the aid of Art, has done that for herself. I was fortunate enough to engage a very superior German artist; and hope to renew my acquaintance with this and many other Levantine scenes, by the arrival of his performances.

Note 40, page 608.

When Marathon became a magic word.

"Siste Viator—heroa calcas!" was the epitaph on the famous Count Merci;—what then must be our feelings when standing on the tumulus of the two hundred (Greeks) who fell on Marathon? The principal barrow has recently been opened by Fauvel: few or no relics, as vases, &c., were found by the excavator. The plain of Marathon was offered to me for sale at the sum of sixteen thousand piastres, about nine hundred pounds! Alas!—"Expende—quot *libras* in duce summo—invenies!"—was the dust of Miltiades worth no more? It could scarcely have fetched less if sold by *weight*.

CANTO THE THIRD.

"Afin que cette application vous forçât de penser à autre chose; il n'y a en vérité de remède que celui-là et le temps."—*Lettre du Roi de Prusse à D'Alembert, Sept. 7, 1776.*

I.

Is thy face like thy mother's, my fair child!
Ada! sole daughter of my house and heart?
When last I saw thy young blue eyes they smiled,
And then we parted,—not as now we part,
But with a hope.—
Awaking with a start,
The waters heave around me; and on high
The winds lift up their voices: I depart,
Whither I know not; but the hour's gone by,
When Albion's lessening shores could grieve or glad mine eye.

II.

Once more upon the waters! yet once more!
And the waves bound beneath me as a steed
That knows his rider. Welcome to their roar!
Swift be their guidance, whereso'er it lead!
Though the strained mast should quiver as a reed,
And the rent canvas fluttering strew the gale,
Still must I on; for I am as a weed,
Flung from the rock, on Ocean's foam, to sail
Where'er the surge may sweep, the tempest's breath prevail.

III.

In my youth's summer I did sing of One,
The wandering outlaw of his own dark mind;
Again I seize the theme, then but begun,
And bear it with me, as the gushing wind
Bears the cloud onwards: in that Tale I find
The furrows of long thought, and dried-up tears,
Which, ebbing, leave a sterile track behind,
O'er which all heavily the journeying years
Plod the last sands of life,—where not a flower appears.

IV.

Since my young days of passion—joy, or pain,
Perchance my heart and harp have lost a string,
And both may jar: it may be, that in vain
I would essay as I have sung to sing.
Yet, though a dreary strain, to this I cling,
So that it wean me from the weary dream
Of selfish grief or gladness—so it fling
Forgetfulness around me—it shall seem
To me, though to none else, a not ungrateful theme.

V.

He, who grown agèd in this world of woe,
In deeds, not years, piercing the depths of life,
So that no wonder waits him; nor below
Can love, or sorrow, fame, ambition, strife,
Cut to his heart again with the keen knife
Of silent, sharp endurance: he can tell
Why thought seeks refuge in lone caves, yet rife
With airy images, and shapes which dwell
Still unimpair'd, though old, in the soul's haunted cell.

VI.

'T is to create, and in creating live
A being more intense, that we endow
With form our fancy, gaining as we give
The life we image, even as I do now.
What am I? Nothing: but not so art thou,
Soul of my thought! with whom I traverse earth,
Invisible but gazing, as I glow
Mix'd with thy spirit, blended with thy birth,
And feeling still with thee in my crush'd feelings' dearth.

VII.

Yet must I think less wildly:—I *have* thought
Too long and darkly, till my brain became,
In its own eddy boiling and o'erwrought,
A whirling gulf of phantasy and flame:
And thus, untaught in youth my heart to tame,
My springs of life were poison'd. 'T is too late!
Yet am I changed; though still enough the same
In strength to bear what time can not abate,
And feed on bitter fruits without accusing Fate.

VIII.

Something too much of this:—but now 't is past,
And the spell closes with its silent seal.
Long absent Harold re-appears at last;
He of the breast which fain no more would feel,
Wrung with the wounds which kill not, but ne'er heal;
Yet Time, who changes all, had alter'd him
In soul and aspect as in age: years steal
Fire from the mind as vigour from the limb;
And life's enchanted cup but sparkles near the brim.

IX.

His had been quaff'd too quickly, and he found
The dregs were wormwood; but he fill'd again,
And from a purer fount, on holier ground,
And deem'd its spring perpetual; but in vain!
Still round him clung invisibly a chain
Which gall'd for ever, fettering though unseen,
And heavy though it clank'd not; worn with pain,
Which pined although it spoke not, and grew keen,
Entering with every step he took through many a scene.

X.

Secure in guarded coldness, he had mix'd
Again in fancied safety with his kind,
And deem'd his spirit now so firmly fix'd
And sheath'd with an invulnerable mind,
That, if no joy, no sorrow lurk'd behind;
And he, as one, might 'midst the many stand
Unheeded, searching through the crowd to find
Fit speculation; such as in strange land
He found in wonder-works of God and Nature's hand.

XI.

But who can view the ripen'd rose, nor seek
To wear it? who can curiously behold
The smoothness and the sheen of beauty's cheek,
Nor feel the heart can never all grow old?
Who can contemplate Fame, through clouds unfold
The star which rises o'er her steep, nor climb?
Harold, once more within the vortex, roll'd
On with the giddy circle, chasing Time,
Yet with a nobler aim than in his youth's fond prime.

XII.

But soon he knew himself the most unfit
Of men to herd with Man; with whom he held
Little in common; untaught to submit
His thoughts to others, though his soul was quell'd
In youth by his own thoughts; still uncompell'd,
He would not yield dominion of his mind
To spirits against whom his own rebell'd;
Proud though in desolation; which could find
A life within itself, to breathe without mankind.

XIII.

Where rose the mountains, there to him were friends;
Where roll'd the ocean, thereon was his home;
Where a blue sky, and glowing clime, extends,
He had the passion and the power to roam;
The desert, forest, cavern, breaker's foam,
Were unto him companionship; they spake
A mutual language, clearer than the tome
Of his land's tongue, which he would oft forsake
For Nature's pages glass'd by sunbeams on the lake.

XIV.

Like the Chaldean, he could watch the stars,
Till he had peopled them with beings bright
As their own beams; and earth, and earth-born jars,
And human frailties, were forgotten quite:
Could he have kept his spirit to that flight
He had been happy; but this clay will sink
Its spark immortal, envying it the light
To which it mounts, as if to break the link
That keeps us from yon heaven which woos us to its brink.

XV.

But in Man's dwellings he became a thing
Restless and worn, and stern and wearisome,
Droop'd as a wild-born falcon with clipt wing,
To whom the boundless air alone were home:
Then came his fit again, which to o'ercome,
As eagerly the barr'd-up bird will beat
His breast and beak against his wiry dome
Till the blood tinge his plumage, so the heat
Of his impeded soul would through his bosom eat.

XVI.

Self-exiled Harold wanders forth again,
With naught of hope left, but with less of gloom;
The very knowledge that he lived in vain,
That all was over on this side the tomb,
Had made Despair a smilingness assume,
Which, though 't were wild,—as on the plunder'd wreck
When mariners would madly meet their doom
With draughts intemperate on the sinking deck,—
Did yet inspire a cheer, which he forebore to check.

XVII.

Stop!—for thy tread is on an Empire's dust!
An Earthquake's spoil is sepulchred below!
Is the spot mark'd with no colossal bust?
Nor column trophied for triumphal show?
None; but the moral's truth tells simpler so,
As the ground was before, thus let it be;—
How that red rain hath made the harvest grow!
And is this all the world has gain'd by thee,
Thou first and last of fields! king-making Victory?

XVIII.

And Harold stands upon this place of skulls,
The grave of France, the deadly Waterloo!
How in an hour the power which gave annuls
Its gifts, transferring fame as fleeting too!
In "pride of place" here last the eagle flew,[1]
Then tore with bloody talon the rent plain,
Pierced by the shaft of banded nations through;
Ambition's life and labours all were vain;
He wears the shatter'd links of the world's broken chain.

XIX.

Fit retribution! Gaul may champ the bit
And foam in fetters;—but is Earth more free?
Did nations combat to make *One* submit;
Or league to teach all kings true sovereignty?
What! shall reviving Thraldom again be
The patch'd up idol of enlighten'd days?
Shall we, who struck the Lion down, shall we
Pay the Wolf homage? proffering lowly gaze
And servile knees to thrones? No; *prove* before ye praise!

XX.

If not, o'er one fallen despot boast no more!
In vain fair cheeks were furrow'd with hot tears
For Europe's flowers long rooted up before
The trampler of her vineyards; in vain years
Of death, depopulation, bondage, fears,
Have all been borne, and broken by the accord
Of roused-up millions: all that most endears
Glory, is when the myrtle wreathes a sword
Such as Harmodius drew on Athens' tyrant lord.[2]

XXI.

There was a sound of revelry by night,
And Belgium's capital had gather'd then
Her Beauty and her Chivalry, and bright
The lamps shone o'er fair women and brave men;
A thousand hearts beat happily; and when
Music arose with its voluptuous swell,
Soft eyes look'd love to eyes which spake again,
And all went merry as a marriage-bell;[3]
But hush! hark! a deep sound strikes like a rising knell!

XXII.

Did ye not hear it?—No; 't was but the wind,
Or the car rattling o'er the stony street;
On with the dance! let joy be unconfined;
No sleep till morn, when Youth and Pleasure meet
To chase the glowing Hours with flying feet—
But, hark!—that heavy sound breaks in once more,
As if the clouds its echo would repeat;
And nearer, clearer, deadlier than before!
Arm! arm! it is—it is—the cannon's opening roar!

XXIII.

Within a window'd niche of that high hall
Sate Brunswick's fated chieftain; he did hear
That sound the first amidst the festival,
And caught its tone with Death's prophetic ear;
And when they smiled because he deem'd it near,
His heart more truly knew that peal too well
Which stretch'd his father on a bloody bier,
And roused the vengeance blood alone could quell:
He rushed into the field, and, foremost fighting, fell.

XXIV.

Ah! then and there was hurrying to and fro,
And gathering tears, and tremblings of distress,
And cheeks all pale, which but an hour ago
Blush'd at the praise of their own loveliness;
And there were sudden partings, such as press
The life from out young hearts, and choking sighs
Which ne'er might be repeated: who would guess
If ever more should meet those mutual eyes,
Since upon night so sweet such awful morn could rise!

XXV.

And there was mounting in hot haste: the steed,
The mustering squadron, and the clattering car,
Went pouring forward with impetuous speed,
And swiftly forming in the ranks of war;
And the deep thunder peal on peal afar;
And near, the beat of the alarming drum
Roused up the soldier ere the morning star;
While throng'd the citizens with terror dumb,
Or whispering, with white lips—"The foe! They come! they come!"

XXVI.

And wild and high the "Cameron's gathering" rose,
The war-note of Lochiel, which Albyn's hills
Have heard, and heard, too, have her Saxon foes:
How in the noon of night that pibroch thrills
Savage and shrill! But with the breath which fills
Their mountain-pipe, so fill the mountaineers
With the fierce native daring which instils
The stirring memory of a thousand years,
And Evan's, Donald's fame rings in each clansman's ears![4]

XXVII.

And Ardennes waves above them her green leaves,[5]
Dewy with nature's tear-drops, as they pass,
Grieving, if aught inanimate e'er grieves,
Over the unreturning brave,—alas!
Ere evening to be trodden like the grass
Which now beneath them, but above shall grow
In its next verdure, when this fiery mass
Of living valour, rolling on the foe,
And burning with high hope, shall moulder cold and low.

XXVIII.

Last noon beheld them full of lusty life,
Last eve in Beauty's circle proudly gay,
The midnight brought the signal-sound of strife,
The morn the marshalling in arms,—the day
Battle's magnificently-stern array!
The thunder-clouds close o'er it, which when rent
The earth is cover'd thick with other clay,
Which her own clay shall cover, heap'd and pent,
Rider and horse,—friend, foe,—in one red burial blent!

XXIX.

Their praise is hymn'd by loftier harps than mine;
Yet one I would select from that proud throng,
Partly because they blend me with his line,
And partly that I did his sire some wrong,
And partly that bright names will hallow song;
And his was of the bravest, and when shower'd
The death bolts deadliest the thinn'd files along,
Even where the thickest of war's tempest lower'd,
They reach'd no nobler breast than thine, young, gallant Howard!

XXX.

There have been tears and breaking hearts for thee,
And mine were nothing, had I such to give;
But when I stood beneath the fresh green tree,
Which living waves where thou didst cease to live,
And saw around me the wide field revive
With fruits and fertile promise, and the Spring
Come forth her work of gladness to contrive,
With all her reckless birds upon the wing,
I turn'd from all she brought to those she could not bring.[6]

XXXI.

I turn'd to thee, to thousands, of whom each
And one as all a ghastly gap did make
In his own kind and kindred, whom to teach
Forgetfulness were mercy for their sake;
The Archangel's trump, not glory's, must awake
Those whom they thirst for; though the sound of Fame
May for a moment soothe, it cannot slake
The fever of vain longing, and the name
So honour'd, but assumes a stronger, bitterer claim.

XXXII.

They mourn, but smile at length: and, smiling, mourn:
The tree will wither long before it fall;
The hull drives on, though mast and sail be torn;
The roof-tree sinks, but moulders on the hall
In massy hoariness; the ruin'd wall
Stands when its wind-worn battlements are gone;
The bars survive the captive they enthral;
The day drags through though storms keep out the sun;
And thus the heart will break, yet brokenly live on:

XXXIII.

Even as a broken mirror, which the glass
In every fragment multiplies; and makes
A thousand images of one that was,
The same, and still the more, the more it breaks;
And thus the heart will do which not forsakes,
Living in shatter'd guise, and still, and cold,
And bloodless, with its sleepless sorrow aches,
Yet withers on till all without is old,
Showing no visible sign, for such things are untold.

XXXIV.

There is a very life in our despair,
Vitality of poison,—a quick root
Which feeds these deadly branches; for it were
As nothing did we die; but Life will suit
Itself to Sorrow's most detested fruit,
Like to the apples on the Dead Sea's shore,[7]
All ashes to the taste: Did man compute
Existence by enjoyment, and count o'er
Such hours 'gainst years of life,—say, would he name threescore?

XXXV.

The Psalmist number'd out the years of man:
They are enough: and if thy tale be *true*,
Thou, who didst grudge him even that fleeting span,
More than enough, thou fatal Waterloo!
Millions of tongues record thee, and anew
Their children's lips shall echo them, and say—
"Here, where the sword united nations drew,
Our countrymen were warring on that day!"
And this is much, and all which will not pass away.

XXXVI.

There sunk the greatest, nor the worst of men,
Whose spirit antithetically mixt
One moment of the mightiest, and again
On little objects with like firmness fixt,
Extreme in all things! hadst thou been betwixt,
Thy throne had still been thine, or never been;
For daring made thy rise as fall: thou seek'st
Even now to re-assume the imperial mien,
And shake again the world, the Thunderer of the scene!

XXXVII.

Conqueror and captive of the earth art thou!
She trembles at thee still, and thy wild name
Was ne'er more bruited in men's minds than now
That thou art nothing, save the jest of Fame,
Who woo'd thee once, thy vassal, and became
The flatterer of thy fierceness, till thou wert
A god unto thyself; nor less the same
To the astounded kingdoms all inert,
Who deem'd thee for a time whate'er thou didst assert.

XXXVIII.

Oh, more or less than man—in high or low,
Battling with nations, flying from the field;
Now making monarchs' necks thy footstool, now
More than thy meanest soldier taught to yield:
An empire thou couldst crush, command, rebuild,
But govern not thy pettiest passion, nor,
However deeply in men's spirits skill'd,
Look through thine own, nor curb the lust of war,
Nor learn that tempted Fate will leave the loftiest star.

XXXIX.

Yet well thy soul hath brook'd the turning tide
With that untaught innate philosophy,
Which, be it wisdom, coldness, or deep pride,
Is gall and wormwood to an enemy.
When the whole host of hatred stood hard by,
To watch and mock thee shrinking, thou hast smiled
With a sedate and all-enduring eye;—
When Fortune fled her spoil'd and favourite child,
He stood unbow'd beneath the ills upon him piled.

XL.

Sager than in thy fortunes; for in them
Ambition steel'd thee on too far to show
That just habitual scorn, which could contemn
Men and their thoughts; 't was wise to feel, not so
To wear it ever on thy lip and brow,
And spurn the instruments thou wert to use
Till they were turn'd unto thine overthrow;
'T is but a worthless world to win or lose;
So hath it proved to thee, and all such lot who choose.

XLI.

If, like a tower upon a headlong rock,
Thou hadst been made to stand or fall alone,
Such scorn of man had help'd to brave the shock;
But men's thoughts were the steps which paved thy throne,
Their admiration thy best weapon shone;
The part of Philip's son was thine, not then
(Unless aside thy purple had been thrown)
Like stern Diogenes to mock at men;
For sceptred cynics earth were far too wide a den.[8]

XLII.

But quiet to quick bosoms is a hell,
And *there* hath been thy bane; there is a fire
And motion of the soul which will not dwell
In its own narrow being, but aspire
Beyond the fitting medium of desire;
And, but once kindled, quenchless evermore,
Preys upon high adventure, nor can tire
Of aught but rest; a fever at the core,
Fatal to him who bears, to all who ever bore.

XLIII.

This makes the madmen who have made men mad
By their contagion! Conquerors and Kings,
Founders of sects and systems, to whom add
Sophists, Bards, Statesmen, all unquiet things
Which stir too strongly the soul's secret springs,
And are themselves the fools to those they fool;
Envied, yet how unenviable! what stings
Are theirs! One breast laid open were a school
Which would unteach mankind the lust to shine or rule:

XLIV.

Their breath is agitation, and their life
A storm whereon they ride, to sink at last,
And yet so nursed and bigoted to strife,
That should their days, surviving perils past,
Melt to calm twilight, they feel overcast
With sorrow and supineness, and so die;
Even as a flame unfed, which runs to waste
With its own flickering, or a sword laid by,
Which eats into itself, and rusts ingloriously.

XLV.

He who ascends to mountain-tops, shall find
The loftiest peaks most wrapt in clouds and snow;
He who surpasses or subdues mankind,
Must look down on the hate of those below.
Though high *above* the sun of glory glow,
And far *beneath* the earth and ocean spread,
Round him are icy rocks, and loudly blow
Contending tempests on his naked head,
And thus reward the toils which to those summits led.

XLVI.

Away with these! true Wisdom's world will be
Within its own creation, or in thine,
Maternal Nature! for who teems like thee,
Thus on the banks of thy majestic Rhine?
There Harold gazes on a work divine,
A blending of all beauties; streams and dells,
Fruit, foliage, crag, wood, cornfield, mountain, vine,
And chiefless castles breathing stern farewells
From gray but leafy walls, where Ruin greenly dwells.

XLVII.

And there they stand, as stands a lofty mind,
Worn, but unstooping to the baser crowd,
All tenantless, save to the crannying wind,
Or holding dark communion with the cloud.
There was a day when they were young and proud,
Banners on high, and battles pass'd below;
But they who fought are in a bloody shroud,
And those which waved are shredless dust ere now,
And the bleak battlements shall bear no future blow.

XLVIII.

Beneath these battlements, within those walls,
Power dwelt amidst her passions; in proud state
Each robber chief upheld his armed halls,
Doing his evil will, nor less elate
Than mightier heroes of a longer date.
What want these outlaws conquerors should have?[9]
But History's purchased page to call them great?
A wider space, an ornamented grave?
Their hopes were not less warm their souls were full as brave.

XLIX.

In their baronial feuds and single fields,
What deeds of prowess unrecorded died!
And Love, which lent a blazon to their shields,
With emblems well devised by amorous pride,
Through all the mail of iron hearts would glide;
But still their flame was fierceness, and drew on
Keen contest and destruction near allied,
And many a tower for some fair mischief won,
Saw the discolour'd Rhine beneath its ruin run.

L.

But Thou, exulting and abounding river!
Making thy waves a blessing as they flow
Through banks whose beauty would endure for ever
Could man but leave thy bright creation so,
Nor its fair promise from the surface mow
With the sharp scythe of conflict,—then to see
Thy valley of sweet waters, were to know
Earth paved like Heaven; and to seem such to me
Even now what wants thy stream?—that it should Lethe be.

LI.

A thousand battles have assail'd thy banks,
But these and half their fame have pass'd away,
And Slaughter heap'd on high his weltering ranks:
Their very graves are gone, and what are they?
Thy tide wash'd down the blood of yesterday,
And all was stainless, and on thy clear stream
Glass'd with its dancing light the sunny ray;
But o'er the blacken'd memory's blighting dream
Thy waves would vainly roll, all sweeping as they seem.

LII.

Thus Harold inly said, and pass'd along,
Yet not insensibly to all which here
Awoke the jocund birds to early song
In glens which might have made even exile dear:
Though on his brow were graven lines austere,
And tranquil sternness which had ta'en the place
Of feelings fierier far but less severe,
Joy was not always absent from his face,
But o'er it in such scenes would steal with transient trace.

LIII.

Nor was all love shut from him, though his days
Of passion had consumed themselves to dust.
It is in vain that we would coldly gaze
On such as smile upon us; the heart must
Leap kindly back to kindness, though disgust
Hath wean'd it from all worldlings: thus he felt,
For there was soft remembrance, and sweet trust
In one fond breast, to which his own would melt,
And in its tenderer hour on that his bosom dwelt.

LIV.

And he had learn'd to love,—I know not why,
For this in such as him seems strange of mood,—
The helpless looks of blooming infancy,
Even in its earliest nurture; what subdued,
To change like this, a mind so far imbued
With scorn of man, it little boots to know;
But thus it was; and though in solitude
Small power the nipp'd affections have to grow,
In him this glow'd when all beside had ceased to glow.

LV.

And there was one soft breast, as hath been said,
Which unto his was bound by stronger ties
Than the church links withal: and, though unwed,
That love was pure, and far above disguise,
Had stood the test of mortal enmities
Still undivided, and cemented more
By peril, dreaded most in female eyes;
But this was firm, and from a foreign shore
Well to that heart might his these absent greetings pour!

1.

The castled crag of Drachenfels[10]
Frowns o'er the wide and winding Rhine,

Whose breast of waters broadly swells
Between the banks which bear the vine,
And hills all rich with blossom'd trees,
And fields which promise corn and wine,
And scatter'd cities crowning these,
Whose far white walls along them shine,
Have strew'd a scene, which I should see
With double joy wert *thou* with me.

2.

And peasant girls, with deep blue eyes,
And hands which offer early flowers,
Walk smiling o'er this paradise;
Above, the frequent feudal towers
Through green leaves lift their walls of gray,
And many a rock which steeply lowers,
And noble arch in proud decay,
Look o'er this vale of vintage-bowers;
But one thing want these banks of Rhine,—
Thy gentle hand to clasp in mine!

3.

I send the lilies given to me;
Though long before thy hand they touch,
I know that they must wither'd be,
But yet reject them not as such;
For I have cherish'd them as dear,
Because they yet may meet thine eye,
And guide thy soul to mine even here,
When thou behold'st them drooping nigh,
And know'st them gather'd by the Rhine,
And offer'd from my heart to thine!

4.

The river nobly foams and flows,
The charm of this enchanted ground,
And all its thousand turns disclose
Some fresher beauty varying round:
The haughtiest breast its wish might bound
Through life to dwell delighted here;
Nor could on earth a spot be found
To nature and to me so dear,
Could thy dear eyes in following mine
Still sweeten more these banks of Rhine!

LVI.

By Coblentz, on a rise of gentle ground,
There is a small and simple pyramid,
Crowning the summit of the verdant mound;
Beneath its base are heroes' ashes hid,
Our enemy's—but let not that forbid
Honour to Marceau! o'er whose early tomb
Tears, big tears, gush'd from the rough soldier's lid,
Lamenting and yet envying such a doom,
Falling for France, whose rights he battled to resume.

LVII.

Brief, brave, and glorious was his young career,—
His mourners were two hosts, his friends and foes,
And fitly may the stranger lingering here
Pray for his gallant spirit's bright repose;
For he was Freedom's champion, one of those,
The few in number, who had not o'erstept
The charter to chastise which she bestows
On such as wield her weapons; he had kept
The whiteness of his soul, and thus men o'er him wept.[11]

LVIII.

Here Ehrenbreitstein, with her shatter'd wall[12]
Black with the miner's blast, upon her height
Yet shows of what she was, when shell and ball
Rebounding idly on her strength did light:
A tower of victory, from whence the flight
Of baffled foes was watch'd along the plain:
But Peace destroy'd what War could never blight,
And laid those proud roofs bare to Summer's rain—
On which the iron shower for years had pour'd in vain

LIX.

Adieu to thee, fair Rhine! How long delighted
The stranger fain would linger on his way!
Thine is a scene alike where souls united
Or lonely Contemplation thus might stray;
And could the ceaseless vultures cease to prey
On self-condemning bosoms, it were here,
Where Nature, nor too sombre nor too gay,
Wild but not rude, awful yet not austere,
Is to the mellow Earth as Autumn to the year.

LX.

Adieu to thee again! a vain adieu!
There can be no farewell to scene like thine,
The mind is colour'd by thy every hue;
And if reluctantly the eyes resign
Their cherish'd gaze upon thee, lovely Rhine!
'Tis with the thankful glance of parting praise;
More mighty spots may rise—more glaring shine,
But none unite in one attaching maze
The brilliant, fair, and soft,—the glories of old days,

LXI.

The negligently grand, the fruitful bloom
Of coming ripeness, the white city's sheen,
The rolling stream, the precipice's gloom,
The forest's growth, and Gothic walls between,
The wild rocks shaped as they had turrets been
In mockery of man's art; and these withal
A race of faces happy as the scene,
Whose fertile bounties here extend to all,
Still springing o'er thy banks, though Empires near them fall.

LXII.

But these recede. Above me are the Alps,
The palaces of Nature, whose vast walls
Have pinnacled in clouds their snowy scalps,
And throned Eternity in icy halls
Of cold sublimity, where forms and falls
The avalanche—the thunderbolt of snow!
All that expands the spirit, yet appals,
Gather around these summits, as to show
How Earth may pierce to Heaven, yet leave vain man below.

LXIII.

But ere these matchless heights I dare to scan,
There is a spot should not be pass'd in vain,—
Morat! the proud, the patriot field! where man
May gaze on ghastly trophies of the slain,
Nor blush for those who conquer'd on that plain;
Here Burgundy bequeath'd his tombless host,
A bony heap, through ages to remain,
Themselves their monument; the Stygian coast
Unsepulchred they roam'd, and shriek'd each wandering ghost.[13]

LXIV.

While Waterloo with Cannæ's carnage vies,
Morat and Marathon twin names shall stand
They were true Glory's stainless victories,
Won by the unambitious heart and hand
Of a proud, brotherly, and civic band,
All unbought champions in no princely cause
Of vice-entail'd Corruption; they no land
Doom'd to bewail the blasphemy of laws
Making kings' rights divine, by some Draconic clause.

LXV.

By a lone wall a lonelier column rears
A gray and grief-worn aspect of old days;
'Tis the last remnant of the wreck of years,
And looks as with the wild bewilder'd gaze
Of one to stone converted by amaze,
Yet still with consciousness; and there it stands
Making a marvel that it not decays,
When the cöeval pride of human hands,
Levell'd Aventicum, hath strew'd her subject lands.[14]

LXVI.

And there—oh! sweet and sacred be the name!—
Julia—the daughter, the devoted—gave
Her youth to Heaven; her heart, beneath a claim
Nearest to Heaven's, broke o'er a father's grave.
Justice is sworn 'gainst tears, and hers would crave
The life she lived in; but the judge was just,
And then she died on him she could not save.
Their tomb was simple, and without a bust,
And held within their urn one mind, one heart, one dust. [15]

LXVII.

But these are deeds, which should not pass away,
And names that must not wither, though the earth
Forgets her empires with a just decay,
The enslavers and the enslaved, their death and birth;
The high, the mountain-majesty of worth,
Should be, and shall, survivor of its woe,
And from its immortality look forth
In the sun's face, like yonder Alpine snow, [16]
Imperishably pure beyond all things below.

LXVIII.

Lake Leman woos me with its crystal face, [17]
The mirror where the stars and mountains view
The stillness of their aspect in each trace
Its clear depth yields of their far height and hue:
There is too much of man here, to look through
With a fit mind the might which I behold;
But soon in me shall Loneliness renew
Thoughts hid, but not less cherish'd than of old,
Ere mingling with the herd had penn'd me in their fold.

LXIX.

To fly from, need not be to hate, mankind:
All are not fit with them to stir and toil,
Nor is it discontent to keep the mind
Deep in its fountain, lest it overboil
In one hot throng, where we become the spoil
Of our infection, till too late and long
We may deplore and struggle with the coil,
In wretched interchange of wrong for wrong
'Midst a contentious world, striving where none are strong

LXX.

There, in a moment, we may plunge our years
In fatal penitence, and in the blight
Of our own soul, turn all our blood to tears,
And colour things to come with hues of Night;
The race of life becomes a hopeless flight
To those that walk in darkness: on the sea,
The boldest steer but where their ports invite,
But there are wanderers o'er Eternity
Whose bark drives on and on, and anchor'd ne'er shall be.

LXXI.

Is it not better, then, to be alone,
And love Earth only for its earthly sake?
By the blue rushing of the arrowy Rhone, [18]
Or the pure bosom of its nursing lake,
Which feeds it as a mother who doth make
A fair but froward infant her own care,
Kissing its cries away as these awake!—
Is it not better thus our lives to wear,
Than join the crushing crowd, doom'd to inflict or bear?

LXXII.

I live not in myself, but I become
Portion of that around me; and to me
High mountains are a feeling, but the hum
Of human cities torture: I can see
Nothing to loathe in nature, save to be
A link reluctant in a fleshly chain,
Class'd among creatures, when the soul can flee,
And with the sky, the peak, the heaving plain
Of ocean, or the stars, mingle, and not in vain.

LXXIII.

And thus I am absorb'd, and this is life:
I look upon the peopled desert past,
As on a place of agony and strife,
Where, for some sin, to Sorrow I was cast,
To act and suffer, but remount at last
With a fresh pinion; which I feel to spring,
Though young, yet waxing vigorous, as the blast
Which it would cope with, on delighted wing,
Spurning the clay-cold bonds which round our being cling.

LXXIV.

And when, at length, the mind shall be all free
From what it hates in this degraded form,
Reft of its carnal life, save what shall be
Existent happier in the fly and worm,—
When elements to elements conform,
And dust is as it should be, shall I not
Feel all I see, less dazzling, but more warm?
The bodiless thought? the Spirit of each spot?
Of which, even now, I share at times the immortal lot?

LXXV.

Are not the mountains, waves, and skies, a part
Of me and of my soul, as I of them?
Is not the love of these deep in my heart
With a pure passion? should I not contemn
All objects, if compared with these? and stem
A tide of suffering, rather than forego
Such feelings for the hard and worldly phlegm
Of those whose eyes are only turn'd below,
Gazing upon the ground, with thoughts which dare not glow?

LXXVI.

But this is not my theme ; and I return
To that which is immediate, and require
Those who find contemplation in the urn,
To look on One, whose dust was once all fire,
A native of the land where I respire
The clear air for a while—a passing guest,
Where he became a being,—whose desire
Was to be glorious ; 't was a foolish quest,
The which to gain and keep, he sacrificed all rest.

LXXVII.

Here the self-torturing sophist, wild Rousseau,
The apostle of affliction, he who threw
Enchantment over passion, and from woe
Wrung overwhelming eloquence, first drew
The breath which made him wretched; yet he knew
How to make madness beautiful, and cast
O'er erring deeds and thoughts a heavenly hue
Of words, like sunbeams, dazzling as they past
The eyes, which o'er them shed tears feelingly and fast.

LXXVIII.

His love was passion's essence—as a tree
On fire by lightning ; with ethereal flame
Kindled he was, and blasted ; for to be
Thus, and enamour'd, were in him the same.
But his was not the love of living dame,
Nor of the dead who rise upon our dreams,
But of ideal beauty, which became
In him existence, and o'erflowing teems
Along his burning page, distemper'd though it seems.

LXXIX.

This breathed itself to life in Julie, *this*
Invested her with all that's wild and sweet;
This hallow'd, too, the memorable kiss [19]
Which every morn his fever'd lip would greet,
From hers, who but with friendship his would meet;
But to that gentle touch, through brain and breast
Flash'd the thrill'd spirit's love-devouring heat :
In that absorbing sigh perchance more blest
Than vulgar minds may be with all they seek possest.

LXXX.

His life was one long war with self-sought foes,
Or friends by him self-banish'd; for his mind
Had grown Suspicion's sanctuary, and chose
For its own cruel sacrifice the kind,
'Gainst whom he raged with fury strange and blind,
But he was phrensied,—wherefore, who may know?
Since cause might be which skill could never find;
But he was phrensied by disease or woe
To that worst pitch of all, which wears a reasoning show.

LXXXI.

For then he was inspired, and from him came
As from the Pythian's mystic cave of yore,
Those oracles which set the world in flame,
Nor ceased to burn till kingdoms were no more:
Did he not this for France? which lay before
Bow'd to the inborn tyranny of years?
Broken and trembling to the yoke she bore,
Till by the voice of him and his compeers,
Roused up to too much wrath, which follows o'ergrown fears?

LXXXII.

They made themselves a fearful monument!
The wreck of old opinions—things which grew,
Breathed from the birth of time : the veil they rent,
And what behind it lay, all earth shall view.
But good with ill they also overthrew,
Leaving but ruins, wherewith to rebuild
Upon the same foundation, and renew
Dungeons and thrones, which the same hour refill'd,
As heretofore, because ambition was self-will'd.

LXXXIII.

But this will not endure, nor be endured!
Mankind have felt their strength, and made it felt.
They might have used it better, but, allured
By their new vigour, sternly have they dealt
On one another ; pity, ceased to melt
With her once natural charities. But they,
Who in oppression's darkness caved had dwelt,
They were not eagles, nourish'd with the day ;
What marvel then, at times, if they mistook their prey?

LXXXIV.

What deep wounds ever closed without a scar?
The heart's bleed longest, and but heal to wear
That which disfigures it; and they who war
With their own hopes, and have been vanquish'd, bear
Silence, but not submission : in his lair
Fix'd Passion holds his breath, until the hour
Which shall atone for years ; none need despair:
It came, it cometh, and will come,—the power
To punish or forgive—in *one* we shall be slower.

LXXXV.

Clear, placid Leman ! thy contrasted lake,
With the wild world I dwelt in, is a thing
Which warns me, with its stillness, to forsake
Earth's troubled waters for a purer spring.
This quiet sail is as a noiseless wing
To waft me from distraction ; once I loved
Torn ocean's roar, but thy soft murmuring
Sounds sweet as if a Sister's voice reproved,
That I with stern delights should e'er have been so moved.

LXXXVI.

It is the hush of night, and all between
Thy margin and the mountains, dusk, yet clear,
Mellow'd and mingling, yet distinctly seen,
Save darken'd Jura, whose capt heights appear
Precipitously steep; and drawing near,
There breathes a living fragrance from the shore,
Of flowers yet fresh with childhood; on the ear
Drops the light drip of the suspended oar,
Or chirps the grasshopper one good-night carol more;

LXXXVII.

He is an evening reveller, who makes
His life an infancy, and sings his fill ;
At intervals, some bird from out the brakes
Starts into voice a moment, then is still.
There seems a floating whisper on the hill;
But that is fancy, for the starlight dews
All silently their tears of love instil,
Weeping themselves away, till they infuse
Deep into nature's breast the spirit of her hues.

LXXXVIII.

Ye stars! which are the poetry of heaven,
If in your bright leaves we would read the fate
Of men and empires,—'tis to be forgiven,
That in our aspirations to be great,
Our destinies o'erleap their mortal state,
And claim a kindred with you ; for ye are
A beauty, and a mystery, and create
In us such love and reverence from afar,
That fortune, fame, power, life, have named themselves a star.

LXXXIX.

All heaven and earth are still—though not in sleep,
But breathless, as we grow when feeling most;
And silent, as we stand in thoughts too deep:—
All heaven and earth are still: From the high host
Of stars, to the lull'd lake and mountain-coast,
All is concenter'd in a life intense,
Where not a beam, nor air, nor leaf is lost,
But hath a part of being, and a sense
Of that which is of all Creator and defence.

XC.

Then stirs the feeling infinite, so felt
In solitude, where we are *least* alone;
A truth, which through our being then doth melt,
And purifies from self: it is a tone,
The soul and source of music, which makes known
Eternal harmony, and sheds a charm,
Like to the fabled Cytherea's zone,
Binding all things with beauty;—'t would disarm
The spectre Death, had he substantial power to harm.

XCI.

Not vainly did the early Persian make
His altar the high places and the peak
Of earth-o'ergazing mountains,[20] and thus take
A fit and unwall'd temple, there to seek
The Spirit, in whose honour shrines are weak,
Uprear'd of human hands. Come, and compare
Columns and idol-dwellings, Goth or Greek,
With Nature's realms of worship, earth and air,
Nor fix on fond abodes to circumscribe thy pray'r!

XCII.

The sky is changed?—and such a change! Oh night,
And storm, and darkness, ye are wondrous strong,
Yet lovely in your strength, as is the light
Of a dark eye in woman! Far along,
From peak to peak, the rattling crags among
Leaps the live thunder! Not from one lone cloud,
But every mountain now hath found a tongue,
And Jura answers, through her misty shroud,
Back to the joyous Alps, who call to her aloud!

XCIII.

And this is in the night:—Most glorious night!
Thou wert not sent for slumber! let me be
A sharer in thy fierce and far delight,—[21]
A portion of the tempest and of thee!
How the lit lake shines, a phosphoric sea,
And the big rain comes dancing to the earth!
And now again 't is black,—and now, the glee
Of the loud hills shakes with its mountain-mirth,
As if they did rejoice o'er a young earthquake's birth.

XCIV.

Now, where the swift Rhone cleaves his way between
Heights which appear as lovers who have parted
In hate, whose mining depths so intervene,
That they can meet no more, though broken-hearted;
Though in their souls, which thus each other thwarted,
Love was the very root of the fond rage
Which blighted their life's bloom, and then departed:—
Itself expired, but leaving them an age
Of years all winters,—war within themselves to wage.

XCV.

Now, where the quick Rhone thus hath cleft his way,
The mightiest of the storms hath ta'en his stand:
For here, not one, but many, make their play,
And fling their thunder-bolts from hand to hand,
Flashing and cast around: of all the band,
The brightest through these parted hills hath fork'd
His lightnings,—as if he did understand,
That in such gaps as desolation work'd,
There the hot shaft should blast whatever therein lurk'd.

XCVI.

Sky, mountains, river, winds, lake, lightnings! ye!
With night, and clouds, and thunder, and a soul
To make these felt and feeling, well may be
Things that have made me watchful; the far roll
Of your departing voices, is the knoll
Of what in me is sleepless,—if I rest.
But where of ye, oh tempests! is the goal?
Are ye like those within the human breast?
Or do ye find, at length, like eagles, some high nest?

XCVII.

Could I embody and unbosom now
That which is most within me,—could I wreak
My thoughts upon expression, and thus throw
Soul, heart, mind, passions, feelings, strong or weak,
All that I would have sought, and all I seek,
Bear, know, feel, and yet breathe — into *one* word,
And that one word were Lightning, I would speak;
But as it is, I live and die unheard,
With a most voiceless thought, sheathing it as a sword.

XCVIII.

The morn is up again, the dewy morn,
With breath all incense, and with cheek all bloom,
Laughing the clouds away with playful scorn,
And living as if earth contain'd no tomb,—
And glowing into day: we may resume
The march of our existence: and thus I,
Still on thy shores, fair Leman! may find room
And food for meditation, nor pass by
Much, that may give us pause, if ponder'd fittingly.

XCIX.

Clarens! sweet Clarens! birthplace of deep Love!
Thine air is the young breath of passionate thought;
Thy trees take root in Love; the snows above
The very Glaciers have his colours caught,
And sun-set into rose-hues sees them wrought
By rays which sleep there lovingly: the rocks,
The permanent crags, tell here of Love, who sought
In them a refuge from the worldly shocks,
Which stir and sting the soul with hope that woos, then mocks.

C.

Clarens! by heavenly feet thy paths are trod,—
Undying Love's who here ascends a throne
To which the steps are mountains; where the god
Is a pervading life and light,—so shown
Not on those summits solely, nor alone
In the still cave and forest; o'er the flower
His eye is sparkling, and his breath hath blown
His soft and summer breath, whose tender power
Passes the strength of storms in their most desolate hour.

CI.

All things are here of *him;* from the black pines,
Which are his shade on high, and the loud roar
Of torrents, where he listeneth, to the vines
Which slope his green path downward to the shore,
Where the bow'd waters meet him, and adore,
Kissing his feet with murmurs; and the wood,
The covert of old trees, with trunks all hoar,
But light leaves, young as joy, stands where it stood,
Offering to him, and his, a populous solitude.

CII.

A populous solitude of bees and birds,
And fairy-form'd and many-colour'd things,
Who worship him with notes more sweet than words,
And innocently open their glad wings
Fearless and full of life: the gush of springs,
And fall of lofty fountains, and the bend
Of stirring branches, and the bud which rings,
The swiftest thought of beauty, here extend,
Mingling, and made by Love, unto one mighty end.

CIII.

He who hath loved not, here would learn that lore,
And make his heart a spirit; he who knows
That tender mystery, will love the more,
For this is Love's recess, where vain men's woes,
And the world's waste, have driven him far from those,
For 't is his nature to advance or die:
He stands not still, but or decays, or grows
Into a boundless blessing, which may vie
With the immortal lights, in its eternity!

CIV.

'T was not for fiction chose Rousseau this spot,
Peopling it with affections; but he found
It was the scene which passion must allot
To the mind's purified beings; 't was the ground
Where early Love his Psyche's zone unbound,
And hallow'd it with loveliness: 't is lone,
And wonderful, and deep, and hath a sound,
And sense, and sight of sweetness; here the Rhone
Hath spread himself a couch, the Alps have rear'd a throne.

CV.

Lausanne! and Ferney! ye have been the abodes
Of names which unto you bequeath'd a name;[22]
Mortals, who sought and found, by dangerous roads,
A path to perpetuity of fame:
They were gigantic minds, and their steep aim
Was, Titan-like, on daring doubts to pile
Thoughts which should call down thunder, and the flame
Of Heaven, again assail'd, if Heaven the while
On man and man's research could deign do more than smile.

CVI.

The one was fire and fickleness, a child,
Most mutable in wishes, but in mind
A wit as various,—gay—grave—sage—or wild—
Historian, bard, philosopher, combined;
He multiplied himself among mankind,
The Proteus of their talents: But his own
Breathed most in ridicule,—which, as the wind
Blew where it listed, laying all things prone,—
Now to o'erthrow a fool, and now to shake a throne.

CVII.

The other, deep and slow, exhausting thought,
And hiving wisdom with each studious year,
In meditation dwelt, with learning wrought,
And shaped his weapon with an edge severe,
Sapping a solemn creed with solemn sneer;
The lord of irony,—that master-spell,
Which stung his foes to wrath, which grew from fear,
And doom'd him to the zealot's ready Hell,
Which answers to all doubts so eloquently well.

CVIII.

Yet, peace be with their ashes,—for by them,
If merited, the penalty is paid;
It is not ours to judge,—far less condemn;
The hour must come when such things shall be made
Known unto all,—or hope and dread allay'd
By slumber, on one pillow,—in the dust,
Which, thus much we are sure, must lie decay'd;
And, when it shall revive, as is our trust,
T will be to be forgiven, or suffer what is just.

CIX.

But let me quit man's works, again to read
His Maker's, spread around me, and suspend
This page, which from my reveries I feed,
Until it seems prolonging without end.
The clouds above me to the white Alps tend,
And I must pierce them, and survey whate'er
May be permitted, as my steps I bend
To their most great and growing region, where
The earth to her embrace compels the powers of air.

CX.

Italia! too, Italia! looking on thee
Full flashes on the soul the light of ages,
Since the fierce Carthaginian almost won thee,
To the last halo of the chiefs and sages,
Who glorify thy consecrated pages;
Thou wert the throne and grave of empires; still,
The fount at which the panting mind assuages
Her thirst of knowledge, quaffing there her fill,
Flows from the eternal source of Rome's imperial hill.

CXI.

Thus far have I proceeded in a theme
Renew'd with no kind auspices:—to feel
We are not what we have been, and to deem
We are not what we should be,—and to steel
The heart against itself; and to conceal,
With a proud caution, love, or hate, or aught,—
Passion or feeling, purpose, grief, or zeal,—
Which is the tyrant spirit of our thought,
Is a stern task of soul:—No matter,—it is taught.

CXII.

And for these words, thus woven into song,
It may be that they are a harmless wile,—
The colouring of the scenes which fleet along,
Which I would seize, in passing, to beguile
My breast, or that of others, for a while.
Fame is the thirst of youth,—but I am not
So young as to regard men's frown or smile,
As loss or guerdon of a glorious lot;
I stood and stand alone,—remember'd or forgot.

CXIII.

I have not loved the world, nor the world me;
I have not flatter'd its rank breath, nor bow'd
To its idolatries a patient knee,—
Nor coin'd my cheek to smiles,—nor cried aloud
In worship of an echo; in the crowd
They could not deem me one of such; I stood
Among them, but not of them; in a shroud
Of thoughts which were not their thoughts, and still could,
Had I not filed my mind, which thus itself subdued.[24]

CXIV.

I have not loved the world, nor the world me,—
But let us part fair foes; I do believe,
Though I have found them not, that there may be
Words which are things,—hopes which will not deceive,
And virtues which are merciful, nor weave
Snares for the failing: I would also deem
O'er other's griefs that some sincerely grieve;
That two, or one, are almost what they seem,—
That goodness is no name, and happiness no dream.

CXV.

My daughter! with thy name this song begun—
My daughter! with thy name thus much shall end—
I see thee not,—I hear thee not,—but none
Can be so wrapt in thee; thou art the friend
To whom the shadows of far years extend:
Albeit my brow thou never shouldst behold,
My voice shall with thy future visions blend,
And reach into thy heart,—when mine is cold,—
A token and a tone, even from thy father's mould.

CXVI.

To aid thy mind's developement,—to watch
Thy dawn of little joys,—to sit and see
Almost thy very growth,—to view thee catch
Knowledge of objects,—wonders yet to thee!
To hold thee lightly on a gentle knee,
And print on thy soft cheek a parent's kiss,—
This, it should seem, was not reserved for me;
Yet this was in my nature:—as it is,
I know not what is there, yet something like to this.

CXVII.

Yet, though dull Hate as duty should be taught,
I know that thou wilt love me; though my name
Should be shut from thee, as a spell still fraught
With desolation,—and a broken claim:
Though the grave closed between us,—'t were the same,
I know that thou wilt love me; though to drain
My blood from out thy being were an aim,
And an attainment,—all would be in vain,—
Still thou would'st love me, still that more than life retain.

CXVIII.

The child of love,—though born in bitterness,
And nurtured in convulsion. Of thy sire
These were the elements,—and thine no less.
As yet such are around thee,—but thy fire
Shall be more temper'd, and thy hope far higher.
Sweet be thy cradled slumbers! O'er the sea,
And from the mountains where I now respire,
Fain would I waft such blessing upon thee,
As, with a sigh, I deem thou might'st have been to me!

NOTES TO CANTO THE THIRD.

NOTE 1, page 615.

In "pride of place" here last the eagle flew.

"In pride of place" is a term of falconry, and means the highest pitch of flight. See Macbeth, &c.

"An eagle towering in his pride of place," &c.

NOTE 2, page 615.

Such as Harmodius drew on Athens' tyrant lord.

See the famous song on Harmodius and Aristogiton. The best English translation is in "Bland's Anthology," by Mr. (now Lord Chief Justice) Denman,—

"With myrtle my sword will I wreathe," &c.

NOTE 3, page 615.

And all went merry as a marriage-bell.

On the night previous to the action, it is said that a ball was given at Brussels.

NOTE 4, page 615.

And Evan's, Donald's, fame rings in each clansman's ears.

Sir Evan Cameron, and his descendant Donald, the "gentle Lochiel" of the "forty-five."

NOTE 5, page 615.

And Ardennes waves above them her green leaves.

The wood of Soignies is supposed to be a remnant of the forest of Ardennes, famous in Boiardo's "Orlando," and immortal in Shakespeare's "As you like it." It is also celebrated in Tacitus, as being the spot of successful defence by the Germans against the Roman encroachments. I have ventured to adopt the name connected with nobler associations than those of mere slaughter.

NOTE 6, page 617.

I turn'd from all she brought to those she could not bring.

My guide from Mont St. Jean over the field seemed intelligent and accurate. The place where Major Howard fell was not far from two tall and solitary trees (there was a third, cut down, or shivered in the battle), which stand a few yards from each other at a pathway's side. Beneath these he died and was buried. The body has since been removed to England. A small hollow for the present marks where it lay, but will probably soon be effaced; the plough has been upon it, and the grain is. After pointing out the different spots where Picton and other gallant men had perished, the guide said, "Here Major Howard lay: I was near him when wounded." I told him my relationship, and he seemed then still more anxious to point out the particular spot and circumstances. The place is one of the most marked in the field, from the peculiarity of the two trees above mentioned. I went on horseback twice over the field, comparing it with my recollection of similar scenes. As a plain, Waterloo seems marked out for the scene of some great action, though this may be mere imagination: I have viewed with attention those of Platea, Troy, Mantinea, Leuctra, Chæronea, and Marathon; and the field around Mont St. Jean and Hougoumont appears to want little but a better cause, and that undefinable but impressive halo which the lapse of ages throws around a celebrated spot, to vie in interest with any or all of these, except, perhaps, the last mentioned.

NOTE 7, page 617.

Like to the apples on the Dead Sea's shore.

The (fabled) apples on the brink of the lake Asphaltes were said to be fair without, and, within, ashes. *Vide* Tacitus, Histor. lib. v. 7.

Note 8, page 618.

For sceptred cynics earth were far too wide a den.

The great error of Napoleon, "if we have writ our annals true," was a continued obtrusion on mankind of his want of all community of feeling for or with them; perhaps more offensive to human vanity than the active cruelty of more trembling and suspicious tyranny. Such were his speeches to public assemblies as well as individuals; and the single expression which he is said to have used on returning to Paris after the Russian winter had destroyed his army, rubbing his hands over a fire, "This is pleasanter than Moscow," would probably alienate more favour from his cause than the destruction and reverses which led to the remark.

Note 9, page 618.

What want these outlaws conquerors should have?

"What wants that knave that a king should have?" was King James's question on meeting Johnny Armstrong and his followers in full accoutrements.—See the ballad.

Note 10, page 620.

The castled crag of Drachenfels.

The castle of Drachenfels stands on the highest summit of "The Seven Mountains," over the Rhine banks; it is in ruins, and connected with some singular traditions: it is the first in view on the road from Bonn, but on the opposite side of the river; on this bank, nearly facing it, are the remains of another, called the Jew's Castle, and a large cross commemorative of the murder of a chief by his brother. The number of castles and cities along the course of the Rhine on both sides is very great, and their situations remarkably beautiful.

Note 11, page 621.

The whiteness of his soul, and thus men o'er him wept.

The monument of the young and lamented General Marceau (killed by a rifle-ball at Alterkirchen, on the last day of the fourth year of the French republic) still remains as described. The inscriptions on his monument are rather too long, and not required: his name was enough; France adored, and her enemies admired; both wept over him. His funeral was attended by the generals and detachments from both armies. In the same grave General Hoche is interred, a gallant man also in every sense of the word; but though he distinguished himself greatly in battle, *he* had not the good fortune to die there: his death was attended by suspicions of poison. A separate monument (not over his body, which is buried by Marceau's) is raised for him near Andernach, opposite to which one of his most memorable exploits was performed, in throwing a bridge to an island on the Rhine. The shape and style are different from that of Marceau, and the inscription more simple and pleasing:—"The Army of the Sambre and Meuse to its Commander-in-Chief, Hoche." This is all, and as it should be. Hoche was esteemed among the first of France's earlier generals, before Buonaparte monopolised her triumphs. He was the destined commander of the invading army of Ireland.

Note 12, page 621.

Here Ehrenbreitstein, with her shattered wall.

Ehrenbreitstein, *i.e.* "the broad stone of honour," one of the strongest fortresses in Europe, was dismantled and blown up by the French at the truce of Leoben. It had been, and could only be, reduced by famine or treachery. It yielded to the former, aided by surprise. After having seen the fortifications of Gibraltar and Malta, it did not much strike by comparison; but the situation is commanding. General Marceau besieged it in vain for some time, and I slept in a room where I was shown a window at which he is said to have been standing observing the progress of the siege by moonlight, when a ball struck immediately below it.

Note 13, page 622.

Unsepulchred they roam'd, and shriek'd each wandering ghost.

The chapel is destroyed, and the pyramid of bones diminished to a small number by the Burgundian legion in the service of France; who anxiously effaced this record of their ancestors' less successful invasions. A few still remain, notwithstanding the pains taken by the Burgundians for ages (all who passed that way removing a bone to their own country), and the less justifiable larcenies of the Swiss postilions, who carried them off to sell for knife-handles; a purpose for which the whiteness imbibed by the bleaching of years had rendered them in great request.

Of these relics I ventured to bring away as much as may have made a quarter of a hero, for which the sole excuse is, that if I had not, the next passer by might have perverted them to worse uses than the careful preservation which I intend for them.

Note 14, page 622.

Levell'd Aventicum, hath strew'd her subject lands.

Aventicum, near Morat, was the Roman capital of Helvetia, where Avenches now stands.

Note 15, page 623.

And held within their urn one mind, one heart, one dust.

Julia Alpinula, a young Aventian priestess, died soon after a vain endeavour to save her father, condemned to death as a traitor by Aulus Cæcina. Her epitaph was discovered many years ago;—it is thus:—"Julia Alpinula: Hic jaceo. Infelicis patris infelix proles. Deæ Aventiæ Sacerdos. Exorare patris necem non potui: Male mori in fatis ille erat. Vixi annos XXIII."—I know of no human composition so affecting as this, nor a history of deeper interest. These are the names and actions which ought not to perish, and to which we turn with a true and healthy tenderness, from the wretched and glittering detail of a confused mass of conquests and battles, with which the mind is roused for a time to a false and feverish sympathy, from whence it recurs at length with all the nausea consequent on such intoxication.

Note 16, page 623.

In the sun's face, like yonder Alpine snow.

This is written in the eye of Mont Blanc (June 3rd, 1816), which even at this distance dazzles mine.—(July 20th.) I this day observed for some time the distinct reflection of Mont Blanc and Mont Argentiere in the calm of the lake, which I was crossing in my boat; the distance of these mountains from their mirror is sixty miles.

Note 17, page 623.

Lake Leman woos me with its crystal face.

The following touching stanza forms part of the beautiful lines which about this time the poet addressed to his sister:—

"I did remind thee of our own dear lake,
By the old hall which may be mine no more.
Leman's is fair; but think not I forsake
The sweet remembrance of a dearer shore:
Sad havoc Time must with my memory make
Ere *that* or *thou* can fade these eyes before;
Though, like all things which I have loved, they are
Resign'd for ever, or divided far."

Note 18, page 623.

By the blue rushing of the arrowy Rhone.

The colour of the Rhone at Geneva is blue, to a depth of that which I have never seen equalled in water, salt or fresh, except in the Mediterranean and Archipelago.

Note 19, page 624.

This hallow'd, too, the memorable kiss.

This refers to the account in his "Confessions" of his passion for the Comtesse d'Houdetot (the mistress of St. Lambert), and his long walk every morning, for the sake of the single kiss which was the common salutation of French acquaintance. Rousseau's description of his feelings on this occasion may be considered as the most passionate, yet not impure, description and expression of love that ever kindled into words; which, after all, must be felt, from their very force, to be inadequate to the delineation: a painting can give no sufficient idea of the ocean.

Note 20, page 626.

"*Not vainly did the early Persian make*
His altar the high places and the peak
Of earth-o'ergazing mountains."

It is to be recollected, that the most beautiful and impressive doctrines of the divine Founder of Christianity were delivered, not in the *Temple*, but on the *Mount*. To waive the question of devotion, and turn to human eloquence,—the most effectual and splendid specimens were not pronounced within walls. Demosthenes addressed the public and popular assemblies. Cicero spoke in the forum. That this added to their effect on the mind of both orator and hearers, may be conceived from the difference between what we read of the emotions then and there produced, and those we ourselves experience in the perusal in the closet. It is one thing to read the "Iliad" at Sigæum and on the tumuli, or by the springs, with Mount Ida above, and the plain, and rivers, and Archipelago around you; and another to trim your taper over it in a snug library—*this* I know. Were the early and rapid progress of what is called Methodism to be attributed to any cause beyond the enthuiasm excited by its vehement faith and doctrines (the truth or error of which I presume neither to canvass nor to question), I should venture to ascribe it to the practice of preaching in the *fields*, and the unstudied and extemporaneous effusions of its teachers. The Mussulmans, whose erroneous devotion (at least in the lower orders) is most sincere, and therefore impressive, are accustomed to repeat their prescribed orisons and prayers, wherever they may be, at the stated hours—of course, frequently in the open air, kneeling upon a light mat (which they carry for the purpose of a bed or cushion as required); the ceremony lasts some minutes, during which they are totally absorbed, and only living in their supplication: nothing can disturb them. On me the simple and entire sincerity of these men, and the spirit which appeared to be within and upon them, made a far greater impression than any general rite which was ever performed in places of worship, of which I have seen those of almost every persuasion under the sun—including most of our own sectaries, and the Greek, the Catholic, the Armenian, the Lutheran, the Jewish, and the Mahometan. Many of the negroes, of whom there are numbers in the Turkish empire, are idolators, and have free exercise of their belief and its rites; some of these I had a distant view of at Patras; and, from what I could make out of them, they appeared to be of a truly Pagan description, and not very agreeable to a spectator.

Note 21, page 626.

A portion of the tempest and of thee.

The thunder-storm to which these lines refer occurred on the 13th of June, 1816, at midnight. I have seen, among the Acroceraunian mountains of Chimari, several more terrible, but none more beautiful.

Note 22, page 628.

Of names which unto you bequeath'd a name.

Voltaire and Gibbon.

Note 23, page 629.

Had I not filed my mind, which thus itself subdued.

—"If it be thus,
For Banquo's issue have I *filed* my mind." *Macbeth.*

CANTO THE FOURTH.

TO JOHN HOBHOUSE, Esq., A.M. F.R.S., &c.

My dear Hobhouse,

After an interval of eight years between the composition of the first and last cantos of Childe Harold, the conclusion of the poem is about to be submitted to the public. In parting with so old a friend, it is not extraordinary that I should recur to one still older and better,—to one who has beheld the birth and death of the other, and to whom I am far more indebted for the social advantages of an enlightened friendship, than—though not ungrateful—I can, or could be, to Childe Harold, for any public favour reflected through the poem on the poet,—to one, whom I have known long, and accompanied far, whom I have found wakeful over my sickness and kind in my sorrow, glad in my prosperity and firm in my adversity, true in counsel and trusty in peril,—to a friend often tried and never found wanting;—to yourself.

In so doing, I recur from fiction to truth; and in dedicating to you, in its complete or at least concluded state, a poetical work which is the longest, the most thoughtful and comprehensive of my compositions, I wish to do honour to myself by the record of many years' intimacy with a man of learning, of talent, of steadiness, and of honour. It is not for minds like ours to give or to receive flattery; yet the praises of sincerity have ever been permitted to the voice of friendship; and it is not for you, nor even for others, but to relieve a heart which has not elsewhere, or lately, been so much accustomed to the encounter of good-will as to withstand the shock firmly, that I thus attempt to commemorate your good qualities, or rather the advantages which I have derived from their exertion. Even the recurrence of the date of this letter, the anniversary of the most unfortunate day of my past existence, but which cannot poison my future while I retain the resource of your friendship, and of my own faculties, will henceforth have a more agreeable recollection for both, inasmuch as it will remind us of this my attempt to thank you for an indefatigable regard, such as few men have experienced, and no one could experience without thinking better of his species and of himself.

It has been our fortune to traverse together, at various periods, the countries of chivalry, history, and fable—Spain, Greece, Asia Minor, and Italy; and what Athens and Constantinople were to us a few years ago, Venice and Rome have been more recently. The poem also, or the pilgrim, or both, have accompanied me from first to last; and perhaps it may be a pardonable vanity which induces me to reflect with complacency on a composition which in some degree connects me with the spot where it was produced, and the objects it would fain describe; and however unworthy it may be deemed of those magical and memorable abodes, however short it may fall of our distant conceptions and immediate impressions, yet as a mark of respect for what is venerable, and of feeling for what is glorious, it has been to me a source of pleasure in the production, and I part with it with a kind of regret, which I hardly suspected that events could have left me for imaginary objects.

With regard to the conduct of the last canto, there will be found less of the pilgrim than in any of the preceding, and that little slightly, if at all, separated from the author speaking in his own person. The fact is, that I had become weary of drawing a line which every one seemed determined not to receive: like the Chinese in Goldsmith's "Citizen of the World," whom nobody would believe to be a Chinese, it was in vain that I asserted, and imagined that I had drawn, a distinction between the author and the pilgrim; and the very anxiety to preserve this difference, and disappointment at finding it unavailing, so far crushed my efforts in the composition, that I determined to abandon it altogether—and have done so. The opinions which have been, or may be, formed on that subject, are *now* a matter of indifference; the work is to depend on itself, and not on the writer; and the author, who has no resources in his own mind beyond the reputation, transient or permanent, which is to arise from his literary efforts, deserves the fate of authors.

In the course of the following canto it was my intention, either in the text or in the notes, to have touched upon the present state of Italian literature, and perhaps of manners. But the text, within the limits I proposed, I soon found hardly sufficient for the labyrinth of external objects, and the consequent reflections; and for the whole of the notes, excepting a few of the shortest, I am indebted to yourself, and these were necessarily limited to the elucidation of the text.

It is also a delicate, and no very grateful task, to dissert upon the literature and manners of a nation so dissimilar; and requires an attention and impartiality which would induce us—though perhaps no inattentive observers, nor ignorant of the language or customs of the people amongst whom we have recently abode—to distrust, or at least defer our judgment, and more narrowly examine our information. The state of literary, as well as political party, appears to run, or to *have* run, so high, that for a stranger to steer impartially between them is next to impossible. It may be enough, then, at least for my purpose, to quote from their own beautiful language—"Mi pare che in un paese tutto poetico, che vanta la lingua la più nobile ed insieme la più dolce, tutte tutte le vie diverse si possono tentare, e che sinche la patria di Alfieri e di Monti non ha perduto l' antico valore, in tutte essa dovrebbe essere la prima." Italy has great names still—Canova, Monti, Ugo Foscolo, Pindemonti, Visconti, Morelli, Cicognara, Albrizzi, Mezzophanti, Mai, Mustoxidi, Aglietti, and Vacca, will secure to the present generation an honourable place in most of the departments of art, science, and belles lettres; and in some the very highest: Europe—the World—has but one Canova.

It has been somewhere said by Alfieri, that "La pianta uomo nasce più robusta in Italia che in qualungue altra terra—e che gli stessi atroci delitti che vi si commettono ne sono una prova." Without subscribing to the latter part of his proposition—a dangerous doctrine, the truth of which may be disputed on better grounds, namely, that

the Italians are in no respect more ferocious than their neighbours—that man must be wilfully blind, or ignorantly heedless, who is not struck with the extraordinary capacity of this people, or, if such a word be admissible, their *capabilities*, the facility of their acquisitions, the rapidity of their conceptions, the fire of their genius, their sense of beauty, and, amidst all the disadvantages of repeated revolutions, the desolation of battles, and the despair of ages, their still unquenched "longing after immortality,"—the immortality of independence. And when we ourselves, in riding round the walls of Rome, heard the simple lament of the labourers' chorus, "Roma! Roma! Roma! Roma non è più come era prima," it was difficult not to contrast this melancholy dirge with the bacchanal roar of the songs of exultation still yelled from the London taverns, over the carnage of Mont St. Jean, and the betrayal of Genoa, of Italy, of France, and of the world, by men whose conduct you yourself have exposed in a work worthy of the better days of our history. For me,—

"Non movero mai corda
Ove la turba di sue ciance assorda."

What Italy has gained by the late transfer of nations, it were useless for Englishmen to inquire, till it becomes ascertained that England has acquired something more than a permanent army and a suspended Habeas Corpus; it is enough for them to look at home. For what they have done abroad, and especially in the South, "Verily they *will have* their reward," and at no very distant period.

Wishing you, my dear Hobhouse, a safe and agreeable return to that country whose real welfare can be dearer to none than to yourself, I dedicate to you this poem in its completed state; and repeat once more how truly I am ever,

Your obliged and affectionate friend,

Venice, Jan. 2, 1818. BYRON.

I.

I STOOD in Venice, on the Bridge of Sighs;
A palace and a prison on each hand:
I saw from out the wave her structures rise
As from the stroke of the enchanter's wand:
A thousand years their cloudy wings expand
Around me, and a dying Glory smiles
O'er the far times, when many a subject land
Look'd to the wingèd Lion's marble piles,
Where Venice sate in state, throned on her hundred isles!

II.

She looks a sea Cybele, fresh from ocean,[1]
Rising with her tiara of proud towers
At airy distance, with majestic motion,
A ruler of the waters and their powers:
And such she was;—her daughters had their dowers
From spoils of nations, and the exhaustless East
Pour'd in her lap all gems in sparkling showers.
In purple was she robed, and of her feast
Monarchs partook, and deem'd their dignity increased.

III.

In Venice Tasso's echoes are no more,
And silent rows the songless gondolier:
Her palaces are crumbling to the shore,
And music meets not always now the ear:
Those days are gone—but Beauty still is here.
States fall, arts fade—but Nature doth not die,
Nor yet forget how Venice once was dear,
The pleasant place of all festivity,
The revel of the earth, the masque of Italy!

IV.

But unto us she hath a spell beyond
Her name in story, and her long array
Of mighty shadows, whose dim forms despond
Above the dogeless city's vanish'd sway;
Ours is a trophy which will not decay
With the Rialto; Shylock and the Moor,
And Pierre, cannot be swept or worn away—
The keystones of the arch! though all were o'er,
For us repeopled were the solitary shore.

V.

The beings of the mind are not of clay;
Essentially immortal, they create
And multiply in us a brighter ray
And more belov'd existence: that which Fate
Prohibits to dull life, in this our state
Of mortal bondage, by these spirits supplied,
First exiles, then replaces what we hate;
Watering the heart whose early flowers have died,
And with a fresher growth replenishing the void.

VI.

Such is the refuge of our youth and age,
The first from Hope, the last from Vacancy;
And this worn feeling peoples many a page,
And, may be, that which grows beneath mine eye:
Yet there are things whose strong reality
Outshines our fairy-land; in shape and hues
More beautiful than our fantastic sky,
And the strange constellations which the Muse
O'er her wild universe is skilful to diffuse:

VII.

I saw or dream'd of such,—but let them go,—
They came like truth, and disappear'd like dreams;
And whatsoe'er they were—are now but so;
I could replace them if I would: still teems
My mind with many a form which aptly seems
Such as I sought for, and at moments found;
Let these too go—for waking Reason deems
Such over-weening phantasies unsound,
And other voices speak, and other sights surround.

VIII.

I've taught me other tongues—and in strange eyes
Have made me not a stranger; to the mind
Which is itself, no changes bring surprise;
Nor is it harsh to make, nor hard to find
A country with—ay, or without mankind;
Yet was I born where men are proud to be,
Not without cause; and should I leave behind
The inviolate island of the sage and free,
And seek me out a home by a remoter sea,

IX.

Perhaps I loved it well: and should I lay
My ashes in a soil which is not mine,
My spirit shall resume it—if we may
Unbodied choose a sanctuary. I twine
My hopes of being remember'd in my line
With my land's language: if too fond and far
These aspirations in their scope incline,—
If my fame should be, as my fortunes are,
Of hasty growth and blight, and dull Oblivion bar

X.

My name from out the temple where the dead
Are honoured by the nations—let it be—
And light the laurels on a loftier head!
And be the Spartan's epitaph on me—
"Sparta hath many a worthier son than he."[2]
Meantime I seek no sympathies, nor need;
The thorns which I have reaped are of the tree
I planted,—they have torn me,—and I bleed:
I should have known what fruit would spring from such a seed.

XI.

The spouseless Adriatic mourns her lord;
And, annual marriage now no more renew'd,
The Bucentaur lies rotting unrestored,
Neglected garment of her widowhood!
St. Mark yet sees his lion where he stood
Stand, but in mockery of his wither'd power,
Over the proud Place where an Emperor sued,
And monarchs gazed and envied in the hour
When Venice was a queen with an unequall'd dower

XII.

The Suabian sued, and now the Austrian reigns—
An Emperor tramples where an Emperor knelt;
Kingdoms are shrunk to provinces, and chains
Clank over sceptred cities; nations melt
From power's high pinnacle, when they have felt
The sunshine for a while, and downward go
Like lauwine loosen'd from the mountain's belt;
Oh for one hour of blind old Dandolo!
Th' octogenarian chief, Byzantium's conquering foe.

XIII.

Before St. Mark still glow his steeds of brass,
Their gilded collars glittering in the sun;
But is not Doria's menace come to pass?
Are they not *bridled!*—Venice, lost and won,
Her thirteen hundred years of freedom done,
Sinks, like a sea-weed, into whence she rose!
Better be whelm'd beneath the waves, and shun,
Even in destruction's depth, her foreign foes,
From whom submission wrings an infamous repose.

XIV.

In youth she was all glory,—a new Tyre,—
Her very by-word sprung from victory,
The "Planter of the Lion," which through fire[3]
And blood she bore o'er subject earth and sea:

Though making many slaves, herself still free,
And Europe's bulwark 'gainst the Ottomite;
Witness Troy's rival, Candia! Vouch it, ye
Immortal waves that saw Lepanto's fight!
For ye are names no time nor tyranny can blight.

XV.

Statues of glass—all shiver'd—the long file
Of her dead Doges are declined to dust;
But where they dwelt, the vast and sumptuous pile
Bespeaks the pageant of their splendid trust;
Their sceptre broken, and their sword in rust,
Have yielded to the stranger: empty halls,
Thin streets, and foreign aspects, such as must
Too oft remind her who and what enthrals,
Have flung a desolate cloud o'er Venice' lovely walls.

XVI.

When Athens' armies fell at Syracuse,
And fetter'd thousands bore the yoke of war,
Redemption rose up in the Attic Muse,[4]
Her voice their only ransom from afar:
See! as they chant the tragic hymn, the car
Of the o'ermaster'd victor stops, the reins
Fall from his hands—his idle scimitar
Starts from its belt—he rends his captive's chains,
And bids him thank the bard for freedom and his strains.

XVII.

Thus, Venice, if no stronger claim were thine,
Were all thy proud heroic deeds forgot,
Thy choral memory of the Bard divine,
Thy love of Tasso, should have cut the knot
Which ties thee to thy tyrants; and thy lot
Is shameful to the nations,—most of all,
Albion! to thee: the Ocean queen should not
Abandon Ocean's children; in the fall
Of Venice think of thine, despite thy watery wall.

XVIII.

I loved her from my boyhood—she to me
Was as a fairy city of the heart,
Rising like water-columns from the sea,
Of joy the sojourn, and of wealth the mart;
And Otway, Radcliffe, Schiller, Shakspeare's art,[5]
Had stamped her image in me, and even so,
Although I found her thus, we did not part,
Perchance even dearer in her day of woe,
Than when she was a boast, a marvel, and a show.

XIX.

I can repeople with the past—and of
The present there is still for eye and thought,
And meditation chasten'd down, enough;
And more, it may be, than I hoped or sought;
And of the happiest moments which were wrought
Within the web of my existence, some
From thee, fair Venice! have their colours caught
There are some feelings Time can not benumb,
Nor Torture shake, or mine would now be cold and dumb.

XX.

But from their nature will the tannen grow[6]
Loftiest on loftiest and least shelter'd rocks,
Rooted in barrenness, where nought below
Of soil supports them 'gainst the Alpine shocks
Of eddying storms; yet springs the trunk, and mocks
The howling tempest, till its height and frame
Are worthy of the mountains from whose blocks
Of bleak, gray granite, into life it came,
And grew a giant tree;—the mind may grow the same.

XXI.

Existence may be borne, and the deep root
Of life and sufferance make its firm abode
In bare and desolated bosoms: mute
The camel labours with the heaviest load,
And the wolf dies in silence,—not bestow'd
In vain should such example be; if they,
Things of ignoble or of savage mood,
Endure and shrink not, we of nobler clay
May temper it to bear,—it is but for a day.

XXII.

All suffering doth destroy, or is destroy'd,
Even by the sufferer; and, in each event,
Ends:—Some, with hope replenish'd and rebuoy'd,
Return to whence they came—with like intent,
And weave their web again; some, bow'd and bent,
Wax gray and ghastly, withering ere their time,
And perish with the reed on which they leant;
Some seek devotion, toil, war, good or crime,
According as their souls were form'd to sink or climb.

XXIII.

But ever and anon of griefs subdued
There comes a token like a scorpion's sting,
Scarce seen, but with fresh bitterness imbued;
And slight withal may be the things which bring
Back on the heart the weight which it would fling
Aside for ever: it may be a sound—
A tone of music—summer's eve—or spring—
A flower—the wind—the ocean—which shall wound,
Striking the electric chain wherewith we are darkly bound;

XXIV.

And how and why we know not, nor can trace
Home to its cloud this lightning of the mind,
But feel the shock renew'd, nor can efface
The blight and blackening which it leaves

Which out of things familiar, undesign'd,
When least we deem of such, calls up to view
The spectres whom no exorcism can bind
The cold — the changed — perchance the dead — anew,
The mourn'd, the loved, the lost — too many! — yet how few!

XXV.

But my soul wanders; I demand it back
To meditate amongst decay, and stand
A ruin amidst ruins; there to track
Fall'n states and buried greatness, o'er a land
Which *was* the mightiest in its old command,
And *is* the loveliest, and must ever be
The master-mould of Nature's heavenly hand,
Wherein were cast the heroic and the free,
The beautiful, the brave—the lords of earth and sea,

XXVI.

The commonwealth of kings, the men of Rome!
And even since, and now, fair Italy!
Thou art the garden of the world, the home
Of all Art yields, and Nature can decree;
Even in thy desert, what is like to thee?
Thy very weeds are beautiful, thy waste
More rich than other climes' fertility;
Thy wreck a glory, and thy ruin graced
With an immaculate charm which cannot be defaced.

XXVII.

The moon is up, and yet it is not night—
Sunset divides the sky with her—a sea
Of glory streams along the Alpine height
Of blue Friuli's mountains; Heaven is free
From clouds, but of all colours seems to be
Melted to one vast Iris of the West,
Where the Day joins the past Eternity;
While, on the other hand, meek Dian's crest
Floats through the azure air — an island of the blest![7]

XXVIII.

A single star is at her side, and reigns
With her o'er half the lonely heaven; but still
Yon sunny sea heaves brightly, and remains
Roll'd o'er the peak of the far Rhætian hill,
As Day and Night contending were, until
Nature reclaim'd her order:—gently flows
The deep-dyed Brenta, where their hues instil
The odorous purple of a new-born rose,
Which streams upon her stream, and glass'd within it glows,

XXIX.

Fill'd with the face of heaven, which, from afar,
Comes down upon the waters; all its hues,
From the rich sunset to the rising star,
Their magical variety diffuse:
And now they change; a paler shadow strews
Its mantle o'er the mountains; parting day
Dies like the dolphin, whom each pang imbues
With a new colour as it gasps away,
The last still loveliest, till—'tis gone—and all is gray.

XXX.

There is a tomb in Arqua;—rear'd in air,
Pillar'd in their sarcophagus, repose
The bones of Laura's lover: here repair
Many familiar with his well-sung woes,
The pilgrims of his genius. He arose
To raise a language, and his land reclaim
From the dull yoke of her barbaric foes:
Watering the tree which bears his lady's name
With his melodious tears, he gave himself to fame.

XXXI.

They keep his dust in Arqua, where he died;[8]
The mountain-village where his latter days
Went down the vale of years; and 'tis their pride—
An honest pride—and let it be their praise,
To offer to the passing stranger's gaze
His mansion and his sepulchre; both plain
And venerably simple, such as raise
A feeling more accordant with his strain
Than if a pyramid form'd his monumental fane.

XXXII.

And the soft quiet hamlet where he dwelt
Is one of that complexion which seems made
For those who their mortality have felt,
And sought a refuge from their hopes decay'd
In the deep umbrage of a green hill's shade,
Which shows a distant prospect far away
Of busy cities, now in vain display'd,
For they can lure no further; and the ray
Of a bright sun can make sufficient holiday,

XXXIII.

Developing the mountains, leaves, and flowers,
And shining in the brawling brook, where-by,
Clear as its current, glide the sauntering hours
With a calm languor, which, though to the eye
Idlesse it seem, hath its morality.
If from society we learn to live,
'Tis solitude should teach us how to die;
It hath no flatterers; vanity can give
No hollow aid; alone—man with his God must strive:

XXXIV.

Or, it may be, with demons, who impair[9]
The strength of better thoughts, and seek their prey
In melancholy bosoms, such as were
Of moody texture from their earliest day,
And loved to dwell in darkness and dismay,
Deeming themselves predestined to a doom
Which is not of the pangs that pass away;
Making the sun like blood, the earth a tomb,
The tomb a hell, and hell itself a murkier gloom.

XXXV.

Ferrara! in thy wide and grass-grown streets,
Whose symmetry was not for solitude,
There seems as 't were a curse upon the seats
Of former sovereigns, and the antique brood
Of Este, which for many an age made good
Its strength within thy walls, and was of yore
Patron or tyrant, as the changing mood
Of petty power impell'd, of those who wore
The wreath which Dante's brow alone had worn before.

XXXVI.

And Tasso is their glory and their shame.
Hark to his strain! and then survey his cell!
And see how dearly earn'd Torquato's fame,
And where Alfonso bade his poet dwell.
The miserable despot could not quell
The insulted mind he sought to quench, and blend
With the surrounding maniacs, in the hell
Where he had plunged it. Glory without end
Scatter'd the clouds away—and on that name attend

XXXVII.

The tears and praises of all time, while thine
Would rot in its oblivion—in the sink
Of worthless dust, which from thy boasted line
Is shaken into nothing; but the link
Thou formest in his fortunes bids us think
Of thy poor malice, naming thee with scorn—
Alfonso! how thy ducal pageants shrink
From thee! if in another station born,
Scarce fit to be the slave of him thou mad'st to mourn:

XXXVIII.

Thou! form'd to eat, and be despised, and die,
Even as the beasts that perish, save that thou
Hadst a more splendid trough and wider sty:
He! with a glory round his furrow'd brow,
Which emanated then, and dazzles now,
In face of all his foes, the Cruscan quire,
And Boileau, whose rash envy could allow
No strain which shamed his country's creaking lyre,
That whetstone of the teeth—monotony in wire!

XXXIX.

Peace to Torquato's injured shade! 't was his
In life and death to be the mark where Wrong
Aim'd with her poison'd arrows; but to miss.
Oh, victor unsurpass'd in modern song!
Each year brings forth its millions; but how long
The tide of generations shall roll on,
And not the whole combined and countless throng
Compose a mind like thine? though all in one
Condensed their scatter'd rays, they would not form a sun.

XL.

Great as thou art, yet parallel'd by those,
Thy countrymen, before thee born to shine,
The Bards of Hell and Chivalry: first rose
The Tuscan father's comedy divine;
Then, not unequal to the Florentine,
The southern Scott, the minstrel who call'd forth
A new creation with his magic line,
And, like the Ariosto of the North,
Sang ladye-love and war, romance and knightly worth.

XLI.

The lightning rent from Ariosto's bust[10]
The iron crown of laurel's mimic'd leaves;
Nor was the ominous element unjust,
For the true laurel-wreath which Glory weaves
Is of the tree no bolt of thunder cleaves,
And the false semblance but disgraced his brow
Yet still, if fondly Superstition grieves,
Know, that the lightning sanctifies below
Whate'er it strikes;—yon head is doubly sacred now!

XLII.

Italia! oh Italia! thou who hast
The fatal gift of beauty, which became
A funeral dower of present woes and past,
On thy sweet brow is sorrow plough'd by shame,
And annals graved in characters of flame.
Oh God! that thou wert in thy nakedness
Less lovely or more powerful, and couldst claim
Thy right, and awe the robbers back, who press
To shed thy blood, and drink the tears of thy distress;

XLIII.

Then might thou more appal; or, less desired,
Be homely and be peaceful, undeplored
For thy destructive charms; then, still untired,
Would not be seen the armèd torrents pour'd
Down the deep Alps; nor would the hostile horde
Of many-nationed spoilers from the Po
Quaff blood and water; nor the stranger's sword
Be thy sad weapon of defence, and so,
Victor or vanquish'd, thou the slave of friend or foe.[1]

XLIV.

Wandering in youth, I traced the path of him,[12]
The Roman friend of Rome's least mortal mind,
The friend of Tully: as my bark did skim
The bright blue waters with a fanning wind,
Came Megara before me, and behind
Ægina lay, Piræus on the right,
And Corinth on the left; I lay reclined
Along the prow, and saw all these unite
In ruin, even as he had seen the desolate sight;

XLV.

For Time hath not rebuilt them, but uprear'd
Barbaric dwellings on their shatter'd site,
Which only make more mourn'd and more endear'd
The few last rays of their far-scatter'd light,
And the crush'd relics of their vanish'd might.
The Roman saw these tombs in his own age,
These sepulchres of cities, which excite
Sad wonder, and his yet surviving page
The moral lesson bears, drawn from such pilgrimage.

XLVI.

That page is now before me, and on mine
His country's ruin added to the mass
Of perish'd states he mourn'd in their decline,
And I in desolation: all that *was*
Of then destruction *is;* and now, alas!
Rome—Rome imperial, bows her to the storm,
In the same dust and blackness, and we pass
The skeleton of her Titanic form,[13]
Wrecks of another world, whose ashes still are warm.

XLVII.

Yet, Italy! through every other land
Thy wrongs should ring, and shall, from side to side;
Mother of Arts! as once of arms; thy hand
Was then our guardian, and is still our guide;
Parent of our Religion! whom the wide
Nations have knelt to for the keys of heaven!
Europe, repentant of her parricide,
Shall yet redeem thee, and, all backward driven,
Roll the barbarian tide, and sue to be forgiven.

XLVIII.

But Arno wins us to the fair white walls,
Where the Etrurian Athens claims and keeps
A softer feeling for her fairy halls.
Girt by her theatre of hills, she reaps
Her corn, and wine, and oil, and Plenty leaps
To laughing life, with her redundant horn.
Along the banks where smiling Arno sweeps
Was modern luxury of Commerce born,
And buried Learning rose, redeem'd to a new morn

XLIX.

There, too, the Goddess loves in stone, and fills
The air around with beauty; we inhale
The ambrosial aspect, which, beheld, instils
Part of its immortality; the veil
Of heaven is half undrawn; within the pale
We stand, and in that form and face behold
What Mind can make, when Nature's self would fail;
And to the fond idolaters of old
Envy the innate flash which such a soul could mould:

L.

We gaze and turn away, and know not where,
Dazzled and drunk with beauty, till the heart
Reels with its fulness; there—for ever there—
Chained to the chariot of triumphal Art,
We stand as captives, and would not depart.
Away!—there need no words, nor terms precise,
The paltry jargon of the marble mart,
Where Pedantry gulls Folly—we have eyes:
Blood—pulse—and breast, confirm the Dardan Shepherd's prize.

LI.

Appeared'st thou not to Paris in this guise?
Or to more deeply blest Anchises? or,
In all thy perfect goddess-ship, when lies
Before thee thy own vanquish'd Lord of War?
And gazing in thy face as toward a star,
Laid on thy lap, his eyes to thee upturn,
Feeding on thy sweet cheek! while thy lips are
With lava kisses melting while they burn,
Shower'd on his eyelids, brow, and mouth, as from an urn!

LII.

Glowing, and circumfused in speechless love,
Their full divinity inadequate
That feeling to express, or to improve,
The gods become as mortals, and man's fate
Has moments like their brightest; but the weight
Of earth recoils upon us;—let it go!
We can recall such visions, and create,
From what has been, or might be, things which grow
Into thy statue's form, and look like gods below.

LIII.

I leave to learnèd fingers, and wise hands,
The artist and his ape, to teach and tell
How well his connoisseurship understands
The graceful bend, and the voluptuous swell:
Let these describe the undescribable:
I would not their vile breath should crisp the stream
Wherein that image shall for ever dwell;
The unruffled mirror of the loveliest dream
That ever left the sky on the deep soul to beam.

LIV.

In Santa Croce's holy precincts lie
Ashes which make it holier, dust which is
Even in itself an immortality,
Though there were nothing save the past, and this
The particle of those sublimities
Which have relapsed to chaos:—here repose
Angelo's, Alfieri's bones,[14] and his,
The starry Galileo, with his woes;
Here Machiavelli's earth return'd to whence it rose.

LV.

These are four minds, which, like the elements,
Might furnish forth creation:—Italy!
Time, which hath wrong'd thee with ten thousand rents
Of thine imperial garment, shall deny,
And hath denied, to every other sky,
Spirits which soar from ruin:—thy decay
Is still impregnate with divinity,
Which gilds it with revivifying ray;
Such is the great of yore, Canova is to-day.

LVI.

But where repose the all Etruscan three—
Dante, and Petrarch, and, scarce less than they,
The Bard of Prose, creative spirit! he
Of the Hundred Tales of love—where did they lay
Their bones, distinguish'd from our common clay
In death as life? Are they resolved to dust,
And have their country's marbles nought to say?
Could not her quarries furnish forth one bust?
Did they not to her breast their filial earth entrust?

LVII.

Ungrateful Florence! Dante sleeps afar,[15]
Like Scipio, buried by the upbraiding shore;
Thy factions, in their worse than civil war,
Proscribed the bard whose name for evermore
Their children's children would in vain adore
With the remorse of ages; and the crown
Which Petrarch's laureate brow supremely wore,
Upon a far and foreign soil had grown,
His life, his fame, his grave, though rifled—not thine own.

LVIII.

Boccaccio to his parent earth bequeath'd
His dust,[16]—and lies it not her Great among,
With many a sweet and solemn requiem breathed
O'er him who form'd the Tuscan's siren tongue?
That music in itself, whose sounds are song,
The poetry of speech? No;—even his tomb
Uptorn, must bear the hyæna bigot's wrong,
No more amidst the meaner dead find room,
Nor claim a passing sigh, because it told for *whom*

LIX.

And Santa Croce wants their mighty dust;
Yet for this want more noted, as of yore
The Cæsar's pageant, shorn of Brutus' bust,
Did but of Rome's best Son remind her more:
Happier Ravenna! on thy hoary shore,
Fortress of falling empire! honour'd sleeps
The immortal exile;—Arqua, too, her store
Of tuneful relics proudly claims and keeps,
While Florence vainly begs her banished dead, and weeps.

LX.

What is her pyramid of precious stones?
Of porphyry, jasper, agate, and all hues
Of gem and marble, to encrust the bones
Of merchant-dukes? the momentary dues
Which, sparkling to the twilight stars, infuse
Freshness in the green turf that wraps the dead,
Whose names are mausoleums of the Muse,
Are gently prest with far more reverend tread
Than ever paced the slab which paves the princely head.

LXI.

There be more things to greet the heart and eyes
In Arno's dome of Art's most princely shrine,
Where Sculpture with her rainbow sister vies;
There be more marvels yet—but not for mine;
For I have been accustom'd to entwine
My thoughts with Nature rather in the fields,
Than Art in galleries: though a work divine
Calls for my spirit's homage, yet it yields
Less than it feels, because the weapon which it wields

LXII.

Is of another temper, and I roam
By Thrasimene's lake, in the defiles
Fatal to Roman rashness, more at home;
For there the Carthaginian's warlike wiles
Come back before me, as his skill beguiles
The host between the mountains and the shore,
Where Courage falls in her despairing files,
And torrents, swoll'n to rivers with their gore,
Reek through the sultry plain, with legions scatter'd o'er.

LXIII.

Like to a forest fell'd by mountain winds;
And such the storm of battle on this day,
And such the frenzy, whose convulsion blinds
To all save carnage, that, beneath the fray,
An earthquake reel'd unheededly away!
None felt stern Nature rocking at his feet,
And yawning forth a grave for those who lay
Upon their bucklers for a winding sheet;
Such is the absorbing hate when warring nations meet!

LXIV.

The Earth to them was as a rolling bark
Which bore them to Eternity; they saw
The Ocean round, but had no time to mark
The motions of their vessel; Nature's law,
In them suspended, reck'd not of the awe
Which reigns when mountains tremble, and the birds
Plunge in the clouds for refuge, and withdraw
From their down-toppling nests; and bellowing herds
Stumble o'er heaving plains, and man's dread hath no words.

LXV.

Far other scene is Thrasimene now;
Her lake a sheet of silver, and her plain
Rent by no ravage save the gentle plough;
Her aged trees rise thick as once the slain
Lay where their roots are; but a brook hath ta'en—
A little rill of scanty stream and bed—
A name of blood from that day's sanguine rain;
And Sanguinetto tells ye where the dead
Made the earth wet, and turn'd the unwilling waters red.

LXVI.

But thou, Clitumnus! in thy sweetest wave
Of the most living crystal that was e'er
The haunt of river nymph, to gaze and lave
Her limbs where nothing hid them, thou dost rear

Thy grassy banks whereon the milk-white steer
Grazes; the purest god of gentle waters!
And most serene of aspect, and most clear;
Surely that stream was unprofaned by slaughters,
A mirror and a bath for Beauty's youngest daughters!

LXVII.

And on thy happy shore a Temple still,
Of small and delicate proportions, keeps,
Upon a mild declivity of hill,
Its memory of thee; beneath it sweeps
Thy current's calmness; oft from out it leaps
The finny darter with the glittering scales,
Who dwells and revels in thy glassy deeps;
While, chance, some scatter'd water-lily sails
Down where the shallower wave still tells its bubbling tales.

LXVIII.

Pass not unblest the Genius of the place!
If through the air a zephyr more serene
Win to the brow, 'tis his; and if ye trace
Along his margin a more eloquent green,
If on the heart the freshness of the scene
Sprinkle its coolness, and from the dry dust
Of weary life a moment lave it clean
With Nature's baptism,—'tis to him ye must
Pay orisons for this suspension of disgust.

LXIX.

The roar of waters!—from the headlong height
Velino cleaves the wave-worn precipice;
The fall of waters! rapid as the light
The flashing mass foams shaking the abyss;
The hell of waters! where they howl and hiss,
And boil in endless torture; while the sweat
Of their great agony, wrung out from this
Their Phlegethon, curls round the rocks of jet
That gird the gulf around, in pitiless horror set,

LXX.

And mounts in spray the skies, and thence again
Returns in an unceasing shower, which round,
With its unemptied cloud of gentle rain,
Is an eternal April to the ground,
Making it all one emerald:—how profound
The gulf! and how the giant element
From rock to rock leaps with delirious bound,
Crushing the cliffs, which, downward worn and rent,
With his fierce footsteps, yield in chasms a fearful vent

LXXI.

To the broad column which rolls on, and shows
More like the fountain of an infant sea
Torn from the womb of mountains by the throes
Of a new world, than only thus to be
Parent of rivers, which flow gushingly,
With many windings, thro' the vale:—Look back!
Lo! where it comes like an eternity,
As if to sweep down all things in its track,
Charming the eye with dread,—a matchless cataract,[17]

LXXII.

Horribly beautiful! but on the verge,
From side to side, beneath the glittering morn,
An Iris sits, amidst the infernal surge,[18]
Like Hope upon a death-bed, and, unworn
Its steady dyes, when all around is torn
By the distracted waters, bears serene
Its brilliant hues with all their beams unshorn:
Resembling, 'mid the torture of the scene,
Love watching Madness with unalterable mien.

LXXIII.

Once more upon the woody Appenine,
The infant Alps, which—had I not before
Gazed on their mightier parents, where the pine
Sits on more shaggy summits, and where roar
The thundering lauwine[19]—might be worshipp'd more;
But I have seen the soaring Jungfrau rear
Her never-trodden snow, and seen the hoar
Glaciers of bleak Mont Blanc both far and near,
And in Chimari heard the thunder-hills of fear,

LXXIV.

Th' Acroceraunian mountains of old name;
And on Parnassus seen the eagles fly
Like spirits of the spot, as 't were for fame,
For still they soar'd unutterably high:
I've looked on Ida with a Trojan's eye;
Athos, Olympus, Ætna, Atlas, made
These hills seem things of lesser dignity,
All, save the lone Soracte's height display'd,
Not *now* in snow, which asks the lyric Roman's aid

LXXV.

For our remembrance, and from out the plain
Heaves like a long-swept wave about to break,
And on the curl hangs pausing: not in vain
May he, who will, his recollections rake,
And quote in classic raptures, and awake
The hills with Latian echoes; I abhorr'd
Too much, to conquer for the poet's sake,
The drill'd dull lesson, forced down word by word[20]
In my repugnant youth, with pleasure to record

LXXVI.

Aught that recalls the daily drug which turn'd
My sickening memory; and, though Time hath taught
My mind to meditate what then it learn'd,
Yet such the fix'd inveteracy wrought

By the impatience of my early thought,
That, with the freshness wearing out before
My mind could relish what it might have sought,
If free to choose, I cannot now restore
Its health; but what it then detested, still abhor.

LXXVII.

Then farewell, Horace; whom I hated so,
Not for thy faults, but mine; it is a curse
To understand, not feel thy lyric flow,
To comprehend, but never love thy verse,
Although no deeper Moralist rehearse
Our little life, nor Bard prescribe his art,
Nor livelier Satirist the conscience pierce,
Awakening without wounding the touch'd heart,
Yet fare thee well—upon Soracte's ridge we part.

LXXVIII.

Oh Rome! my country! city of the soul!
The orphans of the heart must turn to thee,
Lone mother of dead empires! and control
In their shut breasts their petty misery.
What are our woes and sufferance? Come and see
The cypress, hear the owl, and plod your way
O'er steps of broken thrones and temples, Ye!
Whose agonies are evils of a day—
A world is at our feet as fragile as our clay.

LXXIX.

The Niobe of nations! there she stands,
Childless and crownless, in her voiceless woe;
An empty urn within her wither'd hands,
Whose holy dust was scatter'd long ago;
The Scipios' tomb contains no ashes now;
The very sepulchres lie tenantless
Of their heroic dwellers: dost thou flow,
Old Tiber! through a marble wilderness?
Rise, with thy yellow waves, and mantle her distress.

LXXX.

The Goth, the Christian, Time, War, Flood, and Fire,
Have dealt upon the seven-hill'd city's pride;
She saw her glories star by star expire,
And up the steep barbarian monarchs ride,
Where the car climb'd the capitol; far and wide
Temple and tower went down, nor left a site:—
Chaos of ruins! who shall trace the void,
O'er the dim fragments cast a lunar light,
And say, "here was, or is," where all is doubly night?

LXXXI.

The double night of ages, and of her,
Night's daughter, Ignorance, hath wrapt, and wrap
All round us; we but feel our way to err;
The ocean hath its chart, the stars their map,
And Knowledge spreads them on her ample lap;
But Rome is as the desert, where we steer
Stumbling o'er recollections; now we clap
Our hands, and cry "Eureka!" it is clear—
When but some false mirage of ruin rises near.

LXXXII.

Alas! the lofty city! and alas!
The trebly hundred triumphs! and the day [21]
When Brutus made the dagger's edge surpass
The conqueror's sword in bearing fame away;
Alas, for Tully's voice, and Virgil's lay,
And Livy's pictured page!—but these shall be
Her resurrection; all beside—decay.
Alas, for Earth, for never shall we see
That brightness in her eye she bore when Rome was free!

LXXXIII.

Oh thou, whose chariot roll'd on Fortune's wheel,
Triumphant Sylla! Thou, who didst subdue
Thy country's foes ere thou wouldst pause to feel
The wrath of thy own wrongs, or reap the due
Of hoarded vengeance till thine eagles flew
O'er prostrate Asia;—thou, who with thy frown
Annihilated senates—Roman, too,
With all thy vices, for thou didst lay down
With an atoning smile a more than earthly crown—

LXXXIV.

The dictatorial wreath,—couldst thou divine [22]
To what would one day dwindle that which made
Thee more than mortal? and that so supine
By aught than Romans Rome should thus be laid?
She who was named Eternal, and array'd
Her warriors but to conquer—she who veil'd
Earth with her haughty shadow, and display'd,
Until the o'er-canopied horizon fail'd,
Her rushing wings—Oh! she who was Almighty hail'd!

LXXXV.

Sylla was first of victors; but our own
The sagest of usurpers, Cromwell; he
Too swept off senates while he hew'd the throne
Down to a block—immortal rebel! See
What crimes it costs to be a moment free
And famous through all ages! but beneath
His fate the moral lurks of destiny;
His day of double victory and death
Beheld him win two realms, and, happier, yield his breath.

LXXXVI.

The third of the same moon whose former course
Had all but crown'd him, on the selfsame day
Deposed him gently from his throne of force,
And laid him with the earth's preceding clay, [23]
And show'd not Fortune thus how fame and sway,
And all we deem delightful, and consume
Our souls to compass through each arduous way,

Are in her eyes less happy than the tomb?
Were they but so in man's, how different were his
doom!

LXXXVII.

And thou, dread statue! yet existent in
The austerest form of naked majesty,
Thou who beheldest, 'mid the assassins' din,
At thy bathed base the bloody Cæsar lie,
Folding his robe in dying dignity,
An offering to thine altar from the queen
Of gods and men, great Nemesis! did he die,
And thou, too, perish, Pompey? have ye been
Victors of countless kings, or puppets of a scene?

LXXXVIII.

And thou, the thunder-stricken nurse of Rome!
She-wolf! whose brazen-imaged dugs impart
The milk of conquest yet within the dome
Where, as a monument of antique art,
Thou standest:—Mother of the mighty heart,
Which the great founder suck'd from thy wild teat,
Scorch'd by the Roman Jove's ethereal dart,
And thy limbs blacked with lightning—dost thou
yet [forget?
Guard thine immortal cubs, nor thy fond charge

LXXXIX.

Thou dost;—but all thy foster-babes are dead—
The men of iron; and the world hath rear'd
Cities from out their sepulchres: men bled
In imitation of the things they fear'd, [steer'd,
And fought and conquer'd, and the same course
At apish distance; but as yet none have,
Nor could, the same supremacy have near'd,
Save one vain man, who is not in the grave,
But, vanquish'd by himself, to his own slaves a slave,

XC.

The fool of false dominion—and a kind
Of bastard Cæsar, following him of old
With steps unequal; for the Roman's mind
Was modell'd in a less terrestrial mould,
With passions fiercer, yet a judgment cold,
And an immortal instinct which redeem'd
The frailties of a heart so soft, yet bold.
Alcides with the distaff now he seem'd
At Cleopatra's feet,—and now himself he beamed,

XCI.

And came, and saw, and conquered! But the man
Who would have tamed his eagles down to flee,
Like a train'd falcon, in the Gallic van,
Which he, in sooth, long led to victory,
With a deaf heart which never seemed to be
A listener to itself, was strangely framed;
With but one weakest weakness—vanity:
Coquettish in ambition, still he aim'd— [claim'd?
At what? Can he avouch—or answer what he

XCII.

And would be all or nothing—nor could wait
For the sure grave to level him; few years
Had fix'd him with the Cæsars in his fate,
On whom we tread: For *this* the conqueror rears
The arch of triumph! and for this the tears
And blood of earth flow on as they have flow'd,
An universal deluge, which appears
Without an ark for wretched man's abode,
And ebbs but to reflow!—Renew thy rainbow, God

XCIII.

What from this barren being do we reap?
Our senses narrow, and our reason frail,
Life short, and truth a gem which loves the deep,
And all things weigh'd in custom's falsest scale;
Opinion an omnipotence,—whose veil
Mantles the earth with darkness, until right
And wrong are accidents, and men grow pale
Lest their own judgments should become too
bright,
And their free thoughts be crimes, and earth have
too much light.

XCIV.

And thus they plod in sluggish misery,
Rotting from sire to son, and age to age,
Proud of their trampled nature, and so die,
Bequeathing their hereditary rage
To the new race of inborn slaves, who wage
War for their chains, and rather than be free,
Bleed gladiator-like, and still engage
Within the same arena where they see
Their fellows fall before, like leaves of the same tree.

XCV.

I speak not of men's creeds—they rest between
Man and his Maker—but of things allow'd,
Averr'd, and known,—and daily, hourly seen—
The yoke that is upon us doubly bow'd,
And the intent of tyranny avow'd,
The edict of Earth's rulers, who are grown
The apes of him who humbled once the proud,
And shook them from their slumbers on the throne;
Too glorious, were this all his mighty arm had done.

XCVI.

Can tyrants but by tyrants conquer'd be,
And Freedom find no champion and no child
Such as Columbia saw arise when she
Sprung forth a Pallas, arm'd and undefiled?
Or must such minds be nourish'd in the wild,
Deep in the unpruned forest, 'midst the roar
Of cataracts, where nursing Nature smiled
On infant Washington? Has Earth no more
Such seeds within her breast, or Europe no such
shore?

XCVII.

But France got drunk with blood to vomit crime,
And fatal have her Saturnalia been
To Freedom's cause, in every age and clime;
Because the deadly days which we have seen,
And vile Ambition, that built up between
Man and his hopes an adamantine wall,
And the base pageant last upon the scene,
Are grown the pretext for the eternal thrall
Which nips life's tree, and dooms man's worst—his second fall.

XCVIII.

Yet, Freedom! yet thy banner, torn, but flying,
Streams like the thunder-storm *against* the wind;
Thy trumpet voice, though broken now and dying,
The loudest still the tempest leaves behind;
Thy tree hath lost its blossoms, and the rind,
Chopp'd by the axe, looks rough and little worth,
But the sap lasts—and still the seed we find
Sown deep, even in the bosom of the North;
So shall a better spring less bitter fruit bring forth.

XCIX.

There is a stern round tower of other days,[24]
Firm as a fortress, with its fence of stone,
Such as an army's baffled strength delays,
Standing with half its battlements alone,
And with two thousand years of ivy grown,
The garland of eternity, where wave
The green leaves over all by time o'erthrown;—
What was this tower of strength? within its cave
What treasure lay so lock'd, so hid?—A woman's grave.

C.

But who was she, the lady of the dead,
Tomb'd in a palace? Was she chaste and fair?
Worthy a king's—or more—a Roman's bed?
What race of chiefs and heroes did she bear?
What daughter of her beauties was the heir?
How lived—how loved—how died she? Was she not
So honour'd—and conspicuously there,
Where meaner relics must not dare to rot,
Placed to commemorate a more than mortal lot?

CI.

Was she as those who love their lords, or they
Who love the lords of others? such have been
Even in the olden time, Rome's annals say.
Was she a matron of Cornelia's mien,
Or the light air of Egypt's graceful queen,
Profuse of joy—or 'gainst it did she war,
Inveterate in virtue? Did she lean
To the soft side of the heart, or wisely bar
Love from amongst her griefs?—for such the affections are.

CII.

Perchance she died in youth: it may be, bow'd
With woes far heavier than the ponderous tomb
That weigh'd upon her gentle dust, a cloud
Might gather o'er her beauty, and a gloom
In her dark eye, prophetic of the doom
Heaven gives its favourites—early death; yet shed
A sunset charm around her, and illume
With hectic light, the Hesperus of the dead,
Of her consuming cheek the autumnal leaf-like red.

CIII.

Perchance she died in age—surviving all,
Charms, kindred, children—with the silver gray
On her long tresses, which might yet recall,
It may be, still a something of the day
When they were braided, and her proud array
And lovely form were envied, praised, and eyed
By Rome—But, whither would Conjecture stray?
Thus much alone we know—Metella died,
The wealthiest Roman's wife: Behold his love or pride!

CIV.

I know not why—but standing thus by thee
It seems as if I had thine inmate known,
Thou Tomb! and other days come back on me
With recollected music, though the tone
Is changed and solemn, like the cloudy groan
Of dying thunder on the distant wind;
Yet could I seat me by this ivied stone
Till I had bodied forth the heated mind
Forms from the floating wreck which Ruin leaves behind;

CV.

And from the planks, far shatter'd o'er the rocks,
Built me a little bark of hope, once more
To battle with the ocean and the shocks
Of the loud breakers, and the ceaseless roar
Which rushes on the solitary shore
Where all lies founder'd that was ever dear:
But could I gather from the wave-worn store
Enough for my rude boat, where should I steer?
There woos no home, nor hope, nor life, save what is here.

CVI.

Then let the winds howl on! their harmony
Shall henceforth be my music, and the night
The sound shall temper with the owlets' cry,
As I now hear them, in the fading light
Dim o'er the bird of darkness' native site,
Answering each other on the Palatine,
With their large eyes, all glistening gray and bright,
And sailing pinions.—Upon such a shrine
What are our petty griefs?—let me not number mine.

CVII.

Cypress and ivy, weed and wallflower grown
Matted and mass'd together, hillocks heap'd

On what were chambers, arch crush'd, column strown
In fragments, choked up vaults, and frescos steep'd
In subterranean damps, where the owl peep'd,
Deeming it midnight:—Temples, baths, or halls?
Pronounce who can; for all that Learning reap'd
From her research hath been, that these are walls—
Behold the Imperial Mount! 'tis thus the mighty falls.[25]

CVIII.

There is the moral of all human tales;[26]
'T is but the same rehearsal of the past,
First Freedom, and then Glory—when that fails,
Wealth, vice, corruption—barbarism at last.
And History, with all her volumes vast,
Hath but *one* page—'t is better written here,
Where gorgeous Tyranny hath thus amass'd
All treasures, all delights, that eye or ear,
Heart, soul could seek, tongue ask—Away with words: draw near,

CIX.

Admire, exult—despise—laugh, weep,—for here
There is such matter for all feeling:—Man!
Thou pendulum betwixt a smile and tear,
Ages and realms are crowded in this span,
This mountain, whose obliterated plan
The pyramid of empires pinnacled,
Of Glory's gewgaws shining in the van
Till the sun's rays with added flame were fill'd!
Where are its golden roofs? where those who dared to build?

CX.

Tully was not so eloquent as thou,
Thou nameless column with the buried base!
What are the laurels of the Cæsar's brow?
Crown me with ivy from his dwelling-place.
Whose arch or pillar meets me in the face,
Titus or Trajan's? No—'t is that of Time:
Triumph, arch, pillar, all he doth displace
Scoffing; and apostolic statues climb
To crush the imperial urn, whose ashes slept sublime,[27]

CXI.

Buried in air, the deep blue sky of Rome,
And looking to the stars: they had contain'd
A spirit which with these would find a home,
The last of those who o'er the whole earth reign'd,
The Roman globe, for after none sustain'd,
But yielded back his conquests:—he was more
Than a mere Alexander, and, unstain'd
With household blood and wine, serenely wore
His sovereign virtues—still we Trajan's name adore.[28]

CXII.

Where is the rock of Triumph, the high place
Where Rome embraced her heroes? where the steep
Tarpeian? fittest goal of Treason's race,
The promontory whence the Traitor's Leap
Cured all ambition. Did the Conquerors heap
Their spoils here? Yes; and in yon field below,
A thousand years of silenced factions sleep—
The Forum, where the immortal accents glow,
And still the eloquent air breathes—burns with Cicero!

CXIII.

The field of freedom, faction, fame, and blood:
Here a proud people's passions were exhaled,
From the first hour of empire in the bud
To that when further worlds to conquer fail'd;
But long before had Freedom's face been veil'd,
And Anarchy assumed her attributes;
Till every lawless soldier who assail'd
Trod on the trembling Senate's slavish mutes,
Or raised the venal voice of baser prostitutes.

CXIV.

Then turn we to our latest tribune's name,
From her ten thousand tyrants turn to thee,
Redeemer of dark centuries of shame—
The friend of Petrarch—hope of Italy—
Rienzi! last of Romans! While the tree [29]
Of freedom's wither'd trunk puts forth a leaf,
Even for thy tomb a garland let it be—
The forum's champion, and the people's chief—
Her new-born Numa thou—with reign, alas! too brief.

CXV.

Egeria! sweet creation of some heart
Which found no mortal resting-place so fair
As thine ideal breast; whate'er thou art
Or wert,—a young Aurora of the air,
The nympholepsy of some fond despair;
Or, it might be, a beauty of the earth,
Who found a more than common votary there
Too much adoring; whatsoe'er thy birth,
Thou wert a beautiful thought, and softly bodied forth.

CXVI.

The mosses of thy fountain still are sprinkled
With thine Elysian water-drops; the face
Of thy cave-guarded spring, with years unwrinkled,
Reflects the meek-eyed genius of the place,
Whose green wild margin now no more erase
Art's works; nor must the delicate waters sleep,
Prison'd in marble, bubbling from the base
Of the cleft statue, with a gentle leap
The rill runs o'er, and round, fern, flowers, and ivy creep,

CXVII.

Fantastically tangled: the green hills
Are clothed with early blossoms, through the grass
The quick-eyed lizard rustles, and the bills
Of summer-birds sing welcome as ye pass;
Flowers fresh in hue, and many in their class,
Implore the pausing step, and with their dyes
Dance in the soft breeze in a fairy mass;
The sweetness of the violet's deep blue eyes,
Kiss'd by the breath of heaven, seems coloured by its skies.

CXVIII.

Here didst thou dwell, in this enchanted cover,
Egeria! thy all heavenly bosom beating
For the far footsteps of thy mortal lover;
The purple Midnight veil'd that mystic meeting
With her most starry canopy, and seating
Thyself by thine adorer, what befell?
This cave was only shaped out for the greeting
Of an enamour'd Goddess, and the cell
Haunted by holy Love—the earliest oracle!

CXIX.

And didst thou not, thy breast to his replying,
Blend a celestial with a human heart;
And Love, which dies as it was born, in sighing,
Share with immortal transport? could thine art
Make them indeed immortal, and impart
The purity of heaven to earthly joys,
Expel the venom and not blunt the dart—
The dull satiety which all destroys—
And root from out the soul the deadly weed which cloys?

CXX.

Alas! our young affections run to waste,
Or water but the desert; whence arise
But weeds of dark luxuriance, tares of haste,
Rank at the core, though tempting to the eyes,
Flowers whose wild odours breathe but agonies,
And trees whose gums are poison; such the plants
Which spring beneath her steps as Passion flies
O'er the world's wilderness, and vainly pants
For some celestial fruit forbidden to our wants.

CXXI.

Oh Love! no habitant of earth thou art—
An unseen seraph, we believe in thee,
A faith whose martyrs are the broken heart,
But never yet hath seen, nor e'er shall see
The naked eye, thy form, as it should be;
The mind hath made thee, as it peopled heaven,
Even with its own desiring phantasy,
And to a thought such shape and image given,
As haunts the unquench'd soul—parch'd—wearied—wrung—and riven.

CXXII.

Of its own beauty is the mind diseased,
And fevers into false creation:—where,
Where are the forms the sculptor's soul hath seized?
In him alone. Can Nature show so fair?
Where are the charms and virtues which we dare
Conceive in boyhood and pursue as men,
The unreach'd Paradise of our despair,
Which o'er-informs the pencil and the pen,
And overpowers the page where it would bloom again?

CXXIII.

Who loves, raves—'tis youth's frenzy—but the cure
Is bitterer still; as charm by charm unwinds
Which robed our idols, and we see too sure
Nor worth nor beauty dwells from out the mind's
Ideal shape of such; yet still it binds
The fatal spell, and still it draws us on,
Reaping the whirlwind from the oft-sown winds;
The stubborn heart, its alchemy begun,
Seems ever near the prize,—wealthiest when most undone.

CXXIV.

We wither from our youth, we gasp away—
Sick—sick; unfound the boon—unslaked the thirst,
Though to the last, in verge of our decay,
Some phantom lures, such as we sought at first—
But all too late,—so are we doubly curst.
Love, fame, ambition, avarice—'t is the same,
Each idle—and all ill—and none the worst—
For all are meteors with a different name,
And Death the sable smoke where vanishes the flame.

CXXV.

Few—none—find what they love or could have loved;
Though accident, blind contact, and the strong
Necessity of loving, have removed
Antipathies—but to recur, ere long,
Envenom'd with irrevocable wrong;
And Circumstance, that unspiritual god
And miscreator, makes and helps along
Our coming evils with a crutch-like rod,
Whose touch turns Hope to dust,—the dust we all have trod.

CXXVI.

Our life is a false nature—'t is not in
The harmony of things,—this hard decree,
This uneradicable taint of sin,
This boundless upas, this all-blasting tree,
Whose root is earth, whose leaves and branches be
The skies which rain their plagues on men like dew—
Disease, death, bondage, all the woes we see—
And worse, the woes we see not—which throb through
The immedicable soul, with heart-aches ever new.

CXXVII.

Yet let us ponder boldly—'t is a base[30]
Abandonment of reason to resign
Our right of thought—our last and only place
Of refuge; this, at least, shall still be mine:
Though from our birth the faculty divine
Is chain'd and tortured—cabin'd, cribb'd, confined,
And bred in darkness, lest the truth should shine
Too brightly on the unpreparèd mind,
The beam pours in, for time and skill will couch the blind.

CXXVIII.

Arches on arches! as it were that Rome,
Collecting the chief trophies of her line,
Would build up all her triumphs in one dome,
Her Coliseum stands; the moonbeams shine
As 't were its natural torches, for divine
Should be the light which streams here, to illume
This long-explored but still exhaustless mine
Of contemplation; and the azure gloom
Of an Italian night, where the deep skies assume

CXXIX.

Hues which have words, and speak to ye of heaven
Floats o'er this vast and wondrous monument,
And shadows forth its glory. There is given
Unto the things of earth, which Time hath bent,
A spirit's feeling, and where he hath leant
His hand, but broke his scythe, there is a power
And magic in the ruin'd battlement,
For which the palace of the present hour
Must yield its pomp, and wait till ages are its dower.

CXXX.

Oh Time! the beautifier of the dead,
Adorner of the ruin, comforter
And only healer when the heart hath bled—
Time! the corrector where our judgments err,
The test of truth, love,—sole philosopher,
For all beside are sophists, from thy thrift,
Which never loses though it doth defer—
Time, the avenger! unto thee I lift
My hands, and eyes, and heart, and crave of thee a gift:

CXXXI.

Amidst this wreck, where thou hast made a shrine
And temple more divinely desolate,
Among thy mightier offerings here are mine,
Ruins of years—though few, yet full of fate:—

If thou hast ever seen me too elate,
Hear me not; but if calmly I have borne
Good, and reserved my pride against the hate
Which shall not whelm me, let me not have worn
This iron in my soul in vain—shall *they* not mourn?

CXXXII.

And thou, who never yet of human wrong
Left the unbalanced scale, great Nemesis!
Here, where the ancient paid thee homage long—
Thou, who didst call the Furies from the abyss,
And round Orestes bade them howl and hiss
For that unnatural retribution—just,
Had it but been from hands less near—in this
Thy former realm, I call thee from the dust!
Dost thou not hear my heart?—Awake! thou shalt, and must.

CXXXIII.

It is not that I may not have incurr'd
For my ancestral faults or mine the wound
I bleed withal, and, had it been conferr'd
With a just weapon, it had flowed unbound;
But now my blood shall not sink in the ground;
To thee I do devote it—*thou* shalt take
The vengeance, which shall yet be sought and found,
Which if *I* have not taken for the sake——
But let that pass—I sleep, but thou shalt yet awake.

CXXXIV.

And if my voice break forth, 't is not that now
I shrink from what is suffer'd: let him speak
Who hath beheld decline upon my brow,
Or seen my mind's convulsion leave it weak;
But in this page a record will I seek.
Not in the air shall these my words disperse,
Though I be ashes; a far hour shall wreak
The deep prophetic fulness of this verse,
And pile on human heads the mountain of my curse!

CXXXV.

That curse shall be Forgiveness.—Have I not—
Hear me, my mother Earth! behold it, Heaven!—
Have I not had to wrestle with my lot?
Have I not suffer'd things to be forgiven?
Have I not had my brain sear'd, my heart riven,
Hopes sapp'd, name blighted, Life's life lied away?
And only not to desperation driven,
Because not altogether of such clay
As rots into the souls of those whom I survey.

CXXXVI.

From mighty wrongs to petty perfidy
Have I not seen what human things could do?
From the loud roar of foaming calumny
To the small whisper of the as paltry few,
And subtler venom of the reptile crew,
The Janus glance of whose significant eye,
Learning to lie with silence, would *seem* true,
And without utterance, save the shrug or sigh,
Deal round to happy fools its speechless obloquy.

CXXXVII.

But I have lived, and have not lived in vain:
My mind may lose its force, my blood its fire,
And my frame perish even in conquering pain;
But there is that within me which shall tire
Torture and Time, and breathe when I expire;
Something unearthly, which they deem not of,
Like the remembered tone of a mute lyre,
Shall on their soften'd spirits sink, and move
In hearts all rocky, now the late remorse of love.

CXXXVIII.

The seal is set.—Now welcome, thou dread power!
Nameless, yet thus omnipotent, which here
Walk'st in the shadow of the midnight hour
With a deep awe, yet all distinct from fear:
Thy haunts are ever where the dead walls rear
Their ivy mantles, and the solemn scene
Derives from thee a sense so deep and clear
That we become a part of what has been,
And grow unto the spot, all-seeing but unseen.

CXXXIX.

And the buzz of eager nations ran,
In murmur'd pity, or loud-roar'd applause,
As man was slaughter'd by his fellow man.
And wherefore slaughter'd? wherefore, but because
Such was the bloody Circus' genial laws,
And the imperial pleasure.—Wherefore not?
What matters where we fall to fill the maws
Of worms—on battle-plains or listed spot?
Both are but theatres where the chief actors rot.

CXL.

I see before me the Gladiator lie:
He leans upon his hand—his manly brow
Consents to death, but conquers agony,
And his droop'd head sinks gradually low—
And through his side the last drops, ebbing slow
From the red gash, fall heavy, one by one,
Like the first of a thunder-shower; and now
The arena swims around him—he is gone,
Ere ceased the inhuman shout which hail'd the wretch who won.

CXLI.

He heard it, but he heeded not—his eyes
Were with his heart, and that was far away;[31]
He reck'd not of the life he lost nor prize,
But where his rude hut by the Danube lay,
There were his young barbarians all at play,
There was their Dacian mother—he, their sire,
Butcher'd to make a Roman holiday—

All this rush'd with his blood—Shall he expire
And unavenged?—Arise! ye Goths, and glut your ire!

CXLII.

But here, where Murder breathed her bloody steam;
And here, where buzzing nations choked the ways,
And roar'd or murmur'd like a mountain stream
Dashing or winding as its torrent strays;
Here, where the Roman million's blame or praise
Was death or life, the playthings of a crowd,
My voice sounds much—and fall the stars' faint rays
On the arena void—seats crush'd—walls bow'd—
And galleries, where my steps seem echoes strangely loud.

CXLIII.

A ruin—yet what ruin! from its mass
Walls, palaces, half-cities, have been rear'd;
Yet oft the enormous skeleton ye pass,
And marvel where the spoil could have appeared.
Hath it indeed been plunder'd, or but clear'd?
Alas! developed, opens the decay,
When the colossal fabric's form is near'd;
It will not bear the brightness of the day,
Which streams too much on all years, man, have reft away.

CXLIV.

But when the rising moon begins to climb
Its topmost arch, and gently pauses there;
When the stars twinkle through the loops of time,
And the low night-breeze waves along the air
The garland-forest, which the gray walls wear,
Like laurels on the bald first Cæsar's head;[32]
When the light shines serene but doth not glare,
Then in this magic circle raise the dead:
Heroes have trod this spot—'t is on their dust ye tread.

CXLV.

"While stands the Coliseum, Rome shall stand;[33]
"When falls the Coliseum, Rome shall fall;
"And when Rome falls—the World." From our own land
Thus spake the pilgrims o'er this mighty wall
In Saxon times, which we are wont to call
Ancient; and these three mortal things are still
On their foundations, and unalter'd all;
Rome and her Ruin past Redemption's skill,
The World—the same wide den—of thieves, or what ye will.

CXLVI.

Simple, erect, severe, austere, sublime—
Shrine of all saints and temple of all gods,
From Jove to Jesus—spared and blest by time;[34]
Looking tranquillity, while falls or nods
Arch, empire, each thing round thee, and man plods
His way through thorns to ashes—glorious dome!
Shalt thou not last?—Time's scythe and tyrants' rods
Shiver upon thee—sanctuary and home
Of art and piety—Pantheon!—pride of Rome!

CXLVII.

Relic of nobler days, and noblest arts!
Despoil'd yet perfect, with thy circle spreads,
A holiness appealing to all hearts—
To art a model; and to him who treads
Rome for the sake o. ages, Glory sheds
Her light through thy sole aperture; to those
Who worship, here are altars for their beads;
And they who feel for genius may repose
Their eyes on honour'd forms, whose busts around them close.[35]

CXLVIII.

There is a dungeon, in whose dim drear light[36]
What do I gaze on? Nothing: Look again!
Two forms are slowly shadow'd on my sight—
Two insulated phantoms of the brain:
It is not so; I see them full and plain—
An old man, and a female young and fair,
Fresh as a nursing mother, in whose vein
The blood is nectar;—but what doth she there,
With her unmantled neck, and bosom white and bare?

CXLIX.

Full swells the deep pure fountain of young life,
Where *on* the heart and *from* the heart we took
Our first and sweetest nurture, when the wife,
Blest into mother, in the innocent look,
Or even the piping cry of lips that brook
No pain and small suspense, a joy perceives
Man knows not, when from out its cradled nook
She sees her little bud put forth its leaves—
What may the fruit be yet?—I know not—Cain was Eve's.

CL.

But here youth offers to old age the food,
The milk of his own gift:—it is her sire
To whom she renders back the debt of blood
Born with her birth. No; he shall not expire
While in those warm and lovely veins the fire
Of health and holy feeling can provide
Great Nature's Nile, whose deep stream rises higher
Than Egypt's river:—from that gentle side
Drink, drink and live, old man! heaven's realm holds no such tide.

CLI.

The starry fable of the milky way
Has not thy story's purity; it is
A constellation of a sweeter ray,
And sacred Nature triumphs more in this
Reverse of her decree, than in the abyss
Where sparkle distant worlds:—Oh, holiest nurse
No drop of that clear stream its way shall miss
To thy sire's heart, replenishing its source
With life, as our freed souls rejoin the universe.

CLII.

Turn to the Mole which Hadrian rear'd on high,[37]
Imperial mimic of old Egypt's piles,
Colossal copyist of deformity,
Whose travell'd phantasy from the far Nile's
Enormous model, doom'd the artist's toils
To build for giants, and for his vain earth,
His shrunken ashes, raise this dome: How smiles
The gazer's eye with philosophic mirth,
To view the huge design which sprung from such a birth!

CLIII.

But lo! the dome—the vast and wondrous dome,
To which Diana's marvel was a cell—
Christ's mighty shrine above his martyr's tomb!
I have beheld the Ephesian's miracle—
Its columns strew the wilderness, and dwell
The hyæna and the jackal in their shade;
I have beheld Sophia's bright roofs swell
Their glittering mass i' the sun, and have survey'd
Its sanctuary the while the usurping Moslem pray'd;

CLIV.

But thou, of temples old, or altars new,
Standest alone—with nothing like to thee—
Worthiest of God, the holy and the true.
Since Zion's desolation, when that He
Forsook His former city, what could be,
Of earthly structures, in His honour piled,
Of a sublimer aspect? Majesty,
Power, Glory, Strength, and Beauty, all are aisled
In this eternal ark of worship undefiled.

CLV.

Enter: its grandeur overwhelms thee not
And why? it is not lessen'd; but thy mind,
Expanded by the genius of the spot,
Has grown colossal, and can only find
A fit abode wherein appear enshrined
Thy hopes of immortality; and thou
Shalt one day, if found worthy, so defined,
See thy God face to face, as thou dost now
His Holy of Holies, nor be blasted by His brow.

CLVI.

Thou movest—but increasing with the advance,
Like climbing some great Alp, which still doth rise,
Deceived by its gigantic elegance;
Vastness which grows—but grows to harmonise—
All musical in its immensities;
Rich marbles—richer painting—shrines where flame
The lamps of gold—and haughty dome which vies
In air with Earth's chief structures, though their frame
Sits on the firm-set ground—and this the clouds must claim.

CLVII.

Thou seest not all; but piecemeal thou must break,
To separate contemplation, the great whole;
And as the ocean many bays will make,
That ask the eye—so here condense thy soul
To more immediate objects, and control

Thy thoughts until thy mind hath got by heart
Its eloquent proportions, and unroll
In mighty graduations, part by part,
The glory which at once upon thee did not dart,

CLVIII.

Not by its fault—but thine: Our outward sense
Is but of gradual grasp—and as it is
That what we have of feeling most intense
Outstrips our faint expression; even so this
Outshining and o'erwhelming edifice
Fools our fond gaze, and greatest of the great
Defies at first our Nature's littleness,
Till, growing with its growth, we thus dilate
Our spirits to the size of that they contemplate.

CLIX.

Then pause, and be enlighten'd; there is more
In such a survey than the sating gaze
Of wonder pleased, or awe which would adore
The worship of the place, or the mere praise
Of art and its great masters, who could raise
What former time, nor skill, nor thought could plan;
The fountain of sublimity displays
Its depth, and thence may draw the mind of man
Its golden sands, and learn what great conceptions can.

CLX.

Or, turning to the Vatican, go see
Laocoon's torture dignifying pain—
A father's love and mortal's agony
With an immortal's patience blending:—Vain
The struggle; vain, against the coiling strain
And gripe, and deepening of the dragon's grasp,
The old man's clench; the long envenom'd chain
Rivets the living links,—the enormous asp
Enforces pang on pang, and stifles gasp on gasp.

CLXI.

Or view the Lord of the unerring bow,
The God of life, and poesy, and light—
The Sun in human limbs array'd, and brow
All radiant from his triumph in the fight;
The shaft hath just been shot—the arrow bright
With an immortal's vengeance; in his eye
And nostril beautiful disdain, and might
And majesty, flash their full lightnings by,
Developing in that one glance the Deity.

CLXII.

But in his delicate form—a dream of Love,
Shaped by some solitary nymph, whose breast
Long'd for a deathless lover from above,
And madden'd in that vision—are exprest
All that ideal beauty ever bless'd
The mind with in its most unearthly mood,
When each conception was a heavenly guest—
A ray of immortality—and stood,
Starlike, around, until they gather'd to a god!

CLXIII.

And if it be Prometheus stole from heaven
The fire which we endure, it was repaid
By him to whom the energy was given
Which this poetic marble hath array'd
With an eternal glory—which, if made
By human hands, is not of human thought;
And Time himself hath hallow'd it, not laid
One ringlet in the dust—nor hath it caught
A tinge of years, but breathes the flame with which 't was wrought.

CLXIV.

But where is he, the Pilgrim of my song,
The being who upheld it through the past?
Methinks he cometh late and tarries long.
He is no more—these breathings are his last;
His wanderings done, his visions ebbing fast,
And he himself as nothing:—if he was
Aught but a phantasy, and could be class'd
With forms which live and suffer—let that pass—
His shadow fades away into Destruction's mass.

CLXV.

Which gathers shadow, substance, life, and all
That we inherit in its mortal shroud,
And spreads the dim and universal pall
Through which all things grow phantoms; and the cloud
Between us sinks and all which ever glow'd,
Till glory's self is twilight, and displays
A melancholy halo scarce allow'd
To hover on the verge of darkness; rays
Sadder than saddest night, for they distract the gaze.

CLXVI.

And send us prying into the abyss,
To gather what we shall be when the frame
Shall be resolved to something less than this
Its wretched essence; and to dream of fame,
And wipe the dust from off the idle name
We never more shall hear,—but never more,
Oh, happier thought! can we be made the same:
It is enough in sooth that *once* we bore
These fardels of the heart—the heart whose sweat was gore.

CLXVII.

Hark! forth from the abyss a voice proceeds,
A long low distant murmur of dread sound,

Such as arises when a nation bleeds
With some deep and immedicable wound;
Through storm and darkness yawns the rending ground,
The gulf is thick with phantoms, but the chief
Seems royal still, though with her head discrown'd,
And pale, but lovely, with maternal grief
She clasps a babe, to whom her breast yields no relief.

CLXVIII.

Scion of chiefs and monarchs, where art thou
Fond hope of many nations, art thou dead?
Could not the grave forget thee, and lay low
Some less majestic, less beloved head?
In the sad midnight, while thy heart still bled,
The mother of a moment, o'er thy boy,
Death hush'd that pang for ever: with thee fled
The present happiness and promised joy
Which fill'd the imperial isles so full it seem'd to cloy.

CLXIX.

Peasants bring forth in safety.—Can it be,
Oh thou that wert so happy, so adored!
Those who weep not for kings shall weep for thee,
And Freedom's heart, grown heavy, cease to hoard,
Her many griefs for ONE; for she had pour'd
Her orisons for thee, and o'er thy head
Beheld her Iris.—Thou, too, lonely lord,
And desolate consort—vainly wert thou wed!
The husband of a year! the father of the dead!

CLXX.

Of sackcloth was thy wedding garment made;
Thy bridal's fruit is ashes: in the dust
The fair-hair'd Daughter of the Isles is laid,
The love of millions! How we did entrust
Futurity to her! and, though it must
Darken above our bones, yet fondly deem'd
Our children should obey her child, and bless'd
Her and her hoped-for seed, whose promise seem'd
Like star to shepherds' eyes:—'t was but a meteor beam'd.

CLXXI.

Woe unto us, not her; for she sleeps well:
The fickle reek of popular breath, the tongue
Of hollow counsel, the false oracle,
Which from the birth of monarchy hath rung
Its knell in princely ears, till the o'erstung
Nations have arm'd in madness, the strange fate [38]
Which tumbles mightiest sovereigns, and hath flung
Against their blind omnipotence a weight
Within the opposing scale, which crushes soon or late,—

CLXXII.

These might have been her destiny; but no,
Our hearts deny it: and so young, so fair,
Good without effort, great without a foe;
But now a bride and mother—and now *there!*
How many ties did that stern moment tear!
From thy Sire's to his humblest subject's breast
Is link'd the electric chain of that despair,
Whose shock was as an earthquake's, and opprest
The land which loved thee so that none could love thee best.

CLXXIII.

Lo, Nemi! navell'd in the woody hills [39]
So far, that the uprooting wind which tears
The oak from his foundation, and which spills
The ocean o'er its boundary, and bears
Its foam against the skies, reluctant spares
The oval mirror of thy glassy lake;
And, calm as cherish'd hate, its surface wears
A deep cold settled aspect nought can shake,
All coil'd into itself and round, as sleeps the snake.

CLXXIV.

And near Albano's scarce divided waves
Shine from a sister valley;—and afar
The Tiber winds, and the broad ocean laves
The Latian coast where sprung the Epic war,
"Arms and the Man," whose re-ascending star
Rose o'er an empire:—but beneath thy right
Tully reposed from Rome:—and where yon bar
Of girdling mountains intercepts the sight
The Sabine farm was till'd, the weary bard's delight.[40]

CLXXV.

But I forget,—My Pilgrim's shrine is won,
And he and I must part,—so let it be—
His task and mine alike are nearly done;
Yet once more let us look upon the sea;
The midland ocean breaks on him and me,
And from the Alban Mount we now behold
Our friend of youth, that Ocean, which when we
Beheld it last by Calpe's rock unfold
Those waves, we follow'd on till the dark Euxine roll'd

CLXXVI.

Upon the blue Symplegades: long years—
Long, though not very many, since have done
Their work on both; some suffering and some tears
Have left us nearly where we had begun:
Yet not in vain our mortal race hath run,
We have had our reward—and it is here:
That we can yet feel gladden'd by the sun,
And reap from earth, sea, joy almost as dear
As if there were no man to trouble what is clear.

CLXXVII.

Oh! that the Desert were my dwelling-place,
With one fair Spirit for my minister,
That I might all forget the human race
And hating no one, love but only her!
Ye Elements!—in whose ennobling stir
I feel myself exalted—Can ye not
Accord me such a being? Do I err
In deeming such inhabit many a spot?
Though with them to converse can rarely be our lot

CLXXVIII.

There is a pleasure in the pathless woods,
There is a rapture on the lonely shore,
There is society where none intrudes,
By the deep Sea, and music in its roar:
I love not Man the less, but Nature more,
From these our interviews, in which I steal
From all I may be, or have been before,
To mingle with the Universe, and feel
What I can ne'er express, yet cannot all conceal.

CLXXIX.

Roll on, thou deep and dark blue Ocean—roll!
Ten thousand fleets sweep over thee in vain;
Man marks the earth with ruin—his control
Stops with the shore;—upon the watery plain
The wrecks are all thy deed, nor doth remain
A shadow of man's ravage, save his own,
When, for a moment, like a drop of rain,
He sinks into thy depths with bubbling groan,
Without a grave, unknell'd, uncoffin'd, and unknown.

CLXXX.

His steps are upon thy paths,—thy fields
Are not a spoil for him,—thou dost arise
And shake him from thee; the vile strength he wields
For earth's destruction thou dost all despise,
Spurning him from thy bosom to the skies,
And send'st him, shivering in thy playful spray
And howling, to his Gods, where haply lies
His petty hope in some near port or bay,
And dashest him again to earth:—there let him lay.

CLXXXI.

The armaments which thunderstrike the walls
Of rock-built cities, bidding nations quake,

And monarchs tremble in their capitals,
The oak leviathans, whose huge ribs make
Their clay creator the vain title take
Of lord of thee, and arbiter of war;
These are thy toys, and, as the snowy flake,
They melt into thy yeast of waves, which mar
Alike the Armada's pride, or spoils of Trafalgar.

CLXXXII.

Thy shores are empires, changed in all save thee—
Assyria, Greece, Rome, Carthage, what are they?
Thy waters wasted them while they were free,
And many a tyrant since; their shores obey
The stranger, slave, or savage; their decay
Has dried up realms to deserts:—not so thou,
Unchangeable save to thy wild waves' play—
Time writes no wrinkle on thine azure brow—
Such as creation's dawn beheld, thou rollest now

CLXXXIII.

Thou glorious mirror, where the Almighty's form
Glasses itself in tempests; in all time,
Calm or convulsed—in breeze, or gale, or storm,
Icing the pole, or in the torrid clime
Dark-heaving;—boundless, endless, and sublime—
The image of Eternity—the throne
Of the Invisible; even from out thy slime
The monsters of the deep are made; each zone
Obeys thee; thou goest forth, dread, fathomless, alone.

CLXXXIV.

And I have loved thee, Ocean! and my joy
Of youthful sports was on thy breast to be
Borne, like thy bubbles, onward: from a boy
I wanton'd with thy breakers—they to me
Were a delight; and if the freshening sea
Made them a terror—'t was a pleasing fear,
For I was as it were a child of thee,
And trusted to thy billows far and near,
And laid my hand upon thy mane—as I do here.

CLXXXV.

My task is done—my song hath ceased—my theme
Has died into an echo; it is fit
The spell should break of this protracted dream.
The torch shall be extinguish'd which hath lit
My midnight lamp—and what is writ is writ,—
Would it were worthier! but I am not now
That which I have been—and my visions flit
Less palpably before me—and the glow
Which in my spirit dwelt is fluttering, faint, and low

CLXXXVI.

Farewell! a word that must be, and hath been—
A sound which makes us linger;—yet—farewell!
Ye! who have traced the Pilgrim to the scene
Which is his last, if in your memories dwell
A thought which once was his, if on ye swell
A single recollection, not in vain
He wore his sandal-shoon and scallop-shell;
Farewell! with *him* alone may rest the pain,
If such there were—with *you*, the moral of his strain!

NOTES TO CANTO THE FOURTH.

NOTE 1, page 634.

She looks a sea Cybele, fresh from ocean.

Sabellicus, describing the appearance of Venice, has made use of the above image, which would not be poetical were it not true.—"Quo fit ut qui superne urbem contempletur, turritam telluris imaginem medio Oceano figuratam se putet inspicere."

NOTE 2, page 635.

"*Sparta hath many a worthier son than he.*"

The answer of the mother of Brasidas, the Lacedœmonian general, to the strangers who praised the memory of her son.

NOTE 3, page 635.

The "Planter of the Lion."

That is, the Lion of St. Mark, the standard of the republic, which is the origin of the word Pantaloon—Piantaleone, Pantaleon, Pantaloon.

NOTE 4, page 636.

Redemption rose up in the Attic Muse.

The story is told in Plutarch's "Life of Nicias."

NOTE 5, page 636.

And Otway, Radcliffe, Schiller, Shakspeare's art.

"Venice Preserved;" "Mysteries of Udolpho;" the "Ghost-Seer, or Armenian;" the "Merchant of Venice;" "Othello."

NOTE 6, page 636.

But from their nature will the tannen grow.

Tannen is the plural of *tanne*, a species of fir peculiar to the Alps, which only thrives in very rocky parts, where scarcely soil sufficient for its nourishment can be found. On these spots it grows to a greater height than any other mountain tree.

NOTE 7, page 637.

Floats through the azure air, an island of the blest.

The above description may seem fantastical or exaggerated to those who have never seen an Oriental or an Italian sky, yet it is but a literal and hardly sufficient delineation of an August evening (the eighteenth), as contemplated in one of many rides along the banks of the Brenta, near La Mira.

NOTE 8, page 638.

They keep his dust in Arquà, where he died.

Petrarch retired to Arquà immediately on his return from the unsuccessful attempt to visit Urban V. at Rome, in the year 1370, and, with the exception of his celebrated visit to Venice in company with Francesco Novello da Carrara, he appears to have passed the four last years of his life between that charming solitude and Padua. For four months previous to his death he was in a state of continual languor, and in the morning of July the 19th, in the year 1374, was found dead in his library chair with his head resting upon a book. The chair is still shown amongst the precious relics of Arquà, which, from the uninterrupted veneration that has been attached to every thing relative to this great man from the moment of his death to the present hour, have, it may be hoped, a better chance of authenticity than the Shakspearian memorials of Stratford-upon-Avon.

Every footstep of Laura's lover has been anxiously traced and recorded. The house in which he lodged is shown in Venice. The inhabitants of Arezzo, in order to decide the ancient controversy between their city and the neighbouring Ancisa, where Petrarch was carried when seven months old, and remained until his seventh year, have designated by a long inscription the spot where their great fellow-citizen was born. A tablet has been raised to him at Parma, in the chapel of St. Agatha, at the cathedral, because he was archdeacon of that society, and was only snatched from his intended sepulture in their church by a *foreign* death. Another tablet, with a bust, has been erected to him at Pavia, on account of his having passed the autumn of 1368 in that city, with his son-in-law Brossano. The political condition which has for ages precluded the Italians from the criticism of the living, has concentrated their attention to the illustration of the dead.

NOTE 9, page 638.

Or, it may be, with demons, who impair.

The struggle is to the full as likely to be with demons as with our better thoughts. Satan chose the wilderness for the temptation of our Saviour. And our unsullied John Locke preferred the presence of a child to complete solitude.

NOTE 10, page 639.

The lightning rent from Ariosto's bust,
The iron crown of laurel's mimick'd leaves.

Before the remains of Ariosto were removed from the Benedictine church to the library of Ferrara, his bust, which surmounted the tomb, was struck by lightning, and a crown of iron laurels melted away. The transfer of these sacred ashes, on the 6th of June, 1801, was one of the most brilliant spectacles of the short-lived Italian republic; and to consecrate the memory of the ceremony, the once famous fallen *Intrepidi* were revived and reformed into the Ariostean academy. The large public place throughout which the procession paraded, was then for the first time called Ariosto Square. The author of the "Orlando" is jealously claimed as the Homer, not of Italy, but Ferrara. The mother of Ariosto was of Reggio, and the house in which he was born is carefully distinguished by a tablet with these words: "Qui nacque Ludovico Ariosto il giorno 8. di Settembre dell' anno 1474." But the Ferrarese make light of the accident by which their poet was born abroad, and claim him exclusively for their own. They possess his bones, they show his arm-chair, and his inkstand, and his autographs. The house where he lived, the room where he died, are designated by his own replaced memorial, and by a recent inscription.

NOTE 11, page 639.

Victor or vanquish'd, thou the slave of friend or foe.

The two stanzas xlii. and xliii. are, with the exception of a line or two, a translation of the famous sonnet of Filicaja:—"Italia, Italia, O tu cui feo la sorte!"

NOTE 12, page 639.

Wandering in youth, I traced the path of him.

The celebrated letter of Servius Sulpicius to Cicero, on the death of his daughter, describes as it then was, and now is, a path which I often traced in Greece, both by sea and land, in different journeys and voyages. "On my return from Asia, as I was sailing from Ægina towards Megara, I began to contemplate the prospect of the countries around me: Ægina was behind, Megara before me; Piræus

on the right, Corinth on the left: all which towns, once famous and flourishing, now lie overturned and buried in their ruins. Upon this sight, I could but think presently within myself, Alas! how do we poor mortals fret and vex ourselves if any of our friends happen to die or be killed, whose life is yet so short, when the carcasses of so many noble cities lie here exposed before me in one view."—See Middleton's *Cicero*, vol. ii. p. 371.

NOTE 13, page 640.

The skeleton of her Titanic form.

It is Poggio, who, looking from the Capitoline Hill upon ruined Rome, breaks forth in the exclamation, "Ut nunc omni decore nudata, prostrata jacet, instar gigantei cadaveris corrupti atque undique exesi."

NOTE 14, page 641.

Here repose
Angelo's, Alfieri's bones.

Alfieri is the great name of this age. The Italians, without waiting for the hundred years, consider him as "a poet good in law."—His memory is the more dear to them, because he is the bard of freedom; and because, as such, his tragedies can receive no countenance from any of their sovereigns. They are but very seldom, and but very few of them, allowed to be acted. It was observed by Cicero, that nowhere were the true opinions and feelings of the Romans so clearly shown as at the theatre. In the autumn of 1816, a celebrated improvisatore exhibited his talents at the Opera-house of Milan. The reading of the theses handed in for the subjects of his poetry was received by a very numerous audience, for the most part in silence, or with laughter; but when the assistant, unfolding one of the papers, exclaimed *The apotheosis of Victor Alfieri*, the whole theatre burst into a shout, and the applause was continued for some moments. The lot did not fall on Alfieri; and the Signor Sgricci had to pour forth his extemporary common-places on the bombardment of Algiers. The choice, indeed, is not left to accident quite so much as might be thought from a first view of the ceremony; and the police not only takes care to look at the papers beforehand, but in case of any prudential after thought, steps in to correct the blindness of chance. The proposal for deifying Alfieri was received with immediate enthusiasm, the rather because it was conjectured there would be no opportunity of carrying it into effect.

NOTE 15, page 641.

Ungrateful Florence! Dante sleeps afar.

Dante was born at Florence, in the year 1261. He fought in two battles, was fourteen times ambassador, and once prior of the republic. When the party of Charles of Anjou triumphed over the Bianchi, he was absent on an embassy to Pope Boniface VIII., and was condemned to two years' banishment, and to a fine of 8000 lire; on the non-payment of which he was further punished by the sequestration of all his property The republic, however, was not content with this satisfaction, for in 1772 was discovered in the archives at Florence a sentence, in which Dante is the eleventh of a list of fifteen condemned in 1302 to be burnt alive. The pretext for this judgment was a proof of unfair barter, extortions, and illicit gains; and with such an accusation, it is not strange that Dante should have always protested his innocence, and the injustice of his fellow-citizens. His appeal to Florence was accompanied by another to the Emperor Henry; and the death of that sovereign in 1313 was the signal for a sentence of irrevocable banishment. He had before lingered near Tuscany with hopes of recall; then travelled into the north of Italy, where Verona had to boast of his longest residence; and he finally settled at Ravenna, which was his ordinary but not constant abode until his death. The refusal of the Venetians to grant him a public audience, on the part of Guido Novello da Polenta, his protector, is said to have been the principal cause of this event, which happened in 1321. He was buried at Ravenna, in a handsome tomb, which was erected by Guido, restored by Bernardo Bembo in 1483, prætor for that republic which had refused to hear him, again restored by Cardinal Corsi, in 1692, and replaced by a more magnificent sepulchre, constructed in 1780 at the expense of the Cardinal Luigi Valenti Gonzaga.

NOTE 16, page 641.

Boccaccio to his parent earth bequeath'd
His dust.

Boccaccio was buried in the church of St. Michael and St. James, at Certaldo, a small town in the Valdelsa, which was by some supposed the place of his birth. There he passed the latter part of his life in a course of laborious study, which shortened his existence; and there might his ashes have been secure, if not of honour, at least of repose. But the "hyena bigots" of Certaldo tore up the tombstone of Boccaccio, and ejected it from the holy precincts of St. Michael and St. James. The occasion, and, it may be hoped, the excuse, for this ejectment was the making of a new floor for the church; but the fact is, that the tombstone was taken up and thrown aside at the bottom of the building. Ignorance may share the sin with bigotry. It would be painful to relate such an exception to the devotion of the Italians for their great names, could it not be accompanied by a trait more honourably conformable to the general character of the nation. The principal person of the district, the last branch of the house of Medicis, afforded that protection to the memory of the insulted dead which her best ancestors had dispensed upon all contemporary merit. The Marchioness Lenzoni rescued the tombstone of Boccaccio from the neglect in which it had some time lain, and found for it an honourable elevation in her own mansion. She has done more: the house in which the poet lived has been as little respected as his tomb, and is falling to ruin over the head of one indifferent to the name of its former tenant. It consists of two or three little chambers, and a low tower, on which Cosmo II. affixed an inscription. This house she has taken measures to purchase, and proposes to devote to it that care and consideration which are attached to the cradle and to the roof of genius.

NOTE 17, page 643.

Charming the eye with dread,—a matchless cataract.

I saw the Cascata del Marmore of Terni twice, at different periods; once from the summit of the precipice, and again from the valley below. The lower view is far to be preferred, if the traveller has time for one only; but in any point of view, either from above or below, it is worth all the cascades and torrents of Switzerland put together: the Staubach, Reichenbach, Pisse Vache, fall of Arpenaz, &c., are rills in comparative appearance. Of the fall of Schaffhausen, I cannot speak, not yet having seen it.

NOTE 18, page 643.

An Iris sits, amidst the infernal surge.

Of the time, place, and qualities of this kind of iris, the reader will see a short account, in a note to "Manfred." The fall looks so much like "the hell of waters," that Addison thought the descent alluded to the gulf by which Alecto plunged into the infernal regions. It is singular enough, that two of the finest cascades in Europe should be artificial—this of the Velino, and the one at Tivoli. The traveller is strongly recommended to trace the Velino, at least as high as the little lake, called *Pie' di Lup*. The Reatine territory was the Italian Tempe (Cicer. *Epist. ad Attic.* xv. lib. iv.), and the ancient naturalists (Plin. *Hist.*

Nat. lib. ii. cap. lxii.), amongst other beautiful varieties, remarked the daily rainbows of the lake Velinus. A scholar of great name has devoted a treatise to this district alone. See *Ald. Manut. de Reatina Urbe Agroque, ap. Sallengre,* Thesaur. tom. i. p. 773.

NOTE 19, page 643.

The thundering lauwine.

In the greater part of Switzerland, the avalanches are known by the name of lauwine.

NOTE 20, page 643.

The drill'd dull lesson, forced down word by word.

These stanzas may probably remind the reader of Ensign Northerton's remarks: "D—n Homo," &c.; but the reasons for our dislike are not exactly the same. I wish to express that we become tired of the task before we can comprehend the beauty; that we learn by rote before we can get by heart; that the freshness is worn away, and the future pleasure deadened and destroyed, by the didactic anticipation, at an age when we can neither feel nor understand the power of compositions which it requires an acquaintance with life, as well as Latin and Greek, to relish, or to reason upon. For the same reason, we never can be aware of the fulness of some of the finest passages of Shakspeare ("To be or not to be," for instance), from the habit of having them hammered into us at eight years old, as an exercise, not of mind, but of memory: so that when we are old enough to enjoy them, the taste is gone, and the appetite palled. In some parts of the Continent, young persons are taught from more common authors, and do not read the best classics till their maturity. I certainly do not speak on this point from any pique or aversion towards the place of my education. I was not a slow, though an idle boy; and I believe no one could, or can be, more attached to Harrow than I have always been, and with reason;—a part of the time passed there was the happiest of my life; and my precepter, the Rev. Dr. Joseph Drury, was the best and worthiest friend I ever possessed, whose warnings I have remembered but too well, though too late when I have erred,—and whose counsels I have but followed when I have done well or wisely. If ever this imperfect record of my feelings towards him should reach his eyes, let it remind him of one who never thinks of him but with gratitude and veneration—of one who would more gladly boast of having been his pupil, if by more closely following his injunctions, he could reflect any honour upon his instructor.

NOTE 21, page 644.

The trebly hundred triumphs! and the day.

Orosius gives 320 for the number of triumphs. He is followed by Panvinius; and Panvinius by Mr. Gibbon and the modern writers.

NOTE 22, page 644.

The dictatorial wreath,—couldst thou divine.

Certainly, were it not for these two traits in the life of Sylla, alluded to in this stanza, we should regard him as a monster unredeemed by any admirable quality. The *atonement* of his voluntary resignation of empire may perhaps be accepted by us, as it seems to have satisfied the Romans, who if they had not respected must have destroyed him. There could be no mean, no division of opinion; they must have all thought, like Eucrates, that what had appeared ambition was a love of glory, and that what had been mistaken for pride was a real grandeur of soul.

NOTE 23, page 645.

And laid him with the earth's preceding clay.

On the 3rd of September Cromwell gained the victory of Dunbar: a year afterwards he obtained "his crowning mercy" of Worcester; and a few years after, on the same day, which he had ever esteemed the most fortunate for him, died.

NOTE 24, page 646.

There is a stern round tower of other days.

Alluding to the tomb of Cecilia Metella, called Capo di Bove.

NOTE 25, page 647.

Behold the Imperial Mount! 't is thus the mighty falls.

The Palatine is one mass of ruins, particularly on the side towards the Circus Maximus. The very soil is formed of crumbled brickwork. Nothing has been told, nothing can be told, to satisfy the belief of any but a Roman antiquary.

NOTE 26, page 647.

There is the moral of all human tales.

The author of the life of Cicero, speaking of the opinion entertained of Britain by that orator and his contemporary Romans, has the following eloquent passage:—"From their railleries of this kind, on the barbarity and misery of our island, one cannot help reflecting on the surprising fate and revolutions of kingdoms; how Rome, once the mistress of the world, the seat of arts, empire, and glory, now lies sunk in sloth, ignorance, and poverty, enslaved to the most cruel as well as to the most contemptible of tyrants, superstition and religious imposture: while this remote country, anciently the jest and contempt of the polite Romans, is become the happy seat of liberty, plenty, and letters; flourishing in all the arts and refinements of civil life; yet running perhaps the same course which Rome itself had run before it: from virtuous industry to wealth; from wealth to luxury; from luxury to an impatience of discipline, and corruption of morals: till, by a total degeneracy and loss of virtue, being grown ripe for destruction, it falls a prey at last to some hardy oppressor, and, with the loss of liberty, losing every thing that is valuable, sinks gradually again into its original barbarism."

NOTE 27, page 647.

To crush the imperial urn, whose ashes slept sublime.

The column of Trajan is surmounted by St. Peter; that of Aurelius by St. Paul.

NOTE 28, page 647.

His sovereign virtues—still we Trajan's name adore.

Trajan was *proverbially* the best of the Roman princes (*Eutrop.* l, viii. c. 5.); and it would be easier to find a sovereign uniting exactly the opposite characteristics, than one possessed of all the happy qualities ascribed to this emperor. "When he mounted the throne," says the historian Dion, "he was strong in body, he was vigorous in mind; age had impaired none of his faculties; he was altogether free from envy and from detraction; he honoured all the good, and he advanced them; and on this account they could not be the objects of his fear, or of his hate; he never listened to informers; he gave not way to his anger; he abstained equally from unfair exactions and unjust punishments; he had rather be loved as a man than honoured as a sovereign; he was affable with his people, respectful to the senate, and universally beloved by both; he inspired none with dread, but the enemies of his country."—*Hist. Rom.*, l, lxiii. c. 6, 7.

NOTE 29, page 648.

Rienzi! last of Romans!

The name and exploits of Rienzi must be familiar to the reader of Gibbon.

NOTE 30, page 649.

Yet let us ponder boldly—'tis a base.

"At all events," says the author of the Academical Questions, "I trust, whatever may be the fate of my own speculations, that philosophy will regain that estimation which it ought to possess. The free and philosophic spirit of our nation has been the theme of admiration to the world. This was the proud distinction of Englishmen, and the luminous source of all their glory. Shall we then forget the manly and dignified sentiments of our ancestors, to prate in the language of the mother or the nurse about our good old prejudices? This is not the way to defend the cause of truth. It was not thus that our fathers maintained it in the brilliant periods of our history. Prejudice may be trusted to guard the outworks for a short space of time, while reason slumbers in the citadel; but if the latter sink into a lethargy, the former will quickly erect a standard for herself. Philosophy, wisdom, and liberty support each other: he who will not reason is a bigot; he who cannot, is a fool; and he who dare not, is a slave."—Vol. i. pref. p. 14, 15.

NOTE 31, page 650.

Were with his heart, and that was far away.

Whether the wonderful statue which suggested this image be a laquearian gladiator, which, in spite of Winkelmann's criticism, has been stoutly maintained; or whether it be a Greek herald, as that great antiquary positively asserted*; or whether it is to be thought a Spartan or barbarian shield-bearer, according to the opinion of his Italian editor; it must assuredly seem *a copy* of that masterpiece of Ctesilaus, which represented "a wounded man dying, who perfectly expressed what there remained of life in him." Montfaucon and Maffei thought it the identical statue; but that statue was of bronze. The Gladiator was once in the Villa Ludovizi, and was bought by Clement XII. The right arm is an entire restoration of Michael Angelo.

NOTE 32, page 651.

Like laurels on the bald first Cæsar's head.

Suetonius informs us that Julius Cæsar was particularly gratified by that decree of the senate which enabled him to wear a wreath of laurel on all occasions. He was anxious, not to show that he was the conqueror of the world, but to hide that he was bald. A stranger at Rome would hardly have guessed at the motive, nor should we without the help of the historian.

NOTE 33, page 651.

While stands the Coliseum, Rome shall stand.

This is quoted in the "Decline and Fall of the Roman Empire," as a proof that the Coliseum was entire, when seen by the Anglo-Saxon pilgrims at the end of the seventh, or the beginning of the eighth, century.

* Either Polifontes, herald of Laius, killed by Œdipus; or Cepreas, herald of Euritheus killed by the Athenians when he endeavoured to drag the Heraclidæ from the altar of mercy, and in whose honour they instituted annual games, continued to the time of Hadrian; or Anthemocritus, the Athenian herald, killed by the Megarenses, who never recovered the impiety. See *Storia delle Arti*, &c. tom. ii. pp. 203, 204, 205, 206, 207, lib. ix. cap. ii.

NOTE 34, page 651.

From Jove to Jesus—spared and blest by time.

"Though plundered of all its brass, except the ring which was necessary to preserve the aperture above; though exposed to repeated fires; though sometimes flooded by the river, and always open to the rain, no monument of equal antiquity is so well preserved as this rotundo. It passed with little alteration from the Pagan into the present worship; and so convenient were its niches for the Christian altar, that Michael Angelo, ever studious of ancient beauty, introduced their design as a model in the Catholic church."—Forsyth's *Italy*, p. 137, 2nd edit.

NOTE 35, page 651.

Their eyes on honour'd forms, whose busts around them close.

The Pantheon has been made a receptacle for the busts of modern great, or, at least, distinguished, men. The flood of light which once fell through the large orb above on the whole circle of divinities, now shines on a numerous assemblage of mortals, some one or two of whom have been almost deified by the veneration of their countrymen.

NOTE 36, page 651.

There is a dungeon, in whose dim drear light.

This and the three next stanzas allude to the story of the Roman daughter, which is recalled to the traveller by the site, or pretended site, of that adventure, now shown at the church of St. Nicholas *in Carcere*.

NOTE 37, page 652.

Turn to the Mole which Hadrian rear'd on high.

The Castle of St. Angelo.

NOTE 38, page 654.

Nations have arm'd in madness, the strange fate.

Mary died on the scaffold; Elizabeth of a broken heart; Charles V. a hermit; Louis XIV. a bankrupt in means and glory; Cromwell of anxiety; and, "the greatest is behind," Napoleon (1818) lives a prisoner. To these sovereigns a long but superfluous list might be added of names equally illustrious and unhappy.

NOTE 39, page 654.

Lo, Nemi! navell'd in the woody hills.

The village of Nemi was near the Arician retreat of Egeria, and, from the shades which embosomed the temple of Diana, has preserved to this day its distinctive appellation of *The Grove*. Nemi is but an evening's ride from the comfortable inn of Albano.

NOTE 40, page 654.

The Sabine farm was till'd, the weary bard's delight.

The whole declivity of the Alban hill is of unrivalled beauty, and from the convent on the highest point, which has succeeded to the temple of the Latian Jupiter, the prospect embraces all the objects alluded to in this stanza: the Mediterranean; the whole scene of the latter half of the Æneid, and the coast from beyond the mouth of the Tiber to the headland of Circæum and the Cape of Terracina.

www.ingramcontent.com/pod-product-compliance
Lightning Source LLC
LaVergne TN
LVHW021048110826
845150LV00001B/8

9781425568580